Lecture Notes in Computer Science 11258

Commenced Publication in 1973
Founding and Former Series Editors:
Gerhard Goos, Juris Hartmanis, and Jan van Leeuwen

More information about this series at http://www.springer.com/series/7412

Jian-Huang Lai · Cheng-Lin Liu
Xilin Chen · Jie Zhou · Tieniu Tan
Nanning Zheng · Hongbin Zha (Eds.)

Pattern Recognition and Computer Vision

First Chinese Conference, PRCV 2018
Guangzhou, China, November 23–26, 2018
Proceedings, Part III

Springer

Editors
Jian-Huang Lai
Sun Yat-sen University
Guangzhou, China

Cheng-Lin Liu
Institute of Automation
Chinese Academy of Sciences
Beijing, China

Xilin Chen
Institute of Computing Technology
Chinese Academy of Sciences
Beijing, China

Jie Zhou
Tsinghua University
Beijing, China

Tieniu Tan
Institute of Automation
Chinese Academy of Sciences
Beijing, China

Nanning Zheng
Xi'an Jiaotong University
Xi'an, China

Hongbin Zha
Peking University
Beijing, China

ISSN 0302-9743   ISSN 1611-3349 (electronic)
Lecture Notes in Computer Science
ISBN 978-3-030-03337-8   ISBN 978-3-030-03338-5 (eBook)
https://doi.org/10.1007/978-3-030-03338-5

Library of Congress Control Number: 2018959435

LNCS Sublibrary: SL6 – Image Processing, Computer Vision, Pattern Recognition, and Graphics

This Springer imprint is published by the registered company Springer Nature Switzerland AG
The registered company address is: Gewerbestrasse 11, 6330 Cham, Switzerland

Preface

Welcome to the proceedings of the First Chinese Conference on Pattern Recognition and Computer Vision (PRCV 2018) held in Guangzhou, China!

PRCV emerged from CCPR (Chinese Conference on Pattern Recognition) and CCCV (Chinese Conference on Computer Vision), which are both the most influential Chinese conferences on pattern recognition and computer vision, respectively. Pattern recognition and computer vision are closely inter-related and the two communities are largely overlapping. The goal of merging CCPR and CCCV into PRCV is to further boost the impact of the Chinese community in these two core areas of artificial intelligence and further improve the quality of academic communication. Accordingly, PRCV is co-sponsored by four major academic societies of China: the Chinese Association for Artificial Intelligence (CAAI), the China Computer Federation (CCF), the Chinese Association of Automation (CAA), and the China Society of Image and Graphics (CSIG).

PRCV aims at providing an interactive communication platform for researchers from academia and from industry. It promotes not only academic exchange, but also communication between academia and industry. In order to keep track of the frontier of academic trends and share the latest research achievements, innovative ideas, and scientific methods in the fields of pattern recognition and computer vision, international and local leading experts and professors are invited to deliver keynote speeches, introducing the latest advances in theories and methods in the fields of pattern recognition and computer vision.

PRCV 2018 was hosted by Sun Yat-sen University. We received 397 full submissions. Each submission was reviewed by at least two reviewers selected from the Program Committee and other qualified researchers. Based on the reviewers' reports, 178 papers were finally accepted for presentation at the conference, including 24 oral and 154 posters. The acceptance rate is 45%. The proceedings of the PRCV 2018 are published by Springer.

We are grateful to the keynote speakers, Prof. David Forsyth from University of Illinois at Urbana-Champaign, Dr. Zhengyou Zhang from Tencent, Prof. Tamara Berg from University of North Carolina Chapel Hill, and Prof. Michael S. Brown from York University.

We give sincere thanks to the authors of all submitted papers, the Program Committee members and the reviewers, and the Organizing Committee. Without their contributions, this conference would not be a success. Special thanks also go to all of the sponsors and the organizers of the special forums; their support made the conference a success. We are also grateful to Springer for publishing the proceedings and especially to Ms. Celine (Lanlan) Chang of Springer Asia for her efforts in coordinating the publication.

We hope you find the proceedings enjoyable and fruitful reading.

September 2018

Tieniu Tan
Nanning Zheng
Hongbin Zha
Jian-Huang Lai
Cheng-Lin Liu
Xilin Chen
Jie Zhou

Organization

Steering Chairs

Tieniu Tan	Institute of Automation, Chinese Academy of Sciences, China
Hongbin Zha	Peking University, China
Jie Zhou	Tsinghua University, China
Xilin Chen	Institute of Computing Technology, Chinese Academy of Sciences, China
Cheng-Lin Liu	Institute of Automation, Chinese Academy of Sciences, China
Long Quan	Hong Kong University of Science and Technology, SAR China
Yong Rui	Lenovo Group

General Chairs

Tieniu Tan	Institute of Automation, Chinese Academy of Sciences, China
Nanning Zheng	Xi'an Jiaotong University, China
Hongbin Zha	Peking University, China

Program Chairs

Jian-Huang Lai	Sun Yat-sen University, China
Cheng-Lin Liu	Institute of Automation, Chinese Academy of Sciences, China
Xilin Chen	Institute of Computing Technology, Chinese Academy of Sciences, China
Jie Zhou	Tsinghua University, China

Organizing Chairs

Liang Wang	Institute of Automation, Chinese Academy of Sciences, China
Wei-Shi Zheng	Sun Yat-sen University, China

Publicity Chairs

Huimin Ma	Tsinghua University, China
Jian Yu	Beijing Jiaotong University, China
Xin Geng	Southeast University, China

International Liaison Chairs

Jingyi Yu	ShanghaiTech University, China
Pong C. Yuen	Hong Kong Baptist University, SAR China

Publication Chairs

Zhouchen Lin   Peking University, China
Zhenhua Guo   Tsinghua University, China

Tutorial Chairs

Huchuan Lu   Dalian University of Technology, China
Zhaoxiang Zhang   Institute of Automation, Chinese Academy of Sciences, China

Workshop Chairs

Yao Zhao   Beijing Jiaotong University, China
Yanning Zhang   Northwestern Polytechnical University, China

Sponsorship Chairs

Tao Wang   iQIYI Company, China
Jinfeng Yang   Civil Aviation University of China, China
Liang Lin   Sun Yat-sen University, China

Demo Chairs

Yunhong Wang   Beihang University, China
Junyong Zhu   Sun Yat-sen University, China

Competition Chairs

Xiaohua Xie   Sun Yat-sen University, China
Jiwen Lu   Tsinghua University, China

Website Chairs

Ming-Ming Cheng   Nankai University, China
Changdong Wang   Sun Yat-sen University, China

Finance Chairs

Huicheng Zheng   Sun Yat-sen University, China
Ruiping Wang   Institute of Computing Technology, Chinese Academy
                     of Sciences, China

Program Committee

Haizhou Ai   Tsinghua University, China
Xiang Bai   Huazhong University of Science and Technology, China

Xiaochun Cao	Institute of Information Engineering, Chinese Academy of Sciences, China
Hong Chang	Institute of Computing Technology, China
Songcan Chen	Chinese Academy of Sciences, China
Xilin Chen	Institute of Computing Technology, China
Hong Cheng	University of Electronic Science and Technology of China, China
Jian Cheng	Chinese Academy of Sciences, China
Ming-Ming Cheng	Nankai University, China
Yang Cong	Chinese Academy of Science, China
Dao-Qing Dai	Sun Yat-sen University, China
Junyu Dong	Ocean University of China, China
Yuchun Fang	Shanghai University, China
Jianjiang Feng	Tsinghua University, China
Shenghua Gao	ShanghaiTech University, China
Xinbo Gao	Xidian University, China
Xin Geng	Southeast University, China
Ping Guo	Beijing Normal University, China
Zhenhua Guo	Tsinghua University, China
Huiguang He	Institute of Automation, Chinese Academy of Sciences, China
Ran He	National Laboratory of Pattern Recognition, China
Richang Hong	Hefei University of Technology, China
Baogang Hu	Institute of Automation, Chinese Academy of Sciences, China
Hua Huang	Beijing Institute of Technology, China
Kaizhu Huang	Xi'an Jiaotong-Liverpool University, China
Rongrong Ji	Xiamen University, China
Wei Jia	Hefei University of Technology, China
Yunde Jia	Beijing Institute of Technology, China
Feng Jiang	Harbin Institute of Technology, China
Zhiguo Jiang	Beihang University, China
Lianwen Jin	South China University of Technology, China
Xiao-Yuan Jing	Wuhan University, China
Xiangwei Kong	Dalian University of Technology, China
Jian-Huang Lai	Sun Yat-sen University, China
Hua Li	Institute of Computing Technology, Chinese Academy of Sciences, China
Peihua Li	Dalian University of Technology, China
Shutao Li	Hunan University, China
Wu-Jun Li	Nanjing University, China
Xiu Li	Tsinghua University, China
Xuelong Li	Xi'an Institute of Optics and Precision Mechanics, Chinese Academy of Sciences, China
Yongjie Li	University of Electronic Science and Technology of China, China
Ronghua Liang	Zhejiang University of Technology, China
Zhouchen Lin	Peking University, China

Cheng-Lin Liu	Institute of Automation, Chinese Academy of Sciences, China
Huafeng Liu	Zhejiang University, China
Huaping Liu	Tsinghua University, China
Qingshan Liu	Nanjing University of Information Science and Technology, China
Wenyin Liu	Guangdong University of Technology, China
Wenyu Liu	Huazhong University of Science and Technology, China
Yiguang Liu	Sichuan University, China
Yue Liu	Beijing Institute of Technology, China
Guoliang Lu	Shandong University, China
Jiwen Lu	Tsinghua University, China
Yue Lu	East China Normal University, China
Bin Luo	Anhui University, China
Ke Lv	Chinese Academy of Sciences, China
Huimin Ma	Tsinghua University, China
Zhanyu Ma	Beijing University of Posts and Telecommunications, China
Deyu Meng	Xi'an Jiaotong University, China
Qiguang Miao	Xidian University, China
Zhenjiang Miao	Beijing Jiaotong University, China
Weidong Min	Nanchang University, China
Bingbing Ni	Shanghai Jiaotong University, China
Gang Pan	Zhejiang University, China
Yuxin Peng	Peking University, China
Jun Sang	Chongqing University, China
Nong Sang	Huazhong University of Science and Technology, China
Shiguang Shan	Institute of Computing Technology, Chinese Academy of Sciences, China
Linlin Shen	Shenzhen University, China
Wei Shen	Shanghai University, China
Guangming Shi	Xidian University, China
Fei Su	Beijing University of Posts and Telecommunications, China
Jian Sun	Xi'an Jiaotong University, China
Jun Sun	Fujitsu R&D Center Co., Ltd., China
Zhengxing Sun	Nanjing University, China
Xiaoyang Tan	Nanjing University of Aeronautics and Astronautics, China
Jinhui Tang	Nanjing University of Science and Technology, China
Jin Tang	Anhui University, China
Yandong Tang	Shenyang Institute of Automation, Chinese Academy of Sciences, China
Chang-Dong Wang	Sun Yat-sen University, China
Liang Wang	National Laboratory of Pattern Recognition, China
Ruiping Wang	Institute of Computing Technology, Chinese Academy of Sciences, China
Shengjin Wang	Tsinghua University, China
Shuhui Wang	Institute of Computing Technology, Chinese Academy of Sciences, China

Contents – Part III

Face Recognition and Analysis

Feature Extraction and Selection

Machine Learning

Document Analysis

Chinese Painting Rendering by Adaptive Style Transfer

Wanxin Zou[1], Xutao Li[1]([⊠]), and Sengping Li[2]

[1] Department of Electronic Engineering, Shantou University, Shantou 515063, China
{wxzou,lixt}@stu.edu.cn
[2] Department of Mechanical and Electronic Engineering, Shantou University,
Shantou 515063, China
spli@stu.edu.cn

Abstract. Chinese painting is distinct from other art in that the painting elements are exhibited by complex water-and-ink diffusion and shows gray, white and black visual effect. Rendering such a water-and-ink painting with polychrome style is a challenging problem. In this paper, we propose a novel style transfer method for Chinese painting. We firstly decompose the Chinese painting with adaptive patches based on its structure, and locally colorize the painting. Then, the colorized image is used for guiding the process of texture transfer that is modeled in Markov Random Field (MRF). More precisely, we improve the classic texture transfer algorithm by modifying the compatibility functions for searching the optimal matching, with the chromatism information. The experiment results show that proposed adaptive patches can well preserve the original content while match the example style. Moreover, we present the transfer results with our method and recent style transfer algorithms, in order to make a comparison.

Keywords: Chinese painting rendering · Style transfer
Adaptive patch-based texture transfer · Markov Random Field

1 Introduction

As a traditional art in China, Chinese painting differs from other art in its expressive brush strokes and ink diffusion. To ideally render water-and-ink painting, many researchers attempted to use computer simulation for such complicated texture generation [13, 15]. In this paper, we aim to render Chinese painting with other artistic style, which is regarded as a style transfer problem.

Style transfer is to synthesize an image that combines the structure of a original image with the artistic style of the example image. In this work, it

Supported by NSFC No. 61471229/61573233. and Department of Education of Guangdong Province (2015KCXTD018/2017KCXTD015).

J.-H. Lai et al. (Eds.): PRCV 2018, LNCS 11258, pp. 3–14, 2018.
https://doi.org/10.1007/978-3-030-03338-5_1

is a process of migrating a style from an example image to Chinese painting, which can be generally regarded as transferring two different painting style. In animation production and video post-production fields, style transfer and related approaches are highly interested as they facilitate generating different scenes [9,12]. Although various methods have been proposed for this issue, style transfer task has not been well-defined. The core difficulty is how to distinguish style feature from semantic content in an image, including all visual attributes such as texture, strokes, color and shading.

Previous study offers two distinct methods for style transfer: One is generalization of classic texture synthesis approaches, such as the works in [2,3], in which optimal patches of a single image are expected to be found based on local similarity. An alternative technique for style transfer problem emerged in recent years, defining content and style representation of two images and using Convolutional Neural Networks (CNN) to merge the corresponding content and style [7].

Our work is motivated by patch-based texture synthesis approaches. In spite of traditional patch-based texture synthesis methods made an impressive success for style transfer, the limitations should be overcome. For example, the local texture synthesis is accomplished in the same and fixed size patches throughout the whole image, where the size of the patch is a tradeoff between the style and the content to be preserved in the output image. The size of patch should be large enough to exhibit the patterns that characterize the example style, yet small enough to reconstruct the realistic content of original image. Another limitation is that traditional constrains in transferring consider only luminance and local neighboring similarity of target image, without color information. Hence, we propose a style transfer method for Chinese painting which is able to overcome the limitations. The main contributions of this work are summarized as follows:

- We adaptively divide target Chinese painting into patches based on its local similarity for texture synthesis, in stead of using patches of constant size, so as to achieve a realistic reconstruction of the original image while present most noticeable example style;
- Constraints are modified in the process of texture synthesis, where color is considered as a relevant factor guiding local texture transfer. It may guarantee the validity in transfer process, where the futile texture is prevented.

2   Related Works on Style Transfer

Style transfer can be considered as a special case of texture synthesis, where the content image influences the regular synthesis process. In the literatures of traditional texture synthesis and transfer, example-based methods are to generate a texture image by computing non-parametric sampling from a given example style image based on Markov Random Field (MRF). One of the earliest works in [2] by Efros and Leung takes a pixel to be synthesized by random sampling from a set of candidate pixels that are selected from an example texture image. This process is repeated for every output pixel by growing from the initial region until all the output pixels have been already synthesized. Intuitively, the neighborhood size should be equal to the texture element sizes. Otherwise, the output texture may be too random or regular pattern may be reduced. The quality and speed of these pixel-based approaches [2,14] were improved by path-based one. In [3], a patch-quilting procedure for texture synthesis is proposed, and then extended it to texture transfer. Patch-based texture transfer is similar to pixel-based one, except that instead of synthesizing pixels, it copies patches.

The work in [8] suggested texture optimization as texture synthesis method beyond pixel-based and patch-based algorithms. The algorithm synthesizes an output texture in the units of pixels, but unlike previous pixel-based methods that synthesize pixels one by one in a greedy fashion, this technique considered all pixels together, determining pixel values by minimizing a quadratic energy function. This energy function has been modified by the latest work in [4] to match the transfer task better. In details, both content and example style image were restricted by a segmentation mask adding to the energy function, in order to determine which parts to be transferred and preserved.

Recently, an impressive work of style transfer is using Convolutional Neural Networks (CNN)[7]. Their methods adopt a pre-tranined CNN to extract features from both the style and the content images, respectively.

Motivated by [5], which consider an explicit probability density modeling of the problem and computes an approximate Maximum a Posteriori(MAP) solution based on an iterative optimization of Belief Propagation or Graph cuts, we propose a novel style transfer method for Chinese painting. Unlike the traditional patch-based algorithm in [3], we propose an adaptive patch for style transfer. Especially given that our target image in this work is black-and-white Chinese painting with expressive content, we improve classic style transfer algorithms by modifying the optimal match condition to overcome such a challenge.

3   Problem Description

Traditionally, Chinese painting (water-and-ink) is presented by ink diffusion of different degree on the Xuan paper. The objects are in a wide range of scale, painted by complex and expressive brush strokes. In other words, while some scene objects are always painted with rough brushwork, the key objects are painted in detail with subtle brushwork. For example, in Fig. 1(a), the distant mountains are roughly painted by great water-and-ink diffusion but the fisherman and the texture of the mountains nearby are exhibited subtly by slight ink spreading. Moreover, ink diffusion can be also used for rendering Chinese painting as "color", such as the representation of cloud and shading.

Our goal is to transfer other artistic styles such as impressionism and post-impressionism to Chinese painting. Consequently, we propose a style transfer method that adopts an adaptive patch for patch-based texture transfer, and colorization to guide the process of style transfer. At first, we give the problem definition of style transfer for Chinese painting.

Given a Chinese painting $C : \Omega_C \in \mathbb{R}^3$, and a style image $S : \Omega_S \in \mathbb{R}^3$ with certain style. We aim to synthesis an image C_{out} which captures the style of S while preserves the semantic content of C. This can be considered as finding a mapping $f : \Omega_C \rightarrow \Omega_S$ which comfirms each element $X \in \Omega_C$ with a corresponding element $Y = f(X) \in \Omega_S$.

Applying a similar idea for patch-based texture transfer, the correspondence mapping f should be a piecewise constant translation mapping on region $P = \{P_i\}_{i=1}^n$ of Ω_C. In order to extract the style feature of S while preserving the structure of C, the region P should be obtained based on the painting elements of C, and the texture as well as color of S should be taken into account for the optimal corresponding $f(x)$. Especially, to transfer the style elegantly, smoothness is required on the boundary between neighboring regions.

4   Style Transfer for Chinese Painting

In this section we detail the proposed style transfer algorithm. In order to meet the requirements mentioned above, our approach can divided into three main steps:

- Adaptively decompose Ω_C into n regions P;
- Locally render Ω_C according to the color of S;
- Find the optimal mapping f based on MRF model;

Moreover, corresponding experiment results are presented to illustrate the performance of each step. We note that our style transfer is accomplished in YUV color space, since we consider both luminance and chrominance in the process of texture transfer.

4.1   Adaptive Decomposition for Chinese Painting

We firstly recall that in patch-based texture transfer, the original image to be rendered is decomposed into fixed size patches, and assign one node of a Markov network. Generally, if the size of patches are small (for example the size of 8×8), the content of original image can be ideally reconstructed yet the style of the example style image is nearly obvious; on the contrary, if large patches have been chosen for texture synthesis, the considerable details of original image are lost. To reconstruct the realistic content of original Chinese painting while inheriting the example style, we divide the original image into adaptive-size patches based on its structure and pixel distribution.

Let decomposition starts with one single region $P_i \in \Omega_C$, of size $m \times m$. Each region P_i is divided into four equal squares, with each size of $\frac{m}{2} \times \frac{m}{2}$, if pixel value $X_i = (x_1, x_2, \ldots x_{m \times m}) \in P_i$ satisfies:

$$D(X_i) > \sigma \text{ or } m > \omega \tag{1}$$

where σ is the threshold; $D(X_i) = (\max(X_i) - \min(X_i))$ presents the difference between the maximum and minimum value in region P_i, and ω is the maximum patch size allowed in the quadtree.

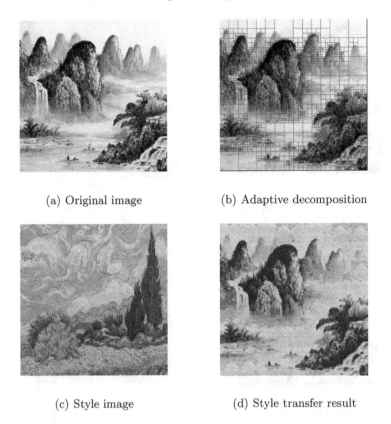

(a) Original image   (b) Adaptive decomposition

(c) Style image   (d) Style transfer result

Fig. 1. Illustration of adaptive decomposition (Color figure online)

The local variance of a quadtree cell decides whether a cell is divided into four cells, which depends the details in C. As illustrated in Fig. 1(b), the more delicate elements in the original image are divided into the more smaller patches to be transferred, such as the trees and fisherman nearby. Thus, the content of original image can be perfectly preserved in texture synthesis, while the style feature can be reflected as much as possible, as showed in Fig. 1(d). Obviously, our decomposition only depends on the structure of original image, rather than the stopping criteria for quadtree splitting in [6].

In Fig. 2, we present a comparison of between our adaptive patches and Image Quilting with fixed-size patches in [3]. To make it clear, We choose the smallest size of patch allowed in two algorithms, and highlight two specific differences in the results by red rectangles. It can be observed that two persons on the bridge and the curved roof of pavilion reconstructed by our method are more clearer than those reconstructed by Image Quilting as showed in Fig. 2(c) and Fig. 2(d). These results present that our adaptive patches preserves the original content better than fixed-size patches.

(a) Original image   (b) Style image

(c) Our method   (d) Image Quilting [3]

Fig. 2. Comparison of adaptive patches and fixed-size patches: Our method with adaptive patches and the minimal size of patches is 4×4 as showed in (c); (d) present the result of Image Quilting algorithm with patches of fixed size 8×8. (Color figure online)

4.2   Locally Color Transfer

Color style transfer is an essential step in style transfer which has usually been done separately after texture transfer in classic approaches. Due to that the brightness and darkness in Chinese painting are exhibited by complex ink diffusion, the colors are usually gray, black and white, while the other artistic style is generally colorful. Without chrominance information, the color fidelity of example style cannot be guaranteed during reconstructing C_{out}. It is worse that the futile texture may appear which is not conform to semantic content of the original image. Thus, instead of transferring texture only in luminance, we consider the chrominance information.

Here, we preprocess colorization for original Chinese painting before texture transfer. Specific colors in S are extracted as color seeds for local rendering through colorization method suggested in [10]. Then, the rendered image $\tilde{C}$ guides the texture transfer as one of criteria in chrominance. In detail, we search

(a) Original image (b) Style image

(c) Our method (d) Image Quilting [3] (e) Split and Match [6]

Fig. 3. Illustration of locally color transfer: Our result is more reasonable than the one of Image Quilting method, since there is futile texture on the farmland by Image Quilting [3]. And the color gamut of our result is more similar to the color gamut of style image compared to the results of Split and Match method [6]. (Color figure online)

for the optimal match for texture transfer in luminance as well as chrominance (in YUV color space), which is described in next 4.3.

Similarly, we show the transfer results in Fig. 3. It is noted that if consider luminance as the only matching condition for texture transfer, the futile texture are synthesized, as showed in Fig. 3(d). From semantic understanding, the color of farmland should be yellow or green, but Image Quilting algorithm (and other classic methods that only consider luminance) synthesizes blue and white texture. As presented in Fig. 3(c), compared with the traditional algorithms, our method can obtain a reasonable output image since the chrominance is considered. In addition, the color gamut of our result is more similar to the color gamut of style image than the results of Split and Match method shown in 3(e). It is indicated that the color style can be better extracted with chromatism information.

4.3 Optimal Match

As mentioned above, both the original image and example style image are divided into patches where each patch is one node of a Markov network. With the framework of Markov Random Field (MRF), the problem of patch-based style transfer can be solved through computing the Maximum Posteriori from a well chosen joint probability distribution on all patches [5]. Thus, the optimal mapping f can finally be found with MRF model.

The MRF model in our work is illustrated in Fig. 4, which can be found that the links on original image connect adaptive patches rather than fixed size patches. We search for the optimal match for each patch by finding maximum a posteriori (MAP), which is equally maximizing the joint probability over the X_i and Y_i, that can be written as

$$Pr(X_1, X_2, \ldots X_N, Y_1, Y_2, \ldots Y_N) = \prod_{(i,j) \in N} \Psi_{i,j}(X_i, X_j) \prod_{k \in N} \Phi_k(X_k, Y_k), \quad (2)$$

where $\Psi_{i,j}(X_i, X_j)$ are pairwise interaction potentials between neighboring nodes i and j, while $N(i, j)$ denotes the neighbors of patches. $\Psi_{i,j}(X_i, X_j)$ ensures that neighboring patches are similar in their overlapping region and it can be written as

$$\Psi_{i,j}(X_i, X_j) = \exp(-E(X_i, X_j)) \quad (3)$$

where $E(X_i, X_j) = \|X_i - X_j\|^2$ is the error term of the overlapping region between two patches. $\Phi_k(X_k, Y_k)$ are the data penalty functions given by

$$\Phi_k(X_k, Y_k) = \exp(-\theta(X_k, Y_k)). \quad (4)$$

where θ is the weighted error term between the newly chosen block and the old blocks. As discussed in 3.3, we use colorized image $\tilde{C}$ to guide the texture transfer, hence, $\theta[X_k, Y_k]$ is defined as

$$\theta(X_k, Y_k) = \alpha d(X_k, Y_k)_{Ori} + \beta d(X_k, Y_k)_{Ch} + \mu d(X_k, Y_k)_L. \quad (5)$$

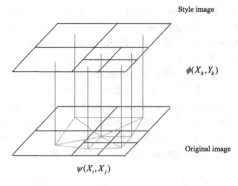

Fig. 4. Markov network for our work: Each node in the network describes a local adaptive patch of original or example image.

(a) Original image   (b) Style image   (c) Style transfer result

Fig. 5. Transfer results on different style examples: Original Chinese painting (left column), example style images (middle column), and the style transfer result (right column).

We modify the criterion in [3] by adding $d(X_k, Y_k)_{Ch}$, presenting the square error of patches between rendered image $\tilde{C}$ and example style image S. $d(X_k, Y_k)_{Ori}$ is the square error of the overlapping regions in the original image C, and $d(X_k, Y_k)_L$ is the square error term of patches between original image and style image in luminance. α, β and μ are three positive weights that no bigger than 1 (respectively fixed to 0.2, 0.2 and 0.6 in all experiments).

Finally, we achieve an optimal boundary of adjacent patches to remove visibly artificial seams. This minimal cost path through the overlap region can be done with dynamic programming [1]. Other transfer results with respect to different example style are presented in Fig. 5. With different style, our algorithm is able to transfer example style while ideally reconstruct the content of the original painting.

5   Comparison of Our Method and Other Approaches

In this section, we would like to make a comparison between our method and recent style transfer approaches.

As shown in Fig. 6, we present the experimental results with our method and a popular method Convolutional Neural Network (CNN) with the parameter setting in [7]. Both our method and CNN achieve ideal reconstruction for

(a) Original image   (b) Style image   (c) Our method   (d) CNN [7]

Fig. 6. Comparison with CNN approach: Original Chinese paintings (first column), different style images (second column), our results (third column), and results of CNN approach (last column). (Color figure online)

original content. The subtle texture feature of the style images can be captured with our method such as the wavy strokes in Van Gogh's Starry night. Even the detail texture element like the yellow and white points are preserved in our result, which hardly appear in CNN transfer results. And the color gamut of our results is more closer to the color gamut of style images, compared with the results of CNN. This is due to that in the style transfer process, we choose the optimal patches in the original style image as the generated patches in stead of extracting the abstract style feature. While CNN uses deep and abstract style representation, it loses low-level pixel features of the style image. Moreover, CNN has the trade-off problem of style and content matching, which has been mentioned in [7]. Similarly, the transfer method in [11] applies MRF prior defining the loss function for CNN to control the abstract style layout yet our algorithm improves compatibility functions of MRF to generates style directly from the style image, rather than extracting the abstract style step by step.

As we mentioned in Sect. 4.1, our adaptive decomposition for the content image only depends on the local variance, while the recent work by Frigo et al., in [6] also regards the similarity between the content image and the style image as the decomposition criterion. Most importantly, compare with Split and

Match method transfers color style separately after texture transfer, we combine texture transfer and color style transfer, by guiding the texture transfer process with chromatism information. As depicted in Fig. 3, our result maintains the original color style of the style image including green, blue and yellow color. Yet the results of Split and Match method almost miss yellow color feature. The color gamut of our result is more closer to the color gamut of style image.

6 Conclusion

In this paper, we regard the rendering problem of Chinese painting as a style transfer issue and propose a new style transfer method for Chinese painting. Based on the characters of Chinese painting where the painting elements are always have obviously distinct scale, adaptive-size patches are applied for texture transfer in our approach. Additionally, we modify the constraints in texture transfer based on MRF model, considering color information of both style image and colorized original image. The local colors of style image are extracted as color seeds for rendering the black-and-white Chinese painting, which helps to guide the process of texture transfer.

The experimental results of each step are presented to clearly illustrate the improvement by our proposed algorithm. The results suggest that decomposing target Chinese painting with adaptive patches to be transferred is able to well preserve the original content while transferring example style, and the color style can be captured with chromatism information. Finally, we discuss the comparison of our method and other state-of-the-art style transfer methods, including patch-based approach and CNN framework.

References

1. Davis, J.: Mosaics of scenes with moving objects. In: IEEE Computer Society Conference on Computer Vision and Pattern Recognition, p. 354 (1998)
2. Efros, A.A., Leung, T.K.: Texture synthesis by non-parametric sampling. In: The Proceedings of the Seventh IEEE International Conference on Computer Vision, p. 1033 (2002)
3. Efros, A.A., Freeman, W.T.: Image quilting for texture synthesis and transfer. In: Proceedings of Siggraph, pp. 341–346 (2001)
4. Elad, M., Milanfar, P.: Style transfer via texture synthesis. IEEE Trans. Image Process. **26**(5), 2338 (2017)
5. Freeman, W.T., Pasztor, E.C., Carmichael, O.T.: Learning low-level vision. Int. J. Comput. Vis. **40**(1), 25–47 (2000)
6. Frigo, O., Sabater, N., Delon, J., Hellier, P.: Split and match: example-based adaptive patch sampling for unsupervised style transfer. In: Computer Vision and Pattern Recognition, pp. 553–561 (2016)
7. Gatys, L.A., Ecker, A.S., Bethge, M.: Image style transfer using convolutional neural networks. In: IEEE Conference on Computer Vision and Pattern Recognition, pp. 2414–2423 (2016)
8. Kwatra, V., Essa, I., Bobick, A., Kwatra, N.: Texture optimization for example-based synthesis. ACM Trans. Graph. **24**(3), 795–802 (2005)

9. Kyprianidis, J.E., Collomosse, J., Wang, T., Isenberg, T.: State of the "art": a taxonomy of artistic stylization techniques for images and video. In: Iberoamerican Optics Meeting and Latin American Meeting on Optics, Lasers, and Applications (2013)
10. Levin, A., Lischinski, D., Weiss, Y.: Colorization using optimization. ACM Trans. Graph. **23**(3), 689–694 (2004)
11. Li, C., Wand, M.: Combining Markov random fields and convolutional neural networks for image synthesis. In: Proceedings of the IEEE Conference on Computer Vision and Pattern Recognition, pp. 2479–2486 (2016)
12. Li, C., Wand, M.: Precomputed real-time texture synthesis with Markovian generative adversarial networks. In: Leibe, B., Matas, J., Sebe, N., Welling, M. (eds.) ECCV 2016. LNCS, vol. 9907, pp. 702–716. Springer, Cham (2016). https://doi.org/10.1007/978-3-319-46487-9_43
13. Way, D.L., Lin, Y.R., Shih, Z.C.: The synthesis of trees in chinese landscape painting using silhouette and texture strokes. J. WSCG **10**, 499–506 (2002)
14. Wei, L.Y., Levoy, M.: Fast texture synthesis using tree-structured vector quantization, pp. 479–488 (2000)
15. Wong, H.T.F., Ip, H.H.S.: Virtual brush: a model-based synthesis of chinese calligraphy. Comput. Graph. **24**(1), 99–113 (2000)

The Accurate Guidance for Image Caption Generation

Xinyuan Qi, Zhiguo Cao[✉], Yang Xiao, Jian Wang, and Chao Zhang

National Key Lab of Science and Technology of Multispetral
Information Processing, School of Automation,
Huazhong University of Science and Technology, Wuhan 430074, Hubei, China
{silliam_qi, zgcao, Yang_Xiao, M201572352,
zhangC_22}@hust.edu.cn

Abstract. Image caption task has been focusing on generating a descriptive sentence for a certain image. In this work, we propose the accurate guidance for image caption generation, which guides the caption model to focus more on the principle semantic object while making human reading sentence, and generate high quality sentence in grammar. In particular, we replace the classification network with object detection network as the multi-level feature extracter to emphasize what human care about and avoid unnecessary model additions. Attention mechanism is utilized to align the feature of principle objects with words in the semantic sentence. Under these circumstances, we combine the object detection network and the text generation model together and it becomes an end-to-end model with less parameters. The experimental results on MS-COCO dataset show that our methods are on part with or even outperforms the current state-of-the-art.

Keywords: Image caption · Object detection · Attention mechanism
Deep learning

1 Introduction

Image caption task aims at automatically generating a descriptive sentence to describe the content of an image with an English sentence [1]. With the explosive increase in digital images and the rapid development in deep learning, teaching machines to understand images as humans is drawing great interests. At the outset, computer vision task aims at classifying the category of a single image (image classification). Hereafter, researchers try to locate the position of objects in more complicated scenes (object detection). After that, researchers further want to distinguish the category of per-pixel (semantic segmentation). Along with this fruitful development route, researchers owe it to comprehending the semantic information of the picture better and better. Meanwhile, another understanding of the images' semantic information is to describe an image's content with a human-like sentence (image caption). This idea is closer to human's habit when there is a scene in front of their eyes. While caption task seems obvious for human beings, it is much more difficult for machine since it requires the 'translation' model to capture several semantic information from a certain image. Such as scenes,

© Springer Nature Switzerland AG 2018
J.-H. Lai et al. (Eds.): PRCV 2018, LNCS 11258, pp. 15–26, 2018.
https://doi.org/10.1007/978-3-030-03338-5_2

objects, attributes, relative position and so on. Another challenge of caption task is to generate descriptive sentence meeting the grammar rules.

Fig. 1. This is an example picture in MS-COCO dataset. The caption ground truth is "Several surfers riding a small wave into the beach". The proportion of principal object (humans and surfboards) is well low. There are too much redundant information, such as sky, which will make it harder for attention mechanism to align the principal object with the noun composition in the descriptive sentence.

Recently, Neural network methods [2, 3] dominate the literature in image captioning. The encoder-decoder architecture in Neural Machine Translation [4] inspire these methods very much. In contrast to original Neural Machine Translation model, image caption model replace the recurrent neural network (RNNs) with convolutional neural network (CNNs) as encoder. CNNs encode the input image into a feature vector, which represents the semantic information of the image. Then a sequence modeling approach (e.g., Long Short-Term Memory (LSTM) [5]) decodes the semantic feature vector into a sequence of words. Such architecture applies to the vast majority of image caption model.

The method to combine CNNs and RNNs together directly will result that the information of the input image decreases by iterations. In this situation, researchers start to utilize image guidance [3], attributes [6] or region attention [7] as the extra input into LSTM decoder for better performance. The original intention comes from visual attention, which has been known in Psychology and Neuroscience for a long time. Attention mechanism highly relies on the quality of the input image. If there are too much redundant information in the image, it will be hard for attention mechanism to capture the principal information. As shown in Fig. 1, the proportion of principal objects (humans and surfboards) is very low. CNNs-encoder usually reduce the dimension of feature vector a lot, which will make it harder for attention mechanism to capture the information for subject, object and other noun composition. In this condition, if we insist on applying attention mechanism to the whole image like [7], caption model may not know what to describe.

In Natural Language Processing, scientists take the noun composition in a sentence as the focus, which people care more about. In image caption task, the noun composition corresponds to the principal object in an image. To help image caption model to capture the principal object more accurate, we propose to get help from object detection task. Object detection task has been studied for a long time. CNNs framework is widely used and rapidly developed in object detection task, such as R-CNN [11], Fast-RCNN [12], Faster-RCNN [13]. These models are able to capture principal objects in the image very well. So we propose to make use of the feature of object detection methods to encode the image and generate guidance for the language generate model. We call it as accurate guidance. This advance also means to combine the higher level of semantic information in computer vision task with the semantic meaning in human-reading sentence.

We implement our model based on a single state-of-the-art object detection network Faster-RCNN [13], for accuracy and speed. Simultaneously, our model can be trained end-to-end, which will make the object detection module to adjust itself to suit for the image caption task. We take the Google NIC [7] as the baseline and compare our methods with popular attention models on the commonly used MS-COCO dataset [9] with publicly available splits of training, validation and testing sets. We evaluate methods on standard metrics. Our proposed methods outperform all of them and achieve state-of-the-art across different evaluation metrics.

The main contributions of our paper are as follows. First, we propose accurate guidance mechanism to help the caption model capture the principal object more precisely and infer their relationships from global information simultaneously. Second, the proposed method utilize a single object detection network as the multi-level feature extracter and demonstrates a less complicated way to achieve end-to-end training of attention-based captioning model, whereas state-of-the-art methods [3, 6, 19] involve LSTM hidden states or image attributes for attention, which compromises the possibility of end-to-end optimization.

2   Related Work

Recent successes of deep neural networks in machine translation catalyze the adoption of neural networks [8] in solving image caption problems. Early works of neural networks-based image caption include the multimodal RNN [10] and LSTM [5]. In these methods, neural networks are used to both image-text embedding and sentence generating.

Attention mechanism has recently attracted considerable interest in LSTM-based image captioning [3, 6]. Xu et al. [7] proposed to integrate visual attention through the hidden state of LSTM model. You et al. [6] propose to fusion visual attributes extracted from images with the input or output of LSTM. These methods achieve state-of-the-art performance but they highly rely on the quality of the pre-specified visual attributes. Our method also use attention mechanism. Different from the predecessors, we consider the object detection-dependent attention to generate high quality guidance rather than search at the whole noisy image. It is an adaptive method to obtain high quality features.

Reinforcement Learning has recently been introduced into image caption task [20] and achieved state-of-the-art performance due to optimize the evaluation metrics directly. These methods are generally applicable training approach not the improvement for the caption model. Thus, we don't compare with them but believe that our model will gain much higher performance with Reinforcement Learning.

[19] first proposes to utilize object detection method in image caption task. However, it utilize Fast-RCNN to detect and VGG net [15] to locate. The caption model is very redundant. While generating guidance, it keep the region of its bounding box unchanged and set remaining regions to mean value of the training set for each object in image. This process will bring much interference to the caption model. Our method solves these puzzles by taking the single object detection network as the multi-level feature extracter. In this way, our method is a clean architecture for the ease of end-to-end learning.

3   Methods

Our accurate guidance model includes a multi-level feature extraction module (MFEM) and a principal object guiding LSTM (po-gLSTM). Figure 2 shows the structure of our model. We first describe how to use object detection network as MFEM to simultaneously extract the features of the whole image (fea_w) and principle objects (fea_o) in Sect. 3.1. Then, we introduce our po-gLSTM which will take advantage of the multi-level feature to guide the LSTM to describe the image more precise in Sect. 3.2.

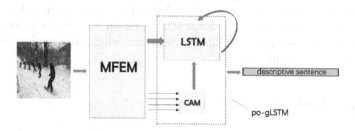

Fig. 2. The structure of our accurate guidance model

3.1   Multi-level Feature Extraction Module

Figure 3 shows the framework of multi-level feature extraction module. The MFEM consists of two parts: (1) fea_o extraction network (above the red dotted line); (2) fea_w extraction network (below the red dotted line). It is a variant of Faster-RCNN [13]. In order to capture the principle objects better, for an input image I, we suppose to utilize object detection network to find the potential objects and extract fea_o, which denoted as $fea_o = \{obj_1, \ldots, obj_N\}$ and formulated as formula (1). N is the number of potential objects. RPN (Region Proposal Network) splits the principle object parts from the whole image. $CNN_{\theta 2}$ is to further extract the features after RPN.

$$fea_0 = CNN_{\theta 2}\{RPN[CNN_{\theta 1}(I)]\} \tag{1}$$

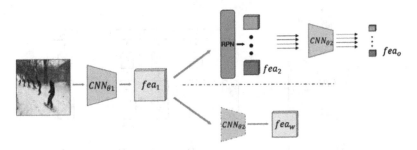

Fig. 3. The structure of the MFEM (Color figure online)

Simultaneously, we also need fea_w so that the po-gLSTM can get the information of scenes and infer the relationship between objects. In this situation, the original output of Faster-RCNN framework does not meet the conditions. Thus, we try to fix it's framework so that it can extract fea_w at the same time. As shown in the part below the red dotted line in Fig. 3, we get a copy of the feature after $CNN_{\theta 1}$ and take it into $CNN_{\theta 2}$ directly. Then we get an imitation classification network followed with fea_w, formulated as formula (2).

$$fea_w = CNN_{\theta 2}[CNN_{\theta 1}(I)] \qquad (2)$$

Notice that the $CNN_{\theta 2}$ with dotted border (below the red dotted line) is the same with the $CNN_{\theta 2}$ with solid border (above the red dotted line). We do not increase the model parameters but obtain fea_w successfully. Faster-RCNN argues the size of input image should be larger than 600 pixel × 600 pixel. For reducing the model parameters, we replace its' fully connected layer with the Global Average Pooling layer to embedding fea_w and resize it to fit the size of the principle object guiding LSTM's input, formulated as follows:

$$x_0 = Pool_{ave}(fea_w) \qquad (3)$$

x_0 is utilized to initialize decoder in Sect. 3.2. Here, we have already gotten the multi-level feature of the input image. The multi-level feature carries the multi-level semantic information. As later experiments will demonstrate, multi-level feature extraction module will help the model to focus more on the principle objects and achieve better performance.

3.2   Principal Object Guiding LSTM (po-gLSTM)

As shown in Fig. 4, the function of po-gLSTM is to decode the multi-level semantic information of the image and generate corresponding descriptive sentence. In this section, we will first introduce the condition attention module to obtain the principle object information for the current word. Then we will introduce how to make use of the principle object information to guide the LSTM to generate sentence. Both of above, we treat them as a whole and call it as po-gLSTM.

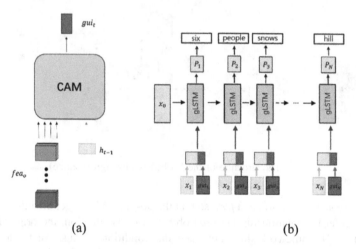

(a)   (b)

Fig. 4. (a) CAM is the condition Attention Module, which is to generate guidance information (gui_t) by principle object features (fea_0) and the information of hidden layer at previous step (h_{t-1}). (b) This sketch map shows how to utilize x_0 and gui_t to generate descriptive sentence. Both of (a) and (b) make up the po-gLSTM.

Condition Attention Module

With the multi-level feature extraction module, fea_o and fea_w of an input image will be extracted easily. Each word in caption is represented by a one-hot vector and the captioning sentence is a sequence of input vectors $(x_1, \ldots, x_T)$. Same as previous methods, we utilize fea_w to initialize the decoder (LSTM), the decoder then computes a sequence of hidden states $(h_1, \ldots, h_t)$ and a sequence of outputs $(y_1, \ldots, y_t)$. The primer decoder only accesses fea_w (encoded as x_0) once at the beginning of the learning process, which will loss most of the information of image I by iterations, and output incorrect words or stop too early. To avoid this, we proposed to utilize condition attention module (CAM) [6] to stress the role of principle objects and supply necessary information lost by iterations. CAM is formulated as followed:

$$a_t^i = Wtanh(W_{ao}obj_i + W_{ah}h_{t-1})i = 1, \ldots, N \tag{4}$$

$$\alpha_t = softmax(a_t) \tag{5}$$

$$gui_t = \sum_{i=1}^{N} \alpha_t^i obj_i \tag{6}$$

W, W_{ao}, W_{ah} are learnable parameters. N is the number of principle object in an image. a_t^i is the relevance of obj_i and h_{t-1}. The elements of α_t is utilized to combine the guiding information (principle objects). gui_t is the guidance at iteration t.

With attention mechanism, model will know "where to see" while generating every word. We also make a visualization of attention mechanism to prove it in later experiment.

Guiding LSTM

The generated sentence by the LSTM model may lose track of the original image content since it only accesses the image content once at the beginning of the learning process, and forgets the image even after a short time. To make use of gui_t mentioned above and supplement the forgotten information if necessary, we propose to utilize an extension of the LSTM model, named the guiding LSTM (gLSTM) [3], which extracts semantic information from the input image and feeds it into the LSTM model every time step as extra information. Its' gate and memory cell can be formulated as follows:

$$i'_t = \sigma\left(W'_i\left[h'_{t-1}, x'_t, gui_t\right]\right) \tag{7}$$

$$f'_t = \sigma\left(W'_f\left[h'_{t-1}, x'_t, gui_t\right]\right) \tag{8}$$

$$o'_t = \sigma\left(W'_o\left[h'_{t-1}, x'_t, gui_t\right]\right) \tag{9}$$

$$\widetilde{C'_t} = tanh\left(W'_c\left[h'_{t-1}, x'_t, gui_t\right]\right) \tag{10}$$

$$C'_t = f'_t C'_{t-1} + i'_t \widetilde{C'_t} \tag{11}$$

$$h'_t = o'_t * tanh\left(C'_t\right) \tag{12}$$

$$x'_{t+1} = W'_{emb}\left(\log softmax\left(W'_h h'_t\right)\right) \tag{13}$$

Where W'_s denote learnable weighs, $*$ represent element-wise multiplication, $\sigma(\cdot)$ is the sigmoid function, $tanh(\cdot)$ is the hyperbolic tangent function, x'_t stands for input at t-th iteration, i'_t for the input gate, f'_t for the forget gate, o'_t for the output gate, C'_t for state of the memory cell, h'_t for the hidden state.

o'_t decides what to forget in C'_t. Its' decision is up to h'_{t-1} and x'_t. In original LSTM, when o'_t decides that forgetting some information is helpful for x'_{t+1}, it will be impossible for $x'_{t'}(t' > t+1)$ to utilize the forgotten information. The longer the descriptive sentence, the worse the condition like this is.

gLSTM is able to supplement the forgotten information if necessary. Condition attention module will also help to pick the most helpful principle object for x'_{t+1}. And we call our gLSTM with principle object condition attention module as op-gLSTM. Somebody may doubt weather emphasizing the principle object so much is helpful. Our experiment will verify that the model can infer the relationship better with stronger principle object information and it will cause no trouble for extracting the scene from fea_w.

One benefit of op-gLSTM is that it allows the language model to learn semantic attention automatically through the back-propagation of the training loss. While [19] only utilize objects and locations, other semantic information, such as scenes and motion relationship, is discarded.

4   Experiments

4.1   Dataset and Experiment Setup

Dataset

We use MS-COCO dataset [9] in our experiments. The dataset contains 123287 images respectively and each is annotated with 5 sentences using Amazon Mechanical Turk. There are 80 classes included in the dataset. We use 113287 images for training, 5000 images for validation and 5000 images for testing.

Experiment Setup

The inputting image is resized to 600 pixel × 600 pixel. The training process contains three stages: (1) pre-train the object detection network (Faster RCNN) on MS-COCO dataset. (2) combine the multi-level feature extract module (a variant of the pre-trained Faster RCNN) with our po-gLSTM and train the po-gLSTM to equip it with the ability to decode. (3) train the integral model end-to-end to help our multi-level feature extract module and po-gLSTM fusion better. Four standard evaluation metrics, e.g. BLUE, METEOR, ROUGE_L, and CIDER, are used evaluate the property of the generated sentence.

4.2   Comparison Between Different CNNs Encoders

Encoder is used to extract the semantic feature of the input image. The property of the extracted feature is decisive to our caption model. To explore which encoder is more proper, we use three different CNNs in our experiments, including 50-layer and 101-layer ResNets [14] and 16-layer VGGNet [15]. Table 1 shows the experimental result.

Table 1.   Results of different CNNs encoders. All values are reported as percentage (%).

CNNs encoders	MS-COCO dataset						
	B1	B2	B3	B4	M	R	C
Ours-VGG16	70.9	53.1	38.4	27.4	23.5	51.3	88.0
Ours-RESNET50	72	54.4	39.8	28.9	24.1	52.3	90.8
Ours-RESNET101	**72.9**	**55.6**	**41.0**	**29.9**	**24.7**	**53.1**	**96**

The experimental results show that deeper CNNs achieves higher scores on all metrics. This indicates that deeper CNNs can capture better semantic features, which contain more and better information for descriptive sentence generation. The guidance of deeper CNNs is much more accurate.

4.3   Comparison to the State-of-the-Art

Several related models have been proposed in Arxiv preprints since the original submission of this work. We also include these in Table 2 for comparison.

Table 2 shows the comparison results. Our models, both VGG16-based and RESNET101-based, outperform other models at the same scale in most metrics by a large margin, ranging from 1% to 5%. Models with attention mechanism, such as ATT [6], Det+Loc [19] achieve better score than models without attention mechanism, such as NIC [7] and LRCN [16]. Det+Loc [19] also utilize the object detection network whose scores are better than the models with classification network. Notice that, our VGG16-based model gets comparable performance with FC-2 K [20] (Resnet-101 based). Meanwhile, our RESNET101-based model outperforms FC-2 K in all metrics. it's up to 5.1% in CIDER. Det+Loc is an object detection-based model, which utilize beam search (beam size 4) while testing. Without beam search, our VGG16-based model outperforms it in Blue_1 and CIDER and slightly inferior to it in other metrics. Det+Loc. introduce too much redundant information, which results in that its' poorer performance.

Table 2. Results of different caption models. All values are reported as percentage (%).

Caption models	MSCOCO dataset						
	B1	B2	B3	B4	M	R	C
NICs	66.6	46.1	32.9	24.6	–	–	–
LRCN	62.8	44.2	30.4	21.0	–	–	–
m-RNN	67.0	49.0	35.0	25.0	–	–	–
Soft-Attention	70.7	49.2	34.4	24.3	23.9	–	–
Hard-Attention	71.8	50.4	35.7	25.0	23.0	–	–
g-LSTM	67.0	49.1	35.8	26.4	22.7	–	81.3
ATT	70.9	53.7	40.2	**30.4**	24.3	–	–
RA-SF	69.1	50.4	35.7	24.6	22.1	50.1	78.3
(RA-SF)-BEAM10	69.7	51.9	38.1	28.2	23.5	50.9	83.8
(Det.+Loc.)-BEAM4	70.4	53.1	39.2	29.0	23.8	52.1	85.0
FC-2K	–	–	–	28.6	24.1	52.3	90.9
Ours-VGG16	70.9	53.1	38.4	27.4	23.5	51.3	88.0
Ours-RESNET101	**72.9**	**55.6**	**41.0**	29.9	**24.7**	**53.1**	**96**

The results of comparison are strong evidence that (1) the object detection task does have the ability to help with image caption model and our multi-level feature extract module is better suitable for caption task. (2) Our end-to-end model can help the two modules merge to get better performance in caption task.

4.4   Comparison Between Different Beam Search Size

In this section, we introduce Beam Search (BS) to replace Maximum Probability Sampling Mechanism. BS is a heuristic algorithm, which will consider more situations to generate better sentence while testing. The larger the beam size is, the more situation will be considered. We take gLSTM as comparison and Table 3 shows the experimental results.

Table 3. Results of different Beam Size. All values are reported as percentage (%).

Beam size	Model	MS-COCO dataset						
		B1	B2	B3	B4	M	R	C
2	gLSTM	70.2	52.7	38.8	28.7	24.1	51.6	88.5
	Ours-VGG16	**71.7**	**54.3**	**40.3**	**29.8**	**24.2**	**52.2**	**92.5**
3	gLSTM	70.2	52.8	39.1	29.0	24.1	51.6	88.9
	Ours-VGG16	**71.1**	**53.9**	**40.2**	**30.0**	**24.2**	**52.3**	**92.6**
4	gLSTM	69.9	52.6	39.0	29.0	24.0	51.4	88.4
	Ours-VGG16	**70.7**	**53.5**	**39.9**	**30.0**	**24.2**	**52.2**	**92.1**

From Table 3, we can see that the performance of a model varies in different beam size. Simultaneously, our model always outperforms gLSTM and it surpass Det+Loc. at beam size = 4. This is another evidence that our accurate guided model is better than other methods.

4.5   Qualitative Results

Figure 5 shows qualitative captioning results. To emphasize the effectiveness of our accurate guidance model and for fair comparison, we compare our VGG16-based model with the baseline model (NIC).

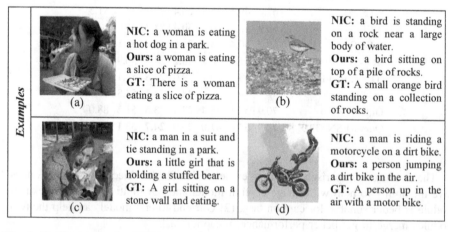

Fig. 5. Qualitative results: **NIC** is the baseline model; **Ours** means our VGG16 based model; **GT** is the ground truth.

The example images include similar colors and rare actions. Our proposed model can better capture objects in the target image, such as "a slice of pizza" in image (a) and "a little girl" in image (b). Our po-gLSTM can better capture the scenes and relationships between objects, such as "on a pile of rocks" in image (b), "in the air" in image (d) and "holding" in image (c), "jumping" in image (d). Assuredly, our model may fail in some cases, such as "bear" in image (c). It is mainly due to there is no class named as "hamburger" while training the object detection network and the hamburger is covered with a white wrapping paper, which is hard for object detection task. If the performance of object detection task gets better, our proposed model can achieve better performance simultaneously. The qualitative result shows that object detection network does do much help to capture the principle objects. Our model does not loss the information of scenes and relationships between objects but it can even do better.

4.6   Visualization of Condition Attention Mechanism

In this section, we visualize the focus of CAM. The brighter part refers to higher attention. Taking the first row as example, our proposed model focus exactly on the bus in the image while generating the word-"bus". When generating "parked", the CAM focus more on where the car and ground contact. This indicates that our po-gLSTM does have the ability to focus on the effective objects all the time (Fig. 6).

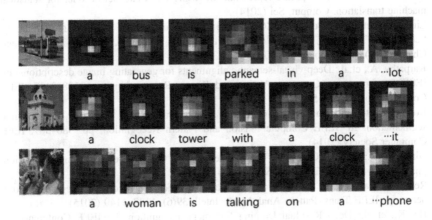

Fig. 6. The visualization of condition attention mechanism on feature maps.

5   Conclusion

In this work, we propose the framework of accurate guidance for image caption. It combines a variety of object detection network (MFEM) and gLSTM with the help of attention mechanism (po-LSTM). We show in our experiments that the proposed methods significantly improve the baseline method and outperform the current state-of-the-art on MS-COCO dataset, which supports our argument of explicit consideration of getting help from object detection task.

References

1. Kulkarni, G., et al.: BabyTalk: understanding and generating simple image descriptions. In: IEEE Conference on Computer Vision and Pattern Recognition, pp. 1601–1608. IEEE Computer Society (2011)
2. Donahue, J., et al.: Long-term recurrent convolutional networks for visual recognition and description. IEEE Trans. Pattern Anal. Mach. Intell. **39**(4), 677–691 (2015)
3. Jia, X., et al.: Guiding the long-short term memory model for image caption generation. In: IEEE International Conference on Computer Vision, pp. 2407–2415. IEEE Computer Society (2015)
4. Bahdanau, D., et al.: Neural machine translation by jointly learning to align and translate. Comput. Sci. (2014)
5. Hochreiter, S., et al.: Long short-term memory. Neural Comput. **9**(8), 1735–1780 (1997)
6. You, Q., et al.: Image Captioning with Semantic Attention. In: IEEE Computer Vision and Pattern Recognition, pp. 4651–4659. IEEE Computer Society (2016)
7. Xu, K., et al.: Show, attend and tell: neural image caption generation with visual attention. Comput. Sci. 2048–2057 (2015)
8. Cho, K., et al.: Learning phrase representations using RNN encoder-decoder for statistical machine translation. Comput, Sci (2014)
9. Lin, T.-Y., et al.: Microsoft COCO: common objects in context. In: Fleet, D., Pajdla, T., Schiele, B., Tuytelaars, T. (eds.) ECCV 2014. LNCS, vol. 8693, pp. 740–755. Springer, Cham (2014). https://doi.org/10.1007/978-3-319-10602-1_48
10. Karpathy, A., et.al.: Deep visual-semantic alignments for generating image descriptions. In: IEEE Conference on Computer Vision and Pattern Recognition, pp. 3128–3137. IEEE Computer Society (2015)
11. Ross, G., et al.: Rich feature hierarchies for accurate object detection and semantic segmentation. In: IEEE Computer Vision and Pattern Recognition, pp. 580–587. IEEE Computer Society (2014)
12. Girshick, R.: Fast R-CNN. In: IEEE International Conference on Computer Vision, pp. 1440–1448. IEEE Computer Society (2015)
13. Ren, S., et al.: Faster R-CNN: towards real-time object detection with region proposal networks. IEEE Trans. Pattern Anal. Mach. Intell. **39**(6), 1137–1149 (2015)
14. He, K., et al.: Deep Residual learning for image recognition. In: IEEE Conference on Computer Vision and Pattern Recognition, pp. 770–778. IEEE Computer Society (2016)
15. Simonyan, K., et al.: Very deep convolutional networks for large-scale image recognition. Comput. Sci. (2014)
16. Donahue, J., et al.: Long-term recurrent convolutional networks for visual recognition and description. IEEE Trans. Pattern Anal. Mach. Intell. **39**(4), 677–691 (2017)
17. Mao, J., et al.: Deep captioning with multimodal recurrent neural networks (m-RNN). arXiv preprint arXiv:1412.6632 (2014)
18. Fu, K., et al.: Aligning where to see and what to tell: image captioning with region-based attention and scene-specific contexts. IEEE Trans. Pattern Anal. Mach. Intell. **39**(12), 2321–2334 (2015)
19. Yang, Z., Zhang, Y.-J., Rehman, S., Huang, Y.: Image captioning with object detection and localization. In: Zhao, Y., Kong, X., Taubman, D. (eds.) ICIG 2017. LNCS, vol. 10667, pp. 109–118. Springer, Cham (2017). https://doi.org/10.1007/978-3-319-71589-6_10
20. Rennie, S.J., et al.: Self-critical sequence training for image captioning. In: IEEE Conference on Computer Vision and Pattern Recognition, pp. 1179–1195. IEEE Computer Society (2017)

Large-Scale Visible Watermark Detection and Removal with Deep Convolutional Networks

Danni Cheng[1], Xiang Li[1(✉)], Wei-Hong Li[2], Chan Lu[1], Fake Li[1], Hua Zhao[1], and Wei-Shi Zheng[2]

[1] Ctrip Group, Shanghai, China
dncheng@Ctrip.com, lixiang651@gmail.com
[2] Sun Yat-sen University, Guangdong, China

Abstract. Visible watermark is extensively used for copyright protection with the wide spread of online image. To verify its effectiveness, there are many researches attempt to detect and remove visible watermark thus it increasingly becomes a hot research topic. Most of the existing methods require to obtain the prior knowledge from watermark, which is not applicable for images with unknown and diverse watermark patterns. Therefore, developing a data-driven algorithm that suits for various watermarks is more significant in realistic application. To address the challenging visible watermark task, we propose the first general deep learning based framework, which can precisely detect and remove a variety of watermark with convolutional networks. Specifically, general object detection methods are adopted for watermark detection and watermark removal is implemented by using image-to-image translation model. Comprehensive empirical evaluation are conducted on a new large-scale dataset, which consists of 60000 watermarked images with 80 watermark classes, the experimental results demonstrate the feasible of our introduced framework in practical. This research aims to increase copyright awareness for the spread of online images. A reminder of this paper is that visible watermark should be designed to not only be striking enough for ownership declaration, but to be more resistant for removal attacking.

Keywords: Visible watermark · Watermark detection
Watermark removal · Deep convolutional networks

1 Introduction

Image, serving as an important information carrier for E-commercial and social media, is widely employed and rapidly spreads nowadays. In modern life, many online images are embedded with visible watermarks for ownership declaration. In order to avoid the misuse of copyrighted images, it requires to perform watermark detection upon images before we use these images. Therefore, it is necessary

J.-H. Lai et al. (Eds.): PRCV 2018, LNCS 11258, pp. 27–40, 2018.
https://doi.org/10.1007/978-3-030-03338-5_3

to develop a watermark detector that is able to automatically and accurately detect visible watermarks in images. Furthermore, as visible watermark plays an important role in copyright protection, for purpose to verify its effectiveness, a number of scientists attempt to attack it by removing watermark from images after detection. Visible watermark detection and removal increasingly becomes a hot research topic [1–6].

Developing robust visible watermark detection and removal methods remain as a challenging task due to the diversification of visible watermarks. More specifically, visible watermarks may consist of texts, symbols or graphic etc, leading to the challenge of extracting discriminative feature from unknown and diverse patterns of watermarks. In addition, the variations of the shape, location, transparency and size of the watermarks in various sorts of watermarked image makes it hard to estimate the area of watermark in practical situation.

Although researchers have extensively explored the visible watermark detection and removal problems [1–6], these works require handcraft feature from images which highly depends on the prior knowledge. Thus, developing a feasible approach that is able to tackle aforemention challenges for watermarked images remains to be an unsolved problem. Recently, despite deep convolutional networks have shown their strong performance on feature representation for computer vision problems through taking advantage of massive image data, there is a lack of deep learning method for watermark detection as well as removal, and a lack of large-scale watermark dataset. Due to this fact, we contribute a large-scale watermark dataset and further utilize deep learning to generalize the detection and removal of unknown and diverse watermark patterns.

In this work, we propose a new visible watermark processing framework consisting of the robust large-scale watermark detection and removal components. Both of watermark detection and removal are build upon deep convolutional networks. Generally speaking, we exploit the trained watermark detector to locate the area where there is a watermark, which will be cropped out and used for the removal. To be more specific, we adopt the framework of current state-of-the-art object detectors as our watermark detection basic network, which is further implemented to be suitable for detecting and locating visible watermarks in images. In the removal procedure, we cast the watermark removal into an image-to-image translation problem, where we propose a full convolutional architecture to transfer the watermarked pixels into the original unmarked pixels effectively. Finally, both components are able to collaborate together to perform visible watermark detection and removal tasks automatically and consistently.

In summary, the main contributions of this work are: (1) It is the first work that formulate the visible watermark detection as an object detection problem and adapt existing detectors to make them suitable for automatic watermark detection. To achieve this, we contribute a new large-scale visible watermark dataset with dense annotations to facilitate the lack of large-scale image dataset for visible watermark detection task. (2) We propose an integrative deep learning based framework to fully address the visible watermark processing problem including detection and removal. Moreover, extensive comparison experiments are conducted to evaluate our proposed framework and the experimental results demonstrate the effectiveness and efficiency of our proposed framework for complex visible watermark detection and removal tasks in real-world scenarios.

2   Related Work

Watermark Detection and Removal. In watermark detection and removal literature, existing methods can be divided into two categories: (a) single image schemes [1–3]. (b) stock images schemes (a large stock of images with same type of watermark) [4,5]. For single image schemes, Santoyo-Garcia et al. [1] proposed to decompose a watermarked image and then distinguish the watermarked area from the structure image. Pei and Zeng [2] utilized Independent Component Analysis (ICA) for watermarked image recovery. These methods have to extract handcraft features from the whole watermarked image, which makes it very inefficient for these methods to be implemented for detecting and removing watermarks with diverse visible patterns. As for stock image schemes, Dekel et al. [4] proposed to estimate the outline sketch and alpha matte of watermarks from a batch of images. In this case, visible watermarks are regarded as foregrounds, whose attributes are required to be the same. Xu et al. [5] proposed an watermark removal technique which assumes the pending images have the same resolution and watermark region as those of training images. Despite the stock-based approaches can estimate the outline of watermark for stock images, these methods are not suitable for detecting and removing watermarks in real-world scenarios where the images are high potentially marked with unknown watermarks or the pattern of watermarks in different images might be distinct. To overcome these challenge, we proposed a new deep learning based framework which can effectively detect and remove watermark with unknown patterns.

Object Detection. Since we formulate the watermark detection as an object detection task in this paper, existing generic object detectors are related to ours. Currently the deep learning based object detection methods can be divided into two-stage approaches [8–10] and one-stage methods [11–15]. Since the one-stage methods take privilege of their high effectiveness and efficiency, they become the mainstream of object detection. For example, YOLOv2 and RetinaNet can obtain the state of art performance in accuracy with high speed (i.e. performing real-time object detection).

Image Inpainting. Related to watermark removal, image inpainting inpaints missing regions in an image, which gains huge benefit from a variety of Generative Adversarial Networks (GAN) based models [16,17]. Different from image inpainting, in visible watermark removal, those pixels in watermarked area are not missing. They instead embedded some background information. Hence, in this work, we utilize the generator architecture to achieve the transformation between watermarked pixels and unmarked pixels, which is proved to be very effective in our work.

3 Methodology

In this work, we aim at automatically and precisely detecting unknown and diverse visible watermarks in images and exploring watermark removal in an effective and efficient way. In this section, we present our visible watermark processing framework. Firstly, a large-scale image dataset for visible watermark processing is introduced. In general, our whole pipeline can be divided into two separate modules: (1) the watermark detection module and (2) the watermark removal module. To be more specific, we illustrate our watermark detection module which is built on the existing deep learning based general object detection methods in Sect. 3.2 and the watermark removal one is detailed in Sect. 3.3. The illustration of our proposed visible watermark processing framework is shown in Fig. 1.

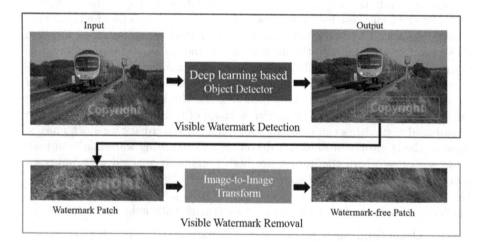

Fig. 1. The pipeline of our visible watermark processing framework. In the period of detection, the goal is to judge whether a image has watermark and locate the water-marked area (the red box). Then, we enlarge the detection boundingbox (the yellow box) and crop the watermarked patch to generate the input for watermark removal. (Color figure online)

3.1 Large-Scale Visible Watermark Dataset

At present there is no watermarked image dataset available for large-scale visible watermark detection and removal. To fill this gap, we contribute a new watermarked image dataset, containing 60000 watermarked images made of 80 watermarks, with 750 images per watermark. Specifically, the original images used in the training and test sets are randomly chosen from the train/val and test sets in PASCAL VOC2012 dataset [18] with replacement respectively. The

80 categories of watermarks cover a vast quantity of patterns, including English and Chinese, which are collected from renowned E-commercial brand, websites, organization, personal, and etc (see Fig. 2(a)). The entire watermarks are transfered into binary image with alpha channel for opacity setting. Furthermore, the size, location and transparency of each watermark in different images are distinct and set randomly. The diversity of watermarks makes our dataset more general (see Fig. 2(b)).

Another important distinction between our dataset and the conventional small-scale watermark dataset [4] is the watermarks in training set are not used for constructing images in test set. To be more particular, in existing watermark dataset, watermarks in training set and test set are exactly the same. This would lead to the situation where the watermark detector trained on such dataset can not work well on detecting unknown watermarks in images, which is impractical. Therefore, to meet the demand of watermark detection in real-world scenarios, in our dataset, watermarks in test set are different from those in training set. More specifically, train set contains 80% sorts of watermark and the test set includes the remaining.

In traditional pattern recognition tasks, object annotation is a time-consuming and tedious procedure. During generating watermarked image, we save the location size of the embedded watermark and original image at the same time. With our large-scale visible watermark dataset, it is possible to develop a significant deep learning based framework for facilitating visible watermark tasks.

(a) Examples of watermarks from our dataset   (b) Examples of images from our dataset

Fig. 2. The diversity of our proposed large-scale watermark dataset.

3.2   Visible Watermark Detection

Visible watermark detection, one of fundamental topics in the computer vision field, is essential for various important applications, such as intellectual property protection in e-commerce, copyright declaration for business intelligence, and visual online advertising, etc. In this work, instead of directly exploiting an existed watermark detector to detect watermarks at the beginning of our watermark processing framework, we consider to develop a new and more robust one.

From the machine learning perspective, watermark detection can be viewed as an two classification task, where the cropped image patches are classified into the watermark or background category. However, in real-world scenarios, images always contain various contents and the pattern, content, location, size, number of the watermarks in images are unknown. Developing a robust method to detect watermarks in images in the wild is inherent challenging and remains unsolved. In this paper, we formulate watermark detection as an object detection problem. Generally speaking, the recent deep learning based algorithms for generic object detection, e.g. Faster RCNN [10] YOLO [11,12], RetinaNet [15] are appropriate for our detection task.

Figure 1 shows the proposed deep learning based framework for watermark detection in images. To be more specific, our model takes as input a watermarked image and estimates the probabilities of all candidates with different scale and ratio at all location in the image classified as the area which is tightly covered by a watermark. Considering that the efficiency of watermark method is one of most important criterions in watermark detection, we adopt the one-stage detection methods in our watermark detection framework.

Thanks to the large-scale watermark dataset proposed in this work, our proposed watermark detector can be trained effectively. More importantly, our proposed method can detect watermarks in images effectively and efficiently under unknown condition such as the unknown watermarks in images and so on.

3.3 Visible Watermark Removal

Once the watermarks in images are accurately detected, the detection results can be used for further image-based watermarks processing such as watermark removal, watermark recognition, etc. In this work, we mainly investigate the former task, the watermark removal, and develop image transformation based method for it.

Image transformation, where an image transformation model takes as input an image and generate a different image to facilitate specific tasks, is one of the popular computer vision topics. Examples like image denoising, super-resolution, image style translation, etc., have taken significant steps since convolutional neural network serves as an indispensable foundation for these works. Inspired by the success of image transformation using deep learning technique [16,19], we propose an effective visible watermark removal system based on deep neural networks.

As shown in Fig. 3, the system consists of two components: watermark removal network and loss network. Each watermarked patch x is fed into the watermark removal network to obtain the estimated watermark free patch $\tilde{y}$. Then the $L1$ loss and perceptual loss are calculated based on the ground truth and the estimated patches.

The whole network is trained to minimize the loss function via the combination of the two during training. During the test procedure, merely a forward transformation is required via passing watermarked patch through the watermark removal network.

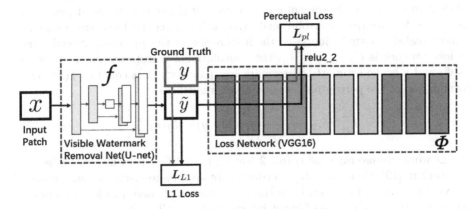

Fig. 3. The illustration of our proposed system for visible watermark removal. We leverage the U-net architecture for transferring visible watermarked patch into the watermark free one. The difference between the outputed watermark free patch and the ground truth watermark free patch is calculated using $L1$ loss, and perceptual loss is exploited for measuring the perceptual features of visible watermark. Therefore, the total loss of the watermark removal module during training process comprise the $L1$ loss and the perceptual one. The loss network for calculating perceptual loss is pretrained on ImageNet for image classification, which remains fixed during the training process.

Network Architectures. Rather than transfering a whole image pixel-to-pixel, our work focuses on partial transformation task (i.e. transfer a specific patch of a image). More specifically, pixels inside the detected area are expected to be recovered to unmarked condition, while those in unmarked area in the watermarked image will remain unchanged. Specifically, we adapt the architecture of our removal network as that of the U-net [7]. This network is mirror symmetrical in structure, with skip connection between corresponding blocks. In this way, the shallow features near to the input get combination with those high-level features so that the low-level features such as location and texture of input image can be preserved.

Objective Function. The $L1$ loss penalizes the pixel distance between the ground truth and the output, which has been proved to have good performance in matching the pixel value of the input with those of the ground truth, and synthesizing the output [16]. Hence it is adopted in our network and is denoted as L_{L1}.

$$L_{L1}(x, y) = \|f(x) - y\|_1, \tag{1}$$

where x denoted as an input watermarked patch detected and cropped from an watermarked image, y refers to the ground truth patch without watermark. $f(x)$

is the output of U-net. As $L1$ loss is calculated based on per-pixel value in a whole image, it will be huge when each pixel has a small change and the image has little difference in visual. Besides, as the perceptual loss, which has been proved to be efficient in capturing the semantic information of the source image, depends on high level feature from convolutional layer, using perceptual loss can result in a more realistic output. Supposed the feature size of the j_{th} convolutional layer of loss network is $C_j \times H_j \times W_j$, the convolutional transformation is denoted as Φ_j and $\tilde{y}$ is the estimated watermark free patch which is equal to $f(x)$. The formulation of the perceptual loss can be expressed as:

$$L_{pl}^{\Phi,j}(\tilde{y}, y) = \frac{1}{C_j H_j W_j} \|\Phi_j(\tilde{y}) - \Phi_j(y)\|_2^2. \tag{2}$$

In our work, we leverage the **relu2_2** feature from VGG-16, which is similar to the work in [19]. Consequently, in order to obtain a more visual pleasure results for visible watermark removal, we combine benefits of these two loss functions, which can keep the details of input information as well as the perceptual information. Thus, the objective function of our removal network is:

$$L_{whole} = L_{L1} + \alpha L_{pl}^{\Phi,relu2\_2}, \tag{3}$$

where $\alpha \geq 0$ is a weight for regularizing the effect of $L1$ loss and perceptual loss.

4   Experiments

In order to evaluate our proposed framework, we conduct comprehensive experiments on our large-scale visible watermark dataset introduced in Sect. 3.1. In this work, both components in our proposed framework, the watermark detection and removal modules, are evaluated and the experiments are conducted on a computer cluster equipped with NVIDIA Tesla K80 GPU with 12 GB memory. The experimental details of these two components are illustrated and analyzed individually. It should be noted that existed methods cannot handle images with unknown watermark patterns, thus they are not suitable for the case that we deal with in this paper.

4.1   Visible Watermark Detection

Settings. We presume the proposed watermark detection framework can take any recent deep learning algorithms for generic object detection. In our work, one two-stage method Faster RCNN [10] and two one-stage methods YOLOv2 [12] and RetinaNet [15] are adopted to verify our assumption. In order to make the generic object detector suitable for watermarks detection in images, we adapt the number of class to two (i.e. watermark or background), and follow the training strategy on object detection [10,12,15] to train our watermark detection networks.

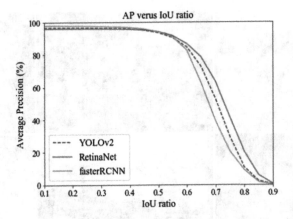

Fig. 4. Evaluation of Intersection over Union (IoU) parameter settings for watermark detection performance (AP)

Table 1. Evaluation of visible watermark detection

Method	$AP_{50:95}$	AP_{50}	AP_{75}
Faster RCNN	40.0	94.0	20.5
YOLOv2	69.9	93.4	29.4
RetinaNet	**72.0**	**94.1**	**41.4**

As we fomulate visible watermark detection as an object detection task, we follow the standard object detection evaluation metric to validate the effectiveness of our visible watermark detector, which is the Average Precision (AP) under defined Intersection over union (IoU).

Results and Analysis. Figure 4 shows the AP curves versus IoU threshold of the watermark detection models using Faster RCNN [10], YOLOv2 [12] and RetinaNet [15]. From the figure, it is clear to see that the AP of the visible watermark detection models stays at around 100% when IOU is smaller than 0.4 and the difference between these three models are very small. This promising results imply that the visible watermark model which is obtained by finetuning existing object detection model on our visible watermark dataset can be effective on detecting unknown visible watermark patterns. With the IoU increasing, the AP curves drop dramatically. However, this has limited influence on our work as watermark detection does not require very precise location of watermark bounding box in real-world scenarios. Furthermore, it is evident that the watermark detection model using one-stage method RetinaNet improves AP significantly over Faster RCNN and YOLOv2. This indicates that the focal loss introduced in RetinaNet can result in a more precise detection results for the small and unapparent visible watermarks target.

To have a rounded analysis, we present the results of visible watermark detection in Table 1. The value of $AP_{50:95}$, AP_{50} and AP_{75} are listed, where $AP_{50:95}$

Fig. 5. Visualization of detection examples on our large-scale watermark dataset with RetinaNet. The red box with the predicted watermark confidence score shown on the top of the box is predicted by our watermark detection model using RetinaNet, while the blue box shown on the bottom of the blue box is the goundtruth with IoU ratio between the groundtruth box and the predicted one. (Color figure online)

is the average of AP under IoU threshold ranging from 0.5 to 0.95. These results validate the excellent performance of RetinaNet.

In order to evaluate the performance of our watermark detector, we visualize the watermark detection results of some testing examples in our collected dataset and show them in Fig. 5. The results in the figure indicate that our watermark detector is strong enough to detect those watermarks with different scales, transparency, location and various pattern from background clutter. It verifies that fomulating the visible watermark detection as an object detection task is feasible.

4.2   Removal

Settings. For visible watermark removal, we build up our U-net with four down-sampling blocks. Specifically, the input patch and the ground truth one are cropped from the marked image and the source one according to the predicted watermark bounding box of our watermark detection model using RetinaNet. Here, the center of both cropped marked and ground truth patches center at the center of the detected watermark bounding box and the size is 1.5 times larger than that of the predicted watermark bounding box to ensure that the watermark target can be included in the cropped patches. We further round the size of both cropped patches (i.e. height and width of the patches) to be a multiplier of 16, which is required to meet the input requirement of the U-net. During training, we adopt Adam optimization algorithm with initializing the learning rate as 2e−4, and the batch size is set to be 1. The α for regulating perceptual loss and L1 loss is adjusted to 1e−6.

The metrics which we adopt to evaluate the effects of watermark removal is the same as that of [4], including Peak Signal to Noise Ratio (PSNR) and Structural dissimilarity Image Index (DSSIM), both of which are adopted to measure the similarity between the predict watermark free patch and the ground truth one.

Table 2. Evaluation of visible watermark removal

Metrics	Input	Perceptual loss	L1 loss	Ours
PSNR	20.65	29.86	30.42	**30.86**
DSSIM	0.103	0.051	0.045	**0.043**

Results and Analysis. We calculate the average value of PSNR and DSSIM over the whole test set. Table 2 gives the PSNR and DSSIM of our model using different types of loss. As shown in Table 2, our removal model can have significant improvement in comparison over the input image. Besides, the results of the combination of the L1 loss and perceptual loss is shown to be better than those of single type of loss.

As shown in Fig. 6, despite the pattern of watermarks in images shown from the first row to the fourth row is quite diverse, our watermark removal algorithm performs well on removing visible watermarks. More specifically, some watermarks are some English words or letters, while some of them are the combination of English words, Logo and etc. However, our proposed method is able to extract the invariant feature of the watermarks and generate the image patches which is almost the same as the original ones. In addition, we report the removal results of our model using different sorts of loss, which are subtle distinct. The results in Fig. 6 indicate that our model using the loss combining the L1 loss as well as perceptual loss can exploit the strength of both loss to wipe out the visible watermarks and meanwhile keep the fine details of the source images, yielding powerful reconstruction performance.

We also conduct experiments to compare the performance of different architectures. Observing the results of the encoder-decoder architecture mentioned

Input   Ground truth   Perceptual Loss   L1 Loss   Ours

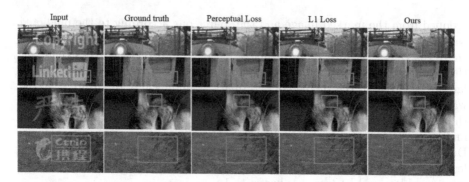

Fig. 6. Different losses induce different removal results. The last three column shows the output results trained under a different loss.

in [16] (The encoder-decoder is created by severing the skip connections in the U-Net), we find that it alters the global brightness and there exists local watermark residual in local area. Thus the watermarked patch is hard to be restored to get similar to its watermark free condition. The outputs of U-net architectures are more similar to the ground truth patches, which is applicable for our removal task. The results in Fig. 7 demonstrate that our U-net architecture is more effective, as it does not break surrounding information by allowing low-level information to be shortcut across the network.

Input   Ground truth   Encoder-decoder   Ours

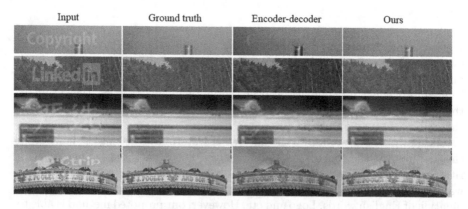

Fig. 7. Example results of different architectures and images of the groundtruth. These experimental results demonstrate that the U-net architecture can be more effective for visible watermark removal.

4.3 Discussions

Our experiments show that our proposed framework can effectively deal with the large-scale visible watermark tasks. For watermark detection, our watermarks detection model using one-stage method RetinaNet perform very well on detecting visible watermark. During watermark removal, the size of bounding box is expanded to a little larger than the size of the detected watermark patch to alleviate the effect of partial detection, and our network can adaptively transform the marked pixels to watermark free ones and do not corrode the other pixels at the same time. Therefore, setting a small IoU threshold to capture the watermarked patches as much as possible, and then expanding and inputing these patches into our removal net, can ensure the performance of our proposed framework.

5   Conclusion

This paper presents a new deep learning based framework for large-scale visible watermark processing tasks, which consist of two components: (1) watermark detection, which is fomulated as an object detection task. (2) watermark removal, which is transferred into an image-to-image translation problem. Besides, we build a large-scale visible watermark dataset for training and evaluating deep learning based framework for watermark detection, watermark removal and so on. In addition, extensive experiments are conducted to verify the feasible of our proposed pipeline. Experimental results show that our proposed framework is effective on watermark detection and removal.

Acknowledgment. Danni Cheng and Xiang Li equally contributed to this work. The authors would like to thank Dongcheng Huang and Xiaobin Chang's valuable advice on paper writing.

References

1. Santoyo-Garcia, H., Fragoso-Navarro, E., Reyes-Reyes, R., et al.: An automatic visible watermark detection method using total variation. In: IWBF 2017 (2017)
2. Pei, S.C., Zeng, Y.C.: A novel Image recovery algorithm for visible watermarked images. IEEE Trans. Inf. Forensics Secur. **1**, 543–550 (2006)
3. Huang, C.H., Wu, J.L.: Attacking visible watermarking schemes. IEEE Trans. Multimed. **6**(1), 16–30 (2004)
4. Dekel, T., Rubinstein, M., Liu, C., et al.: On the effectiveness of visible watermarks. In: CVPR 2017 (2017)
5. Xu, C., Lu, Y., Zhou, Y.: An automatic visible watermark removal technique using image inpainting algorithms. In: ICSAI 2017 (2017)
6. Qin, C., He, Z., Yao, H.: Visible watermark removal scheme based on reversible data hiding and image inpainting. Sig. Process.: Image Commun. **60**, 160–172 (2018)
7. Ronneberger, O., Fischer, P., Brox, T.: U-Net: convolutional networks for biomedical image segmentation. In: MICCAI 2015 (2015)
8. Girshick, R., Donahue, J., Darrell, T., et al.: Rich feature hierarchies for accurate object detection and semantic segmentation. In: CVPR 2014 (2014)
9. Girshick, R.: Fast R-CNN. In: ICCV 2015 (2015)
10. Ren, S., He, K., Girshick, R., et al.: Faster R-CNN: towards real-time object detection with region proposal networks. In: NIPS 2015 (2015)

11. Redmon, J., Divvala, S., Girshick, R., et al.: You only look once: unified, real-time object detection. In: CVPR 2016 (2016)
12. Redmon, J., Farhadi, A.: YOLO9000: better, faster, stronger. In: CVPR 2017 (2017)
13. Redmon, J., Farhadi, A.: YOLOv3: an incremental improvement. arXiv preprint (2018)
14. Liu, W., et al.: SSD: single shot multibox detector. In: Leibe, B., Matas, J., Sebe, N., Welling, M. (eds.) ECCV 2016. LNCS, vol. 9905, pp. 21–37. Springer, Cham (2016). https://doi.org/10.1007/978-3-319-46448-0_2
15. Lin, T.Y., Goyal, P., Girshick, R., et al.: Focal loss for dense object detection. In: ICCV 2017 (2017)
16. Isola, P., Zhu, J.Y., Zhou, T., et al.: Image-to-image translation with conditional adversarial networks. In: CVPR 2017 (2017)
17. Pathak, D., Krahenbuhl, P., Donahue, J., et al.: Context encoders: feature learning by inpainting. In: CVPR 2016 (2016)
18. Everingham, M., Eslami, S.M.A., Van Gool, L.: The pascal visual object classes challenge: a retrospective. IJCV **111**(1), 98–136 (2015)
19. Johnson, J., Alahi, A., Fei-Fei, L.: Perceptual losses for real-time style transfer and super-resolution. In: Leibe, B., Matas, J., Sebe, N., Welling, M. (eds.) ECCV 2016. LNCS, vol. 9906, pp. 694–711. Springer, Cham (2016). https://doi.org/10.1007/978-3-319-46475-6_43

Learning to Generate Realistic Scene Chinese Character Images by Multitask Coupled GAN

Qingxiang Lin[1], Lingyu Liang[1], Yaoxiong Huang[1], and Lianwen Jin[1,2(✉)]

[1] School of Electronic and Information Engineering,
South China University of Technology, Guangzhou, China
lhlqx2014@gmail.com, lianglysky@gmail.com, hwang.yaoxiong@gmail.com,
lianwen.jin@gmail.com
[2] SCUT-Zhuhai Institute of Modern Industrial Innovation,
South China University of Technology, Zhuhai, China

Abstract. Scene text recognition, is challenging due to the large appearance variances of the scene character. Recently, deep learning technique has shown its power for scene text recognition, but it requires enormous annotated data for training and it is time-consuming to manually obtain abundant data for all the categories of characters. This paper proposes a new architecture, called multitask coupled generative adversarial network (MtC-GAN), for scene Chinese character recognition (SCCR). The MtC-GAN consists of coupled GAN networks for scene character style transfer and classifier networks trained by the style-transferred data generated by the coupled GAN. To make the generated data be realistic enough for SCCR, we train the multitask networks using a new loss function that combines the constrains of encoders, generators and classifiers simultaneously. Experiments show that the proposed MtC-GAN framework is general and flexible to improve the accuracy for SCCR.

Keywords: Scene Chinese character recognition
Generative adversarial networks · Multitask training

1 Introduction

Scene text recognition (STR) has been drawing ever-increasing research interests in recent years given its potential for many applications, such as autonomous driving [1,2], license plate recognition [3,4] and industrial automation [5,6]. Although traditional optical character recognition has been extensively studied, naively adapting the technique to STR may fail to perform well, especially for scene Chinese character recognition (SCCR). The main challenge of SCCR lies in the large appearance variances of the scene character caused by style, font, resolution, illumination, projection transformation or partially occluded.

Recently, deep learning technique has been introduced into the field of STR [7–9]. The deep neural networks (DNN) consists of hierarchical nonlinear transformation, and is allowed to learn the feature and classifier with great invariant

© Springer Nature Switzerland AG 2018
J.-H. Lai et al. (Eds.): PRCV 2018, LNCS 11258, pp. 41–51, 2018.
https://doi.org/10.1007/978-3-030-03338-5_4

and discriminate properties. The developed system with DNN structure obtains the state-of-the-art performance for SCCR. However, it requires enormous annotated data to train and fine-tune the DNN-based system. Although large-scale benchmark databases have been constructed for STR and SCCR [10], it is still time-consuming to obtain abundant labels, and the large categories of SCCR may also suffer from data imbalance. For instance, in the recently proposed CTW dataset [10], Chinese character samples of common categories can exceed the 17000 entries, whereas some rare categories contain only one sample. Therefore, it would be significant to generate scene Chinese character images for SCCR using DNN architecture.

The generation of scene Chinese character images can be divided into rule-based and learning-based methods. For the rule-based scheme, Campos et al. [11] generated English characters to train a character-level English scene text classifier; Jaderberg et al. [12] create a synthetic word data generator through physical rendering process to train a whole-word-based English scene text classifier; Gupta et al. [13] proposed a fast and scalable engine to generate synthetic images of text in clutter which further consider the local 3D scene geometry, and then train a text localisation network. The abovementioned methods which are limited by their rule-based nature seems to hardly simulate all the important variances in the real-world. For example, the work of [13] is limited by the segmentation and depth prediction of background images.

The learning-based method is mostly motivated by the GAN architecture [14], which can estimate the target distribution, and then generate similar images to the real ones. Although the previous X-GAN framework can have many advantages, it can't be ensured that each samples generated by GAN methods can preserve annotation information, and the naively synthetic data generated by GAN method may fail to improve the prediction performance due to these bad samples.

To tackle this problem, we propose a multitask coupled GAN framework for scene Chinese character recognition, which generates realistic scene Chinese character and improves the classification accuracy by the generated data simultaneously. The MtC-GAN consists of coupled GAN networks for scene character style transfer and classifier networks trained by the style-transferred data generated by the coupled GAN. To make the generated data be realistic enough for scene Chinese character recognition, we propose a new loss that combines the constrains of encoders, generators and classifiers simultaneously. Experiments show that the synthetic data by our method have great visual consistency to the realistic data. Furthermore, classifiers with different deep structures, like ResNet18 [15], ResNet34 [15] or VGG16 [16], can obtain apparent performance improvement, which indicate that the proposed multitask coupled GAN framework is general and flexible to improve the accuracy for SCCR.

The contributions of our work can be summarized as follows:

- A multitask coupled GAN learning framework for SCCR, which is general and flexible to generate realistic data and improve the accuracy of the classifier by generated data simultaneously without extra human annotation efforts;

- A new loss that combines the constrains of encoders, generators and classifiers to regularize the learning of the multitask coupled GAN.
- We qualitatively and quantitatively assess the classifier performance to demonstrate the effectiveness of the proposed method.

2   Related Works

Scene text image generation is a challenging task given the presence of complex background and font diversity. Many researchers have proposed the generation of realistic scene text images. Campos et al. [11] generated English character images to train a character-level English scene text classifier. Jaderberg et al. [12] create a synthetic word data generator through physical rendering process to train a whole-word-based English scene text classifier. Gupta et al. [13] proposed a fast and scalable engine to generate clutter-text synthetic images considering local 3D scene geometry, and then train a text localisation network. However, these methods are limited by their rule-based nature. For instance, the method in [13] is limited by the segmentation and depth prediction of background images. Unlike the abovementioned methods, we propose a learning-based method to generate realistic scene Chinese character images and further improve the recognition performance.

As one of the most considerable improvements on the research of deep generative models [17,18], GANs [14] are being intensively studied by the deep learning and computer vision communities alike. A GAN basically consists of generator and discriminator networks, where the former generates samples to increase the discriminator error rate, and the latter aims to distinguish real from synthetic images. This adversarial training allows the generator to estimate the target distribution and then generate similar images to the real ones. Mathematically, the standard GAN training aims to solve the following optimization problem:

$$\min_{G} \max_{D} V(D,G) = E_{x \sim p_{data}(x)}[\log D(x)] + E_{z \sim p_z(z)}[\log(1 - D(G(z)))] \quad (1)$$

To extend the abilities of GANs, Mirza et al. [19] proposed a conditional GAN to direct data generation by conditioning both the generator and discriminator on additional information. This type of GAN has been successfully used in plenty of applications, such as image super-resolution [20,21], image style transfer [22–25], domain adaptation [26], etc.

Furthermore, conditional GANs are suitable for image-to-image translation, which has been applied for different purposes including the generation of maps from aerial photos and colorization of grayscale images. Conditional GAN is well suited for this task and many researchers have achieved great success based on it. Likewise, Isola et al. [22] proposed the pix2pix model to learn the mapping from input to output images using paired images. Zhu et al. proposed Cycle-GAN [23] based on a cycle consistency loss to break the limit of training with paired images. Liu et al. [25] proposed an unsupervised image-to-image translation (UNIT) network assuming a shared latent space. Azadi et al. [27] proposed the multi-content GAN(MCGAN) for few-shot font style transfer. Shrivastava et al. [28] proposed a simulated and unsupervised SimGAN to enhance the realism of an image simulator while preserving annotation data and demonstrated a high performance with no labeled real data. Zhao et al. [29] proposed a dual-agent GAN(DA-GAN) to enhance the realism of a face simulator output by using unlabeled real-face images while preserving identity information. Our proposed multitask coupled GAN combines the advantages of the UNIT network [25] and DA-GAN [29] to improve the quality of synthetic images and consequent classifier performance.

3   Multitask Coupled GAN

3.1   Source Data

We first propose a synthetic character generator that retrieves simple Chinese character images through font rendering, affine transformation, and perspective transformation. We denote the synthetic data generated in this way as source data x_s. By using diverse TrueType and OpenType font files obtained from the Internet, we generate plenty of simple Chinese character images with annotation information. In addition, we use real image dataset published by Yuan et al. [10] and denote it as x_t. We aim to simultaneously reduce the difference between x_s and x_t and improve the performance of a scene Chinese character classifier.

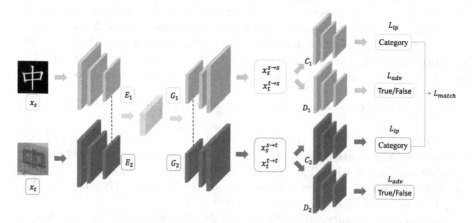

Fig. 1. Diagram of the proposed multitask coupled GAN architecture. E_1 and E_2 are two encoding functions that map images to latent codes. G_1 and G_2 are generation functions that map latent codes to images. D_1 and D_2 are adversarial discriminators for the respective domains. C_1 and C_2 are classifiers for the respective domains. L_{ip}, L_{adv} and L_{match} are the identity perception, adversarial, and matching losses, respectively. The dash lines denote weight sharing.

3.2   Coupled Generator

The same Chinese characters can present appearance variations in natural images arising from complex backgrounds and writing styles. Still, humans can easily recognize these characters, suggesting that the same characters written with different styles might share high-level semantic characteristics in the human brain. This semantic similarity can be represented by a map from characters with different styles into the same latent space, and an inverse map from a latent space into different domain images. Consequently, if the same characters with different styles are mapped into a latent space, we can generate corresponding images in two domains using autoencoders. To this end, we use concepts of coupled GAN [30] and UNIT network [25] to establish a shared latent-space assumption through a weight-sharing constraint. The architecture of the proposed MtC-GAN model is illustrated in Fig. 1 and relies on a UNIT network, where generator loss L_{unit} is formulated as:

$$L_{unit} = L_{VAE_1}(E_1, G_1) + L_{GAN_1}(E_1, G_1, D_1) + L_{CC_1}(E_1, G_1, E_2, G_2) +$$
$$L_{VAE_2}(E_2, G_2) + L_{GAN_2}(E_2, G_2, D_2) + L_{CC_2}(E_2, G_2, E_1, G_1) \quad (2)$$

where L_{VAE} denotes the variational autoencoder loss, L_{CC} denotes the cycle-consistent loss [23], L_{GAN} denotes the standard adversarial loss [14]. and D, G, and E denote adversarial discriminators, generators and encoders, respectively. More details on the loss functions can be found in [25]. The loss constraint can only add realism to synthesized images in appearance, but hardly preserves annotation information well. However, to use the synthesized data for improving classification performance, the synthesized images should preserve annotation information. Therefore, we include identity perception loss L_{ip} that is a multi-class cross-entropy loss to preserve annotation information. Then, we update the generator parameters by minimizing the following loss:

$$L_G = L_{unit} + \lambda_1 L_{ip} \quad (3)$$

where hyperparameter λ_1 control the weights of the objective terms. This combined loss both enhances the realism of synthetic images and preserves annotation data.

3.3   Multitask Discriminator

The discriminator aims to distinguish real from synthesized images. Its loss is given by:

$$L_{adv} = \log D_1(x_s) + \log(1 - D_1(G_1(E_2(x_t)))) +$$
$$\log D_2(x_t) + \log(1 - D_2(G_2(E_1(x_s)))) \quad (4)$$

In addition, we train a classifier to preserve label information of the generated data using identity perception loss L_{ip} defined as:

$$L_{ip} = \sum_n -Y_s \log D_{c_1}(x_s) + \sum_n -Y_t \log D_{c_1}(G_1(E_2(x_t))) +$$
$$\sum_n -Y_t \log D_{c_2}(x_t) + \sum_n -Y_s \log D_{c_2}(G_2(E_1(x_s))) \qquad (5)$$

where D_{c_1} and D_{c_2} are the probabilities of class n output by classifier C_1 and C_2, respectively. Y_s and Y_t are the labels of x_s and x_t, respectively. The definitions above derive in a multitask training that preserves label information of the synthetic data. In addition, we can generate any amount of training data for training supervised models.

To further constrain classifiers C_1 and C_2, we define a matching loss, formulated as:

$$L_{match} = \sum_i |D_{c_1}(x_s) - D_{c_2}(G_2(E_1(x_s)))| + |D_{c_2}(x_t) - D_{c_1}(G_1(E_2(x_t)))| \quad (6)$$

Where i is the class index. This loss improves the classifier performance. Likewise, we define another constraint in the generator to improve the quality of the generated data by training the discriminator to minimize combined loss:

$$L_D = L_{adv} + \gamma_1 L_{ip} + \gamma_2 L_{match} \qquad (7)$$

where hyperparameters γ_1 and γ_2 weigh the corresponding objective terms.

We optimize MtC-GAN by alternatively optimizing multitask discriminator and coupled generator for each training iteration until the whole network converge.

4   Experiments and Results

We evaluated the performance of the proposed MtC-GAN mainly on the CTW dataset [10]. Although the most commonly used metric for determining the quality of generative models is the inception score [31], it does not suit our objective of using the generated data to improve the classifier performance. Instead we use two complementary evaluation metrics. First, similar to [28], we deploy the 'Visual Turing Test' to evaluate the visual quality of the generated images. Second, we use generated data to train a classifier, and compare the performance among classifiers with different generation methods.

4.1   GAN Training

We used a recently released Chinese text detection and recognition dataset, the CTW dataset [10]. It is split into training, validation and testing dataset, where the validation dataset was used for evaluating all the experiments. Similar to [10], we only consider recognition of the top 1000 most frequently observed character categories. In addition, we evaluated a simple classifier to determine the enhancement provided by the generated images. Specifically, the classifier that we used is the ResNet18 [15], whereas the architecture of generator and discriminator was the same as that of the UNIT network [25]. The encoders consisted of 3 convolutional layers as the front-end and 4 basic residual blocks [15] as the back-end. The generators consisted of 4 basic residual blocks as the front-end and 3 transposed convolutional layers as the back-end. The discriminators consist of 6 convolutional layers. Then, an Adam solver [32] was adopted for the MtC-GAN with learning rate of 0.0002, $\lambda_1 = 1$, $\gamma_1 = 1$, $\gamma_2 = 5$.

4.2   Generated Image Quality

In this section, we deployed the 'Visual Turing Test' [28] to quantitatively evaluate the visual quality of the generated images and designed a simple user study where subjects were asked to classify images as being either real or synthetic. Each subject observed a random selection of 40 real and 40 synthetic character images that were randomly presented, and was asked to label the character images as either real or synthetic. We used the classification accuracy for quantitative evaluation, whose outcomes are shown in Table 1. The classification accuracy among subjects was 57%, which is very close to a random selection, i.e., 50%. Consequently, we considered that the subjects were unable to distinguish between real and synthetic images.

Table 1. Results of the 'Visual Turing test' where subjects classified real and synthetic images. The average classification accuracy among subjects was **57%**, close to the **50%** of random selection.

	Selected as real	Selected as synthetic
Ground truth real	225	175
Ground truth synthetic	169	231

Figure 2 shows examples of characters generated using the proposed method that served to quantitatively evaluate its outcomes.

4.3   Classifier Performance

The goal of this study was to use generated data for improving the classifier performance, and thus the classification accuracy was our main concern. Table 2 lists the classification accuracy using different generation methods. We can see that, naively learning from synthetic data can undermine classification accuracy due to the difference between synthetic and real image distributions, whereas the proposed MtC-GAN generation method achieves the best performance among

source characters
generated characters
target characters

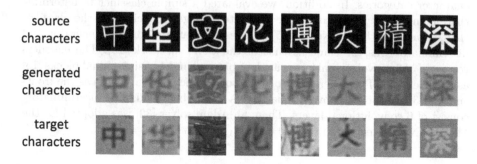

Fig. 2. The generated images using multitask coupled GAN. From top to bottom: source characters, generated characters, target characters.

Table 2. Classification accuracy of different generation methods

Generation method	Classification accuracy
Real data only	76.3%
Real data + source data(x_s)	75.5%
Real data + synthtext2014 [12]	78.5%
Rael data + synthtext2016 [13]	78.2%
Real data + SimGAN [28]	77.2%
Real data + CycleGAN [23]	77.8%
Real data + UNIT [25]	78.5%
Real data + proposed MtC-GAN	**80.7%**

Table 3. Classification accuracy of different classifiers with and without the generated images

Classifier	Real data	Real data+MtC-GAN
ResNet18 [15]	76.3%	**80.7%**
ResNet34 [15]	78.5%	**82.2%**
VGG16 [16]	81.3%	**83.5%**

the compared methods, suggesting that multitask training can improve the classifier performance.

To further verify the effectiveness of the proposed method, we use different classifiers, whose accuracies are listed in Table 3. Every classifiers using data generated from the proposed MtC-GAN exhibits the best performance. Furthermore, the ResNet18 with multitask training can have better performance than the ResNet34 [15] without multitask training. It shows that if we can generate images which are realistic enough, we can train a shallow network enjoying the comparable performance with a deep one.

5 Conclusions

We propose a multitask coupled GAN (MtC-GAN) for realistic annotation-preserving image synthesis. The generated scene Chinese character images improve the performance of character classifiers. Both qualitative and quantitative evaluations demonstrate the effectiveness of the proposed MtC-GAN method and its superior performance. The experimental results also suggest that if we can generate images which are realistic enough, we can train a shallow network enjoying the comparable performance with a deep one.

Acknowledgement. This research was supported in part by GD-NSF (No. 2017A030312006), the National Key Research and Development Program of China (No. 2016YFB1001405), the National Natural Science Foundation of China (No.: 61673182, 61771199, 61502176), GDSTP (No.: 2014A010103012, 2017A010101027), GZSTP (No. 201607010227) and Fundamental Research Funds for the Central Universities (No. 2017BQ058).

References

1. Bojarski, M., et al.: End to end learning for self-driving cars. arXiv preprint arXiv:1604.07316 (2016)
2. Chen, X., Ma, H., Wan, J., Li, B., Xia, T.: Multi-view 3D object detection network for autonomous driving. In: IEEE CVPR, vol. 1, p. 3 (2017)
3. Björklund, T., Fiandrotti, A., Annarumma, M., Francini, G., Magli, E.: Automatic license plate recognition with convolutional neural networks trained on synthetic data. In: 2017 IEEE 19th International Workshop on Multimedia Signal Processing (MMSP), pp. 1–6. IEEE (2017)
4. Masood, S.Z., Shu, G., Dehghan, A., Ortiz, E.G.: License plate detection and recognition using deeply learned convolutional neural networks. arXiv preprint arXiv:1703.07330 (2017)
5. Amato, G., Carrara, F., Falchi, F., Gennaro, C., Meghini, C., Vairo, C.: Deep learning for decentralized parking lot occupancy detection. Expert Syst. Appl. **72**, 327–334 (2017)
6. Song, X., Kanasugi, H., Shibasaki, R.: DeepTransport: prediction and simulation of human mobility and transportation mode at a citywide level. In: IJCAI, pp. 2618–2624 (2016)

7. Shi, B., Wang, X., Lyu, P., Yao, C., Bai, X.: Robust scene text recognition with automatic rectification. In: Proceedings of the IEEE Conference on Computer Vision and Pattern Recognition, pp. 4168–4176 (2016)
8. Shi, B., Bai, X., Yao, C.: An end-to-end trainable neural network for image-based sequence recognition and its application to scene text recognition. IEEE Trans. Pattern Anal. Mach. Intell. **39**(11), 2298–2304 (2017)
9. Cheng, Z., Bai, F., Xu, Y., Zheng, G., Pu, S., Zhou, S.: Focusing attention: towards accurate text recognition in natural images. In: 2017 IEEE International Conference on Computer Vision (ICCV), pp. 5086–5094. IEEE (2017)
10. Yuan, T.-L., Zhu, Z., Xu, K., Li, C.-J., Hu, S.M.: Chinese text in the wild. arXiv preprint arXiv:1803.00085 (2018)
11. De Campos, T.E., Babu, B.R., Varma, M.: Character recognition in natural images (2009)
12. Jaderberg, M., Simonyan, K., Vedaldi, A., Zisserman, A.: Synthetic data and artificial neural networks for natural scene text recognition. arXiv preprint arXiv:1406.2227 (2014)
13. Gupta, A., Vedaldi, A., Zisserman, A.: Synthetic data for text localisation in natural images. In: Proceedings of the IEEE Conference on Computer Vision and Pattern Recognition, pp. 2315–2324 (2016)
14. Goodfellow, I., et al.: Generative adversarial nets. In: Advances in Neural Information Processing Systems, pp. 2672–2680 (2014)
15. He, K., Zhang, X., Ren, S., Sun, J.: Deep residual learning for image recognition. In: Proceedings of the IEEE Conference on Computer Vision and Pattern Recognition, pp. 770–778 (2016)
16. Simonyan, K., Zisserman, A.: Very deep convolutional networks for large-scale image recognition. arXiv preprint arXiv:1409.1556 (2014)
17. Kingma, D.P., Welling, M.: Auto-encoding variational Bayes. arXiv preprint arXiv:1312.6114 (2013)
18. Rezende, D.J., Mohamed, S., Wierstra, D.: Stochastic backpropagation and approximate inference in deep generative models. arXiv preprint arXiv:1401.4082 (2014)
19. Mirza, M., Osindero, S.: Conditional generative adversarial nets. arXiv preprint arXiv:1411.1784 (2014)
20. Ledig, C., et al.: Photo-realistic single image super-resolution using a generative adversarial network. arXiv preprint (2016)
21. Yu, X., Porikli, F.: Ultra-resolving face images by discriminative generative networks. In: Leibe, B., Matas, J., Sebe, N., Welling, M. (eds.) ECCV 2016. LNCS, vol. 9909, pp. 318–333. Springer, Cham (2016). https://doi.org/10.1007/978-3-319-46454-1_20
22. Isola, P., Zhu, J.Y., Zhou, T., Efros, A.A.: Image-to-image translation with conditional adversarial networks. arXiv preprint (2017)
23. Zhu, J.Y., Park, T., Isola, P., Efros, A.A.: Unpaired image-to-image translation using cycle-consistent adversarial networks. arXiv preprint arXiv:1703.10593 (2017)
24. Yi, Z., Zhang, H., Tan, P., Gong, M.: DualGan: unsupervised dual learning for image-to-image translation. arXiv preprint (2017)
25. Liu, M.-Y., Breuel, T., Kautz, J.: Unsupervised image-to-image translation networks. In: Advances in Neural Information Processing Systems, pp. 700–708 (2017)
26. Ganin, Y., et al.: Domain-adversarial training of neural networks. J. Mach. Learn. Res. **17**(1), 2030–2096 (2016)

27. Azadi, S., Fisher, M., Kim, V., Wang, Z., Shechtman, E., Darrell, T.: Multi-content GAN for few-shot font style transfer. arXiv preprint arXiv:1712.00516 (2017)
28. Shrivastava, A., Pfister, T., Tuzel, O., Susskind, J., Wang, W., Webb, R.: Learning from simulated and unsupervised images through adversarial training. In: The IEEE Conference on Computer Vision and Pattern Recognition (CVPR), vol. 3, p. 6 (2017)
29. Zhao, J., et al.: Dual-agent GANs for photorealistic and identity preserving profile face synthesis. In: Advances in Neural Information Processing Systems, pp. 65–75 (2017)
30. Liu, M.-Y., Tuzel, O.: Coupled generative adversarial networks. In: Advances in Neural Information Processing Systems, pp. 469–477 (2016)
31. Salimans, T., Goodfellow, I., Zaremba, W., Cheung, V., Radford, A., Chen, X.: Improved techniques for training GANs. In: Advances in Neural Information Processing Systems, pp. 2234–2242 (2016)
32. Kinga, D., Adam, J.B.: A method for stochastic optimization. In: International Conference on Learning Representations (ICLR) (2015)

A Recognition Method of the Similarity Character for Uchen Script Tibetan Historical Document Based on DNN

Xiaojuan Wang[1], Weilan Wang[1(✉)], Zhenjiang Li[1], Yiqun Wang[1], Yuehui Han[2], and Zhanjun Hao[3]

[1] Key Laboratory of China's Ethnic Languages and Information Technology of Ministry of Education, Northwest Minzu University, Lanzhou, Gansu 730000, China
wangweilan@xbmu.edu.cn
[2] College of Mathematics and Computer Science, Northwest Minzu University, Lanzhou, Gansu 730000, China
[3] College of Computer Science and Engineering, Northwest Normal University, Lanzhou, Gansu, China
[4] Library of Northwest Minzu University, Lanzhou, Gansu 730000, China

Abstract. In order to improve the similarity character recognition of Tibetan historical document, this paper applied the Depth Neural Network (DNN) to similar characters recognition of Tibetan historical document, and proposed a recognition method of the similarity character for Uchen Script Tibetan based on deep learning. The effective feature learning and recognition are automatically carried out by DNN. We also introduced a sample labeling method of Tibetan historical document of Uchen Script using unsupervised clustering and constructing sample sets of the similar characters. Compared with the traditional methods such as Support Vector Machine (SVM) and Naive Bayes Classifier (NBC) based on gradient features through simulation experiment, our method can achieve better performance. The proposed method can learn feature effectively and avoid the disadvantages of manual feature selection and extraction, and it can improve recognition rate greatly. With the increasing of training samples, the recognition rate was improved more significantly. The experimental results show that the proposed method used for similar characters of Tibetan historical document Uchen Script recognition, higher recognition rate can be obtained.

Keywords: Deep neural network (DNN) · Deep learning
Convolutional neural network (CNN) · Tibetan
Similar character of Uchen script

1 Introduction

The characters of Tibetan historical document cover modern Tibetan and Sanskrit Tibetan, so the number of characters is more than 7,000. The similarity between characters of Tibetan historical document is high and there are a lot of similar characters, such as "ཨ", "ཀ", "ཁ", "ས", "ཤ", "ད", "ཟ", etc., which bring a larger technical

© Springer Nature Switzerland AG 2018
J.-H. Lai et al. (Eds.): PRCV 2018, LNCS 11258, pp. 52–62, 2018.
https://doi.org/10.1007/978-3-030-03338-5_5

difficulty to character recognition. In addition, many Tibetan historical documents are carved on the woodblock, which was engraved by hands, so the nicks are usually uneven. Therefore, the late manual inkiness is uneven, for example, the deep groove has less ink, leading to a loss part strokes of character of historical documents; Or a loss of strokes caused by the Image preprocessing of the ancient books, for example, "ཅ" "ས" "ཁ" are changed into "◼" "◼" "◼", which undoubtedly increases the difficulty of character recognition of Tibetan ancient books. At present, there is a lack of researches on the image and character recognition of Tibetan ancient books.

SVM method [1], hidden Markov model [2] and so on are more widely used in character recognition. Convolution neural network is a deep neural network which has a local connection between layers and which was put forward by American scholar LeCun. After the appearance of convolution neural network (CNN), using a variety of types of deep neural network models to analyze and recognize documents has become a research hotspot in this field. CNN has been successfully used in many areas, such as the recognition of handwritten digits, English characters, Chinese character and so on. Among 107 papers collected in ICFHR meeting held in late October 2016, whose image analysis and retrieval [3], text line segmentation [4], feature extraction [5], classification recognition processing [6] and other links involved in Chinese, English, Japanese, Mongolian, Arab, Bangladesh, etc., and more than half of the papers applied the deep learning technology. The Tibetan language includes modern Tibetan language (also known as Tibetan language or local Tibetan language) and Sanskrit Tibetan language (the Tibetan transferring form of Sanskrit). The print form of modern Tibetan characters has been studied a lot, such as professor Ou Zhu at Tibet University, professor Huang Heming at Qinghai Normal University, professor Li Yongzhong at Jiangsu University of Science and Technology, etc. And the team of professor Ding Xiaoqing at Tsinghua University studied, researched and developed the Tibetan character recognition system of practical multifont printing of more than 592 characters [7, 8], which has been well applied. The literature [9–13] shows that, for handwritten character recognition, the statistical characteristics of characters are the best, and for the off-line handwritten Chinese character recognition, gradient feature has a high recognition rate [14–16]. The researchers successfully applied the convolution neural network to digit recognition [17, 18] and character recognition [19, 20] in the natural scene, and pointed out that the convolution neural network could learn the characteristics which are better than artificial design [21, 22]. The literature [23] applied the deep convolution neural network to the recognition of offline handwritten similar characters, and the recognition rate is more significantly improved than traditional method. Therefore, this thesis proposes to use the deep convolution neural network to conduct the recognition of similar Tibetan characters. In contrast, there is no report about the application of deep convolutional neural network in the character recognition research of Tibetan ancient books.

Due to the irreproducibility of Tibetan ancient books, sample extraction of Tibetan characters can only be extracted from the document and image itself of Tibetan ancient books, and the project team has realized the preprocessing, binarization and layout analysis of document and image of Tibetan ancient books, and completed the document character segmentation. Due to the printing requirement of "soft character fine alignment and fine carving" in the Phyi dar of Tibetan Buddhism, most of the Buddhist texts adopted Uchen Script. The striking feature of Uchen Script is that the top stroke of each letter is horizontal and straight, and the base line of the character arrangement is on a straight line. See Fig. 1. The baseline (baseline 1, baseline 2, etc. expressed by the dotted line in Fig. 1) is adopted to further segment into the vowel part above the baseline. For example, baseline 1 is adopted to express the character "▼", "◥" and so on above the baseline; The part under the baseline, such as "◢", "◪", "◪", etc. There are fewer types of characters above the baseline, about a dozen types, and there are also fewer types of similar characters. This thesis mainly studies the similar characters of the characters under the baseline.

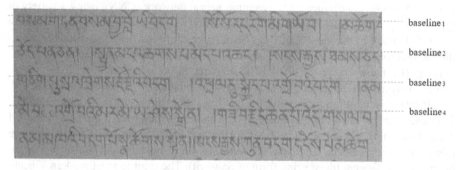

Fig. 1. Document image of Tibetan ancient books (a part)

2 Construct Sample Set of Similar Characters

In view of the current situation that there is no character sample of Tibetan ancient books, the following methods are proposed to classify and label the similar character sets.

In view of the Tibetan characters which have been segmented early, first of all, their characteristics are extracted, and three features about extraction in this paper are:

(1) Gradient 8 direction characteristics (64 D)
    First of all, the character image of Tibetan ancient books is normalized to 136 × 50, and in order to ensure the less distortion of the image, bicubic interpolation is adopted for the deformation process. Then the uniform grid of 4 × 2 is used to evenly divide the original image into 8 small grids according to the size, and then the gradient feature of character pixels in each small grid is calculated. Then, the gradient is decomposed into 8 directions in accordance with the method of Bai to form 8 D gradient direction characteristics [24], and then 8 small grids features are combined to get 64-dimensional gradient direction characteristics.

(2) Features of 8 × 8 grid (64 D)
    In the first place, the character image of Tibetan ancient books is transformed into 64 × 64, and in order to ensure a less distortion of the image, the deformation process adopts bicubic interpolation. Then, the original image is evenly divided

into 64 small grids by using the even grid of 8 × 8, and later, the percentage of the characters in each small grid in the total pixel is calculated, and the characteristics of 64-dimension are obtained.

(3) Peripheral features of characters (64 D)

The grids which are divided and extracted by using feature (2) to continue to extract the pixel periphery features from top to bottom, from bottom to top, from left to right and from right to left. The features of four directions are combined into one-dimensional features, and 64 small grids have a total of 64-D features.

After integrating the above three characteristics, there are a total of 192 D feature dimensions. Through principal component analysis, the dimension is reduced to 80 D features. k-means clustering is used to record the filename of each character and the corresponding relationship of the distance of each centroid. According to the sorting characters in the class, the former k characters which are divided into the same class and which are in a close range are divided into similar characters, constituting a set of similar characters. MATLAB is used to copy the image of similar characters in the same file, and the distance information is added before the image's original file name. Then, according to the sort of file name, the image of the same category of characters can be gathered as far as possible (Fig. 2).

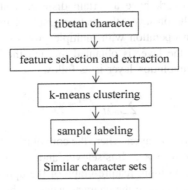

Fig. 2. Construction process of similar character set of Tibetan Uchen script

3   Convolution Neutral Network (CNN)

Convolution neural network (CNN) is a neural network which is specially used to deal with similar network structure data, such as image data which can be considered as a two-dimensional pixel grid. CNN shows a high recognition rate in 2 D image recognition application, and its network structure is highly invariant to translation, scaling, tilting or other forms of deformation. CNN directly conducts the learning and character classification for the characteristics of original image, and it doesn't need too much preprocessing and feature extraction of the original character image, so it is an end-to-end recognition system, which effectively avoid the defects of losing the details of similar characters caused by artificial feature extraction and feature selection in advance. This thesis adopts the following CNN network structure, as shown in Fig. 3.

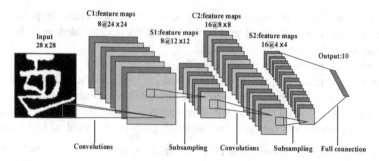

Fig. 3. CNN network structure

Convolution neural network is composed of the convolution layer and the sampling layer, and each layer is composed of multiple feature maps. Each pixel (neuron) of convolution layer is connected with a local area of the upper layer, and it can be viewed as a local feature detector. Each neuron can extract primary visual features such as direction line segments, angular point, etc. At the same time, this local connection makes the network have fewer parameters, which is beneficial to training. There is usually a sampling layer behind the convolution layer, in order to reduce the resolution of the image, and the network have a certain displacement, scaling and distortion invariance. For the convolution layer, the feature graph of the previous layer is conducted with a convolution operation with multiple group of convolution masks and then the feature graph of the layer is obtained through the activation function. The calculation form of the convolution layer is as follows:

$$a_j^l = \sigma\left(\sum_{i \in M_j} a_i^{l-1} * w_{ij}^l + b_j^l\right) \tag{1}$$

In Eq. (1), l is the number of layers where the convolution layer is; w is convolution kernel, which is a template of 5×5. b is setover, and σ is activation function, that is $1/(1 + e^{-x})$. M_j represents an input feature graph of the upper layer.

The sampling layer is to sample the characteristics of the upper convolution layer and get the same number of feature graphs. The training of convolution neural network is the same as that of traditional neural network, and it adopts stochastic gradient descent. The input layer is a character image of Tibetan ancient books, whose size is 28×28. C1 layer is the first convolution layer, which has eight feature graphs of 24×24, and one pixel (node or neuron) in each feature graph is interconnected with a region of 5×5 corresponding to the input layer. S1 layer is a lower sampling layer containing 8 feature graphs of 12×12, and each node in the feature graph is interconnected with a region of 2×2 corresponding to the feature graph in the C1 layer. C2 is the second convolution layer with 16 feature graphs, and the size of each feature graph is 8×8. The connection between S1 and C2 plays an important role in feature extraction. S2 is the second sampling layer with 16 feature graphs, and the size of each feature graph is 4×4. The last layer is the output layer with 10 nodes, corresponding to the output category, and it has a full connection with S2 layer.

4   Experiment and Result Analysis

4.1   Experiment Data

In this paper, the experimental data is the two groups of similar characters under the baseline of Tibetan characters, and each group contains 10 Tibetan character categories. The first group is a set of similar characters formed by Tibetan vertical stacks, and it is composed of "■", "■", "■", "■", "■", "■", "■", "■", "■" and "■". It is represented by G1, and there are a total of 5215 experimental samples.

The second group is a set of similar characters which are composed of complete consonant characters, and it is composed of "■", "■", "■", "■", "■", "■", "■", "■", "■", "■". It is represented by G2, and there are a total of 24,700 experimental samples.

In order to compare the performance of CNN in the recognition of Tibetan similar characters, CNN is compared with Naive Bayes Discriminant classifier and support vector machine classifier. For Naive Bayes discriminant and SVM classification, first of all, gradient 8 direction features described in Sect. 2 are extracted to get 64 D feature vector of each sample, and then the feature vector is used to discriminate and classify. For CNN, the image of the Tibetan characters is directly compressed to the image with a resolution of 28 × 28, so as to reduce the parameters of CNN, and thus improve the training speed of the network.

4.2   Experiment Process

In the network training process shown in Fig. 3, the error reverse transform and the gradient random descent method are adopted to update the parameter w and b.

J(w, b) is used to express the error function, and the expression of updating parameters with the gradient descent method is as follows:

$$w := w - \alpha \frac{\partial J(w, b)}{\partial w} \tag{2}$$

$$b := b - \alpha \frac{\partial J(w, b)}{\partial b} \tag{3}$$

α is the descent rate control parameter, and the selection of α in the experiment is determined by adopting the test method. Finally, selecting $\alpha = 1.5$ as the descent rate parameter of the system.

In order to observe the influence of different α on recognition rate, first of all, other parameters are fixed, for example, the times of circuit training are 30, because smaller number of circuit training times can save the training time, but it is enough to reflect the impact of α on the recognition rate. Different α and corresponding identification error rate are shown in Table 1.

The value of α during the experimental process is conducted according to the order from top to bottom in Table 1. The error rate in Table 1 shows that the error rate is the smallest when $\alpha = 1.5$, and it is 0.2339.

Table 1. Different α and corresponding recognition error rate

α	Error rate
0.01	0.7440
0.25	0.7440
0.6	0.3706
0.9	0.2817
1.5	**0.2339**
2	0.2798
1.8	0.2716
1.6	0.2651
1.4	0.2679

4.3 Experimental Results and Analysis

The experiment adopts CNN network structure shown in Fig. 3 and uses 64 D gradient feature to conduct Naive Bayes and SVM classification. In this paper, G1 and G2 sets are conducted with K-fold cross validation (K = 10), namely, each similar set is evenly divided into 10 parts: T1, T2, T3...... T10. Each part is taken as a test set each time, and the other 9 parts are regarded as the training set. The error rate results of G1 and G2 sets are shown in Tables 2 and 3 respectively. The experimental results show that, compared with Naive Bayes and SVM recognition method, the method based on deep neural network has a lower error rate. The reason for the poor performance of SVM and Naive Bayes is that the identification information of similar Tibetan characters is lost in the process of feature extraction.

Table 2. A comparison of error rate of 10-fold cross-validation on G1 set

Classifier	NBC	SVM	CNN
Error rate of T1	0.1288	0.0250	**0.0212**
Error rate of T2	0.1288	0.0327	**0.0192**
Error rate of T3	0.1308	0.0308	**0.0269**
Error rate of T4	0.1288	0.0327	**0.0173**
Error rate of T5	0.1385	0.0423	**0.0154**
Error rate of T6	0.1115	0.0365	**0.0231**
Error rate of T7	0.1385	0.0212	**0.0154**
Error rate of T8	0.1212	0.0250	**0.0154**
Error rate of T9	0.1231	0.0346	**0.0192**
Error rate of T10	0.1654	0.0404	**0.0231**
Average error rate	0.1315	0.0321	**0.0196**

The experimental results show that, compared with Naive Bayes and SVM recognition method, the method based on deep neural network has a lower error rate.

Table 3. A comparison of error rate of 10-fold cross-validation on G2 set

Classifier	NBC	SVM	CNN
Error rate of T1	0.0526	0.0158	**0.0117**
Error rate of T2	0.0530	0.0154	**0.0134**
Error rate of T3	0.0453	0.0109	**0.0097**
Error rate of T4	0.0555	0.0170	**0.0134**
Error rate of T5	0.0951	0.0146	**0.0121**
Error rate of T6	0.0632	0.0166	**0.0162**
Error rate of T7	0.0567	0.0142	**0.0105**
Error rate of T8	0.0551	0.0153	**0.0109**
Error rate of T9	0.0579	**0.0117**	0.0130
Error rate of T10	0.0587	0.0178	**0.0117**
Average error rate	0.0593	0.0149	**0.0123**

The reason for the poor performance of SVM and Naive Bayes is that the identification information of similar Tibetan characters is lost in the process of feature extraction.

In order to illustrate the recognition performance of this paper method, The average error rate comparison of different classifiers on G1 and G2 sets is shown in Fig. 4.

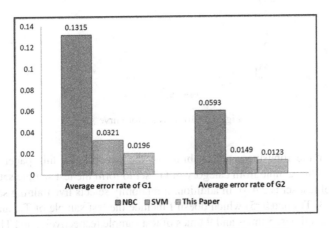

Fig. 4. Error rate of different classifiers on G1 and G2 set

Figure 4 shows this paper's method does not need human intervention in the process of training and recognition, is a kind of end-to-end approach, as well as under the condition of less training samples to achieve ideal effect.

Figures 5 and 6 shows the error curve of T10 of G1 and T10 of G2. It can be seen that CNN has smaller error in similar character recognition with the increase of the iterations.

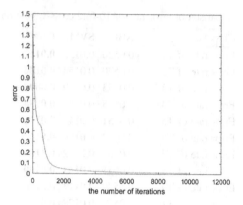

Fig. 5. T10 of G1 error curve

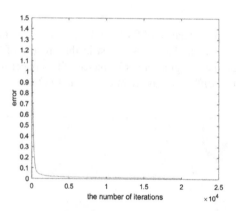

Fig. 6. T10 of G2 error curve

To further the robustness and stability of the network, In this paper randomly selects 1/10 of the sample from category of G2 set to form the test sample set (Te), and the number of test set is 2,470. In addition, it randomly selects five training sample sets (Tr1, Tr2, Tr3, Tr4 and Tr5) which doesn't include the test sample of Te, and the size are 1, 2 times, 3 times, 5 times and 9 times of test sample respectively, and The number of training sample sets is 2470, 4940, 7410, 12350, and 22230. The recognition error rate of these five sets of data is shown in Table 4.

Table 4. A comparison of error rate of different training samples in G2 set

Classifier	NBC	SVM	CNN
Error rate of Tr1-Te (2470-2470)	0.0628	0.0190	0.0510
Error rate of Tr2-Te (4940-2470)	0.0789	0.0202	0.0255
Error rate of Tr3-Te (7410-2470)	0.0846	0.0182	0.0227
Error rate of Tr4-Te (12350-2470)	0.0494	0.0153	0.0166
Error rate of Tr5-Te (22230-2470)	0.0526	0.0158	**0.0146**

Table 4 shows that with the increase of the sample size, the error rate of the recognition method based on the deep neural network gradually decreases, but the error rate of NBC and SVM method fluctuates up and down. It's clear that the network is more stable for the different sample collection, and the system has more robust robustness.

5 Conclusion

This thesis proposes that using convolution neural network to automatically learn and recognize the characteristics of similar characters of Uchen Script in Tibetan ancient books. At the same time, the similar characters of Tibetan ancient books constructed in this paper are adopted to train the model parameters, and the experimental results show that, compared with the traditional methods: (1) Deep convolution neural network can automatically learn the effective features and identify them from the pixel level, which avoids losing details caused by artificial selection and extraction of features and improves the recognition rate; (2) With the increase of the number of training samples, deep convolution neural network has a remarkable performance in reducing the error recognition rate, and the increase of training samples has an obvious effect on enhancing the recognition rate of deep neural network.

Acknowledgment. This work was supported by the National Science Foundation (No. 61772430), Program for Leading Talent of State Ethnic Affairs Commission, the Fundamental Research Funds for the Central University of Northwest Minzu University (No. 31920170142), and also supported by the Gansu Provincial first-class discipline program of Northwest Minzu University.

References

1. Gaur, A., Yadav, S.: Handwritten Hindi character recognition using k-means clustering and SVM. In: International Symposium on Emerging Trends and Technologies in Libraries and Information Services, pp. 65–70. IEEE (2015)
2. Sharma, A., Kumar, R., Sharma, R.K.: HMM based online handwritten Gurmukhi character recognition. Mach. Graph. Vis. **19**(4), 439–449 (2010)
3. Sudholt, S., Fink, G.A.: PHOCNet: a deep convolutional neural network for word spotting in handwritten documents. In: 15th ICFHR, pp. 277–282 (2016)
4. Moysset, B., Louradour, J., Kermorvant, C., Wolf, C.: Learning text-line localization with shared and local regression neural networks. In: 15th ICFHR, pp. 1–6 (2016)
5. Krishnan, P., Dutta, K., Jawahar, C.V.: Deep feature embedding for accurate recognition and retrieval of handwritten text. In: 15th ICFHR, pp. 289–294 (2016)
6. Sun, Z., Jin, L., Xie, Z., Feng, Z., Zhang, S.: Convolutional multi-directional recurrent network for offline handwritten text recognition. In: 15th ICFHR, pp. 240–245 (2016)
7. Wang, W., Ding, X., Chen, L., Wang, H.: Research on modern Tibetan language recognition in print. Comput. Eng. **29**(3), 37–39 (2003)
8. Pan, W.S., Jin, L.W., Feng, Z.Y.: Recognition of Chinese characters based on multiscale gradient and deep neural network. J. Beijing Univ. Aeronaut. Astronaut. **41**(4), 751–756 (2015)

9. Chen, K., Seuret, M., Wei, H., Liwicki, M., Hennebert, J., et al.: Ground truth model, tool, and dataset for layout analysis of historical documents. In: Proceedings of SPIE-IS&T, vol. 9402 940204-2. http://proceedings.spiedigitallibrary.org. Accessed 19 May 2015

10. Wei, H., Chen, K., Ingold, R., et al.: Hybrid feature selection for historical document layout analysis. In: 14th International Conference on Frontiers in Handwriting Recognition (ICFHR), pp. 87–92. IEEE (2015)

11. Likforman-Sulem, L., Zahour, A., Taconet, B.: Text line segmentation of historical documents: a survey. Int. J. Doc. Anal. Recognit. **9**(2), 123–138 (2007)

12. Kesiman, M.W.A., Valy, D., Burie, J.C., Paulus, E., Sunarya, I.M.G.: Southeast Asian palm leaf manuscript images: a review of handwritten text line segmentation methods and new challenges. J. Electron. Imaging **26**(1), 1–15 (2017)

13. Xiao, X., Yang, Y., Ahmad, T., Jin, L., Chang, T.: Design of a very compact CNN classifier for online handwritten Chinese character recognition using DropWeight and global pooling. In: ICDAR (2017)

14. Le, A.D., Nakagawa, M.: Training an end-to-end system for handwritten mathematical expression recognition by generated patterns. In: ICDAR (2017)

15. Wu, Y.-C., Yin, F., Chen, Z., Liu, C.-L.: Handwritten Chinese text recognition using separable multi-dimensional recurrent neural network. In: ICDAR (2017)

16. LeCun, Y., Boser, B., Denker, J.S., et al.: Handwritten digit recognition with a back-propagation network. In: Advances in Neural Information Processing Systems, Denver, United States, pp. 396–404 (1990)

17. Netzer, Y., Wang, T., Coates, A., et al.: Reading digits in natural images with unsupervised feature learning. In: NIPS Workshop on Deep Learning and Unsupervised Feature Learning, Granada, Spain (2011)

18. Sermanet, P., Chintala, S., LeCun, Y.: Convolutional neural networks applied to house numbers digit classification. In: Proceedings of IEEE International Conference on Pattern Recognition, Tsukuba, Japan, pp. 3288–3291 (2012)

19. Coates, A., Carpenter, B., Case, C., et al.: Text detection and character recognition in scene images with unsupervised feature learning. In: Proceedings of IEEE International Conference on Document Analysis and Recognition, Beijing, China, pp. 440–445 (2011)

20. Wang, T., Wu, D.J., Coates, A., et al.: End-to-end text recognition with convolutional neural networks. In: Proceedings of IEEE International Conference on Pattern Recognition, Tsukuba, Japan, pp. 3304–3308 (2012)

21. Jin, L., Zhong, Z., Yang, Z., et al.: Application of deep learning in handwritten Chinese character recognition. J. Automat. **42**(8), 1125–1141 (2016)

22. Liu, C.L.: Normalization-cooperated gradient feature extraction for handwritten character recognition. IEEE Trans. Pattern Anal. Mach. Intell. **29**(8), 1465–1469 (2007)

23. Zhao, Y., Tao, D., Zhang, S., et al.: Similar Chinese character recognition based on deep neural network under big data. J. Commun. **321**(9), 184–189 (2014)

24. Bai, Z.L., Huo, Q.: A study on the use of 8-directional features for online handwritten Chinese character recognition. In: Proceedings of the 8th International Conference on Document Analysis and Recognition, pp. 262–266. IEEE, Seoul (2005)

Research on the Method of Tibetan Recognition Based on Component Location Information

Yuehui Han[1,2], Weilan Wang[1(✉)], Yiqun Wang[1],
and Xiaojuan Wang[1]

[1] Key Laboratory of China's Ethnic Languages and Information Technology of
Ministry of Education, Northwest Minzu University,
Lanzhou 730000, Gansu, China
wangweilan@xbmu.edu.cn
[2] College of Mathematics and Computer Science, Northwest Minzu University,
Lanzhou 730000, Gansu, China

Abstract. The recognition of Tibetan is of great significance to the study of Tibetan culture while the progress of Tibetan character recognition is lagging behind. Especially when there are not a large number of available training samples, Tibetan character recognition is very difficult. So we propose a recognition method for Tibetan characters based on component location information without a large number of training samples. The proposed method includes three main parts: (1) The segmentation of character and the extraction of component which contain location information in the character; (2) Features extraction and classifier design; (3) The superposition of component after recognition and the retrieval of character. The testing results are: the recognition rate of single component is 98.4%, the recognition rate of multilevel component is 97.2%. It indicates that the method has a good effect on the recognition of Tibetan character, and it is helpful for the recognition of Tibetan documents.

Keywords: Tibetan recognition · Character segment
Component combination · Classifier design

1 Introduction

Tibetan is a minority nationality character which is used by 5 million Tibetan people in China. There are two views on the origin of Tibetan character: One view is that the Tibetan was created by a minister Tumi Sabza of Srongtsen Gampo's in the seventh Century. Another view is that the Tibetan was evolved from Zhang zhung character. Tibetan is a special kind of phonetic character, whose longitudinal unit is a character, and a character consists of at most 4 components. Syllables are the basic spelling units. Each syllable consists of at most 4 characters, as shown in Fig. 1.

Compared with other languages, the progress of Tibetan recognition research is relatively backward. However, the gap is gradually narrowing under the efforts of a lot of scholars.

© Springer Nature Switzerland AG 2018
J.-H. Lai et al. (Eds.): PRCV 2018, LNCS 11258, pp. 63–73, 2018.
https://doi.org/10.1007/978-3-030-03338-5_6

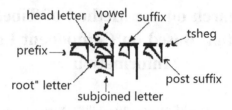

Fig. 1. Example of Tibetan structure

In Printed Tibetan: Hua Wang carried on the preliminary study of Tibetan recognition form the preprocessing, text line segmentation, feature selection and classifier design [1]. By using the segmentation method based on the connected domain and the extraction of the stroke feature based on the grid, Zhu Ou increased the recognition rate of the Tibetan [2]. In order to improve the recognition rate, Yulei Wang extracted the features of Tibetan characters based on Fractal Moments and improved rough mesh method [3]. Yuzhen Baima proposed projection method based on network lattice which is suitable for Tibetan recognition [4]. Wei Zhou proposed a Tibetan recognition method based on geometry analysis of component [5]. In Handwritten Tibetan: Heming Huang established the first off-line handwritten Tibetan recognition system [6]. Xiaojuan Cai proposed a feature extraction algorithm for off-line handwritten Tibetan characters based on multi projection normalization, which further improved the recognition rate [7]. By using HMM based on stroke type and the position relation between strokes to improve the recognition performance [8], Weilan Wang designed a complete online handwritten Tibetan recognition system [9], proposed a Tibetan Sanskrit handwritten sample generation method based on component combination [10]. Longlong Ma proposed a semi-automatic component annotation method for online handwritten Tibetan character database [11], a Tibetan component representation learning method for component-based online handwritten Tibetan character recognition [12], and a component segmentation-based recognition method for online handwritten Tibetan syllables [13]. We propose a recognition method for Tibetan characters based on component location information without a large number of training samples. The rest of this paper is organized as follows.

Section 2 introduces printed Tibetan characters and components. Section 3 gives the component segmentation method. The method of feature extraction and classifier design is given in Sect. 4. Section 5 gives recognition process and result analysis. Section 6 offers concluding remarks.

2 Tibetan Characters and Tibetan Components

Tibetan is a special kind of alphabetic writing that a character contains 1 to 4 components which are superposed up and down. Most Tibetan recognition work is based on characters, while the recognition work based on components is rarely. There are 534 printed Tibetan characters used frequently, while 231 components in totally. And the 231 component contains 51 single components, 180 deformation combination components. As for non-single that changes have taken place in the deformation combination, so we take combination components as a whole, as shown in Table 1 and Fig. 2. In fact based on components is a very useful method for Tibetan recognition work especially when the training sample is insufficient. Tibetan characters have strict distribution rules, which can help separation component easily. Based on component can also help reduce the number of classification. Character is recognized by retrieving Tibetan characters database after the components are recognized.

Table 1. Example of Tibetan characters database.

ID	Tibet	TibetOrder	Sort	Code
144	ཨྲ	82	1	41
145	ཨྲ	82	2	3
146	ཨྲ	82	3	161

Table 1 is a character example in Tibetan characters database, "TibetOrder" is the sequence number of the character in database, "Tibet" is a character, "ID" is the database record number, "Sort" is the layer information of a component in a character, and "Code" is the sequence number of component in the template. Figure 2 is all Tibetan components which contain 51 single components and 180 deformation combination components.

We proposed a recognition method for Tibetan characters based on components location information. The stages of the proposed method are shown as follow.

(1) After the size transformation, the segmentation of the above vowel, the segmentation of the below vowel and the segmentation of intermediate component, the component containing location information are obtained.
(2) Feature extraction and classifier design.
(3) Calculate the matching degree using the Euclidean distance, screen out the top-ten matching degree and the corresponding components.
(4) According to the recognition result of each component, retrieve and find out the corresponding character in database.

3   Component Segmentation

Component segmentation based on the writing standard of Tibetan character, which follow the sequence of above vowel, below vowel and intermediate component. The component segmentation process is shown in Fig. 1.

In Fig. 3, "Above" indicates above vowel, "Below" represent below vowel and "Single" indicates single intermediate component, "Double" refers to double intermediate component.

Fig. 2. All Tibetan components we used.

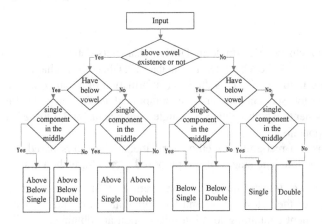

Fig. 3. Component segmentation process

3.1 Above Vowel Segmentation

The above vowel is located on the baseline of the Tibetan character, the top 1/4 part of an image. The above of the baseline is empty without above vowel. The specific algorithms are as follows.

Step 1: Above vowel judgment.

The statistical number of handwriting points in the 1/5 section above the image, and the numbers is replaced by "sup". Column projection on the 1/5 section above the image, Statistical the numbers that Greater than zero, and the numbers is replaced by "tnum". The method of judgment is shown in Fig. 4, "Cnum" represent the numbers of columns. Experimental verification, when T is 5, there is the best result.

Step 2: Find the segmentation point.

Image line projection, and the point near "Rnum/4", which has minimum projection value and has the maximum rate is the segmentation point. "Rowsnum" indicate the numbers of lines.

Step 3: Above vowel segmentation.

Image segmentation based on segmentation point. Example of above vowel segmentation is shown in Fig. 5.

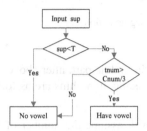

Fig. 4. Above vowel judgment

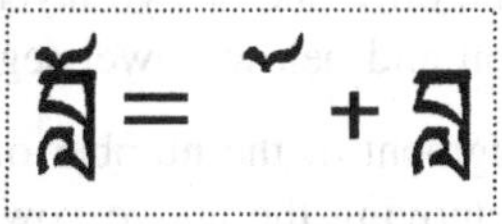

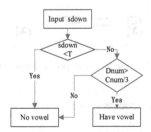

Fig. 5. Example of above vowel segmentation

3.2   Below Vowel Segmentation

The below vowel is located in the underneath, 1/4 part of image. The specific algorithms are as follows.

Step 1: Below vowel judgment.

The statistical number of handwriting points in the bottom 1/5 section of the image is replaced by s*down*. Column projection on the 1/5 section bottom the image, Statistical the numbers that Greater than zero, and the numbers is replaced by "dnum". The method of judgment is shown in Fig. 6.

Fig. 6. Below vowel judgment

The numbers of "Cnum" indicate the number of columns.

Step 2: Find the segmentation point.

Projection in the right half of the image, and the point near "4*Rnum/5", the segmentation point is supposed to have minimum projection value. "Rnum" indicate the numbers of lines.

Step 3: Below vowel segmentation.

Starting from the right side of the image, if connected to a below vowel, disconnect based on the segmentation point. If not connected, search the segmentation path along the contour of below vowel. Figure 7 is the Example of below vowel segmentation.

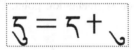

Fig. 7. Example of below vowel segmentation

Intermediate component Segmentation

There are only one or two layers of components in middle part, after above vowel segmentation and below vowel segmentation. The specific algorithms are as follows.

Step 1: Judgment of the number of layers.

After removing the above vowel and below vowel, assume the number of hand-writing points in the top half of the image is N, in the bottom half of the image is M. Single component if $M/N < T_3$, the middle part is called single component, and it is called double component under the condition of $M/N > T_3$. The experiment proves that the result is best when M is 0.9.

Step 2: Find the segmentation point.

Projection the image, and the point near the middle position of the image, which has minimum projection value is the segmentation point.

Step 3: Intermediate component segmentation.

Image segmentation is based on segmentation point. Example of intermediate component segmentation is shown in Fig. 8.

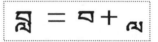

Fig. 8. Intermediate component segmentation

3.3   Special Circumstances Process

(1) Sometimes the segmentation of above vowels may makes mistakes, as is shown in Fig. 9. In this case we can use the minimum rectangle to extract the correct top component. As is shown in Fig. 10.

(2) Sometimes the deformation combination of some components will be considered as a single component, which is shown in Fig. 11. So we consider the result of the deformed combination as a component and increase the number of components in the template.

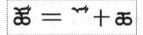 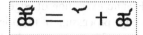

Fig. 9. Error segmentation example   **Fig. 10.** Correct segmentation example

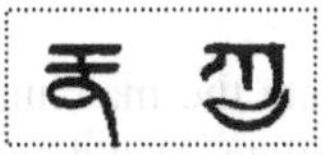

Fig. 11. Component deformation combination

4 Feature Extraction and Classifier Design

4.1 Component Feature Extraction

168 features are extracted altogether, and the images involved are original component image, remove position information image, skeleton image and edge image. As is shown in Fig. 12(a)–(d). All image normalization, 100 rows and 50 columns.

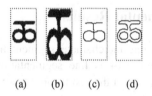

(a)   (b)   (c)   (d)

Fig. 12.   (a) (b) (c) (d) Image used to extract feature

The feature extraction algorithm of the component is as follows.

Step 1: Feature extraction of original image

The original image refers to the component image come form template or character segmentation. The original image contains the location information of the component distribution. And the distribution information of different components is different. Four features are extracted from the original image: The ratio of black pixel points, the number of rows with black pixel points, the position of first and the last row with black pixel points.

Step 2: Feature extraction of remove position information image

After minimum rectangle frame processing, image extends to the original size. And the image is divided into 16 parts using an elastic grid. 23 features are extracted from the remove position information image: The ratio of black pixel points, position of grid line and the position of first black pixel point per line in each part.

Step 3: Feature extraction of skeleton image

After skeleton processing of the original image, we get the skeleton image. 41 features are extracted from the skeleton image: rough periphery and inner profile.

Step 4: Feature extraction of edge image

After edge processing of the original image, we get the edge image. And the image is divided into 25 parts averagely. Statistical directional line information in each part and 100 features are extracted.

4.2 Classifier Design

Euclidean distance is used to calculate the matching degree between the test components and the components in the template. D_i indicate the matching degree between the test components and the i-th components in the template. And the range of number "i" is 1 to 231. As shown in (1).

$$D_i = \sum_{j=1}^{m} (x_j - x_{i,j})^2 \tag{1}$$

Where m indicate the total number of feature values, x_j and $x_{i,\,j}$ represents the j-th feature value of test component and the j-th feature value of i-th components in the template.

5   Analysis of Experimental Results

The method is carried out after line and character segmentation. Figure 13 is a part of the Tibetan document image. Figure 14 is line segmentation results. Figure 15 is the recognition results of Fig. 14(a), and the results are "གདན་ས་བཀྲ་ཤིས་ལྷུན་པོ།". It can be seen from the recognition example that our method has a satisfactory recognition result. For the experiments 100 Tibetan printed document images are used, and the recognition rate of single component is 98.4%, the recognition rate of multilevel component is 97.2%.

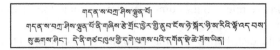

Fig. 13. Tibetan printed document example

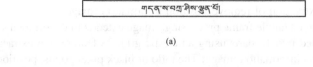

(a)

(b)   (c)

Fig. 14. (a) (b) (c) line segmentation results

Character	Component segmentation result	Recognition results Top1 ->Top10									
ག	ག	ག	ས	ན	ནུ	ཀ	དྲ	ཤ	ཥ	ལ	ཨ
ད	ད	ད	ཉ	ད	ཀ	ར	ཀྱ	ག	ཡ	ར	ན
ན	ན	ན	ནུ	ཏ	ན	ས	ད	ཏ	ཟ	ག	ཏ
·	·	·	ཙ	ཚ	ཀ	ᘇ	རྒྱ	ᘡ	ᘭ	ᘭ	ᘶ
ས	ས	ས	པ	ག	ལ	ས	ཉ	ཤ	ད	ཥ	འ
·	·	·	ཙ	ᘇ	ཀ	ཚ	རྒྱ	ᘭ	ᘳ	ᘭ	ᘶ
བ	བ	བ	ཕ	ཐ	ད	ན	ཟ	ཟྭ	ཆ	ས	འ
ཀྱ	ཀྱ	ཀྱ	ཟ	ཀྱ	ཥ	ན	ད	བ	ནྱ	ᘭ	ས
·	·	·	ᘇ	ཙ	ཀ	ཚ	རྒྱ	ᘡ	ᘭ	ᘭ	ᘶ
ཉི	ཉ ི	ཉ	ᘱ	ᘯ	ᘲ	ᘲ	ᘮ	ᘮ	ᘲ	ᘸ	ᘼ
ས	ས	ས	ལ	པ	ག	ས	ཥ	ད	ཉ	ལ	འ
·	·	·	ᘇ	ᘈ	ཀ	ᘊ	རྒྱ	ᘭ	ᘳ	ᘭ	ᘲ
སྐྱ	ལ ྲ ྑ	སྐྱ	ᘉ	ལ	ᘋ	ᘌ	ᘍ	ᘎ	ᘏ	ᘐ	ᘑ
ན	ན	ན	ནྲ	ན	ཏ	ས	ག	ཏ	ད	ནྲ	ས
·	·	·	ᘇ	ᘈ	ཀ	ᘊ	རྒྱ	ᘭ	ᘳ	ᘭ	ᘲ
པྲ	ᘟ ᘠ	པྲ	པྲ	པྲ	ᘢ	པྲ	ᘤ	ᘥ	པ	ᘧ	ᘨ
།	།	།	·	ན	ག	ཏ	ད	ག	ཥ	ᘭ	ᘶ

Fig. 15. Recognition example

After analysis, we can see that there are two main reasons for wrong recognition. One is caused by the line or character segmentation error, which may cause some character information to lose or increasing noise. And another is caused by components segmentation error, which segmentation points are judged mistakenly. Wrong segmentation point cause wrong segmentation results and lead to wrong recognition results certainly, which is the reason why multi-layer character recognition rate is lower than single-layer character.

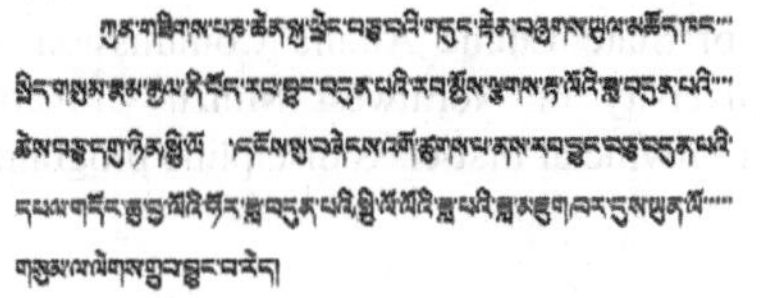

ཀུན་གཞིན་འབྲས་ཆེན་སྐུ་བཞི་བདུང་ཏྲེན་ནརྩུགས་ལ་མཆོད་དང་…
སྐྲིད་གསུམ་རྣམ་རྒྱལ་ནི་ཕྲོད་རབ་བྲང་འདུན་རབ་སྟོབ་གྲགས་ཀ་འོ་ཞི་རྒྱ་འདུན་པའི་…
ཆེམ་འབྲད་དུ་ཉི་ནུ་ཤྱོ། ། རྲིས་ལ་འབྲེ་ལྲ་འགྲ་རྣམ་ལ་ཀྲ་རབ་རྒྱལ་འདུན་པའི་…
དཔལ་ས་གདོན་ཤྲ་ཕྲ་ཡོངི་ཕྲ་རྒྱ་བདུ་ཤ་པའི་ཐ་ཡཚི་པ་ལ་རྐུ་རྣལ་ད…
གཤུས་ལ་ཡོགས་ལ་རྒྱ་ལྲུང་བ་རྲོ།

དྲུའི་ཕྱས་ཀྲུབ་གྲུ་ནུ། ཀྲུ་རྒྱོ་དྲ་ཀི་རྒྱུ་རྩུ་དྲ་ནུ། ། གང་ཤུ་ཟྲི་ཚོ་གི་ཀ་རྲུ་ལ་ཕྲུ་ལ་ནྲ་ཀུ་ཡ་ཀ་ཤ་གྲུ་རྒྱུ་ཀ་ལ་ཤ་ནྲ་རྲ་འ…
དྲ་རྲུ་ཚུ།ཤ་ཤ་ན་བ་ནུ་ཡ་ཀ་ཀ་ཡྲ་ན་རྲ་ཚ་ཚ་ཀ་ཡ་ཕྲ་ནྲ་རྲ་ནུ་ཀ་ཀ་ཡྲ་ཀ་རྲི་ཀ་རྲ་ཐ་ཀ…
དྲི་དྲི་ཕྲི་ཀ་རྲ་ན་ག་ཕྲི་ཤ་ཀྲི་ཕྲི་ཀ་ཤ་རྲ་ཀ་ཤ་ཐ་ཡ་ཀ་ར་ར་ཀྲ་ན་ཀ།ཀ་ན་ག་ན་ར་རྒྱ་ཀྲུ་ཤ…
ཀྲུ་ ཕྲི་ཤ་ཀྲུ། ཀ་རྲི་ཀྲ་ཀ་ཡ།ཤ་ན་ཀྲི་ཀྲུ་ཡྲི་ཤི།ཤ་ན་ཀྲི་ཀ་ཤ་ཀྲི་ཕྲི་ཕྲུ་ཀྲི་ཀྲུ་ཡྲི།ཀ་ན་ཀྲི་ཀྲི་ཀྲུ་ཤི…
ཤ་ན་ནྲ་ཀྲུ་ཀི་ཤྲི།ཤ་ན་ཀྲུ་ན་ན་ཀྲུ།ཤ་ན་ན་ཀྲུ་ཤ་ཕྲི་ཕྲུ་ཕྲི་རྲ་ནྲ་རྲི།

Fig. 16. Black body 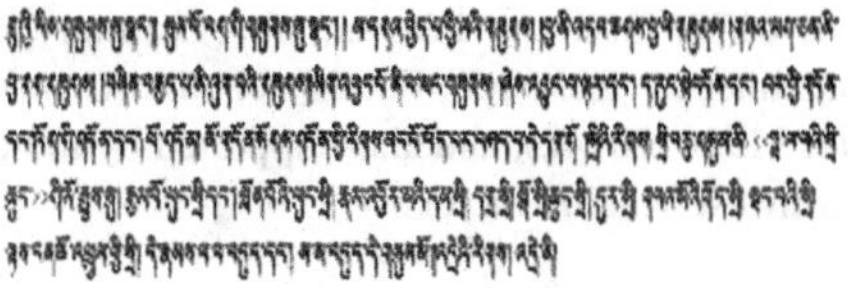   **Fig. 17.** Long body

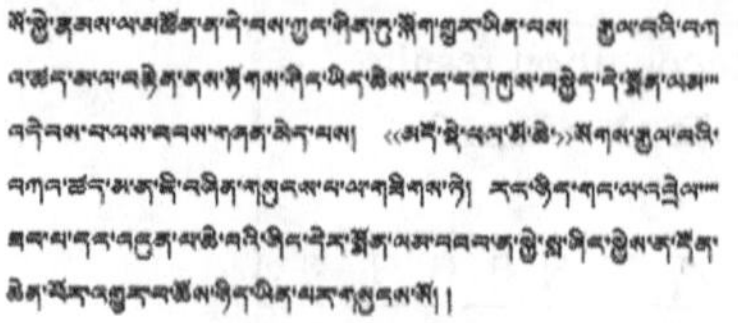

ཨོ་སྐུ་རྣམས་ལ་མཆོག་ཏུ་དགའ་བའི་ཀུན་ཡིད་ཀུ་ཙིག་ཀྲུང་ཨིག་ལས། རྒྱལ་བའི་ལན།
འདུལ་འམ་ལ་ནི་ནེ་ནགས་ཉ་ནགས་ཉེན་ཨིག་ཙིམ་ལ་ནལ་ན་ཀྲུ་ལ་ལ་བྱེ་ན་ཐེག་ལས་
འདི་ནས་ལ་ལ་ས་ལ་ལ་ལ་ན་ནན་ཉ་ཨིན་ལ། 《ཨིན་ཙི་ལ་ལ་ཨིན་ཨ》 སྐ་ལ་རྒྱ་ལ་ན།
བ་ག་ན་ཙན་ལ་ན་ལ་བྱི་ན་ཉི་ན་རྒྱ་ལ་ལ་ལ་ལ་ན་ཉི་ན་ཉ། ར་ན་ཉི་ལ་ན་ལ་ན་ཉི་ལ་—
ཧ་ལ་ལ་ན་ན་ཙ་ལ་ན་ལ་ན་ཨི་ཨིན་ནི་ན་ཉ་ཉ་ལ་ལ་ན་ལ་ན་ཉ་རྒྱ་ཨིན་ཉ་ཉ་ན་ཉ།
ཉི་ན་ལ་ལ་ཙ་ན་ཙ་ལ་ཉ་ན་ཨི་ལ་ན་ཉ་ན་ལ་ཉ། །

ར་ན་ས། །ར་ན་ཉ་ཉ་ཉ་ལ་ཉ་ན་ཉ་ཉ་ན། །ཨ་ན་ཉ་ཉ་ཉ་ཉ་ཉ་ན་ཉ་ཉ། །ཉ་ན་ཙ་ན—
ཉ་ན་ཉ་ཉ་ལ་ན་ན་ན། ། ཉ་ན་ཉ་ན་ཉ་ཉ་ཉ་ན་ཉ་ན། །ན་ན་ཉ། ཉ་ན་ཉ་ཉ་ན་ཉ། ཉ་ན་ཉ་ཉ—
ཉ། ཉ་ན་ཉ་ན་ཉ་ཉ། ཉ་ན་ཉ་ན་ཉ་ཉ་ན་ན་ཉ་ན་ཉ་ན་ཉ་ཉ་ཉ་ཉ་ཉ་ཉ། ཉ་ན་ཉ—
ཉ་ན་ན་ན། ༼ཉ་ན་ཉ་ན་ན་ཉ༽ ཉ་ན་ཉ་ན་ན།

Fig. 18. Round body 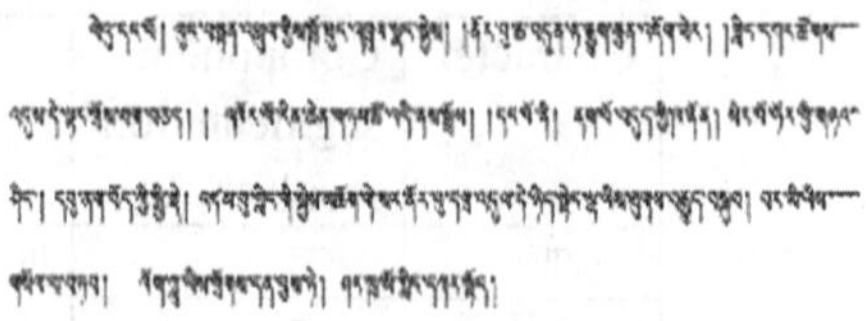   **Fig. 19.** Bamboo body

We also tested four other Tibetan fonts that include Black body (see Fig. 16), Long body (see Fig. 17), Round body (see Fig. 18) and Bamboo body (see Fig. 19), which recognition rate is 96.3%, 92.1%, 95.8% and 93.3% in the 50 sets of test samples. From the test results, we can see that the recognition effect of Black body and Round body is better than Long body and bamboo body. This is because that the change of Long body and Bamboo body is larger than that of Black body and Round body compared with the commonly used Tibetan fonts, which is the template we use. So it is easy to make mistakes when components are segmented, which lead to the component contain noise or some information lost. And then the result of the character recognition is wrong. Although these Tibetan fonts are slightly different from the commonly used Tibetan fonts, but the recognition rate has not been greatly affected. This also can prove that the characteristics extracted are effective.

6 Conclusions

This paper propose a recognition method for Tibetan characters based on component location information when lack a large number of training samples. The main work includes: the extraction of component which contain location information, features extraction based on four kinds of images, classifier training, superposition of component and the retrieval of character based on component location information database. The single-layer character recognition rate for this method is 98.4%, and 97.2% for multi-layer character. It is found that the effect of component segmentation directly affects the recognition of character. So the optimization of component segmentation algorithm is the focus of further research.

Acknowledgements. This work was supported by the National Science Foundation (No. 61772430), the Program for Leading Talent of State Ethnic Affairs Commission, the Fundamental Research Funds for the Central University of Northwest Minzu University (No. 31920170142), and also supported by the Gansu Provincial first-class discipline program of Northwest Minzu University.

References

1. Wang, H., Ding, X.Q.: Multi-font printing Tibetan character recognition. J. Chin. Inf. Process. **17**(6), 47–52 (2003)
2. Drup, N., Ren, P., Sanglangjie, D.: Study on printed Tibetan character recognition. Comput. Eng. Appl. **48**(1), 55–62 (2009)
3. Li, Y.Z., Wang, Y.L., Liu, Z.Z.: Study on printed Tibetan character recognition technology. J. Nanjing Univ. **48**(1), 55–62 (2012)
4. Baima, Y.Z.: Research on feature extraction of Tibetan characters. Comput. Knowl. Technol. **28**(1), 6362–6364 (2013)
5. Zhou, W., Chen, L.: Tibetan recognition based on geometric shape analysis. Comput. Eng. Appl. **48**(18), 201–205 (2012)
6. Huang, H.M.: Research on recognition of off-line handwritten Tibetan character, pp. 19–34. Southeast University (2014)
7. Cai, X.J., Huang, H.M.: Feature extraction of offline handwritten Tibetan characters based on multiple projections. Comput. Technol. Dev. **26**(3), 93–96 (2016)
8. Liang, B., Wang, W.L., Qian, J.J.: Application of hidden Markov model in on-line recognition of handwritten Tibetan characters. Microelectron. Comput. **26**(4), 98–100 (2009)
9. Research on online handwritten Tibetan recognition input: W.L. Wang. Sci. Technol. Achiev. China **11**, 36–38 (2012)
10. Wang, W.L., Lu, X.B., Cai, Z.Q.: Online handwritten sample generated based on component combination for Tibetan-Sanskrit. J. Chin. Inf. Process. **31**(5), 64–73 (2017)
11. Ma, L.L., Wu, L.: Semi-automatic Tibetan component annotation from online handwritten Tibetan character database by optimizing segmentation hypotheses. In: 12th International Conference on Document Analysis and Recognition, pp. 1340–1344 (2013)
12. Ma, L.L., Wu J.: A Tibetan component representation learning method for online handwritten Tibetan character recognition. In: 14th International Conference on Frontiers in Handwriting Recognition, pp. 317–322 (2014)
13. Ma, L.L., Wu, J.: Online handwritten Tibetan syllable recognition based on component segmentation method. In: 13th International Conference on Document Analysis and Recognition. pp. 46–50 (2015)

Research on Text Line Segmentation of Historical Tibetan Documents Based on the Connected Component Analysis

Yiqun Wang[1], Weilan Wang[1(✉)], Zhenjiang Li[1], Yuehui Han[1,2],
and Xiaojuan Wang[1]

[1] Key Laboratory of China's Ethnic Languages and Information Technology
of Ministry of Education, Northwest Minzu University,
Lanzhou 730000, Gansu, China
wangweilan@xbmu.edu.cn
[2] College of Mathematics and Computer Science, Northwest Minzu University,
Lanzhou 730000, Gansu, China

Abstract. Text line segmentation is one of the critical content in handwriting documents recognition especially in the historical documents' analysis and recognition. Because of the low quality and the complexity of these documents (background noise, scattered character, touching components between consecutive lines), automatic text line segmentation remains to be a hot spot for researching. In this paper we propose a new method to segment the text line from the historical Tibetan scripture "kangjur" of the Beijing version on the paper by means of woodcut. This method first performs document image skew detection and correction, using projection profiles to get the baseline of text line, then the connected component is allocated to text line according to the location relationship. For some connected components, analyzing their location and sharp to assign these connected components correctly. This method using connected component instead of pixels, avoiding the noise generated by splitting characters. Experiments show that this method is effective in copes with touching text lines and promising in text line segmentation from historical Tibetan document.

Keywords: Historical Tibetan document · Kangjur · Text line segmentation
Component analysis · Location · Sharp

1 Introduction

The Tibetans have a large number of historical documents; most of them are stored in temples. Those historical documents are exist in the form of scriptures for a very long time. It is urgent to protect and reuse them by using digital technology because of the deterioration of the quality of the historical documents. Using Optical Character Recognition (OCR) technology to converts the historical Tibetan documents into text files. The text files stored in the services is not only appropriate preserved but also convenient for reusing those precious historical documents. In document processing field, the segmentation is essential for document recognition which it needs several steps of binarization, layout analysis, text blocks extraction, text lines and words segmentation

© Springer Nature Switzerland AG 2018
J.-H. Lai et al. (Eds.): PRCV 2018, LNCS 11258, pp. 74–87, 2018.
https://doi.org/10.1007/978-3-030-03338-5_7

and character recognition. The degraded historical documents (e.g. ink stains, torn pages, overlapped/touching character, broken stroke etc.) make a challenge for the text line segmentation task. The variation of the interline distance and the baselines undulation between lines or even along the same text line. The touching characters between adjacent text lines appear frequently in Tibetan documents. The whole characters may be divided into several parts because of broken stroke. All above greatly complicates the task of the text lines segmentation from historical handwritten document.

In this paper, we focus on the extraction of text lines from historical Tibetan documents and we propose a method based on the analysis of the location and shape of the connected component. This method cannot totally solve the problem of segmentation, but we try to reduce the error as much as possible to extract text line complete. For text line extraction of historical Tibetan documents, a few researche have been done such as: based on baseline detection method [1] and contour curve tracking method [2]. Other common text line extraction methods also include: projection-based method [3], Hough-transform [4], smearing method [5], clustering approach [6, 7].

In [1] the baseline is getting by template matching, pruning the salient strokes and closing operation, then touching characters is detecting and splitting, the text-line is extracted according to baseline and split position, this method can deal with the touching characters and fluctuating text lines. However, this method does not consider broken strokes, so it is inadequate for some historical document image with a large number of broken strokes.

In [2] the text line segmentation method based on contour tracking is proposed. The text line is extracted by the contour from the document image which comes from the constructed connected component. The method combine the barycentre coordinates of the connected component to form the curve line and the separated components are assigned to the corresponding text line by the barycentre gravity later. The text line is obtained by the contour curve of the text line. This method is innovative but the performance is not satisfactory when a document image with many touching characters is segmented.

Projection-based method [3] is most commonly used for the text line segmentation especially in printed or slightly document. The projection value is computed by summing the values of pixel in the foreground in horizontal axis of each line. The text lines is segmented by straight lines with suitable positions and directions, this method is not suitable for historical Tibetan document as there is no obvious line gap. According to the layout of the Tibetan Scripture "Kangjur", the direction of the text lines is approximately horizontal parallel, so this method can be used to find the baseline of the text lines.

Hough-based method [4] is proper to detect text lines which are usually parallel in certain areas. Smearing method [5] enlarged area of black pixels, the white space between the black pixels is filled with black pixels if their distance is within a predefined threshold. But this method is not suitable for historical Tibetan document. Because some vertical stroke is overlong that smearing horizontal will produce more touching components.

Clustering method [6, 7] usually divides a picture into several connected components, blocks or other units according to some features, and then aggregates these units to form alignments according to some rules. Considering that there are a lot of touching characters in historical Tibetan documents, it is very difficult to assign the characters to the correct text lines in this way. Thus, this method is not suitable for text line segmentation from historical Tibetan documents.

The paper is organized as follows: in Sect. 2, our method is described. In Sect. 3 the proposed method to segment text lines is detailed. Section 4 present the experimental results and discuss. Section 5 describes conclusions and future work.

2 Our Method

Tibetan character can be regarded as a kind of string composed of basic characters and characters in the vertical direction [8] (see Fig. 1). The authentic historical Tibetan document not only have lots of touching characters between adjacent lines as the height of the character is inconsistent but also have lots of broken strokes than other languages. The touching characters between adjacent line, the separated upper and lower vowels and the broken strokes make the text-line segmentation more complex (see Fig. 2). At present, there is no satisfactory segmentation method for the authentic historical Tibetan document of wooden printing.

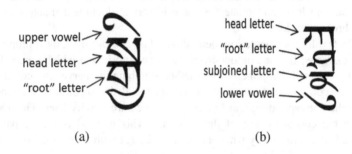

(a)   (b)

Fig. 1. (a) Character with upper vowel (b) character with lower vowel.

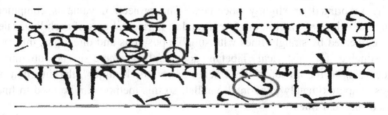

Fig. 2. Partial image with slanted baseline, separated character, overlong and touching characters.

We can see the characters in the historical Tibetan document are very close to each other because of the limited area of the document and there is no obvious gap between adjacent lines. The historical document images have large number of touching and overlapped characters and variety of broken strokes which are the main challenge to extract text lines accurately.

In order to extract the text-line completely from handwritten, degraded, historical Tibetan documents, we present a text-line segmentation method which combine the row projection location analysis and shape analysis of connection components. Our method stems from the idea that the text line is composed of a set of location related components. The task of text line segmentation is to find such a set of components and extract them from the document image to form a text line.

Our method detects the input document image whether the image is skew or not and perform skew correction if it is. Then the position of baseline is obtained using projection method as the text line is approximately horizontal after skew correction.

The connected component is allocated to text line according to the location relationship between the component and segmentation line by their location information. For some connected components, it is difficult to assign them to the corresponding text line only depends on location. Generally speaking, these components are broken strokes, separate vowels, symbols, touch characters, noise, and so on. Therefore, it is necessary to make a further analysis of the location and shape of these connected components in order to correctly determine their attributes. Combining location and shape information to determine which text line these connected components should belong to will be more accurate, especially for complex documents. At last, the components belong to the same alignment are merged to recover the text line.

Here is the architecture we extract text-lines from Tibetan historical documents shown in Fig. 3.

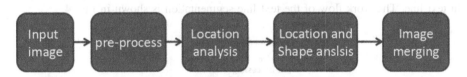

Fig. 3. The text line segmentation process.

Our method includes four stages:

1. Pre-processing: We detect whether the input image is skew. If the image is skewed, the skew correction is done to make the text lines in the image horizontally parallel. Then, the information about height of character is got which will be used to estimate the feature of characters in next stage. At last the position of baseline is detected using the projection method.
2. Location analysis: According to the baseline position we obtained before, the text line region is extracted from the input image as a rectangle, and divide the region into upper part and lower part according to the baseline position of the current baseline. The upper part is undoubtedly part of the current text line, but the lower part contains some components of the next text line. Next, the projection method is used to find the optimal segmentation line (SL) which is the row's location with minimum pixels in the lower part. Then the connected component in the lower part is divided into three classes according to whether it intersects with the SL. Some connected components are belongs to current text line or next text line certainly but

the others cannot easily determine which text line they belong to, so further analysis is needed.

3. Location and Shape analysis: By judging whether there is intersection point with SL, the connected components with uncertain attribution is divided into one class. By analyzing the location information and shape information of the connected component in this class, we classify it into the correct text lines, especially for the touching characters between the text lines, we use some features and rules to detect and separate them.

4. Image merging: Through the Location and Shape analysis (LSA) of the connected components, the connected components belonging to the current text line have been marked out. Combining these connected components to form the lower part of the current text line, and then splicing the upper and lower parts to form a complete image of the current text line.

3   Text Line Segmentation

The proposed text line segmentation method base on the projection, location and shape analysis of connected components for historical Tibetan handwritten document deals with the following challenges: (i) parts of neighboring text lines may be connected; (ii) overlong character and touching character in text line; (iii) the separated vowel may be appeared either above or below the text line and (iv) the broken strokes of characters in text line. The work flow of the text line segmentation is shown in Fig. 4.

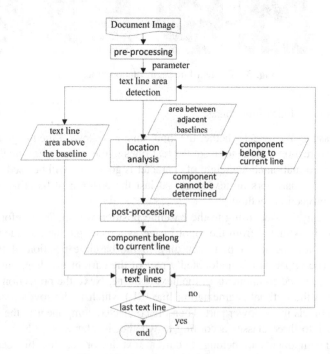

Fig. 4. Proposed method framework.

3.1   Pre-processing

The pre-processing stage consists of three steps. First, whether the input image is skew is detected, the document image is skew corrected if the image is skew. The angle of the skew correction is determined by the length of the border detection line, the method rotates the image from -2 angle to +2 angle at step 0.1, and detects the sum of the length of the edge lines of the four borders, the maximum sum corresponding angle is the correction angle. An example is shown in Fig. 5. Then, average character height (AH) and the average component height (ACH) for the whole document image are calculated and the bordering box is removed. Last, the baseline position of each text line is obtained by row projection profile method, and the number of locations equals the number of text lines. An example is shown in Fig. 6.

(a) the document image is skew   (b) after skew correction

Fig. 5. The input document image is skew (a) and the document image after skew correction (b).

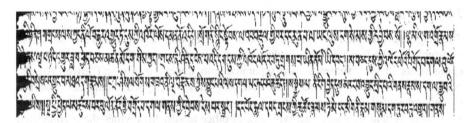

Fig. 6. Row projection diagram of binary document image.

3.2   Location Analysis

This stage includes two steps. At the first step, the projection method is used to get the initial row position of the text line that is the line of beginning (LB) then extract the area between LB and the baseline location of the current text line as the upper part of the current text line image, and this part is denoted as "upper image" (see Fig. 7. black part). The next step will analyze the image ("lower part") between the baseline of current text line and the next baseline. Firstly, the statistical method is used to find the optimal segmentation line (SL) which is the row's location with minimum pixels. Next, by using relative location relations between components and SL, the connected components domain is divided into three sub-domains, which are denoted as "Subsetcur", "Subsetlow" and "Subsetcs" respectively.

"Subsetcur" contains all components which totally are located above the SL (see Fig. 7. green part) and "Subsetlow" contains all components which are located below the SL (see Fig. 7. blue part). "Subsetcs" contains all the components which have the intersected points with the SL, this subset have various components that need to be analyzed in different manners by the proposed method in the next stage (see Fig. 7. red part).

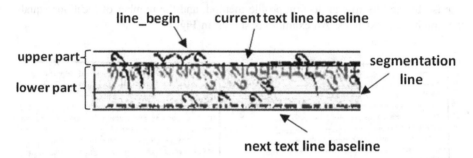

Fig. 7. An example of partitioning the connected components by the relationship between the component and the segmentation line. The black part is upper image, the lower part is the region between current baseline and next text line' baseline, the green part means "subsetcur", the red part means "subsetcs" and the blue part means "subset low". (Color figure online)

3.3 Sharp-Analysis

This stage analyzes the location and shape of the components which is in the "subsetcs" to determine whether it belongs to the current text line or not. The categories of these components in the "subsetcs" are separated into upper vowels and lower vowels, broken strokes ,overlong characters, touching and overlapped characters, and bar shaped connected components. All connected components in "subsetcs" have a common property that they intersect with SL, in other words, SL divides these connected components into upper and lower parts. In order to assign connected components to the corresponding text lines accurately, we need to extract some features of these connected components, such as the height of connected components (H), the height above the SL (HA), the pixel per row for the part above the SL (PPRA), the height below the SL (HB), the pixel per row for the part below the SL (PPRB), and the ratio of the foreground area to the minimum rectangular bounding area (RFB).

The PPRA is calculated as follows: (value 1 for foreground and 0 for background pixels)

$$PPRA = \sum_{x=1}^{width} \sum_{y=1}^{HA} I(x,y)/HA \; if \; I(x,y) = 1 \tag{1}$$

The PPRB is calculated as follows:

$$PPRB = \sum_{x=1}^{width} \sum_{y=1}^{HB} I(x,y)/HB \; if \; I(x,y) = 1 \tag{2}$$

The RFB is defined as follows:

$$RFB = \sum_{x=1}^{width} \sum_{y=1}^{height} I(x,y)/width * height \; if \; I(x,y) = 1 \tag{3}$$

The location and shape analysis (LSA) procedure consists of two steps. At the first step, the feature obtained above are used to determine whether the connected components lying in subsetcs are belong to the current text line or not according to the following conditions.

In the first step, the method take advantage of the feature we obtained above and the average character height (AH) and the average component height (ACH) which are got at first stage to classify them into three categories by rules. The first category have the connected components which are assigned to the next text line. One category consists of components that in this step cannot determine the attribution of text lines, and these components will be analyzed shapes in the next step. The last category includes the components of the current text line, usually consisting of overlong characters, symbols, and touching characters. The touching character will be segmented and retain the component belonging to the current text line.

The broken strokes and separated vowels were selected by conditions 4. The condition is described fellow:

$$H < ACH \tag{4}$$

The connected component is belongs to the current text line, if some features satisfy the condition below:

$$(H > AH) \; and \; (HA > HB) \tag{5}$$

Identify the connected component with height exceeds the height threshold which is defined as:

$$HT = 1.5 * AH \tag{6}$$

The connected components which satisfied the above conditions include the overlong characters (see Fig. 8, a b c), the touching characters(see Fig. 8, d e) and the bar-shaped connected components which generally are Tibetan character symbol(see Fig. 8, f).

The bar-shaped connected components usually are symbol which is belong to current text line. Such component will be selected if the following condition is satisfied:

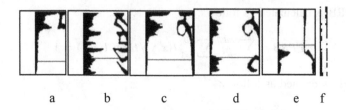

a   b   c   d   e   f

Fig. 8. The image of overlong character, the overlong characters (a b c), the touching characters (d e) and the bar-shaped connected components (f).

$$RFB > 0.5 \tag{7}$$

The touching character are as long as the overlong character (see the Fig. 6a b c and d e). Choose the touching character according to the following constraint.

$$PPRB > 1.2 * PPRA \tag{8}$$

The LSA first step work flow is shown in Fig. 9

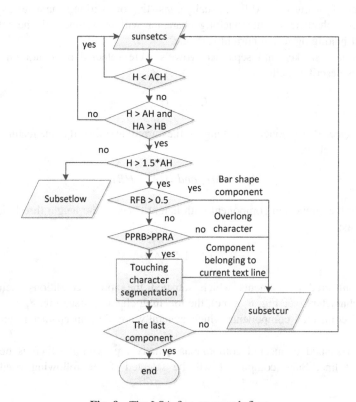

Fig. 9. The LSA first step work flow

The second step continues to deal with connected components still in subsetcs, which are broken strokes (see Fig. 10, a b c d), separated lower vowels belonging to the current text line (see Fig. 10, e f g), and upper vowels belonging to the next text line (see Fig. 10, h i j).

This step has three works to do:

1. Calculate the centroid and the skeleton of connect components, then detect the intersection between skeleton and the line located by the centroid, and calculated the numbers and the coordinate positions of the intersected points.

2. For the connected components with only one intersected point (see Fig. 11 a b c d), move it from subsetcs to the subsetcur if its centroid position is above the segmented line, or it belongs to subsetlow if its centroid position is below the segmented line.

3. For the connected components with two intersected points, the skeleton is segmented into the upper part and the lower part according to the line located by the centroid and the coordinate of two intersected points. The number of pixels in the two parts is counted respectively. Connected components are assigned to subsetcur if the pixels in the lower part is more than that in the upper part (see Fig. 11 e f g), otherwise, the connected components will belong to subsetlow(see Fig. 11 h i j).

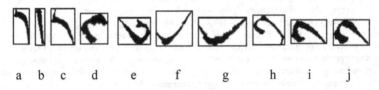

    a   b   c   d   e   f   g   h   i   j

Fig. 10. The connected components of broken strokes, separated lower vowels and separated upper vowels

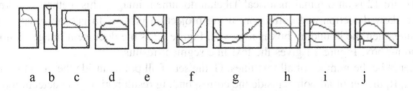

    a   b   c   d   e   f   g   h   i   j

Fig. 11. The skeleton diagram with line located by the centroid

3.4 Merging Image

Since all the connected components that belong to the current text line have been marked in the subsetcur, so the lower part of the current text line is generated by the subsetcur. The complete image of the current text line image is got by merge the upper part and lower part. The input image subtracts the current text line image from the position of the LB to produce a image that is the input image for the next text line.

4   Experimental Results and Discussion

The experimental dataset are from the historical Tibetan scripture "kangjur" of the Beijing version on the paper by means of woodcut. The scripture "kangjur" of the Beijing version have more than 60 thousand images, the dataset just have 1696 text lines from 212 images which is selected at random. The method presented in this paper is implemented in matlab.

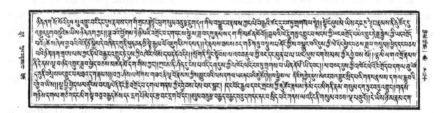

Fig. 12. The input image

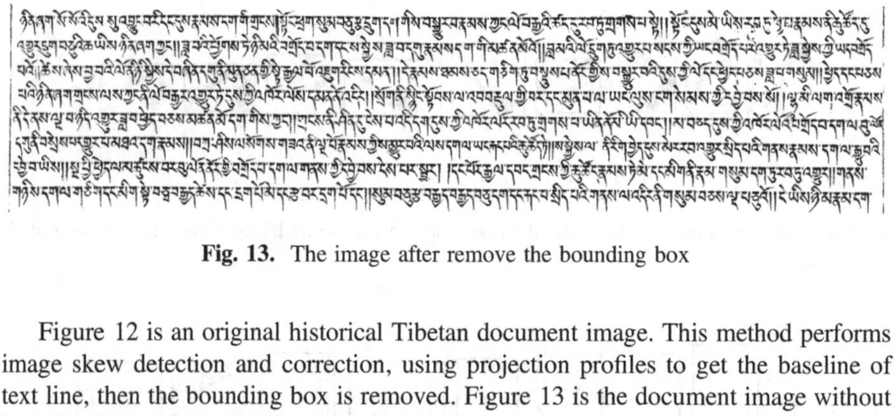

Fig. 13. The image after remove the bounding box

Figure 12 is an original historical Tibetan document image. This method performs image skew detection and correction, using projection profiles to get the baseline of text line, then the bounding box is removed. Figure 13 is the document image without bounding box. Figure 14 gives the text line segment results.

Let N be the number of all text lines, G_j the set of all points inside the ground truth region, R_i the set of all points inside the corresponding result region. The detection rate (DR) and the recognition accuracy rate(RA) are defined as follows:

$$DR = \frac{G \cap R}{G}, RA = \frac{G \cap R}{G} \tag{9}$$

Because text line segmentation is an important part of OCR recognition system, the ideal situation is that the text lines only contains all the components belonging to the text line, and it does not lose any component and does not have any component that do not belong to them. Therefore, we propose completeness rate to measure the segmentation effect. The definition of integrity is as follows:

$$CR = \frac{\sum N_i}{N} \quad N_i = 1, \ if \ G_i = R_i, otherwise \ N_i = 0 \qquad (10)$$

Table 1 shows the performance of contour curve tracking method and our method. Comparing with the contour curve tracking method, our method has a considerable improvement in each evaluation value.

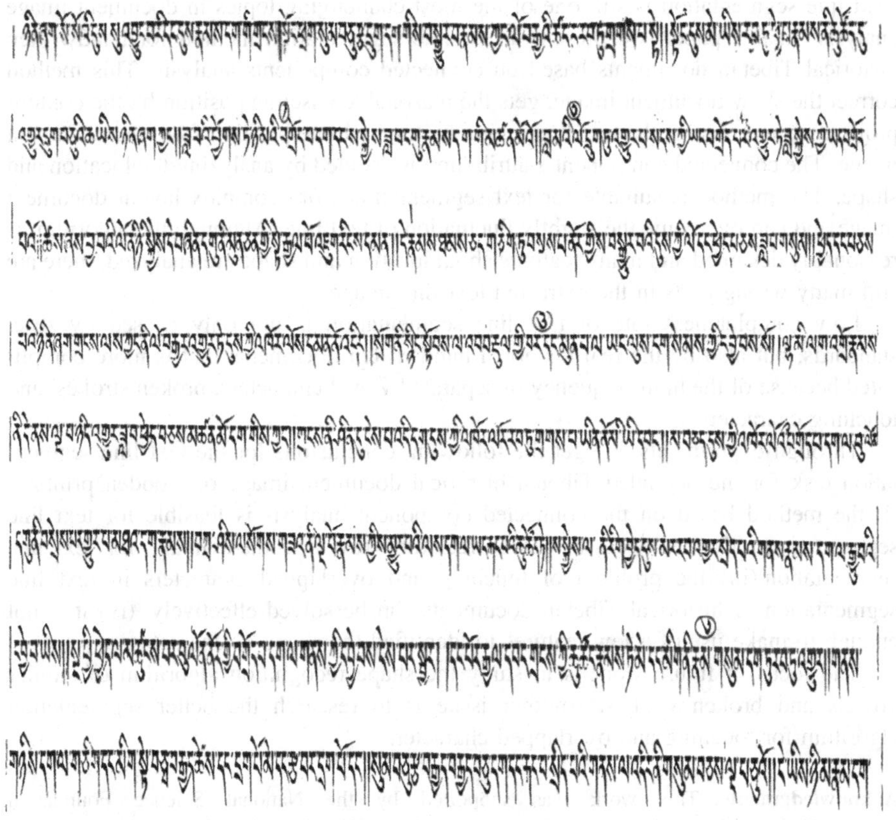

Fig. 14. Result of text line segmentation

Table 1. The performance of contour curve tracking method and our method

Method	N	DR	RA	CR
Contour curve tracking	2196	82.79%	80.09%	33.23%
Our method	2196	91.17%	90.23%	37.51%

Experimental results show that almost all the components belonging to the wrong text line are caused by broken strokes and separated lower vowels. And this method is very efficient to detect the touching characters in adjacent text lines. There are 874 touching characters in the dataset of the 212 pictures, and 840 of them are detected successfully, the touching character's detect ratio is 98.4%.

5   Conclusion and Further Work

Text line segmentation is still one of the most challenging topics in document image analysis. In this paper, we present a text line segmentation method for handwritten historical Tibetan documents based on connected components analysis. This method correct the skew document image, gets the reasonable baseline position by the contour projection, and obtains the text line region by the baseline position from the document image. The connected component's attribution is decided by analyzing the location and shape. The method is suitable for text segmentation from complex layout document image and can overcome the slightly fluctuation of text line. Although the algorithm is reasonably designed and many features about location and shape are analyzed, there are still many wrong parts in the extracted text line image.

Low completeness rate of text line segmentation is not only caused by strict standards, but also by the real historical handwritten documents that is more complicated because of the high frequency of separated vowel characters, broken strokes, and touching characters.

Through experiments, we get the following conclusions for the text line segmentation task for the degraded Tibetan historical document image of wooden printing: (i) the method based on the connected component analysis is feasible for text line segmentation. (ii) it is necessary to correct the skew document image for text line segmentation.(iii) the problem of touching and overlapped characters in text line segmentation of historical Tibetan documents can be solved effectively. (iv) it is not enough to make use of a few features to identified the shape of character.

The focus of future work is to study the shape recognition algorithm of similar vowels and broken strokes. Another issue is to research the better segmentation algorithm for touching and overlapped character.

Acknowledgments. This work was supported by the National Science Foundation (No.61772430), the Program for Leading Talent of State Ethnic Affairs Commission, the Fundamental Research Funds for the Central University of Northwest Minzu University (No. 31920170142), and also supported by the Gansu Provincial first-class discipline program of Northwest Minzu University.

References

1. Li, Y., Ma, L., Duan, L., Wu, J.: A text-line segmentation method for historical tibetan documents based on baseline detection. In: Yang, J., et al. (eds.) CCCV 2017. CCIS, vol. 771, pp. 356–367. Springer, Singapore (2017). https://doi.org/10.1007/978-981-10-7299-4_29
2. Zhou, F., Wang, W., Lin, Q.: A novel text line segmentation method based on contour curve tracking for tibetan historical documents. Recogn. Artif. Intell. **32**(10), 1854025 (2018). Image Processing
3. Manmatha, R., Rothfeder, J.L.: A scale space approach for automatically segmenting words from historical handwritten documents. IEEE Trans. Pattern Anal. Mach. Intell. **27**(8), 1212–1225 (2005)
4. Bar-Yosef, I., Hagbi, N., Kedem, K., Dinstei, I.: Line segmentation for degraded handwritten historical documents. In: 10th ICDAR, pp. 1161–1165 (2009)
5. Likforman-Sulem, L., Zahour, A., Taconet, B.: Text line segmentation of historical documents: a survey. Int. J. Doc. Anal. Recogn. **9**(2), 123–138 (2007)
6. Garz, A., Fischer, A., Bunke, H., Ingold, R.: A binarization-free clustering approach to segment curved text lines in historical manuscripts. In: International Conference on Document Analysis and Recognition, pp. 1290–1294 (2013)
7. Zahour, A., Likforman-Sulem, L., Boussalaa, W., Taconet, B.: Text line segmentation of historical arabic documents. In: 9th International Conference Document Analysis and Recognition, vol. 1, pp. 138–142 (2007)
8. Baima, Y.Z.: Research on feature extraction of tibetan characters. Comput. Knowl. Technol. **9**, 6362–6364 (2013)

Online Handwriting Tibetan Character Recognition Based on Two-Dimensional Discriminant Locality Alignment

Zhengqi Cai[1,2] and Weilan Wang[1(✉)]

[1] Key Laboratory of China's Ethnic Languages and Information Technology of Ministry of Education, Northwest Minzu University, Lanzhou 730000, Gansu, People's Republic of China
caizhengqi@126.com, wangweilan@xbmu.edu.cn
[2] College of Mathematics and Computer Science, Northwest Minzu University, Lanzhou 730000, Gansu, People's Republic of China

Abstract. Discriminant Locality Alignment (DLA) has been successfully applied in handwriting character recognition. In this paper, a new manifold based subspace learning algorithm, which is called Two-dimensional Discriminant Locality Alignment (2DDLA) algorithm, is proposed for online handwriting Tibetan character recognition (OHTCR). The proposed algorithm integrates the idea of DLA and two-dimensional feature extraction algorithm. At first, extracting direction feature matrix and edge feature matrix of Tibetan character respectively, they are together formed original feature matrix. Then, in part optimization stage, for each character sample, a local patch is built by the given sample and its neighbors, and an object function is designed to preserve local discriminant information. Third, in whole alignment stage, the alignment trick is used to align all part optimizations to the whole optimization. The projection matrix can be obtained by solving a standard eigen-decomposition problem. Finally, a SMQDF classifier is used training and recognition. Experimental results demonstrate that 2DLDA is superior to LDA and IMLDA in terms of recognition accuracy. In addition, 2DLDA can overcome the matrix singular problem and small sample size problem in OHTCR.

Keywords: Online handwriting recognition · Tibetan character recognition Two-dimensional discriminant locality alignment (2DDLA) · Subspace learning

1 Introduction

With the acceleration of Tibetan information process, the demand of Tibetan character recognition system is becoming more and more prominent. At present, handwriting Tibetan character recognition (HTCR) has made great progress in both research and practical application [1–6]. However, the recognition of Tibetan character is different from handwriting recognition of other languages, it poses a special challenge due to a complex structure, wide varieties in writing style, a large character set and many instances of highly similar characters. Figure 1 illustrates some samples of handwriting

© Springer Nature Switzerland AG 2018
J.-H. Lai et al. (Eds.): PRCV 2018, LNCS 11258, pp. 88–98, 2018.
https://doi.org/10.1007/978-3-030-03338-5_8

Tibetan character. Unconstrained online HTCR is still an open problem remaining to be solved, for it is still challenging to reach high recognition rate.

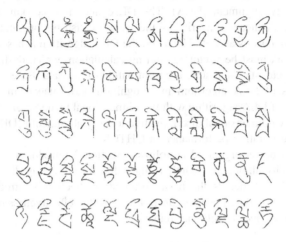

Fig. 1. Some samples of handwriting Tibetan character

As shown in Fig. 1, many Tibetan characters are almost identical to other characters except for only a small different. However, the small difference can be lost during the feature extraction process. So the discriminate information extraction is crucial for improvement of the recognition performance. In OHTCR, dimensionality reduction is the process of transforming data from a high dimensional space to a low dimensional space to reveal the intrinsic structure of the distribution of data. It plays a crucial role in the field of computer vision and pattern recognition as a way of dealing with the "curse of dimensionality". In past decades, a large number of dimensionality reduction algorithms have been proposed and studied. Among them, principal components analysis (PCA) [7] and Fisher's linear discriminant analysis (LDA) [8] are two of the most popular linear dimensionality reduction algorithms.

PCA maximizes the mutual information between original high dimensional Gaussian distributed data and projected low dimensional data. PCA is optimal for reconstruction of Gaussian distributed data. However, it is not optimal for classification problems. LDA overcomes this shortcoming by utilizing the class label information. It finds the projection directions that maximize the trace of the between-class scatter matrix and minimize the trace of the within-class scatter matrix simultaneously. However, LDA is only a suboptimal model which suffers from the class separation problem. The objective of LDA can be formulated as maximizing the sum of all the pairwise distances between different classes, which will overemphasize the large distance of the already well-separated classes, and confuse the small distance classes that are close in the original feature space. Li and Yuan [9] proposed a new method of feature extraction using two-dimensional linear discriminant analysis (2DLDA), and directly uses the matrix to extract the discriminant feature without a vectorization procedure, it has a great advantage over the one-dimensional method in calculation and processing efficiency.

Zhang [10] proposed a local linear dimensionality reduction algorithm called discriminative locality alignment (DLA). The DLA takes into account the locality of samples, deals with the nonlinearity of the samples distribution, and preserves the discriminability of classes as well. However, the DLA algorithm is based on the vector space, and the data must be vectorized during calculation, which destroys the spatial distribution characteristics and structure information of the data. Based on the stability and effectiveness of DLA algorithm in recognition performance, in this paper, we combine the idea of DLA algorithm with two-dimensional feature extraction algorithm, and proposes a two-dimensional discriminative locality alignment (2DDLA) algorithm to improve the recognition performance in OHTCR.

The rest of paper is organized as follows. Section 2 introduces two-dimensional discriminant locality alignment (2DDLA) algorithm for extracting discriminative features for OHTCR and details the basic formulation. Section 3 introduces SMQDF classifier. We perform experiments in Sect. 4 to show the effectiveness of the proposed method and Sect. 5 gives concluding remark.

2 Two-Dimensional Discriminative Locality Alignment

2DDLA aims to extract discriminative information from patches. To achieve this goal, one patch is first built for each sample. Each patch includes a sample and its within-class nearest samples and its between-class nearest samples. Then an objective function is designed to preserve the local discriminative information of each patch. Finally, all the part optimizations are integrated together to form a global coordinate according to the alignment trick. The projection matrix can be obtained by solving a standard Eigen decomposition problem.

2.1 Part Optimization

Suppose we have a set of samples $X = [X_1, X_2, \cdots X_N]$ from C different classes, $X_i \in R^{m \times n}$. For a given sample X_i, we select k_1 nearest neighbors from the samples of the same class with X_i and name them as the neighborhoods of a same class: $X_{i^1}, \cdots, X_{i^{k_1}}$, we also select k_2 nearest neighbors from samples of different classes with X_i, and name them as neighborhoods of different classes: $X_{i_1}, \cdots, X_{i_{k_2}}$. By putting them together, we can build the local patch for X_i as $\Pi_i = [X_i, X_{i^1}, \cdots, X_{i^{k_1}}, X_{i_1}, \cdots, X_{i_{k_2}}]$. For each patch, the corresponding output in the low-dimensional space is denoted by $\Gamma_i = [Y_i, Y_{i^1}, \cdots, Y_{i^{k_1}}, Y_{i_1}, \cdots, Y_{i_{k_2}}]$.

In the low-dimensional space, we expect that distances between the given sample and its within-class samples are as small as possible, while distances between the given sample and its between-class samples are as large as possible. So we have

$$arg \min_{Y_i} \sum_{j=1}^{k_1} ||Y_i - Y_{i^j}||_F^2 \tag{1}$$

$$arg \max_{Y_i} \sum_{p=1}^{k_2} ||Y_i - Y_{i_p}||_F^2 \tag{2}$$

where $||\cdot||_F$ denotes the Frobenius norm for a matrix.

Since the patch formed by the local neighborhood can be regarded approximately linear, we formulate the part discriminator by using the linear manipulation as follows:

$$arg \min_{Y_i}(\sum_{j=1}^{k_1} ||Y_i - Y_{i^j}||_F^2 - \beta \sum_{p=1}^{k_2} ||Y_i - Y_{i_p}||_F^2) \tag{3}$$

where β is a scaling factor ($\beta \in [0,1]$). The coefficients vector is defined as:

$$W_i = [\overbrace{1, \cdots, 1}^{k_1}, \overbrace{-\beta, \cdots, -\beta}^{k_2}] \tag{4}$$

Then the Eq. (3) reduces to:

$$
\begin{aligned}
arg \min_{Y_i} &\left(\sum_{j=1}^{k_1} ||Y_i - Y_{i^j}||_F^2 W_i(j) + \sum_{p=1}^{k_2} ||Y_i - Y_{i_p}||_F^2 W_i(p + k_1) \right) \\
= arg \min_{Y_i} &\left(\sum_{j=1}^{k_1+k_2} ||Y_{F_i\{1\}} - Y_{F_i\{j+1\}}||_F^2 W_i(j) \right) \\
= arg \min_{Y_i} &\, tr(\Gamma_i (L \otimes I_n)(diag(W_i) \otimes I_n)(R \otimes I_n)(\Gamma_i)^T) \\
= arg \min_{\Gamma_i} &\, tr(\Gamma_i T_i \Gamma_i^T)
\end{aligned}
\tag{5}
$$

where $tr(\cdot)$ denotes the trace operator, the operator $\otimes$ denotes the Kronecker product of matrix, $F_i = \{i, i^1, \cdots, i^{k_1}, i_1, \cdots, i_{k_2}\}$ is the index set for the ith patch, $e_{k_1+k_2} = [1, \cdots 1]^T \in R^{k_1+k_2}$, $I_{k_1+k_2}$ is a $(k_1 + k_2) \times (k_1 + k_2)$ identity matrix, $R = [-e_{k_1+k_2}, I_{k_1+k_2}]^T$, $L = \begin{bmatrix} -e_{k_1+k_2}^T \\ I_{k_1+k_2} \end{bmatrix}$, and

$$T_i = (L \otimes I_n)(diag(W_i) \otimes I_n)(R \otimes I_n) \tag{6}$$

2.2 Whole Alignment

After the part optimization step, we unify the optimizations together as a whole one by assuming that the coordinate for the i'th patch $\Gamma_i = [Y_i, Y_{i^1}, \cdots, Y_{i^{k_1}}, Y_{i_1}, \cdots, Y_{i_{k_2}}]$ is selected from the global coordinate $\Gamma = [Y_1, Y_2, \cdots, Y_N]$, such that $\Gamma_i = \Gamma S_i$, where $S_i \in R^{(N \times n) \times ((k_1 + k_2 + 1) \times n)}$ is the selection matrix and an entry is defined as follows:

$$(S_i)_{pq} = \begin{cases} I_n & if & p = F_i(q) \\ 0_n & else \end{cases} \tag{7}$$

Then Eq. (7) can be rewritten as

$$arg \min_{\Gamma} tr(\Gamma S_i T_i S_i^T \Gamma_i^T) \tag{8}$$

By summing over all the part optimizations described as Eq. (8), we can obtain the whole alignment as

$$\begin{aligned} & arg \min_{\Gamma} \sum_{i=1}^{N} tr(\Gamma S_i T_i S_i^T \Gamma^T) \\ & = arg \min_{\Gamma} tr((\Gamma \sum_{i=1}^{N} S_i T_i S_i^T)\Gamma^T) \\ & = arg \min_{\Gamma} tr(\Gamma L \Gamma^T) \end{aligned} \tag{9}$$

where $L = \sum_{i=1}^{N} S_i T_i S_i^T \in R^{N \times N}$ is the alignment matrix.

To obtain the linear and orthogonal projection matrix W, such as $Y = W^T X$, Eq. (9) is deformed as follows:

$$arg \min_{W} tr(W^T X L X^T W), \text{ s.t. } W^T W = I \tag{10}$$

The transformation matrix W that minimizes the objective function is given by the minimum eigenvalue solution to the standard eigenvalue problem,

$$XLX^T P = \lambda P \tag{11}$$

3 SMQDF

3.1 MQDF

MQDF [11] classifier's discriminate function is formulated as

$$\begin{aligned} f(Y, \omega_j) = & \sum_{i=1}^{k} \frac{[(Y - \mu_j)^T \zeta_i^{(j)}]^2}{\lambda_i^j} + \sum_{i=k+1}^{m} \frac{[(Y - \mu_j)^T \zeta_i^{(j)}]^2}{\lambda} \\ & + \sum_{i=1}^{k} \log\lambda_i^{(j)} + \sum_{i=k+1}^{m} \log\lambda \qquad j = 1, 2, \dots, C \end{aligned} \tag{12}$$

where, Y is input feature vector, m is line number of feature matrix, μ_j denotes the mean vector of class ω_j, $\lambda_i^{(j)}$ and $\zeta_i^{(j)}$ denote the ith larger eigenvalue and the corresponding eigenvector of the covariance matrix of class ω_j, respectively. k is the number of dominant principal eigenvectors that are kept in MQDF, λ is experiment parameter.

We can obtain the classified result based on the following criterion: If $f(Y, \omega_i) = \min_{1 \leq j \leq C} f(Y, \omega_j)(C$ is class number), then we believe that input pattern Y belongs to the ω_i class.

3.2 SMQDF

MQDF classifier is widely used in the area of character recognition. However, it only applies to feature vector, and it is not appropriate for feature matrix. For this reason, SMQDF (second modified quadratic discriminate function) classifier is generated by improving MQDF classifier, its discriminate function as shown in the follow formula (13). We take it as a baseline classifier.

$$f(Y, \omega_j) = \sum_{i=1}^{m-1} \frac{((Y - \mu_j)^T \zeta_i^{(j)})^T ((Y - \mu_j)^T \zeta_i^{(j)})}{\lambda_i^{(j)}} + \frac{((Y - \mu_j)^T \zeta_m^{(j)})^T ((Y - \mu_j)^T \zeta_m^{(j)})}{\lambda}$$

$$+ \sum_{i=1}^{m-1} \log \lambda_i^{(j)} + \log \lambda \quad j = 1, 2, \ldots, C$$

$$(13)$$

where, Y is feature matrix, m is positive integer, When classifies, Y belongs to the class whose $f(Y, \omega_i)$ is minimum. To compensate for the estimation error of parameters on limited training samples, the minor eigenvalues are replaced with a constant λ. It can be set to a class-independent constant or class-dependent constant. Here we set λ to be class-independent for its superior performance. λ is computed by

$$\lambda = \frac{1}{c * d} \sum_{j=1}^{c} \sum_{i=1}^{d} \lambda_i^{(j)} \tag{14}$$

4 Experiment Results

4.1 Experiment Data

We evaluated the recognition performance of 2DDLA on a databases of handwritten Tibetan characters, collected by our group, contains the handwriting samples of 7240 characters, 5000 samples per class [12]. In order to reduce the computing cost, we only selected 562 frequently used characters, 2000 samples per class for training and 500 samples per class for testing.

For character image pre-processing and feature extraction, we adopt the same methods as in [6]. Each character image is normalized to 48×96 pixels, the directional features and edge features are extracted. The resulting 60×12 feature matrix is projected onto a 12×12 subspace learned by 2DDLA, then the baseline classifier SMQDF is designed on this 12×12 subspace.

4.2 Choice of Parameters for 2DLDA

Since the parameters setup for 2DDLA is essential for its performance, we carried out the 2DDLA parameter optimization experiments before for OHTCR. In the model of 2DDLA, there are three parameters: k_1, k_2 and β, where k_1 is the number of the samples from identical class in the given patch, k_2 is the number of the samples from other classes in the same given patch, and parameter β is the scale parameter. In order to find a proper range for the dominant parameters k_1, k_2 and β in 2DDLA, we will investigate the effects of the three model parameters on the recognition rates in the validation phase based on our collected database.

Suppose n is the training sample number in each class (n = 2000), N is the total training sample number (N = $562 \times 2000 = 1024000$), and C is class number ($C = 562$). Then, k_1 and k_2 could be chosen in the range of $[1, n-1]$ and $[0, N-n]$ respectively. Therefore, $1 \leq k_1 \leq 1999$, $0 \leq k_2 \leq 1022000$, and $0 \leq \beta \leq 1$.

To evaluate the effects of the three model parameters, firstly, we analyze the effect of the scale parameter β, by fixing patch building parameters k_1 and k_2 to arbitrary values. For a given pair parameters k_1 and k_2, we can obtain the recognition rate curve with respect to β, as shown in Fig. 1. Base on the figures, we observe that the best recognition rates are obtained when β is neither too small nor too larger.

Secondly, we analyze the effects of patch building parameters k_1 and k_2, by fixing scale parameter $\beta = 0.1$. When we vary k_1 and k_2 simultaneously, the best recognition rate with the corresponding to β can be acquired. Table 1 shows that the details of the best recognition rate. Figure 2 shows that best recognition rate with the corresponding $k_1 = 50$ and $k_2 = 300$ in this experiment (Fig. 3).

Table 1 shows that, the best combination of k_1, k_2, and β are $k_1 = 50$, $k_2 = 300$, $\beta = 0.1$ and $k_1 = 100$, $k_2 = 300$, $\beta = 0.3$, with the corresponding accuracy 99.38%. Considering the computing cost, in the following experiments, we use the best combination of k_1, k_2, and β is 50, 300, 0.1 respectively.

4.3 Evaluation Experiments

To evaluation the performance of 2DDLA in SHCCR, we compare the performance of 2DDLA, LDA, IMLDA [13] and 2DLDA in terms of recognition rate over SMQDF classifier [6]. The experimental results are summarized in Table 2. We can see that the proposed method obtains higher top 1 and top 10 recognition rate than other method.

From Table 2, it is shown that the recognition rates of 2DDLA are significantly higher than that of IMLDA and 2DLDA respectively. It also shows the discriminate information extraction performance is very competitive in OHTCR.

To illustrate the effects of the 2DDLA, Fig. 4 shows some sample that are mis-recognized by IMLDA and 2DLDA, but can be corrected by 2DDLA.

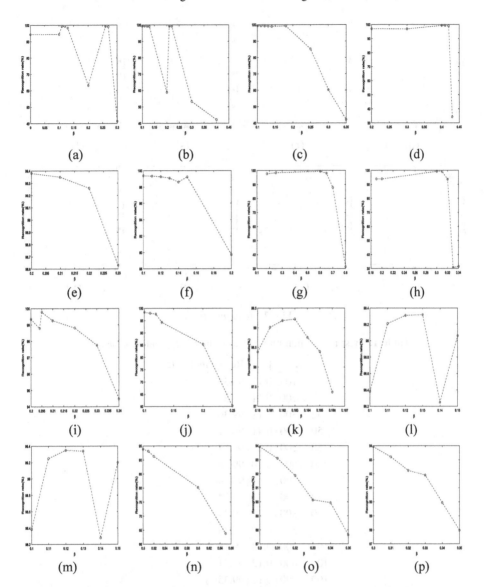

Fig. 2. For a given pair parameters k_1 and k_2, the best recognition rate with the corresponding to β. (a) $k_1 = 32$, $k_2 = 100$, (b) $k_1 = 32$, $k_2 = 200$, (c) $k_1 = 32$, $k_2 = 300$, (d) $k_1 = 50$, $k_2 = 100$, (e) $k_1 = 50$, $k_2 = 200$, (f) $k_1 = 50$, $k_2 = 300$, (g) $k_1 = 80$, $k_2 = 100$, (h) $k_1 = 80$, $k_2 = 200$, (i) $k_1 = 80$, $k_2 = 300$, (j) $k_1 = 100$, $k_2 = 300$, (k) $k_1 = 100$, $k_2 = 500$, (l) $k_1 = 100$, $k_2 = 800$, (m) $k_1 = 100$, $k_2 = 990$, (n) $k_1 = 300$, $k_2 = 500$, (o) $k_1 = 300$, $k_2 = 800$, (p) $k_1 = 300$, $k_2 = 990$, (q) $k_1 = 500$, $k_2 = 800$, (r) $k_1 = 500$, $k_2 = 1000$, (s) $k_1 = 500$, $k_2 = 1200$, (t) $k_1 = 500$, $k_2 = 1500$, (u) $k_1 = 800$, $k_2 = 1500$, (v) $k_1 = 800$, $k_2 = 2500$, (w) $k_1 = 800$, $k_2 = 3800$, (x) $k_1 = 1000$, $k_2 = 300$

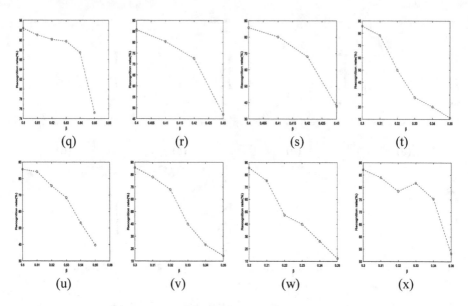

Fig. 2. (*continued*)

Table 1. Best recognition rate (%) with the corresponding k_1 and k_2.

K_1	K_2	β	Recognition rates
32	100	0.11	99.36
32	200	0.11	99.36
32	300	0.11	99.36
50	100	0.41	99.37
50	200	0.21	99.37
50	300	0.10	99.38
80	100	0.61	99.34
80	200	0.31	99.34
80	300	0.21	99.34
100	300	0.30	98.38
100	500	0.18	99.18
100	800	0.12	99.31
100	990	0.12	99.35
300	500	0.50	93.93
300	800	0.30	93.93
300	990	0.30	93.93
500	800	0.60	92.41
500	1000	0.40	85.73
500	1200	0.40	85.72
500	1500	0.30	85.73
800	1500	0.50	85.62
800	2500	0.3	85.62
800	3800	0.2	85.62
1000	3000	0.3	87.19

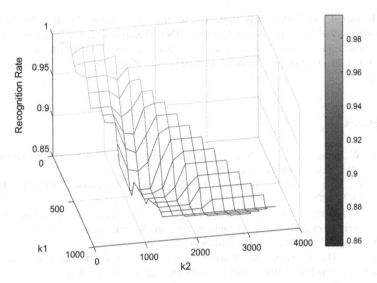

Fig. 3. Recognition rate vs. k_1 and k_2

Table 2. Best recognition rates (%) of three methods.

Methods	Top 1	Top 10
IMLDA	55.56	92.73
2DLDA	83.73	98.21
2DDLA	85.9	99.38

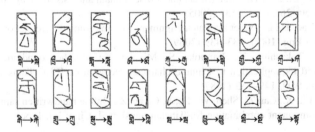

Fig. 4. Some misrecognized by SMQDF, but corrected by compound distance method

5 Conclusion

In this paper, we present a new method, called two-dimensional discriminative locality alignment (2DDLA). Compare with IMLDA and 2DLDA, the proposed method has better recognition rate. It inherits all the advantages of DLA and can overcome the matrix singular problem and small sample size problem in OHTCR.

Acknowledgment. This work was supported by the Fundamental Research Funds for the Central University of Northwest Minzu University (No. 31920170142), the Program for Leading Talent of State Ethnic Affairs Commission, the National Science Foundation (No. 61375029), and supported by the Gansu Provincial first-class discipline program of Northwest Minzu University.

References

1. Wang, W., Ding, X., Qi, K.: Study on similar character in Tibetan character recognition. J. Chin. Inf. Process. **16**(4), 60–65 (2002)
2. Wang, H., Ding, X.: Multi-font printed Tibetan character recognition. J. Chin. Inf. Process. **17**(6), 47–52 (2003)
3. Wang, W., Qian, J., Duojie, Z., Ma, M., Qi, K., Duo, L., et al.: A method of online handwritten Tibetan characters recognition. State Intellectual Property Office of the Peoples Republic of China (2011). ZL200910128595.8
4. Huang, H., Da, F., Hang, X.: Wavelet transform and gradient direction based feature extraction method for offline handwritten Tibetan letter recognition. J. Southeast Univ. **30** (1), 27–31 (2014)
5. Ma, L.L., Wu, J.: A Tibetan component representation learning method for online handwritten Tibetan character recognition. In: Proceedings of the 14th ICFHR, pp. 317–322 (2014)
6. Wang, W., Qian, J., Wang, D., Duojie, Z.: Online handwriting recognition of Tibetan characters based on the statistical method. J. Commun. Comput. **8**(2011), 188–200 (2011)
7. Jolliffe, I.T.: Principal Component Analysis. Springer, New York (1986). https://doi.org/10. 1007/978-1-4757-1904-8
8. Fisher, R.A.: The use of multiple measurements in taxonomic problems. Ann. Eugen. **7**, 179–188 (1936)
9. Li, M., Yuan, B.: 2D-LDA: a statistical linear discriminant analysis for image matrix. Pattern Recognit. Lett. **26**(5), 527–532 (2005)
10. Zhang, T., Tao, D., Li, X., et al.: Patch alignment for dimensionality reduction. IEEE Trans. Knowl. Data Eng. **10**(2), 433–439 (2009)
11. Kimura, F., Takashina, K., Tsuruoka, S., Miyake, Y.: Modified quadratic discriminant functions and its application to Chinese character recognition. IEEE Trans. Pattern Anal. Mach. Intell. **9**(1), 149–153 (1987)
12. Wang, W., Lu, X., Cai, Z., Shen, W., Fu, J., Caike, Z.: Online handwritten sample generated based on component combination for Tibetan-Sanskrit. J. Chin. Inf. Process. **31**(5), 64–73 (2017)
13. Qian, J., Wang, J.: A novel approach for online handwriting recognition of Tibetan characters. In: Proceedings of IMECS 2010, pp. 1–4 (2010)

Complex Printed Uyghur Document Image Retrieval Based on Modified SURF Features

Aliya Batur[1], Patigul Mamat[2], Wenjie Zhou[1], Yali Zhu[1], and Kurban Ubul[1(✉)]

[1] School of Information Science and Engineering,
Xinjiang University, Urumqi 830046, China
kurbanu@xju.edu.cn
[2] School of Mathematics and Information,
Hotan Normal College, Hotan 848000, China

Abstract. As an important part of information retrieval, it is important to improve the accuracy of document image retrieval system. This paper proposes a document image retrieval method based on modified SURF features. Firstly, FAST+SURF features are extracted from the image, and then the similarity degree is retrieved by using different kinds of distances and matching points respectively. With the change of size, angle and illumination, the FLANN bidirectional matching and KD-Tree +BBF matching are implemented for its feature points; finally, based on these two kinds of retrieval methods, various Uyghur document image databases that have been collected and retrieved are searched. The experimental results indicated that both search methods can achieve accurate search requirements, but in computational complexity based on the matching number of retrieval is more convenient. At the same time, the comparison experiment proves that the proposed method is superior to the original feature in the retrieval time.

Keywords: SURF feature · FALNN bidirectional match
KD-Tree and BBF match · Complex document image retrieval

1 Introduction

With the rapid development of multimedia information technology, document images have become the main information resource, which also causes the explosive growth of document image. How to obtain document image content efficiently has become a hot research topic in domestic and overseas research. Xiaoxiao et al. [1] compared 64-dimensional vectors to describe the feature points that were more suitable for image data processing. Two modified SVM algorithms were used to extract information from matched images and compare with traditional SVM algorithm. Zhao et al. [2] first extracted the 64-dimensional SURF feature points, and based on the FLANN algorithm for bidirectional matching, matching pairs for PROSAC analysis, excluding mis-matched pairs to improve the image matching accuracy, and effectively reduce the matching time. Cheon et al. [3] proposed an enhanced Fast Robustness Feature (e-SURF) algorithm to save memory and increase speed. Zhang et al. [4] proposed an

© Springer Nature Switzerland AG 2018
J.-H. Lai et al. (Eds.): PRCV 2018, LNCS 11258, pp. 99–111, 2018.
https://doi.org/10.1007/978-3-030-03338-5_9

modified matching algorithm based on SURF (Speeded Up Robust Features) feature point matching, which combined SURF and RANSAC (Random Sample Consensus) algorithm. Chen et al. [5] proposed to improve the detection of SURF key points, extract the feature points of the image detail region, and achieve accurate matching based on KD-Tree bidirectional matching. Luo et al. [6] modified the SURF descriptor using the DAISY descriptor, and matched the target image with nearest neighbor distance ratio (NNDR), with a maximum matching rate of 95.78%. Wang et al. [7] proposed a robust feature (SURF) based on improved accelerated fast image matching algorithm, The RELIEF-F algorithm is used to reduce and simplify the improved SURF descriptors to achieve image registration, and finally the improved algorithm is verified by the experiments of real-time and robustness.

This paper analyzes the Uyghur complex document image without layout analysis, proposes to the modified SURF features to achieve the key points extraction, and to achieve effective retrieval from the large-scale image database. The algorithmic flow of this paper is shown as in Fig. 1.

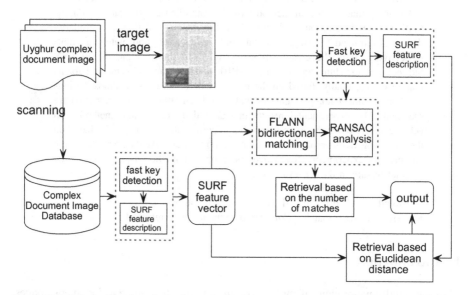

Fig. 1. The block diagram of Uyghur printed complex document image retrieval based on modified SURF feature.

2 Fast and SURF Feature Extraction

The process of fast robust feature extraction (SURF) is similar to SIFT, and consists of two parts: key point detection and feature description. However, it maintains the same image size and changes the size and scale of the box filter in multiples relationship. Based on the integral image, the proportional space is filtered so that the feature detection takes much less time than SIFT. And the key points detected in the scale space have the size translational robustness. In the feature description, the Haar wavelet response value in the fan-shaped area is calculated, the main direction of the key points is determined, and the computational complexity is reduced.

However, shortening time parameter is not ideal for the complicated document images of text and video. Therefore, in order to quickly detect the key points of the image in the complex layout, the author makes full use of pixel gray level information, detects the corners based on the FAST algorithm, and describes the sub-description with the SURF descriptor to form the 64 dimension FAST and SURF feature, effectively shortening the features Extraction time [8]. The Flow chart of modified SURF feature key point detection is shown in the following Fig. 2.

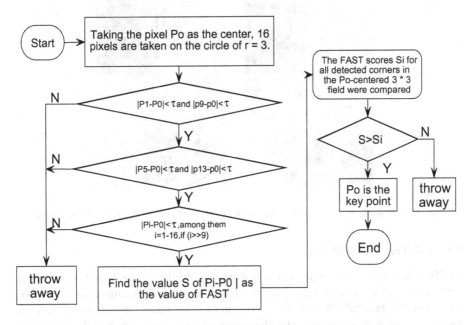

Fig. 2. Flow chart of modified SURF feature key point detection

3   Fast and SURF Feature Matching Analysis

To improve the matching speed of Uyghur complex document images, the author implements two-way fast approximate nearest neighbor (FLANN) matching for different layout images, and compares the results with KD-Tree and BBF matching results, from the performance of matching system to establish a retrieval system, and realize the effective retrieval of Uyghur complex document images.

3.1   Bidirectional FLANN Match

Due to the SURF feature vector is a high-dimensional vector, the matching process is equivalent to the nearest neighbor search problem in high-dimensional space, and the operation is complex. Therefore, this paper starts from the rapidness of FLANN matching, and matches in two directions successively to get the location information of matching pair. By comparing the location of the matching point to determine whether it is correct. In order to effectively remove the mismatched point pairs, the author uses the RANSAC algorithm to calculate the distance between the matched points and the projection matrix, and compares it with the threshold value, effectively eliminating the outer points and improves the matching accuracy. The original image FALNN bidirectional matching results are shown in Fig. 3.

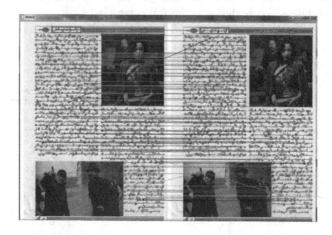

Fig. 3. Schematic diagram of modified SURF features bidirectional FLANN matching

3.2 KD-Tree and BBF Match

KD-Tree is a tree structure for realizes K-nearest neighbor search and matching in large-scale high-dimensional eigenvector space. Its research mainly consists of two parts, namely, the establishment of tree structure and the nearest neighbor search. With the increase of image feature vector dimension, the KD-Tree search ability is greatly reduced. Therefore, starting from the modified KD-Tree, this paper finds the nearest neighbor distance within the limit of maximum backtracking times, and compares the distance ratio with a predetermined threshold to determine whether it is a matching key point [9]. In this paper, the process of improving KD-Tree matching by improving 64-dimensional SURF features is shown in Fig. 4.

The matching efficiency of the matching system under different transformation conditions is evaluated by the matching rate, the correct matching rate and the false matching rate, and its mathematical expression is as follows:

$$\text{Match rate} = \frac{\text{The total number of matched pairs}}{\text{The total number of feature points detected}} \tag{1}$$

$$\text{Correct match rate} = \frac{\text{The total number of correct matched}}{\text{The total number of matched pairs}} \tag{2}$$

$$\text{Mismatch rate} = \frac{\text{The total number of error matched}}{\text{The total number of matched pairs}} \qquad (3)$$

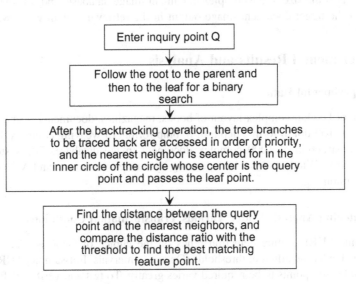

Fig. 4. The description of modified KD-Tree match

4 Uyghur Complex Document Image Retrieval Method

In this paper, the distance-based similarity measure and the matching number-based similarity measure are used. Four eigenvector distance similarity measures algorithms are selected and they are as follows:

$$\text{Euclidean distance} = \sqrt{(x_1 - x_2)^2 + (y_1 - y_2)^2} \qquad (4)$$

$$\text{Manhattan distance} = |x_1 - x_2| + |y_1 - y_2| \qquad (5)$$

$$\text{Chebyshev distance} = \max(|x_1 - x_2|, |y_1 - y_2|) \qquad (6)$$

$$\text{Cosine distance} = \frac{x_1 x_2 + y_1 y_2}{\sqrt{x_1^2 + y_1^2} \times \sqrt{x_2^2 + y_2^2}} \qquad (7)$$

In the retrieval system that based on the matching number, the correct number of matches between the document image and each image in the image database is calculated from the correct number of matches, and then the number of correct matches between each image in the image database is sorted and sorted in descending order to effectively retrieve the document image. The more similar complex document images, the greater the number of matches. The calculation of retrieval system is:

$$\text{Retrieval rate} = \frac{N - S}{N - 1} * 100\% \tag{8}$$

Where N is the size of the complex document image database, and S is the position number of the target document image output in the retrieval system window.

5 Experimental Results and Analysis

5.1 Experimental Data

Collection of Uyghur complex layout of books, magazines, documents, scanned with a resolution of 100 dpi to form a depth of 8. bmp format of weaving complex document images, construction of 1000 complex document image database. The system is in 4 GB memory, Windows7_64 bit operating system environment, and Visual Studio 2010 programming.

5.2 Matching Analysis Under Various Transformation Conditions

The original SURF feature detection relies on the choice of Octaves, Intervals, and thresholds. Under the different thresholds (Octaves, Intervals, Init-sample, THRES), the number of feature points to be acquired varies greatly. To test and verify the feasibility of FAST and SURF features, the original SURF features were extracted at (4, 4, 2, 0.0004f) thresholds for complex text documents, in order to obtain the same layout with different sizes, and compared with FAST and SURF Features for performance analysis. The experimental results are shown in Table 1.

Table 1. Number of FAST+SURF key points and time statistics of different sizes image under different threshold [10].

Image size	Feature					
	Performance	SIFT	SURF	FAST (50) +surf	FAST (100) +surf	FAST (150) +surf
803 × 1145	Key points	3276	3537	9767	7195	4960
	Occupation time (S)	30.405	15.866	0.021	0.01	0.009
1606 × 2290	Key points	10320	11516	22028	9414	9299
	Occupation time (S)	105.450	51.141	0.031	0.019	0.017
3212 × 4581	Key points	27820	38115	52967	17764	7839
	Occupation time (S)	250.492	162.491	0.082	0.04	0.035

In order to detect the robustness of the extracted features to the rotation, scale and illumination transformation, the modified SURF eigenvectors of the Uyghur complex document image with the size of 1606 × 2290 were extracted under different transformations. Based on FLANN bidirectional matching, KD-Tree and BBF matches the number of exact match pairs. When the threshold $\gamma = 0.1$, the results of FLANN bidirectional matching and KD-Tree and BBF under the dimensional transformation are shown in Table 2.

Table 2. Uyghur document image different matching results of FAST+SURF features under scale transform condition [10].

	FLANN bidirectional matching			KD-Tree and BBF match		
	Whole	1:1/2	1:1/4	Whole	1:1/2	1:1/4
The total number of key points	9414	4369	2082	9414	4369	2082
The total number of matching pairs	1145	454	200	9335	4264	2017
Correctly matched pairs	759	363	172	7582	4151	573
Correct match rate (%)	66.29	79.96	86	81.22	97.35	28.40

As can be seen from Table 2 that the image area decreases, the number of feature points detected decreases, and the total number of matches also cut back. Therefore, for thousands of key points, the stability of FLANN bidirectional matching is stronger than KD-Tree and BBF matching. To test and verify the rotation invariance of the selected features, the complex document images are rotated anticlockwise or clockwise in different angular ranges, and matching based on different matching algorithms. The experimental results are shown in Table 3.

Table 3. Two kinds of FAST (100)+SURF feature points matching results under Uyghur document image rotation transform

FLANN bidirectional matching					
	0°	+5°	+10°	−5°	−10°
The total number of key points	9414	10373	10614	9339	10423
The total number of matching pairs	1145	1213	1164	1070	1254
Correctly matched pairs	759	791	757	752	785
Correct match rate (%)	66.29	65.21	65.03	70.28	62.60
KD-Tree and BBF match					
	0°	+5°	+10°	−5°	−10°
The total number of key points	9414	10373	10614	9339	10423
The total number of matching pairs	9335	6044	6691	6005	6794
Correctly matched pairs	7582	1802	2112	2015	1845
Correct match rate (%)	81.22	29.81	31.56	33.56	27.16

Rotating the image of a complex text document in the anti-clockwise or clockwise direction can enlarges the image area. Therefore, the number of the detected key points is appropriately increased and the position of the key point is changed. From Table 3, it can be seen that FLANN bidirectional matching performance is better than KD-Tree and BBF matching under the condition of rotation transformation. In order to verify the robustness of the feature under light conversion conditions, the brightness of the original document image is adjusted. The experimental results are shown in Table 4.

Table 4. Two types of FAST (100)+SURF feature points matching results with Uyghur document image illumination transform

FLANN bidirectional matching					
	0	*20*	*40*	*−20*	*−40*
The total number of key points	9414	9882	9411	8963	9647
The total number of matching pairs	1145	1073	1139	999	952
Correctly matched pairs	759	749	758	803	784
Correct match rate (%)	66.29	69.80	66.55	80.38	82.35
KD-Tree and BBF match					
	0	*20*	*40*	*−20*	*−40*
The total number of key points	9414	9882	9411	8963	9647
The total number of matching pairs	9335	4892	4931	5591	5789
Correctly matched pairs	7582	3556	1869	3499	3281
Correct match rate (%)	81.22	72.69	37.90	62.58	56.68

The change of illumination is the lightness and darkness of the image. From Table 4, it can be seen that the KD-Tree and BBF matching performance is better than FLANN matching under the key point matching under light conversion conditions, and the matching number is large and the matching rate is high.

5.3   Analysis of Search Results

Due to the large size of the original image collected, the number of feature points obtained by feature extraction is too large, which has a great influence on the number of final matching points. Therefore, in order to assess the performance of the retrieval system, two modifications were made to the overall Uyghur complex document image database by compressing each image and cutting each image into 256 * 256 size, as shown in Fig. 5, and constructed two kinds of Uyghur complex document image database.

In Fig. 5, Fig. 5(b) is sheared image from Fig. 5(a). For the above two improved Uyghur complicated document image databases, based on the number of matches, Euclidean distance and cosine distance similarity measures, the user-specific target document images are retrieved. The retrieval test results are shown in Tables 5 and 6.

(a) Compressed image sample   (b) Sheared image sample

Fig. 5. The sample instance of modified database

Table 5. The statistical results of the sheared Uyghur document image retrieval experiment

Retrieve performance indicators	Match the number of search	Euclidean distance search	Cosine distance search
Retrieval rate	100%	100%	100%
Total search time (s)	1000	854	861
Average index time (s)	1	0.854	0.861

Table 6. The statistical results of the compressed Uyghur document image retrieval experiment

Retrieve performance indicators	Match the number of search	Euclidean distance search	Cosine distance search
Retrieval rate	100%	100%	100%
Total search time (s)	1636	599	607
Average index time (s)	1.636	0.599	0.607

It can be seen from Table 5 above that all three retrieval methods in the cut-structured Uyghur complex document database achieve a retrieval rate of 100%, but the search occupancy time is different. The matching needs to find the nearest neighbor and the next nearest neighbor matching point of each key point, and it need to compare the distance ratio with the first threshold to determine whether they match. Therefore, the system consumes more time than the distance similarity metric retrieval algorithm. The experimental results of compressed Uyghur document image are indicated in Table 6.

It can be seen from Table 6 that the retrieval system based on the number of matches consumes more time than the distance similarity metric retrieval system. For the two databases, matching number based retrieval system, the more the number of image feature points is, the greater the number of matching and the greater the system matching index time. In terms of similarity measure of distance between feature vectors, although the number of vector images in compressed image is larger, the output target document image can be searched within a shorter time than the cut image.

In this paper, in order to further validate the effectiveness of the FAST and SURF algorithm proposed in this paper, a cut-file image database of 256 * 256 size Arabic, Chinese, Tibetan and natural images is collected, each of which has a size of 1000 frames. The sample example is shown in Fig. 6 below:

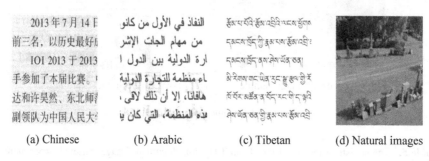

(a) Chinese   (b) Arabic   (c) Tibetan   (d) Natural images

Fig. 6. Comparative experimental database sample diagram

A number of examples of the experimental sample were transformed, such as size (2, 4, 8), illumination (20, 40, 60, −20, −40, −60), and rotation angle (5°, 10°, −5°, −10°) transformation, the retrieval results under different transformations are compared with the retrieval experiments of the Uyghur-cut complex document images, Validate the validity of the retrieval algorithm. The comparison result of the experimental results of retrieving the output target image is shown in Fig. 7(a) to (c).

As can be seen from Fig. 7, the letters of Uyghur, Arabic and Tibetan are more irregular than those of Chinese characters, and the differences in the gray-level values of the neighborhood pixels vary greatly. The Chinese language has horizontal and vertical Coherence; the difference in gray value is small. Therefore, the retrieval rate of Chinese query images after many transformations is larger than that of other databases. There are many transformations on the query, and the average indexing time for finding the target image based on the modified retrieval system is 0.013 (0.018), 0.041 (middle), 0.043 (hide) and 0.003 (natural) respectively. Compared with the average retrieval time of the retrieval system of the original features, it is 35.38 (original), 27.81 (a), 15.61 (middle), 16.05 (hide), 123.33 (natural) times. It can be seen that the retrieval system of FAST+SURF features makes it easy to find the target image quickly and accurately, which shows that this article proposes the effective and reliable method of improving ideas.

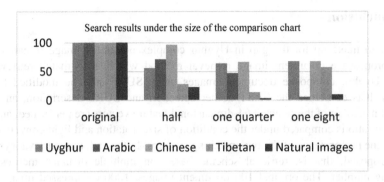

(a) Comparison of experimental results retrieved in five databases under dimensional transformation

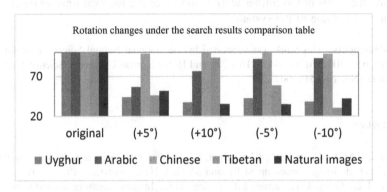

(b) Comparison of experimental results retrieved in five databases under rotation transformation

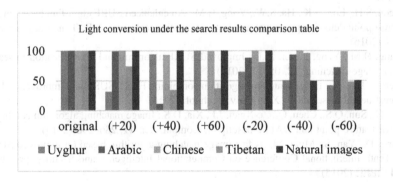

(c) Comparison of experimental results retrieved in five databases under light conversion

Fig. 7. Comparison of modified FAST and SURF retrieval platform under various transformations experimental results comparison chart

6 Conclusion

In order to make up for the gap in Uyghur complex document image research, this paper proposes a document image retrieval method which is to match retrieval of printed Uyghur composite document images using SURF and the modified SURF features. It is combined the FAST corner detection and SURF description, and two kinds of matching of the selected 64-dimensional feature vectors are performed, and the matching ratio is compared under the condition of size, rotation and light conversion to analyze the performance of the two matching systems. In the end, two retrieval systems were proposed, that is, retrieval scheme based on multiple distance metrics and matching number. The original 100 document images, 1000 compressed images and 1000 document images are retrieved respectively. The matched number of searches takes more time than the distance-based search, but it has a good retrieval rate. Therefore, the focus of the further work is to reduce the retrieval time while ensuring the high retrieval rate of the system.

Acknowledgments. This work was supported by the National Natural Science Foundation of China (No. 61563052, 61363064, 61163028), and Hotan Normal University Scientific Research Plan Project (No. 1076515160).

References

1. Xiaoxiao, M.A., Gang, Y.U., Changchun, L.I.: A data processing algorithm for unmanned aerial vehicle images based on SURF and SVM. J. Henan Polytech. Univ. (2017)
2. Zhao, L.L., Geng, G.H., Kang, L.I., A-Jing, H.E.: Images matching algorithm based on SURF and fast approximate nearest neighbor search. Appl. Res. Comput. **30**(3), 921–923 (2013)
3. Cheon, S.H., Eom, I.K., Ha, S.W., Yong, H.M.: An enhanced SURF algorithm based on new interest point detection procedure and fast computation technique. J. R.-Time Image Process. 1–11 (2016)
4. Zhang, H.M., Yang, L., Li, M.L.: Improved SURF algorithm and its application in seabed relief image matching. **12**, 05017 (2017)
5. Chen, J., Han, X.: Image matching algorithm combining FAST-SURF and improved k-d tree nearest neighbor search. J. Xian Univ. Technol. (2016)
6. Luo, N., Sun, Q.S., Chen, Q., Ze-Xuan, J.I., Xia, D.S.: Image matching algorithm combining SURF feature point and DAISY descriptor. Comput. Sci. **41**, 286–290 (2014)
7. Wang, D., Yan, S., Ming, M.: A fast image matching algorithm based on improved SURF. In: Tenth International Conference on Computational Intelligence and Security, pp. 3643–3647 IEEE (2015)
8. Weisheng, A.N, Rangming, Y.U., Yuling, W.U.: Image registration algorithm based on FAST and SURF. Comput. Eng. (2015)
9. Dong, H., Han, D.Y.: Research of image matching algorithm based on SURF features. In: International Conference on Computer Science and Information Processing, pp. 581–584 IEEE (2012)
10. Batur, A.: Research on Uyghur printed complex document image retrieval based on local feature. Xinjiang University (2017)

11. Ren, K., Hu, M.: Color image registration algorithm based on improved SURF. J. Electron. Meas. Instrum. (2016)
12. Ma, Y.L.S.: Research on image based on improved SURF feature matching. In: Seventh International Symposium on Computational Intelligence and Design, pp. 581–584. IEEE (2015)
13. El-Gayar, M.M., Soliman, H., Meky, N.: A comparative study of image low level feature extraction algorithms. Egypt. Inform. J. **14**(2), 175–181 (2013)
14. Huang, L., Chen, C., Shen, H., He, B.: Adaptive registration algorithm of color images based on SURF. Measurement **66**, 118–124 (2015)
15. Zheng, C., Jin, W., Fang, F., Tang, C., Ling, Y.: Robust visual tracking algorithm based on structural multi-scale features adaptive fusion in co-training. In: International Conference on Information Science and Control Engineering, pp. 588–592. IEEE (2016)
16. Pandey, R.C., Singhm, S.K., Shukla, K.K., Agrawal, R.: Fast and robust passive copy-move forgery detection using SURF and SIFT image features. In: International Conference on Industrial and Information Systems, pp. 1–6. IEEE (2015)
17. Darve, N.R., Theng, D.P.: Image processing on eye image using SURF feature extraction. **3297**, 2738–2741 (2015)
18. Horak, K.: Classification of SURF image features by selected machine learning algorithms. In: International Conference on Telecommunications and Signal Processing, pp. 636–641 (2017)
19. Shanmugam, B., Rathinavel, R., Perumal, T., Subbaiyan, S.: An efficient perceptual of CBIR system using MIL-SVM classification and SURF feature extraction. Int. Arab. J. Inf. Technol. **14**(4), 428–435 (2017)

Deep Word Association: A Flexible Chinese Word Association Method with Iterative Attention Mechanism

Yaoxiong Huang[1], Zecheng Xie[1], Manfei Liu[1], Shuaitao Zhang[1], and Lianwen Jin[1,2(✉)]

[1] School of Electronic and Information Engineering,
South China University of Technology, Guangzhou, China
hwang.yaoxiong@gamil.com, zcheng.xie@gamil.com, manfei.l.liu@gamil.com,
z.shuaitao@gamil.com, lianwen.jin@gamil.com
[2] SCUT-Zhuhai Institute of Modern Industrial Innovation,
South China University of Technology, Zhuhai, China

Abstract. Word association is to predict the subsequent words and phrase, acting as a reminder to accelerate the text-editing process. Existing word association models can only predict the next word inflexibly through a given word vocabulary or a simply back-off N-gram language model. Herein, we propose a deep word association system based on attention mechanism with the following contributions: (1) To the best of our knowledge, this is the first investigation of an attention-based recurrent neural network for word association. In the experiments, we provide a comprehensive study on the attention processes for the word association problem; (2) An novel approach, named DropContext, is proposed to solve the over-fitting problem during attention training procedure; (3) Compared with conventional vocabulary-based methods, our word association system can generate an arbitrary-length string of words that are reasonable; (4) Given information on different hierarchies, the proposed system can flexibly generate associated words accordingly.

Keywords: Word association · Attention mechanism
Recurrent neural network · Chinese · DropContext

1 Introduction

Given a word, phrase, or sentence of arbitrary length, word association requires a machine to predict the following word, phrase, or even sentence that the user would like to express, acting as a reminder to accelerate the text-editing process. Word association is widely used in daily life, such as text input to smartphones, the auto-fill of fields in a web browser, and question/answer systems, which can not only save time and effort but also prevent spelling errors by providing users with a list of the most relevant words. Specifically, when a word is input by a user, the word association system provides a list of candidate words for the user

© Springer Nature Switzerland AG 2018
J.-H. Lai et al. (Eds.): PRCV 2018, LNCS 11258, pp. 112–123, 2018.
https://doi.org/10.1007/978-3-030-03338-5_10

to select and then updates the associated word list until the user has finished the text editing task.

In the community, methods have been presented for the advancement of word association. Generally, custom systems use a vocabulary or statistical information for word association. PAL [1], the first word association system, predicted the most frequent words that match the given words, completely ignoring any useful context information. Profet [2] (for Swedish) and WordQ [3] (for English) used both word unigrams and bigrams to improve the word association but still suffered from a lack of context information, which would easily lead to syntactically inappropriate words. Considering the inflexibility of the above-mentioned systems, an approach that models the complex context information of the given words is significantly important for the word association problem. In recent years, neural networks [4–6] have demonstrated outstanding ability in language models (LMs). In particular, recurrent neural network LMs (RNNLMs) [7] use long-term temporal dependencies without a strong conditional independence assumption. As RNNLMs become more popular, Sutskever et al. [8] developed a simple variant of the RNN that can generate meaningful sentences by learning from a character-level corpus. Zhang and Lapata [9] have conducted some interesting work and use RNNs to generate Chinese poetry. Furthermore, the ability to train deep neural networks provides a more sophisticated method of exploiting the underlying context information of the sentence, thereby making the prediction more accurate [10].

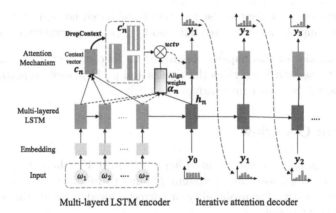

Fig. 1. The proposed word association system consists of two parts: (1) a multi-layered LSTM encoder that learns a hierarchy of semantic features from the input text corpus $w = w_1, \cdots, w_T$. and (2) an iterative attention decoder module (with DropContext) that iteratively updates attentions and refines current predictions. Note that y_0 is uniform distribution and y_N predicts the finally results.

LSTM has the ability to remember the past information, but it is quite limited and thus easily leads to prediction failure [11]. Therefore, the attention mechanism has gained popularity recently in training neural networks [12]; it allows models to learn the alignments between different modalities. The alignments may be between the frame level and text in the speech recognition task [13], or between the source words and translation in the neural machine translation problem [14], allowing the network focus more on the important part of the input. To the best of our knowledge, it is the best choice for natural language processing, e.g., word association problem.

The performance of the current neural network is highly dependent on the greedy learning of model parameters via many iterations based on a properly designed network architecture [15]. During the training phase, it is easy to encounter a problem of over-fitting. Many previous works have been dedicated to solving this problem, e.g., Dropout [16] and DropConnect [17]. Nevertheless, they were not appropriate for the attention mechanism.

Inspired by the aforementioned papers and works, we proposed a word association system that integrates multi-layered LSTM with iterative attention mechanism. The primary contributions of the network can be summarized as follows:

- Attention mechanism is integrated to allow the proposed system to iteratively review context information as well as historical prediction.
- A novel training strategy, namely DropContext, is proposed to alleviate the over-fitting problem during the learning process.
- Given certain information of different hierarchies, the network can generate words of arbitrary length, flexibly. The richer the information provided, the more meaningful words are associated.
- The effectiveness of the proposed system is validated not only by word association on huge Chinese corpus, but also by a poem generating experiment.

The remainder of this paper is organized as follows: Sect. 2 presents a system overview. Section 3 describes the results and performance evaluation of our proposed model. Section 4 summarizes our work.

2   System Overview

Given the training text corpus $\boldsymbol{w} = w_1, \cdots, w_T$ in V, where V is the word dictionary, our word association system f, aims to minimize the loss function $L(\boldsymbol{w})$ as the negative log probability of correctly predicting all the associated words in the text corpus:

$$L(\boldsymbol{w}) = -\frac{1}{T} \sum_t log f(w_t, w_{t-1}, \cdots, w_{t-n+1}; \theta) + R(\theta) \qquad (1)$$

where T is the total length of the corpus and $R(\theta)$ is a regularization term. Figure 1 describe the detailed architecture of our word association system. Given the training corpus $\boldsymbol{w} = w_1, \cdots, w_T$, we first project each the word w_t in the corpus to a distributed feature vector in the word embedding layer. The multi-layered LSTM then sequentially takes these embeddings as well as the past hidden state as input and outputs the corresponding context vector. Next, part of the context vector is randomly discarded in the DropContext layer. Finally, the updated context vector and final hidden state of the encoder are fed into the iterative attention decoder, iteratively updates the attentions and refines the current predictions. At the end of the decoder, the fully connected layer with a *softmax* layer will produce a probability distribution over all the words in the vocabulary.

2.1 Word Embedding

Word embedding is the concept of projecting each word in a vocabulary to a distributed word feature vector. Word embedding plays an important role in language modeling [18]. As pointed out by Bengio et al. [4], word embedding helps a network to fight the curse of dimensionality with distributed representations. Through word embedding, semantically similar words, such as 'cat' and 'dog', are expected to have a similar embedding feature; thus, a training sample that contains 'cat' can easily be projected to the case of 'dog' and vice versa. Accordingly, word embedding reduces the number of training samples requirement and, more importantly, alleviates the curse of dimensionality. Additionally, word embedding, i.e., the feature vector of each word, is directly learned from the corpora and is naturally trained with neural networks, such as RNN and LSTM, in an end-to-end manner. Given the advantages of word embedding, we used it for word representation at the bottom of our word association system, as shown in Fig. 1, to be jointly trained with the encoder and iterative attention decoder.

2.2 Iterative Attention Decoder (IAD)

In the previous works, the attention-based decoder only 'glance' at the source information once, and may make an inappropriate decision. Therefore, we herein employ an iterative attention decoder to our system, giving us a chance to 'view' the source information again and refine the current predictions.

From the multi-layered LSTM encoder, we obtain the source hidden state c_n with a T dimension, which is the same as the number of the input words. Additionally, a current target hidden state h_n is output from the decoder. Therefore, we can formulate the iterative attention decoder as:

$$y_n = \mathrm{IAD}(c_n, y_{n-1}) \tag{2}$$

where y_{n-1} is the last output of the IAD system. Note that, when $n = 1$, y_0 is uniform distribution, and Eq. (2) is updated for N times in the form of a recurrent neural network.

Inspired by the work of Luong [12], we attempt to employ a context vector c_n that captures relevant input information to aid in the prediction of y_n, and Eq. (2) can be executed in two step:

(1) We calculate the aligned weights $\boldsymbol{\alpha}_n$ according to the source context vector $\boldsymbol{c}_n$ and the current target hidden state $\boldsymbol{h}_n$:

$$\alpha_n^s = \frac{\exp(\gamma_n^s)}{\sum_{t=1}^{T} \exp(\gamma_n^t)} \tag{3}$$

where s is the dimension index of both $\boldsymbol{\alpha}_n$ and $\boldsymbol{\gamma}_n$. Here, the content-based score γ_n^t can be denoted as:

$$\gamma_n^t = \boldsymbol{v}_a^\top \tanh(\boldsymbol{W}_a [\boldsymbol{h}_n^\top ; \boldsymbol{c}_n^t]) \tag{4}$$

Note that, both $\boldsymbol{v}_a^\top$ and $\boldsymbol{W}_a$ are learnable parameters and $[\cdot]$ is the concatenation operation. Subsequently, we adopt the soft attention mechanism [19] where the updated context vector uctv_t is defined as the weighted sum of the source context vector.

$$\text{uctv}_t = \sum_{t=1}^{T} \alpha_n^t c_n^t \tag{5}$$

(2) The decoder iteratively updates the attentions and refines the current predictions using a recurrent neural network:

$$\boldsymbol{y}_n = \text{RNN}(\text{uctv}_t, \boldsymbol{y}_{n-1}) \tag{6}$$

where the RNN is implemented by a variant of recurrent neural network: Gated Recurrent Unit (GRU) [20]. Compared with LSTM, GRU only contains two gating units that modulate the flow of information, therefore, costing lower consumption.

In the last time step, the fully connected layer with a *softmax* layer will produce a probability distribution over all the words in the vocabulary.

2.3   DropContext (DC)

To overcome the over-fitting problem of attention model, we propose DropContext, a new training strategy, to enhance the efficiency of the learning process of attention model, as shown in the black dotted line in Fig. 1.

Suppose that we have the source context vector $\boldsymbol{c}_n$, which is a set of T-dimensional vectors, thus we can update the context vector with DropContext layer:

$$c_n^{'} = \text{DC}(\boldsymbol{c}_n) \tag{7}$$

Many attempts have been performed to execute the DropContext layer in our early work, considering the balance between performance and consumption. Our DropContext layer is implemented in two steps. First, we construct a T-dimensional drop-mask $\mathbf{M}$, which is randomly initialized by the drop-ratio θ:

$$\mathbf{M} = \{m_t = \mathbb{I}\{\zeta > \theta\}, t = 1, 2, \cdots, T\} \tag{8}$$

where $\mathbb{I}\{\cdot\} = 1$ when the condition is true and otherwise zero. It is noteworthy that ζ can follow any distribution, e.g., Gaussian distribution ora exponential distribution. In this paper, ζ follows a uniform distribution.

Subsequently, we update the source context vector by the element-wise product between c_n and $\mathbf{M}$:

$$c_n' = c_n \odot \mathbf{M} \tag{9}$$

We have to claim that, after introducing the DropContext layer, we only need to replace c_n with c_n' in Eqs. (4) and (5) for the iterative attention decoder.

2.4 Word Association

By integrating the multi-layered LSTM encoder and iterative attention decoder with the prediction layer, from the bottom to the top, we construct a word association system. Formally, the word association system employs the chain rule to model joint probabilities over word sequences:

$$p(w_1, ..., w_N) = \prod_{i=1}^{N} p(w_i | w_1, ..., w_{i-1}) \tag{10}$$

where the context of all the previous words is encoded with LSTM and updated as the predicted word is added. The probability of words is generated through the *Softmax* layer.

The process of associating words of arbitrary length is shown in Fig. 2. Our word association system takes the words of a given sequence as the input. The system then associates the next word by generating a probability distribution over all the given words, as the number upon the black lines shown in Fig. 2. Therefore, we can sort the predicted words in descending order of probability.

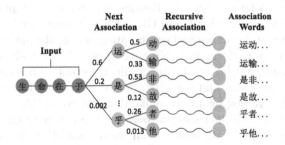

Fig. 2. Schematic diagram of word association. Given the beginning words as input, our word association system predicts a list of candidate words. By recursively adding these candidate words into the input, our word association system can associate sentence of arbitrary length, which is syntactically reasonable. Note that, the numbers upon the black lines represent the probability of the next word.

We adopt the first or top three in the list as the input for the next time step, and associate the following words in the same way. Finally, the system provides candidate associated sentences and their own probability. As described in Fig. 2, after taking the the initial words, our word association system produces a list of candidate words. By associating words in a recursive manner, our word association system manages to generate syntactically reasonable sentences of arbitrary length.

3   Experiments

3.1   Dataset

There is lack of benchmark dataset for the research on word association. Typically, researchers employ their own text corpus to generate the language model. To present an objective evaluation of our word association system, we use two publicly available text corpora, CLDC corpus [21] collected by the Institute of Applied Linguistics, and the Three Hundred Tang Poems (THTP corpus) [22].

For the CLDC corpus, we extracted the available data and filtered extremely rare Chinese characters and characters in other languages. The dataset contains 3455 classes and is divided into two groups, with approximately 70% of data used for training and the remainder for testing. Consequently, the training set contains 59,019,610 words and the test set contains 25,294,119 words.

The THTP corpus consists of 310 poems written by 77 famous poets during the Tang dynasty. For convenience, the punctuation has been removed from the poems. The dataset has approximately 20,000 words and consists of 2,497 classes, including a special symbol that indicates the end of a sentence.

3.2   Implementation Details

The proposed multi-layered LSTM encoder consists of two layers with the hidden size of 512, which are unrolled for 10 steps. Additionally, we also use dropout with probability 0.5 for our LSTMs. Besides, the iterative attention decoder is implemented with an attention-based GRU, whose hidden size is 512. To strike a balance between performance and consumption, we set the maximum iteration N as 3 for the little performance gain with larger N. We train the system in an end-to-end manner using stochastic gradient descent with a weight decay of 0.0005, momentum of 0.9, and gradient clipping set to 10. The initial learning rate is set to 0.1, followed by a polynomial decay of power 0.5.

In this paper, we use the canonical performance metric of language models, namely the perplexity [23], to evaluate our word association system. Perplexity measures the average number of branches of the predicted text, the reciprocal of which can be seen as the average probability of each word. Formally, perplexity is calculated as:

$$\text{perplexity} = \sqrt[K]{\frac{1}{e^{(-\sum \log(p(w)))}}} \tag{11}$$

where $p(w)$ is the probability of each word in the test set and K is the total number of words that appeared in the test set. It is noteworthy that the word association system with a low perplexity generally performs better than those with a higher perplexity. Besides, we also perform many visualizations of the experiment result, which are more obvious.

3.3 Effectiveness of the DropContext Layer

In this section, we perform a detailed analysis on the performance of our proposed DropContext method. In Table 1, we compare the performance of the system with different drop-ratios. When the drop-ratio is 0.0, no DropContext is available in our model and it is set as the baseline in our experiments. As the drop-ratio increases, the gap between train loss and test loss became smaller, and the system performance improves, i.e., the perplexity and testing loss of the system decreases. We can conclude that, by introducing the DropContext, the over-fitting during the training procedure can be alleviated. However, the system performance decreases afterward when the drop-ratio is lager than 0.4. This is because when the drop-ratio is too large, too much context information will be discarded in the training procedure, which will confuse the decoder and render our system difficult to converge.

Table 1. Influence of drop-ratio

Drop-ratio	0.0 (baseline)	0.2	0.4	0.6	0.8
Train loss	2.63	4.13	**4.37**	4.45	4.89
Test loss	4.79	3.92	**3.86**	3.89	4.42
Perplexity	120.36	50.40	**47.46**	48.91	83.10

3.4 Effectiveness of the Iterative Attention Decoder

In this section, we compare the proposed iterative attention model with a regular LSTM-based model similar to that reported by Merity et al. [5]. The regular LSTM-based model consists of two LSTM layers, with the hidden size of 512, which is the same as the multi-layer LSTM encoder in our system. The difference between the regular LSTM-based model and our model is that each hidden state of the former is followed by the fully connected layer and a softmax layer. This means that once a word is input, the system can only make a 'decision' (prediction) once. Note that, both of them are trained with the CLDC corpus.

As shown in Table 2, the regular LSTM-based model (denoted as R-LSTM) achieves a perplexity of 62.80. By introducing the iterative attention decoder, our model (denoted as IA-LSTM) achieves a much lower perplexity of 47.46. We can conclude that adding iterative attention mechanism can lead to a better performance.

Table 2. Perplexity and test loss on the CLDC corpus

Method	Perpelxity	Test loss
R-LSTM [5]	62.80	4.14
IA-LSTM	47.46	3.86

Additionally, Fig. 3 shows several examples on how the proposed iterative attention decoder iteratively updates the attentions and refines the current predictions. As we can see, although the model may make an inexact prediction at the beginning, it can update the attentions to focus on the last few words and make a more reasonable prediction. This is also corresponds to common sense that the associated words are more related with their adjacent words [24].

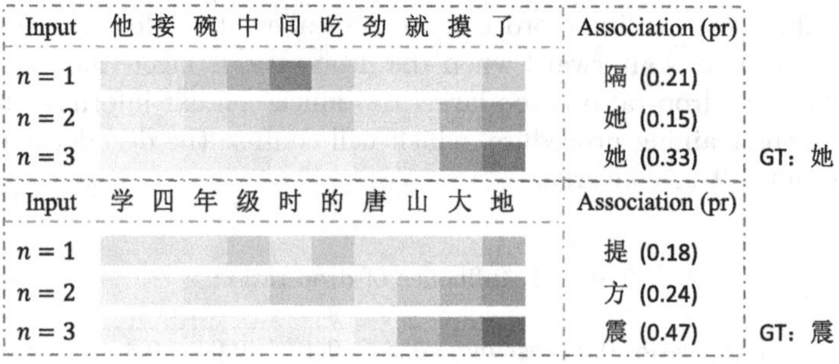

Fig. 3. Examples on how the proposed iterative attention decoder iteratively updates attentions and refines current predictions. At each time-step n, the current association word is listed. Each result is followed by the corresponding probability. Words in red are the most appropriate ones. Note that we use red squares to display the attention weight of each word, the deeper the color is, the greater the weight is.

3.5   Output Visualization of Word Association System

Our word association system generates an arbitrary length string of associated words. The more information is provided to the system, the more meaningful words will be generated. As shown in Fig. 4(a), given different numbers of words as beginning, our system associates sentences with completely different meanings. When only less information is available, the system randomly generates the sentences. However, when given more detailed information, the system associates a sentence that is quite relevant to the given words. In Fig. 4(b), the words in the first line are the input to the word association system and the subsequent lines are the associated sentences of different lengths. Note that regardless of the length of the associated sentences, they are reasonable and meaningful.

(a)

(b)

Fig. 4. Output of word association system. In (a), there are three kinds of inputs to the system, ordered by the amount of information in Chinese. In (b), there are three different lengths of output for the same input to the system. The associated sentence is syntactically reasonable for any arbitrary length. The tiny English sentence right below the Chinese sentence is the corresponding translation.

Fig. 5. Result of the model trained with the THTP corpus (shown in poetry format). Given arbitrary words, our system associates a meaningful poem with the Tang poem style.

3.6 Generating Poems

To verify the significance of our word association system, an poetry generating experiment is conducted using the THTP corpus. In the testing phase, a contiguous piece of a sentence is input to the word association system, and the system attempts to associate a poem accordingly.

To generate a poem, as shown in Fig. 5, arbitrary words are given to the association system. Staring with the given words, the system produces a meaningful poem of the Tang poem style. Furthermore, the associated poem is incredibly 'real' that it is difficult to distinguish whether it is one of the original poems in the dataset.

4 Conclusion

In this paper, we presented a flexible Chinese word association method which consists of a multi-layer LSTM encoder and an iterative attention decoder. Experiments show that the attention mechanism can improve the performance of Chinese word association system. Besides, the iterative attention decoder implemented in our system can iteratively uses its previous prediction to update attentions and to refine current predictions. Moreover, by adopting the DropContext layer in our proposed model, over-fitting can be avoided during the training procedure, which is proved to be better converged. Additionally, we showed that our system can generate syntactically reasonable associated words of arbitrary length and tends to associate more meaningful yet relative words when given more context information. Finally, we verify the significance of our word association system through an interesting poem generating experiment.

Acknowledgement. This research is supported in part by GD-NSF (no. 2017A030312006), the National Key Research and Development Program of China (No. 2016YFB1001405), NSFC (Grant No.: 61673182, 61771199), and GDSTP (Grant No.: 2014A010103012, 2017A010101027), GZSTP(no. 201607010227).

References

1. Swiffin, A.L., Pickering, J.A., Arnott, J.L., Newell A.F.: PAL: an effort efficient portable communication aid and keyboard emulator. In: ACRT, pp. 197–199 (1985)
2. Carlberger, A., Carlberger, J., Magnuson, T., Hunnicutt, M.S., Palazuelos-Cagigas, S.E., Navarro, S.A.: Profet, a new generation of word prediction: an evaluation study. In: Proceedings, ACL Workshop on Natural Language Processing for Communication Aids, pp. 23–28 (1997)
3. Shein, F., Nantais, T., Nishiyama, R., Tam, C., Marshall, P.: Word cueing for persons with writing difficulties: WORDQ. In: Proceedings of CSUN 16th Annual Conference on Technology for Persons with Disabilities (2001)
4. Bengio, Y., Ducharme, R., Vincent, P., Jauvin, C.: A neural probabilistic language model. J. Mach. Learn. Res. **3**(Feb), 1137–1155 (2003)
5. Merity, S., Keskar, N.S., Socher, R.: Regularizing and optimizing LSTM language models. CoRR, abs/1708.02182 (2017)
6. Yang, Z., Dai, Z., Salakhutdinov, R., Cohen, W.W.: Breaking the softmax bottleneck: a high-rank RNN language model. In: ICLR (2018)
7. Mikolov, T., Karafiát, M., Burget, L., Cernockỳ, J., Khudanpur, S.: Recurrent neural network based language model. In: INTERSPEECH, vol. 2, pp. 3 (2010)
8. Sutskever, I., Martens, J., Hinton, G.E.: Generating text with recurrent neural networks. In: ICML, pp. 1017–1024 (2011)
9. Zhang, X., Lapata, M.: Chinese poetry generation with recurrent neural networks. In: EMNLP, pp. 670–680 (2014)
10. Hinton, G., Deng, L.: Deep neural networks for acoustic modeling in speech recognition: the shared views of four research groups. IEEE Signal Process. Mag. **29**(6), 82–97 (2012)
11. Jenckel, M., Bukhari, S.S., Dengel, A.: Training LSTM-RNN with imperfect transcription: limitations and outcomes. In: Proceedings of the 4th International Workshop on Historical Document Imaging and Processing, pp. 48–53. ACM (2017)

12. Luong, M.-T., Pham, H., Manning, C.D.: Effective approaches to attention-based neural machine translation. CoRR, abs/1508.04025 (2015)
13. Chorowski, J.K., Bahdanau, D., Serdyuk, D., Cho, K., Bengio, Y.: Attention-based models for speech recognition. In: NIPS, pp. 577–585 (2015)
14. Dzmitry B., Cho, K., Bengio, Y.: Neural machine translation by jointly learning to align and translate. In: ICLR (2015)
15. Yang, W., Jin, L., Tao, D., Xie, Z., Feng, Z.: DropSample: a new training method to enhance deep convolutional neural networks for large-scale unconstrained handwritten chinese character recognition. Pattern Recognit. **58**, 190–203 (2016)
16. Hinton, G.E., Srivastava, N., Krizhevsky, A., Sutskever, I., Salakhutdinov, R.R.: Improving neural networks by preventing co-adaptation of feature detectors 3 July 2012. CoRR, abs/1207.0580 (2016)
17. Wan, L., Zeiler, M., Zhang, S., Le Cun, Y., Fergus, R.: Regularization of neural networks using DropConnect. In: ICML (2013)
18. Chen, S.F., Goodman, J.: An empirical study of smoothing techniques for language modeling. In: ACL, pp. 310–318. ACL (1996)
19. Show, attend and tell: neural image caption generation with visual attention. In: ICML (2015)
20. Cho, K., et al.: Learning phrase representations using RNN encoder-decoder for statistical machine translation. CoRR, abs/1406.1078 (2014)
21. Chinese linguistic data consortium. The Contemporary Corpus developed by State Language Commission P. R. China, Institute of Applied Linguistics (2009). http://www.chineseldc.org. Accessed 22 Oct 2016
22. Wikipedia. Three Hundred Tang Poems (2018). https://en.wikipedia.org/wiki/Three_Hundred_Tang_Poems
23. Jurafsky, D., James, H.: Speech and language processing an introduction to natural language processing, computational linguistics, and speech (2000)
24. Brown, P.F., Desouza, P.V., Mercer, R.L., Pietra, V.J.D., Lai, J.C.: Class-based N-gram models of natural language. Comput. Linguist. **18**, 467–479 (1992)

Face Recognition and Analysis

Face Recognition Based on Multi-view

Ensemble Learning

Wenhui Shi and Mingyan Jiang$^{(\boxtimes)}$

School of Information Science and Engineering, Shandong University,
Qingdao 266237, China
jiangmingyan@sdu.edu.cn

Abstract. Face recognition is an important research area in human-computer. To solve the problem about the inaccuracy and incompleteness of feature extraction and recognition, an ensemble learning method on face recognition is proposed in this paper. This method is a combination of a variety of feature extraction and classification ensemble technology. In feature extraction, wavelet transform and edge detection are used for extracting features. In classification recognition, the K nearest neighbor (KNN) classifier, wavelet neural network (WNN) and support vector machine (SVM) are used for preliminary identification. Each classifier corresponds to a feature method and then the classification of the three views are constructed. The final output results are integrated by voting strategy. Experimental results show that this method can improve the identification rate compared with the single classifier.

Keywords: Face recognition · Multi-view · Feature extraction
Ensemble learning · Voting

1 Introduction

Biometric authentication is a kind of personal identification, which is performed using the characteristics of the human body by computer [1]. Face recognition is an example of using biometric to authenticate. Compared with the other biological features such as iris and fingerprint, the acquisition of face image is more convenient and the equipment is more hidden. As a method of using effective information for identification, face recognition has been widely used in many aspects in the past few decades [2].

In the past few decades, face recognition technology has become more and more concerned by researchers in the world. Especially since recent years, the research and application of face recognition technology has made great progress and a large number of academic papers have been published every year [3]. Some websites and APP use face login and face registration. In the last year, the iPhone X produced by Apple Inc uses the face recognition function. At the same time, there are many commercial face recognition system into the market, such as law enforcement advanced video surveillance, surveillance portal control and so on.

As a complex pattern recognition problem [4], face recognition involves many disciplines, including image processing, mathematics, physiology, computer vision,

© Springer Nature Switzerland AG 2018
J.-H. Lai et al. (Eds.): PRCV 2018, LNCS 11258, pp. 127–136, 2018.
https://doi.org/10.1007/978-3-030-03338-5_11

etc. Because of the influence of many factors, face recognition is a technique with high complexity. In order to deal with these complex problems, some good methods are needed in feature extraction and recognition.

How can we extract features of the face accurately? Feature extraction is a key step in face recognition, which determines the results of recognition directly. It is affected by many aspects, including posture, expression, age, etc. [5]. The extracted features should reflect the identity as much as possible. It is inaccurate if we just use a single method to extract feature, then the recognition results are unsatisfactory. We can obtain more complete features by combining a variety of methods to extract features and lay the foundation for the recognition of the back. There are many methods to extract features. Reference [6] has proposed a method based on Canny operator to detect edges. The wavelet transform has a good time-frequency localization properties, so it is suitable for image processing. Reference [7] used stationary wavelet transform (SWT) to extract features from MR brain images.

In addition to feature extraction, the design of classifier also has great influence on the performance of face recognition algorithm. Different classification can make different results. In general, feature recognition usually adopts single classifier such as SVM [8], neural network and so on. However, it is unable to ensure the accuracy and stability of the results only relying on a single classifier for recognition. Thus, multiple classifiers are combined by the integration technology [9] to improve the generalization ability and reliability of the classification system. When designing an integrated system, the selection of a single classifier is critical, which is the first factor affecting the performance. The selected single classifier need to be stable and diverse. Secondly, the strategy of ensemble method is the second influencing factor. Reference [10] has used weighted majority voting classifier combination for relation extraction from biomedical sentences.

We proposed a method of ensemble learning for face recognition in this paper. Canny operator, wavelet transform were used to extract features of the images itself and transformation domain in this method [11]. Then we utilized three simple and common classifiers the KNN, SVM and WNN to identify. A classifier combined a feature extraction method and the classification of the three views were constructed subsequently. The voting strategy was adopted to integrate decision finally.

2 Classifier

The classifier can affect the final result, and we will introduce several classifiers used in this chapter.

2.1 KNN (k Nearest Neighbor Classifier)

The K nearest neighbor classifier is an effective classifier in pattern recognition [12].

It uses the known categories of the nearest neighbor samples to judge the unknown sample, which is suitable for dealing with overlapping or crossover samples. Specific steps are as follow: Calculate the distance of the sample (also as known similarity) to be sorted and the known samples in the feature space. This is the key to the method. Then find the k samples that are closest to the unknown sample. Count the category of k samples, and find the category which has the largest number. Finally classify the unknown sample into this category.

2.2   SVM (Support Vector Machine)

Support Vector Machine [8] has great advantages in solving nonlinear classification. The basic principle is to transform the input space into the high-dimensional space by non-linear mapping. The samples can be divided linearly, in which case the optimal interface can be obtained.

Suppose the known training sets are $C = \{(x_i, y_i)\}$, where $x_i \in R^n$, $y_i \in \{-1, 1\}$, (i = 1,2,...,l). For linear transformation of x, the equation of linear separation is $wx_i + b = 0$. The surface that satisfies $y_i(w^T x_i + b) - 1 \geq 0$. The surface that satisfies $y_i(w^T x_i + b) - 1 \geq 0$ and $\|w\|^2$ is the optimal classification surface.

Under this condition, it can be transformed into an optimization problem:

$$\min_{\alpha} \frac{1}{2} \sum_{i=1}^{j} \sum_{j=1}^{l} y_i y_j \alpha_i \alpha_j K(x_i, x_j) - \sum_{j=1}^{l} \alpha_j \tag{1}$$

Then the discriminant function can be determined according to the optimal solution α and the threshold b determined from the training samples:

$$f(x) = \text{sgn}(\sum_{x_i \in S_i}^{n} \alpha_i y_i K(x_i, x) + b) \tag{2}$$

Where α is Lagrange multiplier, $K(x_i, x)$ is the kernel function.

We can construct multiple classifiers to solve the multiple class problems. On the one hand, the SVM multi-class classifier can be realized by combining multiple two-class classifiers. On the other hand, the objective function can be modified to merge the problem of multiple classification surfaces into an optimization problem.

2.3   WNN (Wavelet Neural Network)

Wavelet neural network is the combination of wavelet transform and artificial neural network. It not only includes the local time-frequency characteristics and multi-scale decomposition characteristics of wavelet transform, but also contains the self-learning, adaptive and fault-tolerant ability of neural network [13]. Simply speaking, the wavelet function is used to replace the function in hidden layer on the basic of the BP neural network. The signal of wavelet neural network is transmitted forward, and error is transmitted backward at the same time.

The output of WNN is given by:

$$y(k) = \sum_{j=1}^{l} \omega_{jk} * h_j((\sum_{i=1}^{k} \omega_{ij} x_i - b_j)/a_j) \tag{3}$$

Where h_j is the mother wavelet function; a_j is the scaling factor and b_j is the translation factor.

The error function is used as the fitness function to verify the degree of parameters correction:

$$Error = \sum_{k=1}^{m} (y(k) - D(k))^2 / 2 \tag{4}$$

Where $D(k)$ is the expected output of the network.

We need to adjust the parameters according to the error. There are many methods for parameter revision and the gradient descent method is the most common in the wavelet neural network. However, it converges slowly and is easy to fall into the minimum. In this paper, we use the method of adding momentum item to modify the local parameters:

$$\omega_{ij}(i+1) = \omega_{ij}(i) + \Delta\omega_{ij}(i+1) + k(\omega_{ij}(i) - \omega_{ij}(i-1)) \tag{5}$$

$$a_j(i+1) = a_j(i) + \Delta a_j(i+1) + l * (a_j(i) - a_j(i-1)) \tag{6}$$

$$b_j(i+1) = b_j(i) + \Delta b_j(i+1) + l * (b_j(i) - b_j(i-1)) \tag{7}$$

3   Multi-view Ensemble Learning

3.1   The Multi-view Ensemble Learning Model

The classification technique of ensemble learning is a combination of multiple classifiers to enhance the reliability and generalization of system. In order to identify face images better, different feature extraction methods and identification classifiers are adopted in this study. The recognition model is shown in Fig. 1.

View 1 (LDA + KNN)
In this view, LDA is used to obtain the features with fewer dimensions and then we use KNN to identify the features.

LDA [11] also called Fisher Linear Discriminant, is a supervised algorithm that reduces the dimension. The principle is: The data with label can be projected to a lower dimension by mapping, the projecting points in the same class are as close as possible, and the distance between different classes are as large as possible. Thus the data after projection can be distinguish by category.

View 2 (Edge detection + SVM)
As an edge detection method, Canny operator has good anti-noise performance and detection accuracy [14]. In this view, we use Canny operator to obtain the edge information of the image. The gradient amplitude and direction of images can be calculated after the Gaussian smoothing. We can use non-maximal suppression and double threshold processing to get the final edge.

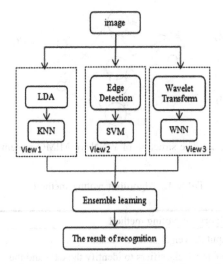

Fig. 1. The multi-view ensemble learning model.

After obtaining the edge features, we utilize SVM to classify to get the results. Face recognition is a typical multi-class identification problem. The support vector machine has strong generalization ability and good recognition rate for face recognition on pattern classification.

View 3 (Wavelet Transform + WNN)
Firstly, we used the wavelet transform to deal the image. It is well known that the wavelet transform has the ability of multi-scale expression. We use the two-dimensional discrete wavelet transform in this model and it can be realized by one-dimensional wavelet transform. The transformed image is divided into four parts: The LL part is an image with approximate coefficient that contains the major feature of the image. LH, HL and HH are images with detail coefficient that contain the details of the image. Among them, HH has high frequency both in horizontal direction and vertical direction, LH has low frequency in horizontal direction and high frequency in vertical direction, HL has high frequency in horizontal direction and low frequency in vertical direction.

In WNN, we adopt the three-layer feed-forward neural network shown in Fig. 2. This kind of wavelet neural network has one hidden layer.

3.2   Ensemble Learning Method

When designing an integrated system, multiple classifiers need to be integrated to achieve good integration [15]. And the selection of ensemble method affects the final results. There are many methods to integrate. Among them, the bagging as the most intuitive method has a surprisingly good performance. Table 1 shows the voting method.

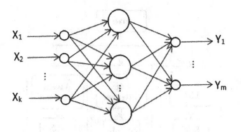

Fig. 2. The structure of WNN for MIMO system.

Table 1. Algorithm: voting method.

Algorithm: voting method

Input: Given N unlabeled data

Use the T classifiers to identify the data and the classification results are:

$$C = \{C_1, C_2, ..., C_M\}$$

where M is the total number of categories.

Suppose

$$\varphi_{i,j} = \begin{cases} 1 & \textit{if } T_i \textit{ is recognized as } C_j \\ 0 & \textit{otherwise} \end{cases}$$

represents the vote result of C_j by the classifier T_i.

The total voting result for each classifier is obtained by:

$$\phi_j = \sum_{i=1}^{T} \varphi_{i,j} \quad j = 1, 2, ..., M$$

Select the class with the highest total voting result as the final category:

$$C_j = \max \phi_j$$

The voting results can be divided into three categories:

The Unanimous Voting: the result of ensemble learning is the class on which all classifiers are consistent. In other words, if KNN, SVM and WNN are identified as the same output, the final result will be this output.

The Plurality Voting: the ensemble result is the class on which more than one half of the classifiers are consistent. For example, if KNN and WNN are identified as the same output A, the SVM is identified as another output B, then the final result is output A.

The Weighted Voting: If the outputs of the three classifiers are different, the output of the classifier which has the highest recognition rate will be the final result. In this experiment, the recognition rate of WNN is higher than KNN and SVM, so the final result is derived from the WNN.

4 Experiments

In order to verify the feasibility of this algorithm, the experiment is carried out in ORL face database. In this paper, we select 320 images of human face in ORL face database consisting of 32 people. The size of each image is 92 × 112 pixels with a grayscale of 256. Some of the face images are shown in Fig. 3. We select 5 images of each person that are 160 images as the training samples, and the rest of the images are used as test samples.

Fig. 3. Some sample images in ORL database.

In view 1, we obtain 160 dimensional features after the process of LDA. Then we classify the features according to the K nearest neighbor classifier. There are many methods to calculate the distance between the sorted samples and the known samples, such as the Euclidean distance, the Minkowski distance, the Manhattan distance, and so on. Here, we use the Euclidean distance. And we choose 5 neighbors through the experiment finally.

In view 2, the two-dimensional Gaussian function is served as the noise filter in Canny operator. Then we use the LIBSVM-FarutoUltimate toolbox to construct SVM classification after obtain the edge features. This toolbox provides a series of auxiliary functions for parameter searching, processing and result visualization, which are more convenient to use. Different inner product kernel functions in SVM will form different algorithms. In this model, we use sigmoid kernel function.

In view 3, in order to improve the speed, we adopt the wavefast function in wavelet toolbox. The Fig. 4 is the original image and its wavelet transform. The left image is the original image, and the right image is a 1-scale wavelet transform. As can be seen from the figure, the low frequency part retains the approximate information, and the high frequency part retains some edge information and noise. In the wavelet neural network, the morlet wavelet shown in Fig. 5 is exploited as the activation function in hidden layer.

Fig. 4. The original image and its wavelet transform.

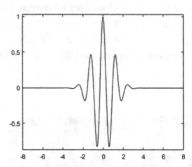

Fig. 5. Morlet wavelet function.

Table 2 shows the recognition rate of the ensemble learning method proposed in this paper. The single classifier is also used to identify the same data set. It can be seen that the recognition rate is lowest when using KNN. Compared with the single classifier, the recognition rate of ensemble learning method has been improved obviously.

Table 2. Average accuracy rates on ORL.

Methods	Rates (%)
LDA + KNN	86.88
Edge detection + SVM	90
Wavelet transform + WNN	91.88
Ensemble learning	96.88

In order to increase the contrast, we select some images from the FERET database randomly. Each person has 7 different images. In the experiment, four images of each person are used for training set randomly and the remaining 3 images of each person are used for testing set. Some of the face images are shown in Fig. 6. Table 3 shows the recognition rate on this small data set. We can see that the ensemble learning method has the highest recognition rate.

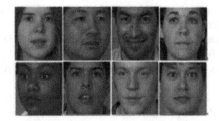

Fig. 6. Some sample images in FERET database.

Table 3. Average accuracy rates on FERET.

Methods	Rates (%)
LDA + KNN	88.54
Edge detection + SVM	92.71
Wavelet transform + WNN	93.75
Ensemble learning	97.91

5   Conclusions

In this paper, combining multiple feature extraction and classification techniques, we propose a method of multi-view ensemble learning in face recognition. A variety of methods are used to extract features, which avoids the incompleteness of information and represents the feature more fully. The classification uses SVM, KNN, WNN as the base classifier to identity respectively. Multi-view results are integrated with voting strategy to ensure the accuracy of identification results. The experimental results show that our method has impressive recognition accuracy on face database.

Future work includes implementing the parallelism of the algorithm to compensate the complexity. In addition, there is a need for further reduction in running time. I believe that face recognition technology will be more prefect, stable and powerful in the near future.

Acknowledgement. This research was financially supported by the National Science Foundation of China (Grant No. 61771293).

References

1. Murillo-Escobar, M.A., Cruz-Hernández, C., Abundiz-Pérez, F., López-Gutiérrez, R.M.: A robust embedded biometric authentication system based on fingerprint and chaotic encryption. Expert Syst. Appl. **42**(21), 8198–8211 (2015)
2. Schroff, F., Kalenichenko, D., Philbin, J.: FaceNet: a unified embedding for face recognition and clustering. In: 2015 IEEE Conference on Computer Vision and Pattern Recognition (CVPR), pp. 815–823. IEEE Press, Boston (2015)

3. Kleinsmith, A., Bianchi-Berthouze, N.: Affective body expression perception and recognition: a survey. IEEE Trans. Affect. Comput. **4**(1), 15–33 (2013)
4. Zipfel, C.: Plant pattern-recognition receptors. Trends Immunol. **35**(7), 345–351 (2014)
5. Drira, H., Ben Amor, B., Srivastava, A., Daoudi, M., Slama, R.: 3D face recognition under expressions, occlusions, and pose variations. IEEE Trans. Pattern Anal. Mach. Intell. **35**(9), 2270–2283 (2013)
6. Zhang, X., Zhang, Y., Zheng, R.: image edge detection method of combining wavelet lift with Canny operator. Procedia Eng. **1**(15), 1335–1339 (2011)
7. Zhang, Y., Dong, Z., Liu, A., Wang, S., Ji, G., Zhang, Z., Yang, J.: Magnetic resonance brain image classification via stationary wavelet transform and generalized eigenvalue proximal support vector machine. J. Med. Imaging Health Inform. **5**(7), 1395–1403 (2015)
8. Gu, B., Sheng, V.S., Tay, K.Y., Romano, W., Li, S.: Incremental support vector learning for ordinal regression. IEEE Trans. Neural Netw. Learn. Syst. **26**(7), 1403–1416 (2014)
9. He, Y., Wu, H., Zhong, R.: Face recognition based on ensemble learning with multiple LBP features. Appl. Res. Comput. **35**(1), 292–295 (2018)
10. Remya, K.R., Ramya, J.S.: Using weighted majority voting classifier combination for relation classification in biomedical texts. In: 2014 International Conference on Control, Instrumentation, Communication and Computational Technologies(ICCICCT), pp. 1205–1209. IEEE Press, Kanyakumari (2014)
11. Martis, R.J., Acharya, U.R., Min, L.C.: ECG beat classification using PCA, LDA, ICA and discrete wavelet transform. Biomed. Signal Process. Control **8**(5), 437–448 (2013)
12. Zhao, Y., You, X., Yu, S.: Multi-view manifold learning with locality alignment. Pattern Recognit. **78**, 154–166 (2018)
13. Ardestani, M., Zhang, X., Wang, L., Lian, Q., Liu, Y.: Human lower extremity joint moment prediction: a wavelet neural network approach. Expert Syst. Appl. **41**(9), 4422–4433 (2014)
14. Guiming, S., Jidong, S.: Remote sensing image edge-detection based on improved Canny operator. In: 2016 8th IEEE International Conference on Communication Software and Networks (ICCSN), pp. 652–656. IEEE Press, Beijing (2016)
15. Xu, W., Shen, Y., Bergmann, N.: Sensor-assisted multi-view face recognition system on smart glass. IEEE Trans. Mob. Comput. **17**(1), 197–210 (2018)

Conditional Face Synthesis for Data Augmentation

Rui Huang[1,2,3], Xiaohua Xie[1,2,3(✉)], Jianhuang Lai[1,2,3],
and Zhanxiang Feng[1,2,3]

[1] School of Data and Computer Science, Sun Yat-sen University, Guangzhou, China
`xiexiaoh6@mail.sysu.edu.cn`
[2] Guangdong Key Laboratory of Information Security Technology, Guangzhou, China
[3] Key Laboratory of Machine Intelligence and Advanced Computing, Ministry of Education, Guangzhou, China

Abstract. Conditional face synthesis has been an appealing yet challenging problem in computer vision. It has a wide range of applications. However, few works attempt to leverage the synthesized face images for data augmentation and improve performance of recognition model. In this paper, we propose a conditional face synthesis framework that combines a variational auto-encoder with a conditional generative adversarial network, for synthesizing face images with specific identity. Our approach has three novel aspects. First, we propose to leverage the synthesized face images to do data augmentation and train a better recognition model. Second, we adopt multi-scale discriminators to enable high-quality image generation. Third, we adopt identity-preserving loss and classification loss to ensure identity invariance of synthesized images, and use feature matching loss to stabilize the GAN training. With extensive qualitative and quantitative evaluation, we demonstrate that face images generated by our approach are realistic, discriminative and diverse. We further show that our approach can be used for data augmentation and train superior face recognition models.

Keywords: Conditional face synthesis · Data augmentation
Generative adversarial network

1 Introduction

Since deep learning is data-driven methods, ample data have been utilized to train high performance models in various computer vision tasks, such as image classification [14], face recognition [20] and so on. However, There are many realistic scenarios which limit data are available. The deep neural networks is prone to overfit in the training set and yield pool generalization ability.

X. Xie—This project is supported by the Natural Science Foundation of China (61702566, 61672544) and Tip-top Scientific and Technical Innovative Youth Talents of Guangdong special support program (No. 2016TQ03X263).

© Springer Nature Switzerland AG 2018
J.-H. Lai et al. (Eds.): PRCV 2018, LNCS 11258, pp. 137–149, 2018.
https://doi.org/10.1007/978-3-030-03338-5_12

Aaron   Adrienne   Alyson   David

Fig. 1. Synthesized faces. Given an identity label and a randomly sampled latent vector, generating diverse face images with specific identity.

As a generative problem in computer vision, image synthesis is appealing yet challenging. In the past few years, it has received great research interests and has a wide range of applications, such as image generation [3], face attribute editing [5], image translation [19], face completion [4], image super-resolution [15] among others. However, exist works seldom utilize the synthesized images for further recognition or detection tasks, like face recognition. In this work, we propose to leverage the synthesized face images for data augmentation and improve performance of recognition model.

Traditional data augmentation techniques [14], like translation, rotation, horizontal flip and random crop, can introduce some known intra-class variance. These techniques are proved to be valid, but the transformations are limit and constant. We argue that we can learn a generative model to do data augmentation. Through a trained model, we can generate images with more abundant intra-class variance.

This work mainly focuses on conditional face synthesis, i.e., given an identity label and a randomly sampled latent vector, generating face images with specific identity, as illustrated in Fig. 1. We hope that synthesized face image have following characteristics: (1) Images are photo-realistic, diverse and rich in intra-class variance, such as pose, illumination and expression. (2) Images must preserve identity so that they can be used for face recognition.

Inspired by CVAE-GAN [3], we propose a conditional face synthesis framework that combines a variational auto-encoder with a conditional generative adversarial network, for synthesizing face images with specific identity. However, we find that using traditional discriminator structure and adversarial loss function will lead to many problems. First, the GAN training is unstable because of the gradient vanishing problem. Then the quality of synthesized face images are poor. Moreover, synthesized images are easy to loss identity information which is the key for recognition task. To tackle these problems, we first adopt multi-scale discriminators [19] to enable high-quality image generation. Specifically, we use multiple discriminators that have the same network structure but handle different image scales to improve image quality. Second, we adopt identity-preserving loss and classification loss to ensure identity invariance of synthesized images. Third, we use feature matching loss to stabilize the GAN training.

In summary, This paper makes the following contributions.

1. We propose a conditional face synthesis framework that combines a variational auto-encoder with a conditional generative adversarial network, for synthesizing face images with specific identity. Furthermore, we leverage the synthesized face images to do data augmentation and train a better recognition model.
2. We adopt multi-scale discriminators to enable high-quality image generation, adopt identity-preserving loss and classification loss to ensure identity invariance of synthesized images, and use feature matching loss to stabilize the GAN training.
3. With extensive qualitative and quantitative evaluation, we demonstrate that face images generated by our approach are realistic, discriminative and diverse. Furthermore, we show that our approach can be used for data augmentation and train superior face recognition models.

2   Related Work

In the last few years, deep generative models have made significant breakthroughs in face synthesis. Since deep neural network is able to learn powerful feature representations, These methods can capture complex data distributions and generate more realistic images than traditional methods. The mainstream face generative models can be roughly divided into two categories: Variational Auto-encoder (VAE) [6] and Generative Adversarial Network (GAN) [2,3,7,11,19].

Variational Auto-encoder (VAE) [6] is one of the most popular approaches to unsupervised learning of complicated distributions. It is actually a pair of connected networks: an encoder and a decoder/generator. The encoder maps an input image to a latent representation, and the decoder/generator converts it back to the original input. With the reparameterization trick [6], VAE is able to be optimized using stochastic gradient descent. However, since VAE uses l2 loss or l1 loss as reconstruction loss, the images generated by VAE often suffer from fuzzy effect.

Generative Adversarial Network (GAN) has attracted significant attention on the research of deep generative models [2,3,7,11,19]. GAN consists of a discriminator D and a generator G that D and G compete in a minimax two-player game. Huang et al. [11] proposed a Two-Pathway Generative Adversarial Network (TP-GAN) for synthesising photorealistic frontal view face from profile. This work perceives global structures and local details simultaneously. To improve the quality of generated images, Wang et al. [19] adopted multi-scale generator and discriminator architectures, as well as improved adversarial loss. Arjovsky et al. [2] adopted Earth Mover Distance to measure the similarity between two distributions, which stabilize the GAN training and alleviate mode-collapse phenomenon to a certain extent.

Bao et al. [3] presents variational generative adversarial networks (CVAE-GAN) for synthesizing images in fine-grained categories. Their work is related to our work. But compared with their method, our method has the following differences: (1) We introduce identity-preserving loss to ensure identity invariance of synthesized images. (2) We adopt multi-scale and multi-task discriminators to enable high-quality image generation.

3 Approach

In this section, we first review the vanilla generative adversarial network (Sect. 3.1). Then we introduce the overall of our conditional face synthesis framework (Sect. 3.2). Next, we describe the detailed network architecture of our method (Sect. 3.3). Finally, we introduce the object functions of the proposed method and the training pipeline (Sect. 3.4).

3.1 Generative Adversarial Network

Generative Adversarial Network (GAN) consists of a discriminator D and a generator G that D and G compete in a minimax two-player game. Specifically, a discriminator D tries to distinguish a real image from a synthesized one, while a generator G tries to capture the data distribution and generate images that can fool D. Specifically, D and G play the following two-player minimax game with value function $V(D, G)$:

$$\min_G\max_D V(D, G) = E_{x \sim p_d(x)}[log D(x)] + E_{z \sim p_z(z)}[log(1 - D(G(z)))] \quad (1)$$

3.2 Problem Formulation

In this section, we elaborate the proposed conditional face synthesis framework. Given an identity label c and a randomly sampled latent vector z, our goal is to generate face images with specific identity. The overall framework is visualized in Fig. 2. Our method consists of four components: (1) encoder network E, (2) generative network G, (3) discriminative network D, (4) identity-preserving network FR. Next, we introduce the function of each component.

The encoder network E is similar to the encoder of VAE. By learning a distribution $P(z|x)$, E first maps the image x to the mean and covariance, and then obtains the latent representation z by reparameterization trick [6]. The generative network G is similar to the generator of conditional GAN [16]. By learning a distribution $P(x|z, c)$, G generates a image $G(z, c)$ given a identity label c and a randomly sampled latent vector z. Specifically, The latent representation z_{encode} is obtained from E and the latent representation z_{random} is sampled from normal gaussian distribution. The generated images are x_{encode} and x_{random}, respectively. Different from the traditional discriminator, we adopt multi-task learning for discriminative network D. D distinguishes real/fake faces and performs identity classification, i.e., estimate the posterior $P(c|x)$, simultaneously. In order to leverage synthesized face images for face recognition task, it is crucial to keep the identity invariance of synthesized images. We thus introduce an identity-preserving network FR to ensure identity invariance through feature matching manner.

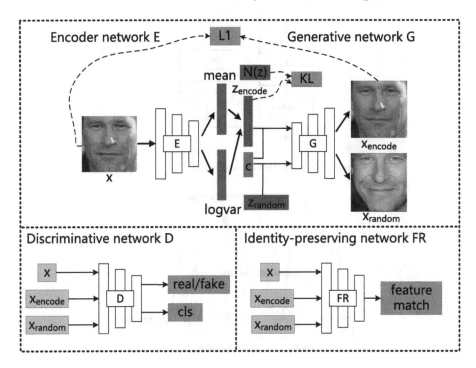

Fig. 2. The overall framework of our conditional face synthesis method. Our method consists of four components: (1) encoder network E, (2) generative network G, (3) discriminative network D, (4) identity-preserving network FR.

3.3   Network Architecture

The encoder network E consists of four residual blocks with 2x downsampling. The architecture of residual block is shown in Fig. 3. The generative network G consists of 6 deconvolution layers with 2x upsampling.

The discriminative network D consists of six convolution layers with 2x downsampling. Different from traditional GAN that the discriminator only distinguishes real/fake images, we adopt multi-task learning for D. D distinguishes real/fake faces and performs identity classification simultaneously. Specifically, our discriminator produces two probability distributions, i.e., $D :$ $x \rightarrow \{D_{src}(x), D_{cls}(x)\}$, where $D_{src}(x)$ is the probability that discriminator regards the input as true, and $D_{cls}(x)$ is the posterior for identity classification.

Recent work [19] shows that the discriminator needs a large receptive field to produce a high-quality image. Inspired by [19], we introduce multi-scale discriminators to distinguish real/fake images from different scales. As illustrated in Fig. 4, we use two discriminators D^1 and D^2. Each has the same network structure but handle images from different scales. The discriminator with coarse scale has large receptive field, which helps to keel global structure information. The discriminator with fine scale has small receptive field, which helps to produce details.

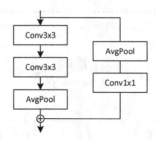

Fig. 3. The architecture of residual block [23].

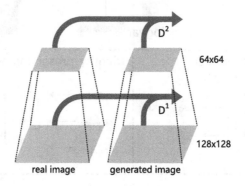

Fig. 4. Illustration of multi-scale discriminators.

3.4 Object Function

The object function used in our approach is a weighted sum of five individual loss functions. Next, we will describe each loss function, respectively.

Adversarial Loss. Traditional GAN uses cross entropy as adversarial loss. Actually at the early stage of training, the distributions of real/fake images may not overlap with each other. So it is easy for D to distinguish real/fake images. This leads to gradient vanishing problem [1]. To stabilize the training process, we use Wasserstein GAN with gradient penalty [2,8] as adversarial loss. It takes the form:

$$
\begin{aligned}
\mathcal{L}_{adv}(G, D^k) =& E_x[D^k_{src}(x)] - E_{z,c}[D^k_{src}(G(z_{encode}, c))]- \\
& E_{z,c}[D^k_{src}(G(z_{random}, c))] - \lambda_{gp}E_{\hat{x}}[(\|\nabla_{\hat{x}}D^k_{src}(\hat{x})\|_2 - 1)^2]
\end{aligned}
\tag{2}
$$

where $D^k_{src}(\cdot)$ denotes the output probability from k-th discriminator. $\hat{x}$ is the linear interpolation between real and fake samples. λ_{gp} is the weight of gradient penalty and we use $\lambda_{gp} = 1.0$ for all experiments.

Feature Match Loss. To stabilize the GAN training, we adopt feature match loss to train generator. Specifically, the feature match loss tries to minimize the distance of intermediate features from multi-scale discriminators between real and fake images. We denote the i-th layer feature of k-th discriminator as $D_{(i)}^k$. The feature match loss is defined as follows:

$$\mathcal{L}_{FM}(G, D^k) = \sum_{i=1}^{T} \frac{1}{N_i} [\|D_{(i)}^k(x) - D_{(i)}^k(G(z_{encode}, c))\|_1 + \qquad (3)$$
$$\|D_{(i)}^k(x) - D_{(i)}^k(G(z_{random}, c))\|_1]$$

where T is the number of layers used for feature matching. N_i is the number of elements in i-th layer. Here we use features of the last three convolution layers.

Pixel Reconstruction Loss. When passing an input image x through E and G, we can get a generated img $G(z_{encode}, c)$. We hope that $G(z_{encode}, c)$ can reconstruct the input x as far as possible. Hence, we adopt pixel-wise L1 loss to maintain structure information:

$$\mathcal{L}_{pixel} = \|x - G(z_{encode}, c)\|_1 \qquad (4)$$

In addition, the encoder network E maps input x to the mean(μ) and covariance(ϵ). We apply KL loss to ensure that the latent representation obeys normal gaussian distribution:

$$\mathcal{L}_{KL} = \frac{1}{2}(\mu^T \mu + sum(exp(\epsilon) - \epsilon - 1)) \qquad (5)$$

Classification Loss. For an arbitrary face image, we hope D can not only distinguish real/fake, but also predict the identity. In detail, the classification loss is defined as

$$\mathcal{L}_{cls}^r(D^k) = E_{x,c}[-log D_{cls}^k(c|x)]$$
$$\mathcal{L}_{cls}^f(G, D^k) = E_{z,c}[-(log D_{cls}^k(c|G(z_{encode}, c)) + log D_{cls}^k(c|G(z_{random}, c)))] \qquad (6)$$

where $D_{cls}^k(c|x)$ represents the posterior for identity classification from k-th discriminator. By minimizing this objective, D tries to classify a real image to its corresponding identity, and G tries to generate a image with specific identity.

Identity-Preserving Loss. In order to leverage synthesized face images for face recognition task, it is crucial to keep the identity invariance of synthesized images. We imitate the perceptual loss [12] widely used in image style transfer. Specifically, with a pre-trained face recognition model Light CNN9 [20], we learn to match the intermediate features between real and fake images that have the same identity. The identity-preserving loss is calculated as follows:

$$\mathcal{L}_{id} = \|FR(x) - FR(G(z_{encode}, c))\|_1 + \|FR(x) - FR(G(z_{random}, c))\|_1 \qquad (7)$$

where $FR(\cdot)$ is the output of penultimate fc layer of Light CNN9. Since Light CNN9 is dedicated to face recognition, its intermediate features contain rich

---

Algorithm 1. The training pipeline

Require: initial network parameters $\{\theta_E, \theta_G, \theta_D, \theta_{FR}\}$, hyper-parameters $\lambda_{cls} = 1, \lambda_{FM} = 1, \lambda_{pixel} = 10, \lambda_{KL} = 0.01, \lambda_{id} = 1$
Ensure: optimal network parameters $\{\theta_E, \theta_G, \theta_D\}$
1: Sample a batch from real data $\{x, c\} \sim P_r$
2: $z_{encode} \leftarrow E(x)$
3: Sample random noise from normal gaussian distribution $z_{random} \sim P_z$
4: $\mathcal{L}_D = \sum_k [-\mathcal{L}_{adv}(G, D^k) + \lambda_{cls} \mathcal{L}_{cls}^r(D^k)]$
5: $\mathcal{L}_{E,G} = \sum_k [\mathcal{L}_{adv}(G, D^k) + \lambda_{cls} \mathcal{L}_{cls}^f(G, D^k) + \lambda_{FM} \mathcal{L}_{FM}(G, D^k)] + \lambda_{pixel} \mathcal{L}_{pixel} + \lambda_{KL} \mathcal{L}_{KL} + \lambda_{id} \mathcal{L}_{id}$
6: $\theta_D \leftarrow \theta_D - \nabla_{\theta_D}(\mathcal{L}_D)$
7: $\theta_{E,G} \leftarrow \theta_{E,G} - \nabla_{\theta_{E,G}}(\mathcal{L}_{E,G})$
8: If not converge, back to step 1; else stop iteration.

---

identity information. So it's reasonable to keep identity invariance by such feature matching manner. During the training process, we freeze the parameters of Light CNN9 and only propagate the gradients back to E and G. We note that a similar loss is used in [11].

Overall Object Function. Finally, the overall object function is a weighted sum of loss functions defined above:

$$\mathcal{L}_D = \sum_k [-\mathcal{L}_{adv}(G, D^k) + \lambda_{cls} \mathcal{L}_{cls}^r(D^k)]$$

$$\mathcal{L}_{E,G} = \sum_k [\mathcal{L}_{adv}(G, D^k) + \lambda_{cls} \mathcal{L}_{cls}^f(G, D^k) + \lambda_{FM} \mathcal{L}_{FM}(G, D^k)] \qquad (8)$$

$$+ \lambda_{pixel} \mathcal{L}_{pixel} + \lambda_{KL} \mathcal{L}_{KL} + \lambda_{id} \mathcal{L}_{id}$$

where $\lambda_{cls}, \lambda_{FM}, \lambda_{pixel}, \lambda_{KL}, \lambda_{id}$ are hyper-parameters to control the importance of each loss. We use $\lambda_{cls} = 1, \lambda_{FM} = 1, \lambda_{pixel} = 10, \lambda_{KL} = 0.01, \lambda_{id} = 1$ for all experiments. The whole training pipeline is shown in Algorithm 1.

4   Experiments

To validate the effectiveness of our approach, we evaluate our model qualitatively and quantitatively on FaceScrub [17] and LFW [9] datasets. We train our model on FaceScrub and test the model on LFW.

At preprocess stage, we perform face detection and get the facial landmarks using the multi-task cascaded CNN [22]. Then we align the faces by similarity transformation based on facial landmarks. The sizes of real and synthesized images are 128×128. All the input are horizontal flip randomly.

For E and G, we use ReLU as activation function. The instance normalization is applied after each convolution layer. For multi-scale discriminators, we use two discriminators D^1 and D^2, where the input of D^1 is 128×128, and the input of D^2 is 64×64. We use Leaky ReLU ($\lambda = 0.01$) as activation function.

In our experiments, the dimension of latent representation is 256. Our model is implemented using deep learning framework pytorch. The models are optimized using Adam [13] with $\beta_1 = 0.5$ and $\beta_2 = 0.999$. We train all models with a learning rate of 0.0002 for the first 100 epochs and linearly decay the learning rate to 0 over the next 100 epochs. Training takes about 36 h on four NVIDIA 1080Ti GPU.

4.1 Qualitative Evaluation

Visualization Comparison. In this section, we compare the proposed method with CVAE and CGAN qualitatively. For CVAE, we remove the discriminative network D and only keep the pixel reconstruction loss $\mathcal{L}_{pixel}$ and KL loss $\mathcal{L}_{KL}$. For CGAN, we remove the encoder network E as well as the pixel reconstruction loss and KL loss, i.e., set λ_{pixel} and λ_{KL} as 0. For fair comparison, we use the same network structure and training data. All methods use G to generate images.

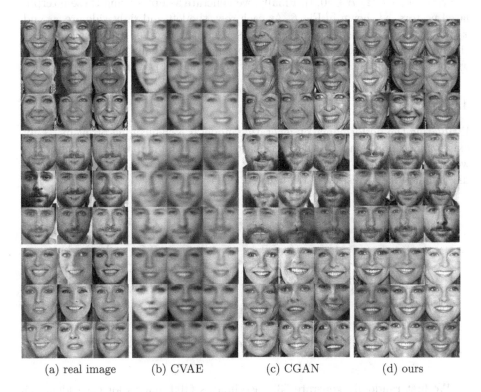

| (a) real image | (b) CVAE | (c) CGAN | (d) ours |

Fig. 5. Visualization results of each method. (a) Real images of 3 different identities. (b) Results of CVAE. It's blur and lack of identity information. (c) Results of CGAN, which losses some structure information in some regions. (d) Our results, which is realistic, diverse and identity-preserving.

At test stage, we first randomly sample a identity c and a latent vector $z \sim N(0, I)$, and then pass them through G to generate a image with identity c. The visualization results of each method are shown in Fig. 5. We can see that images generated by CVAE are very blur. The reason is that CVAE merely uses the l1 reconstruction loss. Then images generated by CGAN often loss structure information in some regions, which is because of the absence of encoder. On the contrary, images generated by our approach are realistic and contain abundant intra-class variance, such as pose and expression. Furthermore, our method can keep the identity well. This shows the effectiveness of our approach.

Latent Representation Interpolation. To validate that our method can learn continuous and general latent space, we perform interpolation for latent representation. Specifically, we first randomly choose two faces of the same identity x_1 and x_2, and then get latent vectors z_1 and z_2 through encoder network E. Next, we obtain a series of latent vectors by linear interpolation, i.e., $z = \alpha z_1 + (1 - \alpha)z_2, \alpha \in [0, 1]$. Finally, we generate samples using these interpolated vectors, as shown in Fig. 6. At each row, the left and right side are x_1 and x_2, respectively. The interpolation results are in the middle. It can be seen that the facial pose, expression and skin color change gradually from left to right, which shows that the latent space learnt by our model is continuous.

4.2 Quantitative Evaluation

Evaluating the performance of generative model is a challenging problem. Many existing methods in face synthesis evaluate images by human, which is a laborious work and lack of objectivity. Following [3], we evaluate the model on image discriminability, realism and diversity.

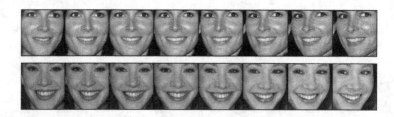

Fig. 6. The result of latent representation interpolation

We first randomly generate 53k face images (100 images for each identity) using our method, CVAE and CGAN, respectively. To validate the discriminability of generated images, we train a face classification model using real data. Here we choose Light CNN29 [20] as a basic model, whose structure is similar to Light CNN9 but deeper than it. With the pre-trained classification model, we calculate the top-1 accuracy of images generated by each method. Table 1 shows the results. Since CVAE merely uses the l1 reconstruction loss. It can't ensure identity invariance. So the accuracy is very poor. Our method achieve the best top-1 accuracy, showing significant margin than CVAE and is closing to real data (99.56% vs 99.69%). This suggests that images generated by our method is discriminative. It can be noted that CGAN also achieve high accuracy. We guess it's the contribution of identity-preserving loss. To validate this assumption, We remove the identity-preserving loss (set λ_{id} as 0), and retrain the model. We find that the accuracy drops dramatically (from 99.56% to 79.50%), which demonstrates that the identity-preserving loss plays a crucial role in keeping identity information.

We adopt inception score [18] to evaluate the realism and diversity of generated images. Specifically, we first train a face recognition model on CASIA-Webface [21] dataset, and then use $exp(E_x KL(p(y|x) \| p(y)))$ as metric. If the model can generate more photo-realistic and diverse images, the inception score will be higher. From Table 1 we can see that our method achieve the highest score and is closing to the real data.

Table 1. Quantitative evaluation of image discriminability, realism and diversity.

-	Real image	CVAE	CGAN	Ours	Ours (w/o $\mathcal{L}_{id}$)
Top-1 accuracy	99.69%	29.13%	98.35%	**99.56%**	79.50%
Inception score	48.86 ± .79	20.81 ± .21	43.95 ± .46	**45.17 ± .59**	44.14 ± .45

4.3 Data Augmentation

The ultimate goal of this paper is to utilize generated images to train better face recognition models. In this section, we further demonstrate that our method can be used for data augmentation. We use FaceScrub as training set and LFW as testing set.

Following [3], we exploit two data augmentation strategies: (1) Generating more faces of existing identities. (2) Generating faces of new identities by mixing existing identity label. For strategy 1, we generate 200 images for each person in training set and get totally 100k images. For strategy 2, we first randomly sample 5k new identities by linearly interpolating three existing identity label, and then generate 100 images for each new identity, getting totally 500k images. The generated images are combined with original FaceScrub dataset to train face recognition model. The models used in this experiment are Light CNN29 [20] and Concentrate Loss [10].

At the testing stage, we use the output of penultimate fc layer as face feature. We adopt cosine similarity as metric for Light CNN29 and euclidean distance for Concentrate Loss. We compare the LFW accuracy with and without data augmentation, as shown in Table 2. We can observe that, Light CNN29 gets 1.30% improvement (from 92.23% to 93.53%) with existing ID augmentation and 0.90%

improvement (from 92.23% to 93.13%) with new ID augmentation. Consistently, Concentrate Loss gets 1.10% improvement (from 93.12% to 94.22%) with existing ID augmentation and 1.08% improvement (from 93.12% to 94.20%) with new ID augmentation. This demonstrates that our method can be used for data augmentation effectively and bring improvement for face recognition.

Table 2. Results of data augmentation

-	Data size	Light CNN29	Concentrate loss
Without data augmentation	90K	92.23%	93.12%
Existing ID augmentation	90K + 100K	93.53%	94.22%
New ID augmentation	90K + 500K	93.13%	94.20%

5   Conclusion

In this paper, we propose a conditional face synthesis framework that combines a variational auto-encoder with a conditional generative adversarial network, for synthesizing face images with specific identity. To improve image quality, we adopt multi-scale discriminators. Furthermore, we incorporate identity-preserving loss and classification loss to ensure identity invariance of synthesized images, and use feature matching loss to stabilize the GAN training. Experimental results demonstrate that our approach not only produces realistic, discriminative and diverse images but also is available for data augmentation.

References

1. Arjovsky, M., Bottou, L.: Towards principled methods for training generative adversarial networks. arXiv preprint arXiv:1701.04862 (2017)
2. Arjovsky, M., Chintala, S., Bottou, L.: Wasserstein generative adversarial networks. In: International Conference on Machine Learning, pp. 214–223 (2017)
3. Bao, J., Chen, D., Wen, F., Li, H., Hua, G.: CVAE-GAN: fine-grained image generation through asymmetric training. arXiv preprint arXiv:1703.10155 (2017)
4. Chen, Z., Nie, S., Wu, T., Healey, C.G.: High resolution face completion with multiple controllable attributes via fully end-to-end progressive generative adversarial networks. arXiv preprint arXiv:1801.07632 (2018)
5. Choi, Y., Choi, M., Kim, M., Ha, J.W., Kim, S., Choo, J.: StarGAN: unified generative adversarial networks for multi-domain image-to-image translation. arXiv preprint arXiv:1711.09020 (2017)
6. Doersch, C.: Tutorial on variational autoencoders. arXiv preprint arXiv:1606.05908 (2016)
7. Goodfellow, I., et al.: Generative adversarial nets. In: Advances in Neural Information Processing Systems, pp. 2672–2680 (2014)
8. Gulrajani, I., Ahmed, F., Arjovsky, M., Dumoulin, V., Courville, A.C.: Improved training of wasserstein gans. In: Advances in Neural Information Processing Systems, pp. 5769–5779 (2017)

9. Huang, G.B., Ramesh, M., Berg, T., Learned-Miller, E.: Labeled faces in the wild: a database for studying face recognition in unconstrained environments. Technical Report 07–49, University of Massachusetts, Amherst (2007)

10. Huang, R., Xie, X., Feng, Z., Lai, J.: Face recognition by landmark pooling-based CNN with concentrate loss. In: IEEE International Conference on Image Processing, pp. 1582–1586 (2017)

11. Huang, R., Zhang, S., Li, T., He, R., et al.: Beyond face rotation: global and local perception GAN for photorealistic and identity preserving frontal view synthesis. arXiv preprint arXiv:1704.04086 (2017)

12. Johnson, J., Alahi, A., Fei-Fei, L.: Perceptual losses for real-time style transfer and super-resolution. In: Leibe, B., Matas, J., Sebe, N., Welling, M. (eds.) ECCV 2016. LNCS, vol. 9906, pp. 694–711. Springer, Cham (2016). https://doi.org/10.1007/978-3-319-46475-6_43

13. Kingma, D.P., Ba, J.: Adam: a method for stochastic optimization. arXiv preprint arXiv:1412.6980 (2014)

14. Krizhevsky, A., Sutskever, I., Hinton, G.E.: ImageNet classification with deep convolutional neural networks. In: Advances in Neural Information Processing Systems, pp. 1097–1105 (2012)

15. Ledig, C., et al.: Photo-realistic single image super-resolution using a generative adversarial network, 2016. arXiv preprint arXiv:1609.04802 (2017)

16. Mirza, M., Osindero, S.: Conditional generative adversarial nets. arXiv preprint arXiv:1411.1784 (2014)

17. Ng, H.W., Winkler, S.: A data-driven approach to cleaning large face datasets. In: 2014 IEEE International Conference on Image Processing (ICIP), pp. 343–347. IEEE (2014)

18. Salimans, T., Goodfellow, I., Zaremba, W., Cheung, V., Radford, A., Chen, X.: Improved techniques for training GANs. In: Advances in Neural Information Processing Systems, pp. 2234–2242 (2016)

19. Wang, T.C., Liu, M.Y., Zhu, J.Y., Tao, A., Kautz, J., Catanzaro, B.: High-resolution image synthesis and semantic manipulation with conditional GANs. arXiv preprint arXiv:1711.11585 (2017)

20. Wu, X., He, R., Sun, Z., Tan, T.: A light CNN for deep face representation with noisy labels. arXiv preprint arXiv:1511.02683 (2015)

21. Yi, D., Lei, Z., Liao, S., Li, S.Z.: Learning face representation from scratch. arXiv preprint arXiv:1411.7923 (2014)

22. Zhang, K., Zhang, Z., Li, Z., Qiao, Y.: Joint face detection and alignment using multitask cascaded convolutional networks. IEEE Signal Process. Lett. **23**(10), 1499–1503 (2016)

23. Zhu, J.Y., et al.: Toward multimodal image-to-image translation. In: Advances in Neural Information Processing Systems, pp. 465–476 (2017)

Face Image Illumination Processing Based on GAN with Dual Triplet Loss

Wei Ma[1], Xiaohua Xie[1,2,3(✉)], Jianhuang Lai[1,2,3], and Junyong Zhu[1,2,3]

[1] Sun Yat-sen University, Guangzhou, China
mawei23@mail2.sysu.edu.cn
{stsljh,xiexiaoh6,zhujuny5}@mail.sysu.edu.cn
[2] Guangdong Key Laboratory of Information Security Technology, Guangzhou, China
[3] Key Laboratory of Machine Intelligence and Advanced Computing, Ministry of Education, Beijing, China

Abstract. It is generally known that the illumination could seriously affect the performance of face analysis algorithms. Moreover, in most practical applications, the illumination is usually uncontrolled. A number of methods have been put forward to tackle the problem of illumination variations in face images, but they always only work on facial region and need to segment faces in advance. Furthermore, many illumination processing methods only demonstrate on grayscale images and require strict alignment of face images, resulting in limited applications in the real world. In this paper, we propose a face image illumination processing method based on the Generative Adversarial Network (GAN) with dual triplet loss. Through considering the inter-domain similarity and intra-domain difference between the generated images and the real images, we put forward the dual triplet loss. At the same time, we introduce the self-similarity constraint of the images in the target illumination field. Experiments on the CMU Multi-PIE face datasets demonstrate that the proposed method preserve the facial details well when relighting. The experiment of 3D face reconstruction also verifies the effectiveness of the proposed method.

Keywords: Face image · Illumination processing
Generative adversarial nets · Dual triplet loss

1 Introduction

Because of the great development of biometric recognition and machine learning, face analysis technologies, such as face detection, face recognition and 3D face reconstruction, have received great attention. Nowadays, in a highly constrained environment, many classical algorithms have been able to achieve nearly perfect performance. However, in the real world, the imaging environment in most applications is uncontrolled. For example, the user's posture or expression are not a neutral state, the illumination condition changes and so on. Compared

© Springer Nature Switzerland AG 2018
J.-H. Lai et al. (Eds.): PRCV 2018, LNCS 11258, pp. 150–161, 2018.
https://doi.org/10.1007/978-3-030-03338-5_13

with other interference factors, illumination has a greater impact on many face analysis algorithms. Therefore, the normalization of illumination is crucial for exploring the method of illumination invariant.

Over the years, a large number of methods on illumination invariance have been put forward. The invariant feature method is proposed to get the illumination invariant feature of images. Among them, Xie et al. [3] divided face images into large scale and small scale, and processed them separately. Recently, Wang et al. [4] proposed robust principal component analysis to eliminate the shadow produced by high-frequency features based on Xie's work. All these methods have achieved impressive results in the removal of soft shadows, but they are not effective in dealing with problems such as hard edge shadow caused by self occlusion. At the same time, these technologies can not be extended to color space, resulting in limited application in the real world.

With the development of 3D technology and deep learning, many researchers turn to use them to solve the illumination problems. Zhao et al. [5] propose a method for minimizing illumination difference by unlighting a 3D face texture via albedo estimation using lighting maps. Hold-Geoffroy et al. [6] trained a convolutional neural network to deduce the illumination parameters and reconstruct the illumination environment map. These methods are powerful and accurate. However, they are easily limited by data collection and unavoidable highly computing cost. In addition, most of the existing methods only focus on dealing with the carefully segmented face regions, which are not robust to the whole face images.

Inspired by the successful application of the Generative Adversarial Network in transfer learning [8] and domain adaptation [9], we propose to reformulate the face image illumination processing problem as a style translation task with a Generative Adversarial Network (GAN) in [10]. By using the circle reversible iterative scheme and via the multi-scale adversarial learning, we build the mapping from any complex illumination field to a target illumination field and its inverse mapping to effectively achieve the normalization of illumination without affecting any other non-illumination features of the image. In this paper, by analyzing the distance relationship between the generated image and the real image, an improved illumination processing method based on the dual triplet loss is proposed in order to better retain the details of the image and improve the quality of the generated image.

Overall, our contributions are as follows:

- We propose an improved illumination processing method based on Generative Adversarial Nets with dual triplet loss.
- We put forward the dual triplet loss through considering the inter-domain similarity and intra-domain difference between the generated images and the real images.
- We introduce the self-similarity constraint of the images in the target illumination field and add two image similarity indexes, SSIM and PSNR, to supplement the measure of similarity.

– We demonstrate that the proposed method can outperforms the state-of-the-arts realistic visualization results on non-strictly aligned color face images and eliminate the ill effects caused by illumination.

2 The Proposed Approach

2.1 Overall Network Framework

The overall network framework of our generative adversarial nets is shown in Fig. 1. The same as [10], our network consists of one generator and a pair of multi-scale discriminators with the same network structure but different classification constraint. We train G to translate an input image x under any lighting conditions into an expected lighting image $\tilde{x}'$ conditioned on the target illumination label c', $G(x, c') \rightarrow \tilde{x}'$. And then reconstruct $\tilde{x}'$ to the input image conditioned on the original illumination label c using the same G, $G(\tilde{x}', c) \rightarrow \tilde{x}$. The discriminator $D1$ distinguishes between the synthesized output images $\tilde{x}'$ and the real ones x, and classify the illumination category $\tilde{c}'$. The classification loss of real images used to optimize $D1$, and the fake images' used to optimize G. Similar but different, $D2$ distinguishes between $\tilde{x}'$ and a randomly selected picture y' of maybe anybody's under target illumination condition and recognizes the identity $\tilde{l}'$ to optimize G and $D2$.

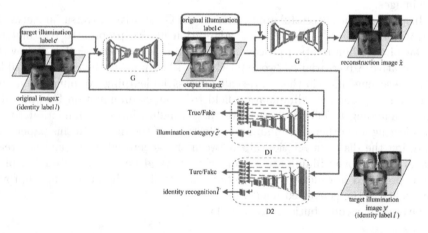

Fig. 1. Basic network architecture for face image illumination processing based on GAN with dual triplet loss.

2.2 Inter-domain Similarity and Intra-domain Difference

According to our research idea, face images under the same illumination conditions are divided into the same domain and our goal is to learn the mapping from any other illumination domain to the target illumination domain, which refs the positive standard illumination in this paper. As shown in Fig. 2(a), the images before and after illumination normalization belong to different illumination domains, but their non-illumination information are same, which we call "inter-domain similarity". At the same time, the different images after normalization belong to the same illumination domain, but their non-illumination information are different, which we call "intra-domain difference".

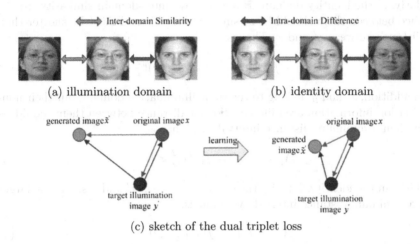

(a) illumination domain   (b) identity domain

(c) sketch of the dual triplet loss

Fig. 2. Sketch of inter-domain similarity, intra-domain difference and the dual triplet loss.

Besides, as shown in Fig. 2(b). If we treat the non-illumination information as a symbol of the domain division, the two images before and after the normalization belong to the same identity domain, but their illumination information are different. That is, the two images have intra-domain difference now. Similarly, for any two different images after illumination normalization, they belong to different identity domains, but their illumination information are consistent. That is, the two images have inter-domain similarity now.

2.3   Dual Triplet Loss

Inspired by the thought of the triplet loss [11], we propose to construct a dual triplet loss based on the intra-domain difference and inter-domain similarity between the generated image and the real image. As is shown in Fig. 2(c).

The dual triplet loss include two triplet loss, each is composed of the original image x, the generated image $\tilde{x}'$ after illumination normalization and the real image y' captured randomly from the target illumination domain. The first triplet loss takes y' as anchor and takes $\tilde{x}'$ and x as positive and negative sample respectively. The second triplet loss takes x as anchor and takes $\tilde{x}'$ and y' as positive and negative sample respectively.

Define $f(x)$, $f(\tilde{x}')$ and $f(y')$ are the features of x, $\tilde{x}'$ and y' extracted from our multi-scale discriminant network. In the illumination domain, x and $\tilde{x}'$ have inter-domain similarity. So the distance between them should be as small as possible and must be shorter than the distance between y' and x. That is:

$$\|f(x) - f(\tilde{x}')\|_2^2 - \|f(x) - f(y')\|_2^2 < 0 \tag{1}$$

Similarly, in the identity domain, $\tilde{x}'$ and y' have inter-domain similarity. So the distance between them should be as small as possible and must be shorter than the distance between y' and x. That is:

$$\|f(y') - f(\tilde{x}')\|_2^2 - \|f(y') - f(x)\|_2^2 < 0 \tag{2}$$

In addition, $\tilde{x}'$ and y' belong to the same illumination domain, but their non-illumination information are different. So, the distance between them should be larger than a minimum distance interval Δ_1. That is:

$$\Delta_1 - \|f(y') - f(\tilde{x}')\|_2^2 < 0 \tag{3}$$

Similarly, in the identity domain, the distance between $\tilde{x}'$ and x should be larger than a minimum distance interval Δ_2. That is:

$$\Delta_2 - \|f(x) - f(\tilde{x}')\|_2^2 < 0 \tag{4}$$

In summary, the formula for calculating the loss function of dual triplet constraints is:

$$
\begin{aligned}
L_{dual-tri} &= \mathbb{E}[\|f(x) - f(\tilde{x}')\|_2^2 - \|f(x) - f(y')\|_2^2]_+ \\
&+ \mathbb{E}[\|f(y') - f(\tilde{x}')\|_2^2 - \|f(y') - f(x)\|_2^2]_+ \\
&+ \mathbb{E}[\Delta_1 - \|f(y') - f(\tilde{x}')\|_2^2]_+ + \mathbb{E}[\Delta_2 - \|f(x) - f(\tilde{x}')\|_2^2]_+
\end{aligned} \tag{5}
$$

where $[\bullet]_+$ is a brief description of $max[\bullet, 0]$, which indicates that the loss is valid only when the result value of $[]$ is greater than 0, otherwise it is recorded as 0. The threshold distance Δ_1 is set as the minimum value of the feature distance between any two face images in the target illumination domain of the current training batch. Similarity, Δ_2 is set to the minimum value of the distance between any two face images in the original identity domain.

2.4   Self-similarity Constraint and Reconstruction Loss

The ideal function of the generate network is transferring the input image to the target illumination and keeping the non-illumination information unchanged. Therefore, if we use any real image of target illumination domain as input, the generated image should be the same as the original, namely "self-similarity. Because the illumination scene of them are already the target illumination and don't need to be transferred.

Similar to the definition of the reconstruction loss in the previous article, we use the L1 distance to measure the error between the input and output image at first. The self-similarity constraint can be defined as

$$L_{rec-y'} = \mathbb{E}\|y' - G(y', c)\|_1 \tag{6}$$

L1 distance calculation is the sum of the absolute values of the corresponding pixel difference of all pixels between two images. The advantage is that it is convenient to calculate and can ignore the influence of the abnormal value in the image data, which is relatively stable and robust. But its disadvantage is also obvious, that is, the space between the pixels and their neighborhood is omitted, which may lead to the loss of high frequency information such as texture and detail. Based on the confirmation in [10], we use SSIM [12] and PSNR [13] to supplement the L1 distance in the image reconstruction constraint. Define:

$$
\begin{aligned}
L_{SSIM}(x_1, x_2) &= 1 - SSIM(x_1, x_2) \\
&= 1 - \frac{(2\mu_{x_1}\mu_{x_2} + c_1)(2\sigma_{x_1 x_2} + c_2)}{(\mu_{x_1}^2 + \mu_{x_2}^2 + c_1)(\sigma_{x_1}^2 + \sigma_{x_2}^2 + c_2)}
\end{aligned} \tag{7}
$$

$$
\begin{aligned}
L_{PSNR}(x_1, x_2) &= 1 - \frac{PSNR(x_1, x_2)}{30} \\
&= 1 - \frac{1}{3} \log \frac{MAX_x{}^2}{MSE(x_1, x_2)}
\end{aligned} \tag{8}
$$

where MAX_x is the maximum possible pixel value of the image. $MSE(x_1, x_2)$ is the mean squared error of x_1 and x_2. μ_{x_1}, μ_{x_2}, and σ_{x_1}, σ_{x_2} are the average and variance of x_1 and x_2 respectively. $\sigma_{x_1 x_2}$ is the covariance of x_1 and x_2. $c_1 = (0.01L)^2$ and $c_2 = (0.03L)^2$ are two variables to stabilize the division with weak denominator, in which L is the dynamic range of the pixel-values (1 in this paper). Special to note is that we use an empirical value of 30 to normalize the PSNR value.

Then the final cycle consistency loss of the generator can be written as

$$
\begin{aligned}
L_{rec-all} &= L_{rec-new} + \alpha_1 L_{rec-y'-new} \\
&= \mathbb{E}\|x - x_{rec}\|_1 + \alpha_2(L_{SSIM}(x, x_{rec}) + L_{PSNR}(x, x_{rec})) \\
&+ \alpha_1(L_{rec-y'} + \alpha_3(L_{SSIM}(y', G(y', c)) + L_{PSNR}(y', G(y', c))))
\end{aligned} \tag{9}
$$

We use $\alpha_2 = 0.5$, $\alpha_3 = 0.5$ and $\alpha_1 = 2$ in all of our experiments.

2.5 Loss Function

Base Loss. To stabilize the training process and generate higher quality images, we use Wasserstein GAN objective with gradient penalty as [8, 10, 14, 15]. Define $\breve{x}_1$ and $\breve{x}_2$ are sampled uniformly along a straight line between a pair of real image and generated image, as well as a pair of target illumination image and generated image. The discriminator network $D1$ and $D2$ update their parameters by minimizing the following loss:

$$L_{adv1} = \mathbb{E}[D1_{src}(x)] - \mathbb{E}[D1_{src}(G(x,c'))] - \lambda_{gp}\mathbb{E}[(\|\nabla_{\breve{x}_2}D1_{src}(\breve{x}_1)\|_2 - 1)^2]$$
$$(10)$$
$$L_{adv2} = \mathbb{E}[D2_{src}(y')] - \mathbb{E}[D2_{src}(G(x,c'))] - \lambda_{gp}\mathbb{E}[(\|\nabla_{\breve{x}_2}D2_{src}(\breve{x}_2)\|_2 - 1)^2]$$
$$(11)$$

where we use $\lambda_{gp} = 10$ for all experiments.

For an input image x whose identity label is l and a target illumination label c', our goal is to translate x into an output image $\tilde{x}'$, which is properly classified by $D1$ to c' and recognized by $D2$ to l. The classification loss for illumination and identity classification task can be defined uniformly as

$$L_{cls1} = \mathbb{E}[log D1_{cls}(\hat{c}|\hat{x})] \tag{12}$$

$$L_{cls2} = \mathbb{E}[log D2_{cls}(\hat{c}|\hat{x})] \tag{13}$$

where $\hat{x}$ represents the image to be classified and the item $\hat{c}$ represents the proper label $\hat{x}$ should be in this classification task.

Loss Function for Generator. Define the illumination label and identity label of the synthesized output image as $\tilde{c}'$ and $\tilde{l}'$. So, the base objective functions to optimize G can be written as

$$\begin{aligned} L_{G-base} &= L_{adv1}(x, G(x,c')) + L_{adv2}(y', G(x,c')) \\ &+ \alpha_4 L_{cls1}(\tilde{c}', c) + \alpha_5 L_{cls2}(\tilde{l}', l) \end{aligned} \tag{14}$$

where α_4 and α_5 are hyper-parameters that control the relative importance of illumination classification and identity recognition losses respectively, compared to the adversarial loss. We set $\alpha_4 = 1$ and $\alpha_5 = 1$. According to Eqs. (14, 9, 5), the overall objective functions to optimize G can be written as

$$L_G = L_{G-base} + \alpha_6 L_{rec-all} + \alpha_7 L_{dual-tri} \tag{15}$$

The detailed description of all the individual loss functions was postpone above. We use $a_6 = 10$ and $a_7 = 10$ in all of our experiments.

Loss Function for Discriminator. The networks parameters of $D1$ and $D2$ can be optimized by minimizing a specifically designed adversarial loss L_{adv1}, L_{adv2} and the aforementioned classification loss L_{cls1}, L_{cls2} of the real one's respectively:

$$L_{D1} = -L_{adv1}(x, G(x,c')) + \alpha_8 L_{cls1}(\tilde{c}', c) \tag{16}$$

$$L_{D2} = -L_{adv2}(y', G(x,c')) + \alpha_9 L_{cls2}(\tilde{l}', l') \tag{17}$$

we set a_8 and a_9 as 1 in our experiments.

2.6   Model Training

We summarize the details of our algorithm training procedure in Algorithm 1. And we use the same history updating strategy as [10]. Moreover, we set $K_d = 5$, $K_g = 1$, $T = 1000$ and $lr_G = lr_D = 0.0001$ in the first 500 iterations, which both decay to 0 linearly in the following iterations.

Algorithm 1. Face Image Illumination Processing Based on the Dual Triplet Loss

---

Input: Real images x, identity label l, illumination label c and target illumination label c'. Images with target illumination y', identity label l'. Max number of steps T, number of the two discriminator network update per step k_d, number of generative network updates per step K_g, the learning rate of lr_G and lr_D.

Output: The network parameters

```
 1  for i = 1 : T do
 2      for k = 1 : k_d do
 3          Sample a batch of real images x and target illumination images y';
 4          Get G(x, c') with current network;
 5          If the history buffer is not null, update the batch content with half a
            batch images sampling from the buffer;
 6          Update network parameters of D1 by taking a Adam step on batch loss
            L_D1 in Eq. (16);
 7          Update network parameters of D2 by taking a Adam step on batch loss
            L_D2 in Eq. (17);
 8          Sample half a batch images from the original G(x, c') and add to the
            history buffer.
 9      end
10      for k = 1 : k_g do
11          Sample a batch of real images x and target illumination images y';
12          Get G(x, c') and G(y', c) with current network;
13          Reconstruct G(G(x, c'), c) and update network parameters of G by
            taking a Adam step on batch loss L_G in Eq. (15)
14      end
15  end
```

---

3 Experimental Results and Analysis

Experiments were conducted on the CMU Multi-PIE Face Database [1] to verify the effectiveness of the proposed methods. Notably, all the images in this dataset are color images, which is always a challenge on illumination normalization for traditional methods. In our experiments, we restrict our attention merely to the frontal face images with neutral expression. All images are simply aligned and resized to 128×128 pixels, among which the first 2000 pictures were used for test and the others used for training.

3.1 Comparisons of the Visual Quality with Other Methods

For convenience, we denote our previous base method in [10] as GAN-base and denote this paper's method as GAN-DTL. In Fig. 3, we compare the visual results of normalized images between the proposed GAN-DTL method, GAN-base method and two baseline algorithms: NPL-QI [17] and ITI [18]. Same as other traditional methods, these two baseline algorithms can only process gray images and require strict alignment of face images. However, even on gray images, they don't work well. For example, the NPL-QI method can't handle the extreme illumination conditions such as the first group and the third group. There is a general loss of detail in face after processing of the ITI method. And these two methods are not effective in dealing with the self occlusion of nose in the second groups. In contrast, our GAN-DTL method and GAN-base method achieve the best normalization performance and preserve more facial details and almost all appearance information, such as the hairstyle and hair color. At the same time, our GAN-DTL method provides a higher visual quality of normalization results on all kinds of test images. Different skin colors were preserved closer to the original ones, especially obvious on the first group image. And the details of eyeglass frame and whiskers in the third group are preserved more perfect. The result indicated that the proposed GAN-DTL method can preserve the details of generated images better and improve the quality of generated images.

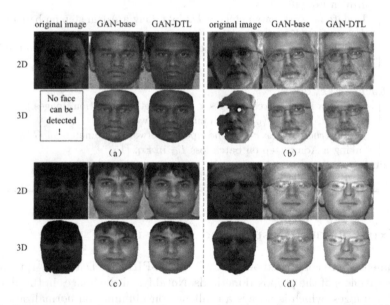

Fig. 3. Quantitative evaluation results comparison between the proposed GAN-DTL method, GAN-base method and two baseline algorithms.

3.2   Comparisons of the Ablation Study

We conduct ablation studies to show the superiority of our GAN-DTL method. We carry out the experiment on our 2000 test images. Take the face image of the same face under the target illumination as benchmark, we calculate the SSIM value and PSNR value of the original image, the generated image of GAN-base and the generated image of GAN-DTL respectively. And take the mean value according to the original illumination category then, which are drawn in black, blue and red curves in Fig. 4 respectively. As we can see, our GAN-DTL method improves the evaluation results to a new height. The total average value of the SSIM is raised from 0.550 of the GAN-base method to 0.736 and the total average of the PSNR is raised from 16.048 to 21.324, which is consistent with the evaluation of the visual effect.

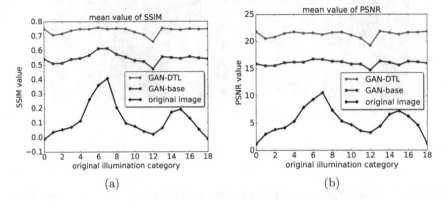

Fig. 4. Comparisons of the ablation study SSIM and PSNR. (Color figure online)

3.3 Test of Face Algorithm Application

We use the online 3D face reconstruction from a single image algorithm [19] which is put forward by the team of nottingham university in 2017. As is shown in Fig. 5. As the initial 3D reconstructed image is not a positive angle of view, the angle and size of the pictures are slightly deviated when they are manually rotated to the front view. But it obviously does not affect the experimental comparison. In group (a), as the original image is in the dark light condition and the skin color of the face is black, the face can not be detected in the 3D reconstruction. In group (b), due to the uneven illumination of original images, the location of facial landmarking is not allowed, resulting in partial deletion of reconstructed 3D models. Similarly, in group (c) and group (d), the face region segmentation of the original image is inaccurate due to the influence of illumination on the location of facial landmarking, and the rough edge produced by the shadow in the chin area. However, in the four sets of images, the 3D model can be built very well and smoothly for the generated images after our GAN-DTL and GAN-base method illumination normalization. And our GAN-DTL method achieve the best results and illustrate the effectiveness of the proposed method in real-world applications.

4 Conclusion

In this paper, we propose a face image illumination processing method based on Generative Adversarial Nets with dual triplet loss. Through considering

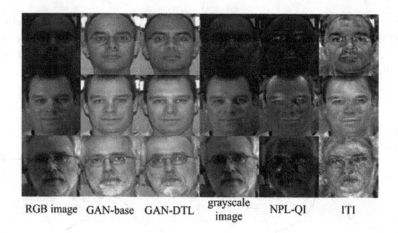

RGB image   GAN-base   GAN-DTL   grayscale image   NPL-QI   ITI

Fig. 5. 3D face reconstruction from a single image.

the inter-domain similarity and intra-domain difference between the generated images and the real images, we put forward the dual triplet loss. At the same time, we introduce the self-similarity constraint of the target illumination images and add two image similarity indexes, SSIM and PSNR, to supplement the measure of similarity. Experiments on the CMU Multi-PIE face datasets demonstrate that the proposed method preserve the details of generated images and improve the quality of generated images. The 3D face reconstruction experiment shows that the face images after our methods processing can eliminate the ill effects caused by illumination, and illustrates the effectiveness of the proposed methods in real-world applications.

Acknowledgment. This project is supported by the Natural Science Foundation of China (61672544, 61702566), Fundamental Research Funds for the Central Universities (No. 161gpy41), and the Tip-top Scientific and Technical Innovative Youth Talents of Guangdong special support program (No. 2016TQ03X263).

References

1. Gross, R., et al.: Multi-pie. Image Vis. Comput. **28**(5), 807–813 (2010)
2. Adini, Y., Moses, Y., Ullman, S.: Face recognition: the problem of compensating for changes in illumination direction. IEEE Trans. Pattern Anal. Mach. Intell. **19**(7), 721–732 (1997)
3. Xie, X., et al.: Normalization of face illumination based on large-and small-scale features. IEEE Trans. Image Process. **20**(7), 1807–1821 (2011)
4. Wang, H., Ye, M., Yang, S.: Shadow compensation and illumination normalization of face image. Mach. Vis. Appl. **24**(6), 1121–1131 (2013)
5. Zhao, X., et al.: Minimizing illumination differences for 3D to 2D face recognition using lighting maps. IEEE Trans. Cybern. **44**(5), 725–736 (2014)
6. Hold-Geoffroy, Y., et al.: Deep outdoor illumination estimation. In: IEEE Conference on Computer Vision and Pattern Recognition, vol. 1, no. 2 (2017)

7. Wu, Z., Deng, W.: One-shot deep neural network for pose and illumination normalization face recognition. In: 2016 IEEE International Conference on Multimedia and Expo (ICME). IEEE (2016)
8. Choi, Y., Choi, M., Kim, M., et al.: StarGAN: unified generative adversarial networks for multi-domain image-to-image translation (2017)
9. Patel, V.M., et al.: Visual domain adaptation: a survey of recent advances. IEEE Sig. Process. Mag. **32**(3), 53–69 (2015)
10. Anonymous: Face image illumination processing based on generative adversarial nets. In: 24th International Conference on Pattern Recognition (ICPR) (2018)
11. Schroff, F., Kalenichenko, D., Philbin, J.: FaceNet: a unified embedding for face recognition and clustering. In: Proceedings of the IEEE Conference on Computer Vision and Pattern Recognition (2015)
12. Wang, Z., et al.: Image quality assessment: from error visibility to structural similarity. IEEE Trans. Image Process. **13**(4), 600–612 (2004)
13. Hore, A., Ziou, D.: Image quality metrics: PSNR vs. SSIM. In: 2010 20th International Conference on Pattern recognition (ICPR). IEEE (2010)
14. Martin, A., Chintala, S., Bottou, L.: Wasserstein generative adversarial networks. In: International Conference on Machine Learning (2017)
15. Gulrajani, I., et al.: Improved training of Wasserstein GANs. Advances in Neural Information Processing Systems (2017)
16. Phillips, P.J., et al.: Overview of the face recognition grand challenge. In: IEEE Computer Society Conference on Computer Vision and Pattern Recognition 2005. CVPR 2005, vol. 1. IEEE (2005)
17. Xie, X., et al.: Non-ideal class non-point light source quotient image for face relighting. Signal Process. **91**(4), 1048–1053 (2011)
18. Liu, J., et al.: Illumination transition image: parameter-based illumination estimation and re-rendering. In: 19th International Conference on Pattern Recognition, 2008. ICPR 2008. IEEE (2008)
19. Jackson, A.S., et al.: Large pose 3D face reconstruction from a single image via direct volumetric CNN regression. In: 2017 IEEE International Conference on Computer Vision (ICCV). IEEE (2017)

Face Detection and Encryption for Privacy Preserving in Surveillance Video

Suolan Liu$^{(\boxtimes)}$, Lizhi Kong, and Hongyuan Wang$^{(\boxtimes)}$

Changzhou University, Changzhou 213164, Jiangsu, China
lan-liu@163.com, hywang@cczu.edu.cn

Abstract. A number of techniques have recently been proposed for privacy preserving in video surveillance. Most of them are irreversible or have interference effect to the observation and recognition of human activities. In this paper, we address these issues by developing an effective method including face detection and encryption. In face detection, skin-color based approach fusing with fuzzy clustering is produced to detect facial candidates coarsely, and then we refine face by using SVM classifier. In face encryption, a reversible hybrid encryption (decryption) scheme based on spatial and value scrambling models is proposed. Simulation results verify the proposed mechanism can effectively detect and obscure faces while leaving the activities comprehensible and has high key sensibility for reducing the probability of attacking.

Keywords: Privacy preserving · Video surveillance · Face detection
Face encryption · Reversible

1 Introduction

Nowadays, video surveillance has become one of the most important auxiliary means in the field of public security monitoring. Video surveillance systems are widely deployed in many public places such as banks, supermarkets, airports, roads and residential areas [1–3]. Everyone is constantly being watched no matter whether you feel like it or not. However, in [4] a report about government surveillance revelations by NAS contractor Edward have raised new concerns about how best to preserve American's privacy in the digital age. What is personal privacy? One approach defines it in property terms as any information which the individual has certain decisional right [5]. Thus one's facial image, actions, location or copyrighted material are personal-partly, because they "belong" to the individual. Among these privacies, facial image is crucial and has highly close relationship with the others, because it can be directly used in face recognition technology to identify the monitored person's identity [2, 3]. In general, privacy preserving measures based on video surveillance can be taken from two aspects [6, 7]. On the one hand, we should enhance law making and law enforcement to regulate videos collection, storage and usage to avoid malicious infringement and disclosure of individual information. On the other hand, it is necessary to take effectively technical measures to protect the data and information, such as using cryptography theories and computer vision algorithms [2, 3, 7]. Cryptography methods mainly focus on encrypting the whole frame images into an unreadable form

© Springer Nature Switzerland AG 2018
J.-H. Lai et al. (Eds.): PRCV 2018, LNCS 11258, pp. 162–172, 2018.
https://doi.org/10.1007/978-3-030-03338-5_14

so that every unauthorized person cannot recover the original video [8]. The traditional encryption algorithms mainly include symmetric cryptographic algorithm and asymmetric cryptographic algorithm. This kind of methods is fit to processing videos for secure transmission over a communication line instead of real-time security monitoring and alarming for some particular activities recognition (e.g. fall and fights, etc.). Therefore encryption of the image as a whole may not be the most fixable method for this application. Recently, privacy preserving method based on computer vision has been a hot topic in the research field. Most of the preserving mechanisms are focused on partly modify the moving targets in the surveillance scenes [8, 9]. Target detection algorithms are used to localize the sensitive regions (e.g. face, eyes) and other methods are applied to obscure or conceal the selected regions, such as video masking, black boxes and replacing techniques. However, these methods are usually irreversible. Objective to recover the original video whenever needed for authorized person, we should apply reversible image processing methods with low computational complexity to meet the requirement of fast and real-time processing and preserving.

In this paper, we address the above-mentioned issues of privacy preserving in surveillance video by fusing image-processing method with encryption and decryption techniques. In particular, the proposed scheme consists of two steps including face detection and scrambling with the purpose of obscuring human face and monitoring his activities without revealing his identity at the same time.

The remaining of this paper is organized as follows. In Sect. 2, we review previous work related to pedestrian face detection, image encryption and decryption algorithms. Section 3 describes the proposed framework. The overview of the scheme is presented. Face detection approach and image encryption based on pixels spatial and value features scrambling models are given. In Sect. 4, simulations and experimental results are reported. Furthermore, we discuss the security of our proposed scheme. Finally, we conclude our work in Sect. 5.

2 Related Works

At present, video surveillances are widespreadly set up for the purpose of ensuring security and smart life. From this point of view, one may like surveillance to be carried out with not be willing to reveal any individual information. As the most informative part of human, face is usually used for identification. Therefore, obscuring or concealing face technique becomes an urgent demand for video surveillance with privacy preserving. Face detection is the first step of this application. Many of the current face detection techniques contain two major modules including face localization and verifying by extracting 'facial' features. To accurately localize face region, some prior information of human face are required. Skin color and face geometry make explicit use as apparent properties. Human skin color is one of the most robust face features and can be efficiently applied to find the pixels belonged to human skin in a scene. Roughly, physical-based methods and statistical-based methods are two basic kinds of skin color-based face localization approaches. Furthermore, statistical-based approached can be grouped into parametric approaches and non-parametric approaches. In parametric approaches, mean values, covariance matrices, Gaussian or mixtures of

Gaussians are used to build parametric face skin distribution models. For instances, in [10] Pujol et al. developed a fuzzy system to detect facial region by computing and fusing image variances from three color spaces of RGB, HSV and YCbCr. For the considering of error detections, a method of detecting where truly face locates is further proposed to eliminate these similar regions, such as the neck and hands. Experiments showed about 93% correct face detection rate in brief backgrounds and stable light conditions. In RGB space, Zhen et al. [11] built a maximum entropy model called the first order model (FOM) for parameter estimating human face. And then belief propagation algorithm was used to obtain fast selection and exact location for facial skin region. But the output of detection was in a gray scale skin map and the special region was not exactly located and marked. In non-parametric approaches, histogram, Bayesian approach and neural networks are usually developed to distinguish "face" or "non-face". In [12], authors applied the histograms of oriented gradients (HOG) as skin feature extraction clue and a feed-forward neural network was trained to classify the face from candidates. They tested the performance of their proposed scheme in sequences of color images and achieved an accuracy of 91.4%. The recent research of convolutional neural networks (CNNs) as the hottest algorithm in application of videos has proposed different solutions for incorporating the face detection and human recognition. Lu et al. [13] proposed using Clarifai net [14] and VGG-D model [15] to extract features and fuse them before fine-tuning. A binary classification by support vector machine (SVM) was conducted to realize face detection. Experimental results on three public datasets verify its state-of-the-art performance. Although great progress has made in recent years, face detection is still confronted with many challenges and cannot handle the large variations in different poses, occlusion, illumination condition and face in poor-quality video sequences.

As reported in [8], Boult proposed to protect privacy by using and adapting encryption techniques and combining them with intelligent video processing methods. The main contribution showed as cryptographically invertible obscuration only for authorized users in possession of the decryption key. Image encryption methods have been increasingly applied to meet security demands in video surveillance. The traditional encryption algorithms mainly include symmetric cryptographic algorithm and asymmetric cryptographic algorithm. Data encryption standard (DES), Triple data encryption standard (TDEA), Rivest Cipher5 (RC5) and International data encryption algorithm (IDEA) are typically symmetric cryptographic algorithms, while RSA (proposed by Ron Rivest, Adi Shamir and Leonard Adleman in 1977), ELGAMAL, RABIN, Diffe-Hellman and Elliptic curve cryptography (ECC) are asymmetric cryptographic algorithms. Video processing requires meeting its need such as fast and high-level efficiency. Therefore these traditional encryption algorithms may not be the most desirable algorithms for encrypting video frames with large size. By analyzing recent reports and publications, encryption schemes for image application may be grouped into three categories including pixel-position permutation, value permutation and hybrid scrambling methods. Arnold transform, Fibonacci transform and Hilbert transform are position permutation approaches with the disadvantage of not being able to change the original histogram. They only rearrange the positions of the image pixels rather than the pixel values. Once the histogram is revealed, exhaustion method can be used to find the original image. Value permutation-based algorithms such as Virginia encryption [16], chaotic map [17] and gravitational transform [18] aim at changing value by setting some parameters in advance. However, contour of original image can always be found in the encrypted image, which may cause security issues. Hybrid scrambling methods are produced by combing the advantages of the two former methods. In [19], to property compromise between imperceptibility and robustness of logo image encryption, Roy et al. proposed to fuse redundant discrete wavelet transform (RDWT) with Arnold scrambling and furtherly reshape it. Qin et al. [20] presented a novel image hash securely generated scheme by diving the image into several quantizes and scrambling the variances of pixel values. Testing results showed good performances with respect to perceptual robustness and discrimination. In [21], a hybrid encryption scheme based on quaternion hartley transform (QHT) and two-dimensional logistic map are suggested to enhance the security level. Simulation results verified that the novel scheme not only had satisfied security level but also had certain robustness against cropping and noise disturbance.

3 The Proposed Method

In this section, we describe the proposed privacy preserving method based on two steps: face detection and face encryption. The framework is shown in Fig. 1. In our scheme, first, we develop cascaded classifiers to extract face from coarse-to-fine. Then, a hybrid encryption approach based on spatial and value scrambling models are used to change and rearrange pixels in facial region. The following subsections will discuss the procedure detailedly.

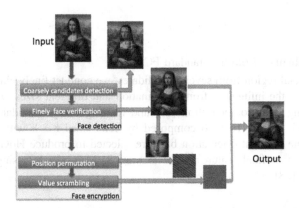

Fig. 1. Framework of our proposed scheme

3.1 Face Detection

Since most of the monitoring devices provide RGB video streams, approaches developed in this paper are based on RGB applications. Skin color model can be used to coarsely search facial candidates. Obviously, RGB has the negative property of each coordinate (red, green and blue) is subject to luminance effects from light changes, which may cause misclassification of skin and non-skin regions. Reported researches show that skin color models work effectively only on the chrominance subspaces such as Cb-Cr [22, 23] and Hue-Saturation (H-S) [24]. Inspired by the work in [25, 26], in our approach skin candidates are produced using fuzzy c-means clustering (FCM) based on pixel local properties termed as LFCM in Cb-Cr subspace. In [27], the standard FCM is used to localize skin-like regions. However, they only consider pixel value instead of other useful information, such as the relationships between pixels, which play important roles in discriminating the category of a pixel. With this in mind, we improve FCM by considering attributions from 8-neighbor pixels of a point. Therefore, the conditional probability of a pixel x_i categorized into the jth class can be expressed as:

$$f(j_i|\eta_i) = \frac{e^{\beta\delta_i(j)}}{\sum_{i=1}^c e^{\beta\delta_i(j)}}, i = 1, 2\cdots, N \tag{1}$$

where j_i means that the pixel x_i is classified into jth class. η_i is the class label from 8 neighbors. $\delta_i(j)$ is the statistical number of 8-neighbor pixels belonged to jth class. β is the weight factor, $\beta \geq 0$. We set $\beta = 0.5$ in all of our tests in Sect. 4. The following criterion can be used to discriminate the pixel's category:

$$j^* = arg \max u_{ij}, i = 1, \cdots, N; j = 1, \cdots, c \tag{2}$$

where u_{ij} is the fuzzy membership value and can be calculated by the following formula:

$$u_{ij} = u'_{ij} \times f(j_i|\eta_i) \tag{3}$$

u'_{ij} can be obtained from the standard FCM.

To refine facial region from several candidates, we conduct finely classification by SVM. To reduce the influences from illumination and different sizes, we do preprocessing including light compensation [27] and resizing every candidate to 64 * 64. Define the block size as 16 * 16 composed by cells sized 8 * 8 with moving step 8 * 8. Next, nine gradient orientation bins are selected to produce HoG features and concatenate them as final feature vector to train SVM model by using polynomial kernel function [28].

3.2 Face Encryption

Once face region is properly detected, the next step is scrambling it for security and privacy protection. Note that the encrypted face should be able to be recovered as needed [29]. Motived by this requirement, a reversible hybrid encryption (decryption) scheme is proposed in this section, which uses Arnold transform in spatial position permutation [30] combining with gravitational transforms termed as GTs in value permutation [18] to encrypt and decrypt human facial region. In our numerical setting, to facilitate Arnold transform, facial region is located in a bounding box sized N*N. The facial region image is expressed as $f(x_i, y_i)$. In mathematics, the hybrid encryption operation is described as follows:

$$F(x_o, y_o) = G\{A(f(x_i, y_i))\}(x_o, y_o) \tag{4}$$

where $F(x_o, y_o)$ represents the output. The symbol "A" means Arnold transform (ART), "G" denotes GTs.

Furthermore, the facial image is imported to Arnold transform function [18], which is defined as:

$$A_N : \begin{bmatrix} x_i' \\ y_j' \end{bmatrix} = mod\left(\begin{bmatrix} 1, 1 \\ 1, 2 \end{bmatrix} \begin{bmatrix} x_i \\ y_j \end{bmatrix}, N \right) \tag{5}$$

where (x_i, y_j) and $\left(x_i', y_j'\right)$ are the coordinates before and after position permutation A_N.

The GTs can be given as:

$$G : \left[\gamma \frac{m_r \times m_{x_i', y_j'}}{\left(x_r - x_i'\right)^2 + \left(y_r - y_j'\right)^2 + k^2} \right] mod256 \oplus V\left(x_i', y_j'\right) \tag{6}$$

γ is gravitational coefficient and assigned a large positive number in experiments. $m_r = 1$ is the quality of unit particle which location is (x_r, y_r). k is an adjusting parameter to ensure $\left(x_r - x_i'\right)^2 + \left(y_r - y_j'\right)^2 + k^2 > 0$. $m_{x_i', y_j'}$ is the quality of the pixel point $\left(x_i', y_j'\right)$ with pixel value $V\left(x_i', y_j'\right)$. Note that V can be a three-tuple corresponding to components of color images.

4 Numerical Simulations and Discussion

The main idea of our work is to develop a reversible method for human face obscuring while having no interference to recognizing and monitoring their activities. To verify the performance of the proposed scheme, we do experiments by choosing several video clips with life scenarios. The operations in the processes of face detection, encryption and decryption will be conducted in Matlab running on a laptop.

4.1 Test One

In this test, the original testing image shown in Fig. 2(a) contains two faces with variations in illumination, position, orientation and accessories. As displayed in Fig. 2 (b), our approach can effectively detect faces with a certain range of skin color changes. Even though the left-side person is lowing the head, his facial region is properly localized. For the right-side person, accessories such as sunglasses greatly increase the difficulties of face refining, which may result in partial detection of human face.

However, our algorithm can successfully suppress this kind of influence and detect the whole face region. Obviously, the effectiveness of this part will greatly facilitate the next step of encryption.

(a) original image   (b) facial localization

Fig. 2. An example of face detection

In Table 1, we list the encrypted results by setting different parameters. For the sake of conducting fair comparisons, in GTs we set the unit particle's position as mean values for each facial position and assign the adjusting parameter k = 100. The first list displays the closeup of the detected faces; in the second list the ART results with different numbers of iterations are presented. We show the GTs results based on ART position permutation in the third list. The final encrypted results are displayed on the original images in the last list. From Table 1, one may find that with the changes of iterations from 3 to 80, the position scrambling effects show better from vision. Note that, once the number of iterations increases to a certain extent, it becomes a decryption operation. On the other hand, with the increase of gravitational coefficient the permutation of pixel values show more uniform and indistinguishable.

4.2 Test Two

A frame image contains multiple faces from different views coupled with cluttering background is utilized to test the robustness and security of our proposed scheme.

For the purpose of strengthening the security, in this test we set encrypt key as KEY4 as following: the number of iterations is 150 and three different sets of parameters for GTs corresponding to 3 channels [18] are applied. For red, $m_{x_i'y_j'} = 85 \times x_i'^2 + y_j'^3 + 230$, $\gamma = 9 \times 10^{14}$; for green, $m_{x_i'y_j'} = 60 \times x_i'^2 + y_j'^3 + 175$, $\gamma = 11.8 \times 10^{15}$; for blue, $m_{x_i'y_j'} = 115 \times x_i'^2 + y_j'^3 + 70$, $\gamma = 10.5 \times 10^{13}$. The cipher-image is displayed in Fig. 3(c). As can be seen that even though the image shows small scaled faces and one of the actors in his profile, our method still achieves good detection rates and localizes the core areas of all faces.

To verify the key sensibility of the proposed method, we select the face from "Monica" shown in Fig. 4(a) and try to recover the encrypted image in Fig. 4(b) by using different decryption keys. Firstly, we decrypt it by using KEY5 of incorrect iterations as 90 for inverse ART operation, but no change to other parameters. The decrypted result displays in Fig. 4(c). Furthermore, we utilize only incorrect keys for inverse GTs operation with $m_{x_i'y_j'} = 50 \times x_i'^2 + y_j'^3 + 60$, $\gamma = 9 \times 10^{13}$ for all 3 channels

Table 1. Scrambling processings and encrypted results

Closeup of face	ART	GTs follow-ing ART	Encrypted results
			KEY1: For ART, the number of iterations is 3; For GTs, $m_{x'_i y'_j} = 50 \times x_i'^2 + y_j'^3 + 80, \gamma = 10^{13}$
			KEY2: For ART, the number of iterations is 50; For GTs, $m_{x'_i y'_j} = 70 \times x_i'^2 + y_j'^3 + 100,$ $\gamma = 10^{14}$
			KEY3: For ART, the number of iterations is 80; For GTs, $m_{x'_i y'_j} = 90 \times x_i'^2 + y_j'^3 + 150,$ $\gamma = 10^{15}$

(a) original image   (b) face detection result   (c) encrypted result

Fig. 3. An example of multiple faces detection and encryption

as KEY6 and show the result in Fig. 4(d). Figure 4(e) is decrypted image with correct keys. Concludely, Figs. 4(c) and (d) indicate that the cipher-image can withstand some potential attacks. Experimental results show the high key sensibility in our scrambling scheme.

4.3   Discussion

Correlation coefficient between plain-image and cipher-image can be used to quantify the performance of an encryption algorithm. The lower correlation coefficient indicates that the encryption algorithm can better hide the feature information of the plain-image.

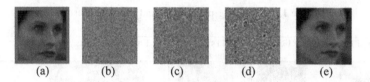

Fig. 4. Test results of key sensibility on a face

In this way, it will become more difficult to be attacked. Here we analyze the performance of the proposed algorithm by calculating the correlation coefficients of red, green and blue color channels respectively. The correlation coefficient between two-dimensional image matrix A and B can be defined as:

$$
C_{AB} = \frac{\left| \sum_{i=1}^{N} \sum_{j=1}^{N} \left(A_{i,j} - mean(A) \right) \left(B_{i,j} - mean(B) \right) \right|}{\sqrt{\sum_{i=1}^{N} \sum_{j=1}^{N} \left(A_{i,j} - mean(A) \right)^2 \times \sum_{i=1}^{N} \sum_{j=1}^{N} \left(B_{i,j} - mean(B) \right)^2}} \tag{5}
$$

Where $mean(x)$ is the mean value.

Table 2 displays the correlation coefficient by using different keys. For Test One, we calculate the correlation coefficient between plain-image (Fig. 2(a)) and cipher-images (displayed in the forth list of Table 1). For Test Two, we calculate the correlation coefficient between cipher-image (Fig. 4(b)) and decrypted images (Figs. 4(c) and (d)).

From Table 2 one may find that for Test One most correlation coefficients are low as approximately zero. It indicates that the relevance between plain-image and cipher-image is very weak. From the aspect of encryption sensitivity, it means that the algorithm presented in this paper has superior sensitivity. Conversely, for Test Two while KEY5 is used to decrypt the cipher-image, correlation coefficient varies from 0.0243 to 0.0618, which shows high relevance. The reason for this phenomenon is the incomplete decryption of spatial position. However, we can see that once KEY6 is applied to decrypt, the average correlation coefficient is dramatically reduced from 0.0400 to 0.0061. As expected, localize and encrypt multiple faces in a picture is more challenging, but our proposed scheme is able to perform quite well with satisfied anti-attack property.

Table 2. Correlation coefficient between the red (r), green (g) and blue (b) color channels

Correlation coefficient		C_{rr}	C_{rg}	C_{rb}	C_{gr}	C_{gg}	C_{gb}	C_{br}	C_{bg}	C_{bb}	**Average**
Test one	KEY1	0.0007	0.0021	0.0015	0.0009	0.0018	0.0011	0.0014	0.0006	0.0023	**0.0014**
	KEY2	0.0013	0.0007	0.0003	0.0024	0.0007	0.0015	0.0008	0.0002	0.0009	**0.0010**
	KEY3	0.0004	0.0018	0.0021	0.0026	0.0015	0.0003	0.0020	0.0014	0.0031	**0.0017**
Test two	KEY5	0.0317	0.0243	0.0430	0.0357	0.0532	0.0618	0.0351	0.0426	0.0322	**0.0400**
	KEY6	0.0079	0.0050	0.0071	0.0068	0.0082	0.0064	0.0047	0.0038	0.0046	**0.0061**

5 Conclusion

We have proposed a practical privacy preserving technique for the application of video surveillance. Faces corresponding to privacy sensitive information are detected and encrypted. We aim to conceal faces while not interfere the observation and recognition of human activities using in intelligent monitoring and alarm systems. Our method is reversible for revealing faces whenever needed to the authorized person. Simulation results demonstrate that the proposed scheme can successively detect and obscure faces while leaving the activities comprehensible. Finally, the performance evaluation with key sensibility shows that the developed mechanism can withstand some potential attacks.

Acknowledgment. This work is supported by National Natural Science Foundations of China (No. 61572085, 61502058), Jiangsu Joint Research Project of Industry, Education and Research (No. BY2016029-15) and Changzhou Science and Technology Support Program (Social Development) Project (No. CE20155044).

References

1. Otto, C., Wang, D., Jain, A.: Clustering millions of faces by identity. IEEE Trans. Pattern Anal. Mach. Intell. **2**(40), 1–14 (2018)
2. Torre, M., Granger, E., Gorodnichy, D.: Adaptive skew-sensitive ensembles for face recognition in video surveillance. Pattern Recognit. **11**(48), 3385–3406 (2015)
3. Radtke, P., Granger, E., Sabourin, R.: Skew-sensitive boolean combination for adaptive ensembles: an application to face recognition in video surveillance. Inf. Fusion **15**(20), 31–48 (2014)
4. Maddern, M., Rainie, L.: Americans' attitudes about privacy, security and surveillance. http://www.pewinternet.org/2015/05/20/americans-attitudes-about-privacy-security-and-surveillance/
5. Haggerty, K., Ericson, R.: Varieties of personal information as influences on attitudes toward surveillance. http://web.mit.edu/gtmarx/www/vancouver.html
6. Bonetto, M., Korshunov, P., Ramponi, G.: Privacy in mini-drone based video surveillance. In: Workshop on De-Identification for Privacy Protection in Multimedia, vol. 4, pp. 2464–2469 (2015)
7. Dufaux, F., Ebrahimi, T.: Scrambling for privacy protection in video surveillance systems. IEEE Trans. Circuits Syst. Video Technol. **8**(18), 1168–1174 (2008)
8. Boult, T.: PICO: privacy through invertible cryptographic obscuration. In: Proceedings of the Computer Vision for Interactive and Intelligent Environment, pp. 27–38, October, 2005
9. Carrillo, P., Kalva, H., Magliveras, S.: Compression independent reversible encryption for privacy in video surveillance. J. Inf. Secur. **1**, 1–13 (2009)
10. Pujol, F., Pujol, M.: Face detection based on skin color segmentation using fuzzy entropy. Entropy **26**(10), 1–22 (2017)
11. Zhen, H., Daoudi, M., Jedynak, B.: Blocking adult images based on statistical skin detection. Electron. Lett. Comput. Vis. Image Anal. **2**(4), 1–14 (2004)

172 S. Liu et al.

12. Aulestia, P.S., Talahua, J.S., Andaluz, V.H., Benalcázar, M.E.: Real-time face detection using artificial neural networks. In: Lintas, Alessandra, Rovetta, S., Verschure, P.F.M.J., Villa, A.E.P. (eds.) ICANN 2017. LNCS, vol. 10614, pp. 590–599. Springer, Cham (2017). https://doi.org/10.1007/978-3-319-68612-7_67

13. Lu, X., Duan, X.: Feature extraction and fusion using deep convolutional neural networks for face detection. Math. Probl. Eng. **3**(2), 1–9 (2017)

14. Zeiler, M.D., Fergus, R.: Visualizing and understanding convolutional networks. In: Fleet, D., Pajdla, T., Schiele, B., Tuytelaars, T. (eds.) ECCV 2014. LNCS, vol. 8689, pp. 818–833. Springer, Cham (2014). https://doi.org/10.1007/978-3-319-10590-1_53

15. Simonyan, K., Zisserman, A.: Very deep convolutional networks for large-scale image recognition. https://arxiv.org/abs/1409.1556

16. He, M., Qiang, S.: Novel image scrambling algorithm based on changing pixel values. Appl. Res. Comput. **12**(29), 4635–4638 (2012)

17. Belazi, A., Hermassi, H., Rhouma, R., Belghith, S.: Algebraic analysis of a RGB image encryption algorithm based on DNA encoding and chaotic map. Nonlinear Dyn. **4**(76), 1989–2004 (2014)

18. Liu, S., Yue, C., Wang, H.: An improved hybrid encryption scheme for RGB images. Int. J. Adv. Sci. Technol. **4**(95), 37–44 (2016)

19. Roy, S., Pal, A.: A robust blind hybrid image watermarking scheme in RDWT-DCT domain using Arnold scrambling. Multimed. Tools Appl. **2**(76), 1–40 (2017)

20. Qin, C., Sun, M., Chang, C.: Perceptual hashing for color image based of hybrid extracting of structural features. Signal Process. **142**, 194–205 (2017)

21. Li, J.: Hybrid color and grayscale images encryption scheme based on quaternion hartley transform and logistic map in gyrator domain. J. Opt. Soc. Korea **3**(20), 42–54 (2016)

22. Gundimada, S., Tao, L., Asari, V.: Face detection technique based on intensity and skin color distribution. In: International Conference on Image Processing, pp. 1413–1416, November 2004

23. Qing, L., Min, L.: Face detection using skin color and location relation. Comput. Eng. Des. **13**, 3396–3398 (2008)

24. Sabottka, K., Pitas, I.: Segmentation and tracking of faces in color images. In: International Conference on Automatic Face & Gesture Recognition, Vermont, pp. 236–241 (1996)

25. Anwar, N., Rahman, A.: RGB-H-CbCr skin colour model for human face detection. http://pesona.mmu.edu.my/~johnsee/research/papers/files/rgbhcbcr_m2usic06.pdf

26. Lu, J., Yuan, X., Yahagi, T.: A method of face recognition based on fuzzy c-means clustering and associated sub-NNs. IEEE Trans. Neural Netw. **1**(18), 150–160 (2007)

27. Hsu, R., Mottaleb, M.: Face detection in color image. IEEE Trans. Pattern Anal. Mach. Intell. **5**(24), 696–706 (2012)

28. Patilkulkarni, S., Lakshmi, H.: Vanishing moments of a wavelet system and feature set in face detection problem for color images. J. Comput. Appl. **16**(66), 36–42 (2013)

29. Liu, Z., Li, Q.: Image encryption based on random scrambling of the amplitude and phase in the frequency domain. Opt. Eng. **8**(48), 1–6 (2009)

30. Li, C., Lin, D., Lu, J.: Cryptanalyzing an image-scrambling encryption algorithm of pixel bits. IEEE Trans. Multimed. **3**(24), 64–71 (2017)

Content-Aware Face Blending by Label Propagation

Lingyu Liang and Xinglin Zhang[✉]

South China University of Technology, Guangzhou, China
`lianglysky@gmail.com,zhxlinse@gmail.com`

Abstract. Facial blending is critical for various facial editing applications, whose goal is to transfer the facial appearance of the reference to the target in seamless manners. However, when there are significant illumination or color differences between the reference and the target, visual artifacts may be probably introduced into the result. To tackle this problem, we propose content-aware masks that adaptively adjust the facial lighting and blended region to achieve seamless face blending. To generate the content-aware masks with good visual consistency, we formulate it as a label propagation process from a semi-supervised learning perspective, where the intensity of the initialized masks are propagated to the whole masks based on the local visual similarity of the images. Then, we construct a content-aware face blending framework that consists of three stages. Firstly, the facial region of the reference and the target are aligned according to the detected facial landmarks. Secondly, a facial quotient image and a binary mask are obtained as the initialized masks, and the content-aware masks for illumination and region adjustment are generated using the label propagation model with different guided feature. Finally, we combine the reference to the target using the generated masks to produce the face blending effects. Experimental results show the effectiveness and robustness of our methods for different image-based facial rendering tasks.

Keywords: Image-based rendering · Label propagation · Face transfer

1 Introduction

Facial image photo-realistic rendering is a novel computational photographic technique [12] to achieve facial effects that can be used for many applications, such as advertisement, movie production, digital entertainment, personalized photo editing and identity protection. Among the various current rendering

This research was supported in part by the National Natural Science Foundation of China under Grant No. 61502176, 61872151, the Natural Science Foundation of Guangdong Province under Grant No. 2016A030313480, the Pearl River S&T Nova Program of Guangzhou under Grant No. 201806010088 and Fundamental Research Funds for the Central Universities (No. 2017BQ058).

J.-H. Lai et al. (Eds.): PRCV 2018, LNCS 11258, pp. 173–182, 2018.
https://doi.org/10.1007/978-3-030-03338-5_15

techniques [14], this paper specifically focuses on the facial appearance transfer problem of the image-based portrait rendering.

Facial appearance transfer is the critical component of various facial editing tasks, including face replacement [4,13], face swapping [1,7,18,19], face reenactment [5,16] and age progression [6]. It aims to transfer the facial appearance of the reference to the target with good visual consistency.

It is challenging to achieve seamless face transfer. Most previous methods are based on the facial mask, and the facial property matching (like lighting or color) between a target and a reference. Pérez et al. [13] proposed the Poisson seamless cloning by the guided interpolation in the gradient domain. Dale et al. [4] used a novel graph-cut method that estimates the optimal seam on the face mesh to obtain video face replacement. Bitouk et al. [1] used the shading model based on a linear combination of spherical harmonics to adjust facial color and lighting for face swapping. Recently, Garrido et al. [5] proposed the automatic face reenactment system that replaces the face of an actor with the face of a user using a color adjustment with the Poisson blending [13].

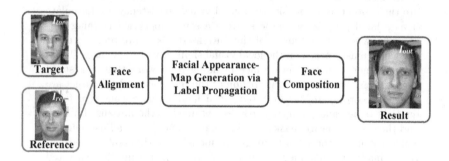

Fig. 1. The framework of the face transfer to blend the facial region of the reference to the target, which is based on facial appearance-map generated by adaptive label propagation.

The framework of the facial appearance transfer is shown in Fig. 1, which aims to transfer the facial region of the aligned reference to the target to produce the blended portrait. It consists of three stages: face alignment, facial appearance-map generation, and face composition.

Due to the complex appearance differences between the faces, however, a simple facial mask with Gaussian feathering may cause visual artifacts on the boundary of the transferred region; even the Poisson image editing [13] may fail to perform well when there is a large lighting or color difference between the target and reference, as shown in Fig. 4. To tackle the problem of illumination and region variances, this paper proposes a facial appearance map with good illumination-aware and region-aware properties for seamless facial appearance transfer. Inspired by Liang's work on face enhancement [11], we formulate the facial appearance map generation as a label propagation process [20] from a semisupervised learning perspective [2]. Since the face blending problem is different from the face enhancement problem in [11], we propose an adaptive label propagation model with a new regularization structure and guided features to achieve seamless face transfer.

Based on the adaptive facial appearance map, we construct the facial appearance transfer framework containing three stages. Firstly, the facial region of the reference is aligned to the target according to the detected facial landmarks. Secondly, a facial quotient image [10,15] and a binary mask are generated, and then the guided label propagation model is used to diffuse the initial features of the quotient image and the binary mask to obtain the adaptive facial appearance-map for illumination and mask adjustment, respectively. Finally, we use the appearance-maps to seamlessly transfer the reference to the target. Experimental results show the effectiveness and robustness of our methods compared with the previous methods for various image based facial rendering tasks, such as face replacement and face dubbing in [1,4,13].

The main contributions of the paper are summarized as follows: (1) An adaptive label propagation model with guided features to generate the illumination-aware and region-aware facial appearance map for seamless face transfer; (2) A facial appearance transfer framework based on the adaptive facial appearance map, which achieves various image-based face blending effects, such as face replacement and face dubbing.

2 Facial Appearance Transfer Framework

2.1 Face Alignment

In face alignment, we aims to match the reference I_{ref} and the target I_{tar} to obtain the transformed reference I'_{ref} and the wrapped target I'_{tar} for appearance-map generation and face composition.

Firstly, we use the Viola-Jones face detector [17] and the active shape model (ASM) [3] to locate the 86 landmarks in the facial components of the reference S_{ref} and the target S_{tar}, respectively. Secondly, the transformed appearance I'_{ref} and shape S'_{ref} of the reference are obtained by matching the reference I_{ref} to the target I_{tar} using the affine transformation with the landmarks. Finally, we wrapped the target by the multilevel B-splines approximation (MBA) [9] according to the transformed shape of the reference S'_{ref}, i.e. the appearance of the wrapped target $I'_{tar} = f_{MBA}(I_{tar}, S_{tar}, S'_{ref})$. For more technical detail of MBA, we refer the readers to the article [9].

2.2 Facial Appearance-Map Generation

In face blending, directly pasting the face region of the reference to the target probably fail to perform well. According to our observation, apparent visual artifacts may be introduced to the results even through the gradient-domain Poisson cloning [13] is used when the reference and the target have large lighting or color variances. To tackle this problems, we construct two different types of facial appearance-maps (T_{quot} and T_{mask}) that perform adaptive illumination and region adjustments of the reference for seamless face transfer.

Inspired by Liang's recent work [11] for face enhancement, we formulate the facial appearance-map generation as a label propagation process, which diffuses the features within the initialized facial map to obtain the whole map. Since the two appearance-maps require different diffusion processes, we integrate different regularization structures with different guided features to the label propagation model for the corresponding map diffusion.

Specifically, the appearance-map T_{quot} aims to relight the reference so that the illumination and the color of the reference appearance is consistent to the target, and it uses the quotient image [15] as the initialization. Unlike the original quotient image that only handles the region within the faces, the diffused the quotient appearance-map T_{quot} facilitates to relight the face with consistent background illumination.

The appearance-map T_{mask} is to adaptively select the facial region of the relighted reference for seamless face transfer with smooth region transition, which use the binary mask of the facial landmarks as the initial map.

The benefit of the diffusion-based map generation is twofold. Firstly, it is fault-tolerant to the small inaccurate landmark detection, since the final map value is determined by the label propagation process instead of the initialized value. Secondly, the map is adapted to the complex facial boundary and texture variance of the region by using different regularization structures and guided features. More detail of the structure and initialization of the label propagation model for T_{quot} and T_{mask} will be presented in Sect. 3.

2.3   Face Composition

To produce the output I_{out} of face transfer, we replace the facial region of the target I_{tar} with the facial region of I'_{ref} using the generated facial map T_{quot}, T_{mask} as follows:

$$I_{out} = I'_{ref} \circ T_{quot} \circ T_{mask} + I_{tar} \circ (J - T_{mask}), \tag{1}$$

where $\circ$ denotes the element wise product operation, and J is the all-ones matrix with the same dimension of T_{mask}. The results of face blending are shown in Fig. 1, where the corresponding generated masks T_{quot} and T_{mask} are shown in Fig. 2.

3   Facial Appearance-Map Generation

3.1   Adaptive Label Propagation Model

The appearance-map for face transfer is formulated as a label propagation model with an adaptive regularization structure and guided features, which generates the whole map by propagating the value of the initial map to the others according to the pixel similarity.

Specifically, the facial appearance-map T with n pixels is mapped into a graph $\mathbf{g} = (\mathcal{V}, \mathcal{E})$ of n nodes, where the node v_p corresponds to the pth map location, and the edge e_{pq} links the node pair (p, q) with the pixel similarity W_{pq}. We initialize the node value by R (more details of R are in Sect.3.2), and obtain the appearance-map T by propagating the initial value of R through the graph according to the pixel-wise edge similarity given by the affinity matrix W.

The label propagation for appearance-map can be formulated as the minimization of the following quadratic cost functional:

$$Z(T) = \sum_p S_{pp}(T_p - R_p)^2 + \frac{\lambda}{2} \sum_{p,q} W_{pq}(T_p - T_q)^2 + \lambda\epsilon \sum_p T_p^2$$

The first term is the data term to constrain the diffusion region, where S is an $n \times n$ diagonal matrix given by $S_{pp} = 1$ in the constraint region, otherwise $S_{pp} = 0$. The third term is a small added regularization term that prevents degeneration.

The second term is the smoothing term to determine the local smoothness property of the generated map T, where λ is used to balance the relative weights of the data term and the smoothness term; the weight matrix W_{pq} is non-zero iff v_p and v_q are "neighbors", and its value measures the similarity between the nodes (pixels). In this paper, we use the typical value $\lambda = 1$ and $\epsilon = 0.0001$ for all the experiments.

The smoothness term has a closely relationship with graph Laplacian L_g. Specifically, D is a diagonal matrix with $D_{pp} = \sum_q W_{pq}$, and $L_g = D - W$ is the un-normalized graph Laplacian. A more compact form of the cost function can be obtained as following:

$$Z(T) = \|S(T - R)\|^2 + \lambda T^\top (L_g + \epsilon I)T. \tag{2}$$

The derivative of the cost is

$$\begin{aligned} \frac{1}{2} \frac{\partial Z(T)}{\partial T} &= S(T - R) + \lambda(L_g + \epsilon I)T \\ &= (S + \lambda L_g + \lambda\epsilon I)T - SR, \end{aligned} \tag{3}$$

T can be obtained when the derivative is set to 0:

$$T = (S + \lambda L_g + \lambda\epsilon I)^{-1}SR = L^{-1}SR, \tag{4}$$

which is a linear equation about a symmetric, positive-definite Laplacian matrix L. It can be solved efficiently by the conjugate gradient descent with the multi-level preconditioning [8].

Also, Eq. 4 can be solved using a Jacobi iteration, which is similar to the iterative label propagation proposed by Zhu and Ghahramani [20] and Liang's mask propagation model [11], except for the weight matrix that controls the diffusion property.

To obtain the appearance map of face transfer, we construct a new kernel structure with guided features for the weight matrix W of appearance-map diffusion.

3.2   Diffusions of Facial Appearance-Map

The edge-aware property of the optimization-based label propagation model is mostly controlled by the smoothness term, specifically the similarity metric of the weight matrix W_{pq}. To produce the appearance-map for face transfer, we design a new kernel structure with guided features:

$$W_{pq} = \frac{c_{pq}G'_{pq}}{\|G_p - G_q\|^\alpha + \varepsilon},$$
(5)

where G and G' are the guided features to control the local property of the map diffusion, c and α are the parameters to adjust the sensitivity of the guided features, ε is a small constant to avoid division by zero (typically $\varepsilon = 0.0001$). The appearance-map T_{quot} and T_{mask} can be generated by different initialization $R_{\{quot,mask\}}$ and weight matrix $W_{\{quot,mask\}}$ with the corresponding guided features and parameters.

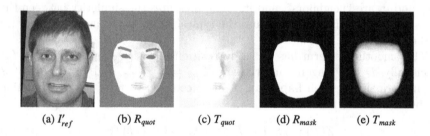

(a) I'_{ref} (b) R_{quot} (c) T_{quot} (d) R_{mask} (e) T_{mask}

Fig. 2. Diffusions of facial appearance-map T_{quot} and T_{mask} based on adaptive label propagation with different guided features.

The appearance-map T_{quot} aims to adjust the illumination of the reference according to the target based on the facial shading model of the quotient image [15], as shown in Fig. 2(c). To produce T_{quot}, we set $R_{quot} = \frac{f_{aWLS}(I'_{tar})}{f_{aWLS}(I'_{ref})}$, where R_{quot} is the quotient image of the matched target I'_{tar} and reference I'_{ref} using Liang's adaptive weighted least squares filter f_{aWLS} [10] for edge-aware smoothing, as shown in Fig. 2(b). For the weight matrix W_{quot}, we set $\alpha = 1$ and $G = logL'_{ref}$, where L'_{ref} is the luminance of I'_{ref} (Fig. 2(a)); the value of cG' is small within the facial region and large in the background so that makes the features of the quotient image diffuse across the significant edges within the facial region to the whole image.

The appearance-map T_{mask} is responsible to paste the facial region of the reference to the target with smooth transition between different regions. For

T_{mask}, we set R_{quot} as a binary mask according to the facial landmarks, as shown in Fig. 2(d). To produce T_{mask} with adaptive region boundary, we set $\alpha = 1.2$, $G = log L'_{ref}$ and $c = 0.5$ with $G' = J$, where L'_{ref} is the luminance of I'_{ref} and J is the all-one matrix. The map diffusion is controlled by the gradient of the guided feature G, which assures the smooth transition of the blended region between I'_{ref} and I_{tar}, as shown in Fig. 2(e).

4 Experiments

4.1 Basic Evaluation

The evaluations for facial appearance-map are shown in Figs. 2 and 3. The results show that the generated T_{quot} efficiently propagates the quotient value from the constrained regions of R_{quot} to the other regions, like eyes, eyebrows and background, and preserves the illumination consistence in the blended face. The appearance-map T_{mask} is generated with smooth transition, which is adapted to the region boundary between the face regions of the faces. The illumination-aware and region-aware diffusion of T_{quot} and T_{mask} ensure the robustness of the appearance transfer for faces with different properties, as shown in the experiments of face transfer.

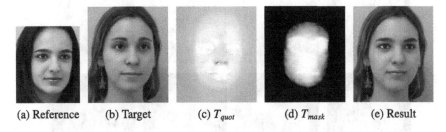

(a) Reference   (b) Target   (c) T_{quot} (d) T_{mask} (e) Result

Fig. 3. Facial appearance-map for quotient-based illumination diffusion (T_{quot}) and blending mask diffusion (T_{mask}) using the proposed label propagation with corresponding guided feature.

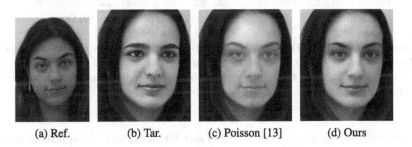

(a) Ref.   (b) Tar.   (c) Poisson [13]   (d) Ours

Fig. 4. Comparison with Poisson image cloning [13] for faces with large differences in age, color and lighting.

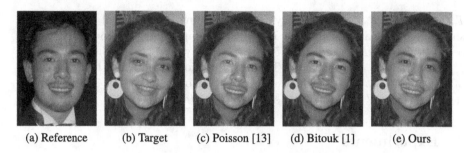

(a) Reference   (b) Target   (c) Poisson [13]   (d) Bitouk [1]   (e) Ours

Fig. 5. Comparison with Bitouk et al. [1] for face replacement using reference target pair with different gender and roll rotation.

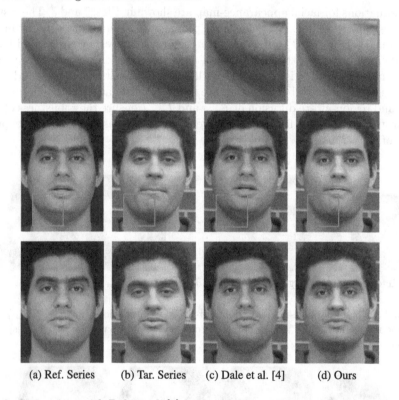

(a) Ref. Series   (b) Tar. Series   (c) Dale et al. [4]   (d) Ours

Fig. 6. Comparison with Dale et al. [4] for face dubbing, aims to transfer the series of the face appearance of the reference to the target. Comparison of the close-up images in the top rows illustrate that our method obtain better illumination consistency to the target than Dale's [4]

The basic experimental evaluations of face blending with the appearance-map were performed for the face pairs with significant different appearance properties, such as lighting, color, age and gender, as shown in Figs. 4, 5 and 6. The test images were taken from the FEI face database or the internet. The good visual consistency of the results indicate the effectiveness and robustness of our method.

4.2 Comparison with Related Methods

We also made comparison with the related methods for face replacement [1, 13]. Figure 4 shows the comparison with the Poisson cloning [13]. Due to the dependency of the gradient and boundary of the blended region, the results of [13] are sensitive to the lighting and color differences of the faces. In contrast, our method obtains natural face blending effects. Comparison with Bitouk's method in Fig. 5 further validates the effectiveness of our diffusion-based model.

We made the comparison between Dale's [4] and our method for face dubbing, which aims to transfer the series of the face appearance of the reference to the target. The results indicate that both the methods can achieve good visual consistency in a global manner, as shown in Fig. 6. The close-up images of the local region in the first rows of Fig. 6, however, show the subtle differences. Dale's method [4] tends to transfer the lighting property of the reference to the target, while ours tends to preserve the original appearance property of the target, which is complementary to [4].

5 Conclusion

This paper proposes a label propagation model with adaptive regularization to achieve facial blending with good visual consistency. Specifically, the illumination-aware and region-aware facial appearance maps are generated by diffusion with different guided features. Experiments illustrate the effectiveness and robustness of our methods for face replacement and face dubbing.

References

1. Bitouk, D., Kumar, N., Dhillon, S., Belhumeur, P., Nayar, S.K.: Face swapping: automatically replacing faces in photographs. ACM Trans. Graph. **27**(3), 39 (2008)
2. Chapelle, O., Schölkopf, B., Zien, A.: Semi-Supervised Learning. MIT Press, Cambridge (2006)
3. Cootes, T.F., Taylor, C.J., Cooper, D.H., Graham, J.: Active shape models-their training and application. Comput. Vis. Image Underst. **61**(1), 38–59 (1995)
4. Dale, K., Sunkavalli, K., Johnson, M.K., Vlasic, D., Matusik, W., Pfister, H.: Video face replacement. ACM Trans. Graph. **30**(6), 130 (2011)
5. Garrido, P., Valgaerts, L., Rehmsen, O., Thormahlen, T., Perez, P., Theobalt, C.: Automatic face reenactment. In: Proceedings of CVPR, pp. 4217–4224 (2014)
6. Kemelmacher-Shlizerman, I., Suwajanakorn, S., Seitz, S.: Illumination-aware age progression. In: Proceedings of CVPR, pp. 3334–3341 (2014)
7. Korshunova, I., Shi, W., Dambre, J., Theis, L.: Fast face-swap using convolutional neural networks. In: Proceedings of ICCV, pp. 3677–3685 (2017)
8. Krishnan, D., Fattal, R., Szeliski, R.: Efficient preconditioning of laplacian matrices for computer graphics. ACM Trans. Graph. **32**(4), 142 (2013)

9. Lee, S., Wolberg, G., Shin, S.Y.: Scattered data interpolation with multilevel B-splines. IEEE Trans. Vis. Comput. Graph. **3**(3), 228–244 (1997)
10. Liang, L., Jin, L.: A new face relighting method based on edge-preserving filter. IEICE Trans. Inf. Syst. **E96-D**(12), 2904–2907 (2013)
11. Liang, L., Jin, L., Liu, D.: Edge-aware label propagation for mobile facial enhancement on the cloud. IEEE Trans. Circuits Syst. Video Technol. **27**(1), 125–138 (2017)
12. Lukac, R.: Computational Photography: Methods and Applications. CRC Press, Boca Raton (2010)
13. Pérez, P., Gangnet, M., Blake, A.: Poisson image editing. ACM Trans. Graph. **22**, 313–318 (2003)
14. Reinhard, E., Efros, A.A., Kautz, J., Seidel, H.P.: On visual realism of synthesized imagery. Proceedings of IEEE **101**(9), 1998–2007 (2013)
15. Shashua, A., Riklin-Raviv, T.: The quotient image: class-based re-rendering and recognition with varying illuminations. IEEE Trans. Pattern Anal. Mach. Intell. **23**(2), 129–139 (2001)
16. Thies, J., Zollhöfer, M., Nießner, M., Valgaerts, L., Stamminger, M., Theobalt, C.: Real-time expression transfer for facial reenactment. ACM Trans. Graph. **34**(6), 183 (2015)
17. Viola, P., Jones, M.: Robust real-time face detection. Int. J. Comput. Vis. **57**(2), 137–154 (2004)
18. Zhang, Y., Zheng, L., Thing, V.L.: Automated face swapping and its detection. In: IEEE International Conference on Signal and Image Processing, pp. 15–19 (2017)
19. Zhou, P., Han, X., Morariu, V.I., Davis, L.S.: Two-stream neural networks for tampered face detection. In: Proceedings of CVPR Workshops, pp. 1831–1839 (2017)
20. Zhu, X., Ghahramani, Z.: Learning from labeled and unlabeled data with label propagation (2002)

Facial Expression Recognition Based on Region-Wise Attention and Geometry Difference

Heran Du[1,2,3], Huicheng Zheng[1,2,3(✉)], and Mingjing Yu[1,2,3]

[1] School of Data and Computer Science, Sun Yat-sen University, Guangzhou, China
zhenghch@mail.sysu.edu.cn
[2] Key Laboratory of Machine Intelligence and Advanced Computing,
Ministry of Education, Guangzhou, China
[3] Guangdong Key Laboratory of Information Security Technology,
135 West Xingang Road, Guangzhou 510275, China

Abstract. Facial expression is usually considered as a face movement process. People can easily distinguish facial expressions via subtle facial changes. Inspired by this, we design two models that are expected to better recognize facial expressions by capturing subtle changes in the face. First, we consider to re-calibrate the response of different facial regions to highlight several special facial areas. According to this idea, we constructed cross-channel region-wise attention network (CCRAN), which can underline the important information and mine the correlations between different facial regions effectively. Moreover, we use the feature subtraction method to obtain geographical facial difference information. Based on this idea, we constructed temporal geometric frame difference network (TGFDN), which accepts the facial landmark points as input. These points are extracted from the facial expression frames. This network can effectively extract the slight changes of geographical information on the expression sequences. Through properly fusing these two networks, we have achieved competitive results on the CK+ and Oulu-CASIA databases.

Keywords: Facial expression recognition · Attention mechanisms
Temporal difference

1 Introduction

Facial expressions are part of the human body's language. It is a physical and psychological response commonly used to convey feelings. Therefore facial expression recognition (FER) in the human-computer interaction is very important. In order to conduct the interaction, the machine needs to recognize the human facial expression to perceive their feeling. Considering that the expression often contains rich emotional information, the application of this task is very extensive.

© Springer Nature Switzerland AG 2018
J.-H. Lai et al. (Eds.): PRCV 2018, LNCS 11258, pp. 183–194, 2018.
https://doi.org/10.1007/978-3-030-03338-5_16

FER is generally considered as a classification problem. Many people have done a lot of research in this field before. Overall, these studies can be divided into two categories: frame-based methods and sequence-based methods [1, 7, 15, 20, 24, 28]. Because facial expressions are generally considered as a movement process, extracting useful temporal and spatial features is very helpful for facial expression recognition. Therefore, the recognition methods based on the image sequence are generally considered to be superior to the methods based on a still single frame [7, 15].

However, the above methods are mainly based on the entire human face. In facial expression recognition tasks, the major changes in expression are often concentrated in several subtle facial regions. Humans can accurately recognize the category of expression through several key areas of the face, such as forehead, mouth, and brow. Therefore, the weights in different areas of the feature maps should be different.

In this paper, we first propose cross-channel region-wise attention network (CCRAN), trying to find the relationship between the different regions of the feature map. We hope to improve the network's ability to express specific image regions by introducing the cross-channel region-wise squeeze and excitation (CCSE) branch. Through this branch, we expect to re-calibrate features and enhance the image regional sensitivity of the network without introducing additional information.

Furthermore, we also propose temporal geometric frame difference network (TGFDN) to extract the temporal features from the facial landmarks. This network can effectively capture facial morphological changes and accurately describe facial movement characteristics. By performing feature extraction and frame difference for the landmarks of each frame separately, the network can extract low-level facial expression movement information from the landmarks. The result of the landmark difference is concatenated along the time axis and then input into the subsequent layers to further extract the high-level expression features. At the end of that, we can obtain the geometry information and movement characteristics of facial expressions.

The main contributions of this paper are divided into three parts.

- We propose CCRAN model, which accepts continuous frames as input, enhancing the network ability to recognize facial expressions by adding cross-channel region-wise attention mechanisms to the network.
- We propose TGFDN model, which can extract the inter-frame difference information from the facial landmarks points and can describe the motion process of expressions accurately.
- Finally, we fuse these two networks. The integrated deep spatial-temporal network takes into account geometry-appearance, regional-global, intra-frame and inter-frame information synthetically, improving the accuracy of expression recognition effectively.

2   Related Work

2.1   FER Based on Traditional Methods

Before the large-scale use of the deep learning-based method, it is a common practice to use hand-crafted features for facial expression recognition. These methods can be further divided into three kinds of methods based on local features extraction, facial action units (FAUs), and spatio-temporal information, respectively. Traditional methods based on local features, such as HOG, SIFT, LBP, and BoW have been extended to video. These methods also have their 3D cases [11,15,23,25,31]. In FAU based methods [12,13], facial action coding system (FACS) is used to detect and analyze FAUs to classify facial expressions. The methods based on spatio-temporal information are represented by the work of Liu et al. [15]. They have proposed an expressionlet-based spatio-temporal manifold descriptor.

2.2   FER Based on Deep Methods

In recent years, deep convolutional neural networks have achieved great success in image classification [4,5,27], object detection and localization [3,16,21,22], semantic segmentation [3,17], and other computer vision fields. Corresponding to these tasks, in the field of facial expression recognition, Liu et al. propose 3DCNN-DAP [14], which is based on 3D-CNN, constructing a deformable parts learning component to capture the expression features. Further, Jung et al. [8] trained two small deep networks with facial landmarks and image sequences separately. To achieve the better result, they performed joint fine tuning method to fuse these two networks. Based on this structure, Zhang et al. [29] introduce recurrent neural network to further analyze the facial landmarks. Ding et al. [2] use a large pre-trained face recognition network to help train a simple facial expression recognition network through a regularization mechanism. Based on this, Ofodile et al. [19] further improved the accuracy by introducing the motion trajectory of the landmark points into the network. In addition, Kim et al. [10] attempted to use a small deep encoder-decoder network pre-trained on a face database to obtain a contrastive representation between expression face and neutral face, which helps to distinguish expressions.

3   Approach

In summary, the proposed method uses a combination of two simple networks. First, we construct the TGFDN to capture the geographical inter-frame motion information. Then we use CCRAN to extract local appearance information in consecutive frames of the expression. Finally, these two networks are properly combined to improve the performance of facial expression recognition.

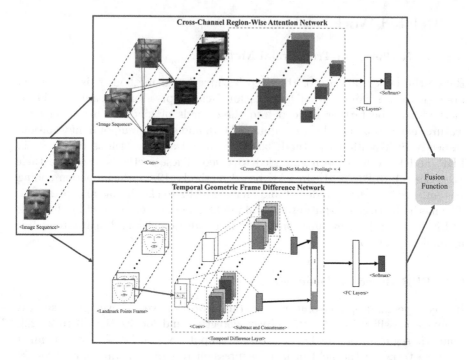

Fig. 1. Overview of our proposed architecture. The upper part of the figure shows the structure of CCRAN. The image sequence is fed into the network directly. Using a simple bottleneck (a convolution layer, a ReLU activation layer, and a batch normalization layer), the channels are increased to 64. After that, four cross-channel region-wise attention (CCRA) blocks are interleaved with four pooling layers and then followed by a fully connected layer to get logits. The lower part of the figure shows the structure of TGFDN. Facial landmark points are extracted from the frame sequence, reshaped into a matrix in which each row stores the coordinates of a point. Then the landmark matrices are fed into convolution layers separately. After the feature subtraction and difference concatenation, a fully connected layer is used to obtain logit values.

3.1 Cross-Channel Region-Wise Attention Network

In recent years, adding short connections to the network has proven to be an effective way to increase the efficiency of network information propagation [4,6,26]. So we use a simple CNN-Resnet structure as our backbone, which receives t frames of expression as input. The network includes four residual blocks interleaved with four pooling layers, and a fully connected layer at the end. Each residual block contains two convolutional layers. A batch normalization layer and a ReLU activation layer are between them, as shown in Fig. 3(a).

The whole Resnet block shown in Fig. 3(a) can be regarded as a unit that does not change the size and channels. The main problem with the backbone is that the convolutional operation takes equal considerations for the entire feature map and are less sensitive to subtle local changes. So we have joined the

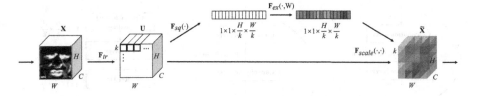

Fig. 2. Overview of the cross channel squeeze and excitation process.

cross-channel region-wise attention branch on the basis Resent block of this network. This branch draws on the squeeze and excitation network [5] and can be trained end-to-end, including a cross-channel squeeze and a cross-channel excitation operation as shown in Fig. 2.

The purpose of the squeeze operation is to compress the information of all feature maps within a layer into a one-dimensional vector. Specifically, we first compress all feature maps into a single feature map using average pooling. Then we use a $k \times k$ filter to do average pooling again on this entire compressed feature map. Each region of the compressed feature map is compressed to one value. We then flatten these values into a one-dimensional vector. The vector obtained in this way takes into account the context between the channels and the facial regions. Formally, a two-dimensional matrix $z \in \mathbb{R}^{\frac{H}{k} \times \frac{W}{k}}$ is generated by squeezing U through cross-channel $k \times k \times C$ sized average pooling window, where the z_{ij} is calculated by:

$$z_{ij} = F_{sq}(U) = \frac{1}{k \times k \times C} \sum_{c=1}^{C} \sum_{h=i \cdot k}^{i \cdot k+k-1} \sum_{w=j \cdot k}^{j \cdot k+k-1} u_c(i,j) \tag{1}$$

We further extract the contextual relationships between the regions contained in the vector through the excitation operation. Like SE-net [5], in order to reduce the complexity of the model while reducing over-fitting, we use two fully-connected layers as a bottleneck. One layer is the dimension-reduction layer, and the other is the dimension-restoring layer. Between these two layers, we use a ReLU as the activation layer to get more nonlinearity, so as to better fit and mine the complex correlations between different regions. We will use this branch to integrate with the original Resnet block. As we have shown in Fig. 3.

We obtain CCRAN by using the block in Fig. 3(b) to replace the block in Fig. 3(a). It can be seen from Fig. 3(b) that the cross-channel SE branch we proposed can be added flexibly to the original network structure. Here, we join the cross-channel SE branch before the identity addition operation.

3.2 Temporal Geometric Frame Difference Network

The entire network includes a temporal difference layer and two fully connected layers as shown in the upper part of Fig. 1. The TGFDN network receives the sequence of facial landmarks as input. We select t-frame facial landmarks to

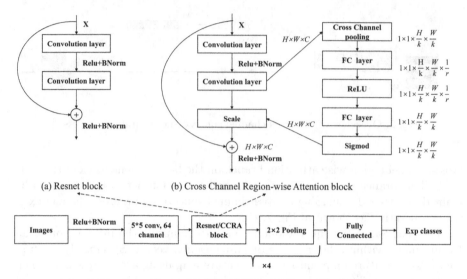

(a) Resnet block

(b) Cross Channel Region-wise Attention block

(c) Cross-Channel Region-wise Attention Network with two different block

Fig. 3. Overview of the CCRAN architecture: (a) resnet block, (b) cross channel region-wise attention block, (c) the backbone network with two kinds of block.

describe the expression features. In Fig. 1, the landmarks selected for each frame are arranged in a matrix where each row stores the xy-coordinates of a point. Then t matrices are stacked and input into the network at the same time.

In the temporal difference layer, we use a convolutional operation to extract features frame-by-frame. The kernel size is $n \times 1$. Let $X = [x_1, x_2, \ldots, x_t]$ denote the input facial landmarks, where x_t refers to the landmark points extracted from the t-th facial expression frame. The set $U = [u_1, u_2, \ldots, u_t]$ represents a set of convolution kernels and $V = [v_1, v_2, \ldots, v_t]$ denotes the features extracted via convolution operation. Features v_t are extracted from x_t using its corresponding convolution kernels u_t,

$$v_t^s = u_t^s * x_t \tag{2}$$

where $*$ denotes convolution, while v_t^s denotes the s-th feature map of v_t and u_t^s represents the s-th kernel of u_t. The convolution operation is followed by a batch normalization layer and a ReLU activation layer. Then, we use the feature obtained in this frame minus the features obtained in the previous frame to obtain frame difference. After that, we concatenate all the differences and flatten them into the one-dimensional vector. Formally, Z represents the concatenation output, and C is the concatenation operation. Here we have:

$$Z = C(u_2 - u_1, u_3 - u_2, \ldots, u_t - u_{t-1}) \tag{3}$$

Then, the difference layers are passed through the two fully connected layers and finally classified using softmax function. The discussion on convolution kernel size and the hyper-parameter t is detailed in Sect. 4.4.

3.3   Model Fusion

We fuse the two networks together through a fusion function referring to the fusion method of Zhang et al. [29].

$$O(x) = \sum_{i=0}^{1} a_i(\beta A_i(x) + P_i(x)) \tag{4}$$

$P_i(x)$ $(0 < P_i(x) < 1)$ is the output of the softmax layer in the CCRAN and TGFDN. $P_0(x)$ comes from CCRAN and $P_1(x)$ comes from TGFDN. $A_i(x)$ is sorted according to the predicted value of each expression in $P_i(x)$. In addition, β $(0 \leq \beta \leq 1)$ acts as a weight parameter. When the value of β is close to 1, the fusion function will give priority to the sorting result of different expressions. When the value of β is close to 0, the fusion function will be a simple weighted-sum function. Finally, a_i is the balance factor between different models. We empirically set a_i to 0.5 and β to 0.1. This function considers the sorting results of the softmax output and actual value of the softmax output simultaneously.

4   Experiments

We evaluated the performance of our model on two widely used databases, including CK+ [18] and Oulu-CASIA [30]. The process and details of the experiments are shown in this section.

4.1   Implementation Details

The structure of CCRAN is I64-[B(5,64)+P2] × 4-FC1024-S7. I64 means that the size of input frames is 64 × 64, and B(5,64) refers to a cross-channel SE block with 64 channels and filters of size 5 × 5. Moreover, P2 refers to a 2 × 2 max pooling layer and FC1024 means a fully connected layer with 1024 nodes. The structure of TGFDN is L(68,2)-C((1,3),16)-FD-FC600-S7. L(68,2) means that landmarks of a frame are reshaped to 68 × 2 for input, and C((1,3),16) means a convolution operation with 16 output channels and filters of size 1 × 3. Moreover, FD means a frame subtraction layer and FC600 means a fully connected layer with 600 nodes. At last S7 is the softmax layer with seven outputs (in CK+ database).

4.2   Databases and Protocols

The CK+ Database. The CK+ database [18] is a representative database of facial expression recognition tasks. This database has a total of 539 sequences of facial expressions, corresponding to 123 subjects with different ages and genders. Among them, 327 expression sequences are marked and correspond to seven types: anger, contempt, disgust, fear, happiness, sadness, and surprise. Each expression sequence begins with a plain frame (neutral expression) and ends with the peak frame of expression. We follow the usual protocol of using 10-fold cross validation [8,15] for testing.

The Oulu-CASIA VIS Database. There are 80 individuals in this database. Each individual has six expressions, including anger, disgust, fear, happiness, sadness, and surprise. So the database has a total of 480 expression sequences. Like the CK+ database, we use 10-fold cross validation as our experimental method.

4.3   Data Preprocessing and Augmentation

The duration of the expression is not the same, but our network needs to accept a fixed-length image sequence as input. Therefore, we use the average sampling method to regularize the expression sequence along the time axis. From these sampled frames, the faces are detected, cropped and reshaped into 64 × 64. What's more, we use dlib [9] to further extract 68 facial landmarks. Then we regularize all the facial landmark points using the method described in [8]. We also follow the method of Jung et al [8], making data augmentation to the training data to alleviate the overfitting problem.

4.4   Experiment Results

Comparison with Other Methods. On the CK+, we can see that our method is very close to state-of-the-art [29] and better than three pre-trained models. The method with * in Table 1 indicates that these methods use the face recognition database for pre-training and the facial expression database for fine-tuning, which introduces additional information to improve the result. On the Oulu-CASIA database, our method has also achieved very good results. The recognition ability of the fused network is higher than VGG-16 pre-trained network. Moreover, the recognition result obtained by CCRAN, which only uses the image frame as input, is surprisingly higher than the DTAGN, which uses both image frames and landmark points as input for recognition on the Oulu-CASIA database. It should be noted that there is no contradiction between our approach and the state-of-the-art [29]. It is very likely to further improve the performance by simply integrating the CCRA mechanism and the frame difference mechanism into the network to form a complementary relationship with our method.

Analysis and Discussion

Region-Wise Squeeze-and-Excitation Blocks. As we can see in Table 2, by adding the cross-channel region-wise attention (CCRA) mechanism to the Resnet block, the network performs better on two databases. This result shows that re-calibration of the different region in feature maps can effectively help the network to learn facial expression features.

Facial Landmark Selection. The coordinates of facial landmarks extracted using the dlib [9] can only be integers, which are not accurate and can cause noise in the result. If the sampling frequency of expression frames is too high, the noise

Table 1. Comparisons of different methods on the CK+ and Oulu-CASIA database (where * indicates that the model use face recognition database for pre-training).

Method	Accuracy(CK+)	Accuracy(Oulu)
3DCNN [14]	85.9%	-
3DCNN-DAP [14]	92.4%	-
DTAN [8]	91.44%	74.38%
DTGN [8]	92.35%	74.17%
DTAGN(Weighted Sum) [8]	96.94%	80.62%
DTAGN(Joint) [8]	97.25%	81.46%
PHRNN-MSCNN [29]	98.50%	86.25%
VGG-16 Fine-Tune* [2]	89.9%	83.26%
FN2EN* [2]	96.8%	87.71%
GCNet* [10]	97.93%	86.39%
CCRAN	95.48%	81.58%
TGFDN	94.55%	77.38%
CCRAN-TGFDN	98.11%	83.54%

Table 2. Comparisons between resnet block and cross-channel region-wise attention block on the CK+ and Oulu-CASIA database.

Method	Explanation	Accuracy(CK+)	Accuracy(Oulu)
Baseline	Resnet block	94.39%	79.91%
CCRAN	CCRA block	95.48%	81.58%

Table 3. Comparisons between different input number and filter size of TGFDN on the CK+ and Oulu-CASIA database.

Input Size	Filter size	Accuracy(CK+)	Accuracy(Oulu)
7-frames	1×3	93.68%	74.12%
3-frames	2×2	92.99%	75.54%
3-frames	1×1	93.61%	77.13%
3-frames	1×3	94.55%	77.38%

will be large after frame difference operation. As shown in Table 3, we can see that using landmarks with only three frames ($t = 3$) for recognition has achieved better result than that with 7 frames. In addition, we also tried different filter sizes in the network. Through the display in Table 3, we can see that the results using 2×2 size filters on CK+ and Oulu-CASIA are significantly lower than the other two convolution kernels. We think the reason is that the correlation between the x-coordinate and the y-coordinate of the face landmark points is relatively small. So a single-column-size filter performs better.

Table 4. Confusion matrix of CK+ database.

	Anger	Contempt	Disgust	Fear	Happy	Sadness	Surprise
Anger	**97.78**	0	1.69	0	0	0	0
Contempt	2.22	**94.44**	0	0	0	3.57	0
Disgust	0	0	**98.31**	0	0	0	0
Fear	0	0	0	**92**	0	0	0
Happy	0	0	0	4	**100**	0	0
Sadness	0	5.56	0	4	0	**96.43**	0
Surprise	0	0	0	0	0	0	**100**

Table 5. Confusion matrix of Oulu-CASIA database.

	Anger	Disgust	Fear	Happy	Sadness	Surprise
Anger	**78.75**	20	0	0	8.75	0
Disgust	12.50	**70**	12.5	0	2.5	0
Fear	0	0	**80**	2.5	2.5	8.75
Happy	1.25	0	6.25	**97.5**	1.25	0
Sadness	7.50	8.75	6.25	0	**85**	1.25
Surprise	0	1.25	6.25	0	0	**90**

Confusion Matrix. Tables 4 and 5 show the confusion matrices for our algorithm on the CK+ and Oulu-CASIA databases, respectively. The abscissa of the table represents prediction results and the ordinate represents labels. We can see that in the CK+ and Oulu-CASIA databases, the performance of our model for the fear is relatively poor, but the performance for happy and surprise is good.

5   Conclusion

In this paper, we try to improve the accuracy of expression recognition by capturing subtle facial movements. We propose CCRAN to extract the continuous, region-based, spatial appearance expression information and construct TGFDN to obtain temporal, global-based geographic expression features. After we fused these two networks, our model achieved better results on two different databases. In addition, other popular network structure may also explore the relationship between different areas of the feature map by simply adding the cross-channel region-wise attention mechanism. Therefore, our method is novel, effective, and general.

Acknowledgments. This work was supported by National Natural Science Foundation of China (U1611461), Special Program for Applied Research on Super Computation of the NSFC-Guangdong Joint Fund (the second phase, No. U1501501), and Science and Technology Program of Guangzhou (No. 201803030029).

References

1. Bartlett, M.S., Littlewort, G., Fasel, I., Movellan, J.R.: Real time face detection and facial expression recognition: development and applications to human computer interaction. In: IEEE Conference on Computer Vision and Pattern Recognition Workshop, vol. 5, pp. 53–53. IEEE (2003)
2. Ding, H., Zhou, S.K., Chellappa, R.: FaceNet2ExpNet: regularizing a deep face recognition net for expression recognition. In: IEEE International Conference on Automatic Face and Gesture Recognition, pp. 118–126. IEEE (2017)
3. Girshick, R., Donahue, J., Darrell, T., Malik, J.: Rich feature hierarchies for accurate object detection and semantic segmentation. In: Proceedings of the IEEE Conference on Computer Vision and Pattern Recognition, pp. 580–587 (2014)
4. He, K., Zhang, X., Ren, S., Sun, J.: Deep residual learning for image recognition. In: Proceedings of the IEEE Conference on Computer Vision and Pattern Recognition, pp. 770–778 (2016)
5. Hu, J., Shen, L., Sun, G.: Squeeze-and-excitation networks. arXiv preprint arXiv:1709.01507 (2017)
6. Huang, G., Liu, Z., van der Maaten, L., Weinberger, K.Q.: Densely connected convolutional networks. In: IEEE Conference on Computer Vision and Pattern Recognition, pp. 2261–2269 (2017)
7. Jeni, L.A., Lőrincz, A., Szabó, Z., Cohn, J.F., Kanade, T.: Spatio-temporal event classification using time-series kernel based structured sparsity. In: Fleet, D., Pajdla, T., Schiele, B., Tuytelaars, T. (eds.) ECCV 2014. LNCS, vol. 8692, pp. 135–150. Springer, Cham (2014). https://doi.org/10.1007/978-3-319-10593-2_10
8. Jung, H., Lee, S., Yim, J., Park, S., Kim, J.: Joint fine-tuning in deep neural networks for facial expression recognition. In: IEEE International Conference on Computer Vision, pp. 2983–2991. IEEE (2015)
9. Kazemi, V., Josephine, S.: One millisecond face alignment with an ensemble of regression trees. In: IEEE Conference on Computer Vision and Pattern Recognition, pp. 1867–1874. IEEE (2014)
10. Kim, Y., Yoo, B., Kwak, Y., Choi, C., Kim, J.: Deep generative-contrastive networks for facial expression recognition. arXiv preprint arXiv:1703.07140 (2017)
11. Klaser, A., Marszałek, M., Schmid, C.: A spatio-temporal descriptor based on 3D-gradients. In: British Machine Vision Conference, p. 275-1. British Machine Vision Association (2008)
12. Liu, M., Li, S., Shan, S., Chen, X.: AU-aware deep networks for facial expression recognition. In: IEEE International Conference and Workshops on Automatic Face and Gesture Recognition, pp. 1–6. IEEE (2013)
13. Liu, M., Li, S., Shan, S., Chen, X.: AU-inspired deep networks for facial expression feature learning. Neurocomputing 159, 126–136 (2015)
14. Liu, M., Li, S., Shan, S., Wang, R., Chen, X.: Deeply learning deformable facial action parts model for dynamic expression analysis. In: Cremers, D., Reid, I., Saito, H., Yang, M.-H. (eds.) ACCV 2014. LNCS, vol. 9006, pp. 143–157. Springer, Cham (2015). https://doi.org/10.1007/978-3-319-16817-3_10
15. Liu, M., Shan, S., Wang, R., Chen, X.: Learning expressionlets on spatio-temporal manifold for dynamic facial expression recognition. In: IEEE Conference on Computer Vision and Pattern Recognition, pp. 1749–1756. IEEE (2014)
16. Liu, W., et al.: SSD: single shot multibox detector. In: Leibe, B., Matas, J., Sebe, N., Welling, M. (eds.) ECCV 2016. LNCS, vol. 9905, pp. 21–37. Springer, Cham (2016). https://doi.org/10.1007/978-3-319-46448-0_2

17. Long, J., Shelhamer, E., Darrell, T.: Fully convolutional networks for semantic segmentation. In: Proceedings of the IEEE Conference on Computer Vision and Pattern Recognition, pp. 3431–3440 (2015)
18. Lucey, P., Cohn, J.F., Kanade, T., Saragih, J., Ambadar, Z., Matthews, I.: The extended Cohn-Kanade dataset (CK+): a complete dataset for action unit and emotion-specified expression. In: IEEE Computer Society Conference on Computer Vision and Pattern Recognition Workshops, pp. 94–101. IEEE (2010)
19. Ofodile, I., et al.: Automatic recognition of deceptive facial expressions of emotion. arXiv preprint arXiv:1707.04061 (2017)
20. Pantic, M., Rothkrantz, L.J.: Facial action recognition for facial expression analysis from static face images. IEEE Trans. Syst. Man Cybern. Part B (Cybern.) **34**(3), 1449–1461 (2004)
21. Redmon, J., Divvala, S., Girshick, R., Farhadi, A.: You only look once: unified, real-time object detection. In: Proceedings of the IEEE Conference on Computer Vision and Pattern Recognition, pp. 779–788 (2016)
22. Ren, S., He, K., Girshick, R., Sun, J.: Faster R-CNN: towards real-time object detection with region proposal networks. In: Advances in Neural Information Processing Systems, pp. 91–99 (2015)
23. Scovanner, P., Ali, S., Shah, M.: A 3-dimensional sift descriptor and its application to action recognition. In: ACM International Conference on Multimedia, pp. 357–360. ACM (2007)
24. Shan, C., Gong, S., McOwan, P.W.: Conditional mutual infomation based boosting for facial expression recognition. In: British Machine Vision Conference (2005)
25. Sikka, K., Wu, T., Susskind, J., Bartlett, M.: Exploring bag of words architectures in the facial expression domain. In: Fusiello, A., Murino, V., Cucchiara, R. (eds.) ECCV 2012. LNCS, vol. 7584, pp. 250–259. Springer, Heidelberg (2012). https://doi.org/10.1007/978-3-642-33868-7_25
26. Srivastava, R.K., Greff, K., Schmidhuber, J.: Highway networks. arXiv preprint arXiv:1505.00387 (2015)
27. Szegedy, C., et al.: Going deeper with convolutions. In: IEEE Conference on Computer Vision and Pattern Recognition. IEEE (2015)
28. Zeng, Z., Pantic, M., Roisman, G.I., Huang, T.S.: A survey of affect recognition methods: audio, visual, and spontaneous expressions. IEEE Trans. Pattern Anal. Mach. Intell. **31**(1), 39–58 (2009)
29. Zhang, K., Huang, Y., Du, Y., Wang, L.: Facial expression recognition based on deep evolutional spatial-temporal networks. IEEE Trans. Image Process. **26**(9), 4193–4203 (2017)
30. Zhao, G., Huang, X., Taini, M., Li, S.Z., Pietikälnen, M.: Facial expression recognition from near-infrared videos. Image Vis. Comput. **29**(9), 607–619 (2011)
31. Zhao, G., Pietikainen, M.: Dynamic texture recognition using local binary patterns with an application to facial expressions. IEEE Trans. Pattern Anal. Mach. Intell. **29**(6), 915–928 (2007)

Score-Guided Face Alignment Network Under Occlusions

Xiang Yan, Huabin Wang$^{(\boxtimes)}$, Qi Wang, Jinjie Song, and Liang Tao

Key Laboratory of Intelligent Computing and Signal Processing of Ministry of
Education, Anhui University, Hefei 230031, China
xiang199286@gmail.com, {wanghuabin,taoliang}@ahu.edu.cn,
1054588756@qq.com, 3470755438@qq.com

Abstract. Recent state-of-the-art landmark localization task are dominated by heatmap regression and fully convolutional network. In spite of its superior performance in face alignment, heatmap regression method has a few drawbacks in nature, such as do not follow shape constraint and sensitivity to partial occlusions. In this paper, we proposed a score-guided face alignment network that simultaneously outputs a heatmap and corresponding score map for each landmark. Rather than treating all predicted landmarks equally, a weight is assigned to each landmark based on the two relational maps. In this way, more reliable landmarks with strong local information are assigned large weights and the landmarks with small weights that may stay with occlusions can be inferred with the help of the reliable landmarks. Meanwhile, an exemplar-based shape dictionary is designed to take advantage of these landmarks with high score to infer the landmark with small score. The shape constraint is implicitly applied in this way. Thus our method demonstrates superior performance in detecting landmarks with extreme occlusions and improving overall performance. Experiment results on 300 W and COFW dataset show the effectiveness of the proposed method.

Keywords: Face alignment · Fully convolutional network · Occlusion

1 Introduction

Face alignment [5,25,40], aslo known as facial landmark detection, which aims to find the locations of a set of predefined facial landmarks (e.g., mouth, eyes, nose, cheek and so on) in a face image. It is a crucial pre-processing step for face recognition [16,26,27], expression recognition [3,13], face analysis [21] and so on. As a well established problem in computer vision, researchers have proposed many methods and made significant progress in face alignment. Recently, heatmap regression method [4,6,10] has shown superior performance on face alignment. However, Face alignment under occlusions still remains unsettled. Especially, when face images suffer from heavy occlusions, the performance of face alignment drops severely.

© Springer Nature Switzerland AG 2018
J.-H. Lai et al. (Eds.): PRCV 2018, LNCS 11258, pp. 195–206, 2018.
https://doi.org/10.1007/978-3-030-03338-5_17

To address face alignment under occlusions, several methods are proposed to tackle face alignment under partial occlusions. The method of [7] divides face into a 3×3 grid and only draw features from the 1/9 of facial region to several separate regressors. The work in [29] proposes a robust cascaded regression framework to handle large facial pose and occlusion. The landmark locations and the landmark visibility probability are updated stage by stage. The method of [18] treat face alignment as an appearance-shape model problem. They learn two dictionaries which are relational, one for the appearance of human face and one for the facial shape. By the two relational dictionaries, the face appearance is employed to infer occlusion and suppress the influence of occluded landmarks. The work in [33] cascades several Deep Regression networks (DR) and De- corrupt Auto-encoders (DA) to explicitly handle partial occlusion problem. In contrast with previous methods that only predict occlusion, the proposed De-corrupt Auto-encoders can recover the occluded facial appearance. They divide the facial landmarks to seven components, each specific DA is able to recover the occluded appearance. Although these methods have shown superior performance in aligning occluded faces, they have limited scalability and robustness. First is the lack of large-scale ground truth occlusion annotation for images in the wild. The task of providing occlusion annotation is often time-consuming, involving a considerable amount of tedious manual work. Another challenge is in the inherent complex facial appearance. Generally, the performance of appearance-shape dictionary depends on whether the image patterns reside within the variations described by the face appearance dictionary. Therefore, it shows limited robustness in unconstrained environment where appearance variations are too wide and complicated. In addition, recovering the occluded appearance is not without diffculties.

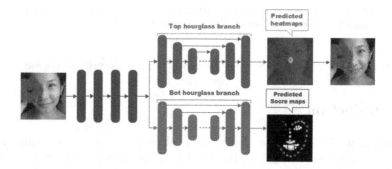

Fig. 1. Papers main idea: Given a face image as input, our network simultaneously outputs heatmaps and score maps. Due to part occlusions, the occluded landmark cannot be located precisely. Observe that the score for the occluded parts is much lower than that of the non-occluded parts in score maps. Based on the two relational maps, the occluded landmarks can be refined with the help of non-occluded landmark by exploiting geometric constraints of face shape.

In this paper, we propose a novel score-guided face alignment network to deal face with large occlusions. The key innovation of our method is score map which is able to dynamically select more reliable landmarks and use these reliable landmarks to refine the landmarks with small score. See Fig. 1 for a graphical representation of our paper's main idea. The proposed network outputs heatmaps and score maps. The occluded part is obvious in score map and has small score than non-occluded part. Rather than treat all landmarks equally, we assign a weight to each landmark based on heatmaps and score maps and the occluded landmark can be refined with the help of the non-occluded landmarks. More specifically, due to the partial occlusion, the occluded landmark cannot be located precisely. However, the non-occluded landmark can be located precisely. Since the non-occluded landmarks have lager weights than occluded landmarks. An exemplar-based shape dictionary act as shape priors can be utilized to search most similar shapes to reconstruct the face shapes based on the weights of landmarks.

The main contributions of our method can be summarized as follows:

1. We propose a novel face alignment network that simultaneously outputs heatmaps and score maps, which is more robust to occlusions. Note that no occlusion annotations are used.
2. Rather than treating all landmarks equally, we introduce score map to assign weight to each landmark. In this way, more reliable landmarks with large weights can help to refine the occluded landmarks with small weights.

2   Related Work

Prior to deep learning, cascade regression [9,17,18,22,23,37] is a popular method in face alignment, it starts with an initial facial shape and refine the shape in a cascaded manner. For each regressor, it learns a mapping function from shape-indexed features to the shape increment. The authors of [31] proposed a method named Supervised Descnet Method (SDM) to learn cascade regressors with strong handcrafted features such as SIFT. The work in [23] proposes learning local binary features by using random forests. Thanks to the sparse binary features, its speed can achieve 3000 FPS. To reduce the influence of inaccurate shape initializations, In [37] a coarse to fine search method is proposed. It begins with a coarse search over a shape pool and employs the coarse solution to finer search of shapes. The authors of [38] reformulates the popular cascaded regression scheme into a cascaded compositional learning (CCL) problem. It divides all training samples into several domains. Each domain-specific cascaded regressor handle one domain. The final shape is a composition of shape estimations across multiple predictions. The method of [11] trains multi-view cascaded regression models using a fuzzy membership weighting strategy, which improving the fault-tolerant of cascade regression. Although cascade regression has achieved good performances on the wild databases, inaccurate shape initializations, independent regressors and handcrafted features still may be sub-optimal for face alignment.

This conventional cascade regression, however, has been greatly reshaped by convolutional neural networks (ConvNets). Recent face alignment methods have universally adopted ConvNets as their main building block, largely replacing hand crafted features. The work in [36] uses multi-stage deep networks to detect facial landmarks in a coarse to fine manner. The authors of [35] formulates a novel tasks-constrained deep model to jointly optimize landmark detection together with the recognition of heterogeneous but subtly correlated facial attributes which improves the performance of landmark detection. The work in [34] employs Autoencoder netwroks (CFAN) that combined several stacked auto-encoder networks in a cascaded manner. The authors of [28] proposes a convolutional recurrent neural network architecture. The feature extraction stage is replaced with a convolutional network, the fitting stage is replaced with the Recurrent Neural NetWork. The work in [30] employs an Attention LSTM (A-LSTM) and an Refinement LSTM (R-LSTM), which sequentially selects the attention center by A-LSTM and refines the landmarks around the attention-center by R-LSTM. The authors of [19] presents a deep regression architecture with two stage reinitialization to explicitly deal with the initialization problem by face detection. FAN [6] employs stacked hourglass Network with a state-of-the-art residual block to solve the 2D&3D Face Alignment problem. The work in [10] formulate a novel Multi-view Hourglass Model which tries to jointly estimate both semi-frontal and profile facial landmarks.

3   Methodology

3.1   Network Architecture

Here, we describe our network architecture based on hourglass [20] backbone. The input is a face image with spatial resolution 128×128. The network starts a 7×7 convolutional layer with stride 2 and padding 3 to process the image to spatial resolution 64×64, followed by three residual blocks [14] to increase feature channels. Then the network is split in two sub-branches. The top sub-branch is a hourglass network, which is a symmetric top-down and bottom-up full convolutional network. Then two residual blocks process the feature maps to 128 channels. After that, nearest neighbor upsampling is used to increase the spatial resolution to 128×128, followed by a residual block and a convolutional layer with 1×1 kernels to produce heatmaps. The bottom sub-branch has the same network structure with the top sub-branch. Batch Normalization is used to before all convolutional layers expect the first convolutional layer with kernels 7×7. ReLU is the activation function. In summary, the input of network is a face image with spatial resolution 128×128. The network output N heatmaps and N score maps, where N is the number of landmarks. Each landmark corresponds to a heatmap and a score map (Fig. 2).

3.2   Score Map and Heatmap

Heatmaps are extensive used in landmark localization tasks. The model outputs N heatmaps where N is the number of landmarks. The pixel with the high- est

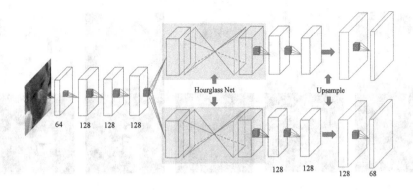

Fig. 2. An illustration of our network architecture.

value is used as the predicted landmark location. Great progress has been made by heatmaps. However, the landmarks with partial occlusion and complex background still cannot be precisely located. To deal with occlusions, we introduce score maps to assign weight to each landmark and suppress the influence of occlusions. During training, Heatmap for one landmark is created by putting a Gaussian peak at ground truth location of the landmark. While the score maps are binary maps, the values within a certain radius around the ground truth locations are set to 1 and the value for the remaining are set to 0. See Fig. 3 for example outputs produced by our network. The non-occluded face part has higher score than the occluded-part in score map. Rather than treating all landmarks equally, we weight each landmark based on their values in score maps. In this way, more reliable landmarks with strong local information are assigned high weights. The landmarks with small weights that may stay with occlusions can be refined with the help of reliable landmarks. Based on the two relational maps, the process of assigning weight can be written via the equation

$$w_i = \frac{\sum_{k=X_i-r}^{X_i+r} \sum_{t=Y_i-r}^{Y_i+r} score_i(k,t)}{(2*r+1)^2}. \tag{1}$$

where $score_i(k,t)$ is the value of coordinate (k,t) in i-th score map. X_i and Y_i are the predicted locations of i-th landmark.

3.3   Face Shape Reconstruction

Based on the two relational maps, the weight of each landmark can be determined. For the non-occluded face images, the heatmaps and score maps assign high weights to each landmark. The final predicted face shape is the locations decoded from heatmaps. For the heavy occluded face images, score maps only can check out these inaccurate landmarks with small weights, these landmarks still cannot be accurately located. Intuitively, the predicted face shape should

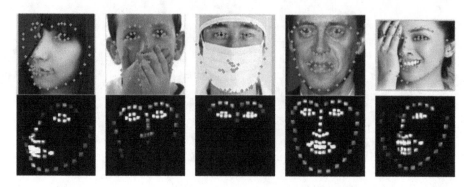

Fig. 3. Example outputs produced by our proposed network. First row shows landmark locations decoded by heatmaps. Second row shows the proposed score maps. Observe that the occluded landmarks cannot be precisely located in most cases. The non-occluded parts in score maps have higher score and are clearer than the occluded parts.

look like a face shape. Human vision has ability to predict good face shape by exploiting geometric constraints. Motivated by this, these inaccurate landmarks caused by occlusions can be refined by searching the most similar face shapes based on non-occluded landmarks, which is feasible and simple.

However, searching from all training samples is time-consuming. There are a lots of similar face shapes which are redundant. Assuming there are M training samples in train set. When M is large, searching from all training samples would be time-consuming. Follow [18], We apply K-SVD [1] on all training shapes to get N representative face shapes and use these face shapes as a shape dictionary D_S. Searching from D_S will be more effective. The searching process is formally written as

$$min_{s_1 \cdots s_k} \| W^S S - (W^S S \odot W^S D_S) \|_2^2 \tag{2}$$

where $W^S = diag(w_1, \cdots, w_N, w_1, \cdots, w_N)$ is the weight matrix and the w_i is the weight of the i-th landmark calculated via Eq. 1. The goal of W is to force the search process to emphasize on the landmarks with high weights and ignore the landmark with small weights. $s_1 \cdots s_k$ are the k nearest exemplar shapes of the non-occluded landmarks. After that, the occlusions landmarks can be reconstructed by the k nearest exemplar shapes and the reconstruction coefficients can be computed by least squares method (Fig. 4).

3.4 Training Details

During training, to prevent overfitting, all training samples are augmented by random in-plane rotation (from -30° to $+30^o$), translation, scale (from 0.9 to 1.2), flip and adding color jittering. The network input is a RGB image of size 128×128. The network is optimized by RMSProp with an initial learning rate of 0.0001 and drop to 0.00005 after 20 epochs. All models are trained using

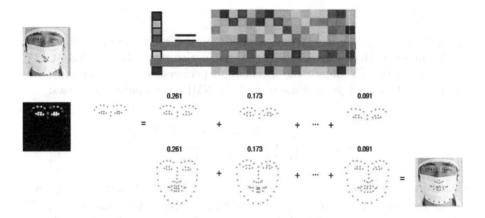

Fig. 4. Face shape reconstruction by the k nearest exemplar shapes.

PyTorch with a Nvidia 1080-Ti GPU card with a mini-batch size of 10 for 80 epochs. The loss function is defined as

$$Loss = \frac{1}{2}\sum_{n=1}^{N}\sum_{k=1}^{K}\|H_k - \hat{H}_k\|_2^2 + \frac{\lambda}{2}\sum_{n=1}^{N}\sum_{k=1}^{K}\|S_k - \hat{S}_k\|_2^2 \qquad (3)$$

where N is the number of training samples,H_k and $\hat{H}_k$ are the predicted heatmaps and the ground-truth heatmaps. S_k and $\hat{S}_k$ are the predicted score map and ground-truth score map. λ is a hyperparameter to balance the loss functions. During inference, the predicted landmark locations $\hat{Z}_k$ is decoded from the predicted heatmap H_k by taking the locations with the maximum value as follows,

$$\hat{Z}_k = \arg\max_{p} H_k(p) \qquad (4)$$

4 Experiments

4.1 Datasets

For training, 300-W is the most widely-used in-the-wild dataset for 2D face alignment. All face images are labeled by 68 landmarks. The training set consists of AFW [39] dataset, HELEN [15] training set and LFPW [2] training set, there are 3148 face images in total. For testing, we report the results on LFPW testing set, Helen testing set and IBUG dataset. To verify the effectiveness of our method on occluded faces, we evaluate COFW [7,12] testing set. The COFW dataset is a challenging dataset with severe facial occlusions and large facial pose collected from web. There are 1345 face images in training set and 507 face images in testing set. All face images are labeled by 29 landmarks. Since our model is trained on images with 68 landmarks, Follow [12], we use the COFW with 68 landmarks for testing. Note that we only use COFW testing set for evaluation.

4.2   Metrics

Given the predicted landmark locations and ground-truth landmark locations, the Normalized Mean Error (NME) or cumulative error distribution (CED) curves employed to evaluate the localization performance. The normalization is normalized by inter-pupil distance and the NME is computed as follows:

$$error = \frac{1}{M} \sum_{i=1}^{M} \frac{\frac{1}{N} \sum_{j=1}^{N} \|p_{i,j}^{pred} - p_{i,j}^{gt}\|_2}{\|p_{i,l} - p_{i,r}\|_2} \tag{5}$$

where M is the number of testing images, N is the number of landmarks. $p_{i,l}, p_{i,r}$ are the locations of left eye center and right eye center in i-th face image. $p_{i,j}^{pred}$ is the predicted location of landmark location of the j-th landmark in i-th face image. $p_{i,j}^{gt}$ is the ground-truth location of landmark location of the j-th landmark in i-th face image.

4.3   Evaluation Results on 300W

The 300-W [24] testing set consists of common set and challenging set. The com- mon set are Helen testing set and LFPW testing set. The challenging set is the IBUG dataset. Table 1 show the resluts on 300 W dataset. We compare our method with eleven state-of-the-art face alignment methods with RCPR [7], CFAN [34], ESR [8], SDM [31], LBF [22], CFSS [37], TCDCN [35], DNN [32], MD- M [28], RAR [30], TR-DRN [19]. Our method outperform most of these methods except RAR.

4.4   Evaluation Results on COFW

To verify the effectiveness of our method on various occluded face images, we test our method on COFW [7,12] dataset. The CED curves are shown in Fig. 5. It can be seen our baseline still outperform all other methods by a large margin. That is because our method benefits from heatmap regression and network architecture. By adding occlusion inference and face reconstruction, the NME error decreases from 6.29% to 5.78%. The success rate increases from 94.67% to 97.83%. Moreover, we analyse the evaluation on only the visible landmarks, our method and baseline show similar results on NME error and success rate. It can be concluded that heatmap regression method achieves excellent performance in detecting non-occluded face part. While evaluation on all the landmarks, benefit from score map to assign weight to each landmark and refine the occluded region by face reconstruction, our method show better results than baseline both in NME error and success rate.

Table 1. Landmark detection results on different subsets of the 300-W dataset in terms of the NME averaged over all the test samples.

Method	Common set	Challenging set	Full set
RCPR	6.18	17.26	8.35
SDM	5.57	15.40	7.52
ESR	5.28	17.00	7.58
CFAN	5.50	16.78	7.69
DeepReg	4.51	13.80	6.31
LBF	4.95	11.98	6.32
CFSS	4.73	9.98	5.76
TCDCN	4.80	8.60	5.54
DDN	-	-	5.59
MDM	4.83	10.14	5.88
RAR	4.12	8.35	4.94
TR-DRN	4.36	7.56	4.99
SIR	4.29	8.14	5.04
Ours	4.16	7.54	4.78

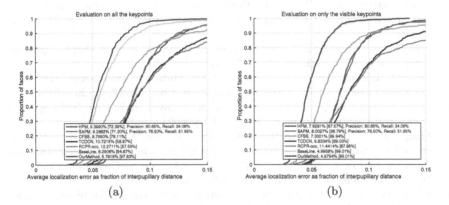

Fig. 5. Comparison of different models on the COFW dataset: (a) evaluation on all the keypoints, (b) evaluation on only the visible keypoints.

5   Conclusion

In this paper, we propose a score-guided face alignment network which is robust to occlusions. The network simultaneously outputs a heatmap and corresponding score map for each landmark. Based on the two relational maps, more reliable landmark are assigned large weights and landmarks with small weights can be inferred with the help of the reliable landmarks. Experiment results on 300 W and COFW dataset show the effectiveness of the proposed method and showed significant performance improvements over the state-of-the-arts.

References

1. Aharon, M., Elad, M., Bruckstein, A.: K-SVD: an algorithm for designing over-complete dictionaries for sparse representation. IEEE Trans. Sig. Process. **54**(11), 4311–4322 (2006)
2. Belhumeur, P.N., Jacobs, D.W., Kriegman, D.J., Kumar, N.: Localizing parts of faces using a consensus of exemplars. In: Computer Vision and Pattern Recognition (CVPR), pp. 545–552 (2011)
3. Bettadapura, V.: Face expression recognition and analysis: the state of the art (2012). arXiv preprint arXiv:1203.6722
4. Bulat, A., Tzimiropoulos, G.: Convolutional aggregation of local evidence for large pose face alignment (2016)
5. Bulat, A., Tzimiropoulos, G.: Binarized convolutional landmark localizers for human pose estimation and face alignment with limited resources. In: The IEEE International Conference on Computer Vision (ICCV), vol. 1, p. 4 (2017)
6. Bulat, A., Tzimiropoulos, G.: How far are we from solving the 2D and 3D face alignment problem? (and a dataset of 230,000 3D facial landmarks). In: International Conference on Computer Vision (ICCV), vol. 1, p. 4 (2017)
7. Burgos-Artizzu, X.P., Perona, P.: Robust face landmark estimation under occlusion. In: International Conference on Computer Vision (ICCV), pp. 1513–1520 (2013)
8. Cao, X., Wei, Y., Wen, F., Sun, J.: Face alignment by explicit shape regression. Int. J. Comput. Vis. **107**(2), 177–190 (2014)
9. Deng, J., Liu, Q., Yang, J., Tao, D.: M3 CSR: Multi-view, multi-scale and multi-component cascade shape regression. Image Vis. Comput. **47**, 19–26 (2016)
10. Deng, J., Trigeorgis, G., Zhou, Y., Zafeiriou, S.: Joint multi-view face alignment in the wild (2017). arXiv preprint arXiv:1708.06023
11. Feng, Z.H., Kittler, J., Christmas, W., Huber, P., Wu, X.J.: Dynamic attention-controlled cascaded shape regression exploiting training data augmentation and fuzzy-set sample weighting. In: 2017 IEEE Conference on Computer Vision and Pattern Recognition (CVPR), pp. 3681–3690. IEEE (2017)
12. Ghiasi, G., Fowlkes, C.C.: Occlusion coherence: detecting and localizing occluded faces (2015). arXiv preprint arXiv:1506.08347
13. Guo, Y., Zhao, G., Pietikäinen, M.: Dynamic facial expression recognition with atlas construction and sparse representation. IEEE Trans. Image Process. **25**(5), 1977–1992 (2016)
14. He, K., Zhang, X., Ren, S., Sun, J.: Deep residual learning for image recognition. In: Computer Vision and Pattern Recognition (CVPR), pp. 770–778 (2016)
15. Le, V., Brandt, J., Bourdev, L., Bourdev, L., Huang, T.S.: Interactive facial feature localization. In: European Conference on Computer Vision (ECCV), pp. 679–692 (2012)
16. Li, D., Zhou, H., Lam, K.M.: High-resolution face verification using pore-scale facial features. IEEE Trans. Image Process. **24**(8), 2317–2327 (2015)
17. Liu, Q., Deng, J., Tao, D.: Dual sparse constrained cascade regression for robust face alignment. IEEE Trans. Image Process. **25**(2), 700–712 (2016)

18. Liu, Q., Deng, J., Yang, J., Liu, G., Tao, D.: Adaptive cascade regression model for robust face alignment. IEEE Trans. Image Process.(TIP) **26**(2), 797–807 (2017)
19. Lv, J.J., Shao, X., Xing, J., Cheng, C., Zhou, X., et al.: A deep regression architecture with two-stage re-initialization for high performance facial landmark detection. In: Computer Vision and Pattern Recognition (CVPR), vol. 1, p. 4 (2017)
20. Newell, A., Yang, K., Deng, J.: Stacked hourglass networks for human pose estimation. In: Leibe, B., Matas, J., Sebe, N., Welling, M. (eds.) ECCV 2016. LNCS, vol. 9912, pp. 483–499. Springer, Cham (2016). https://doi.org/10.1007/978-3-319-46484-8_29
21. Ranjan, R., Sankaranarayanan, S., Castillo, C.D., Chellappa, R.: An all-in-one convolutional neural network for face analysis. In: 2017 12th IEEE International Conference on Automatic Face and Gesture Recognition (FG 2017), pp. 17–24. IEEE (2017)
22. Ren, S., Cao, X., Wei, Y., Sun, J.: Face alignment via regressing local binary features. IEEE Trans. Image Process.(TIP) **25**(3), 1233 (2016)
23. Ren, S., Cao, X., Wei, Y., Sun, J.: Face alignment at 3000 fps via regressing local binary features. In: Proceedings of the IEEE Conference on Computer Vision and Pattern Recognition, pp. 1685–1692 (2014)
24. Sagonas, C., Tzimiropoulos, G., Zafeiriou, S., Pantic, M.: 300 faces in-the-wild challenge: the first facial landmark localization challenge. In: Conference on Computer Vision Workshops (CVPRW), pp. 397–403 (2014)
25. Sun, Y., Wang, X., Tang, X.: Deep convolutional network cascade for facial point detection. In: Computer Vision and Pattern Recognition (CVPR), pp. 3476–3483 (2013)
26. Tai, Y., Yang, J., Zhang, Y., Luo, L., Qian, J., Chen, Y.: Face recognition with pose variations and misalignment via orthogonal procrustes regression. IEEE Trans. Image Process. **25**(6), 2673–2683 (2016)
27. Taigman, Y., Yang, M., Ranzato, M., Wolf, L.: DeepFace: closing the gap to human-level performance in face verification. In: Proceedings of the IEEE Conference on Computer Vision and Pattern Recognition, pp. 1701–1708 (2014)
28. Trigeorgis, G., Snape, P., Nicolaou, M.A., Antonakos, E., Zafeiriou, S.: Mnemonic descent method: a recurrent process applied for end-to-end face alignment. In: Computer Vision and Pattern Recognition (CVPR), pp. 4177–4187 (2016)
29. Wu, Y., Ji, Q.: Robust facial landmark detection under significant head poses and occlusion. In: Proceedings of the IEEE International Conference on Computer Vision, pp. 3658–3666 (2015)
30. Xiao, S., Feng, J., Xing, J., Lai, H., Yan, S., Kassim, A.: Robust facial landmark detection via recurrent attentive-refinement networks. In: Leibe, B., Matas, J., Sebe, N., Welling, M. (eds.) ECCV 2016. LNCS, vol. 9905, pp. 57–72. Springer, Cham (2016). https://doi.org/10.1007/978-3-319-46448-0_4
31. Xiong, X., Torre, F.D.L.: Supervised descent method and its applications to face alignment. In: Computer Vision and Pattern Recognition (CVPR), pp. 532–539 (2013)
32. Yu, X., Zhou, F., Chandraker, M.: Deep deformation network for object landmark localization. In: Leibe, B., Matas, J., Sebe, N., Welling, M. (eds.) ECCV 2016. LNCS, vol. 9909, pp. 52–70. Springer, Cham (2016). https://doi.org/10.1007/978-3-319-46454-1_4
33. Zhang, J., Kan, M., Shan, S., Chen, X.: Occlusion-free face alignment: deep regression networks coupled with de-corrupt autoencoders. In: Computer Vision and Pattern Recognition (CVPR), pp. 3428–3437 (2016)

34. Zhang, J., Shan, S., Kan, M., Chen, X.: Coarse-to-fine auto-encoder networks (CFAN) for real-time face alignment. In: Fleet, D., Pajdla, T., Schiele, B., Tuytelaars, T. (eds.) ECCV 2014. LNCS, vol. 8690, pp. 1–16. Springer, Cham (2014). https://doi.org/10.1007/978-3-319-10605-2_1

35. Zhang, Z., Luo, P., Loy, C.C., Tang, X.: Facial landmark detection by deep multi-task learning. In: Fleet, D., Pajdla, T., Schiele, B., Tuytelaars, T. (eds.) ECCV 2014. LNCS, vol. 8694, pp. 94–108. Springer, Cham (2014). https://doi.org/10.1007/978-3-319-10599-4_7

36. Zhou, E., Fan, H., Cao, Z., Jiang, Y., Yin, Q.: Extensive facial landmark localization with coarse-to-fine convolutional network cascade. In: IEEE International Conference on Computer Vision Workshops (ICCVW), pp. 386–391 (2013)

37. Zhu, S., Li, C., Chen, C.L., Tang, X.: Face alignment by coarse-to-fine shape searching. In: Computer Vision and Pattern Recognition (CVPR), pp. 4998–5006 (2015)

38. Zhu, S., Li, C., Loy, C.C., Tang, X.: Unconstrained face alignment via cascaded compositional learning. In: Proceedings of the IEEE Conference on Computer Vision and Pattern Recognition, pp. 3409–3417 (2016)

39. Zhu, X., Ramanan, D.: Face detection, pose estimation, and landmark localization in the wild. In: Computer Vision and Pattern Recognition (CVPR), pp. 2879–2886. IEEE (2012)

40. Zhu, X., Lei, Z., Liu, X., Shi, H., Li, S.Z.: Face alignment across large poses: a 3D solution. In: Proceedings of the IEEE Conference on Computer Vision And Pattern Recognition, pp. 146–155 (2016)

Robust Face Detector with Fully Convolutional Networks

Yingcheng Su, Xiaopei Wan, and Zhenhua Guo[✉]

Graduate School at Shenzhen, Tsinghua University, Shenzhen, China
zhenhua.guo@sz.tsinghua.edu.cn

Abstract. Many of the exist face detection algorithms are based on the generic object detection methods and have achieved desirable results. However, these methods still struggle in solving the problem of partial occluded face detection. In this paper, we introduce a simple and effective face detector which uses a fully convolutional networks (FCN) for face detection in a single stage. The proposed FCN model is used for pixel-wise prediction instead of anchor mechanism. In addition, we also apply a long short term memory (LSTM) architecture to enhance the contextual infomation of feature maps, making the model more robust to occlusion. Besides, we use a light-weighted neural network PVANet as the backbone, which greatly reduces the computational burden. Experimental results show that the proposed method achieves competitive results with state-of-the-art face detectors on the common face detection benchmarks, including the FDDB, WIDER FACE and MAFA datasets, what's more, it is much more robust to the detection of occluded faces.

Keywords: Face detection · FCN · LSTM · Occlusion

1 Introduction

Face detection has always been a research hotspot as it is a crucial step of many facial applications, such as face alignment, face recognition, etc. Since the pioneering work of Viola-Jones face detector [1], a lot of face detection methods have been proposed. The hand-crafted features [2,3] usually rely on prior knowledge leading to poor performance in complex scenes, especially faces with occlusion.

In recent years, convolutional neural networks (CNNs) have great success in the field of computer vision, including image classification [4,5] and object detection [6–9], etc. The Object detection algorithms such as fast [6]/faster [7] R-CNN, SSD [9], YOLO [8] continue to make new breakthroughs in both speed and precision. Face detection is a special case of object detection. Many face detection approaches are based on object detection methods [10–13] and achieve promising results. However, these anchor-based methods are badly rely on the

Z. Guo—The work is partially supported by the Natural Science Foundation for China (NSFC) (No. 61772296) and Shenzhen fundamental research fund (Grant Nos. JCYJ20160531194840025 and JCYJ20170412170438636).

Fig. 1. Our face detector is robust to heavy occlusion and large appearance.

number of matching proposals. If the faces are partial occluded, it's very likely that the models would miss the proposals of occluded faces or be confused by the features of occluded faces. The cascaded network [17,18] is another type of CNNs-based face detection approach. Several small CNNs are cascaded to detect faces in a coarse-to-fine manner. In spite of very fast speed, these shallow networks failed to represent robust image features to handle faces with occlusion.

Inspired by [20], we consider face detection problem as the combination of binary classification and bounding box regression. In this paper, we propose a fast and efficient face detector that only need two steps for face detection. First, a FCN is used to do the pixel-wise classification and bounding box regression. Then, the produced face predictions are sent to Non-Maximum Suppression (NMS) to yield final results. By making such dense predictions, the model has strong robustness to faces with occlusion. In addition, considering the highly-correlated of adjacent regions of the feature map, we use an in-network recurrent architecture to encode rich context information of the feature map. Even if the face is partial occluded, the model can make the correct predictions from the non-occluded part. An example of our detection results can be found in Fig. 1.

The main contribution of this paper can be summarized as:

- We propose a novel FCN-based face detection method that directly make dense predictions in feature maps. The proposed method is fast, accurate and quite simple, which only consist of two step: a forward propagation of the FCN and a NMS merging.
- We use a recurrent architecture to connect the context information of the feature maps, improving the model's capacity of detecting faces with occlusion.

- The proposed method achieves competitive results in FDDB, WDIER Face datasets, and outperforms state-of-the-art methods in occluded faces datasets like MAFA.

2 Related Work

Before the revolution of deep learning, Face detection has been widely studied. Numerous face detector are based on traditional machine learning methods. The pioneering work of Viola-Jones [1] utilizes Adaboost with Haar-like feature to train a cascade model to detect face and get real-time performance. Since then the studies of face detection focus on designing more efficient features [22,23] and more powerful classifiers [26,27]. Deformable pattern models (DPM) [25] are employed for face detection task and achieve promising results. Liao et al. [24] proposed normalized pixel difference (NPD) features and constructed a deep quadratic tree to handle unconstrained face detection. However, these hand-crafted features always require prior assumptions which would be untenable in complex scenarios, leading to low precision in the challenging face datasets, such as WIDER Face and MAFA.

In recent years, the CNN-based face detectors achieved remarkable performance. Li et al. [17] use cascaded CNNs for face detection. Zhang et al. [18] propose Multi-task cascaded CNNs (MTCNN) to detect face and align face, simultaneously. Qin et al. [19] integrate the training of cascaded CNNs into a framework for end-to-end training, which greatly improves the performance of cascaded networks. Faceness [28] generates face parts responses from attribute-aware networks to detect faces under occlusion and unconstrained pose variation. However, this method needs to label facial attributes of different facial parts and generate face proposals according to facial part response maps, which is complicated and time consuming.

There are also a variety of face detection methods that inherit the achievements from generic object detection methods. Face R-CNN [12] is based on Faster R-CNN and adopts center loss [29] to minimize the intra-class distances of the deep features. It also utilizes some training tricks such as online hard example mining and multi-scale training. CMS-RCNN [10] uses contextual information for face detection. DeepIR [13] concatenate features of multiple layers to improve face detection performance. Hu et al. [16] build image pyramids and defines multiple templates to find tiny faces. SSH [14] establishes detection modules on different feature maps to detect face in a single stage. SFD [15] focuses on scale-invariance by using a new anchor matching strategy. Zhu et al. [30] analyze the anchor matching mechanism with the proposed expected max overlap (EMO) score and introduce new designed anchors to find more tiny faces. All these anchor-based methods have obtained promising results. However, we know that the scale of faces is continuous. The anchor mechanism makes the scale discrete, which may lead to the low matching rate of hard samples, especially occluded faces. A naive way to increase the number of matching anchors is to increase the total number of anchors. But this will result in heavily computational burden.

DenseBox [20] is another kind of object detection method. Different from the above anchor-based methods, DenseBox utilizes a FCN to perform pixel-wise predictions. By doing the upsampling operation to keep a high-resolution output, it has great advantages in handling the detection of small objects. The approach of dense prediction can also improve the robustness of detecting heavy occluded objects. UnitBox [21] further presents a new intersection-over-union (IoU) loss for bounding box prediction. Yet there are some drawbacks of Unit-Box. On one hand, an up-sample layer is used to perform linear interpolation to resize the feature map to the original image size. Although it can detects smaller faces, the computational cost is unacceptable. On the other hand, the feature maps are upsampled 16 times for pixel-wise classification, which may bring artifacts. In this paper, we propose a novel face detector that utilizes a FCN framework to do the dense prediction on the feature maps whose size is just 1/4 of the original image size. The FCN architecture consists of a bottom-up path and a top-down path similar to [20,31]. Inspired by [32], we further employ an in-network recurrence mechanism to explore meaningful information of the convolutional feature maps and improve the robustness of detecting faces with occlusion, leading to state-of-the-art detection performance.

3   Proposed Method

The proposed face detector is trained to directly predict the existence of faces and their locations from full images instead of dividing the detection task into bounding box proposal and classification. A fully convolutional neural network is used to do the pixel-wise dense prediction of faces. The post-processing of our method is quit simple, which only contains thresholding and NMS.

3.1   Base Framework

As we know from [33] that feature maps of different layer represent different semantic information. The shallow layers have high spatial resolution responding to corners and edge/color conjunctions, which is good for spatial localization. The deep layers have lower spatial resolution but more class-specific which is good for classification. Inspired by recent works [20,31,34], we adopt a neural network that contains a top-down architecture with lateral connection to fuse features from different layers.

Our network architecture is shown in Fig. 2. We use PVANet [35] as the backbone. The bottom-up pathway is the feed-forward computation of the backbone ConvNet generating four levels of feature maps, whose sizes are 1/4, 1/8, 1/16 and 1/32 of the original image, respectively. We define that layers producing the output maps of the same size are in the same network stage. Since the deeper layer should have stronger features, the last layer of each stage is chosen to connect with deeper layer with the same output size. It is very difficult to detect tiny object by low resolution features. The top-down pathway increases the resolution by upsampling operations while keeps the semantic information. Each upsample operation is at a scaling step of 2. The top-down pathway features are enhanced by features from the bottom-top pathway via lateral connections. By doing such lateral connections, the network can maintain both geometrical and semantic information. As shown in Fig. 2, we use a 1×1 conv layer to preprocess the lateral features and merge different features by concat layer. Then a 1×1 conv layer and a 3×3 conv layer are used to further cut down half of the number of channels and produce the output of this merging stage, respectively. The size of the final feature maps is only 1/4 of the original image, making the network computation-efficient. The network is then split into two branches, one for classification and the other one for bounding box regression.

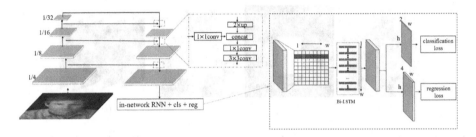

Fig. 2. An overview of our network architecture

3.2 In-Network Recurrence Architecture

Recurrent neural network (RNN) is often applied in scenarios with sequences of inputs such as video, audio, text lines to encode the contextual information. Recent work [32] has shown that the sequential context information is good for text detection. Motivated from this work, we believe that RNN may also benefit for face detection, especially detecting faces with occlusion. We note that features of the face area are highly-correlated, so we can use this correlation via recurrent structure to make correct predictions of the occluded part of face. Besides, the regression task predicts a 4-D distance vector (the distances between the current pixel and the four bounds of the ground truth box), and there is also a strong correlation among the distance vectors of adjacent pixels. RNN can encode these contextual information recurrently using its hidden layers. Formally, The internal state of RNN at t moment is given by

$$H_t = \varphi(H_{t-1}, X_t) \tag{1}$$

where $X_t \in R^{3 \times 3 \times C}$ is the input sequential features from t-th sliding-window (3×3) as shown in Fig. 2. The sliding window slides from left to right at a stride of 1, generating $t = 1, 2, ...W$ sequential inputs for each row. W is the width of the input feature map. In this paper, we adopt the bi-directional long short-term memory (Bi-LSTM) architecture for the RNN layer just as [32] do. The Bi-LSTM allows the model to encode the contextual features in both directions. The outputs of the two inverse LSTMs is then merged by a concat layer, followed by a 1×1 conv layer to cut down the number of channels.

3.3   Label Generation

We consider the face area is a rectangle. The classification task is to predict a binary score map $\in \{0, 1\}$ which indicates the negative area and positive area. The positive area of the rectangle on the score map is designed to be roughly a shrunk version of the original rectangle. For each edge, we shrink it by moving its two endpoints inward along by 0.2 of its length, illustrated in Fig. 3(a). The regression task is to predict a 4 channels of distance map as shown in Fig. 3(d). The ground truth distance map is generated by calculating a 4-D distance vector for each pixel with a value of 1 on the score map, illustrated in Fig. 3(c).

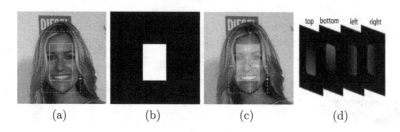

(a)   (b)   (c)   (d)

Fig. 3. Label generation. (a) Face bounding box (green dashed) and the shrunk rectangle (green solid); (b) score map; (c) pixel-wise distances generation; (d) 4 channels of distances of each pixel to rectangle boundaries. (Color figure online)

4   Training

In this section, we introduce our training details, including loss function, training dataset, data augmentation and other implementation details.

4.1   Loss Functions

Considering that there is a class imbalance problem, we restrict the number of positive pixels and negative pixels during training, making them numerically equal. This can be done by hard examples mining. We simply use softmax loss for the classification. The regression task is optimized by IoU loss, more details can be found in [21]. These two tasks are joint optimized equally. The multi-task loss is formulated as

$$L = L_{cls} + L_{IoU} \qquad (2)$$

We empirical note that model optimized by Eq. 2 has a problem in locating tiny faces, leading to lots of false positives. We solve this problem by employing a focal loss to focus training on locating tiny face. The new loss function can be rewritten as

$$L = L_{cls} + \alpha S^{-\gamma} L_{IoU} \qquad (3)$$

where S is the face area, α and γ are two constant. In our experiments, we empirically set $\alpha = 4, \gamma = 0.5$.

4.2   Training Dataset and Data Augmentation

We use the WIDER FACE training set which contrains 12,880 images to train our model. In order to get better results, we also apply the following data augmentation techniques: (1) **Scale modification.** Each image is random scaling in a range between [0.6, 2] via bilinear interpolation. (2) **Random crop.** We randomly crop a square patch from the image. And the size of the image patch is 640×640. For images with shorter side less than 640 pixels, we firstly pad the images with 0, making their shorter side greater than 640. (3) **Horizontal flip.** After random crop, we obtain 640×640 image patch, and then we horizontally flip it with probability of 0.5.

4.3   Other Implementation Details

Online hard examples mining is employed to boost the performance of the model. For the parameter initialization, the parameters of the backbone are initialized from the corresponding pre-trained models. We use PVANet as the backbone in our experiments. Other additional layers are randomly initialized with the "xavier" method. All models are trained by SGD with a single GPU. The mini-batch sizes of models are 6, because of the GPU memory limitation. Weight decay is 1e–5 and momentum is 0.9. Our networks are trained for 500 K iterations. The initial learning rate is 0.001 and drops by a factor of 5 after 200 K iterations. During inference, the score threshold is set to 0.01 and NMS with a threshold of 0.3 is performed on the predicted bounding boxes.

5   Experiments

5.1   Evaluation on Benchmark

We compare the proposed method with existing methods on two common face detection benchmarks: FDDB, WIDER FACE.

FDDB. It contains 2845 images with 5171 annotated faces. The Evaluation criteria include discrete score and continuous score. We compare our face detector against the state-of-the-art methods. Figure 4 shows the results. Our Face detector achieves competitive results with SFD [15] and outperforms other methods, indicating that our method can robustly detect unconstrained faces.

WIDER FACE. It contains 32203 images with a total of 393703 annotated faces with different scales, poses and occlusions. The data set is divided into training (40%), testing (50%) and validation (10%) set. Faces in the testing and validation set are split into three kinds of difficulty (easy, medium and hard). It is one of the most challenging face data sets. Our face detector is trained on WIDER FACE training set and tested on both validation and test set. We set the long side of the test image to 800, 1120, 1400, 1760 and 1920 for multi-scale

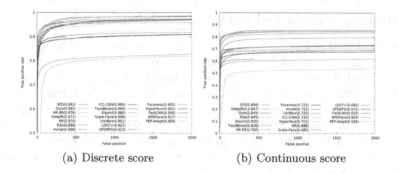

(a) Discrete score   (b) Continuous score

Fig. 4. Evaluation on FDDB

testing. Figure 5 illustrates the precision-recall curves along with AP scores. Our face detector outperforms other recent published methods including Zhu et al. [30], SFD [15], SSH [14] on the validation set and achieves competitive results with Zhu et al.'s [30], which demonstrate that the proposed method has a strong capacity in detecting small and hard faces.

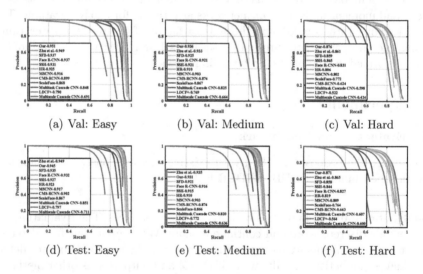

(a) Val: Easy   (b) Val: Medium   (c) Val: Hard

(d) Test: Easy   (e) Test: Medium   (f) Test: Hard

Fig. 5. Precision-recall curves on WIDER FACE validation and test sets.

5.2   Robustness to Occlusion

We further explore the ability of our detector in detecting occluded faces. To demonstrate the effectiveness of LSTM, we carry out comparative experiments with Two models: PVA, PVA+LSTM, where PVA uses PVANet [35] as the backbone without Bi-LSTM architecture. Two occluded face data sets are used for this purpose, i.e. WIDER FACE validation set with artificial occlusion and MAFA with real occlusion. We also compare our method with other algorithms that release their trained models and testing codes such as MTCNN [18], SFD [15], SSH [14].

Faces with Artificial Occlusion. In this experiment, We generate a new occluded face data set by blacking a rectangle area on every faces of the WIDER FACE validation set. The rectangle black is randomly distributed in the left, right and bottom side of the face, accounting for 40% area of the face annotated box. Examples of occluded images are shown in Fig. 6. Table 1 shows the results of different methods. It's clear that our two models outperform other methods. We note that adding LSTM or not makes little difference. The main reason is that the WIDER Face contain lots of tiny face, the role of encoding the context information of the RNN structure is weakened after adding the artificial occlusion.

Fig. 6. Examples of WIDER FACE validation set with Occlusion

Table 1. Comparison of different models on the WDIER FACE validation set with artificial occlusion.

Methods	AP (easy)	AP (medium)	AP (hard)
MTCNN [18]	0.565	0.526	0.361
SSH [14]	0.801	0.768	0.625
SFD [15]	0.835	0.798	0.621
PVA	0.881	0.850	0.723
PVA+LSTM	0.881	0.851	0.720

Faces with Real Occlusion. MAFA data set contains 30,811 image with 35,806 faces collected from the Internet. Most of the faces are occluded by mask. We only use the testing set which contains 4,935 images to evaluate our face detector. The long side of all testing images is set to 1280. Table 2 shows the results of different methods. Our base models without LSTM have already outperform other methods. And the LSTM structure further improves the robustness of our face detectors in detecting faces with real occlusion.

Table 2. Comparison of different models on the MAFA data set.

Methods	MTCNN [18]	SSH [14]	SFD [15]	LLE-CNNs [36]	PVA	PVA+LSTM
AP	0.570	0.643	0.724	0.764	0.768	0.781

5.3 Inference Time

Although our method achieves great performance, its speed is not compromised. We employ PVANet, a light-weighted neural network, as the backbone, which greatly reduces the computational burden. We measure the speed using a GTX 1080Ti GPU and Intel Xeon E5-2620 v4@2.1 GHz CPU. Table 3 shows the inference time and AP with respect to different input sizes of our face detector. The max size stands for the long side of the input image while keeping the aspect ratio.

Table 3. The inference time and AP with respect to different input sizes

Max size	800	1120	1440	1760	1920
AP (hard)	0.723	0.829	0.863	0.873	0.872
Time (ms)	60.7	83.9	124.9	172.9	195.0

6   Conclusions

In this paper, we propose a novel FCN-based face detector which is simple and efficient. Unlike other anchor-based methods, our face detector performs dense prediction on a single feature map, which is inherent robust in detecting occluded faces. By using the in-network RNN structure, our face detector is superior to handle the detection of occluded faces. Besides, the size of the final feature map is only 1/4 of the original image, reducing the computational cost while achieving remarkable results in detecting small faces. The experiments demonstrate that the proposed method achieves the state-of-the-art performance on the challenging face detection benchmarks, especially for small faces and occluded faces.

References

1. Viola, P., Jones, M.J.: Robust real-time face detection. IJCV **57**(2), 137–154 (2004)
2. Dalal, N., Triggs, B.: Histograms of oriented gradients for human detection. In: 2005 IEEE Computer Society Conference on Computer Vision and Pattern Recognition, CVPR, vol. (1), pp. 886–893. IEEE (2005)
3. Ojala, T., Pietikainen, M., Harwood, D.: Performance evaluation of texture measures with classification based on Kullback discrimination of distributions. In: 1994 Proceedings of the 12th IAPR International Conference on Pattern Recognition, Computer Vision and Image Processing, vol. 1, pp. 582–585. IEEE (1994)
4. Simonyan, K., Zisserman, A.: Very deep convolutional networks for large-scale image recognition. arXiv preprint arXiv:1409.1556 (2014)
5. Szegedy, C., Vanhoucke, V., Ioffe, S., et al.: Rethinking the inception architecture for computer vision. In: Proceedings of the IEEE Conference on Computer Vision and Pattern Recognition, pp. 2818–2826 (2016)
6. Girshick, R.: Fast R-CNN. arXiv preprint arXiv:1504.08083 (2015)
7. Ren, S., He, K., Girshick, R., et al.: Faster R-CNN: towards real-time object detection with region proposal networks. In: Advances in neural information processing systems, pp. 91–99 (2015)
8. Redmonm, J., Divvala, S., Girshick, R., et al.: You only look once: unified, real-time object detection. In: Proceedings of the IEEE Conference on Computer Vision and Pattern Recognition, pp. 779–788 (2016)
9. Liu, W., Anguelov, D., Erhan, D., et al.: SSD: single shot multibox detector. In: Leibe, B., Matas, J., Sebe, N., Welling, M. (eds.) ECCV 2016. LNCS, vol. 9905, pp. 21–37. Springer, Cham (2016). https://doi.org/10.1007/978-3-319-46448-0_2
10. Zhu, C., Zheng, Y., Luu, K., Savvides, M.: CMS-RCNN: contextual multi-scale region-based CNN for unconstrained face detection. In: Bhanu, B., Kumar, A. (eds.) Deep Learning for Biometrics. ACVPR, pp. 57–79. Springer, Cham (2017). https://doi.org/10.1007/978-3-319-61657-5_3
11. Jiang, H., Learned-Miller, E.: Face detection with the faster R-CNN. In: 2017 12th IEEE International Conference on Automatic Face and Gesture Recognition (FG 2017), pp. 650–657. IEEE (2017)
12. Wang, H., Li, Z., Ji, X., et al.: Face R-CNN. arXiv preprint arXiv:1706.01061 (2017)
13. Sun, X., Wu, P., Hoi, S.C.H.: Face detection using deep learning: an improved faster RCNN approach. arXiv preprint arXiv:1701.08289 (2017)
14. Najibi, M., Samangouei, P., Chellappa, R., et al.: SSH: single stage headless face detector. In: Proceedings of the IEEE Conference on Computer Vision and Pattern Recognition, pp. 4875–4884 (2017)
15. Zhang, S., Zhu, X., Lei, Z., et al.: S^{3}FD: single shot scale-invariant face detector. arXiv preprint arXiv:1708.05237 (2017)
16. Hu, P., Ramanan, D.: Finding tiny faces. In: 2017 IEEE Conference on Computer Vision and Pattern Recognition (CVPR), pp. 1522–1530 (2017)
17. Li, H., Lin, Z., Shen, X., et al.: A convolutional neural network cascade for face detection. In: Proceedings of the IEEE Conference on Computer Vision and Pattern Recognition, pp. 5325–5334 (2015)
18. Zhang, K., Zhang, Z., Li, Z.: Joint face detection and alignment using multitask cascaded convolutional networks. IEEE Sig. Process. Lett. **23**(10), 1499–1503 (2016)
19. Qin, H., Yan, J., Li, X., et al.: Joint training of cascaded CNN for face detection. In: Proceedings of the IEEE Conference on Computer Vision and Pattern Recognition, pp. 3456–3465 (2016)

20. Ronneberger, O., Fischer, P., Brox, T.: U-Net: convolutional networks for biomedical image segmentation. In: Navab, N., Hornegger, J., Wells, W.M., Frangi, A.F. (eds.) MICCAI 2015. LNCS, vol. 9351, pp. 234–241. Springer, Cham (2015). https://doi.org/10.1007/978-3-319-24574-4_28

21. Yu, J., Jiang, Y., Wang, Z., et al.: UnitBox: an advanced object detection network. In: Proceedings of the 2016 ACM on Multimedia Conference, pp. 516–520. ACM (2016)

22. Yang, B., Yan, J., Lei, Z., et al.: Aggregate channel features for multi-view face detection. In: IEEE International Joint Conference on Biometrics (IJCB), pp. 1–8 (2014)

23. Zhu, Q., Yeh, M.C., Cheng, K.T., et al.: Fast human detection using a cascade of histograms of oriented gradients. In: IEEE Conference on Computer Vision and Pattern Recognition, vol. 2, pp. 1491–1498 (2006)

24. Liao, S., Jain, A.K., Li, S.Z.: A fast and accurate unconstrained face detector. IEEE Trans. Pattern Anal. Mach. Intell. **38**(2), 211–223 (2016)

25. Felzenszwalb, P.F., Girshick, R.B., McAllester, D., et al.: Object detection with discriminatively trained part-based models. IEEE Trans. Pattern Anal. Mach. Intell. **32**(9), 1627–1645 (2010)

26. Brubaker, S.C., Wu, J., Sun, J., et al.: On the design of cascades of boosted ensembles for face detection. Int. J. Comput. Vis. **77**(1–3), 65–86 (2008)

27. Pham, M.T, Cham, T.J.: Fast training and selection of HAAR features using statistics in boosting-based face detection. In: IEEE International Conference on Computer Vision (ICCV), pp. 1–7 (2007)

28. Yang, S., Luo, P., Loy, C.C., et al.: From facial parts responses to face detection: a deep learning approach. In: Proceedings of the IEEE International Conference on Computer Vision, pp. 3676–3684 (2015)

29. Wen, Y., Zhang, K., Li, Z., Qiao, Y.: A discriminative feature learning approach for deep face recognition. In: Leibe, B., Matas, J., Sebe, N., Welling, M. (eds.) ECCV 2016. LNCS, vol. 9911, pp. 499–515. Springer, Cham (2016). https://doi.org/10.1007/978-3-319-46478-7_31

30. Zhu, C., Tao, R., Luu, K., et al.: Seeing small faces from robust anchor's perspective. arXiv preprint arXiv:1802.09058 (2018)

31. Zhou, X., Yao, C., Wen, H., et al.: EAST: an efficient and accurate scene text detector. arXiv preprint arXiv:1704.03155 (2017)

32. Tian, Z., Huang, W., He, T., He, P., Qiao, Y.: Detecting text in natural image with connectionist text proposal network. In: Leibe, B., Matas, J., Sebe, N., Welling, M. (eds.) ECCV 2016. LNCS, vol. 9912, pp. 56–72. Springer, Cham (2016). https://doi.org/10.1007/978-3-319-46484-8_4

33. Zeiler, M.D., Fergus, R.: Visualizing and understanding convolutional networks. In: Fleet, D., Pajdla, T., Schiele, B., Tuytelaars, T. (eds.) ECCV 2014. LNCS, vol. 8689, pp. 818–833. Springer, Cham (2014). https://doi.org/10.1007/978-3-319-10590-1_53

34. Lin, T.Y., Dollr, P., Girshick, R., et al.: Feature pyramid networks for object detection. In: IEEE Conference on Computer Vision and Pattern Recognition (CVPR), vol. 1, no. 2, p. 4 (2017)

35. Kim, K.H., Hong, S., Roh, B., et al.: PVANET: deep but lightweight neural networks for real-time object detection. arXiv preprint arXiv:1608.08021 (2016)

36. Ge, S., Li, J., Ye, Q., et al.: Detecting masked faces in the wild with LLE-CNNS. In: The IEEE Conference on Computer Vision and Pattern Recognition (2017)

Nuclear Norm Based Superposed Collaborative Representation Classifier for Robust Face Recognition

Yongbo Wu and Haifeng Hu[✉]

School of Electronics and Information Technology, Sun Yat-Sen University,
Guangzhou, China
wuyb6@mail2.sysu.edu.cn, huhaif@mail.sysu.edu.cn

Abstract. In this paper, we propose a novel robust face recognition framework named nuclear norm based superposed collaborative representation classifier (NNSCRC) to handle illumination variations, occlusion and undersampled problems in face recognition. Specifically, we develop a superposed linear collaborative representation classifier for robust face recognition by representing the query image in terms of a superposition of the class centroid, the shared intra-class difference, and the low rank error. By representing a face image as the class centroid and the shared intra-class difference, our model can effectively enhance the face recognition performance on undersampled databases. In addition, since the occlusion and illumination variations generally lead to a low-rank error image, we use nuclear norm matrix regression to obtain these low-rank errors, which makes our model able to reconstruct the test image better. Extensive experiments are performed on Extended Yale-B and AR databases, which show the effectiveness of NNSCRC in robust face recognition.

Keywords: Robust face recognition · Nuclear norm
Superposed collaborative representation

1 Introduction

Face recognition (FR) has received extensive research during last thirty years and numerous FR methods have been developed [7,8,13,15,17,24]. Classical FR algorithms including principal component analysis (PCA) [19], linear discriminant analysis (LDA) [3] and laplacianface [10] try to employ subspace learning method to represent the intrinsic characteristics of faces. At the same time, many types of image features like scale-invariant feature transform (SIFT) [16], local binary pattern (LBP) [1], speeded-up robust features (SURF) [2] and histogram of oriented gradient (HOG) [21] have been introduced into FR algorithms, while the final recognition result can be easily obtained based on these feature representations. However, these feature descriptors are hand-crafted and always

© Springer Nature Switzerland AG 2018
J.-H. Lai et al. (Eds.): PRCV 2018, LNCS 11258, pp. 219–232, 2018.
https://doi.org/10.1007/978-3-030-03338-5_19

require many prior knowledge, which limits the improvement of recognition performance.

Regression analysis based methods have also aroused broad interests in face recognition community. For example, Naseem et al. proposed a linear regression classification (LRC) [15] by reconstructing a query image as the linear combination of dictionary faces. Wright et al. proposed a sparse representation based classification algorithm (SRC) [22] for robust face recognition using a sparse constraint. By representing a face image with a sparse linear combination of the dictionary faces, SRC believed that the query image will be reconstructed by the training samples in the same class. However, when the number of training samples is limited, sparsity between classes may lead to misleading solutions. Zhang et al. [25] analyzed the principle of SRC and believed that collaborative representation is more effective than sparsity constraint. Based on ridge regression, they introduced a collaboration representation classifier (CRC) which lead to better FR accuracy and lower complexity than SRC. After that, many improved versions of CRC algorithm have been proposed to further improve the performance of FR. For example, Wang et al. [20] used a relaxed collaborative representation (RCR) by considering locality constraints. Huang et al. [11] introduced group sparse classifier (GSC) which tries to incorporate the class labels to boost FR performance. IRGSC [26] further introduced group sparse classifier with adaptive weights learning, and had achieved good performance in robust face recognition.

Recently, Yang et al. [23] proposed nuclear norm based matrix regression (NMR) classification framework for occlusion face recognition and had achieved good recognition performance. However, NMR relies heavily on the completeness of database. When the number of training samples is limited, NMR suffers from misleading coding coefficients of incorrect classes. More recently, superposed linear representation based classification (SLRC) [9] model was proposed to further improve the robustness of CRC. SLRC decomposed the training sample of CRC into prototype and variation parts, and proposed a superposed linear representation that encodes the test sample as a superposition of the prototype and variation dictionaries. In SLRC, the author simply assumed that the test image can be reconstructed by class-central of corresponding class and the shared intra-class differences. However, when there are unknow illumination variations or occlusion in the test image, the SLRC model will not work effectively since it cannot reconstruct the image properly.

In order to address the limitations of NMR and SLRC, we propose a novel model called nuclear norm based superposed collaborative representation classifier (NNSCRC). In our model, a query image can be decomposed as a class centroid, a shared sample-to-centroid difference and a low rank error image. The main contributions of this paper are outlined as follows:

- We propose a new framework named nuclear norm based superposed collaborative representation classifier for robust face recognition where a test face image can be reconstructed as a superposed of class centroid, intra-class difference and low rank error. The new model can address the misleading coding coefficients of incorrect classes when the dataset is undersampled, since it has decomposed the image as a class centroid and sample-to-centroid difference. Alternating direction method of multipliers (ADMM) algorithm has been used to obtain the optimal solution of proposed model.

- By introducing a nuclear norm constraint, the low-rank part, generally the occlusion or illumination variations in the image, will be separated out from the dictionary reconstruction. Thus, the NNSCRC model is robust to occlusion or illumination variations.
- NNSCRC model is robust to single sample per person (SSPP) face recognition problem. Specifically, when there is only one train image available in each class, we can borrow the intra-class variations from the subjects outside the gallery since these variations are usually similar across different subjects. The variations between query image and gallery images can be represented by these intra-class variations properly, which will improve the performance of SSPP face recognition.
- Experimental results on Extended Yale-B and AR databases show the proposed NNSCRC model achieves better performance than state-of-the-art regression based methods for illumination variations, occlusion and undersampled face recognition.

The remainder of this paper is organized as follows: Sect. 2 reviews the related works. Section 3 introduces the proposed nuclear norm based superposed collaborative representation classifier (NNSCRC). In Sect. 4, we conduct experiments on two popular face databases and compare our model with the state-of-the-art regression based methods. Finally, Sect. 5 concludes this paper.

2   Related Works

In this section, we briefly review the regression based methods and introduce SLRC method in detail, which is related to our model.

Regression based methods have long been a research hotspot in face recognition community. Started by SRC, which represents a query image as a sparse reconstruction of dictionary images, many regression based approaches like CRC have been proposed in succession and have achieved good performance in face recognition task. Collaborative representation based methods believe that l_2-norm constraint is more important than l_1-norm constraint in classifier. They use training samples to reconstruct the test sample and believe the training samples in the same class will become the major components in the reconstruction process. Although these regression based methods have achieved good performance on general face recognition, their generalization ability to illumination variations, occlusion and undersampled face recognition problems is still weak.

Recently, superposed linear representation based classification (SLRC) [9] is proposed to decompose the collaborative dictionary in a manner similar to the decomposed representation in LDA. Specifically, given a sample x from one of the classes in the training set, SLRC assume it can be naturally reconstructed by two parts:

$$x = c_{(x)} + (x - c_{(x)}) \tag{1}$$

where $c_{(x)}$ is the centroid of corresponding class, and $x - c_{(x)}$ is the intra-class difference from the sample to its class centroid. SLRC has achieved promise performance when the test images have similar attributes to the training images. However, when there are unknow variations in the test image such as illumination changes or occlusion, the SLRC model will not work properly since it cannot reconstruct these variations in test image.

Considering these limitations, we propose a novel framework to incorporate the nuclear norm constraint into superposed linear representation based classification, which not only makes use of the general variation information of training samples, but also improves the robustness to unknow illumination changes and occlusions. The proposed model will be introduced in detail in the next section.

3   Nuclear Norm Based Superposed Collaborative Representation Classifier (NNSCRC)

Although CRC methods have received great success in face recognition, it still suffers from undersampled and occlusion problems. Firstly, when the training images are insufficient or unrepresentative, the test sample has to be reconstructed by the samples of other classes, which usually generates misleading coding coefficients. Secondly, when there are illumination changes or occlusion in the test images, the reconstructed error will be dominated by these noise, which will also lead to erroneous results. In order to overcome these difficulties, we propose a novel robust face recognition framework called nuclear norm based superposed collaborative representation classifier (NNSCRC). We will introduce our NNSCRC model in detail and provide the optimization algorithm of NNSCRC in this section.

3.1   NNSCRC Model

Inspired by NMR [23] and SLRC [9], we represent a test image as a superposition of three parts, i.e., the class centres, the shared intra-class differences, and the

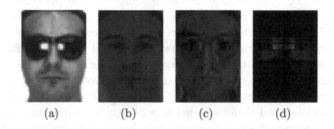

(a)   (b)   (c)   (d)

Fig. 1. In the proposed NNSCRC model, we try to reconstruct a test image as a linear superposition of the class centroid, the shared intra-class differences, and the low-rank error. (a) the original test image (b) the class centroid image (c) the shared intra-class differences image (shown in absolute value) (d) the low-rank error image (shown in absolute value)

low-rank error, as shown in Fig. 1. Specifically, given a test image Y, we assume it can be reconstructed by the mentioned three parts, which can be formulated as:

$$Y = \mathcal{P}(\alpha) + \mathcal{V}(\beta) + B. \tag{2}$$

where $\mathcal{P}(\alpha) = \alpha_1 P_1 + \alpha_2 P_2 + ... + \alpha_n P_n$, $\mathcal{V}(\beta) = \beta_1 V_1 + \beta_2 V_2 + ... + \beta_n V_n$, and P_i is the central of class i, V_i is the variation dictionary of class i. α_i, β_i are the corresponding reconstruction coefficients of class i. B is the low rank error image. To obtain the optimal reconstruction coefficients $\hat{\alpha}$ and $\hat{\beta}$, we can naturally construct the objective function as:

$$\begin{bmatrix} \hat{\alpha} \\ \hat{\beta} \end{bmatrix} = \arg\min \left\| y - [P, V] \begin{bmatrix} \alpha \\ \beta \end{bmatrix} - b \right\|_2^2 + \lambda_1 \left\| \begin{bmatrix} \alpha \\ \beta \end{bmatrix} \right\|_2^2 + \lambda_2 \|B\|_*, \tag{3}$$

where $P \in \mathbb{R}^{d \times k}$ is the prototype dictionary and $V \in \mathbb{R}^{d \times n}$ is the variation dictionary, d is the dimension of face image, k represents the class number and n is the number of training images. $\|B\|_*$ represents the nuclear norm of low rank error B, and b is the vectorization of matrix B. α, β are the coefficient vectors to be determined. λ_1, λ_2 are the penalty parameters. The prototype dictionary P consists of centroid from all classes, and the variation dictionary V consists of intra-class difference from the sample to its class centroid. The construction of dictionaries P and V is similar to [9]. For most collaborative representation based methods, undersampled training images usually lead to misleading coding coefficients. The main reason is that when the training images is insufficient, the difference between test image and corresponding prototype class need to be make up by images from other class, which make the major components of reconstruction might be found in the error class. By integrating superposed linear representation classifier with nuclear norm, our model can address the problem of misleading coefficients and enhance the robustness to illumination changes and occlusion. The reasons are listed as follows:

Firstly, we introduce a superposed linear representation into our model, which constructs a prototype dictionary P and a variation dictionary V. When the dataset is undersampled, the shared variation dictionary V will make up the difference between the test image and the corresponding prototype class. The major components of reconstructed test image will be the class centroid of corresponding class, the intra-class variations from all classes, and the low rank error, which makes our model can handle the misleading coefficients problem.

Secondly, since occlusion and illumination changes generally lead to a low-rank error image, we apply a nuclear norm constrained matrix to characterize this structured noise (see Fig. 1(d)). When there are unknow occlusion or illumination changes in the test image, the nuclear norm constrained error term will represents this kind of noise properly, which makes the NNSCRC model can work effectively.

3.2   Algorithm of NNSCRC

We provide the theoretical solution of NNSCRC in this section. Since Eq. (3) is not always a convex function, we cannot solve it with traditional methods like augmented Lagrange Multipliers (ALM). Notice that it satisfies the condition of Alternating Direction Method of Multipliers (ADMM) [4], which will been proved in Sect. 3.3, we use ADMM algorithm to solve the optimization problem. Specifically, we first introduce a matrix variable C and rewrite Eq. (3), which form the object function as:

$$J(\alpha, \beta, B, C) = \min_{\alpha, \beta, B, C} \|y - [P, V] \begin{bmatrix} \alpha \\ \beta \end{bmatrix} - b\|_2^2 + \lambda_1 \| \begin{bmatrix} \alpha \\ \beta \end{bmatrix} \|_2^2$$
$$+ \lambda_2 \|C\|_*, \qquad s.t. \ C - B = 0. \tag{4}$$

Denote

$$f(\alpha, \beta, B) = \|y - [P, V] \begin{bmatrix} \alpha \\ \beta \end{bmatrix} - b\|_2^2 + \lambda_1 \| \begin{bmatrix} \alpha \\ \beta \end{bmatrix} \|_2^2. \tag{5}$$

Then the Lagrange form of $J(\alpha, \beta, B, C)$ is

$$L_\rho(\alpha, \beta, B, C) = f(\alpha, \beta, B) + \lambda_2 \|C\|_* + tr(Z^T(C - B)) + \frac{\rho}{2}\|C - B\|_F^2$$
$$= f(\alpha, \beta, B) + \lambda_2 \|C\|_* + \frac{\rho}{2}\|C - B + \frac{1}{\rho}Z\|_F^2 - \frac{1}{2\rho}\|Z\|_F^2. \tag{6}$$

where $\rho > 0$ is the Lagrangian multiplier, and Z is the dual variable. The obtain of the optimal solution contains the following three iterative processes.

Fix Z, α, β, B to Solve C. At k-th iterative, when Z, α, β, B is fixed, Eq. (6) can be rewritten as

$$J_1(C) = \arg\min_C \lambda_2 \|C\|_* + \frac{\rho}{2}\|C - B_k + \frac{1}{\rho}Z_k\|_F^2. \tag{7}$$

Let $Q = B_k - \frac{1}{\rho}Z_k \in \mathbb{R}^{m_1 \times m_2}$, where $rank(Q) = r$. We apply singular value decomposition to Q as:

$$Q = U_{m_1 \times r} \Sigma V_{m_2 \times r}^T, \tag{8}$$

where $\Sigma = diag(\sigma_1, \sigma_2, ..., \sigma_r)$ and $\sigma_1, \sigma_2, ..., \sigma_r$ are positive singular values. $U_{m_1 \times r}$ and $V_{m_2 \times r}$ are corresponding matrices with orthogonal columns. According to [5], the iterative solution of C_{k+1} can be expressed as

$$C_{k+1} = U_{m_1 \times r}(\{max(0, \sigma_j - \frac{\lambda_2}{\rho})\}_{1 \le j \le r})V_{m_2 \times r}^T. \tag{9}$$

Fix Z, C to Solve α, β and B. At k-th iterative, when Z, C is fixed, Eq. (6) can be rewritten as

$$J_2(\alpha, \beta, B) = \min_{\alpha, \beta, B} f(\alpha, \beta, B) + \frac{\rho}{2}\|C_{k+1} - B + \frac{1}{\rho}Z_k\|_F^2$$
$$= \min_{\alpha, \beta, B} \|y - [P, V] \begin{bmatrix} \alpha \\ \beta \end{bmatrix} - b\|_2^2 + \lambda_1 \| \begin{bmatrix} \alpha \\ \beta \end{bmatrix} \|_2^2 \tag{10}$$
$$+ \frac{\rho}{2}\|C_{k+1} - B + \frac{1}{\rho}Z_k\|_F^2.$$

Define $\boldsymbol{H}_k = \boldsymbol{C}_{k+1} + \frac{1}{\rho}\boldsymbol{Z}_k \in \mathbb{R}^{m_1 \times m_2}$, $\boldsymbol{h}_k = Vec\{\boldsymbol{H}\} \in \mathbb{R}^{m_1 m_2 \times 1}$, the optimal solution can be obtained by setting the derivative of $J_2(\boldsymbol{\alpha}, \boldsymbol{\beta}, \boldsymbol{b})$ with respect to $\boldsymbol{\alpha}$, $\boldsymbol{\beta}$, and $\boldsymbol{b}$ to zero respectively. Therefore, we have the optimal solution of $\boldsymbol{\alpha}$, $\boldsymbol{\beta}$ and $\boldsymbol{B}$ at k-th iterative as

$$\boldsymbol{\alpha}_{k+1} = (\boldsymbol{P}^T \boldsymbol{P} + 2\lambda_1 \boldsymbol{I})^{-1} \boldsymbol{P}^T (\boldsymbol{y} - \boldsymbol{b}_{k+1} - \boldsymbol{V}\boldsymbol{\beta}_k), \tag{11}$$

$$\boldsymbol{\beta}_{k+1} = (\boldsymbol{V}^T \boldsymbol{V} + 2\lambda_1 \boldsymbol{I})^{-1} \boldsymbol{V}^T (\boldsymbol{y} - \boldsymbol{b}_{k+1} - \boldsymbol{P}\boldsymbol{\alpha}_{k+1}), \tag{12}$$

$$\boldsymbol{b}_{k+1} = \frac{1}{2+\rho}(2\boldsymbol{y} - 2\boldsymbol{P}\boldsymbol{\alpha} - 2\boldsymbol{V}\boldsymbol{\beta} + \rho\boldsymbol{h}_k). \tag{13}$$

Fix $\boldsymbol{\alpha}, \boldsymbol{\beta}, \boldsymbol{C}$ and $\boldsymbol{B}$ to Solve $\boldsymbol{Z}$. According to [4], the optimal solution of $\boldsymbol{Z}$ at iteration k can be directly obtained by

$$\boldsymbol{Z}_{k+1} = \boldsymbol{Z}_k + \rho(\boldsymbol{C}_{k+1} - \boldsymbol{B}_{k+1}). \tag{14}$$

With the iteration optimal solution in Sect. 3.2, we can finally obtain the optimal solution of $J(\boldsymbol{\alpha}, \boldsymbol{\beta}, \boldsymbol{B}, \boldsymbol{C})$ by alternate iteration. Finally, the optimal reconstruction coefficients are:

$$\hat{\boldsymbol{\alpha}} = \boldsymbol{\alpha}_{k+1}, \quad \hat{\boldsymbol{\beta}} = \boldsymbol{\beta}_{k+1}. \tag{15}$$

3.3   Classification Strategy of NNSCRC

Given test image Y, we need to decide which class it belongs to for face recognition task. By using NNSCRC algorithm, we can obtain the reconstruction coefficients $\hat{\boldsymbol{\alpha}}$ and $\hat{\boldsymbol{\beta}}$. We use the reconstruction residual in each class as the criterion for classification. Specifically, the residual of test image Y is

$$r_i(\boldsymbol{Y}) = \left\| \boldsymbol{Y} - [\boldsymbol{P}, \boldsymbol{V}] \begin{bmatrix} \delta_i(\hat{\boldsymbol{\alpha}}) \\ \hat{\boldsymbol{\beta}} \end{bmatrix} - \boldsymbol{B} \right\|_2, \ i = 1, ..., k. \tag{16}$$

Where $\delta_i(\hat{\boldsymbol{\alpha}}) \in \mathbb{R}^n$ is a new vector whose only nonzero entries are the entries in $\hat{\boldsymbol{\alpha}}$ that are associated with class i. Note that when we calculate the residual, we use intra-class variation matrix of all classes to reconstruct the test image Y, because these intra-class variation are often shareable across different subjects. This is also one of the reason that our model is suitable for SSPP task. From Eq. (16), we can find that the normal variations and error image are separated out from the original query image, which can remove the influence of illumination changes and occlusions. Based on the reconstruction residual, we can decide the class label by

$$class(\boldsymbol{Y}) = \arg\min_i r_i(\boldsymbol{Y}). \tag{17}$$

4   Experiments

In this section, we perform extensive experiments on two publicly available face datasets to demonstrate the effectiveness of NNSCRC. Section 4.1 first gives the experimental settings of our experiments. In Sect. 4.2, we evaluate NNSCRC for FR with different training sizes under controlled conditions. Section 4.3 verifies the robustness of NNSCRC to illumination changes and occlusion face recognition. Section 4.4 compares our method with existing methods for face recognition task under real face disguise. Finally, in Sect. 4.5, face recognition experiment with single sample per person has been performed.

4.1 Experimental Settings

We apply Aleix Martinez and Robert Benavente (AR) dataset [14] and the Extended Yale B (ExYaleB) dataset [12] to test the effectiveness and robustness of proposed model. The AR dataset contains over 4000 images of 126 individuals (70 men and 56 women). The faces in AR dataset contain variations such as lighting conditions, expressions and occlusions. Some examples of face images in AR database are shown in Fig. 2. For this dataset, we randomly seclect 100 subjects (50 men and 50 women) for our experiments. The Extended Yale B face dataset contains 38 human subjects under 9 poses and 64 illumination conditions. The 64 samples of each subject are acquired in a particular pose, which are all frontal view facial images. Figure 3 shows some facial images in ExYaleB database. All face images marked with P00 are used in our experiments.

Fig. 2. Facial image samples in AR database

Fig. 3. Facial image samples in the Extended Yale B face database

The proposed model is compared to state-of-the-art regression based representation methods including NMR [23], WGSC [18], RCRC [6], RSRC [22], and IRGSC [26]. For NNSCRC, the Lagrangian multiplier ρ is set to 1, and the parameter λ_1, λ_2 are both traversed in {0.01, 0.05, 0.1, 0.5, 1, 5, 10} to obtain best result. For all the comparative methods, the related parameters are set to the values suggested by the authors.

4.2   Face Recognition with Different Sample Sizes

We first validate the performance of NNSCRC without occlusion on ExYaleB database. In order to explore the effect of sample size on experimental results, we randomly split the dataset into two parts. One part is used as the dictionary, which contains $n(=10, 20, 30, 40, 50)$ images for each person, and the other part is used for testing. The results are shown in Fig. 4, which compares our method with the state-of-the-art method, IRGSC. Two most classical regression based face recognition methods including CRC and SRC have also been used for comparison.

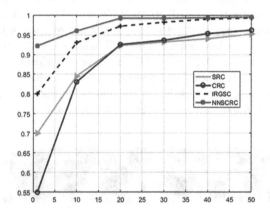

Fig. 4. Face recognition with different sample sizes on ExYaleB database

From Fig. 4, we can find that the performances of all methods improved when the sample size increases. Though the test faces suffers from illumination problems, for all groups of sample size, our NNSCRC model outperforms SRC and CRC for over five percentage, which shows our model is more robust to illumination variations compared to original collaborative representation methods. IRGSC achieves higher accuracy than SRC and CRC because it use the reconstruction residuals to obtain the feature weights, which can reduce the influence of the pixel errors. However, there are still some variations between train images and test images which will influence the reconstruction and classification, and these variations cannot easily removed by the adaptive weights in IRGSC. In comparison, our model still achieves higher accuracy than IRGSC for all groups of sample sizes. The main reason is that our model can reconstruct the variations by using the variation dictionary which is constructed by all classes. The nuclear norm constraint can also handle the illumination variations problem, which make NNSCRC achieve better performance compared to IRGSC.

4.3 Face Recognition with Occlusion

To validate the robustness of proposed NNSCRC model to occlusion, we conduct two types of experiments on ExYaleB dataset, including random block occlusion experiment and random face occlusion experiment.

Random Block Occlusion. We select 20 samples per subject in ExYaleB dataset for training, and 20 for testing. Similar to the work in IRGSC, for each test image, we randomly select a location in the image and replace 10–60% pixels using a black block. Figure 5 shows the examples of different percentage of occlusions. The recognition rates of different methods are shown in Table 1. From Table 1, we can see that for all group of block occlusion, our method achieve the best performance compared with state-of-the-art regression based methods. Note that for 60% occlusion, our method still achieves 80.3% recognition rate, which is 7.7% higher than IRGSC. NMR has worse performance compared to IRGSC because it simply ignores the general variations, which will also influence the reconstruction error. By considering the general variations and the low-lank error, the proposed model can achieve better performance than other methods.

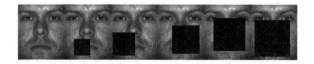

Fig. 5. Samples with different percentage of pixel corruption (0%–60%)

Table 1. Recognition accuracy of different methods versus different percentage of block occlusion

Occlusion (%)	10	20	30	40	50	60
RSRC	98.6	96.2	95.2	93.5	69.7	56.4
RCRC	99.0	97.9	96.7	94.3	81.2	62.0
WGSC	94.1	93.4	85.3	73.9	57.1	41.3
NMR	99.0	98.0	95.9	92.5	81.1	69.3
IRGSC	99.1	98.2	96.7	94.2	83.8	72.6
NNSCRC	**99.4**	**98.4**	**96.7**	**94.7**	**87.5**	**80.3**

Random Face Occlusion. In this experiment, we replace 10–50% pixels of each test images with other face images. As shown in Fig. 6, both the location of occlusion position and the occlusion face images are randomly selected. Table 2 lists the recognition accuracy of different methods. As can be seen, our method still achieve better performance compared to others methods. The recognition

Fig. 6. Samples with different percentage of face occlusion (0%–50%)

Table 2. Recognition accuracy of different methods versus different percentage of face occlusion

Occlusion (%)	10	20	30	40	50
RSRC	96.9	95.6	91.2	88.6	72.9
WGSC	97.6	96.4	90.2	84.0	67.8
NMR	98.9	95.3	93.8	83.1	72.1
IRGSC	99.1	96.4	94.1	89.2	81.7
NNSCRC	**99.3**	**97.2**	**96.0**	**91.4**	**83.2**

rate of our model is a little lower than that of random block occlusion, which is due to the reason that face occlusion is not strictly low rank. Still, our model outperforms about 2% than IRGSC under large percentage face occlusion, which indicates the effectiveness of NNSCRC to address occlusions.

4.4   Face Recognition with Real Disguise

To evaluate the robustness of our model to real possible disguise, we further conduct experiments on AR dataset. As shown in Fig. 2, there are some samples with sunglasses or scarves in AR database, which reflects the real FR conditions in practical application. This kind of occlusion is irregular, thus brings a large challenge for FR tasks. In our experiment, the face images of these 100 persons were separated into 2 sessions according to the shooting time of photos. For each person, we select 3 images in session 1 which has no illumination changes or occlusion problem as training samples. 1200 face images are used for test, which are divided into 4 groups as: 300 face images with illumination changes and sunglasses in session 1, and 300 face images with illumination changes and scarves in session 1, and the same divided in session 2.

The experiment results of competing methods are listed in Table 3. Clearly, the NNSCRC method achieves better result in all 4 groups of experiments compared with WGSC, RCRC, RSRC, and NMR. WGSC has the worst performance, while WGSC tried to regress the query images only with the training samples, and failed to consider the influence caused by occlusion. RCRC tries to solve the problem of occlusion, and in fact achieves better performance than WGSC. Note that our model outperform NMR by around 14%, which indicates that by introducing a superposed linear collaborative representation to NMR model, our model can enhance the robustness of face recognition effectively.

Table 3. Recognition rates (%) of different methods on AR database

Classifier	Session 1		Session 2	
	Sunglasses	Scarves	Sunglasses	Scarves
WGSC	66.3	62.7	32.0	36.3
RSRC	89.3	32.3	57.3	12.7
RCRC	80.3	70.3	46.3	42.0
NMR	72.3	72.3	35.3	45.3
NNSCRC	**90.0**	**79.7**	**59.7**	**50.7**

4.5   Face Recognition with Single Sample per Person

We further conduct experiments on ExYaleB dataset to evaluate the robustness of our model to single sample per person (SSPP) face recognition. 20 persons in ExYaleB are used for SSPP test and the other persons are used to construct intra-class variations. We use the first image of these 20 persons in ExYaleB dataset as gallery, and select 30 images each person as probe set. The results are shown in Table 4. As can be seen, the recognition rate of NNSCRC is 9.9% and 3.9% higher than that of NMR and IRGSC respectively. Though NMR and IRGSC can handle the problem of differences between query and gallery images in some kind, both of them suffers from the misleading coding coefficients of incorrect classes when there is only one sample per subject. Different from these methods, our model can borrow the intra-class variations from other subjects which are not in the gallery set because these variations are usually similar across different subjects. Clearly, the NNSCRC method achieves much better result than NMR and IRGSC since NNSCRC can borrow the intra-class variations from other subjects, which demonstrate our model is capable for SSPP face recognition task.

Table 4. SSPP FR accuracy of different methods on ExYaleB database

	NMR	IRGSC	NNSCRC
Accuracy	79.3	85.3	**89.2**

5   Conclusion

In this paper, we present a NNSCRC model for robust face recognition task. In the proposed framework, a superposed collaborative representation is adopted to obtain robust representation of reconstruct face images. By representing a face image as a superposed of a class centroid, a shared sample-to-centroid difference and a low rank error, our method can address the misleading coding coefficients of incorrect classes when the dataset is undersampled. Specially, when there is only a single sample per class available, the proposed model can still have promised performance by acquiring the intra-class variation base from the generic subjects outside the gallery. Furthermore, our model is robust to occlusion and illumination changes by introducing nuclear norm constrained. Experiments on the famous Extended Yale-B and AR databases show the superiority of our model compared with the state-of-the-art regression based face recognition methods.

Acknowledgement. This work was supported in part by the National Natural Science Foundation of China (61673402, 61273270, 60802069), the Natural Science Foundation of Guangdong Province (2017A030311029, 2016B010123005, 2017B090909005), the Science and Technology Program of Guangzhou of China (201704020180, 201604020024) and the Fundamental Research Funds for the Central Universities of China.

References

1. Ahonen, T., Hadid, A., Pietikainen, M.: Face description with local binary patterns: application to face recognition. IEEE Trans. Pattern Anal. Mach. Intell. **28**(12), 2037–2041 (2006)
2. Bay, H., Ess, A., Tuytelaars, T., Gool, L.V.: Speeded-up robust features (SURF). Comput. Vis. Image Underst. **110**(3), 346–359 (2008)
3. Belhumeur, P.N., Hespanha, J.P., Kriegman, D.J.: Eigenfaces vs. fisherfaces: recognition using class specific linear projection. In: Buxton, B., Cipolla, R. (eds.) ECCV 1996. LNCS, vol. 1064, pp. 43–58. Springer, Heidelberg (1996). https://doi.org/10.1007/BFb0015522
4. Boyd, S., Parikh, N., Chu, E., Peleato, B., Eckstein, J.: Distributed optimization and statistical learning via the alternating direction method of multipliers. Found. Trends Mach. Learn. **3**(1), 1–122 (2010)
5. Cai, J.F., Candès, E.J., Shen, Z.: A singular value thresholding algorithm for matrix completion. SIAM J. Optim. **20**(4), 1956–1982 (2008)
6. Cai, S., Zhang, L., Zuo, W., Feng, X.: A probabilistic collaborative representation based approach for pattern classification. In: IEEE Conference on Computer Vision and Pattern Recognition, pp. 2950–2959 (2016)
7. Chien, J.T., Wu, C.C.: Discriminant waveletfaces and nearest feature classifiers for face recognition. IEEE Trans. Pattern Anal. Mach. Intell. **24**(12), 1644–1649 (2003)
8. Choi, S.I., Lee, S.S., Sang, T.C., Shin, W.Y.: Face recognition using composite features based on discriminant analysis. IEEE Access **6**, 13663–13670 (2018)
9. Deng, W., Hu, J., Guo, J.: Face recognition via collaborative representation: its discriminant nature and superposed representation. IEEE Trans. Pattern Anal. Mach. Intell. **40**, 1 (2017)
10. He, X., Yan, S., Hu, Y., Niyogi, P., Zhang, H.J.: Face recognition using Laplacianfaces. IEEE Trans. Pattern Anal. Mach. Intell. **27**, 328–340 (2005)
11. Huang, J., Nie, F., Huang, H., Ding, C.: Supervised and projected sparse coding for image classification. In: Twenty-Seventh AAAI Conference on Artificial Intelligence, pp. 438–444 (2013)
12. Lee, K.C., Ho, J., Kriegman, D.J.: Acquiring linear subspaces for face recognition under variable lighting. IEEE Trans. Pattern Anal. Mach. Intell. **27**(5), 684–698 (2005)

13. Lu, J., Liong, V.E., Zhou, X., Zhou, J.: Learning compact binary face descriptor for face recognition. IEEE Trans. Pattern Anal. Mach. Intell. **37**(10), 2041–2056 (2015)

14. Martinez, A.M.: The AR face database. CVC Technical report 24 (1998)

15. Naseem, I., Togneri, R., Bennamoun, M.: Linear regression for face recognition. IEEE Trans. Pattern Anal. Mach. Intell. **32**(11), 2106–2112 (2010)

16. Ng, P.C., Henikoff, S.: Sift: predicting amino acid changes that affect protein function. Nucl. Acids Res. **31**(13), 3812–3814 (2003)

17. Pentland, A., Moghaddam, B., Starner, T.: View-based and modular eigenspaces for face recognition. In: 1994 Proceedings of IEEE Conference on Computer Vision and Pattern Recognition, pp. 84–91 (1994)

18. Tang, X., Feng, G., Cai, J.: Weighted group sparse representation for undersampled face recognition. Neurocomputing **145**(18), 402–415 (2014)

19. Turk, M., Pentland, A.: Face recognition using eigenfaces. In: IEEE Computer Society Conference on Computer Vision and Pattern Recognition, pp. 586–591 (1991)

20. Wang, S.: Relaxed collaborative representation for pattern classification. In: IEEE Conference on Computer Vision and Pattern Recognition, pp. 2224–2231 (2012)

21. Wang, X.: An HOG-LBP human detector with partial occlusion handling. In: Proceedings of IEEE International Conference on Computer Vision, Kyoto, Japan, September, vol. 30, no. 2, pp. 32–39 (2009)

22. Wright, J., Yang, A.Y., Ganesh, A., Sastry, S.S., Ma, Y.: Robust face recognition via sparse representation. IEEE Trans. Pattern Anal. Mach. Intell. **31**(2), 210–227 (2008)

23. Yang, J., Luo, L., Qian, J., Tai, Y., Zhang, F., Xu, Y.: Nuclear norm based matrix regression with applications to face recognition with occlusion and illumination changes. IEEE Trans. Pattern Anal. Mach. Intell. **39**(1), 156–171 (2016)

24. Yang, M., Zhang, L., Yang, J., Zhang, D.: Regularized robust coding for face recognition. IEEE Trans. Image Process. **22**(5), 1753–1766 (2013)

25. Zhang, L., Yang, M.: Sparse representation or collaborative representation: which helps face recognition? In: International Conference on Computer Vision, pp. 471–478 (2011)

26. Zheng, J., Yang, P., Chen, S., Shen, G., Wang, W.: Iterative re-constrained group sparse face recognition with adaptive weights learning. IEEE Trans. Image Process. **26**(5), 2408–2423 (2017)

Face Image Set Recognition Based on Bilinear Regression

Wen-Wen Hua[1] and Chuan-Xian Ren[1,2(✉)]

[1] School of Mathematics, Sun Yat-sen University, Guangzhou 510275, China
huaww@mail2.sysu.edu.cn, rchuanx@mail.sysu.edu.cn
[2] Shenzhen Research Institute of Sun Yat-sen University, Shenzhen 518000, China

Abstract. Image sets-based face recognition receives growing research interest in pattern recognition and machine learning. The most challenging problem focuses on how to formulate a computable and discriminative model by using given data sets. In this paper, we propose a new method, which is called Bilinear Regression Classifier (BLRC) for short, to address the image sets-based face recognition problem. BLRC classifies a given test set by choosing the category that simultaneously maximizes the unrelated subspace and minimize the related subspace. In particular, the unrelated subspace is used to characterize the distances between the query set and the unrelated image sets, while the related subspace is used to characterize the distances between the query set and the related sets. In our work, the Mahalanobis metric, rather than the Euclidean metric, is exploited to compute the subspace distance. The subspace coefficient vectors are obtained by solving an Elastic-Net regularized regression model. Extensive experiments are conducted on several benchmark datasets to evaluate the real recognition performance of the new method. The results show that our BLRC method obtains competitive accuracies with some state-of-the-art methods.

Keywords: Face recognition · Image sets · Linear regression

1 Introduction

Face recognition has traditionally been posed as the problem of identifying a face from a single image. Good performance is usually rely on smartly designed classifiers. A number of classifiers were proposed, such as the Nearest Neighbor (NN) [4], A Local Support Vector Machine Approach [12], Sparse Representation-based Classifier [16] and Linear Regression Classification (LRC) [11]. These classifiers use a single test sample for classification and assume that images are taken

C.-X. Ren—This work is supported in part by the Science and Technology Program of Shenzhen under Grant JCYJ20170818155415617, the National Natural Science Foundation of China under Grants 61572536, and the Science and Technology Program of GuangZhou under Grant 201804010248.

J.-H. Lai et al. (Eds.): PRCV 2018, LNCS 11258, pp. 233–244, 2018.
https://doi.org/10.1007/978-3-030-03338-5_20

in controlled environments. Their classification performance is generally dependent on the representation of individual test samples. However, facial appearance changes dramatically under variations in pose, illumination, expression, etc., and images captured under controlled conditions may not suffice for reliable recognition under the more varied conditions, that occur in real surveillance and video retrieval applications. Recently there has been growing interest in face recognition from image sets. Rather than supplying a single query image, the system supplies a set of images of the same unknown individual, and we expect that rich information provided in the image sets can improve the recognition rate.

Image sets classification algorithms include parametric methods [1,8,14] and non-parametric methods [2,3,5–7,9,13,17]. Parametric method, firstly use the probability density functions to represent the image sets, then they use distance of divergence functions to measure the similarity between the image set (probability distribution), and they finally classify the test image set into the category which the closest image collection belongs. There are various difficulties in parametric methods, and the recognition performance is usually unsatisfactory. In recent years, researchers have focused on nonparametric methods that are independent of models. These methods do not have any assumptions about the distribution of image sets. Typical example of such methods is subspace algorithm.

This paper makes a brief review on dual linear regression classification (DLRC), then proposes the bilinear regression classification (BLRC) for image set retrieval. For BLRC algorithm, we first give the concept of uncorrelated subspace. Then, we introduce two strategies to constitute the unrelated subspace. Next, we calculate related distance metric and unrelated distance metric. Last, we introduce a combination metric for two new classifiers based on two constitution strategies of the unrelated subspace. Experimental results shows that the performance of BLRC is better than DLRC and several state-of-the-art classifiers for some benchmark.

2   Dual Linear Regression Classification

Suppose a and b be height and width of an image. Let two sets of (down-scaled) face images be represented by

$$X = [x_1, x_2, \cdots, x_m], \tag{1}$$

$$Y = [y_1, y_2, \cdots, y_n], \tag{2}$$

where x_i $(i = 1, 2, \cdots, m)$ and y_j $(j = 1, 2, \cdots, n)$ are column vectors of size ab.

Column vectors of the image set X and the image set Y determine a subspace respectively, and an image located at the intersection of the two subspaces. That is, the "virtual" face image can be assumed vector V should be a linear combination of the column vectors of two image sets respectively. To calculate the distance between two image sets, our task is to find the "virtual" face V and Coefficient vectors $\alpha = (\alpha_1, \alpha_2, \cdots, \alpha_m)^T$, $\beta = (\beta_1, \beta_2, \cdots, \beta_n)^T$ such that

$$V = X\alpha = Y\beta. \tag{3}$$

Considering that we have all down-scaled images standardized into unit vectors, we further require that

$$\sum_{i=1}^{m} \alpha_i = \sum_{j=1}^{n} \beta_j = 1. \tag{4}$$

When $\hat{x}_i = x_i - x_m$ $(i = 1, 2, \cdots, m-1)$, $\hat{y}_j = y_j - y_n$ $(j = 1, 2, \cdots, n-1)$. We have

$$V = [\hat{x}_1, \hat{x}_2, \cdots, \hat{x}_{m-1}]\hat{\alpha} + x_m = [\hat{y}_1, \hat{y}_2, \cdots, \hat{y}_{n-1}]\hat{\beta} + y_n, \tag{5}$$

where $\hat{\alpha} = (\alpha_1, \alpha_2, \cdots, \alpha_{m-1})^T$, $\hat{\beta} = (\beta_1, \beta_2, \cdots, \beta_{n-1})^T$. Assume that there is a approximate solution $\gamma = (\alpha_1, \alpha_2, \cdots, \alpha_{m-1}, \beta_1, \beta_2, \cdots, \beta_{n-1})^T \in \mathbb{R}^{(m+n-2)\times 1}$ for the equation

$$y_n - x_m = \hat{XY}\gamma, \tag{6}$$

where $\hat{XY} = [\hat{x}_1, \hat{x}_2, \cdots, \hat{x}_{m-1}, -\hat{y}_1, -\hat{y}_2, \cdots, -\hat{y}_{n-1}]$.

After obtaining the estimated value of the regression coefficient γ, the "virtual" face image may be represented by the image set X and the image set Y respectively. Specifically, the "virtual" face image V_X reconstructed from the image set X is

$$V_X = [\hat{x}_1, \hat{x}_2, \cdots, \hat{x}_{m-1}][\hat{\gamma}_1, \hat{\gamma}_2, \cdots, \hat{\gamma}_{m-1}]^T + x_m, \tag{7}$$

while the "virtual" face image V_Y reconstructed from the image set Y is

$$V_Y = [\hat{y}_1, \hat{y}_2, \cdots, \hat{y}_{n-1}][\hat{\gamma}_m, \hat{\gamma}_{m+1}, \cdots, \hat{\gamma}_{m+n-2}]^T + y_n. \tag{8}$$

Obviously, difference between the two reconstructed "virtual" face images is essentially the residual of the linear regression equation. Since the difference between the image set X and the image set Y can be expressed by calculating the difference between the two reconstructed "virtual" face images, we can use the residual of the linear regression equation to estimate the similarity of the two image sets subspace X, Y, namely

$$D(X, Y) = \|V_Y - V_X\| = \|(y_n - x_m) - \hat{XY}\hat{\gamma}\|. \tag{9}$$

If the $D(X, Y)$ value is smaller, the two image sets are closer to each other.

3   Bilinear Regression Classification

Inspired by DLRC, this section proposes bilinear regression classification. We show a simple flowchart in Fig. 1. The main contents of this section are organized as follows. First, the concept of unrelated subspaces is presented in Subsect. 3.1. Second, two strategies of constituting the unrelated subspace are described in Subsect. 3.2. Then, both related metric and unrelated metrics are computed in Subsect. 3.3. Last, the final distance metric for classification called combination metric, is described in Subsect. 3.4.

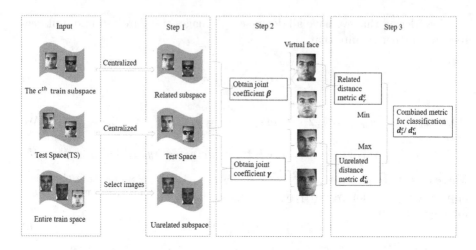

Fig. 1. The flowchart of the proposed BLRC

3.1 Definition of Unrelated Image Set Subspace

Definition 1. *Suppose that there are C-classes image set in the training set, there are a total of M test image sets in the test set. For each image set in the test set, it is assumed that we need to calculate the distance between the test image set and the cth image set, where $c = 1, 2 \cdots C$, and the cth image set in the training image set has N_c image samples. If there is a set U, U also contains N_c samples, and these N_c samples are from the other $C - 1$ classes except for the cth class, then set U is called the unrelated image set subspace of the above test image set.*

According to Definition 1, we need to select N_c image samples from the remaining $C - 1$ class samples that exclude c^{th} category to construct the unrelated image set subspace. In next subsection we will describe how to construct unrelated image set subspace.

3.2 Constructions of the Unrelated Subspace

The cth image set X^c in the training image set is represented as follows:

$$X^c = [x_1^c, x_2^c, \cdots, x_{N_c}^c] \in \mathbb{R}^{q \times N_c}. \tag{10}$$

That means that the cth image set in the training set defines a subspace, which can be represented by X^c.

The subspace X determined by all images on the training set is as follows:

$$X = [X^1, X^2, \cdots, X^C] \in \mathbb{R}^{q \times l}, \tag{11}$$

in which $l = \sum_{c=1}^{C} N_c$.

The overall mean of training image set X is

$$X_{mean} = \frac{1}{l} \sum_{c=1}^{C} \sum_{i=1}^{N_c} x_i^c. \tag{12}$$

The mean of the cth image set on training image sets is $X_{mean}^c = \frac{1}{N_c} \sum_{i=1}^{N_c} x_i^c$. Images in class c are centralized as $\hat{x}_i^c = x_i^c - X_{mean}^c (c = 1, 2, \cdots, C; i = 1, 2, \cdots; N_c)$, then the centralized training image set $\hat{X}$ is formulated as follows:

$$\hat{X} = [x_1^1, x_2^1, \cdots, x_{N_1}^1, \cdots, x_{N_C}^c] \in \mathbb{R}^{q \times l}. \tag{13}$$

Similarly, the image subspace determined by the test image set Y presented by

$$Y = [y_1, y_2, \cdots, y_n] \in \mathbb{R}^{q \times n}. \tag{14}$$

For image set Y, $y_{mean} = \frac{1}{n} \sum_{i=1}^{n} y_i$, centralized as $\hat{y}_i = y_i - y_{mean}$ $(i = 1, 2, \cdots, n)$, and then the centralized testing image set $\hat{Y}$ is formulated as follows:

$$\hat{Y} = [\hat{y}_1, \hat{y}_2, \cdots, \hat{y}_n]. \tag{15}$$

Strategy 1. When calculating the manhatta distance between the test image set and the cth image set, the distance between y_{mean} and a training sample X_i can be computed as:

$$d_i = |X_i - y_{mean}| (i = 1, 2, \cdots, l). \tag{16}$$

The distance metric set D of the training image set X and y_{mean} is as follows:

$$D = [d_1, d_2, \cdots, d_l] \in \mathbb{R}^{1 \times l}. \tag{17}$$

First, we remove the elements corresponding to the cth class from D as $\hat{D} \in R^{1 \times (L - N_c)}$. Then we sort the elements in $\hat{D}$ in ascend order and select N_c samples $x_i^p (p \neq c)$ from X, which corresponds to the smallest N_c distances from $\hat{D}$ to constitute the unrelated subspace U_c.

$$U_c = [u_1^c, u_2^c \cdots u_{N_C}^c] \in \mathbb{R}^{q \times N_c}. \tag{18}$$

The classifier based on strategy 1 will be called bilinear regression classification-I (BLRC-I).

Strategy 2. When calculating the distance between the test image set and the cth training image set, assuming that training image set X and test image set Y determine a "virtual" face image space. Different from strategy 1, Strategy 2 does not directly calculate the distance between each image in the training image set X and the center y_{mean} of the test image set. Instead, it calculates the distance between the projection of each image in the training image set on the "virtual" face space and the center of the test image set y_{mean}.

In order to obtain the joint coefficient vector of the two image sets $\hat{X}$ and $\hat{Y}$, the joint image set E and the test vector e can be constituted as:

$$E = [\hat{X}, -\hat{Y}] \in \mathbb{R}^{q \times (l+n)}, \tag{19}$$

$$e = y_{mean} - x_{mean}. \tag{20}$$

Suppose that $\theta \in \mathbb{R}^{(L+n) \times 1}$ is the joint coefficient vector of $\hat{X}$ and $\hat{Y}$, which can be calculated by solving the optimization problem

$$\hat{\theta} = \arg \min_{\theta} \| e - E\theta \|^2 + \lambda_1 \|\theta\|_2^2 + \lambda_2 \|\theta\|_1, \tag{21}$$

where $\lambda_1 > 0, \lambda_2 > 0$ and $\lambda_1 + \lambda_2 = 1$.

After solving the regression coefficient $\hat{\theta}$. Then, the Mahalanobis distance between the projection of each image in the training image set X on the "virtual" face space and the center of the test image set can be expressed by the following equation:

$$d_i = |\hat{X}_i \hat{\theta}_i - y_{mean}| (i = 1, 2, \cdots, l). \tag{22}$$

The distance metric set D is formulated by

$$D = [d_1, d_2, \cdots, d_l] \in \mathbb{R}^{1 \times l}. \tag{23}$$

First, we remove the elements corresponding to the cth class from D as $\hat{D} \in R^{1 \times (L-N_c)}$. Then we sort the elements in $\hat{D}$ in ascend order and select N_c samples $x_i^p (p \neq c)$ from X, which corresponds to the smallest N_c distances from $\hat{D}$ to constitute the unrelated subspace U_c,

$$U_c = [u_1^c, u_2^c, \cdots, u_{N_C}^c] \in \mathbb{R}^{q \times N_c}. \tag{24}$$

The classifier based on strategy 2 will be called bilinear regression classification-II (BLRC-II).

3.3   Related and Unrelated Distance Metric

Related Distance Metric. In Subsect. 3.2, we have obtained the class mean X_{mean}^c for each class in the training set. After centralized processing, the training image set of class c can be converted to

$$\hat{X}_c = [\hat{x}_1^c, \hat{x}_2^c, \cdots, \hat{x}_{N_c}^c] \in \mathbb{R}^{q \times N_c}. \tag{25}$$

Now we need to calculate the distance between the test image set $\hat{Y}$ and the cth image set $\hat{X}_c$ in the training set. To obtain the joint regression coefficients of the two image sets, the joint image set S_r^c and test vector s_r^c can be constituted as:

$$S_r^c = [\hat{X}_c, -\hat{Y}] \in \mathbb{R}^{q \times (N_c+n)}, \tag{26}$$

and

$$s_r^c = y_{mean} - x_{mean}^c. \tag{27}$$

Assume that $\gamma^c \in \mathbb{R}^{(N_c+n)\times 1}$ is the joint regression coefficient of $\hat{X}_c$ and $\hat{Y}$. According to the regression equation $s_r^c = S_r^c \gamma^c$, we can see that the solution of $\gamma^c \in R^{(N_c+n)\times 1}$ is

$$\hat{\gamma}^c = \left(S_r^{cT} S_r^c + \lambda I\right)^{-1} S_r^{cT} s_r^c. \tag{28}$$

Then, the reconstructed "virtual" face image r_1 obtained from the cth training image set $\hat{X}_c$ is

$$r_1 = \hat{X}_c [\gamma_1^c, \gamma_2^c, \cdots, \gamma_{N_c}^c]^T + x_{mean}^c. \tag{29}$$

The reconstructed "virtual" face image r_2 obtained from the test image set Y is

$$r_2 = \hat{Y} [\gamma_{N_c+1}^c, \gamma_{N_c+2}^c, \cdots, \gamma_{N_c+n}^c]^T + y_{mean}. \tag{30}$$

Finally, the distance between r_1 and r_2 can be used to represent the distance between the test image set and the cth image set in the training set, which is expressed by

$$d_r^c = \|r_1 - r_2\| = \|s_r^c - S_r^c \gamma^c\|. \tag{31}$$

That is, the residual of the linear regression equation $s_r^c = S_r^c \gamma^c$ can be used to represent the distance between the test image set and the cth image set in the training set.

Unrelated Distance Metric. The unrelated image set subspace U_c of the test image set has been obtained in Sect. 3.2. The mean vector of U_c is

$$u_{mean}^c = \frac{1}{N_c} \sum_{i=1}^{N_c} u_i^c. \tag{32}$$

After centralization, the unrelated image set subspace U_c can be converted to

$$\hat{U}_c = [\hat{u}_1^c, \hat{u}_2^c, \cdots, \hat{u}_{N_c}^c] \in \mathbb{R}^{q \times N_c}. \tag{33}$$

Now we need to calculate the distance between the test image set $\hat{Y}$ and the unrelated image set subspace U_c. To obtain the joint regression coefficients of two image sets, the joint image set S_u^c and test vector s_u^c can be constituted as

$$S_u^c = [\hat{U}_c, -\hat{Y}] \in \mathbb{R}^{q \times (N_c+n)}, \tag{34}$$

and

$$s_u^c = y_{mean} - u_{mean}^c. \tag{35}$$

Assume that $\delta^c \in \mathbb{R}^{(N_c+n)\times 1}$ is the joint regression coefficient of $\hat{U}_c$ and $\hat{Y}$. According to the regression equation $s_u^c = S_r^c \delta^c$, it indicates that the solution of $\delta^c \in \mathbb{R}^{(N_c+n)\times 1}$ is

$$\hat{\delta}^c = \left(S_u^{cT} S_u^c + \lambda I\right)^{-1} S_u^{cT} s_u^c. \tag{36}$$

Then, the reconstructed "virtual" face image r_1 obtained from the unrelated image set subspace $\hat{U}_c$ is

$$r_1 = \hat{U}_c [\delta_1^c, \delta_2^c, \cdots, \delta_{N_c}^c]^T + u_{mean}^c. \tag{37}$$

The reconstructed "virtual" face image r_2 obtained from the test image set Y is

$$r_2 = \hat{Y}[\delta_{N_c+1}^c, \delta_{N_c+2}^c, \cdots, \delta_{N_c+n}^c]^T + y_{mean}. \tag{38}$$

Finally, the distance between r_1 and r_2 can be used to represent the distance between the test image set and the unrelated image set subspace, which is expressed by

$$d_u^c = \|r_1 - r_2\| = \|s_u^c - S_u^c \delta^c\|. \tag{39}$$

That is, the residual of the linear regression equation $s_u^c = S_u^c \delta^c$ can be used to represent the distance between the test image set and the unrelated image set subspace.

3.4   Combined Distance Metric

After obtaining the related distance metric d_r^c and the unrelated distance metric d_u^c, we can construct a discriminative criterion by combine the two metric results in a suitable manner. It is obvious that if the test image set belongs to category c, we hope that the distance between the test image set $\hat{Y}$ and the cth image set $\hat{X}_c$ is closer, that is, the d_r^c is as small as possible. on the other hand, it is desirable to make the feature representations between the test image set $\hat{Y}$ and the unrelated image set $\hat{U}_c$ further, that is, the d_u^c is as large as possible. So we propose a new metric d_p^c as

$$d_p^c = \frac{d_r^c}{d_u^c}. \tag{40}$$

The smaller the value of d_p^c, the greater similarity between the test image set and the cth image set. In other words our face image set recognition criterion selects the image set category c when d_p^c takes the minimum value, i.e.

$$\min_{c^*} \{d_p^c \mid c = 1, 2, \cdots, C\}. \tag{41}$$

4   Experimental Results

This section provides extensive experimental results to evaluate the performance of two proposed classifiers: BLRC-I and BLRC-II. These experiments are conducted by using several benchmark datasets, i.e., image-based face recognition on the LFW face database [18] and AR face database [10], video-based face recognition on Honda/UCSD face database [8].

4.1   Experiments on LFW

LFW face database were captured in unconstrained environments such that there will be large variations in face images including pose, age, race, facial expression, lighting, occlusions, and background, etc. We use the aligned version of the LFW database, LFW-a to evaluate the recognition performance.

LFW-a contains more than 5,000 subjects. Each subject including images of the same individual in different poses. Note that all the images in LFW-a are of size 250×250. We manually crop the images into size of 90×78 (by removing 88 pixel margins from top, 72 from bottom, and 86 pixel margins from both left and right sides). An subset of LFW containing 62 persons, each people has more than 20 face images, is used for evaluating the algorithms. Our experimental setting is identical to that in [3]. The first 10 images of each subject are selected to form the training set, while the last 10 images are used as the probe images.

The proposed classifiers are compared with methods including sparse approximated nearest points (SANP) [5,6], affine hull based image set distance (ASIHD) [2], convex hull based image set distance (CSIHD) [2], manifold discriminant analysis (MDA) [13], Dual Linear Regression Based Classification for Face Cluster Recognition (DLRC) [3] and Pairwise Linear Regression Classification for Image Set Retrieval (PLRC) [19]. All methods use the down-scaled images of size of 10×10 and 15×10 as in [3]. The classification results of all methods are illustrated in Table 1. For the images with size of 10×10, the proposed BLRC-I achieves identical performances with the MDA and PLRC-I method, and the recognition rate is 93.55%, which exceeds other classifiers. For BLRC-II, the recognition rate is 98.39%, obtains the best recognition rate compared with other methods. For images with size of 15×10, BLRC-I reaches 96.77% recognition rate, BLRC-II, recognition rate is as high as 98.39%. The effects of BLRC-II are higher than those of other classifiers as shown in Table 1.

Table 1. The recognition rates (RR) on LFW database.

Method	10×10	15×10
SANP	85.48	92.55
ASIHD	87.10	95.16
CSIHD	90.32	93.55
MDA	93.55	95.16
DLRC	91.94	95.16
PLRC-I	93.55	96.77
PLRC-II	95.16	96.77
BLRC-I	93.55	96.77
BLRC-II	**98.39**	**98.39**

4.2 Experiments on AR

In this section, we study the performance of the proposed classifiers by using the well-known AR database. There are over 4000 face images of 126 subjects (70 men and 56 women) in the database. The face images of each individual contain different expressions, lighting conditions, wearing sun glasses and wearing scarf. We use the cropped AR database that includes 2600 face images of 100 individuals, First, we manually crop images into a size of 90×70 (by removing 38 pixel margins from top, 39 from bottom, and 24 pixel margins from left and 25 pixel margins right sides). Then downscale the clipped image to get 40×40 resolutions. In the experiments, the first 13 images of each subject are selected to form a training image set, and the remaining 13 images are composed of test image sets.

For this database, the proposed classifiers are compared with following state-of-the-art approaches: SANP [5,6], ASIHD [2], CSIHD [2], DLRC [3] and PLRC [19]. The recognition rates of different classifiers have been presented in Table 2. Experimental results show that compared with other algorithms, the recognition accuracy of the BLRC-I and BLRC-II for image set recognition is as high as 97.98%, which shows obvious improvement on the classification performance.

Table 2. The recognition rates (RR) on AR database.

Methods	RR
SANP	77.00
ASIHD	87.67
CSIHD	84.67
DLRC	96.00
PLRC-I	95.00
PLRC-II	97.33
BLRC-I	**97.98**
BLRC-II	**97.98**

4.3 Honda/UCSD Face Database

The Honda/UCSD dataset contains 59 video clips of 20 subjects [8], all but one have at least 2 videos. 20 videos are called training videos and the remainder 39 test videos. The lengths of videos vary from 291 to 1168 frames. In order to maintain the comparability of the experimental results, we use face images consistent with other proceeding work [6].

This dataset has been used extensively for image-based face recognition, the accuracy has reached 100% or close to 100%. Therefore, researchers have turned to experiment on the settings using a small amount frames. We carry out the experiment using the first 50 frames in each video for this database. The shared database by [5] is used. For the video clips that contain less than 50 frames, all frames are selected in the experiment. The following methods are chosen for comparison: DCC [7], MMD [15], MDA [13], AHISD [2], CHISD [2], MSM [17], SANP [5,6], DLRC [3] and PLRC [19]. Table 3 lists all recognition rates of these classifiers on this database. We find that the recognition rates of BLRC-I,

AHISD, RNP, DLRC and PLRC-I are all equal 87.18%, which is much better than those of DCC and MMD methods. The BLRC-II classifier obtains the highest accuracy 92.31% for this database, which is obviously superior to the results of other types of recognition algorithms.

Table 3. The recognition rates (RR) on Honda/UCSD database.

Methods	RR
DCC	70.92
MMD	69.32
MDA	82.05
ASIHD	87.18
CSIHD	82.05
MSM	74.36
SANP	84.62
DLRC	87.18
PLRC-I	87.18
PLRC-II	89.74
BLRC-I	87.18
BLRC-II	**92.31**

5   Conclusion

In this paper, bilinear regression classification method (BLRC) is proposed for face image set recognition. Compared to DLRC, BLRC increases the unrelated subspace for classification. Based on different methods of constituting the unrelated subspace, two classifiers are proposed in this paper. In order to validate the performance of two classifiers, some experiments are evaluated on three database for face image set classification tasks. All experimental results confirm the effectiveness of two proposed classification algorithms.

References

1. Arandjelovic, O., Shakhnarovich, G., Fisher, J., Cipolla, R., Darrell, T.: Face recognition with image sets using manifold density divergence. In: IEEE Computer Society Conference on Computer Vision and Pattern Recognition, pp. 581–588 (2005)
2. Cevikalp, H., Triggs, B.: Face recognition based on image sets. In: Computer Vision and Pattern Recognition, pp. 2567–2573 (2010)
3. Chen, L.: Dual linear regression based classification for face cluster recognition. In: Computer Vision and Pattern Recognition, pp. 2673–2680 (2014)
4. Cover, T., Hart, P.: Nearest neighbor pattern classification. IEEE Press (1967)

5. Hu, Y., Mian, A.S., Owens, R.: Sparse approximated nearest points for image set classification, vol. 42, no. 7, pp. 121–128 (2011)
6. Yiqun, H., Mian, A.S., Owens, R.: Face recognition using sparse approximated nearest points between image sets. IEEE Trans. Pattern Anal. Mach. Intell. **34**(10), 1992–2004 (2012)
7. Kim, T.K., Kittler, J., Cipolla, R.: Discriminative learning and recognition of image set classes using canonical correlations. IEEE Trans. Pattern Anal. Mach. Intell. **29**(6), 1005 (2007)
8. Lee, K.C., Ho, J., Yang, M.H., Kriegman, D.: Video-based face recognition using probabilistic appearance manifolds. In: IEEE Conference on Computer Vision and Pattern Recognition, pp. 313–320 (2003)
9. Mahmood, A., Mian, A., Owens, R.: Semi-supervised spectral clustering for image set classification. In: Computer Vision and Pattern Recognition, pp. 121–128 (2014)
10. Martínez, A.M., Kak, A.C.: PCA versus LDA. IEEE Trans. Pattern Anal. Mach. Intell. **23**(2), 228–233 (2001)
11. Naseem, I., Togneri, R., Bennamoun, M.: Linear regression for face recognition. IEEE Trans. Pattern Anal. Mach. Intell. **32**(11), 2106–2112 (2010)
12. Sch, C., Laptev, I., Caputo, B.: Recognizing human actions: a local SVM approach. In: International Conference on Pattern Recognition, pp. 32–36 (2004)
13. Wang, R., Chen, X.: Manifold discriminant analysis. In: IEEE Conference on Computer Vision and Pattern Recognition, pp. 429–436 (2009)
14. Wang, R., Guo, H., Davis, L.S., Dai, Q.: Covariance discriminative learning: a natural and efficient approach to image set classification. In: IEEE Conference on Computer Vision and Pattern Recognition, pp. 2496–2503 (2012)
15. Wang, R., Shan, S., Chen, X., Gao, W.: Manifold-manifold distance with application to face recognition based on image set. In: IEEE Conference on Computer Vision and Pattern Recognition, pp. 1–8 (2008)
16. Wright, J., Ganesh, A., Zhou, Z., Wagner, A., Ma, Y.: Demo: robust face recognition via sparse representation. In: IEEE International Conference on Automatic Face and Gesture Recognition, pp. 1–2 (2009)
17. Yamaguchi, O., Fukui, K., Maeda, K.: Face recognition using temporal image sequence. In: 1998 Proceedings of IEEE International Conference on Automatic Face and Gesture Recognition, pp. 318–323 (1998)
18. Zhu, P., Zhang, L., Hu, Q., Shiu, S.C.K.: Multi-scale patch based collaborative representation for face recognition with margin distribution optimization. In: European Conference on Computer Vision, pp. 822–835 (2012)
19. Feng, Q., Zhou, Y., Lan, R.: Pairwise linear regression classification for image set retrieval. In: IEEE Conference on Computer Vision and Pattern Recognition, pp. 4865–4872 (2016)

Semi-supervised Learning of Deep Difference Features for Facial Expression Recognition

Can Xu, Ruyi Xu, Jingying Chen[✉], and Leyuan Liu

National Engineering Research Center for E-Learning,
Central China Normal University, Wuhan, China
chenjy@mail.ccnu.edu.cn

Abstract. Facial expression recognition (FER) is an important means of detecting human emotions and is widely applied in many fields, such as affective computing and human-computer interaction. Currently, several methods for FER heavily rely on large amounts of manually labeled data, which are costly and not available in real-world applications. To address this problem, this paper proposes a semi-supervised method based on the deep difference features. First, a cascaded structure is introduced to the original safe semi-supervised SVM (S4VM) to solve the multi-classification task. Then, multiple deep different features are fed to the cascaded S4VM to train the six basic facial expressions using the information of the unlabeled data safely. Extensive experiments show that the proposed method achieved encouraging results on public databases even when using a small labeled sample set.

Keywords: Facial expression recognition · Deep learning · Cascaded S4VM
Semi-supervised method

1 Introduction

Analyzing facial expressions is one of the most important methods of human emotion recognition and facial expressions are defined as the corresponding facial changes in response to a person's inner emotional state and intentions [1]. Nowadays, automatic facial expression recognition (FER) has miscellaneous applications, such as affective computing, interactive games, social psychology, synthetic animation, and intelligent robots [2].

Automatic FER systems can be divided into two categories: those that based on static images and those that based on dynamic image sequences [3]. The static-based method only contains information of the currently input image, while the sequence-based method can use temporal information from multi frames to identify the expression. FER systems receive static images or dynamic sequences as input and then output the corresponding expression category. This work focuses on methods based on the key frames extracted from dynamic image sequences.

In the past two decades, many attempts have been made to recognize facial expressions, and the effectiveness of these attempts depends largely on the size of the labeled training set. A large-scale training set can better reflect the real distribution of samples and hence acquire a better generalization error. However, manual annotation is

© Springer Nature Switzerland AG 2018
J.-H. Lai et al. (Eds.): PRCV 2018, LNCS 11258, pp. 245–254, 2018.
https://doi.org/10.1007/978-3-030-03338-5_21

demanding, time consuming and expensive [4]. A semi-supervised method can simultaneously use labeled and unlabeled data to improve the classification performance with small datasets, reduce the workload of manual labeling and enhance the practicability of FER [5].

There have been few attempts to recognize facial expressions using a semi-supervised method. Existing methods can be roughly divided into two categories: semi-supervised learning (SSL) [6–8] and semi-supervised clustering [9–11]. SSL exploits the distribution of the unlabeled data to enhance training. Semi-supervised clustering sets the pairwise constraints with labeled data for cluster analysis. In 2004, Cohen et al. [6] were the first to apply SSL to facial expression recognition. They trained probabilistic classifiers with labeled and unlabeled data based on Bayesian networks and achieved an average recognition accuracy of 74.8% on the Cohn-Kanade dataset. Hady et al. [7] mentioned a learning framework to exploit the unlabeled data by the combination of the Co-Training and the one-against-one output-space decomposition approach, which uses Tri-Class SVMs as binary classifiers. The average recognition accuracy on the four basic expressions of the Cohn-Kanade dataset was 86.95%. Jiang et al. [8] focused on the problem of multi-pose facial expression recognition by bringing transfer learning into SSL. Liu et al. [9] addressed the expression recognition in the wild under a semi-supervised frame that combined reference manifold learning with Semi-Supervised Non-negative Matrix Factorization to select discriminant unlabeled data for enhanced training. Liliana et al. [10] proposed a semi-supervised clustering method based on Fuzzy C-means (FCM) to consider the level of ambiguity of facial expressions. Araujo et al. [11] mentioned a semi-supervised temporal clustering method and applied it to the complex problem of facial emotion categorization.

Although the unlabeled samples are helpful to construct the exact model for facial expression classification, experiments show that the effect of some SSL methods is even worse than simply using the methods employed for labeled samples [12, 13]. To address this problem, Li and Zhou presented the safe semi-supervised vector machine (S4VM) [14] to explore multiple candidate low-density separators, estimate the decision boundary closest to the real situation and ensure the best classification effect. The researchers define S4VM as a safe semi-supervised classifier whose performance never degenerates, even when using unlabeled data.

Inspired by Li and Zhou, this work proposes a semi-supervised learning method based on the DPND feature. The DPND feature proposed in our previous work [15] extract the deep representations of the peak (the fully expressive) frame and the neutral frame, respectively, and use the difference between them to represent the facial expression. In this paper, to further improve the robustness, a set of DPND features is extracted from each facial expression sequence which select the key frames near to the cluster centroids. Then, a cascaded semi-supervised classifier is constructed to classify facial expressions with both labeled and unlabeled samples. The final classification result of each sequence is decided by the voting of all key-frame pairs.

The rest of this paper is organized as follows. The details of the semi-supervised FER method are presented in Sect. 2. The experimental setup is described in detail, and the experiment results are given in Sect. 3. Section 4 concludes the paper.

2 The Proposed Method

In this section, the proposed semi-supervised FER approach will be described in detail. The proposed method consists of two main parts: (1) Multiple DPND feature extraction from expression sequences and (2) construction of a cascaded semi-supervised classifier for FER.

2.1 Multiple DPDN Feature Extraction

To address the FER problem, researchers have proposed many elaborate features to represent facial expressions during past decades [16]. However, some recent works show that features learned from millions of training samples by deep learning outperform manually designed features in face-related tasks, such as face detection [17] and face recognition [18]. Encouraged by these advancements, the popular VGG-16 [19] is adopted as the network architecture for deep representation extraction in this study. The VGG-16 is pre-trained on the VGG face dataset, which contains 2.6 M face images from 2,622 subjects. When face images are put into the VGG-16, the output of neuron responses by one of the intermediate layers of the VGG-16 network can be extracted as images' deep representation. In this paper, the DPND feature is employed to describe the change between the neutral frame and the peak frame as our previous work [15]:

$$f_{DPND} = \left(f^P - f^N\right)/N \tag{1}$$

where f^P and f^N are deep representation features extracted from the peak frame and neutral frame, respectively, and N is the normalized factor. The DPND feature can effectively retain facial expression information while eliminating individual differences and environmental noises.

For some standard facial expression datasets, such as CK+ [20], in which each sequence begins with the neutral expression and ends with the peak expression, the DPND feature can be easily obtained by the deep representation feature of the beginning frame and the end frame. However, the neutral frame and the peak frame of an expression sequence are not directly available in some datasets, such as the BU-4DFE [21]. To extract the DPND feature from expression sequences, a joint method of K-means clustering and rank-SVM is presented.

However, a single DPND feature [15] from each sequence to represent the facial expression has two limitations: first, the extraction of key frames has a certain randomness due to the random initialization of cluster centroids; second, the extracted key frames can only approximately represent the neutral frames and peak frames. In order to further improve the robustness, in this work, a set of DPND features is extracted from each facial expression sequence which select the key frames near to the cluster centroids obtained using K-means. The final classification result of each sequence is decided by the voting of all key-frame pairs. In this way, the multiple DPND feature can effectively avoid the problem caused by the inaccurate selection of key frames. And the subsequent experiments prove that, compared to the single DPND feature, the multiple DPND feature can indeed improve the accuracy of FER.

2.2   Construct a Cascaded Multi-class Classifier for FER

In this subsection, a cascaded classifier is introduced to the S4VM construct to recognize the six basic facial expressions using the proposed DPND feature. The original S4VM proposed by Li and Zhou [14] is an inductive binary classifier. For applying it to FER tasks, a set of S4VMs is combined with a cascaded structure, and each S4VM divides a kind of facial expression from the given dataset. A brief introduction of S4VM is first given.

Safe Semi-Supervised Support Vector Machine (S4VM). Let $\mathcal{X}$ be the input space and $\mathcal{Y} = \{\pm 1\}$ be the label space. A set of labeled data as $\{x_i, y_i\}_{i=1}^{l}$ and a set of unlabeled data are given as $\{\hat{x}_j\}_{j=1}^{u}$. Semi-Supervised learning SVM (S3VM) aims to find a decision function $f : \mathcal{X} \to \{\pm 1\}$ and a label assignment on unlabeled instances $y = \{y_{l+1}, \ldots, y_{l+u}\} \in \mathcal{B}$ such that the following objective function is minimized,

$$h(f, \hat{y}) = \frac{\|f\|_H}{2} + C_1 \sum_{i=1}^{l} l(y_i, f(x_i)) + C_2 \sum_{j=1}^{u} l(\hat{y}_j, f(\hat{x}_j)) \tag{2}$$

S4VM focuses on the safeness of SSL algorithms. Its main idea is to generate multiple low-density separators to approximate the ground truth decision boundary and maximize the improvement in performance of inductive SVMs for any candidate separator. To generate a pool of diverse separators $\{f_t\}_{t=1}^{T}$, the following function is minimized:

$$\min_{\{f, \hat{y}_t \in \mathcal{B}\}_{t=1}^{T}} \sum_{t=1}^{T} h(f_t, \hat{y}_t) + M\Omega(\{\hat{y}_t\}_{t=1}^{T}), \tag{3}$$

where T is the number of separators, Ω is a penalty coefficient about the diversity of separators, and M is a large constant to ensure diversity. A variety of methods can be adopted to solve this optimization problem, such as global simulated annealing search and representative sampling.

To learn a label assignment y such that the performance against the inductive SVM, y^{svm}, is improved, the worst-case improvement over inductive SVM is maximized and $\bar{y}$ is denoted as the optimal solution:

$$\bar{y} = \underset{y}{\arg\max} \ \underset{\hat{y}}{\min} \ gain(y, \hat{y}, y^{svm}) - loss(y, \hat{y}, y^{svm}) \tag{4}$$

where $gain(y, \hat{y}, y^{svm})$ and $loss(y, \hat{y}, y^{svm})$ are the gained and lost accuracies compared to the inductive SVM, respectively. It has been shown that the accuracy of $\bar{y}$ is never worse than that of y^{svm} and achieves the maximal performance improvement over that of y^{svm} in the worst cases.

Multi-class Classification with the Cascaded S4VM. The original S4VM is typically designed for binary classification problems; thus, S4VM must be extended into a multi-class classifier for FER. The most common strategies are called one-against-one and one-against-all, however, S4VM, as an inductive method, cannot use one-against-one to construct a multi-class classification, while adoption of one-against-all is ineffective due to the same large training set for each binary classification.

This paper constructs multi-class classification based on a cascaded structure [22, 23], which can hold inductive and effective to unlabeled data. In detail, the training set that contains labeled and unlabeled data is put into the cascaded classifier, and samples of the specified class are picked out for each S4VM classifier. The identified unlabeled data and the corresponding labeled data are removed from the training set, while the remaining samples are passed to the next S4VM classifier.

It is worth noting that the performance of multi-class classifiers varies widely according to different cascaded order. To design a more effective cascaded classifier, the order of the S4VM classifiers is determined according to a discriminant measure of labeled data. The ratio of the inner-class distance and the inter-class distance is defined as the separable measure:

$$S_p = \frac{D_{pp}}{\sum_{q \neq p} D_{pq}} \tag{5}$$

where $D_{pq} = \frac{1}{|p||q|} \sum_{i \in p, j \in q} d_{ij}$ is the average distance between any two samples in the class p and q. The class p is separated from the training set according to the ascending order of S_p. The corresponding classes are sorted to $p_1, p_2, \ldots, p_m$. Then, a classifier with a cascaded structure is constructed, such as that shown in Fig. 1.

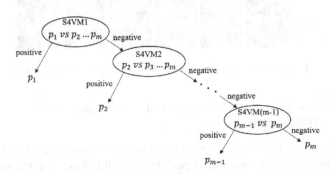

Fig. 1. Multi-class classification based on a cascaded structure.

Samples of class p_1 are assigned to the positive category, and samples of the rest classes are assigned to the negative category; then, the first sub-binary classifier S4VM1 is trained. After that, samples of class p_1 are removed from the training set. Similarly, samples of class p_2 are assigned to the positive category, and the rest of the samples are assigned to the negative category; then, the second sub-binary classifier SVM2 is trained until all the sub-classifiers are trained. Finally, a cascaded S4VM is obtained.

3   Experiments

3.1   Experimental Protocol

To evaluate the effectiveness of the proposed algorithm, two public sequence-based datasets, CK+ [20] and BU-4DFE [21], were chosen for the experiment; the CK+ dataset has been used in [10]. The details of these two datasets are listed in Table 1. In our experiment, only six basic expressions (angry, disgust, fear, happy, sad and surprise) were considered, and we extracted a subset of 53 subjects from the CK+ and a subset of 64 subjects from the BU-4DFE. Some samples of the two databases are shown in Fig. 2. For the CK+ dataset, the DPND feature is the difference between the deep representation feature of the first frame and the last frame; for BU-4DFE, the DPND feature is extracted from the facial sequences directly by our proposed method.

Table 1. Details of the CK+, BU-4DFE dataset.

Dataset	Subjects	Sequences	Gender(F/M)	Age	Ethnicity
CK+	97	486	65%/35%	18–30	Multiethnic
BU-4DFE	101	606	56%/44%	18–70	Multiethnic

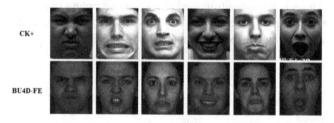

Fig. 2. Exemplar expression images in the CK+, BU-4DFE dataset.

3.2   Comparison Among the Multiple DPND, the Single DPND and the DPR Feature

In order to show the effectiveness of the DPND feature, we compared it with the static feature that the deep representations of peak frames (DPR feature) extracted from the VGG-16 network. Then, the proposed cascaded S4VM was employed to evaluate the effects of the different features. For BU-4DFE, the multiple DPND feature was extracted from a set of key-frame pairs near to the cluster centroids. It is noteworthy that the labeled samples only accounted for 10% of the training set in the experiment. The average accuracies of the different features are listed in Table 2. The results indicate that the accuracy of the single DPND feature on the CK+ and BU-4DFE are 8.5% and 21% higher than that of the DPR feature, and the performance of the multiple DPND feature is 3.4% higher than that of the single DPND feature on the BU-4DFE, which strongly proves the excellence of the DPND feature, especially the multiple DPND feature.

Table 2. Average accuracy of the DPND and DPR features.

Feature	CK+	BU-4DFE
Multiple DPND	——	71.8%
Single DPND	89.4%	68.4%
DPR	80.9%	47.4%

3.3   Comparisons with the State-of-the-Art Method

In this subsection, we compare the proposed method (the cascaded S4VM with the DPND feature) with the current state-of-the-art method [10] on the CK+ dataset. The method [10] is based on an SSL algorithm. It first employed an Active Appearance Model to detect human facial points for feature extraction and then utilized semi-supervised Fuzzy C-Means to work as the classifier system; we refer to the method as SSFCM. It selected 329 images of eight emotions from the CK+ dataset, of which 63% were used as a training set and the remaining samples were used for testing. The average accuracies of the proposed method and SSFCM method are shown in Table 3. The proposed method outperforms the SSFCM method [10] even though the SSFCM method selected the peak frames out from the sequences manually and used more labeled data than our method.

Table 3. Average accuracies of the proposed method and the current state-of-the-art method on the CK+.

Method	CK+
Proposed method	89.4%
SSFCM	80.7%

3.4   Comparison with the Supervised Classification

In this subsection, we aimed to use the CK+ and BU-4DFE dataset to evaluate the capability of the SSL method for FER. To this end, the proposed cascaded S4VM and SVM were used as expression classifiers and SVM was considered the baseline because it has been demonstrated as a successful approach for FER tasks. The performance of the cascaded S4VM was calculated based on its outputs, including the list of generated labels for unlabeled data. Using the same data, SVM was applied as a fully supervised version of the cascaded S4VM (see Table 4) for comparison of the semi-supervised learning and supervised learning. The results demonstrate that although a small proportion of each dataset was labelled (10%), the accuracy of the cascaded S4VM for FER on the CK+ and BU-4DFE are 5% and 12% higher than that of SVM.

For more evaluation, the accuracy of the cascaded S4VM was considered with different amounts of labeled data (10%, 12.5%, 17%, 20%, 25% and 50%), as shown in Fig. 3. In all these experiments, the cascaded S4VM achieved better accuracy than SVM, especially in the case of few labelled data, which confirms the cascaded S4VM's efficiency. The results illustrate that combined with information from labeled and unlabeled samples, the cascaded S4VM can predict the distribution of data more reasonably and then adjust the decision boundary to improve the classification accuracy. Figure 3 also shows that as the number of labeled data increases, the accuracy of the cascaded S4VM and SVM also increase and match.

Table 4. Accuracy of the cascaded S4VM compared to SVM.

Dataset (10%)	SVM	Cascaded S4VM
CK+	84.9%	89.4%
BU-4DFE	59.9%	71.8%

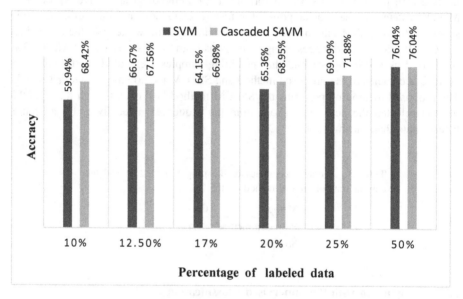

Fig. 3. Accuracy with different percentages of labelled data.

4 Conclusion

In this paper, we propose a semi-supervised method based on the multiple DPND feature for FER. The DPND feature tends to emphasize the facial parts that are changed in the transition from the neutral to the expressive face and to eliminate differences in individual face identities and environmental noises. In this work, the multiple DPND feature are extracted from each sequence to improve the robustness of feature representation. Then, a cascaded semi-supervised classifier is constructed to recognize six basic facial expressions using both labeled and unlabeled data. The proposed method achieves an accuracy of 89.4% on the CK+ dataset and an accuracy of 71.8% on the BU-4DFE dataset when only 10% of the training samples are labeled. The encouraging results on public databases suggests that our method has strong potential to recognize facial expressions in real-world applications.

Acknowledgment. This work was supported by Research funds from the National Key Research and Development Program of China (No. 2018YFB1004500, No. 2018YFB1004504), Research Funds of CCNU from the Colleges' Basic Research and Operation of MOE (No. CCNU17ZDJC04) Humanities and Social Sciences Foundation of the Ministry of Education (No. 14YJAZH005), National Natural Science Foundation of China (No. 61702208), and Natural Science Foundation of Hubei Province (No. 2017CFB504).

References

1. Li, S.Z., Jain, A.K.: Handbook of Face Recognition, vol. 132, no. 3, pp. 470–487. Springer, Heidelberg (2011)
2. Fang, T., Zhao, X., Ocegueda, O., Shah, S.K.: 3D facial expression recognition: a perspective on promises and challenges. In: IEEE International Conference on Automatic Face & Gesture Recognition and Workshops, vol. 28, pp. 603–610. IEEE (2011)
3. Lopes, A.T., Aguiar, E.D., Souza, A.F.D., Oliveira-Santos, T.: Facial expression recognition with convolutional neural networks: coping with few data and the training sample order. Pattern Recogn. **61**, 610–628 (2016)
4. Jiang, B., Jia, K., Sun, Z.: Research on the algorithm of semi-supervised robust facial expression recognition. In: Yoshida, T., Kou, G., Skowron, A., Cao, J., Hacid, H., Zhong, N. (eds.) AMT 2013. LNCS, vol. 8210, pp. 136–145. Springer, Cham (2013). https://doi.org/10.1007/978-3-319-02750-0_14
5. Jadidi, Z., Muthukkumarasamy, V., Sithirasenan, E., Singh, K.: Flow-based anomaly detection using semi supervised learning. In: International Conference on Signal Processing and Communication Systems, pp. 1–5. IEEE (2016)
6. Cohen, I., Cozman, F.G., Sebe, N., Cirelo, M.C., Huang, T.S.: Semi supervised learning of classifiers: theory, algorithms, and their application to human-computer interaction. IEEE Trans. Pattern Anal. Mach. Intell. **26**(12), 1553–1566 (2004)
7. Hady, M.F.A., Schels, M., Schwenker, F., Palm, G.: Semi-supervised facial expressions annotation using co-training with fast probabilistic tri-class SVMs. In: Diamantaras, K., Duch, W., Iliadis, Lazaros S. (eds.) ICANN 2010. LNCS, vol. 6353, pp. 70–75. Springer, Heidelberg (2010). https://doi.org/10.1007/978-3-642-15822-3_8
8. Jiang, B., Jia, K.: Semi-supervised facial expression recognition algorithm on the condition of multi-pose. J. Inf. Hiding Multimed. Sig. Process. **4**(3), 138–146 (2013)
9. Liu, M., Li, S., Shan, S., Chen, X.: Enhancing expression recognition in the wild with unlabeled reference data. In: Lee, K.M., Matsushita, Y., Rehg, J.M., Hu, Z. (eds.) ACCV 2012. LNCS, vol. 7725, pp. 577–588. Springer, Heidelberg (2013). https://doi.org/10.1007/978-3-642-15822-3_8
10. Liliana, D.Y., Widyanto, M.R., Basaruddin, T.: Human emotion recognition based on active appearance model and semi-supervised fuzzy C-means. In: International Conference on Advanced Computer Science and Information Systems, pp. 439–445. IEEE (2017)
11. Araujo, R., Kamel, M.S.: A semi-supervised temporal clustering method for facial emotion analysis. In: IEEE International Conference on Multimedia and Expo Workshops, pp. 1–6. IEEE (2014)

12. Wang, L., Chan, K.L., Zhang, Z.: Bootstrapping SVM active learning by incorporating unlabelled images for image retrieval. In: Proceedings of 2003 IEEE Computer Society Conference on Computer Vision and Pattern Recognition, vol. 1, pp. I-629–I-634. IEEE (2003)

13. Chapelle, O., Sindhwani, V., Keerthi, S.S.: Optimization techniques for semi-supervised support vector machines. J. Mach. Learn. Res. **9**(1), 203–233 (2008)

14. Li, Y.F., Zhou, Z.H.: Towards making unlabeled data never hurt. IEEE Trans. Pattern Anal. Mach. Intell. **37**(1), 175–188 (2015)

15. Chen, J., Xu, R., Liu, L.: Deep peak-neutral difference feature for facial expression recognition. Multimed. Tools Appl. **77**(2), 1–17 (2018)

16. Corneanu, C.A., Oliu, M., Cohn, J.F., Escalera, S.: Survey on RGB, 3D, thermal, and multimodal approaches for facial expression recognition: history, trends, and affect-related applications. IEEE Trans. Pattern Anal. Mach. Intell. **38**(8), 1548–1568 (2016)

17. Li, H., Lin, Z., Shen, X., Brandt, J., Hua, G.: A convolutional neural network cascade for face detection. In: Computer Vision and Pattern Recognition, pp. 5325–5334. IEEE (2015)

18. Hu, G., Yang, Y., Yi, D., Kittler, J., Christmas, W., Li, S.Z., et al.: When face recognition meets with deep learning: an evaluation of convolutional neural networks for face recognition, pp. 384–392 (2015)

19. Parkhi, O.M, Vedaldi, A., Zisserman, A.: Deep face recognition. In: Proceedings of the British Machine Vision Conference (BMVC), pp. 1–12 (2015)

20. Tian, Y.L., Kanade, T., Cohn, J.F.: Recognizing action units for facial expression analysis. IEEE Trans. Pattern Anal. Mach. Intell. **23**(2), 97 (2001)

21. Yin, L., Wei, X., Sun, Y., Wang, J., Rosato, M.J.: A 3D facial expression database for facial behavior research. In: International Conference on Automatic Face and Gesture Recognition, vol. 2006, pp. 211–216. IEEE (2006)

22. Saatci, Y., Town, C.: Cascaded classification of gender and facial expression using active appearance models. In: International Conference on Automatic Face and Gesture Recognition, vol. 47, pp. 393–398. IEEE (2006)

23. Li, L., Gao, Z.P., Ding, W.Y.: Fuzzy multi-class support vector machine based on binary tree in network intrusion detection. In: International Conference on Electrical and Control Engineering, vol. 28, pp. 1043–1046. IEEE (2010)

Feature Extraction and Selection

Noise Level Estimation for Overcomplete Dictionary Learning Based on Tight Asymptotic Bounds

Rui Chen[1(✉)] and Changshui Yang[2]

[1] Tianjin University, Tianjin, China
ruichen@tju.edu.cn
[2] Peking University, Beijing, China
csyang@pku.edu.cn

Abstract. In this paper, we address the problem of estimating Gaussian noise level from the trained dictionaries in update stage. We first provide rigorous statistical analysis on the eigenvalue distributions of a sample covariance matrix. Then we propose an interval-bounded estimator for noise variance in high dimensional setting. To this end, an effective estimation method for noise level is devised based on the boundness and asymptotic behavior of noise eigenvalue spectrum. The estimation performance of our method has been guaranteed both theoretically and empirically. The analysis and experiment results have demonstrated that the proposed algorithm can reliably infer true noise levels, and outperforms the relevant existing methods.

Keywords: Dictionary learning · Sample covariance matrix
Random matrix theory · Noise level estimation

1 Introduction

The dictionary learning is a matrix factorization problem that amounts to finding the linear combination of a given signal $\mathbf{Y} \in \mathbb{R}^{N \times M}$ with only a few atoms selected from columns of the dictionary $\mathbf{D} \in \mathbb{R}^{N \times K}$. In an overcomplete setting, the dictionary matrix $\mathbf{D}$ has more columns than rows $K > N$, and the corresponding coefficient matrix $\mathbf{X} \in \mathbb{R}^{K \times M}$ is assumed to be sparse. For most practical tasks in the presence of noise, we consider a contamination form of the measurement signal $\mathbf{Y} = \mathbf{D}\mathbf{X} + \mathbf{w}$, where the elements of noise $\mathbf{w}$ are independent realizations from the Gaussian distribution $\mathcal{N}(0, \sigma_n^2)$. The basic dictionary learning problem is formulated as:

$$\min_{\mathbf{D}, \mathbf{X}} \|\mathbf{Y} - \mathbf{D}\mathbf{X}\|_F^2 \quad s.t. \ \|\mathbf{x}_i\|_0 \leq L \ \forall i \tag{1}$$

Therein, L is the maximal number of non-zero elements in the coefficient vector $\mathbf{x}_i$. Starting with an initial dictionary, this minimization task can be solved by the popular alternating approaches such as the method of optimal directions (MOD) [1] and K-SVD [2]. The dictionary training on noisy samples can incorporate the denoising together

© Springer Nature Switzerland AG 2018
J.-H. Lai et al. (Eds.): PRCV 2018, LNCS 11258, pp. 257–267, 2018.
https://doi.org/10.1007/978-3-030-03338-5_22

into one iterative process [3]. For a single image, the K-SVD algorithm is adopted to train a sparsifying dictionary and the developed method in [3] denoises the corrupted image by alternating between the update stages of the sparse representations and the dictionary. In general, the residual errors of learning process are determined by noise levels. Noise incursion in a trained dictionary can affect the stability and accuracy of sparse representation [4]. So the performance of dictionary learning highly depends on the estimation accuracy of unknown noise level σ_n^2 when the noise characteristics of trained dictionaries are unavailable.

The main challenge of estimating the noise level lies in effectively distinguishing the signal from noise by exploiting sufficient prior information. The most existing methods have been developed to estimate the noise level from image signals based on specific image characteristics [5–8]. Generally, these works assume that a sufficient amount of homogeneous areas or self-similarity patches are contained in natural images. Thus empirical observations, singular value decomposition (SVD) or statistical properties can be applied on carefully selected patches. However, it is not suitable for estimating the noise level in dictionary update stage because only few atoms for sparse representation cannot guarantee the usual assumptions. To enable wider applications and less assumptions, more recent methods estimate the noise level based on principal component analysis (PCA) [9, 10]. These methods underestimate the noise level since they only take the smallest eigenvalue of block covariance matrix. Although later work [11] has made efforts to tackle these problems by spanning low dimensional subspace, the optimal estimation for true noise variance is still not achieved due to the inaccuracy of subspace segmentation. As for estimating the noise variance techniques, the scaled median absolute deviation of wavelet coefficients has been widely adopted [12]. Leveraging the results from random matrix theory (RMT), the median of sample eigenvalues is also used as an estimator of noise variance [13]. However, these estimators are no longer consistent and unbiased when the dictionary matrix has high dimensional structure.

To solve the aforementioned problems, we propose to accurately estimate the noise variance in a trained dictionary by using exact eigenvalues of a sample covariance matrix. The proposed method can also be applied to estimate the noise level for the noisy image. As a novel contribution, we construct the tight asymptotic bounds of extreme eigenvalues to separate the subspaces between the signal and the noise based on random matrix theory (RTM). Moreover, in order to eliminate the possible bias caused the high-dimensional settings, a corrected estimator is derived to provide the consistent inference on the noise variance for a trained dictionary. Based on these asymptotic results, we develop an optimal variance estimator which can well deal with the settings with different sample sizes and dimensions. The practical usefulness of our method is numerically illustrated.

2   Tight Bounds for Noise Eigenvalue Distributions

In this section, we analyze the asymptotical distribution of the ratio of extreme eigenvalues of a sample covariance matrix based on the limiting RTM law. Then a tight bound is derived.

2.1   Eigenvalue Subspaces of Sample Covariance Matrix

We consider the sparse approximation of each observed sample $\mathbf{y}_i \in \mathbb{R}^N$ with s prototype atoms selected from learned dictionary $\mathbf{D}$. With respect to the sparse model (1), we aim at estimating the noise level σ_n^2 for an elementary trained dictionary $\mathbf{D}_s$ containing a subset of the atoms $\{\mathbf{d}_i\}_{i=1}^s$. Note that $\mathbf{D}_s = \mathbf{D}_S^0 + \mathbf{w}_S$, where $\mathbf{D}_S^0$ denotes original dictionary and $\mathbf{w}_S$ is the additive Gaussian noise. At each iterative step, the noise level σ_n^2 goes gradually to zero when updating towards true dictionary $\mathbf{D}_S^0$ [14]. The known noise variance is helpful to avoid noise incursion and determine the sample size, the sparsity degree and even the performance of the true underlying dictionary [15]. To derive the relationship between the eigenvalues and noise level, we first construct the sample covariance matrix of dictionary $\mathbf{D}_s$ as follows:

$$\Sigma_S = \frac{1}{s-1} \sum_{i=1}^s (\mathbf{d}_i - \overline{\mathbf{d}})(\mathbf{d}_i - \overline{\mathbf{d}})^{\mathrm{T}}, \quad \overline{\mathbf{d}} = \frac{1}{s} \sum_{i=1}^s \mathbf{d}_i \tag{2}$$

According to (2), the square matrix $\sum_s$ has N dimensions with the sparse condition $N \gg s$. Based on the symmetric property, this matrix is decomposed into the product of three matrices: an orthogonal matrix $\mathbf{U}$, a diagonal matrix and a transpose matrix $\mathbf{U}^T$, which can be selected by satisfying $\mathbf{U}^T\mathbf{U} = \mathbf{I}$. Here, this transform process is written as:

$$\mathbf{U}^{\mathrm{T}}\Sigma_S\mathbf{U} = \mathbf{diag}(\lambda_1, \ldots, \lambda_m, \lambda_{m+1}, \ldots, \lambda_N) \tag{3}$$

Given $\lambda_1 \geq \lambda_2 \geq \ldots \geq \lambda_N$, we exploit the eigenvalue subspaces to enable the separation of atoms from noise. To be more specific, we divide the eigenvalues into two sets $\mathbf{S} = \mathbf{S}_1 \cup \mathbf{S}_2$ by finding the appropriate bound in a spiked population model [16]. Most structures of an atom lie in low-dimension subspace and thus the leading eigenvalues in set $\mathbf{S}_1 = \{\lambda_i\}_{i=1}^m$ are mainly contributed by atom itself. The redundant-dimension subspace $\mathbf{S}_2 = \{\lambda_i\}_{i=m+1}^N$ is dominated by the noise. Because the atoms contribute very little to this later portion, we take all the eigenvalues of $\mathbf{S}_2$ into consideration to estimate the noise variance while eliminating the influence of trained atoms. Moreover, the random variables $\{\lambda_i\}_{i=m+1}^N$ can be considered as the eigenvalues of pure noise covariance matrix $\Sigma_{\mathbf{w}}$, whose dimensions are N.

2.2   Asymptotic Bounds for Noise Eigenvalues

Suppose the sample matrix $\Sigma_{\mathbf{w}}$ has the form $(s-1)\Sigma_{\mathbf{w}} = \mathbf{HH}^{\mathrm{T}}$, where the sample entries of $\mathbf{H}$ are independently generated from the distribution $\mathcal{N}(0, \sigma_n^2)$. Then the real matrix $\mathbf{M} = \mathbf{HH}^{\mathrm{T}}$ follows a standard Wishart distribution [17]. The ordered eigenvalues of $\mathbf{M}$ are denoted by $\overline{\lambda}_{\max}(\mathbf{M}) \geq \cdots \geq \overline{\lambda}_{\min}(\mathbf{M})$. In the high dimensional situation: $N/s \to \gamma \in [0, \infty)$ as $s, N \to \infty$, the Tracy-Widom law gives the limiting distribution of the largest eigenvalue of the large random matrix $\mathbf{M}$ [18]. Then we have the following asymptotic expression:

$$\Pr\left\{\frac{\bar{\lambda}_{\max}/\sigma_n^2 - \mu}{\xi} \le z\right\} \to F_{TW1}(z) \tag{4}$$

where $F_{TW1}(z)$ indicates the cumulative distribution function with respect to the Tracy-Widom random variable. In order to improve both the approximation accuracy and convergence rate, even only with few atom samples, we need choose the suitable centering and scaling parameters μ, ξ [19]. By the comparison between different values, such parameters are defined as

$$\begin{cases} \mu = 1/s \cdot \left(\sqrt{s-1/2} + \sqrt{N-1/2}\right)^2 \\ \xi = 1/s \cdot \left(\sqrt{s-1/2} + \sqrt{N-1/2}\right)\left(\frac{1}{\sqrt{s-1/2}} + \frac{1}{\sqrt{N-1/2}}\right)^{1/3} \end{cases} \tag{5}$$

The empirical distribution of the eigenvalues of the large sample matrix converges almost surely to the Marcenko-Pastur distribution on a finite support [20]. Based on the generalized result in [21], when $N \to \infty$ and $\gamma \in [0, \infty)$, with probability one, we derive limiting value of the smallest eigenvalue as

$$\bar{\lambda}_{\min}/\sigma_n^2 \to (1 - \sqrt{\gamma})^2 \tag{6}$$

According to the asymptotic distributions described in the theorems (4) and (6), we further quantify the distribution of the ratio of the maximum eigenvalue to minimum eigenvalue in order to detect the noise eigenvalues. Let T_1 be a detection threshold. Then we find T_1 by the following expression:

$$\begin{aligned} \Pr\left\{\frac{\bar{\lambda}_{\max}}{\bar{\lambda}_{\min}} \le T_1\right\} &= \Pr\left\{\frac{\bar{\lambda}_{\max}}{\sigma_n^2} \le T_1 \cdot \frac{\bar{\lambda}_{\min}}{\sigma_n^2}\right\} \approx \Pr\left\{\frac{\bar{\lambda}_{\max}}{\sigma_n^2} \le T_1 \cdot \left(1 - \sqrt{N/s}\right)^2\right\} \\ &= \Pr\left\{\frac{\bar{\lambda}_{\max}/\sigma_n^2 - \mu}{\xi} \le \frac{T_1 \cdot \left(1 - \sqrt{N/s}\right)^2 - \mu}{\xi}\right\} \approx F_{TW1}\left\{\frac{T_1 \cdot \left(1 - \sqrt{N/s}\right)^2 - \mu}{\xi}\right\} \end{aligned} \tag{7}$$

Note that there is no closed-form expression for the function F_{TW1}. Fortunately, the values of F_{TW1} and the inverse F_{TW1}^{-1} can be numerically computed at certain percentile points [16]. For a required detection probability α_1, this leads to

$$\frac{T_1 \cdot \left(1 - \sqrt{N/s}\right)^2 - \mu}{\xi} = F_{TW1}^{-1}(\alpha_1) \tag{8}$$

Plugging the definitions of μ and ξ into the Eq. (8), we finally obtain the threshold

$$T_1 = \frac{s\left(\sqrt{s-1/2} + \sqrt{N-1/2}\right)^2}{\left(\sqrt{s} - \sqrt{N}\right)^2} \cdot \left(\frac{\left(\sqrt{s-1/2} + \sqrt{N-1/2}\right)^{-2/3}}{(s-1/2)^{1/6}(N-1/2)^{1/6}} \cdot F_{TW1}^{-1}(\alpha_1) + 1\right) \tag{9}$$

When the detection threshold T_1 is known in the given probability, it means that an asymptotic upper bound can also be obtained for determining the noise eigenvalues of the matrix $\Sigma_{\mathbf{w}}$ because the equality $\lambda_{m+1}/\lambda_N = \bar{\lambda}_{\max}/\bar{\lambda}_{\min}$ holds. In general, the noise eigenvalues in the set $\mathbf{S}_2$ surround the true noise variance as it follows the Gaussian distribution. The estimated largest eigenvalue λ_{m+1} should be no less than σ_n^2. The known smallest eigenvalue λ_N is no more than σ_n^2 by the theoretical analysis [11]. The location and value of λ_{m+1} in $\mathbf{S}$ are obtained by checking the bound $\lambda_{m+1} \leq T_1 \cdot \lambda_N$ with high probability α_1. In addition, λ_1 cannot be selected as noise eigenvalue λ_{m+1}.

3 Noise Variance Estimation Algorithm

3.1 Bounded Estimator for Noise Variance

Without requiring the knowledge of signal, the threshold T_1 can provide good detection performance for finite s, N even when the ratio N/s is not too large. Based on this result, more accurate estimation can be obtained by averaging all elements in $\mathbf{S}_2$. Hence, the maximum likelihood estimator of σ_n^2 is

$$\hat{\sigma}_n^2 = \frac{1}{N-m} \sum_{j=m+1}^{N} \lambda_j \tag{10}$$

In the low dimensional setting where N is relatively small compared with s, the estimator $\hat{\sigma}_n^2$ is consistent and unbiased as $s \to \infty$. It follows asymptotically normal distribution as

$$\sqrt{s}(\hat{\sigma}_n^2 - \sigma_n^2) \to \mathcal{N}(0, \ t^2), \quad t^2 = \frac{2\sigma_n^4}{N-m} \tag{11}$$

When N is large with respect to the sample size s, the sample covariance matrix shows significant deviations from the underlying population covariance matrix. In this context, the estimator $\hat{\sigma}_n^2$ might have a negative bias, which leads to overestimation of true noise variance [22, 23]. We investigate the distribution of another eigenvalue ratio. Namely, the ratio of the maximum eigenvalue to the trace of the eigenvalues is

$$U = \frac{\lambda_{m+1}}{1/(N-m) \cdot \text{tr}(\Sigma_{\mathbf{w}})} = \frac{\lambda_{m+1}}{1 \big/ (N-m) \cdot \sum_{j=m+1}^{N} \lambda_j} \tag{12}$$

According to the result in (4), the ratio U also follows a Tracy-Widom distribution as both N, $s \to \infty$. The denominator in the definition of U is distributed as an independent $\sigma_n^2 \chi_N^2/N$ random variable, and thus has $\text{E}(\hat{\sigma}_n^2) = \sigma_n^2$ and $\text{Var}(\hat{\sigma}_n^2) = 2\sigma_n^4/(N \cdot s)$. It is easy to show that replacing σ_n^2 by $\hat{\sigma}_n^2$ results in the same limiting distribution in (4). Then we have

$$\Pr\left\{\frac{\lambda_{m+1}/\hat{\sigma}_n^2 - \mu}{\xi} \leq z\right\} \to F_{\text{TW1}}(z) \tag{13}$$

Unfortunately, the asymptotic approximation present in (13) is inaccurate for small and even moderate values of N [24]. This approximation is not a proper distribution function. The simulation observations imply that the major factor contributing to the poor approximation is the asymptotic error caused by the constant ξ [24]. Therefore, a more accurate estimate for the standard deviation of $\lambda_{m+1}/\hat{\sigma}_n^2$ will provide a significant improvement. For finite samples, we have

$$E\left(\frac{\lambda_{m+1}}{\sigma_n^2}\right) = \mu, \quad E\left(\frac{\lambda_{m+1}^4}{\sigma_n^4}\right) = \mu^2 + \xi^2 \tag{14}$$

Using these asymptotic results, we get the corrected deviation

$$\xi' = \sqrt{\frac{N \cdot s}{2 + N \cdot s}\left(\xi^2 - \frac{2}{N \cdot s}\mu^2\right)} \tag{15}$$

Note that this formula in (15) has corrected the overestimation in the high dimensional setting. thus the better approximation for the probabilities of the ratio is

$$\Pr\left\{\frac{\lambda_{m+1}/\hat{\sigma}_n^2 - \mu}{\xi'} \geq z\right\} \approx 1 - F_{\text{TW1}}(z) \tag{16}$$

The determination of the distribution for the ratio U is devoted to the correction of the variance estimator. In order to complete the detection of the large deviations of the initial estimator $\hat{\sigma}_n^2$, we provide a procedure to set the threshold T_2. Based on the result in (16), an approximate expression for the overestimation probability is given by

$$\Pr\left\{\frac{\hat{\sigma}_n^2}{\lambda_{m+1}} \leq T_2\right\} = \Pr\left\{\frac{\lambda_{m+1}/\hat{\sigma}_n^2 - \mu}{\xi'} \geq \frac{1/T_2 - \mu}{\xi'}\right\} \approx 1 - F_{\text{TW1}}\left(\frac{1/T_2 - \mu}{\xi'}\right) \tag{17}$$

Hence, for a desired probability level α_2, the above equation can be numerically inverted to find the decision threshold. After some simplified manipulations, we obtain

$$T_2 = \frac{1}{\xi' \cdot F_{\text{TW1}}^{-1}(1 - \alpha_2) + \mu} \tag{18}$$

Asymptotically, the spike eigenvalue λ_{m+1} converges to the right edge of the support $\sigma_n^2(1 + \sqrt{N/s})$ as N, s go to infinity. According to the expression in (18), this function turns out to have a simple approximation $T_2 = 1/\mu$ in the high probability case. Then the upper bound $T_2 \cdot \lambda_{m+1}$ for the known $\hat{\sigma}_n^2$ yields a bias estimation. Finally, the following expectation holds true:

$$E\left(\frac{\mu \cdot T_2 \cdot \lambda_{m+1}}{1+\sqrt{N/s}}\right) \approx \sigma_n^2 \ll \hat{\sigma}_n^2 \tag{19}$$

By analyzing the statistical result in (19), the correction for $T_2 \cdot \lambda_{m+1}$ can be approximated as the better estimator than $\hat{\sigma}_n^2$ because this bias-corrected estimator is closer to the true variance under the high dimensional conditions. If $\hat{\sigma}_n^2$ can satisfy the requirement of no excess of the bound $T_2 \cdot \lambda_{m+1}$, the sample eigenvalues are consistent estimates of their population counterparts. Hence, the optimal estimator is given by

$$\hat{\sigma}_*^2 = \min\left\{ \hat{\sigma}_n^2, \ \frac{\mu \cdot T_2 \cdot \lambda_{m+1}}{1+\sqrt{N/s}} \right\} \tag{20}$$

3.2   Implementation

Based on the construction of two thresholds, we propose a noise estimation algorithm for dictionary learning as follows:

Algorithm 1 Noise Estimation for Dictionary Learning

1: **Input:** Noisy dictionary $\mathbf{D}_s$, the dimension N, the sample number s, the probability levels α_1 and α_2.

2: **Compute** the eigenvalues $\{\lambda_i\}_{i=1}^N$ of the sample covariance matrix Σ_s, and order $\lambda_1 \geq \lambda_2 \geq ... \geq \lambda_N$.

3: **Compute** two thresholds T_1 and T_2.

4: **for** $i=1:N-1$ **do**

    if $\lambda_{i+1} \leq T_1 \cdot \lambda_N$ **then**

        Obtain the location $m+1=i+1$, $\lambda_{m+1}=\lambda_{i+1}$ and **break**

    end if

  end for

5: **Estimate** an initial noise variance $\hat{\sigma}_n^2$ using (10).

6: **Compare** the values of two estimators of (20) and select the minimum as an optimal estimator $\hat{\sigma}_*^2$.

7: **Output:** noise level estimation $\sigma_n^2 = \hat{\sigma}_*^2$.

---

4   Numerical Experiments

The proposed estimation method is evaluated on two benchmark datasets: Kodak [7] and TID2008 [9]. The subjective experiment is to compare our method with three state-of-the-art estimation methods by Liu et al. in [8], Pyatykh *et al.* in [9] and Chen *et al.* in [11], which are relevant in SVD domain. The testing images are added to the

independent white Gaussian noise with deviation level 10 and 30, respectively. We set
the probabilities α_1, $\alpha_2 = 0.97$ and choose $N = 256$, $s = 3$. In general, a higher noise
estimation accuracy leads to a higher denoising quality. We use the K-SVD method to
denoise the images [3]. Figures 1 and 2 show the results using our method outperform
other competitors. Moreover, our peak signal-to-noise ratios (PSNRs) are nearest to
true values, 32.03 dB and 27.01 dB, respectively.

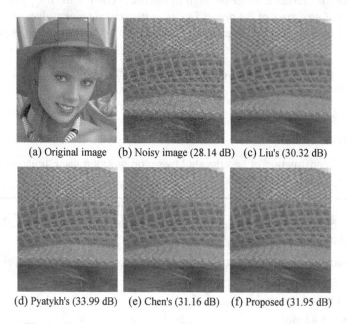

(a) Original image   (b) Noisy image (28.14 dB)   (c) Liu's (30.32 dB)

(d) Pyatykh's (33.99 dB)   (e) Chen's (31.16 dB)   (f) Proposed (31.95 dB)

Fig. 1. Denoising results on the *Woman* image using K-SVD.

To quantitatively evaluate the accuracy of noise estimation, the average of standard
deviations, mean square error (MSE), mean absolute difference (MAD) are computed
by randomly selecting 1500 image patches from 20 testing images. The results shown
in Table 1 indicate that the proposed method is more accurate and stable than other
methods. Next, we compare our optimal estimator $\hat{\sigma}_*^2$ with $\hat{\sigma}_n^2$ and other two existing
estimators in the literatures. The simulated realization of a sample covariance matrix is
followed a Gaussian distribution with different variances. As presented in Table 2, the
performance of $\hat{\sigma}_*^2$ is invariably better than other estimators. To test robustness of our
estimation method, we further obtain the empirical probabilities of the estimated
eigenvalues at typical confidence levels. Figure 3 illustrates that two asymptotic
bounds can achieve very high success probabilities.

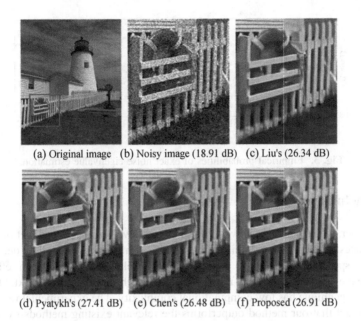

(a) Original image   (b) Noisy image (18.91 dB)   (c) Liu's (26.34 dB)

(d) Pyatykh's (27.41 dB)   (e) Chen's (26.48 dB)   (f) Proposed (26.91 dB)

Fig. 2. Denoising results on the *House* image using K-SVD.

Table 1. Estimation results of different methods (Best results are highlighted).

σ_n	Liu's [8]	Pyatykh's [9]	Chen's [11]	Proposed
1	2.18	1.34	0.59	**1.16**
5	7.30	3.83	5.41	**5.27**
10	13.86	7.19	11.83	**10.19**
15	16.72	13.91	15.92	**15.17**
20	20.99	18.75	20.62	**19.90**
25	26.64	23.29	24.34	**25.06**
30	32.38	27.27	31.98	**30.12**
MAD	3.30	1.59	0.98	**0.15**
MSE	4.84	3.22	1.39	**0.03**

Table 2. Estimation results of four estimators (Best results are highlighted).

σ_n	$\hat{\sigma}_{\text{median}}$ [23]	$\hat{\sigma}_{\text{US}}$ [13]	$\hat{\sigma}_n$	$\hat{\sigma}_*$
1	1.27	1.99	1.14	**1.06**
5	4.59	5.27	6.24	**5.18**
10	8.76	11.28	**9.97**	9.94
15	15.22	14.29	16.17	**14.93**
20	20.85	19.14	20.96	**20.10**
25	25.87	25.98	26.31	**25.28**
30	30.59	30.37	31.16	**30.11**
MAD	0.64	0.78	0.86	**0.12**
MSE	0.52	0.72	0.99	**0.02**

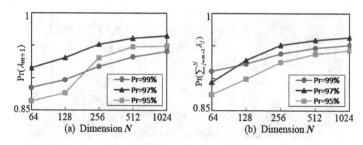

Fig. 3. Empirical probabilities of exact noise eigenvalue estimation.

5 Conclusions

In this paper, we have shown how to infer the noise level from a trained dictionary. The eigen-spaces of the signal and noise are transformed and separated well by determining the eigen-spectrum interval. In addition, the developed estimator can effectively eliminate the estimation bias of a noise variance in high dimensional context. Our noise estimation technique has low computational complexity. The experimental results have demonstrated that our method outperforms the relevant existing methods over a wide range of noise level conditions.

References

1. Engan, K., Aase, S., Husoy, J.: Method of optimal directions for frame design. In: Proceedings of International Conference on Acoustics, Speech, and Signal Pattern Process (ICASSP), pp. 2443–2446 (1999)
2. Aharon, M., Elad, M., Bruckstein, A.: K-SVD: an algorithm designing overcomplete dictionaries for sparse representation. IEEE Trans. Signal Process. **54**(11), 4311–4322 (2006)
3. Elad, M., Aharon, M.: Image denoising via sparse and redundant representations over learned dictionaries. IEEE Trans. Image Process. **15**(12), 3736–3745 (2006)
4. Sahoo, S., Makur, A.: Enhancing image denoising by controlling noise incursion in learned dictionaries. IEEE Signal Process. Lett. **22**(8), 1123–1126 (2015)
5. Li, D., Zhou, J., Tang, Y.: Noise level estimation for natural images based on scale-invariant kurtosis and piecewise stationarity. IEEE Trans. Image Process. **26**(2), 1017–1030 (2017)
6. Hashemi, M., Beheshti, S.: Adaptive noise variance estimation in BayesShrink. IEEE Signal Process. Lett. **17**(1), 12–15 (2010)
7. Tang, C., Yang, X., Zhai, G.: Noise estimation of natural images via statistical analysis and noise injection. IEEE Trans. Circuit Syst. Video Technol. **25**(8), 1283–1294 (2015)
8. Liu, W., Lin, W.: Additive white gaussian noise level estimation in SVD domain for images. IEEE Trans. Image Process. **22**(3), 872–883 (2013)
9. Pyatykh, S., Hesser, J., Zhang, L.: Image noise level estimation by principal component analysis. IEEE Trans. Image Process. **22**(2), 687–699 (2013)
10. Liu, X., Tanaka, M., Okutomi, M.: Single-image noise level estimation for blind denoising. IEEE Trans. Image Process. **22**(12), 5226–5237 (2013)

11. Chen, G., Zhu, F., Heng, P.: An efficient statistical method for image noise level estimation. In: Proceedings of the International Conference on Computer Vision (ICCV), pp. 477–485 (2015)
12. Donoho, L., Johnstone, I.: Ideal spatial adaptation by wavelet shrinkage. Biometrika **81**, 425–455 (1994)
13. Ulfarsson, M., Solo, V.: Dimension estimation in noisy PCA with SURE and random matrix theory. IEEE Trans. Signal Process. **56**(12), 5804–5816 (2008)
14. Gribonval, R., Jenatton, R., Bach, F.: Sparse and spurious: dictionary learning with noise and outliers. IEEE Trans. Inf. Theory **61**(11), 6298–6319 (2015)
15. Jung, A., Eldar, Y., Gortz, N.: On the minimax risk of dictionary learning. IEEE Trans. Inf. Theory **62**(3), 1501–1515 (2016)
16. Johnstone, I.M.: On the distribution of the largest eigenvalue in principal components analysis. Ann. Stat. **29**(2), 295–327 (2001)
17. Chiani, M.: On the probability that all eigenvalues of Gaussian, Wishart, and double Wishart random matrices lie within an interval. IEEE Trans. Inf. Theory **63**(7), 4521–4531 (2017)
18. Karoui, N.E.: A rate of convergence result for the largest eigenvalue of complex white Wishart matrices. The Annals of Probability **34**(6), 2077–2117 (2006)
19. Ma, Z.M.: Accuracy of the Tracy-Widom limits for the extreme eigenvalues in white Wishart matrices. Bernoulli **18**(1), 322–359 (2012)
20. Marcenko, V.A., Pastur, L.A.: Distribution of eigenvalues for some sets of random matrices. Math. USSR-Sb. **1**(4), 457–483 (1967)
21. Bai, Z., Silverstein, J.: Spectral Analysis of Large Dimensional Random Matrices, 2nd edn. Springer, New York (2010). https://doi.org/10.1007/978-1-4419-0661-8
22. Kritchman, S., Nadler, B.: Determining the number of components in a factor model from limited noisy data. Chem. Int. Lab. Syst. **94**(1), 19–32 (2008)
23. Passemier, D., Li, Z., Yao, J.: On estimation of the noise variance in high dimensional probabilistic principal component analysis. J. R. Stat. Soc. B **79**(1), 51–67 (2017)
24. Nadler, B.: On the distribution of the ratio of the largest eigenvalue to the trace of a Wishart matrix. J. Multivar. Anal. **102**, 363–371 (2011)

Perceptual Compressive Sensing

Jiang Du, Xuemei Xie$^{(\boxtimes)}$, Chenye Wang, and Guangming Shi

School of Artificial Intelligence, Xidian University, Xi'an 710071, China
jiangdu@ieee.org, xmxie@mail.xidian.edu.cn, cywang_dd@163.com,
gmshi@xidian.edu.cn

Abstract. Compressive sensing (CS) works to acquire measurements at sub-Nyquist rate and recover the scene images. Existing CS methods always recover the scene images in pixel level. This causes the smoothness of recovered images and lack of structure information, especially at a low measurement rate. To overcome this drawback, in this paper, we propose perceptual CS to obtain high-level structured recovery. Our task no longer focuses on pixel level. Instead, we work to make a better visual effect. In detail, we employ perceptual loss, defined on feature level, to enhance the structure information of the recovered images. Experiments show that our method achieves better visual results with stronger structure information than existing CS methods at the same measurement rate.

Keywords: Compressive sensing · Perceptual loss
Fully convolutional network · Low-level computer vision
Semantic reconstruction

1 Introduction

Nowadays, information is one of the most important component in human world. Visual information takes up most of the percentage. There are billions of images and videos around our daily life. Computer vision has underwent huge resurgence in recent years, since deep learning has made a significant difference in this field. Researchers have shown that deep learning has made breakthrough achievements in the following two broad categories. The first category is the high-level computer vision tasks. For example, image and video classification or recognition [26,27], object detection [8,29], image caption [19], and visual tracking [21]. The second category is low-level reconstruction tasks. For example, denoising [17,35], super-resolution [16], style transfer [13], and optical flow estimation [10].

Researches on inverse problems in imaging [20,22] have been carried on for decades, which cover various low-level computer vision tasks. Compressive sensing (CS) [2,3,5] is a typical inverse problem in imaging. Conventional CS works to recover the signal by optimization algorithms [4,7]. However, this model is hard to be implemented and costs much computational complexity. The application of deep neural networks in inverse problems in imaging makes it possible

© Springer Nature Switzerland AG 2018
J.-H. Lai et al. (Eds.): PRCV 2018, LNCS 11258, pp. 268–279, 2018.
https://doi.org/10.1007/978-3-030-03338-5_23

that the CS measurements can be recovered real-time. Data-driven CS [14,24,25] learns the recovery network from the training data. Adp-Rec [36] jointly train the coder-decoder and brings significant improvement on reconstruction quality. Fully convolutional measurement network (FCMN) [6] firstly measures and recovers full images. However, all the above methods focus on pixel level, and ignore the high-level structure information. This makes the reconstructed results look smooth and have unsatisfactory visual effect. To overcome the drawback, we consider to add high-level perceptual information to CS. So the question is, how to add high-level perceptual information on the low-level CS task.

Design of loss function is a promising solution for perceptual recovery. Study on loss functions for low-level computer vision tasks has provided a variety of approaches. For example, mean square error (MSE) loss, L1 loss [17], NRMSE loss [33] and constraint loss [39]. Recently, perceptual loss [13] has been proposed and employed in many reconstruction tasks, such as style transfer [13] and super-resolution [16]. They are a combination of low-level detailed information and high level semantic information. Perceptual loss is widely used to achieve these goals. It is because perceptual loss is defined in feature space, which can convert the ability of extracting high-level semantic information to recovery network. Thus, the recovered images will contain rich structure information. Inspired by the above applications, we propose perceptual CS, which focuses more on sensing and recovering structure information. We use FCMN [6] as base network to measure and recover scene images, and adopt perceptual loss to train it. We surprisingly find that this framework is capable of capturing and recovering the structure information, especially at extremely low measurement rate, where the measurements can merely contain very limited amount of information.

The contribution of this paper is that, we propose perceptual CS, which can measure and recover the structure information of scene images. It should be noted that, only one deconvolution layer and one Res-block are used in our framework as an illustration. One can employ a deeper network if necessary.

Moreover, perceptual CS indicates an universal architecture. One can change the loss network using pre-trained or dynamic feature extractors for more specific tasks. In this paper, we use VGG [32] as an example. Our code is available on github[1] for further reproduction.

The organization of the rest part of this paper is as follows. Section 2 introduces some related works of this paper. Section 3 describes the technical design and theoretical analysis of the proposed framework. Section 4 presents experimental results of perceptual CS and gives detailed analysis. Section 5 draws the conclusion.

2   Related Work

2.1   Compressive Sensing

CS [5,15,34] proves signal can be reconstructed after being sampled at sub-Nyquist rates as long as the signal is sparse in a certain domain. Reconstructing

---

[1] https://github.com/jiang-du/Perceptual-CS.

signal from measurements is an ill-posed problem. Traditional CS usually solves an optimization problem, which leads to high computational complexity.

Recently, deep neural networks (DNNs) has been applied to CS tasks [6,14, 23–25,36]. These DNN-based methods can be divided into two categories depending on whether measurement and reconstruction process are trained jointly. The first category trains the recovery network while the measurement part is fixed, like SDA [25], ReconNet [14], and DeepInverse [24]. SDA [25] first applies deep learning approach to solve the CS recovery problem, which uses fully-connected layers in the recovery part. ReconNet [14] uses a fully-connected layer along with convolutional layers to recover signals block by block. While, DeepInverse [24] uses pure convolutional layers. The random Gaussian fashion of the measurement part would mismatch the learned recovery part.

The second category jointly trains the measurement part and the recovery part, such as Deepcodec [23], Adaptive [36], and FCMN [6]. These methods totally overcome the problem that the measurement part is independent from the recovery part. Deepcodec [23] is a framework where both measurement and approximate inverse process are learned end-to-end by a deep fully-connected encoder-decoder network. In [36], a fully-connected layer as the measurement matrix along with a super-resolution network as the recovery part is trained. FCMN [6] firstly uses a fully convolutional network where the measurement part is implemented with an overlapped convolution operation. All these methods recover the scene image on pixel level. They ignore the structure information of images.

2.2 Perceptual Loss

Recently, perceptual loss [13] is widely used in many image reconstruction tasks [9,11,13,16,30,38]. It can recover the image with better visual effect since it is defined on feature space. Typically, perceptual loss calculates the Euclidean distance between the features maps of the reconstructed images and the labels from the same layer of the same pre-trained classification network. Perceptual loss reflects the similarity in the feature level between the label and output images, which makes the reconstructed images retain high-level structure information. In contrast, per-pixel loss focuses on similarity in pixel level, which only preserves low-level pixel information.

Perceptual loss achieves more excellent performance than per-pixel loss in most of image restoration tasks. For example, Johnson et al. [13] use perceptual loss for style transfer and super resolution. The output images have sharper edges compared to per-pixel loss. SRGAN [16] trained by perceptual loss generates more photo-realistic super-resolved images than by MSE loss. When used in image inpainting [30], perceptual loss produces satisfactory results due to the addition of high-level context. Additionally, perceptual loss helps to remain finer details for image editing [38]. Inspired by the advantages of perceptual loss in preserving structure and detail, we attempt to apply it to CS field and it accordingly performs well.

3   Perceptual CS Framework

In this section, we mainly introduce the technical design of the perceptual CS framework. The architecture is shown in Fig. 1. It consists of two parts: *compressive sensing network* and *perceptual loss network*. The compressive sensing network originally performs reconstruction in pixel-wise manner. With the perceptual loss network added, the perceptual CS network preserves the structure information of the recovered images. With the help of perceptual recovery, the proposed network is able to acquire high-level perceptual information.

The compressive sensing network measures and recovers the full scene images. The full image processing fashion provides an enough receptive field that makes it possible to perform perceptual reconstruction. While, in the perceptual loss network, we employ a classification network, VGG19, as an auxiliary network. It plays the role of extracting the perceptual information of the images.

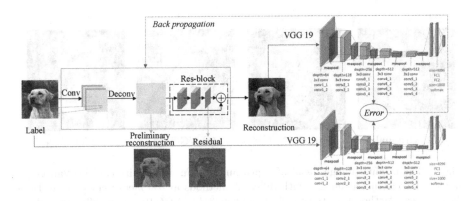

Fig. 1. The architecture of perceptual CS network.

3.1   Full Image Compressive Sensing Network

In most existing CS methods, the scene image is measured and recovered block by block, and each block is reshaped into a column vector. This breaks the structure of the full image. Besides, the computational complexity of the existing methods will extremely increase when the size of the image becomes larger. For example, when an image with the size of $n \times n$ is measured, the memory consumption of the sensing matrix can be up to $S(n) = O(n^4)$. Thus, it is nearly impossible to design a large sensing matrix, let alone measuring the full image. This is because the mapping from the scene image to the measurements is fully-connected, leading to an extremely large-scale parameter nightmare.

Inspired by fully convolutional measurement network (FCMN) [6], we employ a fully convolutional architecture to measure and recover the scene images in the proposed framework, which can get rid of the disaster of the exploding number of parameters. The first convolution layer plays the role of measurement matrix, with kernel size 32 and stride 16. This indicates that the size of measurement matrix is 32×32 and the sliding step is 16 pixels. The deconvolution layer right after the measurement part transforms the dimension of feature map back to the same as input image. Moreover, the fully convolutional architecture can preserve the correspondence among pixels (instead of reshaping into column vector). In this way, block-effect has been largely removed in the recovered images due to the overlapped convolutional measurement. This preserves the structure information of the whole image. Furthermore, the full image method makes it possible to use perceptual loss for semantic reconstruction.

Although the convolution and deconvolution layers can recover the image, for better visual effect, we enhance the proposed framework with residual learning. In detail, we add one residual block and it works quite well, as is shown in Fig. 2(b). One can add more residual blocks for further improvements if necessary.

(a) Original	(b)FCMN [6]	(c) VGG$_{2\_2}$	(d) VGG$_{3\_4}$

Fig. 2. The original image 'head of a peasant woman with white cap' by Van Gogh and the reconstructed images with different methods at 4% measurement rate. Here the proposed method uses the conv2_2 and conv3_4 of VGG19 [32] as different scale of loss respectively.

3.2   Perceptual Reconstruction for Compressive Sensing

In the proposed network, we focus on the perceptual recovery. In the classic CS task, the recovery network approximates the error in the pixel-wise space. To extract the structure information, we recover the scene image in feature-level space. Instead of MSE loss, we consider the perceptual loss, which focuses on perceptual recovery.

MSE loss: In classic CNN-based CS, the loss function is usually defined with pixel-wise loss:

$$l_{pixel}(w) = \|f\{x, w\} - x\|_2^2. \tag{1}$$

This pixel-wise loss will force the image to have the minimized average Euclidean distance between the reconstruction images $f\{x, w\}$ and the labels x. Here, w represents the parameters of the whole network, including the measurement and the recovery parts. Although MSE loss in (1) can help to achieve the reconstructed images with high peak signal-to-noise ratio (PSNR), the reconstructed images usually look smooth and the structure information is not clear. We can see in Fig. 2(b) that the face and the hat of the person is very smooth compared with the original image in Fig. 2(a). Especially the wrinkle on the face cannot be clearly seen.

Perceptual Loss: Considering the current popular classification network works by extracting the features in an image, we can take this advantage into our proposed method. Thus, we apply the perceptual loss. It is formulated as

$$l_{feat}^{\phi,j}(w) = \|\phi_j(f\{x,w\}) - \phi_j(x)\|_2^2 , \qquad (2)$$

where $\phi_j(x)$ denotes the feature map of the j-th layer of VGG19 with the input image x. Different from (1), a typical kind of perceptual loss is defined with the (squared, normalized) Euclidean distance between the feature maps generated from the reconstructed image and the label. Actually, when applying CS at a very low measurement rate, we do not care much about the detailed texture of it. Correspondingly, we emphasize the importance of the structural information. As is shown in Fig. 2(c) and (d), the structure information recovered better, especially the hat of the person has richer structure information compared with Fig. 2(b).

In practical, we define the loss function on $VGG_{2.2}$ or $VGG_{3.4}$ of VGG19 (actually pooling 2 or pooling 3) as examples. The results can be addressed in Fig. 2(c) and (d). The feature map of bottom layers contains detailed low-level information and the top layers have more high-level semantic features. We can also choose other layers by different requirements. In this paper, We do not apply perceptual loss by too high level layers because in terms of compressive sensing, higher level drops too much information that it is nearly impossible to inverse, even if pre-trained.

4   Experiments with Analysis

In this section, we conduct the experiments to illustrate the performance of the proposed perceptual CS framework. We test our framework with a standard dataset [14] containing 11 grayscale images. We also compare the reconstruction results with some typical CS methods. Furthermore, we take some reconstruction results as examples to make a detailed analysis of the performance of the proposed method.

Experiment Setup. The learning rate is set to 10^{-8} when perceptual loss is defined on $VGG_{2.2}$, and 10^{-9} when perceptual loss is defined on $VGG_{3.4}$. The bench size is set to 5 while training. For each measurement rate, the iteration time is 10^6. We use the caffe [12] framework for network training and MATLAB for testing. Our computer is equipped with Intel Core i7-6700K CPU with frequency of 4.0 GHz, 4 NVidia GeForce GTX Titan XP GPUs, 128 GB RAM, and the framework runs on the Ubuntu 16.04 operating system. The training dataset consists of 800 pieces of images with size 256×256 down sampled and cropped from 800 images in DIV2K dataset [1].

Results with Analysis. The following is the analysis of the experimental results at different measurement rates.

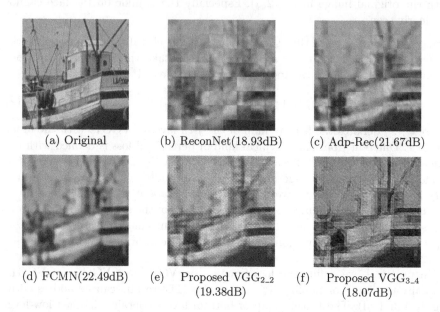

(a) Original	(b) ReconNet(18.93dB)	(c) Adp-Rec(21.67dB)
(d) FCMN(22.49dB)	(e) Proposed VGG$_{2\_2}$ (19.38dB)	(f) Proposed VGG$_{3\_4}$ (18.07dB)

Fig. 3. Boats at measurement rate 1%. (b) and (c) are of block-wise. (d) is of full-image. They all use MSE loss. (e) and (f) are improved by using perceptual loss [2]. Perceptual CS brings stronger structure information compared with FCMN.

The explanation from Fig. 3 at measurement rate 1% is as follows.

(1) Block effect occurs in Fig. 3(b) and (c) by block-wise methods such as Recon-Net [14] and Adp-Rec [36].
   Based on the standard ReconNet [14], the improved ReconNet [18] adds several tricks such as adaptive measurement and adversarial loss. Its performance is even lower than Adp-Rec [36].
(2) Figure 3(d) has no block artifacts in FCMN [6] where fully-convolutional measurement is employed. This work achieves the state-of-the-art results in terms of PSNR and SSIM.
   In this experiment, all existing CS-based image reconstruction works rely on MSE loss. While, FCMN [6] makes perceptual loss promising.
(3) Perceptual loss in Fig. 3(e) and (f) enhances structure information, even if PSNR is lower compared with Fig. 3(d).

The explanation of measurement rate at 4% in Fig. 4 is as follows:

(1) Block effect also occurs in Fig. 4(c) in DR^2-Net [37].
   DR^2-Net achieves highest PSNR among random Gaussian methods, since it adds several Res-blocks that fully convergence in the reconstruction stage.

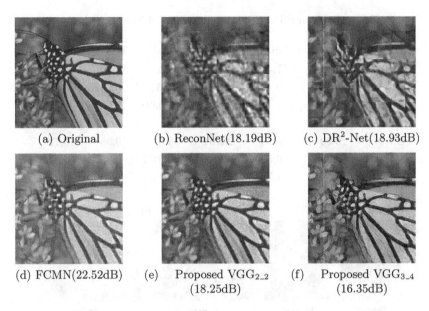

(a) Original   (b) ReconNet(18.19dB)   (c) DR²-Net(18.93dB)

(d) FCMN(22.52dB)   (e)   Proposed VGG$_{2\_2}$ (f)   Proposed VGG$_{3\_4}$
                                  (18.25dB)   (16.35dB)

Fig. 4. Monarch at measurement rate 4%. (b) and (c) are of block-wise. (d) is of full-image. They all use MSE loss. (e) and (f) are improved with perceptual loss. They have stronger structure information than the state-of-the-art result in FCMN. Specially, we can see in the red circle of (f), compared with (a) and (d), that even blurry image can be enhanced. (Color figure online)

(2) The method with adaptive measurement for Fig. 4(d) adopts one Res-block, achieving the highest PSNR. The comparison among several typical methods including DR²-Net is in Fig. 4, where FCMN [6] with full image gets the best result in terms of PSNR.

It should be pointed out that only one Res-block is used in both FCMN [6] and the proposed framework in this paper. One can add more Res-blocks for further improvement.

(3) With just one Res-block, perceptual loss in Fig. 4(e) and (f) works well, which improves FCMN [6]. Structure information is kept. In some case, even wake structure can become strong (see Fig. 4(f) compared to Fig. 4(a) and (d)).

It should be noted that, even if PSNR is worse with perceptual loss, the structure information is clearly reconstructed.

Evaluation of Perceptual CS. To evaluate the performance of the proposed method, we evaluate quality of the reconstructed images with PSNR and SSIM. Furthermore, we also use Mean Opinion Score (MOS) [28] to test the visual effect of these methods. In this metric, an image is scored by 26 volunteers and the final score is the average value. The quality ranking is represented by scores from 1 to 5, where 1 denotes lowest quality and 5 denotes the highest. All the test images are ranked randomly before being scored and they are displayed group

Table 1. Mean PSNR, SSIM and MOS of different methods

MR = 1%	ReconNet	DR²-Net	Adp-Rec	FCMN	VGG₂₋₂	VGG₃₋₄
PSNR	17.27	17.44	20.32	**21.27**	18.30	16.80
SSIM	0.4083	0.4291	0.5031	**0.5447**	0.2478	0.2565
MOS	1.0734	1.1188	1.8496	2.6328	2.6818	2.9510
MR = 4%						
PSNR	19.99	20.80	**24.01**	23.87	19.38	16.72
SSIM	0.5287	0.5804	0.7021	**0.7042**	0.3522	0.4729
MOS	1.5979	1.7237	3.0489	3.4230	3.4755	3.3566

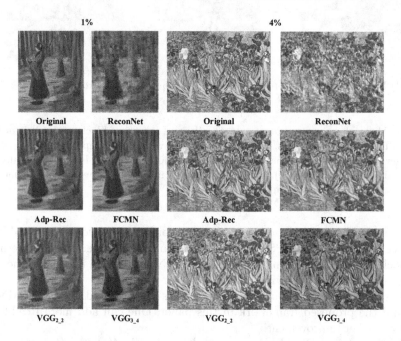

Fig. 5. The reconstructed results of ReconNet [14], Adp-Rec [36], FCMN [6], and the proposed method using the conv2_2 and conv3_4 of VGG19 [32] with measurement rate 1% and 4% and their corresponding original scene image.

by group. Each group has six reconstruction images, in different methods. All participants take this test on the same computer screen, from the same angle and distance. Here the distance from the screen to the tested persons is 50 cm and the eyes of those persons are of the same height of the center of the screen.

The detailed comparison results of mean PSNR, SSIM and MOS is shown in Table 1. we can draw the following conclusion. Our method achieves the highest MOS rating. The PSNR and SSIM value of typical methods is higher, since their loss function is defined as the Euclidean distance between the output and label.

While, perceptual CS concentrates more on the visual effect. Thus, it is helpful for MOS, instead of PSNR and SSIM.

Moreover, we give some examples of color images. In terms of color channels, we measure and recover the RGB channels respectively, and then combine them to a whole color image. The results of perceptual CS with color images are shown in Fig. 5. Of course, we give the comparison with existing methods. We can see obviously from the figure that the visual effect of perceptual CS is quite well.

In terms of hardware implementation, we follow the approach of the existing work proposed in [31] in which sliding window is used to measure the scene. Similarly, we can replace the random Gaussian measurement matrix with the learned pre-defined parameters in the convolution layer of the measurement network. The reconstruction part is not on optical device, so only the measurement part needs to be implemented with the approach above.

5   Conclusion

In this paper, we propose perceptual CS for sensing and recovering structured scene images. The proposed framework managed to recover structure information from CS measurements. Our work is of profound significance, which may open a door towards alternative to semantic sensing and recovery.

Acknowledgements. This work is supported by Natural Science Foundation (NSF) of China (61836008, 61472301, 61632019), and the Foundation for Innovative Research Groups of the National Natural Science Foundation of China (No. 61621005).

References

1. Agustsson, E., Timofte, R.: NTIRE 2017 challenge on single image super-resolution: dataset and study. In: IEEE Conference on Computer Vision and Pattern Recognition (CVPR) Workshops, vol. 3, p. 2 (2017)
2. Baraniuk, R.G.: Compressive sensing [lecture notes]. IEEE Sig. Process. Mag. **24**(4), 118–121 (2007). https://doi.org/10.1109/MSP.2007.4286571
3. Baraniuk, R.G.: More is less: signal processing and the data deluge. Science **331**(6018), 717–719 (2011)
4. Candes, E.J., Tao, T.: Decoding by linear programming. IEEE Trans. Inf. Theory **51**(12), 4203–4215 (2005)
5. Donoho, D.L.: Compressed sensing. IEEE Trans. Inf. Theory **52**(4), 1289–1306 (2006). https://doi.org/10.1109/TIT.2006.871582
6. Du, J., Xie, X., Wang, C., Shi, G., Xu, X., Wang, Y.: Fully convolutional measurement network for compressive sensing image reconstruction. Neurocomputing (2018). https://doi.org/10.1016/j.neucom.2018.04.084
7. Figueiredo, M.A.T., Nowak, R.D., Wright, S.J.: Gradient projection for sparse reconstruction: application to compressed sensing and other inverse problems. IEEE J. Sel. Top. Sig. Process. **1**(4), 586–597 (2008)
8. He, K., Gkioxari, G., Dollar, P., Girshick, R.: Mask R-CNN. In: IEEE International Conference on Computer Vision (ICCV), October 2017

9. Huang, R., Zhang, S., Li, T., He, R.: Beyond face rotation: global and local perception GAN for photorealistic and identity preserving frontal view synthesis. In: IEEE Conference on Computer Vision and Pattern Recognition (CVPR), pp. 2458–2467, July 2017

10. Ilg, E., Mayer, N., Saikia, T., Keuper, M., Dosovitskiy, A., Brox, T.: FlowNet 2.0: evolution of optical flow estimation with deep networks. In: IEEE Conference on Computer Vision and Pattern Recognition (CVPR), July 2017

11. Isola, P., Zhu, J.Y., Zhou, T., Efros, A.A.: Image-to-image translation with conditional adversarial networks. In: IEEE Conference on Computer Vision and Pattern Recognition (CVPR), July 2017

12. Jia, Y., et al.: Caffe: convolutional architecture for fast feature embedding. In: Proceedings of the 22nd ACM International Conference on Multimedia, MM 2014, pp. 675–678. ACM, New York (2014). https://doi.org/10.1145/2647868.2654889

13. Johnson, J., Alahi, A., Fei-Fei, L.: Perceptual losses for real-time style transfer and super-resolution. In: Leibe, B., Matas, J., Sebe, N., Welling, M. (eds.) ECCV 2016. LNCS, vol. 9906, pp. 694–711. Springer, Cham (2016). https://doi.org/10.1007/978-3-319-46475-6_43

14. Kulkarni, K., Lohit, S., Turaga, P., Kerviche, R., Ashok, A.: ReconNet: non-iterative reconstruction of images from compressively sensed measurements. In: IEEE Conference on Computer Vision and Pattern Recognition (CVPR), pp. 449–458, June 2016

15. Kunis, S., Rauhut, H.: Random sampling of sparse trigonometric polynomials, II. Orthogonal matching pursuit versus basis pursuit. Found. Comput. Math. **8**(6), 737–763 (2008)

16. Ledig, C., et al.: Photo-realistic single image super-resolution using a generative adversarial network. In: IEEE Conference on Computer Vision and Pattern Recognition (CVPR), July 2017

17. Lefkimmiatis, S.: Non-local color image denoising with convolutional neural networks. In: 2017 IEEE Conference on Computer Vision and Pattern Recognition (CVPR), pp. 5882–5891. IEEE (2017)

18. Lohit, S., Kulkarni, K., Kerviche, R., Turaga, P., Ashok, A.: Convolutional neural networks for non-iterative reconstruction of compressively sensed images. IEEE Trans. Comput. Imaging **4**(3), 326–340 (2018)

19. Lu, J., Yang, J., Batra, D., Parikh, D.: Neural baby talk. In: Proceedings of the IEEE Conference on Computer Vision and Pattern Recognition, pp. 7219–7228 (2018)

20. Lucas, A., Iliadis, M., Molina, R., Katsaggelos, A.K.: Using deep neural networks for inverse problems in imaging: beyond analytical methods. IEEE Sig. Process. Mag. **35**(1), 20–36 (2018). https://doi.org/10.1109/MSP.2017.2760358

21. Luo, W., Sun, P., Zhong, F., Liu, W., Zhang, T., Wang, Y.: End-to-end active object tracking via reinforcement learning. In: Dy, J., Krause, A. (eds.) Proceedings of the 35th International Conference on Machine Learning. Proceedings of Machine Learning Research, PMLR, stockholmsmässan, Stockholm, Sweden, 10–15 July 2018, vol. 80, pp. 3286–3295 (2018)

22. McCann, M.T., Jin, K.H., Unser, M.: Convolutional neural networks for inverse problems in imaging: a review. IEEE Sig. Process. Mag. **34**(6), 85–95 (2017). https://doi.org/10.1109/MSP.2017.2739299

23. Mousavi, A., Dasarathy, G., Baraniuk, R.G.: DeepCodec: adaptive sensing and recovery via deep convolutional neural networks. In: 2017 55th Annual Allerton Conference on Communication, Control, and Computing (Allerton), p. 744, October 2017. https://doi.org/10.1109/ALLERTON.2017.8262812

24. Mousavi, A., Baraniuk, R.G.: Learning to invert: signal recovery via deep convolutional networks. In: IEEE International Conference on Acoustics, Speech and Signal Processing, pp. 2272–2276 (2017)

25. Mousavi, A., Patel, A.B., Baraniuk, R.G.: A deep learning approach to structured signal recovery. In: Communication, Control, and Computing, pp. 1336–1343 (2016)

26. Rahmani, H., Mian, A., Shah, M.: Learning a deep model for human action recognition from novel viewpoints. IEEE Trans. Pattern Anal. Mach. Intell. **40**(3), 667–681 (2018). https://doi.org/10.1109/TPAMI.2017.2691768

27. Ranjan, R., et al.: Deep learning for understanding faces: machines may be just as good, or better, than humans. IEEE Sig. Process. Mag. **35**(1), 66–83 (2018). https://doi.org/10.1109/MSP.2017.2764116

28. ITU-R Recommendatios: Recommendation 500-10; methodology for the subjective assessment of the quality of television pictures. ITU-R Rec. BT. 500-10 (2000)

29. Redmon, J., Farhadi, A.: YOLOv3: an incremental improvement. arXiv preprint arXiv:1804.02767 (2018)

30. Shen, W., Liu, R.: Learning residual images for face attribute manipulation. In: IEEE Conference on Computer Vision and Pattern Recognition (CVPR), pp. 1225–1233, July 2017

31. Shi, G., Gao, D., Song, X., Xie, X., Chen, X., Liu, D.: High-resolution imaging via moving random exposure and its simulation. IEEE Trans. Image Process. **20**(1), 276–282 (2011). https://doi.org/10.1109/TIP.2010.2052271

32. Simonyan, K., Zisserman, A.: Very deep convolutional networks for large-scale image recognition. arXiv preprint arXiv:1409.1556 (2014)

33. Sun, J., Li, H., Xu, Z., et al.: Deep ADMM-Net for compressive sensing MRI. In: Advances in Neural Information Processing Systems, pp. 10–18 (2016)

34. Tropp, J.A., Gilbert, A.C.: Signal recovery from random measurements via orthogonal matching pursuit. IEEE Trans. Inf. Theory **53**(12), 4655–4666 (2007)

35. Xie, X., Du, J., Shi, G., Hu, H., Li, W.: An improved approach for visualizing dynamic vision sensor and its video denoising. In: Proceedings of the International Conference on Video and Image Processing, ICVIP 2017, pp. 176–180. ACM, New York (2017). https://doi.org/10.1145/3177404.3177411

36. Xie, X., Wang, Y., Shi, G., Wang, C., Du, J., Han, X.: Adaptive measurement network for CS image reconstruction. In: Yang, J., et al. (eds.) CCCV 2017. CCIS, vol. 772, pp. 407–417. Springer, Singapore (2017). https://doi.org/10.1007/978-981-10-7302-1_34

37. Yao, H., Dai, F., Zhang, D., Ma, Y., Zhang, S., Zhang, Y.: DR^2-net: deep residual reconstruction network for image compressive sensing. arXiv preprint arXiv:1702.05743 (2017)

38. Yeh, R.A., Chen, C., Lim, T.Y., Schwing, A.G., Hasegawa-Johnson, M., Do, M.N.: Semantic image inpainting with deep generative models. In: IEEE Conference on Computer Vision and Pattern Recognition (CVPR), pp. 6882–6890, July 2017

39. Zhang, J., Ghanem, B.: ISTA-Net: interpretable optimization-inspired deep network for image compressive sensing. In: Proceedings of the IEEE Conference on Computer Vision and Pattern Recognition, pp. 1828–1837 (2018)

Differential and Integral Invariants Under Möbius Transformation

He Zhang[1,2(✉)], Hanlin Mo[1,2], You Hao[1,2], Qi Li[1,2], and Hua Li[1,2]

[1] Key Laboratory of Intelligent Information Processing,
Institute of Computing Technology, Chinese Academy of Sciences, Beijing, China
zhanghe@ict.ac.cn
[2] University of Chinese Academy of Sciences, Beijing, China

Abstract. One of the most challenging problems in the domain of 2-D image or 3-D shape is to handle the non-rigid deformation. From the perspective of transformation groups, the conformal transformation is a key part of the diffeomorphism. According to the Liouville Theorem, an important part of the conformal transformation is the Möbius transformation, so we focus on Möbius transformation and propose two differential expressions that are invariable under 2-D and 3-D Möbius transformation respectively. Next, we analyze the absoluteness and relativity of invariance on them and their components. After that, we propose integral invariants under Möbius transformation based on the two differential expressions. Finally, we propose a conjecture about the structure of differential invariants under conformal transformation according to our observation on the composition of above two differential invariants.

Keywords: Conformal transformation · Möbius transformation
Differential invariant · Integral invariant

1   Introduction

One of the most challenging problems in the domain of 2-D image or 3-D shape is to handle the non-rigid deformation, especially in the situation of anisotropy, which is universal in the real world. In the viewpoint of transformation groups, the isometric transformation is a prop subgroup of the conformal transformation, which is a prop subgroup of the diffeomorphism. Obviously, the anisotropic non-rigid transformation exceeds the boundary of isometric transformation and contains conformal transformation. Based on the Erlangen program of Klein, geometry is a discipline that studies the properties of space that remain unchanged under a particular group of transformation. In order to solve the anisotropic transformation problem, it is necessary to find the invariants under the conformal transformation.

The original motivation of conformal mapping is how to flatten the map of globe, and the Mercator projection produce an angle-preserving map that is very useful for navigation. More generally, the conformal geometry focuses on

© Springer Nature Switzerland AG 2018
J.-H. Lai et al. (Eds.): PRCV 2018, LNCS 11258, pp. 280–291, 2018.
https://doi.org/10.1007/978-3-030-03338-5_24

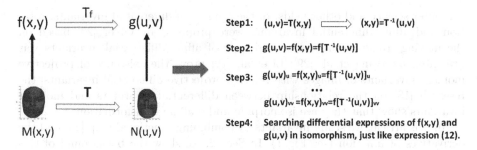

Fig. 1. A brief flowchart of the method.

the shape in which the only measure is angle instead of usually length. The descriptions of conformal mapping contain angle preservation [5,12,26], metric rescaling [21,27], preservation of circles [14,28], etc. Some key ideas reside in the conformal surface geometry are Dirac equation [6], Cauchy-Riemann equation [22], Möbius transformations [27,28], Riemann mapping [9,10,33,35], Ricci flow [34], etc. The conformal geometry lies between the topology geometry and the Riemannian geometry, it studies the invariants of the conformal transformation group. The *conformal structures* [9,10] based on the theories of Riemann surfaces are invariants under conformal transformation. According to conformal geometry [7], the *shape factor* [10] and *conformal module* [35] are conformal invariants. Moreover, the *conformal inner product* [26] defined by an inner product of function is also changeless under conformal transformation. According to the Liouville Theorem [8,20], the Möbius transformation plays an important role in conformal mapping.

The definition of Möbius transformation [25] shows that it is compounded by a series of simple transformations: Translation, Stretching, Rotation, Reflection and Inversion. In the domain of invariants under translation, stretching and rotation transformations, the Geometric moment invariants (GMIs) [32] and the ShapeDNA [17] show a general method to generate the moment invariants; Hu et al. [13] proposed a general construction method of surface isometric moment invariants based on the intrinsic metric. In the domain of invariants under reflection transformation, the chiral invariants [36] show the moment invariants based on the generating functions of ShapeDNA [17]. In the domain of invariants under conformal transformation, Hu [12] proposed limited conformal invariants based on geodesic tangent vectors. In the domain of invariants under Möbius transformation, the expression $(H^2 - K)dA$ proposed by Blaschke [1] is proved to be a conformal invariant by Chen [4]; based on the *Gauss-Bonnet* Theorem, White [30] proposed that $\int_M H^2 dA$ is a global conformal invariant if M is an oriented and closed surface. The *Gauss-Bonnet* Theorem associates the differential expression (Gaussian curvature) of the surface S with its topological invariant $\chi(S)$ (the Euler's characteristic). This great theorem motivates us to explore the differential invariants under the Möbius transformation since the differential expressions play essential roles in some procedures of physics, mathematics, computer science and other fields. In the domain of differential invariants, rotation and affine differential invariants were proposed by Olver [23] based on the moving frame method; a special type of affine differential invariants was presented by Wang et al. [29]; Li et al. [19] prove the existence of projective moment invariants of images with relative projective differential invariants; the research [18] on the relationship between differential invariants and moment invariants show that they are isomorphic under affine transformation.

In this article, we study invariants by combining functional map [24] and the derivatives of function (see Fig. 1). In Sect. 2, we show the background of this paper. In Sect. 3, we propose the invariants under Möbius transformation. In Sect. 4, we show another Möbius invariant from the functional view. Finally, we propose a conjecture about the structure of differential invariants under conformal transformation. The main contributions of this paper are as follows.

- We propose two differential expressions that are invariant under 2-D and 3-D Möbius transformation respectively. According to the Liouville Theorem, the 3-D differential invariant is a conformal invariant.
- Based on the analysis on absoluteness and relativity of invariance about the two differential expressions and their components, we propose integral invariants under Möbius transformation.
- We propose a conjecture about the composition of differential invariants under conformal transformation.

2   Notion and Background

2.1   Notion

The formulation in this paper is same with the functional maps framwork [24]. Assuming M and N are two manifolds, a bijective mapping $T : M \to N$ induces the transformation $T_F : \mathcal{F}(M, \mathbb{R}) \to \mathcal{F}(N, \mathbb{R})$ of derived quantities, where $\mathcal{F}(\cdot, \mathbb{R})$ is scalar function defined on manifold. It means that any function $f : M \to \mathbb{R}$ have a counterpart function $g : N \to \mathbb{R}$ and $g = f \circ T^{-1}$.

To make the invariants under Möbius transformation clear, we partially modify original definition and theorem in this paper with this formulation.

2.2   Theoretic Background

According to the Liouville Theorem [20], the only conformal mapping in $R^n (n > 2)$ are Möbius transformation [11,15,25]. Furthermore, the Generalized Liouville Theorem shows that any conformal mapping defined on $D(D \in \overline{\mathbb{R}}^n, n > 2)$ must be a restriction of Möbius transformation.

Theorem 1 (Generalized Liouville Theorem [8]). *Suppose that D, D' are domains in $\overline{\mathbb{R}}^n$ and that $T : D \to D'$ is a homeomorphism. If $n = 2$, then T is 1-quasiconformal if and only if T or its complex conjugate is a meromorphic function of a complex variable in D. If $n \geq 3$, then T is 1-quasiconformal if and only if T is the restriction to D of a Möbius transformation, i.e., the composition of a finite number of reflections in $(n - 1)$-spheres and planes.*

Next, we will show the common expressions of Möbius transformation in different dimensions $(n \geq 2)$.

In the filed of complex analysis, a Möbius transformation could be expressed as

$$T(z) = \frac{az + b}{cz + d}, \tag{1}$$

where $a, b, c, d, z \in \mathbb{C}$, $ad - bc \neq 0$. Based on the Liouville Theorem [20], every Möbius transformation in higher dimensions could be given with the form

$$T(x) = b + \frac{\gamma A(x - a)}{\| x - a \|_2^\epsilon}, \tag{2}$$

where $x, a, b \in \mathbb{R}^n$, ϵ is 0 or 2, $\gamma \in \mathbb{R}$ and $A \in \mathbb{R}_{n \times n}$ is an orthogonal matrix. The choice of ϵ decides if $T(x)$ contains inversion transformation, and the sign of $det(A)$ decides if $T(x)$ contains reflection transformation.

More generally, a Möbius transformation could be composed of a series of simple transformations (Fig. 2), the definition of Möbius transformation is as below.

Original Data   Reflection   Stretching   Rotation   Inversion

Fig. 2. Some elementary transformations of Möbius transformation.

Definition 1 (Möbius transformation [25]). *A n-dimension Möbius transformation is a homomorphism of $\overline{\mathbb{R}}^n$ (the one-point compactification of $\mathbb{R}^n$), it is a mapping $T : \overline{\mathbb{R}}^n \to \overline{\mathbb{R}}^n$ that is a finite composition of the following elementary transformations ($x \in \mathbb{R}^n$):*

(1) Translation: $T_a(x) = x + a$, $a \in \mathbb{R}^n$.
(2) Stretching: $S_s(x) = sx$, $s \in \mathbb{R}$ and $s > 0$.
(3) Rotation: $Rot_R(x) = Rx$, $R \in \mathbb{R}_{n \times n}$ and R is an orthogonal matrix.
(4) Reflection about plane $P(a, t)$: $Ref_{a,t}(x) = x - 2(a^T x - t)a$, $a \in \mathbb{R}^n$ is the normal vector of $P(a, t)$, $t \in \mathbb{R}$ is the distance from the origin to $P(a, t)$.
(5) Inversion about sphere $S^{n-1}(a, r)$: $I_{a,r}(x) = a + \dfrac{r^2(x - a)}{\| x - a \|_2^2}$, $a \in \mathbb{R}^n$ is the inversion center, r is the inversion radius.

3 Möbius Invariants

3.1 Inversion Invariants

In order to derive the differential invariant under inversion transformation $I_{a,r}$, in the 2-D situation we assume that the $T_{I_{a,r}}$ map the function $f(x,y)$ on domain $D \subset \overline{\mathbb{R}}^n$ to $g(u,v)$ on domain $D' \subset \overline{\mathbb{R}}^n$, where $(u,v) = I_{a,r}(x,y)$ and $g(u,v) = f(x,y)$, this means that the coordinates transformations under $I_{a,r}$ are as follows.

$$u = a_x + \frac{r^2(x - a_x)}{(x - a_x)^2 + (y - a_y)^2} \tag{3}$$

$$v = a_y + \frac{r^2(y - a_y)}{(x - a_x)^2 + (y - a_y)^2} \tag{4}$$

At the same time, it means that the coordinates transformations under $I_{a,r}^{-1}$ are as follows.

$$x = a_x + \frac{r^2(u - a_x)}{(u - a_x)^2 + (v - a_y)^2} \tag{5}$$

$$y = a_y + \frac{r^2(v - a_y)}{(u - a_x)^2 + (v - a_y)^2} \tag{6}$$

Based on $g(u,v) = f(x,y)$ and the Eqs. (5) and (6), we obtain the relationships between the partial derivatives of $g(u,v)$ and $f(x,y)$ as follows.

$$g_u = f_x x_u + f_y y_u \tag{7}$$

$$g_v = f_x x_v + f_y y_v \tag{8}$$

$$g_{uu} = (f_{xx}x_u + f_{xy}y_u)x_u + f_x x_{uu} + (f_{yx}x_u + f_{yy}y_u)y_u + f_y y_{uu} \tag{9}$$

$$g_{uv} = (f_{xx}x_v + f_{xy}y_v)x_u + f_x x_{uv} + (f_{yx}x_v + f_{yy}y_v)y_u + f_y y_{uv} \tag{10}$$

$$g_{vv} = (f_{xx}x_v + f_{xy}y_v)x_v + f_x x_{vv} + (f_{yx}x_v + f_{yy}y_v)y_v + f_y y_{vv} \tag{11}$$

Then we obtain a 2-D equation under the inversion transformation, it is

$$\frac{g_{uu} + g_{vv}}{g_u^2 + g_v^2} = \frac{f_{xx} + f_{yy}}{f_x^2 + f_y^2} \tag{12}$$

This means that

$$\frac{f_{xx} + f_{yy}}{f_x^2 + f_y^2} \tag{13}$$

is a differential invariant under inversion transformation. We use the same method in 3-D situation and obtain a differential invariant under the inversion transformation, it is

$$\frac{f_A + f_B}{(f_x^2 + f_y^2 + f_z^2)^2} \tag{14}$$

where

$$f_A = (f_{xx} + fyy + fzz)(f_x^2 + f_y^2 + f_z^2)$$
$$f_B = f_x^2 f_{xx} + f_y^2 f_{yy} + f_z^2 f_{zz} + 2f_x f_{xy} f_y + 2f_x f_{xz} f_z + 2f_y f_{yz} f_z \tag{15}$$

3.2   The Boundary of Invariance

We have shown that (13) and (14) are differential invariants under inversion transformation. It is obvious that they are invariants under translation transformation. We prove that (13) and (14) are also differential invariants under rotation, stretching and reflection transformations (see Appendix A[1] for a proof). According to the definition of Möbius transformation, we conclude that the differential expression (13) is a differential invariant under 2-D Möbius transformation. Furthermore, with the Generalized Liouville Theorem we obtain that (14) is a conformal invariant.

3.3   Absoluteness and Relativity of Invariance

If expression Inv_T is an invariant under transformation T, the transformed expression Inv_T' satisfies

$$Inv_T' = W_T \cdot Inv_T \tag{16}$$

where W_T is an expression related to T. In this context, Inv_T is an absolute invariant if $W_T \equiv 1$, otherwise, Inv_T is a relative invariant. Base on the analysis in 3.2, (13) is an absolute invariant under Möbius transformation and (14) is an absolute invariant under conformal transformation. Next, we will show the numerator and denominator of (13) or (14) are relative invariants.

In the derivation of 2-D inversion invariants, we obtain that $W_{I_{a,r}} = ||J||^{-1}$ for the numerator and denominator of (13), this means

$$g_{uu} + g_{vv} = ||J||^{-1}(f_{xx} + f_{yy}) \tag{17}$$

$$g_u^2 + g_v^2 = ||J||^{-1}(f_x^2 + f_y^2) \tag{18}$$

where $|J|$ is the determinant of Jacobian matrix of transformation $I_{a,r}$, $||J||$ is the absolute valve of $|J|$. In 3-D situation, we obtain $W_{I_{a,r}} = ||J||^{-\frac{4}{3}}$ for the numerator and denominator of (14). In the stretching transformation, we obtain $W_S = ||J||^{-1}$ in 2-D situation, and $W_S = ||J||^{-\frac{4}{3}}$ in 3-D situation. We also obtain that $W_T = 1$ for the numerator and denominator of (13) or (14) under translation, rotation and reflection transformations.

The result of absoluteness and relativity of invariance on (13) and (14) is shown in Table 1.

3.4   Multiscale and Quantity

Assuming $f(x, y)$ is a regular parameter surface S defined on D, if T_F transform $f(x, y)$ defined on D to $g(u, v)$ defined on D' and $g(u, v) = f(x, y)$, based on the change of variable theorem [16] for multiple integrals and Table 1 we obtain that

$$\iint_{D'} (g_{uu} + g_{vv})dudv = \iint_D W_T(f_{xx} + f_{yy})||J_T||dxdy = \iint_D (f_{xx} + f_{yy})dxdy \tag{19}$$

---

[1] https://github.com/duduhe/Differential-and-integral-invariants-under-Mobius-transformation/blob/master/Appendix.pdf.

Table 1. The form of W_T under transformations

Expression	Translation	Stretching	Rotation	Reflection	Inversion
(13) and (14)	1	1	1	1	1
Num[a]/den of (13)	1	$\|\|J\|\|^{-1}$	1	1	$\|\|J\|\|^{-1}$
Num/den[b] of (14)	1	$\|\|J\|\|^{-\frac{4}{3}}$	1	1	$\|\|J\|\|^{-\frac{4}{3}}$

[a]Num means the numerator of fraction.
[b]Den means the denominator of fraction.

$$\iint_{D'} (g_u^2 + g_v^2)dudv = \iint_D W_T(f_x^2 + f_y^2)\|\|J_T\|\|dxdy = \iint_D (f_x^2 + f_y^2)dxdy \quad (20)$$

where $\|\|J_T\|\|$ is the area extension factor, so we obtain that

$$\iint_D (f_{xx} + f_{yy})dxdy \quad (21)$$

$$\iint_D (f_x^2 + f_y^2)dxdy \quad (22)$$

are integral invariants under 2-D Möbius transformation. In the same way, we obtain that

$$\iiint_D (f_x^2 + f_y^2 + f_z^2)^{\frac{3}{2}}dxdydz \quad (23)$$

$$\iiint_D (f_A + f_B)^{\frac{3}{4}}dxdydz \quad (24)$$

are integral invariants under 3-D conformal transformation.

Actually a differential expression Inv_T of function f defined on domain D_f accurately characterize f at point of D_f, it provides extremely wide space to describe the function f.

Multiscale of Invariants. Assuming $F_i(Inv_T)$ is a function of Inv_T, a general method to construct descriptors in different scale is the integral of $\int_{D_j} F_i(Inv_f)dA$ on region $D_j(D_j \subset D_f)$ with different size, and when $D_j = D_f$ the result is a global invariant, for example, the Willmore energy $\int(H^2-K)dA$ [1] applied in the theory of surfaces [31], digital geometry processing [2] and other fields.

In this view, the only difference between invariant with specify-scale and global invariant is the definition domain, the construction method of specify-scale invariant is same with global invariant. The former could be elaborately modified by selecting domain of integration in different applications.

Quantity of Invariants. A general method to construct a large number of invariants is using various functions $F_i(Inv_T)$ with these functions are independent of each other [3]. We just show a simple method to construct integral invariants based on differential invariants and integral, in addition, more invariant forms can be constructed with differential invariants. Next, we give a possible form of invariants under Möbius transformation:

$$\iint_D \frac{(f_{xx} + f_{yy})^{n+1}}{(f_x^2 + f_y^2)^n} dx dy \tag{25}$$

$$\iint_D \frac{(f_x^2 + f_y^2)^{n+1}}{(f_{xx} + f_{yy})^n} dx dy \tag{26}$$

$$\iiint_D \frac{(f_A + f_B)^{\frac{3}{4}(n+1)}}{(f_x^2 + f_y^2 + f_z^2)^{\frac{3}{2}n}} dx dy dz \tag{27}$$

$$\iiint_D \frac{(f_x^2 + f_y^2 + f_z^2)^{\frac{3}{2}(n+1)}}{(f_A + f_B)^{\frac{3}{4}n}} dx dy dz \tag{28}$$

if the denominators of (25), (26), (27), (28) are not zero.

3.5   Another Conformal Invariant

The expression $(H^2 - K)dA$ proposed by Biacchke [1] has been proved to be an invariant under Möbius transformation [4, 30]. It differs from our method in two important respects: the domain of transformation and the number of functions participated in invariants (see detailed expression at Appendix B).

4   Conjecture of Conformal Invariants

We have shown that (13) is a Möbius invariant and (14) is a conformal invariant. However, the fascinating part of (13) or (14) is that the differential expressions

$$f_x^2 + f_y^2 \quad or \quad f_x^2 + f_y^2 + f_z^2 \tag{29}$$

$$f_{xx} + f_{yy} \quad or \quad f_{xx} + f_{yy} + f_{zz} \tag{30}$$

$$f_x^2 f_{xx} + f_y^2 f_{yy} + f_z^2 f_{zz} + 2f_x f_{xy} f_y + 2f_x f_{xz} f_z + 2f_y f_{yz} f_z \tag{31}$$

are differential invariants under rigid transformation. Based on this observation and the fact that the differential expressions play important roles in transformation, we have a bold conjecture about the structure of differential invariants under conformal transformation.

Conjecture: The differential invariants under conformal transformation are composed of differential invariants under rigid transformation in a self-consistent manner.

One of the possible self-consistent forms in n-dimensional Euclidean space may be

$$\sum_{i=1}^{n-1} \frac{\prod_{j=1}^{a_i} DRI_j}{(f_{x_1}^2 + f_{x_2}^2 + \cdots + f_{x_n}^2)^{n-1}} \tag{32}$$

where DRI is differential invariant under rigid transformation.

5   Experimental Results

We choose a human face model from TOSCA database and treat the z-coordinate value of vertexes of the triangle mesh as a function f defined on x-coordinate and y-coordinate, i.e. $z = f(x, y)$. With least square method, the coordinates of a vertice and its 1-ring neighbors were used to estimate parameters in Taylor expansion of f at the vertice; in order to guarantee the accuracy of descriptor calculation, we only consider vertexes that are located inside the mesh and have enough 1-ring neighbors. After that, we calculate a descriptor at the vertice and the descriptor is composed by (13), (25) and (26) with different $n(\geq 0)$. Moreover, in integral invariants, the area A_{vert} around a vertex is determined by Mixed Voronoi cell.

We deform the definition domain of f with reflection, stretching, rotation and inversion transformation(Fig. 3). In reflection transformation, $a = (1, 0)$ and $t = 0$; the s in stretching transformation is 2; in rotation transformation the original data is rotated $90°$ counterclockwise; in inversion transformation the inversion center is $(0, 1000)$ and inversion radius is 500 (see more explanation about experiments at Appendix C).

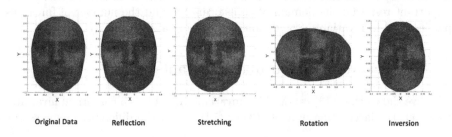

| Original Data | Reflection | Stretching | Rotation | Inversion |

Fig. 3. Elementary transformations of Möbius transformation on human face model.

5.1   Stability of Invariants

In this experiment we choose $n = 0$, 1 and the integral invariants is calculated at the local area of each vertex. After we obtain a 5-dimension descriptor at vertexes of the five mesh in Fig. 3, we calculate the average error of each dimension of the descriptor. In addition, we choose an isometric invariant at the vertex, the Laplacian operator, to compare with above invariants. The average error of each dimension is calculated by the following formula

$$Err = \frac{1}{N} \sum_i \frac{|Inv_{T;i} - Inv_{O;i}|}{|Inv_{T;i}| + |Inv_{O;i}|} \times 100\% \tag{33}$$

where $Inv_{O;i}$ is the value of invariant at vertex i on original data, $Inv_{T;i}$ is the value of invariant at vertex i on deformed data, and N is the total number of vertexes participated in the calculation. The result of this experiment is in Table 2, it shows that (13), (25) and (26) are invariants under Möbius transformations.

Table 2. The average error of Laplacian operator and Möbius invariants.

Expression	Reflection	Stretching	Rotation	Inversion
$f_{xx} + f_{yy}$	0	6.00×10^1	4.82×10^{-13}	8.82×10^1
$\frac{f_{xx}+f_{yy}}{f_x^2+f_y^2}$	0	1.20×10^{-12}	1.33×10^{-12}	1.98×10^{-3}
$\iint_D (f_{xx} + f_{yy})dxdy$	0	4.38×10^{-13}	4.82×10^{-13}	1.69×10^{-1}
$\iint_D (f_x^2 + f_y^2)dxdy$	0	1.21×10^{-12}	1.27×10^{-12}	1.69×10^{-1}
$\iint_D \frac{(f_{xx}+f_{yy})^2}{f_x^2+f_y^2}dxdy$	0	1.24×10^{-12}	1.47×10^{-12}	1.70×10^{-1}
$\iint_D \frac{(f_x^2+f_y^2)^2}{f_{xx}+f_{yy}}dxdy$	0	2.39×10^{-12}	2.58×10^{-12}	1.70×10^{-1}

5.2 Discrimination of Invariants

In this experiment we use the 5-dimension descriptor of vertex at original to match its corresponding vertex in the deformed mesh with nearest neighbor rule, the metric between vertexes is standardized Euclidean distance. The error rate (percentage) of this experiment is in Table 3.

Table 3. The error rate (percentage) of Möbius invariants in vertex matching.

Reflection	Stretching	Rotation	Inversion
0	0	0	0.87

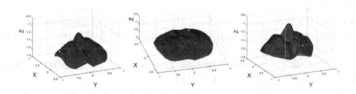

Fig. 4. Some situations where vertex matching fails.

In conformal deformation scenario, this experiment shows the potential of Möbius invariants in matching task. Figure 4 shows some matching-fail situations, where the white point is the real position and the red point is the matching vertex. The reason for most matching failures is that the original white vertex and deformed red vertex have similar functional distribution environments.

6   Conclusions

In this article, we propose two differential invariants under 2-D and 3-D Möbius transformation respectively, in particular, the 3-D expression is a conformal invariant according to the Liouville Theorem. After that, we analyze the absoluteness and relativity of invariance on the two expressions and their components, and we show an integral construction method that targets to the multiscale and quantity of invariant, the experimental results show that the invariants proposed in this paper perform well. Furthermore, we show another Möbius invariant from the functional view. Finally, we propose a conjecture about the structure of differential invariants under conformal transformation.

This article shows a method of combining functional map and derivatives of function to study conformal invariant, more research about the differential invariants under conformal transformation is necessary in the future. In addition to practical application solutions based on Möbius invariants, questing the generative structure of conformal differential invariant is also an interesting topic.

Acknowledgment. The authors would like to thank Dr. Antti Rrasila of Aalto University for providing help on how to distinguish Möbius invariants and conformal invariants.

This work was partly funded by National Key R&D Program of China (No. 2017YFB1002703) and National Natural Science Foundation of China (Grant No. 60873164, 61227802 and 61379082).

References

1. Biaschke, W.: Vorlesungen über differentialgeometrie iii (1929)
2. Bobenko, A.I., Schröder, P.: Discrete Willmore flow (2005)
3. Brown, A.B.: Functional dependence. Trans. Am. Math. Soc. **38**(2), 379–394 (1935)
4. Chen, B.Y.: An invariant of conformal mappings. Proc. Am. Math. Soc. **40**(2), 563–564 (1973)
5. Corman, E., Solomon, J., Ben-Chen, M., Guibas, L., Ovsjanikov, M.: Functional characterization of intrinsic and extrinsic geometry. ACM Trans. Graph. (TOG) **36**(2), 14 (2017)
6. Crane, K., Pinkall, U., Schröder, P.: Spin transformations of discrete surfaces. ACM Trans. Graph. (TOG) **30**(4), 104 (2011)
7. Farkas, H.M., Kra, I.: Riemann surfaces. In: Farkas, H.M., Kra, I. (eds.) Riemann Surfaces. GTM, vol. 71, pp. 9–31. Springer, New York (1992). https://doi.org/10.1007/978-1-4612-2034-3_2
8. Gehring, F.W.: Topics in quasiconformal mappings. In: Vuorinen, M. (ed.) Quasiconformal Space Mappings. LNM, vol. 1508, pp. 20–38. Springer, Heidelberg (1992). https://doi.org/10.1007/BFb0094236
9. Gu, X., Wang, Y., Yau, S.T.: Computing conformal invariants: period matrices. Commun. Inf. Syst. **3**(3), 153–170 (2003)
10. Gu, X., Yau, S.T.: Surface classification using conformal structures, p. 701. IEEE (2003)
11. Haantjes, J.: Conformal representation of an N-dimensional euclidean space with a non-definite fundamental form on itself (1937)
12. Hu, P.: A class of isometric invariants and their applications (in Chinese). Ph.D. thesis, Institute of Computing Technology, Chinese Academy of Sciences, May 2011
13. Hu, P., Li, H., Lin, Z.: A construction method for surface isometric invariants. J. Syst. Sci. Math. Sci. **9**, 006 (2009)

14. Kharevych, L., Springborn, B., Schröder, P.: Discrete conformal mappings via circle patterns. ACM Trans. Graph. (TOG) **25**(2), 412–438 (2006)
15. Kühnel, W., Rademacher, H.B.: Liouville's theorem in conformal geometry. J. de mathématiques pures et appliquées **88**(3), 251–260 (2007)
16. Lax, P.D.: Change of variables in multiple integrals. Am. Math. Mon. **106**(6), 497–501 (1999)
17. Li, E., Huang, Y., Xu, D., Li, H.: Shape DNA: basic generating functions for geometric moment invariants. arXiv preprint arXiv:1703.02242 (2017)
18. Li, E., Li, H.: Isomorphism between differential and moment invariants under affine transform. arXiv preprint arXiv:1705.08264 (2017)
19. Li, E., Mo, H., Xu, D., Li, H.: Image projective invariants. IEEE Trans. Pattern Anal. Mach. Intell., 1 (2018). https://ieeexplore.ieee.org/document/8353142
20. Liouville, J.: Extension au cas des trois dimensions de la question du tracé géographique. Applications de l'analyse à la géométrie, pp. 609–617 (1850)
21. Luo, F.: Combinatorial Yamabe flow on surfaces. Commun. Contemp. Math. **6**(05), 765–780 (2004)
22. Mullen, P., Tong, Y., Alliez, P., Desbrun, M.: Spectral conformal parameterization. Comput. Graph. Forum **27**(5), 1487–1494 (2008)
23. Olver, P.J.: Equivalence, Invariants and Symmetry. Cambridge University Press, Cambridge (1995)
24. Ovsjanikov, M., Ben-Chen, M., Solomon, J., Butscher, A., Guibas, L.: Functional maps: a flexible representation of maps between shapes. ACM Trans. Graph. (TOG) **31**(4), 30 (2012)
25. Rasila, A.: Introduction to quasiconformal mappings in n-space. In: Proceedings of the International Workshop on Quasiconformal (2006)
26. Rustamov, R.M., Ovsjanikov, M., Azencot, O., Ben-Chen, M., Chazal, F., Guibas, L.: Map-based exploration of intrinsic shape differences and variability. ACM Trans. Graph. (TOG) **32**(4), 72 (2013)
27. Springborn, B., Schröder, P., Pinkall, U.: Conformal equivalence of triangle meshes. ACM Trans. Graph. (TOG) **27**(3), 77 (2008)
28. Vaxman, A., Müller, C., Weber, O.: Conformal mesh deformations with möbius transformations. ACM Trans. Graph. (TOG) **34**(4), 55 (2015)
29. Wang, Y., Wang, X., Zhang, B.: Affine differential invariants of functions on the plane. J. Appl. Math. **2013** (2013). https://www.hindawi.com/journals/jam/2013/868725/cta/
30. White, J.H.: A global invariant of conformal mappings in space. Proc. Am. Math. Soc. **38**(1), 162–164 (1973)
31. Willmore, T.J.: Surfaces in conformal geometry. Ann. Glob. Anal. Geom. **18**(3–4), 255–264 (2000)
32. Xu, D., Li, H.: Geometric moment invariants. Pattern Recogn. **41**(1), 240–249 (2008)
33. Xu, J., Kang, H., Chen, F.: Content-aware image resizing using quasi-conformal mapping. Vis. Comput. **34**(3), 431–442 (2018)
34. Yu, X., Lei, N., Wang, Y., Gu, X.: Intrinsic 3D dynamic surface tracking based on dynamic Ricci flow and teichmüller map. In: Proceedings of the IEEE International Conference on Computer Vision, vol. 2017, pp. 5400–5408 (2017)
35. Zeng, W., Gu, X.D.: Registration for 3D surfaces with large deformations using quasi-conformal curvature flow. In: Computer Vision and Pattern Recognition (CVPR) (2011)
36. Zhang, H., Mo, H., Hao, Y., Li, S., Li, H.: Fast and efficient calculations of structural invariants of chirality. arXiv preprint arXiv:1711.05866 (2017)

Automatic Classifier Selection Based on Classification Complexity

Liping Deng[1], Wen-Sheng Chen[1,2], and Binbin Pan[1,2(✉)]

[1] College of Mathematics and Statistics, Shenzhen University, Shenzhen 518060,
People's Republic of China
{chenws,pbb}@szu.edu.cn
[2] Guangdong Key Laboratory of Media Security, Shenzhen University,
Shenzhen 518060, People's Republic of China

Abstract. Choosing a proper classifier for one specific data set is important in practical application. Automatic classifier selection (CS) aims to recommend the most suitable classifiers to a new data set based on the similarity with the historical data sets. The key step of CS is the extraction of data set feature. This paper proposes a novel data set feature that characterizes the classification complexity of problems, which has a close connection with the performance of classifiers. We highlight two contributions of our work: firstly, our feature can be computed in a low time complexity; secondly, we theoretically show that our feature has connection with generalization errors of some classifiers. Empirical results indicate that our feature is more effective and efficient than the existing data set features.

Keywords: Automatic classifier selection · Data set feature
Data set similarity

1 Introduction

Classification is one of the most important tasks in machine learning. A great number of classifiers were putted forward in recent decades to tackle various kinds of classification problems arose in real world, such as support vector machine, decision tree, AdaBoost, artificial neural networks, and so on. Does there exist a classifier that significantly performs better than any other classifiers on most of data sets? Some literatures have done in-depth investigations on this problem. The No Free Lunch Theorem [1] tells us that there does not exist such classifier. If classifier $\mathcal{A}_1$ outperforms $\mathcal{A}_2$ on some data sets, then there must exist as many other data sets on which $\mathcal{A}_2$ outperforms $\mathcal{A}_1$. In [2], authors analyzed the performances of three classifiers on some data sets and they did not observe which classifier is significantly better than the others. Furthermore, [3] conducted classification experiments using 179 classifiers and 121 data sets and showed that there is no optimal classifier. These results indicate that classifiers have preference on different types of data sets. Therefore, which classifier(s) would be selected for a given classification problem?

© Springer Nature Switzerland AG 2018
J.-H. Lai et al. (Eds.): PRCV 2018, LNCS 11258, pp. 292–303, 2018.
https://doi.org/10.1007/978-3-030-03338-5_25

One idea is to use cross validation for all possible classifiers to find the best classifier. However, this procedure is time-consuming. An efficient alternative approach is automatic classifier selection based on data set similarity [4–7,10], or classifier selection (CS) for short. We believe that the performances of classifiers on similar data sets should be close. Since different data sets may vary in sample size, dimensions, classes and attributes, how to measure the similarity between data sets is a critical step of CS. The common method is to extract data set feature by designing a feature extraction function (or called meta-learning) and then compute the similarity between these features. There is an intrinsic relationship between classifier performance and data set feature [9]. Therefore, the recommendation heavily depends on the effectiveness of data set feature. Furthermore, the feature should be calculated in a low time complexity, which is a bottleneck of CS.

A number of data set features have proposed. These features are extracted from different aspects of a data set: (i) statistics and information theory (SI) [7,10]; (ii) model structure (MS) [5]; (iii) problem complexity (PC) [4]; (iv) landmarking (LM) [6]. Especially, PC and LM characterize the classification complexity of problems (we call it *complexity*) using a set of geometrical metrics or basic classifiers. The complexity is expected to highly correlate to the performances of classifiers [11]. In other words, the performances of classifiers on data sets that have similar complexity should be close. Therefore, complexity plays a vital role in CS. However, the data set features extracted by PC and LM have two shortages: (i) time-consuming; (ii) no theoretical connection with performances of classifiers. It is observed that PC and LM did not perform well in some literatures [5,7], which means that they cannot characterize the complexity accurately.

To remedy the aforementioned shortcomings of PC and LM, this paper uses a set of geometrical and statistical metrics to describe the complexity of two-class data set, then these metrics are united as data set feature. We use KNN classifier as recommendation algorithm for CS. For multi-class classification problem, we split the problem into two-class problems using one-vs-one strategy. Compared with PC and LM, our work has improvements in two aspects: computation efficiency and theoretical guarantee. Empirical results demonstrate the effectiveness and efficiency of our method.

The rest of the paper is structured as follows. We briefly introduce the related works in Sect. 2. Section 3 presents our data set feature. The classifier selection algorithm is given in Sect. 4. Empirical investigations are discussed in Sect. 5 and conclusions are drew in Sect. 6.

2   Related Work

The key problem of CS is feature extraction. To the best of our knowledge, there are four kinds of features.

Statistical Feature: This feature can be categorized into two kinds. The first kind describes the data set using a group of statistical and information theory characteristics [10]. The second kind is based on summary statistics. Song [7] characterizes the data set structure by computing the frequencies of itemsets generated from binary data sets. Non-binary data set needs to be transformed to binary data set, which would be time-consuming when the attributes of data set are continuous.

Problem Complexity Feature: Twelve measures are designed to describe the geometrical complexity of decision boundary of two-class problems [11]. Cano [12] claimed that some of the measures have little connection with the performances of classifiers. Bernado [4] selected six measures to characterize data set.

Landmarking Feature: This feature [6] utilizes the performances of a set of basic classifiers (called *landmarkers*) to describe the data set. Therefore, the similar features indicate that data sets may belong to the subspace of the same performance. The chosen landmarkers must be significantly different.

Model Structure Feature: The statistical information of a model generated from data set is collected as feature. In this category, decision tree is usually considered [5], from which we gather a set of statistics like maximum/minimum number of nodes, length of longest/shortest branches, and so on.

The aforementioned features belong to experimental origin. However, a theoretical investigation would be more persuasive. Furthermore, these features are computationally expensive.

3   Proposed Feature

In this section, we firstly propose several metrics of complexity for CS. Then the theoretical connections between two metrics and generalization errors of some classifiers are investigated. Finally, we present our data set feature and similarity measurement criterion.

3.1   Metrics of Complexity

Given a two-class data set $\mathcal{D} = \{(\mathbf{x}_1, y_1), (\mathbf{x}_2, y_2), \ldots, (\mathbf{x}_n, y_n)\}$ in input space $\mathcal{X}$, where $\mathbf{x}_i$, $i = 1, 2, \cdots, n$ are data points, and y_i is the binary class label, i.e., $y_i \in \{1, -1\}$. Let $\mathbf{y} = [y_1, y_2, \cdots, y_n]^\top$ represents the vector formed with n labels. We use n_- and n_+ to represent the amount of samples labeled -1 or 1, respectively. Note that $n_- + n_+ = n$.

For a given kernel function $k(\mathbf{x}, \mathbf{y}) = \langle \phi(\mathbf{x}), \phi(\mathbf{y}) \rangle$, where ϕ is a nonlinear mapping that maps $\mathbf{x} \in \mathcal{X}$ to a reproduce kernel hilbert space (RKHS) $\mathcal{H}$, an $n \times n$ kernel matrix $\mathbf{K}$ is generated from $\mathcal{D}$ as

$$K_{ij} = \langle \phi(\mathbf{x}_i), \phi(\mathbf{x}_j) \rangle, i, j = 1, 2, \cdots, n.$$

$\mathbf{K}$ is a symmetric positive and semi-definite matrix that totally preserves the geometrical structure of $\mathcal{D}$. Our five metrics of complexity are based on $\mathbf{K}$.

Kernel Alignment. This metric, which is known as centered kernel target alignment (KA) [13], is defined as

$$KA(\mathbf{K}_c, \mathbf{yy}^\top) = \frac{\langle \mathbf{K}_c, \mathbf{yy}^\top \rangle_F}{\sqrt{\langle \mathbf{K}_c, \mathbf{K}_c \rangle_F \langle \mathbf{yy}^\top, \mathbf{yy}^\top \rangle_F}}, \tag{1}$$

where $\mathbf{K}_c$ is a centralized kernel matrix of $\mathbf{K}$, $\langle \cdot, \cdot \rangle_F$ denotes Frobenius inner-product and $\mathbf{yy}^\top$ is called the target matrix. $KA \in [0, 1]$ since $\langle \mathbf{K}_c, \mathbf{yy}^\top \rangle_F \geqslant 0$.

The numerator of (1) can be expanded as

$$\langle \mathbf{K}_c, \mathbf{yy}^\top \rangle_F = \mathbf{y}^\top \mathbf{K}_c \mathbf{y} = \sum_{i=1}^{n} \sum_{j=1}^{n} y_i y_j (K_c)_{ij}$$

$$= \sum_{y_i = y_j} (K_c)_{ij} - \sum_{y_i \neq y_j} (K_c)_{ij}.$$

Therefore, KA measures the difference between the within-class and between-class distances of data set. A bigger KA indicates that the corresponding data set is more separable. The most time-consuming calculations of KA are the centralization of $\mathbf{K}$ and $\langle \mathbf{K}_c, \mathbf{K}_c \rangle_F$, which take $O(n^2)$ time complexity.

Kernel Space-Based Separability. The centers of two classes in $\mathcal{H}$ are calculated as

$$\phi_- = \frac{1}{n_-} \sum_{y_i = -1} \phi(\mathbf{x}_i),$$

$$\phi_+ = \frac{1}{n_+} \sum_{y_i = 1} \phi(\mathbf{x}_i), \tag{2}$$

respectively. KS [14] is defined as

$$KS(\mathbf{K}, \mathbf{y}) = \frac{std_- + std_+}{\|\phi_- - \phi_+\|_2}, \tag{3}$$

where

$$std_- = \sqrt{\frac{\sum_{y_i = -1} \langle \phi(\mathbf{x}_i) - \phi_-, \mathbf{e} \rangle^2}{n_- - 1}},$$

$$std_+ = \sqrt{\frac{\sum_{y_i = 1} \langle \phi(\mathbf{x}_i) - \phi_+, \mathbf{e} \rangle^2}{n_+ - 1}}, \tag{4}$$

are the standard deviations of two classes projected along the direction $\mathbf{e} = \frac{\phi_- - \phi_+}{\|\phi_- - \phi_+\|_2}$ respectively, and $\|\cdot\|_2$ denotes 2-norm of vector.

KS $\in (0, +\infty]$ actually describes the samples' distribution along direction $\phi_- - \phi_+$. A smaller KS means that the data set is more separable. KS needs $O(n^2)$ time complexity.

Overlap Region. We propose a metric that compute the ratio of the overlapped region of two classes to the total region of two classes along direction $\mathbf{e}$, denoted as ROR. Suppose that the projected data of one class fall into $[a_1, b_1]$, where a_1, b_1 are the minimum and maximum values of the projected data, and the other class falls into $[a_2, b_2]$. Let $U = [a_1, b_1] \cap [a_2, b_2]$ and $V = [a_1, b_1] \cup [a_2, b_2]$ be intersection and union of these two intervals, respectively. ROR is defined as

$$\text{ROR} = \begin{cases} 0, & U = \emptyset, \\ \frac{\max(U) - \min(U)}{\max(V) - \min(V)}, & U \neq \emptyset, \end{cases} \tag{5}$$

where $\min(\cdot)$ and $\max(\cdot)$ are the maximum and minimum values of interval respectively and $\emptyset$ represents empty set. ROR $\in [0, 1]$ since U is a subset of V. When data set is linear separable, ROR is expected to zero. However, ROR will increase if data set is nonlinear separable. ROR also needs $O(n^2)$ time complexity.

Test of Equality of Means. Now we treat kernel matrix $\mathbf{K}$ as a similarity matrix. The following measure depends on the assumption that the similarity among within-class data is higher than between-class data. We first introduce two vectors extracted from $\mathbf{K}$:

$$\begin{aligned} \mathbf{k}_W &= \{K_{ij} | i < j \wedge y_i = y_j\}, \\ \mathbf{k}_B &= \{K_{ij} | i < j \wedge y_i \neq y_j\}. \end{aligned} \tag{6}$$

We denote $n_W = \frac{n_-(n_--1)}{2} + \frac{n_+(n_-+1)}{2}$ and $n_B = n_- n_+$ represent the size of vectors $\mathbf{k}_W$ and $\mathbf{k}_B$ respectively. We see that $\mathbf{k}_W$ is the collection of within-class similarity and $\mathbf{k}_B$ is the collection of between-class similarity.

TEM [15] is defined as a variant of t-test to evaluate the equality of means of $\mathbf{k}_W$ and $\mathbf{k}_B$:

$$\text{TEM}(\mathbf{K}, \mathbf{y}) = \frac{1}{n} \left| \frac{\bar{k}_W - \bar{k}_B}{\sqrt{\frac{\sigma_W^2}{n_W} + \frac{\sigma_B^2}{n_B}}} \right|, \tag{7}$$

where $\bar{k}_W$ and σ_W^2 denote the mean and variance of $\mathbf{k}_W$ respectively, and $\bar{k}_B$ and σ_B^2 denote the mean and variance of $\mathbf{k}_B$ respectively. TEM is very sensitive to the nonlinearity of decision boundary. A larger TEM reflects that the data set is more likely to be linearly separable. Here we normalized TEM by multiplying the reciprocal of n to eliminate the influence of sample size. TEM only utilizes the upper triangle elements of $\mathbf{K}$, which needs $O(n^2)$ time complexity.

Test of Equality of Variances. Let $\mathbf{k}_{WB} = \mathbf{k}_W \cup \mathbf{k}_B$ be the union of $\mathbf{k}_W$ and $\mathbf{k}_B$. We define three new vectors as follows:

$$\begin{aligned} \mathbf{z}_W &= |\mathbf{k}_W - \tilde{\mathbf{k}}_W|, \\ \mathbf{z}_B &= |\mathbf{k}_B - \tilde{\mathbf{k}}_B|, \\ \mathbf{z}_{WB} &= |\mathbf{k}_{WB} - \tilde{\mathbf{k}}_{WB}|, \end{aligned} \tag{8}$$

where $|\cdot|$ represents element-wise absolute value, $\tilde{\mathbf{k}}_W$, $\tilde{\mathbf{k}}_B$ and $\tilde{\mathbf{k}}_{WB}$ are the medians of $\mathbf{k}_W$, $\mathbf{k}_B$ and $\mathbf{k}_{WB}$ respectively. TEV [15] is defined using Brown-Forsythe test to measure the equality of variances of $\mathbf{k}_W$ and $\mathbf{k}_B$,

$$\text{TEV}(\mathbf{K}, \mathbf{y}) = (1 - \frac{2}{n}) \frac{n_W (\bar{z}_W - \bar{z}_{WB})^2 + n_B (\bar{z}_B - \bar{z}_{WB})^2}{\sum_{i=1}^{n_W} [(z_W)_i - \bar{z}_W]^2 + \sum_{i=1}^{n_B} [(z_B)_i - \bar{z}_B]^2}, \quad (9)$$

where $\bar{z}_B$, $\bar{z}_W$ and $\bar{z}_{WB}$ are the mean values of vectors $\mathbf{z}_B$, $\mathbf{z}_W$ and $\mathbf{z}_{WB}$ respectively, $(z_W)_i$ and $(z_B)_i$ represent the ith element of $\mathbf{z}_W$ and $\mathbf{z}_B$. The idea behind TEV is that if $\mathbf{k}_W$ and $\mathbf{k}_B$ have the same variance, then the data set should be difficult to separate. The high value of TEV rejects the hypothesis of equal variance and indicates compact within-class and mutually distant between-class distribution [15]. Here we also normalize TEV by multiplying $1/n$.

Like TEM, TEV also needs $O(n^2)$ time complexity, but TEV needs extra $O(n^2)$ to search the medians.

3.2   Theoretical Analysis

We theoretically investigate the relationship between metrics KA, KS and generalization errors.

Theorem 1. KA *is defined as (1). Let* $R(h) = \Pr[yh < 0]$ *be the error rate of Parzen window predictor*

$$h(\mathbf{x}') = \frac{E_{\mathbf{x}}[y k_c(\mathbf{x}, \mathbf{x}')]}{\sqrt{E[k_c^2]}} \quad (10)$$

in binary classification. k_c *is the centered kernel function and* $E[\cdot]$ *is an expectation operator. Suppose that* $k(\mathbf{x}, \mathbf{x}) \leqslant S^2$ *for all* $\mathbf{x}$. *Then for any* $\delta > 0$, *the following inequality holds with probability at least* $1 - \delta$:

$$R(h) \leqslant 1 - \left(\text{KA}(\mathbf{K_c}, \mathbf{y}\mathbf{y}^\top) - 18\beta \left[\frac{3}{n} + 4\sqrt{\frac{\log \frac{6}{\delta}}{2n}} \right] \right) \cdot \frac{1}{\Gamma}, \quad (11)$$

where $\Gamma = \max_{\mathbf{x}'} \sqrt{\dfrac{E_{\mathbf{x}}[k_c^2(\mathbf{x}', \mathbf{x})]}{E_{\mathbf{x}, \mathbf{x}'}[k_c^2(\mathbf{x}', \mathbf{x})]}}$, $\beta = \max(\dfrac{S^2}{E[k_c^2]}, \dfrac{S^2}{E[k_c'^2]})$ *and* $k'(\mathbf{x}_i, \mathbf{x}_j) = y_i y_j$.

Proof. According to Theorem 12 in [13], we have

$$\text{KA}(k_c, k_c') \geqslant \text{KA}(\mathbf{K_c}, \mathbf{y}\mathbf{y}^\top) - 18\beta \left[\frac{3}{n} + 4\sqrt{\frac{\log \frac{6}{\delta}}{2n}} \right],$$

where $\text{KA}(k_c, k_c') = \dfrac{E[k_c k_c']}{\sqrt{E[k_c^2] E[k_c'^2]}}$. Unifying Theorem 13 in [13]

$$R(h) \leqslant 1 - \text{KA}(k_c, k_c') \cdot \frac{1}{\Gamma},$$

We obtain the inequation (11) directly.

Theorem 2. [14] KS *is defined as (3). There is a separating hyperplane*

$$h(\mathbf{x}) = \mathbf{e} \cdot \phi(\mathbf{x}) - \mathbf{e} \cdot \frac{std_-\phi_+ + std_+\phi_-}{std_- + std_+}, \tag{12}$$

such that the upper bound of training error of data set $\mathcal{D}$ is

$$\mathrm{KSerr} = \frac{\mathrm{KS}(\mathbf{K}, \mathbf{y})^2}{1 + \mathrm{KS}(\mathbf{K}, \mathbf{y})^2}. \tag{13}$$

Theorem 1 tells us that if there is a high KA and Γ is not too large, then the upper bound of generalization error of (10) on $\mathcal{D}$ is small. Theorem 2 indicates if KS is small, then the upper bound of training error of (12) on $\mathcal{D}$ is small, thus we can expect a low generalization error [14].

3.3   Data Set Feature

Based on the above analysis, we define data set feature as follows:

$$\mathbf{v} = [\mathrm{KA}, 1 - \mathrm{KSerr}, 1 - \mathrm{ROR}, \mathrm{TEM}, \mathrm{TEV}]. \tag{14}$$

The computation of $\mathbf{v}$ has a time complexity of $O(n^2)$. KA, KS and ROR mainly focus on the distributions and the degree of overlap of two classes from a geometrical point of view, while statistical tests (TEM, TEV) are used to characterize the nonlinearity of decision boundary. Employing different kernel functions would produce different features. We adopt Euclidean distance as similarity criterion:

$$\rho(\mathcal{D}, \mathcal{D}') := \|\mathbf{v} - \mathbf{v}'\|_2 = \sqrt{\sum_{i=1}^{5}(v_i - v_i')^2}. \tag{15}$$

The smaller $\rho(\mathcal{D}, \mathcal{D}')$ means that the similarity between data sets $\mathcal{D}$ and $\mathcal{D}'$ is higher.

4   Classifier Selection

Suppose that historical data sets $\mathcal{D}_1, \ldots, \mathcal{D}_m$ and testing data set $\mathcal{D}$ are two-class problems. Our CS algorithm is shown in Algorithm 1.

4.1   Recommendation Algorithm

In step 2 of Algorithm 1, we use KNN classifier as $\mathcal{A}_R$, where the data set similarity is the distance between data set features. Assuming $\mathcal{D}_j, j = 1, 2, \cdots, K$ are the K most similar data sets for $\mathcal{D}$, the recommended classifier is selected as: (i) for each $\mathcal{D}_j$, we assign a rank to candidate classifiers according to its performances on this problem. The classifier with the best performance has rank 1, while the classifier with the worst performance has rank m. Classifiers with

---

Algorithm 1. CS for Two-class Problems

Input: historical data sets $\mathcal{D}_1, \ldots, \mathcal{D}_m$, candidate classifiers $\mathcal{A}_1, \ldots, \mathcal{A}_\ell$, testing data set $\mathcal{D}$

Output: classifier $\mathcal{A}^*$

1: Evaluate the performances of candidate classifiers on historical data sets using 10-fold cross validation.
2: Design a recommendation algorithm $\mathcal{A}_R$ based on similarity and the performances.
3: Extract the data set features $\mathbf{v}_1, \ldots, \mathbf{v}_m$ and $\mathbf{v}$ as (14).
4: Compute the data set similarities using (15).
5: Output a best classifier $\mathcal{A}^*$ for $\mathcal{D}$ using $\mathcal{A}_R$.

---

the same performance have the same average rank; (ii) let $R_{i,j}, i = 1, 2, \cdots, \ell$ denote the rank of classifier $\mathcal{A}_i$ on $\mathcal{D}_j$, then the rank of classification algorithm $\mathcal{A}_i$ on $\mathcal{D}$ is computed as

$$R_{i,\mathcal{D}} = \frac{1}{K} \sum_{\mathcal{D}_j \in N_c(\mathcal{D})} R_{i,j}, j = 1, 2, \cdots, K, \tag{16}$$

where $N_c(\mathcal{D})$ is a set contains the K most similar data sets of $\mathcal{D}$. In the end, the classifier with the lowest rank is the recommended classifier.

4.2 Multi-class Classification Problem

Our feature only suitable for two-class data sets. We handle multi-class problems as follow.

> **Step 1:** Suppose that data set $\mathcal{D}$ has c classes. We split $\mathcal{D}$ into $m = \frac{c(c-1)}{2}$ two-class problems using one-vs-one strategy.
> **Step 2:** For each sub-problem, we recommend one classifier based on Algorithm 1.
> **Step 3:** The final decision is determined by using voting strategy.

The merit of this method is that we can select the most suitable classifier for each sub-problem, which would make the classification accuracy higher than that of the single classifier.

5 Experiments

We evaluate the proposed feature with three state-of-the-art features with respect to computational efficiency and recommendation performance.

5.1 Experimental Setup

Data Sets. We selected 67 classification problems from the UCI repository which include 49 historical data sets and 18 testing data sets (Table 1). Among

Table 1. Summary of testing data sets in terms of attributes, sample size and classes.

ID	Name	Att.	Ins.	Classes	ID	Name	Att.	Ins.	Classes
1	abalone	8	4117	3	10	page-blocks	10	5473	5
2	car	6	1728	4	11	seeds	7	210	3
3	contrac	9	1473	3	12	segment	18	2310	7
4	dermatology	34	366	6	13	st-landsat	36	6534	6
5	hayes-roth	5	132	3	14	st-vehicle	18	846	4
6	hill-valley	100	1212	2	15	synthetic-control	60	600	6
7	hill-valley-noise	100	1212	2	16	teaching	5	151	3
8	iris	4	154	3	17	waveform	21	2000	3
9	nursery	8	12598	4	18	wine	13	178	3

the historical data sets, the multi-class data sets are split into two-class data sets using one-vs-one technique, then those data sets that are easy to classify or have severely unbalanced/small samples in each class are deleted. We totally have 84 two-class historical data sets. The attributes of data sets are normalized into $[-1, 1]$.

Candidate Classifiers. We employ 20 candidate classifiers. Some candidate classifiers are KNN, LDA, logistics regression, SVM (linear, polynomial kernel, RBF kernel), naive bayes, decision tree C4.5, random forest, Bagging (tree) and AdaBoost (tree). These classifiers are run with the MATLAB statistic toolbox except SVM uses LIBSVM software.

The remaining classifiers are nearest mean classifier, Fisher's least square linear discriminant, BP neural network, linear perceptron, Bayesian classifier, Gaussians mixture model, Parzen classifier, Parzen density classifier and radial basis neural network classifier, which are adopted from PrTools toolbox 5.0. We run all codes on MATLAB 2017a on Windows operating system with Inter(R) Core(TM) i5-6500 CPU @3.20GHz processer.

Comparative Classifiers. We evaluate 24 classifiers on testing data sets which include 20 candidate classifiers and 4 data set features.

- statistical feature (F_s) [7];
- problem complexity feature (F_p) [4];
- landmarking feature (F_l) [6] with landmarkers KNN, C4.5, LR and NB;
- our data set feature using polynomial kernel (F_{poly}). We set $d = 3$.

The attributes of 4 data set features are normalized into $[0, 1]$. F_s, F_p and F_l adopt the CS framework in Algorithm 1. For each testing data set, 10% samples of each class are dropped as testing samples and the rests are used for training (the testing data set in Algorithm 1). The classification model of recommended classifier on training samples are trained using 10-fold cross validation. For the

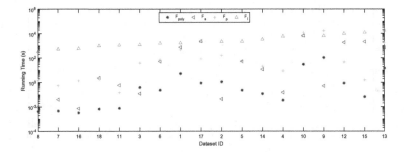

Fig. 1. Running times (s) of F_{poly}, F_s, F_p and F_l on testing data sets. The total times are $160.11s$, $14662.85s$, $31602.10s$ and $77109.74s$, respectively.

sake of fairness, we also evaluate the performance of candidate classifiers on multi-class testing data sets using splitting and voting strategy.

Performance Metrics. We employ classification accuracy (CA), average recommendation performance ratio (ARPR) [8] and non-parameter statistical tests [16] to evaluate the performance of data set features.

5.2   Computational Efficiency

We collected the computation times of 4 data set features on 18 testing data sets (Fig. 1). The recorded time of each data set is the sum of times of its subproblems. From Fig. 1, we see that our feature has the fastest computational speed, which spent 160 seconds on overall data sets. However, F_s, F_p and F_l have unacceptable low speeds. Although F_s outperformed our features on data sets 2, 3, and 9, we found that these data sets have discrete variables. For continuous variables, the efficiency of F_s would be degraded rapidly. Therefore, our feature outperforms F_s, F_p and F_l in terms of efficiency.

5.3   Performance Comparisons

In this section, we compare our F_{poly} with three state-of-the-art data set features: F_s, F_p and F_l, as well as 20 candidate classifiers. The comparisons of CA, ARPR and statistical test are listed in Table 2. We observe that F_{poly} has the highest CA and ARPR.

   To check the statistical difference between different methods, we calculated the average rank of each feature and shown it in the last row of Table 2. F_{poly} has the lowest average rank 1.36, followed by F_s. F_p has the worst average rank. The Friedman statistic is distributed according to the F-distribution with $(4-1) = 3$ and $(4-1) \times (18-1) = 51$ degrees of freedom. The value of Friedman statistic is 11.64 and the critical value of $F(3, 51)$ is 2.79 at 0.05 significance level. Thus, the null hypothesis is rejected. Then we applied the Nemenyi test for pairwise

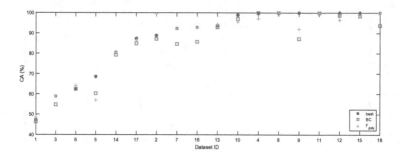

Fig. 2. CA (%) of *best*, BC and F_{poly}. *best* represents the CA of the best candidate classifier.

comparisons. The critical different is 1.11 which means that F_{poly} is significantly better than F_p and F_l.

Finally, we compare the CA of F_{poly} with that of the best candidate classifier and Bayesian classifier (BC) which has the highest ACA among 20 classifiers, shown in Fig. 2. We see that the CA of F_{poly} are very close to the CA of the best candidate classifier except on data sets 7 and 18. F_{poly} is equal to or higher than the best candidate classifier on 11 data sets. F_{poly} has the same CA as or outperforms BC in 14 out of 18 cases. On the 4 data sets that BC outperforms F_{poly}, we see that the CA of BC and F_{poly} are very close.

6   Conclusion

The difficulties of CS mainly stem from the similarity measurement among data sets. So far, people resolve this problem by characterizing data set feature and turn to comparing the similarity of features. In this paper, we proposed a new data set feature to describe the classification complexity of data set. Different

Table 2. CA (%) of F_{poly}, F_s, F_p and F_l on testing data sets. The first column shows the ID of data sets. The last row reports the average rank of each CS algorithm. $\mathcal{A}_{best}$ and $\mathcal{A}_{worst}$ indicate the best and worst CA of candidate classifiers.

ID	F_{poly}	F_s	F_p	F_l	$\mathcal{A}_{best}$	$\mathcal{A}_{worst}$	ID	F_{poly}	F_s	F_p	F_l	$\mathcal{A}_{best}$	$\mathcal{A}_{worst}$
1	**48.56**	46.63	41.59	43.99	47.36	44.47	12	**96.54**	95.67	96.10	95.67	100	98.27
2	**99.42**	74.85	76.02	91.81	88.89	77.19	13	**94.38**	93.59	91.72	90.63	93.75	90.47
3	**58.90**	58.22	50.00	54.79	58.90	53.42	14	**80.49**	74.39	75.61	74.39	80.49	74.39
4	**97.14**	94.29	88.57	94.29	100	100	15	**98.33**	**98.33**	**98.33**	95.00	100	98.33
5	**57.02**	**57.02**	52.07	52.07	68.60	52.89	16	**92.86**	78.57	**85.71**	71.43	92.86	78.57
6	**64.17**	**64.17**	50.83	55.83	66.94	48.33	17	**86.43**	81.41	83.92	84.42	87.44	78.89
7	**92.31**	**92.31**	76.92	84.62	92.31	69.23	18	100	100	93.75	100	100	93.75
8	100	100	100	100	100	100							
9	**92.12**	80.22	78.36	79.29	100	86.01	ACA	**86.35**	82.44	79.54	81.23		
10	**95.59**	94.30	92.28	93.93	98.90	95.96	ARPR	**0.99**	0.95	0.90	0.93		
11	100	100	100	100	100	85.71	Rank	**1.36**	2.44	3.19	3.00		

from previous works, our feature has merits like low computational complexity and theoretical support. We built a CS framework using the proposed feature. Experimental results show that our feature is effective and efficient. Our method outperforms three data set features, which means that the proposed feature can help to choose suitable classifiers for new classification problems.

Acknowledgements. This work was supported by the National Natural Science Foundation of China under Grant 61602308.

References

1. Wolpert, D.H.: The lack of a priori distinction between learning algorithms. Neural Comput. **8**(7), 1341–1390 (1996)
2. Maciá, N., Bernadó-Mansilla, E., Orriols-Puig, A., Kam, H.T.: Learner excellence biased by data set selection: a case for data characterisation and artificial data sets. Pattern Recogn. **46**(3), 1054–1066 (2013)
3. Cernadas, E., Amorim, D.: Do we need hundreds of classifiers to solve real world classification problems? J. Mach. Learn. Res. **15**(1), 3133–3181 (2014)
4. Bernado-Mansilla, E., Ho, T.K.: Domain of competence of XCS classifier system in complexity measurement space. IEEE Trans. Evol. Comput. **9**(1), 82–104 (2008)
5. Peng, Y., Flach, P.A., Soares, C., Brazdil, P.: Improved dataset characterisation for meta-learning. In: Lange, S., Satoh, K., Smith, C.H. (eds.) DS 2002. LNCS, vol. 2534, pp. 141–152. Springer, Heidelberg (2002). https://doi.org/10.1007/3-540-36182-0_14
6. Pfahringer, B., Bensusan, H., Giraud-Carrier, C.G.: Meta-learning by landmarking various learning algorithms. In: Seventeenth International Conference on Machine Learning, vol. 11, no. 9, pp. 743–750. Morgan Kaufmann Publishers Inc. (2000)
7. Song, Q., Wang, G., Wang, C.: Automatic recommendation of classification algorithms based on data set characteristics. Pattern Recogn. **45**(7), 2672–2689 (2012)
8. Wang, G., Song, Q., Zhu, X.: An improved data characterization method and its application in classification algorithm recommendation. Appl. Intell. **43**(4), 892–912 (2015)
9. Kotthoff, L.: Algorithm selection for combinatorial search problems: a survey. In: Bessiere, C., De Raedt, L., Kotthoff, L., Nijssen, S., O'Sullivan, B., Pedreschi, D. (eds.) Data Mining and Constraint Programming. LNCS (LNAI), vol. 10101, pp. 149–190. Springer, Cham (2016). https://doi.org/10.1007/978-3-319-50137-6_7
10. Kalousis, A., Theoharis, T.: NOEMON: design, implementation and performance results of an intelligent assistant for classifier selection. Intell. Data Anal. **3**(5), 319–337 (1999)
11. Ho, T.K., Basu, M.: Complexity measures of supervised classification problems. IEEE Trans. Pattern Anal. Mach. Intell. **24**(3), 289–300 (2002)
12. Cano, J.R.: Analysis of data complexity measures for classification. Expert Syst. Appl. **40**(12), 4820–4831 (2013)
13. Cortes, C., Mohri, M., Rostamizadeh, A.: Algorithms for learning kernels based on centered alignment. J. Mach. Learn. Res. **13**(2), 795–828 (2012)
14. Nguyen, C.H., Tu, B.H.: An efficient kernel matrix evaluation measure. Pattern Recogn. **41**(11), 3366–3372 (2008)
15. Chudzian, P.: Evaluation measures for kernel optimization. Pattern Recogn. Lett. **33**(9), 1108–1116 (2012)
16. Demšar, J.: Statistical comparisons of classifiers over multiple data sets. J. Mach. Learn. Res. **7**(1), 1–30 (2006)

Gradient-Based Representational Similarity Analysis with Searchlight for Analyzing fMRI Data

Xiaoliang Sheng, Muhammad Yousefnezhad, Tonglin Xu,
Ning Yuan, and Daoqiang Zhang[✉]

College of Computer Science and Technology,
Nanjing University of Aeronautics and Astronautics, Nanjing 211106, China
dqzhang@nuaa.edu.cn

Abstract. Representational Similarity Analysis (RSA) aims to explore similarities between neural activities of different stimuli. Classical RSA techniques employ the inverse of the covariance matrix to explore a linear model between the neural activities and task events. However, calculating the inverse of a large-scale covariance matrix is time-consuming and can reduce the stability and robustness of the final analysis. Notably, it becomes severe when the number of samples is too large. For facing this shortcoming, this paper proposes a novel RSA method called gradient-based RSA (GRSA). Moreover, the proposed method is not restricted to a linear model. In fact, there is a growing interest in finding more effective ways of using multi-subject and whole-brain fMRI data. Searchlight technique can extend RSA from the localized brain regions to the whole-brain regions with smaller memory footprint in each process. Based on Searchlight, we propose a new method called Spatiotemporal Searchlight GRSA (SSL-GRSA) that generalizes our ROI-based GRSA algorithm to the whole-brain data. Further, our approach can handle some computational challenges while dealing with large-scale, multi-subject fMRI data. Experimental studies on multi-subject datasets confirm that both proposed approaches achieve superior performance to other state-of-the-art RSA algorithms.

Keywords: RSA · Gradient · Searchlight · Whole-brain fMRI data

1 Introduction

One of the most significant challenges in brain decoding is finding some more effective ways of using multi-subject and whole-brain fMRI data. Representational Similarity Analysis (RSA) is one of the fundamental approaches in fMRI analysis and evaluates similarities between different cognitive tasks [1–3]. Here, one subject is scanned while watching different visual stimuli. With different pairs of stimuli, the brain generates corresponding patterns of neural activities, and then the RSA calculates the similarities between the neural activity patterns of different stimuli. This process obtains Representational Similarity Matrix (RSM), and the matrix encodes the similarity structure. The goal of the method is to explore the correlation between different cognitive tasks. Figure 1 shows the computation of the representational similarity matrix (RSM).

© Springer Nature Switzerland AG 2018
J.-H. Lai et al. (Eds.): PRCV 2018, LNCS 11258, pp. 304–315, 2018.
https://doi.org/10.1007/978-3-030-03338-5_26

RSA can be casted as a multi-task regression problem. Classical RSA is based on basic linear approaches, e.g., Ordinary Least Squares (OLS) or General [1, 2]. Indeed, these methods are restricted to a linear model, each data contains a large number of voxels, and the number of voxels far exceeds the time points. The methods mentioned cannot obtain satisfactory results on fMRI datasets. Moreover, the data is difficult to be converted into a matrix by this method [4], and it could reduce the stability and robustness of the final analysis when the Signal-to-Noise Ratio (SNR) is low [7].

For OLS and GLM, they face a problem of overfitting. The current approaches consider that the regularization can avoid overfitting. For example, Least Absolute Shrinkage and Selection Operator (LASSO) method employs norm $\ell 1$ to address the regression problem [9], whereas Ridge Regression method uses the norm $\ell 2$ to deal with the mentioned problem [8]. As an alternative approach, the Elastic Net method handle above issue by employing $\ell 1$ and $\ell 2$ norms [10].

In general, The RSA provides a way to compare different representational geometries across subjects, brain regions, measurement modalities, and even species. Since the similarity structure can be estimated from the imaging data even if the coding model is not constructed, RSA is suitable not only for model testing but also for exploratory research [3]. Indeed, RSA is initially used as a tool to study visual representations [2, 5, 6], semantic representations [12, 13], and lexical representations [14]. Further, RSA is utilized to reveal the network about dimensions of social-information representations [15, 16].

As an alternative to region-of-interest based analysis, researchers introduce the 'searchlight' approach that performs multivariate analysis on sphere-shaped groups of voxels centered on each brain voxel one by one [1]. Nowadays, fMRI brain image datasets have a large number of subjects. Thus the whole-brain datasets are high-dimensional. In the current general RSA algorithm, the data is difficult to be converted into a matrix by this method and the inverse of the voxel matrix cannot be avoided. Besides, the optimization of RSA is difficult when the number of voxels is too large. Fortunately, modern RSA algorithm can optimize the solution process in comparison to traditional RSA method [17]. One of the modern RSA methods utilizes the searchlight technique, which is applied to EMEG [14]. As a novel application, the searchlight RSA method can be utilized to analyze the structure of moral violations space [11].

In this paper, we propose a new RSA method based on gradient descent called Gradient Representational Similarity Analysis (GRSA). The Gradient RSA algorithm can handle the RSA problem by calculating the solution of LASSO using stochastic gradient descent. It can solve the mapping feature matrix by using stochastic gradient descent method with iteration to obtain an optimal result and explore the similarity between different neural activity patterns. Another key contribution of this paper is a novel application for Searchlight. GRSA is a tool for analyzing whether localized brain regions encode cognitive similarities. Using searchlight, we propose a new method called spatiotemporal searchlight GRSA (SSL-GRSA). In Sect. 3.2, we focus on this approach with an aim to link searchlight analysis with GRSA. We develop this model by using a spatiotemporal searchlight GRSA algorithm which can generalize our ROI-based GRSA algorithm to the whole-brain data.

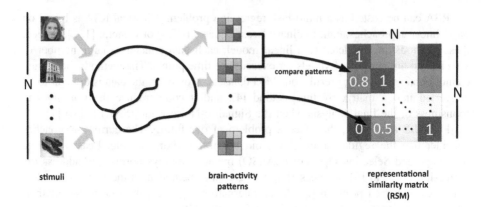

Fig. 1. Computation of the representational similarity matrix (RSM). The matrix encodes the similarity structure. Each block in the RSM is a correlation distance between activation patterns of a pair of experimental conditions (or stimuli). The elements on the main diagonal of the matrix are one by definition. In the non-diagonal part of RSM, a larger value indicates that two stimuli have a high similarity, and the small value implies that the two stimuli are not similar.

2   Representational Similarity Analysis (RSA)

The application of RSA is based on a general linear model (GLM). This method assumes that the neural pattern of fMRI responses is related to stimuli events.

$$Y^{(\ell)} = X^{(\ell)}B^{(\ell)} + \epsilon^{(\ell)} \tag{1}$$

where $Y^{(\ell)} = \{y_{ij}\} \in \mathbb{R}^{T \times V}, 1 \le i \le T, 1 \le j \le V$ denotes the fMRI time series from ℓ-th subject, T is the number of time points and V is the number of brain voxels. Design matrix is denoted by $X^{(\ell)} = \{x_{ik}\} \in \mathbb{R}^{T \times P}, 1 \le i \le T, 1 \le k \le P$. The design matrix is obtained by the convolution of the time series of the stimuli with a typical hemodynamic response function (HRF). Here, P denotes the number of distinct categories of stimuli, $B^{(\ell)} = \{\beta_{kj}\} \in \mathbb{R}^{P \times V}, \beta_{kj} \in \mathbb{R}, 1 \le k \le P, 1 \le j \le V$ denotes the matrix of estimated regressors, and β_{kj} is an amplitude reflecting the response of j-th voxel to the k-th stimulus. This paper assumes that the neural activities of each subject are column-wise standardized, i.e., $Y^{(\ell)} \sim \mathcal{N}(0, 1)$. Indeed, RSA method is looking for the following objective function:

$$\min_{B^{(\ell)}} \left\| Y^{(\ell)} - X^{(\ell)}B^{(\ell)} \right\|_F^2 - r\left(B^{(\ell)}\right) \tag{2}$$

where $r\left(B^{(\ell)}\right)$ is the regularization term for ℓ-th subject. Notably, the regularization term is zero $(r(B^{(\ell)}) = 0)$ for non-regularized methods, including OLS and GLM. The term $r(B^{(\ell)})$ is $\alpha\|B\|_F^2$ for Ridge Regression, $\alpha\|B\|_1$ for LASSO method, $\alpha\rho\|B\|_1 + \frac{\alpha(1-\rho)}{2}\|B\|_F^2$ for Elastic Net method.

In order to generalize RSA for multi-subject fMRI datasets, we calculate the mean of the regressors matrices across subjects:

$$B^* = \frac{1}{S}\sum_{\ell=1}^{S} B^{(\ell)} \tag{3}$$

where S denotes the number of subjects, and each row of $B^* \in \mathbb{R}^{P \times V} = \{\beta_1^*,\ldots,\beta_p^*\}, \beta_k^* \in \mathbb{R}^V$ illustrates the extracted neural signature belonging to k-th category of cognitive tasks.

Three metrics will be used to evaluate the performance of RSA methods. As the first metric, we calculate the mean of square error for analyzing the accuracy of regression:

$$MSE = \frac{1}{TSV}\sum_{\ell=1}^{S}\sum_{i=1}^{T}\sum_{j=1}^{V}\left(x_{ij}^{(\ell)} - \sum_{k=1}^{P} d_{ik}^{(\ell)}\beta_{kj}^{(\ell)}\right)^2 \tag{4}$$

The next two techniques evaluate between-class correlation and between-class covariance of the regressors matrices:

$$CR = \frac{1}{S}\sum_{\ell=1}^{S} \max_{\substack{1 \leq i \leq P \\ i < j \leq P}}\left\{Corr\left(\beta_{i.}^{(\ell)},\beta_{j.}^{(\ell)}\right)\right\} \tag{5}$$

$$CV = \frac{1}{S}\sum_{\ell=1}^{S} \max_{\substack{1 \leq i \leq P \\ i < j \leq P}}\left\{Cov\left(\beta_{i.}^{(\ell)},\beta_{j.}^{(\ell)}\right)\right\} \tag{6}$$

where $\beta_{i.}^{(\ell)}, \beta_{j.}^{(\ell)}$ are rows of $B^{(\ell)}$, function $Corr$ is the Pearson correlation, and function Cov calculates the covariance between two vectors. All of these three metrics must be minimized for an ideal solution [7, 17].

3 Gradient Representational Similarity Analysis (GRSA)

fMRI brain data is high-dimensional. In fMRI, each data contains a large number of voxels, and the number of voxels far exceeds the time points. Meanwhile, the presence of similarity of different features leads to some redundant information. Feature selection can solve this problem. Therefore, we use the $\ell 1$ norm here. The objective function is optimized as follows:

$$J\left(B^{(\ell)}\right) = \min_{B^{(\ell)}} L\left(B^{(\ell)}\right) + r\left(B^{(\ell)}\right) \tag{7}$$

where the typical loss functions considered here are squared Frobenius error, i.e., $L\left(\mathbf{B}^{(\ell)}\right) = \left\|\mathbf{Y}^{(\ell)} - \mathbf{X}^{(\ell)} \cdot \mathbf{B}^{(\ell)}\right\|_F^2$, and $r\left(\mathbf{B}^{(\ell)}\right)$ is the $\ell 1$ norm defined as $\alpha\|\mathbf{B}\|_1$. The problem of this approach is that the computation complexity is tremendous when there are a large number of features. And this method is merely applies to the linear model.

3.1 Optimization

In this section, we attempt to propose a method that is not restricted to a linear model and can reduce the time complexity on high-dimensional data. Here, we propose an effective approach that utilizes Stochastic Gradient Descent (SGD) for optimizing the LASSO objective function. In order to efficiently optimize (7), one solution is to calculate the gradient of (7) which is needed in Stochastic Gradient Descent (SGD) algorithm. The step of gradient optimization is as follows:

$$\nabla J\left(\mathbf{B}_t^{(\ell)}\right) = \frac{\partial}{\partial \mathbf{B}_t^{(\ell)}} J\left(\mathbf{B}^{(\ell)}\right) \tag{8}$$

$$\mathbf{B}_{t+1}^{(\ell)} = \mathbf{B}_t^{(\ell)} - \alpha^t \nabla J\left(\mathbf{B}_t^{(\ell)}\right) \tag{9}$$

where $\nabla J\left(\mathbf{B}_t^{(\ell)}\right)$ denotes the gradient of $J\left(\mathbf{B}^{(\ell)}\right)$ from t-th iteration. The step of iteration of $\mathbf{B}^{(\ell)}$ denoted as (9). α^t is the self-adaptive learning rate, which is defined as follows:

$$\alpha^t = \frac{\alpha}{\sqrt{t+1}} \tag{10}$$

Here, $t \in \mathbb{R}$ is the number of iterations. α^t denotes the updated learning rate of t-th iteration. Since different features have different ranges of values, the iteration could be very slow. In order to apply this algorithm to fMRI brain datasets, the SGD algorithm randomly selects a batch of the time points instead of the whole time points to update the model parameters. So each time of learning is fast and the model parameters can be updated online. This paper uses GRSA approach for estimating the optimized solution. GRSA can reduce the time complexity when applied to fMRI brain datasets, and explore the similarity between different neural activity patterns by iterative optimal algorithm. Our method can rapidly reduce the time complexity and have smaller memory footprint in each process. This application of GRSA could be used not only in the linear model but also in the non-linear model.

3.2 Spatiotemporal Searchlight GRSA (SSL-GRSA)

Finding the most effective method for analyzing multi-subject fMRI data is a long-standing and challenging problem. Since the scarcity of data for each subject and the differences of brain anatomy and functional response between different subjects, researchers have an increasing interest in human cognitive fMRI research.

Multi-subject fMRI datasets contain two group datasets, i.e., Region of Interests (ROI) based datasets, and whole-brain datasets. The ROI-based method analyzes the representation structure in a set of predefined brain regions. However, other brain regions also have representational structures that are suitable for the prediction of our model. Whole-brain data can be used to figure out what information is represented in a region of the human brain. People want to find some more effective ways to analyze whole-brain data. Searchlight analysis provides a way to map cube-shaped groups of voxels across the whole brain continuously [1]. Therefore, we propose a method that combines the ideas of the GRSA model and searchlight-based technique to analyze multi-subject whole-brain fMRI data. A searchlight version of GRSA is conceptually new. Therefore, we refer to our method as Searchlight GRSA (SSL-GRSA).

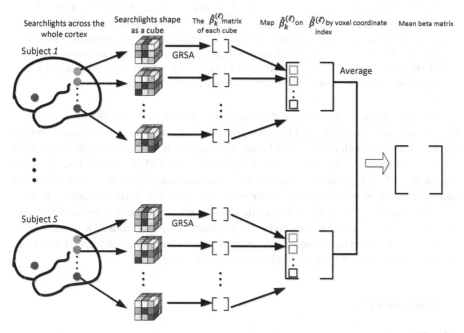

Fig. 2. Process of Spatiotemporal Searchlight GRSA (SL-GRSA). The whole-brain data of each subject is divided into K cubes (searchlights) with a specified size. Here, this size is fixed as $3 \times 3 \times 3$. Then, the GRSA approach applies to each cube to generate K local matrices denoted by $\hat{\beta}_k^{(\ell)}$. In the end, we splice those K local $\hat{\beta}_k^{(\ell)}$ matrices into a complete $\hat{\beta}^{(\ell)}$ matrix according to the coordinates of voxels. The mean matrix is obtained by averaging over all matrices $\hat{\beta}^{(\ell)}$.

$\hat{Y}^{(\ell)} \in \mathbb{R}^{v_x \times v_y \times v_z \times T}$ of four dimension is fMRI time series data from ℓ-th subject where $1 \leq \ell \leq S$ and S is the number of subjects. The tuple (x, y, z) refers to the standard axes, whereas v_x, v_y, v_z refer to the number of voxels along the corresponding axis respectively, and T is the number of time samples in units of repetition time (TR). The process of our searchlight method is as follows: Firstly, a sliding cube is selected and the cube at a specific time covers a contiguous region of voxels. The selected snapshots of the cube need to be adjacent and avoid overlapping. Then, the voxels of the whole-brain is then analyzed by spatial local analysis in each cube. GRSA method is applied to cube groups of voxels in a line. Therefore, the ROI method can be extended to the whole-brain data. The process of our method is depicted in Fig. 2.

Table 1. The datasets.

Title	ID	Task type	S	P	T	Scan	TR	TE
Visual object recognition	R105	Visual	6	8	121	G3T	2500	30
Word and object processing	R107	Visual	49	4	164	S3T	2000	28
Weather prediction without feedback	W011	Decision	14	4	236	S3T	2000	25
Selective stop signal task	W017	Decision	8	6	546	S3T	2000	25
Weather prediction	W052	Decision	13	2	450	S3T	2000	20

This paper utilizes five datasets, shared by Open fMRI (http://openfmri.org). S is the number of subject, P denotes the number of stimulus categories, T is the number of scans in unites of scans in unites of TRs (Time of Repetition), V_{ROI} denotes the number of voxels in ROI. In the column of Scan, G = General Electric, or S = Siemens in 3 T. TR is Time of Repetition in millisecond and TE denotes Echo Time in millisecond.

For standard Searchlight-based RSA method, the study first used the scene image as task stimuli for experiment, and then used the Searchlight method to find brain regions related to the perception of human brain. The results show that using the searchlight method, we can find the active brain regions in the FMRI data related to scene recognition of each subject. Compared with standard searchlight RSA, our method is competitive and performs better with the same cube size. It's worth mentioning that we only load necessary data according to the mini batch to maintain a reduced memory footprint in each process. We extend the application of GRSA from ROI to the whole-brain. Further, we create a novel approach that addresses some computational challenges while dealing with large-scale, multi-subject fMRI data.

4 Experiments

4.1 Datasets

This paper utilizes five datasets, shared by Open fMRI (http://openfmri.org), for running empirical studies. All datasets are separately preprocessed by FSL 5.0.10 (https://fsl.fmrib.ox.ac.uk), i.e., slice timing, anatomical alignment, normalization, smoothing. Here, we use two groups of datasets, i.e., Region of Interests (ROI) based datasets, and whole-brain datasets. Here, we analyze some specific parts of brain images in ROI-based data, where these parts are manually selected based on the original papers of each data. In this paper, we use 'R' prefix for the ROI-based dataset and a 'W' prefix is used for denoting the whole-brain data.

Technically, the whole-brain datasets include all of the neural activities which are registered to a standard space, i.e., Montreal Neurological Institute (MNI) 152 space $T1$ with voxel size 4 mm. Before applying our approach to each fMRI dataset, the dataset is normalized, i.e., $Y^{(\ell)} \sim \mathcal{N}(0,1)$, which allows us to obtain desirable experiment result. The technical information of these datasets is shown in Table 1.

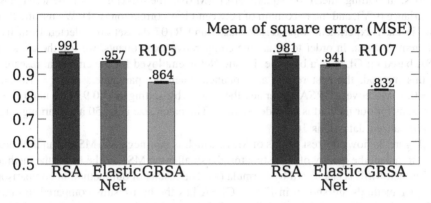

Fig. 3. The standard deviation of MSE for all RSA methods in the Fig. 3 is lower than 10^{-2}.

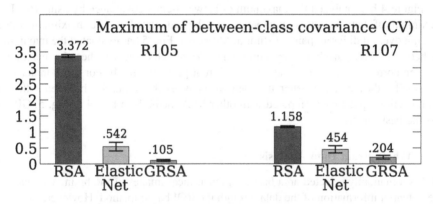

Fig. 4. Maximum of between-class covariance (*CV*) across subjects.

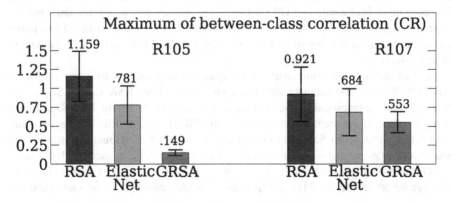

Fig. 5. Maximum of between-class correlation (*CR*) across subjects.

4.2   ROI Data Analysis

In this section, we analyze the performance of our method results by calculating three metrics, including mean of square error (MSE), the maximum of between-class covariance (CV), and the maximum of between-class correlation (CR). We use the ROI data in each experiment, thus R105 dataset and R107 dataset are selected from five different datasets. In order to create the comparative experiments, we use the classical RSA based on GLM as a baseline. Elastic Net is employed for the empirical research. In this method, the best results are obtained when the parameters are $\alpha = 1.0$ and $\rho = 0.5$. Moreover, GRSA generates the results by setting $\alpha = 0.9$. The number of iterations for our method is considered 1000. The batch size is set 50 and learning rates of normalized datasets is 10^{-3}.

Figure 3 shows the test results of MSE, which is non-negative. MSE is an indicator used to reflect the quality of the estimator. the smaller the MSE is, the better the method is. Further, MSE is calculated by Formula (4). The results of our method in comparison to other methods are shown in Fig. 3. GRSA has the best results compared to other RSA methods. The standard deviation of MSE for all RSA methods in the Table 2 is lower than 10^{-2}.

Figure 4 has analyzed the maximum of between-class covariance by using (6). The maximum of between-class covariance can be calculated as the maximum value ranging over all different pairs of stimuli. Moreover, Fig. 5 has evaluated the maximum of between-class correlation by employing (5) in which it searches the maximum Pearson correlation coefficient amongst different pairs of stimuli. For those indicators, the smaller they are, the better the method analyzes the similarity between different neural activity patterns. Compared with other RSA methods in Fig. 4 or Fig. 5, GRSA has the best results.

4.3   Whole-Brain Data Analysis

ROI is a manually selected area based on anatomical images of the brain. We analyze the potential information of the data through the ROI based method. However, a certain type of information is not necessarily confined to only one specific brain region, and could be included in several areas. Therefore, the analysis of the whole-brain data becomes more important. The GRSA method is applied to whole-brain data and this approach can explore the relationship between different cognitive tasks. In this paper, the whole-brain datasets are used in our method, i.e., W011 dataset, W017 dataset and W052 dataset.

In this section, we implement the comparative experiments by some traditional methods. We use the ordinary Spatiotemporal Searchlight RSA (SSL-RSA) as the baseline. For the empirical study, Spatiotemporal Searchlight Elastic Net (SSL- Elastic Net) is utilized. As mentioned before, both SSL-RSA and RSA share the same parameters. And so do SSL- Elastic Net and Elastic Net. Previously mentioned, the main challenges are the high dimension of data and the issue of memory footprint.

Our approach can address these challenges and has good performance. The cube size can be set arbitrarily. Thus, all Searchlight RSA methods take the same cube size set as $3 \times 3 \times 3$. In fact, the best result is obtained by using this cube size. The result of each contrast experiment is showed in Tables 2 and 3.

In each comparative experiment, we evaluate all the methods by using CV and CR. The formulas of these two indicators have already been mentioned in the previous section. Table 2 has analyzed the maximum of between-class covariance whereas.

Table 2. Maximum of between-class covariance (*CV*) across subjects (max±std)

Datasets	SSL-RSA	SSL-elastic net	SSL-GRSA
W011	0.415 ± 0.125	0.265 ± 0.046	**0.208 ± 0.042**
W017	0.462 ± 0.062	0.237 ± 0.186	**0.143 ± 0.143**
W052	1.831 ± 0.184	0.396 ± 0.143	**0.237 ± 0.052**

Table 3. Maximum of between-class correlation (*CR*) across subjects (max±std)

Datasets	SSL-RSA	SSL-elastic net	SSL-GRSA
W011	0.785 ± 0.033	**0.507 ± 0.042**	0.609 ± 0.202
W017	0.849 ± 0.124	0.441 ± 0.052	**0.358 ± 0.082**
W052	0.866 ± 0.071	0.471 ± 0.104	**0.407 ± 0.151**

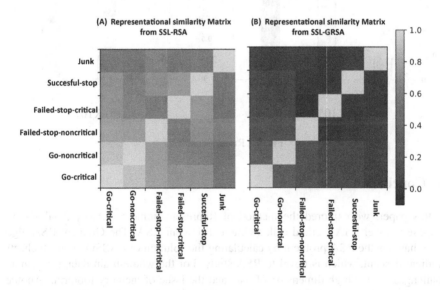

Fig. 6. Comparing correlation of a traditional method and SSL-GRSA method by using W017

Table 3 evaluated the maximum of between-class correlation. As depicted in the result Table 2, SSL-GRSA has generated better performance in comparison with other methods. Further, as Table 3 demonstrates, the performance of the maximum of between-class correlation is significantly lower except for W011, which confirms that our method is better.

Base on W017 data, Fig. 6 depicts the comparison of correlation of a traditional method and SSL-GRSA method. Each small block shows the similarity of the related category of stimuli with respect to the corresponding row and column. Therefore, we compare the between-class correlation of SSL-GRSA with the traditional methods. SSL-GRSA provides the best similarity analysis compared with other methods.

4.4 Runtime Analysis

This section analyzes the runtime of the proposed method and compares it to the runtime of other RSA methods. Here, the analysis is based on the ROI datasets. For convenience, the runtime of other methods is scaled based on GRSA, that is, the runtime of GRSA is regarded as a unit. As illustrated in Fig. 7, the Elastic Net is the slowest one whereas traditional RSA beats others. Since GRSA utilizes a min-batch of time-points, it runs faster than the regularized method. As a conclusion, the performance of GRSA is more efficient. It is worth mentioning that the runtime of the whole brain dataset has the same tendency.

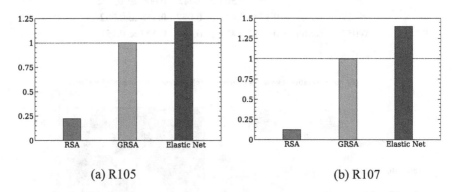

(a) R105   (b) R107

Fig. 7. Runtime analysis

5   Conclusion

In this paper, we explored the method of Representational Similarity Analysis. we propose a novel RSA method called Gradient descent RSA. The Gradient-RSA algorithm handles the RSA problem by calculating the solution of LASSO using stochastic gradient descent, which is novel to RSA study. For the whole-brain data, the primary challenges are the high dimension of data and the issue of memory footprint. Another primary contribution of this paper is a new application in Searchlight. Based on Searchlight, the application of our GRSA method is extended from the localized brain regions to the whole-brain region. Further, Our methods show improved results over standard competing methods. In the future work, our method can be applied to more large-scale, multi-subject fMRI datasets, and further optimized by other new approaches to obtain better performance.

Acknowledgements. This work was supported in part by the National Natural Science Foundation of China under Grant (61876082, 61861130366, 61703301, and 61473149), the Fundamental Research Funds for the Central Universities and the Foundation of Graduate Innovation Center in NUAA (kfjj20171609).

References

1. Kriegeskorte, N., Goebel, R., Bandettini, P.: Information-based functional brain mapping. Proc. Natl. Acad. Sci. U. S. A. **103**(10), 3863–3868 (2006)
2. Connolly, A.C., et al.: The representation of biological classes in the human brain. J. Neurosci. **32**(8), 2608–2618 (2012)
3. Kriegeskorte, N., Mur, M., Bandettini, P.A.: Representational similarity analysis-connecting the branches of systems neuroscience. Front. Syst. Neurosci. **2**, 4 (2008)
4. Yousefnezhad, M., Zhang, D.: Anatomical pattern analysis for decoding visual stimuli in human brains. Cogn. Comput. **10**(2), 284–295 (2018)
5. Peelen, M.V., Caramazza, A.: Conceptual object representations in human anterior temporal cortex. J. Neurosci. **32**(45), 15728–15736 (2012)
6. Kravitz, D.J., Peng, C.S., Baker, C.I.: Real-world scene representations in high-level visual cortex: it's the spaces more than the places. J. Neurosci. **31**(20), 7322–7333 (2011)
7. Cai, M.B., Schuck, N.W., Pillow, J.W., Niv, Y.: A Bayesian method for reducing bias in neural representational similarity analysis. In: Advances in Neural Information Processing Systems, pp. 4951–4959 (2016)
8. Hoerl, A.E., Kennard, R.W.: Ridge regression: biased estimation for nonorthogonal problems. Technometrics **12**(1), 55–67 (1970)
9. Yuan, M., Lin, Y.: Model selection and estimation in regression with grouped variables. J. R. Stat. Soc.: Ser. B (Stat. Methodol.) **68**(1), 49–67 (2006)
10. Zou, H., Hastie, T.: Regularization and variable selection via the elastic net. J. R. Stat. Soc.: Ser. B (Stat. Methodol.) **67**(2), 301–320 (2005)
11. Wasserman, E.A., Chakroff, A., Saxe, R., Young, L.: Illuminating the conceptual structure of the space of moral violations with searchlight representational similarity analysis. NeuroImage **159**, 371–387 (2017)
12. Handjaras, G., et al.: How concepts are encoded in the human brain: a modality independent, category-based cortical organization of semantic knowledge. Neuroimage **135**, 232–242 (2016)
13. Huth, A.G., Nishimoto, S., Vu, A.T., Gallant, J.L.: A continuous semantic space describes the representation of thousands of object and action categories across the human brain. Neuron **76**(6), 1210–1224 (2012)
14. Su, L., Fonteneau, E., Marslen-Wilson, W., Kriegeskorte, N.: Spatiotemporal searchlight representational similarity analysis in EMEG source space. In: 2012 International Workshop on Pattern Recognition in Neuroimaging (PRNI), pp. 97–100. IEEE (2012)
15. Tamir, D.I., Thornton, M.A., Contreras, J.M., Mitchell, J.P.: Neural evidence that three dimensions organize mental state representation: rationality, social impact, and valence. Proc. Natl. Acad. Sci. **113**(1), 194–199 (2016)
16. Chavez, R.S., Heatherton, T.F.: Representational similarity of social and valence information in the medial pFC. J. Cogn. Neurosci. **27**(1), 73–82 (2015)
17. Oswal, U., Cox, C., Lambon-Ralph, M., Rogers, T., Nowak, R.: Representational similarity learning with application to brain networks. In: International Conference on Machine Learning, pp. 1041–1049 (2016)

Feature Aggregation Tree: Capture Temporal Motion Information for Action Recognition in Videos

Bing Zhu[✉]

Beijing Laboratory of Intelligent Information Technology,
School of Computer Science, Beijing Institute of Technology (BIT),
Beijing 100081, People's Republic of China
zhubing@bit.edu.cn

Abstract. We propose a model named Feature Aggregation Tree to capture the temporal motion information in videos for action recognition. Feature Aggregation Tree constructs a logical motion sequence by considering the concrete semantics of features and mining feature combinations in a video. It will save different feature combinations and then use the bayesian model to calculate the conditional probabilities of frame-level features based on the previous features to aggregate features. It doesn't matter about the length of the video. Compared with the existing feature aggregation methods that try to enhance the descriptive capacity of features, our model has the following advantages: (i) It considers the temporal motion information in a video, and predicts the conditional probability by using the bayesian model. (ii) It can deal with arbitrary length of the video, rather than uniform sampling or feature encoding. (iii) It is compact and efficient compared to other encoding methods, with significant results compared to baseline methods. Experiments on the UCF101 dataset and HMDB51 dataset demonstrate the effectiveness of our method.

Keywords: Action recognition · Feature learning
Feature aggregation

1 Introduction

Human action recognition [1] is one of the fundamental researches in the field of computer vision, which has great significance and application prospects in video retrieval, video recommendation and video surveillance. In recent years, many researches mainly focuse on two aspects. One is how to extract a more discriminative spatio-temporal description for the video. The other is how to aggregate frame-level features to a video-level feature, which gives more attention to efficient feature organization strategies.

© Springer Nature Switzerland AG 2018
J.-H. Lai et al. (Eds.): PRCV 2018, LNCS 11258, pp. 316–327, 2018.
https://doi.org/10.1007/978-3-030-03338-5_27

In terms of feature description, most of the existing video feature representations for action recognition are mainly learned by two different types of networks: one is two-stream network [2,3] and the other is 3D convolutional neural network [4–6]. The trend of networks is to learn better video features which can capture both spatial and temporal information in videos. And we need a strategy to handle long videos with arbitrary frames, which can aggregate frame-level features to a representation for the whole video.

In terms of feature aggregation, one strategy is selecting a key frame or several key frames to represent the entire action video [7–9]. This strategy can achieve satisfactory results when a video contains only one action instance, but it is not so useful in the videos containing multiple categories action instances. Another common strategy is to encode frame features, such as vectors of locally aggregated descriptors (VLAD) [10], fisher vectors (FV) [11,12] and bag of words (BoW) [13,14]. While these strategies cannot capture the temporal information of the entire video. In addition, in the neural network methods, the temporal pooling operation is usually used to compress the features of a video [3,15,16], e.g. the mean and the max pooling. There are also some recent works trying to modify the traditional pooling strategies to further improve the recognition performance, such as adascan [17] and ActionVLAD [18], which attaches frame features to different wight values. However, the pooling strategies don't consider the order of frames, which ignore the temporal information. Besides the CNNs, the LSTM network is also considered to use attention mechanism to learn the weight of different each frame [19–21]. But because of the complexity of the training process, LSTM doesn't become a mainstream method.

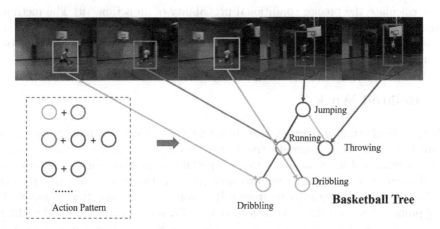

Fig. 1. We propose Feature Aggregation Tree to represent actions in videos. For example, Action "Basketball" can be grouped by "running", "dribbling", "jumping" and "throwing". We construct a "basketball" tree to record action primitives nodes and excavate the action pattern between two action primitives.

To better understand what an action is performing, temporal information is as important as spatial information. However, no matter hand-crafted features or deep features, are all frame-level, which don't make full use of the temporal information of the entire video. To better use the temporal information, we need to understand the component of actions firstly. The hierarchical definition proposed by Moeslund [22] divides the actions into three levels, e.g. the lower level definition is "action primitive", the middle level definition is "action" which is an ordered combination of primitives, while the concept of high-level definition of "behavior" is the logical combination of actions, which is a complex advanced semantics. Taking the action of basketball as an example, shown in Fig. 1, playing basketball can be broken down into several action primitives like "running", "dribbling", "jumping" and "throwing"and these primitives are organized in a temporal order. Actions have different meanings in different orders, such as "running-throwing" means playing basketball, while "running-jumping" means high jump or long jump. And these temporal information involved in the patterns will be helpful in action recognition. The method ActionVLAD with the similar idea proves the effectiveness. In this work, we propose a novel method named Feature Aggregation Tree (FA-Tree) to learn video features for action recognition, which is based on the knowledge of frequent patterns and association rules in the field of data mining [23].

The main contribution of this work is that we propose a novel FA-Tree for action recognition, which has the following advantages: (i) The method treats frame-level features as action primitives, and aggregate them into action patterns. Taking the temporal information of primitives into account, FA-Tree organizes patterns with different orders to better represent a complete action, and then calculate the precise conditional probability of an action. (ii) The method can deal with arbitrary length of the video, rather than uniform sampling or feature encoding. (iii) The model is compact and efficient, and has achieved good results on two datasets.

2   Related Work

Action Feature Representation. In recent years, more and more researchers want to extract more discriminative features to represent a video, which should contain temporal information as well as spatial information. Some hand-crafted traditional features [1,24,25] are proposed from 2D to 3D, and their description ability has been significantly improved. It is worthy mentioning that Wang et al. [26] proposed improved Dense Trajectories (iDT), which is the best hand-crafted feature at present but it is computationally intensive. Simonyan and Zisserman [3] proposed the two-stream network, which decomposed a video into appearance and motion streams, and trained two networks respectively. Considering that the input of 2D convolutional neural networks is always an image so it lacks the temporal information, the 3D neural network uses the video segment as the input [4–6].

Video Feature Aggregation. One approach is to select a key frame or a key segment to replace the entire video when predicting the action category. Cao et al. [7] extracted the key frame with manifold learning based on the optical flow graph for action recognition. Liu et al. [8,9] used supervised learning and unsupervised clustering methods to extract key segments in action videos.

Another approach is feature encoding. Some methods use the bag of words model (BoW) [14] to extract some local spatio-temporal descriptor, and encode them into dictionaries to make templates [13,15,27,28]. Latev et al. [27] described a video with BoW that encoded HoG and HoF features. Ji et al. [5] also used BoW in their method. Similar to BoW are the methods such as VLAD [10,18] and Fisher Vector [11–13]. Wang et al. [15] proposed the improved Dense Trajectories(iDT) approach, which combined dense trajectories, histogram by using Fisher Vector to encode. By combining iDT [26] features and Fisher Vector [29] algorithm, Peng et al. [13] discussed fusing first and then encoding or encoding first and then fusing, and finally found the latter method is better. Tang et al. [30] proposed a more flexible approach using a variable duration HMM [31] that factored each video into latent states with variable durations.

Now the popular strategy in the neural network is to compress the information of different frames in a video into a fixed summary vector by using pooling operation [3,4,15,16]. The mean pooling and the max pooling are common choices, i.e. taking average or maximum values of each feature vector, such as C3D [4] adopts the average value of each feature in every dimension. However, these pooling methods consider each frame equally, which is not robust to the noisy information. As there may be some noisy frames in the video, these noisy frames will cause some losses and ultimately lead to error judgments. Some recent works try to modify pooling strategy for action recognition, such as ActionVLAD [18] and adascan [17].

Frequent Pattern Tree. Our Feature Aggregation Tree, which want to mine action pattern in a video, is inspired by Frequent Pattern Tree. Han et al. [32] introduced the Frequent Pattern Tree structure for storing crucial information about mining frequent patterns in transaction and time-series databases. They also developed the FP-Growth algorithm for efficient and scalable mining on both long and short frequent patterns. Chang et al. [33] proposed an incremental data mining algorithm based on FP-Growth using the concept of heap tree to address the issue of incremental updating of frequent itemsets. Aditya and Pradana [34] leveraged the FP-Growth algorithm to find the customer buying habits on market basket in organic medicine store. Dharmaraajan and Dorairangaswamy [35] utilized the FP-Growth algorithm to classify user behavior in identifying the patterns of the browsing and navigation data of web users.

3   Approach

In this section, we will describe the details of Feature Aggregation Tree. As is outlined in Fig. 2, we extract frame-level features by the C3D network and then regard these features as action primitives, which are the results of the softmax

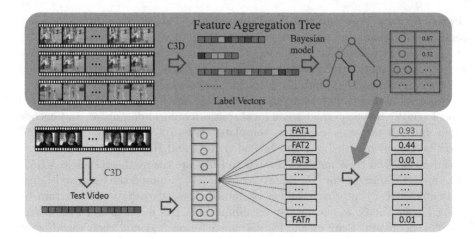

Fig. 2. When constructing the Feature Aggregation Tree (above), we extract the frame-level features by C3D network, and than get feature labels to make up label vectors. We use these label vectors to constuct Feature Aggregation Tree model and calculate the probabilities of each node and each pattern. When testing (below), we predict the test video label by matching each FA-Tree and calculating the probability.

layer. The next step is aggregating primitives into patterns to construct Feature Aggregation Tree. In a FA-Tree, each node corresponds to the conditional probability that the node appears, which we use the bayesian model to calculate. In the following we first describe how to construct Feature Aggregation Tree (Sect. 3.1) and then discuss the strategies for calculate the probability of each action pattern (Sect. 3.2).

3.1 How to Construct FA-Tree

In this part, we will give some definitions about the FA-Tree firstly. Specifically, devide the entire dataset D into different subsets, such as $D = \{S_1, S_2, \cdots, S_k\}$. Videos in every subset S_i have the same category label i, i is from 1 to k. And every subset S_i will generate one FA-Tree. Let $S_i = \{v_1, v_2, \cdots, v_j\}$, where v means a label vector, as every video corresponds to a label vector by C3D network, and j is the number of videos in subset S_i. Just like what is shown in Fig. 2. For each video, each frame in the video is regarded as an element in the label vector. Here we name one label in the vector as "item", and two different label pair as "pattern". Item set is $F = \{f_1, f_2, \cdots, f_m\}$ and pattern set is $P = \{p_1, p_2, \cdots, p_n\}$.

The first step is using the unique operation to deal with the same consecutive items. Because in our approach, we just consider different item pairs to mine association rules. The second step is to set support and confidence thresholds. Because there will be some noisy labels in the vector after the softmax layer, we set the minimum item support threshold (MIST) to remove these noisy labels when the frequence of one item is lower than the threshold. The other threshold is named minimum pattern confidence threshold (MPCT), which is set to choose the root node of a FA-Tree. When we construct a FA-Tree, the root node must be the actual label of this category. So we need to sort items by MIST, and MPCT determines that in top 0.05 or 0.1 rate of all items, we can choose the actual label as the root node. In Sect. 4.2, the data were uniformly sampled in experiments to help set the thresholds.

In addition, when constructing a FA-Tree, we have fully considered the temporal information in a video. Because in the processing step, we have not changed the positions of items. So the remaining items are organized in the order as the original video. The construction of a FA-Tree is divided into three steps. First, those items whose frequence is higher than MPCT are selected as the root node. Second, each label vector is divided into patterns to generate frequent pattern set. Third, for each root node, we connect the items that appear before root node in the left branch, and those after the root node in the right branch. The specific algorithm is shown as below.

Algorithm 1. Pseudo-code of the Construction of Feature Aggregation Tree

---

Input: Action label vector subset $S_i = \{v_1, v_2, \cdots, v_j\}$, $MIST$, $MPCT$

Output: Feature Aggregation Tree $FA - Tree$

1 Scan S_i once. Collect items higher than $MIST$ to group F. Construct the pattern set P. Sort F by support frequence in the descending order, and choose items higher than $MPCT$ to be the $Root$ of a FA-Tree ;

2 Scan the pattern set P;

3 **for** *each vector in V_j* **do**

4   **for** *each pattern in P* **do**

5   **if** *item p appears before Root* **then**

6   **if** *Root has a left child node p* **then**

7   the frequence of p add 1;

8   **else**

9   reach to the left child node of $Root$ recursively, create a new node p, and let its frequence be 1, linked to its parent node and recorded in the list;

10   **else**

11   the same step as before except right instead of left;

12   **if** *there is no p in the pattern* **then**

13   create new $Root$ and repeat step 2

14 **final** ; return $FA - Tree$;

Given a simple FA-Tree as an example in Fig. 3. The letter 'a' means 'action' while the subscript of 'a' is the result of the softmax layer. The item set is $\{a_2, a_1, a_{20}\}$ and the pattern set is $\{[a_{20}, a_2], [a_2, a_1], [a_2, a_{20}], [a_1, a_{20}]\}$. When the root is a_2, we make a_{20} to be its left child node and a_1 to be its right child node. When we extract the pattern $[a_2, a_{20}]$, we find a_2 already has the right child node, so let a_{20} be the right child node of a_1.

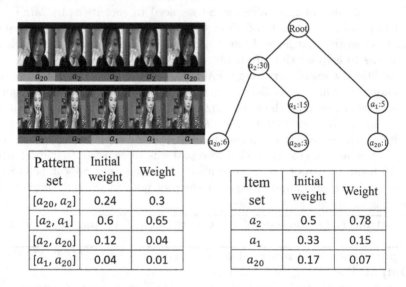

Pattern set	Initial weight	Weight
$[a_{20}, a_2]$	0.24	0.3
$[a_2, a_1]$	0.6	0.65
$[a_2, a_{20}]$	0.12	0.04
$[a_1, a_{20}]$	0.04	0.01

Item set	Initial weight	Weight
a_2	0.5	0.78
a_1	0.33	0.15
a_{20}	0.17	0.07

Fig. 3. We construct a simple AF-Tree as an example. Initial weights are calculated by the statistical approach while weights are calculated by the bayesian model.

FA-Tree is a highly compressed structure that stores all the information of action patterns, and the memory space occupied by FA-Tree is proportional to the depth and width of the tree. For the depth of the tree, it generally depends on the complexity of label vectors, as well as the quality of classifier. For example, the more chaotic the label vector is, the deeper the tree will be. The width of the tree indicates that there are not only one root node. FA-Tree is compact because the size of the tree is usually much smaller than the original label vector set.

3.2 How to Design FA-Tree Probability Estimation

After constructing a FA-Tree, we initialize the weights of each node with the simple statistical approach. The definition of weights is shown as below. For each single item, its weight means the probability that it belongs to one action. For each pattern, its weight means the probability product of a two-item combination and this combination belongs to one action. The weight can be thought as the contribution of items and patterns to the whole video. However, simple statistical approach can not get precise weights in our experiments, Table 1. So we use the bayesian model to predict weights, the formula is shown as:

$$P(C_{cls}|l_i) = \frac{P(l_i|C_{cls})P(C_{cls})}{P(l_i)},$$

where C_{cls} means the category of one action, l_i means the ith label in a video label vector. $P(l_i)$ is given by softmax classifier. $P(C_{cls})$ and $P(l_i|C_{cls})$ are calculated by data statistics. So we can update $P(C_{cls}|l_i)$ to have a more precise weight. And the weight will be saved in the node of a FA-Tree.

The FA-Tree is used to compute the probability of the whole video by finding the matched patterns in the test video. We will introduce the probability formula for calculating the video probability, which is as follows:

- Set the node weight parameter μ, pattern weight parameter γ.
- The patterns extracted from a label vector has N nodes and M patterns, referred to as p_{node} and $p_{pattern}$ respectively.

The probability that a test label vector passed by a FA-Tree can be expressed as:

$$P(v, FA - Tree) = \sum_{i=1}^{N} \mu_i p_i^{node} + \sum_{j=1}^{M} \gamma_j p_j^{pattern} + c,$$

where v represents the test video label vector; μ and γ are the weight parameters corresponding to p; c is a penalty, which plays a similar role as bias.

As is shown in Fig. 3, we get the initial weights with the statistical approach. Given that this AF-Tree belongs to action "ApplyLipstick", which is label 2. If the assumption is $P(C_{cls=2}) = 0.76$, and $P(a_2), P(a_1), P(a_{20})$ are given by softmax, we can calculate the weights as the figure.

4   Experiments

4.1   Dataset

UCF101. UCF101 [36] is a dataset which is cut from real action videos in YouTube. It contains a total of 101 action categories and 13320 videos. We use split 1 for the experiment, including 9537 training videos and 3783 test videos, whose total hours up to 27 h.

HMDB51. HMDB51 [37] is collected from a variety of sources, most of which come from movies, and a small percentage from public databases such as Prelinger files, YouTube and Google Video. The dataset contains 6849 segments, which are divided into 51 action categories with at least 101 segments for each category.

4.2   FA-Tree Construction

In the experiment, we use the first split of HMDB51 dataset to show the process of parameter setting. Each video is divided into segments with the length of 16 frames and 50% overlap between segments. We use these video segments as the input of the 3D convolutional neural network [4] and we will get the classification result of each feature after the softmax layer. Therefore, for each action video, we can get a label vector which is made up by some different labels. We accumulate all the vectors of the same category action in one subset.

To get the item set and pattern set, first, we select 80% training data to predict the remaining 20% and we repeat this step 5 times. We randomly select some data in HMDB51, and finally select about 4500 videos to construct Feature Aggregation Trees. When observing these label vectors, some noisy data need to be removed. We just set the threshold MIST, and items below the thresholds are all excluded. The MIST is set to be 0.05 and the MPCT is set to be 0.1.

In the process of probability estimation, we set c as a penalty coefficient which is shown in the formula of the Sect. 3.2. We also test whether we should set the penalty factor c, which is shown in Table 1. The table (left) records accuracies without the bayesian model and the penalty coefficient c. While the first three columns in the table (right) record accuracies without the bayesian model but with c. And the last column in the table (right) records accuracies with the bayesian model and c.

Table 1. Accuracy (%) comparison between FA-Tree with PN (right) and without PN (left) on the HMDB51 dataset

	Rank-1	Rank-2	Rank-3		Rank-1	Rank-2	Rank-3	Bayesian
Split 1	56.9	69.9	75.0	Split 1	57.0	69.8	75.4	67.7
Split 2	53.3	67.5	72.3	Split 2	53.5	68.2	73.8	63.4
Split 3	55.4	69.2	74.7	Split 3	55.5	69.7	74.8	66.8

When experimenting on the HMDB51 dataset, if we only use the C3D features and all weight of items and patterns are initialized, we can calculate the accuracy of Rank-2 is 69.80%. This shows that the Feature Aggregation Tree can really capture the latent motion information in the video. The reason why these segments can not achieve the highest score is that the predictions are mainly limited to using only the simple softmax. So after using the bayesian model we get the result lower than Rank-2 but higher than Rank-1.

4.3 FA-Tree Comparison Experiment

In this part, we consider Fisher Vector [11,13] and VLAD [10] to be the baseline method. In addition, we also consider the mean pooling and the max pooling, as well as RNN-FV [38] and ST-VLMPF [39]. The experimental results are in Table 2.

The result of FA-Tree is better than the baseline methods, which proves the effectiveness of our method. It is worthy mentioning that, compared with the improvement on the UCF101 dataset, the result is more obvious on the HMDB51 dataset because the labels in the UCF101 dataset are more ordered. However in the HMDB51 dataset, the FA-Tree can find enough action patterns from chaotic labels to represent the actions and ultimately improve the accuracy.

Table 2. Accuracy (%) comparison between mean pooling, max pooling and FA-Tree on the UCF101 dataset and the HMDB51 dataset

Strategies	UCF101	HMDB51
iFV [11]	79.8	49.0
VLAD [10]	81.4	49.1
RNN-FV [38]	82.3	52.9
Mean pooling	82.7	51.6
Max pooling	83.3	52.5
ST-VLMPF [39]	86.2	56.3
FA-Tree	**86.9**	**66.2**

4.4 Comparison with the State-of-the-Art

In Table 3, we show a comparison of our FA-Tree with the state-of-the-art methods on both datasets. Our method with MIFS feature achieves 94.6% on the UCF101 dataset and 74.2% on the HMDB51 dataset.

Table 3. Accuracy (%) comparison of our method with the state-of-the-art methods

Approach	UCF101	HMDB51
Wang et al. [26]	85.9	57.2
Tran et al. [4]	82.6	52.5
Simonyan et al. [3]	88.0	59.4
Peng et al. [13]	87.9	61.1
Wang et al. [16]	90.3	63.2
Wang et al. [2]	94.2	69.4
Kar et al. [17]	93.2	66.9
Girdhar et al. [18]	93.6	69.8
Duta et al. [39]	93.6	69.5
Our Method + MIFS [40]	**94.6**	**74.2**

5 Conclusion

We propose a novel model - the Feature Aggregation Tree to capture the temporal motion information in action videos. The FA-Tree connects frame-level features with the specific meanings of action primitives, and mines action patterns in the action sequence. We use the bayesian model to calculate the conditional probability of patterns. The experimental results on the UCF101 dataset and HMDB51 dataset demonstrate the effectiveness of our method.

References

1. Laptev, I., Lindeberg, T.: On space-time interest points. Int. J. Comput. Vis. **64**(2–3), 107–123 (2005)
2. Wang, L., et al.: Temporal segment networks: towards good practices for deep action recognition. ACM Trans. Inf. Syst. **22**(1), 20–36 (2016)
3. Simonyan, K., Zisserman, A.: Two-stream convolutional networks for action recognition in videos. In: International Conference on Neural Information Processing Systems, pp. 568–576 (2014)
4. Tran, D., Bourdev, L., Fergus, R., Torresani, L., Paluri, M.: Learning spatiotemporal features with 3D convolutional networks, pp. 4489–4497 (2014)
5. Ji, S., Xu, W., Yang, M., Yu, K.: 3D convolutional neural networks for human action recognition. IEEE Trans. Pattern Anal. Mach. Intell. **35**(1), 221–231 (2013)
6. Varol, G., Laptev, I., Schmid, C.: Long-term temporal convolutions for action recognition. IEEE Trans. Pattern Anal. Mach. Intell. **PP**(99), 1 (2016)
7. Cao, X., Ning, B., Yan, P., Li, X.: Selecting key poses on manifold for pairwise action recognition. IEEE Trans. Ind. Inform. **8**(1), 168–177 (2012)
8. Liu, L., Shao, L., Zhen, X., Li, X.: Learning discriminative key poses for action recognition. IEEE Trans. Cybern. **43**(6), 1860–1870 (2013)
9. Jiang, Z., Lin, Z., Davis, L.S.: Recognizing human actions by learning and matching shape-motion prototype trees. IEEE Trans. Pattern Anal. Mach. Intell. **34**(3), 533–547 (2012)
10. Jegou, H., Douze, M., Schmid, C., Perez, P.: Aggregating local descriptors into a compact image representation, pp. 3304–3311 (2010)
11. Perronnin, F., Sánchez, J., Mensink, T.: Improving the fisher kernel for large-scale image classification. In: Daniilidis, K., Maragos, P., Paragios, N. (eds.) ECCV 2010. LNCS, vol. 6314, pp. 143–156. Springer, Heidelberg (2010). https://doi.org/10.1007/978-3-642-15561-1_11
12. Sydorov, V., Sakurada, M., Lampert, C.H.: Deep fisher kernels - end to end learning of the fisher kernel GMM parameters, pp. 1402–1409 (2014)
13. Peng, X., Wang, L., Wang, X., Qiao, Y.: Bag of visual words and fusion methods for action recognition: comprehensive study and good practice. Comput. Vis. Image Underst. **150**(C), 109–125 (2016)
14. Li, F.F., Perona, P.: A Bayesian hierarchical model for learning natural scene categories, pp. 524–531 (2005)
15. Wang, H., Dan, O., Verbeek, J., Schmid, C.: A robust and efficient video representation for action recognition. Int. J. Comput. Vis. **119**(3), 219–238 (2016)
16. Wang, L., Qiao, Y., Tang, X.: Action recognition with trajectory-pooled deep-convolutional descriptors, pp. 4305–4314 (2015)
17. Kar, A., Rai, N., Sikka, K., Sharma, G.: AdaScan: adaptive scan pooling in deep convolutional neural networks for human action recognition in videos. In: Proceedings of the IEEE Conference on Computer Vision and Pattern Recognition, pp. 3376–3385 (2017)
18. Girdhar, R., Ramanan, D., Gupta, A., Sivic, J., Russell, B.: ActionVLAD: learning spatio-temporal aggregation for action classification, pp. 3165–3174 (2017)
19. Sharma, S., Kiros, R., Salakhutdinov, R.: Action recognition using visual attention. arXiv preprint arXiv:1511.04119 (2015)
20. Ng, Y.H., Hausknecht, M., Vijayanarasimhan, S., Vinyals, O., Monga, R., Toderici, G.: Beyond short snippets: deep networks for video classification, vol. 16, no. 4, pp. 4694–4702 (2015)

21. Donahue, J., et al.: Long-term recurrent convolutional networks for visual recognition and description, pp. 677–691 (2015)
22. Moeslund, T.B., Hilton, A., Krüger, V.: A survey of advances in vision-based human motion capture and analysis. Comput. Vis. Image Underst. 104(2), 90–126 (2006)
23. Han, J., Kamber, M.: Data Mining: Concepts and Techniques, Data Mining Concepts Models Methods & Algorithms, 2nd edn, vol. 5, no. 4, pp. 1–18 (2011)
24. Scovanner, P., Ali, S., Shah, M.: A 3-dimensional sift descriptor and its application to action recognition, pp. 357–360 (2007)
25. Kläser, A., Marszalek, M., Schmid, C.: A spatio-temporal descriptor based on 3D-gradients. In: British Machine Vision Conference 2008, Leeds, September 2008
26. Wang, H., Schmid, C.: Action recognition with improved trajectories. In: IEEE International Conference on Computer Vision, pp. 3551–3558 (2014)
27. Laptev, I., Marszalek, M., Schmid, C., Rozenfeld, B.: Learning realistic human actions from movies, pp. 1–8 (2008)
28. Wang, H., Ullah, M.M., Klaser, A., Laptev, I., Schmid, C.: Evaluation of local spatio-temporal features for action recognition. In: BMVC 2009-British Machine Vision Conference, p. 124:1. BMVA Press (2009)
29. Perronnin, F., Dance, C.: Fisher kernels on visual vocabularies for image categorization, pp. 1–8 (2007)
30. Tang, K., Fei-Fei, L., Koller, D.: Learning latent temporal structure for complex event detection, pp. 1250–1257 (2012)
31. Vezzani, R., Baltieri, D., Cucchiara, R.: HMM based action recognition with projection histogram features. In: Ünay, D., Çataltepe, Z., Aksoy, S. (eds.) ICPR 2010. LNCS, vol. 6388, pp. 286–293. Springer, Heidelberg (2010). https://doi.org/10.1007/978-3-642-17711-8_29
32. Han, J., Pei, J., Yin, Y., Mao, R.: Mining frequent patterns without candidate generation: a frequent-pattern tree approach. Data Min. Knowl. Discov. 8(1), 53–87 (2004)
33. Chang, H.-Y., Lin, J.-C., Cheng, M.-L., Huang, S.-C.: A novel incremental data mining algorithm based on FP-growth for big data. In: 2016 International Conference on Networking and Network Applications (NaNA), pp. 375–378. IEEE (2016)
34. Aditya, P.: Market basket analysis using FP-growth algorithm in organic medicine store. Skripsi, Fakultas Ilmu Komputer (2016)
35. Dharmaraajan, K., Dorairangaswamy, M.: Analysis of FP-growth and Apriori algorithms on pattern discovery from weblog data. In: IEEE International Conference on Advances in Computer Applications (ICACA), pp. 170–174. IEEE (2016)
36. Soomro, K., Zamir, A.R., Shah, M.: UCF101: a dataset of 101 human actions classes from videos in the wild. arXiv preprint arXiv:1212.0402 (2012)
37. Kuehne, H., Jhuang, H., Garrote, E., Poggio, T., Serre, T.: HMDB: a large video database for human motion recognition, pp. 2556–2563 (2011)
38. Lev, G., Sadeh, G., Klein, B., Wolf, L.: RNN fisher vectors for action recognition and image annotation. In: Leibe, B., Matas, J., Sebe, N., Welling, M. (eds.) ECCV 2016. LNCS, vol. 9910, pp. 833–850. Springer, Cham (2016). https://doi.org/10.1007/978-3-319-46466-4_50
39. Duta, I.C., Ionescu, B., Aizawa, K., Sebe, N., et al.: Spatio-temporal vector of locally max pooled features for action recognition in videos. In: 30th IEEE Conference on Computer Vision and Pattern Recognition (CVPR 2017), pp. 3205–3214. IEEE (2017)
40. Lan, Z., Lin, M., Li, X., Hauptmann, A.G., Raj, B.: Beyond Gaussian pyramid: multi-skip feature stacking for action recognition, pp. 204–212 (2015)

Adaptive Ensemble Probabilistic Matrix Approximation for Recommendation

Xingxing Li, Liping Jing$^{(\boxtimes)}$, and Huafeng Liu

Beijing JiaoTong University, Beijing 100044, China
lpjing@bjtu.edu.cn

Abstract. Matrix approximation has been increasingly popular for recommender systems, which have achieved excellent accuracy among collaborative filtering methods. However, they do not work well especially when there are a large set of items with various types and a huge number of users with diverse interests. In this case, the complicated structure of sparse rating matrix introduces challenges to the single global or local matrix approximation. In this paper, we propose an **A**daptive **E**nsemble **P**robabilistic **M**atrix **A**pproximation method (**AEPMA**), which can potentially alleviate the data sparsity and improve the recommendation accuracy. By integrating the global information over the entire rating matrix and local information on subsets of user/item ratings in a stochastic gradient boosting framework, **AEPMA** has the ability to capture the overall structures information and local strong associations in an adaptive weight strategy. A series of experiments on three real-world datasets (Ciao, Epinions and Douban) have shown that **AEPMA** can effectively improve the recommendation accuracy and scalability.

Keywords: Adaptive · Ensemble
Global and Local Matrix Approximation · Matrix approximation

1 Introduction

The variety and number of products provided by companies have increased dramatically. Companies produce a large number of products to meet the needs of customers. Although this gives more options to customers, Customers are facing more and more information, and how to obtain information accurately and effectively has become a dilemma. Recommender systems are becoming more important due to the increasing challenge-information overload. Recommender systems provide users with personalized recommendation service based on their preferences, needs, and past behaviors.

Till now, the widely-used historical data is user-item rating matrix which describes the user's observed preference. Most popular recommendation techniques (e.g., matrix approximation-based (MA) collaborative filtering) are proposed on rating matrix. In order to predict the rating accurately, many global-based methods have been proposed. The traditional matrix ratings prediction

© Springer Nature Switzerland AG 2018
J.-H. Lai et al. (Eds.): PRCV 2018, LNCS 11258, pp. 328–339, 2018.
https://doi.org/10.1007/978-3-030-03338-5_28

based on global information [2,5,9,24] works by studying the latent feature matrix of users/items. Although this method has the advantages of prediction simple and easy to understand the method from math, the interpretability of the recommendation results is low and these methods failed to detect strong associations among a small set of items/users.

In order to solve the problem of the subsets of users' unique interests, researchers adopted local methods [1,25] to predict the missing values of rating matrix. They apply matrix clustering and community detection to matrix approximation methods. The main idea is to partition the large user-item matrix into a set of smaller submatrices, and the usual method for partition is to consider user-based clustering or item-based clustering. However, sub-matrix may appear over-fitting in this local method, and ignore the overall structure on the rating matrix. Now we proposed the new model AEPMA (Adaptive Ensemble Probabilistic Matrix Approximation), which help us sift through all the available global and local information to make accurate matrix rating prediction. The intuition is that, weaker between correlation of two models, more accurate the prediction values for missing value are. So we take both the global and local information into consideration. Simultaneously, we apply a gradient-boosting framework to learn the more accurate values and not sensitive to abnormal points. We learn the weight of different components in the model, which plays an important role in adaptive and effective prediction. More importantly, there is no manual setting of the parameters, both the weight and learning rate.

2   Related Work

Matrix approximation-based collaborative filtering methods have been proposed to alleviate the data missing issue. Some is from the overall structure, RSVD [9] is a standard matrix factorization method inspired by the effective to the domain of collaborative filtering, which is from the domain of natural language processing. Then NMF [24] view the recommendation task as a actual situation, so the components are non-negative and NMF assume the ratings follows the Poisson distribution. Then the Gaussian distribution assumption has been attempted, PMF [2] is a Probabilistic Matrix Factorization model, which define the conditional distribution over the ratings as Gaussian distributions. And later BPMF [5] – a Bayesian extension of PMF, in which the model is using Markov chain Monte Carlo (MCMC) methods for approximate inference.

Although these methods work well, these methods still limited in detecting the overall structure. More recently, model such as ACCAMS [1] focused on local strong correlation. ACCAMS [1] is an additive model of co-clustering, which can partition rating matrix into blocks that are highly similar through a clustering of the rows and columns. SIACC [25] is a extension of ACCAMS, and has a better effect on co-clustering by using a social influence. WEMAREC [4] takes the rating distribution into consideration. And as a weighted and ensemble model, the submatrix is generated using different co-clustering constraints in WEMAREC. Furthermore, LLORMA [3], SMA [25] also focused on using ensembles of factorization to exploit local structure. But these ensembles models only focused on ratings inside clusters and ignore the majority of user ratings outside clusters. Since training data are often insufficient in the detected clusters, the performance of local ensemble models may degrade due to overfitting. To tackle this problem, we address these issues of ratings prediction by applying an ensemble approach, which can incorporate both global and local information.

In this paper, we unify localized relationships in user-item subgroups and common associations among all users and items to improve the recommendation accuracy. The most related works are Probabilistic Matrix Factorization (PMF) and ACCAMS. In AEPMA, the proposed method can learn global information and local information simultaneously, since we can alternate optimization iteration to obtain of the adaptive sample weight. We use stochastic gradient boosting framework to learn more hidden information of the complex rating matrix. More importantly, In the boosting framework, the ensemble models can enhance the recommendation accuracy and stability.

3 The Proposed AEPMA Model

The structure of rating matrix is more and more complicated. The single framework such as PMF can not accurately predict the rating. So we propose a boosting-based matrix approximation for describing the different information of the rating matrix. Because the user-item rating matrix is represented in a global strategy by PMF, such as the whole rating matrix, which ignore the local structure among rating information. In AEPMA, We can capture sufficient information by combining global rating predictions and local rating predictions. Then a stochastic gradient boosting framework is adopted to produce accurate ratings prediction and enhance the recommendation stability. More importantly, we learn adaptive weight for each predictive rating matrix. Which can sufficiently prevent overfitting. Similar to shrinkage in XGBOOST, the learned weights reduce the influence of prediction in each stage and leave space for finer prediction.

3.1 Global and Local Matrix Approximation

We exploit Global and Local Matrix Approximation (GLMA) which is a new probabilistic model which combined global and local information. More importantly, the user-item rating weight can be learned adaptively. And the rating with most suitable global or local model for each user/item should be with large weights. The conditional distribution over the observed ratings for the global and local model can be given as follows:

$$p(X|\mathbf{U}, \mathbf{V}, \sigma, \alpha, \beta) = \prod_{X_{ij} \in \Omega} [\alpha_i^1 \beta_j^1 N(X_{i,j}|S_{ij}, \sigma^2) + \alpha_i^2 \beta_j^2 N(X_{i,j}|U_i^T V_j, \sigma^2)] \quad (1)$$

Where S is the prediction rating by local method ACCAMS, And U, V are the global user, item latent feature vectors, which is inferred from all user-item rating matrix. And α^1, β^1 are the weight vectors of the local model for all user-item ratings, respectively, and accordingly α^2, β^2 are the weight vectors of the global model for all user-item ratings, Thus, α_i^1, β_j^1 reflect the weights of the local model for the ith user and j^{th} item. The local predictions that reflected the unique interests shared among only subsets of users/items should be with large weights, α_i^2, β_j^2 denote the weights of the globally optimized model, the ratings that reflect the overall structures should be with large weight.

For $\alpha^1, \beta^1, \alpha^2, \beta^2$, we choose a Laplacian prior here, because the models with most suitable global or local model for user-item ratings should be with large weight, the variable should be sparse. More importantly, the adaptive weight can make the model learn useful information and avoid overfitting. Thus the log of the posterior distribution over the user and item features and weights can be given as follows:

$$
\begin{aligned}
&\ln p\left(U, V, \alpha, \beta \mid X, \sigma_U, \sigma_V, \sigma, u_\alpha, u_\beta, b_\alpha, b_\beta\right) \\
&\propto \ln \left[p\left(X \mid U, V, \sigma, \alpha, \beta\right) p\left(U \mid \sigma_U\right) p\left(V \mid \sigma_V\right) p\left(\alpha \mid u_\alpha, b_\alpha\right) p\left(\beta \mid u_\beta, b_\beta\right)\right]
\end{aligned} \tag{2}
$$

Where u_α, u_β are the location parameter of the Laplacian distribution, and accordingly b_α, b_β are the scale parameter of the Laplacian distribution. Unfortunately, it is very difficult to solve the above optimization problem directly. In order to simplify the model, we try to obtain the approximate solution using Jensen's inequality, the lower bound of Eq. (2) can be obtained as follows:

$$
\begin{aligned}
l = &\sum_{i=1}^n \sum_{j=1}^m I_{ij} \left[\ln \alpha_i^1 \beta_j^1 N\left(X_{i,j} \mid S_j, \sigma^2\right) + \ln \alpha_i^2 \beta_j^2 N\left(X_{i,j} \mid U_i^T V_j, \sigma^2\right)\right] \\
&- \frac{1}{2\sigma_u^2} \|U\|_F^2 - \frac{1}{2\sigma_v^2} \|V\|_F^2 - n \ln \sigma_u^2 - m \ln \sigma_v^2 \\
&- \frac{1}{b_\alpha} \sum_{k=1}^2 \sum_{i=1}^n \left|\alpha_i^k - u_\alpha\right| - \frac{1}{b_\beta} \sum_{k=1}^2 \sum_{j=1}^m \left|\beta_j - u_\beta\right| - n \ln b_\alpha^2 - m \ln b_\beta^2
\end{aligned} \tag{3}
$$

If we keep the hyperparameters of the prior distribution fixed may easily lead to overfitting. And we want to obtain the adaptive weight of the model, so we estimate the parameters and hyperparameters simultaneously during model training. In order to estimate the hyperparameters, while fixed the rest variables and then iterate until convergence. The hyperparameters can be given as:

$$
\begin{aligned}
\sigma^2 &= \sum_{X_{ij} \in \Omega} \alpha_i \beta_j \left(X_{ij} - R_{ij}\right)^2 \Big/ \sum_{X_{ij} \in \Omega} 1 \\
\sigma_u^2 &= \frac{1}{n} \sum_{X_{ij} \in \Omega} (U_i)^2 \qquad \qquad \sigma_v^2 = \frac{1}{m} \sum_{X_{ij} \in \Omega} (V_j)^2 \\
u_\alpha &= \frac{1}{n} \sum_{X_{ij} \in \Omega} \alpha_i \qquad \qquad u_\beta = \frac{1}{m} \sum_{X_{ij} \in \Omega} \beta_j \\
b_\alpha &= \frac{1}{n} \sum_{X_{ij} \in \Omega} |\alpha_i - u_\alpha| \qquad b_\beta = \frac{1}{m} \sum_{X_{ij} \in \Omega} |\beta_j - u_\beta|
\end{aligned} \tag{4}
$$

3.2 Boosting-Based Matrix Approximation

The structure of rating matrix is more and more complicated, the single framework has trouble discovering abundant hidden information of the rating matrix.

Thus, we propose a boosting-based mixture matrix approximation model- Adaptive Ensemble Probabilistic Matrix Approximation (AEPMA).

In order to describe the different information of the rating matrix, We propose an ensemble mixture matrix approximation approach for rating prediction. In AEPMA model, we learn an additive model X, with K products $\omega_k * R^k$. Thus the prediction rating matrix $\hat{X}$ is presented:

$$\hat{X} = \sum_{k=1}^{K} \omega_k * R^k \tag{5}$$

Where K is the number of individual learner, R^k is the prediction rating matrix of kth individual learner. $R^k = (U^k)^T V^k$, and ω_k is the weight of prediction rating matrix R^k. And (U^k, V^k) is the pair of user, item latent factor vectors.

In order to discover the global structure information and detect local strong association. We let the first learner is GLMA, so we can get the prediction rating S^1, and the other individual learner corresponds to PMF. Thus the optimal prediction rating value is then equal to:

$$\hat{X} = \omega_1 * S^1 + \sum_{k=2}^{K} \omega_k * R^k \tag{6}$$

To achieve the rating matrix approximation, we use the Frobenius norm-based objective function as follows:

$$\min_{U_k, V_k} \left\| X - \omega_1 * S^1 - \sum_{k=2}^{K} \omega_k * U_k^T V_k \right\|_F^2 \tag{7}$$

Residual Matrix Update. AEPMA solves this problem in a gradient boosting manner, which iteratively adds a new individual learner to better approximate the true rating matrix. The partial residual rating matrix is learn from the negative gradient of the loss function. In AEPMA, the negative gradient of the loss function is the difference of the true ratings and the prediction ratings.

To fit the $k - 1$ learner PMF, $R^{k-1} = \omega_{k-1} * U_{k-1}^T V_{k-1}$, with rank r_{k-1} to the residual matrix X^{k-1}. Where the matrix rank r_{k-1} is adaptive, because the distribution of the residual is different. Then The specific residual matrix X^k calculation method is shown in Fig. 1:

Due to the forward stage-wise manner, We constantly iterative add a new model to better approximate rating matrix X. The prediction from previously learned $k-1$ models is fixed, Thus the kth residual rating matrix can be indicated by the previously learned $k - 1$ models. Thus, we can define the residual rating matrix at stage k as:

$$X^k = \begin{cases} X & if\ i = 1 \\ \frac{X - \omega_1 S^1}{\omega_2} & if\ i = 2 \\ \frac{X^{k-1} - \omega_{k-1} R^{k-1}}{\omega_k} & if\ i \geq 3 \end{cases} \tag{8}$$

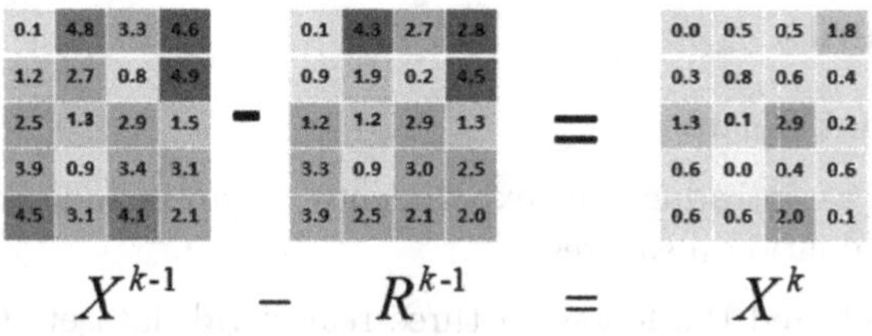

$$X^{k-1} \quad - \quad R^{k-1} \quad = \quad X^k$$

Fig. 1. The residual matrix determined by rating matrix and predictive rating matrix in previous stage.

where ω_k is the weight of kth prediction rating matrix R^k. S^1 is the prediction rating matrix which fitting the GLMA model. And accordingly R^{k-1} is the prediction rating matrix fitting the PMF model, $R^{k-1} = (U^{k-1})^T V^{k-1}$. And (U^{k-1}, V^{k-1}) is the pair of user, item factor latent vectors. Then the input residual rating matrix X^k of the kth individual learner PMF can be written as;

$$X^k = \frac{[[[X - \omega_1 S^1] - \omega_2 R^2] \cdots - \omega_{k-1} R^{k-1}]}{\omega_k} \tag{9}$$

In the kth epoch, according to the Probabilistic Matrix Factorization(PMF) model, we can obtain the user/item factor latent vectors. In our proposed method solves each model of R in a greedy sequential manner, which means that once the solution for R^k is obtained at stage k, it is fixed during the remaining iterations. And in our model, we want to consider the local and global information simultaneously, so the general we choose more than three models.

Adaptive Weight. One important step in the approximate algorithm is to propose adaptive weight. In AEPMA, we assign smaller weight to those components R less explained(large residuals). Let us define the residual probability distribution $P_{ij}^k \ R_{ij}^k - \hat{X}_{ij}^k \sim N(0, \sigma_u^2)$, Then large residuals is far from the mean, in which the corresponding probability is relatively small. Thus the weight of each prediction rating matrix is given by;

$$w_k = \frac{1}{N} \sum_{i,j} \frac{P_{ij}^k}{\sum\limits_{s=1}^{K} P_{ij}^s} \tag{10}$$

In the above equation, higher weight values is assigned to components with smaller residual. In other word, The better the fitting rating matrix, the greater the corresponding weight.

In APEMA, each user-item rating is characterized by a mixture model, and then to predict user-item ratings by the mixture components and the weight of each model. We can predict the user-items ratings as follows:

$$\hat{X} = \omega_1 * R^1 + \omega_2 * R^2 + \omega_3 * R^3 \cdots + \omega_k * R^k \tag{11}$$

4 Experiments

4.1 Experiment Setup

In the following, we introduce our experimental setup include dataset, baseline methods, and evaluation measures.

Datasets. We selected the following three real-world datasets that has widely used for evaluating recommendation algorithm – Ciao, Epinions, and Douban which are usually used in literatures. The rating score is from 1 to 5 score. For each datasets, we randomly split it into five equal sized subsets. Four subsets are used as training set and the left one as testing set in each fold. In the five-fold cross-validation, the result are represented by averaging the results over five different train-test splits. These datasets are summarized in Table 1.

Table 1. Summary of experimental datasets

Dataset	Ciao	Epinions	Douban
♯users	7,375	49,290	129,490
♯items	106,797	139,738	58,541
♯ratings	284,086	284,086	16,830,839
Rating density	0.036%	0.010%	0.222%

Baselines. We compared the recommendation accuracy of our proposed method against various state-of-the-art methods, including PMF [2], BPMF [5], LLORMA [3], WEMAREC [4], ACCAMS [1], SMA [25]. Because in the paper (Low-Rank Matrix Approximation with Stability), the author proposed that the performance of SMA is better than BPMF, LLORMA and WEMAREC. Thus the proposed method (AEPMA) is compared against three state-of-the-art matrix approximation based CF models, which are described as follows:

- **PMF:** A probabilistic matrix factorization, which define the conditional distribution of the observed ratings as Gaussian distribution.
- **RSVD:** A global-based matrix factorization method, in which user/item features are estimated by minimizing the sum-squared error.
- **ACCAMS:** An additive co-clustering model to approximate rating matrix, which can partition rating matrix into blocks that are highly similar through a clustering of the rows and columns. Then using the mean of the values to represent the block missing ratings.
- **SMA:** An low-rank matrix approximation framework, which achieving high stability.

Metrics. The root mean square error (RMSE) and Mean Absolute Error (MAE) is adopted as the evaluation metric for recommendation accuracy. The RMSE is defined as $RMSE = \sqrt{\dfrac{\sum\limits_{X_{ij} \in \mathrm{T}} \left(X_{ij} - \hat{R}_{ij}\right)^2}{|\mathrm{T}|}}$.

where T is the set of ratings in the testing set and $|T|$ is the size of the test ratings. $\hat{R}_{ij}$ is the predicted rating X_{ij} is represented the true rating value from i^{th} user to j^{th} item in the testing set. The MAE is defined by $MAE = \frac{1}{|T|} \sum\limits_{X_{ij} \in T} \left| X_{ij} - \hat{R}_{ij} \right|$.

4.2   Recommendation Performance

Table 2 compares RMSE and MAE in our method with classic matrix approximation method. We can see our method can achieve both lower generalization error and lower expected risk than other methods.

In this experiment, we compare the recommendation accuracy of AEPMA against various state-of-the-art methods, including PMF, RSVD, ACCAMS and SMA. In most of these methods, we use the same parameters values provided in the original papers, and for ACCAMS, we tuned its parameters including the number of users clusters and item cluster, and the number of stencils. In PMF, we set the max-number of iterations as 300 in our experiment. And the regularization parameter on latent is 0.01. In AEPMA, in order to reduce the manual setting of the learning rate, we use adam for stochastic optimization. And we choose 0.001 as stepsize, 0.9, 0.999 as the exponential decay rates for the moment estimates. Then we set the number of individual learners as three. The relative improvements that AEPMA achieves relative to four state-of-the-art methods on three datasets are calculated. As shown in Fig. 2. Obviously, AEPMA performs better than ACCAMS and SMA, which demonstrates that the model with global structure information is better than the only local ensemble matrix approximation methods. Simultaneously, Our method is much better than the only global method PMF and RSVD. From the relative improvements, we can see the SMA is better on the dense dataset (Douban) and perform poor on the sparse datasets (Ciao and Epinions). More importantly, In order to prove that the importance of GLMA method, we compare the performance in terms of MAE, RMSE for PMF+ (global) and ACCAMS+ (local). In the boosting framework, PMF+ is fitting PMF then get S^1, accordingly ACCAMS+ is fitting ACCAMS to get S^1. In additional, our method which using global and local information is better than the method only global on local. And we also find that the model can achieve relatively stable prediction accuracy due to the framework of boosting. A smaller RMSE or MAE value indicate better performance. Because there are too many ratings, a small improvement in RMSE or MAE can have a significant impact on the recommendation result. As shown in Table 2, It can be seen that AEPMA consistently outperforms the global method (PMF, RSVD) and the local method (ACCAMS, SMA), Which means that considering both local and global information is more useful than only considering unilateral influence.

The true datasets have different rating density, For example, The Ciao and Epinions (the rating density is 0.036% and 0.010%) is sparse. Simultaneously, We can see in the Table 2, the recommendation accuracy on sparse dataset is worse than the dense datasets. Thus how to improve the recommendation accuracy of sparse data, is the challenge of the recommendation system. More importantly, ACCAMS is better than SMA on the Ciao and Epinions, but worse than SMA on

Table 2. RMSE and MAE comparison of different methods

Datasets	Metrics	PMF	RSVD	ACCAMS	SMA	PMF+	ACCAMS+	AEPMA
Ciao	RMSE	1.1146	1.4268	1.0540	1.0746	1.0642	1.0339	**1.0121**
	MAE	0.8256	1.0745	0.8084	0.8175	0.8130	0.7846	**0.7788**
Epinions	RMSE	1.3203	1.4772	1.1689	1.1847	1.1710	1.1406	**1.1118**
	MAE	1.1206	1.1411	0.8971	0.9157	0.9112	0.8875	**0.8597**
Douban	RMSE	0.7699	0.7360	0.7309	0.7092	0.7098	0.7261	**0.7038**
	MAE	0.6230	0.5752	0.5818	0.5594	0.5635	0.5779	**0.5574**

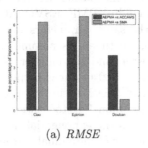
(a) *RMSE*

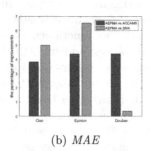
(b) *MAE*

Fig. 2. The relative improvements of AEPMA vs. ACCAMS and SMA in three datasets in terms of (a) RMSE and (b) MAE

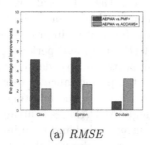
(a) *RMSE*

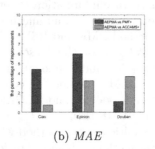
(b) *MAE*

Fig. 3. The relative improvements of AEPMA vs. PMF+ and ACCAMS+ in three datasets in term of (a) RMSE and (b) MAE

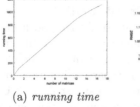
(a) *running time*

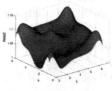
(b) *RMSE*

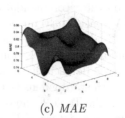
(c) *MAE*

Fig. 4. Effect of Parameters k, s and matrices number on AEPMA

the Douban dataset. In AEPMA, we exploit Global and Local information, and use the boosting framework to learn the hidden information. Thus the proposed AEPMA can outperform on both sparse and dense datasets. Table 2 show that the ensemble-based local methods (ACCAMS, SMA) especially outperforms the global method (PMF, RSVD). Thus we pay attention to the relative improvements that AEPMA achieves to two local baselines on three datasets, as shown in Fig. 2. Obviously, AEPMA performs better than ACCAMS and SMA, which demonstrates the global information benefit the AEPMA model. Figure 2 also reflects that the sparsity of data influence the recommendation accuracy. The relative improvements that AEPMA achieves relative to SMA on sparse datasets (Ciao, Epinions), is superior to the relative improvement to ACCAMS. In other word, The ACCAMS performs better than SMA on sparse dataset, but worse on dense dataset. Because the ACCAMS use the mean of values to the block can lead to overfitting on the dense datasets. In AEPMA, we exploit Global and Local information can fully learn the complicated ratings. More importantly, the boosting framework can improve the model stability and robustness. In the global model such as PMF and RSVD, the same vectors of latent factors inferred from all user-item rating matrix is adopted to describe all users and items, However in many real-world user-item rating matrics, if we think of the global latent factors as "common interests", then subset of users may share "unique interests" that are not reflected by the "common interest". Thus, Fig. 3 investigates the effect of global and local information in our model. We fix the boosting framework and change the S^1. We can see AEPMA is better than PMF+ and ACCAMS+, and ACCAMS+ performs better than PMF+. Because ACCAMS+ trained the model by both global (boosting) and local (S^1) information. But AEPMA can learn the sample weight adaptively to learn sufficient information. Thus AEPMA is superior to ACCAMS+.

Figure 4(a) analyzes the running time with the number of matrices increases. The method AEPMA based on boosting can reduce the bias. And with the number of iterations increasing, the RMSE and MAE can decrease gradually, but running time increases. So in this experiment, we choose a compromise method, the number of matrices is smaller than five. Figure 4(b, c) analyzes the impact of clustering method with different numbers of clusters k and stencils s on Ciao dataset. From Fig. 4(b, c), it can be seen that the performances is destroyed when s is large. The main reason is that large stencils will make overfitting. Meanwhile, we discover that AEPMA is stable under varying k with fixing s. Thus small k is enough to approximate the rating matrix.

5   Conclusions

Traditional matrix approximation based collaborative filtering methods have a major drawback that they perform poorly at detecting strong associations among a small set of closely related items. In this paper, we can capture sufficient information by combining global and local information. More importantly, by placing a Laplacian prior on the user and item weight vectors, we can adaptively learn the sample weight. In the stochastic gradient boosting framework, we can learn the hidden information and enhance the recommendation accuracy and scalability. Experimental study on three real-world datasets demonstrates that proposed AEPMA method can outperform several state-of-art ensemble matrix approximation methods.

References

1. Beutel, A., Ahmed, A., Smola, A.J.: ACCAMS: additive co-clustering to approximate matrices succinctly. In: Proceedings of International Conference on World Wide Web, pp. 119–129 (2016)
2. Salakhutdinov, R., Mnih, A.: Probabilistic matrix factorization. In: Proceedings of International Conference on Machine Learning, pp. 880–887 (2007)
3. Lee, J., Kim, S., Lebanon, G., Singer, Y.: Local low-rank matrix approximation. In: Proceedings of the 30th International Conference on Machine Learning (ICML 2013), pp. 82–90 (2013)
4. Chen, C., Li, D., Zhao, Y., Lv, Q., Shang, L.: WEMAREC: accurate and scalable recommendation through weighted and ensemble matrix approximation. In: Proceedings of the 38th International ACM SIGIR Conference on Research and Development in Information Retrieval (SIGIR 2015), pp. 303–312 (2015)
5. Salakhutdinov, R., Mnih, A.: Bayesian probabilistic matrix factorization using Markov chain Monte Carlo. In: Proceedings of the 25th International Conference on Machine Learning (ICML 2008), pp. 880–887. ACM (2008)
6. Chen, C., Li, D., Lv, Q., Yan, J., Chu, S.M., Shang, L.: MPMA: mixture probabilistic matrix approximation for collaborative filtering. In: Proceedings of the 25th International Joint Conference on Artificial Intelligence (IJCAI 2016), pp. 1382–1388 (2016)
7. Li, D., Chen, C., Lv, Q., Yan, J., Shang, L., Chu, S.: Low-rank matrix approximation with stability. In: Proceedings of the 33rd International Conference on Machine Learning (ICML 2016), pp. 295–303 (2016)
8. Srebro, N., Jaakkola, T.: Weighted low-rank approximations. In: Proceedings of the 20th International Conference on Machine Learning (ICML 2003), pp. 720–727 (2003)
9. Aharon, M., Elad, M., Bruckstein, A.: K-SVD: an algorithm for designing overcomplete dictionaries for sparse representation. IEEE Trans. Signal Process. **54**(11), 4311–4322 (2006)
10. Jing, L., Wang, P., Yang, L.: Sparse probabilistic matrix factorization by Laplace distribution for collaborative filtering. In: Proceedings of the International Conference on Artificial Intelligence, pp. 1771–1777 (2015)
11. Lee, J., Kim, S., Lebanon, G., Singer, Y.: Local low-rank matrix approximation. In: Proceedings of the 30th International Conference on Machine Learning, pp. 82–90 (2013)
12. Mackey, L.W., Jordan, M.I., Talwalkar, A.: Divide-and-conquer matrix factorization. In: Advances in Neural Information Processing Systems, pp. 1134–1142 (2011)
13. Koren, Y.: Factorization meets the neighborhood: a multifaceted collaborative filtering model. In: Knowledge Discovery and Data Mining KDD, pp. 426–434 (2008)
14. Herlocker, J.L., Konstan, J.A., Borchers, A., Riedl, J.: An algorithmic framework for performing collaborative filtering. In: Proceedings of the 22nd International ACM SIGIR Conference on Research and Development in Information Retrieval (SIGIR 1999), pp. 230–237 (1999)

15. Sarwar, B., Karypis, G., Konstan, J., Riedl, J.: Item-based collaborative filtering recommendation algorithms. In: Proceedings of the 10th International Conference on World Wide Web (WWW 2001), pp. 285–295 (2001)

16. Zhang, Y., Zhang, M., Liu, Y., Ma, S.: Improve collaborative filtering through bordered block diagonal form matrices. In: Proceedings of the 36th International ACM SIGIR Conference on Research and Development in Information Retrieval (SIGIR 2013), pp. 313–322 (2013)

17. Lawrence, N.D., Urtasun, R.: Non-linear matrix factorization with Gaussian processes. In: Proceedings of the International Conference on Machine Learning (2009)

18. Mirbakhsh, N., Ling, C.X.: Clustering-based matrix factorization. ArXiv Report arXiv:1301.6659 (2013)

19. Duchi, J., Hazan, E., Singer, Y.: Adaptive subgradient methods for online learning and stochastic optimization. J. Mach. Learn. Res. **12**, 2121–2159 (2011)

20. Moulines, E., Bach, F.R.: Non-asymptotic analysis of stochastic approximation algorithms for machine learning. In: Advances in Neural Information Processing Systems, pp. 451–459 (2011)

21. Polyak, B.T., Juditsky, A.B.: Acceleration of stochastic approximation by averaging. SIAM J. Control. Optim. **30**(4), 838–855 (1992)

22. Sutskever, I., Martens, J., Dahl, G., Hinton, G.: On the importance of initialization and momentum in deep learning. In: Proceedings of the 30th International Conference on Machine Learning (ICML 2013), pp. 1139–1147 (2013)

23. Zeiler, M.D.: ADADELTA: an adaptive learning rate method. arXiv preprint arXiv:1212.5701 (2012)

24. Lee, D.D., Seung, H.S.: Algorithms for non-negative matrix factorization. In: Advances in Neural Information Processing Systems, pp. 556–562 (2001)

25. Li, D., Chen, C., Lv, Q., Yan, J., Shang, L., Chu, SM.: Low-rank matrix approximation with stability (2017)

A Deep Structure-Enforced Nonnegative Matrix Factorization for Data Representation

Yijia Zhou[1] and Lijun Xu[2(✉)]

[1] Dalian Neusoft University of Information,
Dalian 116023, Liaoning, People's Republic of China
zhouyijia@neusoft.edu.cn
[2] Dalian Maritime University,
Dalian 116026, Liaoning, People's Republic of China
lijun_xu@dlmu.edu.cn

Abstract. In this paper, we focus on a deep structure-enforced non-negative matrix factorization (DSeNMF) which represents a large class of deep learning models appearing in many applications. We present a unified algorithm framework, based on the classic alternating direction method of multipliers (ADMM). For updating subproblems, we derive an efficient updating rule according to its KKT conditions. We conduct numerical experiments to compare the proposed algorithm with state-of-the-art deep semi-NMF. Results show that our algorithm performs better and our deep model with different sparsity imposed indeed results in better clustering accuracy than single-layer model. Our DSeNMF can be flexibly applicable for data representation.

Keywords: Deep matrix fatorization · Alternating direction method
Data representation

1 Introduction

Matrix factorization techniques have found great utility in various data-related applications, such as in signal and image processing and in machine learning tasks, primarily because they often help reveal latent features in a dataset. In recent years, Non-negative Matrix Factorization (NMF) is a widely-used method for finding meaningful representations of nonnegative data and has been proven useful in dimension reduction of images, text data and signals, for example. The family of NMF algorithms has been successfully applied to a variety of areas, like environmetrics [1], microarray data analysis [2,3], document clustering [4], face recognition [5,6], speech recognition [7], hyperspectral image unmixing [8,9], blind audio source separation [10], etc. Moreover, NMF has been extended into

Supported by the Fundamental Research Funds for the Central Universities (3132018218).

J.-H. Lai et al. (Eds.): PRCV 2018, LNCS 11258, pp. 340–350, 2018.
https://doi.org/10.1007/978-3-030-03338-5_29

a number of variant forms, allowing for various structures or regularized models, most of which demonstrate distinct advantages in local feature extraction or data representation learning.

The work of Lee and Seung [11] demonstrates that NMF models tend to return part-based sparse representations of data, which has popularized the use of and research on NMF-related techniques. In particular, various NMF-inspired formulations add different regularization or penalty terms to promote desired properties, such as sparsity patterns or orthogonality in addition to nonnegativity (see [12–18], for example). Besides, graph-regularized NMF versions have also been explored. For example, Cai et al. [19] proposed a graph-regularized NMF by incorporating prior information of samples into the typical NMF. This helps to keep the original topological structure of data after being projected into a subspace and usually leads to better clustering results.

Semi Non-negative Matrix Factorization (Semi-NMF) [20], as one of the most popular variants of NMF, was proposed to extend NMF by relaxing the factorized basis matrix to be real values. This practice allows Semi-NMF to learn new lower-dimensional features from the data that have a convenient clustering interpretation and have a wider application in the real world than traditional NMF. Moreover, it has shown that it is equivalent to k-means clustering, and that in fact, this NMF variants are expected to perform better than k-means clustering particularly when the data is not distributed in a spherical manner.

Although there have been extensive variants of NMF, most of them remain to be single-layer models, hence can only capture one level of data features. Most recently, deep learning is becoming increasingly popular and has been demonstrated to be powerful in learning data representation. Inspired by the success of training deep architectures, Multi-layer NMF (see [21,22] for example), Deep Semi-NMF [23], Deep Orthogonal NMF [24], Sparse Deep NMF [25], Deep Nonsmooth NMF [26], etc. have been proposed by stacking one-layer variants of NMF into multiple layers to learn hierarchical relationships among features or hierarchical projections. Since these deep (multi-layer) models can extract high level data representations and yield intuitive interpretations for features generated in each layer, they have been successfully applied to many areas, such as recommender systems [27], image clustering [28], neural network [29], speech separation [30], matrix completion [31], for example. However, these models are only designed for specific problems with certain intuitive structures. In this paper, we focus on a unified deep structure-enforced NMF in data representation, which imposing desired properties (like sparsity, orthogonality, for example) in addition to nonnegativity. A specific algorithmic approach to solve the deep structure-enforced NMF is further studied and can be applicable to a range of easily projectable structures.

This paper is organized as follows. In Sect. 2, we introduce the deep structure-enforced NMF (DSeNMF) and propose a new ADMM-based algorithm framework for solving DSeNMF. Section 3 contains several numerical experiments comparing the proposed algorithm with Deep Semi-NMF and single-layer matrix factorization on MNIST digit dataset. Finally, we conclude this paper in Sect. 4.

2   Deep Structure-Enforced Nonnegative Matrix Fatorization Model

The general structured-enforced matrix factorization (SeMF) model (1) is firstly proposed in the earlier work in [32]. That is, decomposing a given data matrix $M \in \mathbb{R}^{p \times n}$ into two factors $Z \in \mathbb{R}^{p \times k}$ and $H \in \mathbb{R}^{k \times n}$ which belong to $\mathcal{Z}$ and $\mathcal{H}$, respectively,

$$\min_{Z,H} \frac{1}{2} \|M - ZH\|_F^2 \quad \text{s.t.} \quad Z \in \mathcal{Z}, \ H \in \mathcal{H}, \tag{1}$$

where $\| \cdot \|_F$ is Frobenius norm, and $\mathcal{Z}$ and $\mathcal{H}$ are subsets of $\mathbb{R}^{p \times k}$ and $\mathbb{R}^{k \times n}$, respectively. Obviously, the model (1) is a single-layer matrix factorization. Thus, it can only do one-layer feature extraction even utilizing more structures. In practice, it is common that complex data objects have hierarchical features, each of which denotes a different level of abstract understanding of the objects. It is therefore meaningful to develop corresponding models with a deep architecture, which allows to discover the hierarchy of data. It is well known that NMF is widely used both in single-layer and in multi-layer data representation. To this end, we propose a deep structure-enforced version for nonnegative matrix factorization by extending model (1).

Similar to the general multi-layer framework, the Deep Structure-enforced NMF (DSeNMF) model is presented to factorize $M \in \mathbb{R}^{p \times n}$ into the multiplier of m + 1 nonnegative matrices, as follows:

$$\min_{\{Z_i \geq 0\}_{i=1}^m, H_m \geq 0} \frac{1}{2} \|M - Z_1 Z_2 \cdots Z_m H_m\|_F^2 \quad \text{s.t.} \quad Z_i \in \mathcal{Z}_i, \ H_m \in \mathcal{H}, \tag{2}$$

where $Z_1 \in \mathbb{R}^{p \times k_1}$, $\{Z_i \in \mathbb{R}^{k_{i-1} \times k_i}\}_{i=2}^m$, $H_m \in \mathbb{R}^{k_m \times n}$, $\{\mathcal{Z}_i\}_{i=1}^m$ and $\mathcal{H}$ are structure subsets with proper dimensions. In our model, prior knowledge are explicitly enforced as constraint sets $\{\mathcal{Z}_i\}_{i=1}^m$ and $\mathcal{H}$ whose members possess desirable matrix structures allowing "easy projection". In practice, the most useful structures of this kind include, but are not limited to, nonnegativity, normality and various sparsity patterns. Many deep NMF models can be represented by the DSeNMF (2) with different structure constraints, see Sparse Deep NMF, Deep Orthogonal NMF, Deep Semi-NMF as mentioned above, for example.

To make it more intuitive, one can split the model (2) into the following factorizations:

$$M \approx Z_1 H_1,$$
$$H_1 \approx Z_2 H_2,$$
$$\vdots \tag{3}$$
$$H_{m-1} \approx Z_m H_m,$$

where $\{Z_i\}_{i=1}^m$ and $\{H_i\}_{i=1}^m$ satisfy proper constraints, respectively. This formulation can intuitively illustrate that deep model (2) allows for a hierarchy of m layers of implicit representations of data. In other words, not only most multi-layer and deep matrix factorizations is derived from the formulation (3), but also most algorithms for (2) are designed by solving (3) layer by layer. In the beginning of approaches, the objective data matrix are multi-factorized only by solving (3) one round layer by layer. Obviously, these approaches are inefficient since the factor matrices in former layers are useless for subsequent layer factorizations. Therefore, the popular scheme is utilizing the layer by layer technique as initialization or pre-training, then fine-tuning all layers by alternating updating factor matrices one by one. Now, we propose a novel approach based on alternating direction algorithm framework to solve the non-convex problem (2).

2.1   An Alternating Direction Algorithm for the Proposed DSeNMF

As introduced in the work [32,33], an alternating direction and projection method solves single layer structure-enforced matrix factorization (SeMF) efficiently. Motivated by the algorithms in [32,33], we propose a novel way to tackle multi-layer or deep matrix factorizations. To facilitate an efficient use of alternating minimization, we introduce auxiliary variables $\{U_i\}_{i=1}^m$ and V_m in order to separate $\{Z_i\}_{i=1}^m$ and H_m from structure constraints $\{\mathcal{Z}_i\}_{i=1}^m$ and $\mathcal{H}$, respectively. Consider the following model equivalent to (2),

$$
\min_{\{Z_i \geq 0, U_i\}_{i=1}^m, H_m \geq 0, V_m} \frac{1}{2}\|M - Z_1 Z_2 \cdots Z_m H_m\|_F^2
$$

$$
\text{s.t.} \quad Z_i - U_i = 0, \ U_i \in \mathcal{Z}_i, i = 1, \cdots, m, \tag{4}
$$

$$
H_m - V_m = 0, \ V_m \in \mathcal{H},
$$

where $\{U_i\}_{i=1}^m$ and V_m have the same dimension size with $\{Z_i\}_{i=1}^m$ and H_m, respectively. The augmented Lagrangian function of (4) is

$$
\mathcal{L}_A(\{Z_i, U_i, \Lambda_i\}_{i=1}^m, H_m, V_m, \Pi)
$$

$$
= \frac{1}{2}\|M - Z_1 Z_2 \cdots Z_m H_m\|_F^2 +
$$

$$
\sum_{i=1}^m \Lambda_i \bullet (Z_i - U_i) + \Pi \bullet (H_m - V_m) \tag{5}
$$

$$
+ \sum_{i=1}^m \frac{\alpha_i}{2}\|Z_i - U_i\|_F^2 + \frac{\beta}{2}\|H_m - V_m\|_F^2,
$$

where $\{\Lambda_i\}_{i=1}^m, \Pi$ are Lagrangian multipliers with equal-size of $\{Z_i\}_{i=1}^m, H_m$, respectively, and $(\{\alpha_i\}_{i=1}^m, \beta) \geq 0$ are penalty parameters for equality constraints, respectively. Note that the scalar product "$\bullet$" of two equal-size matrices X and Y is the sum of all element-wise products, i.e., $X \bullet Y = \sum_{i,j} X_{ij} Y_{ij}$.

The alternating direction method of multiplier (ADMM) [34,35] for (4) is derived by successively minimizing the augmented Lagrangian function $\mathcal{L}_A$ with respect to $\{Z_i\}_{i=1}^m, H_m, \{U_i\}_{i=1}^m$ and V_m, one at a time while fixing others at their most recent values, and then updating the multipliers after each sweep of such alternating minimization. The introduction of the auxiliary variables $\{U_i\}_{i=1}^m$ and V_m makes it easy to carry out each of the alternating minimization steps. Specifically, these steps can be written in the following forms,

$$Z_j^+ \approx \arg \min_{Z_j \geq 0} \mathcal{L}_A(\{Z_i, U_i, \Lambda_i\}_{i=1}^m, H_m, V_m, \Pi), j = 1, 2, \cdots, m, \quad (6a)$$

$$H_m^+ \approx \arg \min_{H_m \geq 0} \mathcal{L}_A(\{Z_i^+, U_i, \Lambda_i\}_{i=1}^m, H_m, V_m, \Pi), \quad (6b)$$

$$U_j^+ = \mathcal{P}_{\mathcal{Z}_j}(Z_j^+ + \Lambda_j/\alpha_j), j = 1, 2, \cdots, m, \quad (6c)$$

$$V_m^+ = \mathcal{P}_{\mathcal{H}}(H_m^+ + \Pi/\beta), \quad (6d)$$

$$\Lambda_j^+ = \Lambda_j + \alpha_j(Z_j^+ - U_j^+), j = 1, 2, \cdots, m, \quad (6e)$$

$$\Pi^+ = \Pi + \beta(H_m^+ - V_m^+). \quad (6f)$$

where $\mathcal{P}_{\mathcal{Z}_j}$ ($\mathcal{P}_{\mathcal{H}}$) stands for the projection onto the set $\mathcal{Z}_j$ ($\mathcal{H}$) in Frobenius norm, and the superscript "+" is used to denote iterative values at the new iteration.

Updating Rule for Z_j. We fix the rest of the factor matrices and minimize the cost function with respect to Z_j. The Z_j-updating subproblem (6a) actually can be rewritten as

$$\min_{Z_j} \frac{1}{2}\|M - \Phi_j Z_j \Psi_j\|_F^2 + \Lambda_j \bullet (Z_j - U_j) + \frac{\alpha_j}{2}\|Z_j - U_j\|_F^2 \quad (7)$$
$$\text{s.t. } Z_j \geq 0,$$

where $\Phi_j = Z_1 Z_2 \cdots Z_{j-1}$ and $\Psi_j = Z_{j+1} \cdots Z_m H_m$. Let Γ be the lagrangian multiplier for constraint $Z_j \geq 0$, the Lagrangian function of (7) is

$$\mathcal{L} = \frac{1}{2}\|M - \Phi_j Z_j \Psi_j\|_F^2 + \Lambda_j \bullet (Z_j - U_j) + \frac{\alpha_j}{2}\|Z_j - U_j\|_F^2 + \Gamma \bullet Z_j.$$

The partial derivative of $\mathcal{L}$ with respect to Z_j is

$$\frac{\partial \mathcal{L}}{\partial Z_j} = \Phi_j^T \Phi_j Z_j \Psi_j \Psi_j^T + \alpha_j Z_j - \Phi_j^T M \Psi_j^T - \alpha_j U_j + \Lambda_j + \Gamma.$$

Using the Karush-Kuhn–Tucker (KKT) conditions $\Gamma_{ik} Z_{j_{ik}} = 0$, we get the following equations respect to the (i, k)-th element:

$$\left(\Phi_j^T \Phi_j Z_j \Psi_j \Psi_j^T + \alpha_j Z_j - \Phi_j^T M \Psi_j^T - \alpha_j U_j + \Lambda_j\right)_{ik} (Z_j)_{ik} = 0.$$

This equation leads to the following updating rule:

$$(Z_j^+)_{ik} = (Z_j)_{ik} \frac{(\Phi_j^T M \Psi_j^T + \alpha_j U_j - \Lambda_j)_{ik}}{(\Phi_j^T \Phi_j Z_j \Psi_j \Psi_j^T + \alpha_j Z_j)_{ik}}, \quad (8)$$

and it can be rewritten as

$$Z_j^+ = Z_j \odot [(\Phi_j^T M \Psi_j^T + \alpha_j U_j - \Lambda_j) \oslash (\Phi_j^T \Phi_j Z_j \Psi_j \Psi_j^T + \alpha_j Z_j)], \quad (9)$$

where $\odot$ and $\oslash$ denote component multiplications and divisions, respectively.

Updating Rule for H_m. We can derive the H_m-updating rule of (6b) in a similar way. We omit the derivative procedure and directly write updating rule for (i, k)-th component of H_m:

$$(H_m^+)_{ik} = (H_m)_{ik} \frac{(\Phi^\mathrm{T} M + \beta V_m - \Pi)_{ik}}{(\Phi^\mathrm{T} \Phi H_m + \beta H_m)_{ik}}, \tag{10}$$

where $\Phi = Z_1^+ Z_2^+ \cdots Z_m^+$. Namely,

$$H_m^+ = H_m \odot [(\Phi^\mathrm{T} M + \beta V_m - \Pi) \oslash (\Phi^\mathrm{T} \Phi H_m + \beta H_m)], \tag{11}$$

where $\odot$ and $\oslash$ denote component multiplications and divisions, respectively.

Since we update Z_j and H_m by component multiplications and divisions instead of involving inverse matrices, the dominant computational tasks at each iteration are the matrix multiplications. Therefore, our updating scheme posses much lower complexity than inverting matrices.

Based on the formulas in (6), (9) and (11), we can implement the following ADMM algorithmic framework so long as we can compute the projections in steps (6c) and (6d).

Algorithm 1. ADMM Framework for DSeNMF

Input: M, each layer dimension $k_i, i = 1, \cdots, m$, $maxiter > 0$ and $tol > 0$.
Output: $\{Z_i\}_{i=1}^m$ and H_m.
Set $\{\alpha_i\}_{i=1}^m, \beta > 0$.
$H_0 = M$;
for $i = 1$ *to* m **do**
| $Z_i, H_i \leftarrow \mathrm{SeMF}(H_{i-1}, k_i)$ \\ *Initialization.*
end
for $k = 1$ *to* $maxiter$ **do**
| Update $(\{Z_i, U_i, \Lambda_i\}_{i=1}^m, H_m, V_m, \Pi)$ by the formulas in (6), (9) and (11).
| **if** *stopping criterion (12) is met* **then**
| | output $\{Z_i\}_{i=1}^m$ and H_m, and exit.
| **end**
end

We use the following practical stopping criterion: for given tolerance $tol > 0$,

$$\frac{|f_k - f_{k+1}|}{|f_k|} \leq tol, \tag{12}$$

where $f_k = \|X - Z_1^k Z_2^k \cdots Z_m^k H_m^k\|_F$, Z_i^k is the k-th iterate for the variable Z_i, and so on. For the sake of robustness, in our implementation we require that the above condition be satisfied at three consecutive iterations. In other words, we stop the algorithm when data fidelity does not change meaningfully in three consecutive iterations.

3   Experimental Results

In this section we test the proposed model on MNIST dataset to show that our Deep SeNMF is able to learn better high-level representations of data than a single one-layer structure-enforced NMF. In addition, we compare the performance of the proposed DSeNMF with recently Deep Semi-NMF on the task of clustering analysis and consuming time. Note that we consider to impose several sparse constraints on our DSeNMF model (2).

To better understand the proposed model, we introduce three way to impose sparsity on H_m. One is adding sparsity not only during initialization but also in subsequential updating and denote this case as DSeNMF(sparse). The other way is imposing sparsity only in step (6d), that is, using standard NMF to initialize each layer matrix, and is denoted as DSeNMF(semi-sparse). The last one will not impose sparsity and denote this case as DSeMF(no sparse). To illustrate deep model and single-layer factorization distinct, we also consider single-layer structure-enforced matrix factorization and denote as SingleSeMF.

Next, we apply models to the testing data in an unsupervised way to clustering. We opt the digits from 0 to 4 in MNIST which constitute a 784×5139 matrix M. In this test, we choose the number of layers to be 3 and dimension size of each layer is 300, 15 and 50, respectively. Besides, set the maximum number of iteration $maxiter = 500$ and tolerance $tol = 1e-6$. We factorize data matrix M using Deep Semi-NMF (DSemiNMF) in [23], DSeNMF(sparse), DSeNMF(semi-sparse) and SingleSeMF, respectively. Then we cluster columns of the final H_m according to the approach in [23] and output the clustering accuracy as AC.

Table 1. Results comparison with different deep NMF models

Method	DSeNMF (sparse)	DSeNMF (semi-sparse)	DSeNMF (no sparse)	DSemiNMF [23]	SingleSeMF [32]
AC	0.57	0.68	0.48	0.40	0.33
Time(s)	64.18	64.38	66.57	292.54	29.39
RMSE	37.3688	37.3693	37.3676	37.4621	24.0117

In Table 1, we tabulate the average clustering accuracy (AC), average running time (in second) and average root mean square error (RMSE). We see from the table that our deep structure-enforced NMF performs well both in accuracy and in time consuming. It should be note that our algorithm only need about one fifth running time comparing with deep semi-NMF algorithm. In addition, note that the last column in Table 1, we use the SeMF algorithm in [32] to decompose M into multiplication of $Z \in \mathbb{R}^{784 \times 50}$ and $H \in \mathbb{R}^{50 \times 5139}$ which is indeed a single-layer nonnegative matrix factorization. Obviously, SingleSeMF obtain the best data fidelity, but get the worst clustering accuracy meanwhile. It confirms that all the DSeNMF models are able to learn better high-level representations of data than a single one-layer structure-enforced NMF. Among results of our proposed model with three different structure constraints, we note that DSeNMF(sparse) and DSeNMF(semi-sparse) obtain better clustering results than DSeNMF(no sparse) since imposing sparsity on H_m. More interestingly, comparing DSeNMF(sparse) with DSeNMF(semi-sparse), the former gets lower clustering accuracy even though considering sparsity in initialization. It demonstrates that imposing structure constraints earlier could not obtain a better initialization. It makes sense that some properties in real data should be considered step by step rather than completely utilized at the beginning.

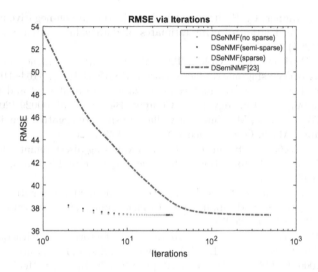

Fig. 1. RMSE comparison with different deep NMF models

Figure 1 presents RMSE curves of four deep models. It shows that our algorithm for solving deep NMF models needs much less (about 50) iterations than the algorithm in [23] (around 500 iterations). It will be evident that our proposed model and algorithm are efficient for the class of deep structured NMF.

4 Conclusion and Future

We have introduced a kind of deep structure-enforced nonnegative matrix factorization and proposed a novel framework for solving the unified model. Although the proposed framework introduces many auxiliary variables, these variables aim to separate from complex structure constraints and split original factor matices. Further, it can facilitate the obtained model equivalently transformed to an ADMM-applicable model which is easy implemented. Numerical experiments also show the efficiency of the proposed algorithm and the applicable of our deep model for data representing problems.

Although deep structured matrix factorization problems are generally highly nonconvex, they widely and variously exist in real-world applications. Our next step is testing the proposed model and algorithm on more datasets and comparing it with other deep NMF algorithms. Another work will be focusing on how different decomposed dimension would affect clustering performance of deep non-negative matrix factorization.

References

1. Paatero, P., Tapper, U.: Positive matrix factorization: a non-negative factor model with optimal utilization of error estimates of data values. Environmetrics **5**(2), 111–126 (1994)
2. Brunet, J.-P., Tamayo, P., Golub, T.R., Mesirov, J.P.: Metagenes and molecular pattern discovery using matrix factorization. PNAS **101**(12), 4164–4169 (2004)
3. Devarajan, K.: Nonnegative matrix factorization: an analytical and interpretive tool in computational biology. PLoS Comput. Biol. **4**(7), e1000029 (2008)
4. Berry, M.W., Browne, M.: Email surveillance using nonnegative matrix factorization. Comput. Math. Organ. Theory **11**(3), 249–264 (2005)
5. Zafeiriou, S., Tefas, A., Buciu, I., Pitas, I.: Exploiting discriminant information in nonnegative matrix factorization with application to frontal face verification. TNN **17**(3), 683–695 (2006)
6. Kotsia, I., Zafeiriou, S., Pitas, I.: A novel discriminant nonnegative matrix factorization algorithm with applications to facial image characterization problems. TIFS **2**(3–2), 588–595 (2007)
7. Zdunek, R., Cichocki, A.: Non-negative matrix factorization with quasi-newton optimization. In: Rutkowski, L., Tadeusiewicz, R., Zadeh, L.A., Żurada, J.M. (eds.) ICAISC 2006. LNCS (LNAI), vol. 4029, pp. 870–879. Springer, Heidelberg (2006). https://doi.org/10.1007/11785231_91
8. Wang, W., Li, S., Qi, H., Ayhan, B., Kwan, C., Vance, S.: Identify anomaly component by sparsity and low rank. In: IEEE Workshop on Hyperspectral Image and Signal Processing: Evolution in Remote Sensor (WHISPERS), Tokyo, Japan (2015)
9. Qu, Y., Guo, R., Wang, W., Qi, H., Ayhan, B., Kwan, C., Vance, S.: Anomaly detection in hyperspectral images through spectral unmixing and low rank decomposition. In: IEEE International Geoscience and Remote Sensing Symposium (IGARSS), Beijing, pp. 1855–1858 (2016)
10. Weninger, F., Schuller, B.: Optimization and parallelization of monaural source separation algorithms in the openBliSSART toolkit. J. Signal Process. Syst. **69**(3), 267–C277 (2012)
11. Lee, D.D., Seung, H.S.: Learning the parts of objects by non-negative matrix factorization. Nature **401**, 788–791 (1999)
12. Hoyer, P.O.: Non-negative sparse coding. In: IEEE Workshop on Neural Networks for Signal Processing, Martigny, Switzerland, pp. 557–565 (2002)
13. Feng, T., Li, S.Z., Shum, H.Y., Zhang, H.J.: Local non-negative matrix factorization as a visual representation. In: Proceedings of the 2nd International Conference on Development and Learning, pp. 178–183 (2002)
14. Hoyer, P.O., Dayan, P.: Non-negative matrix factorization with sparseness constraints. J. Mach. Learn. Res. **5**, 1457–1469 (2004)

15. Montano, A.P., Carazo, J.M., Kochi, K., Lehmann, D., Pascual-Marqui, R.D.: Nonsmooth nonnegative matrix factorization (nsNMF). IEEE Trans. Pattern Anal. **28**(3), 403–415 (2006)

16. Jenatton, R., Obozinski, G., Bach, F.: Structured sparse principal component analysis. In: International Conference on Artificial Intelligence and Statistics (AISTATS) (2010)

17. Peharz, R., Pernkopf, F.: Sparse nonnegative matrix factorization with ℓ_0-constraints. Neurocomputing **80**, 38–46 (2012)

18. Zheng, W.S., Lai, J.H., Liao, S.C., He, R.: Extracting non-negative basis images using pixel dispersion penalty. Pattern Recogn. **45**(8), 2912–2926 (2012)

19. Cai, D., He, X., Han, J.: Locally consistent concept factorization for document clustering. IEEE Trans. Knowl. Data Eng. **23**(6), 902–913 (2011)

20. Ding, C.H., Li, T., Jordan, M.I.: Convex and semi-nonnegative matrix factorizations. IEEE Trans. Pattern Anal. Mach. Intell. **32**(1), 45–55 (2010)

21. Ahn, J.H., Choi, S., Oh, J.: A multiplicative up-propagation algorithm. In: Proceedings of the 21st International Conference on Machine Learning, p. 3 (2004)

22. Song, H.A., Kim, B.K., Xuan, T.L., Lee, S.Y.: Hierarchical feature extraction by multi-layer non-negative matrix factorization network for classification task. Neurocomputing **165**, 63–74 (2015)

23. Trigeorgis, G., Bousmalis, K., Zafeiriou, S., Schuller, B.W.: A deep matrix factorization method for learning attribute representations. IEEE Trans. Pattern Anal. Mach. Intell. **39**(3), 417–429 (2017)

24. Lyu, B., Xie, K., Sun, W.: A deep orthogonal non-negative matrix factorization method for learning attribute representations. In: Liu, D., Xie, S., Li, Y., Zhao, D., El-Alfy, E.S. (eds.) ICONIP 2017. LNCS, vol. 10639, pp. 443–452. Springer, Cham (2017). https://doi.org/10.1007/978-3-319-70136-3_47

25. Guo, Z., Zhang, S.: Sparse deep nonnegative matrix factorization (2017). http://arxiv.org/abs/1707.09316

26. Yu, J., Zhou, G., Cichocki, A., Xie, S.: Learning the hierarchical parts of objects by deep non-smooth nonnegative matrix factorization (2018). http://arxiv.org/abs/1803.07226

27. Xue, H., Dai, X., Zhang, J., Huang, S., Chen, J.: Deep matrix factorization models for recommender systems. In: Proceedings of the 26th International Joint Conference on Artificial Intelligence, Melbourne, Australia, pp. 3203–3209 (2017)

28. Zhao, H., Ding, Z., Fu Y.: Multi-view clustering via deep matrix factorization. In: Thirty-First AAAI Conference on Artificial Intelligence, pp. 2921–2927 (2017)

29. Flenner, J., Hunter, B.: A deep non-negative matrix factorization neural network (2017)

30. Le Roux, J., Hershey, J.R., Weninger, F.: Deep NMF for speech separation. In: IEEE International Conference on Acoustics, Speech and Signal Processing, South Brisbane, Australia, pp. 66–70 (2015)

31. Fan, J., Cheng, J.: Matrix completion by deep matrix factorization. Neural Netw. **98**, 34–41 (2017)

32. Xu, L., Yu, B., Zhang, Y.: An alternating direction and projection algorithm for structure-enforced matrix factorization. Comput. Optim. Appl. **68**(2), 333–362 (2017). https://doi.org/10.1007/s10589-017-9913-x

33. Xu, L., Zhou, Y., Yu, B.: Classification and clustering via structure-enforced matrix factorization. In: Sun, Y., Lu, H., Zhang, L., Yang, J., Huang, H. (eds.) IScIDE 2017. LNCS, vol. 10559, pp. 403–411. Springer, Cham (2017). https://doi.org/10.1007/978-3-319-67777-4_35

34. Glowinski, R., Marroco, A.: Sur lapproximation, par elements finis dordre un, et la resolution, par penalisation-dualite dune classe de problemes de dirichlet non lineaires. Revue francaise dautomatique, informatique, recherche operationnelle. Analyse numerique 9(2), 41–76 (1975)

35. Gabay, D., Mercier, B.: A dual algorithm for the solution of nonlinear variational problems via finite element approximation. Comput. Math. Appl. 2(1), 17–40 (1976)

An Embedded Method for Feature Selection Using Kernel Parameter Descent Support Vector Machine

Haiqing Zhu[1], Ning Bi[1], Jun Tan[1(✉)], and Dongjie Fan[2]

[1] School of Mathematics, Sun Yat-sen University, Guangzhou 510275, China
mcstj@mail.sysu.edu.cn
[2] Center for Urban Science and Progress, New York University,
New York 10012, USA

Abstract. We introduce a novel embedded algorithm for feature selection, using Support Vector Machine (SVM) with kernel functions. Our method, called Kernel Parameter Descent SVM (KPD-SVM), is taking parameters of kernel functions as variables to optimize the target functions in SVM model training. KPD-SVM use sequential minimal optimization, which breaks the large quadratic optimization problem into some smaller possible optimization problem, avoids inner loop on time-consuming numerical computation. Additionally, KPD-SVM optimize the shape of RBF kernel to eliminate features which have low relevance for the class label. Through kernel selection and execution of improved algorithm in each case, we simultaneously find the optimal solution of selected features in the modeling process. We compare our method with algorithms like filter method (Fisher Criterion Score) or wrapper method (Recursive Feature Elimination SVM) to demonstrate its effectiveness and efficiency.

Keywords: Feature selection · Support vector machine
Kernel function

1 Introduction

Feature Selection is a vital issue in machine learning. It is common to apply feature selection methods to classification problems, especially when those original data sets have redundant features [1].

According to [2], there are three main directions for feature selection: filter, wrapper, and embedded methods.

Filter takes statistical analysis to filter out poorly informative features, it is usually done before the samples taken into a classifier. Relief [3] is a typical filter method which is statistically relevant to the target concept and feeds features into the classifier.

Wrapper approach searches the whole set of samples to score feature subset, therefore it naturally entails training and implementation of learning algorithms

© Springer Nature Switzerland AG 2018
J.-H. Lai et al. (Eds.): PRCV 2018, LNCS 11258, pp. 351–362, 2018.
https://doi.org/10.1007/978-3-030-03338-5_30

during the procedure of feature selection, wrappers use different classifier such as naive Bayes [4], neural networks [5] and nearest neighbor [6]. The random forests based wrapper approaches [7,8] are widely used to identify important features from feature subset.

In embedded method, feature selection is embedded into the classifier [9], feature is selected by the internal function of an algorithm such as least absolute shrinkage and selection operator (LASSO) [10] and decision tree [11].

Above methods have their limitation, wrapper algorithms are complex in computation, but usually obtain more accurate results than filter methods [12], the problem of a wrapper is high computational cost because it involves repeated training. The robustness of above methods in high dimension data set is a crucial problem. Therefore some features select approaches constructed by combining multiple classifiers, their robust more than the approaches with a single classifier [13]. In addition, support vector machines (SVM) have been proposed as a wrapper classifier for feature selection [14].

Although standard implementation of SVM shows good performance in classification prediction, it cannot rank each features' importance for feature elimination. Thus we introduce a novel approach which selects features according to the descent path of kernel parameters, indirectly figuring out the importance of each features as well as optimizing the model predicting ability. The method we called Kernel Parameter Descent Support Vector Machine (KPD-SVM), the approach not only optimizes the parameter of SVM, but also obtains a subset of features for specific objective. KPD-SVM will be talked in detail and be compared with other characteristic approaches of feature selection in SVM.

2 Related Works

2.1 Support Vector Machine

In this section, we will simply review the development of SVM method.

Support Vector Machine (SVM) is a strictly math-based machine learning model, raised by Vapnik [15]. The principle of SVM classifier is obvious. It tries to find out the optimal hyperplane for the optimization problem with "soft margin" as follows:

$$\min_{\mathbf{w},b,\xi} \frac{1}{2}\|\mathbf{w}\|^2 + C\sum_{i=1}^{n}\xi_i \tag{1}$$

$$s.t. \quad y_i \cdot (\mathbf{w}^T \cdot \phi(\mathbf{x}_i) + b) \geq (1 - \xi_i) \qquad i = 1,\ldots,n,$$

$$\xi_i \geq 0, \qquad i = 1,\ldots,n$$

Here we denote ξ_i as slack variable. The training data can be transformed into higher dimensional space through kernel function $x \rightarrow \phi(x)$. So the decision function can be rewritten as:

$$f(x) = \sum_{i=1}^{n}\alpha_i y_i \langle \phi(x_i), \phi(x) \rangle + b \tag{2}$$

Since the scalar products $\langle \phi(x), \phi(y) \rangle$ are the only value to be calculated, kernel function

$$K(x, y) = \langle \phi(x), \phi(y) \rangle \tag{3}$$

is used to solve them. As result the optimization problem can be rewritten as:

$$\max_{\alpha} \sum_{i=1}^{n} \alpha_i - \frac{1}{2} \sum_{i,j=1}^{n} \alpha_i \alpha_j y_i y_j K(x_i, x_j) \tag{4}$$

$$s.t. \quad 0 \leq \alpha_i \leq C \quad i = 1, \ldots, n$$

$$\sum_{i=1}^{n} \alpha_i y_i = 0$$

2.2 Feature Selection in SVMs

Typically, there are three methods in SVM based feature selection process, Filter, Wrapper and Embedded [1]. Here we review each of them briefly and stress one representative algorithm of each method, for experimental comparison in next section.

- **Filter Method:** Among all the measurement in Filter method, Fisher Criterion Score (F-Score) is one of the most common indicator to use. It computes the significance of each feature independently of the other feature by comparing that feature's correlation to the output labels. The respective score $F(j)$ of feature j is given by:

$$F(j) = \left| \frac{\mu_j^+ + \mu_j^-}{(\sigma_j^+)^2 + (\sigma_j^-)^2} \right| \tag{5}$$

Where μ_j^+ (μ_j^-)is the mean value for the jth feature in positive(negative) class. And $\sigma_j^+(\sigma_j^-)$ is the standard deviation. When the $F(j)$ is large, it means jth feature has much more information to discriminate itself from other features, which suggests it ranks top of the feature list and would be more likely not to be eliminate and vice versa. The disadvantage of filter method is time consuming and skillful because you need to choose a suitable measurement method.
- **Wrapper Method:** One representative wrapper method is Recursive Feature Elimination SVM (RFE-SVM), which is raised by Guyon [16]. RFE-SVM aims to find out the r-feature subset among the original n-feature set through backward greedy algorithm, which build model by the whole feature at the beginning then cut off one feature according the ranking order. The disadvantage of Wrapper method is that it is more time consuming than filter method because it need to train models on different feature subsets.

- **Embedded Method:** The last method for feature selection is embedded method. The most different novelty between embedded and others is that it conducts the selection in the process of model training. One common embedded method is to add a penalty item to the target function which limits the model complexity [17]. Compared with filter method and wrapper method, we choose embedded method in our model because it is less time consuming.

3 The Proposed Method: KPD-SVM

The principle of proposed method aims to improve the classification performance as well as to eliminate less important features by optimizing parameter/parameters in kernel function. This method use penalty item like $L0 - norm$ or $L1 - norm$ of the parameter to punish the large number of feature we consider in modeling which is more likely to cause over-fitting problems. Through gradient descent algorithm, we can find out the best solution (which means the best classification performance) of the vector of kernel parameters. During this iteration process, we set the parameters whose values are lower than a small criterion as 0. Thus we can deal with the feature selection task.

3.1 Kernel Function

Among the kernel function SVM commonly uses, we pay attention to the following mostly-used kernels:

Gaussian Kernel function we write the kernel function in the form of the summation in each feature:

$$K(x,y) = exp\left(-\sum_{j=1}^{d} \frac{(x_j - y_j)^2}{2\sigma_j^2}\right) \tag{6}$$

where $\sigma = [\sigma_1, \sigma_2, \sigma_3 \ldots, \sigma_n]$ indicates the width of the kernel and determines the kernel shape. d is the number of features. For better demonstration, we denote:

$$\gamma = [\frac{1}{2\sigma_1^2}, \frac{1}{2\sigma_2^2}, \frac{1}{2\sigma_3^2}, \ldots, \frac{1}{2\sigma_d^2}] \tag{7}$$

which leads to

$$K(x,y) = exp\left(-\sum_{j=1}^{d} \gamma_j(x_j - y_j)^2\right) \tag{8}$$

Exponential kernel (Laplace) Similar with Gaussian kernel, it is shown as:

$$K(x,y) = exp\left(-\sum_{j=1}^{d} \gamma_j(x_j - y_j)\right) \tag{9}$$

Polynomial kernel its function as:

$$K(x,y) = (\alpha x^T y + c)^D \tag{10}$$

Here we fix D and let $c = 1$ in our proposed method, hence we only need to consider the vector of α:

$$K(x,y) = ((\sum_{j=1}^{d} \alpha_j x_j y_j) + 1)^D \tag{11}$$

3.2   Target Function in KPD-SVM

According the previous definition, the set of Lagrange multipliers α is considered, and adding the new parameter γ in kernel function and penalty item of model complexity, therefore the optimization problem $\min_{w,b} \frac{1}{2}\|w\|^2$ is minimized with a penalty function and some constrains. Our target function G is as follows:

$$\min_{\alpha,\gamma} G(\alpha, \gamma) = \min_{\alpha} \Psi(\alpha) + \min_{\alpha,\gamma} \Phi(\alpha, \gamma) \tag{12}$$

where the $\Psi(\alpha)$ are transformed from the target optimization function (4) of the standard SVM:

$$\min_{\alpha} \Psi(\alpha) = \min_{\alpha} -\sum_{i=1}^{n} \alpha_i + \frac{1}{2}\sum_{i,j=1}^{n} \alpha_i \alpha_j y_i y_j K(x_i, x_j) \tag{13}$$

$$s.t. \quad 0 \leq \alpha_i \leq C \quad i = 1,\ldots,n$$

$$\sum_{i=1}^{n} \alpha_i y_i = 0$$

and $\Phi(\alpha, \gamma)$ is penalized function, the first item of Eq. (14) is transformed from the second item of Eq. (13), the second item of Eq. (14) is penalized item:

$$\min_{\alpha,\gamma} \Phi(\alpha, \gamma) = \min_{\alpha,\gamma} \frac{1}{2}\sum_{i,s=1}^{n} \alpha_i \alpha_s y_i y_s K(x_i, x_s, \gamma) + C_2 f(\gamma) \tag{14}$$

$$s.t. \quad 0 \leq \alpha_i \leq C \quad i = 1,\ldots,n$$

$$\sum_{i=1}^{n} \alpha_i y_i = 0$$

$$\gamma_j \geq 0 \quad i = 1,\ldots,d$$

where γ_j need to be non-negative and we use $L0 - norm$ as $f(\gamma)$, which is approximately equal to [9]:

$$f(\gamma) = e^T (e - exp(-\beta\gamma)) = \sum_{j=1}^{d} [1 - exp(-\beta\gamma_j)] \tag{15}$$

C_2 is the strength of the penalty of the complexity of our model which is different from C for penalty of training error(slack variable ξ). Also $L0 - norm$ can be replaced with $L1 - norm$ or $L2 - norm$ in our target function.

Because this optimization problem is not convex [17], it may be hard to search the globally optimal solution. So that we propose an algorithm to search a locally optimal solution. Then we use a method to solve this optimization problem in two step [17]:

[Step 1] **Given a set of fixed kernel parameter** γ, calculate the value of α in optimal function $\min_\alpha \Psi(\alpha)$, here sequential minimal optimization(SMO) [18] is a method to solve the SVM QP problem.

For convenience, all quantities that refer to the first multiplier will have a subscript 1, while the other refers to the second multiplier α_2. Without loss of generality, the second multiplier α_2 will be computed firstly. The following bounds W, H apply to α_2 while the target y_1 does not equal the target y_2:

$$W = max(0, \alpha_2 - \alpha_1), H = min(C, C + \alpha_2 - \alpha_1). \tag{16}$$

If the target $y_1 = y_2$, the bounds apply to α_2 is shown as:

$$W = max(0, \alpha_2 + \alpha_1 - C), H = min(C, \alpha_2 + \alpha_1). \tag{17}$$

The second derivative of the objective function $\min_\alpha \Psi(\alpha)$ along the diagonal line can be conducted as:

$$\eta = K(x_1, x_1) + K(x_2, x_2) - 2K(x_1, x_2). \tag{18}$$

Under the normal condition, the objective function is positive definite, there will be a minimum along the direction of the linear constraint, and η is greater than 0. The new minimum is computed along the direction of the constraint as follow:

$$\alpha_2^{opt} = \alpha_2 + \frac{y_2(E_1 - E_2)}{\eta} \tag{19}$$

where $E_i = u_i - y_i, i = 1, 2$ is the error on the i-th training example, as a next step, the constrained minimum is clipped by the bound W, H. Let $s = y_1 y_2$. The optimal α_1 is computed by the optimized and clipped α_2:

$$\alpha_1^{opt} = \alpha_1 + s(\alpha_2 - \alpha_2^{opt}) \tag{20}$$

Under unusual condition, η will not be positive, which can cause the objective function to become indefinite.

[Step 2] **Find out the best** γ **for given fixed** α in step 1, solve the objective function $\min_{\alpha, \gamma} \Phi(\alpha, \gamma)$ using gradient descent algorithm. And if the renewed γ_j is below the criterion we set, eliminate the feature j and loop for next iteration until reaching the stop criterion. For given j the gradient of $F(\gamma_j^*)$ is:

Gaussian

$$\Delta_j \Phi(\gamma^*) = \frac{1}{2} \sum_{i,s=1}^{n} \gamma_j^* (x_{i,j} - x_{s,j})^2 \alpha_i \alpha_s y_i y_s K(x_i, x_s, \gamma^*)$$
$$+ C_2 \beta exp(-\beta \gamma_j^*) \tag{21}$$

Polynomial

$$\Delta_j \Phi(\gamma^{poly}) = \frac{1}{2} \sum_{i,s=1}^{n} D x_{i,j} x_{s,j} \alpha_i \alpha_s y_i y_s K(x_i, x_s, \gamma^{poly}, D-1)$$
$$+ C_2 \beta exp(-\beta \gamma_j^{poly}) \tag{22}$$

To avoid misunderstandings of γ in polynomial kernel and target function, we set γ^{poly} in polynomial kernel. **Exponential Kernel (Laplace)**

$$\Delta_j \Phi(\gamma^*) = \frac{1}{2} \sum_{i,s=1}^{n} (x_{i,j} - x_{s,j}) \alpha_i \alpha_s y_i y_s K(x_i, x_s, \gamma^*)$$
$$+ C_2 \beta exp(-\beta \gamma_j^*) \tag{23}$$

The algorithm adjust the kernel components using gradient descent procedure, specially to parameter γ, which is set to be small to avoid negative at the first iterations.

3.3   Detailed Process of Proposed Algorithm

The pseudo code is shown as below:

Algorithm 1. KPD-SVM

---

kernel selection: we take **Gaussian kernel** as an example.
input:
parameter of gentle update strategy:d_1, d_2, θ;
parameter of update:$\varepsilon_1, \varepsilon_2$
01   **start:** $stop = False,$ $t = 0,$
       $\gamma^* = (\gamma^*)^{[0]},$ $\alpha_1^{[0]}, \alpha_2^{[0]}$
02   WHILE $stop \neq True$
03   train SVM for a given γ^* using SMO
04   FOR $i = 1, \ldots, d_1$
05   compute E_1, E_2, η, s
06          $\alpha_2^{[i+1]} = \alpha_2^{[i]} + \frac{y_2(E_1 - E_2)}{\eta},$
       $\alpha_1^{[i+1]} = \alpha_1^{[i]} + s * (\alpha_2^{[i]} - \alpha_2^{[i+1]})$
07   IF$\|(\alpha_1)^{[t+1]} - (\alpha_1)^{[t]}\| < \varepsilon_1$
       THEN $\alpha^* = (\alpha_1)^{[t+1]}$ Break   ENDIF
08   ENDFOR
09   train SVM for a given α^*
10   FOR $j = 1, \ldots, d_2$
11          $(\gamma_j^*)^{[t+1]} = (\gamma_j^*)^{[t]} - \theta \Delta_j \Phi((\gamma^*)^{[t]})$
12   IF$(\gamma_j^*)^{[t+1]} < \varepsilon_2$
       THEN $(\gamma_j^*)^{[t+1]} = 0$ Break ENDIF
13   ENDFOR
14   IF$(\gamma^*)^{[t]}, (\gamma^*)^{[t+1]}$ meet the requirements of $\zeta_{absolute}, \zeta_{relative}$
15          $stop = True$
16   ENDIF
17   ENDWHILE

---

where

$$\gamma^* = \sqrt{(2\gamma)} = [\frac{1}{\sigma_1}, \frac{1}{\sigma_2}, \ldots, \frac{1}{\sigma_d}] \qquad (24)$$

and

$$F(\gamma^*) = \sum_{i,s=1}^{n} \alpha_i \alpha_s y_i y_s K(x_i, x_j, \gamma^*) + C_2 f(\gamma^*) \qquad (25)$$

In the algorithm, we may consider the following vital step, some details are given as follows:

Kernel Selection, Use the whole features to train model with different kernels (eg. Gaussian, Polynomial) and different parameter (γ, D, c). Calculate the average accuracy of each model with different kernels by cross validations. Then select the kernel with the best performance which is the most appropriate kernel of this data set.

Set Original Value, At the start of algorithm, we give the initial value of α, γ, and some parameter for update.

Calculate α, Based on standard SVM training process and may take SMO algorithm [18] to quickly and efficiently find out the answer α^*.

Update σ and γ, Apply gradient descent algorithm to renew σ_i or γ_i^*, the lines 10–13 of the algorithm shows the iteration process, one by one for fixed the optimal α.

Step size of gradient descent, We set θ as the step size of gradient descend in each iteration.

Elimination criterion, ε is the eliminate threshold which means we eliminate the feature j by setting $\gamma_j^* = 0$ if value γ_j^* is below ε.

Stop criterion, For the stop criterion, we set a relative stop criterion $\zeta_{relative}$ and an absolute stop criterion $\zeta_{absolute}$ in order to balance the time of iterations and the performance of the model. $\zeta_{relative}$ is defined as the ratio $\frac{\|(\gamma^*)^{[t+1]} - (\gamma^*)^{[t]}\|_1}{\|(\gamma^*)^{[t]}\|_1}$ and $\zeta_{absolute}$ is set as $\| (\gamma^*)^{[t]} \|_1$.

3.4   Discussion of Parameter

Our discussion mainly concentrates on one issue: Selection of parameter values in proposed method. Basically, the proposed method outperforms in its process of feature selection and modeling. However, there are some parameters we need to tune for the optimal solution of classification. In [17], it has already concluded that β, ε and $\gamma^{[0]}$ have less influence in the final solution. In terms of the penalty for slack variables, C, we use Leave-One-Out Cross-Validation to find the best value of C in each case.

Complexity Penalty C_2: C_2 is the coefficient of penalty item on the number of feature or model complexity. A large C_2 means a strict limitation to build greatly complicated model. We choose C_2 according to the balance of prediction performances and model complexity.

Step Size θ: θ represents the step size of gradient descend in each iteration.

We want to use an automatically adjusted step size in some cases. Hence,we denote θ_{auto} as $\frac{\varepsilon}{median\{\Delta_j F(\gamma^*)\}}$, $j = 1, \ldots, d$. And we may take $\theta = \min\{\theta_{original}, \theta_{auto}\}$ as step size in each iteration.

Stop Criterion $\zeta_{absolute}, \zeta_{relative}$: With the increasing number of iterations, the $1 - norm$ difference of kernel parameter in t and $t + 1$ iteration goes to convergence, which shows the algorithm can find out the best kernel parameter in certain countable iterations.

4 Experiments

In this section, we apply the proposed method to do experiments in some real-world dataset. Also we will compare our method with F-score and RFE-SVM, which represents the filter and wrapper algorithm in feature selection. The measurements we make comparison are as follows: First, model prediction performance. Second, the number of features in the optimal solution.

4.1 Data Set

The data sets we selected are from UCI Machine Learning Database. Detailed information of each data set is shown as follows:

- **Sonar**: This is the data set used by Gorman and Sejnowski in their study of the classification of sonar signals.
  The data set contains 111 patterns obtained by bouncing sonar signals off a metal cylinder at various angles and under various conditions. And it contains 97 patterns obtained from rocks under similar conditions. The label associated with each record contains the letter "R" if the object is a rock and "M" if it is a mine (metal cylinder).
- **WBC**: The Wisconsin Breast Cancer data set has 569 observations and 30 features. All feature values are recoded with four significant digits. In addition, people who are diagnosed are labeled as M (*malignant tumor*) and the other are marked as B (*benign tumor*).

We basically consider the following three kernel functions: Gaussian, Polynomial, Laplace (Exponential). Then the values of parameters in each kernel function we used are as follows:

- $\sigma_{Gaussian} = (0.0001, 0.0005, 0.001, 0.005, 0.01, 0.05, 0.1, 0.5, 1, 10, 50, 100, 500, 1000)$
- $D = (2, 3, 4, 5, 6, 7, 8, 9, 10, 11, 12, 13, 14, 15)$
- $\sigma_{Laplace} = (0.0001, 0.0005, 0.001, 0.005, 0.01, 0.05, 0.1, 0.5, 1, 10, 50, 100, 500, 1000)$

4.2   Case: Sonar

Basic information of this data set is shown in Table 1.

Table 1. Basic information of Sonar (mines vs. rocks) data set

	Features	Observations	Proportion	Predominant class prop.
Total	60	208	100%	53.4%
Train	60	145	70%	54.5%
Test	60	63	30%	50.8%

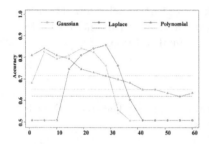

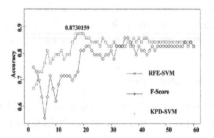

Fig. 1. The accuracy of Gaussian, Laplace and Polynomial in Sonar (horizontal axis represents feature numbers)

Fig. 2. The accuracy of KPD-SVM, F-Scores and RFE-SVM in Sonar (horizontal axis represents feature numbers)

First we carry out kernel selection. Fig. 1 shows the average performances of each kernel function applied in Sonar. Thus we choose Polynomial Kernel in this case.

Figure 2 shows the performance of proposed method KPD-SVM compared with F-Score and RFE-SVM. The optimal feature subset are selected by each method, and the number of these subsets are shown below: Filter(F1-Scores):24, Wrapper(RFE-SVM):18-20, Embedded(KPD-SVM):20.

In conclusion, KPD-SVM outperforms F-Score and RFE-SVM in this Sonar case.

4.3   Case: WBC

Basic information of this data set is shown in Table 2.

First we carry out kernel selection. In WBC we choose Polynomial Kernel in this case. Figure 3 shows the average performances of each kernel function applied in WBC.

The performance of proposed method KPD-SVM compared with F-Score and RFE-SVM shown in Fig. 4. The optimal feature subset are selected by each

Table 2. Basic information of WBC data set

	Features	Observations	Proportion	Predominant class prop.
Total	30	569	100%	62.7%
Train	30	512	90%	63.4%
Test	30	57	10%	52.6%

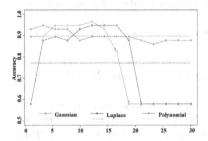

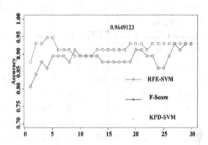

Fig. 3. The accuracy of Gaussian, Laplace and Polynomial in WBC (horizontal axis represents feature numbers)

Fig. 4. The accuracy of KPD-SVM, F-Scores and RFE-SVM in WBC (horizontal axis represents feature numbers)

method, and the number of these subsets are shown below: Filter(F1-Scores):26, Wrapper(RFE-SVM):19, Embedded(KPD-SVM):15.

In conclusion, considering the model prediction accuracy and the model complexity (the number of features), we can say KPD-SVM outperforms in this WBC case.

5 Conclusion

In this paper, we have presented a novel method called Kernel Parameter Descent Support Vector Machine (KPD-SVM) for feature selection using kernel functions. Our embedded method can generalize a well-trained SVM classifier as well as a good solution for feature selecting. In addition, our KPD-SVM method outperforms other methods, like filter method (F-Score) and wrapper method (RFE-SVM). Besides, compared with former embedded algorithm by optimizing kernel parameters [1–4], our method has novelties in stop criterion and step size settings in executions, which performs better in time consuming.

Acknowledgements. We would like to acknowledge Professor Chih-Jen Lin from National Taiwan University for his research on Support Vector Machine and his work on software LIBSVM.

This work was supported by the Guangdong Provincial Government of China through the "Computational Science Innovative Research Team" program and Guangdong Province Key Laboratory of Computational Science at the Sun Yat-sen University, and the National Science Foundation of China (11471012).

References

1. Chandrashekar, G., Sahin, F.: A Survey on Feature Selection Methods. Pergamon Press, Inc., Oxford (2014)
2. Cheriet, M., Kharma, N., Liu, C.L., et al.: Character Recognition Systems: A Guide for Students and Practitioners. Scitech Book News (2007)
3. Kira, K., Rendell, L.A.: A practical approach to feature selection. In: International Workshop on Machine Learning, pp. 249–256. Morgan Kaufmann Publishers Inc., Burlington (1992)
4. Kohavi, R., John, G.H.: Wrappers for feature subset selection. Artif. Intell. **97**(1–2), 273–324 (1997)
5. Sesmero, M.P., Alonso-Weber, J.M., Ledezma, A., et al.: A new artificial neural network ensemble based on feature selection and class recoding. Neural Comput. Appl. **21**(4), 771–783 (2012)
6. Yang, J., Yao, D., Zhan, X., Zhan, X.: Predicting disease risks using feature selection based on random forest and support vector machine. In: Basu, M., Pan, Y., Wang, J. (eds.) ISBRA 2014. LNCS, vol. 8492, pp. 1–11. Springer, Cham (2014). https://doi.org/10.1007/978-3-319-08171-7_1
7. Anaissi, A., Kennedy, P.J., Goyal, M., et al.: A balanced iterative random forest for gene selection from microarray data. Bmc Bioinform. **14**(1), 1–10 (2013)
8. Swan, A.L., Mobasheri, A., Allaway, D., et al.: Application of machine learning to proteomics data: classification and biomarker identification in postgenomics biology. Omics J. Integr. Biol. **17**(12), 595–610 (2013)
9. Blum, A.L., Langley, P.: Selection of relevant features and examples in machine learning. Artif. Intell. **97**(1–2), 245–271 (1997)
10. Tibshirani, R.: Regression shrinkage and selection via the lasso: a retrospective. J. R. Stat. Soc. **73**, 273–282 (2011)
11. Chan, H.P., Kim, S.B.: Sequential random k-nearest neighbor feature selection for high-dimensional data. Expert. Syst. Appl. **42**(5), 2336–2342 (2015)
12. Maldonado, S., Weber, R.: A wrapper method for feature selection using support vector machines. Inf. Sci. **179**(13), 2208–2217 (2009)
13. Tuv, E., Borisov, A., Runger, G., et al.: Feature selection with ensembles, artificial variables, and redundancy elimination. J. Mach. Learn. Res. **10**(3), 1341–1366 (2009)
14. Chen, P., Zhang, D.: Constructing support vector machines ensemble classification method for imbalanced datasets based on fuzzy integral. In: Ali, M., Pan, J.-S., Chen, S.-M., Horng, M.-F. (eds.) IEA/AIE 2014. LNCS (LNAI), vol. 8481, pp. 70–76. Springer, Cham (2014). https://doi.org/10.1007/978-3-319-07455-9_8
15. Vapnik, V.N., Vapnik, V.: Statistical Learning Theory, vol. 1. Wiley, New York (1998)
16. Guyon, I., Gunn, S., Nikravesh, M., et al.: Feature Extraction: Foundations and Applications. Studies in Fuzziness and Soft Computing. Springer, New York (2006). https://doi.org/10.1007/978-3-540-35488-8
17. Maldonado, S., Weber, R., Basak, J.: Simultaneous feature selection and classification using kernel-penalized support vector machines. Elsevier Science Inc. (2011)
18. Platt, J.C.: Sequential minimal optimization: a fast algorithm for training support vector machines. In: Advances in Kernel Methods-Support Vector Learning, pp. 212–223 (1998)

Multimodal Joint Representation for User Interest Analysis on Content Curation Social Networks

Lifang Wu[ID], Dai Zhang[ID], Meng Jian[(✉)][ID], Bowen Yang, and Haiying Liu

Faculty of Information Technology, Beijing University of Technology, Beijing, China
jianmeng648@163.com

Abstract. Content curation social networks (CCSNs), where users share interests by images and their text descriptions, are booming social networks. For the purpose of fully utilizing user-generated contents to analysis user interests on CCSNs, we propose a framework of learning multimodal joint representations of pins for user interest analysis. First, images are automatically annotated with category distributions, which benefit from the network characteristics and represent interests of users. Further, image representations are extracted from an intermediate layer of a fine-tuned multilabel convolutional neural network (CNN) and text representations are obtained with a trained Word2Vec. Finally, a multimodal deep Boltzmann machine (DBM) are trained to fuse two modalities. Experiments on a dataset from Huaban demonstrate that using category distributions instead of single categories as labels to fine-tune CNN significantly improve the performance of image representation, and multimodal joint representations perform better than either of unimodal representations.

Keywords: Multimodal · Content curation social networks
User modeling · Recommender systems

1 Introduction

Content curation social networks (CCSNs) are interest-driven social networks where users can organize and demonstrate multimedia contents they like. Since the most typical CCSN Pinterest became the fastest social network to reach 10M users [4], CCSNs have become popular worldwide. In China, more than 50 Pinterest-like websites such as Huaban, Duitang, Meilishuo, Mogujie and so forth have been published. The rapid development of CCSNs attracts much attention on different research topics, for example, network characteristic analysis [4], user

Supported by National Natural Science Foundation of China 61702022, Beijing Municipal Education Commission Science and Technology Innovation Project KZ201610005012, China Postdoctoral Science Foundation funded project 2017M610027 and 2018T110019.

© Springer Nature Switzerland AG 2018
J.-H. Lai et al. (Eds.): PRCV 2018, LNCS 11258, pp. 363–374, 2018.
https://doi.org/10.1007/978-3-030-03338-5_31

behavior study [5], influence analysis [18], search engine [21], recommender systems [2,9,10,19] and user modeling [1,3,20].

On CCSNs, the carrier of user interests is the basic unit of the network called "pin", which comprises an image and its text description. Most prior works on CCSNs only focused on unimodal data. Yang et al. [19] modeled boards with text representations and recommended boards re-ranked with image representations. Cinar et al. [1] separately predicted categories of pins with either image representations or text representations and fused the results of two modalities by decision fusion. Liu et al. [10] used unimodal representations to respectively generate candidate pins and to re-rank all the candidates. All these methods are late fusion methods which cannot obtain multimodal joint representations.

Multimodal joint representation commonly consists of unimodal representation and multimodal fusion. With regard to image representation, convolutional neural networks (CNNs) have recently achieved many outstanding performances on computer vision. Some works have been done on employing CNNs to represent pins. A key to train CNNs is to create a large labelled dataset. Cinar et al. [1], and You et al. [20] directly used the category of a pin as its label, but this label may be inaccurate as different users may select different categories for a same image. Geng et al. [3] constructed an ontology in fashion domain and trained a multi-task CNN with concepts in ontology, but this methods is hard to be deployed in all domains. Zhai et al. [21] obtained more detailed labels by taking top text search queries on Pinterest, however, the quality and consumption of this annotation highly depends on the performance of the search engine. Inspired by the fact that categories predefined by CCSNs are not independent objects but related notions, we use category distributions based on statistics as labels and fine-tuned a multilabel CNN for image representation.

Many multimodal fusion studies have been carried out on classification and retrieval. Most existed methods are based on discriminative models such as latent Dirichlet allocation [15], CNN [11] and recurrent neural network [12]. Those methods mainly learn the consistency between modalities and can hardly deal with missing input modalities. On the generative side, restricted Bolzmann machine (RBM) [6], deep autoencoder (DAE) [14] and deep Boltzmann machine (DBM) [17] are proved to be feasible to learn both the consistency and complementarity between modalities and can easily deal with the absence of some modalities, however, limited works have been done on fusing features obtained by deep learning with these models. Zhang et al. [22] fused visual features extracted from the 6-th layer of AlexNet and textual features generated by sparse coding of word vectors from a Word2Vec [13] with a DAE. Since DAEs are deterministic models while DBMs are probabilistic models, we trained a multimodal DBM to improve generalization performance.

The proposed framework of learning multimodal joint representations of pins is shown in Fig. 1. For image representation, visual features are extracted from an intermediate layer of the fined-tuned CNN. For text representation, distributed representations of words are learned on corpora and are encoded to represent texts. As our choice, Word2Vec is a frequently used distributed representation for capturing semantic and syntactic relations between words. Mean vector [8] of Word2Vec performs well on text representation and is unsupervised. Our multimodal joint representations is finally generated by a pretrained modified multimodal DBM.

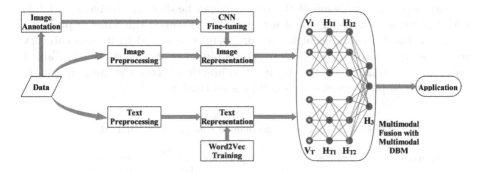

Fig. 1. Framework of learning multimodal joint representations of pins.

We believe that our research is the foundation of further researches on CCSNs such as board and user modeling, with the following contributions:

- We propose an easy-to-accomplish automatic annotate method that accumulate category selections of users to form category distributions of pins and fine-tune a multilabel CNN which significantly improves the category prediction performance.
- Multimodal joint representations of pins we get performs better than the unimodal representations.

The rest of the paper is organized as follows. Section 2 describes the proposed framework in details. Experiments and the corresponding analysis are provided in Sect. 3. And it is followed by conclusions in Sect. 4.

2 Multimodal Joint Representations of Pins

A pin comprise an image and its text description. As shown in Fig. 1, the whole process of multimodal joint representation can be roughly divided into three parts: image representation, text representation and multimodal fusion.

2.1 Image Representation

The aim of image representation is to learn features which not only maintain intrinsic characteristics of images but also relate to user interests on CCSNs. As supervised learning models, CNNs can certainly capture the relationships between images and user interests if user interests on CCSNs are used as labels during the learning process. Not to mention that top layers of CNNs can learn high-level image features, which can be interpreted as color, material, texture, object, scene and so on by some means.

All pins on CCSNs are collected into boards. When a board is created, the owner must select one of categories predefined by CCSNs for it, and all pins in this board will have the same category as the board. Since the category can be considered as the theme of the board, it can be directly treated as a label, which describes a coarse-grained user interest. However, this label is probably weak and noisy, mainly because user preferences may lead to various category selections for a same image since it can be observed that categories in Table 1 are sometimes related notions. To put it in practical terms, the image in Fig. 2a may belong to photography, kids and pets on Huaban.

Table 1. List of all 33 predefined categories on Huaban.

Anime	Apparel	Architecture	Art	Beauty
Cars motorcycles	Data presentation	Design	Desire	DIY crafts
Education	Film music books	Fitness	Food drink	Funny
Games	Geek	Home	Illustration	Industrial design
Kids	Men	Modeling hair	People	Pets
Photography	Quotes	Sports	Tips	Travel places
Web app icon	Wedding events	**Other**		

The most frequently activity on CCSNs is called "re-pin", which means a user collects an image and may add a text description for it from a board of another user into his or hers own board. A "re-pin path" is formed if users are interested in a same image and thus they re-pin it one by one, and all re-pin paths of an image form a "re-pin tree", as illustrated in Fig. 2b. Because any one of the categories in the re-pin tree cannot decide what this image is about but describes a portion of it instead, we use a category distribution to represent interests of an image. The category distribution of a given image I can be computed after counting the categories in the re-pin tree as

$$Interest_I = \left(p_{C_i} = \frac{f_{C_i}}{\sum_{i=1}^{N_C} f_{C_i}} \right) \in [0,1]^{N_C} \tag{1}$$

where f_{C_i} denotes the frequency of the i-th category C_i, N_C is the total number of categories on CCSNs. In practice we set

$$f_{C_i} = 0 \quad \text{if} \quad f_{C_i} < \frac{\sum_{i=1}^{M_C} f_{C_i}}{M_C} \tag{2}$$

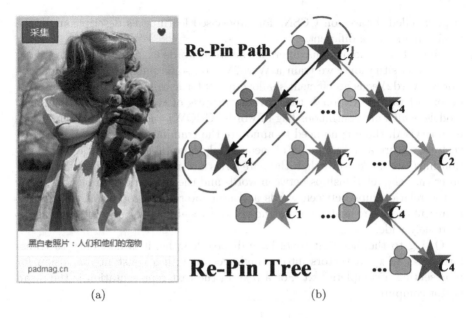

(a)   (b)

Fig. 2. (a): Example of a pin on Huaban. (b): Illustration of a re-pin tree composed of some re-pin paths. Each star represents a pin and C_i nearby is the category of this pin. All pins in the re-pin tree have a same image.

where M_C is the total number of categories occurred in the re-pin tree to filter out spam and make the sequence on behalf of majority opinion.

After automatic image annotation, we then choose a pretrained CNN model to fine-tune for the purpose of accelerate the training process. Most available pretrained CNNs are designed for classifying independent objects, while our model should be a multilabel regressor. Accordingly, we change the loss layer from softmax with logarithmic loss layer to sigmoid with cross entropy loss layer. The loss function is defined as

$$E = -\sum_{i=1}^{N_C} \left[p_{C_i} \ln \hat{p}_{C_i} + (1 - p_{C_i}) \ln (1 - \hat{p}_{C_i}) \right] \tag{3}$$

where p_{C_j} is the percentage in Eq. (1), $\hat{p}_{C_j}$ denotes the corresponding sigmoid output.

After fine-tuning, the weights of the CNN are stored for feature extraction. The activation values of an fully connected (FC) layer will be extracted as the image representations.

2.2 Text Representation

An important aim of text representation is also to discover the relationships between descriptions of pins and categories. However, it is difficult to create a large labelled dataset on CCSNs for supervised learning as descriptions in the re-pin tree may be different.

Since there is no obvious difference between words used on CCSNs and those in common situations, we train a Word2Vec on some public corpora to encode words. Word2Vec is an efficient shallow model for learning distributed representations of words. Although the learning process of either of its two log-linear models, which are continuous bag-of-words (CBOW) and continuous skip-gram, is supervised, there is no need to annotate the training texts. Since the learned vectors capture a large number of meaningful semantic and syntactic word relationships, we make sure that the categories are in the training dictionary in order that the relationships between words and the categories can be considered as the relationships between words and user interests. In addition, distributed representations are scalable even though the vocabulary of natural language is extremely wide.

Owing to the fact that texts have diverse lengths, it is necessary to transform a set of word vectors into a single vector with a constant dimension for representing a complete text. For a text T, the text representation is the mean vector computed as

$$V_T = \frac{1}{M_T} \sum_{i=1}^{M_T} KeyedVector_{Word_i} \tag{4}$$

where $KeyedVector_{Word_i}$ denotes the word vector of the i-th word $Word_i$, M_T is the text length.

2.3 Multimodal Fusion

Different modalities typically have different statistical properties, which makes it difficult to learn a joint representation that capture both consistent and complementary relationships across modalities. A multimodal DBM which combines DBMs by adding a shared hidden layer on top of them can effectively solve this problem. A DBM is structured by stacking RBMs in a hierarchical manner. A RBM is an undirected graphical model with binary-valued visible layer V and binary-valued hidden layer H fully connected to each other defines the energy function

$$\mathrm{E}(V, H; \theta) = -H^T W V - A^T V - B^T H \tag{5}$$

where $\theta = \{W, A, B\}$ denotes the model parameters including the symmetric interaction terms W between two layers, visible layer bias terms A and hidden layer bias terms B.

As illustrated in Fig. 1, we use two-layer DBMs with Gaussian-Bernoulli RBMs, which are a variant of RBMs that can model real-valued vectors, as bottom for both modalities. A Gaussian-Bernoulli RBM with visible units $V = \{v_i\} \in \mathbb{R}^D$ and hidden units $H = \{h_j\} \in \{0,1\}^F$ defines the energy function

$$\mathrm{E}(V, H; \theta) = \sum_{i=1}^{D} \frac{(v_i - a_i)^2}{2\sigma_i^2} - \sum_{i=1}^{D} \sum_{j=1}^{F} \frac{v_i}{\sigma_i} w_{ij} h_j - \sum_{j=1}^{F} b_j h_j \tag{6}$$

where σ_i denotes the standard deviation of the i-th visible unit and $\theta = \{\{w_{ij}\} \in \mathbb{R}^{D \times F}\}, \{a_i\} \in \mathbb{R}^D\}, \{b_j\} \in \mathbb{R}^F\}, (\sigma_i) \in \mathbb{R}^D\}$. During the unsupervised training of the multimodal DBM, modalities can be thought of labels for each other. Since RBMs can be considered as autoencoders, each layer of the multimodal DBM makes a small contribution to eliminate modality-specific correlations. Consequently, the top layer can learn a relatively modality-free representation as opposed to the modality-full input layers. The joint distribution over the multimodal inputs can be written as

$$P(V_I, V_T; \theta) = \sum_{H_{I2}, H_{T2}, H_3} P(H_{I2}, H_{T2}, H_3) \left(\sum_{H_{I1}} P(V_I, H_{I1}, H_{I2}) \right) \left(\sum_{H_{T1}} P(V_T, H_{T1}, H_{T2}) \right) \quad (7)$$

where θ denotes all model parameters.

A pin may has no text description. The multimodal DBM can be used to generate missing text representation by sampling it from the conditional distribution with the standard Gibbs sampler. Finally, activation probabilities of H_3 are used as the multimodal joint representations of pins no matter they have text descriptions or not.

3 Experiment

3.1 Dataset and Implementation Details

All data used in experiments was crawled from Huaban, which is one of typical CCSNs in China. Huaban provides almost the same applications as Pinterest provides, while three main differences between them are: users can "like" pins or boards on Huaban while "like" has been removed by Pinterest; Huaban records both users from whom a pin re-pinned and by whom it initially created while Pinterest only records the direct source; some predefined categories are different and Pinterest has 5 more categories.

We first crawled pins without images of 5957 users and sampled 88 users according to pin counts and categories of their boards. To make our dataset diverse and real, a few cold start and extremely active users have been confirmed in it. We then downloaded the images of sampled users and pins of their like boards. In addition, top 1000 recommended pins of every category was crawled for fine-tuning the CNN, and re-pin paths of all recommended pins was crawled for automatic annotation. In total, the dataset includes 1694 boards and 167747 unique images. All pins was used as supplements for obtaining category distributions of all recommended pins. The average nodes of the incomplete re-pin trees is 47.57.

Labeled images was split into 80% for training and validating and the remaining 20% for testing after label balancing. AlexNet [7] with ImageNet [16] pretrained weights was chosen as a basis. Because AlexNet requires a constant input dimension, the image was first rescaled such that the shorter side was of length 256 pixels, and then the central 256×256 patch of the resulting image was cropped out. As a comparison, we also used the most frequent category as label to fine-tune an multiclass AlexNet. The dimensions of the fc8 layers of both CNNs were change to 33. Image representations was extracted from the FC7 layer of the fine-tuned CNN.

Word2Vec was trained on Wikipedia dumps and Sougou Lab dataset with CBOW and negative sampling. The vector dimension was set to 300. Words with total frequency lower than 5 are ignored. Preprocessing such as traditional Chinese and simplified Chinese conversion, removing punctuation, word tokenize, removing stop words and machine translation has been done on text descriptions of pins.

Image and text features were used for pretraining our multimodal DBM. Dimensions of H_{T1}, H_{T2} and H_{V1} were equal to their corresponding visible inputs, and dimension of H_{V2} and H_3 was set to 2048 for the purpose of compressing the vectors. DBM was pretrained using a greedy layer-wise strategy by learning a stack of modified RBMs. Finally, we ran Gibbs sampler to generate missing text representations and to infer multimodal join representations.

3.2 Analysis of Interests Represented by Pins

Analysis of interests represented by pins is the prerequisite of analysis of interests represented by boards and user interest analysis. The category distribution are interests of the image and can be approximate the interests of the pin, even though some of categories will be enhanced by the text description.

Table 2. Comparison on pin category prediction

Model	Dimension	Dominant category accuracy	Mean nonzero error	Mean error
AlexNet [1]	4096	57.53%	—	—
Word2Vec [1]	300	33.47%	—	—
AlexNet [20]	4096	43.1%	—	—
AlexNet	4096	45.85%	—	—
Multilabel	4096	82.71%	0.1320	0.0141
Word2Vec	300	42.88%	0.3249	0.0415
Multimodal	2048	84.13%	0.1181	0.0119

Multidimensional logical regressions (LRs) were trained on recommended pins for all unimodal and multimodal representations. The results are shown in Table 2, together with the result of the compared AlexNet. Relevant results on 32 [1] and 34 [20] Pinterest categories are also cited as references. Mean nonzero error is the average error between all nonzero categories and corresponding predictions. The dominant category accuracy checks the consistency of the most frequently category between predictions and labels. Comparision of two fine-tuned CNNs shows that our multilabel regressor significantly improves the accuracy.

It is because that category distributions can not only eliminate the interference of related categories but also provide more information to learn than only dominant categories. Although the performance of text representations is not comparable with those of image representations, the complementarity between two modalities helps the multimodal joint representations perform better than the unimodal representations. Our framework can also infer interests of images from other social networks.

3.3 Board Category Recommendation

Every board must be assigned a category nowadays, while some boards have no category as a result of that they were created before the constraint entered into force. However, it is illogical because even if it is hard to select a category for a board about wide interests, "other" in Table 1 can be selected. Consequently, Huaban offers a function that allows any user to select a category for a board which haven't categorized. Board category recommendation will be useful on that occasion, and the first selection and further editing too.

Table 3. Comparison on board category recommendation

Model	Top-1 MRR	MRR
Random	3.03%	12.39%
Text + Cosine similarity	25.65%	38.78%
Image + Multidimensional LR	60.10%	73.41%
Text + Multidimensional LR	38.00%	54.30%
Multimodal + Multidimensional LR	62.35%	74.77%

Same as interests represented by pins, interests represented by boards should not limited in one category. The interest distribution of a board can be computed by averaging all category distributions of its pins. As pins are accumulated, the category preference is reinforced due to the fact that the accumulation process of strong categories are faster than those of weak categories. Our recommended category is the max category in the interest distribution of the board, and the ground truth is the real category of the board. Mean reciprocal rank (MRR) are used as the performance metric. As board category recommendation actually has only one correct selection, we also give the top-1 MRR. Results are organized in Table 3. Cosine similarities between texts and categories are less effective than category distributions obtained with texts, this indicates that there is a gap between semantemes and interests. The multimodal joint representations, which benefit from personalized texts, perform better than image representations. Notice that the recommendation dataset is different from the training dataset, it also proves that our framework has a good generalization ability.

The first selection is a cold start problem, as it only depends on one pin. We then evaluate the influence of pin counts on board category recommendation.

Table 4. Influence of pin count on board category recommendation based on multimodal join representation

Pin count	Top-1 MRR	MRR
=1	7.69%	35.56%
≤4	45.57%	59.68%
≤30	56.53%	69.75%
≤100	59.06%	72.39%
>100	67.11%	78.33%

As shown in Table 4, our recommendation suffers the cold start. However, the theory about preference reinforcement is proved as more pins lead to better performance. Although interests of users are more discrete than interests of boards, we infer that the accumulation process is still effective on user interest analysis.

3.4 Board Recommendation

Well organized boards can be high quality galleries, which makes it easier for users to collect pins. For this reason, CCSNs offer users a board recommendation function. Besides interest distributions, a board can be represent by the mean vector of representations of pins. And similarity between boards can be simply measured with some distance metrics, for example cosine similarity.

Table 5. Comparison on board recommendation

Model	Top-5 MRR	MRR
Category based	2.12%	3.85%
Image + Multidimensional LR	16.08%	18.61%
Text + Multidimensional LR	15.93%	17.95%
Multimodal + Multidimensional LR	17.58%	20.13%
Image + Mean vector	33.66%	35.97%
Text + Mean vector	25.96%	27.49%
Multimodal + Mean vector	35.76%	37.88%

We divided every board in half according to the order of pins, and each half must be similar board for another. The owner of each half will be interested in another half and further re-pin from or like or follow it beyond all doubt. On the basis of this, we consider half of the board as the only correct recommendation result and retrieve the index in the similarity sequence. As Huaban exhibit five pins at the top row of its waterfall flow for common resolution screens, we also demonstrate top-5 MRR. Table 5 shows that results of mean vectors is higher than those of respective interest distributions, simply owing to the additional information. All of our methods significantly improve the results in comparison with the category based filtering. The results also show that multimodal joint representations can model boards better than either of unimodal representations.

4 Conclusion

We propose a framework of learning multimodal joint representations of pins on CCSNs. Experimental results show that multimodal joint representations performs better than either of unimodal representations on interpreting pin-level interests and board-level interests. The obtained representations can be easily used on user modeling and recommender systems for CCSNs. Future work will be focused on extending our framework to model boards and users. In addition, other effective feature extraction methods and multimodal fusion approaches may be taken into account.

References

1. Cinar, Y., Zoghbi, S., Moens, M.F.: Inferring user interests on social media from text and images. In: 2015 IEEE International Conference on Data Mining Workshop (ICDMW), pp. 1342–1347. IEEE (2015)
2. Geng, X., Zhang, H., Bian, J., Chua, T.: Learning image and user features for recommendation in social networks. In: Proceedings of the 2015 IEEE International Conference on Computer Vision (ICCV), pp. 4274–4282. IEEE Computer Society (2015)
3. Geng, X., Zhang, H., Song, Z., Yang, Y., Luan, H., Chua, T.: One of a kind: user profiling by social curation. In: Proceedings of the 22nd ACM International Conference on Multimedia, pp. 567–576. ACM (2014)
4. Gilbert, E., Bakhshi, S., Chang, S., Terveen, L.: "i need to try this!": a statistical overview of pinterest. In: Proceedings of the SIGCHI Conference on Human Factors in Computing Systems, pp. 2427–2436. ACM (2013)
5. Han, J., et al.: Sharing topics in pinterest: understanding content creation and diffusion behaviors. In: Proceedings of the 2015 ACM on Conference on Online Social Networks, pp. 245–255. ACM (2015)
6. Jia, X., Wang, A., Li, X., Xun, G., Xu, W., Zhang, A.: Multi-modal learning for video recommendation based on mobile application usage. In: 2015 IEEE International Conference on Big Data (Big Data) (BIG DATA), pp. 837–842. IEEE (2015)
7. Krizhevsky, A., Sutskever, I., Hinton, G.: Imagenet classification with deep convolutional neural networks. In: Advances in Neural Information Processing Systems 25, pp. 1097–1105. Curran Associates Inc. (2012)
8. Lev, G., Klein, B., Wolf, L.: In defense of word embedding for generic text representation. In: Biemann, C., Handschuh, S., Freitas, A., Meziane, F., Métais, E. (eds.) NLDB 2015. LNCS, vol. 9103, pp. 35–50. Springer, Cham (2015). https://doi.org/10.1007/978-3-319-19581-0_3
9. Li, Y., Mei, T., Cong, Y., Luo, J.: User-curated image collections: modeling and recommendation. In: 2015 IEEE International Conference on Big Data (Big Data), pp. 591–600. IEEE (2015)

10. Liu, D., et al.: Related pins at pinterest: the evolution of a real-world recommender system. In: Proceedings of the 26th International Conference on World Wide Web Companion, pp. 583–592. International World Wide Web Conferences Steering Committee (2017)

11. Ma, L., Lu, Z., Shang, L., Li, H.: Multimodal convolutional neural networks for matching image and sentence. In: 2015 IEEE International Conference on Computer Vision (ICCV) (2015), pp. 2623–2631. IEEE (2015)

12. Mao, J., Xu, J., Jing, Y., Yuille, A.: Training and evaluating multimodal word embeddings with large-scale web annotated images. In: Advances in Neural Information Processing Systems 29, pp. 442–450. Curran Associates, Inc. (2016)

13. Mikolov, T., Sutskever, I., Chen, K., Corrado, G., Dean, J.: Distributed representations of words and phrases and their compositionality. In: Proceedings of the 26th International Conference on Neural Information Processing Systems, vol. 2, pp. 3111–3119. Curran Associates Inc. (2013)

14. Ngiam, J., Khosla, A., Kim, M., Nam, J., Lee, H., Ng, A.: Multimodal deep learning. In: Proceedings of the 28th International Conference on Machine Learning, pp. 529–545. Omnipress (2011)

15. Qian, S., Zhang, T., Xu, C.: Multi-modal multi-view topic-opinion mining for social event analysis. In: Proceedings of the 2016 ACM on Multimedia Conference, pp. 2–11. ACM (2016)

16. Russakovsky, O., Salakhutdinov, R.: Imagenet large scale visual recognition challenge. Int. J. Comput. Vis. **115**, 211–252 (2015)

17. Srivastava, N., Salakhutdinov, R.: Multimodal learning with deep boltzmann machines. J. Mach. Learn. Res. **15**, 2949–2980 (2014)

18. Venkatadri, G., Goga, O., Zhong, C., Viswanath, B., Gummadi, K., Sastry, N.: Strengthening weak identities through inter-domain trust transfer. In: Proceedings of the 25th International Conference on World Wide Web, pp. 1249–1259. ACM (2016)

19. Yang, X., Li, Y., Luo, J.: Pinterest board recommendation for twitter users. In: Proceedings of the 23rd ACM International Conference on Multimedia, pp. 963–966. ACM (2015)

20. You, Q., Bhatia, S., Luo, J.: A picture tells a thousand words-about you! user interest profiling from user generated visual content. Signal Process. **124**, 45–53 (2016)

21. Zhai, A., et al.: Visual discovery at pinterest. In: Proceedings of the 26th International Conference on World Wide Web Companion, pp. 515–524. International World Wide Web Conferences Steering Committee (2017)

22. Zhang, H., Yang, Y., Luan, H., Yan, S., Chua, T.: Start from scratch: towards automatically identifying, modeling, and naming visual attributes. In: Proceedings of the 22nd ACM International Conference on Multimedia, pp. 187–196. ACM (2014)

LTSG: Latent Topical Skip-Gram for Mutually Improving Topic Model and Vector Representations

Jarvan Law, Hankz Hankui Zhuo$^{(\boxtimes)}$, JunHua He, and Erhu Rong

Department of Computer Science, Sun Yat-Sen University, GuangZhou 510006, China
JarvanLaw@gmail.com, zhuohank@mail.sysu.edu.cn,
{hejunh,rongerhu}@mail2.sysu.edu.cn

Abstract. Topic models have been widely used in discovering latent topics which are shared across documents in text mining. Vector representations, word embeddings and topic embeddings, map words and topics into a low-dimensional and dense real-value vector space, which have obtained high performance in NLP tasks. However, most of the existing models assume the results trained by one of them are perfect correct and used as prior knowledge for improving the other model. Some other models use the information trained from external large corpus to help improving smaller corpus. In this paper, we aim to build such an algorithm framework that makes topic models and vector representations mutually improve each other within the same corpus. An EM-style algorithm framework is employed to iteratively optimize both topic model and vector representations. Experimental results show that our model outperforms state-of-the-art methods on various NLP tasks.

Keywords: Topic modeling · Polysemous-word · Word embeddings
Text mining

1 Introduction

Word embeddings, e.g., distributed word representations [16], represent words with low dimensional and dense real-value vectors, which capture useful semantic and syntactic features of words. Distributed word embeddings can be used to measure word similarities by computing distances between vectors, which have been widely used in various IR and NLP tasks, such as entity recognition [23], disambiguation [5] and parsing [21]. Despite the success of previous approaches on word embeddings, they all assume each word has a specific meaning and represent each word with a single vector, which restricts their applications in fields with polysemous words, e.g., "bank" can be either "a financial institution" or "a raised area of ground along a river".

To overcome this limitation, [14] propose a topic embedding approach, namely Topical Word Embeddings (TWE), to learn topic embeddings to characterize various meanings of polysemous words by concatenating topic embeddings

© Springer Nature Switzerland AG 2018
J.-H. Lai et al. (Eds.): PRCV 2018, LNCS 11258, pp. 375–387, 2018.
https://doi.org/10.1007/978-3-030-03338-5_32

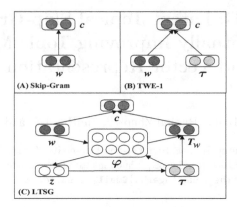

Fig. 1. Skip-Gram, `TWE` and `LTSG` models. Blue, yellow, green circles denote the embeddings of word, topic and context, while red circles in `LTSG` denote the global topical word. White circles denote the topic model part, topic-word distribution φ and topic assignment z. (Color figure online)

with word embeddings. Despite the success of `TWE`, compared to previous multiprototype models [11,20], it assumes that word distributions over topics are provided by off-the-shelf topic models such as `LDA`, which would limit the applications of `TWE` once topic models do not perform well in some domains [19]. As a matter of fact, pervasive polysemous words in documents would harm the performance of topic models that are based on co-occurrence of words in documents. Thus, a more realistic solution is to build both topic models with regard to polysemous words and polysemous word embeddings simultaneously, instead of using off-the-shelf topic models. In this work, we propose a novel learning framework, called Latent Topical Skip-Gram (`LTSG`) model, to mutually learn polysemousword models and topic models. To the best of our knowledge, this is the first work that considers learning polysemous-word models and topic models simultaneously. Although there have been approaches that aim to improve topic models based on word embeddings `MRF-LDA` [24], they fail to improve word embeddings provided words are polysemous; although there have been approaches that aim to improve polysemous-word models `TWE` [14] based on topic models, they fail to improve topic models considering words are polysemous. Different from previous approaches, we introduce a new node T_w, called *global topic*, to capture all of the topics regarding polysemous word w based on topic-word distribution φ, and use the global topic to estimate the context of polysemous word w. Then we characterize polysemous word embeddings by concatenating word embeddings with topic embeddings. We illustrate our new model in Fig. 1, where Fig. 1(A) is the skip-gram model [16], which aims to maximize the probability of context c given word w. Figure 1(B) is the `TWE` model, which extends the skip-gram model to maximize the probability of context c given both word w and topic t, and Fig. 1(C) is our `LTSG` model which aims to maximize the probability of context c given word w and global topic T_w. T_w is generated based on topic-word distribution φ (i.e., the joint distribution of topic embedding τ and word embedding w) and topic embedding τ (which is based on topic assignment z). Through our LTSG model, we can simultaneously learn word embeddings w and global topic embeddings T_w for representing polysemous word embeddings, and topic word distribution φ for mining topics with regard to polysemous words. We will exhibit the effectiveness of our LTSG model in text classification and topic mining tasks with regard to polysemous words in documents.

In the remainder of the paper, we first introduce preliminaries of our LTSG model, and then present our LTSG algorithm in detail. After that, we evaluate our LTSG model by comparing our LTSG algorithm to state-of-the-art models in various datasets. Finally we review previous work related to our LTSG approach and conclude the paper with future work.

2   Preliminaries

In this section, we briefly review preliminaries of Latent Dirichlet Allocation (LDA), Skip-Gram, and Topical Word Embeddings (TWE), respectively. We show some notations and their corresponding meanings in Table 1, which will be used in describing the details of LDA, Skip-Gram, and TWE.

Table 1. Notations of the text collection.

Term	Notation	Definition or description
Vocabulary	$\mathcal{V}$	Set of words in the text collection, $|\mathcal{V}| = W$
Word	w	A basic item from vocabulary indexed as $w \in \{1, 2, \ldots, W\}$
Document	$\mathbf{w}$	A sequence of N words, $\mathbf{w} = (w_1, w_2, \ldots, w_N)$
Corpus	$\mathcal{D}$	A collection of M documents, $\mathcal{D} = \{\mathbf{w}_1, \mathbf{w}_2, \ldots, \mathbf{w}_M\}$
Topic-word	φ	K distributions over vocabulary ($K \times W$ matrix), $|\varphi| = K, |\varphi_k| = W$
Word embedding	v	Distributed representation of $word$, denoted by v_w, $v \in \mathbb{R}^d$
Topic embedding	τ	Distributed representation of $topic$, denoted by τ_k, $\tau \in \mathbb{R}^d$

2.1   Latent Dirichlet Allocation

Latent Dirichlet Allocation (LDA) [2], a three-level hierarchical Bayesian model, is a well-developed and widely used probabilistic topic model. Extending Probabilistic Latent Semantic Indexing (PLSI) [10], LDA adds Dirichlet priors to document-specific topic mixtures to overcome the overfitting problem in PLSI. LDA aims at modeling each document as a mixture over sets of topics, each associated with a multinomial word distribution. Given a document corpus $\mathcal{D}$, each document $\mathbf{w}_m \in \mathcal{D}$ is assumed to have a distribution over K topics. The generative process of LDA is shown as follows,

1. For each topic $k = 1 \to K$, draw a distribution over words $\varphi_k \sim Dir(\beta)$
2. For each document $\mathbf{w}_m \in \mathcal{D}, m \in \{1, 2, \ldots, M\}$
   (a) Draw a topic distribution $\boldsymbol{\theta}_m \sim Dir(\boldsymbol{\alpha})$
   (b) For each word $w_{m,n} \in \mathbf{w}_m, n = 1, \ldots, N_m$
      i. Draw a topic assignment $z_{m,n} \sim Mult(\boldsymbol{\theta}_m), z_{m,n} \in \{1, \ldots, K\}$.
      ii. Draw a word $w_{m,n} \sim Mult(\varphi_{z_{m,n}})$

where $\boldsymbol{\alpha}$ and $\boldsymbol{\beta}$ are Dirichlet hyperparameters, specifying the nature of priors on $\boldsymbol{\theta}$ and φ. Variational inference and Gibbs sampling are the common ways to learn the parameters of LDA.

2.2   The Skip-Gram Model

The Skip-Gram model is a well-known framework for learning word vectors [16]. Skip-Gram aims to predict context words given a target word in a sliding window, as shown in Fig. 1(A).

Given a document corpus $\mathcal{D}$ defined in Table 1, the objective of Skip-Gram is to maximize the average log-probability

$$\mathcal{L}(\mathcal{D}) = \frac{1}{\sum_{m=1}^{M} N_m} \sum_{m=1}^{M} \sum_{n=1}^{N_m} \sum_{-c \leq j \leq c, j \neq 0} \log \Pr(w_{m,n+j}|w_{m,n}), \tag{1}$$

where c is the context window size of the target word. The basic Skip-Gram formulation defines $\Pr(w_{m,n+j}|w_{m,n})$ using the softmax function:

$$\Pr(w_{m,n+j}|w_{m,n}) = \frac{\exp(\boldsymbol{v}_{w_{m,n+j}} \cdot \boldsymbol{v}_{w_{m,n}})}{\sum_{w=1}^{W} \exp(\boldsymbol{v}_w \cdot \boldsymbol{v}_{w_{m,n}})}, \tag{2}$$

where $\boldsymbol{v}_{w_{m,n}}$ and $\boldsymbol{v}_{w_{m,n+j}}$ are the vector representations of target word $w_{m,n}$ and its context word $w_{m,n+j}$, and W is the number of words in the vocabulary $\mathcal{V}$. Hierarchical softmax and negative sampling are two efficient approximation methods used to learn Skip-Gram.

2.3   Topical Word Embeddings

Topical word embeddings (TWE) is a more flexible and powerful framework for multi-prototype word embeddings, where topical word refers to a word taking a specific topic as context [14], as shown in Fig. 1(B). TWE model employs LDA to obtain the topic distributions of document corpora and topic assignment for each word token. TWE model uses topic $z_{m,n}$ of target word to predict context word compared with only using the target word $w_{m,n}$ to predict context word in Skip-Gram. TWE is defined to maximize the following average log probability

$$\mathcal{L}(\mathcal{D}) = \frac{1}{\sum_{m=1}^{M} N_m} \sum_{m=1}^{M} \sum_{n=1}^{N_m} \sum_{-c \leq j \leq c, j \neq 0} \log \Pr(w_{m,n+j}|w_{m,n}) + \log \Pr(w_{m,n+j}|z_{m,n}).$$

$$\tag{3}$$

TWE regards each topic as a pseudo word that appears in all positions of words assigned with this topic. When training TWE, Skip-Gram is being used for learning word embeddings. Afterwards, each topic embedding is initialized with the average over all words assigned to this topic and learned by keeping word embeddings unchanged.

Despite the improvement over Skip-Gram, the parameters of LDA, word embeddings and topic embeddings are learned separately. In other word, TWE just uses LDA and Skip-Gram to obtain external knowledge for learning better topic embeddings.

3   Our LTSG Algorithm

Extending from the TWE model, the proposed Latent Topical Skip-Gram model (LTSG) directly integrates LDA and Skip-Gram by using topic-word distribution φ mentioned in topic models like LDA, as shown in Fig. 1(C). We take three steps to learn topic modeling, word embeddings and topic embeddings simultaneously, as shown below.

Step 1. Sample topic assignment for each word token. Given a specific word token $w_{m,n}$, we sample its latent topic $z_{m,n}$ by performing Gibbs updating rule similar to LDA.

Step 2. Compute topic embeddings. We average all words assigned to each topic to get the embedding of each topic.

Step 3. Train word embeddings. We train word embeddings similar to Skip-Gram and TWE. Meanwhile, topic-word distribution φ is updated based on Eq. (10). The objective of this step is to maximize the following function

$$\mathcal{L}(\mathcal{D}) = \frac{1}{\sum_{m=1}^{M} N_m} \sum_{m=1}^{M} \sum_{n=1}^{N_m} \sum_{-c \leq j \leq c, j \neq 0} \tag{4}$$
$$\log \Pr(w_{m,n+j}|w_{m,n}) + \log \Pr(w_{m,n+j}|T_{w_{m,n}}),$$

where $T_{w_{m,n}} = \sum_{k=1}^{K} \tau_k \cdot \varphi_{k,w_{m,n}}$. τ_k indicates the k-th topic embedding. $T_{w_{m,n}}$ can be seen as a distributed representation of global topical word of $w_{m,n}$.

We will address the above three steps in detail below.

3.1   Topic Assignment via Gibbs Sampling

To perform Gibbs sampling, the main target is to sample topic assignments $z_{m,n}$ for each word token $w_{m,n}$. Given all topic assignments to all of the other words, the full conditional distribution $\Pr(z_{m,n} = k|\mathbf{z}^{-(m,n)}, \mathbf{w})$ is given below when applying collapsed Gibbs sampling [9],

$$\Pr(z_{m,n} = k|\mathbf{z}^{-(m,n)}, \mathbf{w}) \propto \frac{n_{k,w_{m,n}}^{-(m,n)} + \beta}{\sum_{w=1}^{w} n_{k,w}^{-(m,n)} + W\beta} \cdot \frac{n_{m,k}^{-(m,n)} + \alpha}{\sum_{k'=1}^{K} n_{m,k'}^{-(m,n)} + K\alpha}, \tag{5}$$

where $-(m,n)$ indicates that the current assignment of $z_{m,n}$ is excluded. $n_{k,w}$ and $n_{m,k}$ denote the number of word tokens w assigned to topic k and the count of word tokens in document m assigned to topic k, respectively. After sampling all the topic assignments for words in corpus $\mathcal{D}$, we can estimate each component of φ and θ by Eqs. (6) and (7).

$$\hat{\varphi}_{k,w} = \frac{n_{k,w} + \beta}{\sum_{w'=1}^{W} n_{k,w'} + W\beta} \tag{6}$$

$$\hat{\theta}_{d,k} = \frac{n_{m,k} + \alpha}{\sum_{k'=1}^{K} n_{m,k'} + K\alpha} \tag{7}$$

Unlike standard LDA, the topic-word distribution φ is used directly for constructing the modified Gibbs updating rule in LTSG. Following the idea of DRS [7], with the conjugacy property of Dirichlet and multinomial distributions, the Gibbs updating rule of our model LTSG can be approximately represented by

$$\Pr(z_{m,n} = k | \mathbf{w}, \mathbf{z}^{-(m,n)}, \varphi, \alpha) \propto \varphi_{k,w_{m,n}} \cdot \frac{n_{m,k}^{-(m,n)} + \alpha}{\sum_{k'=1}^{K} n_{m,k'}^{-(m,n)} + K\alpha}. \tag{8}$$

In different corpus or applications, Eq. (8) can be replaced with other Gibbs updating rules or topic models, eg. LFLDA [18].

3.2 Topic Embeddings Computing

Topic embeddings aim to approximate the latent semantic centroids in vector space rather than a multinomial distribution. TWE trains topic embeddings after word embeddings have been learned by Skip-Gram. In LTSG, we use a straightforward way to compute topic embedding for each topic. For the kth topic, its topic embedding is computed by averaging all words with their topic assignment z equivalent to k, i.e.,

$$\tau_k = \frac{\sum_{m=1}^{M} \sum_{n=1}^{N_m} \mathbb{I}(z_{m,n} = k) \cdot \boldsymbol{v}_{w_{m,n}}}{\sum_{w=1}^{W} n_{k,w}} \tag{9}$$

where $\mathbb{I}(x)$ is indicator function defined as 1 if x is true and 0 otherwise.

Similarly, you can design your own more complex training rule to train topic embedding like TopicVec [13] and Latent Topic Embedding (LTE) [12].

3.3 Word Embeddings Training

LTSG aims to update φ during word embeddings training. Following the similar optimization as Skip-Gram, hierarchical softmax and negative sampling are used for training the word embeddings approximately due to the computationally expensive cost of the full softmax function which is proportional to vocabulary size W. LTSG uses stochastic gradient descent to optimize the objective function given in Eq. (4).

The hierarchical softmax uses a binary tree (eg. a Huffman tree) representation of the output layer with the W words as its leaves and, for each node, explicitly represents the relative probabilities of its child nodes. There is a unique path from root to each word w and $node(w, i)$ is the i-th node of the path. Let $L(w)$ be the length of this path, then $node(w, 1) = root$ and $node(w, L(w)) = w$. Let $child(u)$ be an arbitrary child of node u, e.g. left child. By applying hierarchical softmax on $\Pr(w_{m,n+j}|T_{w_{m,n}})$ similar to $\Pr(w_{m,n+j}|w_{m,n})$ described in Skip-gram [16], we can compute the log gradient of φ as follows,

$$\frac{\partial \log \Pr(w_{m,n+j}|T_{w_{m,n}})}{\partial \varphi_{k=z_{m,n}, w=w_{m,n}}} = \frac{1}{L(w_{m,n}) - 1} \sum_{i=1}^{L(w_{m,n})-1}$$

$$\left[1 - h_{i+1}^{w_{m,n+j}} - \sigma(T_{w_{m,n}} \cdot v_i^{w_{m,n+j}})\right] \tau_k \cdot v_i^{w_{m,n+j}}, \tag{10}$$

where $\sigma(x) = 1/(1 + \exp(-x))$. Given a path from root to word $w_{m,n+j}$ constructed by Huffman tree, $v_i^{w_{m,n+j}}$ is the vector representation of i-th node. And $h_{i+1}^{w_{m,n+j}}$ is the Huffman coding on the path defined as $h_{i+1}^{w_{m,n+j}} = \mathbb{I}(node(w_{m,n+j}, i+1) = child(node(w_{m,n+j}, i)))$.

Follow this idea, we can compute the gradients for updating the word w and non-leaf node. From Eq. (10), we can see that φ is updated by using topic embeddings τ_k directly and word embeddings indirectly via the non-leaf nodes in Huffman tree, which is used for training the word embeddings.

3.4 An Overview of Our LTSG algorithm

In this section we provide an overview of our LTSG algorithm, as shown in Algorithm 1. In line 1 in Algorithm 1, we run the standard LDA with certain iterations and initialize φ based on Eq. (6). From lines 4 to 6, there are the three steps mentioned in Sect. 3. From lines 7 to 13, φ will be updated after training the whole corpus $\mathcal{D}$ rather than per word, which is more suitable for multi-thread training. Function $f(\xi, n_{k,w})$ is a dynamic learning rate, defined by $f(\xi, n_{k,w}) = \xi \cdot \log(n_{k,w})/n_{k,w}$. In line 16, document-topic distribution $\theta_{m,k}$ is computed to model documents.

4 Experiments

In this section, we evaluate our LTSG model in three aspects, i.e., contextual word similarity, text classification, and topic coherence.

We use the dataset 20NewsGroup, which consists of about 20,000 documents from 20 different newsgroups. For the baseline, we use the default settings of parameters unless otherwise specified. Similar to TWE, we set the number of topics $K = 80$ and the dimensionality of both word embeddings and topic embeddings $d = 400$ for all the relative models. In LTSG, we initialize φ with $init\_nGS = 2500$. We perform $nItrs = 5$ runs on our framework. We perform $nGS = 200$ Gibbs sampling iterations to update topic assignment with $\alpha = 0.01, \beta = 0.1$.

Algorithm 1. Latent Topical Skip-Gram

Input: corpus $\mathcal{D}$, # topics K, size of vocabulary W, Dirichlet hyperparameters α, β, # iterations of LDA for initialization $init\_nGS$, # iterations of framework $nItrs$, # Gibbs sampling iterations nGS.

Output: $\theta_{m,k}, \varphi_{k,w}, \boldsymbol{v}_w, \boldsymbol{\tau}_k, m = 1, 2, \ldots, M; k = 1, 2, \ldots, K; w = 1, 2, \ldots, W$

1: **Initialization.** Initialize $\varphi_{k,w}$ as in Equation (6) with $init\_nGS$ iterations in standard LDA as in Equation (5)
2: $i \leftarrow 0$
3: **while** $(i < nItrs)$ **do**
4:     **Step 1.** Sample $z_{m,n}$ as in Equation (8) with nGS iterations
5:     **Step 2.** Compute each topic embedding τ_k as in Equation (9)
6:     **Step 3.** Train word embeddings with objective function as in Equation (4)
7:     Compute the first-order partial derivatives $\mathcal{L}'(\mathcal{D})$
8:     Set the learning rate ξ
9:     **for** $(k = 1 \rightarrow K)$ **do**
10:         **for** $(w = 1 \rightarrow W)$ **do**
11:             $\varphi_{k,w}^{(i+1)} \leftarrow \varphi_{k,w}^{(i)} + f(\xi, n_{k,w}) \frac{\partial \mathcal{L}'(\mathcal{D})}{\partial \varphi_{k,w}}$
12:         **end for**
13:     **end for**
14:     $i \leftarrow i + 1$
15: **end while**
16: Compute each $\theta_{m,k}$ as in Equation (7)

4.1   Contextual Word Similarity

To evaluate contextual word similarity, we use Stanford's Word Contextual Word Similarities (SCWS) dataset introduced by [11], which has been also used for evaluating state-of-art model [14]. There are totally 2,003 word pairs and their contexts, including 1328 noun-noun pairs, 399 verb-verb pairs, 140 verb-noun, 97 adjective-adjective, 30 noun-adjective, 9 verb-adjective pairs. Among all of the pairs, there are 241 same-word pairs which may show different meaning in the giving context. The dataset provide human labeled similarity scores based on the meaning in the context. For comparison, we compute the Spearman correlation similarity scores of different models and human judgments.

Following the `TWE` model, we use two scores `AvgSimC` and `MaxSimC` to evaluate the multi-prototype model for contextual word similarity. The topic distribution $\Pr(z|w, c)$ will be inferred by using $\Pr(z|w, c) \propto \Pr(w|z) \Pr(z|c)$ with regarding c as a document. Given a pair of words with their contexts, namely (w_i, c_i) and (w_j, c_j), `AvgSimC` aims to measure the averaged similarity between the two words all over the topics:

$$AvgSimC = \sum_{z, z' \in K} \Pr(z|w_i, c_i) \Pr(z'|w_j, c_j) S(\boldsymbol{v}_{w_i}^z, \boldsymbol{v}_{w_j}^{z'}) \tag{11}$$

where $\boldsymbol{v}_w^z$ is the embedding of word w under its topic z by concatenating word and topic embeddings $\boldsymbol{v}_w^z = \boldsymbol{v}_w \oplus \boldsymbol{\tau}_z$. $S(\boldsymbol{v}_{w_i}^z, \boldsymbol{v}_{w_j}^{z'})$ is the cosine similarity between $\boldsymbol{v}_{w_i}^z$ and $\boldsymbol{v}_{w_j}^{z'}$.

MaxSimC selects the corresponding topical word embedding $\boldsymbol{v}_w^z$ of the most probable topic z inffered using w in context c as the contextual word embedding, defined as

$$MaxSimc = S(\boldsymbol{v}_{w_i}^z, \boldsymbol{v}_{w_j}^{z'}) \tag{12}$$

where

$z = \arg\max_z \Pr(z|w_i, c_i)$, $z' = \arg\max_z \Pr(z|w_j, c_j)$.

We consider the two baselines Skip-Gram and TWE. Skip-Gram is a well-known single prototype model and TWE is the state-of-the-art multi-prototype model. We use all the default settings in these two model to train the 20NewsGroup corpus.

Table 2. Spearman correlation $\rho \times 100$ of contextual word similarity on the SCWS dataset.

Model	$\rho \times 100$	
Skip-Gram	51.1	
LTSG-word	53.4	
	AvgSimC	MaxSimC
TWE	52.0	49.2
LTSG	**54.2**	**54.1**

From Table 2, we can see that LTSG achieves better performance compared to the two competitive baseline. It shows that topic model can actually help improving polysemous-word model, including word embeddings and topic embeddings. The meaning of a word is certain by giving its specify context so that MaxSimC is more relative to real application. Then LTSG model achieves more improvement in MaxSimC than AvgSimC compared to TWE, which tells that LTSG could perform better in telling a word meaning in specify context.

4.2 Text Classification

In this sub-section, we investigate the effectiveness of LTSG for document modeling using multi-class text classification. The 20NewsGroup corpus has been divided into training set and test set with ratio 60% to 40% for each category. We calculate macro-averaging precision, recall and F1-score to measure the performance of LTSG.

We learn word and topic embeddings on the training set and then model document embeddings for both training set and testing set. Afterwards, we consider document embeddings as document features and train a linear classifier using Liblinear [8]. We use $\boldsymbol{v}_m$, $\boldsymbol{\tau}_k$, $\boldsymbol{v}_w$ to represent document embeddings, topic embeddings, word embeddings, respectively, and model documents on both topic-based and embedding-based methods as shown below.

Table 3. Evaluation results of multi-class text classification.

Model	Accuracy	Precision	Recall	F1-score
BOW	79.7	79.5	79.0	79.2
LDA	72.2	70.8	70.7	70.7
Skip-Gram	75.4	75.1	74.7	74.9
TWE	81.5	81.2	80.6	80.9
LTSG-theta	74.1	73.1	72.7	72.9
LTSG-topic	74.8	74.0	73.3	73.7
LTSG-word	81.4	81.0	80.4	80.7
LTSG	**82.7**	**82.5**	**81.7**	**82.1**

Table 4. Top words of some topics from LTSG and LDA on 20NewsGroup for $K = 80$.

LTSG	LDA	LTSG	LDA	LTSG	LDA	LTSG	LDA
image	image	jet	printer	stimulation	doctor	anonymous	list
jpeg	files	ink	good	diseases	disease	faq	mail
gif	color	laser	print	disease	coupons	send	information
format	gif	printers	font	toxin	treatment	ftp	internet
files	jpeg	deskjet	graeme	icts	pain	mailing	send
file	file	ssa	laser	newsletter	medical	server	posting
convert	format	printer	type	staffed	day	mail	email
color	bit	noticeable	quality	volume	microorganisms	alt	group
formats	images	canon	printers	health	medicine	archive	news
images	quality	output	deskjet	aids	body	email	nonymous
−75.66	−88.76	−91.53	−119.28	−66.91	−100.39	−78.23	−95.47

- **LTSG-theta.** Document-topic distribution θ_m estimated by Eq. (7).
- **LTSG-topic.** $v_m = \sum_{k=1}^{K} \theta_{m,k} \cdot \tau_k$.
- **LTSG-word.** $v_m = (1/N_m) \sum_{n=1}^{N_m} v_{w_{m,n}}$.
- **LTSG.** $v_m = (1/N_m) \sum_{n=1}^{N_m} v_{w_{m,n}}^{z_{m,n}}$, where contextual word is simply constructed by $v_{w_{m,n}}^{z_{m,n}} = v_{w_{m,n}} \oplus \tau_{z_{m,n}}$.

Result Analysis. We consider the following baselines, bag-of-word (BOW) model, LDA, Skip-Gram and TWE. The BOW model represents each document as a bag of words and use TFIDF as the weighting measure. For the TFIDF model, we select top 50,000 words as features according to TFIDF score. LDA represents each document as its inferred topic distribution. In Skip-Gram, we build the embedding vector of a document by simply averaging over all word embeddings in the document. The experimental results are shown in Table 3.

From Table 3, we can see that, for topic modeling, LTSG-theta and LTSG-topic perform better than LDA slightly. For word embeddings, LTSG-word significantly outperforms Skip-Gram. For topic embeddings using for multi-prototype word embeddings, LTSG also outperforms state-of-the-art baseline TWE. This verifies that topic modeling, word embeddings and topic embeddings can indeed impact each other in LTSG, which lead to the best result over all the other baselines.

4.3 Topic Coherence

In this section, we evaluate the topics generated by LTSG on both quantitative and qualitative analysis. Here we follow the same corpus and parameters setting in Sect. 4.2 for LSTG model.

Quantitative Analysis. Although perplexity (held-out likehood) has been widely used to evaluate topic models, [3] found that perplexity can be hardly to reflect the semantic coherence of individual topics. Topic Coherence metric [17] was found to produce higher correlation with human judgments in assessing topic quality, which has become popular to evaluate topic models [1,4]. A higher topic coherence score indicates a more coherent topic.

We compute the score of the top 10 words for each topic. We present the score for some of topics in the last line of Table 4. By averaging the score of the total 80 topics, LTSG gets −92.23 compared with −108.72 of LDA. We can conclude that LTSG performs better than LDA in finding higher quality topics.

Qualitative Analysis. Table 4 shows top 10 words of topics from LTSG and LDA model on 20NewsGroup. The words in this two models are ranked based on the probability distribution φ for each topic. As shown, LTSG is able to capture more concrete topics compared with general topics in LDA. For the topic about "image", LTSG shows about image conversion on different format, while LDA shows the image quality of different format. In topic "printer", LTSG emphasizes the different technique of printer in detail and LDA generally focus on "good quality" of printing.

5   Releated Work

Recently, researches on cooperating topic models and vector representations have made great advances in NLP community. [24] proposed a Markov Random Field regularized LDA model (MRF-LDA) which encourages similar words to share the same topic for learning more coherent topics. [6] proposed Gaussian LDA to use pre-trained word embeddings in Gibbs sampler based on multivariate Gaussian distributions. LFLDA [18] is modeled as a mixture of the conventional categorical distribution and an embedding link function. These works have given the faith that vector representations are capable of helping improving topic models. On the contrary, vector representations, especially topic embeddings, have been promoted for modeling documents or polysemy with great help of topic models.

For examples, [14] used topic model to globally cluster the words into different topics according to their context for learning better multi-prototype word embeddings. [13] proposed generative topic embedding (TopicVec) model that replaces categorical distribution in LDA with embedding link function. However, these models do not show close interactions among topic models, word embeddings and topic embeddings. Besides, these researches lack of investigation on the influence of topic model on word embeddings.

6   Conclusion and Future Work

In this paper, we propose a basic model Latent Topical Skip-Gram (LTSG) which shows that LDA and Skip-Gram can mutually help improve performance on different task. The experimental results show that LTSG achieves the competitive results compaired with the state-of-art models.

We consider the following future research directions: (I) We will investigate non-parametric topic models [22] and parallel topic models [15] to set parameters automatically and accelerate training using multi threading for large-scale data. (II) We will construct a package which can be convenient to extend with other topic models and word embeddings models to our framework by using the interfaces. (III) We will deal with unseen words in new documents like Gaussian LDA [6].

Acknowledgments. We thank all reviewers for their valuable comments and feedback that greatly improved our paper. Zhuo thanks the National Key Research and Development Program of China (2016YFB0201900), National Natural Science Foundation of China (U1611262), Guangdong Natural Science Funds for Distinguished Young Scholar (2017A030306028), Pearl River Science and Technology New Star of Guangzhou, and Guangdong Province Key Laboratory of Big Data Analysis and Processing for the support of this research.

References

1. Arora, S., et al.: A practical algorithm for topic modeling with provable guarantees. In: ICML, pp. 280–288 (2013)
2. Blei, D.M., Ng, A.Y., Jordan, M.I.: Latent dirichlet allocation. JMLR **3**, 993–1022 (2003)
3. Chang, J., Gerrish, S., Wang, C., Boyd-Graber, J.L., Blei, D.M.: Reading tea leaves: how humans interpret topic models. In: NIPS, pp. 288–296 (2009)
4. Chen, Z., Liu, B.: Topic modeling using topics from many domains, lifelong learning and big data. In: ICML, pp. 703–711 (2014)
5. Collobert, R., Weston, J., Bottou, L., Karlen, M., Kavukcuoglu, K., Kuksa, P.P.: Natural language processing (almost) from scratch. JMLR **12**, 2493–2537 (2011)
6. Das, R., Zaheer, M., Dyer, C.: Gaussian LDA for topic models with word embeddings. In: ACL, pp. 795–804 (2015)
7. Du, J., Jiang, J., Song, D., Liao, L.: Topic modeling with document relative similarities. In: IJCAI 2015, pp. 3469–3475 (2015)

8. Fan, R., Chang, K., Hsieh, C., Wang, X., Lin, C.: LIBLINEAR: a library for large linear classification. JMLR **9**, 1871–1874 (2008)
9. Griffiths, T.L., Steyvers, M.: Finding scientific topics. Proc. Nat. Acad. Sci. **101**(Suppl. 1), 5228–5235 (2004)
10. Hofmann, T.: Probabilistic latent semantic indexing. In: SIGIR 1999, pp. 50–57 (1999)
11. Huang, E.H., Socher, R., Manning, C.D., Ng, A.Y.: Improving word representations via global context and multiple word prototypes. In: ACL, pp. 873–882 (2012)
12. Jiang, D., Shi, L., Lian, R., Wu, H.: Latent topic embedding. In: COLING, pp. 2689–2698 (2016)
13. Li, S., Chua, T., Zhu, J., Miao, C.: Generative topic embedding: a continuous representation of documents. In: ACL (2016)
14. Liu, Y., Liu, Z., Chua, T., Sun, M.: Topical word embeddings. In: AAAI, pp. 2418–2424 (2015)
15. Liu, Z., Zhang, Y., Chang, E.Y., Sun, M.: PLDA+: parallel latent dirichlet allocation with data placement and pipeline processing. ACM TIST **2**(3), 26 (2011)
16. Mikolov, T., Sutskever, I., Chen, K., Corrado, G.S., Dean, J.: Distributed representations of words and phrases and their compositionality. In: NIPS, pp. 3111–3119 (2013)
17. Mimno, D.M., Wallach, H.M., Talley, E.M., Leenders, M., McCallum, A.: Optimizing semantic coherence in topic models. In: EMNLP, pp. 262–272 (2011)
18. Nguyen, D.Q., Billingsley, R., Du, L., Johnson, M.: Improving topic models with latent feature word representations. TACL **3**, 299–313 (2015)
19. Phan, X.H., Nguyen, C., Le, D., Nguyen, M.L., Horiguchi, S., Ha, Q.: A hidden topic-based framework toward building applications with short web documents. IEEE Trans. Knowl. Data Eng. **23**(7), 961–976 (2011)
20. Reisinger, J., Mooney, R.J.: Multi-prototype vector-space models of word meaning. In: NAACL, pp. 109–117 (2010)
21. Socher, R., Bauer, J., Manning, C.D., Ng, A.Y.: Parsing with compositional vector grammars. In: ACL, pp. 455–465 (2013)
22. Teh, Y.W., Jordan, M.I., Beal, M.J., Blei, D.M.: Hierarchical dirichlet processes. J. Am. Stat. Assoc. **101**(476), 1566–1581 (2006)
23. Turian, J.P., Ratinov, L., Bengio, Y.: Word representations: a simple and general method for semi-supervised learning. In: ACL 2010, pp. 384–394 (2010)
24. Xie, P., Yang, D., Xing, E.P.: Incorporating word correlation knowledge into topic modeling. In: NAACL, pp. 725–734 (2015)

Improve the Spoofing Resistance of Multimodal Verification with Representation-Based Measures

Zengxi Huang[1], Zhen-Hua Feng[2], Josef Kittler[2], and Yiguang Liu[3](✉)

[1] School of Computer and Software Engineering,
Xihua University, Chengdu, China
luomul17@hotmail.com
[2] Centre for Vision, Speech and Signal Processing,
University of Surrey, Guildford, UK
[3] College of Computer Science, Sichuan University, Chengdu, China
lygpapers@aliyun.com

Abstract. Recently, the security of multimodal verification has become a growing concern since many fusion systems have been known to be easily deceived by partial spoof attacks, i.e. only a subset of modalities is spoofed. In this paper, we verify such a vulnerability and propose to use two representation-based measures to close this gap. Firstly, we use the collaborative representation fidelity with non-target subjects to measure the affinity of a query sample to the claimed client. We further consider sparse coding as a competing comparison among the client and the non-target subjects, and hence explore two sparsity-based measures for recognition. Last, we select the representation-based measure, and assemble its score and the affinity score of each modality to train a support vector machine classifier. Our experimental results on a chimeric multimodal database with face and ear traits demonstrate that in both regular verification and partial spoof attacks, the proposed method significantly outperforms the well-known fusion methods with conventional measure.

Keywords: Multimodal verification · Spoof attacks
Representation-based measure · Support vector machine

1 Introduction

A generic biometric system has eight vulnerable points that can be exploited by an intruder to gain unauthorized access [1]. Among them, spoof attacks usually present a counterfeited biometric sample (e.g., a gummy fingerprint, a face image/video/mask) to a system sensor, which do not require knowledge about the system's operational mechanism and internal parameters. Spoof attacks are also known as non-zero effort attacks, presentation attacks, and direct attacks. The concept of non-zero effort attacks is relative to zero effort attempts, where an imposter doesn't fabricate the biometric trait of any specific client and merely presents his/her own biometric trait to the system. In the literature, an imposter is generally regarded as an intruder who performs zero effort attempts. In this paper, for clarity and terminological consistence, a legitimate claim,

© Springer Nature Switzerland AG 2018
J.-H. Lai et al. (Eds.): PRCV 2018, LNCS 11258, pp. 388–399, 2018.
https://doi.org/10.1007/978-3-030-03338-5_33

zero effort attempt, and non-zero effort attack are termed as genuine, imposter and spoof, respectively, together with their associated executor/sample/score.

Multimodal systems have been considered intrinsically more secure than unimodal systems based on the intuition that an intruder would have to spoof all the biometric traits to successfully impersonate the targeted client [2]. Such a belief has long been established disregarding the possibility that an intruder is falsely accepted by spoofing only a subset of the biometric traits. The vulnerability of multimodal systems to partial spoof attacks has been shown in the worst-case scenario, where the intruder is assumed to be able to replicate a subset of the biometric traits of a genuine client exactly. Under this assumption, Rodrigues [3] showed experimental results on chimeric multimodal databases with face and fingerprint that multimodal systems can be deceived easily by spoofing only a subset of the modalities, if the fusion rule is not designed with any anti-spoofing measure. Wild et al. [4] showed the sensitivity of multimodal systems to partial spoof attacks with real fake biometric databases.

Some efforts to enhance the security of multimodal systems against partial spoof attacks have already been reported. Rodrigues et al. [5] proposed a modification of the classic likelihood ratio (LLR) method that considers the possibility of spoof attacks and the degree of security to individual trait when modelling score distributions. However, these prior probabilities are application dependent and may not be time invariant, hence are quite difficult to quantify. Rodrigues et al. [3] also proposed the idea of using quality measures to protect against spoof attacks. Intuitively, a fake biometric sample is likely to be of inferior quality. However, biometric quality assessment is still an open issue to most biometrics. Besides, fake biometric sample is not necessarily to be inferior with the emerging image/video synthesis, 3D printing, and materials.

Liveness detection is another kind of approach used to improve the spoofing resistance for a given system. Marasco et al. [6] proposed a multimodal system that incorporates a liveness detection algorithm to reject spoofed samples. If a spoof attempt is indicated, the related modality matching score is ignored. Wild et al. [4] combined the recognition score and liveness measure at score level with a 1-median filtering scheme for enhanced tolerance to spoof attacks. Nevertheless, neither one of hardware-based and software-based liveness detection systems have shown acceptable performance and cost against spoof attacks. Physiological and behavioral characteristics are also employed to enhance multimodal verification security in [7].

This paper is enlightened by the fact that in a partial spoof attack, the recognition scores achieved from non-spoofed modalities are generally near the imposter score distribution center, given that they are also zero effort attempts from a unimodal viewpoint. Unlike the quality- and/or liveness-based methods that focus on the spoofed modalities, we propose to take advantage of non-spoofed modalities. To this end, we put forward a representation-based measure to gauge the affinity of a query sample to a claimed client. This is based on the assumption that a biometric sample would result in inferior sparse representation fidelity if it doesn't lie in any subspace spanned by the samples from the same subject [8–10]. Note that, it is unlikely to exhaustively collect the representative samples per subject to construct a class specific overcomplete dictionary. We propose to build the dictionary together with samples from non-target subjects to collaboratively represent a query sample.

This affinity score could be an additional measure to a traditional verification method. However, we further consider sparse coding as a one-to-many comparison among the claimed client and non-target subjects, and hence explore other sparsity-based measures for verification. We evaluate two measures, namely, sparse coding error (SCE) and sparse contribution rate (SCR), on a multimodal database with face and ear. Encouraging performance of SCE-based and SCR-based Sum fusion methods evidently supports the usage of sparsity-based one-to-many comparisons in multimodal verification. However, SCR shows much more inferior performance in spoof attacks. Last, we assemble the proposed affinity score and SCE score of each modality as an input vector to train a support vector machine (SVM) classifier.

To validate the effectiveness of the proposed method, we construct a chimeric multimodal database with face and ear traits. The proposed method is compared with the well-known multimodal methods like LLR, SVM, and Sum fusion that are based on cosine similarity. The experimental results validate that in both no spoof and partial spoof cases, the proposed method significantly outperforms its competitors. For example, the traditional methods get the best equal error rates (EER) of 8.32% and 11.89% in no spoof and spoof cases, while our method achieves 0.27% and 2.12%. Apparently, the proposed method helps to increase the spoofing resistance of multi-modal systems.

The remainder of the paper is structured as follows. We discuss the approaches to verification based on one-to-many match, and we review the existing methods using sparse coding in Sect. 2. In Sect. 3, we present the sparsity-based affinity and recognition measures, together with the proposed multimodal verification system. In Sect. 4, we describe our chimeric multimodal database and report the corresponding experimental results. The conclusion is drawn in Sect. 5.

2   Related Work

In a biometric verification system, an individual who desires to be recognized claims an identity and presents biometric samples. Then the system conducts a comparison to determine whether the claim is licit or not. Verification is used for positive recognition, where the aim is to prevent multiple people from using the same identity.

Typically, biometric verification systems conduct a one-to-one match that compares a query image against the gallery template(s), whose identity is being claimed. The comparison produces a similarity score. The system accepts the claim if the score is higher than an operating threshold, otherwise rejects it. The operating threshold is determined in the training phase based on the genuine and imposter score distributions. However, it is unlikely to collect all the representative samples of a client that cover all possible variations, for example, expression, pose, illumination, aging, and occlusion in face. Under such circumstances, it cannot be guaranteed that no imposter score is higher than the predefined operating threshold. The system is at a risk of being cracked by intruders. Therefore, the one-to-one match solely based on a predetermined operating threshold is problematic.

Two decades ago, Verlinde et al. [11] proposed a one-to-many match biometric verification method using a k-NN classifier. To the best of our knowledge, this is one of the first attempts to consider non-target subjects for verification in the test phase. Nevertheless, the inferior comparison algorithm like k-NN could probably account for the rare use of one-to-many match in verification. Cohort-based score normalization also takes advantage of non-target subjects but serves the traditional one-to-one match verification [12]. In recent years, we have witnessed the great success of sparse coding techniques in biometric recognition [13–15]. The sparse representation-based classification (SRC) conducts one-to-many comparisons in a sparse coding procedure and is naturally applicable to biometric identification. Note that, along with the initial research of SRC-based face identification in [13], a measure called sparse concentration index (SCI) was applied to reject outliers, i.e. the subjects who do not appear in dictionary.

Inspired by the success of SRC identification and sparsity-based outlier verification, SRC-based comparison has been introduced in speaker verification. In [16], GMM mean supervector is used as feature of an utterance. The L_1-norm value of the representation coefficients associated with the claimed identity is used as genuine score, while the L_1-norm of the coefficients of each other non-target subject are imposter scores. Based on a similar idea, Li et al. [17] created the dictionary using the total variability i-vectors and evaluated three sparsity-based measures for speaker verification, which achieved better results than a SVM baseline.

3   The Proposed Method

3.1   Affinity Measure

In this section, we present a representation-based measure to gauge the affinity of a query sample to a claimed client, based on the assumption that a biometric sample would result in inferior sparse representation fidelity if it doesn't lie in the subspace spanned by the samples from the same subject [8, 9]. Note that, it is unlikely to exhaustively collect the representative samples per subject to construct a class specific overcomplete dictionary. A feasible way is to use non-target subjects to collaboratively represent the query samples [18].

Therefore, we select a number of non-target subjects together with the claimed client. Their gallery samples/features are used to construct an overcomplete dictionary $A = [A_c, A_b] \in R^{M \times N}$ ($M < < N$). The first sub-dictionary $A_c = [a_{c,1}, a_{c,2}, \cdots, a_{c,n}] \in R^{M \times n}$ is composed of the gallery samples of the claimed client, which is a dynamic part of the dictionary. The other sub-dictionary $A_b = [a_1, a_2, a_3, \cdots, a_{(N-n)}] \in R^{M \times (N-n)}$ consists of the samples of non-target subjects. Without any specific instructions, A_b is fixed for all identity verification processes. Given a query sample y, if it is from a genuine client and isn't of inferior quality, y should lie in a subspace spanned by A_c. In this context, y can be sparsely represented by $y = A\alpha$ with high fidelity (see the genuine distribution in Fig. 1), where $\alpha \in R^N$ is the coefficient vector. A sparse solution of α can be obtained by the following optimization problem [13]:

$$\hat{\alpha} = \arg\min \|\alpha\|_1 \text{ s. t. } \|y - A\alpha\|_2 < \varepsilon, \tag{1}$$

where $\|\cdot\|_1$ denotes the L_1-norm, and $\varepsilon > 0$ is a positive constant.

In a partial spoof attack, a query sample of non-spoofed modalities is unlikely to lie in any subspace spanned by the dictionary samples given that the non-target subjects are confidential. In this context, only a solution with inferior collaborative representation fidelity (CRF), described in Eq. (2), can be found by optimizing Eq. (1).

$$F(y) = \|y - A\hat{\alpha}\|_2. \tag{2}$$

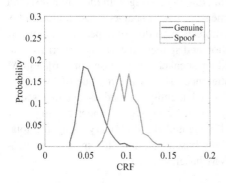 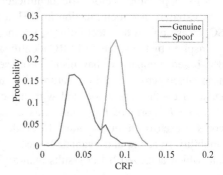

(a) Face distribution in ear spoof case   (b) Ear distribution in face spoof case

Fig. 1. CRF distributions in partial spoof attacks.

Figure 1 shows the CRF distributions on a chimeric multimodal database using face and ear, detailed in Sect. 4. When the ear of a client is spoofed, the intruder needs to show his/her face or an arbitrary face to complete the biometric data enrollment. Such arbitrary face is unlikely to be from the non-target subjects since the combination of the overcomplete dictionary is confidential. In this context, the non-spoofed face is an outlier that does not lie in the subspace spanned by A and hence leads to an inferior CRF score, see in Fig. 1(a). When the face is spoofed, we see similar CRF distribution of the non-spoofed ears in Fig. 1(b). From the perspective of the client, CRF score can be used to represent the affinity of the query sample to it.

3.2 Sparsity-Based Recognition Scores

We consider sparse coding as a competing comparison among the client and non-target subjects, and hence explore other two sparsity-based measures, namely, sparse coding error (SCE) and sparse contribution rate (SCR), for multimodal verification.

Since $\hat{\alpha}$ is achieved in Eq. (1), the SCE value is calculated by

$$E(y) = \|y - A_c\delta_c(\hat{\alpha})\|_2, \tag{3}$$

where $\delta_c: R^N \to R^N$ is the characteristic function that selects the coefficients associated with the claimed client.

The well-known SRC and most of its extensions identify a query sample based on comparing the SCEs of all classes in dictionary. Their superior classification performance validates that SCE is a good candidate to measure the correlation between a query sample and a specific class, as a distance score. Thus, it is reasonable to use SCE for verification.

Wright et al. [13] presented a measure called sparse concentration index (SCI) to reject outliers in face identification. Essentially, the SCI value depends on the class who contributes the most in sparse coding. Given a query sample that isn't an outlier, it generally belongs to the class with the maximal sparse contribution rate (SCR), as defined in Eq. (4). A large value of SCR obtained by a class indicates a greater possibility of the query sample belonging to this class. Therefore, SCR could possibly be used as a similarity score for verification.

$$R(\hat{\alpha}) = \|\delta_c(\hat{\alpha})\|_1 / \|\hat{\alpha}\|_1. \tag{4}$$

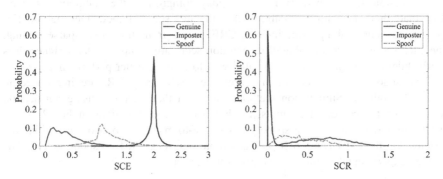

Fig. 2. The distributions of SCE and SCR with Sum fusion on our multimodal dataset.

Figure 2 plots the distributions of SCE and SCR scores obtained on the proposed chimeric multimodal database of face and ear. For convenience to illustrate the effectiveness of SCE and SCR in multimodal verification, we use the Sum rule to fuse face and ear scores. As for SCE, the distribution centers of the genuine and imposter scores are far away from each other with little overlap. Although there is no a clear distribution center peak of the genuine SCR, the overlap is not evident as well. More experimental evidence supporting SCE and SCR is shown in Sect. 4. In addition, Fig. 2 also demonstrates that most spoof scores are located between the distribution centers of genuine and imposter scores. This implies that the multimodal fusion methods based on SCE or SCR are vulnerable to spoof attacks.

Some variants of SCE and SCR have been used in speaker verification and shown to achieve comparable performance with the traditional one-to-one verification. However, in our face and ear unimodal experiments, a genuine client might lose his/her chance to obtain an eligible SCE or SCR score in the competing comparison, owing to the variations in query samples. If it happens, the genuine score will be extremely low. It means that many licitly claimed clients could not pass the verification system by tuning a client specific operating threshold. Instead, more user cooperation will be necessary, which would degrade the user experience. Therefore, for high accuracy and user convenience of identity verification, sparsity-based one-to-many comparisons would be rather preferable in multimodal scenarios rather than in unimodal applications.

3.3 Multimodal Verification

The CRF score that measures the affinity of a query sample to its claimed client can be utilized to enhance the system's resistance to partial spoof attacks in a serial or parallel fusion mode. In a serial fusion mode, multimodal systems firstly examine the CRF scores of each modality to determine whether they are spoofed or not, and then conduct multimodal verification.

However, as shown in Fig. 1, the overlap of the genuine and the spoof CRF score distribution is still rather obvious. A hard CRF threshold would lead to high false acceptance rate (FAR), while a loose one may compromise the multimodal system. Note that, there is a high possibility that the non-spoofed modalities get inferior recognition scores along with inferior CRF scores from the same sparse coding. The CRF score and sparsity-based recognition score are complementary. Hence, it is worthwhile to combine them in a parallel way to achieve better performance.

Two sparsity-based recognition scores, i.e., SCE and SCR, are introduced in Sect. 3.2. Both the Sum fusion methods based on them get promising verification performance in zero effort attempts, as shown by the distributions in Fig. 2. These results support the use of the sparsity-based one-to-many comparison in multimodal systems. On the other hand, SCR is much more inferior to SCE in spoof attacks. The detailed experimental results will be given in Sect. 4.

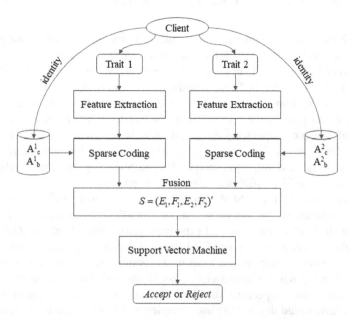

Fig. 3. An overview of the multimodal system architecture.

Last, we select the SCE and CRF scores of each modality to form a score vector for a verification claim. Suppose there are K modalities, e_k and f_k are the SCE and CRF scores of the kth modality. The final score vector can be denoted by $S = (e_1, f_1, e_2, f_2, \cdots, e_K, f_K)'$. In the training phase, we use genuine, imposter, and spoof score samples to train a SVM classifier with RBF kernel. For simplicity but without the loss of generality, an overview of system architecture with two modalities (K = 2) is shown in Fig. 3 to illustrate the proposed method.

The chimeric multimodal database introduced in Sect. 4 contains 79 subjects with 7 gallery samples each. All these samples are used to form an overcomplete dictionary with 553 atoms. We don't have abundance data to discuss how to optimally select the non-target subjects in this paper. Note that, we ignore the issue of score normalization, given that the scores of face and ear are compatible in our experiments.

4 Experiments and Discussion

4.1 Databases

The proposed method is general for verification using multiple biometric traits. In this paper, we construct a chimeric multimodal database with publicly available face and ear databases. All the 79 subjects in USTB III ear database [19] are randomly paired with the first 79 subjects of AR face database [20]. For each subject, the 7 face images without occlusion of Session 1 are used as gallery samples, while the same type of 7 images of Session 2 are used as probe samples. The USTB III is a multi-view ear database with 20 images per subject. We use the same gallery and probe partition rule in [8, 9], where 7 ear gallery images and 13 ear probe images are selected for each subject. In our experiments, the 2 probe images per subject with extreme pose variation are discarded. For each subject on the multimodal database, in the gallery set, 7 face images are uniquely paired with the 7 ear images to form $79 \times 7 = 553$ multimodal samples. In the probe set, each face image is paired with all the ear images to form $79 \times 7 \times 11 = 6083$ multimodal samples.

To simulate the worst-case partial spoof attacks, in a face spoof case, we replace the ear part of a multimodal sample with the image of USTB II ear database (77 subjects, 4 images per subject) [19], In an ear spoof case, we replace the face part with the image of Georgia Tech face database (GT, 50 subjects, 8 images per subject) [21]. Finally, we get 77 subjects, 28 face spoof multimodal samples per subject, and 50 subjects, 88 ear spoof multimodal samples per subject.

In the experiments, we use the features of gallery samples of all 79 subjects to construct the overcomplete dictionary. The SCE, SCR, and CRF scores are derived from the comparison between one-sample and one-set. The numbers of genuine, imposter and spoof score samples are 6083, 474474 (6083×78), and 6556, respectively. As for the competing methods using cosine similarity, we empirically select the best match score from each comparison, hence their score sample numbers are the same.

4.2 Settings

The 2D-DCT method is applied for feature extraction of face and ear images, since it is fast, general, and without specific training. The DCT coefficients are scanned in a zigzag manner starting from the top-left corner of the entire transformed image to form a feature vector with 200 dimensions.

The proposed multimodal method uses SVM with RBF kernel (sigma = 0.25). It is compared with the Sum fusion methods of SCE and SCR, denoted by SUM(sce) and SUM(scr), respectively. The competing multimodal methods include the well-known LLR [22], SVM [23], and Sum fusion methods, which use cosine similarity and are respectively denoted by LLR(cos), SVM(cos), and SUM(cos). SVM(cos) also uses RBF kernel (sigma = 1).

Without specific instructions, half of the genuine, imposter and spoof scores are randomly selected for training, and the remainder are for testing. To alleviate the imbalance of training samples, SVM-based classifiers use 1/10 imposters to train. The LLR(cos) uses half of all kinds of samples to fit Gaussian mixture models for score distribution estimation. We run all experiments 5 times, the results presented here are based on the average from these 5 runs.

5   Results

The metrics like false acceptance rate (FAR), false rejection rate (FRR), equal error rate (EER), and the receiver operating characteristic (ROC) curves are generally used to evaluate methods in regular verification. The spoof FAR (SFAR) is specifically used to note the FAR in spoof attacks.

In the first part of the experiments, we train all the learning-based classifiers without considering the spoof samples, namely Regular training. Figure 4 plots the ROC curves of all competing methods in regular verification. The methods with sparsity-based measures are observed to be significantly better than the methods with traditional measure. Among the former methods, SUM(scr) is obviously inferior to SUM(sce) and the proposed method. The ROC curves and the EERs summarized in Table 1 do not show evident advantage of our method when compared with SUM(sce).

Table 1. Performance in terms of EER (%).

Training	Testing	SUM(cos)	SVM(cos)	LLR(cos)	SUM(sce)	SUM(scr)	Ours
Regular training	Regular	11.83	6.632	6.85	0.20	0.39	0.18
	Spoof attacks	12.44	22.05	21.04	8.73	28.26	4.13
Spoof training	Regular	11.83	8.79	8.32	0.20	0.39	0.27
	Spoof attacks	12.44	11.89	12	8.73	28.26	2.12

Figure 5(a) demonstrates that all these methods without spoof training are vulnerable to partial spoof attacks. Both the EERs of LLR(cos) and SVM(cos) increase by about 15%, and even that of SUM(scr) soars to 28.26%. On the other hand, our method achieves a 4.13% EER, which is less than half of the second best.

In the second part of the experiments, all the learning-based classifiers are trained with genuine, imposter and spoof samples, namely spoof training. We can see from Table 1 that, compared with the former experiments of spoof attacks, both LLR(cos) and SVM(cos) get about 10% improvements, while the EER of ours reduces by half, down to 2.12%. The overwhelming advantage of our method can be seen vividly with the ROC curves plotted in Fig. 5(b). It is quite promising provided that the experiments here are in the worst-case spoof conditions where the fake score distribution of the spoofed modalities is identical to that of genuine.

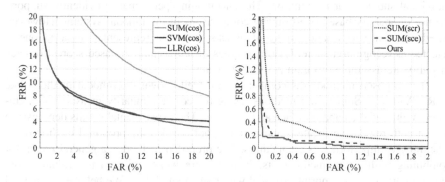

Fig. 4. Performance in regular verification.

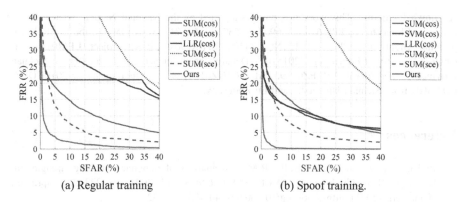

(a) Regular training   (b) Spoof training.

Fig. 5. Performance in partial spoof attacks.

Although LLR(cos) and SVM(cos) also exhibit obvious improvements, they encounter obvious accuracy decline in regular verification, see Table 1. These results show again that the spoof training may bring about unacceptable performance degradation in regular identity verification [2]. As for the proposed method, the EER increases from 0.18% to 0.27%, which is still very low. Above all, the proposed method is able to achieve very low EER in both regular verification and partial spoof attacks.

6 Conclusion

In this paper, aiming to improve the multimodal system's resistance to partial spoof attacks, we proposed the use of collaborative representation fidelity with non-target subjects to measure the affinity of a query sample to a claimed client. We further considered sparse coding as a competing comparison among the claimed client and non-target subjects, and hence explored two sparsity-based measures associated with individual subjects for recognition. The encouraging performance evidently supports the use of sparsity-based one-to-many comparisons in multimodal systems. However, based on their performance in spoof attacks, only the representation-based one is selected as recognition score. Last, two types of representation-based scores for each modality are assembled to train a SVM classifier.

The proposed method was compared with well-known multimodal methods like LLR, SVM, and Sum fusion methods, using the cosine similarity measure, on a chimeric multimodal database of face and ear traits. The experimental results demonstrate that in both regular verification and partial spoof attacks, the proposed method overwhelmingly outperforms its competitors. The proposed method is a general model for combining multiple biometric traits. In the future work, we plan to evaluate more biometric traits like palmprint, iris, and with real spoofed data. We believe the method can be further enhanced by using more robust feature extraction method like CNN-based, and advanced multimodal joint sparse coding techniques [24].

Acknowledgements. This work was partly supported by the National Natural Science Foundation of China (61602390, 61860206007, 61532009, 61571313, 61605054), the EPSRC Programme Grant (FACER2VM) EP/N007743/1, EPSRC/dstl/MURI project EP/R018456/1, Chinese Ministry of Education (Z2015101), Department of Science and Technology of Sichuan Province (2017RZ0009, 2017FZ0029, and 18GJHZ0138), and by funding under 2016CDLZ-G02-SCU from Sichuan University and Lu-Zhou city.

References

1. Ratha, N.K., Connell, J.H., Bolle, R.M.: An analysis of minutiae matching strength. In: Bigun, J., Smeraldi, F. (eds.) AVBPA 2001. LNCS, vol. 2091, pp. 223–228. Springer, Heidelberg (2001). https://doi.org/10.1007/3-540-45344-X_32
2. Biggio, B., Fumera, G., Marcialis, G.L., Roli, F.: Statistical meta-analysis of presentation attacks for secure multibiometric systems. IEEE Trans. Pattern Anal. Mach. Intell. **39**(3), 561–575 (2017)
3. Rodrigues, R.N., Ling, L.L., Govindaraju, V.: Robustness of multimodal biometric fusion methods against spoof attacks. J. Vis. Lang. Comput. **20**(3), 169–179 (2009)

4. Wild, P., Radu, P., Chen, L., et al.: Robust multimodal face and fingerprint fusion in the presence of spoofing attacks. Pattern Recogn. **50**, 17–25 (2016)
5. Rodrigues, R.N., Kamat, N., Govindaraju, V.: Evaluation of biometric spoofing in a multimodal system. In: IEEE International Conference on Biometrics: Theory Applications & Systems, pp. 1–5 (2010)
6. Marasco, E., Johnson, P., Sansone, C., Schuckers, S.: Increase the security of multibiometric systems by incorporating a spoofing detection algorithm in the fusion mechanism. In: Sansone, C., Kittler, J., Roli, F. (eds.) MCS 2011. LNCS, vol. 6713, pp. 309–318. Springer, Heidelberg (2011). https://doi.org/10.1007/978-3-642-21557-5_33
7. Bhardwaj, I., Londhe, N.D., Kopparapu, S.K.: A spoof resistant multibiometric system based on the physiological and behavioral characteristics of fingerprint. Pattern Recogn. **62**, 214–224 (2017)
8. Huang, Z., Liu, Y., Li, C., et al.: A robust face and ear based multimodal biometric system using sparse representation. Pattern Recogn. **46**(8), 2156–2168 (2013)
9. Huang, Z., Liu, Y., Li, C., et al.: An adaptive bimodal recognition framework using sparse coding for face and ear. Pattern Recogn. Lett. **53**, 69–76 (2015)
10. Song, X., Feng, Z.H., Hu, G., Kittler, J., Wu, X.J.: Dictionary integration using 3D morphable face models for pose-invariant collaborative-representation-based classification. IEEE Trans. Inf. Forensics Secur. **13**(11), 2734–2745 (2018)
11. Verlinde, P., Cholet, G.: Comparing decision fusion paradigms using k-NN based classifiers, decision trees and logistic regression in a multi-modal identity verification application. In: AVBPA, pp. 188–193 (1999)
12. Merati, A., Poh, N., Kittler, J.: User-specific cohort selection and score normalization for biometric systems. IEEE Trans. Inf. Forensics Secur. **7**(4), 1270–1277 (2012)
13. Wright, J., Yang, A.Y., Ganesh, A., et al.: Robust face recognition via sparse representation. IEEE Trans. Pattern Anal. Mach. Intell. **31**(2), 210–227 (2009)
14. Cheng, H., Liu, Z., Yang, L., Chen, X.: Sparse representation and learning in visual recognition: Theory and applications. Signal Process. **93**(6), 1408–1425 (2013)
15. Shao, C., Song, X., Feng, Z.H., Wu, X.J., Zheng, Y.: Dynamic dictionary optimization for sparse-representation-based face classification using local difference images. Inf. Sci. **393**, 1–14 (2017)
16. Kua, J., Ambikairajah, E., Epps, J., Togneri, R.: Speaker verification using sparse representation classification. In: IEEE ICASSP, pp. 4548–4551 Prague, Czech Republic, (2011)
17. Li, M., Zhang, X., Yan, Y., Narayanan, S.: Speaker verification using sparse representations on total variability i-vectors. In: 12th Annual Conference of the International Speech Communication Association, Florence, Italy, pp. 2729–2732 (2011)
18. Zhang, L., Yang, M., Feng, X.: Sparse representation or collaborative representation: which helps face recognition? In: ICCV, Barcelona, Spain, pp. 471–478 (2011)
19. University of Science & Technology Beijing (USTB). http://www1.ustb.edu.cn/resb/. Accessed Jan 2016
20. Martinez, A.M., Benavente, R.: The AR Face Database. CVC Technical Report 24 (1998)
21. Georgia Tech Face Database. http://www.anefian.com/research/face_reco.htm. Accessed June 2016
22. Figueiredo, T., Jain, A.K.: Unsupervised learning of finite mixture models. IEEE Trans. Pattern Anal. Mach. Intell. **24**(3), 381–396 (2002)
23. Liu, Y., You, Z., Cao, L.: A novel and quick SVM-based multi-class classifier. Pattern Recogn. **39**(11), 2258–2264 (2006)
24. Yuan, X.T., Liu, X., Yan, S.: Visual classification with multitask joint sparse representation. IEEE Trans. Image Process. **21**(10), 4349–4360 (2012)

Machine Learning

Function-Guided Energy-Precision Optimization with Precision-Rate-Complexity Bivariate Models

Hao Liu[1], Rong Huang[1(✉)], and Zhihai He[2]

[1] College of Information Science and Technology,
Donghua University, Shanghai 201620, China
{liuhao,rong.huang}@dhu.edu.cn
[2] Department of Electrical and Computer Engineering,
University of Missouri, Columbia, MO 65211, USA

Abstract. In an intelligent wireless vision sensor network, an intra encoder is used for the energy-precision optimization with two control parameters: sampling ratio and quantization parameter, which have a direct impact on the coding bit rate, encoder complexity, wireless transmission energy, as well as the server-end object classification precision. Through extensive experiments, we construct the precision-rate-complexity bivariate models to understand the behaviors of the intra encoder and the deep convolutional neural networks, and then characterize the inherent relationship between bit rate, encoding complexity, classification precision and these two control parameters. With these models, we study the problem of optimization control of the wireless vision sensor node so that the node-end energy can be minimized subject to the server-end object classification precision. Our experimental results demonstrate that the proposed control method is able to effectively adjust the energy consumption of the sensor node while achieving the target classification performance.

Keywords: Intra encoder · Energy-precision optimization · Bivariate models
Deep convolutional neural networks

1 Introduction

In an intelligent wireless vision sensor networks (iWVSN), the vision analysis task is performed on the compressed images. Therefore, the reconstruction quality of the compressed image, as well as the encoder design and configuration, will have direct impact on the subsequent vision analysis performance. The latest standardization efforts in compression coding have led to the specification of high efficiency video coding (HEVC) [1]. Studies have been performed to analyze and model the complexity behavior of the HEVC encoder. In [2], the encoding complexity is incorporated into the rate-distortion analysis to reduce the encoder's energy consumption, where the macroblock-level computational complexity of the H.264 encoder is modeled for each prediction mode. Authors in [3] proposed a rate-power allocation scheme for wireless video chat applications, where the transmission parameters are adaptively adjusted based on a power-rate-distortion model.

© Springer Nature Switzerland AG 2018
J.-H. Lai et al. (Eds.): PRCV 2018, LNCS 11258, pp. 403–414, 2018.
https://doi.org/10.1007/978-3-030-03338-5_34

Recently, researchers have recognized the importance of joint design of image compression and vision analysis. For traffic surveillance, an unequal error protection scheme was developed in [4] to increase the vehicle tracking accuracy by allocating more resources to the image region of interest. By classifying macroblocks into different groups in video frames, a rate control method was also proposed for preserving the important local image features [5]. For moving object surveillance, a dynamic rate control scheme was developed in [6] to achieve higher image quality for the regions of interest. For lossy image compression of plant phenotyping, a λ-domain HEVC rate-distortion model was implemented to reduce the object segmentation errors at different bit rates [7].

In this work, we choose the deep convolutional neural networks (DCNN) for object classification of target images at the server end. Deep neural networks are able to construct complex representations and automatically learn a compositional relationship between inputs and outputs, mapping input images to output labels [8]. Once a DCNN is trained using the back-propagation learning procedure, the classification or test is a purely feedforward process [9]. During the past several years, a significant amount of works have been done to push the performance limits of DCNN in vision analysis. However, the join design of image compression, wireless transmission, and DCNN-based object classification has not been studied.

Within the context of iWVSN with DCNN-based target classification, this work has identified two important system control parameters, image sampling ratio (S) and quantization parameter (Q) of the HEVC intra encoder, play a critical role in determining the encoder complexity, coding bit rate, energy consumption in encoding and wireless transmission, reconstructed image quality, and object classification precision. Following an operational approach with extensive experiments, we establish models to characterize the behaviors of coding bit rate, encoding energy, wireless transmission energy, and DCNN classification precision with respect to two control parameters. Based on these models, we then develop optimal resource allocation schemes to minimize the sensor-node energy consumption while achieving the object classification precision.

2 Energy-Precision Control Framework

As discussed in the above, the task objective of the iWVSN is to identify targets. The target images are collected, encoded, transmitted and analyzed for automated classification. As illustrated in Fig. 1, each iWVSN sensor node encodes the target image using the HEVC intra encoder. The compressed bit stream is transmitted over a wireless channel, and then forwarded to the cloud server through Internet. At the server side, the bit stream is decoded to reconstruct the image. The DCNN is then applied to classify this reconstructed image to determine the target class. The iWVSN system is controlled by two important parameters: (1) the sampling ratio S and (2) the quantization parameter Q. Specifically, before encoding, we perform down-sampling on the target image X with a sampling ratio of S. As we know, the sampling ratio S has a direct impact on the following: (1) the encoding complexity which translates into encoder power consumption, (2) the coding bit rate which translates into power consumption in wireless transmission, and (3) the complexity and precision of the DCNN classifier.

The quantization parameter Q has a direct impact on (1) the coding bit rate, (2) the quality of reconstructed images, and (3) the precision of target classification.

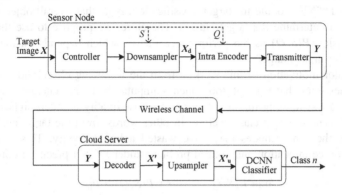

Fig. 1. The module diagram of energy-precision control framework.

HEVC image compression and wireless transmission are two major tasks for each node, consuming most of its energy. With S and Q as the control parameters, $P(S, Q)$ denotes the classification precision in percentage (%), and $R(S, Q)$ denotes the coding bit rate per image in Kbps, and $C(S, Q)$ denotes the average complexity per image in millisecond (ms). The node-end energy consumption includes two additive components: the encoding energy E_c for compressing images, and the transmission energy E_t for sending bit data to a cloud server. The encoding energy E_c is related to the computational complexity $C(S, Q)$ of the encoder, which depends on the two control parameters: S and Q. In other words, we have

$$E_c = \Phi[C(S, Q)] \tag{1}$$

where $\Phi[\cdot]$ is a task-specific mapping the computational complexity or processor cycles into energy consumption. The transmission energy E_t is related to the bit rate $R(S, Q)$ of the compressed image data stream which also depends on (S, Q). Therefore, we write

$$E_t = \Theta[R(S, Q)] \tag{2}$$

where $\Theta[\cdot]$ is also a task-specific mapping which depends on the wireless transmission scheme. In this work, we consider the concise mapping mechanism for $\Phi[\cdot]$ and $\Theta[\cdot]$. In iWVSN, the node-end processor power is stable and the wireless transmission is delay-tolerant. The encoding energy E_c exhibits a linear relation with the computational complexity $C(S, Q)$, and the wireless transmission energy E_t also exhibits a linear relation with the coding bit rate $R(S, Q)$ [10]. In this way, the total amount of energy consumption by the sensor node is given as follows:

$$E(S, Q) = E_c + E_t = p_c \cdot C(S, Q) + e_t \cdot R(S, Q) \tag{3}$$

where the encoding power p_c is a constant in J/ms, and the wireless transmission power e_t is another constant in J/Kbps. At the server end, the HEVC decoder decodes the received bit stream and reconstructs the image. The reconstructed image is then used as input to the DCNN module for target classification. Note that overall objective of the iWVSN is to determine the target classes. Therefore, we propose to use the classification precision $P(S, Q)$ as the performance metric, which depends on the size and quality of the input image.

One major motivation of this work is from the following observation: the vision sensor nodes may have spent too much computational and energy resources in encoding and transmitting the image samples whose quality is much higher than that needed for accurate target classification. In other words, from the target classification perspective, the sensor nodes may have wasted a lot of energy. This leads to the optimal resource allocation and control problem under DCNN precision constraints:

$$\min E(S, Q) \qquad \text{s.t.} \, P(S, Q) \geq P_{\min} \qquad (4)$$

In this work, we aim to minimize the energy consumption of the iWVSN node while achieving the required precision $P_{\min}$ for target classification. To successfully solve the above control problem, we need to establish those precision-rate-complexity models: $P(S, Q)$, $R(S, Q)$ and $C(S, Q)$, which will be presented in the following section.

3   Precision-Rate-Complexity Modeling

Through extensive experiments, we will establish models to characterize the behaviors of rate, complexity, and precision with respect to the two control parameters: S and Q.

3.1   Datasets and Experimental Setup

In this paper, we consider the application scenario of remote wildlife monitoring and protection. A network of vision sensors are deployed to monitor wildlife and human presence in the monitoring region. Triggered by animal motion, the sensor node will capture an image and transmit it to the cloud server for object classification: animal, human, or no-object. For example, if a human is detected in the wildlife protection zone, an alarm will be generated. To test the DCNN classification module, we have assembled a dataset of 1001 images of size 640 × 480, with about 1/3 images for each class. The basic unit of HEVC is a coded tree block (CTB) whose minimum size is 16 × 16 pixels. Let (W, H) and (W_d, H_d) be the (width, height) of the original image X and its down-sampled image X_d, respectively. With a given sampling ratio S, the (width, height) of the down-sampled image X_d can be denoted as follows:

$$(W_d, H_d) = ([W/\sqrt{S}], [H/\sqrt{S}]) \qquad (5)$$

where $[k]$ denotes a multiple of 16 that is closest to k; the width and height of a down-sampled image uniformly increase or decrease. For each target image, we will use the

HEVC intra encoder to compress the image with different sampling ratios S and quantization parameters Q. The candidate values of S are $\Omega_s = \{1, 2, \cdots, 50\}$ and the candidate values of Q are $\Omega_q = \{0, 1, 2, \cdots, 51\}$. In total, we have 50×52 different (S, Q) configurations. In this paper, we assume that the compressed bit stream is correctly received at the server side for successful image decoding and reconstruction. The DCNN is then applied to classify the reconstructed image into one of three classes: Human, Animal, and Background. The DCNN model is previously trained with a large set of labeled images, which are uncompressed and have the original resolution of 640×480.

3.2   Precision-Rate-Complexity Analysis

Note that S and Q are two independently control parameters. We propose to firstly analyze the precision-rate-complexity behaviors with respect to each individual parameter. Once we have understood and established these 1-Dimensional models, we then proceed to establish the joint model with these two control parameters. Figure 2(a) shows the actual $P(S, Q)$ curves at different S and different Q. We can see that for small values of Q, for example, from 0 to 30, the compressed image quality is high, and the precision does not change much. When Q is larger than the threshold (e.g., 30), the precision drop exponentially. This implies that the image quality does not affect the DCNN classification performance if it is above a certain threshold. This example suggests that the sensor node will waste the bits and energy resources if the image quality is already above the threshold since an even higher image quality level does not help the DCNN classification. We can see that the $P(S)$ curves follows a decreasing near-exponential behavior. For actual coding bit rate, Fig. 2(b) plots the actual $R(S, Q)$ curves at different S and different Q, whose average bit rate is 1725 Kbps. These curves show an exponentially decreasing relationship with the increasing S or Q. For a given encoder, its computational complexity is directly related to its encoding time. Figure 2 (c) plots the actual $C(S, Q)$ curves at different S and different Q, whose average complexity is 258 ms. We can see that the quantization parameter Q does not affect the complexity much. Certainly, the complexity will decrease for smaller input images or larger sampling ratios.

3.3   Precision-Rate-Complexity Bivariate Models

A fundamental goal of the precision-rate-complexity modeling is to solve the node-end energy minimization problem under server-end classification precision constraints. By heuristically feeding actual data into the constrained minimization task in (4), the actual distribution of all optimal control parameters can be obtained by exhaustively testing all possible (S, Q) configurations. With all cases, Fig. 3 shows the distribution of actual optimal Q values at different precisions, where a dot denotes an optimal Q value at its precision. It can be seen that all optimal Q values are limited to a range from $Q = 24$ and $Q = 51$. When the smaller Q values vary from 0 to 23, the resulting precision (bit rate, complexity) have no influence on the optimal solution of the energy-precision optimization task, which motivates us neglect some (S, Q) configurations so as to produce more accurate precision-rate-complexity models.

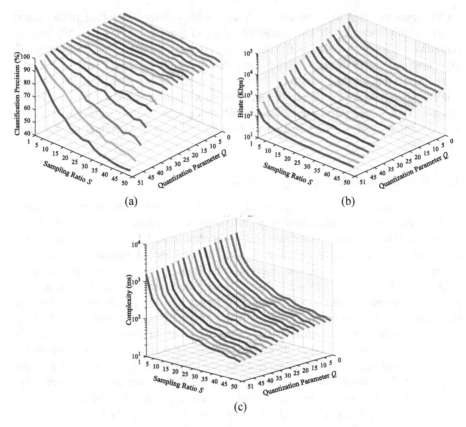

Fig. 2. The actual behaviors of classification precision, coding bit-rate and complexity: (a) $P(S, Q)$ curves, (b) $R(S, Q)$ curves, (c) $C(S, Q)$ curves.

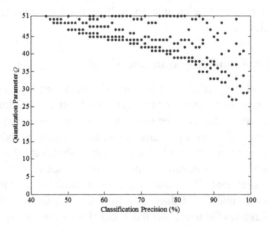

Fig. 3. The distribution of actual optimal Q values.

Based on the experiments, our curve fitting goal may only considers those larger Q values in the range of $[24, 51]$ and all 50 possible values for S. Thus, we have 50×28 possible (S, Q) configurations that needs to be fitted. It can be seen that the curves of actual precision and complexity also exhibits a certain linear behavior, and a first-order polynomial may approximate such a behavior. We relax the maximum value constraint in a smaller fitting space. By comparing various exponential forms and their parameters, the precision-rate-complexity bivariate models can be constructed as follows:

$$P(S, Q) = \beta_{p1} - \beta_{p2} \cdot e^{\beta_{p3} \cdot Q + \beta_{p4} \cdot S} - \beta_{p5} \cdot Q - \beta_{p6} \cdot S \tag{6}$$

$$R(S, Q) = \beta_{r1} \cdot e^{\beta_{r2} \cdot Q + \beta_{r3} \cdot S} + \beta_{r4} \cdot e^{\beta_{r5} \cdot Q + \beta_{r6} \cdot S} \tag{7}$$

$$C(S, Q) = \beta_{c1} \cdot e^{\beta_{c2} \cdot Q + \beta_{c3} \cdot S} + \beta_{c4} \cdot e^{\beta_{c5} \cdot Q + \beta_{c6} \cdot S} + \beta_{c7} \cdot Q + \beta_{c8} \cdot S + \beta_{c9} \tag{8}$$

By continuous approximation, Table 1 reports the optimal parameter values of the precision-rate-complexity bivariate models. With better fitting results, the bivariate models can be used to search the appropriate S and Q for the energy-precision optimization task.

Table 1. The parameters values of precision-rate-complexity bivariate models.

Parameter	Value	Parameter	Value	Parameter	Value
β_{p1}	102.6	β_{r1}	132020	β_{c1}	5850.2
β_{p2}	0.0863	β_{r2}	−0.1059	β_{c2}	−0.01508
β_{p3}	0.1123	β_{r3}	−0.5508	β_{c3}	−0.792
β_{p4}	0.01999	β_{r4}	41189	β_{c4}	1336.5
β_{p5}	−0.04603	β_{r5}	−0.1159	β_{c5}	−0.02882
β_{p6}	0.1242	β_{r6}	−0.04011	β_{c6}	−0.07452
				β_{c7}	−0.5673
				β_{c8}	0.7176
				β_{c9}	23.73

4 Resource Allocation and Energy Minimization

In the above section, we have established models to predict the encoder computational complexity $C(S, Q)$, coding bit rate $R(S, Q)$, and the DCNN precision $P(S, Q)$. Based on these models, we are ready to study the resource allocation problem, answering the following important question: what is the minimum energy consumption that the iWVSN node needs to spend in order to achieve the desired DCNN object classification precision at the server end? As discussed in the above section, the iWVSN resource allocation problem can be formulated by:

$$\min E(S, Q) = p_c \cdot C(S, Q) + e_t \cdot R(S, Q) \quad \text{s.t.} \quad P(S, Q) \geq P_T \tag{9}$$

In the above section, we have obtained analytical models for the encoder complexity $C(S, Q)$, the encoding bit rate $R(S, Q)$, and the DCNN classification precision $P(S, Q)$. We resort to a numerical solution. Specifically, with the precision-rate-complexity bivariate models, we are able to compute the values of $P(S, Q)$, $R(S, Q)$, and $C(S, Q)$ for a dense grid of points (S, Q). We then find the set of grid points which satisfy the precision constraint. Finally, within this set, we find the optimal (S, Q) which has the minimum energy $E(S, Q)$. Figure 4 shows the optimal sampling ratio S^* and encoder quantization parameter Q^* for a given target classification precision P_T. Each dot represents an optimal look-up-table value of S^* or Q^* for a given target precision P_T. The jig-saw effect is caused by the fact that the quantization parameter Q has to be an integer and the input image size has to be a multiple of 16. For easy implementation in actual system control, we propose to approximate optimal sampling ratio $S^*(P_T)$ using a piece-wise linear function as shown in Fig. 4(a) in solid lines, and approximate the optimal encoder quantization parameter $Q^*(P_T)$ using an exponential function as shown in Fig. 4(b):

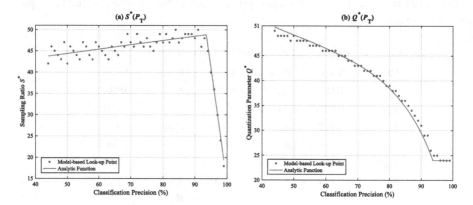

Fig. 4. The look-up-table solution and analytic solution for energy-precision optimization: (a) the $S^*(P_T)$ function; (b) the $Q^*(P_T)$ function.

$$S^*(P_T) = \begin{cases} Round(\omega_1 \cdot P_T + \omega_2), P_T < P_0 \\ Round(\omega_3 \cdot P_T + \omega_4), P_T \geq P_0 \end{cases} \tag{10}$$

$$Q^*(P_T) = Round\left(\tau_1 \cdot e^{\tau_2 \cdot P_T} + \tau_3 \cdot e^{\tau_4 \cdot P_T}\right) \tag{11}$$

where the values of $S^*(P_T)$ belong to $\{1, 2, \cdots, 49, 50\}$, and the values of $Q^*(P_T)$ belong to $\{24, 25, \cdots, 50, 51\}$. The model parameters are listed in Table 2.

Table 2. The coefficients of analytic functions.

Coefficient	Value	Coefficient	Value
ω_1	0.103	τ_1	−0.002
ω_2	39.22	τ_2	0.096
ω_3	−5.4	τ_3	62.01
ω_4	553.3	τ_4	−0.0046
P_0	93.6		

5 Experimental Results

In this section, we conduct experiments to evaluate the proposed method. Our test dataset consists of 1001 uncompressed camera-trap images. The original input image size is 640 × 480 in RGB color format. The DCNN classifier is constructed and trained by using CAFFE which has 5 convolutional layers followed by 3 fully connected layers [11]. The DCNN classifier has been well trained and tested on original target images, where the target images are categorized into three object classes, namely: *Human*, *Animal*, and *Background*. The image sampling ratio S and quantization parameter Q jointly affect the complexity, bit rate, and object classification precision. The candidate values of S are set to be $\{1, 2, 3, ..., 49, 50\}$, and the candidate values of Q are set to be $\{0, 1, 2, ..., 50, 51\}$. For image compression, we adopt the HM-16.7 main profile HEVC intra coding [12]. During simulation, to translate the computational complexity into computational energy, we set the thermal design power (TDP) of the micropro-cessor to be $p_c = 0.14$ J/ms. The transmission power e_t is set to 2.6×10^{-3} Kbps [10].

Figures 5, 6 and 7 show the estimation results by the precision-rate-complexity bivariate models obtained from the above section. Specifically, Fig. 5(a) shows the estimation results for the $P(Q)$ curve at different S. Figure 5(b) shows the estimation results for the $P(S)$ curve for different Q. We can see that the model is able to accurately capture the behavior of actual classification precision. For the estimation performance, we have R - square = 0.9548, and RMSE = 3.057%. Figure 6(a) shows the estimation results for the $R(Q)$ curve at different S. Figure 6(b) shows the estimation results for the $R(S)$ curve for different Q. We can see that this rate model is very accurate with R - square = 0.991. Figure 7(a) shows the estimation results for the $C(Q)$ curves at different S. Figure 7(b) shows the estimation results for the $C(S)$ distributions for dif-ferent Q. We can see that the complexity model is very accurate with R - square = 0.997.

Figure 8(a) shows the minimum energy consumption (in lines with circles) of the iWVSN node to achieve the target DCNN classification precision at the server end using the precision-rate-complexity bivariate model and resource allocation. For comparison, we also include the actual optimal value of minimum energy consumption (in lines with crosses) which are obtained from brute-force search based on experiments with all possible combinations of control parameters (S, Q). We can see that our analysis and optimization approaches the actual optimal values. Figure 8(b) shows the operating bit rate and complexity of the iWVSN node. We can see that, if we allow a very small percentage of performance drop, for example, from dropping the precision from 97% to 96%, we can save the total energy at the iWVSN node by up to 2 times, which is very significant.

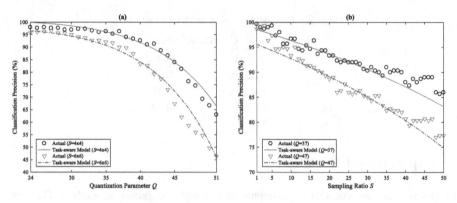

Fig. 5. The fitting results for precision model: (a) $P(Q)$ at different S; (b) $P(S)$ at different Q.

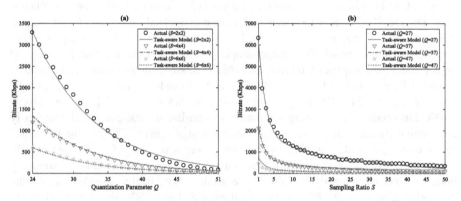

Fig. 6. The fitting results for rate model: (a) $R(Q)$ at different S; (b) $R(S)$ at different Q.

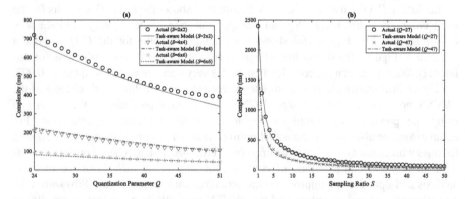

Fig. 7. The fitting results for complexity model: (a) $C(Q)$ at different S; (b) $C(S)$ at different Q.

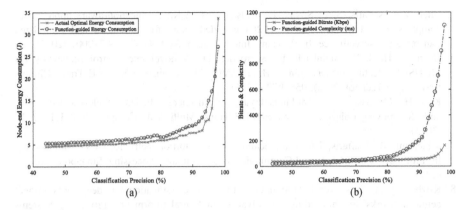

Fig. 8. The actual optimal energy consumption vs. function-guided energy consumption.

6   Conclusion

In this paper, we have studied the resource modeling, allocation, and optimization problem for an intelligent wireless vision sensor network which collects image samples of the targets, encodes and transmits the data to a cloud server for object classification using DCNN. We developed a new framework for energy-precision analysis and optimization. Specifically, we use the HEVC intra encoder for image compression configured with two control parameters: the image sampling ratio and quantization parameter. Through extensive experiments, we construct the precision-rate-complexity bivariate models to understand the behaviors of the HEVC intra encoder and the DCNN, and characterize the inherent relationship between bit rate, encoding complexity, classification precision and these two control parameters. Based on these models, we study the problem of optimization control of the wireless vision sensor node so that the node-end energy can be minimized subject to the server-end object classification precision. Our experimental results demonstrate that the proposed control method is able to effectively adjust the energy consumption of the sensor node while achieving the target classification performance.

Acknowledgments. This work is supported by the Natural Science Foundation of Shanghai (18ZR1400300).

References

1. Pastuszak, G., Abramowski, A.: Algorithm and architecture design of the H.265/HEVC intra encoder. IEEE Trans. Circuits Syst. Video Technol. **26**(1), 210–222 (2016)
2. Li, X., Wien, M., Ohm, J.R.: Rate-complexity-distortion optimization for hybrid video coding. IEEE Trans. Circuits Syst. Video Technol. **21**(7), 957–970 (2011)
3. Chuah, S.P., Tan, Y.P., Chen, Z.: Rate and power allocation for joint coding and transmission in wireless video chat applications. IEEE Trans. Multimed. **17**(5), 687–699 (2015)

4. Chen, Z., Tsaftaris, S.A., Soyak, E., Katsaggelos, A.K.: Application-aware approach to compression and transmission of H.264 encoded video for automated and centralized transportation surveillance. IEEE Trans. Intell. Transp. Syst. **14**(4), 2002–2007 (2013)

5. Chao, J., Huitl, R., Steinbach, E., Schroeder, D.: A novel rate control framework for SIFT/SURF feature preservation in H.264/AVC video compression. IEEE Trans. Circuits Syst. Video Technol. **25**(6), 958–972 (2015)

6. Ko, J.H., Mudassar, B.A., Mukhopadhyay, S.: An energy-efficient wireless video sensor node for moving object surveillance. IEEE Trans. Multi-Scale Comput. Syst. **1**(1), 7–18 (2015)

7. Minervini, M., Tsaftaris, S.A.: Classification-aware distortion metric for HEVC intra coding. In: Proceedings of IEEE Visual Communications and Image Processing, Singapore, pp. 1–4 (2015)

8. Krizhevsky, A., Sutskever, I., Hinton, G.E.: ImageNet classification with deep convolutional neural networks. In: Proceedings of Advances in Neural Information Processing Systems (NIPS), Lake Tahoe, NV, pp. 1097–1105 (2012)

9. Jia, Y., et al.: Caffe: convolutional architecture for fast feature embedding. arXiv preprint arXiv:1408.5093 (2014)

10. Redondi, A., Baroffio, L., Bianchi, L., Cesana, M., Tagliasacchi, M.: Compress-then-analyze versus analyze-then-compress: what is best in visual sensor networks? IEEE Trans. Mob. Comput. **15**(12), 3000–3013 (2016)

11. http://caffe.berkeleyvision.org/installation.html

12. HEVC Software Repository — HM-16.7 Reference Model. https://hevc.hhi.fraunhofer.de/svn/svn_HEVCSoftware/tags/HM-16.7

Point Cloud Noise and Outlier Removal with Locally Adaptive Scale

Zhenxing Mi[1,2] and Wenbing Tao[1,2(✉)]

[1] Shenzhen Huazhong University of Science and Technology Research Institute,
Shenzhen 518057, China
[2] National Key Laboratory of Science and Technology on Multi-spectral Information
Processing, School of Automation, Huazhong University of Science and Technology,
Wuhan 430074, China
{m201772503,wenbingtao}@hust.edu.cn

Abstract. This paper introduced a simple and effective algorithm to remove the noise and outliers in point sets generated by multi-view stereo methods. Our main idea is to discard the points that are geometrically or photometrically inconsistent with its neighbors in 3D space using the input images and corresponding depth maps. We attach a scale value to each point reflecting the influence to the adjacent area of the point and define a geometric consistency function and a photometric consistency function for the point. We employ a very efficient method to find the neighbors of a point using projection. The consistency functions are related to the normal and scale of the neighbors of points. Our algorithm is locally adaptive, feature preserving and easy to implement for massive parallelism. It performs robustly with a variety of noise and outliers in our experiments.

Keywords: Multi-view stereo · Noise filtering · Scale · Local adaptive

1 Introduction

The state of the art in multi-view stereo methods has seen great development in robustness and accuracy these years. However, point sets produced by multi-view stereo methods are usually redundant and inevitably with a lot of noise and outliers due to imperfection of acquisition hardware and algorithms, as is shown in Fig. 1(b). Modern MVS algorithms use different output scene representations, such as depth maps, a point cloud, or a mesh. Depth map scene representation is one of the most popular choices due to the flexibility and scalability [7] but suffers more noise. This poses a great challenge to surface reconstruction.

We can impose strong regularization in MVS methods to reduce outliers, but this will destroy sharp features and may be time consuming. Some denoising methods directly operate on unorganized point cloud and using k nearest neighbors to optimize the position and normal of a reference point [13]. Depth map, however, often provides us with additional information such as connectivity and

© Springer Nature Switzerland AG 2018
J.-H. Lai et al. (Eds.): PRCV 2018, LNCS 11258, pp. 415–426, 2018.
https://doi.org/10.1007/978-3-030-03338-5_35

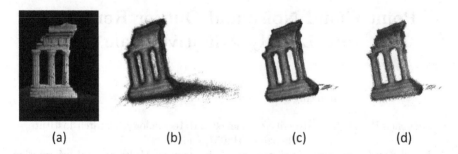

(a)   (b)   (c)   (d)

Fig. 1. We use the multi-view stereo methods MVE [8] to reconstruct a dense 3D point cloud (b) for the Middlebury Temple dataset [11] (a). The output point cloud is very noisy. We denoise the depth maps only use geometric consistency (c). A lot of noise and outliers are removed but there are still some black points from the background retained on the border of the temple. We use geometric consistency and photometric consistency together in (d) and get better result.

scale [3]. Therefore, in our method, we computed a scale value for each point using the input depth maps in image space. The scale value provides valuable information about the surface area each point was acquired from, as discussed by Fuhrmann et al. [3]. With scale information, we can handle datasets containing non-uniform noise and sample resolution.

In our method, we do not discretize the 3D space, avoiding large memory and time usage. We project a reference point to other depth maps and find its neighbors in the image space. The neighbors obtained from image space are not necessarily but most likely to be neighbors in the 3D space. Then we project them back to the 3D space to evaluate the geometric and photometric consistency between the reference point and its neighbors. Our locally adaptive geometric consistency function and photometric consistency are related to the scale of the reference point and it's neighbors. The functions are defined compactly supported, namely, the neighbors used for evaluating the functions must be near the reference point in spatial space. Because of the redundancy of the depth maps, we do not change the position, normal and color of the points but just remove the points that are not consistent with its neighbors. For the sake of efficiency, we employ view selection strategy to identify nearby views using the feature points reconstructed in the previous SFM phase [6,8]. This enables our methods the ability to operate on extremely large photo collections.

Our contributions are:

- An approach using *scale* information to evaluate the geometric and photometric consistency, which is local adaptive feature preserving and more accurate.
- Finding neighbors of reference points in image space by depth map triangulation and projection, which is very efficiency.

In the remainder of this paper, we first review related work (Sect. 2). Then introduce our denoise approach (Sect. 3), perform experiments on a variety of data sets (Sect. 4) and conclude our work (Sect. 5).

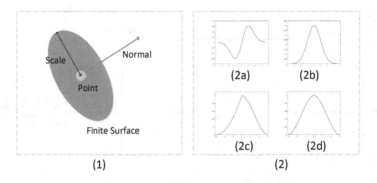

Fig. 2. (1) A point with a scale value represents a finite surface in the spatial space. (2) The shape of the functions $f_x(x)$ (2a), $f_y(y)$ and $f_z(z)$ (2b), $w_x(x)$ (2c) and $w_{yz}(r)$ (2d).

2 Related Work

Here we describe some closely related work in point set denoising, focusing on how they handle point sets generated by images with varying resolution and viewing parameters, what parameters they use and to what extend they are time and memory consuming.

Most multi-view stereo methods integrate a depth map fusion strategy into the depth estimation stage or after the whole reconstruction. They usually enforce visibility and consistency across views. Wu et al. [18] firstly use an indicator function based on visibility cues in [16] to remove outliers. Then they enforce visibility consistency across views. Such method is not sophisticated thus there remains a lot of noise and outliers. Schönberger et al. [10] define a directed graph of consistent pixels with their photometric and geometric consistency support set, then find and fuse the clusters of consistent pixels in this graph. The fused point cloud are of high quality and have little outliers. However, finding clusters is very time consuming and not easy to parallelize. In addition, they use the photometric and geometric consistency terms computed in the MVS procedure of their reconstruction method, which are only available in their approach.

The above methods proposed as part of multi-view stereo methods usually use parameters that are unique in their depth reconstruction and thus their use is restricted. There are also some methods independent of the MVS. Sun et al. [13] directly denoise point clouds using the L_0 norm to preserving sharp features. Wolff et al. [17] take depth maps as input and implicitly uses a surface represented by the input depth maps to check geometric consistency and photometric consistency between each per-view point and other input views. Our method are relevant to their method, projecting the points to the image space of other depth maps. However, we take a completely different, local adaptive strategy to examine consistency using the finite surface represented by points with scale value.

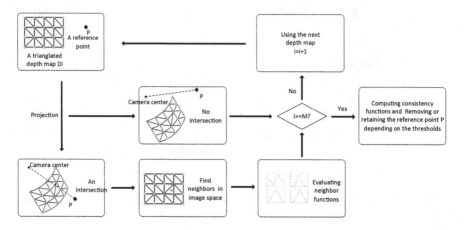

Fig. 3. Our point denoising pipeline: we examine a reference point **p** against other depth maps. A depth map D_i is triangulated in the image space. Then we project the reference point to the depth map and get which triangle it falls into. If no such triangle exist, we do not compute any function and examine **p** against next depth map. If it falls into an triangle, we regard the three vertexes as the neighbor of **p** and use them to evaluate our functions. Our functions are related to the scale of the points. After examining the reference point against all the depth maps, we compare the functions with threshold and decide if the point will be removed.

The quality of the reconstructed surface strongly depends on the quality of the input point set which is inevitably with noise and outliers. Therefore, many surface reconstruction methods explicitly use some strategy to handle the noise and outliers. Poisson surface reconstruction [9] estimate local sampling density and scale the contribution of each point accordingly. However, sampling density is not necessarily related to the sample resolution, and an increased sampling density may simply be caused by data redundancy as discussed in [4]. Fuhrmann et al. [3] construct a discrete, multi-scale signed distance field capable of representing surfaces at multiple levels of detail and produce output surfaces that are adaptive to the scale of the input data. Our methods apply the same depth map triangulation step and compute the scale of every points. Fuhrmann et al. [4] attach the scale value to each sample point and use the weighted average of locally estimated functions to define the implicit surface compactly around the input data. The method is virtually parameter-free for mixed-scale datasets and does not require any global operations. Our method draws inspiration from this method and uses scale value computed from the triangulated depth maps to handle the noise outliers.

3   Denoising and Outlier Removal

In this section, we describe the evaluation of geometric and photometric consistency between a reference point **p** and its neighbors in spatial space. We assume that M input depth maps are given and points in them are equipped with a position, a normal and a color.

3.1 Definition of *Scale*

We define a scale value for each point related to the depth map it comes from. As illustrated in Fig. 3, we first find the adjacent points for a point in the input depth map in image space, and then computed a scale value for each point by averaging the spatial distances between the point and its adjacent points. As discussed by Fuhrmann et al. [3], the scale value provides valuable information about the surface area each point was acquired from. The points in depth maps are not ideal points. Instead, they represent a surface at a particular scale depending on viewing distance, focal length and image resolution [3] as illustrated in Fig. 2. With scale information, we can define local adaptive functions for geometric consistency and photometric consistency to handle datasets containing non-uniform noise and sample resolution.

3.2 Neighbors in Image Space and LCS

To determine the geometric and photometric consistency, every reference point $\mathbf{p}$ has to be examined against its neighbors in the spatial space. Depth maps can provide us with additional information such as connectivity. As illustrated in Fig. 3, We triangulate the depth maps in image space using the method proposed by [3]. Then we project the reference point $\mathbf{p}$ to other depth maps and get the triangles it falls into. The three vertices of the triangle are regarded as the neighbors of the reference point. After the whole projection, we get a set of neighbors $N_{\mathbf{p}} = \{\mathbf{p}_i | i = 1, ..., M\}$ for $\mathbf{p}$. Each of them are equipped with a position $\mathbf{p}_i \in \mathbb{R}^3$, a normal $\mathbf{n}_i \in \mathbb{R}^3$, $\|\mathbf{n}_i\| = 1$, and a scale value $s_i \in \mathbb{R}$. Generally, such neighbors are most likely near the reference point in spatial space. Since our functions are compactly supported, we can ensure that the neighbor points used to evaluate geometric and photometric consistency are actually near the reference point. When examining $\mathbf{p}$ against $\mathbf{p}_i$, we use the local coordinate of $\mathbf{p}$ in the local coordinate system (LCS) of $\mathbf{p}_i$. The local coordinate is $\mathbf{x}_i = R_i \cdot (\mathbf{p} - \mathbf{p}_i)$ with a rotation matrix $R_i = R(\mathbf{n}_i)$ such that $\mathbf{p}_i$ is located in the origin and the normal $\mathbf{n}_i$ coincides with the positive x-axis [4]. The LCS is only up to the position and normal of $\mathbf{p}_i$ so the functions should be invariant to the choice of the LCS orthogonal to the normal.

3.3 Geometric Consistency

Given a reference point $\mathbf{p}$, and a set of neighbors $N_{\mathbf{p}} = \{\mathbf{p}_i | i = 1, ..., M\}$, we define a signed geometric consistency function $F(\mathbf{p})$ as a weighted sum of basis functions, as proposed in the surface reconstruction method [4]:

$$F(\mathbf{p}) = \frac{\sum_i w d_i(\mathbf{x}_i) w n_i(\mathbf{p}_i) f_i(\mathbf{x}_i)}{\sum_i w d_i(\mathbf{x}_i) w n_i(\mathbf{p}_i)}$$

$$W(\mathbf{p}) = \sum_i wd_i(\mathbf{x}_i)wn_i(\mathbf{p}_i) \tag{1}$$

where $\mathbf{x}_i$ is the local coordinate of $\mathbf{p}$ in local coordinate system of (LCS) $\mathbf{p}_i$. The basis function $f_i(\mathbf{x}_i)$ is a signed function which is positive in front of the surface and negative otherwise (similar to a signed distance function). The function $f_i(\mathbf{x}_i)$ and weight $wd_i(\mathbf{x}_i)$, $wn_i(\mathbf{p}_i)$ are parameterized by the ith neighbor's position $\mathbf{p}_i$, normal $\mathbf{n}_i$ and scale s_i. Similar to [4], for each neighbor $\mathbf{p}_i$, we define a basis function that is unit-integral and stretched depending on the scale of the neighbor.

With $\mathbf{x}_i = (x, y, z)$, we use a function $f_x(x)$ that is like the derivative of the Gaussian in the x-coordinate. The standard deviation of $f_x(x)$ is set to the scale of the neighbor, that is $\sigma = s_i$. It is positive when $x > 0$ and negative when $x < 0$. Normalized Gaussians $f_y(y)$, $f_z(z)$ are used orthogonal to the normal in y-coordinate and z-coordinate.

$$f_x(x) = \frac{x}{\sigma^2}e^{\frac{-x^2}{2\sigma^2}}, f_y(y) = \frac{1}{\sigma\sqrt{2\pi}}e^{\frac{-y^2}{2\sigma^2}}, f_z(z) = \frac{1}{\sigma\sqrt{2\pi}}e^{\frac{-z^2}{2\sigma^2}} \tag{2}$$

We define the basis function of the ith neighbor as:

$$f_i(\mathbf{x}_i) = f_x(x)f_y(y)f_z(z) = \frac{x}{\sigma^4 2\pi} \cdot e^{\frac{-1}{2\sigma^2}(x^2+y^2+z^2)} \tag{3}$$

The function meets the condition that it must be unit-integral as discussed before:

$$\int\int\int |f_i(\mathbf{x}_i)|d\mathbf{x}_i = \int|f_x(x)|dx \int f_y(y)dy \int f_z(z)dz = 1 \tag{4}$$

In the following, we define a weighting function $wd_i(\mathbf{x}_i)$ related to the distance between the neighbor $\mathbf{p}_i$. It is designed to ensure that the neighbor used to evaluate $F(\mathbf{p})$ are actually near the reference point $\mathbf{p}$. As illustrated in the Fig. 2, $f_i(\mathbf{x}_i)$ is almost zero beyond 3σ, and thus $wd_i(\mathbf{x}_i)$ is define as 0 beyond 3σ to ensure the compact support. As discussed by Curless and Levoy [1] and Vrubel et al. [14]: if a point has been observed, the existence of a surface between the observer and the point is not possible. Therefore, if $x < 0$, the existence of a reference point behind the neighbor cause conflict. Therefore, we want to reduce the weight quickly. The weighting function $wd_i(\mathbf{x}_i)$ is non-symmetric in x-direction and rotation invariant in y- and z-direction:

$$wd_i(\mathbf{x}_i) = w_x(x) \cdot w_{(yz)}(\sqrt{y^2 + z^2}) \tag{5}$$

$$w_x(x) = \begin{cases} \frac{1}{9}\frac{x^2}{\sigma^2} + \frac{2}{3}\frac{x}{\sigma} + 1 & x \in [-3\sigma, 0) \\ \frac{2}{27}\frac{x^3}{\sigma^3} - \frac{1}{3}\frac{x^2}{\sigma^2} + 1 & x \in (0, 3\sigma] \\ 0 & \text{otherwise} \end{cases} \tag{6}$$

$$w_{yz}(r) = \begin{cases} \frac{2}{27}\frac{r^3}{\sigma^3} - \frac{1}{3}\frac{r^2}{\sigma^2} + 1 & r < 3\sigma \\ 0 & \text{otherwise} \end{cases} \tag{7}$$

$$r = \sqrt{y^2 + z^2} \tag{8}$$

Additionally, to better preserve the sharp features in the point set and avoid over smoothing, we define a weighting function $wn_i(\mathbf{p}_i)$ related to the similarity between the normals of the points.

$$wn_i(\mathbf{p}_i) = \begin{cases} \frac{\mathbf{n}_\mathbf{p}^T \mathbf{n}_i}{\|\mathbf{n}_\mathbf{p}\| \cdot \|\mathbf{n}_i\|} & \mathbf{n}_\mathbf{p}^T \mathbf{n}_i > 0 \\ 0 & \mathbf{n}_\mathbf{p}^T \mathbf{n}_i \leq 0 \end{cases} \tag{9}$$

We define $wn_i(\mathbf{p}_i)$ as 0 if $\mathbf{n}_\mathbf{p}^T \mathbf{n}_i \leq 0$ to eliminate the influence of neighbors that have a much different normal direction with the reference point, which can improve the robustness.

Since $F(\mathbf{p})$ is compactly supported, some extremely isolated outliers with little neighbors will have small $F(\mathbf{p})$. They cannot be filtered if we only make use of $F(\mathbf{p})$. We observe that if a reference point is an outlier with little neighbors, its $W(\mathbf{p})$, the sum of the weighting function, will be very small. In practice, points with a weight below a certain value are also removed, which can filter out extremely isolated outliers.

3.4 Photometric Consistency

In practice, our algorithm can filter out common noise and outliers with geometric consistency function. However, as illustrated by Fig. 1(b) (c), the noisy points near the border of object are hard to remove. Our observation is that such points usually have a blurred color that is quite different from its neighbors. So we define a function $E(\mathbf{p})$ to evaluate the photometric consistency between the reference point $\mathbf{p}$, with a color $\mathbf{c}(\mathbf{p})$, and its neighbors $N_\mathbf{p} = \{\mathbf{p}_i | i = 1, ..., M\}$, whose colors are $\mathbf{c}(\mathbf{p}_i)$. $E(\mathbf{p})$ is defined as

$$E(\mathbf{p}) = \frac{\|\mathbf{c}(\mathbf{p}) - \mathbf{c}'(\mathbf{p})\|}{\|\mathbf{c}(\mathbf{p})\|} \tag{10}$$

where $\mathbf{c}'(\mathbf{p})$ is the temporary color of $\mathbf{p}$ computed by the color of its neighbors. Inspired by the anisotropic and feature-preserving nature of bilateral filtering [2], we compute $\mathbf{c}'(\mathbf{p})$ as

$$\mathbf{c}'(\mathbf{p}) = K(\mathbf{p}) \sum_i W_c(\mathbf{p}_i) W_s(\mathbf{p}_i) \mathbf{c}(\mathbf{p}_i) \tag{11}$$

where $W_c(\mathbf{p}_i)$ is the spatial weighting term, $W_s(\mathbf{p}_i)$ is the signal weighting term and $K(\mathbf{p}) = \frac{1}{\sum_i W_c(\mathbf{p}_i) W_s(\mathbf{p}_i)}$ is the normalization factor. $W_c(\mathbf{p}_i)$ is a spatial Gaussian that decreases the influence of distant neighbors:

$$W_c(\mathbf{p}_i) = \exp(-\|\mathbf{p} - \mathbf{p}_i\|^2 / 2\sigma^2) \tag{12}$$

where $\sigma = s_\mathbf{p}$, which is the scale value of the reference point $\mathbf{p}$. We do not define $W_s(\mathbf{p}_i)$ as Gaussian but just use the normalized dot product of the normals between $\mathbf{p}$ and $\mathbf{p}_i$ for efficiency.

$$W_s(\mathbf{p}_i) = \begin{cases} \frac{\mathbf{n}_\mathbf{p}^T \mathbf{n}_i}{\|\mathbf{n}_\mathbf{p}\| \cdot \|\mathbf{n}_i\|} & \mathbf{n}_\mathbf{p}^T \mathbf{n}_i > 0 \\ 0 & \mathbf{n}_\mathbf{p}^T \mathbf{n}_i \leq 0 \end{cases} \tag{13}$$

The influence of neighbors that have a much different normal direction with the reference point, i.e. $\mathbf{n}_\mathbf{p}^T \mathbf{n}_i \leq 0$, are eliminated.

3.5   Depth Map Selection for Scalability

Our algorithm proposed above does not perform costly optimizations and thus is very efficient and easy to parallel. However, assuming we have N input depth maps with a resolution of K, the time complexity of our algorithm is $O(KN^2)$. It increases quadratically with the number of depth maps N. In practice, we do not consider depth maps whose viewing direction $\mathbf{v}_i$ differs too much from the viewing direction $\mathbf{v}$ under which $\mathbf{p}$ was observed, i.e. $\mathbf{v}_i^T \mathbf{v} < 0$. However, the time complexity still increase quickly when operating extremely large data sets. In order to make our algorithm more scalable, we introduce a view selection method as an option when operating on large data sets. We use SFM points to select nearby depth maps for a reference depth map. The number of shared SFM points between the reference depth map and other depth maps is a good indicator whether the reference point is visible in other depth maps. We calculate the number of shared feature points, sort them from large to small and only examine the points in the reference depth map against the first C depth maps. Now the time complexity is $O(KCN)$, increasing linearly with the number of depth maps N. Since the reference point is not likely visible by the depth maps with few shared SFM points, our algorithm still yields good results with view selection in our experiments.

3.6   Point Filtering Strategy

After evaluating $F(\mathbf{p})$, $W(\mathbf{p})$ and $E(\mathbf{p})$ for a reference point $\mathbf{p}$, we use them to decide whether the point $\mathbf{p}$ will be retained. We *retain* a point if it satisfies all of the following three conditions:

$$-T_\mathbf{p} < F(\mathbf{p}) < T_\mathbf{p}, \quad W(\mathbf{p}) > \alpha, \quad E(\mathbf{p}) < \varepsilon \tag{14}$$

Since $F(\mathbf{p})$ is an locally adaptive function, we define a locally adaptive threshold $T_\mathbf{p} = \beta F(x = s_\mathbf{p}, \sqrt{y^2 + z^2} = s_\mathbf{p}, \sigma = s_\mathbf{p})$ for $F(\mathbf{p})$. Actually, $F(x = s_\mathbf{p}, \sqrt{y^2 + z^2} = s_\mathbf{p}, \sigma = s_\mathbf{p})$ is the function value of a virtual point whose local coordinates are relate to the scale of reference point. This definition can ensure the adaptivity of filtering. β is a constant decided by users to control the degree of filtering. It performs well in feature preserving in our experiments. The threshold of $W(\mathbf{p})$ is a constant α to filter out the extremely isolated outliers. It is related to the number of input depth maps and typically we set it to 25 when there are hundreds of input depth maps. The threshold of $E(\mathbf{p})$ is a constant ε. We typically set it to 0.1, that is, if the difference between the real color and the temporary color is above 10%, we filter the point out. It performs well in eliminating the color blur in the point sets.

4 Results

In this section, we perform evaluation of our algorithm on different types of datasets. In Sect. 4.1 we compare our filtering results with the method proposed by Wolff et al. [17] on several datasets released by Yücer et al. [15]. We use (Screened) Poisson Surface Reconstruction (PSR) [9] for surface reconstruction. In Sect. 4.2 we analyze the performance of our strategy for filtering using the Fountain data set of Strecha et al. [12]. In Sect. 4.3 we check the validity of the photometric consistency function on the Temple Full dataset from the Middlebury benchmark [11].

4.1 Comparison Against the Method of Wolff et al.

Figure 4 shows the results of comparison of our method and the method proposed by Wolff et al. [17] on the datasets released by Yücer et al. [15]. Wolff et al. [17] also takes depth maps as input and use these datasets for the evaluation of their method. We use two of state-of-the-art multi-view stereo methods, the colmap of Schönberger et al. [10] and the MVE of Fuhrmann et al. [5] for the dense multi-view depth reconstruction. While Fuhrmann et al. (MVE) [5] do not integrate a fusion step into the MVS reconstruction, colmap of Schönberger et al. [10] fuse their resulting depth maps into a point cloud. In our experiment, we disable the fusion step in colmap [10] and use its raw depth maps for filtering. We also show the result of the fusion result of colmap [10] for comparison.

We use about 200 input images for the reconstructions of each dataset. For MVE we used the level-2 depth maps (4*downsampling) the same as the experiments of Wolff et al. [17]. We also limit the max image size in colmap to the same resolution as the experiment of MVE for comparison. We run PSR for each point cloud in our experiment after the filtering. As shown in Fig. 4, the outliers of the results of MVE and colmap are very dense so that it is not easy to filter them out. However, our method employ both the $F(\mathbf{p})$ and $W(\mathbf{p})$ in Geometric consistency and thus more robust to such outliers. Comparing to the results of Wolff et al. [17], we get more clean and dense point cloud and little outliers with our method. In all the experiments, the run time of our method and Wolff et al. are almost the same. With the use of scale value, our method are not only perform well in removing outliers but also preserve more sharp features in the point cloud. Since the method of Wolff et al. are actually global, the results of it often retains some outliers while destroying the sharp features.

4.2 Analysis of Filtering Strategy

In this section, we analyze the filtering strategy of our methods using the datasets released by Yücer et al. [15] and the Fountain data set of Strecha et al. [12]. In our experiments, we use the locally adaptive threshold for $T_{\mathbf{p}}$. As is shown in Fig. 4, the result of locally adaptive threshold is more clean nearby the surface of the objects. That is, $F(\mathbf{p})$ with a locally adaptive threshold performs better in feature preserving with the scale information. We also use different constant

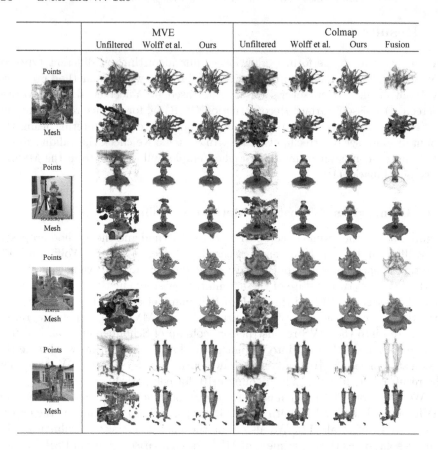

Fig. 4. We use the MVE [5] and colmap [10] to generate the depth maps. After filtering, we use (PSR) [9] to reconstruct a surface for the point cloud. We compare our output point clouds and surfaces with those of Wolff et al. [17]. We also show the result of the fusion method of colmap as a comparison.

threshold of α for $W(\mathbf{p})$. As illustrated by Fig. 5, as the increase of α, the number of outliers in the point cloud decreases quickly because $W(\mathbf{p})$ play an important role in extreme outliers removing.

4.3   Performance of Photometric Consistency

Figure 1 shows the importance of photometric consistency function. The Temple Full dataset from the Middlebury benchmark [11] contains 312 images. Their background are black, so as shown in Fig. 1, the resulting point cloud using MVE contains a mass of black points near the border of the object. These black points are retained when we only apply the photometric consistency. When we integrate the photometric consistency in filtering, most of the black points are removed and the colors of the surface of the object are more uniform.

Fig. 5. The sum of weight, $W(\mathbf{p})$ performs an important role in outliers removing. The α for $W(\mathbf{p})$ in (b), (c), (d), (e) are 0, 2, 4, 6. It is clear that as the increase of α, the number of outliers decreases quickly.

5 Conclusions

We propose a very efficient point cloud denoiser which is locally adaptive. We are mainly inspired by the surface reconstruction method [4]. Since scale and efficiency are common topics in 3D reconstruction, we hope that other people can be inspired by our work and solve some other problems.

Acknowledgment. We would like to thank the reviewers for their time and the valuable comments. This work is supported by the National Natural Science Foundation of China (Grant 61772213) and in part by Grants JCYJ20170818165917438 and 2017010201010121.

References

1. Curless, B., Levoy, M.: A volumetric method for building complex models from range images. In: Proceedings of the 23rd Annual Conference on Computer Graphics and Interactive Techniques, pp. 303–312. ACM (1996)
2. Fleishman, S., Drori, I., Cohen-Or, D.: Bilateral mesh denoising. In: ACM SIGGRAPH, pp. 950–953 (2003)
3. Fuhrmann, S., Goesele, M.: Fusion of depth maps with multiple scales. In: SIGGRAPH Asia Conference, p. 148 (2011)
4. Fuhrmann, S., Goesele, M.: Floating scale surface reconstruction. ACM Trans. Graph. **33**(4), 1–11 (2014)
5. Fuhrmann, S., Langguth, F., Goesele, M.: MVE-A multi-view reconstruction environment. In: GCH, pp. 11–18 (2014)
6. Furukawa, Y., Curless, B., Seitz, S.M., Szeliski, R.: Towards internet-scale multiview stereo. In: 2010 IEEE Conference on Computer Vision and Pattern Recognition (CVPR), pp. 1434–1441. IEEE (2010)
7. Furukawa, Y., Hernández, C., et al.: Multi-view stereo: a tutorial. Found. Trends® Comput. Graph. Vis. **9**(1–2), 1–148 (2015)
8. Goesele, M., Snavely, N., Curless, B., Hoppe, H., Seitz, S.M.: Multi-view stereo for community photo collections. In: IEEE 11th International Conference on Computer Vision, ICCV 2007, pp. 1–8. IEEE (2007)
9. Kazhdan, M., Hoppe, H.: Screened poisson surface reconstruction. ACM Trans. Graph. **32**(3), 29 (2013)
10. Schönberger, J.L., Zheng, E., Frahm, J.-M., Pollefeys, M.: Pixelwise view selection for unstructured multi-view stereo. In: Leibe, B., Matas, J., Sebe, N., Welling, M. (eds.) ECCV 2016. LNCS, vol. 9907, pp. 501–518. Springer, Cham (2016). https://doi.org/10.1007/978-3-319-46487-9_31

11. Seitz, S.M., Curless, B., Diebel, J., Scharstein, D., Szeliski, R.: A comparison and evaluation of multi-view stereo reconstruction algorithms. In: 2006 IEEE Computer Society Conference on Computer Vision and Pattern Recognition, pp. 519–528 (2006)

12. Strecha, C., Hansen, W.V., Gool, L.V., Fua, P., Thoennessen, U.: On benchmarking camera calibration and multi-view stereo for high resolution imagery. In: IEEE Conference on Computer Vision and Pattern Recognition, CVPR 2008, pp. 1–8 (2008)

13. Sun, Y., Schaefer, S., Wang, W.: Denoising point sets via l0 minimization. Comput. Aided Geom. Des. **35**, 2–15 (2015)

14. Vrubel, A., Bellon, O.R., Silva, L.: A 3D reconstruction pipeline for digital preservation. In: IEEE Conference on Computer Vision and Pattern Recognition, CVPR 2009, pp. 2687–2694. IEEE (2009)

15. Yücer, K., Sorkine-Hornung, A., Wang, O., Sorkine-Hornung, O.: Efficient 3D object segmentation from densely sampled light fields with applications to 3D reconstruction. ACM Trans. Graph. **35**(3), 22 (2016)

16. Wei, J., Resch, B., Lensch, H.P.: Multi-view depth map estimation with cross-view consistency. In: BMVC (2014)

17. Wolff, K., et al.: Point cloud noise and outlier removal for image-based 3D reconstruction. In: 2016 Fourth International Conference on 3D Vision (3DV), pp. 118–127. IEEE (2016)

18. Wu, P., Liu, Y., Ye, M., Li, J., Du, S.: Fast and adaptive 3D reconstruction with extensively high completeness. IEEE Trans. Multimed. **19**(2), 266–278 (2017)

Robust Multi-view Subspace Learning Through Structured Low-Rank Matrix Recovery

Jiamiao Xu[2], Xinge You[1,2(✉)], Qi Zheng[2], Fangzhao Wang[2], and Peng Zhang[2]

[1] Research Institute of Huazhong University of Science and Technology in Shenzhen, Shenzhen, China
[2] Huazhong University of Science and Technology, Wuhan 430074, China
{jiamiao_xu,youxg}@hust.edu.cn

Abstract. Multi-view data exists widely in our daily life. A popular approach to deal with multi-view data is the multi-view subspace learning (MvSL), which projects multi-view data into a common latent subspace to learn more powerful representation. Low-rank representation (LRR) in recent years has been adopted to design MvSL methods. Despite promising results obtained on real applications, existing methods are incapable of handling the scenario when large view divergence exists among multi-view data. To tackle this problem, we propose a novel framework based on structured low-rank matrix recovery. Specifically, we get rid of the framework of graph embedding and introduce class-label matrix to flexibly design a supervised low-rank model, which successfully learns a discriminative common subspace and discovers the invariant features shared by multi-view data. Experiments conducted on CMU PIE show that the proposed method achieves the state-of-the-art performance. Performance comparison under different random noise disturbance is also given to illustrate the robustness of our model.

Keywords: Subspace learning · Multi-view learning
Low-rank representation

1 Introduction

In our daily life, people or objects can be captured at different viewpoints or by different sensors. Consequently, one object has multiple representations, this is also known as multi-view data. Multi-view data is generally heterogeneous [4,13] (i.e., intra-class samples from another views may have lower similarity than inter-class samples from the same view), which brings a large challenge to recognition or classification tasks. For this reason, numerous work focusing on multi-view subspace learning (MvSL) appears.

Early work on MvSL aims to learn multiple mapping functions, one for each view, to respectively project multi-view data into a common latent subspace,

© Springer Nature Switzerland AG 2018
J.-H. Lai et al. (Eds.): PRCV 2018, LNCS 11258, pp. 427–439, 2018.
https://doi.org/10.1007/978-3-030-03338-5_36

in which the view divergence can be decreased and the similarity of heterogeneous samples can be measured. Among these approaches, the most well-known unsupervised method is Canonical Correlation Analysis (CCA) [8]. However, CCA can only be applied to two-view scenarios. Multi-view Canonical Correlation Analysis (MCCA) [20] was later proposed to generalize CCA to multi-view situations. Moreover, some state-of-the-art methods (e.g., Generalized Multiview Analysis (GMA) [21], Multi-view discriminant analysis (MvDA) [10] and Multi-view Hybrid Embedding (MvHE) [26]) also have been proposed. Different from MCCA, these methods take into consideration discriminant information, thus improving the representation power of subspace. Despite significant results obtained by them, they fail to work during the testing phase, when the view-related information of test samples is not provided [5].

Low-rank multi-view subspace learning (LRMSL) circumvents this drawback by learning a common mapping function for all views, with the help of low-rank representation (LRR). Compared with aforementioned methods, this type of approaches do not need view-related information in testing process. Based on how the prior knowledge (i.e., view-related information and class-label information) is involved in the training phase, LRMSL approaches can be divided into three categories: unsupervised methods, weakly-supervised methods and supervised methods. Unsupervised methods (e.g., Latent Low-rank Representation (LatLRR) [17]) make no use of these two kinds of information, weakly-supervised methods (e.g., Low-rank Common Subspace (LRCS) [4]) only take into consideration view-related information, whereas supervised methods take full advantage of class-label information (e.g., Supervised Regularization based Robust Subspace (SRRS) [12] and Robust Multi-view Subspace Learning (RMSL) [5]).

LRMSL approaches did make a great progress for multi-view data, but there still exist some problems. The success of low-rank representation bases on the assumption that samples from a same class have higher similarity, but the assumption is invalid for multi-view data. Hence, unsupervised and weakly-supervised methods are incapable of effectively discovering the invariant features shared by multi-view data. Although supervised methods provide a feasible solution, existing methods (e.g., SRRS and RMSL) do not achieve significant improvement. One possible reason is that some graph embedding (e.g., Locally Linear Embedding (LLE) [19] and Locality Preserving Projections (LPP) [7]) can not be applied to multi-view data. This is because these methods require manifolds are locally linear. Unfortunately, this condition is also not met for multi-view data [22,25].

To overcome the problems discussed above, we get rid of the framework of graph embedding and introduce class-label matrix to flexibly design a supervised low-rank model. In the process, a discriminative subspace and the shared information of multi-view data are discovered. Experimental results on face recognition demonstrate the superiority of our method.

The remainder of this paper is organized as follows. Section 2 introduces related work and Sect. 3 presents the proposed method. Optimization is given in Sect. 4. Experimental results are provided in Sect. 5. Finally, Sect. 6 concludes this paper.

2   Related Work

In this section, related work is presented to make interested readers more familiar with the low-rank multi-view subspace learning (LRMSL).

Low-rank Representation (LRR) is a popular approach that has been widely applied in many computer vision and machine learning tasks. In [3], Robust Principle Component Analysis (Robust PCA) was proposed to recover a low-rank component and a sparse component from given data, which assumes that data is homogeneous. To handle data sampled from multiple spaces, Liu *et al.* [15,16] proposed LRR methods which learn a lowest-rank representation at a given dictionary. Besides discovering the global class structure, it also eliminates the influence of noises. Similar to dictionary learning approaches [1,18], the dictionary used in LRR is also expected to be overcomplete. However, this condition is not always easily met. Thus, LatLRR [17] was proposed to construct the dictionary with both observed data and hidden data. In the area of LRR, methods all aim to find an optimal (i.e. structured) representation matrix Z with respect to data X [15,16]. Specifically, assume that we have a dataset $X = [X_1, X_2, \cdots, X_c]$ and a dictionary A, then the optimal representation Z is expected to be block-diagonal as follows:

$$Z^* = \begin{pmatrix} Z_1^* & 0 & 0 & 0 \\ 0 & Z_2^* & 0 & 0 \\ 0 & 0 & \ddots & 0 \\ 0 & 0 & 0 & Z_c^* \end{pmatrix}, \tag{1}$$

where c is number of classes.

Low-rank Multi-view Subspace Learning (LRMSL) uses low-rank representation technology to learn a robust subspace, in which the intrinsic structure of data is preserved. In [4], LRCS was proposed to capture the shared structure from multiple views. SRRS [12] used fisher criterion to learn a discriminant subspace. Considering there are two kinds of structure embedded in multi-view data (i.e. class structure and view structure), Ding *et al.* [5] proposed RMSL to learn two kinds of low-rank structure simultaneously.

3   Robust Low-Rank Multi-view Subspace Learning

3.1   Problem Formulation

Suppose we have a multi-view dataset $X = [X_1, X_2, \cdots, X_n]$, where n is the number of views. $X_k = [X_{k_1}, X_{k_2}, \cdots, X_{k_c}]$ denotes the k-th view data, where c is the number of classes and X_{k_i} represent all samples of the i-th class under the k-th view. Low-rank multi-view subspace learning (LRMSL) aims to find a component mapping function $P \in \mathbb{R}^{d \times p}$ to project multi-view data from d-dimensional space into a p-dimensional subspace $(p \leq d)$, in which projected samples $P^{\mathrm{T}}X$ can be represented as a linear combination of the bases of dictionary A, and the representation matrix exhibits low-rank characteristic. Its objective can be formulated as:

$$\min_{Z,E,P} \|Z\|_* + \lambda_1 \|E\|_1$$
$$s.t. \quad P^{\mathrm{T}}X = AZ + E, \quad P^{\mathrm{T}}P = \mathrm{I}, \tag{2}$$

where E in Eq. (2) is introduced to remove random noise, the orthogonal constraint on P is used to obtain an orthogonal subspace and $\lambda_1 > 0$ can be determined by cross validation.

Equation (2) is a basic framework of LRMSL algorithms. To learn a discriminant subspace, we develop a novel supervised model below.

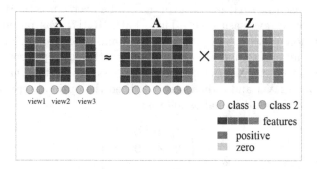

Fig. 1. Illustration of structured low-rank matrix recovery for multi-view data.

3.2 Structured Low-Rank Matrix Recovery

Suppose $A = [A_1, A_2, \cdots, A_c]$ denotes the dictionary, where A_i are the bases of the i-th class. According to the discussion in Sect. 2, structured low-rank matrix Z of multi-view projected samples $P^{\mathrm{T}}X$ can be defined as follows:

$$Z^* \triangleq (Z_1^*, Z_2^*, \cdots, Z_n^*), \tag{3}$$

where Z_k^* is the structured representation matrix of $P^{\mathrm{T}}X_k$, which can be represented as

$$Z_k^* = \begin{pmatrix} Z_{k_1}^* & 0 & 0 & 0 \\ 0 & Z_{k_2}^* & 0 & 0 \\ & & \ddots & 0 \\ 0 & 0 & 0 & Z_{k_c}^* \end{pmatrix}. \tag{4}$$

Obviously, low-rank matrix Z is a structured matrix when each sample from the i-th class can be represented as a linear combination of the dictionary bases from the i-th class. The illustration of the structured low-rank matrix recovery for multi-view data is shown in Fig. 1. As can be seen, intra-class representations are united and inter-class representations are deviated from each other.

To this end, we use class-label matrix $Y = [y_1, y_2, \cdots, y_m]$ to design a supervised model, where m is the number of samples. Assume that $y_k \in \mathbb{R}^{c \times 1}$ is from the j-th class, it can be defined as

$$y_k = \left[\overbrace{0, ..., 0}^{j-1}, 1, \overbrace{0, ..., 0}^{C-j} \right]^{\mathrm{T}}. \tag{5}$$

The objective of the proposed supervised algorithm can be formulated as

$$\min_{Z,E,P} \|Z\|_* + \lambda_1 \|E\|_1$$
$$s.t. \quad P^{\mathrm{T}} X = AZ + E, \quad P^{\mathrm{T}} P = I, \quad YZ = Y_s, \quad e^{\mathrm{T}} Z = e^{\mathrm{T}}, \quad Z \geq 0, \tag{6}$$

where $Y \in \mathbb{R}^{c \times m_1}$ and $Y_s \in \mathbb{R}^{c \times m_2}$ are the class-label matrices of the dictionary A and the dataset X respectively, and e is a column vector with all elements equal to one. $e^{\mathrm{T}} Z = e^{\mathrm{T}}$ in Eq. (6) is used to normalize the representation coefficients (i.e., the sum of each column in Z is equal to one), $Z \geq 0$ is used to guarantee that each element in Z is non-negative. Based on the normalization and non-negative constraints, $YZ = Y_s$ can guarantee that the Z we learned is a structured matrix.

The dictionary A is generally represented by training samples in previous algorithms, thus we replace A with $P^{\mathrm{T}} X$ and we have $Y = Y_s$. Moreover, to improve the generalization performance, we introduce an error term E_L. Then, the objective function (6) can be reformulated as:

$$\min_{Z,E,E_L,P} \|Z\|_* + \lambda_1 \|E\|_1 + \lambda_2 \|E_L\|_F^2$$
$$s.t. \quad P^{\mathrm{T}} X = P^{\mathrm{T}} XZ + E, \quad P^{\mathrm{T}} P = I, \quad Y_s Z = Y_s + E_L, \quad e^{\mathrm{T}} Z = e^{\mathrm{T}}, \quad Z \geq 0, \tag{7}$$

where λ_2 controls the contribution of E_L.

4   Optimization

Through introducing relax variable J, problem (7) can be translated into

$$\min_{J,Z,E,E_L,P} \|J\|_* + \lambda_1 \|E\|_1 + \lambda_2 \|E_L\|_F^2$$
$$s.t. \quad P^{\mathrm{T}} X = P^{\mathrm{T}} XZ + E, \quad P^{\mathrm{T}} P = I, \quad J = Z$$
$$Y_s Z = Y_s + E_L, \quad e^{\mathrm{T}} Z = e^{\mathrm{T}}, \quad Z \geq 0, \tag{8}$$

where the augmented Lagrangian function is formulated as

$$\|J\|_* + \lambda_1 \|E\|_1 + \lambda_2 \|E_L\|_F^2 + tr\left(Y_1^T\left(P^T X - P^T X Z - E\right)\right) + tr\left(Y_2^T\left(Z - J\right)\right)$$
$$+ tr\left(Y_3^T\left(Y_s Z - Y_s - E_L\right)\right) + tr\left(Y_4^T\left(e^T Z - e^T\right)\right)$$
$$+ \frac{\mu}{2}\left(\left\|P^T X - P^T X Z - E\right\|_F^2 + \|Z - J\|_F^2\right) + \frac{\mu}{2}\left(\|Y_s Z - Y_s - E_L\|_F^2 + \left\|e^T Z - e^T\right\|_F^2\right), \tag{9}$$

where Y_1, Y_2, Y_3 and Y_4 are Lagrange multipliers and μ is a positive penalty parameter. There are five parameters in problem (9) to be optimized, and it is difficult to optimize them simultaneously. For this reason, we employ the alternating direction method of multipliers (ADMMs) [6] to alternately optimize J, Z, E, E_L and P one by one through fixing the other variables. For example, during the $t+1$ iteration of optimization, when we optimize J, variables Z, E, E_L and P are regarded as constants, i.e. inherit results of the tth iteration. In detail, we define J_t, Z_t, E_t, $E_{L,t}$, P_t, $Y_{1,t}$, $Y_{2,t}$, $Y_{3,t}$ and $Y_{4,t}$ as variables in the tth iteration, and then we optimize variables in the $t+1$ iteration as follows.

Updating J:

$$J_{t+1} = \arg\min_J \frac{1}{\mu_t}\|J\|_* + \frac{1}{2}\left\|J - \left(Z_t + \frac{Y_{2,t}}{\mu_t}\right)\right\|_F^2. \tag{10}$$

Updating E:

$$E_{t+1} = \arg\min_E \frac{\lambda_1}{\mu_t}\|E\|_1 + \frac{1}{2}\left\|E - \left(P_t^T X - P_t^T X Z_t + \frac{Y_{1,t}}{\mu_t}\right)\right\|_F^2, \tag{11}$$

The two problems above can be optimized by the iterative thresholding approach [14].

Updating E_L:

$$E_{L,t+1} = (2\lambda_2 + \mu_t)^{-1}\left(Y_{3,t} + \mu_t Y_s Z_t - \mu_t Y_s\right). \tag{12}$$

Updating P:

$$P_{t+1} = \left((X - X Z_t)(X - X Z_t)^T\right)^{-1}\left((X - X Z_t)(E_t^T - Y_{1,t}^T/\mu_t)\right). \tag{13}$$

Updating Z:

$$Z = Z_1^{-1} Z_2, \tag{14}$$

where Z_1 and Z_2 are represented as follows:

$$Z_1 = X^T P_t P_t^T X + I + Y_s^T Y_s + e e^T,$$
$$Z_2 = X^T P_t\left(P_t^T X - E_t\right) + J_t + Y_s^T\left(Y_s + E_{L,t}\right) + e e^T$$
$$+ \left(X^T P_t Y_{1,t} - Y_{2,t} - Y_s^T Y_{3,t} - e Y_{4,t}\right)/\mu_t.$$

Algorithm 1. Solving Problem (7) by ADMM

Input: X, Y_s, λ_1 and λ_2;
Initialization: $J = Z = E = E_L = P = 0$,
$\qquad\qquad Y_1 = Y_2 = Y_3 = Y_4 = 0$,
$\qquad\qquad \mu_{max} = 10^6$, $\quad \mu = 10^{-3}$,
$\qquad\qquad \rho = 1.03$, $\quad \epsilon = 10^{-6}$;

While not converged **do**
Step 1. Update J by solving problem (10);
Step 2. Update E by solving problem (11);
Step 3. Update E_L by (12);
Step 4. Update P by (13), and then $P \leftarrow$**orthogonal**(P) [9];
Step 5. Update Z by (14), and then $Z = \max(0, Z)$ [27];
Step 6. Update multipliers and parameter μ by (15);
Step 7. Check the convergence conditions:
$$\left\| P^T X - P^T X Z - E \right\|_\infty < \epsilon,$$
$$\left\| Z - J \right\|_\infty < \epsilon,$$
$$\left\| Y_s Z - Y_s - E_L \right\|_\infty < \epsilon,$$
$$\left\| e^T Z - e^T \right\|_\infty < \epsilon;$$
End while
Output: P, Z, E, E_L.

Afterwards, we update multipliers $\boldsymbol{Y}_1$, $\boldsymbol{Y}_2$, $\boldsymbol{Y}_3$ and $\boldsymbol{Y}_4$ in the following way

$$\boldsymbol{Y}_{1,t+1} = \boldsymbol{Y}_1, t + \mu_t \left(\boldsymbol{P}_{t+1}^T \boldsymbol{X} - \boldsymbol{P}_{t+1}^T \boldsymbol{X} \boldsymbol{Z}_{t+1} - \boldsymbol{E}_{t+1} \right),$$
$$\boldsymbol{Y}_{2,t+1} = \boldsymbol{Y}_2, t + \mu_t \left(\boldsymbol{Z}_{t+1} - \boldsymbol{J}_{t+1} \right),$$
$$\boldsymbol{Y}_{3,t+1} = \boldsymbol{Y}_3, t + \mu_t \left(\boldsymbol{Y}_s \boldsymbol{Z}_{t+1} - \boldsymbol{Y}_s - \boldsymbol{E}_{L,t+1} \right),$$
$$\boldsymbol{Y}_{4,t+1} = \boldsymbol{Y}_4, t + \mu_t \left(\boldsymbol{e}^T \boldsymbol{Z}_{t+1} - \boldsymbol{e}^T \right),$$
$$\mu_{t+1} = \min \left(\rho \mu_t, \mu_{max} \right), \tag{15}$$

where $\rho > 1$ and μ_{max} is a constant. We iteratively update variables and the penalty parameter until the algorithm satisfies the convergence conditions or reaches the maximum iterations. The detailed iteration process is summarized in Algorithm 1.

5 Experiments

In this section, we first specify the evaluation protocol of MvSL algorithms. Following this, one public dataset is introduced and experimental setting is presented. In order to evaluate the performance of the proposed method, three baselines (i.e., PCA [24], LDA [2], LPP [7]) and three state-of-the-art low-rank multi-view subspace learning (LRMSL) algorithms (i.e., LRCS [4], SRRS [12] and RMSL [5]) are selected for comparison.

5.1 Evaluation Protocol

Evaluation protocol of single-view subspace learning (SvSL) methods can not precisely evaluate the performance of multi-view learning algorithms. To this end, similar to [11], we adopt a more convincing evaluation protocol as follows:

$$acc_{v_1}^{v_2} = \frac{\sum\left(x : x \in X_{probe}^{v_2} \wedge \bar{y}=y\right)}{\sum\left(x : x \in X_{probe}^{v_2}\right)}, \qquad mACC = \left(\sum_{v_1=1}^{n}\sum_{v_2=1}^{n} acc_{v_1}^{v_2}\right)/n^2, \qquad (16)$$

where n is the number of views, $acc_{v_1}^{v_2}$ denotes the accuracy when gallery and probe sets are from view v_1 and view v_2 respectively. y and $\bar{y}$ are the true label and the predicted label of data x respectively. In experiments, we average results of all pairwise views as the mean accuracy (mACC).

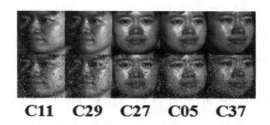

C11   C29   C27   C05   C37

Fig. 2. Exemplar subjects from the CMU PIE dataset. C11, C29, C27, C05 and C37 poses are selected to construct multi-view data. The top row shows clean images and the bottom row shows images with 10% random noise.

5.2 Dataset and Experimental Setting

The CMU Pose, Illumination, and Expression (PIE) Database. (CMU PIE) [23] contains 41,368 images of 68 people with 13 different poses, 43 diverse illumination conditions and 4 various expressions. Five poses (i.e., C11, C29, C27, C05 and C37) are selected to construct multi-view data (see Fig. 2 for exemplar subjects). In experiments, each person at a given pose has 4 images, and images are cropped and resized to 64×64. To make results more convincing, experiments on CMU PIE are repeated ten times by randomly dividing data into training set, validation set and test set, and we report average result as the final accuracy. Hyper-parameters of all approaches are determined by validation set.

5.3 The Superiority of the Proposed Method

The CMU PIE is used to evaluate face recognition across poses. Similar to [4, 5], experiments are conducted in 5 cases, namely case 1: {C27, C29}, case 2: {C27, C11}, case 3: {C05, C27, C29}, case 4: {C37, C27, C11} and case 5:

Table 1. The average recognition accuracy (%) in 5 cases of CMU PIE in terms of mean accuracy (mACC). **Bold** denotes the best performance.

	Case 1	Case 2	Case 3	Case 4	Case 5
PCA [24]	76.6 ± 7.3	66.0 ± 5.7	62.1 ± 5.7	55.1 ± 4.8	55.5 ± 4.1
LDA [2]	64.5 ± 6.6	58.6 ± 4.1	41.0 ± 10.0	45.0 ± 1.8	46.7 ± 3.6
LPP [7]	72.8 ± 7.5	65.5 ± 4.8	62.3 ± 4.6	53.5 ± 3.7	54.0 ± 4.1
LRCS [4]	74.0 ± 6.7	66.1 ± 4.4	68.9 ± 5.5	56.3 ± 3.1	58.1 ± 3.8
SRRS [12]	74.3 ± 6.5	66.8 ± 4.3	69.0 ± 5.2	56.2 ± 3.4	59.4 ± 3.3
RMSL [5]	75.7 ± 7.7	68.0 ± 4.7	70.7 ± 4.4	57.9 ± 3.2	62.0 ± 3.0
Proposed	**83.0 ± 5.9**	**76.7 ± 7.0**	**78.5 ± 5.7**	**67.0 ± 4.5**	**70.9 ± 5.0**

{C37, C05, C27, C29, C11}. In our experiments, 40 people are used as training set, 14 people serve as validation set and the rest comprise the test set.

In the first experiment, we evaluate our performance with three baselines and three state-of-the-art methods. The experimental results are summarized in Table 1. As can be seen, SvSL based methods rank the lowest due to the neglect of the view divergence. Benefited from the consideration of discriminant information, SRRS and RMSL perform better than LRCS. As expected, our method achieves a remarkable improvement compared with RMSL, which we argue can be attributed to the more effectively exploiting discriminant information.

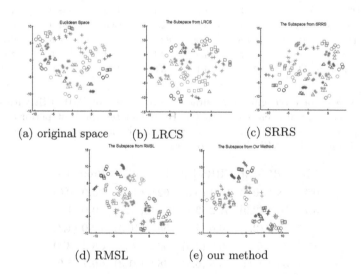

(a) original space   (b) LRCS   (c) SRRS

(d) RMSL   (e) our method

Fig. 3. Illustration of 2D embedding of Euclidean space, the subspace generated by LRCS, SRRS, RMSL and the proposed metho in case 5 of CMU PIE dataset. Different colors denote different classes, and different views are denoted by different markers.

Table 2. The average recognition results (%) in case 5 of CMU PIE. **Bold** denotes the best performance.

Gallery	Probe	PCA [24]	LDA [2]	LPP [7]	LRCS [4]	SRRS [12]	RMSL [5]	Proposed
C37	C37	98.8	99.8	99.1	95.2	98.4	**100.0**	99.8
	C05	70.9	53.6	67.3	71.6	69.3	69.5	**81.4**
	C27	38.8	23.4	35.5	29.1	30.5	37.7	**52.9**
	C29	27.1	18.0	26.3	29.8	28.6	30.4	**45.0**
	C11	25.2	21.3	23.4	28.0	29.8	32.5	**46.3**
C05	C37	73.0	57.3	70.5	80.5	83.2	84.1	**89.3**
	C05	96.1	**100.0**	95.9	85.7	87.9	99.8	99.6
	C27	62.0	40.7	60.5	60.0	63.0	67.3	**75.9**
	C29	32.9	26.4	29.3	47.7	47.3	49.6	**57.9**
	C11	31.6	28.2	28.4	43.2	45.9	45.7	**58.2**
C27	C37	44.3	28.9	41.4	49.3	50.2	48.0	**65.5**
	C05	58.8	42.0	56.3	70.4	72.3	74.3	**78.6**
	C27	84.1	**99.1**	90.0	81.4	85.0	89.1	92.5
	C29	54.1	33.9	51.3	62.3	64.1	66.6	**70.0**
	C11	48.0	28.9	43.8	49.1	50.1	52.1	**65.2**
C29	C37	27.9	22.3	25.4	37.5	38.2	37.3	**50.9**
	C05	34.5	24.6	30.2	42.5	43.8	46.4	**59.5**
	C27	46.6	33.9	52.1	45.5	49.1	48.8	**67.0**
	C29	97.0	**99.8**	97.9	89.6	91.6	98.9	99.5
	C11	75.4	60.5	75.7	83.6	85.9	85.5	**91.3**
C11	C37	25.0	19.3	17.3	33.9	34.8	37.0	**45.7**
	C05	29.3	25.4	20.7	29.6	27.7	31.8	**45.5**
	C27	38.0	21.1	38.8	34.1	32.5	38.0	**49.1**
	C29	73.6	58.6	76.8	82.1	84.3	82.9	**88.9**
	C11	94.6	**99.8**	96.3	89.3	91.8	96.6	97.1
Average		55.5	46.7	54.0	58.1	59.4	62.0	**70.9**
Standard derivation		4.1	3.6	4.1	3.8	3.3	**3.0**	5.0

Table 3. The average recognition accuracy (%) in case 5 of CMU PIE with random noise in terms of mean accuracy (mACC). **Bold** denotes the best performance. the values in parentheses denote the relative performance loss (%) with respect to the random noise scenario. "NR" denotes noise ratio.

NR	LRCS [4]	SRRS [12]	RMSL [5]	Proposed
0%	58.1 (0.0)	59.4 (0.0)	62.0 (0.0)	**70.9** (0.0)
5%	56.4 (2.9)	57.2 (3.7)	60.0 (3.2)	**70.0** (1.3)
10%	56.5 (2.8)	56.6 (4.7)	55.6 (10.3)	**70.0** (1.3)
15%	54.9 (5.5)	56.8 (4.4)	56.2 (9.4)	**68.2** (3.8)
20%	53.4 (8.1)	55.6 (6.4)	48.8 (21.3)	**66.7** (5.9)

To better evaluate performance of the proposed method, detailed results in case 5 of CMU PIE are shown in Fig. 3 and Table 2. As can be seen in Fig. 3, all low-rank subspace learning approaches can remove the view divergence to some extent. However, LRCS, SRRS and RMSL approaches fail to distinguish the yellow class from the green one correctly, whereas these two classes are separated obviously in the subspace generated by our method. As a whole, the embeddings shown in Fig. 3 corroborate the results summarized in Table 1. Moreover, as can be seen in Table 2, one should note that our method does not achieve the best performance when the gallery and the probe data come from the same view. The reason for this phenomenon is that the constraint with respect to intra-view and intra-class samples is only based on low-rank representation. Compared with traditional graph embedded, this is a weak constraint.

At last, we evaluate the robustness of the proposed methods. we add random noise to original images by randomly replacing 5%, 10%, 15% and 20% pixels (see Fig. 2 for exemplar subjects) and report the results in case 5 in Table 3. As can be seen, LRCS, SRRS and RMSL are more sensitive to random noise than our method. Take the 20% random noise scenario as an example, our method only suffers from a relative 5.9% performance drop from its original 70.9% accuracy, whereas the accuracy of RMSL decreases to 48.8% with a relative performance drop nearly 21.3%.

6   Conclusion

In this paper, we proposed an novel framework based on structured low-rank matrix recovery to learn a discriminant subspace for multi-view data. Experiments conducted on CMU PIE show that the proposed method successfully discovers the discriminant information shared by multi-view data, thus improving the performance of subsequent recognition or classification tasks. Moreover, experimental results in the scenario of random noise disturbance indicate that our method is more robust to random noise. In the future, we are interested in develop a nonlinear version of our method to handle more challenge scenarios.

Acknowledgment. This work was supported partially by National Key Technology Research and Development Program of the Ministry of Science and Technology of China (No. 2015BAK36B00), in part by the Key Science and Technology of Shenzhen (No. CXZZ20150814155434903), in part by the Key Program for International S&T Cooperation Projects of China (No. 2016YFE0121200), in part by the Key Science and Technology Innovation Program of Hubei (No. 2017AAA017), in part by the National Natural Science Foundation of China (No. 61571205), in part by the National Natural Science Foundation of China (No. 61772220).

References

1. Agarwal, A., Anandkumar, A., Jain, P., Netrapalli, P., Tandon, R.: Learning sparsely used overcomplete dictionaries. In: Conference on Learning Theory, pp. 123–137 (2014)
2. Belhumeur, P.N., Hespanha, J.P., Kriegman, D.J.: Eigenfaces vs. fisherfaces: recognition using class specific linear projection. IEEE Trans. Pattern Anal. Mach. Intell. **19**(7), 711–720 (1997)

3. Candès, E.J., Li, X., Ma, Y., Wright, J.: Robust principal component analysis? J. ACM (JACM) **58**(3), 11 (2011)
4. Ding, Z., Fu, Y.: Low-rank common subspace for multi-view learning. In: 2014 IEEE International Conference on Data Mining (ICDM), pp. 110–119. IEEE (2014)
5. Ding, Z., Fu, Y.: Robust multi-view subspace learning through dual low-rank decompositions. In: AAAI, pp. 1181–1187 (2016)
6. Gabay, D., Mercier, B.: A dual algorithm for the solution of nonlinear variational problems via finite element approximation. Comput. Math. Appl. **2**(1), 17–40 (1976)
7. He, X., Niyogi, P.: Locality preserving projections. In: Advances in Neural Information Processing Systems, pp. 153–160 (2004)
8. Hotelling, H.: Relations between two sets of variates. Biometrika **28**(3/4), 321–377 (1936)
9. Jhuo, I.H., Liu, D., Lee, D., Chang, S.F.: Robust visual domain adaptation with low-rank reconstruction. In: 2012 IEEE Conference on Computer Vision and Pattern Recognition (CVPR), pp. 2168–2175. IEEE (2012)
10. Kan, M., Shan, S., Zhang, H., Lao, S., Chen, X.: Multi-view discriminant analysis. IEEE Trans. Pattern Anal. Mach. Intell. **38**(1), 188–194 (2016)
11. Li, J., Wu, Y., Zhao, J., Lu, K.: Low-rank discriminant embedding for multiview learning. IEEE Trans. Cybern. **47**, 3516–3529 (2016)
12. Li, S., Fu, Y.: Robust subspace discovery through supervised low-rank constraints. In: Proceedings of the 2014 SIAM International Conference on Data Mining, pp. 163–171. SIAM (2014)
13. Lian, W., Rai, P., Salazar, E., Carin, L.: Integrating features and similarities: flexible models for heterogeneous multiview data. In: AAAI, pp. 2757–2763 (2015)
14. Lin, Z., Chen, M., Ma, Y.: The augmented lagrange multiplier method for exact recovery of corrupted low-rank matrices. arXiv preprint arXiv:1009.5055 (2010)
15. Liu, G., Lin, Z., Yan, S., Sun, J., Yu, Y., Ma, Y.: Robust recovery of subspace structures by low-rank representation. IEEE Trans. Pattern Anal. Mach. Intell. **35**(1), 171–184 (2013)
16. Liu, G., Lin, Z., Yu, Y.: Robust subspace segmentation by low-rank representation. In: Proceedings of the 27th International Conference on Machine Learning (ICML2010), pp. 663–670 (2010)
17. Liu, G., Yan, S.: Latent low-rank representation for subspace segmentation and feature extraction. In: 2011 IEEE International Conference on Computer Vision (ICCV), pp. 1615–1622. IEEE (2011)
18. Mairal, J., Bach, F., Ponce, J., Sapiro, G.: Online dictionary learning for sparse coding. In: Proceedings of the 26th Annual International Conference on Machine Learning, pp. 689–696. ACM (2009)
19. Roweis, S.T., Saul, L.K.: Nonlinear dimensionality reduction by locally linear embedding. Science **290**(5500), 2323–2326 (2000)
20. Rupnik, J., Shawe-Taylor, J.: Multi-view canonical correlation analysis. In: Conference on Data Mining and Data Warehouses (SiKDD 2010), pp. 1–4 (2010)
21. Sharma, A., Kumar, A., Daume, H., Jacobs, D.W.: Generalized multiview analysis: a discriminative latent space. In: 2012 IEEE Conference on Computer Vision and Pattern Recognition (CVPR), pp. 2160–2167. IEEE (2012)
22. Silva, V.D., Tenenbaum, J.B.: Global versus local methods in nonlinear dimensionality reduction. In: Advances in Neural Information Processing Systems, pp. 721–728 (2003)

23. Sim, T., Baker, S., Bsat, M.: The CMU pose, illumination, and expression (PIE) database. In: 2002 Proceedings of Fifth IEEE International Conference on Automatic Face and Gesture Recognition, pp. 53–58. IEEE (2002)

24. Turk, M., Pentland, A.: Eigenfaces for recognition. J. Cogn. Neurosci. **3**(1), 71–86 (1991)

25. Van Der Maaten, L., Postma, E., Van den Herik, J.: Dimensionality reduction: a comparative. J. Mach. Learn. Res. **10**, 66–71 (2009)

26. Xu, J., Yu, S., You, X., Leng, M., Jing, X.Y., Chen, C.: Multi-view hybrid embedding: a divide-and-conquer approach. arXiv preprint arXiv:1804.07237 (2018)

27. Yin, M., Gao, J., Lin, Z., Shi, Q., Guo, Y.: Dual graph regularized latent low-rank representation for subspace clustering. IEEE Trans. Image Process. **24**(12), 4918–4933 (2015)

An Online Learning Approach for Robust Motion Tracking in Liver Ultrasound Sequence

Chunxu Shen[1], Huabei Shi[1], Tao Sun[1], Yibin Huang[3],
and Jian Wu[1,2(✉)]

[1] Tsinghua University, Beijing 100084, China
{scxl6, shbl6, suntl6}@mails.tsinghua.edu.cn,
wuj@sz.tsinghua.edu.cn
[2] Graduate School at Shenzhen, Tsinghua University, Shenzhen 518055, China
[3] Shenzhen Traditional Chinese Medicine Hospital, Shenzhen 518034, China
huangyb2004@126.com

Abstract. Suffering from respiratory motion and drift, radiotherapy requires real-time and accuracy motion tracking to minimize damage to critical structures and optimize dosage delivery to target. In this paper, we propose a robust tracker to minimize tracking error and enhance the quality of radiotherapy based on two-dimensional ultrasound sequences. We firstly develop a scale adaptive kernel correlation filter to compensate deformation. Then the filter with an improved update rule is utilized to predict target position. Moreover, displacement and appearance constrains are elaborately devised to restrict unreasonable positions. Finally, a weighted displacement is calculated to further improve the robustness. Proposed method has been evaluated on 53 targets, yielding 1.13 ± 1.07 mm mean and 2.31 mm 95%ile tracking error. Extensive experiments are performed between proposed and state-of-the-art algorithms, and results show our algorithm is more competitive. Favorable agreement between automatically and manually tracked displacements proves proposed algorithm has potential for target motion tracking in abdominal radiotherapy.

Keywords: Target tracking · Kernel correlation filter · Scale adaptation
Displacement and appearance constrain · Radiotherapy

1 Introduction

Motion in the abdomen is worth accounting for during radiotherapy image guided intervention [1] and focus ultrasound surgery [2]. The motion induced in abdominal organs is mainly due to breathing motion, drift and surgical instruments. Therefore, motion tracking of abdominal target is crucial to minimize the damage to surrounding crucial structure and optimize dosage delivery to target.

Respiratory gating is one of the most conventional approach to deal with abdomen motion, whereas it potentially increases treatment time [3]. Motion modeling like implanting fiducial markers to target region [4] is an alternative method, but it is usually at the expense of healthy tissue. Tracking base on medical image e.g. magnetic

© Springer Nature Switzerland AG 2018
J.-H. Lai et al. (Eds.): PRCV 2018, LNCS 11258, pp. 440–451, 2018.
https://doi.org/10.1007/978-3-030-03338-5_37

resonance (MR), ultrasound (US) generally becomes a superior to localize abdomen target. De Senneville [5] generates an atlas of motion fields based on magnitude data of temperature-sensitive MR acquisitions. They suppose that motion of target region is periodic and can be estimated in the next moment, so it just recovers deformation caused by periodic component. 4D MR [6] is also introduced to respiratory motion reconstruction, but low signal-to-noise ratio and additional high cost must be considered in clinical practice. US is an appealing choice for abdominal target tracking, by contrast, as it has high temporal resolution and sub-millimeter spatial resolution along the beam direction.

Recently several literatures focus on tracking hepatic landmark and reconstructing liver motion of free breathing. Block matching [7], optical flow [8], particle filter [9], image registration and mechanical simulation [10] are widely investigated. Meanwhile temporal regularization [7] and distance metric [10] are also introduced to reject false tracking results. While some results have achieved a great process, many limitations remain to be discussed like tradeoff between real-time and accuracy, as well as robustness for acoustic shadowing and large deformation due to out-of-plane motion.

Our tracking approach is motivated by kernel correlation filter (KCF) [11], which achieves a fast and high performance on Visual Tracker Benchmark [12]. KCF provides an effective solution for translation, but its performance would degrade because of the scale and deformation of targets. Li et al. [13] suggests an effective scale adaptive scheme. Without discussing update strategy adequately, however, better tracking results cannot be remerged in US sequence. Besides, we integrate intensity feature, namely speckle patter, to proposed tracking frame as it includes much information about anatomical structure. In fact, if all the speckle patterns are stable, target motion can be easily reconstructed. Unluckily, speckle patterns are not identical because of out-of-plane motion and acoustic shadowing [14]. Moreover, similarity metrics is another important ingredient in proposed method. While mutual information (MI) has been suggested to be the most suitable metric for US to US match, high computation limits its usage in real-time target tracking. In this work, normalized cross-correlation (NCC) is chosen as it is easy to implement and effective to perform block matching.

In this work, we propose a real-time, robust tracking algorithm to compensate target motion in abdominal radiotherapy. Our contributions mainly focus on four aspects: first, we propose a scale adaptation strategy to alleviate deformation and scale change. Second, an improved update rule for proximate periodic motion is applied to reducing accumulation error in long-term tracking. Third, we integrate displacement and appearance constrains to proposed method in order to restrict unreasonable target prediction. And fourth, we suggest to use weighted displacement to determine target displacement.

2 Method

2.1 The KCF Tracker

In KCF tracker, Henriques et al. [11] suppose that the cyclic shifts version of base sample is approximate the dense samples over the base sample. Take one-dimension data $\mathbf{x} = [x_1, x_2, \ldots, x_n]$ for example, a cyclic shift of $\mathbf{x}$ is defined as

$\mathbf{Px} = [x_n, x_1, x_2, \ldots, x_{n-1}]$. Therefore, all the cyclic shift samples, $\{\mathbf{P}^u\mathbf{x}|u = 0, \ldots, n - 1\}$, can be concatenated to form sample matrix $\mathbf{X}$, which also called circulant matrix as the matrix is purely generated by the cyclic shifts of $\mathbf{x}$. This matrix has a helpful property that all the circulant matrices can be formulated as follows:

$$\mathbf{X} = \mathbf{F}^H diag(\mathbf{Fx})\mathbf{F} \tag{1}$$

Where, $\mathbf{F}$ is the Discrete Fourier Transformation (DFT) matrix. $\mathbf{F}^H$ is the Hermitian transpose of $\mathbf{F}$. Benefit from the decomposition of circulant matrix, it can be used to the solution of linear regression. Moreover, the objective function of linear ridge regression can be written as:

$$\min_{\mathbf{w}} \sum_i^n (f(\mathbf{x}_i) - y_i)^2 + \lambda\|\mathbf{w}\| \tag{2}$$

Where, f is linear combination of basis samples, $f(\mathbf{x}) = \mathbf{w}^T\mathbf{x}$. The ridge regression has a close-form solution, $\mathbf{w} = (\mathbf{X}^T\mathbf{X} + \lambda\mathbf{I})^{-1}\mathbf{X}^T\mathbf{y}$. The solution can be rewritten with Eq. 1, $\hat{\mathbf{w}}^* = \frac{\hat{\mathbf{x}}^* \odot \hat{\mathbf{y}}}{\hat{\mathbf{x}}^* \odot \hat{\mathbf{X}} + \lambda}$. Where, $\hat{\mathbf{x}} = \mathbf{Fx}$ donates the DFT of $\mathbf{x}$; $\hat{\mathbf{x}}^*$ is the complex-conjugate of $\hat{\mathbf{x}}$; $\odot$ denotes element-wise multiplication. So during the process of extracting patches explicitly and solving a general regression problem, this step can save much computational cost. In order to construct a more powerful classifier in case of non-linear regression, Henriques et al. [11] adopt a kernel tracker, $f(\mathbf{z}) = \mathbf{w}^T\mathbf{z} = \sum_{i=1}^n \alpha_i \mathcal{K}(\mathbf{z}, \mathbf{x}_i)$. Then dual space confident α can be learned as follows:

$$\hat{\alpha}^* = \frac{\hat{\mathbf{y}}}{\hat{\mathbf{k}}^{\mathbf{xx}} + \lambda} \tag{3}$$

$\mathbf{k}^{\mathbf{xx}}$ is defined as kernel correlation. Similar to the linear classifier, the dual coefficients are learned in Fourier domain. $\mathbf{y}$ is a regression target vector in Fourier domain and has the same size with $\mathbf{x}$; λ is regularization weight in ridge regression. Note that the search window, which is the size of $\mathbf{x}$, has 2.5 times the size of the target in the implementation of KCF. In case of Gaussian kernel function, the kernel correlation can be denoted as:

$$\mathbf{k}^{\mathbf{xx}'} = \exp\left(-\frac{1}{\sigma^2}\left(\|\mathbf{x}\|^2 + \|\mathbf{x}'\|^2\right) - 2\mathbf{F}^{-1}(\hat{\mathbf{x}} \odot \hat{\mathbf{x}}'^*)\right) \tag{4}$$

Where $\mathbf{F}^{-1}$ denotes inverse Fourier transform.

In detection step, the regression function Eq. 5 is applied to predict the position of target where the maximum regression value locates.

$$\hat{\mathbf{f}}(\mathbf{z}) = \left(\hat{\mathbf{k}}^{\tilde{\mathbf{x}}\mathbf{z}}\right)^* \odot \hat{\alpha} \tag{5}$$

Where $\tilde{\mathbf{x}}$ denotes basic data template to be learned in the model; $\mathbf{z}$ is the candidate patch, which has the same size and location with $\mathbf{x}$ in next frame. When we transform

$\hat{f}(z)$ back into the spatial domain, the translation with respect to the maximum response is considered as the displacement of the tracked target.

2.2 Scale Adaptive KCF

Deformations and scale variations of targets is potential to increase the tracking error and reduce robustness, even fail. However, these negative factors are common in abdominal targets. In our clinical practice, there are two situations leading to target deformation. First, with the contraction and relaxation of the diaphragm in free breathing situation [15], the hepatic targets would suffer from deformation. Second, because of free breathing and drift, the appearance of cross section between ultrasound beam and targets would change. In this part, we propose a scale adaptive strategy to compensate these deformations and scale variations.

Suppose that the size of search window sets as $s_T = (s_x, s_y)$, we define a scaling pool $\eta = \{\eta_1, \eta_2, \ldots, \eta_m\}$ to expand search range to different scale space, which can be donated as $\tilde{s}_T = \{(\eta_i s_x, \eta_j s_y) | \eta_i, \eta_j \in \eta, \}$. Because the dot-product requires the search window with the fixed size in kernel correlation filter, we resize $\tilde{s}_T$ into the fixed size of s_T using bilinear-interpolation. Note that our proposed scale adaptive method is different from Li's work [13], which adopts $\breve{s}_T = \{\eta_i s_T | \eta_i \in \eta\}$. Therefore, the response $R(\eta_i, \eta_j)$ in difference scale space can be calculated.

$$R(\eta_i, \eta_j) = F^{-1}\hat{f}(z(\eta_i, \eta_j)) \tag{6}$$

Where $z(\eta_i, \eta_j)$ is the sample patch resampled by scaling pool and the size of $z(\eta_i, \eta_j)$ is $(\eta_i s_x, \eta_j s_y)$, which is subsequently resized to the fixed size of s_T.

2.3 Improved Update Rule for Approximate Periodic Motion

According to Eq. 5, there are two sets of coefficient should be update. One is dual space coefficient α, another is basic template $\tilde{x}$. Original update rule is realized by combining new filter with old one linearly as Eq. 7 illustrates.

$$\begin{cases} \tilde{x}_{t+1} = \mu \, \tilde{x}_{t+1} + (1 - \mu) \, \tilde{x}_t \\ \hat{\alpha}_{t+1} = \mu \, \hat{\alpha}_{t+1} + (1 - \mu) \, \hat{\alpha}_t \end{cases} \tag{7}$$

Where μ is the linear interpolation factor.

While the update rule above achieves impressive success for nature video tracking, it is so sensitive that cannot support for long-term tracking in our work. An explanation is that Eq. 7 pays more attention to learn new characteristics from a new image. Once ultrasound images suffer from noise severely, like acoustic shadowing and speckle decorrelation, the performance of online classifier could degrade largely. With prior knowledge that motion of liver is approximate periodic in free breathing, the target in first frame would also appear in subsequent sequence. Therefore, an improved update rule for long-term tracking of approximate periodic motion is proposed as Eq. 8 shows:

$$\begin{cases} \tilde{\mathbf{x}}_{t+1} = \beta\,\tilde{\mathbf{x}}_1 + (1 - \beta - \mu)\,\tilde{\mathbf{x}}_{t+1} + \mu\,\tilde{\mathbf{x}}_t \\ \hat{\alpha}_{t+1} = \beta\,\hat{\alpha}_1 + (1 - \beta - \mu)\,\hat{\alpha}_{t+1} + \mu\,\hat{\alpha}_t \end{cases} \tag{8}$$

Where β is recurrence factor.

2.4   Restricting Unreasonable Target Prediction

Though NCC has been a popular similarity measure in specking tracking, it still suffers from acoustic shadowing, speckle decorrelation and other artifacts. Here, in order to alleviate these adverse effect, we provide displacement and appearance constrains to restrict unreasonable target prediction.

Displacement Constrain. In clinical ultrasound image guided abdominal radiotherapy, we notice that the target displacement in two consecutive frames is very small (<3 mm, acquisition frequency is 13–23 Hz). So a displacement cost function is employed to restrict unreasonable prediction. Suppose that $\mathbf{D} = \left(\Delta\mathbf{x}(\eta_i,\eta_j), \Delta\mathbf{y}(\eta_i,\eta_j)\right)$ is the displacement prediction and $\mathbf{R}(d_{ij}|d_{ij} \in D)$ is corresponding response map, therefore, the response with displacement constrain can be expressed by:

$$\mathbf{R}_{\text{dis}}(\eta_i,\eta_j) = \mathbf{R}(\eta_i,\eta_j) \odot \exp\left(-\frac{\Delta\mathbf{x}^2 + \Delta\mathbf{y}^2}{\sigma_{\text{dis}}}\right) \tag{9}$$

Where σ_{dis} is the bandwidth of displacement constrain.

Appearance Constrain. For alleviating the unreasonable matching from NCC, we also employ a set of confidence response to determine target displacement instead of selecting the displacement that the best response locates. Supposing the threshold of confidence response is θ_{app}, the appearance constrain can be expressed as Eq. 10 shows.

$$\mathbf{R}_{\text{dis}}^{\text{app}}(\eta_i,\eta_j) = \begin{cases} \mathbf{R}_{\text{dis}}(\eta_i,\eta_j), & \text{if } \mathbf{R}_{\text{dis}} \geq \max\{\mathbf{R}_{\text{dis}}\} \cdot \theta_{app} \\ 0, & \text{others} \end{cases} \tag{10}$$

With constrains of displacement and appearance, the best scale space can be determined by maximize the average response $\overline{\mathbf{R}_{\text{dis}}^{\text{app}}(\eta_i,\eta_j)}$ in Eq. 10:

$$\arg\max \overline{\mathbf{R}_{\text{dis}}^{\text{app}}(\eta_i,\eta_j)} \tag{11}$$

2.5   Weighted Displacement

Motivated by Carletti's work [9], a weighted displacement is calculated to enhance the robustness of proposed tracking algorithm. The displacements used to calculate weighted displacement are from Eq. 10, namely $r_{ij} \in \mathbf{R}_{dis}^{app}(\eta_i, \eta_j)$. Finally the target displacement can be determined in adjacent frames.

$$\bar{\mathbf{d}} = \frac{\sum_{i=1}^{M}\sum_{j=1}^{N} r_{ij}\mathbf{d}_{ij}}{\sum_{i=1}^{M}\sum_{j=1}^{N} r_{ij}} \tag{12}$$

Note that $\bar{\mathbf{d}}$ is the displacement in best scale space, we get the real displacement $\bar{\mathbf{d}}_r$ by performing scale inverse transformation with scale parameters from Eq. 11. Therefore, by combining the target position in last frame $\mathbf{p}_{old}$ and displacement $\bar{\mathbf{d}}_r$, new target position $\mathbf{p}_{new}$ in current frame can be determined.

$$\mathbf{p}_{new} = \mathbf{p}_{old} + \bar{\mathbf{d}}_r \tag{13}$$

Finally, the overall algorithm is summarized into Algorithm 1

Algorithm 1. Overall of proposed tracking algorithm

Require:
   The template of tracked target, $\tilde{\mathbf{x}}$;
   The dual space coefficient, $\boldsymbol{\alpha}$;
   The newly search window, $\mathbf{y}$;
   The last target position, $\mathbf{p}_{old}$;
Ensure:
   The updated template of tracked target, $\tilde{\mathbf{x}}$;
   The updated dual space coefficient, $\boldsymbol{\alpha}$;
   The new target position, $\mathbf{p}_{new}$;
1: **for** every $(\eta_i s_x, \eta_j s_y)$ in $\tilde{\mathbf{s}}_T$ **do**
2:    Sample the new search window $\mathbf{z}(\eta_i \eta_j)$ based on size $(\eta_i s_x, \eta_j s_y)$ and
      resize it to $\mathbf{s}_T$ with bilinear interpolation
3:    Calculate the corresponding response $\mathbf{R}(\eta_i \eta_j)$ in different scale space with Eqn. 5
4:    Apply displacement and appearance constrains with Eqn.9 and Eqn.10
5:    Get the best scale space and corresponding scale parameters
6:    Calculate the weighted displacement $\bar{\mathbf{d}}$ in best scale space with Eqn.11
7: **end for**
8:    Get the real displacement $\bar{\mathbf{d}}_r$ with scale parameters
9:    Get the new target position $\mathbf{p}_{new}$ with Eqn.13.
10: Get the new $\tilde{\mathbf{x}}$ and $\boldsymbol{\alpha}$ base on the new position $\mathbf{p}_{new}$ with Eqn.3.
11: Update $\tilde{\mathbf{x}}$ and $\boldsymbol{\alpha}$ with Equation 8.
12: **return** update $\tilde{\mathbf{x}}$ and $\boldsymbol{\alpha}$;

---

3   Experiments and Results

3.1   Dataset and Parameter Settings

Datasets and Resource. Our 2D liver ultrasound sequences are provided by MICCAI 2015 Challenge on Liver Ultrasound Tracking (CLUST) [16] training database, and it consists of five different datasets CIL, ETH, ICR, MED1 and MED2. Each dataset is acquired by different scanner with different image resolution (0.30–0.55 mm) and acquisition frequency (13–23 Hz). Besides, our code is implemented using MATLAB R2017b on an Intel Core i7-4910MQ CPU @ 2.90 GHz.

Parameter Settings. The parameters in our algorithm come from two parts. One is from the original KCF tracker and we adopt the default parameters as [11] recommends. The learning rate λ in Eqs. 2 and 3 sets to 10^{-4} ; the σ used in Gaussian function Eq. 4 sets to 0.2; the linear interpolation factor μ in Eq. 8 sets to 0.1; and the size of search window is 2.5 times to the size of target. Another part is from our contributions, which is used to ensure proposed tracker more accuracy and robust. We adopt scaling pool with the suggestion from our experienced radiologist $\eta = \{0.85, 0.90, 0.95, 1.00, 1.05, 1.10, 1.15\}$. And the recurrence factor β in Eq. 8, bandwidth of displacement σ_{dis} in Eq. 9 and the threshold of confidence response θ_{app} in Eq. 10 set to 0.15, 10 and 0.95 respectively. Parameters are same for all following experiments.

Note that proposed method needs image patches as initialization. Therefore, we generate a rectangular region manually with the guidance of experienced radiologist in the first frame. During online tracking process, the center of rectangular region is recorded and then used to evaluate tracking performance.

3.2   Tracking Results

We employ Euclidean distance suggested by Organizers of CLUST [16] to evaluate the tracking performance. In our experiments, we compute errors between each manual annotation and the output of proposed algorithm, and then mean, standard deviation (SD), 95%ile and maximum errors are counted. Additionally, processing speed is estimated by counting frames that are tracked per second (FPS).

Performance Evaluation on CLUST. Firstly, we evaluate the performance of proposed tracking algorithm using the five datasets of CLUST database. The number of objects means the total objects being tracked in corresponding dataset. The following Table 1 shows the tracking error distribution of each dataset and the total 2D ultrasound sequences respectively.

Comparison Proposed with Baseline Algorithm. Then a performance comparison experiment is performed between proposed and baseline algorithm, and the results are shown in Fig. 1.

Compared with baseline algorithm, proposed method achieves state-of-the-art results with mean decreasing by 78.8% (from 5.33 mm to 1.13 mm), 95%ile error decreasing by 77.1% (from 10.08 mm to 2.31 mm) and maximum error deceasing by 82.8% (from 66.10 mm to 11.37 mm) respectively.

Table 1. A summary for performance evaluation on CLUST. All tracking errors are in millimeters and processing speed is presented by frames per second.

Dataset	No. objects	Mean	SD	95%ile	Maximum	FPS
CIL	3	0.99	1.16	2.02	3.61	20.33
ETH	16	0.89	0.60	1.73	4.18	23.57
ICR	12	1.00	0.54	2.31	6.23	23.14
MED1	19	1.39	1.62	2.74	11.37	22.21
MED2	3	1.38	2.04	3.01	7.88	31.00
Total	53	1.13	1.07	2.31	11.37	23.22

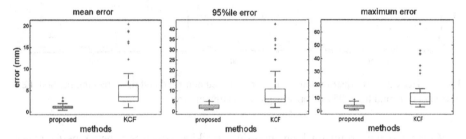

Fig. 1. Tracking errors comparison between proposed and baseline algorithm on CLUST. Left is mean tracking error; middle is 95%ile error; right is maximum error.

Comparison Proposed with State-of-the-art Algorithms. Extensive comparison experiments are performed among our tracker and some state-of-the-art trackers. The following Table 2 gives a summary of tracking error distribution. It is worth mentioning that we compare these algorithms whose tracking performance is also evaluated on CLUST training database. Compared with TMG [17], RMTwS [17] and Hybrid [18], proposed algorithm achieves a competitive accuracy with maximum tracking error decreasing by 40.4%–47.8%, which means it would provide a more effective guidance for clinical operation. Experimental results also indicate our tracker is more real time than the existing state-of-the-art trackers.

Table 2. Comparison of published results with our tracking results. All tracking errors are in millimeters and processing speed is presented by frames per second.

Algorithms	Mean	SD	95%ile	Maximum	FPS
Proposed	1.13	1.07	2.31	11.37	17–34
TMG [17]	1.17	0.89	2.61	21.78	8–23
RMTwS [17]	1.12	0.81	2.19	21.78	3–16
Hybrid [18]	0.80	0.80	1.85	19.08	8–32

3.3   Experimental Analysis

In this section, we first perform an ablation analysis to understand the benefit of scale adaptive strategy. Then a detailed parameters analysis are performed to find out the effectiveness of improved update rule (Eq. 8) and appearance/displacement (Eqs. 9 and 10) constraints.

Ablation Study About Scale Adaptive Strategy. Deformation is common in liver ultrasound sequence. In this part, we perform a comparison experiment between non-rigid (with Eq. 6) and rigid (without Eq. 6) tracking. Results are shown in Fig. 2.

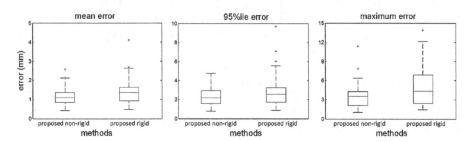

Fig. 2. Tracking error distributions (mm) for proposed non-rigid and rigid tracking method. Left is mean error; middle is 95%ile error, right is maximum error.

Compared with rigid tracking, non-rigid tracking achieves a better performance with mean decreasing by 20.4% (from 1.42 mm to 1.13 mm), 95%ile error decreasing by 19.5% (from 2.87 mm to 2.31 mm) and maximum error deceasing by 18.1% (from 13.88 mm to 11.37 mm) respectively. That means non-rigid deformation should be considered seriously in precise radiotherapy.

Figure 3 shows an instance to compare the results from non-rigid and rigid tracking. The target position calculated by rigid tracking yields larger deviations, by contrast, the positions from proposed method are more accurate and robust.

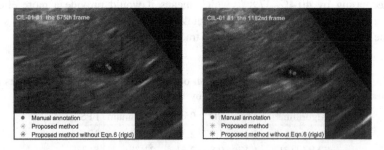

Fig. 3. An example for showing deviation between non-rigid and rigid tracking. Images are both from CIL-01 #1 in CLUST. Left is the 675th frame and right is the 1182nd frame.

Parameters Analysis. There are four parameters, $[\eta, \sigma_{dis}, \theta_{app}, \beta]$, needing more discussion. Among them, scaling pool η can be designed when the deformation of target is estimated. And we also can determine σ_{dis} by magnitude of target motion and frequency of image acquisition. However, θ_{app} and β are assigned empirically. In this part, we investigate the effect when we change the threshold of confidence response and recurrence factor. Without loss of generality, we choose $\theta_{app} \in [0.90, 0.95, 1.00]$ and $\beta \in [0.10, 0.15, 0.20]$ to perform parameters analysis on CLUST training database. Here, mean and 95%ile tracking errors, as regardful indicators for our project, are chosen to evaluate the results of parameters analysis. Results are shown in Fig. 4 and Table 3.

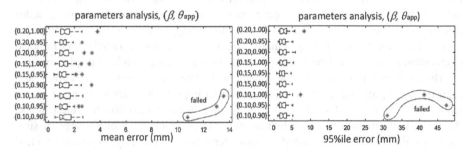

Fig. 4. The results of parameters analysis on CLUST. Left is results of mean error and right is results of 95%ile error with parameters (β, θ_{app}) changing.

Table 3. Statistic results of mean and 95%ile errors (mm) with (β, θ_{app}) changing.

(β, θ_{app})	(0.10,0.90)	(0.10,0.95)	(0.10,1.00)	(0.15,0.90)	(0.15,0.95)
mean	1.45	1.43	1.53	1.24	1.13
95%ile	3.23	3.36	3.54	2.54	2.31
(β, θ_{app})	(0.15,1.00)	(0.20,0.90)	(0.20,0.95)	(0.20,1.00)	
mean	1.26	1.24	1.18	1.32	
95%ile	2.65	2.56	2.43	2.78	

Therefore, recurrence factor is a crucial parameter in proposed algorithm. A smaller β has a terrible effect on long-term tracking (like $\beta = 0.10$, see Fig. 4). But a larger one would also enlarge tracking error by unduly limiting learning ability for proposed method. Besides, a smaller or larger θ_{app} are not a wise chose, which would potentially introduce more unreasonable position or be not adaptive for artifacts well respectively. Therefore, (0.15, 0.95) is a better combination for accuracy and robust tracking in our project.

4 Conclusion and Discussion

In this paper, we present a 2D real-time tracking approach, which consists four steps namely (1) initial target regions selection, (2) tracking with scale adaptive kernel correlation filter, (3) displacement and appearance constrains, and (4) weighted displacement. The initial target regions are generated by our experienced radiologist. Then we train an online classifier to predict targets position. Because deformation of targets can lead to error accumulation in learning phase, we employ adaptive scale strategy to mitigate this adverse effect. Considering US images suffer from acoustic shadowing and speckle decorrelation, NCC is more susceptible to bias. We employ displacement and appearance constrains to constrict unreasonable position prediction by carefully investigating the motion extents of landmarks in liver under free breathing. Furthermore, with prior knowledge that target motion in liver is approximately periodic under free breathing, we revise the update rule by introducing a recurrence factor to improve robustness in long-term tracking. Finally, inspired by success of particle filter in noise circumstance, we obtain new target positions by calculating weighted displacement.

However, we just adopt single feature to realize target tracking. Accuracy and robustness for proposed method may continue to improve by combining other image features like texture and shape, which is a major research direction for future work. Also, similarity metrics is a core ingredient for target tracking. While a large of similarity metrics have been proposed in computer vision community, there are no clear rules about how to select the most suitable one but to try them in different condition.

There are several avenues of future work that would potentially improve proposed method. Integrating texture feature into our tracking method would be helpful to improve accuracy. And adaptive recurrence factor strategy will be investigated to improve robustness for long-time tracking.

In conclusion, we propose an online learning approach for robust and real-time motion tracking in liver ultrasound sequences and evaluate it on five different datasets. Favorable agreement between automatically and manually tracked displacements, along with real-time processing speed prove that proposed algorithm has potential for target motion tracking in abdominal radiotherapy.

Acknowledgement. This work is supported in part by Knowledge Innovation Program of Basic Research Projects of Shenzhen under Grant JCYJ20160428182053361, in part by Guangdong Science and Technology Plan under Grant 2017B020210003 and in part by National Natural Science Foundation of China under Grant 81771940, 81427803.

References

1. Riley, C., Yang, Y., Li, T., Zhang, Y., Heron, D.E., Huq, M.S.: Dosimetric evaluation of the interplay effect in respiratory-gated RapidArc radiation therapy. Med. Phys. **41**, 011715 (2014)
2. Jenne, J.W., Preusser, T., Günther, M.: High-intensity focused ultrasound: principles, therapy guidance, simulations and applications. Zeitschrift Für Medizinische Physik **22**, 311–322 (2012)

3. Okada, A., et al.: A case of hepatocellular carcinoma treated by MR-guided focused ultrasound ablation with respiratory gating. Magn. Reson. Med. Sci. Mrms Off. J. Jpn. Soc. Magn. Reson. Med. **5**, 167 (2006)
4. Kothary, N., Dieterich, S., Louie, J.D., Chang, D.T., Hofmann, L.V., Sze, D.Y.: Percutaneous implantation of fiducial markers for imaging-guided radiation therapy. AJR Am. J. Roentgenol. **192**, 1090–1096 (2009)
5. de Senneville, B.D., Mougenot, C., Moonen, C.T.: Real-time adaptive methods for treatment of mobile organs by MRI-controlled high-intensity focused ultrasound. Magn. Reson. Med. **57**, 319–330 (2007)
6. Rank, C.M., et al.: 4D respiratory motion-compensated image reconstruction of free-breathing radial MR data with very high undersampling. Magn. Reson. Med. **77**, 1170 (2016)
7. De Luca, V., Tschannen, M., Székely, G., Tanner, C.: A learning-based approach for fast and robust vessel tracking in long ultrasound sequences. In: Mori, K., Sakuma, I., Sato, Y., Barillot, C., Navab, N. (eds.) MICCAI 2013. LNCS, vol. 8149, pp. 518–525. Springer, Heidelberg (2013). https://doi.org/10.1007/978-3-642-40811-3_65
8. Chuang, B., Hsu, J.H., Kuo, L.C., Jou, I., Su, F.C., Sun, Y.N.: Tendon-motion tracking in an ultrasound image sequence using optical-flow-based block matching. Biomed. Eng. Online **16**, 47 (2017)
9. Carletti, M., Dall'Alba, D., Cristani, M., Fiorini, P.: A robust particle filtering approach with spatially-dependent template selection for medical ultrasound tracking applications. In: 11th International Conference on Computer Vision Theory and Applications, pp. 522–531. SCITE Press, Rome (2016)
10. Royer, L., Krupa, A., Dardenne, G., Le, B.A., Marchand, E., Marchal, M.: Real-time target tracking of soft tissues in 3D ultrasound images based on robust visual information and mechanical simulation. Med. Image Anal. **35**, 582–598 (2017)
11. Henriques, J.F., Caseiro, R., Martins, P., Batista, J.: High-speed tracking with kernelized correlation filters. IEEE Trans. Pattern Anal. Mach. Intell. **37**, 583–596 (2015)
12. Wu, Y., Lim, J., Yang, M.H.: Online object tracking: a benchmark. In: IEEE Conference on Computer Vision and Pattern Recognition, pp. 2411–2418. IEEE press, Portland (2013)
13. Li, Y., Zhu, J.: A scale adaptive kernel correlation filter tracker with feature integration. In: Agapito, L., Bronstein, Michael M., Rother, C. (eds.) ECCV 2014. LNCS, vol. 8926, pp. 254–265. Springer, Cham (2015). https://doi.org/10.1007/978-3-319-16181-5_18
14. Liang, T., Yung, L., Yu, W.: On feature motion decorrelation in ultrasound speckle tracking. IEEE Trans. Med. Imaging **32**, 435–448 (2016)
15. Lei, P., Moeslein, F., Wood, B.J., Shekhar, R.: Real-time tracking of liver motion and deformation using a flexible needle. Int. J. Comput. Assist. Radiol. Surg. **6**, 435–446 (2011)
16. Luca, V.D., et al.: The 2014 liver ultrasound tracking benchmark. Phys. Med. Biol. **60**, 5571–5599 (2015)
17. Ozkan, E., Tanner, C., Kastelic, M., Mattausch, O., Makhinya, M., Goksel, O.: Robust motion tracking in liver from 2D ultrasound images using supporters. Int. J. Comput. Assist. Radiol. Surg. **12**, 941–950 (2017)
18. Williamson, T., Cheung, W., Roberts, S.K., Chauhan, S.: Ultrasound-based liver tracking utilizing a hybrid template/optical flow approach. Int. J. Comput. Assist. Radiol. Surg. **13**, 1–11 (2018)

Set-to-Set Distance Metric Learning on SPD Manifolds

Zhi Gao, Yuwei Wu$^{(\boxtimes)}$, and Yunde Jia

Beijing Laboratory of Intelligent Information Technology,
School of Computer Science, Beijing Institute of Technology (BIT),
Beijing 100081, People's Republic of China
{gaozhi_2017,wuyuwei,jiayunde}@bit.edu.cn

Abstract. The Symmetric Positive Definite (SPD) matrix on the Riemannian manifold has become a prevalent representation in many computer vision tasks. However, learning a proper distance metric between two SPD matrices is still a challenging problem. Existing metric learning methods of SPD matrices only regard an SPD matrix as a global representation and thus ignore different roles of intrinsic properties in the SPD matrix. In this paper, we propose a novel SPD matrix metric learning method of discovering SPD matrix intrinsic properties and measuring the distance considering different roles of intrinsic properties. In particular, the intrinsic properties of an SPD matrix are discovered by projecting the SPD matrix to multiple low-dimensional SPD manifolds, and the obtained low-dimensional SPD matrices constitute a set. Accordingly, the metric between two original SPD matrices is transformed into a set-to-set metric on multiple low-dimensional SPD manifolds. Based on the learnable alpha-beta divergence, the set-to-set metric is computed by summarizing multiple alpha-beta divergences assigned on low-dimensional SPD manifolds, which models different roles of intrinsic properties. The experimental results on four visual tasks demonstrate that our method achieves the state-of-the art performance.

Keywords: SPD manifold · Metric learning · Set-to-set metric
Multiple manifolds

1 Introduction

The Symmetric Positive Definite (SPD) matrix has become a prevalent representation in many visual tasks, such as face recognition [12], action recognition [30], and object detection [25]. It utilizes the second-order or higher-order statistics information to capture the desirable feature distribution. There are several works try to model a more discriminative SPD matrix [16,27,28] from local features. Meanwhile, calculating the distance metric in the SPD manifold is a crucial problem coming along with the SPD matrix representation. Due to the no-Euclidean structure of SPD manifolds, the Euclidean metric can't be applied

J.-H. Lai et al. (Eds.): PRCV 2018, LNCS 11258, pp. 452–464, 2018.
https://doi.org/10.1007/978-3-030-03338-5_38

directly on it. In this paper, we focus on a robust metric learning method on SPD manifolds.

Many efforts have been devoted to the SPD matrix metric, such as the Affine Invariant Metric (AIM) [19], Log-Euclidean Metric (LEM) [2], Bregman divergence [14], Stein divergence [21], and alpha-beta divergence [3,4,22]. Given a concrete metric, metric learning aims at learning proper metric parameters that keep similar pairs close and separate dissimilar pairs. Most of the existing metric learning methods on the SPD manifold learn a discriminative metric on the tangent Euclidean space [11,23,31].

However, how to learn a proper SPD matrix metric is still a challenging problem. The SPD matrix is aggregated from local features, and contains different essential intrinsic properties. Existing SPD matrix metric learning methods [11,23,31] just regard an SPD matrix as a global representation and exploit a direct metric on the complex manifold, ignoring the different roles of intrinsic properties in the SPD matrix. It is unsuitable to treat intrinsic properties equally when they have different roles, *e.g.,* different distribution or significance. Therefore, we argue that an SPD matrix metric modeling different roles of intrinsic properties will achieve a better performance.

In this paper, a novel metric learning method on SPD manifolds is proposed to solve the issues mentioned above. Firstly we discover intrinsic properties of an SPD matrix, and then calculate the SPD matrix metric considering different roles of them. In particular, our method aims to jointly learn multiple low-dimensional projections and a set-to-set metric. As the property discovery can be seen as the feature extraction, we apply multiple low-dimensional manifold projections on the SPD matrix to discover discriminative intrinsic properties. Thus, the distance metric between two original SPD matrices is transformed into the distance metric between the two sets which contain several corresponding projected low-dimensional SPD matrices. The alpha-beta divergences is a learnable SPD matrix metric, so it is applied in our set-to-set metric to be adaptive to the intrinsic property. We assign multiple alpha-beta divergences on different low-dimensional manifolds as the sub-metrics and summarize these sub-metrics discriminatively as the SPD matrix metric. Through this, the different roles of intrinsic properties are involved in the SPD matrix metric. Evaluated by experiments, the proposed learnable metric is extremely helpful to capture meaningful nearest neighbors of different original SPD matrices.

In summary, our contributions are three-fold.

(1) We propose a robust SPD matrix metric learning method of discovering discriminative intrinsic properties and modeling their different roles in metric computation.
(2) We formulate the metric learning as the two-component joint optimization problem, *i.e.,* multiple low-dimensional manifold projections and a set-to-set metric are learned jointly.
(3) We introduce the manifold optimization method which can learn metric parameters to guarantee the robustness of the proposed metric.

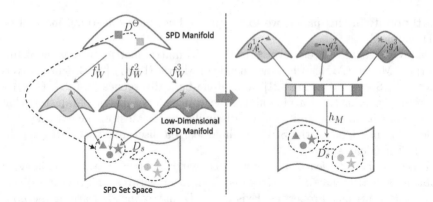

Fig. 1. The flowchart of our SPD matrix metric learning method. Left: multiple projections f_W^1, f_W^2, and f_W^3 used to discover intrinsic properties; Right: the computation of the set-to-set distance D_s which considers different roles of intrinsic properties.

2　The Proposed Method

Throughout this paper, scalars are denoted by the lower-case letters; the vectors are represented by the bold lower-case letters; the matrices are denoted by the upper-case letters; the sets are represented by the bold upper-case letters.

2.1　Problem Definition

This work aims to discover discriminative intrinsic properties in an SPD matrix and compute the distance of SPD matrices considering different roles of discovered properties. The property discovery can be regarded as a feature extraction process that projects an original SPD matrix to multiple low-dimensional SPD manifolds to form a set of the low-dimensional SPD matrices. We propose a set-to-set metric to consider different roles of intrinsic properties. Individual sub-metrics are assigned on low-dimensional manifolds and summarized discriminatively. Consequently, our metric learning method is composed of two components, multiple low-dimensional manifold projections and a set-to-set metric. Given two SPD matrices X_i and X_j, the distance $D^{\Theta}(X_i, X_j)$ is

$$
\begin{aligned}
D^{\Theta}(X_i, X_j) &= D_s(\mathbf{X}_i, \mathbf{X}_j) \\
&= D_s\Big(\{f_W^1(X_i), \cdots, f_W^m(X_i)\}, \{f_W^1(X_j), \cdots, f_W^m(X_j)\}\Big) \\
&= h_M\Big(g_A^1\big(f_W^1(X_i), f_W^1(X_j)\big), \cdots, g_A^m\big(f_W^m(X_i), f_W^m(X_j)\big)\Big),
\end{aligned}
\tag{1}
$$

where $f_W^k(\cdot)$ is the low-dimensional manifold projection, and $\mathbf{X}_i = \{f_W^k(X_i)\}_{k=1}^m$ is the set containing low-dimensional SPD matrices. The distance $D^{\Theta}(X_i, X_j)$ between original SPD matrices X_i and X_j is transformed into a set-to-set distance $D_s(\mathbf{X}_i, \mathbf{X}_j)$, where the sub-metric on the k-th low-dimensional manifold is calculated by $g_A^k(\cdot,\cdot)$ and all sub-metrics of properties are summarized by $h_M(\cdot)$. W, A, M are the projection parameter, the sub-metric parameter, and the summarization parameter, respectively. We exploit a learnable parameter set $\Theta = \{W, A, M\}$ to represent the parameters. The framework of our metric learning method for the SPD matrix is shown in Fig. 1.

The goal of metric learning is to learn the metric parameter Θ from an SPD matrix similar pair set $\mathcal{S}$, a dissimilar pair set $\mathcal{D}$, and their labels Y, where $y_{ij} = 1$ means X_i and X_j are similar, otherwise $y_{ij} = 0$. The metric parameter Θ can be learned by optimizing the loss function $\mathcal{L}(\Theta, \mathcal{S}, \mathcal{D}, Y)$ which is the punishment of both far similar sample pairs and close dissimilar sample pairs. We define $\mathcal{L}(\Theta, \mathcal{S}, \mathcal{D}, Y)$ in the following subsection. Moreover, we impose the manifold constraints on W and M to obtain a more robust metric.

2.2   Multiple Low-Dimensional Manifold Projections

For an SPD matrix sample $X_i \in \mathbb{R}^{n \times n}$, we project X_i to m low-dimensional manifolds to discover the intrinsic properties,

$$X_i^1 = f_W^1(X_i) = W_1^\top X_i W_1$$
$$\cdots \tag{2}$$
$$X_i^m = f_W^m(X_i) = W_m^\top X_i W_m,$$

where $X_i^k \in \mathbb{R}^{p \times p}$ is the k-th low-dimensional SPD matrix, $k \in \{1, 2, \cdots, m\}$. An SPD matrix X_i is projected to a set $\mathbf{X}_i = \{X_i^k\}_{k=1}^m$, which contains several low-dimensional SPD matrices.

We expect that each low-dimensional matrix X_i^k is guaranteed to be still an SPD matrix having the ability of capturing desirable feature distribution, and any two low-dimensional SPD manifolds are unrelated to preserve as much information as possible in the low-dimensional SPD matrix set. The learnable parameter W_k needs to be a column full rank matrix to make X_i^k be an SPD matrix as well. Based on the affine invariance [3,7] of the alpha-beta divergence, we relax the column full rank constraint of W_k to the semi-orthogonal constraint, i.e., $W_k^\top W_k = I_p$. In order to preserve more information in the $\mathbf{X}_i = \{X_i^k\}_{k=1}^m$ set, we expect that any two low-dimensional manifolds have a low relevance. For any $k \neq l$, we set $W_k^\top W_l = \mathbf{0}$, where $\mathbf{0} \in \mathbb{R}^{p \times p}$ is a matrix whose elements are all "0"s, to reduce relevance between X_i^k and X_i^l. These low-dimensional SPD manifolds can be seen as analogies of different PCA subspaces. A total projection matrix W is composed of all W_k, $W = [W_1, W_2, \cdots, W_m] \in \mathbb{R}^{n \times mp}$, in which W_k is a partitioned matrix of W containing p columns. Note that, W is a semi-orthogonal matrix, i.e., $W^\top W = I_{mp}$, which is on the non-Euclidean Stiefel manifold [1].

2.3   The Set-to-Set Metric

Based on multiple manifold projections, the distance $D^\Theta(X_i, X_j)$ of two SPD matrices is transformed into the set-to-set distance $D_s(\mathbf{X}_i, \mathbf{X}_j)$. Firstly

$\{g_A^k(\cdot,\cdot)\}_{k=1}^m$ is exploited to compute sub-metrics on m low-dimensional SPD manifolds, and then $h_M(\cdot)$ is utilized to summarize the m sub-metrics, where A and M are learnable parameters. We use the flexible alpha-beta divergence [3,4,22] as the sub-metric $g_A^k(\cdot,\cdot)$. For two SPD sets $\mathbf{X}_i = \{X_i^k\}_{k=1}^m$, $\mathbf{X}_j = \{X_j^k\}_{k=1}^m$, the distance d_{ij}^k between X_i^k and X_j^k is computed by the k-th alpha-beta divergence,

$$d_{ij}^k = g_A^k(X_i^k, X_j^k) = D^{(\alpha_k,\beta_k)}\left(X_i^k \| X_j^k\right) = \frac{1}{\alpha_k \beta_k} \sum_{u=1}^p log\left(\frac{\alpha_k(\lambda_{iju}^k)^{\beta_k} + \beta_k(\lambda_{iju}^k)^{-\alpha_k}}{\alpha_k + \beta_k}\right),$$
(3)

where λ_{iju}^k is the u-th eigenvalue of $X_i^k(X_j^k)^{-1}$, and (α_k, β_k) is the individual parameter of the k-th alpha-beta divergence. We denote all alpha-beta divergence parameters as a matrix $A = [(\alpha_1,\beta_1),(\alpha_2,\beta_2),...,(\alpha_m,\beta_m)] \in \mathbb{R}^{m \times 2}$, and a distance vector between $\mathbf{X}_i$ and $\mathbf{X}_j$ as $\mathbf{d}_{ij} = [d_{ij}^1, d_{ij}^2, ..., d_{ij}^m] \in \mathbb{R}^{m \times 1}$. Since (α_k, β_k) needs to be adaptive to the k-th low-dimensional manifold, we exploit a learnable strategy to update (α_k, β_k), which is detailed in the next subsection. After computing all sub-metrics, the distance metric $D^\Theta(X_i, X_j)$ between two original SPD matrices X_i and X_j is formulated as

$$D^\Theta(X_i, X_j) = D_s(\mathbf{X}_i, \mathbf{X}_j) = h_M(d_{ij}^1, d_{ij}^2, ..., d_{ij}^m) = \mathbf{d}_{ij}^\top M \mathbf{d}_{ij}$$
$$= \sum_{k=1}^m \sum_{l=1}^m \left(D^{(\alpha_k,\beta_k)}(W_k^\top X_i W_k \| W_k^\top X_j W_k) \cdot M_{kl} \cdot D^{(\alpha_l,\beta_l)}(W_l^\top X_i W_l \| W_l^\top X_j W_l)\right),$$
(4)

where $M \in \mathbb{R}^{m \times m}$ is the metric parameter, and M_{kl} is an element of M in the k-th row and l-th column, reflecting the significance and relationship of properties. If $X_i = X_j$, then $\mathbf{d}_{ij}$ is a zero vector, and $D^\Theta(X_i, X_j) = 0$. If $X_i \neq X_j$, then $\mathbf{d}_{ij}$ is a non-zero vector, and $D^\Theta(X_i, X_j)$ should be larger than 0. The nonnegativity of the metric forces M to be an SPD matrix and $M \in Sym_m^+$.

To learn the parameter Θ, we formulate loss function $\mathcal{L}(\Theta, \mathcal{S}, \mathcal{D}, Y)$ as

$$\min_\Theta \mathcal{L}(\Theta, \mathcal{S}, \mathcal{D}, Y) = \frac{1}{|\mathcal{S}|} \sum_{i,j \in \mathcal{S}} y_{ij} \cdot max\left(D^\Theta(X_i, X_j) - \zeta_s, 0\right)^2$$
$$+ \frac{1}{|\mathcal{D}|} \sum_{i,j \in \mathcal{D}} (1 - y_{ij}) \cdot max\left(\zeta_d - D^\Theta(X_i, X_j), 0\right)^2 \quad (5)$$
$$+ \xi \cdot \gamma(M, M_0).$$

We expect that the distance between similar samples is smaller than a threshold ζ_s, and the distance between dissimilar samples is larger than a threshold ζ_d. We add two coefficients $\frac{1}{|\mathcal{S}|}$ and $\frac{1}{|\mathcal{D}|}$ to solve the imbalance issue of similar and dissimilar sample pairs, where $|\mathcal{S}|$ and $|\mathcal{D}|$ are the pair numbers of sets $\mathcal{S}$ and $\mathcal{D}$. In addition, we add a regularization term $\xi \cdot \gamma(M, M_0)$ on M in Eq. (5). $\gamma(M, M_0) = Tr(MM_0^{-1}) - logdet(MM_0^{-1}) - m$ is the burgman divergence [5,8, 10], where $Tr(\cdot)$ is the trace of a matrix, M_0 is the prior information, and ξ is the trade-off coefficient.

2.4   Optimization

$\mathcal{L}(\Theta, \mathcal{S}, \mathcal{D}, Y)$ in Eq. (5) is not a convex function with respect to W, A, and M. Accordingly, we apply the gradient descent to learn Θ. The gradients are computed as follows.

(1) The gradient of $\mathcal{L}$ with respect to M
The gradient of $\mathcal{L}$ with respect to M can be computed by

$$\nabla_M(\mathcal{L}) = \frac{1}{|\mathcal{S}|} \sum_{i,j \in \mathcal{S}} \mathbf{d}_{ij} \nabla_{D_{ij}^{\Theta}}(\mathcal{L}) \mathbf{d}_{ij}^{\top} + \frac{1}{|\mathcal{D}|} \sum_{i,j \in \mathcal{D}} \mathbf{d}_{ij} \nabla_{D_{ij}^{\Theta}}(\mathcal{L}) \mathbf{d}_{ij}^{\top} + \xi \cdot \nabla_M(\gamma(M, M_0)), \tag{6}$$

where $\nabla_{D_{ij}^{\Theta}}(\mathcal{L})$ is the gradient of $\mathcal{L}$ with respect to $D^{\Theta}(X_i, X_j)$,

$$\nabla_{D_{ij}^{\Theta}}(\mathcal{L}) = 2 \cdot y_{ij} \cdot max(D_{ij}^{\Theta} - \zeta_s, 0) + 2 \cdot (y_{ij} - 1) \cdot max(\zeta_d - D_{ij}^{\Theta}, 0), \tag{7}$$

and $\nabla_M(\gamma(M, M_0))$ is the gradient of $\gamma(M, M_0)$ with respect to M,

$$\nabla_M(\gamma(M, M_0)) = M_0^{-1} - M^{-1}. \tag{8}$$

(2) The gradient of $\mathcal{L}$ with respect to A
The gradients of $\mathcal{L}$ with respect to α_k and β_k in A are

$$\nabla_{\alpha_k}(\mathcal{L}) = \frac{1}{|\mathcal{S}|} \sum_{i,j \in \mathcal{S}} \nabla_{d_{ij}^k}(\mathcal{L}) \cdot \nabla_{\alpha_k}(d_{ij}^k) + \frac{1}{|\mathcal{D}|} \sum_{i,j \in \mathcal{D}} \nabla_{d_{ij}^k}(\mathcal{L}) \cdot \nabla_{\alpha_k}(d_{ij}^k), \tag{9}$$

$$\nabla_{\beta_k}(\mathcal{L}) = \frac{1}{|\mathcal{S}|} \sum_{i,j \in \mathcal{S}} \nabla_{d_{ij}^k}(\mathcal{L}) \cdot \nabla_{\beta_k}(d_{ij}^k) + \frac{1}{|\mathcal{D}|} \sum_{i,j \in \mathcal{D}} \nabla_{d_{ij}^k}(\mathcal{L}) \cdot \nabla_{\beta_k}(d_{ij}^k). \tag{10}$$

$\nabla_{d_{ij}^k}(\mathcal{L})$ is the k-th element of $\nabla_{\mathbf{d}_{ij}}(\mathcal{L})$ which is the gradient of $\mathcal{L}$ with respect to $\mathbf{d}_{ij}$,

$$\nabla_{\mathbf{d}_{ij}}(\mathcal{L}) = \nabla_{D_{ij}^{\Theta}}(\mathcal{L}) \cdot \nabla_{\mathbf{d}_{ij}}(D_{ij}^{\Theta}) = \nabla_{D_{ij}^{\Theta}}(\mathcal{L}) \mathbf{d}_{ij}^{\top}(M^{\top} + M). \tag{11}$$

$\nabla_{\alpha_k}(d_{ij}^k)$ and $\nabla_{\beta_k}(d_{ij}^k)$ are the gradients of d_{ij}^k with respect to α_k and β_k, respectively,

$$\begin{aligned}
\nabla_{\alpha_k}(d_{ij}^k) =& \frac{1}{\alpha_k^2 \beta_k} \sum_{u=1}^{p} \left(\frac{\alpha_k(\lambda_{iju}^k)^{\beta_k} - \alpha_k \beta_k(\lambda_{iju}^k)^{-\alpha_k} log\lambda_{iju}^k}{\alpha_k(\lambda_{iju}^k)^{\beta_k} + \beta_k(\lambda_{iju}^k)^{-\alpha_k}} \right. \\
& \left. - \frac{\alpha_k}{\alpha_k + \beta_k} - log\frac{\alpha_k(\lambda_{iju}^k)^{\beta_k} + \beta_k(\lambda_{iju}^k)^{-\alpha_k}}{\alpha_k + \beta_k} \right),
\end{aligned} \tag{12}$$

$$\nabla_{\beta_k}(d_{ij}^k) = \frac{1}{\alpha_k \beta_k^2} \sum_{u=1}^{p} \left(\frac{\beta_k (\lambda_{iju}^k)^{-\alpha_k} - \alpha_k \beta_k (\lambda_{iju}^k)^{\beta_k} log \lambda_{iju}^k}{\alpha_k (\lambda_{iju}^k)^{\beta_k} + \beta_k (\lambda_{iju}^k)^{-\alpha_k}} \right. \tag{13}$$
$$\left. - \frac{\beta_k}{\alpha_k + \beta_k} - log \frac{\alpha_k (\lambda_{iju}^k)^{\beta_k} + \beta_k (\lambda_{iju}^k)^{-\alpha_k}}{\alpha_k + \beta_k} \right).$$

(3) The gradient of $\mathcal{L}$ with respect to W

The gradient of $\mathcal{L}$ with respect to each W_k is

$$\nabla_{W_k}(\mathcal{L}) = \sum_{i}^{N} \left((X_i)^\top W_k \nabla_{X_i^k}(\mathcal{L}) + X_i W_k \nabla_{X_i^k}(\mathcal{L})^\top \right), \tag{14}$$

where N is the number of training samples, and $N = 2 \times (|\mathcal{S}| + |\mathcal{D}|)$. $\nabla_{X_i^k}(\mathcal{L})$ is the gradient of $\mathcal{L}$ with respect to the low-dimensional SPD matrix X_i^k. The eigenvalue decomposition of $X_i^k (X_j^k)^{-1}$ is $X_i^k (X_j^k)^{-1} = U_{ij}^k \Sigma_{ij}^k (U_{ij}^k)^\top$. Σ_{ij}^k is the diagonal matrix eigenvalues, and λ_{iju}^k is the u-th eigenvalue. The gradients $\nabla_{X_i^k}(\mathcal{L})$ and $\nabla_{X_j^k}(\mathcal{L})$ are

$$\nabla_{X_i^k}(\mathcal{L}) = U_{ij}^k \nabla_{\Sigma_{ij}^k}(\mathcal{L})(U_{ij}^k)^\top (X_i^k)^{-\top}, \tag{15}$$

$$\nabla_{X_j^k}(\mathcal{L}) = (-1) \cdot (X_j^k)^{-\top} (X_i^k)^\top U_{ij}^k \nabla_{\Sigma_{ij}^k}(\mathcal{L})(U_{ij}^k)^\top (X_j^k)^{-\top}, \tag{16}$$

where $\nabla_{\Sigma_{ij}^k}(\mathcal{L})$ is the gradient of Σ_{ij}^k with respect to $\mathcal{L}$. $\nabla_{\Sigma_{ij}^k}(\mathcal{L})$ is a diagonal matrix, and the u-th element is

$$\nabla_{\lambda_{iju}^k}(\mathcal{L}) = \nabla_{d_{ij}^k}(\mathcal{L}) \cdot \nabla_{\lambda_{iju}^k}(d_{ij}^k)$$
$$= \nabla_{d_{ij}^k}(\mathcal{L}) \cdot \frac{1}{\alpha_k \beta_k} \frac{\alpha_k \beta_k (\lambda_{iju}^k)^{\beta_k - 1} - \alpha_k \beta_k (\lambda_{iju}^k)^{-\alpha_k - 1}}{\alpha_k (\lambda_{iju}^k)^{\beta_k} + \beta_k (\lambda_{iju}^k)^{-\alpha_k}}. \tag{17}$$

Since the gradients $\nabla_W(\mathcal{L})$, $\nabla_M(\mathcal{L})$, and $\nabla_A(\mathcal{L})$ are obtained, the metric parameter set Θ can be updated. A is optimized by the standard gradient descent, $A := A - \eta \nabla_A(\mathcal{L})$, where η is the learning rate. W and M are updated by the Riemannian optimization algorithm [1,6,20]. The computation details are presented below,

$$\begin{cases} \nabla_{W_R}(\mathcal{L}) = \nabla_W(\mathcal{L}) - W\frac{1}{2}(W^\top \nabla_W(\mathcal{L}) + \nabla_W(\mathcal{L})^\top W) \\ W := q(W - \eta \nabla_{W_R}(\mathcal{L})) \end{cases}, \tag{18}$$

and

$$\begin{cases} \nabla_{M_R}(\mathcal{L}) = M\frac{1}{2}(\nabla_M(\mathcal{L}) + \nabla_M(\mathcal{L})^\top)M \\ M := M^{\frac{1}{2}} expm\left(-\eta M^{-\frac{1}{2}} \nabla_{M_R}(\mathcal{L})M^{-\frac{1}{2}} \right)M^{\frac{1}{2}} \end{cases}, \tag{19}$$

where $\nabla_{W_R}(\mathcal{L})$ and $\nabla_{M_R}(\mathcal{L})$ are the Riemannian gradients with respect to W and M. In Eq. (18), $q(\cdot)$ is the retraction operation mapping the data back to the Stiefel manifold. $q(W)$ denotes the Q matrix of the QR decomposition to a matrix W, i.e., for the matrix $W \in \mathbb{R}^{n \times p}$, $W = QR$, where $Q \in \mathbb{R}^{n \times p}$ is a semi-orthogonal matrix and $R \in \mathbb{R}^{p \times p}$ is a upper triangular matrix. In Eq. (19), $expm(\cdot)$ is the matrix exponential function. We summarize the learning process of our method in Algorithm 1, w.

Algorithm 1. Trainging Process of Our Method

Input: Training SPD sample pairs $\mathcal{S}$ and $\mathcal{D}$, labels Y. The initial projection matrix W. The initial metric matrix M. The initial alpha-beta divergence parameter A. Learning rate η.

Output: The learned W, M, and A.

1: **while** not converge **do**
2:     For each SPD matrix, compute subspaces by Eq.(2).
3:     For each sample pairs, compute the distance between their sets by Eq.(3) and Eq.(4).
4:     Compute the loss $\mathcal{L}$ by Eq.(5).
5:     Compute the gradient $\nabla_M(\mathcal{L})$ by Eq.(7), Eq.(8), and Eq.(6).
6:     Compute the gradient $\nabla_A(\mathcal{L})$ by Eq.(12), Eq.(13), Eq.(9), and Eq.(10).
7:     Compute the gradient $\nabla_W(\mathcal{L})$ by Eq.(17), Eq.(15), Eq.(16), and Eq.(14).
8:     Update the parameter W by Eq.(18).
9:     Update the parameter A by $A := A - \eta \nabla_A(\mathcal{L})$.
10:     Update the parameter M by Eq.(19).
11: **end while**
12: **return** W, M and A

---

3   Experiments

In order to test the efficiency of our method, we conduct experiments on the object recognition, video-based face recognition, action recognition, and texture classification tasks. Four datasets are utilized: the ETH-80 [15], the MSR-Action3D [17], the YouTube Celebrities (YTC) [13], and the UIUC [18] datasets.

3.1   Datasets and Settings

The ETH-80 is an object image dataset, which contains 80 image sets of eight categories. Each category consists of 10 image sets, and each set includes 41 images captured under different views. In our experiment, all the images of the ETH-80 are resized to 20×20 and denoted by the intensity features. The YTC is a video-based face dataset, collecting 1910 videos of 47 persons. Face regions are detected from each frame by a cascaded face detector and resized to 30×30, followed by the histogram equalized operation, and represented by the gray values. The MSR-Action3D is a 3D action dataset, containing totally 567 videos of 20 actions. There are 20 skeleton joints in the body of actions. In the experiments, each frame is represented by a 120-dimensional feature, which is the 3D coordinate differences of skeleton joints between this frame and its two neighborhood frames. The UIUC material dataset contains 216 samples of 18 categories. We resize each image to 400×400. Then 128-dimensional dense SIFT features are extracted from each image with 4-pixel space concatenated by 27-dimensional RGB color features from 3×3 patches centered at the locations of dense SIFT features.

On the ETH-80, YTC, and UIUC datasets, we compute a covariance matrix C to represent each sample and add a small ridge δI to avoid the matrix singularity, where $\delta = 0.001 \times Tr(C)$. On the MSR-Action3D dataset, we first compute the covariance matrix C with size of 120×120, then transform it to a 121×121 Gaussian distribution SPD matrix, $C = |C|^{-\frac{1}{121}} \begin{bmatrix} C + \mathbf{mm}^T & \mathbf{m} \\ \mathbf{m}^T & 1 \end{bmatrix}$ as the sample representation, where $\mathbf{m}$ is the mean vector of 120-dimensional features. Following the standard protocols [7,11,24,29], for each category, we randomly select half of the samples for training and the rest for testing on the ETH-80, MSR-Action3D, and UIUC datasets. On the YTC dataset, for each person, three videos are randomly selected as the gallery, and six as the probe. In experiments, we set $\xi = 0.01$, $M_0 = I_m$, $\zeta_s = 5$, and $\zeta_d = 100$.

3.2   Evaluation

We exploit the 1-NN classifier to evaluate the performance of all metric learning methods. The following methods are evaluated in our experiments: AIM [19], Stein Divergence [21], LEM [2], SPD-DR [7], CDL [29], RSR-ML [9], LEML [11], and α-CML [31]. AIM, Stein Divergence, and LEM are the basic SPD matrix metrics, measuring the geodesic distance between SPD matrices. SPD-DR implements the dimensionality reduction on the SPD matrix and then applies the AIM or Stein Divergence between samples. CDL is a Riemannian kernel discriminative learning approach on the SPD manifold. RSR-ML employs sparse coding and dictionary learning scheme on the SPD manifold. LEML and α-CML are two LEM based SPD matrix metric learning methods which project SPD matrices to the tangent space and utilize the LEM to compute the distance between them.

Table 1 shows the comparisons of the four visual tasks. In the object recognition task, we set the dimensionality of the low-dimensional manifolds is 10×10 and the number of them is 20, *i.e.*, $m = 20$. We find that LEM has a better performance than AIM, 93.0 vs 85.0, showing that the point on the tangent space is more discriminative. If the manifold point is projected to a low-dimensional discriminative space, *i.e.*, the SPD-DR method, the performance can be improved to 96.0, 0.5 better than LEML. Compared with SPD-DR, our method achieves 97.5, 1.5 higher than it, which shows the power of discovering discriminative properties and their roles.

In the video-based face recognition task, the dimensionality of projected manifolds is 10×10, and the number of them is 40. We achieve 49.2 in this task, 2.5

higher than SPD-DR and 10 percent higher than the basic SPD matrix metrics approximately. However, due to the large variable faces caused by posture, illumination, scale, and occlusion, the performance of linear metric learning methods is far less than it of the nonlinear kernel method CDL. The reason we think is that the samples in the original space are not separable, a more higher-dimensional RKHS space can relieve this problem.

In the action recognition task, the dimensionality of the low-dimensional manifolds is 8×8 and the number of them is 15. Nonlinear kernel methods CDL and RSR-ML achieve 95.4 and 95.0 respectively and have a better performance than the existing metric methods [7,11,31]. In this case, our linear method obtains the comparable performance with CDL and RSR-ML, achieving 95.8. Besides, Wang et al. [26] shows that the nonlinear kernel matrix representation has a better performance than the linear SPD representation, while our accuracy is 3.1 higher than α-CML whose performance is based on the kernel matrix [26] rather than the Gaussian distribution SPD matrix.

In the texture classification task, in our method, we set the dimensionality of the low-dimensional manifolds is 8×8, and there are totally 18 low-dimensional manifolds. We can see that, the three basic SPD matrix metrics i.e., AIM, Stein Divergence, and LEM achieve comparable performance in the UIUC dataset, 35.6, 35.8 and 36.7 respectively. Meanwhile, metric learning methods can bring a remarkable improvement. CDL achieves 54.9, and the accuracy of LEML is 53.9. SPD-DR achieves a better performance 58.3, showing that there are too much noise and information redundancy in the original SPD representation. Our method further improves the result to 60.8 showing that our method can not only remove the noise and information redundancy but also bring the benefits of discovering discriminative intrinsic properties and their different roles.

Table 1. Accuracies (%) on the four visual tasks. Our method is bold in the last line.

Method	Eth-80	YTC	MSR-Action3D	UIUC
AIM [19]	85.0	38.2	84.7	35.6
Stein [21]	-	-	83.5	35.8
LEM [2]	93.0	40.8	84.7	36.7
AIM-DR [7]	96.0	46.7	93.1	58.3
Stein-DR [7]	-	-	94.6	58.1
CDL [29]	94.5	67.5	95.4	54.9
RSR-ML [9]	94.8	-	95.0	-
LEML [11]	95.5	-	92.3	53.9
α-CML [31]	-	-	92.7	-
Ours	**97.5**	**49.2**	**95.8**	**60.8**

4 Conclusions

In this paper, we have proposed a novel metric learning method on the SPD manifold, which can discover discriminative intrinsic properties and computes the metric considering their different roles. We can formulate the SPD manifold metric learning process as the multiple projections and a set-to-set metric joint optimization problem. Moreover, we force the projection matrix and the metric matrix on manifolds, obtaining a robust metric. Extensive experiments have shown that our method outperforms existing metric learning methods on the SPD manifold. As our method is differentiable in the whole process, in the future, we will endow it with deep learning for the desirable nonlinearity.

Acknowledgements. This work was supported by the Natural Science Foundation of China (NSFC) under Grants No. 61702037 and No. 61773062, and Beijing Municipal Natural Science Foundation under Grant No. L172027, in part by Beijing Institute of Technology Research Fund Program for Young Scholars.

References

1. Absil, P.A., Mahony, R., Sepulchre, R.: Optimization Algorithms on Matrix Manifolds. Princeton University Press, Princeton (2009)
2. Arsigny, V., Fillard, P., Pennec, X., Ayache, N.: Log-Euclidean metrics for fast and simple calculus on diffusion tensors. Magn. Reson. Med. **56**(2), 411 (2006)
3. Cherian, A., Stanitsas, P., Harandi, M., Morellas, V., Papanikolopoulos, N.: Learning discriminative $\alpha\beta$-divergences for positive definite matrices. In: Proceedings of the IEEE International Conference on Computer Vision (ICCV), pp. 4270–4279 (2017)
4. Cichocki, A., Cruces, S., Amari, S.: Log-determinant divergences revisited: alpha-beta and gamma log-det divergences. Entropy **17**(5), 2988–3034 (2015)
5. Davis, J.V., Kulis, B., Jain, P., Sra, S., Dhillon, I.S.: Information-theoretic metric learning. In: Proceedings of the International Conference on Machine Learning (ICML), pp. 209–216 (2007)
6. Harandi, M., Fernando, B.: Generalized backpropagation, Étude de cas: Orthogonality. arXiv preprint arXiv:1611.05927 (2016)
7. Harandi, M., Salzmann, M., Hartley, R.: Dimensionality reduction on SPD manifolds: the emergence of geometry-aware methods. IEEE Trans. Pattern Anal. Mach. Intell. **40**, 48–62 (2017)
8. Harandi, M., Salzmann, M., Hartley, R.: Joint dimensionality reduction and metric learning: a geometric take. In: Proceedings of the International Conference on Machine Learning (ICML), pp. 1404–1413 (2017)
9. Harandi, M.T., Sanderson, C., Hartley, R., Lovell, B.C.: Sparse coding and dictionary learning for symmetric positive definite matrices: a kernel approach. In: Fitzgibbon, A., Lazebnik, S., Perona, P., Sato, Y., Schmid, C. (eds.) ECCV 2012. LNCS, pp. 216–229. Springer, Heidelberg (2012). https://doi.org/10.1007/978-3-642-33709-3_16
10. Hoffman, J., Rodner, E., Donahue, J., Kulis, B., Saenko, K.: Asymmetric and category invariant feature transformations for domain adaptation. Int. J. Comput. Vis. **109**(1-2), 28–41 (2014)

11. Huang, Z., Wang, R., Shan, S., Li, X., Chen, X.: Log-Euclidean metric learning on symmetric positive definite manifold with application to image set classification. In: Proceedings of the International Conference on Machine Learning (ICML), pp. 720–729 (2015)
12. Huang, Z., Wang, R., Van Gool, L., Chen, X., et al.: Cross Euclidean-to-Riemannian metric learning with application to face recognition from video. IEEE Trans. Pattern Anal. Mach. Intell. **PP**(99), 1 (2018)
13. Kim, M., Kumar, S., Pavlovic, V., Rowley, H.: Face tracking and recognition with visual constraints in real-world videos. In: Proceedings of the IEEE Conference on Computer Vision and Pattern Recognition (CVPR), pp. 1–8 (2008)
14. Kulis, B., Sustik, M.A., Dhillon, I.S.: Low-rank kernel learning with Bregman matrix divergences. J. Mach. Learn. Res. **10**(1), 341–376 (2009)
15. Leibe, B., Schiele, B.: Analyzing appearance and contour based methods for object categorization. In: Proceedings of The IEEE Conference on Computer Vision and Pattern Recognition (CVPR), vol. 2, pp. II-409 (2003)
16. Li, P., Xie, J., Wang, Q., Zuo, W.: Is second-order information helpful for large-scale visual recognition? In: IEEE International Conference on Computer Vision, pp. 2089–2097 (2017)
17. Li, W., Zhang, Z., Liu, Z.: Action recognition based on a bag of 3D points. In: Proceedings of the IEEE Conference on Computer Vision and Pattern Recognition Workshops (CVPRW), pp. 9–14 (2010)
18. Liao, Z., Rock, J., Wang, Y., Forsyth, D.: Non-parametric filtering for geometric detail extraction and material representation. In: Proceedings of the IEEE Conference on Computer Vision and Pattern Recognition (CVPR), pp. 963–970 (2013)
19. Pennec, X., Fillard, P., Ayache, N.: A Riemannian framework for tensor computing. Int. J. Comput. Vis. **66**(1), 41–66 (2006)
20. Roy, Kumar, S., Mhammedi, Z., Harandi, M.: Geometry aware constrained optimization techniques for deep learning. In: Proceedings of the IEEE Conference on Computer Vision and Pattern Recognition (CVPR), vol. 1 (2018)
21. Sra, S.: A new metric on the manifold of kernel matrices with application to matrix geometric means. In: Advances in Neural Information Processing Systems, pp. 144–152 (2012)
22. Thiyam, D.B., Cruces, S., Olias, J., Cichocki, A.: Optimization of Alpha-Beta Log-Det divergences and their application in the spatial filtering of two class motor imagery movements. Entropy **19**(3), 89 (2017)
23. Vemulapalli, R., Jacobs, D.W.: Riemannian metric learning for symmetric positive definite matrices. arXiv preprint arXiv:1501.02393 (2015)
24. Vemulapalli, R., Pillai, J.K., Chellappa, R.: Kernel learning for extrinsic classification of manifold features. In: Proceedings of The IEEE Conference on Computer Vision and Pattern Recognition (CVPR), pp. 1782–1789 (2013)
25. Wang, H., Wang, Q., Gao, M., Li, P., Zuo, W.: Multi-scale location-aware kernel representation for object detection. In: Proceedings of the IEEE Conference on Computer Vision and Pattern Recognition (CVPR), vol. 1 (2018)
26. Wang, L., Zhang, J., Zhou, L., Tang, C., Li, W.: Beyond covariance: feature representation with nonlinear kernel matrices. In: Proceedings of the IEEE International Conference on Computer Vision (ICCV), pp. 4570–4578 (2015)
27. Wang, Q., Li, P., Zhang, L.: G2DeNet: global Gaussian distribution embedding network and its application to visual recognition. In: IEEE Conference on Computer Vision and Pattern Recognition, pp. 6507–6516 (2017)

28. Wang, Q., Li, P., Zuo, W., Zhang, L.: RAID-G: robust estimation of approximate infinite dimensional Gaussian with application to material recognition. In: Computer Vision and Pattern Recognition, pp. 4433–4441 (2016)
29. Wang, R., Guo, H., Davis, L.S., Dai, Q.: Covariance discriminative learning: a natural and efficient approach to image set classification. In: Proceedings of The IEEE Conference on Computer Vision and Pattern Recognition (CVPR), pp. 2496–2503 (2012)
30. Zhang, T., Zheng, W., Cui, Z., Zong, Y., Li, Y.: Deep manifold-to-manifold transforming network for action recognition. arXiv preprint arXiv:1705.10732 (2017)
31. Zhou, L., Wang, L., Zhang, J., Shi, Y., Gao, Y.: Revisiting metric learning for SPD matrix based visual representation. In: Proceedings of the IEEE Conference on Computer Vision and Pattern Recognition (CVPR), pp. 3241–3249 (2017)

Structure Fusion and Propagation
for Zero-Shot Learning

Guangfeng Lin[✉], Yajun Chen, and Fan Zhao

Xi'an University of Technology, Xi'an 710048, Shaanxi Province,
People's Republic of China
{lgf78103,chenyajun,vcu}@xaut.edu.cn

Abstract. The key of zero-shot learning (ZSL) is how to find the
information transfer model for bridging the gap between images and
semantic information (texts or attributes). Existing ZSL methods usually construct the compatibility function between images and class labels
with consideration of the relevance on the semantic classes (the manifold structure of semantic classes). However, the relationship of image
classes (the manifold structure of image classes) is also very important
for the compatibility model construction. It is difficult to capture the
relationship among image classes due to unseen classes, so that the manifold structure of image classes often is ignored in ZSL. To complement
each other between the manifold structure of image classes and that of
semantic classes information, we propose structure fusion and propagation (SFP) for improving the performance of ZSL for classification. SFP
can jointly consider the manifold structure of image classes and that
of semantic classes for approximating to the intrinsic structure of object
classes. Moreover, the SFP can describe the constraint condition between
the compatibility function and these manifold structures for balancing
the influence of the structure fusion and propagation iteration. The SFP
solution provides not only unseen class labels but also the relationship of
two manifold structures that encodes the positive transfer in structure
fusion and propagation. Experiments demonstrate that SFP can attain
the promising results on the AwA, CUB, Dogs and SUN datasets.

Keywords: Structure fusion and propagation · Manifold structure
Zero-shot learning · Transfer learning

1 Introduction

Although deep learning [32] depending on large-scale labeled data training has
been generally used for visual recognition [31], a daunting challenge still exists
to recognize visual object "in the wild". In fact, in specific applications it is

Supported by NSFC (Program No. 61771386, Program No. 61671376 and Program
No. 61671374), Natural Science Basic Research Plan in Shaanxi Province of China
(Program No. 2016JM6045, Program No. 2017JZ020).

J.-H. Lai et al. (Eds.): PRCV 2018, LNCS 11258, pp. 465–477, 2018.
https://doi.org/10.1007/978-3-030-03338-5_39

impossible to collect all class data for training deep model, so training (seen classes) and testing classes(unseen classes) are often disjoint. The main idea of ZSL is to handle this problem by exploiting the transfer model from the redundant relevance of the semantic description. To recognize unseen classes from seen classes, ZSL needs face to two challenges [3]. One is how to utilize the semantic information for constructing the relationship between unseen classes and seen classes, and other is how to find the compatibility among all kinds of information for obtaining the optimal discriminative characteristics on unseen classes.

ZSL can bridge the gap among the different domains to recognize unseen class objects by semantic embedding of class labels. These semantic embeddings can come from vision (attributes [11]) and language information (text [25]) by the manual annotation, machine learning [29]or data mining [5]. In term of the transformation relationship of different embedding, recent ZSL methods mainly fall into linear embedding, nonlinear embedding and similarity embedding. Linear embedding [1,2,7,13,24] implements the linear transformation method among different embedding spaces for learning the relevance between unseen class objects and class labels. Nonlinear embedding [23,25,28] can realize the nonlinear mapping of the embedding space for building the compatibility function or classifier, which can be learned by deep networks [14,30]. Similarity embedding [3,9,15,19,33] builds the classifier by the similarity metrics, which mostly include structure learning or class-wise similarities. In our approach, the similarity metric is extended from semantic space to image space, we attempt to find the relationship of similarities (manifold structure in the different space) for constraining the compatibility function, and further capture to the positive structure propagation for the significantly improvement of the unseen object classification.

In this paper, our motivation is inspired by structure fusion [16–18] for jointly dealing with two challenges. The intrinsic manifold structure is crucial for object classification. However, in fact, we only can attain the observation data of the manifold structure, which can represent different aspects of the intrinsic manifold structure. For recovering or approximating the intrinsic structure, we can fuse various manifold structures from observation data. Based on the above idea, we try to capture different manifold structures in image and semantic space for improving the recognition performance of unseen classes in ZSL. Therefore, we expect to construct the compatibility function for predicting labels of unseen classes by building the manifold structure of image classes. On the other end, we attempt to find the relevance between the manifold structure of semantic classes and that of image classes in model space for encoding the influence between the negative and positive transfer, and further make the better compatibility function for classifying unseen class objects. Model space corresponding to visual appearances is the jointed projection space of semantic space and image space, and can preserve the respective manifold structure. Figure 1 illustrates the idea of the proposed method conceptually. SFP considers not only semantic and image structures but also the positive structure propagation for ameliorating unseen objects classification, while SynC [3] only focus on manifold structure in semantic space for combining the base classifier in ZSL.

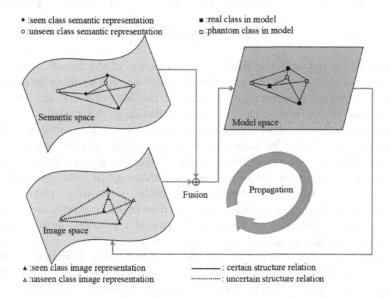

Fig. 1. The illustration of structure fusion and propagation for zero-shot learning. Phantom object classes (the coordinates of classes in the model space are optimized to achieve the best performance of the resulting model for the real object classes in discriminative tasks [3].) and real object classes corresponding to all classes in model space.

In our main contribution, a novel idea have tow aspects to recover or approximate the intrinsic manifold structure from seen classes to unseen classes by fusing the different space manifold structure for handling the challenging unseen classes recognition. Specifically, one constructs the projected manifold structure for real and phantom class in model space, another constrains the compatibility function and the relationship of the manifold structure for the positive structure propagation.

2   Structure Fusion and Propagation

In ZSL, we have training data set $\mathscr{D} = \{(x_n \in R^D, y_n)\}_{n=1}^N$, in which x_n is image representation (it can be extracted based on deep model, and the detail is described in Table 1) and $y_n(n = 1, ..., N)$ is the class label in the seen class set $\mathscr{S} = \{s|s = 1, ..., S\}$. We can denote the unseen class set as $\mathscr{U} = \{u|u = S+1, ..., S+U\}$. $a_c \in R_D$ is the linear transformation vector of the $c \in \{\mathscr{S} \bigcup \mathscr{U}\}$ class.

2.1   Classification Model and Manifold Structure

We construct a pair-wise linear classifier [3] in the visual image feature space, and determinate a estimated label $\hat{y}$ to a feature x by the following formula.

$$\hat{y} = \arg\max_c a_c^T x, \tag{1}$$

here, $a_c \in R^D$ is not only the transformation vector of the feature x, but also the representation of the class c in model. In other words, the above formula can describe the pair-wise linear relation between the feature space and the class label space for characterizing the class representation in the model.

To measure the manifold structure, we can compute the similarity of the related representation in the homogeneous space, which has the same scale and metric. To this end, we respectively build a bipartite graph between unseen classes and seen classes in semantic space and image space (this space includes all image representations). In these bipartite graphs, nodes are corresponding to unseen classes or seen classes, and weights of these nodes connect unseen classes with seen classes. Because we focus on the transfer relation between unseen classes and seen classes, no connection exists in unseen classes or seen classes. Supposing $G_b{<}V_b, E_b{>}$ can denote the manifold structure of semantic classes. Here, $V_b = V_{bs} \bigcup V_{bu}$ and $\emptyset = V_{bs} \bigcap V_{bu}$. E_b includes connections between V_{bs} (seen classes set in semantic space) and V_{bu} (unseen classes set in semantic space); $G_x{<}V_x, E_x{>}$ for the manifold structure of image classes. Here, $V_x = V_{xs} \bigcup V_{xu}$ and $\emptyset = V_{xs} \bigcap V_{xu}$. E_x includes the connections between V_{xs} (seen classes set in image space) and V_{xu} (unseen classes set in image space). Therefore, the similarity of semantic and image space is respectively regarded as the weight between nodes, which can be defined as following.

$$w_{su}^{(b)} = \frac{\exp(-d(b_s, b_u))}{\sum_{u=1}^U \exp(-d(b_s, b_u))}, w_{su}^{(x)} = \frac{\exp(-d(x_s, x_u))}{\sum_{u=1}^U \exp(-d(x_s, x_u))}, \tag{2}$$

here, b_s and x_s are respectively the semantic and image representation (the detail is described in Table 1) of the seen class s, while b_u and x_u are respectively the semantic and image representation of the unseen class u. $w_{su}^{(b)}$ and $w_{su}^{(x)}$ are respectively the weight (the similarity) between the seen class s and the unseen class u in semantic and image representation space. $d(b_s, b_u)$ and $d(x_s, x_u)$ are respectively the distance metric [3] of each space, and can be defined as following.

$$d(b_s, b_u) = (b_s - b_u)^T \Sigma_b^{-1}(b_s - b_u), d(x_s, x_u) = (x_s - x_u)^T \Sigma_x^{-1}(x_s - x_u), \tag{3}$$

here, $\Sigma_b = \sigma_b I$ can be learned from the semantic representation by cross-validation (We alternately divide the training classes set into two part in according with the proportion between the training classes set and the test classes set. One part is to learn the model, and another is to validate the model. We give the range of σ_b, which is form 2^{-5} to 2^5, and select the parameter corresponding to the best result as the value of σ_b.) $\Sigma_x = \sigma_x I$ can be learned from the image representation by cross-validation (It is the same procedure like σ_b learning.).

In image space, the differentiation compared with the semantic space is that x_u is not determined because of unseen classes, while x_s can be obtained from training data by computing the mean value of the seen class. The way to produce the center of the class as a representation is simple for convenient computation, and it is reasonable to preserve the base characteristic of image representation according with the distribution of the same class. x_u can be attained by pre-classification of unseen classes (the detail in the next section).

In (1), a_c is the transformation vector, and also is the class representation in model space. In (2), b_s and b_u is the class representation in semantic space, while x_s and x_u is the class representation in image space. We expect to construct the link among these space by v_s and v_u, which are respectively the phantom class of seen or unseen classes in model. For preserving the manifold structure of two bipartite graphs and aligning the image, the semantic and the model space, we build the optimization formula under the condition of the distortion error minimization, which is defined as following.

$$(a_c, v_u, \boldsymbol{\beta}) = \arg \min_{a_c, v_u, \boldsymbol{\beta}} \|a_c - \sum_{u=1}^{U} \boldsymbol{\beta}^T \left[w_{su}^{(x)} \ w_{su}^{(b)} \right]^T v_u - \sum_{s=1}^{S} \boldsymbol{\gamma}^T \left[w_{ss}^{(x)} \ w_{ss}^{(b)} \right]^T v_s\|_2^2,$$
$$s.t. \quad \boldsymbol{\beta}^T 1 = 1, \boldsymbol{\gamma}^T 1 = 1, 0 \leq \beta_i \leq 1, 0 \leq \gamma_i \leq 1 \quad (i = 1, 2)$$
$$(4)$$

here, $\boldsymbol{\beta} = \left[\beta_1 \ \beta_2\right]^T$, $\boldsymbol{\gamma} = \left[\gamma_1 \ \gamma_2\right]^T$, and $1 = \left[1 \ 1\right]^T$. Because no connection exists between unseen classes or seen classes in tow bipartite graphs, $w_{ss}^{(b)} = 0$ and $w_{ss}^{(x)} = 0$. The analytical solution of (4) can find the relation between a_c and v_u.

$$a_c = \sum_{u=1}^{U} \boldsymbol{\beta}^T \left[w_{su}^{(x)} \ w_{su}^{(b)} \right]^T v_u,$$
$$s.t. \quad \boldsymbol{\beta}^T 1 = 1, 0 \leq \beta_i \leq 1 \quad (i = 1, 2)$$
$$(5)$$

here, $\forall c \in \{1, 2, ..., S + U\}$.

2.2   Phantom Classes and Structure Relation Learning

For obtaining phantom class $v_u (u = 1, ..., U)$ and the manifold structure of the weight coefficient vector β, we further reformulate the optimization formula for one-versus-other classifier [3].

$$(v_1, ..., v_U, \beta) = \arg \min_{v_1,...,v_U,\beta} \sum_{c=1}^{S} \sum_{n=1}^{N} \ell(x_n, \mathbb{I}_{y_n,c}, a_c)$$

$$+ \frac{\lambda}{2} \sum_{c=1}^{S} \|a_c\|_2^2 + \frac{\gamma}{2} \|\beta_1 W^x - \beta_2 W^b\|_2^2, \tag{6}$$

$$s.t. \quad a_c = \sum_{u=1}^{U} \beta^T \left[w_{su}^{(x)} \ w_{su}^{(b)} \right]^T v_u,$$

$$\beta^T \mathbf{1} = 1, 0 \le \beta_i \le 1 \quad (i = 1, 2)$$

here, $w_{su}^{(x)}$ is the element of the matrix W^x, and $w_{su}^{(b)}$ is the element of the matrix W^b. The first term of formula (6) is the squared hinge loss, which can be defined as $\ell(x_n, \mathbb{I}_{y_n,c}, a_c) = \max(0, 1 - \mathbb{I}_{y_n,c} a_c x_n)$. $\mathbb{I}_{y_n,c} \in \{-1, 1\}$ determines whether or not $y_n = c$. The second term of formula (6) is a_c of a regularization tern, which avoids over-fitting problem on the pair-wise linear classifier for modeling the relationship between the class label and the image representation. The third term of formula (6) is the constraint of the manifold structure similarity for preventing the negative structure propagation in image space. The alternating optimization can be implemented for minimizing the formula (6) with respect to $\{v_u\}_{u=1}^{U}$ and β by solving the quadratic programming problem.

To depict the whole process of the structure fusion and propagation mechanism, we show the pseudo code of the proposed SFP algorithm in Algorithm 1.

Algorithm 1. The pseudo code of the SFP algorithm

Input: $\mathscr{D} = \{(x_n \in R^D, y_n)\}_{n=1}^{N}, b_s$ and b_u (input data)
Output: y_P^* (P is the total iteration number)
1: Computes the similarity matrix $W_{(b)}$ on the semantic representation by (2)
2: Setting the similarity matrix $W_{(x)}$ to zero matrix on the image representation
3: **for** $1 < t < P$ **do**
4:     Solving $\{v_u\}_{u=1}^{U}$ and β by alternately optimizing (6)
5:     Computing a_c according to (5)
6:     Computing $\hat{y}$ by (1) and obtaining the class label y_t^* of the unseen class corresponding to the semantic class
7:     Computing the mean value of each image class as the image class representation x_s and x_u
8:     Computing and updating the similarity matrix $W_{(x)}$ on the image representation by (2)
9: **end for**

2.3   Complexity Analysis

Formula (6) can be solved by alternately quadratic programming, which of the complexity includes two parts. In the first part, when β is fixed, formula (6) is related to $\{v_u\}_{u=1}^{U}$ of a quadratic programming problem, which of the complexity is $O(U^3)$ for the worst. In the second part, while $\{v_u\}_{u=1}^{U}$ is fixed, formula (6) is corresponding to β of a quadratic programming problem, which of the complexity is $O(k^3)$ (k is the dimension of β) for the worst. Given the proposed algorithm SFP needs P iterations, it's complexity is $O(PU^3 + Pk^3)$.

3 Experiment

3.1 Datasets

For evaluating the proposed algorithm SFP[1], we carry out the experiment in four challenging datasets, which are Animals with Attributes (AwA) [12], CUB-200-2011 Birds (CUB) [27], Stanford Dogs (Dogs) [4], and SUN Attribute (SUN) [21]. These datasets can be used for fine-grained recognition (CUB and Dogs) or non-fine-grained recognition (AwA and SUN) in ZSL. In semantic space, AwA and CUB respectively are described by att [6], w2v [20], glo [22] and hie [1], while Dogs is represented by w2v [20], glo [22] and hie [1]. SUN is only depicted by att [6]. Table 1 provides the statistics and the extracted features for these datasets. In addition, for conveniently comparing with the state-of-art methods, we adopt image feature provided by [1].

Table 1. Datasets statistics and the extracted feature in experiments.

Datasets	Number of seen classes	Number of unseen classes	Total number of images	Semantic feature/ dimension	Image feature/ dimension
AwA	40	10	30473	att/85, w2v/400, glo/400, hie/about 200	Deep feature based on GoogleNet [26]/1024
CUB	150	50	11786	att/312, w2v/400, glo/400, hie/about 200	Deep feature based on GoogleNet [26]/1024
Dogs	85	28	19499	N/A, w2v/400, glo/400, hie/about 200	Deep feature based on GoogleNet [26]/1024
SUN	645	72	14340	att/102, N/A, N/A, N/A	Deep feature based on GoogleNet [26]/1024

---

[1] Source code: https://github.com/lgf78103/Structure-propagation-for-zero-shot-learning.

3.2   Comparison with the Baseline Methods

In this paper, there are three methods as the baseline for comparing with the proposed SFP method because of the semantic structure mining. The first method is structured joint embedding (SJE) [1], which can build the bilinear compatibility function with consideration of the structured output space for predicting the label of the unseen class. The second method is latent embedding model (LatEm) [28],which can construct the pair-wise bilinear (nonlinear) compatibility function according to model number selection for recognizing unseen classes. The third method is synthesized classifiers (SynC) [3], which can make nonlinear compatibility function with manifold structure in semantic space for combining the base classifier in ZSL. Table 2 shows the performance of the structure fusion and propagation (the proposed SFP method) greatly outperforms that of other three methods.

3.3   Classification and Validation Protocols

Classification accuracy is average value of all test class accuracy in each database. Because the learned model involves four parameters, which are $\lambda, \gamma, \sigma_b$ and σ_x (respectively are in formula (3) in formula (6)). We alternately divide the training classes set into two part in according with the proportion between the training classes set and the test classes set. One part is to learn the model, and another is to validate the model. Firstly, we set σ_b and σ_x to 1, and obtain γ and λ corresponding to the best result in γ (form 2^{-24} to 2^{-9}) and λ (form 2^{-24} to 2^{-9}) by cross validation. Secondly, we learn σ_b and σ_x corresponding to the best result in σ_b and σ_x (form 2^{-5} to 2^5) by cross validation.

3.4   Structure Fusion and Propagation with the Iteration

The main idea of the proposed SFP method shows three contents. In the first content, the manifold structure of images is considered for constructing the compatibility function between the class label and the visual feature. In the second content, the relationship between multi-manifold structures is found for booting the influence of the positive structure. In the last content, it is the most important to propagate the positive structure and fuse multi-manifold structures by the iteration computation. Therefore, we carry out the related experiment for evaluating the effect of the iteration on the structure evolution in AwA. The recognition accuracy can show the approximation degree of the class manifold structure. In other word, the better recognition accuracy is proportional to the more similar relationship between the reconstruction manifold structure and the intrinsic manifold structure of classes. Figure 2 demonstrates the recognition accuracy change with the iteration. In the beginning, the recognition accuracy rapidly increases with the iteration, and then reaches a stable state. It means that structure fusion and propagation with the iteration can advance the recognition accuracy and finally obtain the best state.

Table 2. Comparison of SFP method with SJE [1], LatEm [28] and SynC [3] in each semantic space, average per-class Top-1 accuracy (%) of unseen classes is reported based on the same data configurations, same images and semantic features in AwA. w: the fusion includes att, w2v, glo and hie, while w/o: the fusion contains w2v, glo and hie.

Datasets	Semantic feature	SJE	LatEm	SynC	SFP
AwA	att	66.7	71.9	69.3	**84.3**
	w2v	51.2	61.1	52.9	**77.4**
	glo	58.8	62.9	53.4	**70.5**
	hie	51.2	57.5	52.0	**62.1**
	w	73.9	76.1	78.0	**85.4**
	w/o	60.1	66.2	69.1	**81.4**
CUB	att	50.1	45.5	47.5	**51.8**
	w2v	28.4	31.8	32.3	**32.5**
	glo	24.2	32.5	32.8	**33.3**
	hie	20.6	24.2	22.7	**24.3**
	w	51.7	47.4	48.8	**54.1**
	w/o	29.9	34.9	35.2	**35.3**
Dogs	att	*N/A*	*N/A*	*N/A*	*N/A*
	w2v	19.6	22.6	27.6	**33.3**
	glo	17.8	20.9	21.9	**33.4**
	hie	24.3	25.2	31.1	**32.4**
	w	*N/A*	*N/A*	*N/A*	*N/A*
	w/o	35.1	36.3	36.3	**48.1**
SUN	att	56.1	57.6	62.8	**67.6**

3.5 Comparison with State-of-the-Arts

In term of the image data utilization of unseen classes in testing, we can divide ZSL methods into two categories, which are inductive ZSL and transductive ZSL. Inductive ZSL methods can serially process unseen samples without the consideration of the underlying manifold structure in unseen samples [1,3,28,33], while transductive ZSL can usually use the manifold structure of unseen samples to improve ZSL performance [8,10,15]. SFP can find the structure of unseen classes in image feature space to enhance the transfer model between seen and unseen classes, so SFP belongs to a transductive ZSL method. For a fair comparison, we use deep feature of images based on GoogleNet [26] in contrasting methods, which include our method, one transductive ZSL method (DMaP [15]), and three inductive ZSL methods (SJE [1], LatEm [28] and SynC [3]). To the best of our knowledge, these methods are state-of-the-art methods for ZSL. Table 3 shows their results for ZSL on three benchmark datasets. SFP mostly outperforms the state-of-the-art methods except DMaP on CUB. DMaP focuses on the manifold

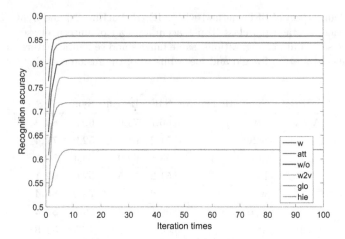

Fig. 2. Average per-class Top-1 accuracy (%) of unseen classes is reported with structure fusion and propagation iteration times on AwA. w: the fusion includes att, w2v, glo and hie, while w/o: the fusion contains w2v, glo and hie

structure consistency between the semantic representation and the image feature, and can better distinguish fine-grained classes. SFP can complement the manifold structure between the semantic representation and the image feature, and better recognize coarse-grained classes. Therefore, integrating two ideas is expected to further improve the ZSL performance in future work.

3.6 Experimental Result Analysis

From the above experiments, we can attain the following observations.

- The semantic description have the different contribution for classifying unseen classes. The supervised attribute tend to obtain the better recognition performance than the unsupervised semantic representation (w2v, glo and hie) in AwA and CUB. In the unsupervised semantic representation, the recognition accuracy of w2v or glo is better than that of hie in AwA and CUB, but the performance of hie is superior to that of w2v or glo in Dogs. This is mainly due to the flexibility and uncertainty of the semantic representation in the unsupervised way.
- The performance of SFP is better than that of other three methods, which are SJE, LatEm, and SynC. However, the performance improvement is different in the various datasets. The obvious improvement can be found in AwA, Dogs and SUN, while the slight improvement can be shown in CUB. The main reason of this situation is related to whether or not effectively to propagate the positive structure in the optimization computation in term of data differences.
- SFP emphasizes on the different manifold structure complement, while DMaP focuses on the various manifold structure consistency. Therefore, the performance of SFP is superior to that of DMaP because the structure complementarity plays the important role for learning transfer model in AwA and

Table 3. Comparison of SFP method with state-of-the-art methods for ZSL, average per-class Top-1 accuracy (%) of unseen classes is reported based on the same data configurations. '+' indicates fusion operation.

Method	Semantic feature	T/I	AwA	CUB	Dogs
SJE	att	I	66.7	50.1	N/A
	w2v	I	51.2	28.4	19.6
LatEm	att	I	71.9	45.5	N/A
	w2v	I	61.1	31.8	22.6
SynC	att	I	69.3	47.5	N/A
	w2v	I	52.9	32.3	27.6
DMaP	att	T	74.9	**61.8**	N/A
	w2v	T	67.9	31.6	38.9
	att+w2v	T	78.6	59.6	N/A
SFP	att	T	84.3	51.8	N/A
	w2v	T	77.4	32.5	33.3
	att+w2v	T	84.7	52.5	N/A
	att+w2v+glo+hie	T	**85.4**	54.1	N/A
	w2v+glo+hie	T	81.4	35.3	**48.1**

Dogs, and the performance of DMaP is better than that of SFP because the structure consistency is a key point for classifying unseen classes in CUB.

- SFP performs better with the positive structure fusion and propagation. SFP has demonstrated great promise in above experiments due to multi-manifold structure consideration and alternated optimization between the weight computation and the manifold structure estimation for ZSL.
- The proposed fusion method can attain the better performance than the non-fusion method because of appropriate complementing each other. w or w/o always performs better on AwA, CUB and Dogs.

4 Conclusion

We have proposed a new ZSL method, which called structure fusion and propagation (SFP). This method can not only directly model the relevance among the manifold structures in semantic and image space, but also dynamically propagate the positive structure by the crossing iteration. Specifically, the proposed SFP method mainly includes four parts. First, nonlinear model constructs the mapping relationship between the class label and the visual image representation. Second, graph describes the relevance between seen classes and unseen classes in semantic or image space. Three, loss function indicates the constrains relationship of multi-manifold structure to balance the structure dependance. Last, structure fusion and propagation is implemented by the crossing iteration computation between phantom classes and weights solving. For evaluating the proposed SFP, we carry out the experiment on AwA, CUB, Dogs and SUN. Experimental results show that SFP can obtain the promising results for ZSL.

References

1. Akata, Z., Reed, S., Walter, D., Lee, H., Schiele, B.: Evaluation of output embeddings for fine-grained image classification. In: IEEE Conference on Computer Vision and Pattern Recognition (CVPR), pp. 2927–2936 (2015)
2. Akata, Z., Perronnin, F., Harchaoui, Z., Schmid, C.: Label-embedding for image classification. IEEE Trans. Pattern Anal. Mach. Intell. **38**(7), 1425–1438 (2016)
3. Changpinyo, S., Chao, W.L., Gong, B., Sha, F.: Synthesized classifiers for zero-shot learning. In: IEEE Conference on Computer Vision and Pattern Recognition(CVPR), pp. 5327–5336 (2016)
4. Deng, J., Krause, J., Fei-Fei, L.: Fine-grained crowdsourcing for fine-grained recognition. In: IEEE Conference on Computer Vision and Pattern Recognition(CVPR), pp. 580–587 (2013)
5. Elhoseiny, M., Saleh, B., Elgammal, A.: Write a classifier: zero-shot learning using purely textual descriptions. In: IEEE International Conference on Computer Vision(ICCV), pp. 2584–2591 (2013)
6. Farhadi, A., Endres, I., Hoiem, D., Forsyth, D.: Describing objects by their attributes. In: IEEE Conference on Computer Vision and Pattern Recognition (CVPR), pp. 1778–1785 (2009)
7. Frome, A., et al.: DeViSE: a deep visual-semantic embedding model. In: Advances in Neural Information Processing Systems (NIPS), pp. 2121–2129 (2013)
8. Fu, Y., Hospedales, T.M., Xiang, T., Gong, S.: Transductive multi-view zero-shot learning. IEEE Trans. Pattern Anal. Mach. Intell. **37**(11), 2332–2345 (2015)
9. Fu, Z., Xiang, T.A., Kodirov, E., Gong, S.: Zero-shot object recognition by semantic manifold distance. In: IEEE Conference on Computer Vision and Pattern Recognition (CVPR), pp. 2635–2644 (2015)
10. Kodirov, E., Xiang, T., Fu, Z., Gong, S.: Unsupervised domain adaptation for zero-shot learning. In: IEEE International Conference on Computer Vision (ICCV), pp. 2452–2460 (2015)
11. Lampert, C.H., Nickisch, H., Harmeling, S.: Learning to detect unseen object classes by between-class attribute transfer. In: IEEE Conference on Computer Vision and Pattern Recognition (CVPR), pp. 951–958 (2009)
12. Lampert, C.H., Nickisch, H., Harmeling, S.: Attribute-based classification for zero-shot visual object categorization. IEEE Trans. Pattern Anal. Mach. Intell. **36**(3), 453–465 (2014)
13. Li, X., Guo, Y., Schuurmans, D.: Semi-supervised zero-shot classification with label representation learning. In: IEEE International Conference on Computer Vision (ICCV), pp. 4211–4219 (2016)
14. Li, Y., Zhang, J., Zhang, J., Huang, K.: Discriminative learning of latent features for zero-shot recognition. In: IEEE Conference on Computer Vision and Pattern Recognition (CVPR), pp. 7463–7471 (2018)
15. Li, Y., Wang, D., Hu, H., Lin, Y., Zhuang, Y.: Zero-shot recognition using dual visual-semantic mapping paths. arXiv preprint arXiv:1703.05002 (2017)
16. Lin, G., Fan, C., Zhu, H., Miu, Y., Kang, X.: Visual feature coding based on heterogeneous structure fusion for image classification. Inf. Fusion **36**, 275–283 (2017)

17. Lin, G., Fan, G., Kang, X., Zhang, E., Yu, L.: Heterogeneous feature structure fusion for classification. Pattern Recognit. **53**, 1–11 (2016)
18. Lin, G., Liao, K., Sun, B., Chen, Y., Zhao, F.: Dynamic graph fusion label propagation for semi-supervised multi-modality classification. Pattern Recognit. **68**, 14–23 (2017)
19. Mensink, T., Gavves, E., Snoek, C.G.M.: Costa: co-occurrence statistics for zero-shot classification. In: IEEE Conference on Computer Vision and Pattern Recognition (CVPR), pp. 2441–2448 (2014)
20. Mikolov, T., Sutskever, I., Chen, K., Corrado, G., Dean, J.: Distributed representations of words and phrases and their compositionality. In: Advances in Neural Information Processing Systems (NIPS), pp. 3111–3119 (2013)
21. Patterson, G., Xu, C., Su, H., Hays, J.: The sun attribute database: beyond categories for deeper scene understanding. Int. J. Comput. Vis. **108**(1), 59–81 (2014)
22. Pennington, J., Socher, R., Manning, C.: Glove: global vectors for word representation. In: Conference on Empirical Methods in Natural Language Processing (EMNLP), pp. 1532–1543 (2014)
23. Qi, G.J., Liu, W., Aggarwal, C., Huang, T.S.: Joint intermodal and intramodal label transfers for extremely rare or unseen classes. IEEE Trans. Pattern Anal. Mach. Intell. **PP**(99), 1 (2016). https://doi.org/10.1109/TPAMI.2016.2587643
24. Romera-Paredes, B., Torr, P.H.: An embarrassingly simple approach to zero-shot learning. In: International Conference on Machine Learning (ICML), pp. 2152–2161 (2015)
25. Socher, R., Ganjoo, M., Sridhar, H., Bastani, O., Manning, C.D., Ng, A.Y.: Zero-shot learning through cross-modal transfer. In: Advances in Neural Information Processing Systems (NIPS), pp. 935–943 (2013)
26. Szegedy, C., et al.: Going deeper with convolutions. In: IEEE Conference on Computer Vision and Pattern Recognition (CVPR), pp. 1–9 (2015)
27. Wah, C., Branson, S., Welinder, P., Perona, P., Belongie, S.: The caltech-ucsd birds200-2011 dataset. California Institute of Technology (2011)
28. Xian, Y., Akata, Z., Sharma, G., Nguyen, Q., Hein, M., Schiele, B.: Latent embeddings for zero-shot classification. In: IEEE Conference on Computer Vision and Pattern Recognition (CVPR), pp. 69–77 (2016)
29. Yu, F.X., Cao, L., Feris, R.S., Smith, J.R., Chang, S.F.: Designing category-level attributes for discriminative visual recognition. In: IEEE Conference on Computer Vision and Pattern Recognition (CVPR), pp. 771–778 (2013)
30. Zhang, C., Peng, Y.: Visual data synthesis via GAN for zero-shot video classification. arXiv preprint arXiv:1804.10073 (2018)
31. Zhang, E., Chen, W., Zhang, Z., Zhang, Y.: Local surface geometric feature for 3D human action recognition. Neurocomputing **208**, 281–289 (2016)
32. Zhang, Y., Zhang, E., Chen, W.: Deep neural network for halftone image classification based on sparse auto-encoder. Eng. Appl. Artif. Intell. **50**, 245–255 (2016)
33. Zhang, Z., Saligrama, V.: Zero-shot learning via joint latent similarity embedding. In: IEEE Conference on Computer Vision and Pattern Recognition (CVPR), pp. 6034–6042 (2016)

A Hierarchical Cluster Validity Based Visual Tree Learning for Hierarchical Classification

Yu Zheng[1,2], Jianping Fan[3], Ji Zhang[4], and Xinbo Gao[2(✉)]

[1] School of Cyber Engineering, Xidian University, Xi'an 710071,
People's Republic of China
[2] School of Electronic Engineering, Xidian University, Xi'an 710071,
People's Republic of China
xbgao@mail.xidian.edu.cn
[3] Department of Computer Science, University of North Carolina, Charlotte,
NC 28223, USA
[4] Institute of Artificial Intelligence and Robotics, Xi'an Jiaotong University,
Xi'an 710049, People's Republic of China

Abstract. For hierarchical learning, one open issue is how to build a reasonable hierarchical structure which characterize the inter-relation between categories. An effective approach is to utilize hierarchical clustering to build a visual tree structure, however, the critical issue of this approach is how to determine the number of clusters in hierarchical clustering. In this paper, a hierarchical cluster validity index (HCVI) is developed for supporting visual tree learning. Before clustering of each level begins, we will measure the impact of different numbers of clusters on visual tree building and select the most suitable number of clusters. The proposed HCVI will control the structure of visual tree neither too flat nor too deep. Based on this visual tree, a hierarchical classifier can be trained for achieving more discriminative capability. Our experimental results have demonstrated that the proposed hierarchical cluster validity index (HCVI) can guide the building of a more reasonable visual tree structure, so that the hierarchical classifier can achieve better results on classification accuracy.

Keywords: Hierarchical cluster validity · Number of clusters
Visual tree · Hierarchical classification

1 Introduction

Recently, hierarchical classification has received enough attention in the field of machine learning [19,30,38,39], and also has been applied successfully in many applications [3,9,40]. In general, hierarchical classification has three advantages: (1) Hierarchical classification has higher classification efficiency. In the testing phase, hierarchical classifier only need to go through fewer node classifiers than

© Springer Nature Switzerland AG 2018
J.-H. Lai et al. (Eds.): PRCV 2018, LNCS 11258, pp. 478–490, 2018.
https://doi.org/10.1007/978-3-030-03338-5_40

flat classifiers [6,37]. (2) Hierarchical classification can effectively deal with the imbalanced data. (3) The structural characteristics of the hierarchical classifier make it possible to obtain higher classification accuracy when dealing with structured data. For hierarchical learning, one open problem is how to build a reasonable hierarchical structure which characterize the inter-relation between categories.

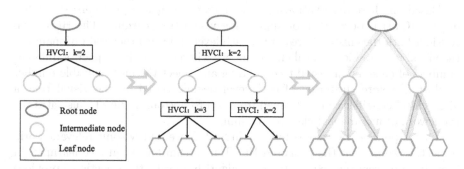

Fig. 1. The framework of hierarchical classifier training. The blue elliptical nodes represent the root nodes; the green circular nodes represent the intermediate nodes; the violet hexagonal nodes represent the leaf nodes. Before clustering, HCVI was utilized to select the optimal number of clusters. This process is applied recursively until the leaf node is reached, and then the hierarchical classifier can be trained over the visual tree from top to bottom. (Color figure online)

In general, the existing approaches for building hierarchical structure can be roughly divided into three types: (1) Semantic tree [12,22,33]. It builds an hierarchical structure by leveraging the semantic ontology in the real world. However, it cannot characterise the inter-relation between categories in the feature space. (2) Label tree [9,23]. To learn a label tree, we need to train a flat one-versus-rest (OVR) binary classifiers first, and then utilize the classification results to build the visual tree. However, the label tree structure always suffer from the imbalanced data and training efficiency. (3) Visual tree [13,30,41]. In general visual tree learning, a large number of categories can be organized hierarchically in a coarse-to-fine fashion with hierarchical clustering. Because the feature space is the common space for classifier training and classification, the visual tree can provide a good environment to characterize the inter-relation between categories. However, the number of cluster centers will profoundly influence the structure of the visual tree. Thus, how to determine the number of clusters is a critical issue.

Therefore, the suitable clustering number of hierarchical clustering is the key to building a reasonable visual tree and training a more discriminative classifier. It is necessary to find a way to effectively evaluate the goodness of clustering in order to select the suitable number of clusters. It is worth noting that the cluster validity index (CVI) is often used to evaluate the success of clustering applications [24,25]. Cluster validity index can be roughly divided into two categories: external cluster validity index and internal cluster validity index. The main difference is whether the external information is used in the cluster validity. Usually, the external information refers to the category labels. For visual tree, the objects of clustering are categories instead of samples, so there is no external information available for visual tree structure. Therefore, only internal cluster validity index can be used to guide the visual tree building.

Based on these observations, in this paper, an hierarchical cluster validity index (HCVI) is developed for supporting visual tree learning. The HCVI will consider both the clustering results of each level and the structural rationality of the visual tree. In hierarchical clustering, we will measure the impact of different numbers of clusters on visual tree building and select the most suitable number of clusters before clustering of each level begins. Based on the visual tree, a hierarchical classifier can be trained from top to bottom. Figure 1 illustrates the framework of hierarchical classifier training.

This paper is organized as follows. In Sect. 2, we review some relevant work. In Sect. 3, we present the proposed HCVI algorithm for visual tree learning. In Sect. 4, we present our experiments for algorithm evaluation. Section 5 provides some conclusions.

2   Related Work

The existing approaches for building hierarchical structure can be divided into three groups: (a) semantic tree; (b) label tree; (c) visual tree. Some researchers utilize the semantic ontology to organize large numbers of categories hierarchically [8,12,22,26,27,33]. Marszalek et al. employ the affiliation between nouns of WordNet to build a semantic tree for visual recognition [26]. Li et al. utilize both image and tag information to discover the semantic image hierarchy, and than employ this hierarchy to encode the inter-categories relations [22]. Fan et al. integrate semantic ontology and multi-task learning to complete the multi-level image annotation [12]. Some researchers build the label tree structure in the feature space [1,9,15,29,36]. Bengio et al. propose a label embedding tree for multi-class tasks [1]. Griffin et al. automatically generate useful taxonomies for learning hierarchical relationships between categories [15]. However, the label tree structure always suffer from the imbalanced data and training efficiency. Therefore, other researchers learn the visual tree by hierarchical clustering directly [28,30,40,41]. Zheng et al. utilize hierarchical affinity propagation clustering and active learning to build the visual tree [40]. Nister et al. built a vocabulary tree by employing hierarchical clustering [28].

Cluster validity index can be roughly divided into two categories: external cluster validity index and internal cluster validity index. External cluster validity is a measure for evaluating the quality of a clustering by employing the ground truth partition [21,24,25]. At present, many external cluster validity indexes have been proposed, such as: Rand Index (RI) [31], Adjusted Rand Index (ARI) [17], Fowlkes and Mallow index (FM) [14], Jaccard Index (JI) [18]. However, in visual tree learning, no ground truth information is available, so the internal cluster validity index should be used. Internal cluster validity index has been widely used in selecting the number of clusters. Calinski et al. proposed the Calinski-Harabasz index (CH), and it defined as the average between- and within- cluster sum of squares [4,24]. Davies et al. proposed the Davies-Bouldin index (DB), and it defined as the sum ratio of within-cluster scatter to between-cluster separation [7]. Rousseeuw proposed the Silhouette index (Si), and it is utilized to evaluate the consistency within clusters of data [32]. Tibshirani et al. focused the well separated clusters and developed a Gap index (Gap) [34]. Dunn proposed the Dunn index (Dunn), and it defined as the ratio between the inter-cluster separation to the intra-cluster compactness [11]. Hartigan proposed the Hartigan index (Har) [5,16].

3   Hierarchical Cluster Validity Index for Visual Tree Learning

In general, both external cluster validity index and internal cluster validity index are used to evaluate the performance of clustering. If we want to use CVI to guide visual tree learning, the most direct method is to find a reasonable CVI and use it to select the suitable number of clusters before each level clustering starts. This approach is appropriate for hierarchical clustering alone. However, although the visual tree is built by employing the hierarchical clustering, its purpose is not to get a good clustering result, but to train a discriminative hierarchical classifier based on it. No matter what CVI is used, it can only select the optimal number of clusters for a single clustering. However, one hierarchical clustering contains many sub-clustering. As computer scientists often say: local greed does not guarantee the global optimum, a satisfactory visual tree structure cannot be obtained through traditional internal CVI guidance. For example: according to CVI, one hierarchical clustering tends to choose fewer clusters at each level, the obtaining visual tree will be deep and narrow, and then the more node classifiers will be trained on one path of hierarchical classifier. Unfortunately, at some times, the more node classifiers passed, the lower the classification accuracy will be.

Based on these understanding, we propose a hierarchical cluster validity index that can measure the clustering validity while taking care of visual tree learning. The vast majority of CVIs are designed based on two key criteria: compactness and separation. The compactness measures the distance between the cluster center and samples in one cluster. Separation measures the pairwise distances between cluster centers. The existing methods have done a good job on these two criteria. Therefore, our hierarchical cluster validity index (HCVI) mainly focuses on visual tree learning. Specifically, we design a parameter based on the clustering results to measure whether the current cluster is suitable for building a visual tree. After that, we combined this parameter with the common CVIs to construct HCVI and employing the HCVI to guide the visual tree building.

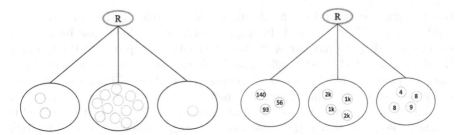

Fig. 2. The overly imbalanced structure of the visual tree. For sub-figure (a), most categories are grouped into one cluster, which leads to category imbalance. For sub-figure (b), Although the categories are relatively balanced, the huge difference in the number of samples in different categories leads to data imbalance.

In the real-world, large numbers of categories are usually imbalanced in the feature space (e.g., some of them have strong inter-category similarities, while others may have weaker inter-category similarities). Therefore, hierarchical clustering also generates an imbalanced visual tree. However, an overly imbalanced structure can also have negative effects on the training of hierarchical classifiers. Figure 2(a) illustrates an overly imbalanced structure. In this figure, each circle represents one category, and one can observe that most categories are grouped into one cluster. It will lead to imbalanced data problems when training hierarchical classifiers over this visual tree. In order to solve this problem, we have developed a parameter to evaluate the category balance, it defined as:

$$\sum_{k=1}^{q}[(\frac{r_k - r_E}{r_E})^2 + 1] \tag{1}$$

where parameter q indicates number of clusters. r_E indicates the average number of categories for one cluster. r_k indicates the number of categories contained in the kth cluster.

This parameter indicates the category balance in the clustering. The larger the parameter, the more imbalanced it is. On the other hand, in visual tree learning, the clustering objects are categories. However, when training hierarchical classifiers over the visual tree, every sample needs to be used for training. Therefore, we also need to consider the sample balance. Figure 2(b) illustrates an overly sample imbalance. One can observe that the number of categories in each cluster is almost equal, but the number of samples in each category varies greatly, which can seriously affect the training of hierarchical classifiers. Therefore, we have developed another parameter to evaluate the sample balance, it defined as:

$$\sum_{k=1}^{q}[(\frac{m_k - m_E}{m_E})^2 + 1] \tag{2}$$

where m_E indicates the average number of samples for one cluster. m_k indicates the number of samples contained in the kth cluster.

In order to measure the category and sample balance simultaneously, we combine these two parameters to generate a balance parameter, it defined as:

$$\delta(q) = \frac{1}{q} \sum_{k=1}^{q} \left(\left(\frac{r_k - r_E}{r_E}\right)^2 + 1\right)\left(\left(\frac{m_k - m_E}{m_E}\right)^2 + 1\right) \tag{3}$$

This parameter measures the balance of the visual tree learning. The smaller the value, the better the balance. We employ the balance parameter in combination with common CVIs as HCVI to measure the clustering effect so that the optimal number of clusters for hierarchical clustering can be selected. Some CVIs are the bigger the better, such as: CH [4], we denote HCVI as $CH/\delta(q)$, meanwhile, others are the smaller the better, such as: DB [7], we denote the HCVI as $DB \cdot \delta(q)$.

4   Experimental Results

4.1   Notation and Definitions

In this section, we introduce the notations used in the experiment [5], and than provide the definitions about HCVIs and internal CVIs, such as: CH [4], DB [7], Si [32], Dunn [11] and Har [16].

In the following, we denote:

n = number of samples;
p = number of variables;
q = number of clusters;
$X = \{x_{ij}\}, i = 1, ..., n j = 1, ..., p$;
$\overline{x}$ = centroid of data matrix X;
C_k = the k-th clusters;
n_k = number of objects in cluste C_k;
c_k = centroid of cluster C_k;
$d(x, y)$ = distance between x and y;
x_i = p-dimensional vector of samples of the i-th object in cluster C_k;
$\|x\| = (x^T x)^{1/2}$;
$W_q = \sum_{k=1}^{q} \sum_{i \in C_k} (x_i - c_k)(x_i - c_k)^T$ is the within-class dispersion matrix;
$B_q = \sum_{k=1}^{q} n_k (c_k - \overline{x})(c_k - \overline{x})^T$ is the between-class dispersion matrix;
$N_t = n(n-1)/2$;
$N_w = \sum_{k=1}^{q} n_k(n_k - 1)/2$;
$N_b = N_t - N_w$;
$S_w = \sum_{k=1}^{q} \sum_{i,j \in C_k, i<j} d(x_i, x_j)$ is sum of the within-cluster distances;

Table 1. Definitions of cluster validity index.

Method	Notation	CVI definition	HCVI definition
Calinski-Harabasz index	CH	$CH = \frac{trace(B_q)/(q-1)}{trace(W_q)/(n-q)}$	$CH/\delta(q)$
Davies-Bouldin index	DB	$DB = \frac{1}{q} \sum\limits_{k=1}^{q} \max\limits_{k \neq l} \left\{ \frac{\chi_k + \chi_l}{d(c_k, c_l)} \right\},$ $\chi_k = \frac{1}{n_k} \sum\limits_{x \in C_k} d(x, c_k),$ $\chi_l = \frac{1}{n_l} \sum\limits_{x \in C_l} d(x, c_l)$	$DB \cdot \delta(q)$
Silhouette index	Si	$Si = \frac{1}{n} \sum\limits_{x=1}^{n} \frac{b(x) - a(x)}{\max\{a(x), b(x)\}},$ $a(x) = \frac{1}{n_i - 1} \sum\limits_{y \in C_i, y \neq x} d(x, y),$ $b(x) = \min\limits_{j, j \neq i} [\frac{1}{n_j} \sum\limits_{y \in C_j} d(x, y)]$	$Si/\delta(q)$
Dunn index	Dunn	$Dunn = \frac{\min\limits_{1 \leq i < j \leq q} (\min\limits_{x \in C_i, y \in C_j} d(x,y))}{\max\limits_{1 \leq k \leq q} (\max\limits_{x, y \in C_k} d(x,y))}$	$Dunn/\delta(q)$
Hartigan index	Har	$Har = (\frac{trace(W_q)}{trace(W_{q+1})} - 1)(n - q - 1)$	$Har \cdot \delta(q)$

$S_b = \sum\limits_{k=1}^{q-1} \sum\limits_{l=k+1}^{q} \sum\limits_{i \in C_k, j \in C_l} d(x_i, y_i)$ is sum of the between-cluster distances.

Based on these notations, Table 1 shows 5 widely used internal cluster validity index and its corresponding hierarchical cluster validity index. The "Method" column gives the full name of these indices, and the "Notation" column gives the abbreviation. The "CVI Definition" column gives the computation formulas of these indices and the "HCVI Definition" column gives the corresponding hierarchical forms.

4.2   Experimental Settings

In order to verify the effectiveness of the proposed balance parameter, we compare the common CVIs and the balance parameter based HCVIs through experiments. We employ K-means as the clustering algorithm for experiment. All the experiments are carried out on Matlab 2015a. In our experiments, DB, CH, Si can be implemented by using the Statistics and Machine Learning Toolbox of Matlab. We implement the Har index by employed part of CVAP toolbox [35]. Our experimental environment is: a single machine with 4 cores and 16GB memory.

4.3   Experiment for Balance Parameter

In this experiment, we evaluate the proposed approach on *Fisheriris* data set. *Fisheriris* data set is one of available data set at UCI machine learning repository [2]. It has 150 samples with 50 samples in each category. The dimension of the original data is 4. To facilitate visualization, we use the first two dimensions of

Table 2. Criterion values of CVIs.

Number of clusters	2	3	4	5	6	7	8
CH	730.92	873.13	1009.93	1190.18	**1230.11**	1196.25	1173.77
DB	**0.36**	0.58	0.70	0.61	0.67	0.69	0.72
Si	**0.84**	0.69	0.67	0.70	0.67	0.64	0.63
Dunn	0.0207	0.0282	0.0340	**0.0654**	0.0504	0.0548	0.0504
Har	**−184.47**	−31.60	60.72	−64.90	318.50	−112.69	63.88

Table 3. Balance parameter of Fisheriris data set.

Number of clusters	2	3	4	5	6	7	8
Balance parameter	1.89	1.57	1.24	1.06	1.40	1.23	1.22

each sample as one sample and the last two dimensions as another. In this way, there are 300 samples in total. In the experiment, we use 5 common CVIs and their corresponding HCVIs to evaluate the clustering results with different number of clusters. It is worth noting that each sample in this experiment represents only one single sample, so HCVIs can only evaluate the sample balance.

Table 2 shows the criterion values of CVIs. The bold value is the optimal criterion values of different CVIs. One can observe that the optimal number of clusters derived from different CVIs is not identical, even though the clustering data is the same. It shows the criteria of different CVIs vary widely. Since we have reconstructed the data set, the original labels has been invalidated, so we cannot evaluate which CVI is better. However, our main purpose is not to find the optimal indicators, but to verify the effectiveness of the balance parameters. Table 3 shows the balance parameter of different number of clusters. From the result, it is obvious that the clustering result is the most balanced when the number of clusters q = 5. From Tables 2 and 3, we can observe that most common CVIs do not pay attention to the balance of clustering, which is the precisely concern of building a visual tree. Therefore, HCVI is a reasonable choice for considering both clustering goodness and balance. Figure 3 illuminates the cluster assignments and the criterion values of CVIs and their corresponding HCVIs. The first two columns show the results of the CVI, and the last two columns show the results of the corresponding HCVI. We can observe that the common CVIs tend to choose fewer clusters, while HCVIs tend to choose more clusters. In particular, the DB and Si indices both consider $q = 2$ as the optimal number of clusters, however, it results in a very imbalanced clustering result. After using the balance parameter, the HCVIs of DB and Si have selected a reasonable cluster number that makes the clustering results more balanced. It is worth noting that the balance parameter does not improve balance of Har index. It shows that the Har index hardly considers the clustering balance as a criterion. In summary, we can conclude that the proposed balance parameter can effectively improve the performance of CVIs in terms of clustering balance.

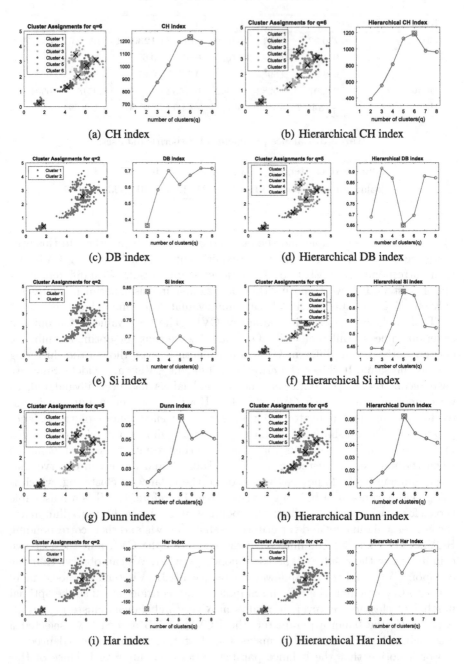

Fig. 3. The cluster assignments and the criterion values of CVIs and their corresponding HCVIs.

4.4   Experiment for Hierarchical Classification

In this section, we evaluate the proposed HVCIs comparing the classification accuracy of different visual tree structures. In the experiment, we employ the proposed HCVI to build visual trees and train hierarchical classifiers based on these visual trees. Our experiment are carried out on two data sets: *CIFAR-100* [20], the *ILSVRC-2012* [8]. CIFAR-100 has 100 image categories and each category contains 600 images. We randomly select 10,000 images, half for training and half for testing. ILSVRC-2012 data set is a subset of ImageNet. It contains 1000 image categories and each category has over 1,000 images. We randomly select 20,000 images, half for training and half for testing. In the experiment, we employ DeCAF features as the image representation [10], and then use PCA to reduce the dimensionality of the DeCAF from 4096 to 128.

Table 4. Classification results on CIFAR-100 and ILSVRC-2012 image set.

Approaches	CIFAR-100	ILSVRC-2012
Semantic tree	22.86	26.39
Label tree	24.51	28.11
Visual tree	25.07	28.16
EVT	28.28	28.59
CH-VT	36.98	33.96
DB-VT	25.46	32.21
Si-VT	30.90	39.12
Dunn-VT	28.08	30.02
Har-VT	29.34	28.10
HCH-VT	38.00	35.03
HDB-VT	29.04	34.46
HSi-VT	29.30	38.35
HDunn-VT	34.74	32.71
HHar-VT	31.54	28.58

In this experiments, we compare the proposed HCVI-visual tree structure with two types of tree structure: CVI-visual tree structure and traditional hierarchical structure. In particular, traditional hierarchical structures contains: semantic tree [27], label tree [15], visual tree [40] and EVT [40]. We train hierarchical classifiers based on these tree structure and compare their classification results. We employ K-means as the clustering algorithm for experiment and the SVM classifier as the node classifiers. The Mean Accuracy (%) is used as the criterion to evaluate the performance of all approaches. The experimental results are shown in Table 4. We can observe that the hierarchical classifiers based on visual trees which utilizing cluster validity indices can achieve better results.

The reason is that the cluster validity indices allows us to get better clustering results, so as to get more discriminative visual trees. In addition, most of HCVIs-based methods have achieved better results, which illustrates the effectiveness of the proposed balance parameter. It's worth noting that CH index based method achieve higher classification accuracy compared to HCH index based method. One possible reason is that the HCH index considers balance too much and ignores the compactness and the separation of clustering. In general, we can obtain more reasonable visual tree structures through the guidance of HCVIs to help train more discriminative hierarchical classifiers.

5   Conclusion

In this paper, a hierarchical cluster validity index (HCVI) is developed to achieve more discriminative solution for visual tree learning, where the hierarchical classifiers can be trained over the visual trees. Our HCVI integrate the proposed balance parameter and the common CVIs. Both the balance of visual tree and the effectiveness of clustering are leveraged to learn more discriminative hierarchical structure. Therefore, the hierarchical classifier can achieve better results. The experimental results have demonstrated that our hierarchical cluster validity index has superior performance as compared with other cluster validity indices on both the clustering balance and the classification accuracy.

Acknowledgments. This work was supported in part by the National Natural Science Foundation of China under (Grant No. 61432014, No. U1605252, No. 61772402, No. 61671339, No. 61571347, and No. 61603233), in part by National High-Level Talents Special Support Program (Leading Talent of Technological Innovation of Ten-Thousands Talents Program) (No. CS31117200001), in part by the National Key Research and Development Program of China (No. 2016QY01W0200), in part by the Key Industrial Innovation Chain Project in Industrial Domain (Grant No. 2016KTZDGY04-02), in part by the Shaanxi Basic Research Projects in Natural Sciences (No. 2017JQ6076).

References

1. Bengio, S., Weston, J., Grangier, D.: Label embedding trees for large multi-class tasks. In: NIPS, pp. 163–171 (2010)
2. Blake, C.L., Merz, C.J.: UCI repository of machine learning databases. Department of Information and Computer Science, University of California, Irvine, CA, vol. 55 (1998). http://www.ics.uci.edu/~mlearn/mlrepository.html
3. Bruse, J.L., et al.: Detecting clinically meaningful shape clusters in medical image data: metrics analysis for hierarchical clustering applied to healthy and pathological aortic arches. IEEE Trans. Biomed. Eng. **64**, 2373–2383 (2017)
4. Caliński, T., Harabasz, J.: A dendrite method for cluster analysis. Commun. Stat.-Theory Methods **3**(1), 1–27 (1974)
5. Charrad, M., Ghazzali, N., Boiteau, V., Niknafs, A.: NbClust package: finding the relevant number of clusters in a dataset. J. Stat. Softw. (2012)

6. Chen, S., Yang, J., Luo, L., Wei, Y., Zhang, K., Tai, Y.: Low-rank latent pattern approximation with applications to robust image classification. IEEE Trans. Image Process. **26**, 5519–5530 (2017)
7. Davies, D.L., Bouldin, D.W.: A cluster separation measure. IEEE Trans. Pattern Anal. Mach. Intell. **2**, 224–227 (1979)
8. Deng, J., Dong, W., Socher, R., Li, L.J., Li, K., Fei-Fei, L.: ImageNet: a large-scale hierarchical image database. In: CVPR, pp. 248–255 (2009)
9. Deng, J., Satheesh, S., Berg, A.C., Li, F.: Fast and balanced: efficient label tree learning for large scale object recognition. In: NIPS, pp. 567–575 (2011)
10. Donahue, J., et al.: DeCAF: a deep convolutional activation feature for generic visual recognition. In: ICML, pp. 647–655 (2014)
11. Dunn, J.C.: Well-separated clusters and optimal fuzzy partitions. J. Cybern. **4**(1), 95–104 (1974)
12. Fan, J., Gao, Y., Luo, H.: Integrating concept ontology and multitask learning to achieve more effective classifier training for multilevel image annotation. IEEE Trans. Image Process. **17**(3), 407–426 (2008)
13. Fan, J., Zhou, N., Peng, J., Gao, L.: Hierarchical learning of tree classifiers for large-scale plant species identification. IEEE Trans. Image Process. **24**(11), 4172–4184 (2015)
14. Fowlkes, E.B., Mallows, C.L.: A method for comparing two hierarchical clusterings. J. Am. Stat. Assoc. **78**(383), 553–569 (1983)
15. Griffin, G., Perona, P.: Learning and using taxonomies for fast visual categorization. In: CVPR, pp. 1–8 (2008)
16. Hartigan, J.A.: Clustering algorithms (1975)
17. Hubert, L., Arabie, P.: Comparing partitions. J. Classif. **2**(1), 193–218 (1985)
18. Jaccard, P.: Étude comparative de la distribution florale dans une portion des alpes et des jura. Bull. Soc. Vaudoise Sci. Nat. **37**, 547–579 (1901)
19. Kalantarian, H., Sideris, C., Sarrafzadeh, M.: A hierarchical classification and segmentation scheme for processing sensor data. IEEE J. Biomed. Health Inform. **21**(3), 672–681 (2017)
20. Krizhevsky, A., Hinton, G.: Learning multiple layers of features from tiny images. Technical report, U. Toronto (2009)
21. Lei, Y., Bezdek, J.C., Romano, S., Vinh, N.X., Chan, J., Bailey, J.: Ground truth bias in external cluster validity indices. Pattern Recogn. **65**, 58–70 (2017)
22. Li, L.J., Wang, C., Lim, Y., Blei, D.M., Fei-Fei, L.: Building and using a semantivisual image hierarchy. In: CVPR, pp. 3336–3343 (2010)
23. Liu, B., Sadeghi, F., Tappen, M., Shamir, O., Liu, C.: Probabilistic label trees for efficient large scale image classification. In: CVPR, pp. 843–850 (2013)
24. Liu, Y., Li, Z., Xiong, H., Gao, X., Wu, J.: Understanding of internal clustering validation measures. In: ICDM, pp. 911–916 (2010)
25. Liu, Y., Li, Z., Xiong, H., Gao, X., Wu, J., Wu, S.: Understanding and enhancement of internal clustering validation measures. IEEE Trans. Cybern. **43**(3), 982–994 (2013)
26. Marszałek, M., Schmid, C.: Constructing category hierarchies for visual recognition. In: Forsyth, D., Torr, P., Zisserman, A. (eds.) ECCV 2008. LNCS, vol. 5305, pp. 479–491. Springer, Heidelberg (2008). https://doi.org/10.1007/978-3-540-88693-8_35
27. Miller, G.A.: WordNet: a lexical database for English. Commun. ACM **38**(11), 39–41 (1995)
28. Nister, D., Stewenius, H.: Scalable recognition with a vocabulary tree. In: CVPR, vol. 2, pp. 2161–2168 (2006)

29. Phan, H., Hertel, L., Maass, M., Koch, P., Mertins, A.: Label tree embeddings for acoustic scene classification. In: ACM MM, pp. 486–490 (2016)
30. Qu, Y., et al.: Joint hierarchical category structure learning and large-scale image classification. IEEE Trans. Image Process. **26**(9), 4331–4346 (2017)
31. Rand, W.M.: Objective criteria for the evaluation of clustering methods. J. Am. Stat. Assoc. **66**(336), 846–850 (1971)
32. Rousseeuw, P.J.: Silhouettes: a graphical aid to the interpretation and validation of cluster analysis. J. Comput. Appl. Math. **20**, 53–65 (1987)
33. Tang, J., Chang, S., Qi, G.J., Tian, Q., Rui, Y., Huang, T.S.: LEGO-MM: learning structured model by probabilistic logic ontology tree for multimedia. IEEE Trans. Image Process. **26**(1), 196–207 (2017)
34. Tibshirani, R., Walther, G., Hastie, T.: Estimating the number of clusters in a data set via the gap statistic. J. R. Stat. Soc.: Ser. B (Stat. Methodol.) **63**(2), 411–423 (2001)
35. Wang, K., Wang, B., Peng, L.: CVAP: validation for cluster analyses. Data Sci. J. **8**, 88–93 (2009)
36. Wu, Q., Tan, M., Song, H., Chen, J., Ng, M.K.: ML-FOREST: a multi-label tree ensemble method for multi-label classification. IEEE Trans. Knowl. Data Eng. **28**(10), 2665–2680 (2016)
37. Yao, C., Liu, Y.F., Jiang, B., Han, J., Han, J.: LLE score: a new filter-based unsupervised feature selection method based on nonlinear manifold embedding and its application to image recognition. IEEE Trans. Image Process. **26**, 5257–5269 (2017)
38. Zhang, L., Shah, S., Kakadiaris, I.: Hierarchical multi-label classification using fully associative ensemble learning. Pattern Recogn. **70**, 89–103 (2017)
39. Zhao, T., et al.: Deep mixture of diverse experts for large-scale visual recognition. IEEE Trans. Pattern Anal. Mach. Intell. (2018)
40. Zheng, Y., Fan, J., Zhang, J., Gao, X.: Hierarchical learning of multi-task sparse metrics for large-scale image classification. Pattern Recogn. **67**, 97–109 (2017)
41. Zhou, N., Fan, J.: Jointly learning visually correlated dictionaries for large-scale visual recognition applications. IEEE Trans. Pattern Anal. Mach. Intell. **36**(4), 715–730 (2014)

Robust Shapelets Learning:
Transform-Invariant Prototypes

Huiqi Deng[1,3], Weifu Chen[1], Andy J. Ma[2,3], Qi Shen[1,4], Pong C. Yuen[3],
and Guocan Feng[1(✉)]

[1] School of Mathematics, Sun Yat-sen University, Guangzhou, China
denghq7@mail2.sysu.edu.cn, {chenwf26,mcsfg}@mail.sysu.edu.cn
[2] School of Data and Computer Science, Sun Yat-sen University, Guangzhou, China
majh8@mail.sysu.edu.cn
[3] Department of Computer Science, Hong Kong Baptist University,
Hong Kong, China
pcyuen@comp.hkbu.edu.hk
[4] Department of Genetics and Genomic Sciences, Icahn School of Medicine
at Mount Sinai, New York, USA
qi.shen@mssm.edu

Abstract. *Shapelets* are discriminative local patterns in time series, which maximally distinguish among different classes. Instead of considering full series, shapelet transformation considers the existence or absence of local shapelets, which leads to high classification accuracy, easy visualization and interpretability. One of the limitation of existing methods is robustness. For example, *Search-based* approaches select sample subsequences as shapelets and those methods intuitively may be not accurate and robust enough. *Learning-based* approaches learn shapelets by maximizing the discriminative ability. However, those methods may not preserve basic shape for visualization. In practice, shapelets are subjected to various geometric transformations, such as translation, scaling, and stretching, which may result in a confusion of shapelet judgement. In this paper, robust shapelet learning is proposed to solve above problems. By learning transform-invariant representative prototypes from all training time series, rather than just selecting samples from the sequences, each time series sample could be approximated by the combination of the transformations of those prototypes. Based on the combination, samples could be easily classified into different classes. Experiments on 16 UCR time series datasets showed that the performance of the proposed framework is comparable to the state-of-art methods, but could learn more representative shapelets for complex scenarios.

Keywords: Robustness · Transform-invariant
Representative prototype

1 Introduction

Time series classification has attracted a lot of attention in many applications, such as finance (e.g. stock market), medical diagnosis (e.g. EEG and ECG),

© Springer Nature Switzerland AG 2018
J.-H. Lai et al. (Eds.): PRCV 2018, LNCS 11258, pp. 491–502, 2018.
https://doi.org/10.1007/978-3-030-03338-5_41

motion capture and speech recognition. Since the order of series and the dependence of close time stamps are crucial in finding the most discriminative features and patterns, it raises great difficulty for algorithms to classify time series data. Recently, a new primitive named *Shapelets* has been generating increasing interests in time series classification (TSC). Shapelets are discriminative continuous snippets of full series, which maximally distinguish among different classes. Hence, shapelets can be treated as representative of some class, and time series classification turns out to be the problem of presence or absence of some shapelets for representing time series data.

Shapelets for time series have attracted many researchers' interest for two main reasons. First, shapelets focus on local variation rather than global variation as traditional algorithms did, which could be more robust to noise and available for early time series prediction. Second, shapelets reveal the inherent attention mechanism of data so that allow for easier summarization and visualization, which provides explanatory insights to the classification problem.

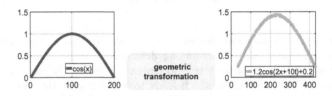

Fig. 1. Demo of deformation. The left column is a cosine curve; the right column is the transformed cosine curve obtained by imposing shift, translation, scaling, stretching transformations and Gaussian noise on the original cosine curve.

Despite the above advantages of shapelets, current shapelets are a little clumsy. We observe that samples in the same class always share a basic shape, while in practice, the basic shape may subject to individual difference and go through various deformations, such as shift, translation, scaling, stretching and so on. As shown in Fig. 1, the cosine curve is actually similar to the transformed cosine curve in term of shape, despite individual noises and slight differences in phase (shift), amplitude (scaling), offset (translation), uniform scaling (stretching).

In this paper, we introduce a new conception, "shapelets prototypes" and propose a transform-invariant robust shapelet learning framework based on dictionary learning theory. The proposed framework aims to learn representative basic shapes that are learned from the transformed subsequences by alternative iteration. In each iteration, robust shapelet learning performs two steps: a) in the alignment step, the best transformation operators are automatically obtained by minimizing the average least square error between the transformed subsequences and current shapelets prototype; b) in the refinement step, the dictionaries are updated to reflect the basic shapes from transformed training series. Figure 2 shows a real-world example from the GunPoint dataset. $S1$ and

$S2$ are learned shapelet prototypes, $T1$–$T3$ are three time series from gun class, and $T4$–$T6$ are examples from no gun class. Here $S1$ represents an action of drawing guns from holsters, and $S2$ represents returning guns to the holsters, which are critical patterns for classifying the two classes. While such actions are subject-dependent, and the corresponding patterns from samples shows a high variety due to individual factors. As seen from Fig. 2, our proposed method can align probe sample to learned prototypes and reveals the inherent knowledge of data. Our contributions can be summarized as:

- We propose a robust shapelet learning framework based on dictionary learning theory, which is invariant to various deformations;
- The discovered shapelet prototypes can explore intrinsic shapes which are more general and expressive.
- Shapelet prototypes well preserve the basic shapes and hence have better interpretability.

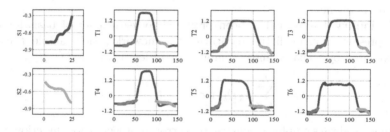

Fig. 2. Illustration of two shapelet prototypes $S1, S2$ (leftmost plots) learned from *GunPoint* dataset. First row $(T1, T2, T3)$ and second row $(T4, T5, T6)$, are instances from Gun class and NoGun class respectively. Each sample mathced prototypes to all segments and projected corresponding segments (red and green) to prototypes by optimal transformation parameters. It can be observed that series in Gun have a better match to prototypes than series in NoGun. (Color figure online)

2   Related Work

Shapelets are discriminative shapes that can be used to classify time series data effectively. Shapelet learning algorithms make classification decision based on the presence or absence of shapelets in representing a time series. Existing shapelet learning methods can be categorized into *search-based* algorithms [7,8,10,13,14] and *learning-based* algorithms [4,12]. The original *search-based* algorithm adopts a brute-force strategy to select shapelets from a large pool of candidate segments and select the most expressive subsequences by various quality criteria, which is time-consuming [14]. In order to reduce the searching time, several algorithms have been proposed to speed up the algorithm by skipping similar segments so that the number of candidates are greatly reduced [7,8,10,13]. Instead of learning the shapelets first, learning-based algorithms try to learn shapelets and classify time series data simultaneously. Grabocka et al. proposed a classification logistic loss function to jointly learn the shapelets and the logistic regression classifier through stochastic gradient descent approach. *Search-based* approaches choose existing subsequences from training time series, while *learning-based* approach sometimes may not preserve the basic shape of shapelets so that may lack of interpretability, as it mainly considered classification ability. In other words, the above methods lack of the ability of learning a transform-invariant prototypes from training series.

Invariance of transformations is important for time-series domain because sequences are easily distorted and always show high variety due to geometric transformations. For examples, scaling (amplitude) and translation (offset) invariance might benefit for seasonal variations of markets with inflation motion caption [9], and shift invariance [15] is essential for the case where time series share similar patterns but in different phase. In addition, uniform scaling invariance is required for heartbeats with measurement periods of different sampling frequency.

Dictionary learning has been proposed to learn a set of basis for compact representation. In dictionary learning frameworks, each sample T can be approximated by a sparse linear combination of learned basis $\{D_k\}_{k=1}^K$.

$$T = \sum_{k=1}^{K} \alpha_k D_k + \epsilon \qquad s.t \; \|\alpha\|_1 \leq c_0, \tag{1}$$

Such models always employ reconstruction error as objective loss function, where basis and representation coefficients are optimized by alternate iteration. Dictionary learning has been proved feasible and desirable in image classification [6], signal reconstruction and representation [1,11]. Further, it has been shown great power in scalable data mining and has strong interpretability and generalization capability [16].

3   Learning Transform Invariant Shapelet Prototypes

Formulations. In this section we adopt a conception of "prototype" D, representative shapes learned from training samples. For a set of subsequences without transformation, the prototype is usually computed based on Euclidean space:

$$\underset{\substack{\alpha^i \in R^K \\ D_k \in R^q}}{\arg\min} \sum_{i=1}^{N} \|T^i - \sum_{k=1}^{K} \alpha_k^i D_k\|^2 + \lambda \sum_{i=1}^{N} \|\alpha^i\|_1 \tag{2}$$

$$s.t. \; \|D_k\|^2 \leq d_0, \quad \text{for } k = 1\ldots,K$$

While it's not appropriate to utilize Euclidean distance by $L2$ norm in many cases, as we often pay more attention to the shape similarity. Even tiny operation in scaling, translation, and stretching may rapidly swamp shape similarity measured by Euclidean distance.

For subsequences with various transformations, we introduce a conception of transformation operator τ, and τ may be a compound of multiple transformations. An intuitive observation is that each sample subsequences is transformed from shared "prototype" dictionary bases D by a corresponding transformation operator:

$$\tau^i(T^i) = \sum_{k=1}^{K} \alpha_k D_k + \epsilon^i \qquad s.t \; \|\alpha\|_1 \le c_0, \tag{3}$$

where each sample has specific transformation operator τ^i. Therefore, the learned dictionaries, removing the effect of transformations, is defined as "prototypes" and could be estimated by minimizing the reconstruction error between the sample subsequence and the aligned reconstruction samples. The reformulation is as follows:

$$\underset{\substack{\alpha^i \in R^K \\ D_k \in R^q \\ \tau^i \in \omega}}{\arg\min} \sum_{i=1}^{N} \left\| \tau^i(T^i) - \sum_{k=1}^{K} \alpha_k^i D_k \right\|^2 + \lambda \sum_{i=1}^{N} \|\alpha^i\|_1$$

$$\text{s.t. } \|D_k\|^2 \le d_0, \quad \text{for } k = 1 \ldots, K. \tag{4}$$

Here prototypes D for series and transformation operator τ^i and codes α^i for each sample need to be optimized.

Transform Definition

The proposed robust shapelet learning framework aims to find the intrinsic local patterns of time series. For a prototype $w \in R^p$, a vector ordered by time stamps, most classical linear transformations can be represented as:

$$T^i = \tau^i(w) + \epsilon_i = a_i w(\mu_i t) + c_i + \epsilon_i, \tag{5}$$

where a_i is a scaling factor, c_i is a translation factor and μ_i is a stretching factor. Here τ_i defines a general transformation, where scaling, translation and stretching operators are its special cases:

- **Scaling operator:** Scaling transformation describes differences in amplitude between $w(t)$ and transformed sequence $T_i(t)$:

$$T_i(t) = a_i w(t) \quad t = 1, \ldots, p \tag{6}$$

- **Translation operator:** Translation transformation describes a translation along y axis from $w(t)$ to transformed sequence $T_i(t)$:

$$T_i(t) = w(t) + c_i \quad t = 1, \ldots, p \tag{7}$$

- **Stretch operator** [3]: Uniform scaling transformation is used for matching sequences with different lengths. Subsequences with different length may require a stretching or shrinking operation due to different tempo or sampling frequency:

$$T_i(t) = w\left(\left\lceil \frac{t}{\mu} \right\rceil\right) \quad t = 1, \ldots, \lceil \mu p \rceil \tag{8}$$

Note that stretching operator defined is motivated by uniform scaling operation through ceiling function [3].

Figure 3 shows the above defined transformations. Similarly, we can define the inverse operators for the above transformations.

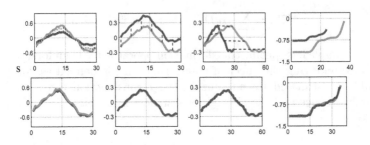

Fig. 3. Difference between transformed subsequence (plotted in red) and original subsequence (blue): Scale operator $a = 1.5$ (leftmost). Translation operator $c = 0.2$ (second column). Stretch operator $\mu = 2$ (third column). Multiple transformations on GunPoint dataset (rightmost). (Color figure online)

4   Model Inference

Optimization objective function is a non-convex problem with respect to the prototypes and transformation operators. We adopt a coordinate descent approach for iteration alternatively. And in each iteration, we perform two steps shown in Algorithm 1: (i) Alignment step: Given current dictionary, updating corresponding transformation operator for each sample subsequences. (ii) Refinement step: Given all transformation operators, the dictionary is updated to reflect the basic shapes learnt from training series.

Alignment Step. Fix the dictionary and sparse coding, i.e., D and α, reconstruction sequence has been determined. We are going to find the optimal alignment (deformation) between original series T^i and reconstruction sequence. To learn the transform parameters, we minimize the mean square error between the reconstruction sequence and subsequence of time series by all possible conversion. It's remarkable that for input segments T^i_j with stretching factor μ, it has an unequal length to the dictionary. So it needs to do an inverse operation μ^{-1}. For a given sparse coding and dictionary, problems can be solve as:

$$\arg\min_{\tau^i} \left\| \tau^i(T^i) - \sum_{k=1}^{K} \alpha^i_k D_k(t) \right\|^2 \tag{9}$$

where $\tau = \{a, \mu, c\}$, superscript and subscript are dropped for clarify. Obviously, a and c are scaling and translation factors with continuous values, μ is a stretch

---

Algorithm 1. Transform Invariant shapelet prototypes learning

---

Input: Initial segments $\{T_i\}_{i=1}^N$, Initial dictionary $D \in R^{K*q}$.
1: **for** $Iter = 1, ..., MaxIter$ do **do**
2:    **for** $i = 1, ..., N$ do **do**
3:       Alignment step:
4:       $\tau_i = $ E.q (9) ;
5:       $T_i' = \tau^i(T^i)$;
6:    **end for**
7:    Refinement step:
8:       $\{\alpha, D, \tau\} = $ E.q (10)
9: **end for**
10: **return** α, D, τ;

---

factor with discrete factor. So fixed μ, optimal a, c can be derived by Least Square methods. Then a grid search will be conducted by all possible μ. With obtained parameters, original subsequence $\tau(T)$ at transformed location are exacted, as well as aligned sequence $S = \tau(T) \in R^q$.

Refinement Step. Fix the transform parameters, i.e., $\tau = \{a, \mu, c\}$, optimize α, D. If transform parameters τ are known, it's easy to get updated segments, i.e., updated $\{\tau^i(T^i)\}_{i=1}^N$, which is transformed with fixed length. The problem then reduces to a traditional dictionary learning problem:

$$\arg\min_{\alpha, D} \sum_{i=1}^N \left\| \tau^i(T^i) - \sum_{k=1}^K \alpha_k^i D_k \right\|^2 + \sum_{i=1}^N \lambda \|\alpha^i\|_1 \tag{10}$$
$$\text{s.t. } \|D_k\|^2 \le c, \quad \text{for } k = 1 \dots, K$$

Coordinate descent is used to solve for dictionary D and sparse coding α.

5 Experiment

5.1 Experiment Setting

Since there are enormous shapelet candidates, we calculated the average sequence to decide the discriminative ability by information gain. And shapes with low discriminative power have been removed so that the volume of candidates would be much smaller (similar, redundant candidates have been discarded), and only valuable candidates were selected as input segments. In training phase, the algorithm was initialized by subsequence matching, where we aligned the initial candidate to all possible segment and extracted the most similar projection. Then, these segments T_i were fed into our transform invariant prototype learning framework and after iterations, a transform-invariant dictionary could be derived. Lastly in testing phase, the sparse representation were conducted based on learned transform-invariant dictionary learning.

Table 1. Statistics of the benchmark time series datasets

	Train/test	Length	Class
Adiac	390/391	176	37
Beef	30/30	470	5
Coffee	28/28	286	2
Diatom	16/306	345	4
ECGFiveDays	23/861	136	2
FaceFour	24/88	350	4
GunPoint	50/150	150	2
ItalyPower	67/1029	24	2
Lighting7	70/73	319	7
MedicalImages	381/760	99	10
MoteStrain	20/1252	84	2
Sony	20/601	70	2
Symbols	25/995	398	6
SytheticC	300/300	60	6
Trace	100/100	275	4
TwoLeadECG	23/1129	82	2

During candidate selection process, it requires the tuning of hyperparameters, which were found through a grid search approach using cross-validation over the training data. The initial number of shape set was searched in a range of $K_1 \in \{0.05, 0.1\} * Q$, and the length of shapelets $q \in \{0.125, 0.25, 0.375, 0.5\} * Q$, where Q is the full series length. During dictionary learning process, the number of atoms in dictionary $K_2 \in \{5, 10, 15\}$, while the sparsity parameter $\lambda \in \{0.1, 1\}$. For efficiency, the operation of the above deformation could be selected flexibly.

5.2   Complexity Analysis

The time complexity of shapelet prototypes learning consists of two parts, one for initialization segments exaction, and the other for transform invariant dictionary learning. For initialization segments exaction, we need to compute a robust shape similarity, instead of optimal transformation operators, between shapelets with length q candidates and all possible segments. Therefore, we adopted a Z-normalization distance with all range of stretching factors, and the cost is $O(Cq)$, where C is the number of stretching factors. Here, the complexity is similar to the Euclidean distance computation, with a constant multiplier.

For transform invariant dictionary learning, the cost part of alignment step is the computing for τ^i, which takes $O(CNq)$, including the complexity of least square solution of scaling, translation factor and grid search on stretching factors.

Refinement step takes $O(KNq)$, including sparse coding and dictionary learning. Therefore, the total complexity for one call to Algorithm 1 is $O(M((C+K)Nq))$, where M is the maximum number of iterations allowed in Algorithm 1. M can be set quite small. In practice, 20 iterations would be sufficient.

5.3   Classification Accuracy

Experiments were performed on the 16 commonly used UCR time series benchmark which could be downloaded from UCR website [2], and the information of the those datasets were listed in Table 1. For the sake of equivalent comparison, we used the same training and testing split for all the methods. And in the experiments, SVM was chosen as the classifier.

There are many shapelet learning algorithms proposed in the last decades. Ref. [5] compared the performance of some popular shapelet learning algorithms. In this work, we compared our algorithm with three state-of-art baselines IGSVM, LTS and FLAG:

- IGSVM [7]: Shapelet-transform algorithm, which uses the linear SVM as classifier and information as shapelet quality measurement.
- LTS [4]: learning time series shapelets algorithm, which learns the shapelets and logistic classifier automatically and jointly.
- FLAG [5]: Learning position of shapelets, which maximizes the ratio of projected data variances between classes by fussed lasso constraints efficiently.

Table 2 shows the classification accuracy of baseline and the proposed method. Our method shows a superiority to IGSVM, FLAG and a comparable performance to LTS, even better prediction accuracy in several dataset. In addition, dictionary learning is desirable for scalable analysis, as well as interpretability.

5.4   Exploratory Data Analysis

One of the strengths of using shapelets as a classification tool is that they provide an easy interpretation and summarization behind data that other classification approaches simply do not. It helps for mining inherent structure. One of the key motivation of our work is to capture an intrinsic structure and knowledge behind data, which is interpretable and unified for data.

To verify the power of transform invariant shapelet learning, we briefly analyze a classical problem in time series data mining domain. On the Gun/NoGun motion capture time series dataset, there are 100 instances from each class. In the Gun class, the actors have their hands by their sides, draw a gun from a hip-mounted holster, point it at a target for approximately one second, and then return the gun to the holster and their hands to their sides. In contrast, in the NoGun class, actors do the similar hands-down, point, hold, and return motion without the gun in their hands and therefore are pointing to a target using the index finger. The classification problem is to distinguish between above two very

Table 2. Classification accuracy on 16 commonly used dataset.

Dataset	Compared methods			
	IGSVM	LTS	FLAG	Ours
Adiac	23.5(4)	51.9(3)	**75.2(1)**	61.8(2)
Beef	**90.0(1)**	76.7(3)	83.2(3)	76.7(3)
Coffee	**100.0(1)**	**100.0(1)**	**100.0(1)**	**100.0(1)**
Diatom	93.1(4)	94.2(3)	**96.4(1)**	95.4(2)
ECGFiveDays	99.0(3)	**100.0(1)**	92.0(4)	**100.0(1)**
FaceFour	**97.7(1)**	94.3(3)	90.9(4)	96.6(2)
GunPoint	**100.0(1)**	99.6(2)	96.7(4)	**100.0(1)**
ItalyPower	93.7(4)	**95.8(1)**	94.6(3)	95.3(2)
Lighting7	63.0(4)	**79.0(1)**	76.7(3)	78.1(2)
MedicalImages	52.2(4)	71.2(2)	**71.4(1)**	70.5(3)
MoteStrain	88.7(2)	**90.0(1)**	88.7(2)	88.7(2)
Sony	92.7(1)	91.0(4)	**92.9(1)**	91.5(3)
Symbols	84.6(4)	94.5(2)	87.5(3)	**97.1(1)**
SytheticC	87.3(4)	97.3(3)	**99.7(1)**	99.0(2)
Trace	98.0(4)	**100.0(1)**	99.0(3)	**100.0(1)**
TwoLeadECG	**100.0(1)**	**100.0(1)**	99.0(4)	**100.0(1)**
AverageRank	2.69	2	2.43	**1.78**

similar action. Moreover, the dataset consists of instances from two actors, who differ in baseline height about 12 in. (translation) and motion 'style', including different movement range (scaling), tempo (stretching). To sum up, the challenges relied on the similarity between two action and the intra-class diversity due to geometric transformation.

As shown in Fig. 4, the original top shapelet trained by [14], represents a "overshot" phenomenon at the end of series. It contains an action corresponding to the arm being lowered back into position. However, at the begin of series, Gun class has a specific shape found by proposed method before a consistent action of raising the arm. That's because action from Gun class has to draw a gun from a holster. Intuitively, it's one of intrinsic feature of Gun class, which differ from NoGun class. However, owing to the intra-class diversity, instances differ in offset, scale and stretching factor. DTW and Z-normalization fail to deal with such variance, so that they failed to explore the latent discriminative power of $S1$, because of the complex transformation. While our transform invariant framework achieved meaningful detection of shapelets. The graphs in Fig. 4 shows a best alignment for $S1$ by projecting it through optimal deformation factors.

Therefore, shapelet found by proposed method reflect the essential difference between classes. Interestingly, once instance take a gun from a holster, we can achieve a earlier judgement or prediction for Gun/NoGun classification problem.

Fig. 4. An illustration for complex transformation from the Gun class, where $TS1$ represents the optimal projection (transformation) from $S1$ to samples.

Acknowledgement. This work is partially supported by the NSFC under grants Nos. 61673018, 61272338, 61703443 and Guangzhou Science and Technology Founding Committee under grant No. 201804010255 and Guangdong Province Key Laboratory of Computer Science.

References

1. Chen, X., Du, Z., Li, J., Li, X., Zhang, H.: Compressed sensing based on dictionary learning for extracting impulse components. Sign. Process. **96**, 94–109 (2014)
2. Chen, Y., et al.: The UCR time series classification archive, July 2015
3. Fu, W.C., Keogh, E., Lau, L.Y., Ratanamahatana, C.A., Wong, C.W.: Scaling and time warping in time series querying. VLDB J. **17**(4), 899–921 (2008)
4. Grabocka, J., Schilling, N., Wistuba, M., Schmidt-Thieme, L.: Learning time-series shapelets. In: Proceedings of the 20th ACM SIGKDD International Conference on Knowledge Discovery and Data Mining, pp. 392–401. ACM (2014)
5. Hou, L., Kwok, J.T., Zurada, J.M.: Efficient learning of timeseries shapelets. In: Thirtieth AAAI Conference on Artificial Intelligence (2016)
6. Kong, S., Wang, D.: A dictionary learning approach for classification: separating the particularity and the commonality. In: Fitzgibbon, A., Lazebnik, S., Perona, P., Sato, Y., Schmid, C. (eds.) ECCV 2012. LNCS, vol. 7572, pp. 186–199. Springer, Heidelberg (2012). https://doi.org/10.1007/978-3-642-33718-5_14
7. Lines, J., Davis, L.M., Hills, J., Bagnall, A.: A shapelet transform for time series classification. In: Proceedings of the 18th ACM SIGKDD International Conference on Knowledge Discovery and Data Mining, pp. 289–297. ACM (2012)
8. Mueen, A., Keogh, E., Young, N.: Logical-shapelets: an expressive primitive for time series classification. In: Proceedings of the 17th ACM SIGKDD International Conference on Knowledge Discovery and Data Mining, pp. 1154–1162. ACM (2011)
9. Paparrizos, J., Gravano, L.: K-shape: efficient and accurate clustering of time series. In: Proceedings of the 2015 ACM SIGMOD International Conference on Management of Data, pp. 1855–1870. ACM (2015)
10. Rakthanmanon, T., Keogh, E.: Fast shapelets: a scalable algorithm for discovering time series shapelets. In: Proceedings of the 2013 SIAM International Conference on Data Mining, pp. 668–676. SIAM (2013)
11. Rubinstein, R., Zibulevsky, M., Elad, M.: Double sparsity: learning sparse dictionaries for sparse signal approximation. IEEE Trans. Sig. Process. **58**(3), 1553–1564 (2010)

12. Shah, M., Grabocka, J., Schilling, N., Wistuba, M., Schmidt-Thieme, L.: Learning DTW-shapelets for time-series classification. In: IKDD Conference on Data Science, p. 3 (2016)
13. Wistuba, M., Grabocka, J., Schmidt-Thieme, L.: Ultra-fast shapelets for time series classification. arXiv preprint arXiv:1503.05018 (2015)
14. Ye, L., Keogh, E.: Time series shapelets: a new primitive for data mining. In: Proceedings of the 15th ACM SIGKDD International Conference on Knowledge Discovery and Data Mining, pp. 947–956. ACM (2009)
15. Zhao, R., Schalk, G., Ji, Q.: Temporal pattern localization using mixed integer linear programming
16. Zheng, G., Yang, Y., Carbonell, J.G.: Efficient shift-invariant dictionary learning. In: KDD, pp. 2095–2104 (2016)

A Co-training Approach for Multi-view Density Peak Clustering

Yu Ling[1,2], Jinrong He[1,2(✉)], Silin Ren[1,2], Heng Pan[1,2], and Guoliang He[3]

[1] College of Information Engineering, Northwest A&F University, Yangling 712100,
Shaanxi, China
hejinrong@nwafu.edu.cn
[2] Key Laboratory of Agricultural Internet of Things, Ministry of Agriculture and
Rural Affairs, Yangling 712100, Shaanxi, China
[3] School of Computer Science, Wuhan University, Wuhan 430072, China

Abstract. In this paper, we propose a multi-view clustering algorithm
based on fast search and find of density peaks. We combined the original clustering algorithm with co-training to handle multi-view data and
implement self-adapting cluster center selecting through cluster fusion.
Based on the assumption that a point would be assigned to the same
cluster in all views, we search for the clustering result that agree across
the views by continually modifying one view with the clustering from
another view. We demonstrate the efficacy of the proposed algorithm on
several test cases.

Keywords: Peak clustering · Multi-view learning · Co-training
Cluster center · Adaptive clustering

1 Introduction

Unlabeled data exist in nature widely, and labeling each sample in a big-scale
data in multi-view learning costs a lot of time and work. Thus, we focus on unsupervised learning. Clustering algorithms are widely used in unsupervised learning, which aim to partition elements based on their similarity. Many clustering
algorithms have been proposed such as K-means clustering algorithm seeking to
minimize the average squared distance between points in the same cluster [1],
spectral clustering [2] dividing the graph up into several subgraphs exploiting
the properties of the Laplacian of the original graph and Density-Based Spatial
Clustering of Applications with Noise (DBSAN) [3] viewing clusters as high-
density areas. In 2014, a clustering algorithm based on fast search and find of

This work was partially supported by the National Natural Science Foundation of China
(61876136), China Postdoctoral Science Foundation (2018M633585), Natural Science
Basic Research Plan in Shaanxi Province of China (2018JQ6060), the Doctoral Starting
up Foundation of Northwest A&F University (2452015302), and Students Innovation
Training Project of China (201710712064).

J.-H. Lai et al. (Eds.): PRCV 2018, LNCS 11258, pp. 503–513, 2018.
https://doi.org/10.1007/978-3-030-03338-5_42

density (DPC) was proposed in [4], which was formed by the idea that cluster centers are characterized by a higher density than their neighbors and by a relatively large distance from points with higher densities. The DPC algorithm has attracted attention by its good performance on automatically excluding outliers and recognizing clusters irrespective of their shape and of the dimensionality of the space.

In real world, we have access to lots of features from single object, and limited information can be obtained through an individual view. Hence, we attempt to obtain more information through observing an object in multiple views. For examples, we can take a photo of an object in different angles or even by different sensors. Different views make up for the lack of information in single-view learning. Motivated by this factor, many multi-view learning methods have been proposed. In [5], Laplacian support vector machines (SVMs) [6] is extended from supervised learning to multi-view semi-supervised learning. Canonical Correlational Analysis (CCA) [7–9], Bilinear Model (BLM) [10] and Partial Least Squares (PLS) [8,11,12] are popular unsupervised approaches in multi-view learning [13]. In 2015, Later Multi-View Linear Discriminant Analysis (MLDA) [14] was proposed through combining CCA and Linear Discriminant Analysis (LDA) [15]. Linear Discriminant Analysis is a single-view learning method seeking an optimal linear transformation that maps data into a subspace. Multi-View Intact Space Learning (MISL) proposed in [16] aims to find a space from several views, which assumes that different views are generated from an intact view. Differing from many multi-view approaches, MISL focuses on the insufficiency of each view. However, we do not pay attention to whether each view is sufficient or not, but focus on how to combine the information of multiple views. Therefore, we focus on co-training [17] which is widely used in multi-view learning.

Recently, many clustering methods are applied in multi-view learning. In 2013, a multi-view method, which combines spectral clustering with co-training is proposed in [18]. In 2015, a Co-Spectral Clustering Based Density Peak is proposed in [19], which replaces k-means in spectral clustering with DPC and combines the exteneded spectral clustering with co-training. In 2016, a Multi-View Subspace Clustering is proposed in [20], which performs subspace clustering on each view simultaneously, meanwhile guarantees the consistence of the clustering structure among different views.

Some clustering methods demand preset number of clusters such as k-means and spectral clustering. In this paper, we extend the cluster centers selection of the orignal DPC with cluster fusion to implement self-adaptive cluster centers selection which remains unsolved in [4]. We propose an adjusted co-training framework for DPC which varies weights of views according to views' aggregation. Combining the extended DPC and adjusted co-training, the proposed approach is runed without sensitive parameters.

2   Related Work

2.1   Co-training

Co-training [17] was proposed for problems of semi-supervised learning setting, in which we have access to both labeled and unlabeled samples in two distinct views. It considered the problem of using a small set of labeled samples to boost the performance of unsupervised learning. It has its basis on two assumptions: each view is sufficient for classification independently, and the views are conditionally independent given the labels.

Given the labeled training set L and the unlabeled training set U, here we outline the process of co-training:

- Create a pool U' of examples with u examples chosen randomly from U
- Loop for k iterations:
  - Use L to train a classifier h_1 that considers only the x_1 portion of x
  - Use L to train a classifier h_2 that considers only the x_2 portion of x
  - Allow h_1 to label p positive and n negative examples from U'
  - Allow h_2 to label p positive and n negative examples from U'
  - Add these self-labeled examples to L
  - Randomly choose $2p + 2n$ examples from U to replenish U'.

2.2   Clustering by Fast Search and Find of Density Peaks

Given the distance between data points, density peaks clustering (DPC) [4] chooses data points surrounded by neighbours with lower local density as cluster centers. For data point p_i, two quantities ρ_i and δ_i need to be calculated. ρ_i indicates the number of points that distances between point p_i and these points are less than the cutoff distance d_c. δ_i indicates the distance between point p_i and its nearest neighbour with higher local density, and δ_i is defined as

$$\delta_i = \min_{j:\rho_j>\rho_i} d_{ij} \tag{1}$$

One can choose d_c so that the average number of neighbors is around 1% to 2% of the total number of points in the data set.

For the point with highest density, δ_i is defined as $\delta_i = \max_j(d_{ij})$. Expect the point with highest density, each point and its nearest neighbour with higher local density are assigned to the same cluster temporarily.

Data points with high ρ and high δ or with high γ defined as $\gamma = \rho\delta$ are selected as cluster center.

To exlude outliers, for each cluster, the algorithm finds a border region, defined as the set of points assigned to that cluster but being within a distance d_c from data points belonging to other clusters. Then the algorithm finds the point with highest density within its border region for each cluster. Its density is denoted by ρ_b. A point is considered part of the cluster core (robust assignation), if their density is higher than ρ_b of its cluster. Otherwise, it is considered part of the cluster halo (suitable to be considered as noise).

3 A Co-training Approach for Multi-view Density Peak Clustering

3.1 Adjusted Co-training Framework

The main idea of the standard co-training is training several classifiers through results produced by themselves. Thus, in the proposed approach, views are modified with their clustering results. In a modified view v'_a, distances between two data points belonging to the same cluster in another view v_b are supposed to decrease according to the aggregation of v_b denoted by A_b, and other distances maintain unchanged. Specifically, given the adjacency matrix D_b of view v_b, we first obtain labels L_b by clustering and calculate modification weight matrix W_b defined as:

$$W_{bij} = \begin{cases} A_b & L_{bi} = L_{bj} \\ 1 & L_{bi} \neq L_{bj} \end{cases} \tag{2}$$

$$A_b = \max \frac{\sum_{L_{bi}=L_{bj}} \frac{D_{bij}}{\max D_{bxy}}}{Size(L_{bi})} \tag{3}$$

In Eq. (3), $Size(L_{bi})$ denotes the size of the cluster which includes data point p_i in view v_b.

The modified view v'_a is defined as

$$v'_{aij} = W_{bij} D_{aij} \tag{4}$$

Similar with the standard co-training, we modify each view with another view's clustering result through some iterations. The modification will be ended when all views' clustering results are the same or $max_i A_i$ is less than a preset threshold T. The brief process of the proposed approach is shown in Fig. 1.

3.2 Cluster Center Selection and Cluster Fusion

A problem remains unsolved in the orignal DPC is how to select cluster centers automatically and accurately. To help select cluster centers, the author introduced a quantity γ defined as $\gamma_i = \delta_i \rho_i$ for each data point i, whose value is enormously large for cluster centers [4]. Since we attempt to produce the clustering result through iterations in our adjusted co-training framework, DPC doesn't have to perform perfectly in cluster centers selection during each iteration. Thus, we simply select points whose γ is higher than the average value of γ as temporary cluster centers to ensure that the expected cluster centers are included in the set of chosen points. After this step, we fuse some excessive clusters based on the border region of cluster center defined in [4].

The boder region of a cluster is originally used to find the cluster halo which can be regarded as outliers [4]. We discard its function for excluding outliers, and instead we apply it in merging excessive clusters produced by the cluster centers selection. In the process of calculating border densities, for each cluster

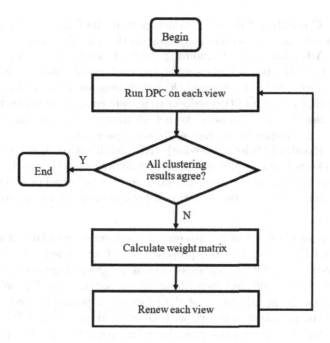

Fig. 1. The brief process of the proposed approach

C_i in we record its border cluster denoted by BC_i within whose border region the border density ρ_{Bi} is obtained, where ρ_{Bi} and BC_i are defined as

$$\rho_{Bi} = \max_{CL_x \neq CL_y, CL_x = C_i} \frac{\rho_x + \rho_y}{2} \tag{5}$$

$$BC_i = arg \max_{CL_y} \frac{\rho_x + \rho_y}{2} \quad (CL_x \neq CL_y, CL_x = C_i) \tag{6}$$

where CL_x denotes the cluster which data point p_x belongs to, and ρ_x denotes the local density of data point p_x.

If the local density of the cluster center in cluster C_i is less than ρ_{Bi}, cluster C_i will be mergerd with BC_i and the center of new cluster will be the orignal center of BC_i.

4 Experiment

4.1 Experiment Setup

To demonstrate the efficiency of the proposed approach, we compare our co-trained density peak clustering approach with following baselines:

- **Best Single View** (BSV) Selecting most informative view where clustering result achieving the highest scores.

- **Feature Concatenation** (FC) Concatenating the features from each view, and then running a clustering algorithm on the joint features.
- **Kernel Addition** (KA) Combining different kernels by adding them. As suggested in [21], this seemly simple approach often leads to near optimal results as compared to more sophisticated approaches for classification. It can be noted that kernel addition reduces to feature concatenation for the special case of linear kernel. In general, kernel addition is same as concatenation of features in the Reproducing Kernel Hilbert Space [18].
- **Kernel Product (element-wise)** (KP) Multiplying the corresponding entries of kernels and applying a clustering algorithm on the resultant matrix. For the special case of Gaussian kernel, element-wise kernel product would be same as simple feature concatenation if both kernels use same width parameter σ [18].

In the section of experiments, we compare performances of DPC with Density Peak Spectral Clustering (DPSC) proposed in [19] combined with above baselines and co-training. DPSC replaces k-means in spectral clustering with DPC to determine number of clusters without preset parameters. The self-adaptive cluster selection is the advantage of the proposed approach as well. Therefore, we compare the proposed approach with DPSC and co-trained DPC instead of spectral clustering or other clustering algorithms requiring sensitive parameters.

4.2   Dataset

- **Synthetic Dataset**
  Our synthetic data consists of 3 views. Each view consists of 2000 data points in two-dimension space $(x_0, x_1, x_2 \in \mathbb{R}^2)$ and four central points $(p_0 = (1,1), p_1 = (-1,-1), p_2 = (1,-1), p_3 = (-1,1))$. The distribution of data points follows

$$||x_i - p_{(i \bmod 4)}||_\infty \leqslant r \qquad (7)$$

  where r is a given range for generating data points randomly. We define the true label of data point x_i as $L_i = i \bmod 4$. We evaluate the proposed approach with a synthesis dataset containing three views as shown in Fig. 2.
- **MNIST Handwritten Digit**
  One real-world dataset is taken from the handwritten digits (0–9) data from the MNIST dataset (Modified National Institute of Standards and Technology database). The dataset is consisted of 1000 examples. Digit images are described in two ways: Histogram of Oriented Gradient (HOG) [22] (view-1) and binaryzation (view-2). This dataset will exam the proposed approach's performance on features extracted with different methods from the same samples.
- **IXMAS Actions Dataset**
  The IXMAS dataset contains recordings of 14 actions from different angles. Images from each angle are regarded as samples in one view. HOG is applied for describing features in views of different angles. This dataset will exam the proposed approach's performance on samples taken from different angles.

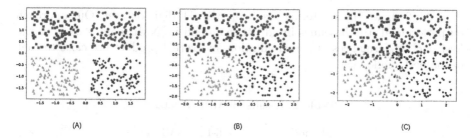

Fig. 2. Three images showing distribution of data points in three views. The range r in view (A) is 0.8; in view (B) is 1.0; and in view (C) is 1.2. Each shape or colour represents one expected cluster.

4.3 Results

The clustering results are evaluated with adjusted rand score (adj-RI) [23] and normalized mutual information score (NMI) [24].

Table 1. Results for synthetic dataset

Method	adj-RI	NMI
BSV DPSC	0.1468	0.6094
BSV DPC	0.4322	0.7328
FC DPSC	0.7828	0.8498
FC DPC	0.7902	0.8681
KA DPSC	0.3850	0.6508
KA DPC	0.4759	0.7359
KP DPSC	0.3306	0.5769
KP DPC	0.5036	0.7484
Co-trained DPSC	0.2298	0.5457
Co-trained DPC	**0.9683**	**0.9712**

Table 1 shows the clustering result on synthetic dataset. Our approach outperforms all baselines by a significant margin. The feature concatenation is the second best one among remaining baselines. Compared with DPSC, the proposed approach integrates information in three views and avoids degradation of performance.

Table 2 shows the clustering result on MINST digit dataset. Our approach outperforms all the baselines in adj-RI score and its NMI score is close to the best one. Performances of kernel addition and kernel product are close to that of the best single view.

Table 2. Results for MNIST dataset

Method	adj-RI	NMI
BSV DPSC	0.3480	0.6271
BSV DPC	0.3633	0.5665
FC DPSC	0.4118	0.6395
FC DPC	0.4164	**0.6649**
KA DPSC	0.3966	0.5931
KA DPC	0.3511	0.5796
KP DPSC	0.3238	0.5315
KP DPC	0.3421	0.6011
Co-trained DPSC	0.3498	0.5637
Co-trained DPC	**0.4797**	0.6456

Table 3 shows the clustering results on IXMAS action dataset. On this dataset, our approach outperforms all baselines by a significant margin. Except the co-trained DPC, other baselines combined with DPC perform worse than the Best Single View combined with DPC do.

Table 3. Results for IXMAS dataset

Method	adj-RI	NMI
BSV DPSC	0.3479	0.6491
BSV DPC	0.3841	0.6550
FC DPSC	0.4214	0.6957
FC DPC	0.3398	0.6250
KA DPSC	0.3960	0.6723
KA DPC	0.3429	0.6353
KP DPSC	0.3238	0.5315
KP DPC	0.3554	0.6422
Co-trained DPSC	0.3746	0.6772
Co-trained DPC	**0.5178**	**0.7495**

Figures 3, 4 and 5 show adj-RI scores in different datasets with increase of the number of iterations. The proposed approach complete clustering by few steps of iteration.

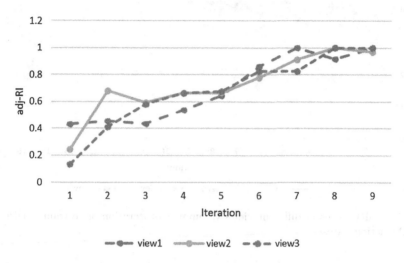

Fig. 3. adj-RI scores in different views vs number of iterations of co-trained DPC for Synthetic dataset

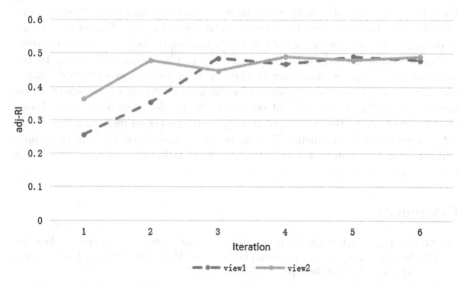

Fig. 4. adj-RI scores in different views vs number of iterations of co-trained DPC for MNIST dataset

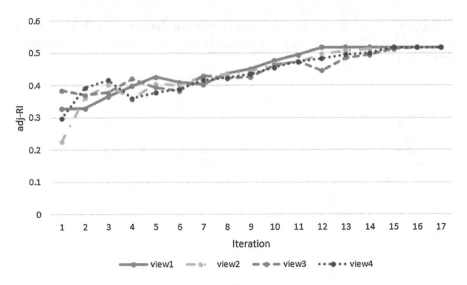

Fig. 5. adj-RI scores in different views vs number of iteration of co-trained DPC for IXMAS action dataset

5   Conculusion

We extend the original density peak clustering method from single-view learning to multi-view learning with the idea of co-training. In our adjusted co-training framework, distances between data points belonging to the same cluster decrease during iteration according to the clustering result for another view. In our adjusted density peak clustering method, cluster centers are selected simply, and then excessive clusters produced by the simple cluster center selection are merged according to densities of points in the border area of clusters. Based on these extensions, the co-trained density peak clustering method outperforms other baselines in experiments. The proposed approach has the ability to integrating information in views and avoiding degradation of performance through few steps of iteration.

References

1. Arthur, D., Vassilvitskii, S.: K-means++: the advantages of careful seeding. In: Eighteenth ACM-SIAM Symposium on Discrete Algorithms. Society for Industrial and Applied Mathematics, pp. 1027–1035 (2007)
2. Shi, J., Malik, J.: Normalized cuts and image segmentation. IEEE Trans. Pattern Anal. Mach. Intell. **22**(8), 888–905 (2000)
3. Ester, M., Kriegel, H.P., Xu, X.: A density-based algorithm for discovering clusters in large spatial databases with noise. In: International Conference on Knowledge Discovery and Data Mining, pp. 226–231. AAAI Press (1996)
4. Rodriguez, A., Laio, A.: Machine learning. Clustering by fast search and find of density peaks. Science **344**(6191), 1492 (2014)

5. Sun, S.: Multi-view laplacian support vector machines. Appl. Intell. **41**(4), 209–222 (2013)
6. Cortes, C., Vapnik, V.: Support-vector networks. Mach. Learn. **20**(3), 273–297 (1995)
7. Cohen, J., Cohen, P., West, S.G., et al.: Applied Multiple Regression/Correlation Analysis for the Behavioral Sciences, 3rd edn, pp. 227–229. L. Erlbaum Associates (2003)
8. Shawe-Taylor, J., Cristianini, N.: Kernel methods for pattern analysis. Publ. Am. Stat. Assoc. **101**(476), 1730–1730 (2004)
9. Hardoon, D.R., Szedmak, S., Shawe-Taylor, J.: Canonical correlation analysis: an overview with application to learning methods. Neural Comput. **16**(12), 2639–2664 (2014)
10. Tenenbaum, J.B., Freeman, W.T.: Separating style and content with bilinear models. Neural Comput. **12**(6), 1247–1283 (2014)
11. Rosipal, R., Krämer, N.: Overview and recent advances in partial least squares. In: Saunders, C., Grobelnik, M., Gunn, S., Shawe-Taylor, J. (eds.) SLSFS 2005. LNCS, vol. 3940, pp. 34–51. Springer, Heidelberg (2006). https://doi.org/10.1007/11752790_2
12. Sharma, A., Jacobs, D.W.: Bypassing synthesis: PLS for face recognition with pose, low-resolution and sketch. In: Computer Vision and Pattern Recognition, pp. 593–600. IEEE (2011)
13. Sharma, A., Kumar, A., Daume, H., et al.: Generalized multiview analysis: a discriminative latent space. In: IEEE Conference on Computer Vision and Pattern Recognition. IEEE Computer Society, pp. 2160–2167 (2012)
14. Sun, S., Xie, X., Yang, M.: Multiview uncorrelated discriminant analysis. IEEE Trans. Cybern. **46**(12), 3272 (2016)
15. Hotelling, H.: Relations Between Two Sets of Variates. Breakthroughs in Statistics, pp. 321–377. Springer, New York (1992)
16. Xu, C., Tao, D., Xu, C.: Multi-view intact space learning. IEEE Trans. Pattern Anal. Mach. Intell. **37**(12), 2531–2544 (2015)
17. Blum, A., Mitchell, T.: Combining labeled and unlabeled data with co-training. In: Eleventh Conference on Computational Learning Theory, pp. 92–100. ACM (1998)
18. Kumar, A., Daumé III, H.: A co-training approach for multi-view spectral clustering. In: International Conference on International Conference on Machine Learning, pp. 393–400. Omnipress (2011)
19. Li, Y., Liu, W., Wang, Y., et al.: Co-spectral clustering based density peak. In: IEEE International Conference on Communication Technology, pp. 925–929. IEEE (2015)
20. Gao, H., Nie, F., Li, X., et al.: Multi-view subspace clustering. In: IEEE International Conference on Computer Vision, pp. 4238–4246. IEEE (2016)
21. Cortes, C., Mohri, M., Rostamizadeh, A.: Learning non-linear combinations of kernels. In: International Conference on Neural Information Processing Systems, pp. 396–404. Curran Associates Inc. (2009)
22. Dalal, N., Triggs, B.: Histograms of oriented gradients for human detection. In: IEEE Computer Society Conference on Computer Vision and Pattern Recognition, CVPR 2005, pp. 886–893. IEEE (2005)
23. Manning, C.D., Raghavan, P., Schütze, H.: An introduction to information retrieval. J. Am. Soc. Inf. Sci. Technol. **61**(4), 852–853 (2008)
24. Hubert, L., Arabie, P.: Comparing partitions. J. Classif. **2**(1), 193–218 (1985). Assortative pairing and life history strategy - a cross-cultural study. Hum. Nat. **20**, 317–330

Boosting Sparsity-Induced Autoencoder: A Novel Sparse Feature Ensemble Learning for Image Classification

Rui Shi, Jian Ji[✉], Chunhui Zhang, and Qiguang Miao

School of Computer Science and Technology, Xidian University,
Xi'an 710071, China
jji@xidian.edu.cn

Abstract. As a model of unsupervised learning, autoencoder is often employed to perform the pre-training of the deep neural networks. However, autoencoder and its variants have not taken the statistical characteristics and the domain knowledge of training set into the design of deep neural networks and have abandoned a lot of features learned from different levels at the pre-training process. In this paper, we propose a novel sparse feature ensemble learning method for natural image classification, named boosting sparsity-induced autoencoder, to fully utilize hierarchical and diverse features. Firstly, a sparsity encourage method is introduced by adding an extra sparsity-induced layer to exploit the representative and intrinsic features of the input. And then, the ensemble learning is taken into consideration of the construction of the model to improve and boost the accuracy and stability of a single model. The classification results on three datasets demonstrate the effectiveness of the proposed method.

Keywords: Sparse representation · Sparsity-induced method
Ensemble learning · Image classification

1 Introduction

The performance of a generic learning algorithm, especially adopted to the classification problem, extremely relies on the quality of learned feature representation of raw input data. Good features not only could remove irrelevant or redundant features coexisting in the original input space, but preserve the essential information for the target tasks. A good feature extractor built for input space, especially using unsupervised learning methods, can be further utilized for computer vision tasks. Deep hierarchical features produced by stacked unsupervised models have been demonstrated to be a powerful tool and appeal to emerging focus [1, 2].

In recent years, the study found that deep learning constructed by the multiple nonlinear transformations can be a powerful feature learning tool. Deep learning has already been broadly used to address image classification tasks [3–6]. As a tool of deep learning with a special architecture, the autoencoder has already been stacked to pre-train a deep neural network using a greedy layer-wise means [7], where each layer is separately initialized by unsupervised pre-training method, and then a fine-tuning way

J.-H. Lai et al. (Eds.): PRCV 2018, LNCS 11258, pp. 514–526, 2018.
https://doi.org/10.1007/978-3-030-03338-5_43

based on backpropagation is used by a supervised learning algorithm [8, 9], leading to solving the lack of expression ability of shallow network.

By restricting the output of the model identical to the input data, autoencoder can be regarded as an identity function which could reconstruct the raw input data composed of an encoding phase and a decoding phase. Meanwhile, sparse representation has proven its significant impact on computer vision [10–12]. The performance of an image classifier can be improved if the input image can be represented by a sparse representation. Ghifary [12] demonstrated that, in most cases, sparse network structures have better classification performance than dense structures. In recent years, the sparse deep model is proposed based on the sparse encoding strategy, sparse regularization term and sparse filtering that have taken the input samples into sparse depth related neural network model.

However, autoencoder and its variants have not taken the statistical characteristics and the domain knowledge of training set into the design of deep networks, and they have abandoned a lot of features learned from different levels. Therefore, autoencoder can only provide a relatively coarse parameters setting and serves as a pre-training method because of the large variance and low generalization ability on the unknown testing dataset. So, how to fully utilize the features existed in the input is one of the most important points in our work. It is well known that an ensemble of multiple classifiers is considered as a practical technique for improving accuracy and stability with comparisons to a single classifier. Ensemble learning employs some weak classifiers, according to some combination rule, to construct a stronger one to obtain significantly reduced generalization error than any weak one. But, two key issues, namely the diversity and accuracy of each classifier and the combination rules of fusion rules [13], are required to be taken into consideration to ensure a better performance.

In this paper, we introduce a novel sparsity-induced autoencoder that can further exploit the representative and intrinsic features of the input. Then, to benefit the ability of the ensemble learning, an ensemble sparse feature learning algorithm based on the novel sparse autoencoder mentioned above, named BoostingAE, is proposed. On the one hand, the completion of the pre-training sparsity-induced autoencoder can obtain a plurality of different levels of abstraction of sparse features; on the other hand, ensemble learning could effectively improve and enhance the recognition rate and stability of single classifier. Experimental results on three different datasets show that the proposed ensemble feature learning method can significantly improve the overall performance.

2   Related Work

2.1   Sparse Representation

Sparse Coding. Sparse coding provides a family of methods for acquiring the condense features in the input. Given only the unlabeled dataset, it can discover the basic functions aimed to capture the higher-level features in the data itself. Despite its close relationship to the traditional sparse coding techniques on image denoising, the main drawback of sparse coding is its high computation cost. Moreover, it is well-known that the sparse coding is not "smooth" [14, 15], which means a tiny variation in input space might result in a significant difference in code space.

Sparse Filtering [16]. In contrast to many existing feature learning models, one of the important properties of sparse filtering is that it only requires one hyper-parameter rather than extensive hyper-parameters tuning for its very simple cost function:

$$\min \sum_{i=1}^{M} \left\| \hat{f}^{(i)} \right\|_1 = \sum_{i=1}^{M} \left\| \frac{\tilde{f}^{(i)}}{\left\| \tilde{f}^{(i)} \right\|_2} \right\|_1 \tag{1}$$

where f represents the learned feature value for input sample, $\tilde{f}$ is defined by ℓ_2 norm of f, and M indicates the sample's number.

Sparse Regularization. Compared with sparse coding, sparse regularization needs to perform an extra separate stage to induce sparsity and encourage sparse representations of input. Various methods of sparsity regularization either employed in deep belief network or autoencoder [17], similar to sparse coding, each of which has been proved the beneficial effects for some particular scene.

2.2 Softmax Regression

Softmax regression is a generalized version of logistic regression applied to classification problems where the class label y can be chosen from more than two values. Assume that there are k labels and m training samples: $\left\{ \left(x^{(1)}, y^{(1)} \right), \left(x^{(2)}, y^{(2)} \right), \ldots, \left(x^{(i)}, y^{(i)} \right) \right\} (i = 1, 2, \ldots, m)$, where x is the input sample, and $y \in \{1, 2, \ldots, k\}$ is the corresponding label.

For every input, the output probability function can be defined as follows:

$$h_\theta(x^i) = \begin{bmatrix} p\left(y^{(i)} = 1 \middle| x^{(i)}; \theta\right) \\ p\left(y^{(i)} = 2 \middle| x^{(i)}; \theta\right) \\ \vdots \\ p\left(y^{(i)} = k \middle| x^{(i)}; \theta\right) \end{bmatrix} = \frac{1}{\sum_{j=1}^{k} e^{\theta_j^T x^{(i)}}} \begin{bmatrix} e^{\theta_1^T x^{(i)}} \\ e^{\theta_2^T x^{(i)}} \\ \vdots \\ e^{\theta_j^T x^{(i)}} \end{bmatrix} \tag{2}$$

where θ is the parameter of the softmax model. For each input, the probability of its category is estimated to be:

$$p\left(y = k \middle| x^{(i)}; \theta\right) = \frac{e^{\theta_j^T x^{(i)}}}{\sum_k e^{\theta_k^T x^{(i)}}} \tag{3}$$

2.3 Ensemble Learning

According to certain combination rule, ensemble learning employs some weak classifiers to construct a stronger one to obtain significantly reduced generalization error than any weak one. Weak learner refers to whose generalization performance on the unknown testing dataset is only slightly better than random guessing. From mathematics, ensemble learning can significantly reduce the variance to achieve more stable performance. In order to get a better integration result, it is necessary to make the individual learner as different as possible, that is to say, there is a high degree of diversity between the base learners, which will be helpful to the performance of ensemble learning.

Boosting method is a widely used method for statistical learning, and severs as an important means of ensemble learning. By changing the weights of training samples, boosting method trains a group of individual learners and gets final decision results with a combination rule of voting.

3 Boosting Sparsity-Induced Autoencoder

To learn more representative and intrinsic features of input, a novel sparsity encourage method is first introduced to build a new autoencoder, called sparsity-induced autoencoder (SparsityAE). Based on SparsityAE and ensemble learning, we further proposed a boosting sparsity-induced autoencoder (BoostingAE), which is capable of utilizing the hierarchical and diverse features, ensuring the accuracy and diversity, and boosting the performance of the single SparsityAE on computer vision tasks.

3.1 Sparsity-Induced Autoencoder

Inspired by the assumptions of the sparse representation and the efficient reconstruction of low-dimension feature representation obtained in the encoding phase of deep models, SparsityAE is proposed, whose structure is shown in Fig. 1.

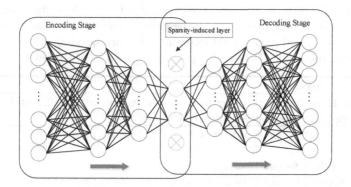

Fig. 1. The topology of the proposed sparsity-induced autoencoder

We feed the encoder by the dataset of high-dimension space. The length of the codes learned by each layer gets less along with the deepening of the encoder. At the end of the encoding phase, we employ a sparsity-induced layer to generate sparse codes. Conversely, the decoding phase deals with the compressed and sparse codes given by sparsity-induced layer. In sparsity-induced layer, the neurons without significant activation value will be set to zero, which could decrease the number of neurons, remove the correlation between attributes and compress the raw inputs.

Let $y_i(i = 1, 2, \ldots N)$ be the original data and x_i be its degraded version, so the input can be mapped to a hidden representation by the formulations as follows:

$$\hat{y}(x_i) = \sigma\left(W'h(x_i) + b'\right) \tag{4}$$

where $\hat{y}_i$ is an approximation of y_i, and $\sigma(\bullet)$ is the mapping function.

To benefit both from the virtues of sparse representation and deep neural networks, we optimize the reconstruction loss regularized by a weight decay and a sparsity-inducing term. The cost function can be designed as follows:

$$L(X, Y; \theta) = \|y_i - \hat{y}(x_i)\|_2^2 / N + \beta \bullet KL(\hat{\rho}\|\rho) \tag{5}$$

where $\theta = \left(W, b, W', b'\right)$ represents weights and bias, $KL(\hat{\rho}\|\rho)$ is the sparse regularization to extract sparse representation, and $\hat{\rho}$ is the average output of hidden neurons:

$$KL(\hat{\rho}\|\rho) = \sum_{j=1}^{|\hat{\rho}|} \rho \log\left(\frac{\rho}{\hat{\rho}_j}\right) + (1 - \rho) \log\left(\frac{1 - \rho}{1 - \hat{\rho}_j}\right) \tag{6}$$

$$\hat{\rho} = (1/N) \sum_{i}^{N} h(x_i) \tag{7}$$

In the training process, for the intractability of the whole image, the model is provided with the original overlapping patches $y_i(i = 1, 2, \ldots, N)$ as the reconstruction, and their corrupted image patches x_i as the polluted input. As long as the training is completed, the learned model could reconstruct the corresponding clean image given any polluted observation. The detailed process is shown in Algorithm 1.

Algorithm 1 SparsityAE

Notation: Ω_i is reconstruction error for x_i, S_i is the reconstruction coefficient for x_i, and $\{y_i\}_1^N$ is the hidden representation for every input.

Input: training set $D = \{x_i\}_1^N$, parameters k (constant) and $\theta = \{W, b, W', b'\}$.

Process:

(1) Compute the S_i for each input $\{x_i\}_1^N$;

(2) Minimize the cost function by the stochastic gradient descent and update θ;

(3) Compute the hidden representation $\{y_i\}_1^N$ for each input, keep the k biggest activation value and others are set to zero, and update S_i and Ω_i;

(4) Repeat the step (2) and (3) until convergence.

Output: reconstruction representation of the input.

3.2 Feature Ensemble Method

Multiple sparse features with different abstraction levels will be obtained using the SparsityAE introduced above; ensemble feature learning could effectively improve the accuracy and stability of a single classifier. Together two points above, a BoostingAE is proposed that uses hierarchical feature obtained in pre-training stage to train multiple classifiers, and integrates the outputs of classifiers with specific fusion rules to get the final prediction of image classification.

To make the whole structure easy to understand, Fig. 2 gives a clear and detailed understanding of BoostingAE, which indicates that by cascading multiple SparsityAEs, BoostingAE is theoretically possible to obtain N compressed sparse features derived from the output of SparsityAEs.

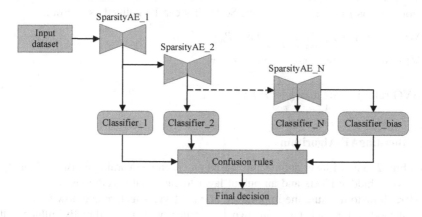

Fig. 2. The topology of the proposed BoostingAE

In our work, training three SparsityAEs and utilizing softmax regression to perform the classification task. First, we train SparsityAE_1 in Fig. 2. Assuming that the original input sample is x, the weight matrix connecting the input layer and the hidden layer is $W^{(1)}$, the bias vector is $b^{(1)}$, so its output can be mapped by Eq. (4):

$$\hat{y}_1 = \sigma\left(x \bullet W^{(1)} + b^{(1)}\right) \tag{8}$$

Regard $\hat{y}_1$ as the input of the second SparsityAE, thus further train SparsityAE_2. Its weight matrix connecting the input layer and the hidden layer is $W^{(2)}$, and bias vector is $b^{(2)}$. With reference to the above operation, SparsityAE_2's output can be further obtained, which also be used as the input of next SparsityAE:

$$\hat{y}_2 = \sigma\left(\hat{y}_1 \bullet W^{(2)} + b^{(2)}\right) \tag{9}$$

Along with the cascaded sparsity-induced autoencoder network, the characteristic attributes which are trained from the current layer will be passed to the next layer by above process, and therefore three SparsityAEs can be trained. At the same time, in the longitudinal direction, the trained classifier model and optimal parameters of each classifier are obtained by training the characteristic attribute at the encoding stage. Further, three classifiers are obtained.

3.3 Combination Method of Voting

After training all base classifiers, final prediction is given by results of three classifiers after integrating with some fusion rules. Here, the Naïve Bayes combination rules [18] are applied which assume that individual classifiers are mutually independent.

We adopt three Naïve Bayes combination methods, namely MAX, MIN, and AVG rules. Given a sample x, and its label y has C possible values. Assuming that the current BoostingAE model consists of N base classifiers, $P_{nj}(x)$ is the probability that the category of x is j in the nth classifier. So label y can be defined as follows:

- MAX rule: $y = \arg \max\limits_{j=1,2,\ldots,C} \max\limits_{n=1,2,\ldots,N} P_{nj}(x)$,
- MIN rule: $y = \arg \max\limits_{j=1,2,\ldots,C} \min\limits_{n=1,2,\ldots,N} P_{nj}(x)$,
- AVG rule: $y = \arg \max\limits_{j=1,2,\ldots,C} \frac{1}{N} \sum\limits_{n=1}^{N} P_{nj}(x)$.

3.4 BoostingAE Algorithm

From Fig. 2, a multi-layer architecture based on ensemble learning consists of an input layer, some hidden layers and an output layer to carry out specific tasks.

Here, how to measure the importance of each layer's feature and how to select the optimal models for each layer are two key issues, which will directly influence the performance of the model. As a main contribution of this paper, we employ Adaboost to supervise the adjustment of parameters and weight coefficients. Algorithm 2 gives the detailed process of the proposed BoostingAE.

Algorithm 2 BoostingAE

Notation: T is the number of base sparse autoencoder, and the algorithm of base learner is SparsityAE.

Input: training set $D = \left\{ \left(x^{(1)}, y^{(1)} \right), \left(x^{(2)}, y^{(2)} \right), \ldots, \left(x^{(m)}, y^{(m)} \right) \right\}$.

Process:

Initialize: assign the default parameters.

Loop: for $k = 1, 2, \ldots, k$

Generate the new dataset D' by bootstrapping the original dataset;

Obtain the trained individual classifier, $g_t = \text{SparsityAE}(D')$.

Output: Obtain ensemble classifier $D' = Uniform(\{g_t\})$.

Compared with traditional sparse stacked autoencoder, BoostingAE's characteristics are shown in following aspects:

- whose construction of base learners is similar to that of AdaBoost, BoostingAE utilizes the cascade serialization mechanism among the base learners, which makes the individual learners are related to each other and also maintain the difference;
- the subsequent layer takes the output of the previous layer as the input to obtain rich feature representation, which makes each learners receive various "training input" at the same time and avoids the waste of computing and storage resources;
- when design individual learners, the topology of each model can be specified separately rather than by a unified model topology. This makes it possible to further increase the diversity of base learners while maintaining the homogeneity of them.

4 Experiments

First of all, we verify the performance of SparsityAE in sparse feature learning. Next, to unbiasedly and accurately show the performance and the stability of BoostingAE on real-world image classification, the experiments are carried out on three widely employed datasets, i.e., MNIST, CIFAR-10, and SVHN. Moreover, some state-of-art methods are employed to provide the comparable results on the same datasets.

4.1 The Sparse Feature Learning of SparsityAE

To validate the performance of SparsityAE in sparse feature learning, we mainly focus on denoising of grey-scale images. From http://decsai.ugr.es/cvg/dbimagenes, a set of natural images are employed as the training set, and a set of standard natural images as the testing set which has been widely used in the image processing.

When it comes to the training process, we randomly pick a clean image y from the dataset and generate its corresponding noisy patch x by corrupting it with a specific strength of additive white Gaussian noise. The training performed, the learned model will be capable of reconstructing the corresponding clean image given any noisy observation. To avoid the local minimum, we adopt the layer-wise pre-training procedure introduced in [7].

Figure 3 shows the comparison between SparsityAE and classic image denoising methods: KSVD [19], BM3D [20], on standard testing images degraded by various noise levels. We tell that when $\sigma = 25$, SparsityAE (magenta line) is competitive, while corrupts for other different, i.e., higher noise strengthens, which is owing to that our model knowing nothing about the noise of level but other methods were provided with such information. The green line shows that if we train the proposed model on several different noise levels, our SparsityAE is more robust to the change of noise levels which means that it can generalize significantly better to higher noise levels.

What's more, we compared the SparsityAE with several state-of-art denoising methods: WNNM [21] and two training based methods: MLP [22], TNRD [23]. The numerical results are shown in Table 1, which is measured by the peak signal to noise ratio (PSNR in dB). The best PSNR result for each image is highlighted in bold.

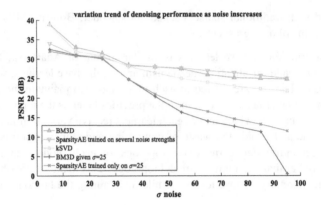

Fig. 3. Denoising performance comparison of various methods with various noise levels (Color figure online)

Table 1. Comparison of the various methods' denoising performance measured by PSNR.

Image	KSVD	BM3D	WNNM	MLP	TNRD	Ours
Lena	31.35	32.08	32.24	32.25	32.00	**32.46**
House	32.14	32.86	33.23	32.56	32.53	**32.96**
C.man	28.72	29.45	29.64	29.61	29.72	**29.98**
Moarch	28.81	29.25	29.85	29.61	**29.85**	29.65
Couple	28.84	29.71	29.82	**29.76**	29.69	29.68
Man	29.09	29.61	29.76	29.88	**30.11**	29.78
Babara	29.60	30.72	**31.24**	29.54	29.41	29.20
Boat	29.32	29.91	30.03	29.97	**30.21**	29.91
Pepper	29.71	30.16	30.42	30.30	30.57	**30.37**

Although images with a lot of repeating structure are ideal for both KSVD and BM3D, we do outperform KSVD, BM3D, and WNNM on every image except Barbara. It is also shown that our SparsityAE is able to compete with MLP and TNPD.

The results illustrated that SparsityAE can not only project the original high dimensional space to a lower dimensional and more intrinsic space from the perspective of dimension-reduction, but capture the more representative sparse feature from multiple layers to make the best use of the information contained in original space.

4.2 BoostingAE for Classification on MNIST

MNIST is a large dataset of handwritten digits that is widely used for image processing and computer vision tasks. It contains 60,000 training images and 10,000 testing images with labels, and the size of a single image is 28×28.

The topology of the SparsityAE on MNIST with three hidden layers is first determined, i.e., $784 \times 500 \times 250 \times 100 \times 10$, which 784 is the size of the image and

10 is the label number. Then, Classifier_1 in Fig. 2 is obtained by pre-training and fine-tuning SparsityAE_1. After that, SparsityAE_2 takes the feature representations learned from SparsityAE_1 as input to get Classifier_2. With the process above, we get the final three base classifiers that will be integrated when all base learners achieve convergence after fine-tuning. With this, the whole BoostingAE model is constructed and trained completely. When it comes to predicting the real samples, three Naïve Bayes combination rules will be respectively used for voting the integrative result of three classifiers to improve the performance.

Table 2 shows that three individual classifiers have better classification results than KNN and SVM because of the introduction of the sparsity-induced layer in SparsityAE. And the BoostingAE with three different fusion rules gets better performance than any individual classifier and achieves 98.37%, 98.43% and 98.87% accuracy rate respectively, which is very close to the result of Lp–norm AE [24]. Moreover, stacked CAE [25] and CASE [26] employ more feature maps obtained by convolutional operations and hidden layers, so our performance is slightly worse than these.

Table 2. Classification results on three datasets.

	MNIST	CIFAR-10	SVHN
KNN	91.32%	84.47%	78.32%
SVM	94.02%	88.45%	83.24%
Lp–norm AE(KNN) [24]	97.44%	/	67.23%
Lp–norm AE(SVM) [24]	98.64%	/	71.19%
Stacked CAE [25]	99.29%	79.20%	/
CSAE [26]	99.39%	/	/
CDSAE [27]	/	74.18%	/
Classifier_1	96.73%	91.46%	88.46%
Classifier_2	96.35%	91.83%	88.93%
Classifier_3	95.89%	90.96%	87.69%
BoostingAE(MAX)	98.37%	**92.32%**	**89.94%**
BoostingAE(MIN)	98.43%	**91.49%**	**90.35%**
BoostingAE(AVG)	**98.87%**	**92.63%**	**90.87%**

4.3 BoostingAE for Classification on CIFAR-10 and SVHN

CIFAR-10 is a dataset contains ten kinds of color images, each category contains 6000 color images. The training set contains 5000 images of each category, the remaining is used for testing. SVHN dataset can be regarded as the upgrade of MNIST and also contains ten kinds of color images. Both are captured from the real life so the background is more complex and the images are difficult to identify. SVHN is divided into training set, testing set and extra set; the validation set is constructed in a random way: the 2/3 of them is derived from the training set (400 samples per class), and the remaining samples come from the extra set (200 samples per class).

Before the experiment, the original images of CIFAR-10 and SVHN should be transformed from RGB space into grey space, and then normalized. To improve the training efficiency, the mini-batch gradient descent algorithm is used when pre-training and fine-tuning. Considering the unsupervised learning mechanism of autoencoder, both CIFAR-10 and SVHN use a certain proportion of unlabeled samples as training set in pre-training; and in the process of fine-tuning, two datasets require ground-truth to implement the classification. Next, the topology of SparsityAE is determined as $1024 \times 500 \times 250 \times 100 \times 10$. The subsequent operations are similar to those performed on MNIST.

We report the results of comparison methods, individual classifiers and the proposed method in Table 2 and get the similar conclusion as MNIST. Our methods achieve the best results among comparison methods. The results illustrated the BoostingAE could capture more sparse representation and utilize multi-layer features, resulting in the improvement of accuracy and diversity of overall.

5   Conclusion

In this work, we first built SparsityAE by adding an extra sparsity-induced layer, which efficiently abstract the sparse feature representations, and then based on SparsityAE and ensemble learning, we further proposed a BoostingAE model to integrate sparse feature learned from multi-layer, so as to improve the performance of individual sparse encoder, which has been successfully applied to image classification.

The main advantage of our approach is that it could abstract more significantly sparse representations that reflect the distribution of original data better and make full use of the features learned from multi-layer to improve the diversity of base learners. What's more, it also promotes the overall performance after integrating multiple weak learners. Additional experiments on three different datasets validate the effectiveness of the proposed algorithm in image classification.

References

1. Goh, H., Thome, N., Cord, M., Lim, J.H.: Learning deep hierarchical visual feature coding. IEEE Trans. Neural Netw. Learn. Syst. **25**(12), 2212–2225 (2014)
2. Ma, C., Huang, J.B., Yang, X.,Yang, M.H.: Hierarchical convolutional features for visual tracking. In: IEEE International Conference on Computer Vision, pp. 3074–3082. IEEE Computer Society Press, Santiago (2015)
3. Yang, X., Ye, W., Li, X., Lau, R.Y.K., Zhang, X., Huang, X.: Hyperspectral image classification with deep learning models. IEEE Trans. Geosci. Remote Sens. **56**(9), 1–16 (2018)
4. Mei, S., Jiang, R., Ji, J., Sun, J., Peng, Y.: Invariant feature extraction for image classification via multi-channel convolutional neural network. In: International Symposium on Intelligent Signal Processing and Communication Systems, pp. 491–495. IEEE, Japan (2018)

5. Durand, T., Mordan, T., Thome, N., Cord, M.: WILDCAT: weakly supervised learning of deep convnets for image classification, pointwise localization and segmentation. In: IEEE Conference on Computer Vision and Pattern Recognition, pp. 642–651. IEEE Computer Society, Hawaii (2017)

6. Marino, K., Salakhutdinov, R., Gupta, A.: The more you know: using knowledge graphs for image classification. In: IEEE Conference on Computer Vision and Pattern Recognition, pp. 2673–2681. IEEE Computer Society Press, Hawaii (2017)

7. Bengio, Y., Lamblin, P., Popovici, D., Larochelle, H.: Greedy layer-wise training of deep networks. In: International conference on Neural Information Processing Systems, pp. 153–160. MIT Press, Vancouver (2006)

8. Hinton, G.E., Salakhutdinov, R.R.: Reducing the dimensionality of data with neural networks. Science **313**(5786), 504–507 (2006)

9. Wen, W., Wu, C., Wang, Y., Chen, Y., Li, H.: Learning structured sparsity in deep neural networks. In: International conference on Neural Information Processing Systems, pp. 2074–2082. MIT Press, Barcelona (2016)

10. Shahnawazuddin, S., Sinha, R.: Sparse coding over redundant dictionaries for fast adaptation of speech recognition system. Comput. Speech Lang. **43**, 1–17 (2017)

11. Srinivas, M., Lin, Y., Liao, H.Y.M.: Learning deep and sparse feature representation for fine-grained object recognition. In: IEEE International Conference on Multimedia and Expo, pp. 1458–1463. IEEE Press, Hong Kong (2017)

12. Ghifary, M., Kleijn, W.B., Zhang, M.: Sparse representations in deep learning for noise-robust digit classification. In: International Conference on Image and Vision Computing New Zealand, pp. 340–345. IEEE Press, Wellington (2013)

13. Zhang, L., Zhou, W.: Sparse ensembles using weighted combination methods based on linear programming. Pattern Recogn. **44**(1), 97–106 (2011)

14. Wang, J., Yang, J., Yu, K., Lv, F., Huang, T., Gong, Y.: Locality-constrained linear coding for image classification. In: IEEE Conference on Computer Vision and Pattern Recognition, pp. 3360–3367. IEEE Press, San Francisco (2010)

15. Gao, S., Tsang, I.W., Chia, L., Zhao, P.: Local features are not Lonely–Laplacian sparse coding for image classification. In IEEE Conference on Computer Vision and Pattern Recognition, pp. 3555–3561. IEEE Computer Society Press, San Francisco (2010)

16. Ngiam, J., Koh, P.W., Chen, Z., Bhaskar, S., Ng, A.Y.: Sparse filtering. In: International Conference on Neural Information Processing Systems, pp. 1125–1133. MIT Press, Granada (2011)

17. Le, Q.V., Ngiam, J., Coates, A., Lahiri, A., Prochnow, B., Ng, A.Y.: On optimization methods for deep learning. In: 28th International Conference on Machine Learning, pp. 265–272. Omnipress, Bellevue (2011)

18. Kuncheva, L.I.: Combining Pattern Classifiers: Methods and Algorithms, 1st edn. Wiley, Hoboken (2004)

19. Elad, M., Aharon, M.: Image denoising via sparse and redundant representations over learned dictionaries. IEEE Trans. Image Process. **15**(12), 3736–3745 (2016)

20. Dabov, K., Foi, A., Katkovnik, V., Egiazarian, K.: Image denoising by sparse 3D transform-domain collaborative filtering. IEEE Trans. Image Process. **16**(8), 2080–2095 (2007)

21. Gu, S., Zhang, L., Zuo, W., Feng, X.: Weighted nuclear norm minimization with application to image denoising. In: IEEE Conference on Computer Vision and Pattern Recognition, pp. 2862–2869. IEEE Computer Society Press, Columbus (2014)

22. Burger, H.C., Schuler, C.J., Harmeling, S.: Image denoising: can plain neural networks compete with BM3D? In: IEEE Conference on Computer Vision and Pattern Recognition, pp. 2392–2399. IEEE Computer Society Press, Providence (2012)

23. Chen, Y., Pock, T.: Trainable nonlinear reaction diffusion: a flexible framework for fast and effective image restoration. IEEE Trans. Pattern Anal. Mach. Intell. **39**(6), 1256–1272 (2017)

24. Mehta, J., Gupta, K., Gogna, A., Majumdar, A., Anand, S.: Stacked robust autoencoder for classification. In: Hirose, A., Ozawa, S., Doya, K., Ikeda, K., Lee, M., Liu, D. (eds.) ICONIP 2016. LNCS, vol. 9949, pp. 600–607. Springer, Cham (2016). https://doi.org/10.1007/978-3-319-46675-0_66

25. Masci, J., Meier, U., Cireşan, D., Schmidhuber, J.: Stacked convolutional auto-encoders for hierarchical feature extraction. In: Honkela, T., Duch, W., Girolami, M., Kaski, S. (eds.) ICANN 2011. LNCS, vol. 6791, pp. 52–59. Springer, Heidelberg (2011). https://doi.org/10.1007/978-3-642-21735-7_7

26. Luo, W., Li, J., Yang, J.: Convolutional sparse autoencoders for image classification. IEEE Trans. Neural Netw. Learn. Syst. **2017**(99), 1–6 (2017)

27. Chen, S., Liu, H., Zheng, X., Qian, S., Yu, J., Guo, W.: Image classification based on convolutional denoising sparse autoencoder. Math. Probl. Eng. **2017**, 1–16 (2017)

Matrix-Instance-Based One-Pass AUC Optimization

Changming Zhu[1]([✉]) [ID], Chengjiu Mei[1], Hui Jiang[2], and Rigui Zhou[1]

[1] College of Information Engineering, Shanghai Maritime University,
Shanghai 201306, People's Republic of China
{cmzhu,rgzhou}@shmtu.edu.cn, 544306495@qq.com
[2] School of Mechanical Engineering,
University of Shanghai for Science and Technology,
Shanghai 200093, People's Republic of China
huijiang@hotmail.com

Abstract. Area under the receiver operating characteristic curve, i.e., AUC, is a widely used performance measure. Traditional off-line and some online AUC optimization methods should store the entire or part of dataset in memory which is infeasible to process big data or streaming data applications. So some scholars develop one-pass AUC optimization (OPAUC) which is independent from the data size. While OPAUC cannot process matrix instances. So we propose a matrix-instance-based one-pass AUC optimization model, i.e., MOPAUC, to overcome such an issue. Related experiments on some benchmark datasets including five image datasets validate that MOPAUC can improve the average AUC, cost little running time with matrix-instance cases. Furthermore, some parameters including regularization parameters and weights have less influence on the average AUC while step sizes have strong influence.

Keywords: One-pass · Matrix instance · AUC

1 Introduction

1.1 Background

As we all know, the area under the receiver operating characteristic (ROC) curve (i.e., AUC) is an important performance measure and it has been widely used in many tasks [1–5]. According to [6] said, AUC is measured by the losses defined over pairs of instances from different classes which is different from the classical classification and regression problems where the loss function can be gotten by a single training instance. In present, during the procedure of design, many classifiers demand the AUC be maximization [7–9]. Thus, the optimization of AUC is a hot spot of present research. The traditional AUC optimization methods include semi-supervised learning receiver operating characteristic (SSLROC) algorithms which utilize unlabeled test instances in classifier training to maximize AUC

© Springer Nature Switzerland AG 2018
J.-H. Lai et al. (Eds.): PRCV 2018, LNCS 11258, pp. 527–538, 2018.
https://doi.org/10.1007/978-3-030-03338-5_44

[10], direct-AUC which is a boosting method to directly optimizes AUC value as a classification performance measure [11], semi-supervised AUC optimization method with generative models (OptAG) which utilizes generative models to assist the incorporation of unlabeled instances in AUC-optimized classifiers [12]. While all those traditional AUC optimization methods exist two defects. One is that those off-line AUC optimization methods [2,8,10–12] need to store the entire dataset in memory before an optimization procedure is applied while this is infeasible for applications involving big data or streaming data in which a large volume of data come in a short time period. The other is that for some online AUC optimization methods [1,7,9], they find the optimal solution of some performance measures by only scanning the training data once, but these methods still need to store $\sqrt{T}$ instances where T is the number of training instances.

1.2   Proposal

As [6] said, a good AUC optimization method (i.e., one-pass AUC optimization) should be independent from the number of training instances since it is always difficult to expect how many data will be received in the applications. Until now, only few scholars pay attention to one-pass AUC optimization problems. To the best of our knowledge, work [13] is the extended work of [6] which aims to process one-pass AUC optimization and except the scholars of [6] and [13], we have not found any other scholars to pay attention to this field.

Moreover, it is found that in [6] and [13], the used datasets consist vector instances, i.e., each instance $x \in \mathbb{R}^{d \times 1}$ is a d-dimensionality one. This representation can bring a convenience in mathematics. But as we know, in real world applications, more and more instances are represented in matrix form, i.e., a matrix instance $A \in \mathbb{R}^{m \times n}$ and its dimensionality is $m \times n$. Classical matrix datasets include images. Since the model named one-pass AUC (OPAUC) which is developed by [6] and [13] cannot process matrix instances, thus this paper will develop a matrix-instance-based one-pass AUC optimization model, i.e., MOPAUC, so as to process the matrix datasets.

1.3   Difficulty

As we said, MOPAUC can process matrix instances. While the difficulty that extends OPAUC to handle matrix instances is obvious. Once we extend the model of vector-instance-based learning machine to the one of the matrix-instance-based learning machine, we should optimize more parameters due to for a matrix instance, a more classifier weight is needed. How to optimize them is the difficulty which should be conquered. Thus, in our work, in order to solve this difficulty, we adopt gradient descent method and details are given in Sect. 2.

1.4   Contribution and Framework of the Manuscript

The contributions of the MOPAUC are (1) it can process the matrix-instance-based AUC optimization problems; (2) compared with the OPAUC whose required storage is $O(d^2)$ where $d = m \times n$, the storage requirement is reduced to $O(m^2 + n^2)$; (3) it inherits the advantage of OPAUC which is independent from the number of training instances.

What's more, Sect. 2 shows the framework of the developed MOPAUC. Section 3 gives the experiments. The conclusion is given in Sect. 4.

2   Matrix-Instance-Based One-Pass AUC Optimization

There is a matrix instance $A \in \mathbb{R}^{m \times n}$ and its dimensionality is $m \times n$. The class label of each instance is selected from the set $y = \{+1, -1\}$. Here, the instances form the instance space $\mathcal{A}$ while the labels form the label space $\mathcal{Y}$. Denote $\mathcal{D}$ by an unknown distribution over the product space $\mathcal{A} \times \mathcal{Y}$. Let $\mathcal{S} = \{(A_1, y_1), (A_2, y_2), \ldots, (A_T, y_T)\}$ be a series of instances which arrive continuously and each instance arrives identically and independently from $\mathcal{D}$. Moreover, we denote $[n] = \{1, 2, \ldots, n\}$ where the integer $n > 0$ and $\lfloor \alpha \rfloor$ represents the largest integer which is no more than α where the real $\alpha > 0$. Then we adopt $|\mathcal{A}|$ to denote its cardinality.

Now we let $f : \mathcal{A} \to \mathbb{R}$ be a real-valued function, and for $\mathcal{S}$, the AUC of function f is defined as:

$$AUC(f, \mathcal{S}) = \sum_{i=1}^{T} \sum_{j=1}^{T} B. \tag{1}$$

where $B = \frac{(\prod[f(A_i) > f(A_j)] + \frac{1}{2} \prod[f(A_i) = f(A_j)]) \prod[y_i > y_j]}{T_s^+ T_s^-}$, $\prod[\star]$ is the indicator function which returns 1 if the argument is true and 0 otherwise, $T_s^+ = |\{(A_i, y_i) \in \mathcal{S} : y_i = +1\}|$ and $T_s^- = |\{(A_i, y_i) \in \mathcal{S} : y_i = -1\}|$.

Then the optimization of AUC can be turned to optimize the pairwise surrogate losses as follows:

$$\mathcal{L}(f, \mathcal{S}) = \sum_{i=1}^{T} \sum_{j=1}^{T} \frac{\ell(f(A_i) - f(A_j)) \prod[y_i > y_j]}{T_s^+ T_s^-} \tag{2}$$

$$= \sum_{i=1}^{T} \sum_{j=1}^{i-1} \frac{\ell(y_i(f(A_i) - f(A_j))) \prod[y_i \neq y_j]}{T_s^+ T_s^-}.$$

where $\ell : \mathbb{R} \to \mathbb{R}^+$ is a convex function. Then we say in the $\mathcal{D}$, the loss can be computed as bellow.

$$\mathcal{L}(f, \mathcal{D}) = E_{A_i \sim \mathcal{D}^+, A_j \sim \mathcal{D}^-}[\ell(f(A_i) - f(A_j))] \tag{3}$$

$$= E_{(A_i, y_i) \sim \mathcal{D}, (A_j, y_j) \sim \mathcal{D}}[\ell(f(A_i) - f(A_j)) | y_i > y_j].$$

In order to optimize the Eq. (3) in convenience, we let $\ell(t) = (1 - t)^2$. Then for $\mathcal{S}$, its pairwise least square loss is given below.

$$\mathcal{L}(u, v, \mathcal{S}) = \frac{\lambda_1}{2} |u|^2 + \frac{\lambda_2}{2} |v|^2 + \frac{1}{2} \sum_{i=1}^{T} \sum_{j=1}^{i-1} \frac{(1 - y_i u^T (A_i - A_j)^T v)^2}{T_s^+ T_s^-}. \tag{4}$$

where the weights are $u \in \mathbb{R}^{m \times 1}$ and $v \in \mathbb{R}^{n \times 1}$. λ_1 and λ_2 are regularization parameters that control the model complexity. The constant $\frac{1}{2}$ is introduced for simplicity. Moreover, we define that the pairwise least square loss with respect to distribution $\mathcal{D}$ as

$$\mathcal{L}(u, v, \mathcal{D}) = E_{\mathcal{S}}[\mathcal{L}(u, v, \mathcal{S})] = \frac{1}{T} \sum_{t=1}^{T} \mathcal{L}_t(u, v). \tag{5}$$

where

$$\mathcal{L}_t(u, v) = \frac{\lambda_1}{2} |u|^2 + \frac{\lambda_2}{2} |v|^2 + \sum_{i=1}^{t-1} \frac{\prod [y_i \neq y_j](1 - y_i u^T (A_i - A_j)^T v)^2}{2 |i \in [t-1] : y_i y_t = -1|}. \tag{6}$$

Now we can say the minimization of Eq. (6) is the equivalent problem to optimize the AUC of instances $\mathcal{S}$. In order to process this problem, we will adopt the gradient descent method and here, we define $\mathcal{L}_t(u, v) = 0$ when $T_t^+ T_t^- = 0$ where T_t^+ and T_t^- denote the cardinalities of positive and negative instances in $\mathcal{S}_t = \{(A_1, y_1), (A_2, y_2), \ldots, (A_t, y_t)\}$, respectively.

If $y_i = +1$, the gradient of Eq. (6) is

$$\frac{\partial \mathcal{L}_t(u, v)}{\partial u} = \lambda_1 u - A_t v + c_t^- v + [(A_t - c_t^-) v v^T (A_t - c_t^-)^T] u + S_{t_u}^- u. \tag{7}$$

$$\frac{\partial \mathcal{L}_t(u, v)}{\partial v} = \lambda_2 v - A_t^T u + [c_t^-]^T u + [(A_t - c_t^-)^T u u^T (A_t - c_t^-)] v + S_{t_v}^- v. \tag{8}$$

where

$$c_t^- = \sum_{i:i<t, y_i=-1} \frac{A_i}{T_t^-}. \tag{9}$$

$$S_{t_u}^- = \sum_{i:i<t, y_i=-1} \frac{A_i v (A_i v)^T - (c_t^- v)(c_t^- v)^T}{T_t^-}. \tag{10}$$

$$S_{t_v}^- = \sum_{i:i<t, y_i=-1} \frac{(u^T A_i)^T u^T A_i - (u^T c_t^-)^T u^T c_t^-}{T_t^-}. \tag{11}$$

Otherwise, if $y_i = -1$, the gradient of Eq. (6) is

$$\frac{\partial \mathcal{L}_t(u, v)}{\partial u} = \lambda_1 u + A_t v - c_t^+ v + [(A_t - c_t^+) v v^T (A_t - c_t^+)^T] u + S_{t_u}^+ u. \tag{12}$$

$$\frac{\partial \mathcal{L}_t(u, v)}{\partial v} = \lambda_2 v + A_t^T u - [c_t^+]^T u + [(A_t - c_t^+)^T u u^T (A_t - c_t^+)] v + S_{t_v}^+ v. \tag{13}$$

where

$$c_t^+ = \sum_{i:i<t,y_i=+1} \frac{A_i}{T_t^+}. \tag{14}$$

$$S_{t_u}^+ = \sum_{i:i<t,y_i=+1} \frac{A_i v(A_i v)^T - (c_t^+ v)(c_t^+ v)^T}{T_t^+}. \tag{15}$$

$$S_{t_v}^+ = \sum_{i:i<t,y_i=+1} \frac{(u^T A_i)^T u^T A_i - (u^T c_t^+)^T u^T c_t^+}{T_t^+}. \tag{16}$$

Once we compute the gradient $\frac{\partial \mathcal{L}_t(u,v)}{\partial u}$ and $\frac{\partial \mathcal{L}_t(u,v)}{\partial v}$, we can update the classifier weights by

$$u_t = u_{t-1} - \eta_{ut} \frac{\partial \mathcal{L}_t(u_{t-1}, v_{t-1})}{\partial u_{t-1}}. \tag{17}$$

$$v_t = v_{t-1} - \eta_{vt} \frac{\partial \mathcal{L}_t(u_{t-1}, v_{t-1})}{\partial v_{t-1}}. \tag{18}$$

where $u_t(v_t)$ represents the $u(v)$ under t-th iteration. Here each iteration represents one instance arrives. η_{ut} and η_{vt} are the step sizes in the t-th iteration. During the procedure, we should notice that once a new instance arrives, the $T_t^-, c_t^-, S_{t_u}^-, S_{t_v}^-, T_t^+, c_t^+, S_{t_u}^+, S_{t_v}^+$ are also updated. If $y_t = -1$, we have

$$T_t^- = T_{t-1}^- + 1, T_t^+ = T_{t-1}^+, c_t^- = c_{t-1}^- + \frac{1}{T_t^-}(A_t - c_{t-1}^-), \tag{19}$$

$$c_t^+ = c_{t-1}^+, S_{t_u}^+ = S_{t-1_u}^+, S_{t_v}^+ = S_{t-1_v}^+,$$

$$S_{t_u}^- = S_{t-1_u}^- + c_{t-1}^- v(c_{t-1}^- v)^T - c_t^- v(c_t^- v)^T +$$

$$(A_t v(A_t v)^T - S_{t-1_u}^- - c_{t-1}^- v(c_{t-1}^- v)^T)/T_t^-,$$

$$S_{t_v}^- = S_{t-1_v}^- + (u^T c_{t-1}^-)^T u^T c_{t-1}^- - (u^T c_t^-)^T u^T c_t^- +$$

$$((u^T A_t)^T u^T A_t - S_{t-1_v}^- - u^T c_{t-1}^-)^T u^T c_{t-1}^-)/T_t^-.$$

Otherwise, if $y_t = +1$, we have

$$T_t^+ = T_{t-1}^+ + 1, T_t^- = T_{t-1}^-, c_t^+ = c_{t-1}^+ + \frac{1}{T_t^+}(A_t - c_{t-1}^+), \tag{20}$$

$$c_t^- = c_{t-1}^-, S_{t_u}^- = S_{t-1_u}^-, S_{t_v}^- = S_{t-1_v}^-,$$

$$S_{t_u}^+ = S_{t-1_u}^+ + c_{t-1}^+ v(c_{t-1}^+ v)^T - c_t^+ v(c_t^+ v)^T +$$

$$(A_t v(A_t v)^T - S_{t-1_u}^+ - c_{t-1}^+ v(c_{t-1}^+ v)^T)/T_t^+,$$

$$S_{t_v}^+ = S_{t-1_v}^+ + (u^T c_{t-1}^+)^T u^T c_{t-1}^+ - (u^T c_t^+)^T u^T c_t^+ +$$

$$((u^T A_t)^T u^T A_t - S_{t-1_v}^+ - u^T c_{t-1}^+)^T u^T c_{t-1}^+)/T_t^+.$$

Once we get weights u_T and v_T, we can treat u_T and v_T as the weights of classifier with T instances arrive continuously in a short time. For convenience, we summary the algorithm in Table 1.

3   Experiments

3.1   Experiments on Benchmark Datasets

We conduct the experiments on 27 benchmark datasets [14] which can be found in Table 2. Since our MOPAUC can be used for matrix datasets, so we also adopt some image datasets for experiments, they are Coil-20, Letter-Image, ORL, CIFAR-10, and MNIST. For each dataset, we scale the features to $[-1, 1]$ and each multi-class dataset is transformed into a binary one by randomly partitioning classes into two groups, where each group contains the same or similar number of classes. Then in order to validate the effectiveness of MOPAUC, we can also reshape the vector instance into different matrix forms with the way given in [15] and select a feasible form for experiments. Contrariwise, if we conduct other AUC optimization methods which aim to process vector instances, we can vectorize the matrix instances to vector ones. Moreover, we adopt the following methods for comparison. Since some online and off-line AUC optimization methods has been compared in OPAUC [6,13] and it has been validate that OPAUC outperforms those methods, especially some online ones including online AUC optimization with a sequential updating method or with a gradient descent updating method [16], online gradient descent algorithm which optimizes the (weighted) univariate exponential loss or optimizes the (weighted) univariate logistic loss or optimizes the (weighted) univariate least square loss [17], thus we compare some new methods including $OPAUC$ (one-pass AUC [13]), $KOAUC$ (kernel online AUC maximization [1]), $KOIL$ (kernel online imbalanced learning with AUC [7]), $SSAUC_{GM}$ (semi-supervised AUC optimization method with generative models [18]), ELM_{AUC} (off-line binary AUC optimization algorithm [19]), SVM_{pAUC} (support vector algorithms for optimizing the partial area under the ROC curve [20]).

Among these methods, OPAUC, KOAUC, and KOIL are online ones and others are new off-line AUC optimization methods. Since $SSAUC_{GM}$ is a semi-supervised method, so for the experiments about $SSAUC_{GM}$, each dataset is divided into two parts. We choose 30% instances in random as labeled instances and the rest is treated as the unlabeled part. Of course, as we know, more labeled instances brings a better classification performance. But according to our all experimental results which include those not written in this manuscript, even though we adopt 100% labeled instances, the performance of $SSAUC_{GM}$ is still worse than the proposed MOPAUC in average. Thus, we only show the results when 30% instances are chosen in random as the labeled instances here.

Experimental environment is given below. All the computations are performed on a node of compute cluster with 16 CPUs (Intel Core Due 3.0 GHz) running RedHat Linux Enterprise 5 with 48 GB main memory which is similar with the one used in OPAUC. The coding environment is MATLAB 2016.

For each dataset, we choose 80% for training and the rest is used for test. Since some datasets maybe have many instances and limited to our memory, so we select 10000 training instances at random (without replacement) over the whole training data for batch algorithms if training size exceeds 10000. For all online methods, we go through the entire training data only once. Then in terms of the parameter settings for the compared methods, we can refer to each related reference. For our MOPAUC, the parameter setting is similar with the one in OPAUC for fair comparison. Namely, η_{ut} and η_{vt} are selected from the set $2^{[-12:10]}$, the regularization parameters λ_1 and λ_2 are selected from the set $2^{[-10:2]}$, weights u and v are initialized from the set $10^{[-3:3]}$. In order to get the optimal parameters, for each compared method, we carry out 10-fold cross-validation and repeat for ten times so as to get the average optimal results. In other words, the results in the following tables are from ten runs.

Table 3 shows the average testing AUC results for all compared methods on the benchmark datasets after we carry out the experiments for ten runs. From this table, it is found that in terms of testing AUC, our proposed MOPAUC is better than other compared online and off-line AUC optimization methods in average. Moreover, for the used five image datasets, MOPAUC performs best which validates that MOPAUC is feasible for the matrix-instance-based AUC optimization problems. Furthermore, the win/tie/loss counts show that MOPAUC is clearly superior to these online methods, as it wins for most times and never loses. For the other off-line AUC optimization methods, they performs better than MOPAUC sometimes. The reason is that these off-line methods can store the whole dataset so that they have potential for better performances.

What's more, it is found that the proposed MOPAUC outperforms OPAUC on vector instances. The reason for such a result can refer to the relationship between some vector-instance-based learning machines (for example, MHKS, i.e., modification of Ho-Kashyap algorithm with squared approximation of the misclassification errors [21]) and their corresponding matrixized versions (for example, MatMHKS, i.e., matrix-instance-based MHKS [15]). As we know, MHKS is a learning machine to process vector instances directly and MatMHKS which is developed on the base of MHKS is a one to process matrix instances directly. In MHKS, ωx^T is used to label a vector instance x while in MatMHKS, $uA^T v^T$ is used for labeling. Here, ω, u, and v are classifier weights and A is the matrix version of x. As [15] and [22] said, with $uA^T v^T$ used, MatMHKS is treated as MHKS imposed with Kronecker product decomposability constraint and MatMHKS has more constraints than MHKS since MatMHKS should optimize more weights. More constraints bring more prior information such as structural or local contextual information and the information bring a better performance. For that, MatMHKS outperforms MHKS even though they process vector instances. According to the same reason, in terms of the forms of models, the relationship between OPAUC and MOPAUC is same as the one between MHKS and MatMHKS, thus MOPAUC has more constraints than OPAUC, and then MOPAUC has more useful information to design a feasible classifier. That's why our developed MOPAUC outperforms OPAUC on vector instances.

Table 1. Algorithm: MOPAUC

Input: Regularization parameters $\lambda_1 > 0$, $\lambda_2 > 0$, step sizes $\{\eta_{ut}\}_{t=1}^{T}$, $\{\eta_{vt}\}_{t=1}^{T}$
Initialize: Set $T_0^+ = T_0^- = 0$, $c_0^+ = c_0^- = [0]_{m \times n}$, $S_{0_u}^+ = [0]_{m \times m}$,
$S_{0_v}^+ = [0]_{n \times n}$, $S_{0_u}^- = [0]_{m \times m}$, $S_{0_v}^- = [0]_{n \times n}$
1. for t=1,2,...,T do
2.   Arrive a training instance (A_t, y_t)
3.   if $y_t = +1$ then
4. $T_t^+ = T_{t-1}^+ + 1$ and $T_t^- = T_{t-1}^-$
5. $c_t^+ = c_{t-1}^+ + \frac{1}{T_t^+}(A_t - c_{t-1}^+)$ and $c_t^- = c_{t-1}^-$
6.   Update $S_{t_u}^+$, $S_{t_v}^+$, $S_{t_u}^-$, $S_{t_v}^-$ with Eq. (20)
7.   Calculate the gradient of $\mathcal{L}_t(u, v)$
8.   else
9. $T_t^- = T_{t-1}^- + 1$ and $T_t^+ = T_{t-1}^+$
10. $c_t^- = c_{t-1}^- + \frac{1}{T_t^-}(A_t - c_{t-1}^-)$ and $c_t^+ = c_{t-1}^+$
11.   Update $S_{t_u}^+$, $S_{t_v}^+$, $S_{t_u}^-$, $S_{t_v}^-$ with Eq. (19)
12.   Calculate the gradient of $\mathcal{L}_t(u, v)$
13.   end if
14.   Update u_t and v_t with Eqs. (17) and (18)
15. end for
Output: weights u_T and v_T

Table 2. Benchmark datasets

datasets	No. instances	No. features	datasets	No. instances	No. features	datasets	No. instances	No. features
AuC	690	14	PID	768	8	BA	1372	4
BCW	699	9	Satellite Image	6435	36	TSE	5820	32
GeD	1000	24	Shuttle	58000	9	UKM	403	5
Glass	214	9	Sonar	208	60	QSAR	1055	41
Heart	270	13	Thyroid	7200	21	Coil-20	1440	32 × 32
Iris	150	4	Vowel	990	10	Letter-Image	500	24 × 18
Letter	20000	16	Waveform	5000	21	ORL	400	32 × 20
Liver	345	6	Waveform-noise	5000	40	CIFAR-10	60000	32 × 32
Pendigits	7494	16	Wine	178	13	MNIST	60000	28 × 28

Table 3. Testing AUC (mean ± std.) of MOPAUC with compared methods on benchmark datasets. ●/○ indicates that MOPAUC is significantly better/worse than the corresponding method (pairwise t-tests at 95% significance level). The best average AUC for each dataset is shown in bold.

datasets	$MOPAUC$	$OPAUC$	$KOAUC$	$KOIL$	$SSAUC_{GM}$	ELM_{AUC}	SVM_{pAUC}
AuC	**78.07 ± 1.00**	77.50 ± 1.77 ●	77.77 ± 0.54 ●	76.23 ± 1.41 ●	76.44 ± 1.03 ●	74.37 ± 1.12 ●	73.40 ± 1.33 ●
BCW	89.85 ± 1.46	89.44 ± 1.99 ●	88.59 ± 2.76 ●	88.56 ± 1.27 ●	88.58 ± 0.48 ●	88.09 ± 0.30 ○	87.22 ± 1.69 ●
GeD	71.77 ± 0.07	**79.78 ± 1.46** ●	71.74 ± 1.36 ●	70.17 ± 2.10 ●	70.57 ± 0.71 ●	68.27 ± 2.13 ○	67.58 ± 0.26 ●
Glass	**84.58 ± 1.95**	83.03 ± 0.44 ●	83.21 ± 1.25	83.15 ± 1.89 ●	83.46 ± 0.77	82.48 ± 2.48	81.74 ± 2.00
Heart	79.34 ± 0.59	79.79 ± 0.73	**80.20 ± 0.18** ●	77.17 ± 1.17 ●	77.98 ± 0.95 ○	73.79 ± 2.83	72.96 ± 2.14 ○
Iris	**91.37 ± 0.99**	89.70 ± 0.20 ●	89.01 ± 1.75	88.81 ± 2.16	89.22 ± 2.71	88.91 ± 0.93 ○	88.09 ± 0.55
Letter	**86.02 ± 2.76**	81.14 ± 0.64	85.09 ± 0.65 ●	79.65 ± 1.65 ●	81.06 ± 0.21 ●	74.41 ± 2.66 ●	72.84 ± 1.56 ●
Liver	**64.43 ± 2.99**	63.23 ± 0.95 ●	63.61 ± 1.73	63.57 ± 0.84	63.91 ± 2.11	63.28 ± 0.31	62.63 ± 2.30 ○
Pendigits	**91.58 ± 2.70**	90.75 ± 1.71 ●	90.54 ± 1.21 ●	89.40 ± 0.51 ●	89.65 ± 0.70 ●	88.12 ± 0.37 ●	87.30 ± 2.67 ●
PID	**66.30 ± 0.38**	64.84 ± 0.77 ●	64.49 ± 0.30	64.40 ± 2.26 ●	64.33 ± 0.78 ●	63.41 ± 2.42	63.03 ± 2.22
Satellite Image	**77.96 ± 1.46**	75.99 ± 0.62	75.88 ± 0.33 ●	75.30 ± 0.92	75.33 ± 0.58	74.41 ± 1.72 ●	73.79 ± 1.86 ●
Shuttle	**86.38 ± 1.82**	84.54 ± 1.79 ●	83.25 ± 1.63	82.33 ± 2.11	82.36 ± 1.80	81.28 ± 2.91	80.48 ± 1.54
Sonar	**70.94 ± 2.25**	69.41 ± 0.94	69.19 ± 0.36 ●	67.71 ± 1.53 ●	68.22 ± 2.59 ○	65.90 ± 2.80	65.18 ± 0.21 ○
Thyroid	**84.47 ± 0.71**	83.16 ± 0.09 ●	83.79 ± 1.09	84.08 ± 0.84	84.44 ± 0.66 ●	84.22 ± 2.82 ●	83.84 ± 0.99 ●
Vowel	54.73 ± 2.64	53.75 ± 0.78	53.37 ± 1.46	50.54 ± 2.21	51.45 ± 2.21	48.35 ± 0.05	47.31 ± 1.10
Waveform	**72.18 ± 0.55**	71.60 ± 0.33 ●	71.05 ± 1.10 ●	70.18 ± 1.41 ●	70.91 ± 1.82 ●	70.09 ± 0.40 ●	69.26 ± 0.73
Waveform-noise	**77.68 ± 0.48**	76.95 ± 0.56 ●	77.42 ± 1.63	76.70 ± 1.39	77.24 ± 0.02	75.13 ± 0.80	74.65 ± 3.42
Wine	**82.41 ± 0.27**	80.83 ± 1.62 ●	80.61 ± 1.12 ●	81.00 ± 1.43 ●	80.67 ± 2.43 ○	80.26 ± 2.71	79.93 ± 1.88
BA	**91.62 ± 0.94**	88.86 ± 0.24	88.33 ± 1.95 ●	88.42 ± 1.67	88.45 ± 0.57	88.80 ± 1.29 ○	88.02 ± 2.68 ●
TSE	**85.29 ± 1.58**	83.85 ± 2.84 ●	84.46 ± 0.30	85.11 ± 1.57 ●	85.28 ± 0.92 ●	85.04 ± 2.04 ●	84.69 ± 0.34 ●
UKM	**81.71 ± 1.25**	80.69 ± 2.62	79.21 ± 0.43	78.57 ± 0.25	78.91 ± 2.81 ○	77.68 ± 0.79 ○	76.68 ± 2.29 ○
QSAR	**92.51 ± 0.39**	90.33 ± 0.23	89.69 ± 0.41 ●	84.31 ± 2.94	86.53 ± 2.76	79.50 ± 1.51	78.05 ± 2.54
Coil-20	**79.64 ± 1.47**	77.27 ± 1.02 ●	76.84 ± 2.10 ●	76.44 ± 2.99 ●	76.77 ± 0.20 ●	76.10 ± 2.94 ●	75.89 ± 1.98 ●
Letter-Image	**79.64 ± 2.11**	78.31 ± 2.35 ●	78.34 ± 2.48 ●	77.11 ± 2.77 ●	77.37 ± 1.51 ●	75.90 ± 1.19 ●	75.35 ± 0.02 ●
ORL	**83.11 ± 0.54**	82.84 ± 2.04 ●	82.81 ± 2.52 ●	79.56 ± 2.26 ●	81.29 ± 2.94 ●	77.25 ± 0.89 ●	76.00 ± 2.42 ●
CIFAR-10	**94.03 ± 0.31**	93.88 ± 0.14 ●	93.01 ± 2.58 ●	89.45 ± 1.63 ●	78.32 ± 2.65 ●	74.09 ± 0.67 ●	72.47 ± 2.07 ●
MNIST	**93.56 ± 0.36**	92.42 ± 0.21 ●	92.34 ± 0.57 ●	84.32 ± 1.07 ●	78.41 ± 1.83 ●	81.55 ± 0.70 ●	73.30 ± 0.15 ●
win/tie/loss		18 / 9 / 0	16 / 11 / 0	15 / 12 / 0	13 / 10 / 4	11 / 11 / 5	14 / 9 / 4

Moreover, we also compare the average running time of MOPAUC and the other three online AUC optimization methods after we carry out the experiments for ten runs. Table 4 shows the comparison of the running time (in seconds) of MOPAUC and the compared online methods on the used datasets. From this table, it is found that for the datasets except the five image datasets, KOAUC and KOIL can cost least running time in average. The reason is that KOAUC and KOIL optimize on single instance loss, whereas MOPAUC and OPAUC optimize on pairwise loss. Moreover, compared with OPAUC, MOPAUC costs less running time. Especially, for the image datasets, our proposed MOPAUC costs least running time which validate the effectiveness of our method. Indeed, as OPAUC said, its required storage is $O(d^2)$ where $d = m \times n$ while for our MOPAUC, the storage requirement is reduced to $O(m^2 + n^2)$. Furthermore, as [23] said, compared with vector leaning machine, matrix learning machine can reduce the computational complexity and improve the classification performance. The reduction of computational complexity always brings less running time.

Table 4. Comparison of the running time (in seconds) on datasets for the online AUC optimization methods.

datasets	$MOPAUC$	$OPAUC$	$KOAUC$	$KOIL$	datasets	$MOPAUC$	$OPAUC$	$KOAUC$	$KOIL$
AuC	0.10	0.37	0.02	0.01	Thyroid	0.38	2.86	0.74	0.09
BCW	0.03	0.15	0.03	0.01	Vowel	0.19	0.65	0.07	0.16
GeD	0.10	1.08	0.11	0.05	Waveform	0.38	2.86	0.15	0.22
Glass	0.03	0.15	0.01	0.02	Waveform-noise	0.58	10.37	1.09	0.59
Heart	0.32	0.32	0.02	0.09	Wine	1.10	1.10	0.17	0.14
Iris	0.01	0.03	0.01	0.01	BA	0.05	0.10	0.02	0.02
Letter	0.21	1.66	0.07	0.07	TSE	0.52	6.64	1.19	1.75
Liver	0.08	0.23	0.05	0.02	UKM	0.13	0.16	0.02	0.04
Pendigits	0.21	1.66	0.55	0.02	QSAR	10.81	10.90	2.30	0.96
PID	0.13	0.41	0.03	0.06	Coil-20	13.28	6797.67	735.72	1519.31
Satellite Image	0.63	8.40	0.83	1.59	Letter-Image	5.83	1209.84	55.07	81.79
Shuttle	0.12	0.53	0.11	0.10	ORL	9.23	2655.34	58.46	344.08
Sonar	0.88	23.34	4.96	3.15	CIFAR-10	13.28	6797.67	283.49	463.37
MNIST	10.16	3984.67	188.00	856.00					

3.2 Experiments About Parameter Influence

In our proposed MOPAUC, it consists many adjustable parameters including regularization parameters λ_1, λ_2, step sizes η_{ut}, η_{vt}, weights u and v. So here, we discuss the influence of them. Since $\eta_{ut} \in 2^{[-12:10]}$, $\eta_{vt} \in 2^{[-12:10]}$, $\lambda_1 \in 2^{[-10:2]}$, $\lambda_2 \in 2^{[-10:2]}$, $u \in 10^{[-3:3]}$, and $v \in 10^{[-3:3]}$, so we use the following three figures to show the influence. For the convenience of elaboration, we only select four datasets, they are GeD, Letter, CIFAR-10, MNIST. Figure 1 shows the influence of the regularization parameters; Fig. 2 shows the influence of the step sizes; Fig. 3 shows the one of the weights. Each sub-figure in each figure, 2^x and 2^y just represent the power operation. Namely, the parameter is 2^{-10}, 2^6 and so on. For 10^x and 10^y, the meaning is same. According to these three figures, it is found that the regularization parameters and weights have less influence on the average AUC. While the step sizes should not be set to values bigger than 1, whereas there is a relatively big range between $[2^{-12}, 2^{-4}]$ where MOPAUC achieves good results. This conclusion is similar with one given in OPAUC [13].

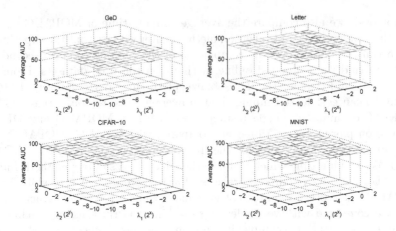

Fig. 1. Influence of regularization parameters.

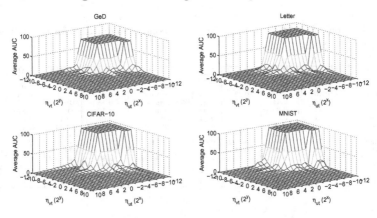

Fig. 2. Influence of step sizes.

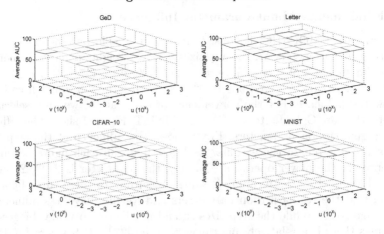

Fig. 3. Influence of weights.

4 Conclusion

AUC is an important performance measure and it is always measured by the losses defined over pairs of instances from different classes. Conducting traditional off-line AUC optimization methods should store the entire dataset in memory which is infeasible for big data or streaming data applications. Online AUC optimization methods need not store the entire dataset, but the present mostly online AUC optimization methods still need to store $\sqrt{T}$ instances yet where T is the number of the entire training dataset. One-pass AUC optimization (OPAUC) is a new online one and it is independent from the number of training instances. While OPAUC is infeasible for matrix datasets including images. So this paper extend the model of OPAUC and develop a matrix-instance-based one-pass AUC optimization model, i.e., MOPAUC, so as to process the matrix datasets. Related experiments on some datasets including the vector ones and matrix ones validate that (1) MOPAUC has a best average testing AUC compared with the online and off-line AUC optimization methods; (2) MOPAUC is superior to some online methods from the statistical view; (3) MOPAUC can cost less running time compared with other online methods for processing image datasets; (4) regularization parameters and weights have less influence on the average AUC for MOPAUC while step sizes have strong influence. If the values of step sizes range from $[2^{-12}, 2^{-4}]$, MOPAUC can achieve good results. If the values are bigger than 1, the average AUC will decreased to be 0. In generally, our proposed MOPAUC can process matrix-instance-based AUC optimization problems without storing the dataset and only scanning the training data once.

Acknowledgment. This work is supported by (1) Natural Science Foundation of Shanghai under grant number 16ZR1414500 (2) National Natural Science Foundation of China under grant number 61602296 and the authors would like to thank their supports.

References

1. Ding, Y., Liu, C.H., Zhao, P.L., Hoi, S.C.H.: Large scale kernel methods for online AUC maximization. In: 2017 IEEE International Conference on Data Mining, pp. 91–100 (2017)
2. Liu, R.H., Hall, L.O., Bowyer, K.W., Goldgof, D.B., Gatenby, R., Ahmed, K.B.: Synthetic minority image over-sampling technique: How to improve AUC for glioblastoma patient survival prediction. In: 2017 IEEE International Conference on Systems, Man, and Cybernetics, pp. 1357–1362 (2017)
3. Jiang, H., Yi, J., Chen, S., Zhu, X.: A multi-objective algorithm for task scheduling and resource allocation in cloud-based disassembly. J. Manuf. Syst. **41**, 239–255 (2016)
4. Fan, Q.Q., Wang, W.L., Yan, X.F.: Multi-objective differential evolution with performance-metric-based self-adaptive mutation operator for chemical and biochemical dynamic optimization problems. Appl. Soft Comput. **59**, 33–44 (2017)
5. Fan, P., Zhou, R.G., Jing, N., Li, H.S.: Geometric transformations of multidimensional color images based on NASS. Inf. Sci. **340**, 191–208 (2016)

6. Gao, W., Jin, R., Zhu, S.H., Zhou, Z.H.: One-pass AUC optimization. In: Proceedings of the 30th International Conference on Machine Learning, pp. 906–914 (2013)
7. Hu, J.J., Yang, H.Q., Lyu, M.R., King, I., So, A.M.C.: Online nonlinear AUC maximization for imbalanced data sets. IEEE Trans. Neural Netw. Learn. Syst. **99**, 1–14 (2017)
8. Khajavi, N.T., Kuh, A.: The covariance selection quality for graphs with junction trees through AUC bounds. In: 54th Annual Allerton Conference on Communication Control and Computing (Allerton), pp. 1252–1258 (2016)
9. Kim, Y.S., Toh, K.A., Teoh, A.B.J., Eng, H.L., Yau, W.Y.: An online AUC formulation for binary classification. Pattern Recogn. **45**(6), 2266–2279 (2012)
10. Wang, S.J., Li, D., Petrick, N., Sahiner, B., Linguraru, M.G., Summers, R.M.: Optimizing area under the ROC curve using semi-supervised learning. Pattern Recogn. **48**(1), 276–287 (2015)
11. Li, Z.L., Zhai, S.D., Xia, T., Wang S.J.: A boosting method for direct AUC optimization. In: 2015 IEEE China Summit and International Conference on Signal and Information Processing (ChinaSIP), pp. 797–801 (2015)
12. Fujino, A., Ueda N.: A semi-supervised AUC optimization method with generative models. In: 2016 IEEE 16th International Conference on Data Mining, pp. 883–888 (2016)
13. Gao, W., Wang, L., Jin, R., Zhu, S.H., Zhou, Z.H.: One-pass AUC optimization. Artif. Intell. **236**, 1–29 (2016)
14. Blake, C.L., Newman, D.J., Hettich, S., Merz C.J.: UCI repository of machine learning databases (2012)
15. Chen, S.C., Wang, Z., Tian, Y.J.: Matrix-pattern-oriented Ho-Kashyap classifier with regularization learning. Pattern Recogn. **40**(5), 1533–1543 (2007)
16. Zhao, P., Hoi, S.C.H., Jin, R., Yang T.: Online AUC maximization. In: Proceedings of the 25th International Conference on Machine Learning, pp. 233–240 (2011)
17. Kotlowski, W., Dembczynski, K., Hüllermeier, E.: Bipartite ranking through minimization of univariate loss. In: Proceedings of the 28th International Conference on Machine Learning, pp. 1113–1120 (2011)
18. Fujino, A., Ueda, N.: A semi-supervised AUC optimization method with generative models. In: IEEE International Conference on Data Mining, pp. 883–888 (2017)
19. Yang, Z.Y., Zhang, T.H., Lu, J.C., Zhang, D.Z., Kalui, D.: Optimizing area under the ROC curve via extreme learning machines. Knowl.-Based Syst. **130**, 74–89 (2017)
20. Narasimhan, H., Agarwal, S.: Support vector algorithms for optimizing the partial area under the ROC curve. Neural Comput. **29**(7), 1919–1963 (2017)
21. Leski, J.: Ho-Kashyap classifier with generalization control. Pattern Recogn. Lett. **24**(14), 2281–2290 (2003)
22. Zhu, C.M., Wang, Z., Gao, D.Q.: New design goal of a classifier: global and local structural risk minimization. Knowl.-Based Syst. **100**, 25–49 (2016)
23. Zhu, C.M.: Double-fold localized multiple matrix learning machine with Universum. Pattern Anal. Appl. **20**(4), 1091–1118 (2017)

Piecewise Harmonic Image Restoration with High Order Variational Model

Bibo Lu[1(✉)], Zhenzhen Huangfu[1], and Rui Huang[2]

[1] Henan Polytechnic University, Jiaozuo 454003, Henan, China
lubibojz@gmail.com
[2] South China Normal University, Guangzhou 510631, Guangdong, China

Abstract. Image denoising is a fundamental problem in image processing and computer vision. A main challenge is to remove noise while preserving features and developing piecewise smoothing image. Piecewise constant and linear image recovery has been focused in the past decades. In this paper, we propose a model recover a class more smoothing image with complex geometrical structure. We first give definition of piecewise harmonic image, which covers a wide range piecewise smoothing image. Then a multiplicative framework for high order variational construction is introduced. Within this framework, we present a geometrical weighted Laplace (GWL) high order model. The proposed model is discussed and compared to some typical related methods. Experimental results on test images show the performance of the proposed method.

Keywords: Image denoising · Piecewise smoothing image
High order · Harmonic function

1 Introduction

In a standard problem of gray scale image denosing problem, the noisy image u_0 corrupted by additive white Gaussian noise is modeled as

$$u_0(x, y) = u(x, y) + \sigma(x, y), \tag{1}$$

where u is the unknown noisy free image and σ is assumed as known noise level: $\int_\Omega (u - u_0)^2 dx dy = \sigma^2$. The goal of image restoration is to remove noise while preserving the important structure features from the observed noisy image u_0 [1]. An usual regularization approach to remove noise by minimizing the following functional:

$$E(u, \lambda) = E(u) + \frac{\lambda}{2} \int_\Omega (u - u_0)^2 dx dy, \tag{2}$$

where $E(u)$ is the regularization term to measure the variation of the noise intensity and $\lambda \geq 0$ is the Lagrange multiplier. The first regularization term on the

Supported by NSFC (U1404103) and Guangdong Engineering Research Center for Data Science.

ⓒ Springer Nature Switzerland AG 2018
J.-H. Lai et al. (Eds.): PRCV 2018, LNCS 11258, pp. 539–549, 2018.
https://doi.org/10.1007/978-3-030-03338-5_45

right-hand side of Eq. (2) is to measure the oscillations using weighted Laplace operator. The second fitting term is to measure the identification between u and u_0. In seminar total variational (TV) method [2], the regularization functional is defined as

$$E_{TV}(u) = \int_\Omega |\nabla u| dx dy, \tag{3}$$

which produces a piecewise constant image while removing noise. However, TV suffers from staircase effect in smoothing transition region [3]. A more smoothing image is also expected in varying image processing fields, inluding computer photography [4], medical image processing [5], image registration [6], Retinex problem [7]. Some operations have been used to construct high order models, such as Laplace operation based YK model [3] and LLT model [5], the Frobenius norm of the Hessian based affine TV model [8], curvature based elastic model [9] mean curvature based model [10] and Gaussian curvature based model [11]. A variable exponent high order variational model was proposed in [12], where the Gaussian convolution was used for detecting edges.

Low order model and high order operators are combined to construct new methods: one part to produce flat image and the other part to generate smoothing transition. In [15], Papafitsoros and Schönlieb considered a general additive high order functional and proved its existence and uniqueness. A popular high order model, total generalized variation (TGV), involves high order derivatives and automatically balances the first to kth derivatives [13]. The second order TGV is defined as following:

$$E(u)_{TGV} = \text{TGV}_\alpha^2 = \alpha_1 \int_\Omega |\nabla u - v| dx dy + \alpha_2 \int_\Omega |\varepsilon(v)| dx dy, \tag{4}$$

where the minimum is taken over the vector fields v and $\varepsilon(v) = \frac{1}{2}(\nabla v + \nabla v^{\text{T}})$ denotes the symmetrized derivative. TGV reduces the staircase effect and leads to piecewise polynomial intensities [14]. The connections between some typical additive high order models are detailed in [15]. Typical non-variational methods includes bilateral filter [16], nonlocal means filter [17,18], guided filter [19] and BM3D [20].

In this paper, we will introduce piecewise harmonic image, which is more smoother beyond the classical piecewise constant image and piecewise linear image. It allow a weak edge between different regions and it is difficult to recovery it. We will present a a new model to address this problem. The rest of this paper is organized as follows. Since our aim is to recover a more smoothing image, Sect. 2 introduce the definition of harmonic image and a new multiplicative framework for model construction. A new high order model is presented and its features are discussed in Sect. 3, Experimental results are shown in Sect. 4 and a brief conclusion is given in Sect. 5.

2 Framework for Piecewise Smoothing Image Recovery

2.1 Piecewise Smoothing Image: From Constant to Harmonic

Let $\Omega_i, i = 1, 2, \cdots, n$, be a partition of Ω. A common piecewise image is defined as

$$u(x, y) = \sum_{i=0}^{m} u_i(x, y), \tag{5}$$

where

$$u_i(x, y) = \begin{cases} \text{smoothing image} & (x, y) \in \Omega_i, \\ 0 & \text{otherwise.} \end{cases} \tag{6}$$

We require that the smoothing image in (6) is continuous and differentiable in every partition Ω_i. An usual way is to use homogeneous polynomial to represent the smoothing function. Therefore, image I is named as a piecewise constant image when $u(i) = c_i$ and a piecewise linear or affine image when $u(i) = a_i x + b_i y + c_i$. TV can recover piecewise constant image successfully. Several high order models have been proposed to recover piecewise linear image.

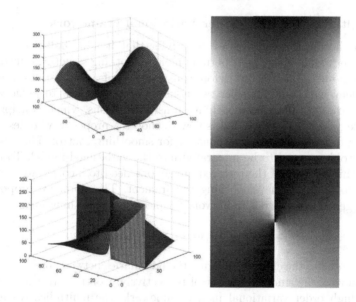

Fig. 1. Two harmonic functions and their corresponding images. The left-up is the shape of the harmonic function $f(x, y) = \frac{x^2}{a^2} - \frac{y^2}{b^2}$ and right-up is its corresponding image. The right-down is the shape of the harmonic function $f(x, y) = \frac{y}{x}$ and right-up is its corresponding image.

In this paper, for the first time, we consider the recovery of a class more smoothing image: piecewise harmonic image. In mathematic, a function f is said to be harmonic if it satisfies the following Laplace equation:

$$\triangle f(x,y) = \frac{\partial^2 f}{\partial x^2} + \frac{\partial^2 f}{\partial y^2} = 0. \tag{7}$$

Except the traditional constant function and the linear ones, many more smoothing function are harmonic. A quadratic one is a special case when $a = b$ for the hyperbolic paraboloid in geometry:

$$f(x,y) = \frac{x^2}{a^2} - \frac{y^2}{b^2}, \tag{8}$$

which describes the shape for a doubly ruled surface in 3D space. Another example is $f(x,y) = \arctan(\frac{y}{x})$, which has a non-vanishing derivatives to infinity. Figure 1 illustrates the the profiles of two harmonic functions and their corresponding images. These two functions and images has a complex and smoothing geometrical structure. Therefore, an image u is said to be a piecewise harmonic if $u(i)$ meets Eq. (7) in partition Ω_i. It permits more wild range smoothing functions beyond polynomial, though it is an extension to the traditional piecewise constant image and linear image. The sharp edges between the piecewise constant are easy to preserved and it is difficult to preserve the edges between the different harmonic regions, as its gradient may be small.

2.2   Multiplicative High Order Variational Framework

Based on the decisions above, we may infer that it is a challenge to recover piecewise harmonic image as it permits more smoothing structures beyond constant region and affine region. Before constructing a feasible variation model to this problem, we should consider two issues. The first is how to judge where is the boundaries of different smoothing transition regions, which is helpful for a reasonable piecewise. The second is how to choose a proper way to describe the smoothing function, which is responsible for smoothing control. The answers to the two problems need to be integrated into the variational model. To improve the smoothing degree of the restored image, one need to incorporate high order operator to describe the smoothing requirement. Therefore, we proposed the following general high order framework for piecewise smoothing image recovery:

$$E(u) = \int_{\Omega} f_{\mathrm{p}}(u, u_i, u_{ij}) f_{\mathrm{s}}(u, u_i, u_{ij}) dx dy, \tag{9}$$

where f_{p} provides the clues for judging the boundaries between piecewise regions and f_{s} conveys the smoothing control respectively. Contrary to the traditional additive high order variational model framework, the multiplicative model is easy to extend to other imaging tasks.

3   Proposed Weighted Laplacian Model

By consider a gray scale image $u(x, y)$ as a surface $S = (x, y, u(x, y))$, we propose the the following geometrical weighted Laplace (GWL) energy functional:

$$E_{\mathrm{GWL}}(u) = \int_{\Omega} \frac{|\triangle u|}{\sqrt{1 + |\nabla u|^2}} dx dy. \tag{10}$$

The kernel in the the energy (10) is a product of two functions and it can be seen as a special case for (9) when choosing $f_p = \dfrac{1}{\sqrt{1+|\nabla u|^2}}$ and $f_s = |u_{xx} + u_{yy}| = |\Delta u|$.

The key of recovery of the piecewise harmonic image is the interaction between two functions.

1. Piecewise. The piecewise effect in a certain partition is guaranteed by edge boundary detector $g = \sqrt{1+|\nabla u|^2}$, which has a remarkable geometrical interpretation:

$$r = \frac{1}{g} = \frac{1}{\sqrt{1+u_x^2+u_y^2}} = \frac{dxdy}{gdxdy} = \frac{A^{\text{domain}}}{A^{\text{surface}}}, \qquad (11)$$

where A^{domain} is the area of the infinitesimal surface in the image domain (x,y), and A^{surface} is its corresponding area on the image surface $(x, y, u(x, y))$. Therefore, r conveys the height variation on the surface as well the intensigy variation on the image data [21]. r is equal 1 for flat surface and its Laplacian is zero too, such structure will be preserved. r is equal 0 near edges, which is helpful to preserve edges.

2. Harmonic. The smoothing harmonic constrain is mainly performed by Laplacian operator Δu. As $g = \sqrt{1+|\nabla u|^2} > 1$, zero Laplacian means the kernel function will be zero too and functional reaches the minimizer in this region. Therefore, smoothing structures will be kept if they can be represented as any harmonic function.

3. Edge preserving. For an ideal typical sharp edge, its Laplace has a famous zero crossing property: near the midpoint of the edge, its second order derivative would cross zero. The kernel function will be 0 as $\Delta u = 0$ and $r = 0$ for a true sharp edge, which will be recognized and well preserved.

Therefore, the proposed model permits discontinuous while preserving piecewise smoothing regions.

Adding an artificial time to the Euler-Lagrange equation derived to (10), we can obtain the following an anisotropic high order nonlinear diffusion equation:

$$u_t = -\Delta\left(\frac{\Delta u}{g|\Delta u|}\right) + \text{div}\left(\frac{|\Delta u|}{g^3}\nabla u\right) - \lambda(u - u_0). \qquad (12)$$

The initial condition is $u(x,0) = u_0$ and its boundary condition is

$$(u_x, u_y)\cdot\boldsymbol{\mu} = 0, \qquad (\gamma_1, \gamma_2)\cdot\boldsymbol{\mu} = 0, \qquad (13)$$

where $\boldsymbol{\mu}$ is the unit outward normal direction to $\partial\Omega$ and γ_1 and γ_2 are defined as

$$\gamma_1 = \left(\frac{\Delta u}{g|\Delta u|}\right)_x + \frac{|\Delta u|u_x}{g^3}, \qquad (14)$$

$$\gamma_2 = \left(\frac{\Delta u}{g|\Delta u|}\right)_y + \frac{|\Delta u|u_y}{g^3}. \qquad (15)$$

The diffusion of Eq. (12) is decided by the interaction of the first order edge detector g and the second order information $\frac{\triangle u}{|\triangle u|}$. Noting $\frac{\triangle u}{|\triangle u|} = \text{sign}\triangle u$, only three values, $-1, 0, 1$ are permitted. When it equals 0, the diffusion stop automatically. It means that the local structure described by the harmonic function maybe preserved. When it equals 1 or -1, the diffusion now depends on the magnitude the boundary detector. The diffusion speed will slow down as the sign of the Laplace operator is scaled by the inverse of a large gradient magnitude. A fast diffusion will be performed in flat region as the image gradient is small and the boundary detector $g \simeq 1$.

As the evolution equation is nonlinear highly, we now consider to solve it by an explicit finite difference method. For time discretion, forward difference is used and the space grid size is set as $h = 1$. Table 1 lists the scheme for time and spatial operators in high order nonlinear Eq. (12).

Table 1. The discrete scheme for operators in high order nonlinear Eq. (12).

Continuous variable	Discrete variable	Discrete scheme
t	$\triangle t$	Time space
u	$u_{i,j}^0$	Initial image
$\triangle u$	$\triangle(u_{i,j})$	$u_{i+1,j} + u_{i-1,j} + u_{i,j+1} + u_{i,j-1} - 4u_{i,j}$
u_x in fourth term	$D_x(u_{i,j})$	$D_x(u_{i,j}) = \frac{u_{i+1,j}-u_{i-1,j}}{2}l$
u_y in fourth term	$D_y(u_{i,j})$	$D_y(u_{i,j}) = \frac{u_{i,j+1}-u_{i,j-1}}{2}$
u_x in third term	$D_x^{\mp} u_{i,j}$	$\mp(u_{i\mp1,j} - u_{i,j})$
u_y in third term	$D_y^{\mp} u_{i,j}$	$\mp(u_{i,j\mp1} - u_{i,j})$

4   Experimental Results

In this section, we conduct several experiments to demonstrate the performance of the high order GWL model. We make comparisons with three related methods. The first one is second order TV method, which is famous for its edge preserving ability. The second method is TGV method, which is implemented by a primal-dual splitting method in [22]. The code is also available: http://www.gipsa-lab. fr/~laurent.condat/software.html. The third one is state of art BM3D method. To do a quantitative comparison, peak signal-to-noise-ratio (PSNR) is used for quantitative comparison. For the proposed method, we set time space $\triangle t = 10^{-2}$ and $\lambda = 0.01$.

The first experimental results on a synthesized piecewise quadratic image are shown in Fig. 2. The test image is composed by two constant functions (one for left side and another for right side), a linea function (up middle and down middle) and a selected quadratic harmonic function for $u(x,y) = \frac{x^2}{16} - \frac{y^2}{16}$ in (8) (middle). The noise level is 10 and the denosing results for the noisy image

Fig. 2. Piecewise quadratic denoised images. The image is composed by two constant functions (one for left side and another for right side), a linea function (up middle and down middle) and a selected quadratic harmonic function for $u(x, y) = \frac{x^2}{16} - \frac{y^2}{16}$. From the left to right, the first row: clean image, noisy image (PSNR = 28.1376), TV result (PSNR = 43.3636). From the left to right, the second row, from the left to right, TGV result(PSNR = 32.3433), BM3D result (PSNR = 47.0606), GWL result (PSNR = 49.3684).

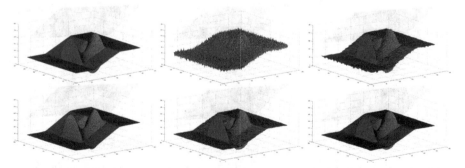

Fig. 3. The induced surfaces of piecewise quadratic denoised images. The order is the same as Fig. 2.

(PSNR = 28.1376) by four methods are shown in 2. The staircase effect is obvious in quadratic region for TV denoised image (PSNR = 43.3636). The TGV denoised image (PSNR = 32.3433) shows a good smoothing ability but blurs

Fig. 4. Piecewise smoothing denoised images beyond quadratic. It is composed of a linear function and a smoothing function $u(x, y) = \arctan(\frac{y}{x})$, whose infinite derivatives are non-vanishing. From the left to right, the first row: clean image, noisy image (PSNR = 28.1221), TV result (PSNR = 43.2176). From the left to right, the second row, from the left to right, TGV result (PSNR = 31.8597), BM3D result (PSNR = 45.4445), GWL result (PSNR = 49.6065).

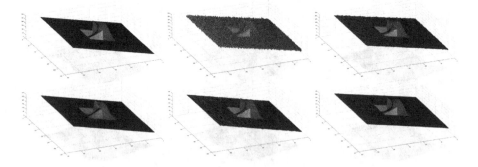

Fig. 5. The induced surfaces of piecewise smoothing denoised images in Fig. 4.

the edges seriously. The staircase effect in linear regions and quadratic regions is unpleasant in visual for BM3D denoised image (PSNR = 47.0606). The proposed GWL method provide an almost perfect denoised image visually and quantitatively (PSNR = 49.3684). The corresponding induced surfaces are displayed in

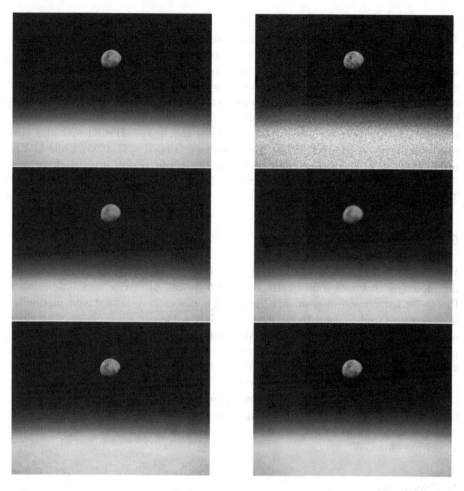

Fig. 6. Nasa denoised image. From the left to right, the first row: clean image, noisy image (PSNR = 22.1151), TV result (PSNR = 40.1939). From the left to right, the second row, from the left to right, TGV result (PSNR = 33.5203), BM3D result, GWL result (PSNR = 42.2764).

Fig. 3. It can be observed that TGV and GWL shows a better smoothing effect than TV and BM3D.

The second test synthesized image has a more complex structures: it is composed of a linear function and a smoothing function $u(x, y) = \arctan \frac{y}{x}$, whose infinite derivatives are non-vanishing. The noise level is 10 and the denosing results for the noisy image (PSNR = 28.1221) by four methods are shown in 4. TV result shows a serious staircase effect for the tangent function region (PSNR = 43.2176). The TGV denoised image (PSNR = 31.8597) blurs the edges heavily again. BM3D performs better than TV and TGV but staircase effect is visual for linear region (PSNR = 45.4445). The proposed GWL method yields a best result among four methods visually and quantitatively (PSNR = 49.6065). The corresponding induced surfaces are displayed in Fig. 5.

The third test image is a picture of moon rise captured from the space station by NASA astronaut Randy Bresnik on August 3, 2017. The noise level is 20 and the denosing results for the noisy image (PSNR = 22.1151) by four methods are shown in Fig. 6. Four methods remove noise in white and black background. The differences between them lie in the moon surface and the smoothing transition regions in the middle of the image. BM3D provides the best detail preservation ability for moon surface (PSNR = 41.3395) while GWL produces a good transition effect between the white region and black region (PSNR = 42.2764). TV still suffers from the staircase (PSNR = 40.1939) and TGV blurs edges (PSNR = 33.5203).

5 Conclusions

We present a high order variational method to recover a class more smoothing piecewise image beyond quadratic, which we call piecewise harmonic image. Piecewise harmonic image covers the popular piecewise constant and piecewise linear images and beyond them, even including some certain function with infinite order non-vanishing derivatives. We construct the new model within a multiplicative variational framework and its kernel is based is based on a geometrical weighted Laplacian operation. The research in this paper shows that we can restore piecewise harmonic image perfectly. Its major limitation is the fact that the natural image do not always contain standard piecewise quadratic geometrical structures. Therefor, improvement on its adaptability to more image is part of our future work. Another important work is to devise an efficient speeding up algorithms for GWL model.

References

1. Chan, T., Shen, J.: Image Processing and Analysis: Variational, PDE, Wavelet, and Stochastic Methods. SIAM Publisher, Philadelphia (2005)
2. Rudin, L., Osher, S., Fatemi, E.: Nonlinear total variation based noise removal algorithms. Physica D **60**, 258–268 (1992)
3. You, Y.L., Kaveh, M.: Fourth-order partial differential equation for noise removal. IEEE Trans. Image Process. **9**(10), 1723–1730 (2000)
4. Tumblin, J., Turk, G.: LCIS: a boundary hierarchy for detail-preserving contrast reduction. In: Proceedings of the SIGGRAPH 1999 Annual Conference on Computer Graphics, Los Angeles, CA, USA, 83–90 (1999)
5. Lysaker, M., Lundervold, A., Tai, X.C.: Noise removal using fourth order partial differential equation with applications to medical magnetic resonance images in space and time. IEEE Trans. Image Process. **12**(12), 1579–1590 (2003)
6. Jewprasert, S., Chumchob, N., Chantrapornchai, C.: A fourth-order compact finite difference scheme for higher-order PDE-based image registration. East Asian J. Appl. Math. **5**(4), 361–386 (2015)

7. Liang, J., Zhang, X.: Retinex by higher order total variation L^1 decomposition. J. Math. Imaging Vis. **52**(3), 345–355 (2015)
8. Yuan, J., Schnörr, C., Steidl, G.: Total-variation based piecewise affine regularization. In: Tai, X.-C., Mørken, K., Lysaker, M., Lie, K.-A. (eds.) SSVM 2009. LNCS, vol. 5567, pp. 552–564. Springer, Heidelberg (2009). https://doi.org/10.1007/978-3-642-02256-2_46
9. Tai, X.C., Hahn, J., Chung, G.J.: A fast algorithm for Euler's elastica model using augmented Lagrangian method. SIAM J. Imaging Sci. **4**(1), 313–344 (2010)
10. Zhu, W., Chan, T.: Image denoising using mean curvature of image surface. SIAM J. Imaging Sci. **51**, 1–32 (2012)
11. Brito-Loeza, C., Chen, K., Uc-Cetina, V.: Image denoising using the Gaussian curvature of the image surface. Numer. Methods Partial. Differ. Equ. **32**(3), 1066–1089 (2016)
12. Bibo, L., Jianlong, W., Zhang, Q.: A variable exponent high-order variational model for noise removal. J. Comput. Inf. Syst. **11**(13), 4605–4614 (2015)
13. Bredies, K., Kunisch, K., Pock, T.: Total generalized variation. SIAM J. Imaging Sci. **3**(3), 492–526 (2010)
14. Wu, Y., Feng, X.: Speckle noise reduction via nonconvex high total variation approach. Math. Probl. Eng. **20**(15), 11 (2015)
15. Papafitsoros, K., Schönlieb, C.B.: A combined first and second order variational approach for image reconstruction. J. Math. Imaging Vis. **48**, 308–333 (2014)
16. Tomasi, C., Manduchi, R.: Bilateral filtering for gray and color images. In: Proceeding of International Conference on Computer Vision, pp. 839–846 (1998)
17. Buades, A., Coll, B., Morel, J.M.: A review of image denoising algorithms with a new one. SIAM J. Multi-Scale Model. Simul. **4**(2), 490–530 (2005)
18. Jin, Q., Grama, I., Kervrann, C., et al.: Nonlocal means and optimal weights for noise removal. SIAM J. Imaging Sci. **10**(4), 1878–1920 (2017)
19. Kaiming, H., Jian, S., Xiaoou, T.: Guided image filtering. IEEE Trans. Pattern Anal. Mach. Intell. **35**(6), 1397–1409 (2013)
20. Dabov, K., Foi, A., Katkovnik, V., Egiazarian, K.: Image denoising by sparse 3D transform-domain collaborative filtering. IEEE Trans. Image Process. **16**(8), 2080–2095 (2007)
21. Sochen, N., Kimmel, R., Malladi, R.: A general framework for low level vision. IEEE Trans. Image Process. **7**, 310–318 (1998)
22. Condat, L.: A primal-dual splitting method for convex optimization involving Lipschitzian, proximable and linear composite terms. J. Optim. Theory Appl. **158**(2), 460–479 (2013)

Dynamic Delay Based Cyclic Gradient Update Method for Distributed Training

Wenhui Hu[✉], Peng Wang, Qigang Wang, Zhengdong Zhou, Hui Xiang,
Mei Li, and Zhongchao Shi

Artificial Intelligence Lab, Lenovo Research, Beijing 100085, China
{huwh1,wangpeng31,wangqg1,zhouzd2,xianghui1,limei8,shizc2}@lenovo.com

Abstract. Distributed training performance is constrained by two factors. One is the communication overhead between parameter servers and workers. The other is the unbalanced computing powers across workers. We propose a dynamic delay based cyclic gradient update method, which allows workers to push gradients to parameter servers in a round-robin order with dynamic delays. Stale gradient information is accumulated locally in each worker. When a worker obtains the token to update gradients, the accumulated gradients are pushed to parameter servers. Experiments show that, compared with the previous synchronous and cyclic gradient update methods, the dynamic delay cyclic method converges to the same accuracy at a faster speed.

Keywords: Distributed training · Deep learning
Cyclic delayed method · Stochastic optimization

1 Introduction

Deep learning trains deep neural networks with huge volumes of data. The training process is compute-intensive. It can take weeks or months with one modern GPU. Many researchers employ distributed training to accelerate the training process with a server cluster [1].

Model parallelism and data parallelism are two commonly adopted paradigms for distributed training. Model parallelism splits the model into different parts and allocates each part to one GPU [2]. Although model parallelism can speed up the training process with parallel computing, it has two drawbacks which limit its application. The first drawback is scalability, which means it is hard to create a generic model parallelism solution which splits arbitrary model into balanced parts, allocates to adequate GPUs and achieves sublinear scaling ratio. The second drawback is that model parallelism has high communication-to-computation ratio and the communication overhead may counteract the performance gain. Data parallelism is more widely adopted for its simplicity and generality. The training dataset is usually large and easy to split into sub-datasets. Each GPU hosts a replica of the model and trains it with its sub-dataset concurrently.

© Springer Nature Switzerland AG 2018
J.-H. Lai et al. (Eds.): PRCV 2018, LNCS 11258, pp. 550–559, 2018.
https://doi.org/10.1007/978-3-030-03338-5_46

Various architectures have been proposed for data parallelism, e.g. parameter server (PS) [3], peer-to-peer, ring-based structure [4]. PS architecture has been proved to be effective and are widely adopted [5,6]. There are two entities defined in the PS architecture: parameter servers and workers. Parameter servers are responsible for collecting gradient updates from workers and calculating new model parameters with received gradients. Workers pull latest parameters from parameter servers, train their model replicas with their sub-datasets, calculate gradients, and push gradients to parameter servers. The gradient update method between parameter servers and workers can be roughly classified into synchronous method and asynchronous method. For synchronous method, all workers push gradients to parameter servers in every training iteration. This method is robust, fast and has been proved to be equivalent to the standard stochastic gradient descent (SGD) in single GPU training. But the synchronous method has two issues. One is traffic burst when all workers push gradients at roughly the same time. The other one is that if workers are not homogeneous, the slowest one will slow down the overall training process. Asynchronous methods have been proposed to overcome these issues [7]. However, asynchronous methods may suffer from slower convergence or divergence issues due to stale gradients [8].

In this paper, we propose a method to delay the gradient updates between parameter servers and workers dynamically. Experimental results show that our method increases the distributed training throughput, reduces the network bandwidth requirement, and achieves almost the same accuracy as the synchronous method.

2   Related Works

Many previous works target at reducing the communication overhead in distributed training. Chen et al. [9] propose a double buffering technique which shows the delayed update works well. Seide et al. [10] and Strom et al. [11] use an 1-bit SGD method which adds delay to gradient updates. Lin et al. [12] propose a gradient threshold algorithm, which throttles small gradient updates and accumulates them locally. These gradient sparsification technologies can reduce the communication volume and they are validated by experiments. But the convergence of these implicit delayed methods are not proved in theory. Agarwal et al. [7] propose explicitly delayed gradient update methods to reduce the communication frequency. For convex optimization problem, it has been theoretically proved that the delayed gradient update can be asymptotically negligible and the convergence rate scales as $\mathcal{O}\left(1/\sqrt{nT}\right)$ for n-node cluster after T iterations. However, this cyclic delayed method suffers from the unbalanced worker computing power issues. In the next section, we introduce a dynamic delay based algorithm to overcome these problems and improve the performance.

3   Dynamic Delay Based Cyclic Gradient Update Method

We propose a dynamic delay based cyclic gradient update method, which extends the previous cyclic delayed method. A dynamic delay is applied to the gradient update of each worker. The delay is calculated from the real-time global gradient updating status. This method decouples the cyclic period and actual delays of workers.

The conventional cyclic delayed architecture computes the stochastic gradients in parallel and updates the model parameters in sequence. The worker i computes the gradient $g_i(t - \tau) = \nabla F[x(t - \tau)]$ from the stale parameters $x(t - \tau)$ of τ updates before. The central parameter server obtains $g_i(t - \tau)$ from worker i, computes the updated model $x(t + 1)$ and pushes it back only to worker i. Meanwhile, other workers do their computations on the stale parameters other than the latest $x(t + 1)$. The delay τ comes from the sequential updating of the parameters among the workers, where $\tau = n - 1$ for a n worker cluster in the simplest case. The errors coming from τ is a second order effect, which makes the penalty of delay asymptotically negligible [7].

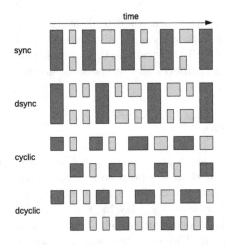

Fig. 1. Runtime illustration with two workers (Color figure online)

The behavior of each worker can be roughly classified into two phases: a communication phase for gradient synchronization, and a computation phase for gradient calculation and accumulation. Although it is possible to overlap part of the backward computation phase with the communication phase for a single worker, the cyclic method focuses more on overlapping the computation phase of a worker with the communication phases of other workers.

In our proposed method, an additional delay is introduced to improve the throughput performance. Each worker maintains an independent local training pool. When a worker is in computation phase, it keeps doing local training and

Algorithm 1.1. Dynamic delay cyclic method

1: Initialize x_0, $t \leftarrow 0$ and $x_{-1} \leftarrow x_0$
2: **for all** $n < N$ **do**
3:     $\tilde{G} \leftarrow 0$
4:     **while** $t < T$ **do**
5:         **while** mod $(t, N) \neq n$ **do**
6:             Wait
7:         **end while**
8:         Push $x_t \leftarrow x_{t-1} - \tilde{\eta}_t \tilde{G}$
9:         Pull $\tilde{x} \leftarrow x_t$
10:        $t \leftarrow t + 1$, $\tilde{G} \leftarrow 0$
11:        **for** $\tilde{d} < D$ **do**
12:            Compute $\tilde{g} = \nabla f(\tilde{x})$
13:            Accumulate $\tilde{G} \leftarrow \tilde{G} + \tilde{g}$, $\tilde{x} \leftarrow \tilde{x} - \tilde{\eta}_t \tilde{g}$
14:            **if** mod $(t, N) = n$ **then**
15:                Break
16:            **end if**
17:        **end for**
18:    **end while**
19: **end for**

gradient accumulation. Mini-batches of the dataset are fetched continuously to train the local model replica. The following communication phase is dynamically postponed until the worker obtains the token. The delay is adaptive, which helps to maintain a good load balance. A powerful worker does more training (and hence processes more training data examples) in its computation phase and a weak worker does less.

Figure 1 shows the runtime illustration of different gradient update methods. Blue blocks denote communication phases, and green blocks denote training operations. The width denotes the duration of different operations in the runtime, which is variational because of the imbalance of workloads. In the synchronous method (sync), a strong worker has to wait for a weak worker in every communication phase. The delayed synchronous method (dsync) postpones the synchronizations with a fixed amount of local computations. This additional delay alleviates the load imbalance and reduces the communication volume. In the cyclic method, the round-robin communication phases prevents the network traffic burst. However the computation phases are not fully utilized if the workers are heterogeneous. Additional computations of the strong workers are introduced in our dynamic delay cyclic method (dcyclic), where the computation phase is prolonged to overlap the communication phase of other workers. The dynamic delay makes full use of every worker's computation power while minimizing the network traffic.

The dynamic delay cyclic method is described in Algorithm 1.1, where the local variables on the workers are decorated with a tilde. N denotes the number of workers, T denotes the maximum global step, and D denotes the maximum amount of accumulations, i.e. the limitation on the delay of the communication phase in every training iteration. x denotes the weights, g denotes the gradients and G denotes the accumulations. The global step t serves as the token for the synchronization communication and is maintained by the PS. The subscript -1 of x is introduced for convenience, which is unnecessary in the implementation. Each worker implements two operations. One is the communication operation (remote push-to/pull-from the PS), the other one is the local computation operation (computing/accumulating of gradients).

The communication operation is based on the cyclic delayed method [7]. All workers cooperate in a round-robin order. The worker obtaining the communication token performs the communication operation, including the pushing of gradients and the pulling of updated weights. Then the global step t increases by one, in which case the token is relayed to the next worker.

The dynamic delay occurs in the computation phase of the worker. Compared to the single gradient computation in the conventional cyclic architecture, our dynamic cyclic method enables additional gradient computations and accumulations before the worker obtains the token. In the meanwhile, the amount of accumulations is adaptive in runtime, which is limited by the predefined largest delay D. When $D = 1$, this method falls back to the conventional cyclic delay method [7]. When $D > 1$, local updates and gradient accumulations are activated. In the computation phase when the worker processes new mini-batches, it keeps monitoring the global step t. As soon as it obtains the communication token, the worker aborts the remnant local operations in order to do the communication operation at the earliest.

The dynamic delay cyclic method brings two benefits. One is the optimized throughput (e.g. in examples/second) due to gradient accumulations. By doing as many training as possible in the computation phase, device utilization is improved. As a result, the total processing time for the same quantity of examples is decreased. The other benefit is the convergence conservation. Being able to abort the computation helps to suppress the actual delay and the staleness of gradients, even when the predefined D is large. This helps to achieve the convergence state.

4   Experimental Results

In this section, the dynamic delay cyclic method is evaluated with two large-scale datasets.

4.1   Datasets and Experiment Setup

Two datasets are selected for the evaluations. One is the ILSVRC2012 [13] dataset, which focuses on the image object classification. The training set contains 1.2 million images and the validation set contains 150 thousand images. Both of them are labeled with the presence or absence of 1000 object categories. The ResNet-V2-50 [14] model is adopted for the classification task. The other dataset is the union of the 10^9 Word Parallel Corpus for training and the updated development set of the News Crawl for validation from the WMT'15 [15]. The training corpus consists of over 22 million sentences, and the validation corpus consists of 3 thousand sentences. Both focus on the recurring translation task on the French–English pair. The Seq2Seq model [16] is adopted for the translation task.

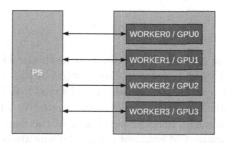

Fig. 2. Experiment setup. Workers are bound to different GPUs inside one node. All workers connect directly to the PS on the other node. The traffic goes over the network in the same manner as a distributed cluster

Two computing nodes are utilized for all experiments. Both nodes are equipped with dual Intel Xeon E5-2600v4 CPUs, 512 GB memory and a Mellanox 40 Gbit/s network adapter. One node has 4 NVIDIA Tesla P100 GPUs, and the other node has no GPU. The distributed computing environment is simulated with these two nodes by making use of the GPU affinity as illustrated in Fig. 2. The worker procedures are bound to different GPUs, in the meanwhile the PS procedure is launched on the other node. PS and workers communicate through the network adapter, in the same way as a real distributed cluster.

4.2 Algorithm and Implementation

We compare our method with the cyclic and the delayed synchronous methods, and take the vanilla synchronous method as the baseline. Workers in the cyclic method update the parameters in a round-robin order [7]. In the vanilla synchronous method, the weights on the PS are updated by gradients received from all workers at around the same time. In the delayed synchronous method, the gradients are accumulated and applied to the local model replicas first. And then the gradient update to the PS works similarly with the vanilla synchronous method.

We implement these four methods with the PS architecture [17], where the server maintains the parameters and the workers do the computations. The data manipulation is automatically managed by TensorFlow [6] from the implicit insertion of nodes to the computation graph.

The ResNet-V2-50 model is trained with the Nesterov accelerated gradient (NAG) method [18,19] with a batch size of 32, a momentum of 0.9 and a learning rate of 0.005 in 80 epochs. The learning rate is exponentially decayed with a factor of 0.1 every 20 epochs. The learning rate warmup [20] is implemented in the synchronous methods in order to accelerate the convergence. The vanilla SGD is used to train the Seq2Seq model in 1 epoch with a batch size of 64. The learning rate starts at 0.02 and decays every 0.01 epoch with a decay factor of 0.99. The learning rate warmup is not utilized in the training of the Seq2Seq model.

4.3   Results

We first investigate the performance of different methods. The convergence rates of train (dashed) and validation (solid) are plotted in Fig. 3. The columns from left to right show the synchronous (blue), the delayed synchronous (green), the cyclic (red) and the dynamic delay cyclic (cyan) methods. The top-5 error of the ResNet model is on the top, and the perplexity of the Seq2Seq model is at the bottom. The actual amount of gradient accumulations are tuned to be the same during the training of each model.

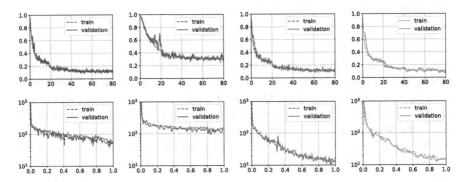

Fig. 3. (Color online) The convergence after definite epochs. The top row presents the top-5 error of the ResNet model, and the bottom shows the perplexity of the Seq2Seq model. The columns indicate the synchronous (blue), the delayed synchronous (green), the cyclic (red) and the dynamic delay cyclic (cyan) methods from left to right. The dashed lines denotes the training and the solid lines denotes the validation. (Color figure online)

In the ResNet model, the cyclic methods achieve the same performance with the synchronous method. The rate of convergence is not impacted by the inherent gradient staleness from the round-robin order. The additional gradient accumulations limit the rate of convergence in the delayed synchronous method. Nevertheless, it takes little effect on the dynamic-cyclic method.

In the Seq2Seq model, the cyclic methods perform better than the synchronous methods, where the perplexity converges quickly to a lower value in the limited number of epochs. The additional accumulations impacts the convergence rate negatively in the delayed synchronous method. The result shows

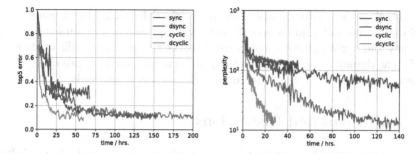

Fig. 4. (Color online) The wall-clock time of different methods. On the left shows the top-5 error of ResNet, and on the right shows the perplexity of Seq2Seq. The vanilla synchronous SGD (blue) is taken as the baseline. The cyclic method (red) finishes after a long time due to the low device utilization. The delayed synchronous SGD (green) obtains slow convergence in the limited number of epochs. The dynamic delay cyclic method (cyan) converges faster in less wall-clock time because of its high throughput. (Color figure online)

that the dynamic delay method is more robust to the staleness of the gradient information than the delayed synchronous method.

The gradient accumulations improve the throughput performance significantly. In the delayed methods, the synchronizations are postponed by the local operations on the workers. This delay reduces the communication-to-computation ratio and increases the utilization of the computing device, which leads to a higher throughput as illustrated in Fig. 4. Large datasets are trained to the same convergence rate at a faster speed with the dynamic delay cyclic method.

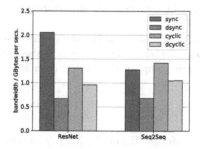

Fig. 5. (Color online) The actual network bandwidth consumption under different update methods. To achieve the same state of convergence, the dynamic delay cyclic method requires less network traffic than the vanilla synchronous and cyclic methods. (Color figure online)

The network traffic is reduced with the dynamic delay cyclic method. The delay reduces the communication frequency and the total communication volume. In the cyclic methods, the PS responds to only one worker at a time.

The rolling of the communication token prevents the traffic burst issue in the synchronous methods and reduces the network requirements. In our experiments, the delay and cyclic methods significantly reduce the network traffic as shown in Fig. 5. The dynamic delay cyclic method preserves the convergence and requires less network traffic than the synchronous and the cyclic methods.

5 Conclusions and Discussions

We propose a dynamic delay based cyclic gradient update method, which benefits from the cyclic gradient update architecture and the local gradient accumulations. The network traffic burst is relieved from the round-robin updating order, and the communication volume and frequency is suppressed by the explicit delay of gradient updates. This method keeps the rate of convergence from the restricted duration between synchronizations, and improves the throughput performance by the dynamic extension of the actual delay. The wall-clock time is reduced in the training of large datasets.

The cyclic methods take full use of the gradients computed from every mini-batch of examples. The gradients are not only employed to update local model replicas, but also accumulated to update the global model on the PS. A fixed (perhaps with decay) learning rate is more applicable for these aggressive methods.

The actual delay is bounded to prevent the convergence problem rising from the gradient staleness. The PS cycles the refresh of the local replicas among all workers in the cluster. The duration of the computation phase scales linearly with the number of workers, which comes from the round-robin nature of the cyclic methods. An oversize delay may limit the convergence rate because of the gradient staleness. An optimized delay restriction should be selected to accelerate the training and preserve the convergence simultaneously.

Acknowledgements. We would like to acknowledge the computation power support from the appliance group in the laboratory. We would also like to thank Mr. Zhenhua Liu from the computer vision group for the fruitful discussion.

References

1. Dean, J., Corrado, G., Monga, R., et al.: Large scale distributed deep networks. In: NIPS (2012)
2. Krizhevsky, A.: One weird trick for parallelizing convolutional neural networks. arXiv:1404.5997 (2014)
3. Li, M., et al.: Scaling distributed machine learning with the parameter server. In: OSDI 2014, pp. 583–598 (2014)
4. Zhang, H., et al.: Poseidon: an efficient communication architecture for distributed deep learning on GPU clusters. arXiv:1706.03292 (2017)
5. Chen, T., et al.: MXNet: a flexible and efficient machine learning library for heterogeneous distributed systems. arXiv:1512.01274 (2015)

6. Abadi, M., Barham, P., Chen, J.M., et al.: TensorFlow: a system for large-scale machine learning. In: 12th USENIX Symposium on Operating Systems Design and Implementation (OSDI 2016), pp. 265–283 (2016)
7. Agarwal, A., Duchi, J.C.: Distributed delayed stochastic optimization. In: NIPS 2011, 4247 (2011)
8. Ho, Q., et al.: More effective distributed ML via a stale synchronous parallel parameter server. In: NIPS 2012, pp. 2141–2149 (2012)
9. Chen, X., Eversole, A., Li, G., Yu, D., Seide, F.: Pipelined back-propagation for context-dependent deep neural networks. In: Interspeech 2012 (2012)
10. Seide, F., Fu, H., Droppo, J., Li, G., Yu, D.: 1-bit stochastic gradient descent and application to data-parallel distributed training of speech DNNs. In: Interspeech 2014 (2014)
11. Strom, N.: Scalable distributed DNN training using commodity GPU cloud computing. In: Interspeech 2015 (2015)
12. Lin, Y., Han, S., Mao, H., Wang, Y., Dally, W.J.: Deep gradient compression: reducing the communication bandwidth for distributed training. In: ICLR 2018 (2018)
13. Russakovsky, O., Deng, J., Su, H., et al.: ImageNet large scale visual recognition challenge. Int. J. Comput. Vis. **115**(3), 211–252 (2015)
14. He, K., Zhang, X., Ren, S., Sun, J.: Delving deep into rectifiers: surpassing human-level performance on imagenet classification. In: Proceedings of the 2015 IEEE International Conference on Computer Vision (ICCV), pp. 1026–1034 (2015)
15. Bojar, O., Buck, C., Federmann, C., et al.: Findings of the 2015 workshop on statistical machine translation. In: Tenth Workshop on Statistical Machine Translation (2015). http://www.statmt.org/wmt15
16. Vinyals, O., Kaiser, L., Koo, T., et al.: Grammar as a foreign language. In: NIPS 2015, pp. 2773–2781 (2015)
17. Li, M., Andersen, D.G., Smola, A.J., Yu, K.: Communication efficient distributed machine learning with the parameter server. In: NIPS 2014, pp. 19–27 (2014)
18. Qian, N.: On the momentum term in gradient descent learning algorithms. Neural Netw. **12**(1), 145–151 (1999)
19. Nesterov, Y.: A method of solving a convex programming problem with convergence rate $\mathcal{O}\left(1/k^2\right)$. Soviet Math. Doklady **27**(2), 372–376 (1983)
20. Goyal, P., Dollár, P., Girshick, R., et al.: Accurate, large minibatch SGD: training ImageNet in 1 hour. arXiv:1706.02677 (2017)

Semi-supervised Dictionary Active Learning for Pattern Classification

Qin Zhong[1,2], Meng Yang[1(✉)], and Tiancheng Zhang[2]

[1] School of Data and Computer Science, Sun Yat-sen University,
Guangzhou, China
zhongqin0820@163.com, yangm6@mail.sysu.edu.cn
[2] School of Computer Science and Engineering, Northeastern University,
Shenyang, China
tczhang@mail.neu.edu.cn

Abstract. Gathering labeled data is one of the most time-consuming and expensive tasks in supervised machine learning. In practical applications, there are usually quite limited labeled training samples but abundant unlabeled data that is easy to collect. Semi-supervised learning and active learning are two important techniques for learning a discriminative classification model when labeled data is scarce. However, unlabeled data with significant noises and outliers cannot be well exploited and usually worsen the performance of semi-supervised learning and the performance of active learning also needs a powerful initial classifier learned from the quite limited labeled training data. In order to solve the above issues, in this paper we proposed a novel model of semi-supervised dictionary active learning (SSDAL), which aims to integrate semi-supervised learning and active learning to effectively use all the training data. In particular, two criterions based on estimated class possibility are designed to select the unlabeled data with confident class estimation for semi-supervised learning and the informative unlabeled data for active learning, respectively. Extensive experiments are conducted to show the superior performance of our method in classification applications, e.g., handwritten digit recognition, face recognition and large-scale image classification.

Keywords: Semi-supervised learning · Dictionary learning · Active learning
Pattern classification

1 Introduction

Considering the explosion of digital images in the real world, it is necessary to collect, classify and organize them in a simple, fast and efficient way. In order to use these increasing images as labeled data, automatic image annotation [28] is proposed by establishing statistical models, which can significantly reduce the labor cost of manually annotating images. However, statistical models, which need a large amount of labeled training samples, are not applicable for the case with a quite limited labeled data. How to build an accurate classification model with limited labeled samples for multi-class classification is still an open question.

© Springer Nature Switzerland AG 2018
J.-H. Lai et al. (Eds.): PRCV 2018, LNCS 11258, pp. 560–572, 2018.
https://doi.org/10.1007/978-3-030-03338-5_47

Semi-Supervised learning (SSL) [1–4, 12] are potential solutions to the problem with a quite limited labeled data. SSL utilizes unlabeled samples to enhance the generalization ability of supervised learning. Classical SSL algorithms include Co-Training [2], graph-based semi-supervised learning [3], semi-supervised support vector machines (S3VM) [4] and semi-supervised dictionary learning (SSDL) [5–10, 12]. Recently promising performance has been achieved by jointly learning a dictionary based classifier and the class estimation of unlabeled data. However, it has been pointed by [11] that directly using unlabeled samples may significantly reduce classification performance when there are large amounts of noisy samples and outliers in the unlabeled data.

In order to effectively adopt the unlabeled training samples, which disturb semi-supervised learning methods due to their noise and variations, active learning (AL) [11, 29, 30] methods attract much attention recently. AL trains the model in an interactive way, which is capable of selecting the representative data based on the classification model learned in different iterations. However, the performance of AL quite depends on the effectiveness of the initial classifier.

Semi-supervised learning and active learning are not perfect alone but complementary to each other together. The classifier obtained by SSL, which takes both the labeled and unlabeled samples into account, can act as a good initial classifier; the introduction of AL can eliminate the problem of the model performance reduction caused due to the presence of a large number of noise samples and outliers in the unlabeled samples. Meanwhile, the introduction of AL can also gradually get labeled samples from the unlabeled data set for training without the need to prepare the required large-scale labeled datasets at the beginning. Several methods have been developed to study how to effectively combine SSL and AL. Song et al. [13] proposed an active learning method based on co-training in video annotation. Jiang et al. [14] developed a graph-based SSL method for video concept detection and used active learning to select data-concept pairs for human annotation. Although these combinations have improved the performance, the recently developed powerful semi-supervised dictionary learning (SSDL) models are not well exploited and how to jointly integrate SSDL and AL is still an open question.

In order to solve above issues, in this paper we proposed a novel framework of semi-supervised dictionary active learning (SSDAL) to effectively integrate semi-supervised dictionary learning (SSDL) and active learning (AL). Initially, we use a handful of labeled samples and abundant unlabeled samples to train a SSDL model. Based on that, we introduce AL algorithm to select the informative samples to boost the training. Compared to the original SSDL model, it is not necessary to prepare all the labeled samples at the beginning. Compared with the simple AL algorithm, it has a great advantage in learning from less labeled data and more unlabeled data. The experimental results on the benchmark datasets clearly show the superior performance of the proposed

To summarize, the main contributions of our work are as follows:

- A novel semi-supervised dictionary active learning (SSDAL) framework is proposed to integrate the advantages of SSDL and AL for the first time.

- The representative unlabeled samples selected by AL and the unlabeled samples with confident class estimation are complementary to each other.
- Experiments on the benchmark datasets are conducted, with remarkable performance reported.

The rest of the paper is organized as follows. Section 2 presents a brief review of related work. Section 3 overviews the pipeline of our framework, followed by a discussion of model formulation and optimization in Sect. 4. The experimental results are presented in Sect. 5. Section 6 concludes the paper.

2 Related Work

2.1 Semi-supervised Dictionary Learning

Owing to the impressive performance of sparse representation and dictionary learning [16, 17, 31–34], semi-supervised dictionary learning (SSDL) algorithms [5–10, 12] have been proposed recently.

Most of SSDL methods aim to learn a shared dictionary. Pham et al. [5] incorporated the reconstruction error of both the labeled and unlabeled data with sparsity constraint into a joint objective function. Zhang et al. [6] proposed an online semi-supervised dictionary learning model, in which the reconstruction error of both labeled data and unlabeled data, label consistency and the classification error were integrated into a joint model. Wang et al. [9] proposed a robust dictionary learning method by exploiting the global structure of all labeled and unlabeled data. In these semi-supervised dictionary methods mentioned above, the unlabeled training data is only used to learn a shared dictionary, ignoring to explore the discrimination hidden in the unlabeled data.

In order to utilize the class information of unlabeled data, Shrivastava et al. [7] learnt a class-specific semi-supervised dictionary with estimating the class possibility of unlabeled data. Wang et al. [10] proposed an adaptively unified semi-supervised dictionary learning model which integrated the reconstruction error of both the labeled data and unlabeled data, and classifier learning into a unified framework. Vu et al. [27] proposed a shared dictionary learning by grouping the unlabeled samples via using the coefficient-based relationship between the labeled and unlabeled samples. The methods above try to exploit the discrimination hidden in the unlabeled data. However, the class probability of unlabeled training samples is artificially designed but not derived from the objective function. And the powerful class specific representation ability cannot be used in the shared dictionary learning model.

Recently, Yang et al. [12] proposed a discriminative semi-supervised dictionary learning (DSSDL) method, which achieves superior performance by introducing a regularization of entropy and using an extended dictionary to explore the discrimination embedded in the unlabeled data. However, there are some representative samples (e.g., nearby the border of different classes), which cannot be correctly estimated by DSSDL, preventing the further improvement of DSSDL.

2.2   Active Learning

Active learning (AL) has been widely studied in [11, 29, 30] for its ability to reducing human labor. In the view of sampling strategy, active learning can be roughly divided into three categories [28]: (i) membership query synthesis, (ii) stream-based selective sampling, and (iii) pool-based sampling.

Membership query synthesis assumes that the system can interact with the surrounding environment, e.g., the annotator can be asked to determine the category of some samples and learn the unknown concepts. But the disadvantage of this method is that all unlabeled samples are labeled by the annotator without considering the actual distribution of samples. To solve this issue with a large scale of unlabeled data, stream-based selective sampling introduced. Although the stream-based selective strategy can solve the problems caused by direct query methods to some extent, it often needs to set a fixed threshold to measure the information content of the sample, thus lack the universality of different tasks. Moreover, because of the way it compares, the actual distribution of unlabeled data sets and the difference between the unlabeled data can not be obtained [28].

Pool-based sampling active learning is proposed to overcome the drawbacks above. Lewis et al. [29] solved this by proposing pool-based sampling, which compares the information of unlabeled samples, and then selects the sample with the highest amount of information to ask the annotator. Since the pool-based sampling strategy has inherited the previous two methods and overcome the shortcomings of the above two methods, it has become the most widely studied and used sampling strategy [29, 30]. It has also pointed out by Lin et al. [30] that the sample selection criterion is the another key in AL algorithm, and there exists many sample selection criteria including risk reduction, uncertainty, diversity and so on [28]. The criteria is typically defined according to the classification uncertainty of samples. Specifically, the samples of low classification confidence, together with other informative criteria like diversity, are generally treated as the candidates for model retraining. The accuracy of progressively selecting uncertain unlabeled sample depends on the recognition ability of the desired classifier, which needs to perform well in the case with limited labeled training data.

3   Semi-supervised Dictionary Active Learning

We propose a novel SSDL-based active learning framework which is composed of a SSDL model and an active learning algorithm. Figure 1 illustrates the overall framework. Initially, the training set includes a limited labeled samples and abundant unlabeled samples. Next, we use semi-supervised dictionary learning to train a dictionary, which is supposed to have a good representative ability with a small within-class variation but a bad interclass representative ability. Then we select the most informative sample through active learning technique to retrain the proposed model. For the most informative sample, we introduce a user to annotate it and add it into labeled data set for the next dictionary training until the model converges.

3.1   Model of SSDAL

As many prevailing semi-supervised dictionary learning models [5–10, 12], we focus on the case that the identity of unlabeled training data lies in the training set. In order to overcome the drawbacks of the prevailing semi-supervised learning (e.g., its performance will be worsened by the unlabeled noisy samples and outliers) and active learning (e.g., a powerful initial classifier is needed), we proposed a novel model of semi-supervised dictionary active learning to fully exploit the benefits of both of semi-supervised dictionary learning [12] and active learning.

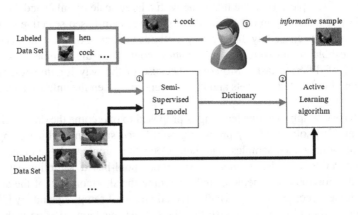

Fig. 1. Illustration of our proposed SSDAL framework. Firstly, the SSDL model is learned with quite limited labeled samples and all of the unlabeled samples. Secondly, we use AL algorithm to select the most *informative* samples iteratively from the unlabeled data set. Thirdly, we introduce a user to label those *informative* samples and add them into labeled data set to update the model with the new labeled samples and the rest of unlabeled data.

Given data points set $A = [A_1, \ldots, A_i, \ldots, A_C, B]$ where A_i denotes the ith-class training data and each column of A_i is a training sample while the remaining $B = [b_1, \ldots, b_i, \ldots, b_N]$ is the N unlabeled training samples from class 1 to C. Let $D = [D_1, \ldots, D_i, \ldots, D_C]$ denote the supervised dictionary initialized by A, while $E = [E_1, \ldots, E_i, \ldots, E_C]$ is an extended dictionary that mainly explore the discrimination of unlabeled training data. Both D_i and E_i are associated to class i, and they are required to well represent i^{th}-class data but with a bad representation ability for all the other classes. As P_{ij} indicates the probabilistic relationship between the jth-unlabeled training sample and i^{th}-class. The model of our proposed SSDAL framework is:

$$\min_{\hat{D},P,X} \sum_{i=1}^{C} \left(\left\|A_i - \hat{D}_i X_i^i\right\|_F^2 + \gamma \left\|X_i^i\right\|_1 + \lambda \left\|X_i^i - M_i\right\|_F^2 \right)$$
$$+ \sum_{j=1}^{N-L} \left(\sum_{i=1}^{C} P_{i,j} \left\|b_j - \hat{D}_i y_j^i\right\|_F^2 + \gamma \left\|y_j^i\right\|_1 \right)$$
$$- \beta \left(- \sum_{j=1}^{N-L} \sum_{i=1}^{C} P_{i,j} \log P_{i,j} \right) \tag{1}$$

s.t. semi supervised learning for confident estimation
active learning for unconfident class estimation

where X_i^i and y_j^i are the coding coefficient matrix of A_i and unlabeled data b_j on the class-specific dictionary $\hat{D}_i = [D_i E_i]$, respectively.

The confidence of the estimated class possibility can be measured by the entropy

$$H(b_i) = - \sum_{i=1}^{C} P_{i,j} \log P_{i,j} \tag{2}$$

The entropy value of Eq. (2) indicates the uncertainty of the class estimation. For instance, if the unlabeled data is definitely assigned to some class (e.g., $P_{i,j} = 1$ for some j when the sample is assigned to the ith class, and $P_{i,j} = 0$ for $j \neq i$), the entropy value will be zero.

3.2   Semi-supervised Dictionary Learning

When the class estimation is confident, the proposed SSDAL model changes to

$$\min_{\hat{D},P,X} \sum_{i=1}^{C} \left(\left\|A_i - \hat{D}_i X_i^i\right\|_F^2 + \gamma \left\|X_i^i\right\|_1 + \lambda \left\|X_i^i - M_i\right\|_F^2 \right)$$
$$+ \sum_{j=1}^{N-L} \left(\sum_{i=1}^{C} P_{i,j} \left\|b_j - \hat{D}_i y_j^i\right\|_F^2 + \gamma \left\|y_j^i\right\|_1 \right) \tag{3}$$
$$- \beta \left(- \sum_{j=1}^{N-L} \sum_{i=1}^{C} P_{i,j} \log P_{i,j} \right)$$

$$s.t. H(b_j) < T$$

where T is a threshold, which is usually set as 0.5. In the dictionary learning, we only use the unlabeled data whose entropy is smaller than the threshold, i.e., their class estimation is relatively confident.

3.3   Active Learning

Considering the combination of active learning, Let $\hat{D}$ denote the output of $[DE]$ in Eq. (1). Set L as the number of labeled samples for active learning. In model's iteration, we can get the probabilistic outputs P for all the unlabeled samples and a class-specific dictionary $\hat{D} = [DE]$. If we want to boost the performance of our model by acquiring some labeled examples, the main issue is how to select the most valuable examples to query the user for labels. Considering that the SSDL model can naturally provide the probabilistic outputs, which is convenient to measure the uncertainty of all unlabeled samples, we adopt the uncertainty measurement to select the most uncertain samples.

For the unlabeled data, there are C candidate classes. Therefore, the semi-supervised dictionary learning provides C classifiers. When multiple learners exist, a widely applied strategy is to select the samples that have the maximum disagreement amongst them. Here the disagreement of multiple learners can also be regarded as an uncertainty measure, and this strategy is categorized into the uncertainty criterion as well. Inspired by [15], we use the uncertainty estimation method that considers the posterior probabilities of the best and the second best predictions, that is,

$$\text{Uncertainty}(x) = P(c_1|x) - P(c_2|x) \qquad (4)$$

where c_1 and c_2 are the classes with the largest and second largest posterior class probabilities, respectively. If their margin is small, it means that the model is more confused on the sample and thus it is with high uncertainty. We use Eq. (3) as the final sample selection strategy in the active learning.

3.4 Classification Model

We utilize different coding models when dealing with the testing sample, e.g., collaborative representation of Eq. (5) for face recognition and the large scale image classification, while local representation of Eq. (6) is used in digit recognition [12].

$$Code\_Classify(b_j, \hat{D}) = argmin_{y_j} \left\| b_j - \hat{D}y_j \right\|_F^2 + \gamma \left\| y_j \right\|_1 \qquad (5)$$

$$Code\_Classify(b_j, \hat{D}) = argmin_{y_j^i} \left\| b_j - \hat{D}_i y_j^i \right\|_F^2 + \gamma \left\| y_j^i \right\|_1, \forall i \qquad (6)$$

where $y_j = [y_j^1, \ldots, y_j^i, \ldots, y_j^c]$ is the coding vector on the whole dictionary, $\hat{D} = [DE]$ is the learned structured dictionary associated with class i, and y_j^i is the coding vector associated to i^{th} class of the jth unlabeled data. Then the final classification is conducted by

$$identity(b) = arg \min_i \{e_i\} \qquad (7)$$

where $e_i = \left\| b - \hat{D}_i y_j^i \right\|_2^2$.

4 Optimization of SSDAL

The optimization of SSDAL is an alternative solving procedure, which includes the selection of unlabeled data and the semi-supervised dictionary learning of Eq. (3). And the semi-supervised dictionary learning can further be divided into two sub-problems by doing class estimation of unlabeled data and discriminative dictionary learning alternatively: updating P by fixing D, E and X, while updating D, E and X alternatively by fixing P [12]. These processes enable the model to converge.

Selection of Unlabeled Data. With the class estimation of all unlabeled data, the ones with confident class estimation will be integrated into the model of discriminative semi-supervised dictionary learning.

For the unlabeled data with unconfident class estimation, we select the most informative samples from the rest of unlabeled data set iteratively via Eq. (4). Then, we introduce a user to label those informative samples and then add them into the annotated dataset.

Update P. By fixing the class-specific dictionary and the corresponding coding coefficient (e.g., D, E, X and y), and let $\varepsilon_j^i = \left\| b_j - \hat{D}_i y_j^i \right\|$. The class probability of jth unlabeled training sample is

$$P_{i,j} = \exp\left\{-\varepsilon_j^i/\beta\right\} / \sum\nolimits_{i=1}^{C} \exp\left\{-\varepsilon_j^i/\beta\right\} \tag{8}$$

Update D, E and X. The unlabeled data, which are not included into the active learning or don't have a confident estimation, their probability of class will be set as zero, i.e., $P_{i,j} = 0$. Then the proposed SSDAL changes to

$$\min_{\hat{D},X} \sum\nolimits_{i=1}^{C} \left(\left\| A_i - \hat{D}_i X_i^i \right\|_F^2 + \gamma \left\| X_i^i \right\|_1 + \lambda \left\| X_i^i - M_i \right\|_F^2 \right)$$
$$+ \sum\nolimits_{j=1}^{N-L} \left(\sum\nolimits_{i=1}^{C} P_{i,j} \left\| b_j - \hat{D}_i y_j^i \right\|_F^2 + \gamma \left\| y_j^i \right\|_1 \right) \tag{9}$$

which can efficiently solved by using the method in Yang et al. [12].

5   Experiments

In this section, extensive experiments were conducted over on the benchmark datasets, such as LFW [24], Web Vision 1.0 [25], USPS [22] and MNIST [23] to demonstrate the effectiveness of our proposed semi-supervised dictionary active learning (SSDAL). The competing methods include several representative supervised dictionary learning methods: SRC [18], FDDL [19], DKSVD [20], LCKSVD [26] and semi-supervised dictionary learning methods: JDL [5], OSSDL [6], S2D2 [7], SSRD [9], SSP-DL [21] and recently proposed DSSDL [12] algorithm. Here we don't include deep learning related models because our base classifier is a dictionary learning related model and the number of labeled samples is too limited to train a good enough deep learning model. The coding of unlabeled training data and testing data in our proposed framework adopts the same coding representation.

The SSDL model used in our framework has three super parameters, λ, γ and β. We set them as $\lambda = 0.01$, $\gamma = 0.001$, $\beta = 0.01$ in all experiments as same as [12].

We evaluate the performance of our proposed SSDAL in the classification accuracy with the same amount of user annotation totally. The classification accuracy is defined as the top one rate for digit recognition and face recognition, with an extra top-5 rate in Web Vision large-scale image classification task.

5.1   Datasets and Results

Face Identification. Following the same experimental setting in [10], we estimate our proposed framework in the LFW database [24], which is a large-scale database consists of 4,174 face images of 143 individuals taken under varying pose, expression, illumination, misalignment and occlusion conditions. Each individual has no less than 11 images and we select the first 10 samples for training data with the remaining samples for testing. We randomly select 2 samples from each class as the initial labeled data, then we set 5 times of user-query iteration, which makes the final amount of labeled data as same as other methods. As shown in Fig. 2, the data is divided into 3 parts, the data not used, the training data, and the test data.

Fig. 2. Illustration of how the data is divided. In this experiment, firstly, the data is randomly divided into 3 parts during the whole training process. Secondly, for training data, we randomly select 2 of them as the initial labeled data (i.e., orange frame) and the rest as unlabeled data. Then, we gradually add the labeled data (i.e., green frame) from the rest of the unlabeled data(i.e., red frame) via AL algorithm to boost our model. After all, we use testing data to test our model. (Color figure online)

We use the same feature in [12] which reduces the feature vectors to 500 dimension. Table 1 lists the identification results of the LFW database, which show clearly that our proposed method achieves the highest recognition rates with the same amount of labeled data among the competing schemes. Compare to DSSDL, the improvement of the performance stems from the integration of active learning algorithm, which can select the most informative samples and no need to get all the labeled data ready.

Digit Recognition. Use the same experimental setting in [12], we evaluate the performance on both the USPS dataset [22] and MNIST dataset [23]. In the USPS dataset, there are 9,298 digital images consisting of 10 classes. We randomly select 110 images

Table 1. The recognition rates (%) on LFW database.

Methods	LFW
SRC	62.2 ± 2.7
DKSVD	56.7 ± 1.8
LC-KSVD	58.6 ± 1.3
FDDL	66.1 ± 1.5
JDL	64.8 ± 2.1
S2D2	65.4 ± 2.1
DSSDL	67.5 ± 1.2
SSDAL	**72.0 ± 0.7**

from each class and then randomly select 2 images as the labeled samples for the initial dictionary training, 58 images as the unlabeled samples and the left as the testing samples. For MNIST dataset, there are 10 classes and 70,000 handwritten digital images totally, 60,000 for training and 10,000 for testing respectively. But we randomly select 200 samples from each class then we randomly select 2 images each class as the labeled samples for the initial dictionary training, 98 images as the unlabeled, and 100 images as the testing samples. The feature we used is the whole image, which was normalized to have unit l_2-norm. We set 18 times user-query iteration, which with 10 labels updated in each iteration. This makes the final labeled data amount as same as other methods, which use 20 labeled images per class for training.

All relevant results for ten independent tests are listed in Table 2, which calculates the mean accuracy and standard deviation. It can be seen that the proposed SSDAL is able to find the informative samples from the unlabeled dataset for next round training and can then utilize information of the selected unlabeled data to improve the classification accuracy. Compare to all the competing methods, our proposed SSDAL achieves the best performance.

Table 2. The recognition rates (%) on USPS and MNIST

Methods	USPS	MNIST
SRC	68.6 ± 2.7	72.9 ± 2.3
DKSVD	67.5 ± 1.8	71.4 ± 1.7
FDDL	85.2 ± 1.2	82.5 ± 1.3
LC-KSVD	76.9 ± 1.3	73.0 ± 1.3
OSSDL	80.8 ± 2.8	73.2 ± 1.8
S2D2	86.6 ± 1.6	77.6 ± 0.8
SSR-D	87.2 ± 0.5	83.8 ± 1.2
SSP-DL	87.8 ± 1.1	85.8 ± 1.2
DSSDL	90.2 ± 0.9	88.3 ± 1.5
SSDAL	**90.9 ± 0.9**	**88.8 ± 1.1**

Web Vision Database 1.0. Web Vision database 1.0 [25] is larger than all the database we evaluated. We use a subset with the same number of classes (i.e., 1,000 classes) as the dataset, which contains 50 samples in each class. For each class, we randomly set 30 samples for train and 20 samples for test. From the training set, we select the first 5 samples as the initial labeled data. Next we set 8 times of user-query iteration. This makes it 13 labeled samples for each class finally.

We extract feature as same as [25] then we reduced it to 300 dimension. The top-1 result and top-5 result of the proposed SSDAL and two most competing methods, such as the supervised LCKSVD and the semi-supervised DSSDL. The results of all methods are listed in Table 3, from which we can observed that the improvements of SSDAL over DSSDL are 1.3% in Top-1 accuracy and 2.7% in Top-5 accuracy. Compared to LCKSVD, the advantages of SSDAL is larger.

Table 3. The recognition rates (%) on web Vision sub-database.

Methods	Top-1	Top-5
LCKSVD	52.6 ± 1.4	71.4 ± 2.9
DSSDL	56.0 ± 1.1	78.0 ± 1.1
SSDAL	**57.3 ± 0.9**	**80.7 ± 1.2**

6 Conclusions

In this paper, we proposed a new model of semi-supervised dictionary active learning (SSDAL), which integrates the state-of-the-art semi-supervised dictionary learning and active learning for the first time. Based on the proposed criterion which based on the estimated class possibility, the unlabeled data with confident class estimation and the representative information are returned into the training of SSDAL. Extensive experiments have shown the superior performance of our proposed framework.

Acknowledgement. This work is partially supported by the National Natural Science Foundation of China (Grant no. 61772568), the Guangzhou Science and Technology Program (Grant no. 201804010288), the Fundamental 535 Research Funds for the Central Universities (Grant no. 18lgzd15), the Shenzhen Scientific Research and Development Funding Program (Grant no. JCYJ20170302153827712).

References

1. Zhu, X.: Semi-supervised learning literature survey. Technical report 1530, Wisconsin-Madison (2005)
2. Blum, A., Mitchell, T.: Combining labeled and unlabeled data with co-training. In: COLT (1998)
3. Zhu, X.: Semi-supervised learning with graphs. In Proceedings of IJCNLP (2005)
4. Sindhwani, V., Keerthi, S.S.: Large scale semi-supervised linear SVMs. In: ACM SIGIR (2006)

5. Pham, D.-S., Svetha, V.: Joint learning and dictionary construction for pattern recognition. In: Proceedings of CVPR (2008)
6. Zhang, G., Jiang, Z., Davis, L.S.: Online semi-supervised discriminative dictionary learning for sparse representation. In: Lee, K.M., Matsushita, Y., Rehg, J.M., Hu, Z. (eds.) ACCV 2012. LNCS, vol. 7724, pp. 259–273. Springer, Heidelberg (2013). https://doi.org/10.1007/978-3-642-37331-2_20
7. Shrivastava, A., Pillai, J.K., Patel, V.M., Chellappa, R.: Learning discriminative dictionaries with partially labeled data. In: Proceedings of ICIP (2012)
8. Babagholami-Mohamadabadi, B., Zarghami, A., Zolfaghari, M., Baghshah, M.S.: PSSDL: probabilistic semi-supervised dictionary learning. In: Blockeel, H., Kersting, K., Nijssen, S., Železný, F. (eds.) ECML PKDD 2013. LNCS (LNAI), vol. 8190, pp. 192–207. Springer, Heidelberg (2013). https://doi.org/10.1007/978-3-642-40994-3_13
9. Wang, H., Nie, F., Cai, W., Huang, H.: Semi-supervised robust dictionary learning via efficient l2,0+-norms minimization. In: Proceedings of ICCV (2013)
10. Wang, X., Guo, X., Li, S.: Adaptively unified semisupervised dictionary learning with active points. In: Proceeding of the ICCV (2015)
11. Li, Y.-F., Zhou, Z.-H.: Towards making unlabeled data never hurt. IEEE Trans. Pattern Anal. Mach. Intell. 37(1), 175–188 (2015)
12. Yang, M., Chen, L.: Discriminative semi-supervised dictionary learning with entropy regularization for pattern classification. In: AAAI (2017)
13. Song, Y., Hua, X.-S., Dai, L.-R., Wang, M.: Semi-automatic video annotation based on active learning with multiple complementary predictors. In: MIR, pp. 97–104 (2005)
14. Jiang, W., Loui, A.: Laplacian adaptive context-based SVM for video concept detection. In: ACMSIGMM Workshop, pp. 15–20 (2011)
15. Joshi, A.J., Porikli, F., Papanikolopoulos, N.: Multi-class active learning for image classification. In: 2009 IEEE Conference on Computer Vision and Pattern Recognition, CVPR 2009. IEEE, pp. 2372–2379 (2009)
16. Yang, M., Dai, D., Shen, L., Gool, L.V.: Latent dictionary learning for sparse representation based classification. In: Proceedings of CVPR (2014)
17. Yang, M., Zhang, L., Yang, J., Zhang, D.: Metaface learning for sparse representation based face recognition. In: Proceedings of ICIP (2010)
18. Wright, J., Yang, A.Y., Ganesh, A., Sastry, S.S., Ma, Y.: Robust face recognition via sparse representation. IEEE TPAMI 31(2), 210–227 (2009)
19. Yang, M., Zhang, L., Feng, X.: Fisher discrimination dictionary learning for sparse representation. In: Proceedings of ICCV (2011)
20. Zhang, Q., Li, B.: Discriminative K-SVD for dictionary learning in face recognition. In: Proceedings of CVPR (2010)
21. Wang, D., Zhang, X., Fan, M., Ye, X.: Semi-supervised dictionary learning via structural sparse preserving. In: Proceedings of AAAI (2016)
22. Hull, J.: A database for handwritten text recognition research. IEEE TPAMI 16(5), 550–554 (1994)
23. LeCun, Y., Bottou, L., Bengio, Y., Haffner, P.: Gradientbased learning applied to document recognition. Proc. IEEE 86(11), 2278–2324 (1998)
24. Wolf, L., Hassner, T., Taigman, Y.: Similarity scores based on background samples. In: Zha, H., Taniguchi, R.-i., Maybank, S. (eds.) ACCV 2009. LNCS, vol. 5995, pp. 88–97. Springer, Heidelberg (2010). https://doi.org/10.1007/978-3-642-12304-7_9
25. Li, W., Wang, L., Li, W., et al.: WebVision database: visual learning and understanding from web data (2017)
26. Jiang, Z., Lin, Z., Davis, L.S.: Label consistent K-SVD: learning a discriminative dictionary for recognition. IEEE TPAMI 35(11), 2651–2664 (2013)

27. Vu, T.H., Monga, V.: Learning a low-rank shared dictionary for object classification. In: International Conference on Image Processing (ICIP) (2016)
28. Settles, B.: Active learning literature survey. Computer Sciences Technical report 1648, University of Wisconsin–Madison (2009)
29. Lewis, D., Gale, W.: A sequential algorithm for training text classifiers. In: Croft, B.W., van Rijsbergen, C.J. (eds.) SIGIR 1994, pp. 3–12. Springer, London (1994). https://doi.org/10. 1007/978-1-4471-2099-5_1. Proceedings of the ACM SIGIR Conference on Research and Development in Information Retrieval
30. Lin, L., Wang, K., Meng, D., et al.: Active self-paced learning for cost-effective and progressive face identification. IEEE Trans. Pattern Anal. Mach. Intell. **PP**(99), 7–19 (2017)
31. Jing, X.Y., Zhang, D.: A face and palmprint recognition approach based on discriminant DCT feature extraction. IEEE Trans. Syst. Man Cybern. Part B Cybern. **34**(6), 2405 (2004)
32. Jing, X.Y., Zhu, X., Wu, F., et al.: Super-resolution person re-identification with semi-coupled low-rank discriminant dictionary learning. IEEE Trans. Image Process. **26**(3), 1363–1378 (2017)
33. Zhu, X., Jing, X.Y., You, X., et al.: Image to video person re-identification by learning heterogeneous dictionary pair with feature projection matrix. IEEE Trans. Inf. Forensics Secur. **PP**(99), 1 (2017)
34. Learning heterogeneous dictionary pair with feature projection matrix for pedestrian video retrieval via single query image. In: AAAI 2017, pp. 4341–4348 (2017)

Multi-feature Shared and Specific Representation for Pattern Classification

Kangyin Ke and Meng Yang[(⊠)]

School of Data and Computer Science, Sun Yat-Sen University, Guangzhou, China
keky@mail2.sysu.edu.cn, yangm6@mail.sysu.edu.cn

Abstract. Sparse representation has been widely applied to pattern classification, where the input is coded as a sparse linear combination of training samples and classified to a category with the minimum reconstruction error. In the recent years, multi-feature representation based classification has attracted widespread attention and most of these methods have showed the superiorities compared to the classification model with single feature. One key issue in multi-feature representation is how to effectively exploit the similarity and distinctiveness of different feature, which is still an open question. In this paper, we present a novel multi-feature shared and specific representation (MFSSR) model, which not only keeps the distinctiveness of different features, but further exploits their similarity with a shared representation coefficient. In addition, different features are weighted differently to reflect their discriminative abilities. Several representative experiments have shown the effectiveness and simplicity of the proposed MFSSR.

Keywords: Multi-feature representation
Shared and specific representation · Pattern classification

1 Introduction

Over the past decade, sparse representation has achieved great success [14] and has been widely applied to various applications, such as face recognition [21,22,24], image classification [25], signal classification [18], and image restoration [12]. The main idea of sparse representation is to approximate a testing sample by a linear combination of training samples and the representation coefficients should be sparse to some extent. Both l_0-norm (i.e., the number of non-zero elements) and l_1-norm (i.e., the count of absolute values of elements) minimizations can be applied to implement sparsity coding. However, considering l_0-norm minimization is an NP-hard problem, most of sparse representation methods employ l_1-norm minimization. And the simplest and standard sparse representation can be regarded as the following regularized linear problem.

$$\min_{\alpha} \|\mathbf{y} - \mathbf{D}\alpha\|_2^2 + \lambda\|\alpha\|_1 \tag{1}$$

© Springer Nature Switzerland AG 2018
J.-H. Lai et al. (Eds.): PRCV 2018, LNCS 11258, pp. 573–585, 2018.
https://doi.org/10.1007/978-3-030-03338-5_48

where $\mathbf{y}$ is the feature vector of testing sample, $\mathbf{D} = [\mathbf{d}_1, \ldots, \mathbf{d}_i, \ldots, \mathbf{d}_n]$ is the dictionary in which $\mathbf{d}_i$ is the feature vector of the ith training sample, and λ is a positive scalar as sparsity penalty parameter.

Based on Eq. (1), Wright et al. [22] proposed the sparse representation based classification (SRC) method for robust face recognition, which not only achieves high classification accuracy, but is also robust to face occlusion. In SRC, the query face image is approximated by a linear combination of all the training samples, and then classified to the category i with the lowest reconstruction error:

$$i = \min_i \|\mathbf{y} - \mathbf{D}_i \widehat{\alpha}_i\|_2^2 \tag{2}$$

where $\mathbf{D}_i$ is the sub-dictionary of ith class, $\widehat{\alpha}_i$ is the coefficient associated with the sub-dictionary $\mathbf{D}_i$.

Compared to single feature, multiple features obviously can provide more effective information [6] to recognize the class of testing sample. Amount of works [4,15] have shown the benefits of complementary information provided by different features. Hence a mass of methods have sprung up to deal with multi-feature representation based classification problems, which can be divided into two categories, namely classifier fusion [17] and feature fusion [2].

Multi-feature sparse representation based methods have emerged in recently years. In [26], a multi-task joint sparse representation based classification method (MTJSRC) is proposed, which adopts a mixed norm regularization on the representation coefficients to enforce the similarity of different features and the sparsity of classes. Considering that multiple features may have different contributions for the representation and classification, [23] proposed a relaxed collaborative representation (RCR) model with a weighted within-class regularization on the coding coefficient. Although promising performance of RCR is reported, the within-class regularization has no direct connection with the final classifier. Very recently, in order to keep the distinctiveness of each feature, a joint similar and specific learning (JSSL) model [9] is proposed, which divides representation coefficients into two parts to balance the similarity and distinctiveness among different features. However, the model of JSSL is a little unnecessary complex due to its double flexility on the coding coefficients.

Fortunately, all the above issues can be solved by designing a suitable multi-feature representation model. Lately, many effective models have been proposed. For example, Luo et al. [11] proposed the consistent and specific multi-view subspace clustering, and Lan et al. [8] learned common and feature-specific patterns for multiple features. In this paper, we propose a multi-feature shared and specific representation (MFSSR) model. In the proposed model, different features have a shared representation for their commonality and different specific representations for their specificity. Moreover, a weighted representation term, which has direct connection with the final classifier, is designed to handle some features with outliers. An efficient solving algorithm is also proposed for the proposed MFSSR. Extensive experiments have been conducted to show the advantages in accuracy and running time.

The rest of this paper is organized as the following. Section 2 reviews some related works. Section 3 introduces the proposed model and its optimization. Section 4 illustrates the experimental results in several representative databases, and Sect. 5 concludes the paper.

2   Brief Review of Related Works

MTJSRC

With multiple types features for joint sparse representation and recognition, the multi-task joint sparse representation based classification (MTJSRC) has been proposed in [26]

$$\min_{\alpha_k} \sum_{k=1}^{K} \|\mathbf{y_k} - \mathbf{D}_k\alpha_k\|_2^2 + \lambda \sum_{j=1}^{C} \|\alpha_j\|_2 \tag{3}$$

where K is the number of different features, C is the number of classes, $\mathbf{y}_k$ denotes the kth feature vector of query samples, $\mathbf{D}_k = [\mathbf{D}_{k,1}, \ldots, \mathbf{D}_{k,j}, \ldots, \mathbf{D}_{k,C}]$ represents the kth-feature dictionary, and $\alpha_j = [\alpha_{1,j}, \ldots, \alpha_{k,j}, \ldots, \alpha_{K,j}]$ is the coefficient associated to class j of all features, where $\alpha_{k,j}$ is associated to the kth feature and the class j. It can seen clearly that, by using a mixed-norm regularization, the representation coefficients of different features can be similar and sparse in terms of classes.

RCR

Different from the mixed-norm regularization of MTJSRC, the relaxed collaborative representation (RCR) model in [23] utilizes a weighted within-class regularization term and a l_2-norm for representation coefficients, assuming that the coding vectors from different features have a small variance. Besides, in order to exploit the discrimination of different features, the weight for each feature can be learned in the stage of coding process. The whole formulation of RCR is as the following.

$$\min_{\alpha_k} \sum_{k=1}^{K} (\|\mathbf{y_k} - \mathbf{D}_k\alpha_k\|_2^2 + \lambda\|\alpha_k\|_2^2 + \tau\omega_k\|\alpha_k - \overline{\alpha}\|_2^2) \tag{4}$$

where $\overline{\alpha}$ is the mean of all α_k. τ and λ are positive scalar constants and ω_k indicates the discrimination of kth features. It can be observed that the similarity between different features is exploited by reducing the variance representation coefficients.

JSSL

Although minimizing the distance between coefficients can exploit the similarity of different features, it is too restrictive since there is also distinctiveness among the coefficients. In order to keep the distinctiveness of them, [9] proposed a joint similar and specific learning (JSSL) model to address the problem. In the model of JSSL, representation coefficients are divided into two parts, namely similar part and specific part. On the one hand, similar part exploits similarity of different features. On the other hand, specific part keeps their distinctiveness. The model of JSSL can be written as the following.

$$\min \sum_{k=1}^{K} \|\mathbf{y}_k - \mathbf{D}_k(\alpha_k^c + \alpha_k^s)\|_2^2 + \tau\|\alpha_k^c - \overline{\alpha}^c\|_2^2 + \sum_{k=1}^{K} \lambda(\|\alpha_k^c\|_1 + \|\alpha_k^s\|_1) \quad (5)$$

where α_k^c and α_k^s are similar part and specific part, respectively. It can be seen that α_k^c achieves similarity between different features by minimizing the distance of their coefficients. Besides, the specific part α_k^s extracted from α_k can keep the distinctiveness of kth feature, which makes their representation more flexible.

MTJSRC assumes that multiple features have the same contributions for the representation and classification, which may not be correct in practice. For RCR, the within-class coding coefficient term has no direct connection with the final classifier, lacking a meaningful illustration on the discriminative dictionary learning model. Although promising performance has been reported by JSSL, there are still several issues. It is not necessary to introduce double flexilities, e.g., $\alpha_k^c - \overline{\alpha}^c$ and α_k^s, because the introduction of α_k^s has represent the speciality. The model of JSSL is complex due to unnecessary unknown variable, e.g., $\overline{\alpha}$. Another drawback of JSSL doens't consider the features with outliers although the specific representation can tolerate noises to some extent.

3   Multi-feature Shared and Specific Representation

3.1   Multi-feature Shared and Specific Representation Model

Similarity and distinctiveness of multiple features are always the main problem considered in multi-feature representation based classification. Both of them are important. On the one hand, the similarity of different features means the same information they keep, which should be exploited to make the classification stable. On the other hand, different features may have extra valuable information, which may improve the recognition performance.

In order to solve the issues presented in Sect. 2, we proposed a novel multi-feature shared and specific representation (MFSSR) model

$$\min_{\alpha^c, \alpha^s, \omega} \sum_{k=1}^{K} \left(\|\mathbf{y}_k - \mathbf{D}_k(\alpha^c + \alpha_k^s)\|_2^2 + \tau\omega_k\|\mathbf{y}_k - \mathbf{D}_k\alpha^c\|_2^2 + \lambda_2\|\alpha_k^s\|_1\right) + \lambda_1\|\alpha^c\|_1 \quad (6)$$

where K is the number of different features and τ, λ_1 and λ_2 are positive scalar constants. $\mathbf{y}_k = [y_k^1; y_k^2; \ldots; y_k^n] \in \mathbb{R}^n$ denotes the kth feature vector of query samples. $\mathbf{D}_k = [\mathbf{d}_k^1, \mathbf{d}_k^2, \ldots, \mathbf{d}_k^m] \in \mathbb{R}^{n \times m}$ represents the kth-feature dictionary. $\alpha^c = [\alpha^{c,1}; \alpha^{c,2}; \ldots; \alpha^{c,m}] \in \mathbb{R}^m$ is the shared coefficient vector of each feature vector $\mathbf{y}_k$ over dictionary $\mathbf{D}_k$. $\alpha_k^s = [\alpha_k^{s,1}; \alpha_k^{s,2}; \ldots; \alpha_k^{s,m}] \in \mathbb{R}^m$ is the specific coefficient vector of the kth feature vector $\mathbf{y}_k$ over the dictionary $\mathbf{D}_k$. ω_k is the weight assigned to the kth feature.

Inspired by JSSL [9], in order to exploit the similarity and distinctiveness of multiple features, we also divide the representation coefficients into two parts. The primary coefficient α_k can be written as the following form

$$\alpha_k = \alpha^c + \alpha_k^s \tag{7}$$

where α^c is the shared part of all features. Different from JSSL, we required the shared coding coefficient be same for different features, i.e., α^c is the shared coding vector for all $\mathbf{y}_k$. The reason is that the specific representation part, i.e., α_k^s has introduced enough flexility, and it is more effective and simpler than that of JSSL.

As the related works mentioned above, RCR introduces a weighted within-class regularization to minimize the distance of coefficients between different features under the assumption that their representation coefficients should be close to some extent. However, the regularization of RCR is too restrictive to keep enough distinctiveness of various features. Compared to RCR, which uses weighted within-class variance of coding vectors to handle bad features, the proposed MFSSR directly weights the class-specific dictionary representation, which is also the criterion of final classification. The benefit of Eq. (6) is that the training phase and testing phase are consistent. In the proposed model, we can learn the weights of different features as the following term.

$$\sum_{k=1}^{K} \omega_k \|\mathbf{y}_k - \mathbf{D}_k \alpha^c\|_2^2 \tag{8}$$

It is obvious that the weight ω_k should be big when $\mathbf{y}_k$ can be well reconstructed by using only the shared coefficient, indicating the kth modality is more distinctive. In order to keep our model more stable, some regularization constraints on ω_k can be adopted. For example, both Karush-Kuhn-Tucker condition and maximum entropy principle can deal with it. In this paper, we use maximum entropy principle to regularize the prior ω_k:

$$-\sum_{k=1}^{K} \omega_k \ln \omega_k > \delta \tag{9}$$

where δ is a positive scalar constant.

3.2 Optimization Algorithm

The objective function (6) can be minimized by alternately updating the shared coefficient α^c, the specific one α_k^s and the weight ω_k until the function converges to local minimum.

Initialization:
We initialize the proposed model by simply setting the shared coefficient and the specific coefficients as zero vectors, and the weights as one.

$$\alpha^c = \mathbf{0}, \alpha_k^s = \mathbf{0}, \omega_k = 1 \tag{10}$$

Updating the Shared Representation:
If we fix the specific coefficient α_k^s and the weight ω_k, the objective function (6) is reduced to Eq. (11).

$$\min_{\alpha^c} \sum_{k=1}^{K} \left(\|(\mathbf{y}_k - \mathbf{D}_k \alpha_k^s) - \mathbf{D}_k \alpha^c\|_2^2 + \tau \omega_k \|\mathbf{y}_k - \mathbf{D}_k \alpha^c\|_2^2 \right) + \lambda_1 \|\alpha^c\|_1 \qquad (11)$$

Obviously, we can combine all the K sub-functions because they share the same coefficient α^c. The minimization of Eq. (11) with respect to α^c can be rewritten as the following function.

$$\min_{\alpha^c}(\| \begin{bmatrix} \mathbf{y}_1 - \mathbf{D}_1 a_1^s \\ \mathbf{y}_2 - \mathbf{D}_2 a_2^s \\ \vdots \\ \mathbf{y}_k - \mathbf{D}_k a_k^s \end{bmatrix} - \begin{bmatrix} \mathbf{D}_1 \\ \mathbf{D}_2 \\ \vdots \\ \mathbf{D}_k \end{bmatrix} \alpha^c \|_2^2 + \tau \| \begin{bmatrix} \sqrt{\omega_1}\mathbf{y}_1 \\ \sqrt{\omega_2}\mathbf{y}_2 \\ \vdots \\ \sqrt{\omega_k}\mathbf{y}_k \end{bmatrix} - \begin{bmatrix} \sqrt{\omega_1}\mathbf{D}_1 \\ \sqrt{\omega_2}\mathbf{D}_2 \\ \vdots \\ \sqrt{\omega_k}\mathbf{D}_k \end{bmatrix} \alpha^c \|_2^2 + \lambda_1 \|\alpha^c\|_1)$$
$$(12)$$

Here all the left two terms in Eq. (12) are differentiable. For convenience, We rewrite Eq. (12) as the following.

$$\min_{\alpha^c}(\mathbf{F}(\alpha^c) + \lambda_1 \|\alpha^c\|_1) \qquad (13)$$

where $\mathbf{F}(\alpha^c)$ represents the left two terms of the objective function (12). Since $\mathbf{F}(\alpha^c)$ is differentiable, The Iterative Projection Method (IPM) [16] can be applied to minimize Eq. (11), as described in Algorithm 1.

Updating the Specific Representation:
We fix the shared coefficient α^c and the weight ω, the specific coefficient α_k^s can be updated by reducing the objective function (6) to Eq. (14)

$$\min_{\alpha_k^s} \left(\|(\mathbf{y}_k - \mathbf{D}_k \alpha^c) - \mathbf{D}_k \alpha_k^s\|_2^2 + \lambda_2 \|\alpha_k^s\|_1 \right) \qquad (14)$$

It is clear that the objective function is similar to Eq. (13), which can be also optimized by The Iterative Projection Method [16].

Updating the Weight:
If the coefficient a^c and a^s are known, under the condition of maximum entropy principle (9), the objective function (6) becomes Eq. (15).

$$\min_{\omega_k} \left(\tau \omega_k \|(\mathbf{y}_k - \mathbf{D}_k \alpha^c)\|_2^2 + \gamma \omega_k \ln \omega_k \right) \qquad (15)$$

The weight ω_k can be derived:

$$\omega_k = \exp\left(-\tau \|\mathbf{y}_k - \mathbf{D}_k \alpha^c\|_2^2 / \gamma \right) \qquad (16)$$

In all, our optimization algorithm alternately updates the shared representation coefficient α^c, the specific coefficients α_k^s and the weights ω_k, until Eq. (6) converges. The summary of the algorithm is described in Algorithm 2. Since each sub-problem in the optimization of Eq. (6) will reduce the objective, Algorithm 2 will converge to a local optimal solution.

Algorithm 1. The coding algorithm of shared coefficient

1: **Input:** $\sigma, \lambda_1 > 0$
2: **Initialization:** $\widetilde{\alpha}^{c(1)} = \mathbf{0}$ and h=1.
3: **while** convergence and maximal iteration number are not reached **do**
    $h = h + 1$
    $\widetilde{\alpha}^{c(h)} = \mathbf{S}_{\lambda_1/\sigma}\big(\widetilde{\alpha}^{c(h-1)} - \frac{1}{2\sigma}\nabla \mathbf{F}(\widetilde{\alpha}^{c(h-1)})\big)$
    where $\nabla \mathbf{F}(\widetilde{\alpha}^{c(h-1)})$ is the derivative of $\mathbf{F}(\alpha^c)$ w.r.t. $\widetilde{\alpha}^{c(h-1)}$, and $\mathbf{S}_{\lambda_1/\sigma}$ is a soft
    threshold operator defined in [16].
4: **Return** $\alpha^c = \widetilde{\alpha}^{c(h)}$.

Algorithm 2. Multi-Feature Shared and Specific Representation (MFSSR)

1: **Input:** $\lambda_1, \lambda_2, \tau, \mathbf{y}_k, \mathbf{D}_k, k = 1, 2, \ldots, K$
2: **Initialization:** $\alpha^c = \mathbf{0}, \alpha_k^s = \mathbf{0}, \omega_k = 1, k = 1, 2, \ldots, K$
3: **while** not converged **do**
    update coefficients α^c following Eq. (12)
    update coefficients α_k^s following Eq. (14)
    update weights ω_k following Eq. (15)
4: **Return** α^c and α_k^s, $k = 1, 2, \ldots, K$

3.3 Classification

When the coding coefficients and the weights are obtained, its label is decided based on the lowest reconstruction error over all K vector:

$$identity = \arg\min_j \sum_{k=1}^{K} \omega_k \|\mathbf{y}_k - \mathbf{D}_{k,j}(\alpha_j^c + \alpha_{k,j}^s)\|_2^2 \tag{17}$$

where $\mathbf{D}_{k,j}$ is the elements of the dictionary $\mathbf{D}_k$ of class j, and α_j^c and $\alpha_{k,j}^s$ are the shared and specific coefficients associated to the sub-dictionary $\mathbf{D}_{k,j}$.

4 Experiments

In this section, we conduct three face recognition (FR) experiments on two benchmark face databases, including the AR database [13] and the Labeled Faces in the Wild (LFW) database [20], to verify the effectiveness of the proposed model. In the experiments, the methods nearest neighbor (NN) [5] and SVM [7] are used as the baseline. In order to further evaluate the effectiveness of MFSSR, several multi-feature representation based classification methods, including MTJSRC [26], RCR [23] and JSSL [9], are compared with the proposed model.

For AR database, the three parameters λ_1, λ_2, γ (the Lagrange multiplier of the entropy constraint) are set as 0.0005, 0.0005, and 0.02, respectively, which are the same for FR without occlusion and FR with disguise. For the experiments of LFW databases, a challenging task in uncontrolled environment, the parameters, such as λ_1, λ_2 and the weights ω are learned from the validation set.

This section is organized as the following. First, we give the experiment of AR with occlusion in Sect. 4.1, which evaluates MFSSR is robust to face occlusion. In Sect. 4.2, we evaluate the performance of MFSSR on LFW database with multiple features as input. Then, in Sect. 4.3, we evaluate the performance of MFSSR on experiment of AR without occlusion. In Sect. 4.4, we focus on the comparison of time complexity and running time with JSSL.

4.1   AR with Occlusion

In this subsection, we perform face recognition based on AR with occlusion. The AR database contains two-session data of 50 male and 50 female subjects. In each session, every person has 7 images with only illumination and expression variations, and 6 with real face occlusion (sunglass or scarf disguise).

In these experiments, 800 images (8 samples per person with only expression variations from two sessions) serve as the training set, while another 200 images with sunglass (or scarf) disguise are used for testing, as shown in Fig. 1(a). Following the experimental setting of RCR [23], we also resize all images to 83 × 64 and partitioned them into 4 × 2 blocks with the size of 20 × 30, as shown in Fig. 1(b). Then, each block is resized to a 600-dim vector, which can be regarded as a feature vector.

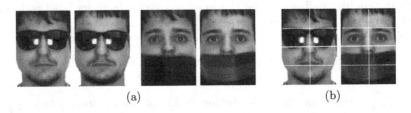

(a)   (b)

Fig. 1. (a) The testing samples with sunglass and scarves in AR database; (b) partitioned testing samples.

The experimental results of these methods are listed in Table 1. Our proposed MFSSR achieves the best performance. SVM and NN, which are not designed for dealing with multi-features, get the worse results compared to other methods. As a multi-feature representation based classification, MTJSRC fails to deal with the problem that there is occlusion variation in some blocks, since it treats each block equally. Inversely, RCR learns weights for different blocks, and hence, the occluded parts are set very small weights, which can reduce the interference of occluded blocks in the stage of classification. JSSL, which adopts the similar within-class regularization, achieves similar results. Compared to RCR and JSSL, MFSSR not only automatically learns the weights for different blocks, but also exploits the similarity of different features by shared representation coefficient. What's more, it keep their distinctiveness by the specific part. Therefore, the proposed MFSSR achieves the best performance.

Table 1. Face recognition rates on AR database with disguise.

Method	Sunglass	Scarf
SVM	53.5%	10.5%
NN	63%	12%
MTJSRC	80.5%	90.5%
RCR	97%	94%
JSSL	96%	94%
MFSSR	**100%**	**97.5%**

4.2 LFW Face Recognition

Labeled Faces in the Wild (LFW) [20], a large-scale database of human face images, is designed for unconstrained FR in uncontrolled environment with variations of pose, illumination, expression, misalignment and occlusion, etc. (shown in Fig. 2). We use one subset of aligned LFW in our experiments. It contains 143 subjects with at least 11 samples per subject. In our experiments, the first 10 samples serve as training data and the rest as testing data. There are four representative features extracted from each sample, including intensity values, low-frequency Fourier feature [19], Gabor magnitude [10] and LBP [1]. In the feature extraction stage, similar the processing method of LDA [3], we first partition each image into 2 × 2 blocks, then extract the enhanced discriminative feature in each block. At last, the features of all blocks are concatenated as the final feature.

The comparison of MFSSR with other methods are presented in Table 2. With no obvious occlusion in all images, there is little difference between the recognition rates of all methods. However, SVM and NN are still worse than other multi-feature representation based classification methods, for the reason that multi-feature methods have the powerful ability to mitigate the correlation between different features, which can greatly improve the performance of classification. And among these methods, the proposed MFSSR gets the best performance, with at least 0.6% improvement over other methods. Compared to JSSL, which also divides representation coefficients into two parts, MFSSR further enforce the similarity among different features.

(a)   (b)

Fig. 2. (a) and (b) are samples in training and testing sets of LFW.

Table 2. Face recognition accuracy on LFW.

SVM	NN	MTJSRC	RCR	JSSL	MFSSR
68.3%	70%	77.4%	79.5%	79.3%	**80.1%**

4.3 AR Without Occlusion

As in RCR [23], the images with only illumination and expression variations are selected, where 700 images (7 samples per person) from Session 1 serve as the training data, while another 700 images (7 samples per person) from Session 2 for the testing data. With no obvious occlusion in these images, we simply divide them into 1 × 4 blocks. Then each block is resized to a vector, as the same of the experiment of AR with occlusion.

The comparison of proposed model with other competing methods is shown in Table 3. It can be observed that MFSSR has about 2% improvement compared with MTJSRC and RCR, though it is slightly worse than JSSL.

Table 3. Face recognition rates on the AR database without occlusion.

SVM	NN	MTJSRC	RCR	JSSL	MFSSR
87.1%	74.7%	95.8%	95.9%	**97.8 %**	**97.7%**

4.4 Time Complexity and Running Time

We verify the efficiency of MFSSR by comparing with JSSL in time complexity and running time.

Suppose that the size of all $\mathbf{D}_k$ are $n \times m$, and the number of testing data is t. All the testing vectors are organized as a matrix. For JSSL updating a_k^c once by Augment Lagrangian Method (ALM), the time complexity of coding is $\mathcal{O}((3K+c)m^3 + Km^2n + 3Kmnt)$. First, Computing Q has complexity $\mathcal{O}(cm^3)$, where c is a positive constant. Second, Computing P_k has complexity $2Km^3$. Third, the time complexity P_kQ is Km^3. Fourth, the computation complexity of $a_{0,k}^c$ is $\mathcal{O}(K(m^2n+2mnt))$. At last, soft threshold operation needs $\mathcal{O}(Kmnt)$. Besides, when updating a_k^s one iteration, the time complexity $\mathcal{O}(3Kmnt)$. In all, the time complexity of JSSL is $\mathcal{O}(q((3K+c)m^3 + Km^2n + 6Kmnt))$, where q is the iteration number.

However, in MFSSR, both a^c and a_k^s are updated by IPM, which is very timesaving. First, updating a^c has complexity of $\mathcal{O}(6Kmnt)$. Then, the time complexity of updating a_k^s is $\mathcal{O}(3Kmnt)$ like JSSL. SO, the coding complexity of MFSSR is $\mathcal{O}(q(9Kmnt))$, where q is the iteration number. It is obvious in the proposed MFSSR is more effective than JSSL.

We conduct the running time experiments by the desktop of 3.5 GHz CPU with a 8 GB RAM. As is seen in Table 4, the proposed MFSSR is more efficient than JSSL in all experiments. For instance, MFSSR is two times faster than JSSL on the LFW database.

Table 4. Average computational time (seconds) coding and classifying one testing sample.

Experiment	AR(sunglass)	AR(scarf)	LFW	AR block
JSSL	0.91	0.92	3.96	0.71
MFSSR	0.63	0.78	1.87	0.45

5 Conclusion

In this paper, we propose a multi-feature shared and specific representation model (MFSSR) for pattern recognition, which further exploit the similarity and distinctiveness of different features for coding and classification. By dividing the coefficients into the shared part and the specific part, the discrimination embedded in multiple features is enhanced through the shared representation, while the distinctiveness of different features is tolerated by the specific representation. An adaptively weighted representation term is also proposed, with excellent performance to image recognition with occlusions. The experimental results on several representative databases demonstrated the advantages of our proposed model in accuracy and efficiency.

Acknowledgement. This work is partially supported by the National Natural Science Foundation of China (Grant no. 61772568), the Guangzhou Science and Technology Program (Grant no. 201804010288), the Fundamental 535 Research Funds for the Central Universities (Grant no. 18lgzd15), the Shenzhen Scientific Research and Development Funding Program (Grant no. JCYJ20170302153827712).

References

1. Ahonen, T., Hadid, A., Pietikäinen, M.: Face recognition with local binary patterns. In: Pajdla, T., Matas, J. (eds.) ECCV 2004. LNCS, vol. 3021, pp. 469–481. Springer, Heidelberg (2004). https://doi.org/10.1007/978-3-540-24670-1_36
2. Ross, A.A., Govindarajan, R.: Feature level fusion of hand and face biometrics (2005)
3. Belhumeur, P.N., Hespanha, J.P., Kriegman, D.J.: Eigenfaces vs. Fisherfaces: recognition using class specific linear projection. IEEE Trans. Pattern Anal. Mach. Intell. **19**(7), 711–720 (1997)
4. Caruana, R.: Multitask learning. Mach. Learn. **28**(1), 41–75 (1997)
5. Cover, T., Hart, P.: Nearest neighbor pattern classification. IEEE Trans. Inform. Theory **13**(1), 21–27 (1967)

6. Hall, D.L., Llinas, J.: An introduction to multisensor data fusion. Proceed. IEEE **85**(1), 6–23 (1997)
7. Heisele, B., Ho, P., Poggio, T.: Face recognition with support vector machines: global versus component-based approach. In: Proceedings Eighth IEEE International Conference on Computer Vision, ICCV 2001, vol. 2, pp. 688–694 (2001)
8. Lan, X., Zhang, S., Yuen, P.C., Chellappa, R.: Learning common and feature-specific patterns: a novel multiple-sparse-representation-based tracker. IEEE Trans. Image Process. **27**(4), 2022–2037 (2018)
9. Li, J., Zhang, D., Li, Y., Wu, J., Zhang, B.: Joint similar and specific learning for diabetes mellitus and impaired glucose regulation detection. Inform. Sci. **384**, 191–204 (2017)
10. Liu, C., Wechsler, H.: Gabor feature based classification using the enhanced fisher linear discriminant model for face recognition. IEEE Trans. Image Process. **11**(4), 467–476 (2002)
11. Luo, S., Zhang, C., Zhang, W., Cao, X.: Consistent and specific multi-view subspace clustering (2018)
12. Mairal, J., Bach, F., Ponce, J., Sapiro, G., Zisserman, A.: Non-local sparse models for image restoration. In: 2009 IEEE 12th International Conference on Computer Vision, pp. 2272–2279, September 2009
13. Martínez, A., Benavente, R.: The AR face database. CVC Technical report 24 (1998)
14. Olshausen, B.A., Field, D.J.: Emergence of simple-cell receptive field properties by learning a sparse code for natural images. Nature **381**(6583), 607–9 (1996)
15. Ozawa, S., Roy, A., Roussinov, D.: A multitask learning model for online pattern recognition. IEEE Trans. Neural Netw. **20**(3), 430 (2009)
16. Rosasco, L., Verri, A., Santoro, M., Mosci, S., Villa, S.: Iterative projection methods for structured sparsity regularization. Computation (2009)
17. Ruta, D., Gabrys, B.: An overview of classifier fusion methods. Comput. Inform. Syst. **7**, 1–10 (2000)
18. Schölkopf, B., Platt, J., Hofmann, T.: Sparse representation for signal classification. In: Proceedings of the Twentieth Conference on Neural Information Processing Systems Advances in Neural Information Processing Systems 19, Vancouver, British Columbia, Canada, December, pp. 609–616 (2006)
19. Su, Y., Shan, S., Chen, X., Gao, W.: Hierarchical ensemble of global and local classifiers for face recognition. IEEE Trans. Image Process. **18**(8), 1885–1896 (2009)
20. Wolf, L., Hassner, T., Taigman, Y.: Similarity scores based on background samples. In: Zha, H., Taniguchi, R., Maybank, S. (eds.) ACCV 2009. LNCS, vol. 5995, pp. 88–97. Springer, Heidelberg (2010). https://doi.org/10.1007/978-3-642-12304-7_9
21. Wright, J., Ma, Y.: Dense error correction via ell^1-minimization. IEEE Trans. Inform. Theory **56**(7), 3540–3560 (2010)
22. Wright, J., Yang, A.Y., Ganesh, A., Sastry, S.S., Ma, Y.: Robust face recognition via sparse representation. IEEE Trans. Pattern Anal. Mach. Intell. **31**(2), 210–227 (2009)
23. Yang, M., Zhang, L., Zhang, D., Wang, S.: Relaxed collaborative representation for pattern classification. In: 2012 IEEE Conference on Computer Vision and Pattern Recognition, pp. 2224–2231, June 2012
24. Yang, M., Zhang, L.: Gabor feature based sparse representation for face recognition with gabor occlusion dictionary. In: Daniilidis, K., Maragos, P., Paragios, N. (eds.) ECCV 2010. LNCS, vol. 6316, pp. 448–461. Springer, Heidelberg (2010). https://doi.org/10.1007/978-3-642-15567-3_33

25. Yang, M., Zhang, L., Yang, J., Zhang, D.: Robust sparse coding for face recognition. In: Computer Vision and Pattern Recognition, pp. 625–632 (2011)
26. Yuan, X.T., Liu, X., Yan, S.: Visual classification with multitask joint sparse representation. IEEE Trans. Image Process. **21**(10), 4349–4360 (2012)

Distillation of Random Projection Filter Bank for Time Series Classification

Yufei Lin[1], Sen Li[1], and Qianli Ma[1,2]($\boxtimes$)

[1] School of Computer Science and Engineering,
South China University of Technology, Guangzhou, China
yufeilincs@foxmail.com, awslee@foxmail.com
[2] Guangdong Key Laboratory of Big Data Analysis and Processing,
Guangzhou, China
qianlima@scut.edu.cn

Abstract. Time series is widely found in various fields such as geoscience, medicine, finance, and social sciences. How to effectively extract the features of time series remains a challenge due to its potentially complex non-linear dynamics. Recently, Random Projection Filter Bank (RPFB) [5] is proposed as a generic and simple approach to extract features from time series data. It generates the features by randomly generating numerous autoregressive filters that are convolved with input time series. Such numerous random filters inevitably have redundancy and lead to the increased computational cost of the classifier. In this paper, we propose a distillation method of RPFB, named D-RPFB, to not only maintain the high level of quantity of the filters, but also reduce the redundancy of the filters while improving precision. We demonstrate the efficacy of the features extracted by D-RPFB via extensive experimental evaluation in three different areas of time series data with three traditional classifiers (i.e., Logistic Regression (LR) [2], Support Vector Machine (SVM) [14] and Random Forest (RF) [8]).

Keywords: Random projection · Filter bank · Time series
Feature extraction

1 Introduction

Time series data are ubiquitous in many practical applications ranging from health care [3], action recognition [10], financial markets [15] to urban traffic control [16]. How to extract the features of time series effectively is a popular research topic [4,5,7,9,13]. However, time series extraction remains a challenging task due to the potentially complex non-linear dynamic system behind the time series.

Recently, Random Projection Filter Bank (RPFB) [5] is proposed as a generic and simple approach to extract features from time series data. RPFB is a set of randomly generated stable autoregressive filters that are convolved with the input time series to generate the features. These features can be used by any

J.-H. Lai et al. (Eds.): PRCV 2018, LNCS 11258, pp. 586–596, 2018.
https://doi.org/10.1007/978-3-030-03338-5_49

conventional machine learning algorithm for solving tasks such as time series prediction, classification with time series data, etc. Different filters in RPFB extract different aspects of the time series, and together they provide a reasonably good summary of the time series.

However, numerous random filters inevitably have redundancy and lead to the increased computational cost of classifier. Moreover, in some cases, redundant features will make the performance of classifier worse. How to reduce redundant features (i.e., estimate the quality of the filter) is an important issue. In this paper, with an aim of reducing the number of redundant filters, we propose a way to distil the filters of RPFB, named D-RPFB, which uses a set of specific rules to filter the filters that are most capable of guiding the classifier to get better performance. D-RPFB can reduce the number of redundant and even potentially mislead filters, thus improving the quality of the features provided to the classifier which directly improves the learning ability of the classifier and obtains a better performance.

2   Preliminaries

There is a crucial process for the distillation of RPFB, which is designed to measure the quality of a specific filter. To do that, we introduce entropy [6]. Considering that entropy is not very common in time series analysis, we first introduce the concept of entropy briefly before proposing our D-RPFB formally.

Entropy [6] is often used in information theory and probability statistics to measure the uncertainty of a variable. Entropy is always a real number larger than 0 but smaller than 1. Its value indicates the degree of uncertainty of random variables. When the entropy is equal to 0, the random variable is completely certain without any randomness. When entropy is equal to 1, the uncertainty of the random variable peaks. This property of entropy makes it possible to use the entropy to measure the classification quality of the classification subset when a classifier uses a single feature extracted by certain filter to classify an instance. The smaller the entropy of a subset, the more the feature extracted by the filter can make the classifier better complete the clustering, and vice versa, the greater the entropy value indicates that the feature extracted by the filter may lead to the confusion of the classification results.

3   Proposed Methods D-RPFB

3.1   Brief Review of Random Projection Filter Bank

The idea behind RPFB is to randomly generate many simple dynamical systems (i.e., $\frac{1}{1-Z'_n z^{-1}}$ denotes a certain simple dynamical system with a given pole Z'_n and z^{-1} denotes the inverse of z-transform [11]) that can approximate optimal dynamical systems with a high accuracy.

In order to do this, what we should do first is to determine the number of filters in the filter bank. After that, given the certain number of filters N, we draw

N random real numbers or the imaginary numbers $Z'_1, \cdots, Z'_n$ from the unit circle to construct a filter bank defined by filter $\phi(z^{-1}) = (\frac{1}{1-Z'_1 z^{-1}}, \cdots, \frac{1}{1-Z'_n z^{-1}})$ which contains N random projection filters. Then, we pass each input time series through every filter in RPFB to do convolution and generate N features corresponding to each time series at each time step. For example, assuming the length of the each input time series is T, we will get $N * T$ features after passing it through RPFB. Finally, we can input the obtained features into different classifiers for conducting time series classification.

3.2   The Distillation of Random Projection Filter Bank

Introduce the Entropy into Time Series. The entropy is used in the traditional decision tree ID3 algorithm [12] for feature selection. That motivates us to use entropy to evaluate the quality of a certain filter. However, in the traditional decision tree ID3 algorithm [12], the entropy is only applicable to a discrete variable. To solve this issue, we use an extra classifier to introduce the entropy into time series and achieve the purpose of evaluating the quality of a certain filter. In general, assuming the length of the each input time series is T, we will get T features through time after passing it through a certain filter. Then, we input the T features into a certain classifier to get the classification result. In this way, for each time series example, we get a classification result which makes a certain filter become a discrete variable. And, we propose evaluation method combined with entropy and classification result to evaluate the quality of a certain filter.

Computation of Subset Uncertainty and Evaluation of Filters. After using RPFB to generate filter, each filter will be executed with the proposed evaluation algorithms to get their evaluation value. The overall algorithm flow is shown in Algorithm 1. First, in the training data set, randomly select the same number of instances in each category to form data set D_m for avoiding unbalanced sample. For each filter in RPFB, randomly select the half number of instances in D_m as training data D_t, the other half as validation data D_v and then pass the train and valid data into the filter, extracting the corresponding features (denoted by F_t and F_v). Then, fitting the classifier with the F_t. When the remaining features F_v are classified by the classifier, each category (totally M category) will produce a corresponding subset D'_m. Each subset D'_m may contain the instances that belong to the subset or contains instances that do not belong to the subset. Thirdly, we can calculate the uncertainty of each subsets D'_m by entropy. If the uncertainty of the subset D'_m is small it means that D'_m contains many instances of the same category, which means that the feature extracted by the filter can guide the classifier to complete the clustering of the time series. However, only clustering results cannot evaluate whether a filter is really efficient because if a subset D'_m contains many instances of the same category that do not belong to D'_m, the feature extracted by the filter is quite bad which misleads the classifier. Therefore, we have to consider the classification accuracy as the second characteristics of each subset D'_m. In this way, the two important measurements, the clustering effect and the classification accuracy are both considered. Both of them are equally important for evaluating the quality of the feature extracted by a filter. Therefore, D-RPFB proposes a method for calculating the evaluation value of a certain filter as follow:

Algorithm 1. The distillation of random projection filter bank

---

Input: Dataset $= (X_{i,1}, Y_{i,1}), \cdots, (X_{i,T_i}, Y_{i,T_i})_{i=1}^{m}$
Output: Classifier $\hat{f}$ and new filter bank ϕ_{new}

1   $l : Y' \times Y \to \mathbb{R}$: Loss function;
2   $\mathcal{F}$: Function space;
3   n : The number of filters in random projection filter banks;
4   ρ : The percentage of remaining filters after the screening filter;
5   Draw $Z'_1, \cdots, Z'_n$ uniformly random within the unit circle.
6   Define filter $\phi(z^{-1}) = (\frac{1}{1-Z'_1 z^{-1}}, \cdots, \frac{1}{1-Z'_n z^{-1}})$.
7   In the training data set, randomly select the same number of instances in each category to form data set D_m.
8   **foreach** $\phi_i(z^{-1})$ *in* $\phi(z^{-1})$ **do**
9   Pass each time series in D_m through filter $\phi_i(z^{-1})$.
10   Randomly select the half number of instances in D_m as training data D_t, the other half as valid data D_v.
11   Input the corresponding features F_t generated by training data D_t in step 9 into the classifier to fit the model. (The type of classifier used here is the same as the f in line 19.)
12   Input the corresponding features F_v generated by valid data D_v into the fitted model got by step 11 to get the classification subsets D'_m.
13   Use Equation (3) to calculate the evaluation $E_{\phi(z^{-1})}$ of the filter $\phi_i(z^{-1})$.
14   **end**
15   Sort all filters according to their evaluation value $E_{\phi(z^{-1})}$.
16   Select the corresponding number of filters based on ρ with higher evaluation values to form new filter banks ϕ_{new}.
17   Pass each time series in training set through every filter in the new filter bank ϕ_{new}.
18   Use the new extracted features $(X'_{i,1:T_i})$ generated by new filter bank ϕ_{new} to construct the estimator, we use regularized empirical risk minimization to solve it and $J(f)$ controls the complexity of the function space:
19      $\hat{f} \leftarrow \arg\min_{f \in \mathcal{F}} \sum_{i=1}^{m} \sum_{t=1}^{T_i} l(f(X'_{i,t}, Y_{i,t})) + \lambda J(f)$
     where l denotes the cross entropy cost function, J can be lasso or ridge regression regularization.
20   Return $\hat{f}$ and ϕ_{new}

$$H(D'_m) = - \sum_{m=1}^{M} p_m \log p_m \qquad (1)$$

$$Recall_{D'_m} = \frac{TP}{TP + FN} \qquad (2)$$

$$E_{\phi(z-1)} = \sum_{m=1}^{M} (1 - H(D'_m)) \times (Recall_{D'_m}) \qquad (3)$$

where $H(D'_m)$ is the entropy of a classification subset of the filter i, M is the total number of category, p_m is proportion of an instance of M category in the classification subset D'_m, TP is the number of the samples classified correctly in this category, $TP + FN$ is the number of the total samples in this category, $Recall_{D'_m}$ is the recall of classification subsets D'_m and $E_{\phi(z-1)}$ is the total evaluation value E of the i filter.

4   Experiment

In order to verify that the proposed D-RPFB can reduce the redundancy of the numerous filters while also keeping or even improving the performance of classification, we evaluate it in three different areas of time series data with three traditional classifiers (i.e., LR, SVM and RF) compared with RPFB. First, we investigate the effect of the proposed evaluation method for measuring the quality of a specific filter. Then, we show the experimental results on other two time series. Finally, we give an analysis of the screening percentage of the filters to empirically decide how many filters should be retained.

4.1   Analyzing the Effect of the Proposed Evaluation on Star Curve Data Set

The proposed evaluation method in the Eq. (3) for measuring the quality of a certain filter plays an important role in our D-RPFB. We first investigate the effect of the proposed evaluation method on the Star curve data set [1]. We assess the effect of the Eq. (3) by answering the question: Can we use the Eq. (3) to get three group filter banks that correspond to an excellent, inferior, and average property and get the corresponding performance on the test set? If this happens, then the proposed evaluation method is considered to be effective.

Our experimental scheme is as follows. Firstly, a sufficient number of filters are generated to form an initial filter group. Then, we input a part of the training data and the initial filter bank into the filter method to get the evaluation of all the filters by Eq. 3). Third, sorting the filter by the respective evaluation value of E, we divide the filter into four intervals according to the evaluation value of E (i.e., $0 < E < 0.25$ for worst, $0.25 < E < 0.5$ for worse, $0.5 < E < 0.75$ for better, $0.75 < E < 1$ for best). Finally, we construct three group filter banks with 200 filters in each that corresponds to excellent, inferior, and average distribution by randomly selecting a specific number of filters in a specific interval to meet the scheme we need. The corresponding distribution is shown in Fig. 1.

Figure 2 shows clearly the ability of the evaluation method to distinguish high quality filters from inferior filters. Generally speaking, the classification error of the inferior distribution is far higher than the classification error rate of the average distribution and the classification errors of the excellent distribution

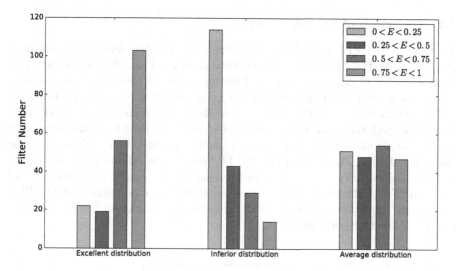

Fig. 1. The number of filters with different evaluation values in the three group of filter banks.

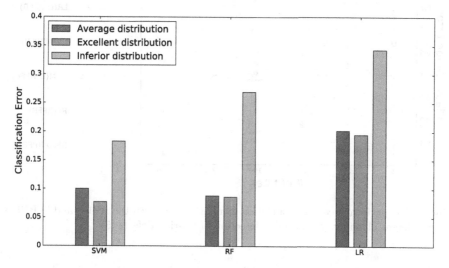

Fig. 2. The performance of classification comparison among three filter banks distribution with three classifiers.

are lower than the average distribution on the three classifiers, which shows that the proposed evaluation method can effectively distinguish high quality and low quality filters.

4.2 Detection of Bearing Defects

To compare D-RPFB and RPFB, we employ the bearing defect detection data set [5] used by the RPFB. We extract 40 time series of length 3333 in each class time series for filtering screening and testing. First, we select 15 time series (3 categories in total 45) in each category to screen the filter. Next, we generate a set of filter banks, each of which will be used in the D-RPFB and RPFB respectively. In RPFB, the filter group will maintain the number of the filters and participate in the classification of time series, and finally produce the classification error rate. In D-RPFB, the filter group will be firstly screened and then participate in the classification of time series. In this case, if the classification error rate of the D-RPFB is the same with that of the RPFB, it can verify that D-RPFB can reduce the number of redundancy and even potentially mislead filters, thus obtaining a better performance.

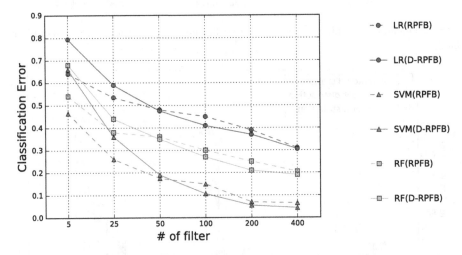

Fig. 3. The performance of classification comparison between the RPFB and D-RPFB with different classifiers on data set detection of bearing defects [5].

In our experiment, we empirically retain 75% filters (i.e., reduced number of filters in RPFB by 25%) in D-RPFB. As shown in Fig. 3, both of D-RPFB and RPFB are decreasing with the increasing of the number of filters. On this data set, the SVM can provide a lower error rate than the LR or RF. This conclusion is consistent in both the D-RPFB and RPFB. On the one hand, the error rate of the RPFB and D-RPFB is relatively high when the number of filters is relatively small. Besides, D-RPFB is worse than PRFB. This implies that the RPFB has a limited ability to summarize the time series when there are only a few filters. Meanwhile, D-RPFB further reduces the number of filters with relatively poor quality by distillation mechanism results in fewer filters, which reduces the accuracy of the D-RPFB. On the other hand, with the increasing of the number of filters, the error rate of the D-RPFB and RPFB has decreased, but the D-RPFB declines more. This is because the D-RPFB has gradually obtained the filter which can accurately summarize the time series through the screening mechanism and remove some filters that can produce a misleading effect. The RPFB, because there is no screening mechanism to distinguish the redundant and misleading filters, the effect of some inefficient filters hinders classifier from getting a better performance.

4.3 Heart Rate Classification

To show more that the D-RPFB can improve the performance of classification, we apply the heart rate data set [5] used in the RPFB. There are two time series with a length of 1800, which belong to category A and B respectively. We firstly divide the time series of category A into 30 short time series with 60 length, 15 of which are training data sets and 15 others are test data sets. Next, we conduct the same operations on the time series of category B. After dividing two long time series, we get 30 training time series (15 of them are category A and the remaining 15 are category B) and 30 test time series (also 15 of them are category A and the remaining 15 are category B). Then, we generate a set of filter banks, each of which will be used in the D-RPFB and RPFB respectively. Finally, again, RPFB uses all the generated filters for classifier. And D-RPFB uses the screened filters for classifier.

In this experiment, we empirically retain 75% filters (i.e., reduced number of filters in RPFB by 25%) in D-RPFB. As shown in Fig. 4, with the small amounts of filters, the performance of D-RPFB is inferior to RPFB again. This implies that there is no need for distillation when the number of filter is very small. However, with the increase of the filters, most of the points on the classification

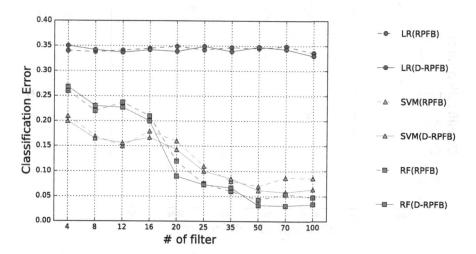

Fig. 4. The performance of classification comparison between the RPFB and D-RPFB with different classifiers on data set heart rate [5].

error curve using the features provided by D-RPFB are under the classification error curve of using the features provided by RPFB, even if some points are not under the classification error curve of RPFB, they are not much higher than in the original method. That is to say, such numerous filters randomly generated by RPFB are indeed redundant and have some misleading filters. D-RPFB distil the filters obtained by RPFB to reduce redundancy or some misleading filters to achieve the high quality of the filters and then input to the classifier, resulting a better performance.

4.4 Analyzing the Choosing of the Screening Percentage of the Filters on Hand Profile Data Set

How many filters can be kept to obtain a good summary of the input time series remains to be a question. The above reported result is under the 75% retainment (i.e., the corresponding percentage of screening is 25%) of the filters case. In this section, we analyze the choosing of the screening percentage of the filters on Hand profile data set [1]. We first generate 200 filters and then adjust the remaining filter ratio by selecting the high ranking filters, obtaining the corresponding results.

As shown in Fig. 5, if the number of filters retained is too small, the features extracted by these filters may not provide a good summary of the input time series, thus resulting a worse performance. With the percentage of retainment is increasing, the performance is better. Combined with the conclusions of experiments 4.2 and 4.3, there is no redundant or misleading information which could

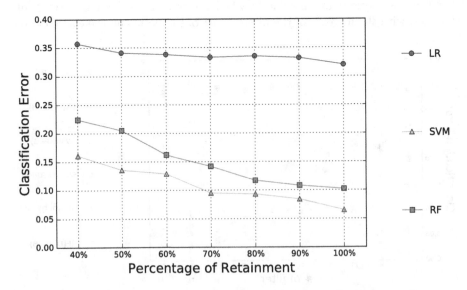

Fig. 5. The performance of classification obtained by using different classifiers under different percentages of retainment on D-RPFB.

harm the performance among such 200 filters. We can see that the original time series has been well summarized at the 80% of retainment (i.e., the corresponding percentage of screening is 20%), because the benefits from retaining more are already very small. Besides, more filters retained mean more running-time consuming when combined with specific classifier. So, in our experiment, we retain the number of filters at the original 80% while making further adjustments and finally retain 75% (i.e., the corresponding percentage of screening is 25%) to get a better performance.

5 Conclusion

In this paper, we proposed the distillation of random projection filter bank (D-PRFB) for time series classification, which is an improvement method of the random projection filter bank (PRFB). Before directly applying the features generated by the randomly generated numerous autoregressive filters that are convolved with the input time series, we add filter screening in the original method for screening the filters that are most capable of guiding the classifier to get better performance. We evaluated the D-PRFB in three different areas of time series data with three traditional classifiers. Extensive experimental results demonstrate that D-RPFB can reduce redundancy and even potentially misleading filters, thus improving the quality of the features provided to the classifier which directly improves the learning ability of the classifier to obtain a better performance.

Acknowledgment. The work described in this paper was partially funded by the National Natural Science Foundation of China (Grant No. 61502174, 61872148), the Natural Science Foundation of Guangdong Province (Grant No. 2017A030313355, 2017A030313358), the Guangzhou Science and Technology Planning Project (Grant No. 201704030051), the Opening Project of Guangdong Province Key Laboratory of Big Data Analysis and Processing (Grant No. 2017014) and the Guangdong University of Finance & Economics Big Data and Educational Statistics Application Laboratory (Grant No. 2017WSYS001).

References

1. Chen, Y., et al.: The UCR time series classification archive, July 2015. www.cs. ucr.edu/~eamonn/time_series_data/
2. Cucchiara, A.: Applied logistic regression. Technometrics **44**(1), 81–82 (1989)
3. Elmoaqet, H., Tilbury, D.M., Ramachandran, S.K.: Multi-step ahead predictions for critical levels in physiological time series. IEEE Trans. Cybern. **46**(7), 1704–1714 (2016)
4. Faloutsos, C., Ranganathan, M., Manolopoulos, Y.: Fast subsequence matching in time-series databases, vol. 23 (1994)
5. Farahmand, A.M., Pourazarm, S., Nikovski, D.: Random projection filter bank for time series data. In: Advances in Neural Information Processing Systems, pp. 6565–6575 (2017)

6. Jaynes, E.T.: Information theory and statistical mechanics. Phys. Rev. **106**(4), 620 (1957)
7. Keogh, E., Chakrabarti, K., Pazzani, M., Mehrotra, S.: Dimensionality reduction for fast similarity search in large time series databases. Knowl. Inform. Syst. **3**(3), 263–286 (2001)
8. Liaw, A., Wiener, M.: Classification and regression by randomForest. R news **2**(3), 18–22 (2002)
9. Lin, J., Keogh, E., Lonardi, S., Chiu, B.: A symbolic representation of time series, with implications for streaming algorithms. In: Proceedings of the 8th ACM SIG-MOD Workshop on Research Issues in Data Mining and Knowledge Discovery, pp. 2–11 (2003)
10. Ma, Q., Shen, L., Chen, E., Tian, S., Wang, J., Cottrell, G.W.: Walking walking walking: action recognition from action echoes. In: International Joint Conference on Artificial Intelligence, pp. 2457–2463 (2017)
11. Oppenheim, A.V., Schafer, R.W.: Discrete-time signal processing **23**(2), 157 (1989)
12. Quinlan, J.R.: Induction of decision trees. Mach. Learn. **1**(1), 81–106 (1986)
13. Susto, G.A., Schirru, A., Pampuri, S., Mcloone, S.: Supervised aggregative feature extraction for big data time series regression. IEEE Trans. Ind. Inform. **12**(3), 1243–1252 (2016)
14. Suykens, J.A., Vandewalle, J.: Least squares support vector machine classifiers. Neural Process. Lett. **9**(3), 293–300 (1999)
15. Xu, Z., Kersting, K., von Ritter, L.: Stochastic online anomaly analysis for streaming time series. In: Proceedings of the 26th International Joint Conference on Artificial Intelligence, pp. 3189–3195 (2017)
16. Zhan, H., Gomes, G., Li, X.S., Madduri, K., Sim, A., Wu, K.: Consensus ensemble system for traffic flow prediction. IEEE Transactions on Intelligent Transportation Systems, 1–12 (2018)

Jointly Sparse Reconstructed Regression Learning

Dongmei Mo[1], Zhihui Lai[1(✉)], and Heng Kong[2]

[1] College of Computer Science and Software Engineering, Shenzhen University,
Shenzhen 518060, China
lai_zhi_hui@163.com
[2] School of Medicine, Shenzhen University, Shenzhen 518060, China

Abstract. Least squares regression and ridge regression are simple and effective methods for feature selection and classification and many methods based on them are proposed. However, most of these methods have small-class problem, which means that the number of the projection learned by these methods is limited by the number of class. In this paper, we propose a jointly sparse reconstructed regression (JSRR) to solve this problem. Moreover, JSRR uses $L_{2,1}$-norm as the basic measurement so that it can enhance robustness to outliers and guarantee joint sparsity for discriminant feature selection. In addition, by integrating the property of robust feature selection (RFS) and principle component analysis (PCA), JSRR is able to obtain the projections that have minimum reconstructed error and strong discriminability for recognition task. We also propose an iterative algorithm to solve the optimization problem. A series of experiments are conducted to evaluate the performance of JSRR. Experimental results indicate that JSRR outperforms the classical RR and some state-of-the-art regression methods.

Keywords: Regression · Feature selection · Joint sparsity · Classification
Robustness

1 Introduction

During the last decades, many methods are proposed for feature selection. Taking the label information into consideration or not, the feature selection methods can be divided into three categories: supervised algorithms, semi-supervised algorithms and unsupervised algorithms. For unsupervised learning, the classical method is principle component analysis (PCA) [1] which projects high dimensional data into a lower dimensional space via seeking the maximum the variance of the data [2]. For supervised learning, linear discriminant analysis (LDA) [3] is the representative method that utilizes label information to learn an optimal matrix that maximizes the between-class scatter and at the same time minimizes the within-class scatter in feature space [4]. Besides, least squares regression (LSR) and ridge regression (RR) are also the classical supervised learning methods.

Although PCA, LDA and LSR are simple and effective in dealing with problems in data analysis and machine learning, they still have a major disadvantage. That is, they

J.-H. Lai et al. (Eds.): PRCV 2018, LNCS 11258, pp. 597–609, 2018.
https://doi.org/10.1007/978-3-030-03338-5_50

do not have sparsity property. Actually, the methods with sparsity are able to learn a series of sparse projections for feature presentation. To solve this problem, the sparse RR [5] as well as elastic net [6] was proposed. These methods are very classical and widely used in many cases. Inspired by them, many regression based methods are also developed to learn sparse approximation projections for feature selection [7–10]. However, these sparse learning methods based on L_1-norm regularization have two drawbacks. First, the L_1-norm based methods do not have joint sparsity. Second, since these methods use L_1-norm regularization on the projections, they need to compute the projection vectors one by one during the procedure of feature selection, which leads to higher training time. Recently, $L_{2,1}$-norm regularization has attracted great attention in the field of feature selection, with which we can obtain joint sparsity to improve the performance of feature selection and classification. Moreover, the $L_{2,1}$-norm based methods are less time-consuming than the methods based on L_1-norm regularization. Nie et al. proposed robust feature selection (RFS) [11] by using $L_{2,1}$-norm on both of loss function and the regularization term. Yang et al. proposed unsupervised discriminative feature selection (UDFS) [12] to extend the $L_{2,1}$-norm regularization to unsupervised learning. Xiang et al. proposed discriminative least squares regression (DLSR) [13] to enlarge the distance between different classes based on the framework of LSR. In addition, many $L_{2,1}$-norm based methods are also proposed to deal with different classification tasks [14–19].

Even though the above $L_{2,1}$-norm based methods are able to obtain jointly sparse projections for discriminative feature selection, they ignore the small-class problem. That is, the number of the learned projections is limited by the number of class. For example, suppose the number of the class is c, RR, RFS and even DSLR cannot obtain more than c projections for feature selection, which indicates that they cannot obtain enough projections if the number of the class is small. In addition, all of the existing methods do not consider the property of supervised and unsupervised learning in a unified regression form.

Based on this regard, in this paper we propose a reconstructed regression method for jointly sparse feature selection. The proposed method called Jointly Sparse Reconstructed Regression (JSRR) integrates the property of RFS and PCA in regression form, by which the joint sparsity is obtained and the small-class problem is solved. Moreover, compared with PCA, JSRR is able to embed the label information in the loss function so as to obtain discriminative projection for feature selection. In summary, the contributions of the proposed JSRR can be described as follows:

(1) JSRR is able to enhance the robustness to outliers by using $L_{2,1}$-norm instead of the L_2-norm as the basic measurement on the loss function. Moreover, it can guarantee the joint sparsity for discriminative feature selection by imposing $L_{2,1}$-norm penalty on the regularization term.
(2) Compared with LSR, RR and their extensions, JSRR can solve the small-class problem, by which it can obtain more than c projections to improve the performance of feature selection and classification.
(3) Compared with PCA, JSRR considers the label information on the loss function, so that it can obtain more discriminative information for effective feature selection.

2 The Proposed Method

In this section, we first present the notation of the variables in this paper and briefly review the classical ridge regression. Then we propose the jointly sparse reconstructed regression (JSRR) for feature selection and give the corresponding optimization procedure.

2.1 Notation

In this paper, we denote all the matrices as bold uppercase italic letters, i.e. X, Y, etc., while vectors are denoted as bold lowercase italic letters, i.e. x, y, etc. and scalars are presented as lowercase italic letters, i.e. i, j, c, n.

The sample matrix is denoted as $X \in R^{d \times n}$, where d is the dimension of the data and n is the number of samples. The label matrix is presented as $Y \in R^{n \times c}$ with $Y_{ij} = 1$ where x_i belongs to j-th class, otherwise, $Y_{ij} = 0$.

2.2 Ridge Regression Revisit

Least squares regression is simple and effective technic for data analysis and classification. The optimization problem of LSR is as follows

$$W^{\#} = \arg\min_{W} ||Y - X^T W||_F^2 \tag{1}$$

where $Y \in R^{n \times c}$ is the label matrix and $X \in R^{d \times n}$ is the sample matrix, $W \in R^{d \times c}$ is the projection matrix used for feature selection.

LSR can obtain its optimal solution only when XX^T is full-rank, that is, it exists the singular problem. To solve this problem, a L_2-norm based penalty is added to the objective function and that comes to the optimization problem of the ridge regression.

$$W^* = \arg\min_{W} ||Y - X^T W||_F^2 + \lambda ||W||_F^2 \tag{2}$$

where λ is the parameter to balance the two terms. The second term in (2) acts as bias term and it can avoid the singular problem in LSR.

2.3 Jointly Sparse Reconstructed Regression

Motivated by the previous work in RFS [11] that using $L_{2,1}$-norm on both of the loss function and regularization term can not only enhance the robustness to outliers but also obtain jointly sparse projections for feature selection. In this paper, we integrate the property of RFS and PCA to design a more complete model to not only inherit the property of RFS and PCA, but also solve the small-class problem in RR or its extensions so as to obtain enough projections to improve the performance of feature selection and classification. The objective function of the proposed JSRR is presented as follows

$$(Q^*, P^*, A^*) = \arg\min_{Q,P,A} \alpha \, \|Y - X^T Q A\|_{2,1} + (1 - \alpha) \, \|X - P Q^T X\|_{2,1} + \beta \, \|Q\|_{2,1}$$

$$s.t \; A A^T = I$$

(3)

where $X \in R^{d \times n}$ is the sample matrix, $Y \in R^{n \times c}$ is label matrix, $A \in R^{k \times c}$ is the orthogonal matrix, $P \in R^{d \times k}$ is the auxiliary matrix and $Q \in R^{d \times k}$ is projection matrix. α and β are the parameters to balance the three terms. $\| \cdot \|_{2,1}$ is the $L_{2,1}$-norm definition.

In (3), the first term is the loss function as in LSR where matrix QA with size $d \times c$ is similar to the matrix $W \in R^{d \times c}$. The difference between JSRR and LSR is that the size of the projection matrix Q in JSRR is $d \times k$ while the projection matrix in LSR or RR is $d \times c$, which means the JSRR can obtain k projections for feature selection while LSR and RR can only obtain at most c projections (note that k is a variable and it can be set as any integer). If we set $k > c$, then JSRR can break through the limitation of the class number and thus solve the small-class problem. Another difference between JSRR and LSR or RR is that JSRR uses $L_{2,1}$-norm as the basic measurement on the loss function, by which the model is more robust to outliers. Compared with RFS, JSRR does not have the small-class problem. Moreover, JSRR can degrade to conceptual framework of RFS when $\alpha = 1$. That is, the second term in (3) is released, JSRR is the $L_{2,1}$-norm based RR that has similar property with RFS. When $\alpha = 0$, JSRR becomes a unsupervised learning method. In this case, JSRR is the joint sparse principle component analysis method as proposed in [19]. Otherwise, if $\alpha \neq 0$ and $\alpha \neq 1$, JSRR holds the property of RFS and PCA, which enhances the robustness to outliers and at the same time obtains sparse principle components (PCs) for feature selection.

In summary, from the objective function of JSRR, we can know that it uses $L_{2,1}$-norm instead of L_2-norm on all terms to enhance robustness to outlier and simultaneously guarantee joint sparsity for discriminative feature selection. Also, since the projection matrix is Q with size $d \times k$, JSRR can obtain k projections instead of c projection to solve the small-class problem so as to obtain enough projections for feature selection and classification. In addition, JSRR enjoys the property of RFS and PCA when $\alpha \neq 1$ and $\alpha \neq 0$, or it can also be used for unsupervised learning when $\alpha = 0$.

2.4   The Optimal Solution

There are three variables in (3) and the optimization problem is not convex, which means that we cannot obtain the optimal solution directly. Therefore, we need to develop an iterative algorithm to solve the optimization problem.

First, from (3), we have

$$\begin{aligned} &\alpha \, \|Y - X^T Q A\|_{2,1} + (1 - \alpha) \| X - P Q^T X\|_{2,1} + \beta \, \|Q\|_{2,1} \\ &= \alpha tr[(Y - X^T Q A)^T D (Y - X^T Q A)] \\ &\quad + (1 - \alpha) tr[(X - P Q^T X)^T D_1 (X - P Q^T X)] + \beta tr(Q^T D_2 Q) \end{aligned}$$

(4)

where $D \in R^{n \times n}$ is a diagonal matrix with the elements represented as

$$D_{ii} = \frac{1}{2||(Y - X^T QA)^i||_2} \tag{5}$$

where $(Y - X^T QA)^i$ denotes the i-th row of the matrix $(Y - X^T QA)$.

Similarly, the elements of diagonal matrix $D_1 \in R^{d \times d}$ and $D_2 \in R^{d \times d}$ are represented as

$$(D_1)_{ii} = \frac{1}{2||(X - PQ^T X)^i||_2} \tag{6}$$

$$(D_2)_{ii} = \frac{1}{2||Q^i||_2} \tag{7}$$

where $(X - PQ^T X)^i$ and Q^i denote the i-th row of the matrix $(X - PQ^T X)$ and Q, respectively.

From (4), we have

$$\begin{aligned}
&\alpha ||Y - X^T QA||_{2,1} + (1 - \alpha) ||X - PQ^T X||_{2,1} + \beta ||Q||_{2,1} \\
&= \alpha tr[(Y - X^T QA)^T D(Y - X^T QA)] \\
&\quad + (1 - \alpha) tr[(\sqrt{D_1}(X - PQ^T X))^T (\sqrt{D_1}(X - PQ^T X))] + \beta tr(Q^T D_2 Q)
\end{aligned} \tag{8}$$

From (8), we can know that the objective function in (3) can be rewritten as the following optimization problem

$$\begin{aligned}
(Q^*, P^*, A^*) = \arg\min_{Q,P,A} &\; \alpha \left\| \sqrt{D}(Y - X^T QA) \right\|_F^2 + (1 - \alpha) \left\| \sqrt{D_1}(X - PQ^T X) \right\|_F^2 + \beta \left\| \sqrt{D_2} Q \right\|_F^2 \\
&s.t \; AA^T = I
\end{aligned} \tag{9}$$

Let $\bar{P} = \sqrt{D_1}P$, $\bar{Q} = \sqrt{D_1}^{-1}Q$, then (9) is equal to

$$\begin{aligned}
(\bar{Q}^*, \bar{P}^*, A^*) = \arg\min_{\bar{Q},\bar{P},A} &\; \alpha \left\| \sqrt{D}(Y - X^T \sqrt{D_1}\bar{Q}A) \right\|_F^2 \\
&+ (1 - \alpha) \left\| \sqrt{D_1}X - \bar{P}\bar{Q}^T \sqrt{D_1}X \right\|_F^2 + \beta \left\| \sqrt{D_2}\sqrt{D_1}\bar{Q} \right\|_F^2 \\
&s.t \; AA^T = I
\end{aligned} \tag{10}$$

By imposing the orthogonal constraint $\bar{P}^T \bar{P} = I$ to (10), we have

$$\begin{aligned}
(\bar{Q}^*, \bar{P}^*, A^*) = \arg\min_{\bar{Q},\bar{P},A} &\; \alpha \left\| \sqrt{D}(Y - X^T \sqrt{D_1}\bar{Q}A) \right\|_F^2 \\
&+ (1 - \alpha) \left\| \sqrt{D_1}X - \bar{P}\bar{Q}^T \sqrt{D_1}X \right\|_F^2 + \beta \left\| \sqrt{D_2}\sqrt{D_1}\bar{Q} \right\|_F^2 \\
&s.t \; AA^T = I, \; \bar{P}^T \bar{P} = I
\end{aligned} \tag{11}$$

Take the optimization problem in (11) as the objective optimization problem in this paper, we can first obtain the optimal solution of $\bar{P}$ and $\bar{Q}$, and then we obtain the optimal solution of P and Q as $P = \sqrt{D_1}^{-1}\bar{P}$, $Q = \sqrt{D_1}\bar{Q}$.

$\bar{Q}$ **Step:** Suppose $\bar{P}$ and A are fixed, there exists an optimal matrix $\bar{P}_\perp$ that guarantees $[\bar{P}, \bar{P}_\perp]$ is a $d \times d$ column orthogonal matrix. From the optimization problem in (11), we have

$$
\begin{aligned}
||\sqrt{D_1}X - \bar{P}\bar{Q}^T\sqrt{D_1}X)||_F^2 &= ||X^T\sqrt{D_1} - X^T\sqrt{D_1}\bar{Q}\bar{P}^T||_F^2 \\
&= ||X^T\sqrt{D_1}[\bar{P}, \bar{P}_\perp] - X^T\sqrt{D_1}\bar{Q}\bar{P}^T[\bar{P}, \bar{P}_\perp]||_F^2 \\
&= ||X^T\sqrt{D_1}\bar{P} - X^T\sqrt{D_1}\bar{Q}\bar{P}^T\bar{P}||_F^2 + ||X^T\sqrt{D_1}\bar{P}_\perp - X^T\sqrt{D_1}\bar{Q}\bar{P}^T\bar{P}_\perp||_F^2 \\
&= ||X^T\sqrt{D_1}\bar{P} - X^T\sqrt{D_1}\bar{Q}||_F^2 + ||X^T\sqrt{D_1}\bar{P}_\perp||_F^2
\end{aligned}
\tag{12}
$$

In (12), since $\bar{P}$ is given and $||X^T\sqrt{D_1}\bar{P}_\perp||_F^2$ is a constant, the optimization problem in (11) becomes

$$
\begin{aligned}
\bar{Q}^* = \arg\min_{\bar{Q}} \alpha\,||\sqrt{D}(Y - X^T\sqrt{D_1}\bar{Q}A)||_F^2 \\
+ (1 - \alpha)\,||X^T\sqrt{D_1}\bar{P} - X^T\sqrt{D_1}\bar{Q}||_F^2 + \beta\,||\sqrt{D_2}\sqrt{D_1}\bar{Q}||_F^2 \\
s.t\ AA^T = I
\end{aligned}
\tag{13}
$$

From (13), we have

$$
\begin{aligned}
&\alpha tr(Y^TDY - 2\bar{Q}^T\sqrt{D_1}XDYA^T + \bar{Q}^T\sqrt{D_1}XDX^T\sqrt{D_1}\bar{Q}) \\
&+ (1 - \alpha)tr(\bar{P}^T\sqrt{D_1}XX^T\sqrt{D_1}\bar{P} - 2\bar{Q}^T\sqrt{D_1}XX^T\sqrt{D_1}\bar{P} + \bar{Q}^T\sqrt{D_1}XX^T\sqrt{D_1}\bar{Q}) \\
&+ \beta tr(\bar{Q}^T\sqrt{D_1}D_2\sqrt{D_1}\bar{Q})] \\
&\quad s.t.\ AA^T = I
\end{aligned}
\tag{14}
$$

By the derivative of (14) with respect to $\bar{Q}$ to be 0, we have

$$
\begin{aligned}
&\alpha(\sqrt{D_1}XDX^T\sqrt{D_1}\bar{Q} - \sqrt{D_1}XDYA^T) \\
&+ (1 - \alpha)(\sqrt{D_1}XX^T\sqrt{D_1}\bar{Q} - \sqrt{D_1}XX^T\sqrt{D_1}\bar{P}) + \beta tr(\sqrt{D_1}D_2\sqrt{D_1}\bar{Q}) = 0
\end{aligned}
\tag{15}
$$

Then, we have

$$
\bar{Q} = [\sqrt{D_1}(\alpha XDX^T + (1 - \alpha)XX^T + \beta D_2)\sqrt{D_1}]^{-1}(\alpha\sqrt{D_1}XDYA^T + (1 - \alpha)\sqrt{D_1}XX^T\sqrt{D_1}\bar{P})
\tag{16}
$$

Since $Q = \sqrt{D_1}\bar{Q}$, then

$$
Q = [\alpha XDX^T + (1 - \alpha)XX^T + \beta D_2]^{-1}(\alpha XDYA^T + (1 - \alpha)XX^T\sqrt{D_1}\bar{P})
\tag{17}
$$

$\bar{P}$ **Step:** Suppose $\bar{Q}$ and A are given, from (14), we have

$$\bar{P}^* = \arg\max_{\bar{P}} \ tr(\bar{P}^T \sqrt{D_1} XX^T \sqrt{D_1} \bar{Q}) \tag{18}$$

Theorem 1. [20] Suppose $G \in R^{c \times k}$ is a matrix with rank of k and $Z \in R^{c \times k}$ is an orthogonal matrix. The optimization problem

$$Z = \arg\min \ tr(Z^T G) \ \ s.t. \ Z^T Z = I_k \tag{19}$$

Algorithm 1 The algorithm of JSRR

Input: The data matrix $X \in R^{d \times n}$, the label matrix $Y \in R^{n \times c}$, the projection number k, the parameter α and β.

　Initialize $A \in R^{k \times c}$, $P \in R^{d \times k}$, $Q \in R^{d \times k}$, $D \in R^{n \times n}$, $D_1 \in R^{d \times d}$ and $D_2 \in R^{d \times d}$.

repeat
　　compute $\bar{Q}$ using (16); update Q using (17); compute $\bar{P}$ using (21); update P using (22);
　　update A using (25); update D using (5); update D_1 using (6); update D_2 using (7);
until converge
Output: $Q \in R^{d \times k}$ with k sparse projections.

---

can be solved by singular value decomposition (SVD) of G, i.e. $G = \breve{U} \breve{D} \breve{V}^T$, then $Z = \breve{U} \breve{V}^T$.

From Theorem 1, we can know that the optimal solution of $\bar{P}$ can be obtain by SVD of $\sqrt{D_1} XX^T \sqrt{D_1} \bar{Q}$, that is,

$$\sqrt{D_1} XX^T \sqrt{D_1} \bar{Q} = UDV^T \tag{20}$$

then

$$\bar{P} = UV^T \tag{21}$$

Since $P = \sqrt{D_1}^{-1} \bar{P}$, we have

$$P = \sqrt{D_1}^{-1} UV^T \tag{22}$$

A **Step:** Suppose $\bar{Q}$ and $\bar{P}$ are given, from (14), we have

$$\begin{aligned} A^* &= \arg\max_{A} \ \alpha tr(AY^T DX^T \sqrt{D_1} \bar{Q}) \\ &\ \ s.t. \ \ AA^T = I \end{aligned} \tag{23}$$

Similarly, according to Theorem 1, we know that the optimal solution of A can be obtain by SVD of $Y^T D X^T \sqrt{D_1} \bar{Q}$, that is,

$$Y^T D X^T \sqrt{D_1} \bar{Q} = \tilde{U} \tilde{D} \tilde{V}^T \tag{24}$$

Then, we have

$$A = \tilde{U} \tilde{V}^T \tag{25}$$

The details of the iterative algorithm that solves optimization problem in (3) are shown in Algorithm 1.

3   Experiments

In this section, several benchmark datasets with varying image types are used to evaluate the performance of the proposed JSRR on feature selection and recognition. These datasets include AR dataset, CMU PIE dataset and LFW dataset. In addition, in all experiments, we compare the proposed JSRR with some classical methods including RR, and some state-of-the-art methods including RFS [11], UDFS [12], DLSR [13] and RIPCA [21].

3.1   Datasets Description

The AR database [22] is consist of over 4000 images from 126 individuals. In our experiment, we use the subsection that contains 2,400 images from 120 individuals. All of these images are normalized to 50×40 pixels. This dataset is used to evaluate the performance of JSRR with varying facial expressions, lighting conditions and occlusions.

The CMU PIE dataset [23] contains 41,368 face images from 68 individuals. We use a subset (C29) which has 1632 images from 68 individuals in our experiment. All of these images are cropped to 32×32 pixels.

Labeled Faces in the Wild (LFW) databases [24] is consist of images from 5,749 subjects in uncontrolled environment. In our experiment, we select 4,324 images from 158 subjects in LFW-a dataset.

Recently, deep learning technique is very famous in the field of machine learning and computer vision. Therefore, to explore the performance of JSRR based on the background of deep learning, we use deep features on LFW dataset instead of original image features as input. Similar to [25], we use deep convolutional neural network (CNN) as feature extractor to obtain deep features. After that, JSRR, RR, RFS, UDFS, DLSR and RIPCA are used to perform further feature selection and extraction. The property of the datasets is summarized in Table 1.

Table 1. Description of datasets.

Datasets	# of Samples	Features	classes
AR	2,400	2,000	120
CMU PIE	1,632	1,024	68
LFW	4,324	1,024	158

3.2 Experimental Setting

In our experiments, PCA is used as pre-processing to perform dimensionality reduction. After that, all methods including the comparative methods and the proposed JSRR are used to perform feature selection and extraction and nearest neighbor (NN) classifier is used for classification. The recognition rate is used as the criteria to evaluate the performance of all methods. Each method independently runs 10 times to conduct feature selection and the mean recognition rate is computed.

For JSRR, since there are two parameters, i.e. α and β, need to optimize, we analyze their values in the area of $[-3,\cdots, 3]$ and $[10^{-3},\cdots, 10^3]$, respectively. For the comparative methods, their parameters are set as the value that introduced in the original paper. For example, the value of the parameter in RFS, UDFS and DLSR is set as $[10^{-3},\cdots, 10^3]$, $[10^{-3},\cdots, 10^3]$ and $[10^{-4},\cdots, 10^1]$, respectively.

3.3 Experimental Results and Comparison

On AR, CMU PIE and LFW dataset, l_1 ($l_1 = 2, 3$), l_2 ($l_2 = 4, 5$) l_3 ($l_3 = 4, 5$) images of each individual are selected for training while the rest of the images are used for testing.

To explore the optimal values of α and β, we report in Fig. 1(a) the recognition rates with varying values of $\alpha \in [-3, -2,\cdots, 3]$ and $\beta \in [10^{-3}, 10^{-2}, \cdots, 10^3]$ on AR database. From Fig. 1(a), we can know that JSRR obtain the best performance while α lies in the area of $[-3, -2, -1]$ and β lies in the area of $[10^{-3}, 10^{-2}, \cdots, 10^3]$. Therefore, we use these values for α and β on all experiments for simplicity.

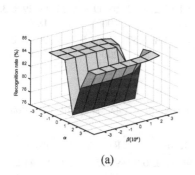

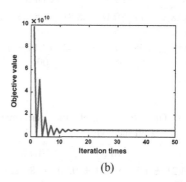

(a)   (b)

Fig. 1. (a) Sensitivity analysis of parameters, (b) convergence curve on AR database.

The average recognition rates with varying dimension on AR and CMU PIE dataset are shown in Fig. 2 while the maximum average recognition versus the dimension and the standard deviation on AR, CUM PIE and LFW dataset are listed in Tables 2, 3 and 4, respectively. The convergence curve of the proposed JSRR on AR dataset is presented in Fig. 1(b).

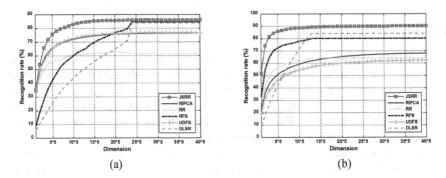

Fig. 2. The recognition rate versus the dimension on (a) AR, (b) CUM PIE dataset.

Table 2. On AR dataset, the performance (recognition rate, standard deviation (%), dimension) of all methods.

l_1	RR	RFS	UDFS	DLSR	RIPCA	JSRR
2	49.62 ± 6.69	80.74 ± 12.00	71.20 ± 5.01	81.74 ± 9.03	71.03 ± 5.02	**83.93 ± 8.25**
	105	120	180	120	195	**195**
3	62.97 ± 5.21	84.54 ± 12.37	76.92 ± 5.12	83.81 ± 10.08	76.70 ± 5.26	**86.08 ± 9.99**
	105	120	180	120	200	**135**

Table 3. On CMU PIE dataset, the performance (recognition rate, standard deviation (%), dimension) of all methods.

l_2	RR	RFS	UDFS	DLSR	RIPCA	JSRR
4	64.28 ± 9.71	80.18 ± 8.81	62.54 ± 10.15	84.15 ± 8.92	68.09 ± 9.33	**90.29 ± 3.58**
	65	65	200	65	200	**185**
5	72.56 ± 8.98	87.40 ± 7.42	72.46 ± 13.57	86.04 ± 6.57	71.82 ± 7.34	**90.75 ± 3.59**
	65	65	200	65	200	**200**

Table 4. On LFW dataset, the performance (recognition rate, standard deviation (%), dimension) of all methods.

l_3	RR	RFS	UDFS	DLSR	RIPCA	JSRR
4	94.21 ± 1.36	98.24 ± 0.00	97.86 ± 0.00	96.34 ± 0.00	98.35 ± 0.00	**98.44 ± 0.04**
	155	155	70	155	130	**170**
5	92.64 ± 3.63	98.53 ± 0.00	98.02 ± 0.00	97.62 ± 0.00	98.64 ± 0.00	**98.70 ± 0.05**
	155	155	90	155	90	**135**

According to the experimental results, we have the following interesting observations:

(1) In all experiments, JSRR obtains the best performance. The potential reason for this phenomenon is that JSRR integrates the property of RFS and PCA, with which it can obtain joint sparse projections for discriminative feature selection and extraction. Furthermore, by considering the label information on the loss function, JSRR is able to enhance the discriminability of the sparse PCs.

(2) On AR and CMU PIE dataset, JSRR, RFS and DLSR obtain better performance than other methods, which indicates that utilizing $L_{2,1}$-norm on loss function and regularization term is able to enhance the robustness and guarantee joint sparsity, such that they are superior for feature selection and classification.

(3) The experimental results demonstrate that JSRR can solve the small-class problem. For example, Fig. 2(b) and Table 3 show that RR, RFS and DLSR obtain the best recognition rate when dimension is 65 (the class number is 68). However, JSRR obtains its highest recognition rate when dimension is 185. It indicates that the number of the projection learned by JSRR is not limited by the number of class, i.e. JSRR can solve the small-class problem.

4 Conclusion

In this paper, we propose a method called jointly sparse reconstructed regression (JSRR) which uses joint $L_{2,1}$-norm as the basic measurement on the objective function. By doing so, JSRR is more robust to outliers than the L_2-norm based methods. Also, it can obtain jointly sparse projection for discriminative feature selection. Different from LSR, RR and their extensions, JSRR is able to solve the small-class problem, which enables it to obtain enough projections to perform feature selection and extraction even though the class number is small. Under some certain conditions, JSRR can degrade to RFS or sparse version of PCA, which indicates that JSRR at least guarantees the effectiveness of RFS and PCA. To solve the optimization problem of JSRR, an iterative algorithm is proposed. Experimental results on three well-known facial datasets demonstrate that JSRR is superior to the classical RR and some state-of-the-art feature selection methods.

Acknowledgment. This work was supported in part by the Natural Science Foundation of China (Grant 61573248, Grant 61773328, Grant 61773328 and Grant 61703283), Research Grant of The Hong Kong Polytechnic University (Project Code:G-UA2B), China Postdoctoral Science Foundation (Project 2016M590812 and Project 2017T100645), the Guangdong Natural Science Foundation (Project 2017A030313367 and Project 2017A030310067), and Shenzhen Municipal Science and Technology Innovation Council (No. JCYJ20170302153434048 and No. JCYJ20160429182058044).

References

1. Yang, J., Zhang, D., Frangi, A.F., Yang, J.: Two-dimensional PCA: a new approach to appearance-based face representation and recognition. IEEE Trans. Pattern Anal. Mach. Intell. **26**, 131–137 (2004)
2. Fan, Z., et al.: Modified principal component analysis: an integration of multiple similarity subspace models. IEEE Trans. Neural Netw. Learn. Syst. **25**, 1538–1552 (2017)
3. Belhumeur, P.N., Hespanha, J.P., Kriegman, D.J.: Eigenfaces vs. fisherfaces: recognition using class specific linear projection. IEEE Trans. Pattern Anal. Mach. Intell. **19**, 711–720 (1997)
4. Zhong, F., Zhang, J., Li, D.: Discriminant locality preserving projections based on L1-norm maximization. IEEE Trans. Neural Netw. Learn. Syst. **25**, 2065–2074 (2014)
5. Tibshirani, R.: Regression shrinkage and selection via the Lasso. J. Roy. Stat. Soc. Ser. B Stat. Methodol. **58**, 267–288 (1996)
6. Zou, H., Hastie, T.: Regularization and variable selection via the elastic net. J. Roy. Stat. Soc. Ser. B. **67**, 301–320 (2005)
7. Majumdar, A., Ward, R.K.: Classification via group sparsity promoting regularization. In: IEEE International Conference on Acoustics, Speech and Signal Processing, pp. 861–864 (2009)
8. Li, C., Shao, Y., Deng, N.: Robust L1-norm two-dimensional linear discriminant analysis. Neural Netw. **65**, 92–104 (2015)
9. Gong, P., Zhang, C., Lu, Z., Huang, J.Z., Ye, J.: A general iterative shrinkage and thresholding algorithm for non-convex regularized optimization problems. In: International Conference on Machine Learning, vol. 28, pp. 37–45 (2013)
10. Xu, Y., Zhang, B., Zhong, Z.: Multiple representations and sparse representation for image classification. Pattern Recognit. Lett. **68**, 9–14 (2015)
11. Nie, F., Huang, H., Cai, X., Ding, C.: Efficient and robust feature selection via joint L2,1-norms minimization. Adv. Neural Inf. Process. Syst. **23**, 1813–1821 (2010)
12. Yang, Y., Shen, H.T., Ma, Z., Huang, Z., Zhou, X.: L2,1-norm regularized discriminative feature selection for unsupervised learning. In: International Joint Conference on Artificial Intelligence, pp. 1589–1594 (2011)
13. Xiang, S., Nie, F., Meng, G., Pan, C., Zhang, C.: Discriminative least squares regression for multiclass classification and feature selection. IEEE Trans. Neural Netw. Learn. Syst. **23**, 1738–1754 (2012)
14. He, R., Tan, T., Wang, L., Zheng, W.: l2,1 regularized correntropy for robust feature selection. In: Computer Vision and Pattern Recognition, pp. 2504–2511 (2012)
15. Shi, X., Yang, Y., Guo, Z., Lai, Z.: Face recognition by sparse discriminant analysis via joint L2,1-norm minimization. Pattern Recognit. **47**, 2447–2453 (2014)
16. Gu, Q., Li, Z., Han, J.: Joint feature selection and subspace learning. In: International Joint Conference on Artificial Intelligence, vol. 55, pp. 1294–1299 (2011)
17. Huang, J., Li, G., Huang, Q., Member, S., Wu, X.: Joint feature selection and classification for multilabel learning. IEEE Trans. Cybern. 1–14 (2017)
18. Yang, J., Chu, D., Zhang, L., Xu, Y., Yang, J.: Sparse representation classifier steered discriminative projection with applications to face recognition. IEEE Trans. Neural Netw. Learn. Syst. **24**, 1023–1035 (2013)
19. Yi, S., Lai, Z., He, Z., Cheung, Y.M., Liu, Y.: Joint sparse principal component analysis. Pattern Recognit. **61**, 524–536 (2017)
20. Zou, H., Hastie, T., Tibshirani, R.: Sparse principal component analysis. J. Comput. Graph. Stat. **15**, 1–30 (2004)

21. Lai, Z., Xu, Y., Yang, J., Shen, L., Zhang, D.: Rotational invariant dimensionality reduction algorithms. IEEE Trans. Cybern. **47**, 3733–3746 (2017)
22. Martinez, A.A., Benavente, R.: The AR face database. CVC Technical report #24 (1998)
23. Sim, T., Baker, S., Bsat, M.: The CMU pose, illumination, and expression database. IEEE Trans. Pattern Anal. Mach. Intell. **25**, 1615–1618 (2003)
24. Huang, G.B., Mattar, M., Berg, T., Learned-Miller, E.: Labeled faces in the wild: a database for studying face recognition in unconstrained environments. Technical report 07-49. University Massachusetts, Amherst (2007)
25. Wen, Y., Zhang, K., Li, Z., Qiao, Y.: A discriminative feature learning approach for deep face recognition. In: Leibe, B., Matas, J., Sebe, N., Welling, M. (eds.) ECCV 2016. LNCS, vol. 9911, pp. 499–515. Springer, Cham (2016). https://doi.org/10.1007/978-3-319-46478-7_31

Multi-scale Attributed Graph Kernel for Image Categorization

Duo Hu, Qin Xu[✉], Jin Tang, and Bin Luo

School of Computer Science and Technology, Anhui University, Hefei, China
michaelhd524@163.com, {xuqin,tj,binluo}@ahu.edu.cn

Abstract. The spatial pyramid matching has been widely adopted for scene recognition and image retrieval. It splits the image into sub-regions and counts the local features within the sub-region. However, it has not captured the spatial relationship between the local features located in the sub-region. This paper proposes to construct the multi-scale attributed graphs which involve the vocabulary label to characterize the spatial structure of the local features at different scales. We compute the distances of any two attributed graph corresponding to the image grids and find the optimal matching to aggregate. Then we poll the distances of graphs at different scales to build the kernel for image classification. We conduct our method on the Caltech 101, Caltech 256, Scene Categories, and Six Actions datasets and compare with five methods. The experiment results demonstrate that our method can provide a good accuracy for image categorization.

Keywords: Image classification · Multi-scale attributed graph
Graph distance

1 Introduction

Image Categorization, which has a quite wide range of applications, such as face recognition, scene classification and pedestrian tracking, is a challenging task in computer vision. It is undoubtedly of great theoretical and practical significance to study the robust and accurate image classification algorithm. How to find the correct classification of an unlabel image from a large scale image database has been a research spot for several decades and numerous methods have been developed.

The approach bag of words (BoW) has been widely used in image classification [1–3]. BoW based methods use image visual features (e.g. SIFT [4]) to build a dictionary of visual words and computing a histogram for each image for recognition. However, the BoW method does not contain spatial and structural information of the image. In this respect, one limitation of the BoW approach is that it can not encode the spatial distribution of visual words within an image.

To characterize the spatial layout of the local features, the spatial pyramid [5] divides the image into different regions at different levels and computes a

© Springer Nature Switzerland AG 2018
J.-H. Lai et al. (Eds.): PRCV 2018, LNCS 11258, pp. 610–621, 2018.
https://doi.org/10.1007/978-3-030-03338-5_51

BoW for each region, and the final image descriptor as the concatenation of the histograms from all regions. For the same reason, latent pyramidal regions (LPR) [6] are trained by combining the benefits of spatial pyramid representation using nonlinear feature coding and latent SVM. Yang et al. [7] proposed the linear spatial pyramid matching using sparse coding (ScSPM) and Wang et al. [8] proposed the locality-constrained linear coding method to improve the ScSPM method by adding the local constraints. In order to obtain the vector based on BoW with certain invariance, Cao etc. presented two methods of linear BoW and annular BoW to improve the robustness to some degree [9].

In recent years, graph matching algorithms have been applied to solve image classification [10,11]. One of the most popular methods to perform graph matching is the graph edit distance [12–15]. Jouili et al. [12] used Hungarian method with a vector which encodes vertices and edges of the same representation to compute a suboptimal cost of edit distance. Zhou et al. [16] proposed a deformable graph matching method to match graphics that are subject to global rigid and non rigid geometric constraints. The bag of graph [13] and bag of visual graphs [14] combines the spatial locations of interest points and their labels defined in terms of the traditional visual-word codebook to define a set of connected graphs, then defines descriptors for image classification based on graph local structures. Lee et al. [17] generalizes the formula of hyper-graph matching to cover arbitrary sequence of feature relations and obtained a new graph matching algorithm by reinterpreting the concept of random walk on hyper-graph. Zhang et al. [18] proposed a saliency-guided graphlet selection algorithm for image categorization. In the multi-graph-view respects, Wu et al. [19] proposes a multi-graph-view model to represent and classify complex targets. Mousavi et al. [20] generated a graph pyramid based on the selected graph summarization algorithm to provide the required information for classification.

The matching node embeddings [21] is presented as the graph kernel based on the pyramid match kernel. It restricts the matchings only between vertices that share same labels. However, the interest points have not assigned labels. Thus this method is not competent for the graph based on interest points without tags. Our approach takes this into account that applying the weighted Hungarian method to find the most similar graph, that can be a good way to overcome this problem.

In this paper, we propose to construct a multi-scale attributed graph model for image classification, where the spatial structure relation between the interest points of the image at different scales are captured. The graphs are pruned to give more efficient structure information for categorization. At each scale, the distance of the attributed graphs are calculated to find the optimal matched graphs. Final the distances are accumulated with weight to built the kernel for SVM.

The rest of the paper is organized as follows. We first present the proposed multi-scale attributed graph for image representation in Sect. 2, and then compute the distance between the attributed graphs corresponding to image grids in Sect. 3. In Sect. 4, the kernel for classification is built by accumulating the distances between the matched graphs. The experimental results on four public datasets are presented and discussed in Sect. 5. Finally, conclusions are drawn in Sect. 6.

2   The Multi-scale Attributed Graph Model for Image Representation

To describe the structure and spatial features of the images at different scales, we define multi-scale attributed graphs $G^l = (V^l, E^l, A^l)$, where l denotes the scale or level factor, the nodes set $V^l = \{v_1, v_2, \cdots, v_n\}$ corresponds to the image feature points $F = \{f_1, f_2, \cdots, f_n\}$, which obtained by extracting the SIFT features of the images in our experiment, the edges set $E^l = \{e_{ij}\}$ are constructed by delaunay triangulation, and A^l denotes the attribute of the node set V^l, for a node v_i, its attribute is defined as,

$$A_{v_i}^l = \{av_i, degree(v_i), \{ae_i\}\} \tag{1}$$

where av_i is the label of node v_i which corresponds to the feature point f_i. In terms of the widely used bag of words, we assign a vocabulary label to each node, $degree(v_i)$ is the degree of the node v_i, $\{ae_i\}$ is the attribute set of all the edges which are adjacent to the node v_i. There exist many methods for constructing graph based on images, such as k-nearest neighbor graph [22] and deep learning hash [23]. We use the delaunay triangulation method here for its stability and efficiency. To characterize the image structure at different scale, we split an image into a sequence of grids at each scale $l \in (0, \ldots, L)$, such that a total of $S = 2^{sl}$ image grids are obtained, where s is the dimension of the images. For each grid, we construct an attributed graph on the feature points, as shown in Fig. 1. These graphs form the multi-scale structure representation of an image.

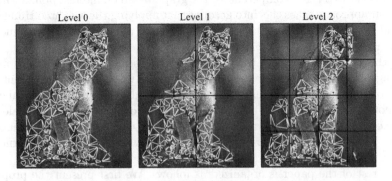

Fig. 1. The multi-scale attributed graph extraction from an cougar body.

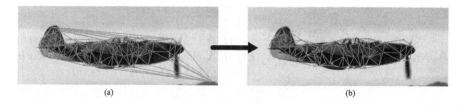

(a)   (b)

Fig. 2. The graph model for an image in Caltech 101. (a) The delaunay triangulation graph on the feature points; (b) Our graph constructed after pruning.

Since the images have not been preprocessed as segmentation or salient analysis, the images usually have the objective, background and noise. The multi-scale attributed graphs built from the original image will contains the additional structure information which is not related to the objective. For example, Fig. 2(a) shows the attributed graph constructed from an image in Caltech 101 at level 0. We can see that one point in the background in the lower right corner of the image is connected to feature of the aircraft. Furthermore, the feature points of the tail and the head of the aircraft are also connected. However, these edges are useless to reflect the structure of the aircraft and not helpful for image classification. Therefore, we consider to prune the graph, specifically, remove the edges which connect the points with long distance and short distance, as shown in Fig. 2(b). Let m be the value of the longest edge of the constructed graphs for one image, we delete the edges longer than βm and shorter than αm, where $0 < \alpha < \beta < 1$. In the experiments, we choose $\alpha = 0.1$ and $\beta = 0.6$. Because experiments show that the short edges can not improve the classification but increase the computational complexity. We can effectively avoid the error structure with the complicated background, and focus on the local structure of the image by pruning edges and constructing the multi-scale attributed graphs. Moreover, the graph after pruning becomes sparse and computational efficient.

3   Graph Distance Based on Node Attributes

To match the multi-scale structure between two images, we compute the distance between the multi-scale graphs constructed from two images. The graph distance is obtained based on the node attributes using the heterogeneous euclidean overlap metric (HEOM) [12], which can handle the numeric and symbolic attributes of nodes. The distance of two nodes v_i and v_j is defined as their distance between the node attribute $\mathbf{A}_i$ and $\mathbf{A}_j$,

$$d(\mathbf{A}_i, \mathbf{A}_j) = \sqrt{\sum_{k=0}^{N} q(\mathbf{A}_i(k), \mathbf{A}_j(k))^2} \qquad (2)$$

where N refers the length of the longest node signature of v_i and v_j, and

$$q(\mathbf{A}_i(k), \mathbf{A}_j(k)) = \begin{cases} \frac{|\mathbf{A}_i(k) - \mathbf{A}_j(k)|}{range} & if \ \mathbf{A}_i(k) \ and \ \mathbf{A}_j(k) \ are \ both \ numeric \\ R(\mathbf{A}_i(k), \mathbf{A}_j(k)) & if \ \mathbf{A}_i(k) \ and \ \mathbf{A}_j(k) \ are \ both \ symbolic \\ 1 & if \ \mathbf{A}_i(k) \ or \ \mathbf{A}_j(k) \ is \ missing \end{cases} \tag{3}$$

where

$$R(\mathbf{A}_i(k), \mathbf{A}_j(k)) = \begin{cases} 0 & if \ \mathbf{A}_i(k) = \mathbf{A}_j(k) \\ 1 & otherwise \end{cases} \tag{4}$$

and *range* is used to normalize the distance of the numeric attribute.

The distance between an attributed graph corresponding to the grid i in image I_1 and an attributed graph corresponding to the grid j in image I_2 at the same scale is computed as [12]:

$$D(G_1(i), G_2(j)) = \frac{\bar{M}}{|\mathbf{M}|} + ||G_1(i)| - |G_2(j)|| \tag{5}$$

where $\bar{M}$ is the optimum graph matching cost of two attributed graphs $G_1(i)$ and $G_2(j)$, the $\mathbf{M}$ is the distance matrix of two attributed graphs that each element of matrix corresponds to the distance between a vertex of graph $G_1(i)$ and a vertex of graph $G_2(j)$. The node matching between two attributed graphs $G_1(i)$ and $G_2(i)$ is carry out by the hungarian method. Then the optimum graph matching cost $\bar{M}$ is computed by calculating the sum of the distance between two correspondence points. $|\mathbf{M}|$ is a normalization constant that refers to the number of matched vertices. $|G_1(i)|$ is the number of vertices in graph $G_1(i)$. The Eq. (5) represents the matching cost normalized by the matching size, and is effected by the sizes of the two graphs.

4   Multi-scale Attributed Graph Kernel Computation

When the distances between any two attributed graphs corresponding to two grids in the different images are computed at a scale, for convenience, we use the efficient hungarian method to find the optimal matched graphs correspond to two different images and get c distances $\{D_1, D_2, \cdots, D_c\}$ between the matched graphs. Inspired by the concept of graph kernel [24], which compares and counts the common subgraphs between two graphs. We compute a kernel by accumulating the distances between the matched graphs from two images, i.e.

$$\kappa(G_1^l, G_2^l) \propto exp(-\frac{\sum_{i=1}^{c} w_i \cdot D_i}{c}) \tag{6}$$

where w_i is the reciprocal of the total number of vertices of the matched graphs corresponding to two grids.

The final kernel is then the sum of all the level kernels,

$$K(G_1, G_2) = \sum_{l=0}^{L} \frac{1}{2^{L-l}} \kappa(G_1^l, G_2^l) \tag{7}$$

where the weight associated with level l is set to $\frac{1}{2^{L-l}}$, which are inversely proportional to the number of the grids which increases as the level increases. The multi-scale attributed graph match kernel we built is a positive semidefinite kernel matrix which can be used by SVM for classification. We summarize the proposed image categorization model in Algorithm 1.

Algorithm 1. The Multi-scale Attributed Graph Kernel algorithm.

Input: H category-labeled training images $\{I^1, I^2, \ldots, I^H\}$;

Output: The multi-scale attributed graph match kernel;

---

(1) Split each image into a sequence of grids at each scale $l \in (0, \ldots, L)$;

(2) Use the delaunay triangulation method to characterize the image structure at different scale, built the multi-scale attributed graphs;

(3) Remove the long edges and short edges of the constructed graphs;

(4) Compute the distance between the multi-scale graphs based on the node attributes, use the hungarian method to find the optimal matched graph;

(5) Build the multi-scale attributed graph match kernel by accumulating the distances between the multi-scale matched graphs from two images.

---

5 Experiments

In this section, we conduct comparative experiments on four benchmark datasets: Caltech 101 [27], Caltech 256 [28], Scene Categories [29], and Six Actions [30]. The performance of the proposed multi-scale attributed graph match kernel is evaluated and compared with traditional bag of words (BoW) [3], the spatial pyramids (SP) [5], BoVG-SP [14], fine-grained dictionary learning (FDL) [25] and word spatial arrangement (WSA) [32] respectively. The experimental results are summarized and analyzed. All experiments are implemented in Matlab 8.6 and executed on a Intel Core i7-6700 3.4 GHz CPU with 16 GB of memory and no effort made to optimize algorithm speed.

5.1 Dataset

The Scene Categories dataset is composed of fifteen scene categories. Each category has 200 to 400 images, and average image size is 300×250 pixels. In experiments, we randomly select 40 images of each class for training and 20 images per class for testing to evaluate the impact of different approaches in image categories.

The Caltech 101 dataset consists of a total of 9146 images, split between 101 different object categories. Each object category contains between 40 and 800 images on average. Each image is about 300×200 pixels in dimension. We use SIFT detector, a codebook of size 300 and 30 images per class for training and the rest for testing.

The Caltech 256 dataset is collected in a similar manner of Caltech 101 which split into a set of 256 object categories containing a total of 30607 images.

The Six Actions dataset collect about 2400 images in total for six action queries, each action class contains about 400 images and the size of each class are 200×200 pixels.

5.2   Baseline

This paper adopts the method in [3] as the baseline approach. The 128-D SIFT descriptors are used for feature extraction and the experiment uses K-means method to get the codebook of size 300. With the increase of scale l, the effect of characterizing image structure is better, but when the scale is larger than 3, the number of grids is too large, the complexity of the algorithm is greatly increased but the improvement of accuracy is limited. Thus the scale level of the multi-scale attributed graph is set to $L = 3$. The LIB-SVM [31] is employed for classification training.

5.3   Results

Table 1 shows the classification results on four datasets. As we can see our method and FDL produce the higher classification accuracy than other methods. Our method achieves highest recognition rates on Scene Categories, Caltech 101 and Six Actions dataset. Taking Scene Categories for example, it is clear that the classification accuracy of MsAG is 79.67%, which is higher than others.

Table 1. Categorization accuracies on four datasets

Dataset	BoW	SP	BOVG-SP	FDL	WSA	MsAG
Scene Categories	69.00%	73.33%	78.00%	82.96%	78.43%	79.67%
Caltech 101	26.43%	34.75%	38.75%	43.73%	39.74%	44.56%
Caltech 256	9.92%	15.70%	16.19%	19.93%	16.08%	18.52%
Six Actions	77.50%	82.50%	83.33%	85.67%	85.16%	86.02%

Figure 3 shows a confusion matrix between the fifteen scene categories, confusion occurs between the classes like kitchen, bedroom, living room, and also between some natural classes, such as coast and open country. The curves in Fig. 4 shows the classification accuracy for different training set sizes on Caltech 101. We partition the dataset into train images (5, 10, 15, 20, 25 and 30 images per class) and test images (limit the number of test images to 30 per class). The figure shows that the accuracy increases with the training size. Our approach has always been better than the other methods when the number increases from 5 to 30. In Fig. 5, the experimental results on Six Actions show that the results of our method is consistent with that on Caltech 101.

Then we compare the classification accuracies of each method for different codebook sizes, the FDL and WSA methods do not involve codebook, so we do

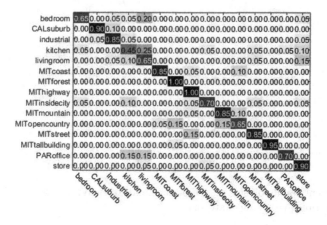

Fig. 3. Confusion matrix for the Scene Category dataset. Average classification rates for individual classes are listed along the diagonal. The entry in the ith row and j^{th} column is the percentage of images from class i that were misidentified as class j.

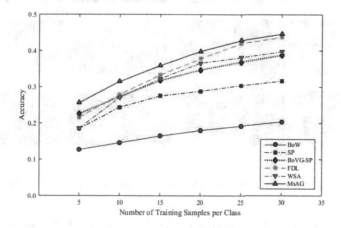

Fig. 4. Classification accuracy for different training set sizes on Caltech 101.

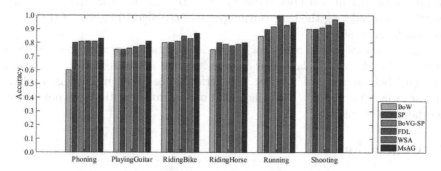

Fig. 5. Performance of BoW, SP, BoVG-SP, FDL, WSA and MsAG on Six Actions.

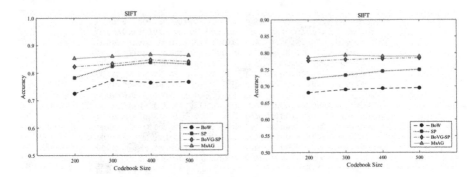

Fig. 6. Different codebook size on the performance of BoW, SP, BoVG-SP and MsAG on (a) Six Actions, (b) Scene Category.

Fig. 7. Partial results of image classification on the Six Actions database.

not compare them in this experiment. As shown on Fig. 6, classification accuracy increases when the codebook size increases from 200 to 500 and remains obtain similar results on both datasets when the size is lager than 300. Comparatively, considering the time consumption of the algorithm, we set the size of the codebook to 300.

Figure 7 shows partial results of image classification on Six Actions database using the MsAG, which show that our method had better recognition accuracy on each label category. Meanwhile, the performance of our method is stable in similar categories problem. We believe that our approach is still very competitive in other conditions.

6   Conclusion

In this paper, we explore the multi-scale attributed graph construction and matching kernel for image classification. This may provide a further step to utilize the structure information for image recognition. The comparisons on four standard datasets with five approaches, which are BoW, SP, FDL, WSA and BoVG-SP, show the efficiency of our approach.

Our work has been limited the simple edge construction using delaunay triangulation, there are several nature extension that can be taken advantage of. First, we can build different edge sets to form the local structure for image. Second, one can use various graph distance computation for more accurate graph matching.

Acknowledgment. The authors would like to thank the anonymous referees for their constructive comments which have helped improve the paper. The research is supported by the National Natural Science Foundation of China (Nos. 61502003, 71501002, 61472002 and 61671018), Natural Science Foundation of Anhui Province (No. 1608085QF133).

References

1. Penatti, O.A.B., Valle, E., da S. Torres, R.: Encoding spatial arrangement of visual words. In: San Martin, C., Kim, S.-W. (eds.) CIARP 2011. LNCS, vol. 7042, pp. 240–247. Springer, Heidelberg (2011). https://doi.org/10.1007/978-3-642-25085-9_28
2. Boureau, Y.L., Bach, F., Lecun, Y., Ponce, J.: Learning mid-level features for recognition. In: Proceedings of the IEEE Conference on Computer Vision and Pattern Recognition, vol. 26, pp. 2559–2566 (2010)
3. Sivic, J., Russell, B.C., Efros, A.A., et al.: Discovering objects and their location in images. In: Tenth IEEE International Conference on Computer Vision, vol. 1, pp. 370–377 (2005)
4. Lowe, D.G.: Distinctive image features from scale-invariant keypoints. Int. J. Comput. Vis. **60**(2), 91–110 (2004)
5. Lazebnik, S., Schmid, C., Ponce, J.: Beyond bags of features: spatial pyramid matching for recognizing natural scene categories. In: Proceedings of IEEE Conference on Computer Vision and Pattern Recognition, vol. 2, no. (1/2), pp. 2169–2178 (2006)
6. Sadeghi, F., Tappen, M.F.: Latent pyramidal regions for recognizing scenes. In: Fitzgibbon, A., Lazebnik, S., Perona, P., Sato, Y., Schmid, C. (eds.) ECCV 2012. LNCS, vol. 7576, pp. 228–241. Springer, Heidelberg (2012). https://doi.org/10.1007/978-3-642-33715-4_17
7. Yang, J., Yu, K., Gong, Y., et al.: Linear spatial pyramid matching using sparse coding for image classification. In: IEEE Conference on Computer Vision and Pattern Recognition, pp. 1794–1801 (2009)
8. Wang, J., Yang, J., Yu, K., et al.: Locality-constrained linear coding for image classification. In: IEEE Conference on Computer Vision and Pattern Recognition, vol. 119, pp. 3360–3367 (2010)
9. Cao, Y., Wang, C., Li, Z., et al.: Spatial-bag-of-features. In: IEEE Conference on Computer Vision and Pattern Recognition, vol. 238, pp. 3352–3359 (2010)
10. Silva, F.B., Werneck, R.D.O., Goldenstein, S., et al.: Graph-based bag-of-words for classification. In: International Conference on Pattern Recognition, vol. 74, pp. 266–285 (2018)

11. Bunke, H., Allermann, G.: Inexact graph matching for structural pattern recognition. In: International Conference on Pattern Recognition Letters, vol. 1, no. 4, pp. 245–253 (1983)

12. Jouili, S., Mili, I., Tabbone, S.: Attributed graph matching using local descriptions. In: Blanc-Talon, J., Philips, W., Popescu, D., Scheunders, P. (eds.) ACIVS 2009. LNCS, vol. 5807, pp. 89–99. Springer, Heidelberg (2009). https://doi.org/10.1007/978-3-642-04697-1_9

13. Silva, F.B., Tabbone, S., Torres, R.D.S.: Bog: a new approach for graph matching. In: International Conference on Pattern Recognition, pp. 82–87 (2014)

14. Silva, F.B., Goldenstein, S., Tabbone, S., et al.: Image classification based on bag of visual graphs. In: IEEE International Conference on Image Processing, vol. 2010, pp. 4312–4316 (2014)

15. Hashimoto, M., Cesar, R.M.: Object detection by keygraph classification. In: Torsello, A., Escolano, F., Brun, L. (eds.) GbRPR 2009. LNCS, vol. 5534, pp. 223–232. Springer, Heidelberg (2009). https://doi.org/10.1007/978-3-642-02124-4_23

16. Zhou, F., Torre, F.D.L.: Deformable graph matching. In: Proceedings of the IEEE Conference on Computer Vision and Pattern Recognition, vol. 9, pp. 2922–2929 (2013)

17. Lee, J., Cho, M., Lee, K.M.: Hyper-graph matching via reweighted random walks. In: Proceedings of the IEEE Conference on Computer Vision and Pattern Recognition, vol. 42, pp. 1633–1640 (2011)

18. Zhang, L., Hong, R., Gao, Y.: Image categorization by learning a propagated graphlet path. IEEE Trans. Neural Netw. Learn. Syst. **27**(3), 674–685 (2016)

19. Wu, J., Pan, S., Zhu, X., et al.: Multi-graph-view learning for complicated object classification. In: International Conference on Artificial Intelligence, pp. 3953–3959. AAAI Press (2015)

20. Mousavi, S.F., Safayani, M., Mirzaei, A., et al.: Hierarchical graph embedding in vector space by graph pyramid. In: International Conference on Pattern Recognition, vol. 61, pp. 245–254 (2017)

21. Nikolentzos, G., Meladianos, P., Vazirgiannis, M.: Matching node embeddings for graph similarity. In: Proceedings of the 31st Conference on Artificial Intelligence, AAAI, pp. 2429–2435 (2017)

22. Dong, W., Moses, C., Li, K.: Efficient k-nearest neighbor graph construction for generic similarity measures. In: International Conference on World Wide Web, pp. 577–586. ACM (2011)

23. Song, J., Gao, L., Zou, F.: Deep and fast: deep learning hashing with semi-supervised graph construction. Image Vis. Comput. **55**, 101–108 (2016)

24. Harchaoui, Z., Bach, F.: Image classification with segmentation graph kernels. In: Proceedings of IEEE Conference on Computer Vision and Pattern Recognition, vol. 76, pp. 1–8 (2007)

25. Shu, X., Tang, J., Qi, G.J.: Image classification with tailored fine-grained dictionaries. IEEE Trans. Circuits Syst. Video Technol. **28**(2), 454–467 (2018)

26. Grauman, K., Darrell, T.: The pyramid match kernels: discriminative classification with sets of image features. In: Proceedings of the Tenth IEEE International Conference on Computer Vision, vol. 2, pp. 1458–1465 (2005)

27. Li, F.F., Fergus, R., Perona, P.: Learning generative visual models from few training examples: an incremental Bayesian approach tested on 101 object categories. In: IEEE CVPR Workshop on Generative-Model Based Vision, vol. 106, no. 1, pp. 59–70 (2007)

28. Griffin, G., Holub, A., Perona, P.: Caltech-256 object category dataset. In: California Institute of Technology (2007)
29. Li, F.F., Perona, P.: A Bayesian hierarchical model for learning natural scene categories. In: Proceedings of IEEE Conference on Computer Vision and Pattern Recognition, pp. 524–531 (2005)
30. Li, P., Ma, J.: What is happening in a still picture? In: International Conference on Pattern Recognition, pp. 32–36 (2011)
31. Chang, C.C., Lin, C.J.: LIBSVM: a library for support vector machines. ACM Trans. Intell. Syst. Technol. **2**(3), 1–27 (2011)
32. Penatti, O.A.B., Silva, F.B., Valle, E., et al.: Visual word spatial arrangement for image retrieval and classification. In: International Conference on Pattern Recognition, vol. 47, no. 2, pp. 705–720 (2014)

Author Index

Printed in the United States
By Bookmasters

Soft Computing for Knowledge Discovery and Data Mining

Soft Computing for Knowledge Discovery and Data Mining

edited by

Oded Maimon
Tel-Aviv University
Israel

and

Lior Rokach
Ben-Gurion University of the Negev
Israel

Oded Maimon
Tel Aviv University
Dept.of Industrial Engineering
69978 TEL-AVIV
ISRAEL
maimon@eng.tau.ac.il

Lior Rokach
Ben-Gurion University
Dept. of Information System Engineering
84105 BEER-SHEVA
ISRAEL
liorrk@bgu.ac.il

Soft Computing for Knowledge Discovery and Data Mining
Edited by Oded Maimon and Lior Rokach

ISBN 978-1-4419-4351-4   e-ISBN 978-0-387-69935-6

Printed on acid-free paper.

9 8 7 6 5 4 3 2 1

springer.com

Preface

The information age has made it easy to store large amounts of data. Data mining is a new and exciting field that tries to solve the crisis of information overload by exploring large and complex bodies of data in order to discover useful patterns. It is extreme importance because it enables modeling and knowledge extraction from abundance data availability. Therefore theoreticians and practitioners are continually seeking techniques to make the process more efficient, cost-effective and accurate. Among the more promising technique that have emerged in recent years are soft computing methods such as fuzzy sets, artificial neural networks, genetic algorithms. These techniques exploit a tolerance for imprecision, uncertainty and partial truth to achieve tractability, robustness and low cost solutions. This book shows that the soft computing methods extend the envelope of problems that data mining can solve efficiently.

This book presents a comprehensive discussion of the state of the art in data mining along with the main soft computing techniques behind it. In addition to presenting a general theory of data mining, the book provides an in-depth examination of core soft computing algorithms.

To help interested researchers and practitioners who are not familiar with the field, the book starts with a gentle introduction to data mining and knowledge discovery in databases (KDD) and prepares the reader for the next chapters. The rest of the book is organized into four parts. The first three parts devoted to the principal constituents of soft computing: neural networks, evolutionary algorithms and fuzzy logic. The last part compiles the recent advances in soft computing and data mining.

This book was written to provide investigators in the fields of information systems, engineering, computer science, statistics and management, with a profound source for the role of soft computing in data mining. In addition, social sciences, psychology, medicine, genetics, and other fields that are interested in solving complicated problems can much benefit from this book. The book can also serve as a reference book for graduate / advanced undergraduate level courses in data mining and machine learning. Practitioners among the readers may be particularly interested in the descriptions of real-world data mining projects performed with soft-computing.

We would like to thank all authors for their valuable contributions. We would like to express our special thanks to Susan Lagerstrom-Fife and Sharon Palleschi of Springer for working closely with us during the production of this book.

Tel-Aviv, Israel   *Oded Maimon*
Beer-Sheva, Israel   *Lior Rokach*

July 2007

Contents

List of Contributors

Ajith Abraham
Center of Excellence for Quantifiable
Quality of Service (Q2S),
Norwegian University of Science and
Technology,
Trondheim, Norway
ajith.abraham@ieee.org

Arnulfo Azcarraga
College of Computer Studies,
De La Salle University, Manila,
The Philippines
azcarragaa
@canlubang.dlsu.edu.ph

**Ricardo José Gabrielli Barreto
Campello**
Instituto de Ciências Matemáticas e
de Computação,
Universidade de São Paulo
campello@icmc.usp.br

**André Carlos Ponce de Leon
Ferreira de Carvalho**
Instituto de Ciê
ncias Matemá
ticas e de Computação
Universidade de São Paulo
andre@icmc.usp.br

Jorge Casillas
Dept. of Computer Science and
Artificial Intelligence,
University of Granada,
Spain
casillas@decsai.ugr.es

Yixin Chen
Dept. of Computer and Information
Science
The University of Mississippi
MS 38655
ychen@cs.olemiss.edu

Hong Cheng
University of Illinois at Urbana-
Champaign
hcheng3@cs.uiuc.edu

Swagatam Das
Dept. of Electronics and Telecommu-
nication Engineering,
Jadavpur University,
Kolkata 700032,
India.

Christos Dimou
Electrical and Computer Engineering
Dept.
Aristotle University of Thessaloniki,
54 124, Thessaloniki,
Greece
cdimou@issel.ee.auth.gr

Alex A. Freitas
Computing Laboratory,
University of Kent,
Canterbury, Kent, CT2 7NF, UK
A.A.Freitas@kent.ac.uk

Jiawei Han
University of Illinois at Urbana-
Champaign
hanj@cs.uiuc.edu

Eduardo Raul Hruschka
eduardo.hruschka
@pesquisador.cnpq.br

Ming-Huei Hsieh
Dept. of International Business,
National Taiwan University,
Taiwan
mhhsieh@management.ntu.edu.tw

Jonathan Lawry
Artificial Intelligence Group,
Department of Engineering Mathe-
matics,
University of Bristol,
BS8 1TR, UK.
j.lawry@bris.ac.uk

Ana Carolina Lorena
Centro de Matemática,
Computação e Cognição
Universidade Federal do ABC
Rua Catequese, 242,
Santo André, SP, Brazil
ana.lorena@ufabc.edu.br

Oded Maimon
Dept. of Industrial Engineering
Tel-Aviv University
Israel
maimon@eng.tau.ac.il

Francisco J. Martínez-López
Dept. of Marketing, University of
Granada, Spain
fjmlopez@ugr.es

Murilo Coelho Naldi
Instituto de Ciê
ncias Matemá
ticas e de Computação
Universidade de São Paulo
murilocn@icmc.usp.br

Shan-Ling Pan
School of Computing,
National University of Singapore,
Singapore
pansl@comp.nus.edu.sg

Gisele L. Pappa
Computing Laboratory
University of Kent
Canterbury, Kent, CT2 7NF, UK
glp6@kent.ac.uk

Huy Nguyen Anh Pham
Dept. of Computer Science,
298 Coates Hall,
Louisiana State University,
Baton Rouge, LA 70803
hpham15@lsu.edu

Zengchang Qin
Berkeley Initiative in Soft Comput-
ing (BISC),
Computer Science Division,
EECS Department,
University of California,
Berkeley, CA 94720, US.

zqin@eecs.berkeley.edu

Lior Rokach
Dept. of Information System Engineering,
Ben-Gurion University,
Israel
liorrk@bgu.ac.il

Sandip Roy
Dept. of Computer Science and Engineering,
Asansol Engineering College,
Asansol-713304, India.

Alon Schclar
School of Computer Science,
Tel Aviv University,
Tel Aviv 69978,
Israel
shekler@post.tau.ac.il

Rudy Setiono
School of Computing,
National University of Singapore,
Singapore
rudys@comp.nus.edu.sg

Andreas L. Symeonidis
Electrical and Computer Engineering
Dept.
Aristotle University of Thessaloniki,
54 124, Thessaloniki,
Greece
asymeon@iti.gr

Pericles A. Mitkas
Electrical and Computer Engineering
Dept.
Aristotle University of Thessaloniki,
54 124, Thessaloniki,
Greece
mitkas@eng.auth.gr

Evangelos Triantaphyllou
Dept. of Computer Science,
298 Coates Hall,
Louisiana State University,
Baton Rouge, LA 70803
trianta@lsu.edu

Philip S. Yu
IBM T. J. Watson Research Center
psyu@us.ibm.com

G. Peter Zhang
Georgia State University,
Dept. of Managerial Sciences
gpzhang@gsu.edu

Introduction to Soft Computing for Knowledge Discovery and Data Mining

Oded Maimon[1] and Lior Rokach[2]

[1] Department of Industrial Engineering, Tel-Aviv University, Ramat-Aviv 69978, Israel,
maimon@eng.tau.ac.il
[2] Department of Information System Engineering, Ben-Gurion University, Beer-Sheba, Israel,
liorrk@bgu.ac.il

Summary. In this chapter we introduce the Soft Computing areas for Data Mining and the Knowledge Discovery Process, discuss the need for plurality of methods, and present the book organization and abstracts.

1 Introduction

Data Mining is the science, art and technology of exploring data in order to discover insightful unknown patterns. It is a part of the overall process of Knowledge Discovery in Databases (KDD). The accessibility and abundance of information today makes data mining a matter of considerable importance and necessity.

Soft computing is a collection of new techniques in artificial intelligence, which exploit the tolerance for imprecision, uncertainty and partial truth to achieve tractability, robustness and low solution cost. Given the history and recent growth of the field, it is not surprising that several mature soft computing methods are now available to the practitioner, including: fuzzy logic, artificial neural networks, genetic algorithms, and swarm intelligence. The aims of this book are to present and explain the important role of soft computing methods in data mining and knowledge discovery.

The unique contributions of this book is in the introduction of soft computing as a viable approach for data mining theory and practice, the detailed descriptions of novel soft-computing approaches in data mining, and the illustrations of various applications solved in soft computing techniques, including: Manufacturing, Medical, Banking, Insurance, Business Intelligence and others. The book does not include some of the most standard techniques in Data Mining, such as Decision Trees (the reader is welcome to our new book, from 2007, dedicated entirely to Decision Trees). The book include the leading soft computing methods, though for volume reasons it could not cover all methods, and there are further emerging techniques, such as fractal based data mining (a topic of our current research).

Since the information age, the accumulation of data has become easier and storing it inexpensive. It has been estimated that the amount of stored information doubles less than twenty months. Unfortunately, as the amount of electronically stored information increases, the ability to understand and make use of it does not keep pace with its growth. Data Mining is a term coined to describe the process of sifting through large databases for interesting patterns and relationships. The studies today aim at evidence-based modeling and analysis, as is the leading practice in medicine, finance, intelligence and many other fields. Evidently, in the presence of the vast techniques' repertoire and the complexity and diversity of the explored domains, one real challenge today in the data mining field is to know how to utilize this repertoire in order to achieve the best results. The book shows that the soft computing methods extend the envelope of problems that data mining can solve efficiently. The techniques of soft computing are important for researchers in the fields of data mining, machine learning, databases and information systems, engineering, computer science and statistics.

This book was written to provide investigators in the fields of information systems, engineering, computer science, statistics and management, with a profound source for the role of soft computing in data mining. In addition, social sciences, psychology, medicine, genetics, and other fields that are interested in solving complicated problems can much benefit from this book. Practitioners among the readers may be particularly interested in the descriptions of real-world data mining projects performed with soft computing.

The material of this book has been taught by the authors in graduate and undergraduate courses at Tel-Aviv University and Ben-Gurion University. The book can also serve as a reference book for graduate and advanced undergraduate level courses in data mining and machine learning.

In this introductory chapter we briefly present the framework and overall knowledge discovery process in the next two sections, and then the logic and organization of this book, with brief description of each chapter.

2 The Knowledge Discovery process

This book is about methods, which are the core of the Knowledge Discovery process. For completion we briefly present here the process steps. The knowledge discovery process is iterative and interactive, consisting of nine steps.

Note that the process is iterative at each step, meaning that moving back to previous steps may be required. The process has many "artistic" aspects in the sense that one cannot present one formula or make a complete taxonomy for the right choices for each step and application type. Thus it is required to understand the process and the different needs and possibilities in each step.

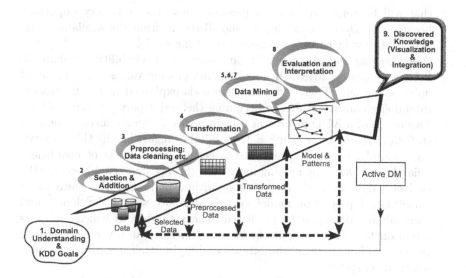

Fig. 1. The Process of Knowledge Discovery in Databases.

The process starts with determining the KDD goals, and "ends" with the implementation of the discovered knowledge. Then the loop is closed - the Active Data Mining part starts. As a result, changes can be made in the application domain (such as offering different features to mobile phone users in order to reduce churning). This closes the loop, and the effects are then measured on the new data repositories, and the KDD process is launched again.

Following is a brief description of the nine-step KDD process, starting with a managerial step:

1. Developing an understanding of the application domain: This is the initial preparatory step. It prepares the scene for understanding what should be done with the many decisions (about transformations, algorithms, representation, etc.). The people who are in charge of a KDD project need to understand and define the goals of the end-user and the environment in which the knowledge discovery process will take place (including relevant prior knowledge). As the KDD process proceeds, there may be even a revision of this step.

   Having understood the KDD goals, the preprocessing of the data starts, defined in the next three steps.

2. Selecting and creating a data set on which discovery will be performed: Having defined the goals, the data that will be used for the knowledge discovery should be determined. This includes finding out what data is available, obtaining additional necessary data, and then integrating all the data for the knowledge discovery into one data set, including the attributes

that will be considered for the process. This process is very important because the Data Mining learns and discovers from the available data. This is the evidence base for constructing the models.

3. Preprocessing and cleansing: In this stage, data reliability is enhanced. It includes data clearing, such as handling missing values and removal of noise or outliers. There are many methods explained in the handbook, from doing almost nothing to becoming the major part (in terms of time consumed) of a KDD project in certain projects. It may involve complex statistical methods or using a Data Mining algorithm in this context. For example, if one suspects that a certain attribute is of insufficient reliability or has many missing data, then this attribute could become the goal of a data mining supervised algorithm, or finding the centroids of clustering. A prediction model for this attribute will be developed, and then missing data can be predicted. The extension to which one pays attention to this level depends on many factors. In any case, studying the aspects is important and often revealing by itself, regarding complex information systems.

4. Data transformation: In this stage, the generation of better data for the data mining is prepared and developed. Methods here include dimension reduction (such as feature selection and record sampling), and attribute transformation (such as discretization of numerical attributes and functional transformation). This step can be crucial for the success of the entire KDD project, and it is usually very project-specific. For example, in medical examinations, the quotient of attributes may often be the most important factor, and not each one by itself. In marketing, we may need to consider effects beyond our control as well as efforts and temporal issues (such as studying the effect of advertising accumulation). However, even if we do not use the right transformation at the beginning, we may obtain a surprising effect that hints to us about the transformation needed (in the next iteration). Thus the KDD process reflects upon itself and leads to an understanding of the transformation needed.

Having completed the above four steps, the following four steps are related to the Data Mining part, where the focus is on the algorithmic aspects employed for each project:

5. Choosing the appropriate Data Mining task: We are now ready to decide on which type and approach of Data Mining to use, for example, classification, regression, or clustering. This mostly depends on the KDD goals, and also on the previous steps. There are two major goals in Data Mining: prediction and description. Prediction is often referred to as supervised Data Mining, while descriptive Data Mining includes the unsupervised and visualization aspects of Data Mining. Most Data Mining techniques are based on inductive learning, where a model is constructed explicitly or implicitly by generalizing from a sufficient number of training examples. The underlying assumption of the inductive approach is that the trained

model is applicable to future cases. The strategy also takes into account the level of meta-learning for the particular set of available data.

6. Choosing the Data Mining algorithm: Having the strategy, we now decide on the tactics. This stage includes selecting the specific method to be used for searching patterns (including multiple inducers). For example, in considering precision versus understandability, the former is better with neural networks, while the latter is better with decision trees. For each strategy of meta-learning there are several possibilities of how it can be accomplished. Meta-learning focuses on explaining what causes a Data Mining algorithm to be successful or not in a particular problem. Thus, this approach attempts to understand the conditions under which a Data Mining algorithm is most appropriate. Each algorithm has parameters and tactics of learning (such as ten-fold cross-validation or another division for training and testing).

7. Employing the Data Mining algorithm: Finally the implementation of the Data Mining algorithm is reached. In this step we might need to employ the algorithm several times until a satisfied result is obtained, for instance by tuning the algorithm's control parameters, such as the minimum number of instances in a single leaf of a decision tree.

8. Evaluation: In this stage we evaluate and interpret the mined patterns (rules, reliability, etc.), with respect to the goals defined in the first step. Here we consider the preprocessing steps with respect to their effect on the Data Mining algorithm results (for example, adding features in Step 4 and repeating from there). This step focuses on the comprehensibility and usefulness of the induced model. In this step the discovered knowledge is also documented for further usage.

The last step is the usage and overall feedback on the patterns and discovery results obtained by the Data Mining:

9. Using the discovered knowledge: We are now ready to incorporate the knowledge into another system for further action. The knowledge becomes active in the sense that we may make changes to the system and measure the effects. Actually the success of this step determines the effectiveness of the entire KDD process. There are many challenges in this step, such as loosing the "laboratory conditions" under which we have operated. For instance, the knowledge was discovered from a certain static snapshot (usually sample) of the data, but now the data becomes dynamic. Data structures may change (certain attributes become unavailable), and the data domain may be modified (such as, an attribute may have a value that was not assumed before).

3 The need for plurality of methods

Data Mining methods are becoming part of general purpose Integrated Information Technology (IIT) software packages. Starting from the data sources (such as operational databases, semi- and non-structured data and reports, Internet sites etc.), then the tier of the data warehouse, followed by OLAP (On Line Analytical Processing) servers and concluding with analysis tools, where Data Mining tools are the most advanced.

We can naively distinguish among three levels of analysis. The simplest one is achieved by report generators (for example, presenting all claims that occurred because of a certain cause last year, such as car theft). We then proceed to OLAP multi-level analysis (for example presenting the ten towns where there was the highest increase of vehicle theft in the last month as compared to with the month before). Finally a complex analysis is carried out for discovering the patterns that predict car thefts in these cities, and what might occur if anti theft devices were installed. The latter is based on modeling of the phenomena, where the first two levels are ways of data aggregation and fast manipulation.

Empirical comparison of the performance of different approaches and their variants in a wide range of application domains has shown that each performs best in some, but not all, domains. This phenomenon is known as the selective superiority problem, which means, in our case, that no induction approach or algorithm can be the best in all possible domains. The reason is that each algorithm contains an explicit or implicit bias that leads it to prefer certain generalizations over others, and it will be successful only as long as this bias matches the characteristics of the application domain.

Results have demonstrated the existence and correctness of this "no free lunch theorem". If one inducer is better than another in some domains, then there are necessarily other domains in which this relationship is reversed. This implies in KDD that for a given problem a certain approach can yield more knowledge from the same data than other approaches.

In many application domains, the generalization error (on the overall domain, not just the one spanned in the given data set) of even the best methods is far above the training set, and the question of whether it can be improved, and if so how, is an open and important one. Part of the answer to this question is to determine the minimum error achievable by any classifier in the application domain (known as the optimal Bayes error). If existing classifiers do not reach this level, new approaches are needed. Although this problem has received considerable attention, no generally reliable method has so far been demonstrated. This is one of the challenges of the DM research – not only to solve it, but even to quantify and understand it better. Heuristic methods can then be compared absolutely and not just against each other.

A subset of this generalized study is the question of which approach and inducer to use for a given problem. To be even more specific, the performance measure need to be defined appropriately for each problem. Though there are some commonly accepted measures it is not enough. For example, if the analyst is looking for accuracy only, one solution is to try each one in turn, and by estimating the generalization error, to choose the one that appears to perform best. Another approach, known as multi-strategy learning, attempts to combine two or more different paradigms in a single algorithm.

The dilemma of what method to choose becomes even greater if other factors such as comprehensibility are taken into consideration. For instance, for a specific domain, neural networks may outperform decision trees in accuracy. However from the comprehensibility aspect, decision trees are considered superior. In other words, in this case even if the researcher knows that neural network is more accurate, the dilemma of what methods to use still exists (or maybe to combine methods for their separate strength).

Induction is one of the central problems in many disciplines such as machine learning, pattern recognition, and statistics. However the feature that distinguishes Data Mining from traditional methods is its scalability to very large sets of varied types of input data. Scalability means working in an environment of high number of records, high dimensionality, and a high number of classes or heterogeneousness. Nevertheless, trying to discover knowledge in real life and large databases introduces time and memory problems.

As large databases have become the norms in many fields (including astronomy, molecular biology, finance, marketing, health care, and many others), the use of Data Mining to discover patterns in them has become potentially very beneficial for the enterprise. Many companies are staking a large part of their future on these "Data Mining" applications, and turn to the research community for solutions to the fundamental problems they encounter.

While a very large amount of available data used to be the dream of any data analyst, nowadays the synonym for "very large" has become "terabyte" or "pentabyte", a barely imaginable volume of information. Information-intensive organizations (like telecom companies and financial institutions) are expected to accumulate pentabyte of raw data every one to two years.

High dimensionality of the input (that is, the number of attributes) increases the size of the search space in an exponential manner (known as the "Curse of Dimensionality"), and thus increases the chance that the inducer will find spurious classifiers that in general are not valid. There are several approaches for dealing with a high number of records including: sampling methods, aggregation, massively parallel processing, and efficient storage methods. This book presents some of the approaches in this direction.

4 The organization of the book

The book has sixteen chapters divided into four main parts, where the first three address the methods and topics that are most identified with soft computing, and then the last part adds advanced and promising methods and areas:

I. Neural network methods: Chapters 2 to 3
II. Evolutionary methods: Chapters 4 to 7

III. Fuzzy logic methods: Chapters 8 to 11
IV. Advanced soft computing methods and areas: Chapters 12 to 16 Including: Swarm intelligence (12), diffusion process (13), and agent technology (14); and the areas of: approximate frequent item-set mining (15), and finally the impact of over-fitting and over-generalization on the classification accuracy in Data Mining (16).

In the following, edited abstracts of the chapters in the book are presented, for the reader map and convenience:

4.1 Neural network methods

The first methodology addressed in the book is **Neural Networks**, which have become elaborated important tools for data mining. Chapter 2 provides an overview of neural network models and their applications to data mining tasks. It also provides historical development of the field of neural networks and present three important classes of neural models including feed forward multilayer networks, Hopfield networks, and Kohonen's self-organizing maps. Modeling issues and applications of these models for data mining are discussed as well.

Then Chapter 3 continues in this direction by specifically addressing **Self-Organizing Maps** (SOMs). SOMs have been useful in gaining insights about the information content of large volumes of data in various data mining applications. As a special form of neural networks, they have been attractive as a data mining tool because they are able to extract information from data even with very little user-intervention (though some is needed). This chapter proposes a methodical and semi-automatic SOM labeling procedure that does not require a set of labeled patterns, and shows an effective alternative. The effectiveness of the method is demonstrated on a data mining application involving customer-profiling based on an international market segmentation study.

4.2 Evolutionary methods

A new family of methods starts in Chapter 4 with a review of **Evolutionary Algorithms** (EAs) for Data Mining. Evolutionary Algorithms are stochastic search algorithms inspired by the process of neo-Darwinian evolution. The motivation for applying EAs to data mining is that they are robust, adaptive search techniques that perform a global search in the solution space. This chapter first presents a brief overview of EAs, focusing mainly on two kinds of EAs, viz. Genetic Algorithms (GAs) and Genetic Programming (GP). Then the chapter reviews the main concepts and principles used by EAs designed for solving several data mining tasks, namely: discovery of classification rules, clustering, attribute selection and attribute construction. Finally, it discusses

Multi-Objective EAs, based on the concept of Pareto dominance, and their use in several data mining tasks.

Then Chapter 5 continues this topic by specifically addressing **Genetic Clustering** for Data Mining. Genetic Algorithms (GAs) have been successfully applied to several complex data analysis problems in a wide range of domains, such as image processing, bioinformatics, and crude oil analysis. The need for organizing data into categories of similar objects has made the task of clustering increasingly important to those domains. This chapter presents a survey of the use of GAs for clustering applications. A variety of encoding (chromosome representation) approaches, fitness functions, and genetic operators are described, all of them customized to solve problems in such an application context.

Chapter 6 addresses the discovering of new rule by induction algorithms with **Grammar-Based Genetic Programming**. Rule induction is a data mining technique used to extract classification rules of the form IF (conditions) THEN (predicted class) from data. The majority of the rule induction algorithms found in the literature follow the sequential covering strategy, which essentially induces one rule at a time until (almost) all the training data is covered by the induced rule set. This strategy describes a basic algorithm composed by several key elements, which can be modified to generate new and better rule induction algorithms. With this in mind, this work proposes the use of a **Grammar-based Genetic Programming** (GGP) algorithm to automatically discover new sequential covering algorithms. The proposed system is evaluated using 20 data sets, and the automatically-discovered rule induction algorithms are compared with four well-known human-designed rule induction algorithms. Results showed that the GGP system is a promising approach to effectively discover new sequential covering algorithms

Another general aspect of data mining issues is introduced in Chapter 7 with **Evolutionary Design** of code-matrices for multi-class problems. Given a dataset containing data whose classes are known, Machine Learning algorithms can be employed for the induction of a classifier able to predict the class of new data from the same domain, performing the desired discrimination. Several machine learning techniques are originally conceived for the solution of problems with only two classes. In multi-class applications, an alternative frequently employed is to divide the original problem into binary subtasks, whose results are then combined. The decomposition can be generally represented by a code-matrix, where each row corresponds to a codeword assigned for one class and the columns represent the binary classifiers employed. This chapter presents a survey on techniques for multi-class problems code-matrix design. It also shows how evolutionary techniques can be employed to solve this problem.

4.3 Fuzzy logic methods

The role of **Fuzzy Sets** in Data Mining is introduced in Chapter 8. This chapter discusses how fuzzy logic extends the envelop of the main data mining tasks: clustering, classification, regression and association rules. The chapter begins by presenting a formulation of the data mining using fuzzy logic attributes. Then, for each task, the chapter provides a survey of the main algorithms and a detailed description (i.e. pseudo-code) of the most popular algorithms.

Continuing with the same area Chapter 9 addresses **Support Vector Machines and Fuzzy Systems.** Fuzzy set theory and fuzzy logic provide tools for handling uncertainties in data mining tasks. To design a fuzzy rule-based classification system (fuzzy classifier) with good generalization ability in a high dimensional feature space has been an active research topic for a long time. As a powerful machine learning approach for data mining and pattern recognition problems, support vector machine (SVM) is known to have good generalization ability. More importantly, an SVM can work very well on a high (or even infinite) dimensional feature space. This chapter presents a survey of the connection between fuzzy classifiers and kernel machines.

KDD in Marketing with **Genetic Fuzzy Systems** is addressed in Chapter 10. This chapter presents a new methodology to marketing (causal) modeling. Specifically it is applied to a consumer behavior model used for the experimentation. The characteristics of the problem (with uncertain data and available knowledge from a marketing expert) and the multi objective optimization make genetic fuzzy systems a good tool for this problem type. By applying this methodology useful information patterns (fuzzy rules) are obtained, which help to better understand the relations among the elements of the marketing system being analyzed (consumer model in this case).

In Chapter 11 the fuzzy theme is continued with a **Framework for Modeling with Words.** The learning of transparent models is an important and neglected area of data mining. The data mining community has tended to focus on algorithm accuracy with little emphasis on the knowledge representation framework. However, the transparency of a model will help practitioners greatly in understanding the trends and idea hidden behind the system. In this chapter a random set based knowledge representation framework for learning linguistic models is introduced. This framework is referred to as label semantics and a number of data mining algorithms are proposed. In this framework, a vague concept is modeled by a probability distribution over a set of appropriate fuzzy labels, which is called as mass assignment. The idea of mass assignment provides a probabilistic approach for modeling uncertainty based on pre-defined fuzzy labels.

4.4 Advanced soft computing methods and areas

A new soft computing methodology is introduced in Chapter 12, which addresses **Swarm Intelligence** algorithms for data clustering. Data mining tasks require fast and accurate partitioning of huge datasets, which may come with a variety of attributes or features. This, in turn, imposes severe computational requirements on the relevant clustering techniques. A family of bio-inspired algorithms, well-known as Swarm Intelligence (SI) has recently emerged that meets these requirements and has successfully been applied to a number of real world clustering problems. This chapter explores the role of SI in clustering different kinds of datasets. It finally describes a new SI technique for partitioning any dataset into an optimal number of groups through one run of optimization. Computer simulations undertaken in this research have also been provided to demonstrate the effectiveness of the proposed algorithm.

In Chapter 13 another type of method for soft computing is revealed, namely **Diffusion method**. This chapter describes a natural framework based on diffusion processes for the multi-scale analysis of high-dimensional data-sets. Many fields of research deal with high-dimensional data sets. Hyper spectral images in remote sensing and in hyper-spectral microscopy, transactions in banking monitoring systems are just a few examples for this type of sets. Revealing the geometric structure of these data-sets is a preliminary step to facilitate their efficient processing. Often, only a small number of parameters govern the structure of the data-set. This number is the true dimension of the data-set and is the motivation to reduce the dimensionality of the set. Dimensionality reduction algorithms try to discover the true dimension of a data set. The diffusion process scheme enables the description of the geometric structures of such sets by utilizing the Newtonian paradigm according to which a global description of a system can be derived by the aggregation of local transitions. Specifically, a Markov process is used to describe a random walk on the data set. The spectral properties of the Markov matrix that is associated with this process are used to embed the data-set in a low-dimensional space. This scheme also facilitates the parameterization of a data-set when the high dimensional data-set is not accessible and only a pair-wise similarity matrix is at hand.

Agent Technology as applied to Data Mining is introduced in Chapter 14. Today's applications are required to extract knowledge from large, often distributed, repositories of text, multimedia or hybrid content. The nature of this quest makes it impossible to use traditional deterministic computing techniques. Instead, various soft computing techniques are employed to meet the challenge for more sophisticated solutions in knowledge discovery. Most notably, Data Mining (DM) is thought of as one of the state-of-the-art paradigms. DM produces useful patterns and associations from large data repositories that can later be used as *knowledge nuggets*, within the context of any application. Individual facets of knowledge discovery, introduced by DM techniques, often need to be orchestrated, integrated and presented to end users in a unified way. Moreover, knowledge has to be exploited and embodied in autonomous software for learning purposes and, hence, a more increased performance. Agent Technology (AT) proves to be a promising paradigm that is suitable for modeling and implementing the unification of DM tasks, as well as for providing autonomous entity models that dynamically incorporate and use existing knowledge. Indeed, a plethora of multi-agent systems (MAS) and other agent-related solutions for knowledge-based systems can be found in the literature, and more specifically in the area of agent-based DM, as it is explained in detail in this chapter.

The issue of error-tolerant item-set is presented in Chapter 15, which addresses **Approximate Frequent Item-set Mining** in the presence of random noise. Frequent item-set mining has been a focused theme in data mining research and an important first step in the analysis of data arising in a broad range of applications. The traditional exact model for frequent item-set requires that every item occur in each supporting transaction. However, real application data is usually subject to random noise or measurement error, which poses new challenges for the efficient discovery of frequent item-set from the noisy data. Mining approximate frequent item-set in the presence of noise involves two key issues: the definition of a noise-tolerant mining model and the design of an efficient mining algorithm. This chapter gives an overview of the approximate item-set mining algorithms in the presence of random noise and examines several noise-tolerant mining approaches.

The impact of over fitting and over generalization on the classification accuracy in Data Mining is addressed in, Chapter 16, the last chapter of the book. Many classification studies often times conclude with a summary table, which presents performance results of applying various data mining approaches on different datasets. No single method outperforms all methods all the time. Further-more, the performance of a classification method in terms of its false-positive and false-negative rates may be totally unpredictable. Attempts to minimize any of the previous two rates, may lead to an increase on the other rate. If the model allows for new data to be deemed as unclassifiable when there is not adequate information to classify them, then it is possible for the previous two error rates to be very low. However, at the same time, the rate of having unclassifiable new examples may be very high. The root to the above critical problem is the over fitting and overgeneralization behaviors of a given classification approach when it is processing a particular dataset.

Although the above situation is of fundamental importance to data mining, it has not been studied from a comprehensive point of view. Thus, this chapter analyzes the above issues in depth. It also proposes a new approach called the Homogeneity-Based Algorithm (or HBA) for optimally controlling the previous three error rates. This is done by first formulating an optimization problem. The key development in this chapter is based on a special way for analyzing the space of the training data and then partitioning it according to the data density of different regions of this space. Next, the classification task is pursued based on the previous partitioning of the training space. In this way, the previous three error rates can be controlled in a comprehensive manner. Some preliminary computational results seem to indicate that the proposed approach has a significant potential to fill in a critical gap in current data mining methodologies.

Part I

Neural Network Methods

Neural Networks For Data Mining

G. Peter Zhang

Georgia State University,
Department of Managerial Sciences,
gpzhang@gsu.edu

Summary. Neural networks have become standard and important tools for data mining. This chapter provides an overview of neural network models and their applications to data mining tasks. We provide historical development of the field of neural networks and present three important classes of neural models including feedforward multilayer networks, Hopfield networks, and Kohonen's self-organizing maps. Modeling issues and applications of these models for data mining are discussed.

Key words: neural networks, regression, classification, prediction, clustering

1 Introduction

Neural networks or artificial neural networks are an important class of tools for quantitative modeling. They have enjoyed considerable popularity among researchers and practitioners over the last 20 years and have been successfully applied to solve a variety of problems in almost all areas of business, industry, and science (Widrow, Rumelhart & Lehr, 1994). Today, neural networks are treated as a standard data mining tool and used for many data mining tasks such as pattern classification, time series analysis, prediction, and clustering. In fact, most commercial data mining software packages include neural networks as a core module.

Neural networks are computing models for information processing and are particularly useful for identifying the fundamental relationship among a set of variables or patterns in the data. They grew out of research in artificial intelligence; specifically, attempts to mimic the learning of the biological neural networks especially those in human brain which may contain more than 10^{11} highly interconnected neurons. Although the *artificial* neural networks discussed in this chapter are extremely simple abstractions of biological systems and are very limited in size, ability, and power comparing biological neural networks, they do share two very important characteristics: 1) parallel processing of information and 2) learning and generalizing from experience.

The popularity of neural networks is due to their powerful modeling capability for pattern recognition. Several important characteristics of neural networks make them suitable and valuable for data mining. First, as opposed to the traditional model-based methods, neural networks do not require several unrealistic *a priori* assumptions about the underlying data generating process and specific model structures. Rather, the modeling process is highly adaptive and the model is largely determined by the characteristics or patterns the network learned from data in the learning process. This data-driven approach is ideal for real world data mining problems where data are plentiful but the meaningful patterns or underlying data structure are yet to be discovered and impossible to be pre-specified.

Second, the mathematical property of the neural network in accurately approximating or representing various complex relationships has been well established and supported by theoretic work (Chen and Chen, 1995; Cybenko, 1989; Hornik, Stinchcombe, and White 1989). This universal approximation capability is powerful because it suggests that neural networks are more general and flexible in modeling the underlying data generating process than traditional fixed-form modeling approaches. As many data mining tasks such as pattern recognition, classification, and forecasting can be treated as function mapping or approximation problems, accurate identification of the underlying function is undoubtedly critical for uncovering the hidden relationships in the data.

Third, neural networks are nonlinear models. As real world data or relationships are inherently nonlinear, traditional linear tools may suffer from significant biases in data mining. Neural networks with their nonlinear and nonparametric nature are more cable for modeling complex data mining problems.

Finally, neural networks are able to solve problems that have imprecise patterns or data containing incomplete and noisy information with a large number of variables. This fault tolerance feature is appealing to data mining problems because real data are usually dirty and do not follow clear probability structures that typically required by statistical models.

This chapter aims to provide readers an overview of neural networks used for data mining tasks. First, we provide a short review of major historical developments in neural networks. Then several important neural network models are introduced and their applications to data mining problems are discussed.

2 A Brief History

Historically, the field of neural networks is benefited by many researchers in diverse areas such as biology, cognitive science, computer science, mathematics, neuroscience, physics, and psychology. The advancement of the filed, however, is not evolved steadily, but rather through periods of dramatic progress and enthusiasm and periods of skepticism and little progress.

The work of McCulloch and Pitts (1943) is the basis of modern view of neural networks and is often treated as the origin of neural network field. Their research is the first attempt to use mathematical model to describe how a neuron works. The main feature of their neuron model is that a weighted sum of input signals is compared to a threshold to determine the neuron output. They showed that simple neural networks can compute any arithmetic or logical function.

In 1949, Hebb (1949) published his book "The Organization of Behavior." The main premise of this book is that behavior can be explained by the action of neurons. He proposed one of the first learning laws that postulated a mechanism for learning in biological neurons.

In the 1950s, Rosenblatt and other researchers developed a class of neural networks called the perceptrons which are models of a biological neuron. The perceptron and its associated learning rule (Rosenblatt, 1958) had generated a great deal of interest in neural network research. At about the same time, Widrow and Hoff (1960) developed a new learning algorithm and applied it to their ADALINE (Adaptive Linear Neuron) networks which is very similar to perceptrons but with linear transfer function, instead of hard-limiting function typically used in perceptrons. The Widrow-Hoff learning rule is the basis of today's popular neural network learning methods. Although both perceptrons and ADALINE networks have achieved only limited success in pattern classification because they can only solve linearly-separable problems, they are still treated as important work in neural networks and an understanding of them provides the basis for understanding more complex networks.

The neural network research was hit by the book "Perceptrons" by Minsky and Papert (1969) who pointed out the limitation of the perceptrons and other related networks in solving a large class of nonlinearly separable problems. In addition, although Minsky and Papert proposed multilayer networks with hidden units to overcome the limitation, they were not able to find a way to train the network and stated that the problem of training may be unsolvable. This work causes much pessimism in neural network research and many researchers have left the filed. This is the reason that during the 1970s, the filed has been essentially dormant with very little research activity.

The renewed interest in neural network started in the 1980s when Hopfield (1982) used statistical mechanics to explain the operations of a certain class of recurrent network and demonstrated that neural networks could be trained as an associative memory. Hopfield networks have been used successfully in solving the Traveling Salesman Problem which is a constrained optimization problem (Hopfield and Tank, 1985). At about the same time, Kohonen (1982) developed a neural network based on self-organization whose key idea is to represent sensory signals as two-dimensional images or maps. Kohonen's networks, often called Kohonen's feature maps or self-organizing maps, organized neighborhoods of neurons such that similar inputs into the model are topologically close. Because of the usefulness of these two types of networks in solving real problems, more research was devoted to neural networks.

The most important development in the field was doubtlessly the invention of efficient training algorithms—called backpropagation—for multilayer perceptrons which have long been suspected to be capable of overcoming the linear separability limitation of the simple perceptron but have not been used due to lack of good training algorithms. The backpropagation algorithm, originated from Widrow and Hoff's learning rule, formalized by Werbos (1974), developed by Parker (1985), Rumelhart Hinton, and Williams (Rumelhart Hinton & Williams, 1986) and others, and popularized by Rumelhart, et al. (1986), is a systematic method for training multilayer neural networks. As a result of this algorithm, multilayer perceptrons are able to solve many important practical problems, which is the major reason that reinvigorated the filed of neural networks. It is by far the most popular learning paradigm in neural networks applications.

Since then and especially in the 1990s, there have been significant research activities devoted to neural networks. In the last 15 years or so, tens of thousands of papers have been published and numerous successful applications have been reported. It will not be surprising to see even greater advancement and success of neural networks in various data mining applications in the future.

3 Neural Network Models

As can be seen from the short historical review of development of the neural network field, many types of neural networks have been proposed. In fact, several dozens of different neural network models are regularly used for a variety of problems. In this section, we focus on three better known and most commonly used neural network models for data mining purposes: the multilayer feedforward network, the Hopfield network, and the Kohonen's map. It is important to point out that there are numerous variants of each of these networks and the discussions below are limited to the basic model formats.

3.1 Feedforward Neural Networks

The multilayer feedforward neural networks, also called multi-layer perceptrons (MLP), are the most widely studied and used neural network model in practice. According to Wong, Bodnovich, and Selvi (1997), about 95% of business applications of neural networks reported in the literature use this type of neural model. Feedforward neural networks are ideally suitable for modeling relationships between a set of predictor or input variables and one or more response or output variables. In other words, they are appropriate for any functional mapping problem where we want to know how a number of input variables affect the output variable(s). Since most prediction and classification tasks can be treated as function mapping problems, the MLP networks are very appealing to data mining. For this reason, we will focus more on feed-forward networks and many issues discussed here can be extended to other types of neural networks.

Model Structure

An MLP is a network consisted of a number of highly interconnected simple computing units called neurons, nodes, or cells, which are organized in layers. Each neuron performs simple task of information processing by converting received inputs into processed outputs. Through the linking arcs among these neurons, knowledge can be generated and stored as arc weights regarding the strength of the relationship between different nodes. Although each neuron implements its function slowly and imperfectly, collectively a neural network is able to perform a variety of tasks efficiently and achieve remarkable results.

Figure 1 shows the architecture of a three-layer feedforward neural network that consists of neurons (circles) organized in three layers: input layer, hidden layer, and output layer. The neurons in the input nodes correspond to the independent or predictor variables that are believed to be useful for predicting the dependent variables which correspond to the output neurons. Neurons in the input layer are passive; they do not process information but are simply used to receive the data patterns and then pass them into the neurons into the next layer. Neurons in the hidden layer are connected to both input and output neurons and are key to learning the pattern in the data and mapping the relationship from input variables to the output variable. Although it is possible to have more than one hidden layer in a multilayer networks, most applications use only one layer. With nonlinear transfer functions, hidden neurons can process complex information received from input neurons and then send processed information to output layer for further processing to generate outputs. In feedforward neural networks, the information flow is one directional from the input to hidden then to output layer and there is no feedback from the output.

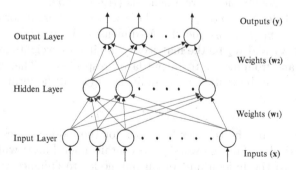

Fig. 1. Multi-layer feedforward neural network

Thus, a feedforward multilayer neural network is characterized by its architecture determined by the number of layers, the number of nodes in each layer, the transfer function used in each layer, as well as how the nodes in each layer connected to nodes in adjacent layers. Although partial connection between nodes in adjacent layers and direct connection from input layer to output layer are possible, the most commonly used neural network is so called fully connected one in that each node at one layer is fully connected only to all nodes in the adjacent layers.

To understand how the network in Figure 1 works, we need first understand the way neurons in the hidden and output layers process information. Figure 2 provides the mechanism that shows how a neuron processes information from several inputs and then converts it into an output. Each neuron processes information in two steps. In the first step, the inputs (x_i) are combined together to form a weighted sum of inputs and the weights (w_i) of connecting links. The 2nd step then performs a transformation that converts the sum to an output via a transfer function. In other words, the neuron in Figure 2 performs the following operations:

$$Out_n = f\left(\sum_i w_i x_i\right), \tag{1}$$

where Out_n is the output from this particular neuron and f is the transfer function. In general, the transfer function is a bounded nondecreasing function. Although there are many possible choices for transfer functions, only a few of them are commonly used in practice. These include

1. the sigmoid (logistic) function, $f(x) = (1 + \exp(-x))^{-1}$,
2. the hyperbolic tangent function, $f(x) = \frac{\exp(x) - \exp(-x)}{\exp(x) + \exp(-x)}$,
3. the sine and cosine function, $f(x) = \sin(x)$, $f(x) = \cos(x)$, and
4. the linear or identity function, $f(x) = x$.

Among them, the logistic function is the most popular choice especially for the hidden layer nodes due to the fact that it is simple, has a number of good characteristics (bounded, nonlinear, and monotonically increasing), and bears a better resemblance to real neurons (Hinton, 1992).

In Figure 1, let $\mathbf{x} = (x_1, x_2, ..., x_d)$ be a vector of d predictor or attribute variables, $\mathbf{y} = (y_1, y_2, ..., y_M)$ be the M-dimensional output vector from the network, and $\mathbf{w_1}$ and $\mathbf{w_2}$ be the matrices of linking arc weights from input to hidden layer and from hidden to output layer, respectively. Then a three-layer neural network can be written as a nonlinear model of the form

$$\mathbf{y} = f_2(\mathbf{w_2} f_1(\mathbf{w_1 x})), \tag{2}$$

where f_1 and f_2 are the transfer functions for the hidden nodes and output nodes respectively. Many networks also contain node biases which are constants added to the hidden and/or output nodes to enhance the flexibility of neural network modeling. Bias terms act like the intercept term in linear regression.

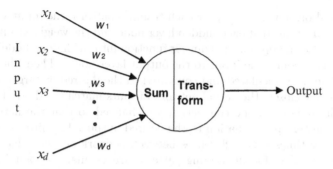

Fig. 2. Information processing in a single neuron

In classification problems where desired outputs are binary or categorical, logistic function is often used in the output layer to limit the range of the network outputs. On the other hand, for prediction or forecasting purposes, since output variables are in general continuous, linear transfer function is a better choice for output nodes. Equation (3) can have many different specifications depending on the problem type, the transfer function, and numbers of input, hidden, and output nodes employed. For example, the neural network structure for a general univariate forecasting problem with logistic function for hidden nodes and identity function for the output node can be explicitly expressed as

$$y_t = w_{10} + \sum_{j=1}^{q} w_{1j} f\left(\sum_{i=1}^{p} w_{ij} x_{it} + w_{0j}\right) \tag{3}$$

where y_t is the observation of forecast variable and $\{x_{it}, i = 1, 2, \ldots, p\}$ are p predictor variables at time t, p is also the number of input nodes, q is the number of hidden nodes, $\{w_{1j}, j = 0, 1, \ldots, n\}$ are weights from the hidden to output nodes and $\{w_{ij}, i = 0, 1, \ldots, p; \; j = 1, 2, \ldots, q\}$ are weights from the input to hidden nodes; α_0 and β_{0j} are bias terms, and f is the logistic function defined above.

Network Training

The arc weights are the parameters in a neural network model. Like in a statistical model, these parameters need to be estimated before the network can be adopted for further use. Neural network training refers to the process in which these weights are determined, and hence is the way the network learns. Network training for classification and prediction problems is performed via supervised learning in which known outputs and their associated inputs are both presented to the network.

The basic process to train a neural network is as follows. First, the network is fed with training examples, which consist of a set of input patterns and their desired outputs. Second, for each training pattern, the input values are weighted and summed at each hidden layer node and the weighted sum is then transmitted by an appropriate transfer function into the hidden node's output value, which becomes the input to the output layer nodes. Then, the network output values are calculated and compared to the desired or target values to determine how closely the actual network outputs match the desired outputs. Finally, the weights of the connection are changed so that the network can produce a better approximation to the desired output. This process typically repeats many times until differences between network output values and the known target values for all training patterns are as small as possible.

To facilitate training, some overall error measure such as the mean squared errors (MSE) or sum of squared errors (SSE) is often used to serve as an objective function or performance metric. For example, MSE can be defined as

$$\text{MSE} = \frac{1}{M}\frac{1}{N}\sum_{m=1}^{M}\sum_{j=1}^{N}(d_{mj} - y_{mj})^2, \tag{4}$$

where d_{mj} and y_{mj} represent the desired (target) value and network output at the mth node for the jth training pattern respectively, M is the number of output nodes, and N is the number of training patterns. The goal of training is to find the set of weights that minimize the objective function. Thus, network training is actually an unconstrained nonlinear optimization problem. Numerical methods are usually needed to solve nonlinear optimization problems.

The most important and popular training method is the backpropagation algorithm which is essentially a gradient steepest descent method. The idea of steepest descent method is to find the best direction in the multi-dimension error space to move or change the weights so that the objective function is reduced most. This requires partial derivative of the objective function with respect to each weight to be calculated because the partial derivative represents the rate of change of the objective function. The weight updating therefore follows the following rule

$$\begin{aligned} w_{ij}^{new} &= w_{ij}^{old} + \Delta w_{ij} \\ \Delta w_{ij} &= -\eta \frac{\partial E}{\partial w_{ij}} \end{aligned} \tag{5}$$

where Δw_{ij} is the gradient of objective function E with respect to weight w_{ij}, and η is called the learning rate which controls the size of the gradient descent step. The algorithm requires an iterative process and there are two versions of weight updating schemes: batch mode and on-line mode. In the batch mode, weights are updated after all training patterns are evaluated, while in the on-line learning mode, the weights are updated after each pattern presentation. The basic steps with the batch mode training can be summarized as initialize the weights to small random values from, say, a uniform distribution

choose a pattern and forward propagate it to obtain network outputs
calculate the pattern error and back-propagate it to obtain partial derivative
of this error with respect to all weights
add up all the single-pattern terms to get the total derivative
update the weights with equation (7)
repeat steps 2-5 for next pattern until all patterns are passed through.

Note that each one pass of all patterns is called an epoch. In general, each weight update reduces the total error by only a small amount so many epochs are often needed to minimize the error. For information on further detail of the backpropagation algorithm, readers are referred to Rumelhart et al. (1986) and Bishop (1995).

It is important to note that there is no algorithm currently available which can guarantee global optimal solution for general nonlinear optimization problems such as those in neural network training. In fact, all algorithms in nonlinear optimization inevitably suffer from the local optima problems and the most we can do is to use the available optimization method which can give the "best" local optima if the true global solution is not available. It is also important to point out that the steepest descent method used in the basic backpropagation suffers the problems of slow convergence, inefficiency, and lack of robustness. Furthermore, it can be very sensitive to the choice of the learning rate. Smaller learning rates tend to slow the learning process while larger learning rates may cause network oscillation in the weight space. Common modifications to the basic backpropagation include adding in the weight updating formula (2) an additional momentum parameter proportional to the last weight change the to control the oscillation in weight changes and (3) a weight decay term that penalizes the overly complex network with large weights.

In light of the weakness of the standard backpropagation algorithm, the existence of many different optimization methods (Fletcher, 1987) provides various alternative choices for the neural network training. Among them, the second-order methods such as BFGS and Levenberg-Marquardt methods are more efficient nonlinear optimization methods and are used in most optimization packages. Their faster convergence, robustness, and the ability to find good local minima make them attractive in neural network training. For example, De Groot and Wurtz (1991) have tested several well-known optimization algorithms such as quasi-Newton, BFGS, Levenberg-Marquardt, and conjugate gradient methods and achieved significant improvements in training time and accuracy.

Modeling Issues

Developing a neural network model for a data mining application is not a trivial task. Although many good software packages exist to ease users' effort in building a neural network model, it is still critical for data miners to understand many important issues around the model building process. It is important to point out that building a successful neural network is a combination of art and science and software alone is not sufficient to solve all problems in the process. It is a pitfall to blindly throw data into a software package and then hope it will automatically identify the pattern or give a satisfactory solution. Other pitfalls readers need to be cautious can be found in Zhang (2007).

An important point in building an effective neural network model is the understanding of the issue of learning and generalization inherent in all neural network applications. This issue of learning and generalization can be understood with the concepts of model bias and variance (Geman, Bienenstock & Doursat, 1992). Bias and variance are important statistical properties associated with any empirical model. Model bias measures the systematic error of a model in *learning* the underlying relations among variables or observations. Model variance, on the other hand, relates to the stability of a model built on different data samples and therefore offers insights on *generalizability* of the model. A pre-specified or parametric model, which is less dependent on the data, may misrepresent the true functional relationship and hence cause a large bias. On the other hand, a flexible, data-driven model may be too dependent on the specific data set and hence have a large variance. Bias and variance are two important terms that impact a model's usefulness. Although it is desirable to have both low bias and low variance, we may not be able to reduce both terms at the same time for a given data set because these goals are conflicting. A model that is less dependent on the data tends to have low variance but high bias if the pre-specified model is incorrect. On the other hand, a model that fits the data well tends to have low bias but high variance when applied to new data sets. Hence a good predictive model should have an "appropriate" balance between model bias and model variance.

As a data-driven approach to data mining, neural networks often tend to fit the training data well and thus have low bias. But the potential price to pay is the overfitting effect that causes high variance. Therefore, attentions should be paid to address issues of overfitting and the balance of bias and variance in neural network model building.

The major decisions in building a neural network model include data preparation, input variable selection, choice of network type and architecture, transfer function, and training algorithm, as well as model validation, evaluation, and selection procedures. Some of these can be solved during the model building process while others must be considered before actual modeling starts.

Neural networks are data-driven techniques. Therefore, data preparation is a critical step in building a successful neural network model. Without an adequate and representative data set, it is impossible to develop a useful data mining model.

There are several practical issues around the data requirement for a neural network model. The first is the data quality. As data sets used for typical data mining tasks are massive and may be collected from multiple sources, they may suffer many quality problems such as noises, errors, heterogeneity, and missing observations. Results reported in Klein and Rossin (1999) suggest that data error rate and its magnitude can have substantial impact on neural network performance. Klein and Rossion believe that an understanding of errors in a dataset should be an important consideration to neural network users and efforts to lower error rates are well deserved. Appropriate treatment of these problems to clean the data is critical for successful application of any data mining technique including neural networks (Dasu and Johnson, 2003).

Another one is the size of the sample used to build a neural network. While there is no specific rule that can be followed for all situations, the advantage of having large samples should be clear because not only do neural networks have typically a large number of parameters to estimate, but also it is often necessary to split data into several portions for overfitting prevention, model selection, evaluation, and comparison. A larger sample provides better chance for neural networks to adequately approximate the underlying data structure.

The third issue is the data splitting. Typically for neural network applications, all available data are divided into an in-sample and an out-of-sample. The in-sample data are used for model fitting and selection, while the out-of-sample is used to evaluate the predictive ability of the model. The in-sample data often are further split into a training sample and a validation sample. The training sample is used for model parameter estimation while the validation sample is used to monitor the performance of neural networks and help stop training and select the final model. For a neural network to be useful, it is critical to test the model with an independent out-of-sample which is not used in the network training and model selection phase. Although there is no consensus on how to split the data, the general practice is to allocate more data for model building and selection although it is possible to allocate 50% vs. 50% for in-sample and out-of-sample if the data size is very large. Typical split in data mining applications reported in the literature uses convenient ratio varying from 70%:30% to 90%:10%.

Data preprocessing is another issue that is often recommended to highlight important relationships or to create more uniform data to facilitate neural network learning, meet algorithm requirements, and avoid computation problems. For time series forecasting, Azoff (1994) summarizes four methods typically used for input data normalization. They are along channel normalization, across channel normalization, mixed channel normalization, and external normalization. However, the necessity and effect of data normalization on network learning and forecasting are still not universally agreed upon. For example, in modeling and forecasting seasonal time series, some researchers (Gorr, 1994) believe that data preprocessing is not necessary because the neural network is a universal approximator and is able to capture all of the underlying patterns well. Recent empirical studies (Nelson, Hill, Remus & O'Connor, 1999; Zhang and Qi, 2002), however, find that pre-deseasonalization of the data is critical in improving forecasting performance.

Neural network design and architecture selection are important yet difficult tasks. Not only are there many ways to build a neural network model and a large number of choices to be made during the model building and selection process, but also numerous parameters and issues have to be estimated and experimented before a satisfactory model may emerge. Adding to the difficulty is the lack of standards in the process. Numerous rules of thumb are available but not all of them can be applied blindly to a new situation. In building an appropriate model, some experiments with different model structures are usually necessary. Therefore, a good experiment design is needed. For further discussions of many aspects of modeling issues for classification and forecasting tasks, readers may consult Bishop (1995), Zhang, Patuwo, and Hu (1998), and Remus and O'Connor (2001).

For network architecture selection, there are several decisions to be made. First, the size of output layer is usually determined by the nature of the problem. For example, in most time series forecasting problems, one output node is naturally used for one-step-ahead forecasting, although one output node can also be employed for multi-step-ahead forecasting in which case, iterative forecasting mode must be used. That is, forecasts for more than two-step ahead in the time horizon must be based on earlier forecasts. On the other hand, for classification problems, the number of output nodes is determined by the number of groups into which we classify objects. For a two-group classification problem, only one output node is needed while for a general M-group problem, M binary output nodes can be employed.

The number of input nodes is perhaps the most important parameter in an effective neural network model. For classification or causal forecasting problems, it corresponds to the number of feature (attribute) variables or independent (predictor) variables that data miners believe important in predicting the output or dependent variable. These input variables are usually pre-determined by the domain expert although variable selection procedures can be used to help identify the most important variables. For univariate forecasting problems, it is the number of past lagged observations. Determining an appropriate set of input variables is vital for neural networks to capture the essential relationship that can be used for successful prediction. How many and what variables to use in the input layer will directly affect the performance of neural network in both in-sample fitting and out-of-sample prediction.

Neural network model selection is typically done with the basic cross-validation process. That is the in-sample data is split into a training set and a validation set. The neural network parameters are estimated with the training sample, while the performance of the model is monitored and evaluated with the validation sample. The best model selected is the one that has the best performance on the validation sample. Of course, in choosing competing models, we must also apply the principle of parsimony. That is, a simpler model that has about the same performance as a more complex model should be preferred. Model selection can also be done with all of the in-sample data. This can be done with several in-sample selection criteria that modify the total error function to include a penalty term that penalizes for the complexity of the model. Some in-sample model selection approaches are based on criteria such as Akaike's information criterion (AIC) or Schwarz information criterion (SIC). However, it is important to note the limitation of these criteria as empirically demonstrated by Swanson and White (1995) and Qi and Zhang (2001). Other in-sample approaches are based on pruning methods such as node and weight pruning (see a review by Reed, 1993) as well as constructive methods such as the upstart and cascade correlation approaches (Fahlman and Lebiere, 1990; Frean, 1990).

After the modeling process, the finally selected model must be evaluated using data not used in the model building stage. In addition, as neural networks are often used as a nonlinear alternative to traditional statistical models, the performance of neural networks needs be compared to that of statistical methods. As Adya and Collopy (1998) point out, "if such a comparison is not conducted it is difficult to argue that the study has taught us much about the value of neural networks." They further propose three evaluation criteria to objectively evaluate the performance of a neural network: (2) comparing it to well-accepted (traditional) models; (3) using true out-of-samples; and (4) ensuring enough sample size in the out-of-sample (40 for classification problems and 75 for time series problems). It is important to note that the test sample served as out-of-sample should not in any way be used in the model building process. If the cross-validation is used for model selection and experimentation, the performance on the validation sample should not be treated as the true performance of the model.

Relationships with Statistical Methods

Neural networks especially the feedforward multilayer networks are closely related to statistical pattern recognition methods. Several articles that illustrate their link include Ripley (1993, 1994), Cheng and Titterington (1994), Sarle (1994), and Ciampi and Lechevallier (1997). This section provides a summary of the literature that links neural networks, particularly MLP networks to statistical data mining methods.

Bayesian decision theory is the basis for statistical classification methods. It provides the fundamental probability model for well known classification procedures. It has been shown by many researchers that for classification problems, neural networks provide the direct estimation of the posterior probabilities under a variety of situations (Richard and Lippmann, 1991). Funahashi (1998) shows that for the two-group d-dimensional Gaussian classification problem, neural networks with at least $2d$ hidden nodes have the capability to approximate the posterior probability with arbitrary accuracy when infinite data is available and the training proceeds ideally. Miyake and Kanaya (1991) shows that neural networks trained with a generalized mean-squared error objective function can yield the optimal Bayes rule.

As the statistical counterpart of neural networks, discriminant analysis is a well-known supervised classifier. Gallinari, Thiria, Badran, and Fogelman-Soulie (1991) describe a general framework to establish the link between discriminant analysis and neural network models. They find that in quite general conditions the hidden layers of an MLP project the input data onto different clusters in a way that these clusters can be further aggregated into different classes. The discriminant feature extraction by the network with nonlinear hidden nodes has also been demonstrated in Webb and Lowe (1990) and Lim, Alder and Hadingham (1992).

Raudys (1998a, b) presents a detailed analysis of nonlinear single layer perceptron (SLP). He shows that by purposefully controlling the SLP classifier complexity during the adaptive training process, the decision boundaries of SLP classifiers are equivalent or close to those of seven statistical classifiers. These statistical classifiers include the Euclidean distance classifier, the Fisher linear discriminant function, the Fisher linear discriminant function with pseudo-inversion of the covariance matrix, the generalized Fisher linear discriminant function, the regularized linear discriminant analysis, the minimum empirical error classifier, and the maximum margin classifier.

Logistic regression is another important data mining tool. Schumacher, Robner and Vach (1996) make a detailed comparison between neural networks and logistic regression. They find that the added modeling flexibility of neural networks due to hidden layers does not automatically guarantee their superiority over logistic regression because of the possible overfitting and other inherent problems with neural networks (Vach Schumacher & Robner, 1996).

For time series forecasting problems, feedforward MLP are general nonlinear autoregressive models. For a discussion of the relationship between neural networks and general ARMA models, see Suykens, Vandewalle, and De Moor (1996).

3.2 Hopfield Neural Networks

Hopfield neural networks are a special type of neural networks which are able to store certain memories or patterns in a manner similar to the brain—the full pattern can be recovered if the network is presented with only partial or noisy information. This ability of brain is often called associative or content-addressable memory. Hopfield networks are quite different from the feedforward multilayer networks in several ways. From the model architecture perspective, Hopfield networks do not have a layer structure. Rather, a Hopfield network is a single layer of neurons with complete interconnectivity. That is, Hopfield networks are autonomous systems with all neurons being both inputs and outputs and no hidden neurons. In addition, unlike in feedforward networks where information is passed only in one direction, there are looping feedbacks among neurons.

Figure 3 shows a simple Hopfield network with only three neurons. Each neuron is connected to every other neuron and the connection strengths or weights are symmetric in that the weight from neuron i to neuron j (w_{ij}) is the same as that from neuron j to neuron i(w_{ji}). The flow of the information is not in a single direction as in the feedforward network. Rather it is possible for signals to flow from a neuron back to itself via other neurons. This feature is often called feedback or recurrent because neurons may be used repeatedly to process information.

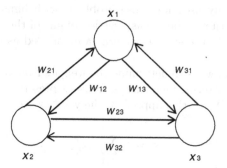

Fig. 3. A three-neuron Hopfield network

The network is completely described by a state vector which is a function of time t. Each node in the network contributes one component to the state vector and any or all of the node outputs can be treated as outputs of the network. The dynamics of neurons can be described mathematically as the following equations:

$$u_i(t) = \sum_{j=1}^{n} w_{ij} x_j(t) + v_i \tag{6}$$

where $u_i(t)$ is the internal state of the ith neuron, $x_i(t)$ is the output activation or output state of the ith neuron, v_i is the threshold to the ith neuron, n is the number of neurons, and $sign$ is the sign function defined as $sign(x)=1$, if $x > 0$ and -1 otherwise. Given a set of initial conditions $\mathbf{x}(0)$, and appropriate restrictions on the weights (such as symmetry), this network will converge to a fixed equilibrium point.

For each network state at any time, there is an energy associated with it. A common energy function is defined as

$$E(t) = -\frac{1}{2}\mathbf{x}(t)^T \mathbf{W} \mathbf{x}(t) - \mathbf{x}(t)^T \mathbf{v} \tag{7}$$

where $\mathbf{x}(t)$ is the state vector, $\mathbf{W}$ is the weight matrix, $\mathbf{v}$ is the threshold vector, and T denote transpose. The basic idea of the energy function is that it always decreases or at least remains constant as the system evolves over time according to its dynamic rule in equations 6 and 7. It can be shown that the system will converge from an arbitrary initial energy to eventually a fixed point (a local minimum) on the surface of the energy function. These fixed points are stable states which correspond to the stored patterns or memories.

The main use of Hopfield's network is as associative memory. An associative memory is a device which accepts an input pattern and generates an output as the stored pattern which is most closely associated with the input. The function of the associate memory is to recall the corresponding stored pattern, and then produce a clear version of the pattern at the output. Hopfield networks are typically used for those problems with binary pattern vectors and the input pattern may be a noisy version of one of the stored patterns. In the Hopfield network, the stored patterns are encoded as the weights of the network.

There are several ways to determine the weights from a training set which is a set of known patterns. One way is to use a prescription approach given by Hopfield (1982). With this approach, the weights are given by

$$\mathbf{w} = \frac{1}{n} \sum_{i=1}^{p} z_i z_i^T \tag{8}$$

where z_i, $i = 1, 2, \ldots, p$ are p patterns that are to be stored in the network. Another way is to use an incremental, iterative process called Hebbian learning rule developed by Hebb (1949). It has the following learning process:

choose a pattern from the training set at random

present a pair of components of the pattern at the outputs of the corresponding nodes of the network

if two nodes have the same value then make a small positive increment to the interconnected weight. If they have opposite values then make a small negative decrement to the weight. The incremental size can be expressed as $\Delta w_{ij} = \alpha z_i^p z_j^p$, where α is a constant rate in between 0 and 1 and z_i^p is the ith component of pattern p.

Hopfield networks have two major limitations when used as a content addressable memory. First, the number of patterns that can be stored and accurately recalled is fairly limited. If too many patterns are stored, the network may converge to a spurious pattern different from all programmed patterns. Or, it may not converge at all. The second limitation is that the network may become unstable if the common patterns it shares are too similar. An example pattern is considered unstable if it is applied at time zero and the network converges to some other pattern from the training set.

3.3 Kohonen's Self-organizing Maps

Kohonen's self-organizing maps (SOM) are important neural network models for dimension reduction and data clustering. SOM can learn from complex, multidimensional data and transform them into a topological map of much fewer dimensions typically one or two dimensions. These low dimension plots provide much improved visualization capabilities to help data miners visualize the clusters or similarities between patterns.

SOM networks represent another neural network type that is markedly different from the feedforward multilayer networks. Unlike training in the feedforward MLP, the SOM training or learning is often called the unsupervised because there are no known target outputs associated with each input pattern in SOM and during the training process, the SOM processes the input patterns and learns to cluster or segment the data through adjustment of weights. A two-dimensional map is typically created in such a way that the orders of the interrelationships among inputs are preserved. The number and composition of clusters can be visually determined based on the output distribution generated by the training process. With only input variables in the training sample, SOM aims to learn or discover the underlying structure of the data.

A typical SOM network has two layers of nodes, an input layer and output layer (sometimes called the Kohonen layer). Each node in the input layer is fully connected to nodes in the two-dimensional output layer. Figure 4 shows an example of an SOM network with several input nodes in the input layer and a two dimension output layer with a 4x4 rectangular array of 16 neurons. It is also possible to use hexagonal array or higher dimensional grid in the Kohonen layer. The number of nodes in the input layer is corresponding to the number of input variables while the number of output nodes depends on the specific problem and is determined by the user. Usually, this number of neurons in the rectangular array should be large enough to allow a sufficient number of clusters to form. It has been recommended that this number is ten times the dimension of the input pattern (Deboeck and Kohonen, 1998)

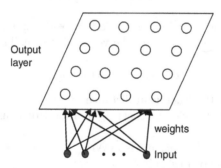

Fig. 4. A 4x4 SOM network

During the training process, input patterns are presented to the network. At each training step when an input pattern $\mathbf{x}$ randomly selected from the training set is presented, each neuron i in the output layer calculates how similar the input is to its weights $\mathbf{w}_i$. The similarity is often measured by some distance between $\mathbf{x}$ and $\mathbf{w}_i$. As the training proceeds, the neurons adjust their weights according to the topological relations in the input data. The neuron with the minimum distance is the winner and the weights of the winning node as well as its neighboring nodes are strengthened or adjusted to be closer to the value of input pattern. Therefore, the training with SOM is unsupervised and competitive with winner-take-all strategy.

A key concept in training SOM is the neighborhood N_k around a winning neuron, k, which is the collection of all nodes with the same radial distance. Figure 5 gives an example of neighborhood nodes for a 5x5 Kohonen layer at radius of 1 and 2.

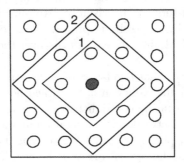

Fig. 5. A 5x5 Kohonen Layer with two neighborhood sizes

The basic procedure in training an SOM is as follows:
initialize the weights to small random values and the neighborhood size large enough to cover half the nodes
select an input pattern **x** randomly from the training set and present it to the network
find the best matching or "winning" node k whose weight vector w_k is closest to the current input vector **x** using the vector distance. That is:

$$\|x - w_k\| = \min_i \|x - w_i\|$$

where $\|.\|$ represents the Euclidean distance
update the weights of nodes in the neighborhood of k using the Kohonen learning rule:

$w_i^{new} = w_i^{old} + \alpha h_{ik}(x - w_i)$ if i is in N_k
$w_i^{new} = w_i^{old}$ if i is not in N_k (10)

where α is the learning rate between 0 and 1 and h_{ik} is a neighborhood kernel centered on the winning node and can take Gaussian form as

$$h_{ik} = \exp\left[-\frac{\|r_i - r_k\|^2}{2\sigma^2}\right] \tag{9}$$

where r_i and r_k are positions of neurons i and k on the SOM grid and σ is the neighborhood radius.

decrease the learning rate slightly

repeat Steps 1—5 with a number of cycles and then decrease the size of the neighborhood. Repeat until weights are stabilized.

As the number of cycles of training (epochs) increases, better formation of the clusters can be found. Eventually, the topological map is fine-tuned with finer distinctions of clusters within areas of the map. After the network has been trained, it can be used as a visualization tool to examine the data structure. Once clusters are identified, neurons in the map can be labeled to indicate their meaning. Assignment of meaning usually requires knowledge on the data and specific application area.

4 Data Mining Applications

Neural networks have been used extensively in data mining for a wide variety of problems in business, engineering, industry, medicine, and science. In general, neural networks are good at solving the following common data mining problems such as classification, prediction, association, and clustering. This section provides a short overview on the application areas.

Classification is one of the frequently encountered data mining tasks. A classification problem occurs when an object needs to be assigned into a predefined group or class based on a number of observed attributes related to that object. Many problems in business, industry, and medicine can be treated as classification problems. Examples include bankruptcy prediction, credit scoring, medical diagnosis, quality control, handwritten character recognition, and speech recognition. Feed-forward multilayer networks are most commonly used for these classification tasks although other types of neural networks can also be used.

Forecasting is central to effective planning and operations in all business organizations as well as government agencies. The ability to accurately predict the future is fundamental to many decision activities in finance, marketing, production, personnel, and many other business functional areas. Increasing forecasting accuracy could facilitate the saving of millions of dollars to a company. Prediction can be done with two approaches: causal and time series analysis, both of which are suitable for feedforward networks. Successfully applications include predictions of sales, passenger volume, market share, exchange rate, futures price, stock return, electricity demand, environmental changes, and traffic volume.

Clustering involves categorizing or segmenting observations into groups or clusters such that each cluster is as homogeneous as possible. Unlike classification problems, the groups or clusters are usually unknown to or not predetermined by data miners. Clustering can simplify a complex large data set into a small number of groups based on the natural structure of data. Improved understanding of the data and subsequent decisions are major benefits of clustering. Kohonen or SOM networks are particularly useful for clustering

Table 1. Data mining applications of neural networks

Data Mining Task	Application Area
Classification	bond rating (Dutta and shenkar, 1993) corporation failure (Zhang et al., 1999; Mckee and Greenstein, 2000) credit scoring (West, 2000) customer retention (Mozer and Wolniewics, 2000; Smith et al., 2000) customer satisfaction (Temponi et al., 1999) fraud detection (He et al., 1997) inventory (Partovi and Anandarajan, 2002) project (Thieme et al., 2000; Zhang et al., 2003) target marketing (Zahavi and Levin, 1997)
Prediction	air quality (Kolehmainen et al., 2001) business cycles and recessions (Qi, 2001) consumer expenditures (Church and Curram, 1996) consumer choice (West et al., 1997) earnings surprises (Dhar and Chou, 2001) economic crisis (Kim et al., 2004) exchange rate (Nag and Mitra, 2002) market share (Agrawal and Schorling, 1996) ozone concentration level (Prybutok et al., 2000) sales (Ansuj et al., 1996; Kuo, 2001; Zhang and Qi, 2002) stock market (Qi, 1999; Chen et al., 2003; Leung et al., 2000; Chun and Kim, 2004) tourist demand (Law, 2000) traffic (Dia, 2001; Qiao et al., 2001)
Clustering	bankruptcy prediction (Kiviluoto, 1998) document classification (Dittenbach et al., 2002) enterprise typology (Petersohn, 1998) fraud uncovering (Brockett et al., 1998) group technology (Kiang et al., 1995) market segmentation (Ha and Park, 1998; Vellido et al., 1999; Reutterer and Natter, 2000; Boone and Roehm, 2002) process control (Hu and Roŝe, 1995) property evaluation (Lewis et al., 1997) quality control (Chen and Liu, 2000) webpage usage (Smith and Ng, 2003)
Association/Pattern Recognition	defect recognition (Kim and Kumara, 1997) facial image recognition (Dai and Nakano, 1998) frequency assignment (Salcedo-Sanz et al., 2004) graph or image matching (Suganthan et al., 1995; Pajares et al., 1998) image restoration (Paik and Katsaggelos, 1992; Sun and Yu, 1995) imgage segmentation (Rout et al., 1998; Wang et al., 1992) landscape pattern prediction (Tatem et al., 2002) market basket analysis (Evans, 1997) object recognition (Huang and Liu, 1997; Young et al., 1997; Li and Lee, 2002) on-line marketing (Changchien and Lu, 2001) pattern sequence recognition (Lee, 2002) semantic indexing and searching (Chen et al., 1998)

tasks. Applications have been reported in market segmentation, customer targeting, business failure categorization, credit evaluation, document retrieval, and group technology.

With association techniques, we are interested in the correlation or relationship among a number variables or objects. Association is used in several ways. One use as in market basket analysis is to help identify the consequent items given a set of antecedent items. An association rule in this way is an implication of the form: IF x, THEN Y, where x is a set of antecedent items and Y is the consequent items. This type of association rule has been used in a variety of data mining tasks including credit card purchase analysis, merchandise stocking, insurance fraud investigation, market basket analysis, telephone calling pattern identification, and climate prediction. Another use is in pattern recognition. Here we train a neural network first to *remember* a number of patterns, so that when a distorted version of a stored pattern is presented, the network associates it with the closest one in its memory and returns the original version of the pattern. This is useful for restoring noisy data. Speech, image, and character recognitions are typical application areas. Hopfield networks are useful for this purpose.

Given an enormous amount of applications of neural networks in data mining, it is difficult if not impossible to give a detailed list. Table 1 provides a sample of several typical applications of neural networks for various data mining problems. It is important to note that studies given in Table 1 represent only a very small portion of all the applications reported in the literature, but we should still get an appreciation of the capability of neural networks in solving wide range of data mining problems. For real-world industrial or commercial applications, readers are referred to Widrow et al. (1994), Soulie and Gallinari (1998), Jain and Vemuri (1999), and Lisboa, Edisbury, and Vellido (2000).

5 Conclusions

Neural networks are standard and important tools for data mining. Many features of neural networks such as nonlinear, data-driven, universal function approximating, noise-tolerance, and parallel processing of large number of variables are especially desirable for data mining applications. In addition, many types of neural networks functionally are similar to traditional statistical pattern recognition methods in areas of cluster analysis, nonlinear regression, pattern classification, and time series forecasting. This chapter provides an overview of neural networks and their applications to data mining tasks. We present three important classes of neural network models: Feedforward multilayer networks, Hopfield networks, and Kohonen's self-organizing maps, which are suitable for a variety of problems in pattern association, pattern classification, prediction, and clustering.

Neural networks have already achieved significant progress and success in data mining. It is, however, important to point out that they also have limitations and may not be a panacea for every data mining problem in every situation. Using neural networks require thorough understanding of the data, prudent design of modeling strategy, and careful consideration of modeling issues. Although many rules of thumb exist in model building, they are not necessarily always useful for a new application. It is suggested that users should not blindly rely on a neural network package to "automatically" mine the data, but rather should study the problem and understand the network models and the issues in various stages of model building, evaluation, and interpretation.

References

Adya M., Collopy F. (1998), How effective are neural networks at forecasting and prediction? a review and evaluation. Journal of forecasting ; 17:481-495.

Agrawal D., Schorling C. (1996), Market share forecasting: an empirical comparison of artificial neural networks and multinomial logit model. Journal of Retailing ; 72:383-407.

Ahn H., Choi E., Han I. (2007), Extracting underlying meaningful features and canceling noise using independent component analysis for direct marketing Expert Systems with Applications, ; 33: 181-191

Azoff E. M. (1994), Neural Network Time Series Forecasting of Financial Markets. Chichester: John Wiley & Sons, .

Bishop M. (1995), Neural Networks for Pattern Recognition. Oxford: Oxford University Press, .

Boone D., Roehm M. (2002), Retail segmentation using artificial neural networks. International Journal of Research in Marketing ; 19:287-301.

Brockett P.L., Xia X.H., Derrig R.A. (1998), Using Kohonen's self-organizing feature map to uncover automobile bodily injury claims fraud. The Journal of Risk and Insurance ; 65: 24

Changchien S.W., Lu T.C. (2001), Mining association rules procedure to support on-line recommendation by customers and products fragmentation. Expert Systems with Applications ; 20:

Chen T., Chen H. (1995), Universal approximation to nonlinear operators by neural networks with arbitrary activation functions and its application to dynamical systems, Neural Networks ; 6:911-917.

Chen F.L., Liu S.F. (2000), A neural-network approach to recognize defect spatial pattern in semiconductor fabrication. IEEE Transactions on Semiconductor Manufacturing ; 13:366-37

Chen S.K., Mangiameli P., West D. (1995), The comparative ability of self-organizing neural networks to define cluster structure. Omega ; 23:271-279.

Chen H., Zhang Y., Houston A.L. (1998), Semantic indexing and searching using a Hopfield net. Journal of Information Science ; 24:3-18.

Cheng B., Titterington D. (1994), Neural networks: a review from a statistical perspective. Statistical Sciences ; 9:2-54.

Chen K.Y., Wang, C.H. (2007), Support vector regression with genetic algorithms in forecasting tourism demand. Tourism Management ; 28:215-226.

Chiang W.K., Zhang D., Zhou L. (2006), Predicting and explaining patronage behavior toward web and traditional stores using neural networks: a comparative analysis with logistic regression. Decision Support Systems ; 41:514-531.

Church K. B., Curram S. P. (1996), Forecasting consumers' expenditure: A comparison between econometric and neural network models. International Journal of Forecasting ; 12:255-267

Ciampi A., Lechevallier Y. (1997), Statistical models as building blocks of neural networks. Communications in Statistics: Theory and Methods ; 26:991-1009.

Crone S.F., Lessmann S., Stahlbock R. (2006), The impact of preprocessing on data mining: An evaluation of classifier sensitivity in direct marketing. European Journal of Operational Research ; 173:781-800

Cybenko G. (1989), Approximation by superpositions of a sigmoidal function. Mathematical Control Signals Systems ; 2:303–314.

Dai Y., Nakano Y. (1998), Recognition of facial images with low resolution using a Hopfield memory model. Pattern Recognition ; 31:159-167.

Dasu T., Johnson T. (2003), Exploratory Data Mining and Data Cleaning. New Jersey: Wiley, .

De Groot D., Wurtz D. (1991), Analysis of univariate time series with connectionist nets: A case study of two classical examples. Neurocomputing ;3:177-192.

Deboeck G., Kohonen T. (1998), Visual Explorations in Finance with Self-organizing Maps. London: Springer-Verlag, .

Delen D., Sharda R., Bessonov M. (2006), Identifying significant predictors of injury severity in traffic accidents using a series of artificial neural networks Accident Analysis and Prevention ; 38:434-444.

Dhar V., Chou D. (2001), A comparison of nonlinear methods for predicting earnings surprises and returns. IEEE Transactions on Neural Networks ; 12:907-921.

Dia H. (2001), An object-oriented neural network approach to short-term traffic forecasting. European Journal of Operation Research ; 131:253-261.

Dittenbach M., Rauber A., Merkl, D. (2002), Uncovering hierarchical structure in data using the growing hierarchical self-organizing map. Neurocompuing ; 48:199-216.

Doganis P., Alexandridis A., Patrinos P., Sarimveis H. (2006), Time series sales forecasting for short shelf-life food products based on artificial neural networks and evolutionary computing. Journal of Food Engineering ; 75:196-204.

Dutot A.L., Rynkiewicz J., Steiner F.E., Rude J. (2007), A 24-h forecast of ozone peaks and exceedance levels using neural classifiers and weather predictions Modelling and Software; 22:1261-1269.

Dutta S., Shenkar S. (1993), "Bond rating: a non-conservative application of neural networks." In Neural Networks in Finance and Investing, Trippi, R., and Turban, E., eds. Chicago: Probus Publishing Company.

Enke D., Thawornwong S. (2005), The use of data mining and neural networks for forecasting stock market returns. Expert Systems with Applications ; 29:927-940.

Evans O.V.D. (1997), Discovering associations in retail transactions using neural networks. ICL Systems Journal ; 12:73-88.

Fahlman S., Lebiere C. (1990), "The cascade-correlation learning architecture." In Advances in Neural Information Processing Systems, Touretzky, D., ed. .

Fletcher R. (1987), Practical Methods of Optimization 2nd. Chichester: John Wiley & Sons, .

Frean M. (1990), The Upstart algorithm: a method for constructing and training feed-forward networks. Neural Computations ; 2:198-209.

Funahashi K. (1998), Multilayer neural networks and Bayes decision theory. Neural Networks ; 11:209-213.

Gallinari P., Thiria S., Badran R., Fogelman-Soulie, F. (1991), On the relationships between discriminant analysis and multilayer perceptrons. Neural Networks ; 4:349-360.

Geman S., Bienenstock E., Doursat T. (1992), Neural networks and the bias/variance dilemma. Neural Computation ; 5:1-58.

Gorr L. (1994), Research prospective on neural network forecasting. International Journal of Forecasting ; 10:1-4.

He H., Wang J., Graco W., Hawkins S. (1997), Application of neural networks to detection of medical fraud. Expert Systems with Applications ; 13:329-336.

Hebb D.O. (1949), The Organization of Behavior. New York: Wiley.

Hinton G.E. (1992), How neural networks learn from experience. Scientific American ;9:145-151.

Hornik K., Stinchcombe M., White H. (1989), Multilayer feedforward networks are universal approximators. Neural Networks ; 2:359–366.

Hopfield J.J. (2558), (1982), Neural networks and physical systems with emergent collective computational abilities. Proceedings of National Academy of Sciences; 79:2554-.

Hopfield J.J., Tank D.W. (1985), Neural computation of decisions in optimization problems. Biological Cybernetics ; 52:141-152.

Hu J.Q., Rose, E. (1995), On-line fuzzy modeling by data clustering using a neural network. Advances in Process Control. , 4, 187-194.

Huang J.S., Liu H.C. (2004), Object recognition using genetic algorithms with a Huang Z. Chen, H., Hsu, C.J. Chen, W.H. and Wu, S., Credit rating analysis with support vector machines and neural networks: a market comparative study. Decision Support Systems ; 37:543-558

Hopfield's neural model (1997). Expert Systems with Applications 1997; 13:191-199.

Jain L.C., Vemuri V.R. (1999), Industrial Applications of Neural Networks. Boca Raton: CRC Press, .

Kiang M.Y., Hu, M.Y., Fisher D.M. (2006), An extended self-organizing map network for market segmentation—a telecommunication example Decision Support Systems ; 42:36-47.

Kiang M.Y., Kulkarni U.R., Tam K.Y. (1995), Self-organizing map network as an interactive clustering tool-An application to group technology. Decision Support Systems ; 15:351-374.

Kim T., Kumara S.R.T., (1997), Boundary defect recognition using neural networks. International Journal of Production Research; 35:2397-2412.

Kim T.Y., Oh K.J., Sohn K., Hwang C. (2004), Usefulness of artificial neural networks for early warning system of economic crisis. Expert Systems with Applications ; 26:583-590.

Kirkos E., Spathis C., Manolopoulos Y., (2007), Data Mining techniques for the detection of fraudulent financial statements. Expert Systems with Applications ; 32: 995-1003.

Kiviluoto K. (1998), Predicting bankruptcy with the self-organizing map. Neuro-computing ; 21:203-224.

Klein B.D., Rossin D. F. (1999), Data quality in neural network models: effect of error rate and magnitude of error on predictive accuracy. Omega ; 27:569-582.

Kohonen T. (1982), Self-organized formation of topologically correct feature maps. Biological Cybernetics ; 43:59-69.

Kolehmainen M., Martikainen H., Ruuskanen J. (2001), Neural networks and periodic components used in air quality forecasting. Atmospheric Environment ; 35:815-825.

Law R. (2000), Back-propagation learning in improving the accuracy of neural network-based tourism demand forecasting. Tourism Management ; 21:331-340.

Lee D.L. (2002), Pattern sequence recognition using a time-varying Hopfield network. IEEE Transactions on Neural Networks ; 13:330-343.

Lewis O.M., Ware J.A., Jenkins D. (1997), A novel neural network technique for the valuation of residential property. Neural Computing and Applications ; 5:224-229.

Li W.J., Lee T., (2002), Object recognition and articulated object learning by accumulative Hopfield matching. Pattern Recognition; 35:1933-1948.

Lim G.S., Alder M., Hadingham P. (1992), Adaptive quadratic neural nets. Pattern Recognition Letters ; 13: 325-329.

Lisboa P.J.G., Edisbury B., Vellido A. (2000), Business Applications of Neural Networks : The State-of-the-art of Real-world Applications. River Edge: World Scientific, .

McCulloch W., Pitts W. (1943), A logical calculus of the ideas immanent in nervous activity. Bulletin of Mathematical Biophysics ; 5:115-133.

Min S.H., Lee J., Han I. (2006), Hybrid genetic algorithms and support vector machines for bankruptcy prediction. Expert Systems with Applications ; 31: 652-660.

Minsky M. L., Papert S. A. (1969), Perceptrons. MA: MIT press, .

Miyake S., Kanaya F. (1991), A neural network approach to a Bayesian statistical decision problem. IEEE Transactions on Neural Networks ; 2:538-540.

Mozer M.C., Wolniewics R. (2000), Predicting subscriber dissatisfaction and improving retention in the wireless telecommunication. IEEE Transactions on Neural Networks ; 11:690-696

Nag A.K., Mitra A. (2002), Forecasting daily foreign exchange rates using genetically optimized neural networks. Journal of Forecasting ; 21:501-512.

Nelson M., Hill T., Remus T., O'Connor, M. (1999), Time series forecasting using neural networks: Should the data be deseasonalized first? Journal of Forecasting ; 18:359-367.

O'Connor N., Madden M.G. (2006), A neural network approach to predicting stock exchange movements using external factors. Knowledge-Based Systems ; 19:371-378.

Paik J.K., Katsaggelos, A.K. (1992), Image restoration using a modified Hopfield neural network. IEEE Transactions on Image Processing ; 1:49-63.

Pajares G., Cruz J.M., Aranda, J. (1998), Relaxation by Hopfield network in stereo image matching. Pattern Recognition ; 31:561-574.

Panda C., Narasimhan V. (2007), Forecasting exchange rate better with artificial neural network. Journal of Policy Modeling ; 29:227-236.

Parker D.B. (1985), Learning-logic: Casting the cortex of the human brain in silicon, Technical Report TR-47, Center for Computational Research in Economics and Management Science, MIT.

Palmer A., Montaño J.J., Sesé, A. (2006), Designing an artificial neural network for forecasting tourism time series. Tourism Management ; 27: 781-790.

Partovi F.Y., Anandarajan M. (2002), Classifying inventory using an artificial neural network approach. Computers and Industrial Engineering ; 41:389-404.

Petersohn H. (1998), Assessment of cluster analysis and self-organizing maps. International Journal of Uncertainty Fuzziness and Knowledge-Based Systems. ; 6:139-149.

Prybutok V.R., Yi J., Mitchell D. (2000), Comparison of neural network models with ARIMA and regression models for prediction of Houston's daily maximum ozone concentrations. European Journal of Operational Research ; 122:31-40.

Qi M. (2001), Predicting US recessions with leading indicators via neural network models. International Journal of Forecasting ; 17:383-401.

Qi M., Zhang G.P. (2001), An investigation of model selection criteria for neural network time series forecasting. European Journal of Operational Research ; 132:666-680.

Qiao F., Yang H., Lam, W.H.K. (2001), Intelligent simulation and prediction of traffic flow dispersion. Transportation Research, Part B ; 35:843-863.

Raudys S. (1998), Evolution and generalization of a single neuron: I., Single-layer perceptron as seven statistical classifiers Neural Networks ; 11:283-296.

Raudys S. (1998), Evolution and generalization of a single neuron: II., Complexity of statistical classifiers and sample size considerations. Neural Networks ; 11:297-313.

Raviwongse R. Allada V., Sandidge T. (2000), Plastic manufacturing process selection methodology using self-organizing map (SOM)/fuzzy analysis. International Journal of Advanced Manufacturing Technology; 16:155-161.

Reed R. (1993), Pruning algorithms-a survey. IEEE Transactions on Neural Networks ; 4:740-747.

Remus W., O'Connor M. (2001), "Neural networks for time series forecasting." In Principles of Forecasting: A Handbook for Researchers and Practitioners, Armstrong, J. S. ed. Norwell:Kluwer Academic Publishers, 245-256.

Reutterer T., Natter M. (2000), Segmentation based competitive analysis with MULTICLUS and topology representing networks. Computers and Operations Research; 27:1227-1247.

Richard, M. (1991), D., Lippmann, R., Neural network classifiers estimate Bayesian *aposteriori* probabilities. Neural Computation ; 3:461-483.

Ripley A. (1993), "Statistical aspects of neural networks." In Networks and Chaos - Statistical and Probabilistic Aspects, Barndorff-Nielsen, O. E., Jensen J. L. and Kendall, W. S. eds. London: Chapman and Hall, 40-123.

Ripley A. (1994), Neural networks and related methods for classification. Journal of Royal Statistical Society, Series B ; 56:409-456.

Roh T. H. (2007), Forecasting the volatility of stock price index. Expert Systems with Applications ; 33:916-922.

Rosenblatt F. (1958), The perceptron: A probabilistic model for information storage and organization in the brain. Psychological Review ; 65:386-408.

Rout S., Srivastava, S.P., Majumdar, J. (1998), Multi-modal image segmentation using a modified Hopfield neural network. Pattern Recognition ; 31:743-750.

Rumelhart D.E., Hinton G.E., Williams R.J. (1986), "Learning internal representation by back-propagating errors." In Parallel Distributed Processing: Explorations in the Microstructure of Cognition Press, Rumelhart, D.E., McCleland,
J.L. and the PDP Research Group, eds. MA: MIT.

Saad E.W., Prokhorov D.V., Wunsch, D.C. II. (1998), Comparative study of stock
trend prediction using time delay, recurrent and probabilistic neural networks.
IEEE Transactions on Neural Networks; 9:456-1470.

Salcedo-Sanz S., Santiago-Mozos R.,Bousono-Calzon, C. (2004), A hybrid Hopfield network-simulated annealing approach for frequency assignment in satellite communications systems. IEEE Transactions on System, Man and Cybernetics, Part B:108-116.

Sarle W.S. (1994), Neural networks and statistical models. Poceedings of the Nine-
teenth Annual SAS Users Group International Conference, Cary, NC: SAS Institute, .

Schumacher M., Robner R., Vach W. (1996), Neural networks and logistic regression: Part I., Computational Statistics and Data Analysis ; 21:661-682.

Smith K.A., Ng, A. (2003), Web page clustering using a self-organizing map of user
navigation patterns. Decision Support Systems ; 35:245-256.

Smith K.A., Willis R.J., Brooks M. (2000), An analysis of customer retention
and insurance claim patterns using data mining: a case study. Journal of the
Operational Research Society; 51:532-541.

Soulie F.F., Gallinari P. (1998), Industrial Applications of Neural Networks. River
Edge, NJ: World Scientific.

Suganthan P.N., Teoh E.K., Mital D.P. (1995), Self-organizing Hopfield network for
attributed relational graph matching. Image and Vision Computing; 13:61-71.

Sun Z.Z., Yu S. (1995), Improvement on performance of modified Hopfield neural
network for image restoration. IEEE Transactions on Image processing; 4:683-
692.

Suykens J.A.K., Vandewalle J.P.L., De Moor B.L.R. (1996), Artificial Neural Networks for Modeling and Control of Nonlinear Systems. Boston: Kluwer.

Swanson N.R., White H. (1995), A model-selection approach to assessing the information in the term structure using linear models and artificial neural networks.
Journal of Business and Economic Statistics; 13;265-275.

Tatem A.J., Lewis H.G., Atkinson P.M., Nixon M.S. (2002), Supre-resolution land
cover pattern prediction using a Hopfield neural network. Remote Sensing of
Environment; 79:1-14.

Temponi C., Kuo Y.F., Corley H.W. (1999), A fuzzy neural architecture for customer satisfaction assessment. Journal of Intelligent & Fuzzy Systems; 7:173-
183.

Thieme R.J., Song M., Calantone R.J. (2000), Artificial neural network decision
support systems for new product developement project selection. Journal of
Marketing Research ; 37:543-558.

Vach W., Robner R., Schumacher M. (1996), Neural networks and logistic regression: Part I. Computational Statistics and Data Analysis; 21:683-701.

Wang T., Zhuang X., Xing X. (1992), Robust segmentation of noisy images using
a neural network model. Image Vision Computing; 10:233-240.

Webb A.R., Lowe D., (1990), The optimized internal representation of multilayer
classifier networks performs nonlinear discriminant analysis. Neural Networks;
3:367-375.

Werbos P.J., (1974), Beyond regression: New tools for prediction and analysis in the behavioral sciences. Ph.D. thesis, Harvard University, 1974.

West D., (2000), Neural network credit scoring models. Computers and Operations Research; 27:1131-1152.

West P.M., Brockett P.L., Golden L.L., (1997), A comparative analysis of neural networks and statistical methods for predicting consumer choice. Marketing Science; 16:370-391.

Widrow B., Hoff M.E., (1960), Adaptive switching circuits, 1960 IRE WESCON Convention Record, New York: IRE Part 4 1960:96-104.

Widrow B., Rumelhart D.E., Lehr M.A., (1994), Neural networks: applications in industry, business and science, Communications of the ACM; 37:93-105.

Wong B.K., Bodnovich T.A., Selvi Y., (1997), Neural network applications in business: A review and analysis of the literature (1988-1995). Decision Support Systems; 19:301-320.

Young S.S., Scott P.D., Nasrabadi, N.M., (1997), Object recognition using multi-layer Hopfield neural network. IEEE Transactions on Image Processing; 6:357-372.

Zhang G.P., (2007), Avoiding Pitfalls in Neural Network Research. IEEE Transactions on Systems, Man, and Cybernetics; 37:3-16.

Zhang G.P., Hu M.Y., Patuwo B.E., Indro D.C., (1999), Artificial neural networks in bankruptcy prediction: general framework and cross-validation analysis. European Journal of Operational Research; 116:16-32.

Zhang G.P., Keil M., Rai A., Mann J., (2003), Predicting information technology project escalation: a neural network approach. European Journal of Operational Research 2003; 146:115–129.

Zhang G.P., Qi M. (2002), "Predicting consumer retail sales using neural networks." In Neural Networks in Business: Techniques and Applications, Smith, K. and Gupta, J.eds. Hershey: Idea Group Publishing, 26-40.

Zhang G.P., Patuwo E.P., Hu M.Y., (1998), Forecasting with artificial neural networks: the state of the art. International Journal of Forecasting; 14:35-62.

Zhang W., Cao Q., Schniederjans M.J., (2004), Neural Network Earnings per Share Forecasting Models: A Comparative Analysis of Alternative Methods. Decision Sciences; 35: 205–237.

Zhu Z., He H., Starzyk J.A., Tseng, C., (2007), Self-organizing learning array and its application to economic and financial problems. Information Sciences; 177:1180-1192.

Improved SOM Labeling Methodology for Data Mining Applications

Arnulfo Azcarraga[1], Ming-Huei Hsieh[2], Shan-Ling Pan[3], and Rudy Setiono[4]

[1] College of Computer Studies, De La Salle University, Manila, the Philippines
azcarragaa@canlubang.dlsu.edu.ph
[2] Department of International Business, National Taiwan University, Taiwan
mhhsieh@management.ntu.edu.tw
[3] School of Computing, National University of Singapore, Singapore
pansl@comp.nus.edu.sg
[4] School of Computing, National University of Singapore, Singapore
rudys@comp.nus.edu.sg

Summary. Self-Organizing Maps (SOMs) have been useful in gaining insights about the information content of large volumes of data in various data mining applications. As a special form of neural networks, they have been attractive as a data mining tool because they are able to extract information from data even with very little user-intervention. However, although learning in self-organizing maps is considered unsupervised because training patterns do not need desired output information to be supplied by the user, a trained SOM often has to be labeled prior to use in many real-world applications. Unfortunately, this labeling phase is usually supervised as patterns need accompanying output information that have to be supplied by the user. Because labeled patterns are not always available or may not even be possible to construct, the supervised nature of the labeling phase restricts the deployment of SOM to a wider range of potential data mining applications. This work proposes a methodical and semi-automatic SOM labeling procedure that does not require a set of labeled patterns. Instead, nodes in the trained map are clustered and subsets of training patterns associated to each of the clustered nodes are identified. Salient dimensions per node cluster, that constitute the basis for labeling each node in the map, are then identified. The effectiveness of the method is demonstrated on a data mining application involving customer-profiling based on an international market segmentation study.

Key words: self-organizing maps, neural networks, classification, clustering

1 Introduction

In many data mining applications, there is limited knowledge about what might be contained in the input data, and very often, the dataset has no veritable structure that will allow for easy searching of information. As such, neural networks are important tools for data mining applications because they are able to learn just from being shown examples of the data, without explicitly being told what to look for, or how the information is structured in the input data.

Neural network models are often categorized as either "supervised" or "unsupervised", based on whether or not the learning method they employ requires some supplementary "desired output" information to accompany each of the training patterns. The most well-known supervised neural network model is the multi-layered perceptron (MLP), with retro-propagation of error as the underlying learning mechanism (Haykin, 1998, Rumelhart *et al.*, 1986). In such systems, network parameters are adjusted during training based on the difference (i.e. error) between the system's response for a given training pattern and the desired output for this pattern.

Among the unsupervised neural network models, the most popular are the Kohonen maps or Self-Organizing Maps (SOMs) (Kohonen, 1995, Kohonen, 1999). In the class of unsupervised neural network models, the underlying learning mechanism is Competitive Learning, the general framework for which is described in (Rumelhart and Zipser, 1986). Other models in this class include the Adaptive Resonance Theory (ART) (Carpenter and Grossberg, 1991) and the Neocognitron (Fukushima, 1980). All these models do not require any supplementary information other than the input data. The input space is partitioned into non-overlapping regions which are delineated based on a process of competition among the nodes in the neural network. For every training pattern that is shown to the network, the single node that is closest to the input pattern, based on some distance measure, earns the right to assimilate the training pattern by adapting its weights as well as the weights of those nodes in its neighborhood.

The SOM methodology dates back to the early 80's (Kohonen, 1982) and has been applied to a wide variety of applications (Kohonen, 1990), which include data mining (Kiang and Kumar, 2001), marketing (Schmitt and Deboeck, 1998, Kuo *et al.*, 2002), investment banking (Kiviluto and Bergius, 1998, Shumsky and Yarovoy, 1998); speech processing (Kohonen, 1990), robotics (Ritter *et al.*, 1992), finance engineering (Serrano-Cinca, 1998, Deboeck, 1998a, Deboeck, 1998b, Resta, 1998), text organization and retrieval (Kohonen *et al.*, 2000, Merkl, 1998), and real-estate applications (Carlson, 1998, Tulkki, 1998).

Prior to its use in some real-world application, a trained SOM has to be labeled - typically using labeling patterns that have accompanying category information. In a bankruptcy analysis application, for example, a set of known cases is used to determine which nodes are sensitive to profiles of companies that have financial difficulties and which nodes are sensitive to profiles of companies that are solvent (Serrano-Cinca, 1998). On the basis of these node labels, a new company is evaluated in terms of its chances of going bankrupt based on its profile. In such a typical SOM application, even if training is unsupervised, the labeling phase is supervised.

Because such labeled patterns are not always available or may not even be possible to construct, this supervised labeling phase of the SOM methodology hinders the deployment of SOM to an even wider range of potential domains of application. Take for example the case of a market survey of potential consumers, with questions pertaining to what consumers look for from a specific line of products. After the set of respondent records is fed to a SOM for training, a separate set of labeled consumer records would be needed to associate each node with some tangible purchasing pattern or behavior. For example, if we want the SOM to assist in identifying which types of responses correspond to what kinds of purchasing behavior, it would be convenient to have access to a set of respondent records with an indication of the type of product that they have actually purchased. With such "labeled" respondent records, we can check each node in the map to see which kinds of respondent records are associated with it, and to label them accordingly. This would then allow the user to do various post-processing tasks, like analyzing the socio-demographic profile of each cluster of nodes (i.e. each cluster of associated respondent records). In turn, this makes for clusters that are identifiable and actionable, with the presumption that clusters become meaningful only when they can be identified and can be acted upon (Wedel and Kamakura, 1998).

Indeed, several special-cases of self-organizing maps that have been deployed for very specific tasks are designed such that the labeling of the nodes does not require a set of pre-labeled patterns. This is the case for SOMs used in text-processing and classification (Merkl, 1998,Kohonen *et al.*, 2000,Azcarraga *et al.*, 2002). In these systems, the words associated with certain dimensions in the weight vectors of the trained SOM are used to label the nodes.

Building on the ideas underlying such systems, we improve on the SOM methodology by proposing a methodical and automatic SOM labeling procedure that does not require any set of labeled patterns. The proposed method is quite general. It can be applied to numerous other areas where self-organizing maps are being employed. For illustration purposes, however, we shall focus the discussions on a SOM-based international market segmentation study.

The rest of the chapter is organized as follows. Section 2 describes in greater detail the SOM methodology and includes some of the most frequently used training and labeling methods. Section 3 describes the unsupervised SOM labeling method that we propose. The application of this labeling method to a SOM-based international market segmentation study is discussed in section 4. Section 5 introduces some non-SOM techniques to validate the results. This is followed by the conclusions and recommendations for future work in section 6.

2 SOM methodology

The SOM methodology is depicted in Figure 1. Pre-processing would typically include dealing with missing data and normalizing input fields within a consistent input range, e.g. 0 to 1. Various other pre-processing steps are done depending on the specific domain of application. When preparing documents as input patterns in text processing and classification, for example, common words known as "stop words" are removed to reduce the dimensionality of the input space. Furthermore, words are reduced to their root form, through a process called "stemming". In the digital archiving of music, where SOMs may be used as an innovative interface for searching through and surfing over a large archive of music files, music files are pre-processed to extract various "features" that characterize the beat, rhythm, timbre, and higher level characteristics such as music genre, vocal quality, types of instruments used, etc. (Mayer *et al.*, 2006).

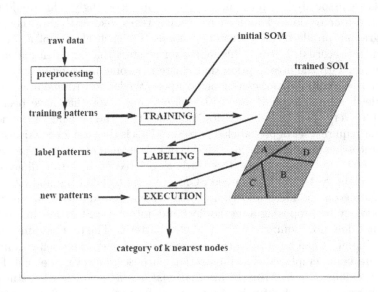

Fig. 1. A general SOM methodology

Once the raw data have been adequately represented in the input space, SOM training is performed. In a SOM system, a map is usually a rectangular grid of nodes, although some SOMs use hexagonal grid structures (Kohonen, 1999, Kohonen, 1990). All input units are connected to each node in the map, and the connection from each input unit i to a node j is represented by a connection weight w_{ij}. Each input unit corresponds to one input field, and typically, all input units draw their values from a binary set (0 or 1), bipolar set (-1 or +1), or from a uniform range of real values (e.g. 0 to 1). The set of values assumed by the individual input units at a certain training cycle

t is denoted by an input vector x^t, with x_i^t referring to the specific value of input unit i at cycle t. Training of the map consists of successively presenting input patterns through the input units and of adapting the various connection weights of each node in the map. At each training cycle t, one training sample x_t is selected at random. Each node then computes its distance/similarity to the current input, using some appropriate distance or similarity measure (e.g. Euclidean distance or cosine of angle between input and node weight vector). The weights w_{ij}^t of all nodes n_i in the neighborhood of the node with the smallest distance (the winning node n_c) are then updated using the following learning rule (Clark and Ravishankar, 1990):

$$w_{ij}^{t+1} = w_{ij}^t + \alpha(t)(x_j^t - w_{ij}^t) \qquad (1)$$

The gain parameter $\alpha(t)$ and the size of the neighborhood decrease with the number of cycles, according to some parameter adjustment function (Ritter et al., 1992).

The more recent version of the training algorithm does away with the neighborhood region. In its place, a gaussian function $G(c, i, t)$ is used so that nodes near the winning node n_c have larger weight changes than those further away (Kohonen, 1999):

$$w_{ij}^{t+1} = w_{ij}^t + \alpha(t)G(c, i, t)(x_j^t - w_{ij}^t) \qquad (2)$$

The function $G(c, i, t)$ is defined by the formula below, where $\sigma(t)$ is a parameter to control the size of the neighborhood of nodes that would have substantial weight changes, and $D(c, i)$ is the grid distance between a given node n_i and the winning node:

$$G(c, i, t) = \exp\left(\frac{-D(c, i)^2}{\sigma(t)^2}\right) \qquad (3)$$

By the end of the training phase, a self-organized map would have emerged. This map is often not useful until each node in the map is labeled. Some SOM applications, however, make do with just visualizing the individual component planes of the map. This is done by rendering the weight of each node's reference vector in 2D as shown in Figure 2. In the figure, each plane corresponds to a certain car feature. These features are the following: fun to drive, acceleration and speed, dealer service, fuel economy, styling, level of technology, luxury features, made to last, prestige, reliability, safety in accidents, sportiness, quality, passenger space, cargo/luggage space.

A total of 2,385 potential customers have been asked to select which three of the 15 car features above are most important to them. Based on the survey responses, a 16×16 SOM was trained and the weights on a per dimension basis are shown. In the SOM literature, these are referred to as "component planes". Each plane has 16×16 smaller squares, with each square representing a node in the 16×16 map. The grey level of each square denotes the weight value of the node for the given dimension. Black squares correspond to zero

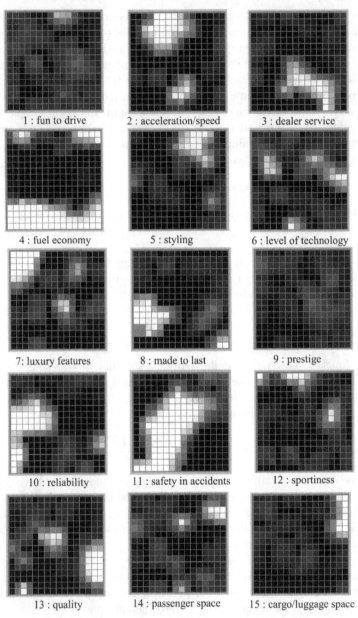

Fig. 2. Component planes for the trained 16×16 SOM, with one component plane for each dimension. Each dimension corresponds to a car feature that potential car buyers look for when buying a car. Lighter shades of grey indicate higher weight values for the given dimension.

or near zero weight values, while white squares denote higher weight values. A high weight value of a node for a given dimension (i.e. car feature) indicates that most of the respondents associated to the node have selected the given car feature as one of three car features they value most.

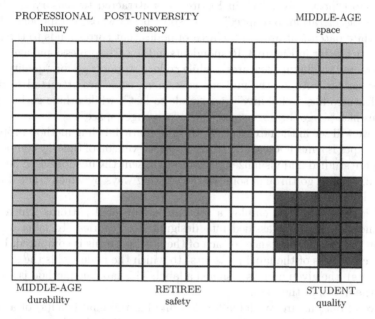

Fig. 3. A hypothetical SOM with clusters of nodes that have been labeled according to the age bracket to which most of its associated label patterns belong.

Deboeck and Kohonen (DeBoeck and Kohonen, 1998) present numerous examples on how component planes are visualized. Basically, the user takes note of the distribution patterns in the map of the weight values for every dimension (or component) and interprets them based on their relation to the clusters observed. To illustrate, suppose that the component planes of Figure 2 correspond to a trained SOM (refer to Figure 3) that has been labeled according to the age brackets of the majority of the associated respondent records. The nodes of the trained SOM have been labeled as: college student (age 18-22), post-university (23-30), early-professional (31-40), mid-age (41-60), and retiree (61-75). The aim of this labeling scheme would be to understand what types of car features attract customers of certain age groups[5].

---

[5] The labeling scheme of Figure 3 is fictitious aimed only at illustrating the use of component planes in relation to labeled maps. However, the component planes of Figure 2 are actual component planes generated for the market segmentation study discussed in section 4.

In this example, the user visually inspects the component planes and notes, for example, that component plane 11 reveals high preference for "safety in accidents" as a car feature among the retiree age-group, as manifested by the patch of white squares corresponding to those nodes associated with the retiree group in the mid-section of the map. Likewise, the young out-of-college age group ("post university" in Figure 3) is attracted to sensory car benefits like "acceleration and speed" and "sportiness" whose component planes show white patches at around the area of nodes that corresponds to the post-university cluster in Figure 3. Respondents in the early-professional age group are attracted to "luxury features", while college students go for "quality" and "dealer service". As for the mid-age customers, some are attracted to durability features like "reliability" and "made to last", while others go for space features like "cargo/luggage space" and "passenger space".

As we will see in the next section, the automatic labeling method proposed in this paper is a methodical and statistics-based version of the way component planes are studied and visualized. Before we present the unsupervised labeling method, we first go through some of the existing ways by which trained maps can be labeled.

The usual way is to employ a separate set of label patterns which have been individually pre-classified into designated categories. To label a given node in the map, its distance to each of the label patterns is computed. Based on the categories of the label pattern(s) to which the node yields the smallest distance(s), the given node is assigned a label. This labeling method is applied to all the nodes in the map.

Several options are available for determining the final label(s) of a node, given its distance d_i to each of the label patterns p_i. If the labels are categorical (e.g. "vowel a" for a phonetic map, "terrorism" for news classification), then given the set β of k label patterns which yield the k smallest distances to node j, some of the labeling methods for assigning a label c to the given node j are as follows:

1. c is any label among patterns in β. If $k = 1$, then c is just the label of pattern p_m that yields the lowest distance d_m;
2. c is the most common label among patterns in β;
3. c is any label appearing at least r times among patterns in β where r is a pre-set percentage of k; and
4. c is a label determined as follows: rank the patterns in β from the nearest to the farthest from node j, and assign them with weights $(k - r + 1)$, where r is their rank. The sum of weights for each label is tallied and the label with the highest total weight is chosen.

There are many variants to these labeling methods. Note that methods 2 and 4 yield a single label for each node, while methods 1 and 3 can assign multiple labels. Furthermore, if labels are assigned continuous values (e.g. "age": 22.3, "grade point average": 3.57), then method 2 is modified by computing the average label instead of choosing the most common label, while method 4 is modified by taking the weighted average of the labels.

Once the map is fully labeled, it is ready for use. Although it varies depending on the task a SOM is supposed to support, one frequent role of the SOM is to assist in the classification of some unknown pattern which has the same input fields as those of the training patterns. Classification is done by computing the distances of the unknown pattern with respect to each of the nodes in the map. The relative distances of the nodes plus their associated categories (labels) would then serve as basis for classifying the unknown pattern. The final classification of the unknown pattern can be as simple as just assigning the category of the node that registers the smallest distance to the unknown pattern.

Depending on the application, the process can be more complicated than a simple classification of an unknown pattern. In some applications, the distances and categories of a whole region of nodes (sometimes the entire map) that are nearest to the unknown pattern are fed to another classification system, along with the associated distances of each node. Or, as in the case of the phonetic map, for example, the trajectory of the nearest nodes while phonemes are fed to the SOM one after another is the basis for segmenting the speech data and for recognizing the spoken words (Kohonen, 1990). In Serrano-Cinca's work (Serrano-Cinca, 1998), this same type of trajectory of nearest nodes is the basis for determining the general liquidity (solvency) and financial health of banks.

3 Unsupervised SOM labeling

We propose a general method for labeling self-organizing maps that does away with pre-labeled patterns. Indeed, in many applications, pre-labeled patterns are not easy to obtain. In fact, if pre-labeled patterns are available, then the supervised neural network models could have been used instead. Unsupervised neural network models are attractive options because they do not require training patterns to be accompanied with the desired classification outcome. But if these unsupervised models would require labeled patterns for labeling the resultant neural network, then the applicability of these models becomes limited. Such is the drawback of self-organizing maps that we are able to fix with a novel labeling method that does not require pre-labeled patterns - not during training, and not even during labeling.

At the onset, we clarify that this unsupervised SOM labeling method is not applicable to every conceivable SOM application. For example, this proposed method may not be used in some applications in image processing, where the input dimensions refer to identical input features (i.e. light intensity) for pixels in different locations of the image. Nor would the method be applicable to some applications in speech processing, where all dimensions might refer to the amplitude at different frequencies of a set of voice signals. Since we use the dimensions as basis for differentiating the clusters, the physical interpretation of each individual dimension must then be distinguishable from each other.

The unsupervised labeling method we describe here would be useful in most other types of applications where each input dimension corresponds to a tangible feature that has some concrete meaning in the application domain. In text processing for example, each input dimension may correspond to some unique word or phrase (bi-grams or tri-grams). In various finance engineering applications, each input dimension may refer to some country-specific macro-economic variable like GNP or inflation rate. Or the input dimensions may correspond to normalized values of company-specific factors such as price-equity ratio, stock price, and market capitalization. In market segmentation studies, input dimensions may correspond to scaled responses to market survey questions such as whether a customer values prompt waiter service or whether a consumer prefers cars that have large passenger space, for example.

The general idea of our proposed unsupervised SOM labeling method consists of five main steps (refer to Figure 3), each of which would be elaborated further below:

1. group all nodes that have similar reference weight vectors using some clustering method;
2. for each cluster of nodes, prune out outlier nodes that are very different from their cluster centroids;
3. for each cluster of nodes (minus the outliers), classify the set of (unlabeled) training patterns as either in-patterns or out-patterns depending on whether or not their nearest node in the map is in the cluster;
4. based on the set of in-patterns and out-patterns of a given cluster, identify the salient dimensions; and
5. on the basis of the salient dimensions, assign a descriptive label to each cluster of nodes that is meaningful in the context of the application domain.

3.1 Step 1: Clustering of node weight vectors

In grouping the nodes into clusters of similar reference weight vectors, one major problem is determining the appropriate number of clusters. This can be resolved by doing a hierarchical clustering of the weight vectors. Various hierarchical methods can be used and these are discussed in standard clustering textbooks (Everitt, 1974, Hartigan, 1975, Spath, 1980). A recent survey was done by Xu and Wunsch (Xu and Wunsch, 2005).

There are basically two types of hierarchical methods: agglomerative and divisive. In agglomerative methods, each node weight vector starts off as individual clusters. At every step, the two most similar clusters are merged into a single cluster and the new cluster center, or centroid, is computed. The merging of clusters continues until the quality of the clusters is satisfactory, that is, no two distinct clusters may be merged and result in a significant increase in the quality of the groupings, according to some measure of clustering quality.

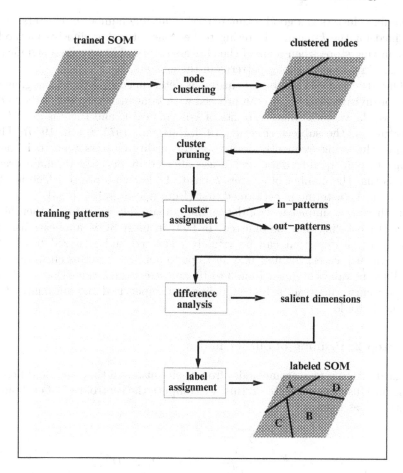

Fig. 4. General unsupervised SOM labeling method.

In divisive methods, all the node weight vectors start off as a single cluster. At each cycle, a partitioning system selects the cluster with the highest variance and breaks it up into two. Weight vectors in the cluster that has just been split are redistributed to the two new clusters. Again, the breaking up of clusters continues until the quality of the groupings has become satisfactory, according to some clustering quality measure.

The quality (usually based on the within-cluster variance) of the resultant groupings is computed every time two clusters are merged in the case of agglomerative methods, or whenever a cluster is split into two in the case of divisive methods. For agglomerative methods, a relatively large increase in the variance among the patterns within a cluster is a good indicator that the two clusters are quite distinct and should not be merged. When this happens, the hierarchical clustering may be stopped at this point, and the number of remaining clusters is a good estimate of the suitable number of clusters to be specified for the k-means clustering to be done later. For divisive methods, the splitting stops when none of the clusters can be split to gain a significant decrease in variance among patterns in the clusters.

Once the suitable number of clusters is determined by either an agglomerative or divisive method, we can proceed with k-means clustering of the SOM node weight vectors. Many variants of k-means exist, and there is abundant literature on the subject (Everitt, 1974, Hartigan, 1975, Spath, 1980). This form of clustering frequently derives better quality clusters, since it is more robust to poor quality data, and is less affected by outliers. Its main drawback is that the number of clusters k has to be known a priori, which is why hierarchical clustering is performed first (Punj and Steward, 1983).

If there is a simpler way of determining a suitable value for k, then hierarchical clustering may be omitted. In fact, in most SOM applications, the number of clusters that can be visually inspected and analyzed has to be small. In such cases, the user may just opt to perform k-means clustering using different values of k, say from 3 to 10, and select the k value that produces the best clustering results. Since labeling is unsupervised and automatic, this is feasible to do.

3.2 Step 2: Pruning of outlier nodes

We next try to remove some nodes from their clusters if they are too different from the cluster centers. To do this, we compute the centroid χ^k of each node cluster Γ^k as follows :

$$\chi_j^k = \frac{\sum\limits_{n_i \in \Gamma^k} w_{ij}}{|\Gamma^k|}, \quad j = 1, 2, \ldots, D \tag{4}$$

where D is the dimensionality of the data and w_{ij} is the jth component of the reference weight vector of node n_i, one of the nodes in Γ^k. The function $|A|$ returns the cardinality of set A. We then compute the distance d_i from each node n_i in Γ^k to its centroid χ^k as :

$$d_i = \sqrt{\sum_{j=1}^{D} \left(w_{ij} - \chi_j^k\right)^2} \tag{5}$$

With the individual node distances to their respective cluster centroids, we are ready to compute the mean μ_d^k of these distances and the standard deviation σ_d^k for each cluster of nodes. Using $z = 1$, we retain a node n_i in its original cluster if

$$\mu_d^k - z \times \sigma_d^k < d_i < \mu_d^k + z \times \sigma_d^k \tag{6}$$

Those nodes with distance from the centroid that differ from the mean by more than one standard deviation are considered *outliers* and are excluded from the cluster. All these nodes that have been dropped from their original clusters can be collectively referred to as "unlabeled nodes". In some applications, this special set of nodes may have some concrete role to play.

3.3 Step 3: Separating in-patterns and out-patterns

Once each node in the map is assigned to a given cluster, the individual training patterns are re-used. Each of these patterns is assigned to the cluster of the node to which the distance is smallest. On the basis of these training pattern assignments, we construct an *in-patterns* set and an *out-patterns* set for each cluster. The in-patterns are those patterns belonging to the given cluster, while the out-patterns are all the other patterns not belonging to the cluster, including those patterns associated with "unlabeled nodes" if any.

3.4 Step 4: Identifying salient dimensions

The next step is to identify those dimensions in a given cluster, referred to as salient dimensions, whose values are significantly different in a statistical sense compared to those in the other clusters. For each cluster, we determine if the mean input value among the in-patterns for a given dimension is significantly higher or lower than the corresponding mean input value among the out-patterns. To identify salient dimensions of each cluster Γ^k, we do the following

1. for each dimension v, compute $\mu_{in}(k, v)$ and $\mu_{out}(k, v)$ as the mean input value for the set of in-patterns $\Phi_{in}(k)$ and out-patterns $\Phi_{out}(k)$, respectively, where p_i is training pattern i and x_{iv} is the v-th component of the input vector of p_i:

$$\mu_{in}(k, v) = \frac{\displaystyle\sum_{p_i \in \Phi_{in}(k)} x_{iv}}{|\Phi_{in}(k)|} \tag{7}$$

$$\mu_{out}(k, v) = \frac{\displaystyle\sum_{p_i \in \Phi_{out}(k)} x_{iv}}{|\Phi_{out}(k)|} \tag{8}$$

2. compute the *difference factor* $df(k, v)$ of each dimension v as

$$df(k, v) = \frac{\mu_{in}(k, v) - \mu_{out}(k, v)}{\mu_{out}(k, v)} \tag{9}$$

3. compute the difference factors mean $\mu_{df}(k)$ and standard deviation $\sigma_{df}(k)$ over all dimensions v; to avoid possible mix-up in the indices, we give the formula for the mean and standard deviation as follows:

$$\mu_{df}(k) = \frac{\sum_{v=1}^{D} df(k,v)}{D} \tag{10}$$

$$\sigma_{df}(k) = \left(\sum_{v=1}^{D} (df(k,v) - \mu_{df}(k,v))^2 / D \right)^{\frac{1}{2}} \tag{11}$$

Using Equations 12, 13 and 14, we are ready to precisely define a salient dimension. A dimension v is a salient dimension for cluster Γ^k if its corresponding difference factor deviates from the mean by at least one standard deviation; that is if

$$df(k,v) \leq \mu_{df}(k) - z \times \sigma_{df}(k) \tag{12}$$

or

$$df(k,v) \geq \mu_{df}(k) + z \times \sigma_{df}(k) \tag{13}$$

with $z = 1$.

3.5 Step 5: Assignment of descriptive labels

Once the salient dimensions are identified for each cluster of nodes, we manually interpret the label combinations and assign domain-specific descriptions as final cluster labels. This step is inherently supervised in most domains of applications. A user has to inspect the salient dimensions and must provide the required descriptive labels. It is interesting to note that in text processing applications, even this final step can be unsupervised, since the words that correspond to the salient dimensions can in fact take the place of a "descriptive label". Note that the association between dimension and words is done automatically during the pre-processing stage.

In cases where there is more than one significant dimension for a given cluster, the absolute value of the difference factors is used to rank the salient dimensions, which would then aid in deciding on an appropriate descriptive label for the cluster. It should also be noted that in some applications, only dimensions that have positive difference factors (i.e. $\mu_{in}(k,v) > \mu_{out}(k,v)$) are meaningful. In such cases, the user may just ignore the negative difference factors when choosing appropriate labels for the cluster. Examples will be given below to illustrate this.

On the issue of input representation, we explained at the onset, that we are assuming dimensions are distinct and they individually represent some tangible feature in the application domain. Note, however, that even if this is not the case, our method would be able to detect the salient dimensions. For some applications, this is all that is needed (i.e. descriptive labels are not necessary).

Another point regarding input representation is that our method is sensitive to "high values" and "low values" when evaluating each dimension for purposes of spotting salient dimensions. Therefore, if the domain of application is such that several ranges of values may have important connotations, then assigning one dimension to each range of values is a better encoding scheme. In the case of age or income brackets, for example, representing each range of values as a separate dimension would allow for labels to be deduced for the specific age or income bracket. Otherwise, if data are entered as normalized values within a certain range (e.g. 0 to 1), then the label will only be in terms of high and low age or income, and will not pertain to specific income or age brackets.

4 Customer profiling: an illustration

Being visual renderings of the input set, self-organized maps open up opportunities for gaining insights and mining critical information from an otherwise unstructured set of data. We illustrate here how a SOM is labeled with the appropriate labels and, once labeled, is used to do an automatic profiling of potential car buyers. The user of the SOM results could, for example, design detailed marketing strategies for very specific niche markets, given the features and qualities that the specific market is attracted to.

We trained a SOM using data collected by MORPACE International in a cross-national consumer survey. The data set covers the top twenty automobile markets in the world consisting of 4,320 eligible new vehicle buyers who bought a car within the past six months during the period September-October 1997. Although the dataset consists of 4,332 samples, only respondents who had purchased or intended to purchase a passenger car were selected for analysis. Furthermore, Chinese-, Russian-, Turkish-, and Indian samples were removed from the dataset for analysis due to the relatively modest qualified sample sizes in those countries. Consequently, a total of 2,385 respondent records from 16 countries were included in the study.

In the survey, automobile benefit-sought behavior was measured by asking respondents to choose up to three benefits (out of 15) that they considered as most important benefits when purchasing a new car. The list of benefits includes "fun to drive", "good acceleration and speed", "good dealer service", "good fuel economy", "good styling", "level of technology", "luxury features", "made to last", "prestige", "reliability", "safety in accidents", "sportiness", "high quality", "passenger space", and "cargo/luggage space".

According to a study (Hsieh, 2002), the dimensionality of the benefits listed above corresponds approximately to the brand concepts[6] proposed by

---

[6] Brand concepts are defined as brand-unique abstract meanings that typically originate from a particular configuration of product features and a firm's efforts to create meaning from these arrangements (Park *et al.*, 1991).

Park, Jaworski and MacInnis (Park *et al.*, 1986). The four dimensions extracted are: (1) the symbolic dimension including prestige, luxury features, styling and quality, (2) the sensory dimension including good acceleration and speed, fun to drive, and sportiness (3) the utilitarian dimension including reliability, durability and safety in accidents, and (4) the economic dimension consisting of fuel economy and dealer service. The relationship between functional/utilitarian, social/symbolic and experiential/sensory needs and consumption has been proven to be significant in various studies (Holbrook and Schindler, 1994). The set of benefits covering the three universal needs along with specific product benefits serve as a rather comprehensive set of benefits that consumers are likely to be seeking.

A 16×16 SOM was trained using the converted binary data from the global samples. By doing an agglomerative hierarchical clustering on the data, we observed that when the number of clusters was fewer than six, relatively distinct clusters were being merged (big increase in inter-cluster variance). But there was really no specific number of clusters that was evidently ideal, so we proceeded with doing k-means clustering using different values of k. We did not probe more than eight clusters since, from a market segmentation point of view, a large number of clusters would be counter-productive. Of the clusters generated, we zeroed in on the initial 6-cluster solution shown in Figure 5.

By virtue of SOM's well-studied characteristics (Wu and Chow, 2005), it can be surmised that clusters 4 and 5 are somewhat related because the nodes that constitute these clusters are positioned spatially close together in the map. On the other hand, clusters 0 and 3 are positioned at opposite ends of the map, indicating that responses to the survey vary more significantly between these two clusters than between other pairs of clusters in the map. It is also worth noting that even if our clustering method does not force nodes in the same cluster to be contiguous in the map, the clusters we derived are patches of nodes that are mostly contiguous in the map, except for the lone cluster 0 node somewhere above cluster 5. The fact that nodes in a cluster tend to be contiguous in the trained map is a result of the weight update procedure done on the nodes reference vectors during training.

Each respondent record in our dataset is matched to the node in the map with a reference weight vector that has the smallest (Euclidean) distance with respect to it. The cluster number of the nearest node is assigned to the respondent record accordingly. Thus, the entire dataset is now subdivided into subsets of respondent records for each cluster (i.e. the set of in-patterns per cluster). The number of respondent records assigned to each cluster is shown in Table 1. In this study, we skipped the pruning step and retained all the nodes in the different clusters as part of the their respective clusters. As will be discussed in the next section, we will be conducting a separate study focused on the pruned off nodes.

Since cluster 2 is a significantly sized cluster, we probed it further by doing a further k-means clustering on just the nodes in this cluster 2. At $k = 3$, we

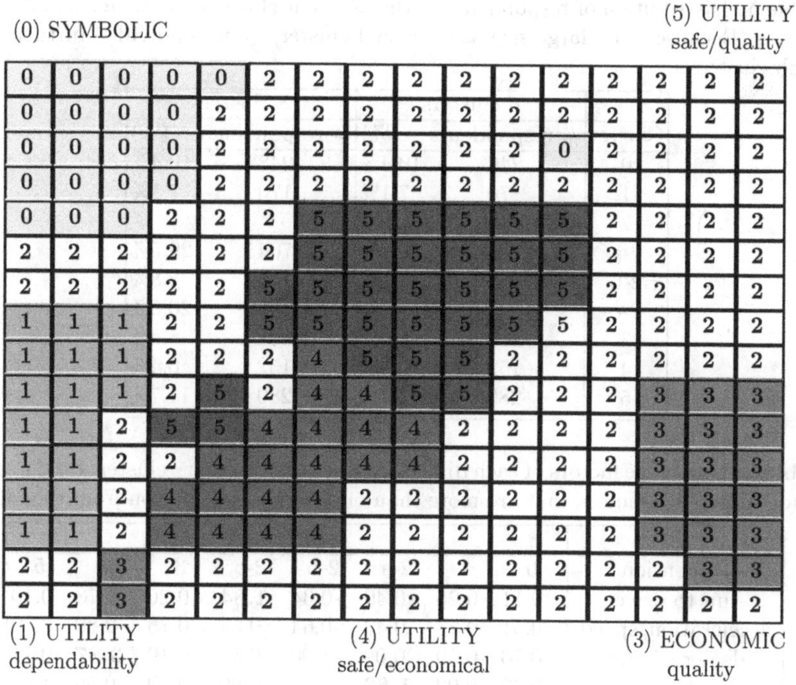

(0) SYMBOLIC

(5) UTILITY
safe/quality

0	0	0	0	0	2	2	2	2	2	2	2	2	2	2	2
0	0	0	0	2	2	2	2	2	2	2	2	2	2	2	2
0	0	0	0	2	2	2	2	2	2	2	0	2	2	2	2
0	0	0	0	2	2	2	2	2	2	2	2	2	2	2	2
0	0	0	2	2	2	5	5	5	5	5	5	2	2	2	2
2	2	2	2	2	2	5	5	5	5	5	5	2	2	2	2
2	2	2	2	2	5	5	5	5	5	5	5	2	2	2	2
1	1	1	2	2	5	5	5	5	5	5	5	2	2	2	2
1	1	1	2	2	2	4	5	5	5	2	2	2	2	2	2
1	1	1	2	5	2	4	4	5	5	2	2	2	3	3	3
1	1	2	5	5	4	4	4	4	2	2	2	2	3	3	3
1	1	2	2	4	4	4	4	4	2	2	2	2	3	3	3
1	1	2	4	4	4	4	2	2	2	2	2	2	3	3	3
1	1	2	4	4	4	4	2	2	2	2	2	2	3	3	3
2	2	3	2	2	2	2	2	2	2	2	2	2	3	3	3
2	2	3	2	2	2	2	2	2	2	2	2	2	2	2	2

(1) UTILITY
dependability

(4) UTILITY
safe/economical

(3) ECONOMIC
quality

Fig. 5. The trained 16 × 16 SOM with a clustering of nodes. Cluster 2 nodes have subsequently been clustered into 3 smaller sub-clusters.

are able to break-up cluster 2 into meaningful sub-clusters. This portion of our market segmentation study, which does a second k-means clustering on the relatively very large cluster from the initial clustering, deviates somewhat from the method outlined in the preceding section. However, the goal is to reach a final clustering of the SOM nodes, and we are consistent as far as this goal is concerned. Note that if we simply do a one-step k-means clustering using $k = 8$, we would not be able to obtain the same quality of clusters that we obtained here.

We then inspect the respondent records in each cluster to generate the profile of benefits-sought in each of the clusters. The frequency distribution of each selected benefit in the entire survey set is first computed. We then compute the frequency distributions for just the individual clusters, after which we compute the difference factors between in-patterns and out-patterns on a per dimension basis. The difference factors between the set of in-patterns and the set of out-patterns for each of the benefit dimensions are shown in Table 2. For each cluster, we also compute the mean and the standard deviation of these difference factors. These would be the basis for deciding which dimensions are salient for each cluster.

Table 1. Distribution of respondents to the different clusters based on six and eight clusters. Because of its large size, the original cluster 2 was subdivided further into 3 sub-clusters.

	6 clusters		8 clusters	
Cluster	# respondents	(%)	# respondents	(%)
0	248	10.4%	248	10.4%
1	170	7.1%	170	7.1%
2	1334	55.9%		
2-a			704	29.5%
2-b			139	5.8%
2-c			491	20.6%
3	201	8.4%	201	8.4%
4	152	6.4%	152	6.4%
5	280	11.7%	280	11.7%

Table 2. Difference factors of each dimension (benefit) for every cluster. Bold figures denote difference factors that are more than one standard deviation from the mean.

	Clusters							
Dimension	0	1	2-a	2-b	2-c	3	4	5
fun to drive	-0.11	-0.25	-0.49	-0.34	**1.84**	-0.20	-0.78	0.10
acceleration/speed	0.51	-0.87	0.43	-0.64	0.55	-0.75	-0.89	0.10
dealer service	-0.76	-0.59	-0.09	-1.00	0.55	0.10	**3.87**	-0.71
fuel economy	-0.39	-0.02	**1.63**	1.08	-0.99	0.59	0.56	-1.00
styling	-0.52	-0.42	**0.92**	-0.51	0.46	-0.11	-0.85	-0.44
level of technology	0.18	-0.50	-0.36	0.12	**1.47**	-0.83	-0.95	0.41
luxury features	**13.25**	-0.90	-0.72	-1.00	-0.58	-0.72	-1.00	0.23
made to last	-0.73	**4.80**	-0.54	-0.62	-0.51	0.02	**2.34**	-0.23
prestige	1.46	-0.56	-0.49	-0.68	0.87	-0.16	-0.71	0.13
reliability	-0.77	**5.18**	0.01	-0.90	-0.09	0.04	-0.66	-0.63
safety in accident	-0.97	-0.56	0.44	-0.68	-0.84	-0.55	**2.05**	**2.49**
sportiness	1.74	-0.40	-0.27	-0.67	0.96	-0.59	-0.45	-0.59
quality	-0.79	-0.54	-0.96	-0.83	-0.09	**11.00**	-1.00	**0.89**
passenger space	-0.24	-0.87	-0.18	**3.98**	0.06	-0.68	-0.66	0.34
cargo/luggage space	-0.42	-0.85	0.12	**8.56**	-0.25	-0.79	-0.83	-0.68
μ	0.76	0.18	-0.04	0.39	0.23	0.42	0.00	0.03
σ	3.55	1.97	0.67	2.59	0.83	0.95	1.52	0.86
$\mu+\sigma$	4.31	2.15	0.64	2.98	1.06	3.38	1.52	0.89

Since this is a market-segmentation study, we refer to the salient dimensions as the "primary benefit(s)" sought by respondents in each cluster. We only considered positive difference factors, because of the nature of the study. We are mainly trying to establish what car features each cluster of consumers is seeking when buying a car, and not so much what they are least interested in. The distinctive meaning of each segment is then determined by assessing the combination of benefits and the importance respondents attach to individual benefits. Eight types of benefit segments were identified, as listed in

Table 3. In the table, we also present "secondary benefits" since they aid in providing a better profile of the kind of benefits the customers are seeking for each cluster. We consider all positive difference factors that are less than one standard deviation from the mean as "secondary benefits".

Table 3. Primary and secondary benefits sought for each cluster with corresponding difference factors.

Cluster	Label	Primary benefits	Secondary benefits
0	SYMBOLIC	luxury features (13.25)	sportiness (1.74) prestige (1.46) acceleration/speed (0.51) level of technology (0.18)
1	UTILITARIAN (dependability)	reliability (5.18) made to last (4.80)	
2-a	ECONOMIC (fuel economy)	fuel economy (1.63) styling (0.92)	safety in accidents (0.44) acceleration/speed (0.43) cargo/luggage space (0.12) reliability (0.01)
2-b	UTILITARIAN (larger space)	cargo/luggage space (8.56) passenger space (3.98)	fuel economy (1.08) level of technology (0.12)
2-c	SENSORY	fun to drive (1.84) level of technology (1.47)	sportiness (0.96) prestige (0.87) acceleration/speed (0.55) dealer service (0.55) styling (0.46) passenger space (0.06)
3	ECONOMIC (quality)	high quality (11.00)	fuel economy (0.59) dealer service (0.10) reliability (0.04) made to last (0.02)
4	UTILITARIAN (safe/economical)	good dealer service (3.87) made to last (2.34) safety in accidents (2.05)	fuel economy (0.56)
5	UTILITARIAN (safe/high quality)	safety in accidents (2.49) high quality (0.89)	level of technology (0.41) passenger space (0.34) luxury features (0.23) prestige (0.13) acceleration/speed (0.10) fun to drive (0.10)

Cluster 2-a, an economic-oriented segment, is dominated by "good fuel economy" and supplemented by "good styling", "safety in accidents", "good acceleration and speed", "cargo/luggage space" and "reliability". Cluster 2-c, which is a "sensory" segment, values benefits such as "fun to drive", "level of technology", "sportiness", "prestige", "good acceleration and speed" and "styling". Respondents who fall under the "symbolic" segment (cluster 0) are those who value "luxury features" and appreciate other symbol-oriented benefits such as "prestige", "sportiness", "good acceleration and speed" and "level of technology". Cluster 3 is the other economic-oriented segment with benefits such as "high quality", "fuel economy", and "good dealer service".

The remaining four segments differ from each other, but all reflect various utilitarian needs. Cluster 1 represents utilitarian benefit seekers who are after "reliability" and "made to last". Clusters 4 and 5 are both concerned with "safety in accidents", except that their respective secondary benefits point to two distinct types of needs. Whereas cluster 4 is a grouping of safety-conscious consumers who value "good dealer service", "made to last" and "good fuel economy", cluster 5 consumers are concerned with "high quality", "level of technology", "passenger space", "luxury features", "prestige", etc. Finally, cluster 2-b is another utilitarian segment that is mainly focused on "space" benefits, including both "passenger space" and "cargo/luggage space".

Note that the component planes shown earlier in Figure 2 are based on the actual trained weights of the SOM we have generated for this study. Knowing the primary and secondary benefits from Table 3, it is easy to work backwards and verify our results. Indeed, when a dimension is a primary benefit for a given cluster, the component plane corresponding to that dimension has a white patch (high weight values) in the section of the map that corresponds to the nodes that make up the given cluster. However, had we relied on just the visual inspection of component planes the way it is usually done, we might be able to manually deduce some of the primary benefits, but the level of detail of Table 3 will be very difficult to match.

We are now ready to construct the demographic profile of each of the eight clusters, including age, gender, marital status, and whether or not a respondent has children under 18. We have done this at the global level as well as at the level of groupings of countries (i.e. continental Europe, Latin America, Anglo-America, East Asia). Interested readers are referred to (Azcarraga *et al.*, 2003) for the marketing context of the study.

Table 4 gives socio-demographic profile of each cluster of car features at the global level in terms of the percent distribution of respondents in each of the car-benefits clusters that were previously identified. From Table 5, we observe that the symbolic segment has a significantly higher proportion of younger consumers in the under-30 age bracket. We expected the sensory segment to be dominated by the younger consumers as well, but this trend is not significant at the global level.

A quite unexpected result is the significantly higher proportion of female consumers who value passenger and cargo space. In the global sample, only 37% of the respondents are female. This proportion increased significantly to 50% for cluster 2-b. Also, married consumers prefer low maintenance attributes and good dealer service. Furthermore, the economic cluster 3 shows a significantly dominant middle age consumer bracket from 30 to 40 years old, and slightly older.

Table 4. Global socio-demographic profile of each benefits-sought cluster (figures are in %).

Clusters		Demographics							
		gender		status		age			
		female	male	single	married	< 30	30-39	40-49	50-59	≥ 60
0	symbolic	35	65	47	53	33	30	23	12	8
1	utilitarian (dependability)	34	66	29	71	19	32	25	14	10
2-a	utilitarian (fuel economy)	38	62	39	61	26	29	23	14	8
2-b	utilitarian (space)	50	50	42	58	24	30	24	12	9
2-c	sensory	33	67	39	61	31	29	20	11	9
3	economic (quality)	38	62	39	61	24	36	24	11	4
4	utilitarian (safe/economical)	41	59	25	75	15	34	24	17	11
5	utilitarian (safe/quality)	38	62	34	66	25	26	26	11	10
All		**37**	**63**	**38**	**62**	**26**	**30**	**23**	**12**	**8**

Table 5. Global socio-demographic profile of each benefits-sought cluster based on net deviation of % proportion from mean. Items labeled as ++ and −− have one standard deviation of positive or negative deviation from the mean. Others are labeled as + or − when the net deviation is more than 5%.

Clusters		Demographics							
		gender		status		age			
		female	male	single	married	< 30	30-39	40-49	50-59	≥ 60
0	symbolic	−	+	+	−	++	−	−	−	−
1	utilitarian (dependability)	−	+	−	+	−−	+	+	+	+
2-a	utilitarian (fuel economy)						−		+	
2-b	utilitarian (space)	++	−−	+	−	−		+		
2-c	sensory	−	+			+		−	−	
3	economic (quality)					−	++	+	−	−
4	utilitarian (safe/economical)	+	−	−−	++	−−	+		+	+
5	utilitarian (safe/quality)			−	+	−	−	+	−	+

The socio-demographic profiles of each cluster are more pronounced when studied at a regional level than at the global level, as can be seen from Table 6. At the global level, the profiles of the various niche markets in the regional levels tend to cancel each other.

For the purpose of illustrating how we are able to mine for insights that may be very useful in marketing applications, for example, we will highlight here a few of the marketing-related results for Continental Europe and Latin America. In Continental Europe, gender does not matter much compared to the other regional-cultural blocs. Whether a consumer is male or female matters only in cluster 2-b, associated with passenger and cargo space. Latin America is where socio-demographics matter the most. For example, proportionately more unmarried (single) consumers go for symbolic, utilitarian (space), and economic benefits, while the married consumers go for dependability and safe-and-economical. Gender matters in all clusters as well, even significantly with dependability and sensory benefits for males, and safe-and-economical and space benefits for females. Age is significantly pronounced in seven of the eight Latin American clusters. It should be noted that like the Anglo-American bloc, the proportion for the above-60 age bracket (retired segment) is significantly higher for three benefits clusters. However, only one

Table 6. Regional socio-demographic profile of each benefits-sought cluster.

	Clusters	Demographics (Anglo-America)								
		gender		status		age				
		female	male	single	married	< 30	30-39	40-49	50-59	≥ 60
0	symbolic	--	++	+	-	+	++		-	++
1	utilitarian (dependability)	-	+	-	+	--	+	+	+	+
2-a	utilitarian (fuel economy)						-		+	
2-b	utilitarian (space)	++	--	+	-		-	+	-	
2-c	sensory	-	+			+		-	-	
3	economic(quality)					-	++	+	-	-
4	utilitarian (safe/economical)	+	-	--	++	--	+		+	+
5	utilitarian (safe/quality)			-	+	-	-	-	-	+

	Clusters	Demographics (Continental Europe)								
		gender		status		age				
		female	male	single	married	< 30	30-39	40-49	50-59	≥ 60
0	symbolic			+	-	++	-	+	-	-
1	utilitarian (dependability)	-	+	--	++	--		+	+	+
2-a	utilitarian (fuel economy)					-				+
2-b	utilitarian (space)	++	--				+			+
2-c	sensory	-	+	+	-	++		-	-	
3	economic (quality)	-	+	+	-	-	++			-
4	utilitarian (safe/economical)			-	+	--	-	+	++	-
5	utilitarian (safe/quality)	+	-			+	-	+	+	-

	Clusters	Demographics (Latin America)								
		gender		status		age				
		female	male	single	married	< 30	30-39	40-49	50-59	≥ 60
0	symbolic	-	+	++	--	++		--	-	-
1	utilitarian (dependability)	--	++	--	++	--	-	+		++
2-a	utilitarian (fuel economy)	++	--	-	+		-		-	++
2-b	utilitarian (space)	++	--	++	--	++	--	-	--	--
2-c	sensory	--	++	-	+	+	+	-	--	-
3	economic (quality)	+	-	++	--		++	-		-
4	utilitarian (safe/economical)	+	-	--	++	--	++			++
5	utilitarian (safe/quality)	-	+	-	+	--	-	++	-	-

	Clusters	Demographics (East Asia)								
		gender		status		age				
		female	male	single	married	< 30	30-39	40-49	50-59	≥ 60
0	symbolic			++	--	++		--		-
1	utilitarian (dependability)	-	+	-	+	--	++		-	-
2-a	utilitarian (fuel economy)	++	-	+	-	+	--		+	
2-b	utilitarian (space)	++	--			+	--	++	-	-
2-c	sensory	--	++	-	+		+	-		+
3	economic (quality)	++	--			+	+			-
4	utilitarian (safe/economical)	+	-	--	++	--	+	+		+
5	utilitarian (safe/quality)	-	+			+	--	+		+

of the three clusters represents the same group of benefits sought, namely "safe and economical" (cluster 4).

In a very succinct manner, a SOM rendering of the marketing information contains a lot of relevant information that are more readily understood when shown in a picture form (Figures 6 and 7) than in the form of a table, as in Table 6. The SOM, once appropriately labeled, does provide various insights depending on the use of the information revealed by the SOM. In Figure 6, we note that luxury features and economic benefits are positioned at opposite corners of the map, reflecting the distinct types of benefits they include. In the middle portion are most of the utilitarian benefits, with the two safety-in-accidents clusters positioned side-by-side each other in the center of the map.

For the Anglo-American bloc, the males are mainly attracted to the symbolic benefit, while a significantly higher proportion of women are attracted to two utilitarian clusters (clusters 2-b and 4) in the mid-section of the map. The married consumers are likewise attracted to cluster 4 (i.e., safety and economic related benefits). As for the age, the young consumers are attracted to the symbolic and sensory clusters, as expected, while the middle-aged consumers are attracted to utilitarian and economic clusters. There is a distinct market among the 60-over consumers in the Anglo-American bloc (which is not evident in Continental Europe and East Asia), in that they gravitate significantly towards the symbolic benefit as well as the two safety-in-accidents benefits (i.e., clusters 4 and 5).

In Figure 7 we use another visual SOM-rendering of the socio-demographic segmentation of a group of countries (East Asia) to reinforce the claim that such "pictures" can be more insightful than the usual tabular presentation of Table 6. Notice how much easier it is to see the over-all picture when the demographics are presented as shown in Figure 7. In addition, the socio-demographic profiles of the Anglo-American and East Asian blocs can be readily compared. In the East-Asian bloc, the males are mainly attracted to the sensory benefits ("level of technology", "fun to drive", etc.), while a significantly higher proportion of women is attracted cluster 2-b (space) and cluster 3 "high quality". The married consumers are attracted to cluster 4 (i.e., safety and economic related benefits). The young consumers under 30 years old are attracted to the symbolic cluster ("luxury features"), while those in the 30-39 range go for "durability", and those in the 40-59 range go for "space".

5 Assessing the quality of the cluster labels

Although the method works well for the market segmentation study discussed above, one may wonder whether other known methods might yield similar results or might provide further evidence that the results are indeed satisfactory. To address this question, we assessed the quality of the clusters and of the identified salient dimensions using various statistical tests and machine learning techniques.

First, we applied Wilks' Lambda F test using MANOVA to test the effect of each of the factors (i.e., eight clusters) on the dependent variables (i.e., 15 benefits) on a pair-wise basis. Wilks' Lambda is a test statistic frequently used in multivariate analysis for mean differences among more than two groups. In our case, this test would establish whether in fact the eight clusters that we have generated are distinct in terms of benefits desired by respondents in each cluster. At significance level .01, the centroid vector representing each cluster was found to be pair-wise different from each of the centroids vectors of all the other clusters. As described earlier, we also saw that each cluster can be associated with a unique set of benefits that would establish its distinctive

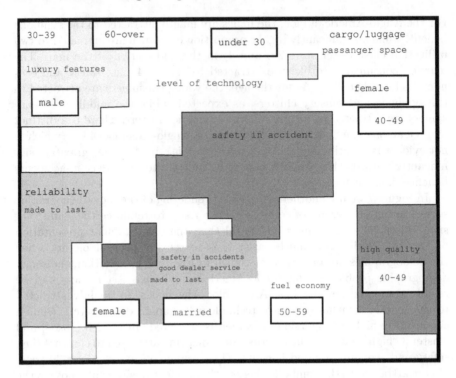

Fig. 6. Labeled SOM with superimposed socio-demographics for the Anglo-American bloc.

character. That we are able to do so further supports our claim that the eight clusters are distinct.

To validate the assignment of primary and secondary benefits to each cluster, we relied on the tests of between-subject effects generated from the same MANOVA to check for significant effect of cluster on each benefit across different clusters. We noted for each cluster all those benefits which are different at significance level .05 from all the seven other clusters. From among these, we further identify those benefits whose means are higher than the over-all mean (all clusters included). Table 7 shows that the benefits identified as outlined above are exactly those listed as either primary or secondary benefits in Table 3, which used difference factors as basis for identifying them. Furthermore, almost all of the primary benefits for each cluster in Table 3 are significantly different from all seven other clusters as shown in Table 7. The only exception is the "fuel economy" primary benefit of cluster 2-a. It has a mean value that is not significantly different from that of cluster 2-b, which also has "fuel economy" as a secondary benefit.

These tests for independence that help us determine which of the dimensions are significantly different for a given cluster are only useful for validating the selection of significant dimensions that we have previously done. If it were

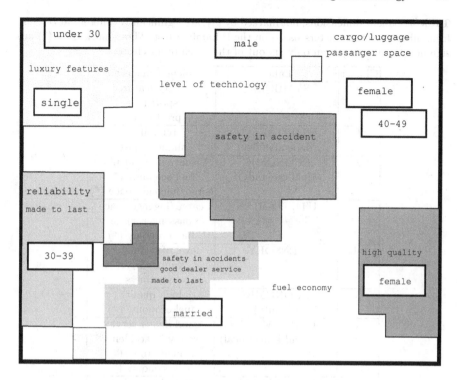

Fig. 7. Labeled SOM with superimposed socio-demographics for the East-Asian bloc.

used as the main technique for identifying the significant dimensions, it is not clear what criteria (cut-off point) should be used to identify the salient dimensions. For example, a given dimension that is extremely high for three and very low for five out of eight clusters may in fact be a "salient dimension" for labeling purposes. Yet, if the cut-off is set at six out of seven other clusters, such a dimension may not be selected as a salient dimension. Also, secondary benefits would have been difficult to identify.

A final validation technique involves the use of C4.5, a very well-established decision tree classifier (Quinlan, 1993). We use C4.5 to automatically build a decision tree that would classify respondent patterns as either belonging to the in-patterns set or the out-patterns set. A very useful feature of C4.5 is that aside from building a decision tree, it is able to extract a set of rules that mimics the decision-making process of the tree. Figure 8 is an example of the extracted rules for cluster 0, after C4.5 has built a decision tree based on the sets of in-patterns and out-patterns for cluster 0. In the rules of Figure 8, class 0 refers to the out-patterns set while class 1 refers to the in-patterns set. Note that C4.5 automatically drops certain rules, which explains why rules 3 to 6 are missing.

Table 7. Salient dimensions, not marked by (*), are significantly different at $\alpha = .05$ from all other seven clusters based on the F Lambda test. Those marked by (*) are significantly different from only six out of the seven other clusters.

Cluster	Label	Salient Dimensions
0	SYMBOLIC	luxury features sportiness prestige (*)
1	UTILITARIAN (dependability)	reliability made to last
2	ECONOMIC (fuel economy)	safety in accidents fuel economy (*) cargo/luggage space (*)
2-a	UTILITARIAN (larger space)	cargo/luggage space passenger space fuel economy (*)
2-b	SENSORY	level of technology fun to drive sportiness
3	ECONOMIC (quality)	high quality fuel economy (*)
4	UTILITARIAN (safe and economical)	good dealer service safety in accidents made to last fuel economy (*)
5	UTILITARIAN (safe and high quality)	safety in accidents high quality luxury features passenger space (*)

We basically would want the extracted rules to confirm that cluster 0 is a "symbolic" cluster, with "luxury features" as the primary benefit. Indeed, this is what C4.5 is able to extract from the decision tree it has built for cluster 0. Clearly, the rules extracted by C4.5 are the kinds of information we need when we want to assign descriptive labels to each cluster in the map. As a validation technique, it does well in confirming that the significant dimensions identified by the proposed methodology are in fact what the C4.5 rules are using in deciding that a pattern belongs to the in-patterns set. In fact, all the significant dimensions we have identified have also appeared prominently in the respective rules extracted by C4.5 (in the interest of space, we are not showing them all here).

Just like for the F tests for significance, it is tempting to conclude that C4.5 can replace the dimension-selection technique based on difference factors. Just to illustrate how it can be quite complicated to do so, we refer to Figure 9 containing the list of extracted C4.5 rules for cluster 2-b. The rules set for cluster 2-b is already the next to the simplest, after that of cluster

```
Rule 1:
        Q7-Luxury-Features = 0
        -> class 0  [99.9%]

Rule 7:
        Q11-Safety-in-Accidents = 1
        -> class 0  [99.4%]

Rule 2:
        Q3-Dealer-Service = 0
        Q5-Styling = 0
        Q7-Luxury-Features = 1
        Q10-Reliability = 0
        Q11-Safety-in-Accidents = 0
        Q13-Quality = 0
        -> class 1  [95.9%]
```

Fig. 8. Extracted rules using C4.5 given the sets of in-patterns (class 1) and out-patterns (class 0) for cluster 0. Clearly, the dimension "luxury features" is the salient dimension for this "symbolic" cluster, thus validating the salient dimension (primary benefit) extracted by our method as shown in Table 3.

0. Those for the other clusters have many more rules with many more dimensions included in the rule conditions. Again, knowing that our method has tagged "passenger space" and "luggage space" as the primary benefits for this cluster, we can confirm the validity of our extracted primary labels. However, if C4.5 were directly used to isolate these two primary benefits, there is no straightforward method for isolating these two dimensions from "fuel economy" for example, which also appears prominently in the rules. Only by assessing the rules together as a set, are we able to discern the truly important variables. This obviously becomes extremely difficult when the set of rules is complex. Furthermore, there is no clear way of ranking the dimensions from the most significant to the least significant, the way it can be done in a very neat manner using difference factors.

There remains one more important point. Although it is quite clear that the two validation methods employed here - statistical and decision-tree - cannot be used as alternatives to our method based on difference factors, it remains a methodological issue whether one or both methods ought to be included in the general unsupervised labeling methodology that we are proposing.

We prefer to leave validation out as an optional phase and to use it only when 1) the user has absolutely no idea as to what constitutes a "reasonable" set of findings; and 2) the results appear counter-intuitive. Basically, the validation techniques, particularly the rule extraction method using C4.5, would be useful to detect some procedural or computational mistakes related to the computation of difference factors, means and standard deviations. However,

```
Rule 5:
        Q4-Fuel-Economy = 1
        Q15-Cargo-Luggage-Space = 1
        -> class 1  [82.9%]

Rule 3:
        Q11-Safety-in-Accidents = 0
        Q14-Passenger-Space = 1
        Q15-Cargo-Luggage-Space = 1
        -> class 1. [71.8%]

Rule 2:
        Q4-Fuel-Economy = 0
        Q14-Passenger-Space = 0
        -> class 0  [99.9%]

Rule 4:
        Q4-Fuel-Economy = 0
        Q11-Safety-in-Accidents = 1
        -> class 0  [99.7%]

Rule 1:
        Q15-Cargo-Luggage-Space = 0
        -> class 0  [97.9%]
```

Fig. 9. Extracted rules using C4.5 given the sets of in-patterns (class 1) and out-patterns (class 0) for cluster 2-b. Although "passenger space" and "cargo/luggage space" which are the cluster's primary benefits from Table 3, do appear prominently in the rules, it is not clear how these two dimensions could have been isolated from the other dimensions (e.g. "fuel economy") just based on the rules extracted for cluster 2-b.

it must be emphasized that since C4.5 comes into the picture after the sets of in-patterns and out-patterns of each cluster have been determined, any error prior to this step would remain undetected.

6 Conclusion

Neural networks are potent data mining models, as they are able to learn just from being shown examples of the data, without explicitly being told what to look for, or how the information is structured in the input heap. Indeed, data mining tools become very useful precisely when there is little knowledge about what might be contained in the input data, and often times, the dataset has no veritable structure to speak of. Among the neural network models, self-organizing maps, which belong to the class of unsupervised neural network learning models, become doubly interesting for data mining applications because this model does not require training data to have accompanying desired-output information that typically would need some tedious user-intervention (which is the case for supervised neural network learning models).

It must be emphasized that although training (learning) in self-organizing maps (SOMs) is unsupervised, the labeling phase is very often a supervised process. The labeling process is supervised in that we rely on labeled patterns that have accompanying desired-output information. Since such labeled patterns are not always available or may not even be possible to construct, the supervised labeling phase of the SOM methodology hinders the deployment of SOMs to a wider range of potential domains of application.

We improved on the SOM methodology by devising a methodical and automatic SOM labeling procedure that does not require a set of labeled patterns. Nodes of the trained map are clustered and the so-called *salient dimensions* in each cluster are automatically identified. Out of these salient dimensions, a "descriptive label" is assigned by the user. Assignment of a descriptive label is still a form of user intervention, but this is no longer at the level of individual labeled patterns.

We have illustrated the effectiveness of the method by applying the unsupervised labeling method to a SOM-based customer-profiling study. The market segmentation application illustrates the usefulness of SOM as a methodology for data mining, through clustering and visualization of unstructured data.

In the market segmentation study, clustering of the benefits-sought data could have been done by a multitude of clustering techniques, and a number of these would probably generate a similar segmentation. However, SOM provides an additional feature: visualization of the clusters on a simple 2D grid that would position the clusters in such a way that those that are near each other, in a spatial sense, pertain to benefits groupings that are fairly similar (i.e. the Euclidean distance of their associated input vectors is small). In addition, we are able to superimpose on this cluster distribution the primary benefits for the different clusters, and the various socio-demographic patterns for the different market niches represented by the clusters.

Acknowledgment

The authors acknowledge the contribution of MORPACE International Inc. in providing the dataset for analysis.

References

Azcarraga AP, Hsieh M, Setiono R, (2003), Visualizing globalization: A SOM approach to customer profiling. In:Proceedings of 24th International Conference on Information Systems (ICIS), Seattle, WA.

Azcarraga A, Yap TN, Tan J, Chua TS, (2002), Evaluating keyword selection methods for WEBSOM text archives, IEEE Transactions on Knowledge and Data Engineering, 16(3): 380–383.

Carlson E, (1998), Real estate investment appraisal of land properties using SOM. In: Deboeck G, Kohonen T (eds), Visual explorations infinance with self-organizing maps, Springer-Verlag, London.

Carpenter GA, Grossberg S, (1991), Pattern-recognition by self-organizing neural networks. MIT Press, Cambridge, MA.

Clark D, Ravishankar K, (1990), A convergence theorem for Grossberg learning, Neural Networks 3(1): 87–92.

Deboeck G, Kohonen T, (1998), Visual explorations in finance with self-organizing maps,Springer-Verlag, London.

Deboeck G, (1998), Picking mutual funds with self-organizing maps. In:Deboeck G, Kohonen T (eds), Visual explorations in finance with self-organizing maps, Springer-Verlag, London.

Deboeck G, (1998), Investment maps of emerging markets. In: Deboeck G, Kohonen T (eds), Visual explorations in finance with self-organizing maps, Springer-Verlag, London.

Everitt B, (1974), Cluster analysis, Heinemann Educational Books, London.

Fukushima K, (1980), Neocognitron: a self-organizing neural network model for a mechanism of pattern recognition unaffected by shift inposition, Biological Cybernetics 36: 121–136.

Hartigan JA, (1975), Clustering algorithms, Wiley-Interscience, New York.

Haykin S, (1998), Neural networks: a comprehensive foundation. Prentice-Hall International, 2nd Edition, Upper Saddle River, NewJersey.

Holbrook MB, Schindler RM, (1994), Age, sex, and attitude toward the pastas predictors of consumers' aesthetic taste for cultural products. Journal of Consumer Research 31: 412–22.

Hsieh MH, (2002), Identifying brand image dimensionality and measuring degree of brand globalization: a cross-national study. Journal of International Marketing 10(2): 46–67.

Kiang MY, Kumar A, (2001), An evaluation of self-organizing map networks as a robust alternative to factor analysis in data mining applications, Information Systems Research 12: 177–194.

Kiviluto K, Bergius P, (1998), Maps for analyzing failures of small andmedium-sized enterprises. In: Deboeck G, Kohonen T (eds), Visual explorations in finance with self-organizing maps,Springer-Verlag, London.

Kohonen T, (2000), Self-organization of a massive document collection, IEEE Transactions on Neural Networks 11(3): 574–585.

Kohonen T, (1982), Self-organized formation of topologically-correct feature maps, Biological Cybernetics 43: 59–69.

Kohonen T, (1990), The self-organizing map, Proceedings of the IEEE 78:1464–1480.

Kohonen T, (1995), Self-organizing maps, Springer-Verlag, Berlin.

Kohonen T, (1999), Kohonen maps, Elsevier, New York.

Kuo RJ, Ho LM, Hu CM, (2002), Integration of self-organizing feature mapand k-means algorithm for market segmentation, Computers and Operations Research 29:1475–1493.

Mayer R, Lidy T, Rauber A, (2006), The map of Mozart, Proc 7th International Conference on Music Information Retrieval, Victoria,Canada, Oct 8-12.

Merkl D, (1998), Text classification with self-organizing maps: some lessons learned, Neurocomputing 21: 61–77.

Park CW, Jaworski BJ, MacInnis DJ, (1986), Strategic brand concept-imagemanagement. Journal of Marketing 50: 135–145.

Park CW, Milberg S, Lawson R, (1991), Evaluation of brand extension:the role of product level similarity and brand concept consistency. Journal of Consumer Research 18: 185–193.

Punj G, Steward DW, (1983), Cluster analysis in marketing research: review and suggestions for applications. Journal of Marketing Research 20: 134–148.

Quinlan R, (1993), C4.5: Programs for machine learning, Morgan Kaufman,San Mateo, CA.

Resta M, (1998), A hybrid neural network system for trading financial markets. In: Deboeck G, Kohonen T (eds), Visual explorations infinance with self-organizing maps, Springer-Verlag, London.

Ritter H, Martinetz T, Schulten K, (1992), Neural computation and self-organizing maps (translated from German), Addison-Wesley, Reading MA.

Rumelhart DE, Zipser D, (1986), Feature discovery by competitive learning. In: Rumelhart DE and McClelland JL (eds) Parallel and Distributed Processing, Vol 1, 151-193. MIT Press, Cambridge, CA.

Rumelhart DE, Hinton GE, Williams RJ, (1986), Learning internal representations by error propagation. In: Rumelhart DE, McClelland JL (eds) Parallel and Distributed Processing, Vol 1. 318-362. MITPress, Cambridge, MA.

Schmitt B, Deboeck G, (1998), Differential patterns in consumer purchase preferences using self-organizing maps: a case study of China. In:Deboeck G, Kohonen T (eds), Visual explorations in finance withself-organizing maps, Springer-Verlag, London.

Serrano-Cinca C, (1998), Let financial data speak for themselves. In:Deboeck G, Kohonen T (eds), Visual explorations in finance with self-organizing maps, Springer-Verlag, London.

Shumsky S, Yarovoy AV, (1998), Self-organizing atlas of Russian banks. In:Deboeck G, Kohonen T (eds), Visual explorations in finance with self-organizing maps, Springer-Verlag, London.

Spath H, (1980), Cluster analysis algorithms, Ellis Horwood, Chichester,England.

Tulkki A, (1998), Real estate investment appraisal of buildings using SOM. In: Deboeck G, Kohonen T (eds), Visual explorations in financewith self-organizing maps, Springer-Verlag, London.

Wedel M, Kamakura W, (1998), Market segmentation: conceptual and methodological foundations, Kluwer Academic Publishers, Boston,MA.

Wu S, Chow T, (2005), PRSOM: A new visualization method by hybridizing multi dimensional scaling and self-organizing Map, IEEE Trans on Neural Networks 16(6): 1362–1380.

Xu R, Wunsch D, (2005), Survey of cluster algorithms, IEEE Trans on Neural Networks, 16(3): 645–678.

Part II

Evolutionary Methods

A Review of Evolutionary Algorithms for Data Mining

Alex A. Freitas

University of Kent, UK, Computing Laboratory, A.A.Freitas@kent.ac.uk

Summary. Evolutionary Algorithms (EAs) are stochastic search algorithms inspired by the process of neo-Darwinian evolution. The motivation for applying EAs to data mining is that they are robust, adaptive search techniques that perform a global search in the solution space. This chapter first presents a brief overview of EAs, focusing mainly on two kinds of EAs, viz. Genetic Algorithms (GAs) and Genetic Programming (GP). Then the chapter reviews the main concepts and principles used by EAs designed for solving several data mining tasks, namely: discovery of classification rules, clustering, attribute selection and attribute construction. Finally, it discusses Multi-Objective EAs, based on the concept of Pareto dominance, and their use in several data mining tasks.

Key words: genetic algorithm, genetic programming, classification, clustering, attribute selection, attribute construction, multi-objective optimization

1 Introduction

The paradigm of Evolutionary Algorithms (EAs) consists of stochastic search algorithms inspired by the process of neo-Darwinian evolution (Back et al. 2000; De Jong 2006; Eiben & Smith 2003). EAs work with a population of individuals, each of them a candidate solution to a given problem, that "evolve" towards better and better solutions to that problem. It should be noted that this is a very generic search paradigm. EAs can be used to solve many different kinds of problems, by carefully specifying what kind of candidate solution an individual represents and how the quality of that solution is evaluated (by a "fitness" function).

In essence, the motivation for applying EAs to data mining is that EAs are robust, adaptive search methods that perform a global search in the space of candidate solutions. In contrast, several more conventional data mining methods perform a local, greedy search in the space of candidate solutions. As a result of their global search, EAs tend to cope better with attribute interactions than greedy data mining methods (Freitas 2002a; Dhar et al. 2000; Papagelis & Kalles 2001; Freitas 2001, 2002c). Hence, intuitively EAs can discover interesting knowledge that would be missed by a greedy method.

The remainder of this chapter is organized as follows. Section 2 presents a brief overview of EAs. Section 3 discusses EAs for discovering classification rules. Section 4 discusses EAs for clustering. Section 5 discusses EAs for two data preprocessing tasks, namely attribute selection and attribute construction. Section 6 discusses multi-objective EAs. Finally, Section 7 concludes the chapter. This chapter is an updated version of (Freitas 2005).

2 An Overview of Evolutionary Algorithms

An Evolutionary Algorithm (EA) is essentially an algorithm inspired by the principle of natural selection and natural genetics. The basic idea is simple. In nature individuals are continuously evolving, getting more and more adapted to the environment. In EAs each "individual" corresponds to a candidate solution to the target problem, which could be considered a very simple "environment". Each individual is evaluated by a fitness function, which measures the quality of the candidate solution represented by the individual. At each generation (iteration), the best individuals (candidate solutions) have a higher probability of being selected for reproduction. The selected individuals undergo operations inspired by natural genetics, such as crossover (where part of the genetic material of two individuals are swapped) and mutation (where part of the generic material of an individual is replaced by randomly-generated genetic material), producing new offspring which will replace the parents, creating a new generation of individuals. This process is iteratively repeated until a stopping criterion is satisfied, such as until a fixed number of generations has been performed or until a satisfactory solution has been found.

There are several kinds of EAs, such as Genetic Algorithms, Genetic Programming, Classifier Systems, Evolution Strategies, Evolutionary Programming, Estimation of Distribution Algorithms, etc. (Back et al. 2000; De Jong 2006; Eiben & Smith 2003). This chapter will focus on Genetic Algorithms (GAs) and Genetic Programming (GP), which are probably the two kinds of EA that have been most used for data mining.

Both GA and GP can be described, at a high level of abstraction, by the pseudocode of Algorithm 1. Although GA and GP share this basic pseudocode, there are several important differences between these two kinds of algorithms. One of these differences involves the kind of solution represented by each of these kinds of algorithms. In GAs, in general a candidate solution consists mainly of values of variables – in essence, data. By contrast, in GP the candidate solution usually consists of both data and functions. Therefore, in GP one works with two sets of symbols that can be represented in an individual, namely the terminal set and the function set. The terminal set typically contains variables (or attributes) and constants; whereas the function set contains functions which are believed to be appropriate to represent good solutions for the target problem. In the context of data mining, the explicit use of a function set is interesting because it provides GP with potentially powerful means of changing the original data representation into a representation that is more suitable for knowledge discovery purposes, which is not so naturally done when using GAs or another EA where only attributes (but not functions) are represented by an individual. This ability of changing the data representation will be discussed particularly on the section about GP for attribute construction.

Note that in general there is no distinction between terminal set and function set in the case of GAs, because GAs' individuals usually consist only of data, not functions. As a result, the representation of GA individuals tend to be simpler than the representation of GP individuals. In particular, GA individuals are usually represented by a fixed-length linear genome, whereas the genome of GP individuals is often represented by a variable-size tree genome – where the internal nodes contain functions and the leaf nodes contain terminals.

Algorithm 1: Generic Pseudocode for GA and GP

1: Create initial population of individuals
2: Compute the fitness of each individual
3: **repeat**
4:    Select individuals based on fitness
5:    Apply genetic operators to selected individuals, creating new individuals
6:    Compute fitness of each of the new individuals
7:    Update the current population (new individuals replace old individuals)
8: **until** (stopping criteria)

When designing a GP algorithm, one must bear in mind two important properties that should be satisfied by the algorithm, namely closure and sufficiency (Banzhaf et al. 1998; Koza 1992). Closure means that every function in the function set must be able to accept, as input, the result of any other function or any terminal in the terminal set. Some approaches to satisfy the closure property in the context of attribute construction will be discussed in Subsection 5.2. Sufficiency means that the function set should be expressive enough to allow the representation of a good solution to the target problem. In practice it is difficult to know *a priori* which functions should be used to guarantee the sufficiency property, because in challenging real-world problems one often does not know the shape of a good solution for the problem. As a practical guideline, (Banzhaf et al. 1998) (p. 111) recommends:

"An approximate starting point for a function set might be the arithmetic and logic operations: PLUS, MINUS, TIMES, DIVIDE, OR, AND, XOR. ... Good solutions using only this function set have been obtained on several different classification problems,... ,and symbolic regression problems."

We have previously mentioned some differences between GA and GP, involving their individual representation. Arguably, however, the most important difference between GAs and GP involves the fundamental nature of the solution that they represent. More precisely, in GAs (like in most other kinds of EA) each individual represents a solution to one particular instance of the problem being solved. In contrast, in GP a candidate solution should represent a generic solution – a program or an algorithm – to the kind of problem being solved; in the sense that the evolved program should be generic enough to be applied to any instance of the target kind of problem.

To quote (Banzhaf et al. 1998), p. 6:

> it is possible to define genetic programming as the direct evolution of *programs or algorithms* [our italics] for the purpose of inductive learning.

In practice, in the context of data mining, most GP algorithms evolve a solution (say, a classification model) *specific for a single data set*, rather than a *generic program* that can be applied to different data sets from different application domains. An exception is the work of (Pappa & Freitas 2006), proposing a grammar-based GP system that automatically evolves full rule induction algorithms, with loop statements, generic procedures for building and pruning classification rules, etc. Hence, in this system the output of a GP run is a *generic* rule induction algorithm (implemented in Java), which can be run on virtually any classification data set – in the same way that a manually-designed rule induction algorithm can be run on virtually any classification data set. An extended version of the work presented in (Pappa & Freitas 2006) is discussed in detail in another chapter of this book (Pappa & Freitas 2007).

3 Evolutionary Algorithms for Discovering Classification Rules

Most of the EAs discussed in this section are Genetic Algorithms, but it should be emphasized that classification rules can also be discovered by other kinds of EAs. In particular, for a review of Genetic Programming algorithms for classification-rule discovery, see (Freitas 2002a); and for a review of Learning Classifier Systems (a type of algorithm based on a combination of EA and reinforcement learning principles), see (Bull 2004; Bull & Kovacs 2005).

3.1 Individual Representation for Classification-Rule Discovery

This Subsection assumes that the EA discovers classification rules of the form "IF (conditions) THEN (class)" (Witten & Frank 2005). This kind of knowledge representation has the advantage of being intuitively comprehensible to the user – an important point in data mining (Fayyad et al. 1996). A crucial issue in the design of an individual representation is to decide whether the candidate solution represented by an individual will be a rule set or just a single classification rule (Freitas 2002a, 2002b).

The former approach is often called the "Pittsburgh approach", whereas the later approach is often called the "Michigan-style approach". This latter term is an extension of the term "Michigan approach", which was originally used to refer to one particular kind of EA called Learning Classifier Systems (Smith 2000; Goldberg 1989). In this chapter we use the extended term "Michigan-style approach" because, instead of discussing Learning Classifier Systems, we discuss conceptually simpler EAs sharing the basic characteristic that an individual represents a single classification rule, regardless of other aspects of the EA.

The difference between the two approaches is illustrated in Figure 1. Figure 1(a) shows the Pittsburgh approach. The number of rules, m, can be either variable, automatically evolved by the EA, or fixed by a user-specified parameter. Figure 1(b) shows the Michigan-style approach, with a single rule per individual. In both Figure 1(a) and 1(b) the rule antecedent (the "IF part" of the rule) consists of a conjunction of conditions. Each condition is typically of the form <Attribute, Operator, Value>, also known as attribute-value (or propositional logic) representation. Examples are the conditions: "Gender = Female" and "Age < 25". In the case of continuous attributes it is also common to have rule conditions of the form <LowerBound, Operator, Attribute, Operator, UpperBound>, e.g.: "30K ≤ Salary ≤ 50K".

In some EAs the individuals can only represent rule conditions with categorical (nominal) attributes such as Gender, whose values (male, female) have no ordering – so that the only operator used in the rule conditions is "=", and sometimes "≠". When using EAs with this limitation, if the data set contains continuous attributes – with ordered numerical values – those attributes have to be discretized in a preprocessing stage, before the EA is applied. In practice it is desirable to use an EA where individuals can represent rule conditions with both categorical and continuous attributes. In this case the EA is effectively doing a discretization of continuous values "on-the-fly", since by creating rule conditions such as "30K ≤ Salary ≤ 50K" the EA is effectively producing discrete intervals. The effectiveness of an EA that directly copes with continuous attributes can be improved by using operators that enlarge or shrink the intervals based on concepts and methods borrowed from the research area of discretization in data mining (Divina & Marchiori 2005).

It is also possible to have conditions of the form <Attribute, Operator, Attribute>, such as "Income > Expenditure". Such conditions are associated with relational (or first-order logic) representations. This kind of relational representation has considerably more expressiveness power than the conventional attribute-value representation, but the former is associated with a much larger search space – which often requires a more complex EA and a longer processing time. Hence, most EAs for rule discovery use the attribute-value, propositional representation. EAs using the relational, first-order logic representation are described, for instance, in (Neri & Giordana 1995; Hekanaho 1995; Woung & Leung 2000; Divina & Marchiori 2002).

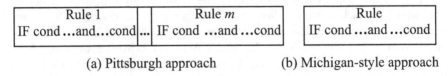

(a) Pittsburgh approach   (b) Michigan-style approach

Fig. 1. Pittsburgh vs. Michigan-style approach for individual representation

Note that in Figure 1 the individuals are representing only the rule antecedent, and not the rule consequent (predicted class). It would be possible to include the predicted class in each individual's genome and let that class be evolved along with its corresponding rule antecedent. However, this approach has one significant drawback, which can be illustrated with the following example. Suppose an EA has just generated an individual whose rule antecedent covers 100 examples, 97 of which have class c_1. Due to the stochastic nature of the evolutionary process and the "blind-search" nature of the generic operators, the EA could associate that rule antecedent with class c_2, which would assign a very low fitness to that individual – a very undesirable result. This kind of problem can be avoided if, instead of evolving the rule consequent, the predicted class for each rule is determined by other (non-evolutionary) means. In particular, two such means are as follows.

First, one can simply assign to the individual the class of the majority of the examples covered by the rule antecedent (class c_1 in the above example), as a conventional, non-evolutionary rule induction algorithm would do. Second, one could use the "sequential covering" approach, which is often used by conventional rule induction algorithms (Witten & Frank 2005). In this approach, the EA discovers rules for one class at a time. For each class, the EA is run for as long as necessary to discover rules covering all examples of that class. During the evolutionary search for rules predicting that class, all individuals of the population will be representing rules predicting the same fixed class. Note that this avoids the problem of crossover mixing genetic material of rules predicting different classes, which is a potential problem in approaches where different individuals in the population represent rules predicting different classes. A more detailed discussion about how to represent the rule consequent in an EA can be found in (Freitas 2002a).

The main advantage of the Pittsburgh approach is that an individual represents a complete solution to a classification problem, i.e., an entire set of rules. Hence, the evaluation of an individual naturally takes into account rule interactions, assessing the quality of the rule *set*. In addition, the more complete information associated with each individual in the Pittsburgh approach can be used to design "intelligent", task-specific genetic operators. An example is the "smart" crossover operator proposed by (Bacardit & Krasnogor 2006), which heuristically selects, out of the N sets of rules in N parents (where $N \geq 2$), a good subset of rules to be included in a new child individual. The main disadvantage of the Pittsburgh approach is that it leads to long individuals and renders the design of genetic operators (that will act on selected individuals in order to produce new offspring) more difficult.

The main advantage of the Michigan-style approach is that the individual representation is simple, without the need for encoding multiple rules in an individual. This leads to relatively short individuals and simplifies the design of genetic operators. The main disadvantage of the Michigan-style approach is that, since each individual represents a single rule, a standard evaluation of the fitness of an individual ignores the problem of rule interaction. In the classification task, one usually wants to evolve a *good set* of rules, rather than a set of *good rules*. In other words, it is important to discover a rule set where the rules "cooperate" with each other. In particular, the rule set should cover the entire data space, so that each data instance should be covered by at least one rule. This requires a special mechanism to discover a diverse set of rules, since a standard EA would typically converge to a population where almost all the individuals would represent the same best rule found by the evolutionary process.

In general the previously discussed approaches perform a "direct" search for rules, consisting of initializing a population with a set of rules and then iteratively modifying those rules via the application of genetic operators. Due to a certain degree of randomness typically present in both initialization and genetic operations, some bad quality rules tend to be produced along the evolutionary process. Of course such bad rules are likely to be eliminated quickly by the selection process, but in any case an interesting alternative and "indirect" way of searching for rules has been proposed, in order to minimize the generation of bad rules. The basic idea of this new approach, proposed in (Jiao et al. 2006), is that the EA searches for good groups (clusters) of data instances, where each group consists of instances of the same class. A group is good to the extent that its data instances have similar attribute values and those attribute values are different from attribute values of the instances in other groups. After the EA run is over and good groups of instances have been discovered by the EA, the system extracts classification rules from the groups. This seems a promising new approach, although it should be noted that the version of the system described in (Jiao et al. 2006) has the limitation of coping only with categorical (not continuous) attributes.

In passing, it is worth mentioning that the above discussion on rule representation issues has focused on a generic classification problem. Specific kinds of classification problems may well be more effectively solved by EAs using rule representations "tailored" to the target kind of problem. For instance, (Hirsch et al. 2005) propose a rule representation tailored to document classification (i.e., a *text* mining problem), where strings of characters – in general fragments of words, rather than full words – are combined via Boolean operators to form classification rules.

3.2 Searching for a Diverse Set of Rules

This subsection discusses two mechanisms for discovering a diverse set of rules. It is assumed that each individual represents a single classification rule (Michigan-style approach). Note that the mechanisms for rule diversity discussed below are not normally used in the Pittsburgh approach, where an individual already represents a set of rules whose fitness implicitly depends on how well the rules in the set cooperate with each other.

First, one can use a niching method. The basic idea of niching is to avoid that the population converges to a single high peak in the search space and to foster the EA to create stable subpopulations of individuals clustered around each of the high peaks. In general the goal is to obtain a kind of "fitness-proportionate" convergence, where the size of the subpopulation around each peak is proportional to the height of that peak (i.e., to the quality of the corresponding candidate solution).

For instance, one of the most popular niching methods is fitness sharing (Goldberg & Richardson 1987; Deb & Goldberg 1989). In this method, the fitness of an individual is reduced in proportion to the number of similar individuals (neighbors), as measured by a given distance metric. In the context of rule discovery, this means that if there are many individuals in the current population representing the same rule or similar rules, the fitness of those individuals will be considerably reduced, and so they will have a considerably lower probability of being selected to produce new offspring. This effectively penalizes individuals which are in crowded regions of the search space, forcing the EA to discover a diverse set of rules.

Note that fitness sharing was designed as a generic niching method. By contrast, there are several niching methods designed specifically for the discovery of classification rules. An example is the "universal suffrage" selection method (Giordana et al. 1994; Divina 2005) where – using a political metaphor – individuals to be selected for reproduction are "elected" by the training data instances. The basic idea is that each data instance "votes" for a rule that covers it in a probabilistic fitness-based fashion. More precisely, let R be the set of rules (individuals) that cover a given data instance i, i.e., the set of rules whose antecedent is satisfied by data instance i. The better the fitness of a given rule r in the set R, the larger the probability that rule r will receive the vote of data instance i. Note that in general only rules covering the same data instances are competing with each other. Therefore, this selection method implements a form of niching, fostering the evolution of different rules covering different parts of the data space. For more information about niching methods in the context of discovering classification rules the reader is referred to (Hekanaho 1996; Dhar et al. 2000).

Another kind of mechanism that can be used to discover a diverse set of rules consists of using the previously-mentioned "sequential covering" approach – also known as "separate-and-conquer". The basic idea is that the EA discovers one rule at a time, so that in order to discover multiple rules the EA has to be run multiple times. In the first run the EA is initialized with the full training set and an empty set of rules. After each run of the EA, the best rule evolved by the EA is added to the set of discovered rules and the examples correctly covered by that rule are removed from the training set, so that the next run of the EA will consider a smaller training set. The process proceeds until all examples have been covered. Some examples of EAs using the sequential covering approach can be found in (Liu & Kwok 2000; Zhou et al. 2003; Carvalho & Freitas 2004). Note that the sequential covering approach is not specific to EAs. It is used by several non-evolutionary rule induction algorithms, and it is also discussed in data mining textbooks such as (Witten & Frank 2005).

3.3 Fitness Evaluation

One interesting characteristic of EAs is that they naturally allow the evaluation of a candidate solution, say a classification rule, as a whole, in a global fashion. This is in contrast with some data mining paradigms, which evaluate a partial solution. Consider, for instance, a conventional, greedy rule induction algorithm that incrementally builds a classification rule by adding one condition at a time to the rule. When the algorithm is evaluating several candidate conditions, the rule is still incomplete, being just a partial solution, so that the rule evaluation function is somewhat shortsighted (Freitas 2001, 2002a; Furnkranz & Flach 2003).

Another interesting characteristic of EAs is that they naturally allow the evaluation of a candidate solution by simultaneously considering different quality criteria. This is not so easily done in other data mining paradigms. To see this, consider again a conventional, greedy rule induction algorithm that adds one condition at a time to a candidate rule, and suppose one wants to favor the discovery of rules which are both accurate and simple (short). As mentioned earlier, when the algorithm is evaluating several candidate conditions, the rule is still incomplete, and so its size is not known yet. Hence, intuitively is better to choose the best candidate condition to be added to the rule based on a measure of accuracy only. The simplicity (size) criterion is better considered later, in a pruning procedure.

The fact that EAs evaluate a candidate solution as a whole and lend themselves naturally to simultaneously consider multiple criteria in the evaluation of the fitness of an individual gives the data miner a great flexibility in the design of the fitness function. Hence, not surprisingly, many different fitness functions have been proposed to evaluate classification rules. Classification accuracy is by far the criterion most used in fitness functions for evolving classification rules. This criterion is already extensively discussed in many good books or articles about classification, e.g. (Hand 1997; Caruana & Niculescu-Mizil 2004), and so it will not be discussed here – with the exception of a brief mention of overfitting issues, as follows. EAs can discover rules that overfit the training set – i.e. rules that represent very specific patterns in the training set that do not generalize well to the test set (which contains data instances unseen during training). One approach to try to mitigate the overfitting problem is to vary the training set at every generation, i.e., at each generation a subset of training instances is randomly selected, from the entire set of training instances, to be used as the (sub-)training or validation set from which the individuals' fitness values are computed (Bacardit et al. 2004; Pappa & Freitas 2006; Sharpe & Glover 1999; Bhattacharyya 1998). This approach introduces a selective pressure for evolving rules with a greater generalization power and tends to reduce the risk of overfitting, by comparison with the conventional approach of evolving rules for a training set which remains fixed throughout evolution. In passing, if the (sub)-training or validation set used for fitness computation is significantly smaller than the original training set, this approach also has the benefit of significantly reducing the processing time of the EA.

Hereafter this section will focus on two other rule-quality criteria (not based on accuracy) that represent different desirables properties of discovered rules in the context of data mining, namely: comprehensibility (Fayyad et al. 1996), or simplicity; and surprisingness, or unexpectedness (Liu et al. 1997; Romao et al. 2004; Freitas 2006).

The former means that ideally the discovered rule(s) should be comprehensible *to the user*. Intuitively, a measure of comprehensibility should have a strongly subjective, user-dependent component. However, in the literature this subjective component is typically ignored (Pazzani 2000; Freitas 2006), and comprehensibility is usually evaluated by a measure of the syntactic simplicity of the classifier, say the size of the rule set. The latter can be measured in an objective manner, for instance, by simply counting the total number of rule conditions in the rule set represented by an individual.

However, there is a natural way of incorporating a subjective measure of comprehensibility into the fitness function of an EA, namely by using an *interactive* fitness function. The basic idea of an interactive fitness function is that the user directly evaluates the fitness of individuals during the execution of the EA (Banzhaf 2000). The evaluation of the user is then used as the fitness measure for the purpose of selecting the best individuals of the current population, so that the EA evolves solutions that tend to maximize the subjective preference of the user.

An interactive EA for attribute selection is discussed e.g. in (Terano & Ishino 1998, 2002). In that work an individual represents a selected subset of attributes, which is then used by a classification algorithm to generate a set of rules. Then the user is shown the rules and selects good rules and rule sets according to her/his subjective preferences. Next the individuals having attributes that occur in the selected rules or rule sets are selected as parents to produce new offspring. The main advantage of interactive fitness functions is that intuitively they tend to favor the discovery of rules that are comprehensible and considered "good" by the user. The main disadvantage of this approach is that it makes the system considerably slower. To mitigate this problem one often has to use a small population size and a small number of generations.

Another kind of criterion that has been used to evaluate the quality of classification rules in the fitness function of EAs is the surprisingness of the discovered rules. First of all, it should be noted that accuracy and comprehensibility do not imply surprisingness. To show this point, consider the following classical hypothetical rule, which could be discovered from a hospital's database: IF (patient is pregnant) THEN (gender is female). This rule is very accurate and very comprehensible, but it is useless, because it represents an obvious pattern.

One approach to discover surprising rules consists of asking the user to specify a set of general impressions, specifying his/her previous knowledge and/or believes about the application domain (Liu et al. 1997). Then the EA can try to find rules that are surprising in the sense of contradicting some general impression specified by the user. Note that a rule should be reported to the user only if it is found to be both surprising and at least reasonably accurate (consistent with the training data). After all, it would be relatively easy to find rules which are surprising and inaccurate, but these rules would not be very useful to the user.

An EA for rule discovery taking this into account is described in (Romao et al. 2002, 2004). This EA uses a fitness function measuring both rule accuracy and rule surprisingness (based on general impressions). The two measures are multiplied to give the fitness value of an individual (a candidate prediction rule).

4 Evolutionary Algorithms for Clustering

There are several kinds of clustering algorithm, and two of the most popular kinds are iterative-partitioning and hierarchical clustering algorithms (Aldenderfer & Blashfield 1984; Krzanowski & Marriot 1995). In this section we focus mainly on EAs that can be categorized as iterative-partitioning algorithms, since most EAs for clustering seem to belong to this category.

4.1 Individual Representation for Clustering

A crucial issue in the design of an EA for clustering is to decide what kind of individual representation will be used to specify the clusters. There are at least three major kinds of individual representation for clustering (Freitas 2002a), as follows.

Cluster description-based representation – In this case each individual explicitly represents the parameters necessary to precisely specify each cluster. The exact nature of these parameters depends on the shape of clusters to be produced, which could be, e.g., boxes, spheres, ellipsoids, etc. In any case, each individual contains K sets of parameters, where K is the number of clusters, and each set of parameters determines the position, shape and size of its corresponding cluster. This kind of representation is illustrated, at a high level of abstraction, in Figure 2, for the case where an individual represents clusters of spherical shape. In this case each cluster is specified by its center coordinates and its radius. The cluster description-based representation is used, e.g., in (Srikanth et al. 1995), where an individual represents ellipsoid-based cluster descriptions; and in (Ghozeil and Fogel 1996; Sarafis 2005), where an individual represents hyperbox-shaped cluster descriptions. In (Sarafis 2005), for instance, the individuals represent rules containing conditions based on discrete numerical intervals, each interval being associated with a different attribute. Each clustering rule represents a region of the data space with homogeneous data distribution, and the EA was designed to be particularly effective when handling high-dimensional numerical datasets.

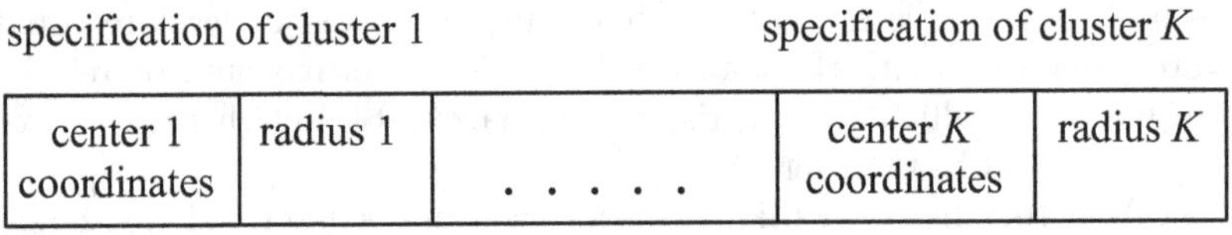

specification of cluster 1   specification of cluster K

center 1 coordinates	radius 1	. . . . .	center K coordinates	radius K

Fig. 2. Structure of cluster description-based individual representation

Centroid/medoid-based representation – In this case each individual represents the coordinates of each cluster's centroid or medoid. A centroid is simply a point in the data space whose coordinates specify the centre of the cluster. Note that there may not be any data instance with the same coordinates as the centroid. By contrast, a medoid is the most "central" representative of the cluster, i.e., it is the data instance which is nearest to the cluster's centroid. The use of medoids tends to be more robust against outliers than the use of centroids (Krzanowski & Marriot 1995) (p. 83). This kind of representation is used, e.g., in (Hall et al. 1999; Estivill-Castro and Murray 1997) and other EAs for clustering reviewed in (Sarafis 2005). This representation is illustrated, at a high level of abstraction, in Figure 3. Each data instance is assigned to the cluster represented by the centroid or medoid that is nearest to that instance, according to a given distance measure. There-fore, the position of the centroids/medoids and the procedure used to assign instances to clusters implicitly determine the precise shape and size of the clusters.

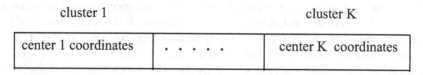

Fig. 3. Structure of centroid/medoid-based individual representation

Instance-based representation – In this case each individual consists of a string of n elements (genes), where n is the number of data instances. Each gene i, $i=1,\ldots,n$, represents the index (id) of the cluster to which the i-th data instance is assigned. Hence, each gene i can take one out of K values, where K is the number of clusters. For instance, suppose that $n = 10$ and $K = 3$. The individual <2 1 2 3 3 2 1 1 2 3> corresponds to a candidate clustering where the second, seventh and eighth instances are assigned to cluster 1, the first, third, sixth and ninth instances are assigned to cluster 2 and the other instances are assigned to cluster 3. This kind of representation is used, for instance, in (Krishma and Murty 1999; Handl & Knowles 2004). A variation of this representation is used in (Korkmaz et al. 2006), where the value of a gene represents not the cluster id of a gene's associated data instance, but rather a link from the gene's instance to another instance which is considered to be in the same cluster. Hence, in this approach, two instances belong to the same cluster if there is a sequence of links from one of them to the other. This variation is more complex than the conventional instance-based representation, and it has been proposed together with repair operators that rectify the contents of an individual when it violates some pre-defined constraints.

Comparing different individual representations for clustering – In both the centroid/medoid-based representation and the instance-based rep-resentation, each instance is assigned to exactly one cluster. Hence, the set of clusters determine a partition of the data space into regions that are mutually exclusive and exhaustive. This is not the case in the cluster description-based representation. In the latter, the cluster descriptions may have some overlap-ping – so that an instance may be located within two or more clusters – and the cluster descriptions may not be exhaustive – so that some instance(s) may not be within any cluster.

Unlike the other two representations, the instance-based representation has the disadvantage that it does not scale very well for large data sets, since each individual's length is directly proportional to the number of instances being clustered. This representation also involves a considerable degree of redundancy, which may lead to problems in the application of conventional genetic operators (Falkenauer 1998). For instance, let $n = 4$ and $K = 2$, and consider the individuals <1 2 1 2> and <2 1 2 1>. These two individuals have different gene values in all the four genes, but they represent the same candidate clustering solution, i.e., assigning the first and third instances to one cluster and assigning the second and fourth instances to another cluster. As a result, a crossover between these two parent individuals can produce two children individuals representing solutions that are very different from the solutions represented by the parents, which is not normally the case in conventional crossover operators used by genetic algorithms. Some methods have been proposed to try to mitigate some redundancy-related problems associated with this kind of representation. For example, (Handl & Knowles 2004) proposed a mutation operator that is reported to work well with this representation, based on the idea that, when a gene has its value mutated – meaning that the gene's corresponding data instance is moved to another cluster – the system selects a number of "nearest neighbors" of that instance and moves all those nearest neighbors to the same cluster to which the mutated instance was moved. Hence, this approach effectively incorporates some knowledge of the clustering task to be solved in the mutation operator.

4.2 Fitness Evaluation for Clustering

In an EA for clustering, the fitness of an individual is a measure of the quality of the clustering represented by the individual. A large number of different measures have been proposed in the literature, but the basic ideas usually involve the following principles. First, the smaller the intra-cluster (within-cluster) distance, the better the fitness. The intra-cluster distance can be defined as the summation of the distance between each data instance and the centroid of its corresponding cluster – a summation computed over all instances of all the clusters. Second, the larger the inter-cluster (between-cluster) distance, the better the fitness. Hence, an algorithm can try to find optimal values for these two criteria, for a given fixed number of clusters. These and other clustering-quality criteria are extensively discussed in the clustering literature – see e.g. (Aldenderfer and Blashfield 1984; Backer 1995; Tan et al. 2006). A discussion of this topic in the context of EAs can be found in (Kim et al. 2000; Handl & Knowles 2004; Korkmaz et al. 2006; Krishma and Murty 1999; Hall et al. 1999).

In any case, it is important to note that, if the algorithm is allowed to vary the number of discovered clusters without any restriction, it would be possible to minimize intra-cluster distance and maximize inter-cluster distance in a trivial way, by assigning each example to its own singleton cluster. This would be clearly undesirable. To avoid this while still allowing the algorithm to vary the number of clusters, a common response is to incorporate in the fitness function a preference for a smaller number of clusters. It might also be desirable or necessary to incorporate in the fitness function a penalty term whose value is proportional to the number of empty clusters (i.e. clusters to which no data instance was assigned) (Hall et al. 1999).

5 Evolutionary Algorithms for Data Preprocessing

5.1 Genetic Algorithms for Attribute Selection

In the attribute selection task the goal is to select, out of the original set of attributes, a subset of attributes that are relevant for the target data mining task (Liu & Motoda 1998; Guyon and Elisseeff 2003). This Subsection assumes the target data mining task is classification – which is the most investigated task in the evolutionary attribute selection literature – unless mentioned otherwise.

The standard individual representation for attribute selection consists simply of a string of N bits, where N is the number of original attributes and the i-th bit, $i=1,\ldots,N$, can take the value 1 or 0, indicating whether or not, respectively, the i-th attribute is selected. For instance, in a 10-attribute data set, the individual "1 0 1 0 1 0 0 0 0 1" represents a candidate solution where only the 1st, 3rd, 5th and 10th attributes are selected. This individual representation is simple, and traditional crossover and mutation operators can be easily applied. However, it has the disadvantage that it does not scale very well with the number of attributes. In applications with many thousands of attributes (such as text mining and some bioinformatics problems) an individual would have many thousands of genes, which would tend to lead to a slow execution of the GA.

An alternative individual representation, proposed by (Cherkauer & Shavlik 1996), consists of M genes (where M is a user-specified parameter), where each gene can contain either the index (id) of an attribute or a flag – say 0 – denoting no attribute. An attribute is considered selected if and only if it occurs in at least one of the M genes of the individual. For instance, the individual "3 0 8 3 0", where $M = 5$, represents a candidate solution where only the 3rd and the 8th attributes are selected. The fact that the 3rd attribute occurs twice in the previous individual is irrelevant for the purpose of decoding the individual into a selected attribute subset. One advantage of this representation is that it scales up better with respect to a large number of original attributes, since the value of M can be much smaller than the number of original attributes. One disadvantage is that it introduces a new parameter, M, which was not necessary in the case of the standard individual representation.

With respect to the fitness function, GAs for attribute selection can be roughly divided into two approaches – just like other kinds of algorithms for attribute selection – namely the wrapper approach and the filter approach. In essence, in the wrapper approach the GA uses the classification algorithm to compute the fitness of individuals, whereas in the filter approach the GA does not use the classification algorithm. The vast majority of GAs for attribute selection has followed the wrapper approach, and many of those GAs have used a fitness function involving two or more criteria to evaluate the quality of the classifier built from the selected attribute subset. This can be shown in Table 1, adapted from (Freitas 2002a), which lists the evaluation criteria used in the fitness function of a number of GAs following the wrapper approach. The columns of that table have the following meaning: *Acc* = accuracy; *Sens, Spec* = sensitivity, specificity; |Sel Attr| = number of selected attributes; |rule set| = number of discovered rules; *Info. Cont.* = information content of selected attributes; *Attr cost* = attribute costs; *Subj eval* = subjective evaluation of the user; |*Sel ins*| = number of selected instances.

Table 1. Diversity of criteria used in fitness function for attribute selection

Reference	Acc	Sens, Spec	|Sel Attr|	|rule set|	Info cont	Attr cost	Subj eval	|Sel ins|
(Bala et al. 1995)	yes		yes					
(Bala et al. 1996)	yes		yes		yes			
(Chen et al. 1999)	yes		yes					
(Cherkauer & Shavlik 1996)	yes		yes	yes				
(Emmanouilidis et al. 2000)	yes		yes					
(Emmanouilidis et al. 2002)		yes	yes					
(Guerra-Salcedo, Whitley 1998, 1999)	yes							
(Ishibuchi & Nakashima 2000)	yes		yes					yes
(Llora & Garrell 2003)	yes							
(Miller et al. 2003)		yes						
(Moser & Murty 2000)	yes		yes					
(Ni & Liu 2004)	yes							
(Pappa et al. 2002)	yes			yes				
(Rozsypal & Kubat 2003)	yes		yes					yes
(Terano & Ishino 1998)	yes			yes			yes	
(Vafaie & DeJong 1998)	yes							
(Yang & Honavar 1997, 1998)	yes					yes		
(Zhang et al 2003)	yes							

A precise definition of the terms used in the titles of the columns of Table 1 can be found in the corresponding references quoted in that table. The table refers to GAs that perform attribute selection for the classification task. GAs that perform attribute selection for the clustering task can be found, e.g., in (Kim et al. 2000; Jourdan 2003). In addition, in general Table 1 refers to GAs whose individuals directly represent candidate attribute subsets, but GAs can be used for attribute selection in other ways. For instance, in (Jong et al. 2004) a GA is used for attribute ranking. Once the ranking has been done, one can select a certain number of top-ranked attributes, where that number can be specified by the user or computed in a more automated way.

Empirical comparisons between GAs and other kinds of attribute selection methods can be found, for instance, in (Sharpe and Glover 1999; Kudo & Skalansky 2000). In general these empirical comparisons show that GAs, with their associated global search in the solution space, usually (though not always) obtain better results than local search-based attribute selection methods. In particular, (Kudo & Skalansky 2000) compared a GA with 14 non-evolutionary attribute selection methods (some of them variants of each other) across 8 different data sets. The authors concluded that the advantages of the global search associated with GAs over the local search associated with other algorithms is particularly important in data sets with a "large" number of attributes, where "large" was considered over 50 attributes in the context of their data sets.

5.2 Genetic Programming for Attribute Construction

In the attribute construction task the general goal is to construct new attributes out of the original attributes, so that the target data mining task becomes easier with the new attributes. This Subsection assumes the target data mining task is classification – which is the most investigated task in the evolutionary attribute construction literature.

Note that in general the problem of attribute construction is considerably more difficult than the problem of attribute selection. In the latter the problem consists just of deciding whether or not to select each attribute. By contrast, in attribute construction there is a potentially much larger search space, since there is a potentially large number of operations that can be applied to the original attributes in order to construct new attributes. Intuitively, the kind of EA that lends itself most naturally to attribute construction is GP. The reason is that, as mentioned earlier, GP was specifically designed to solve problems where candidate solutions are represented by both attributes and functions (operations) applied to those attributes. In particular, the explicit specification of both a terminal set and a function set is usually missing in other kinds of EAs.

Data Preprocessing vs. Interleaving Approach

In the data preprocessing approach, the attribute construction algorithm evaluates a constructed attribute without using the classification algorithm to be applied later. Examples of this approach are the GP algorithms for attribute construction proposed by (Otero et al. 2003; Hu 1998), whose attribute evaluation function (the fitness function) is the information gain ratio – a measure discussed in detail in (Quinlan 1993). In addition, (Muharram & Smith 2004) did experiments comparing the effectiveness of two different attribute-evaluation criteria in GP for attribute construction – viz. information gain ratio and gini index – and obtained results indicating that, overall, there was no significant difference in the results associated with those two criteria.

By contrast, in the interleaving approach the attribute construction algorithm evaluates the constructed attributes based on the performance of the classification algorithm with those attributes. Examples of this approach are the GP algorithms for attribute construction proposed by (Krawiec 2002; Smith and Bull 2003; Firpi et al. 2005), where the fitness functions are based on the accuracy of the classifier built with the constructed attributes.

Single-Attribute-per-Individual vs.
Multiple-Attributes-per-Individual Representation

In several GPs for attribute construction, each individual represents a single constructed attribute. This approach is used for instance by CPGI (Hu 1998) and the GP algorithm proposed by (Otero et al. 2003). By default this approach returns to the user a single constructed attribute – the best evolved individual. However it can be extended to return to the user a set of constructed attributes, say returning a set of the best evolved individuals of a GP run or by running the GP multiple times and returning only the best evolved individual of each run. The main advantage of this approach is simplicity, but it has the disadvantage of ignoring interactions between the constructed attributes.

An alternative approach consists of associating with an individual a set of constructed attributes. The main advantage of this approach is that it takes into account interaction between the constructed attributes. In other words, it tries to construct the *best set* of attributes, rather than the set of *best attributes*. The main disadvantages are that the individuals' genomes become more complex and that it introduces the need for additional parameters such as the number of constructed attributes that should be encoded in one individual (a parameter that is usually specified in an ad-hoc fashion). In any case, the equivalent of this latter parameter would also have to be specified in the above-mentioned "extended version" of the single-attribute-per-individual approach when one wants the GP algorithm to return multiple constructed attributes.

Examples of this multiple-attributes-per-individual approach are the GP algorithms proposed by (Krawiec 2002; Smith & Bull 2003; Firpi et al. 2005). Here we briefly discuss the former two, as examples of this approach. In (Krawiec 2002) each individual encodes a fixed number K of constructed attributes, each of them represented by a tree, so that an individual consists of K trees – where K is a user-specified parameter. The algorithm also includes a method to split the constructed attributes encoded in an individual into two subsets, namely the subset of "evolving" attributes and the subset of "hidden" attributes. The basic idea is that high-quality constructed attributes are considered hidden (or "protected"), so that they cannot be manipulated by the genetic operators such as crossover and mutation. The choice of attributes to be hidden is based on an attribute quality measure. This measure evaluates the quality of each constructed attribute separately, and the best attributes of the individual are considered hidden.

Another example of the multiple-attributes-per-individual approach is the GAP (Genetic Algorithm and Programming) system proposed by (Smith & Bull 2003, 2004). GAP performs both attribute construction and attribute selection. The first stage consists of attribute construction, which is performed by a GP algorithm. As a result of this first stage, the system constructs an extended genotype containing both the constructed attributes represented in the best evolved individual of the GP run and original attributes that have not been used in those constructed attributes. This extended genotype is used as the basic representation for a GA that performs attribute selection, so that the GA searches for the best subset of attributes out of all (both constructed and original) attributes.

Satisfying the Closure Property

GP algorithms for attribute construction have used several different approaches to satisfy the closure property (briefly mentioned in Section 2). This is an important issue, because the chosen approach can have a significant impact on the types (e.g., continuous or nominal) of original attributes processed by the algorithm and on the types of attributes constructed by the algorithm. Let us see some examples.

A simple solution for the closure problem is used in the GAP algorithm (Smith and Bull 2003). Its terminal set contains only the continuous (real-valued) attributes of the data being mined. In addition, its function set consists only of arithmetic operators (+, −, *, %,) – where % denotes protected division, i.e. a division operator that handles zero denominator inputs by returning something different from an error (Banzhaf et al. 1998; Koza 1992) – so that the closure property is immediately satisfied. (Firpi et al. 2005) also uses the approach of having a function set consisting only of mathematical operators, but it uses a considerably larger set of mathematical operators than the set used by (Smith and Bull 2003).

The GP algorithm proposed by (Krawiec 2002) uses a terminal set including all original attributes (both continuous and nominal ones), and a function set consisting of arithmetical operators $(+, -, *, \%, \log)$, comparison operators $(<, >, =)$, an "IF (conditional expression)", and an "approximate equality operator" which compares its two arguments with tolerance given by the third argument. The algorithm did not enforce data type constraints, which means that expressions encoding the constructed attributes make no distinction between, for instance, continuous and nominal attributes. Values of nominal attributes, such as male and female, are treated as numbers. This helps to solve the closure problem, but at a high price: constructed attributes can contain expressions that make no sense from a semantical point of view. For instance, the algorithm could produce an expression such as "*Gender + Age*", because the value of the nominal attribute *Gender* would be interpreted as a number.

The GP proposed by (Otero et al. 2003) uses a terminal set including only the continuous attributes of the data being mined. Its function set consists of arithmetic operators $(+, -, *, \%,)$ and comparison operators $(\geq, \leq)$. In order to satisfy the closure property, the algorithm enforces the data type restriction that the comparison operators can be used only at the root of the GP tree, i.e., they cannot be used as child nodes of other nodes in the tree. The reason is that comparison operators return a Boolean value, which cannot be processed by any operator in the function set (all operators accept only continuous values as input). Note that, although the algorithm can construct attributes only out of the continuous original attributes, the constructed attributes themselves can be either Boolean or continuous. A constructed attribute will be Boolean if its corresponding tree in the GP individual has a comparison operator at the root node; it will be continuous otherwise.

In order to satisfy the closure property, GPCI (Hu 1998) simply transforms all the original attributes into Boolean attributes and uses a function set containing only Boolean functions. For instance, if an attribute A is continuous (real-valued), such as the attribute *Salary*, it is transformed into two Boolean attributes, such as "Is *Salary* $> t$?" and "Is *Salary* $\leq t$?", where t is a threshold automatically chosen by the algorithm in order to maximize the ability of the two new attributes in discriminating between instances of different classes. The two new attributes are named "*positive-A*" and "*negative-A*", respectively. Once every original attribute has been transformed into two Boolean attributes, a GP algorithm is applied to the Boolean attributes. In this GP, the terminal set consists of all the pairs of attributes "*positive-A*" and "*negative-A*" for each original attribute A, whereas the function set consists of the Boolean operators {AND, OR}. Since all terminal symbols are Boolean, and all operators accept Boolean values as input and produce Boolean value as output, the closure property is satisfied.

Table 2 summarizes the main characteristics of the five GP algorithms for attribute construction discussed in this Section.

Table 2. Summary of GP Algorithms for Attribute Construction

Reference	Approach	Individual representation	Datatype of input attrib	Datatype of output attrib
(Hu 1998)	Data preprocessing	Single attribute	Any (attributes are booleanised)	Boolean
(Krawiec 2002)	Interleaving	Multiple attributes	Any (nominal attrib. values are interpreted as numbers)	Continuous
(Otero et al. 2003)	Data preprocessing	Single attribute	Continuous	Continuous or Boolean
(Smith & Bull 2003, 2004)	Interleaving	Multiple attributes	Continuous	Continuous
(Firpi et al. 2005)	Interleaving	Multiple attributes	Continuous	Continuous

6 Multi-Objective Optimization with Evolutionary Algorithms

There are many real-world optimization problems that are naturally expressed as the simultaneous optimization of two or more conflicting objectives (Coello Coello 2002; Deb 2001; Coello Coello & Lamont 2004). A generic example is to maximize the quality of a product and minimize its manufacturing cost in a factory. In the context of data mining, a typical example is, in the data pre-processing task of attribute selection, to minimize the error rate of a classifier trained with the selected attributes and to minimize the number of selected attributes.

The conventional approach to cope with such multi-objective optimization problems using evolutionary algorithms is to convert the problem into a single-optimization problem. This is typically done by using a weighted formula in the fitness function, where each objective has an associated weight reflecting its relative importance. For instance, in the above example of two-objective attribute selection, the fitness function could be defined as, say: "2/3 classification_error + 1/3 Number_of_selected_attributes".

However, this conventional approach has several problems. First, it mixes non-commensurable objectives (classification error and number of selected attributes in the previous example) into the same formula. This has at least the disadvantage that the value returned by the fitness function is not meaningful to the user. Second, note that different weights will lead to different selected attributes, since different weights represent different trade-offs between the two conflicting objectives. Unfortunately, the weights are usually defined in an ad-hoc fashion. Hence, when the EA returns the best attribute subset to the user, the user is presented with a solution that represents just one possible trade-off between the objectives. The user misses the opportunity to analyze different trade-offs.

Of course we could address this problem by running the EA multiple times, with different weights for the objectives in each run, and return the multiple solutions to the user. However, this would be very inefficient, and we would still have the problems of deciding which weights should be used in each run, how many runs we should perform (and so how many solutions should be returned to the user), etc.

A more principled approach consists of letting an EA answer these questions automatically, by performing a global search in the solution space and discovering as many good solutions, with as much diversity among them, as possible. This can be done by using a multi-objective EA, a kind of EA which has become quite popular in the EA community in the last few years (Deb 2001; Coello Coello 2002; Coello Coello & Lamont 2004). The basic idea involves the concept of Pareto dominance. A solution s_1 is said to dominate, in the Pareto sense, another solution s_2 if and only if solution s_1 is strictly better than s_2 in at least one of the objectives and solution s_1 is not worse than s_2 in any of the objectives. The concept of Pareto dominance is illustrated in Figure 4. This figure involves two objectives to be minimized, namely classification error and number of selected attributes (No_attrib). In that figure, solution D is dominated by solution B (which has both a smaller error and a smaller number of selected attributes than D), and solution E is dominated by solution C. Hence, solutions A, B and C are non-dominated solutions. They constitute the best "Pareto front" found by the algorithm. All these three solutions would be returned to the user.

The goal of a multi-objective EA is to find a Pareto front which is as close as possible to the true (unknown) Pareto front. This involves not only the minimization of the two objectives, but also finding a diverse set of non-dominated solutions, spread along the Pareto front. This allows the EA to return to the user a diverse set of good trade-offs between the conflicting objectives. With this rich information, the user can hopefully make a more intelligent decision, choosing the best solution to be used in practice.

At this point the reader might argue that this approach has the disadvantage that the final choice of the solution to be used depends on the user, characterizing a subjective approach. The response to this is that the knowledge discovery process is interactive (Brachman & Anand 1996; Fayyad et al. 1996), and the participation of the user in this process is important to obtain useful results. The questions are *when and how* the user should participate (Deb 2001; Freitas 2004). In the above-described multi-objective approach, based on Pareto dominance, the user participates by choosing the best solution out of all the non-dominated solutions. This choice is made *a posteriori*, i.e., after the algorithm has run and has returned a rich source of information about the solution space: the discovered Pareto front. In the conventional approach – using an EA with a weighted formula and returning a single solution to the user – the user has to define the weights *a priori*, i.e., before

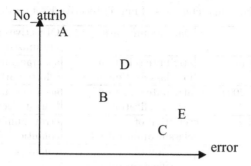

Fig. 4. Example of Pareto dominance

running the algorithm, when the solution space was not explored yet. The multi-objective approach seems to put the user in the loop in a better moment, when valuable information about the solution space is available. The multi-objective approach also avoids the problems of ad-hoc choice of weights, mixing non-commensurable objectives into the same formula, etc.

Table 3 lists the main characteristics of multi-objective EAs for data mining. Most systems included in Table 3 consider only two objectives. The exceptions are the works of (Kim et al. 2000) and (Atkinson-Abutridy et al. 2003), considering 4 and 8 objectives, respectively. Out of the EAs considering only two objectives, the most popular choice of objectives – particularly for EAs addressing the classification task – has been some measure of classification accuracy (or its dual, error) and a measure of the size of the classification model (number of leaf nodes in a decision tree or total number of rule conditions – attribute-value pairs – in all rules). Note that the size of a model is typically used as a proxy for the concept of "simplicity" of that model, even though arguably this proxy leaves a lot to be desired as a measure of a model's simplicity (Pazzani 2000; Freitas 2006). (In practice, however, it seems no better proxy for a model's simplicity is known.) Note also that, when the task being solved is attribute selection for classification, the objective related to size can be the number of selected attributes, as in (Emmanouilidis et al. 2000), or the size of the classification model built from the set of selected attributes, as in (Pappa et al. 2002, 2004). Finally, when solving the clustering task a popular choice of objective has been some measure of intra-cluster distance, related to the total distance between each data instance and the centroid of its cluster, computed for all data instances in all the clusters. The number of clusters is also used as an objective in two out of the three EAs for clustering included in Table 3. A further discussion of multi-objective optimization in the context of data mining in general (not focusing on EAs) is presented in (Freitas 2004; Jin 2006).

Table 3. Main characteristics of multi-objective EAs for data mining

Reference	Data mining task	Objectives being Optimized
(Emmanouilidis et al. 2000)	attribute selection for classification	accuracy, number of selected attributes
(Pappa et al 2002, 2004)	attribute selection for classification	accuracy, number of leafs in decision tree
(Ishibuchi & Namba 2004)	selection of classification rules	error, number of rule conditions (in all rules)
(de la Iglesia 2007)	selection of classification rules	confidence, coverage
(Kim et al. 2004)	classification	error, number of leafs in decision tree
(Atkinson-Abutridy et al. 2003)	text mining	8 criteria for evaluating explanatory knowledge across text documents
(Kim et al. 2000)	attribute selection for clustering	Cluster cohesiveness, separation between clusters, number of clusters, number of selected attributes
(Handl & Knowles 2004)	clustering	Intra-cluster deviation and connectivity
(Korkmaz et al. 2006)	clustering	Intra-cluster variance and number of clusters

7 Conclusions

This chapter started with the remark that EAs are a very generic search paradigm. Indeed, the chapter discussed how EAs can be used to solve several different data mining tasks, namely the discovery of classification rules, clustering, attribute selection and attribute construction. The discussion focused mainly on the issues of individual representation and fitness function for each of these tasks, since these are the two EA-design issues that are more dependent of the task being solved. In any case, recall that the design of an EA also involves the issue of genetic operators. Ideally these three components – individual representation, fitness function and genetic operators – should be designed in a synergistic fashion and tailored to the data mining task being solved.

There are at least two motivations for using EAs in data mining, broadly speaking. First, as mentioned earlier, EAs are robust, adaptive search methods that perform a global search in the solution space. This is in contrast to other data mining paradigms that typically perform a greedy search. In the context of data mining, the global search of EAs is associated with a better ability to cope with attribute interactions. For instance, most "conventional", non-evolutionary rule induction algorithms are greedy, and therefore quite sensitive to the problem of attribute interaction. EAs can use the same knowledge representation (IF-THEN rules) as conventional rule induction algorithms, but their global search tends to cope better with attribute interaction and to discover interesting relationships that would be missed by a greedy search (Dhar et al. 2000; Papagelis & Kalles 2001; Freitas 2002a).

Second, EAs are a very flexible algorithmic paradigm. In particular, borrowing some terminology from programming languages, EAs have a certain "declarative" – rather than "procedural" – style. The quality of an individual (candidate solution) is evaluated, by a fitness function, in a way independent of how that solution was constructed. This gives the data miner a considerable freedom in the design of the individual representation, the fitness function and the genetic operators. This flexibility can be used to incorporate background knowledge into the EA and/or to hybridize EAs with local search methods that are specifically tailored to the data mining task being solved.

Note that declarativeness is a matter of degree, rather than a binary concept. In practice EAs are not 100% declarative, because as one changes the fitness function one might consider changing the individual representation and the genetic operators accordingly, in order to achieve the above-mentioned synergistic relationship between these three components of the EA. However, EAs still have a degree of declarativeness considerably higher than other data mining paradigms. For instance, as discussed in Subsection 3.3, the fact that EAs evaluate a complete (rather than partial) rule allows the fitness function to consider several different rule-quality criteria, such as comprehensibility, surprisingness and subjective interestingness to the user. In EAs these quality criteria can be directly considered during the search for rules. By contrast, in conventional, greedy rule induction algorithms – where the evaluation function typically evaluates a partial rule – those quality criteria would typically have to be considered in a post-processing phase of the knowledge discovery process, when it might be too late. After all, many rule set post-processing methods just try to select the most interesting rules out of all discovered rules, so that interesting rules that were missed by the rule induction method will remain missing after applying the post-processing method.

Like any other data mining paradigm, EAs also have some disadvantages. One of them is that conventional genetic operators – such as conventional crossover and mutation operators – are "blind" search operators in the sense that they modify individuals (candidate solutions) in a way independent from the individual's fitness (quality). This characteristic of conventional genetic operators increases the generality of EAs, but intuitively tends to reduce their effectiveness in solving a specific kind of problem. Hence, in general it is important to modify or extend EAs to use task specific-operators.

Another disadvantage of EAs is that they are computationally slow, by comparison with greedy search methods. The importance of this drawback depends on many factors, such as the kind of task being performed, the size of the data being mined, the requirements of the user, etc. Note that in some cases a relatively long processing time might be acceptable. In particular, several data mining tasks, such as classification, are typically an off-line task, and the time spent solving that task is usually less than 20% of the total time of the knowledge discovery process. In scenarios like this, even a processing time of hours or days might be acceptable to the user, at least in the sense that it is not the bottleneck of the knowledge discovery process.

In any case, if necessary the processing time of an EA can be significantly reduced by using special techniques. One possibility is to use parallel processing techniques, since EAs can be easily parallelized in an effective way (Cantu-Paz 2000; Freitas & Lavington 1998; Freitas 2002a). Another possibility is to compute the fitness of individuals by using only a subset of training instances – where that subset can be chosen either at random or using adaptive instance-selection techniques (Bhattacharyya 1998; Gathercole & Ross 1997; Sharpe & Glover 1999; Freitas 2002a).

An important research direction is to better exploit the power of Genetic Programming (GP) in data mining. Several GP algorithms for attribute construction were discussed in Subsection 5.2, and there are also several GP algorithms for discovering classification rules (Freitas 2002a; Wong & Leung 2000) or for classification in general (Muni et al. 2004; Song et al. 2005; Folino et al. 2006). However, the power of GP is still underexplored. Recall that the GP paradigm was designed to *automatically* discover computer *programs*, or *algorithms*, which should be *generic "recipes"* for solving a given kind of problem, and not to find the solution to one particular instance of that problem (like in most EAs). For instance, classification is a kind of problem, and most classification-rule induction algorithms are generic enough to be applied to different data sets (each data set can be considered just an instance of the kind of problem defined by the classification task). However, these generic rule induction algorithms have been *manually* designed by a human being. Almost all current GP algorithms for classification-rule induction are competing with conventional (greedy, non-evolutionary) rule induction algorithms, in the sense that both GP and conventional rule induction algorithms are discovering classification rules for a single data set at a time. Hence, the output of a GP for classification-rule induction is a set of rules for a given data set, which can be called a "program" or "algorithm" only in a very loose sense of these words.

A much more ambitious goal, which is more compatible with the general goal of GP, is to use GP to *automatically* discover a rule induction *algorithm*. That is, to perform *algorithm induction*, rather than rule induction. The first version of a GP algorithm addressing this ambitious task has been proposed in (Pappa & Freitas 2006), and an extended version of that work is described in detail in another chapter of this book (Pappa & Freitas 2007).

References

Aldenderfer MS & Blashfield RK (1984) *Cluster Analysis* (Sage University Paper Series on Quantitative Applications in the Social Sciences, No. 44) Sage Publications.

Atkinson-Abutridy J, Mellishm C, and Aitken S (2003) A semantically guided and domain-independent evolutionary model for knowledge discovery from texts. *IEEE Trans. Evolutionary Computation 7(6)*, 546-560.

Bacardit J, Goldberg DE, Butz MV, Llora X, Garrell JM (2004). Speeding-up Pittsburgh learning classifier systems: modeling time and accuracy. *Proc. Parallel Problem Solving From Nature (PPSN-2004), LNCS 3242*, 1021-1031, Springer.

Bacardit J and Krasnogor N (2006) Smart crossover operator with multiple parents for a Pittsburgh learning classifier system. *Proc. Genetic & Evolutionary Computation Conf. (GECCO-2006)*, 1441-1448. Morgan Kaufmann.

Backer E (1995) *Computer-Assisted Reasoning in Cluster Analysis*. Prentice-Hall.

Back T, Fogel DB and Michalewicz (Eds.) (2000) *Evolutionary Computation 1: Basic Algorithms and Operators*. Institute of Physics Publishing.

Bala J, De Jong K, Huang J, Vafaie H and Wechsler H (1995) Hybrid learning using genetic algorithms and decision trees for pattern classification. *Proc. Int. Joint Conf. on Artificial Intelligence (IJCAI-95)*, 719-724.

Bala J, De Jong K, Huang J, Vafaie H and Wechsler H (1996) Using learning to facilitate the evolution of features for recognizing visual concepts. *Evolutionary Computation 4(3)*: 297-312.

Banzhaf W (2000) Interactive evolution. In: T. Back, D.B. Fogel and T. Michalewicz (Eds.) *Evolutionary Computation 1*, 228-236. Institute of Physics Pub.

Banzhaf W, Nordin P, Keller RE, and Francone FD (1998) *Genetic Programming ~ an Introduction: On the Automatic Evolution of Computer Programs and Its Applications*. Morgan Kaufmann.

Bhattacharrya S (1998) Direct marketing response models using genetic algorithms. *Proceedings of the 4th Int. Conf. on Knowledge Discovery and Data Mining (KDD-98)*, 144-148. AAAI Press.

Brachman RJ and Anand T. (1996) The process of knowledge discovery in databases: a human-centered approach. In: U.M. Fayyad et al (Eds.) *Advances. in Knowledge Discovery and Data Mining*, 37-58. AAAI/MIT.

Bull L (Ed.) (2004) *Applications of Learning Classifier Systems*. Springer.

Bull L and Kovacs T (Eds.) (2005) *Foundations of Learning Classifier Systems*. Springer.

Cantu-Paz E (2000) *Efficient and Accurate Parallel Genetic Algorithms*. Kluwer.

Caruana R and Niculescu-Mizil A (2004) Data mining in metric space: an empirical analysis of supervised learning performance criteria. *Proc. 2004 ACM SIGKDD Int. Conf. on Knowledge Discovery and Data Mining (KDD-04)*, ACM.

Carvalho DR and Freitas AA (2004). A hybrid decision tree/genetic algorithm method for data mining. *Special issue on Soft Computing Data Mining, Information Sciences 163(1-3)*, pp. 13-35. 14 June 2004.

Chen S, Guerra-Salcedo C and Smith SF (1999) Non-standard crossover for a standard representation - commonality-based feature subset selection. *Proc. Genetic and Evolutionary Computation Conf. (GECCO-99)*, 129-134. Morgan Kaufmann.

Cherkauer KJ and Shavlik JW (1996). Growing simpler decision trees to facilitate knowledge discovery. *Proc. 2nd Int. Conf. on Knowledge Discovery and Data Mining (KDD-96)*, 315-318. AAAI Press.

Coello Coello CA, Van Veldhuizen DA and Lamont GB (2002) *Evolutionary Algorithms for Solving Multi-Objective Problems.* Kluwer.

Coello Coello CA and Lamont GB (Ed.) (2004) *Applications of Multi-objective Evolutionary Algorithms.* World Scientific.

Deb K (2001) *Multi-Objective Optimization Using Evolutionary Algorithms.* Wiley.

Deb K and Goldberg DE (1989). An investigation of niche and species formation in genetic function optimization. *Proc. 2nd Int. Conf. Genetic Algorithms (ICGA-89)*, 42-49.

De Jong K (2006) *Evolutionary Computation: a unified approach.* MIT.

De la Iglesia B (2007) Application of multi-objective metaheuristic algorithms in data mining. *Proc. 3rd UK Knowledge Discovery and Data Mining Symposium (UKKDD-2007)*, 39-44, University of Kent, UK, April 2007.

Dhar V, Chou D and Provost F (2000). Discovering interesting patterns for investment decision making with GLOWER – a genetic learner overlaid with entropy reduction. *Data Mining and Knowledge Discovery 4(4)*, 251-280.

Divina F (2005) Assessing the effectiveness of incorporating knowledge in an evolutionary concept learner. *Proc. EuroGP-2005 (European Conf. on Genetic Programming), LNCS 3447*, 13-24, Springer.

Divina F & Marchiori E (2002) Evolutionary Concept Learning. *Proc. Genetic & Evolutionary Computation Conf. (GECCO-2002)*, 343-350. Morgan Kaufmann.

Divina F & Marchiori E (2005) Handling continuous attributes in an evolutionary inductive learner. *IEEE Trans. Evolutionary Computation, 9(1)*, 31-43, Feb. 2005.

Eiben AE and Smith JE (2003) *Introduction to Evolutionary Computing.* Springer.

Emmanouilidis C, Hunter A and J. MacIntyre J (2000) A multiobjective evolutionary setting for feature selection and a commonality-based crossover operator. *Proc. 2000 Congress on Evolutionary Computation (CEC-2000)*, 309-316. IEEE.

Emmanouilidis C (2002) Evolutionary multi-objective feature selection and ROC analysis with application to industrial machinery fault diagnosis. In: K. Giannakoglou et al. (Eds.) *Evolutionary Methods for Design, Optimisation and Control.* Barcelona: CIMNE.

Estivill-Castro V and Murray AT (1997) Spatial clustering for data mining with genetic algorithms. *Tech. Report FIT-TR-97-10.* Queensland University of Technology. Australia.

Falkenauer E (1998) *Genetic Algorithms and Grouping Problems.* John-Wiley & Sons.

Fayyad UM, Piatetsky-Shapiro G and Smyth P (1996) From data mining to knowledge discovery: an overview. In: U.M. Fayyad et al (Eds.) *Advances in Knowledge Discovery and Data Mining*, 1-34. AAAI/MIT.

Firpi H, Goodman E, Echauz J (2005) On prediction of epileptic seizures by computing multiple genetic programming artificial features. *Proc. 2005 European Conf. on Genetic Programming (EuroGP-2005), LNCS 3447*, 321-330. Springer.

Folino G, Pizzuti C and Spezzano G (2006) GP ensembles for large-scale data classification. *IEEE Trans. Evolutionary Computation 10(5)*, 604-616, Oct. 2006.

Freitas AA and. Lavington SH (1998) *Mining Very Large Databases with Parallel Processing*. Kluwer.

Freitas AA (2001) Understanding the crucial role of attribute interaction in data mining. *Artificial Intelligence Review 16(3)*, 177-199.

Freitas AA (2002a) *Data Mining and Knowledge Discovery with Evolutionary Algorithms*. Springer.

Freitas AA (2002b) A survey of evolutionary algorithms for data mining and knowledge discovery. In: A. Ghosh and S. Tsutsui. (Eds.) *Advances in Evolutionary Computation*, pp. 819-845. Springer-Verlag.

Freitas AA (2002c). Evolutionary Computation. In: W. Klosgen and J. Zytkow (Eds.) *Handbook of Data Mining and Knowledge Discovery*, pp. 698-706.Oxford Univ. Press.

Freitas AA (2004) A critical review of multi-objective optimization in data mining: a position paper. *ACM SIGKDD Explorations, 6(2)*, 77-86, Dec. 2004.

Freitas AA (2005) Evolutionary Algorithms for Data Mining. In: O. Maimon and L. Rokach (Eds.) *The Data Mining and Knowledge Discovery Handbook*, pp. 435-467. Springer.

Freitas AA (2006) Are we really discovering "interesting" knowledge from data? *Expert Update, Vol. 9, No. 1*, 41-47, Autumn 2006.

Furnkranz J and Flach PA (2003). An analysis of rule evaluation metrics. *Proc.20th Int. Conf. Machine Learning (ICML-2003)*. Morgan Kaufmann.

Gathercole C and Ross P (1997) Tackling the Boolean even N parity problem with genetic programming and limited-error fitness. *Genetic Programming 1997: Proc. 2nd Conf. (GP-97)*, 119-127. Morgan Kaufmann.

Ghozeil A and Fogel DB (1996) Discovering patterns in spatial data using evolutionary programming. *Genetic Programming 1996: Proceedings of the 1st Annual Conf.*, 521-527. MIT Press.

Giordana A, Saitta L, Zini F (2004) Learning disjunctive concepts by means of genetic algorithms. *Proc. 10th Int. Conf. Machine Learning (ML-94)*, 96-104. Morgan Kaufmann.

Goldberg DE (1989). *Genetic Algorithms in Search, Optimization and Machine Learning*. Addison-Wesley.

Goldberg DE and Richardson J (1987) Genetic algorithms with sharing for multimodal function optimization. *Proc. Int. Conf. Genetic Algorithms (ICGA-87)*, 41-49.

Guerra-Salcedo C and Whitley D (1998) Genetic search for feature subset selection: a comparison between CHC and GENESIS. *Genetic Programming 1998: Proc. 3rd Annual Conf.*, 504-509. Morgan Kaufmann.

Guerra-Salcedo C, Chen S, Whitley D, and Smith S (1999) Fast and accurate feature selection using hybrid genetic strategies. *Proc. Congress on Evolutionary Computation (CEC-99)*, 177-184. IEEE.

Guyon I and Elisseeff A (2003) An introduction to variable and feature selection. *Journal of Machine Learning Research 3*, 1157-1182.

Hall LO, Ozyurt IB, Bezdek JC (1999) Clustering with a genetically optimized approach. *IEEE Trans. on Evolutionary Computation 3(2)*, 103-112.

Hand DJ (1997) *Construction and Assessment of Classification Rules*. Wiley.

Handl J and Knowles J (2004) Evolutionary multiobjective clustering. *Proc. Parallel Problem Solving From Nature (PPSN-2004), LNCS 3242*, 1081-1091, Springer.

Hekanaho J (1995) Symbiosis in multimodal concept learning. *Proc. 1995 Int. Conf. on Machine Learning (ML-95)*, 278-285. Morgan Kaufmann.

Hekanaho J (1996) Testing different sharing methods in concept learning. *TUCS Technical Report No. 71*. Turku Centre for Computer Science, Finland.

Hirsch L, Saeedi M and Hirsch R (2005) Evolving rules for document classification. *Proc. 2005 European Conf. on Genetic Programming (EuroGP-2005), LNCS 3447*, 85-95, Springer.

Hu YJ (1998). A genetic programming approach to constructive induction. *Genetic Programming 1998: Proc. 3rd Annual Conf.*, 146-151. Morgan Kaufmann.

Ishibuchi H and Nakashima T (2000) Multi-objective pattern and feature selection by a genetic algorithm. *Proc. 2000 Genetic and Evolutionary Computation Conf. (GECCO-2000)*, 1069-1076. Morgan Kaufmann.

Ishibuchi H and Namba S (2004) Evolutionary multiobjective knowledge extraction for high-dimensional pattern classification problems. *Proc. Parallel Problem Solving From Nature (PPSN-2004), LNCS 3242*, 1123-1132, Springer.

Jiao L, Liu J and Zhong W (2006) An organizational coevolutionary algorithm for classification. *IEEE Trans. Evolutionary Computation, Vol. 10, No. 1*, 67-80, Feb. 2006.

Jin, Y (Ed.) (2006) *Multi-Objective Machine Learning*. Springer.

Jong K, Marchiori E and Sebag M (2004) Ensemble learning with evolutionary computation: application to feature ranking. *Proc. Parallel Problem Solving from Nature VIII (PPSN-2004), LNCS 3242*, 1133-1142. Springer, 2004.

Jourdan L, Dhaenens-Flipo C and Talbi EG (2003) Discovery of genetic and environmental interactions in disease data using evolutionary computation. In: G.B. Fogel and D.W. Corne (Eds.) *Evolutionary Computation in Bioinformatics*, 297-316. Morgan Kaufmann.

Kim Y, Street WN and Menczer F (2000) Feature selection in unsupervised learning via evolutionary search. *Proc. 6th ACM SIGKDD Int. Conf. on Knowledge Discovery and Data Mining (KDD-2000)*, 365-369. ACM.

Kim D (2004). Structural risk minimization on decision trees: using an evolutionary multiobjective algorithm. *Proc. 2004 European Conference on Genetic Programming (EuroGP-2004), LNCS 3003*, 338-348, Springer.

Korkmaz EE, Du J, Alhajj R and Barker (2006) Combining advantages of new chromosome representation scheme and multi-objective genetic algorithms for better clustering. *Intelligent Data Analysis 10* (2006),163-182.

Koza JR (1992) *Genetic Programming: on the programming g of computers by means of natural selection*. MIT Press.

Krawiec K (2002) Genetic programming-based construction of features for machine learning and knowledge discovery tasks. *Genetic Programming and Evolvable Machines 3(4)*, 329-344.

Krsihma K and Murty MN (1999) Genetic k-means algorithm. *IEEE Transactions on Systems, Man and Cyberneics - Part B: Cybernetics*, 29(3), 433-439.

Krzanowski WJ and Marriot FHC (1995) *Kendall's Library of Statistics 2: Multivariate Analysis - Part 2. Chapter 10 - Cluster Analysis*, pp. 61-94.London: Arnold.

Kudo M and Sklansky J (2000) Comparison of algorithms that select features for pattern classifiers. *Pattern Recognition 33(2000)*, 25-41.

Liu JJ and Kwok JTY (2000) An extended genetic rule induction algorithm. *Proc. 2000 Congress on Evolutionary Computation (CEC-2000)*. IEEE.

Liu H and Motoda H (1998) *Feature Selection for Knowledge Discovery and Data Mining.* Kluwer.

Liu B, Hsu W and Chen S (1997) Using general impressions to analyze discovered classification rules. *Proc. 3rd Int. Conf. on Knowledge Discovery and Data Mining (KDD-97),* 31-36. AAAI Press.

Llora X and Garrell J (2003) Prototype induction and attribute selection via evolutionary algorithms. *Intelligent Data Analysis 7,* 193-208.

Miller MT, Jerebko AK, Malley JD, Summers RM (2003) Feature selection for computer-aided polyp detection using genetic algorithms. *Medical Imaging 2003: Physiology and Function: methods, systems and applications.* Proc. SPIE Vol. 5031.

Moser A and Murty MN (2000) On the scalability of genetic algorithms to very large-scale feature selection. *Proc. Real-World Applications of Evolutionary Computing (EvoWorkshops 2000). LNCS 1803,* 77-86. Springer.

Muharram MA and Smith GD (2004) Evolutionary feature construction using information gain and gene index. *Genetic Programming: Proc. 7th European Conf. (EuroGP-2003), LNCS 3003,* 379-388. Springer.

Muni DP, Pal NR and Das J (2004) A novel approach to design classifiers using genetic programming. *IEEE Trans. Evolutionary Computation 8(2),* 183-196, April 2004.

Neri F and Giordana A (1995) Search-intensive concept induction. *Evolutionary Computation 3(4),* 375-416.

Ni B and Liu J (2004) A novel method of searching the microarray data for the best gene subsets by using a genetic algorithms. *Proc. Parallel Problem Solving From Nature (PPSN-2004), LNCS 3242,* 1153-1162, Springer.

Otero FB, Silva MMS, Freitas AA and Nievola JC (2003) Genetic programming for attribute construction in data mining. *Genetic Programming: Proc. EuroGP-2003, LNCS 2610,* 384-393. Springer.

Papagelis A and Kalles D (2001) Breeding decision trees using evolutionary techniques. *Proc. 18th Int. Conf. Machine Learning (ICML-2001),* 393-400. Morgan Kaufmann.

Pappa GL and Freitas AA (2006) Automatically evolving rule induction algorithms. *Machine Learning: ECML 2006 – Proc. of the 17th European Conf. on Machine Learning, LNAI 4212,* 341-352. Springer.

Pappa GL and Freitas AA (2007) Discovering new rule induction algorithms with grammar-based genetic programming. *Maimon O and Rokach L (Eds.) Soft Computing for Knowledge Discovery and Data Mining.* Springer.

Pappa GL, Freitas AA and Kaestner CAA (2002) A multiobjective genetic algorithm for attribute selection. *Proc. 4th Int. Conf. On Recent Advances in Soft Computing (RASC-2002),* 116-121. Nottingham Trent University, UK.

Pappa GL, Freitas AA and Kaestner CAA (2004) Multi-Objective Algorithms for Attribute Selection in Data Mining. In: Coello Coello CA and Lamont GB (Ed.) *Applications of Multi-objective Evolutionary Algorithms,* 603-626. World Scientific.

Pazzani MJ (2000) Knowledge discovery from data, *IEEE Intelligent Systems,* 10-13, Mar./Apr. 2000.

Quinlan JR. (1993) *C4.5: Programs for Machine Learning.* Morgan Kaufmann.

Romao W, Freitas AA and Pacheco RCS (2002) A Genetic Algorithm for Discovering Interesting Fuzzy Prediction Rules: applications to science and technology data. *Proc. Genetic and Evolutionary Computation Conf. (GECCO-2002)*, pp. 1188-1195. Morgan Kaufmann.

Romao W, Freitas AA, Gimenes IMS (2004) Discovering interesting knowledge from a science and technology database with a genetic algorithm. *Applied Soft Computing 4(2)*, pp. 121-137.

Rozsypal A and Kubat M (2003) Selecting representative examples and attributes by a genetic algorithm. *Intelligent Data Analysis 7*, 290-304.

Sarafis I (2005) *Data mining clustering of high dimensional databases with evolutionary algorithms*. PhD Thesis, School of Mathematical and Computer Sciences, Heriot-Watt University, Edinburgh, UK.

Sharpe PK and Glover RP (1999) Efficient GA based techniques for classification. *Applied Intelligence 11*, 277-284.

Smith RE (2000) Learning classifier systems. In: T. Back, D.B. Fogel and T. Michalewicz (Eds.) *Evolutionary Computation 1: Basic Algorithms and Operators*, 114-123. Institute of Physics Publishing.

Smith MG and Bull L (2003) Feature construction and selection using genetic programming and a genetic algorithm. *Genetic Programming: Proc. EuroGP-2003, LNCS 2610*, 229-237. Springer.

Smith MG and Bull L (2004) Using genetic programming for feature creation with a genetic algorithm feature selector. *Proc. Parallel Problem Solving From Nature (PPSN-2004), LNCS 3242*, 1163-1171, Springer.

Song D, Heywood MI and Zincir-Heywood AN (2005) Training genetic programming on half a million patterns: an example from anomaly detection. *IEEE Trans. Evolutionary Computation 9(3)*, 225-239, June 2005.

Srikanth R, George R, Warsi N, Prabhu D, Petry FE, Buckles B (1995) A variable-length genetic algorithm for clustering and classification. *Pattern Recognition Letters 16(8)*, 789-800.

Tan PN, Steinbach M and Kumar V (2006) *Introduction to Data Mining*. Addison-Wesley.

Terano T and Ishino Y (1998) Interactive genetic algorithm based feature selection and its application to marketing data analysis. In: Liu H and Motoda H (Eds.) *Feature Extraction, Construction and Selection: a data mining perspective*, 393-406. Kluwer.

Terano T and Inada M (2002) Data mining from clinical data using interactive evolutionary computation. In: A. Ghosh and S. Tsutsui (Eds.) *Advances in Evolutionary Computing: theory and applications*, 847-861. Springer.

Vafaie H and De Jong K (1998) Evolutionary Feature Space Transformation. In: H. Liu and H. Motoda (Eds.) *Feature Extraction, Construction and Selection*, 307-323. Kluwer.

Witten IH and Frank E (2005) *Data Mining: practical machine learning tools and techniques* . 2nd Ed. Morgan Kaufmann.

Wong ML and Leung KS (2000) *Data Mining Using Grammar Based Genetic Programming and Applications*. Kluwer.

Yang J and Honavar V (1997) Feature subset selection using a genetic algorithm. *Genetic Programming 1997: Proc. 2nd Annual Conf. (GP-97)*, 380-385. Morgan Kaufmann.

Yang J and Honavar V (1998) Feature subset selection using a genetic algorithm. In: Liu, H. and Motoda, H (Eds.) *Feature Extraction, Construction and Selection*, 117-136. Kluwer.

Zhang P, Verma B, Kumar K (2003) Neural vs. Statistical classifier in conjunction with genetic algorithm feature selection in digital mammography. *Proc. Congress on Evolutionary Computation (CEC-2003)*. IEEE Press.

Zhou C, Xiao W, Tirpak TM and Nelson PC (2003) Evolving accurate and compact classification rules with gene expression programming. *IEEE Trans. on Evolutionary Computation 7(6)*, 519-531.

Genetic Clustering for Data Mining

Murilo Coelho Naldi[1]
André Carlos Ponce de Leon Ferreira de Carvalho[1]
Ricardo José Gabrielli Barreto Campello[1]
Eduardo Raul Hruschka[2]

Instituto de Ciências Matemáticas e de Computação
Universidade de São Paulo
murilocn@icmc.usp.br, andre@icmc.usp.br, campello@icmc.usp.br,
eduardo.hruschka@pesquisador.cnpq.br

Summary. Genetic Algorithms (GAs) have been successfully applied to several complex data analysis problems in a wide range of domains, such as image processing, bioinformatics, and crude oil analysis. The need for organizing data into categories of similar objects has made the task of clustering increasingly important to those domains. In this chapter, the authors present a survey of the use of GAs for clustering applications. A variety of encoding (chromosome representation) approaches, fitness functions, and genetic operators are described, all of them customized to solve problems in such an application context.

1 Introduction

Clustering is one of the main tasks in Machine Learning, being usually employed when none or little information on the dataset is available. Intuitively, clustering is based on an inductive principle where objects within a cluster are more similar to each other then objects belonging to different clusters. This inductive principle is regarded as the objective function of clustering algorithms. The association of this objective function with a dataset creates an optimization problem (Jain *et al.*, 1999), whose goal depends on the validation employed. The partitions obtained by a clustering algorithm depend on the validation function adopted and the values assigned to the algorithm free-parameters. For some algorithms, the order of presentation of the examples can also affect the partitions produced.

The values for the free parameters are usually defined by trial and error, which may be computationally prohibitive. Finding an optimal or near optimal solution to the problem of partitioning n objects into k clusters has been shown to be *NP*-complete (Kaufman and Rousseeuw, 1990). Therefore, more sophisticated search techniques are necessary in order to be able to find a suitable set of values for the free parameters in a reasonable processing time.

Genetic Algorithms (GAs) are population-based search techniques that combine features of selected solutions in order to evolve them towards a global optimum.

GAs have been successfully used in many different tasks, including clustering. This survey will be organized in a framework describing the alternatives followed by different authors for each aspect of this application. For the application of GAs to a clustering problem, it is necessary to determine the representation of the possible solutions, how these solutions will be evaluated (the fitness function), the genetic operators employed to manipulate these solutions and the values of the free parameters (population size and application rate of the genetic operators). These subjects will be discussed in sections 2, 4 and 5, respectively.

1.1 A Brief Look at Genetic Algorithms

GAs are search and optimization methods inspired by the process of evolution of biological organisms. According to Charles Darwin in *The Origin of Species* (Darwin, 2006), organisms evolve by principles of natural selection and survival of the fittest organisms. John Holland's group from the University of Michigan introduced GAs in the middle of 1976 (Holland, 1975). However, its full use only started almost ten years later (Goldberg, 1989).

In a few words, a GA uses a population of individuals to solve a given problem. Each individual of the population corresponds to a possible solution for the problem. A reproduction based mechanism is applied to the current population, generating a new population. The population usually evolves through several generations until a suitable solution is reached.

According to (Goldberg, 1989), GAs differ from traditional methods of search and optimization mainly in four aspects:

- they can work with a code of the set of parameters and not necessarily with the own parameters;
- they work with several possible solutions and not with a single solution point;
- they use cost information or reward functions and not derivative or other auxiliary knowledge;
- they use probabilistic rules of transition instead of deterministic rules.

GAs start generating an initial population formed by a random group of individuals, which can be seen as first guesses to solve the problem. Supposing that a solution of a problem can be represented by a set of parameters, such parameters are coded into an individual by using a data structure called chromosome (in general a vector or a bit string). The chromosome is composed by a string of genes, where each gene is a coded parameter. The codification of parameters is defined by the programmer.

The initial population is evaluated and, for each individual, a score (named fitness) is given, reflecting the quality of the solution associated to it. In function optimization problems, the fitness is usually equal to the (raw or scaled) value of the objective function of the problem.

By mimicking the "natural selection", a GA probabilistically selects the best individuals whereas the worst are discarded. The selected individuals can be modified by genetic operators such as crossover and mutation, generating descendants for the next generation. This process is named reproduction. The evolutionary procedure is repeated until the population converges to a unique solution that is likely to be an optimal solution. Figure 1 presents a general diagram of a GA life cycle.

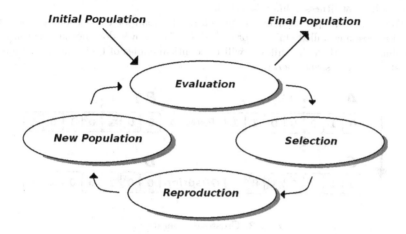

Fig. 1. Genetic Algorithm cycle.

GAs operate on a population of candidates in parallel. Thus, they can simultaneously search different regions of the solutions space. While selection drives the population into the direction of better solutions, crossover and mutation explore new solutions (i.e. new areas of the search space).

Different methods have been proposed to select individuals from a population. The most commonly used method is the roulette wheel sampling. In this method, each individual from the population occupies an area of the roulette wheel proportional to its fitness value. If P individuals are to be selected, the roulette wheel randomly spins P times. For each run, the individual pointed by the roulette wheel is selected. As a result, fitter individuals have higher chances of being selected.

Although largely used, the roulette wheel method does not work with negative fitness values and the expected number of children from a same parent suffers high variance. This problem can be overcome by the Stochastic Universal Sampling (SUS) (Baker, 1987), which ensures a selection of offspring which is closer to what is deserved than roulette wheel selection. The individuals are mapped to contiguous segments, such that each individual's segment is equal in size to its fitness exactly as in roulette-wheel selection. Equally spaced pointers are placed over the segments as many as there are individuals to be selected. Consider P the number of individuals to be selected, then the distance between the pointers are $1/P$ and the position of the first pointer is given by a randomly generated number in the range $[0, 1/P]$, the position of the second pointer is given by a randomly generated number in the range $[1/P, 2/P]$ and so on. SUS samples individuals by spinning the roulette P times for each equally-spaced pointers, instead of spinning randomly for all the segments as occurs in the roulette wheel method.

Other alternative is tournament selection (Mitchell, 1999), in which T (usually, $T = 2$) chromosomes are randomly selected from the population, with the same probability. These chromosomes compete against each other and the chromosome with the highest fitness value is selected.

The crossover operation exchanges parts of a pair of chromosomes, creating new chromosomes called children or offspring (If crossover does not succeed in the probability test, then the children will be identical copies of their parents). Figure 2 illustrates a crossover operation.

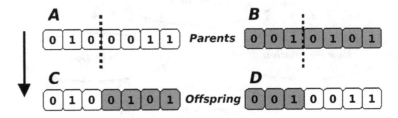

Fig. 2. Crossover operation.

In Figure 2, a cut point is randomly chosen and two chromosomes, A and B, contribute with a subset of their genes for the creation of the offspring C and D. There are several variations of crossover operators, such as the two cut point crossover and the uniform crossover. When the two point crossover is used, the segments between the two randomly chosen cut points are exchanged between the two parents (Goldberg, 1989, Mitchell, 1999), as can be seen in Figure 3.

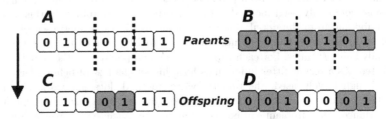

Fig. 3. Two point crossover operation.

For the uniform crossover, a mask is used to define from which parent each offspring inherits each of its genes (Goldberg, 1989, Mitchell, 1999).

The mutation operator aims to increase the variability of the population, allowing the GA to simultaneously search different areas of the solution space. This operator changes at random the value of a chromosome gene, also randomly chosen with a given probability (named mutation rate). Figure 4 shows a mutation operation that changes the value of the forth gene from 0 to 1.

After the creation of the children, the new population is obtained by replacing the original parents by their children. The usual approach involves replacing all parents. This approach is called generational replacement, which combined with elitism gives better results (Goldberg, 1989). An elitist policy means never replacing

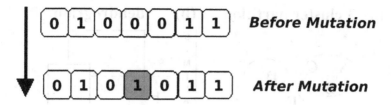

Fig. 4. Mutation operation.

the best parent, or set of parents, by any children worse (e.g. with lower aptitude) than them (Mitchell, 1999).

It's worth noting that the raw fitness (i.e. the fitness obtained directly from the objective function or cost function) may cause problems in most real world problems. Such as, for instance, premature convergence and low resolution of selection in later stages of evolution (when many individuals have high fitness values). Scaling and ranking adjust raw fitness more gently. Scaling adjusts the raw fitness using a linear function $a + bf_{raw}$, where a and b are constants. Ranking sorts chromosomes best-to-worst fashion and assign fitness by interpolating the best (rank $= 1$) individual to the worst (rank $= P$) according to some function, usually linear or exponential. The ranked fitness of the ith individual using a linear function is given by:

$$min + (max - min)\frac{P - rank(i)}{P - 1} \tag{1}$$

This ranking requires $1 \leq max \leq 2$ and $min + max = 2$.

2 Representation

Clustering algorithms can be divided into two main categories: partitional and hierarchical. Partitional clustering algorithms identify the partition that optimizes a given clustering criterion (Jain *et al.*, 1999). Hierarchical clustering algorithms produce a nested series of partitions based on a criterion for either merging (agglomerative algorithms) or splitting (divisive algorithms) clusters based on a similarity measure. Hierarchical clusters may be represented by a *dendrogram*, showing the nested grouping of objects and similarity levels at which groupings change (Jain *et al.*, 1999). An example of a partition (a) and a *dendrogram* (b) for the objects A, B, C, D, E, F, G, is shown in Figure 5.

When applied to partitional clustering problems, some GAs can search for the number of clusters that best fits the dataset structure. As described in Section 1.1, each possible solution is represented in a GA by a vector (chromosome) of numeric values (genes). Different representations have been proposed for clustering using GAs (Cole, 1998). The most frequently used representations for partitional algorithms are:

- **Group-Number**: It is an encoding scheme in which a chromosome is an integer vector of n positions, where n is the number of dataset objects or objects. Each position corresponds to an object, i.e., the ith position (gene) represents the

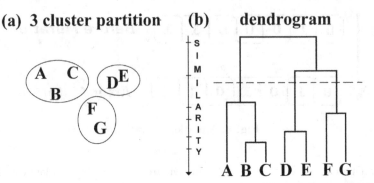

Fig. 5. Main cluster types: (a) partitional and (b) hierarchical.

*i*th dataset object. Provided that a genotype represents a partition formed by *k* clusters, each gene has a value from the alphabet 1,2,3,...,*k*. These values define the cluster labels (Krovi, 1992, Murthy and Chowdhury, 1996, Cowgill *et al.*, 1998). The same encoding scheme is used in (Hruschka and Ebecken, 2003, Hruschka *et al.*, 2004), but the authors additionally propose to store the number of clusters *k* in the genotype.

- **Binary Matrix:** In this case, the chromosome is represented by a $k \times n$ matrix of binary values, where *k* is the number of clusters and *n* is the number of objects in the dataset. If the value of the matrix position $P(C, x)$ is 1, the object *x* belongs to cluster *C*. Otherwise, it does not belong to this cluster (Bezdek *et al.*, 1994).

- **Centroids and Medoids:** The chromosomes are made up of real numbers that represent the coordinates of the cluster centers (Scheunders, 1997, Fränti *et al.*, 1997, Maulik and Bandyopadhyay, 2000, Merz and Zell, 2002, Kivijärvi *et al.*, 2003). If a genotype *i* encodes *k* clusters in a *d* dimensional space, its length is $d \times k$. Lucasius et al. (Lucasius *et al.*, 1993) proposed a related representation, which is based on the position of *k* selected objects (named medoids) from the dataset. Given the set of these medoids, *k* clusters are formed by assigning the remaining $(n - k)$ objects to the nearest medoid. Thus, each partition is encoded with a string of *k* different integers from $1, ..., n$. These integers correspond to the objects according to the order they appear in the dataset. The same representation scheme is adopted in (Estivill-Castro, 1997, Hall *et al.*, 1999, Sheng and Liu, 2004)

- **Labels:** Ma et al. (Ma *et al.*, 2006) proposed an evolutionary algorithm for clustering, named EvoCluster, which encodes a partition in such a way that each gene represents one cluster and contains the labels of the objects grouped into it. Thus, a genotype encoding *k* clusters $(C_1, C_2, ..., C_k)$ of a dataset with *n* objects is formed by *k* genes, each of which stores l_i labels $(l_1 + l_2 + ... + l_k = n)$. The they claim that this encoding scheme is an advantageous alternative over other different schemes. In particular, they argue that the group-number encoding, where each object is encoded as a gene and given a label from 1 to *k*, is not very scalable since the length of each genotype is exactly the number of objects of the training set. Although this assertion is persuasive at a first glance, it is worth noticing that the amount of information that must be stored (and handled) in both encoding schemes previously described is essentially the same, that is,

n object labels (EvoCluster's encoding) or n cluster labels (Group-Number). Therefore, the scalability of EvoCluster in terms of memory requirement does not benefit from its encoding scheme. Actually, the encoding scheme does not seem to be a crucial aspect regarding the practical usefulness of an algorithm when handling large data sets. In the end, the data set itself must be handled somehow (e.g. using efficient data structures for external memory management) and its dimensionality is necessarily larger than that of any encoding scheme.

Figure 6 presents the chromosome for the clusters $\{\{A, C, F\}, \{B, D, E\}\}$, using each of the representations described. The clusters are labeled 1 and 2 and the instances are labeled in the range between A and E. In Figure 6, the chromosome (c) represents two centroids, z_1 and z_2, and their respective hypothetical attribute values from a_1 to a_d.

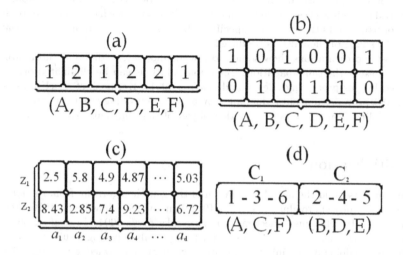

Fig. 6. Examples of (a)Group-Number, (b)Binary Matrix, (c)Centroids and (d) using labels.

In hierarchical clustering, the hierarchy, represented by the *dendrogram*, can be broken at different levels to yield different clustering partitions of the dataset. Thus, a hierarchical cluster can be represented by a set of partitions with its respective representation. Figure 7 shows two possible representations for the *dendrogram* in Figure 5: a set of partitions, represented by Group-Number, and an object oriented approach representation proposed by Greene (Greene, 2003). In the first representation (a), each line is associated with one possible level of partition and each column with a object. The second representation (b) indicates the clusters of the *dendrogram* as nodes in a graph. The cluster associated with each node contains the children clusters and belongs to the cluster represented by its parent node. This relationship is represented by the edges of the graph.

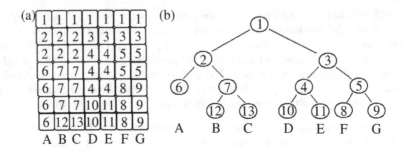

Fig. 7. Hierarchical representations using a set of partitions (a) and object orientation (b).

Another representation, named Cluster Description-Based Representation, was proposed by Freitas (Freitas, 2005). In this representation, each chromosome specifies a set of parameters that precisely specify each cluster. These parameters are related with the shape of the clusters produced.

Most representations show some form of redundancy, as different chromosomes may represent the same partition. Unfeasible solutions can be eliminated or remunerated by pos-processing (Belew and Booker, 1991). Korkmaz et al. (Korkmaz *et al.*, 2006) propose to avoid redundancy by using an encoding scheme in which each gene is a link from an object to another object of the same cluster.

3 Initialization

Many authors build the initial population of the genetic algorithm from random assignments of objects to clusters (Krovi, 1992, Murthy and Chowdhury, 1996, Cowgill *et al.*, 1998, Hruschka and Ebecken, 2003, Hruschka *et al.*, 2004, Ma *et al.*, 2006). Lucasius et al. (Lucasius *et al.*, 1993) suggest to randomly selecting a subset of objects to be the medoids of the initial population when prior knowledge is not available. Similarly, in (Kuncheva and Bezdek, 1997, Estivill-Castro, 1997, Maulik and Bandyopadhyay, 2000, Merz and Zell, 2002, Sheng and Liu, 2004) an initialization scheme is adopted that randomly chooses dataset objects to be initial prototypes of the clusters. The initial centers of the clusters can also be randomly generated (Scheunders, 1997, Fränti *et al.*, 1997, Kivijärvi *et al.*, 2003).

In Tseng and Yang (Tseng and Yang, 2001), the population of strings is randomly generated. The number of $1's$ in the binary strings is uniformly distributed within $[1, k]$, where k is the number of clusters initially generated. Some authors use heuristics to find good initial partitions and avoid invalid clusters (Bezdek *et al.*, 1994).

4 Fitness Function

A fitness function must be defined for the evaluation of the chromosomes. This function is based on the objective function used by traditional clustering algorithms.

Since the objective function has to be rescaled, the fitness function is very often a composition of the objective function and a scaling function (Grefenstette, 2000).

One of the most commonly used fitness function consists on minimizing the sum of squared Euclidean distances of the objects to their respective cluster mean (centroids) (Murthy and Chowdhury, 1996, Maulik and Bandyopadhyay, 2000, Merz and Zell, 2002). This fitness function $f(C_1, C_2, ..., C_k)$ can be formally described by:

$$f(C_1, C_2, ..., C_k) = \sum_{j=1}^{k} \sum_{x \in C_j} ||x - z_j||^2 \qquad (2)$$

where $(C_1, C_2, ..., C_k)$ is the set of k clusters encoded by the genotype, x is a dataset object, and z_j is the mean vector (centroid) of cluster C_j. Similarly, the fitness functions used in the genetic algorithms described in (Fränti et al., 1997, Kivijärvi et al., 2003) aim to minimize the distortion in the clusters. The minimization of such distortion is equivalent to minimize $f(C_1, C_2, ..., C_k)$ defined in Equation (2). More precisely, the distortion dst is a measure of the intra-cluster diversity, which can be defined as:

$$dst = \frac{f(C_1, C_2, ..., C_k)}{n \times m} \qquad (3)$$

where n and m are the numbers of objects and attributes, respectively. Adopting $f(C_1, C_2, ..., C_k)$ defined in Equation (2) and assuming a dataset formed by n objects, the fitness function employed in (Scheunders, 1997) can be written as:

$$f_m(C_1, C_2, ..., C_k) = \frac{n}{f(C_1, C_2, ..., C_k)} \qquad (4)$$

Similar to what is carried out with centroids, the minimization of the distances of the k medoids to all the corresponding objects of the same cluster was proposed also in (Lucasius et al., 1993). Functions presented above are monotonic with the number of cluster and does not optimize it.

Alternative validation criteria have also been used as fitness functions. The validation criteria are in general statistical indexes employed to evaluate the quality of a given partition. Three different approaches can be followed internal, external and relative:

- Internal criteria: measure the quality of a partition using only the original dataset. They measure how well the clusters obtained represent the similarities present in the dataset. A fitness function based on Euclidian distance is an example of internal criterion.
- External criteria: these criteria evaluate the partitions according to a predefined structure, based on what is known about the dataset. This predefined structure can be either a known partition for the dataset or a partition defined a specialist in the data domain.
- Relative criteria: They are employed to compare two or more clustering techniques regarding a particular aspect. They can be used, for example, to compare different clustering algorithms or runs of the same algorithm with different parameter values.

In principle, any relative clustering validity criterion (Jain and Dubes, 1988, Milligan and Cooper, 1985, Halkidi et al., 2001) that is not monotonic with the number of clusters can be potentially used as a fitness function for a genetic algorithm designed to optimize the number of clusters. These criteria have been extensively studied, and some of them have shown good results for several applications. This fact has motivated their use as fitness functions, as it will be seen in this survey. However, it is worth mentioning that the particular features of a given relative validity criterion can make its performance problem dependent (Pal and Bezdek, 1995). The following criteria can optimize the final partition's cluster number.

Variation Ratio Criteria (VRC) (Calinski and Harabasz, 1974) and Silhouette (Rousseeuw, 1987) are two popular relative criteria choices when clustering is combined with GAs (Cowgill *et al.*, 1998, Casillas *et al.*, 2003, Pan *et al.*, 2003, Hruschka and Ebecken, 2003, Hruschka *et al.*, 2004). The values produced by these criteria are independent of the cluster algorithm used and can be employed to estimate the natural number of clusters in a dataset (Milligan and Cooper, 1985).

VRC is based on internal cluster cohesion and external cluster isolation. The internal cohesion is calculated by the within-group sum of square distances (WGSS) and the external isolation by the between-groups sum of square distances (BGSS) (Duda *et al.*, 2001), given by:

$$WGSS = \sum_{i=1}^{n} \sum_{j=i+1}^{n} D_{ij} \tag{5}$$

where n is the total number of objects and i and j are objects with $i \in C$ and $j \in C$, for all clusters C, D_{ij} is the dissimilarity between objects i and j, and

$$BGSS = \sum_{i=1}^{n} \sum_{j=i+1}^{n} D_{ij} \tag{6}$$

where i and j are objects with $i \in C$ and $j \notin C$, for all clusters C. The VRC criterion is given by:

$$VRC = \frac{BGSS}{(k-1)} / \frac{WGSS}{(n-k)} \tag{7}$$

with k being the total number of clusters and n the total number of objects.

Silhouette is based on the distance between objects from the same cluster and their distance to the closest cluster. Consider an object x belonging to a cluster C_a. Let the average dissimilarity of x to all other objects of C_a be denoted by $a(x)$. Next, let the average dissimilarity of x to all objects of a cluster C be represented by $d(x, C)$. After computing $d(x, C)$ for all clusters $C \neq C_a$, the smallest value, $b(x)$, is selected, where $b(x) = \min d(x, C) \forall C \neq C_a$. Thus, the silhouette for object x is given by:

$$s(x) = \begin{cases} 1 - a(x)/b(x), & a(x) < b(x) \\ 0, & a(x) = b(x) \\ b(x)/a(x) - 1, & a(x) > b(x) \end{cases} \tag{8}$$

It is easy to verify that $-1 \leq s(x) \leq 1$. This measure is appropriate when the values of the different attributes exhibit similar inferior and superior limits and the true clusters are compact and disjoint (Rousseeuw, 1987). In addition, if $s(x)$ is equal to zero, then it is not clear whether the instance should have been assigned to its current cluster or to a neighboring one (Everitt *et al.*, 2001). Finally, if the cluster is a singleton, then $s(x)$ is not defined and the most neutral choice is to set

$s(x) = 0$ (Kaufman and Rousseeuw, 1990). The silhouette criterion is given by the average of $s(i)$ over $i = 1, 2, ..., n$.

Two additional validity indexes to guide the genetic search were proposed by Hruschka et al. (Hruschka *et al.*, 2004), one of them is a simplified version of the silhouette. This criterion is based on the computation of distances between objects and cluster centroids, which are the mean vectors of the clusters. More specifically, the term $a(x)$ of Equation (8) becomes the dissimilarity of object x to the centroid of its cluster C_a. Similarly, instead of computing $d(x, C)$ as the average dissimilarity of x to all objects of C, $C \neq C_a$, only the distance between x and the centroid of C must be computed. Alternatively to the original and simplified versions of the silhouette, Hruschka et al. (Hruschka *et al.*, 2004) have shown that the fitness function can be taken as the average of $b(x)/(a(x) + \varepsilon)$ over $i = 1, 2, ..., n$, using the centroid based terms $a(x)$ and $b(x)$ just described. The term ε is necessary to compute $s(x)$ when $a(x)$ is zero, i.e., when all objects of cluster C_a are equal to each other. This modified objective function seems to be more sensitive to slight changes in $a(x)$ and $b(x)$, which in turn may correspond to significant changes in the clustering solution.

S. Bandyopadhyay and U. Maulik (Bandyopadhyay *et al.*, 2001) proposed a validity index $I(k)$ for computing the fitness of a genotype that represents k clusters, that is defined as:

$$I(k) = \left(\frac{1}{k} \cdot \frac{E_1}{E_k} \cdot D_k \right)^p \tag{9}$$

where p is any real number larger than or equal to 1, E_j and D_j are given by the following equations, respectively:

$$E_j = \sum_{j=1}^{k} \sum_{i=1}^{n} \mu_{ji} ||x_i - z_j|| \tag{10}$$

$$D_j = \max_{l,w=1}^{k} ||z_l - z_w|| \tag{11}$$

where n is the total number of objects in the dataset, $[\mu_{ji}]_{k \times n}$ is a partition matrix for the dataset $D = \{x_1, ..., x_n\}$, and z_w is the center of the wth cluster. They report some experiments in which $I(k)$ provides better results than the indexes proposed in (Davies *et al.*, 1979) and (Dunn *et al.*, 1973), which are commonly used as relative validity criteria for clustering. However, in a more recent work (Bandyopadhyay and Maulik, 2002), they decided to use a fitness function based on the Davis-Bouldin (DB) (Davies *et al.*, 1979) index. The DB index for the partitioning of n objects into k clusters is defined as:

$$DB = \frac{1}{k} \sum_{i=1}^{k} R_{C_i} \tag{12}$$

The index for the ith cluster, R_{C_i}, is given by:

$$R_{C_i} = \max_{j \neq i} \{R_{j,i}\} \tag{13}$$

and $R_{j,i}$ measure the within-to-between cluster spread for all pairs of clusters (j, i):

$$R_{j,i} = \frac{e_j + e_i}{v_{j,i}} \tag{14}$$

where e_j is the within cluster variation for the jth cluster and $v_{j,i}$ is the distance between the centers of the jth and the ith clusters.

The fitness function adopted in EvoCluster (Ma et al., 2006) has been conceived to deal with noisy and missing data, as well as to recognize interesting feature values for the clustering process. The fitness of each genotype is assessed by means of two main steps. The first step is dedicated to the discovery of statistically significant association of objects in the partition encoded in the genotype. To this end, some objects from different clusters are randomly selected to form a training set for object discovery. Let a be an attribute, a_j the jth value this attribute takes in the dataset, and obs_{ij} the total number of objects in the dataset that belong to cluster C_i and are characterized by the same attribute value a_j. According to Ma et al. (Ma *et al.*, 2006), $exp_{ij} = (obs_{i+}) \cdot (obs_{+j})/n'$ is the expected number of objects under the assumption that being a member of C_i is independent of whether a object has the value a_j, where obs_{i+}, obs_{+j}, and n' are given by:

$$obs_{i+} = \sum_{j=1}^{g} obs_{ij} \tag{15}$$

$$obs_{+j} = \sum_{i=1}^{k} obs_{ij} \tag{16}$$

$$n' = \sum_{i,j} obs_{ij} \leq n \tag{17}$$

where g is the total number of distinct values for a, k is the number of clusters encoded by the genotype and n is the number of objects. The statistical significance of the association can be evaluated by:

$$z_{ij} = \frac{obs_{ij} - exp_{ij}}{\sqrt{exp_{ij}}} \tag{18}$$

where the maximum likelihood estimate of its asymptotic variance v_{ij} is defined by:

$$v_{ij} = \left(1 - \frac{obs_{i+}}{n'}\right)\left(1 - \frac{obs_{+j}}{n'}\right) \tag{19}$$

Then $sd_{ij} = z_{ij}/(v_{ij})^{1/2}$ has an approximately standard normal distribution and the attribute value can be selected based on a statistically significant cluster dependency. In step 2 of the fitness computation, an uncertainty measure, named weight of evidence, W, is calculated for the values a_j associated with the cluster C_i at a given confidence level. The value of W for an object characterized by a_j to belong to C_i and not to other clusters is given by:

$$W(cluster = C_i/cluster \neq C_i | a_j) = L(C_i : a_j) - L(\neq C_i : a_j) \tag{20}$$

where $L(C_i : a_j)$ is given by:

$$L(C_i : a_j) = log\frac{P(C_i | a_j)}{P(C_i)} \tag{21}$$

For a collection of selected attribute values, the weight of evidence from all observed values is defined as:

$$W\left(cluster = C_i/cluster \neq C_i|a_1...a_j...a_{g'}\right) = \sum_{j=1}^{g'} W\left(cluster = C_i/cluster \neq C_i|a_j\right)$$

$$(22)$$

where g' is the number of selected attribute values. Cluster C_i is inferred if W is maximized. Thus, the predicted value can be compared with the original label of each object encoded in the genotype to determine the reclassification accuracy of the objects not selected in step 1. Finally, the fitness value is calculated based on this accuracy. The authors (Ma et $al.$, 2006) claim that EvoCluster does not require the number of clusters k to be defined in advance. However, this aspect was not fully investigated in the reported experimental evaluation, in which a set of interesting values for k was chosen a priori.

Validation criteria are independent of the representation and the cluster algorithm used.

5 Genetic Operators

Genetic operators are responsible for the modification of the individuals from one population to the next. Such operators may include, for instance, the exchange of parts of the parents, thus allowing the production of new solutions sharing features from both parents. By creating new solutions, genetic operators expand the exploration of the search space, making it possible to reach any of its regions. The main genetic operators are selection crossover and mutation. When GAs are used for clustering, the traditional genetic operators may need to be adapted to fit the chosen clustering representation.

5.1 Selection

As chromosomes are selected based on their relative fitness, the selection type is independent of representation or clustering algorithm. Proportional selection has been used by several authors (Krovi, 1992, Lucasius et $al.$, 1993, Murthy and Chowdhury, 1996, Estivill-Castro, 1997, Cowgill et $al.$, 1998, Maulik and Bandyopadhyay, 2000, Kivijärvi et $al.$, 2003). The simplest approach for proportional selection is the roulette wheel method, described in Section 1.1. Another popular choice is tournament selection, also described in Section 1.1.

Additionally to proportional selection, elitist variants for selecting genotypes are also investigated in (Murthy and Chowdhury, 1996, Fränti et $al.$, 1997, Kivijärvi et $al.$, 2003). A particular kind of elitist strategy is adopted in (Kuncheva and Bezdek, 1997), where the parents and the children are pooled and the best genotypes survive, composing the new population. Similarly, Merz and Zell (Merz and Zell, 2002) derive a new population by selecting the best genotypes out of the pool of parents and children. These selection methods can be viewed as variants of the so-called $(\mu + \lambda)$ selection procedure used in evolution strategies.

5.2 Crossover

Traditional crossover operators act at the chromosome level, ignoring the true shape of the clusters. This may result, for instance, in offspring whose representation is very similar to the parents, but whose corresponding clusters are very different. Therefore, the incorporation of context sensitivity to the crossover operators applied to clustering problems is commonly used, although it is not compulsory (Cowgill *et al.*, 1998, Bandyopadhyay and Maulik, 2002).

The main idea behind context sensitivity is to create crossover operators that can transmit clusters (integrally or partially) from the parents to the offspring, preserving their building blocks.

An example of this type of crossover is the edge-based crossover (Belew and Booker, 1991). In this operator, after the selection of parent two chromosomes, their objects are selected based on the edge of the clusters they belong to. Two objects are connected by the same edge if they are present in the same cluster in both chromosomes. The resulting children are composed of the non-empty intersections of their parent clusters. An example of two parent chromosomes and a possible child chromosome is showed on Figure 8, where cluster $\{C, D\}$ is copied from PC_1, $\{A, E\}$ from PC_2 and $\{B, F\}$ from both parents.

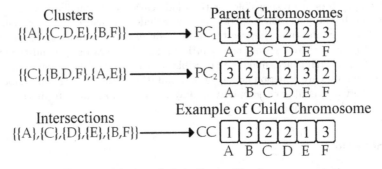

Fig. 8. Two partitions and their Group-Number representations.

Another context-sensitive crossover operator is proposed by Hruschka and Ebecken (Hruschka and Ebecken, 2003) and combines clustering solutions coming from different genotypes. After the selection of two chromosomes (PC_1 and PC_2), $e \in 1, 2, ..., k_1$ clusters are copied from PC_1 to PC_2, assuming that PC_1 represents k_1 clusters. The unchanged clusters of PC_2 are maintained. The modified clusters have their remaining instances allocated to the cluster with the nearest centroid, resulting in the offspring CC_1. The procedure is repeated to generate another offspring, CC_2. However, now, the modified clusters of PC_2 are copied into PC_1. Figure 3 illustrates this crossover, where clusters 2 and 3 are copied from PC_1 to PC_2. The instances of clusters indirectly affected have their value set to zero and are reallocated to the cluster with the nearest centroid later.

The crossover operators used by the EvoCluster algorithm (Ma *et al.*, 2006) can be seen as modified versions of the context-sensitive evolutionary operators of the clustering genetic algorithm (CGA) proposed by Hruschka and Ebecken (Hruschka and Ebecken, 2003). Indeed, in both CGA and EvoCluster, the crossover operators

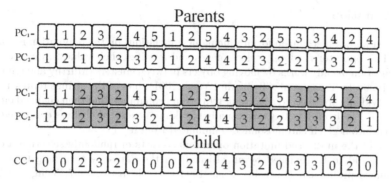

Fig. 9. Example of crossover between the chromosomes PC_1 and PC_2.

were essentially designed to copy (exchange), split, merge, and eliminate groups. Besides some minor details on how these basic operations are performed, there is an important difference regarding the way the operators are applied in each algorithm: the application of EvoCluster's crossover operator can be probabilistically guided by information concerning the quality of the individual clusters in a given partition.

Estivill-Castro et al. (Casillas *et al.*, 2003) use a one-point crossover that is also context sensitive. This operator manipulates the edges of a Minimum Spanning Tree (MST) in which the nodes represent the dataset objects and the edges correspond to proximity indexes between them.

An interesting work, Pasi Fränti et al. (Fränti *et al.*, 1997) use five crossover operators that fundamentally select k centroids from two parents. The random crossover operator randomly chooses $k/2$ centroids from each of the two parents. Duplicate centroids are replaced by averages of repeated draws. In the operator named centroid distance, the clusters are initially sorted according to their distances from the grand mean of the dataset. Next, they are divided into two subsets, namely: central clusters and remote clusters. The central clusters are those closer to the centroid of the dataset, whereas the remote clusters are the remaining ones. An offspring is created by taking the central clusters from parent PC_1 and the remote clusters from parent PC_2. In pairwise crossover, clusters codified in different parents are paired according to the similarities of their centroids. Offspring is then generated by randomly taking one centroid from each pair of clusters. In the largest partition operator, y centroids are selected by a greedy heuristic based on the assumption that larger clusters are more important than smaller ones. Finally, they evaluate the pairwise nearest neighbor crossover operator that considers that the $2k$ centroids from parents PC_1 and PC_2 can be clustered into k clusters that will form the offspring. All the crossover operators previously described by the authors are context-sensitive, except for centroid distance, which can be viewed as a variant of the single point crossover. They argue that the pairwise nearest neighbor operator is the best choice. Another work (Kivijärvi *et al.*, 2003) used the same crossover operators above in addition to a single point crossover operator.

5.3 Mutation

The best known mechanism for producing new variations on the population is mutation. This operator randomly selects genes and modifies their values. In clustering, the mutation usually works by moving objects between clusters (Murthy and Chowdhury, 1996). In Tseng et al. (Tseng and Yang, 2001), bits of the strings representing the individuals are selected according to a given probability, and then changed either from 0 to 1 or from 1 to 0. Conceptually speaking, generated clusters can be either inserted into a given chromosome or eliminated from it.

One of the most used mutation operators consists of randomly selecting a centroid/medoid to be replaced by an object from the dataset - according to a predetermined probability (Lucasius *et al.*, 1993, Estivill-Castro, 1997, Sheng and Liu, 2004, Fränti *et al.*, 1997, Kivijärvi *et al.*, 2003).

Some implementations alter the partition with the insertion/creation and removal/agglomeration of clusters (Hall *et al.*, 1999, Greene, 2003). An example are the two mutation operators used in (Hruschka and Ebecken, 2003, Hruschka *et al.*, 2004). The first operator works only on genotypes that encode more than two clusters. It eliminates a randomly chosen cluster, placing its objects into the nearest remaining clusters (according to their centroids). The second mutation operator splits a randomly selected cluster, which must be formed by at least two objects to be eligible for this operator, into two new ones. The first cluster is formed by the objects closer to the original centroid, whereas the other cluster is formed by those objects closer to the farthest object from the centroid.

Another class of operators is based on the displacement of the clusters centroids on the vectorial space. An operator of this class, proposed by Scheunders (Scheunders, 1997), randomly adds either a negative or a positive constant (-1 or +1) to a randomly chosen component of the centroid of a given cluster. The mutation of clusters centers by the a similar procedure is investigated in (Maulik and Bandyopadhyay, 2000). A number δ in the range $[0, 1]$ is generated with uniform distribution. This number is then used to change the value v of a given gene to $(1 \pm 2\delta)v$, when $v \neq 0$, or to $\pm 2\delta$ when $v = 0$. The signs "+" and "−" occur with equal probability.

A number of GAs combine two or more mutation operators to increase the population diversity. An example is the GA described in (Merz and Zell, 2002), which uses two distinct mutation operators. The first operator assigns a randomly chosen dataset object to substitute a randomly chosen centroid. The second operator randomly selects two clusters C_i and C_j. Then, the object belonging to C_i with the maximum distance from its centroid is chosen to replace the centroid of C_j.

Another example is the algorithm EvoCluster (Ma *et al.*, 2006) which has six mutation operators. Similarly to the operators used in (Hruschka and Ebecken, 2003), these operators essentially split, merge, and eliminate groups. However, differently from the previous operators, EvoCluster's mutation operators can be simultaneously applied to multiple clusters of the same partition. Besides, they can be probabilistically guided by information concerning the quality of the individual clusters in a given partition.

6 Some Related Works and Applications

GAs have been successfully used as clustering techniques in many applications, such as image processing (Hall *et al.*, 1999, Kivijärvi *et al.*, 2003), classification of pixels of satellite image (Bandyopadhyay and Maulik, 2002), gene expression analysis (Pan *et al.*, 2003), crude oil analysis (Murthy and Chowdhury, 1996, Maulik and Bandyopadhyay, 2000) and intrusion detection in computer networks (Liu *et al.*, 2004), just to mention a few.

Several works combine the use of GAs with other clustering techniques, e. g. by employing a GA to select characteristics of the database to be clusted (Ohtsuka *et al.*, 2002) or initial clusters for these techniques (Maulik and Bandyopadhyay, 2000). A method that combines a Bayesian feature selection approach with a clustering genetic algorithm to get classification rules is described in (Hruschka and Ebecken, 2003). In (Hruschka and Ebecken, 2006), a clustering genetic algorithm is applied to extract rules from multilayer perceptrons trained in classification problems.

7 Conclusion

This text presents a survey on the use of Genetic Algorithms for clustering. GAs can represent different types of clustering partitions while being able to adopt a wide variety of fitness functions as objective functions based on clustering validity criteria. The combination of several desirable optimization skills makes GAs able to be applied to many clustering problems from a large number of application areas.

Most of the objective functions involved in clustering and measures employed for clustering validation are based on different inductive biases, which can favor datasets with particular characteristics. Thus, it is worth stressing that the selection of a proper fitness function to the problem in hand is important to obtain the desired results.

Current research has focused on more efficient cluster representations and context sensitive genetic operators. The study of fitness and objective functions is also an important research area on GAs applied to clustering problems.

Acknowledgements

The authors would like to thank CNPq, FAPESP and FINEP for the support received during this work.

References

Baker, J.E., (1987), Reducing bias and inefficiency in the selection algorithm. Proceedings of the Second International Conference on Genetic Algorithms and their Application, pp. 14–21.

Bandyopadhyay, S., Maulik, U., (2001), Nonparametric genetic clustering: Comparison of validity indices. Systems, Man and Cybernetics, Part C, IEEE Transactions on : Applications and Reviews. **31**(1): 120–125.

Bandyopadhyay, S., Maulik, U., (2002), An evolutionary technique based on k-means algorithm for optimal clustering in rn. Inf. Sci. Appl. **146**(1-4): 221–237.

Belew, R.K., Booker, L.B., (1991), eds., Solving Partitioning Problems with Genetic Algorithms. In Belew, R.K., Booker, L.B., eds.: ICGA, Morgan Kaufmann.

Bezdek, J.C., Boggavaparu, S., Hall, L.O., (1994), Bensaid, A., Genetic algorithm guided clustering. Procedings of the First IEEE Conference on Evolutionary Computation: 34–40.

Calinski, T., Harabasz, J., (1974), A dendrite method for cluster analysis. Communications in statistics **3**(1): 1–27.

Casillas, A., de Lena, M.T.G., Martnez, R., (2003), Document clustering into an unknown number of clusters using a genetic algorithm. Lecture Notes in Computer Science **2807**: 43–49.

Cole, R.M., (1998), Clustering with Genetic Algorithms. PhD thesis, Department of Computer Science, University of Western Australia.

Cowgill, M.C., Harvey, R.J., Watson, L.T., (1998), A genetic algorithm approach to cluster analysis. Technical report, Virginia Polytechnic Institute & State University, Blacksburg, VA, USA.

Darwin, C., (2006), The Origin of Species: A Variorum Text. University of Pennsylvania Press.

Davies, D., Bouldin, D.W., (1979), A cluster separation measure. IEEE Transactions of Pattern Analysis and Machine Intelligence **1**: 224–227.

Duda, R., Hart, P., Stork, D., (2001), Pattern Classification. John Wiley & Sons.

Dunn, J., (1973), A fuzzy relative of the isodata process and its use in detecting compact well-separated clusters. J. Cybern **3**: 32–57.

Estivill-Castro, V., (1997), Spatial clustering for data mining with genetic algorithms. Technical report, Australia.

Everitt, B., Landau, S., Leese, M., (2001), Cluster Analysis, Arnold Publishers. Arnold Publishers.

Fränti, P., Kivijärvi, J., Kaukoranta, T., Nevalainen, O., (1997), Genetic algorithms for large scale clustering problems. The Computer Journal **40**: 547–554.

Freitas, A. (2005), Evolutionary Algorithms for Data Mining. in Oded Maimon, Lior Rokach (Eds.), The Data Mining and Knowledge Discovery Handbook, Springer, pp. 435–467.

Goldberg, D., (1989), Genetic Algorithms in Search, Optimization, and Machine Learning. Addison-Wesley.

Greene, W.A., (2003), Unsupervised hierarchical clustering via a genetic algorithm. In: Proceedings of the 2003 Congress on Evolutionary Computation, IEEE Press, pp. 998–1005.

Grefenstette, J., (2000), Proportional selection and sampling algorithms. In: Evolutionary Computation 1. Institute of physics publishing, pp. 172–180.

Halkidi, M., Batistakis, Y., Vazirgiannis, M., (2001), On clustering validation techniques. Intelligent Information Systems Journal **17**(2-3): 107–145.

Hall, L., Ozyurt, B., Bezdek, J., (1999), Clustering with a genetically optimized approach. IEEE Transations on Evolutionary Computation. 3: 103–112.

Holland, J., (1975), Adaptation in Natural and Artificial Systems. University of Michigan Press, Ann Arbor.

Hruschka, E.R., Campello, R.J.G.B., de Castro, L.N., (2004), Improving the efficiency of a clustering genetic algorithm. In: Advances in Artificial Intelligence

- IBERAMIA 2004: 9th Ibero-American Conference on AI, Puebla, Mexico, November 22-25. Proceedings. Volume 3315., Springer-Verlag GmbH, Lecture Notes in Computer Science, pp.861-868.

Hruschka, E.R., Ebecken, N.F.F., (2003), A genetic algorithm for cluster analysis. Intelligent Data Analysis **7**(1): 15–25.

Hruschka, E.R., Ebecken, N.F.F., (2003), A feature selection bayesian approach for extracting classification rules with a clustering genetic algorithm. Applied Artificial Intelligence **17**(5-6): 489–506.

Hruschka, E.R., Ebecken, N.F.F., (2006), Extracting rules from multilayer perceptrons in classification problems: A clustering-based approach. Neurocomputing **70**: 384–397.

Jain, A.K., Murty, M.N., Flynn, P.J., (1999), Data clustering: a review. ACM Computing Surveys **31**(3): 264–323.

Jain, A., Dubes, R., (1988), Algorithms for Clustering Data. Prentice Hall.

Kaufman, L., Rousseeuw, P., (1990), Finding groups in data: An introduction to cluster analysis. Wiley Series in Probability and Mathematical Statistics.

Kivijärvi, J., Fränti, P., Nevalainen, O., (2003), Self-adaptive genetic algorithm for clustering. Journal of Heuristics **9**(2): 113–129.

Korkmaz, E.E., Du, J., Alhajj, R., Barker, K., (2006), Combining advantages of new chromosome representation scheme and multi-objective genetic algorithms for better clustering. Intell. Data Anal. **10**(2): 163–182.

Krovi, R., (1992), Genetic algorithms for clustering: a preliminary investigation. System Sciences, 1992. Proceedings of the Twenty-Fifth Hawaii International Conference on **4**: 540–544.

Kuncheva, L., Bezdek, J.C., (1997), Selection of cluster prototypes from data by a genetic algorithm. Procedings of the 5th European Congress on Intelligent Techniques and Soft Computing, pp. 1683–1688.

Liu, Y., Chen, K., Liao, X., Zhang, W., (2004), A genetic clustering method for intrusion detection. Pattern Recognition **37**(5): 927–942.

Lucasius, C.B., Dane, A.D., Kateman, G., (1993), On k-medoid clustering of large data sets with the aid of a genetic algorithm: background, feasibility and comparison. Analytica Chimica Acta, pp. 647–669.

Ma, P.C.H., Chan, K.C.C., Yao, X., Chiu, D.K.Y., (2006), An evolutionary clustering algorithm for gene expression microarray data analysis. IEEE Trans. Evolutionary Computations **10**(3): 296–314.

Maulik, U., Bandyopadhyay, S., (2000), Genetic algorithm-based clustering technique. Pattern Recognition **33**: 1455 – 1465.

Merz, P., Zell, A., (2002), Clustering gene expression profiles with memetic algorithms. In: PPSN VII: Proceedings of the 7th International Conference on Parallel Problem Solving from Nature, London, UK, Springer-Verlag, pp. 811–820.

Milligan, G.W., Cooper, M.C., (1985), An examination of procedures for determining the number of clusters in a data set. Psychometrika **50**: 159–179.

Mitchell, M., (1999), An introduction to Genetic Algorithms. MIT Press.

Murthy, C.A., Chowdhury, N., (1996), In search of optimal clusters using genetic algorithms. Pattern Recogn. Lett. **17**(8): 825 – 832.

Ohtsuka, A., Kamiura, N., Isokawa, T., Matsui, N., (2002), On detection of confused blood samples using self organizing maps and genetic algorithm. In: Neural Information Processing, 2002. ICONIP '02. Proceedings of the 9th International Conference on. Volume 5., Department of Computer Science and Illinois Genetic Algorithms Laboratory, 2233 – 2238.

Pal, N., Bezdek, J., (1995), On cluster validity for the fuzzy c-means model. IEEE Transactions of Fuzzy Systems 3(3):370–379.

Pan, H., Zhu, J., Han, D., (2003), Genetic algorithms applied to multi-class clustering for gene expression data. Genomics, Proteomics and Bioinformatics 1(4): 279–287.

Rousseeuw, P.J., (1987), Silhouettes: a graphical aid to the interpretation and validation of cluster analysis. Journal of Computational and Applied Mathematics 20:53–65.

Scheunders, P., (1997), A genetic c-means clustering algorithm applied to color image quantization. Pattern Recognition 30(6): 859–866.

Sheng, W., Liu, X., (2004), A hybrid algorithm for k-medoid clustering of large data sets. In: Proceedings of the 2004 IEEE Congress on Evolutionary Computation, Portland, Oregon, IEEE Press, pp. 77–82.

Tseng, L., Yang, S.B., (2001), A genetic approach to the automatic clustering problem. Pattern Recognition 34:415–424.

Discovering New Rule Induction Algorithms with Grammar-based Genetic Programming

Gisele L. Pappa and Alex A. Freitas

Computing Laboratory
University of Kent
Canterbury, Kent, CT2 7NF, UK
glp6, A.A.Freitas@kent.ac.uk
http://www.cs.kent.ac.uk/~aaf

Summary. Rule induction is a data mining technique used to extract classification rules of the form IF (conditions) THEN (predicted class) from data. The majority of the rule induction algorithms found in the literature follow the sequential covering strategy, which essentially induces one rule at a time until (almost) all the training data is covered by the induced rule set. This strategy describes a basic algorithm composed by several key elements, which can be modified and/or extended to generate new and better rule induction algorithms. With this in mind, this work proposes the use of a grammar-based genetic programming (GGP) algorithm to automatically discover new sequential covering algorithms. The proposed system is evaluated using 20 data sets, and the automatically-discovered rule induction algorithms are compared with four well-known human-designed rule induction algorithms. Results showed that the GGP system is a promising approach to effectively discover new sequential covering algorithms.

1 Introduction

In the classification task of data mining, one way of representing the knowledge discovered by the data mining algorithm consists of a set of classification rules, where each rule has the form: IF (conditions) THEN (predicted class). This knowledge representation has the advantage of being intuitively comprehensible to the user (Iglesia *et al.*, 1996).

There are a number of rule induction algorithms that have been proposed to discover such classification rules (Fürnkranz, 1999, Mitchell, 1997). A particularly popular strategy consists of the sequential covering approach, where in essence the algorithm discovers one rule at a time until (almost) all examples are covered by the discovered rules (i.e., match the conditions of at least one rule). Sequential covering rule induction algorithms are typically greedy, performing a local search in the rule space.

An alternative approach to discover classification rules consists of using an evolutionary algorithm (EA), which performs a more global search in the rule space.

Indeed, there are also a number of EAs for discovering a set of classification rules from a given data set (Freitas, 2002).

In this chapter, however, we propose a very different and pioneering way of using an EA in the context of classification rule discovery. We propose a grammar-based genetic programming (GGP) system that *automatically* discovers new sequential covering rule induction *algorithms* (rather than *rules*). The discovered rule induction algorithms are generic and robust enough to be applicable to virtually any classification data set in any application domain, in the same way that a manually-designed rule induction algorithm is generic and robust enough to be applicable to virtually any classification data set.

The proposed method allows the automatic discovery of new rule induction algorithms potentially quite different from conventional, manually-designed rule induction algorithms. Hence, the automatically-discovered rule induction algorithms can avoid some of the human preconceptions and biases embedded in manually-designed rule induction algorithms, possibly leading to more effective algorithms in challenging application domains.

The first version of the proposed GGP system and its corresponding computational results have been previously published in (Pappa and Freitas, 2006). Nonetheless, one limitation of that version is that the evolved rule induction algorithms could cope only with nominal (categorical) attributes, and not with continuous (real-valued) attributes. In this chapter we describe a new, extended version of the system, which can cope with both nominal and continuous attributes. This new characteristic introduced into the system makes it now suitable for a larger variety of classification data sets, and this fact is reflected in the greater number of data sets used to evaluate the system, namely 20 data sets, whereas our first experiments reported in (Pappa and Freitas, 2006) used only 11 data sets. In addition, this chapter shows and discusses in detail one of the rule induction algorithms automatically generated by the GGP system, a result that was not reported in (Pappa and Freitas, 2006).

The remainder of this chapter is organized as follows. Section 2 briefly discusses rule induction algorithms. Section 3 gives a brief overview of GGP. Section 4 introduces the proposed GGP. Section 5 reports the results of several computational experiments. Finally, Section 6 presents the conclusions and describes future research directions.

2 Sequential Covering Rule Induction Algorithms

The sequential covering strategy (also known as separate and conquer) is certainly the most explored and most used strategy to induce rules from data. It was first employed by the algorithms of the AQ family (Michalski, 1969) in the late sixties, and over the years was applied again and again as the basic algorithm in rule induction systems.

The separate and conquer strategy works as follows. It learns a rule from a training set, removes from it the examples covered by the rule, and recursively learns another rule which covers the remaining examples. A rule is said to cover an example e when all the conditions in the antecedent of the rule are satisfied by the example e. For instance, the rule "IF (salary $>$ £ 100,000) THEN rich" covers all the examples in the training set in which the value of salary is greater than £100,000, regardless of the current value of the class attribute of an example. The learning process goes on until a pre-defined criterion is satisfied. This criterion usually requires that all or almost all examples in the training set are covered by a rule.

Algorithms following the sequential covering approach usually differ from each other in four main elements: the representation of the candidate rules, the search mechanisms used to explore the space of candidate rules, the way the candidate rules are evaluated and the pruning method, although the last one can be absent (Fürnkranz, 1999, Witten and Frank, 2005).

Considering the first of these four rule induction algorithms elements, the rule representation has a significant influence in the learning process, since some concepts can be easily expressed in one representation but hardly expressed in others. The most common rule representations used by rule induction algorithms are propositional or first order logic.

The next two elements found in rule induction algorithms determine how the algorithm will explore the space of candidate rules. The first of them, i.e., the search mechanism, is composed by two components: a search strategy and a search method. The search strategy determines the region of the search space where the search starts and its direction, while the search method specifies which specializations/generalizations should be considered.

Broadly speaking, there are three kinds of search strategies: bottom-up, top-down and bi-directional. A bottom-up strategy starts the search with a very specific rule, and iteratively generalizes it. A top-down strategy, in contrast, starts the search with the most general rule and iteratively specializes it. The most general rule is the one that covers all examples in the training set (because it has an empty antecedent, which is always satisfied for any example). At last, a bi-directional search is allowed to generalize or specialize the candidate rules.

Any of these search strategies is complemented with a search method. The search method is a very important part of a rule induction algorithm since it determines which specializations/generalizations will be considered at each specialization/generalizations step. Too many specializations/generalizations are not allowed due to computational time, but too few may disregard good conditions and reduce the chances of finding a good rule. Among the available search methods are the greedy search and the beam search.

The search method is guided by a rule evaluation heuristic, which is the second component found in rule induction algorithms which has influence in the way the rule space is explored. The regions of the search space being explored by a rule induction algorithm can drastically change according to the heuristic chosen to assess a rule while it is being built. Among the heuristics used to estimate the quality of a rule are the information content, information gain, Laplace correction, m-estimate, ls-content, among others (Fürnkranz, 1999).

The first algorithms developed using the sequential covering approach were composed by the three components described so far: a rule representation, a search strategy and a evaluation heuristic. However, these first algorithms searched the data for complete and consistent rule sets. It means they were looking for rules that covered all the examples in the training set (complete) and that covered no negative examples (consistent). These are not common characteristics of any real-world data sets. Hence, pruning methods were introduced to sequential covering algorithms to avoid over-fitting and to handle noisy data.

Pruning methods are divided in two categories: pre- and post-pruning. Pre-pruning methods stop the refinement of the rules before they become too specific or over-fit the data, while post-pruning methods first produce a complete and consistent rule or rule set, and later try to simplify it. When comparing pre- and post-pruning techniques, each of them has its advantages and pitfalls. Though pre-pruning techniques are faster, post-pruning techniques usually produce simpler and more accurate models (at the expense of inefficiency, since some rules are learned and then simply discarded from the model).

In an attempt to solve the problems caused by pre- and post-pruning techniques, some methods combine or integrate them to get the best of both worlds. Some of these systems, for instance, prune each rule right after it is created, instead of waiting for the complete model to be generated (Cohen, 1995).

This section briefly described the main elements which compose a sequential covering rule induction algorithm. Knowledge about these elements and the variety of ways they can be implemented was the base to build the grammar used by the GGP system described in Section 4. For a more complete survey of sequential covering rule induction algorithms and its components the user is referred to (Fürnkranz, 1999, Mitchell, 1997, Witten and Frank, 2005).

3 Grammar-based Genetic Programming

Genetic Programming (GP) (Koza, 1992) is an area of evolutionary computation which aims to automatically evolve computer programs. It works by following Darwin's principle of selection and survival of the fittest, and can be easily adapted to solve a variety of problems. GP's success is backed up by a list of 36 human-competitive solutions, where two created patentable new inventions (gp.org).

Grammar-based Genetic Programming (GGP) is a variation of the classical GP method and, as its name indicates, the main difference among GGP and GP is that the former uses a grammar to create the population of candidate solutions for the targeted problem. The main advantage of using a grammar together with a GP system is that it can include previous knowledge about how the target problem is solved, and so be used to guide the GP search. Moreover, GGP solves a well-known problem in the GP literature, called closure[1].

Grammars (Aho et al., 1986) are simple mechanisms capable of representing very complex structures. Their formal definition was first given by Chomsky in 1950. According to Chomsky, a grammar can be represented by a four-tuple $\{N, T, P, S\}$, where N is a set of non-terminals, T is a set of terminals, P is a set of production rules, and S (a member of N) is the start symbol. The production rules define the language which the grammar represents by combining the grammar symbols.

In this work we are specially interested in context-free grammars (CFG). CFGs are the class of grammars most commonly used with genetic programming, and they are usually described using the Backus Naur Form (BNF) (Naur, 1963).

---

[1] A traditional GP system creates individuals by combining a set of functions and terminals. The closure property states that every function in the GP function set has to be able to process any value it receives as input. For further details see (Banzhaf et al., 1998).

According to the BNF notation, production rules have the form <expr> ::= <expr><op><expr>, and symbols wrapped in "<>" represent the non-terminals of the grammar. Three special symbols might be used for writing the production rules in BNF: "|","[ ]" and "( )". "|" represents a choice, like in <var> ::=$x|y$, where <var> generates the symbol x or y. "[ ]" wraps an optional symbol which may or may not be generated when applying the rule. "( )" is used to group a set of choices together, like in $x ::= k(y|z)$, where x generates k followed by y or z. The application of a production rule from $p \in P$ to some non-terminal $n \in N$ is called a derivation step, and it is represented by the symbol $\Rightarrow$.

Once a grammar that includes background knowledge about the target problem has been defined by the user, a GGP system follows the pseudo-code defined in Algorithm 1.

Algorithm 1: Basic pseudo-code for a GGP system

Define a representation for the individuals

Define parameters such as population size, number of generations, crossover, mutation and reproduction rates

Generate the first GGP population based on the production rules of the grammar

while maximum number of generations not reached **do**

 Evaluate the individuals using a pre-defined fitness function

 Select the best individuals, according to the fitness function, to breed

 Perform crossover, mutation and reproduction operations with the selected individuals, always producing offspring which are also valid according to the defined grammar

Return individual with best fitness

Note that each individual represents a candidate solution to the target problem. Hence, since we use a GGP to automatically evolve rule induction algorithms, each individual is a rule induction algorithm, and the grammar gathers knowledge about how rule induction algorithms were previously developed.

4 Discovering New Rule Induction Algorithms

This section describes an extended version of the GGP method proposed in (Pappa and Freitas, 2006). As explained before, the main difference between the method described here and the one described in (Pappa and Freitas, 2006) is that, while the latter could only cope with nominal attributes, the former can cope with both nominal and numerical attributes.

In summary, the proposed GGP works as follows. It creates the first population of individuals based on the production rules of a grammar, which is used to guide the search for new rule induction algorithms. In this population, each GGP individual represents a complete sequential-covering rule induction algorithm, such as CN2 (Clark and Boswell, 1991). As the GGP system is based on the principle of survival of the fittest, a fitness function is associated with each individual in the population, and used to select a subset of them (through a tournament selection of size 2) to breed and undergo crossover, mutation and reproduction operations. The individuals generated by these operations (which also have to be valid according to the grammar being used) are inserted into a new population, representing a new generation of evolved individuals. The evolution process is carried out until a maximum number of generations is reached.

Note that the main modifications introduced to the system in order to cope with numerical attributes are related to the terminals of the grammar and the way they are implemented. Hence, in this section, we first present the grammar introduced in (Pappa and Freitas, 2006), emphasizing its components which cannot be found in traditional rule induction algorithms, and then we present the modifications necessary to make it cope with numerical attributes. Following the grammar description, we show an example of an individual which can be evolved by the system, and then describe the individuals' evaluation process. Finally, we explain how the evolutionary operators were implemented.

4.1 The grammar

In a GGP system, the grammar is the element which determines the search space of the candidate solutions for a target problem. Hence, in the GGP system proposed here, the grammar contains previous knowledge about how humans design rule induction algorithms, plus some new concepts which were borrowed from other data mining paradigms or created by the authors (and that to the best of the authors' knowledge were never used in the design of sequential-covering rule induction algorithms).

The proposed grammar is presented in Table 1. It uses the BNF terminology introduced earlier, and its *Start* symbol is represented by the non-terminal with the same name. Recall that non-terminals are wrapped into <> symbols, and each of them originates a production rule. Grammar symbols not presented between <> are terminals. In the context of rule induction algorithms, the set of non-terminals and terminals are divided into two subsets. The first subset includes general programming elements, like *if* statements and *for/while* loops, while the second subset includes components directly related to rule induction algorithms, such as *RefineRule* or *PruneRule*.

The non-terminals in the grammar represent high-level operations, like a while loop (*whileLoop*) or the procedure performed to refine a rule (*RefineRule*). The terminals, in turn, represent a very specific operation, like *Add1*, which adds one condition-at-a-time to a candidate rule during the rule refinement process (*RefineRule*). Terminals are always associated with a building block. A building block represents an "atomic operation" (from the grammar's viewpoint) which does not need any more refinements. Building blocks will be very useful during the phase of rule induction code generation, as each of them is associated with a chunk of Java code.

As observed in Table 1, the grammar contains 26 non-terminals (NT), where each NT can generate one or more production rules. Recall that in the BNF notation, used to describe the grammar in Table 1, the symbol "|" separates different production rules, and the symbol "[ ]" wraps an optional symbol (which may or may not be generated when applying the rule). For

Table 1. The grammar used by the GGP (adapted from (Pappa and Freitas, 2006))

```
1-  <Start> ::= (<CreateRuleSet>|<CreateRuleList>) [<PostProcess>].
2-  <CreateRuleSet> ::= forEachClass <whileLoop> endFor
                        <RuleSetTest>.
3-  <CreateRuleList> ::= <whileLoop> <RuleListTest>.
4-  <whileLoop>::= while <condWhile> <CreateOneRule> endWhile.
5-  <condWhile>::= uncoveredNotEmpty |uncoveredGreater
                        (10| 20| 90%| 95%| 97%| 99%) trainEx.
6-  <RuleSetTest> ::= lsContent |confidenceLaplace.
7-  <RuleListTest>::= appendRule | prependRule.
8-  <CreateOneRule>::= <InitializeRule> <innerWhile> [<PrePruneRule>]
                        [<RuleStoppingCriterion>].
9-  <InitializeRule> ::= emptyRule| randomExample| typicalExample |
                        <MakeFirstRule>.
10- <MakeFirstRule> ::= NumCond1| NumCond2| NumCond3| NumCond4.
11- <innerWhile> ::= while (candNotEmpty| negNotCovered)
                        <FindRule> endWhile.
12- <FindRule> ::= (<RefineRule>|<innerIf>) <EvaluateRule>
                        [<StoppingCriterion>] <SelectCandidateRules>.
13- <innerIf> ::= if <condIf> then <RefineRule> else <RefineRule>.
14- <condIf> ::=  <condIfExamples> | <condIfRule>.
15- <condIfRule> ::= ruleSizeSmaller (2| 3| 5| 7).
16- <condIfExamples> ::= numCovExp ( >| <)(90%| 95%| 99%).
17- <RefineRule> ::= <AddCond>| <RemoveCond>.
18- <AddCond> ::= Add1| Add2.
19- <RemoveCond>::= Remove1| Remove2.
20- <EvaluateRule>::= confidence | Laplace| infoContent| infoGain.
21- <StoppingCriterion> ::= MinAccuracy (0.6| 0.7| 0.8)|
                        SignificanceTest (0.1| 0.05| 0.025| 0.01).
22- <SelectCandidateRules> ::= 1CR| 2CR| 3CR| 4CR| 5CR| 8CR| 10CR.
23- <PrePruneRule> ::= (1Cond| LastCond| FinalSeqCond) <EvaluateRule>.
24- <RuleStoppingCriterion> ::= accuracyStop (0.5| 0.6| 0.7).
25- <PostProcess> ::= RemoveRule EvaluateModel| <RemoveCondRule>.
26- <RemoveCondRule> ::= (1Cond| 2Cond| FinalSeq) <EvaluateRule>.
```

instance, the NT *Start* generates four production rules: *CreateRuleList, CreateRuleSet, CreateRuleList PostProcess* and *CreateRuleSet PostProcess*. In total, the grammar has 83 production rules, which were carefully generated after a comprehensive study of the main elements of the pseudo-codes of basic rule induction algorithms, which follow the basic process described in Section 2.

In this section, we focus on the new components of the grammar, which are usually not found in traditional rule induction algorithms. The major "new" components inserted to the grammar are:

- The terminal *typicalExample*, which creates a new rule using the concept of typicality, borrowed from the instance-based learning literature (Zhang, 1992). An example is said to be typical if it is very similar to the other examples belonging to the same class it belongs to, and not similar to the other examples belonging to other classes. In other words, a typical example has high intra-class similarity and low inter-class similarity.

- The non-terminal *MakeFirstRule*, which allows the first rule to be initialized with one, two, three or four attribute-value pairs, selected probabilistically from the training data in proportion to their frequency. Attribute-value pairs are selected subject to the restriction that they involve different attributes (to prevent inconsistent rules such as "sex = male AND sex = female").

- The non-terminal *innerIf*, which allows rules to be refined in different ways (e.g. adding or removing one or two conditions-at-a-time to/from the rule) according to the number of conditions they have, or the number of examples the rule list/set covers.

- Although some methods do use rule look-ahead, i.e., they do insert more than one condition-at-a-time to a set of candidate rules, we did not find in the literature any rule induction algorithm which removes two conditions-at-a-time from a rule. This is implemented by the terminal *Remove2*.

Note that the list above shows a set of single components which are new "building blocks" of rule induction algorithms. These components increase the diversity of the candidate rule induction algorithms considerably, but it is the combination of the "standard" and new components which will potentially contribute to the creation of a new rule induction algorithm different from conventional algorithms.

As it will be discussed in Section 4.3, the individuals generated by following the production rules of the grammar are converted into executable rule induction algorithms by using a GGP/Java interface, which reads out an individual and puts together chunks of code associated with the terminals and non-terminals of the grammar contained in that individual.

Hence, in order to modify the grammar and make it cope with data sets containing numerical attributes, the main modifications are introduced in some chunks of Java code associated with the terminals of the grammar. The terminals whose implementation went through major extensions were the ones responsible for refining rules by adding/removing conditions to/from it. They were extended in a way that they can produce algorithms that represent rule conditions of the form "<attribute, operator, value>", where operator is "=" in the case of nominal attributes, and operator is "≥" or "≤" in the case of numerical attributes.

The approach followed by these terminals to generate rule conditions with numerical attributes is similar to the one implemented by the Ripper and C4.5 algorithms, where the values of a numerical attribute are sorted, and all threshold values considered. The best threshold value is chosen according to

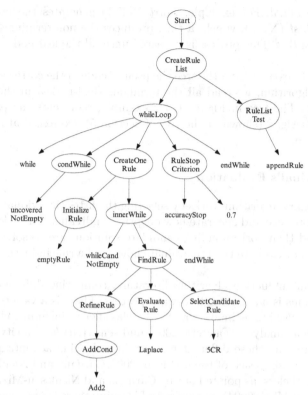

Fig. 1. Example of a GGP Individual (a complete rule induction algorithm)

the information gain associated with that attribute-value pair - see (Witten and Frank, 2005) or (Quinlan, 1993) for details.

By applying the production rules defined by the grammar, the GGP system can generate up to approximately 5 billion different rule induction algorithms (Pappa, 2007). Each of these rule induction algorithms can be represented by an individual in the GGP population. The next section explains how the individuals extracted from the grammar are represented in the proposed GGP system.

4.2 Individual Representation

In a GGP system, each individual represents a candidate solution for the problem being tackled. In this work, each individual represents a complete rule induction algorithm following the sequential covering approach, which can be applied to generate rules for any classification data set.

Figure 1 shows an example of an individual generated by the grammar presented in the previous section. The root of the tree is the non-terminal *Start*. The tree is then derived by the application of production rules for each non-terminal. For example, *Start* (NT 1) generates the non-terminal *CreateRuleList* (NT 3), which in turn produces the non-terminals *whileLoop* and *RuleListTest*. This process is repeated until all the leaf nodes of the tree are terminals.

In order to extract from the tree the pseudo-code of the corresponding rule induction algorithm, we read all the terminals (leaf-nodes) in the tree from left to right. The tree in Figure 1, for example, represents the pseudo-code described in Alg. 2 (shown at the end of Section 5), expressed at a high level of abstraction.

4.3 Individual's Evaluation

An evolutionary algorithm works by selecting the fittest individuals of a population to reproduce and generate new offspring. Individuals are selected based on how good their corresponding candidate solutions are to solve the target problem. In our case, we need to evaluate how good a rule induction algorithm is.

In the rule induction algorithm literature, comparing different classification algorithms is not a straightforward process. There is a variety of metrics which can be used to estimate how good a classifier is, including classification accuracy, ROC analysis (Fawcett, 2003) and sensitivity/specificity. There are studies comparing these different metrics, and showing advantages and disadvantages in using each of them (Flach, 2003, Caruana and Niculescu-Mizil, 2004). Nevertheless, as pointed out by Caruana and Niculescu-Mizil (Caruana and Niculescu-Mizil, 2004), in supervised learning there is one ideal classification model, and "we do not have performance metrics that will reliably assign best performance to the probabilistic true model given finite validation data".

Classification accuracy is still the most common metric used to compare classifiers, although some authors tried to show the pitfalls of using classification accuracy when evaluating induction algorithms (Provost *et al.*, 1998) – specially because it assumes equal misclassification costs and known class distributions – and others tried to introduce ROC analysis as a more robust standard measure. Based on these facts and on the idea of using a simpler measure when first evaluating the individuals produced by the GGP, we chose to use a measure based on accuracy to compose the fitness of the GGP system.

In this framework, a rule induction algorithm RI_A is said to outperform a rule induction algorithm RI_B if RI_A has better classification accuracy in a set of classification problems. Thus, in order to evaluate the rule induction algorithms being evolved, we selected a set of classification problems, and created a meta-training set. The meta-training set consists of a set of data sets, each of them divided as usual into (non-overlapping) training and validation sets.

As illustrated in Figure 2, each individual in the GGP population is decoded into a rule induction algorithm using a GGP/Java interface. The Java code is then compiled, and the resulting rule induction algorithm run in all the

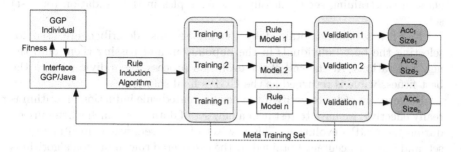

Fig. 2. Fitness evaluation process of a GGP Individual

data sets belonging to the meta-training set. It is a conventional run where, for each data set, a set or list of rules is built using the set of training examples and evaluated using the set of validation examples. It is important to observe that, during preliminary experiments with the GGP, we noticed that it was suffering from a common problem found when solving predictive data mining tasks: over-fitting. As the same training sets were being accessed by the GGP over and over, the produced rule induction algorithms were over-fitting these data sets. We solved this problem with a simple and effective solution borrowed from the literature on GP for data mining (Bhattacharyya, 1998): at each generation, the data used in the training and validation sets of the data sets in the meta-training set are merged and randomly redistributed. This means that, at each generation, the GGP individuals are evaluated in a different set of validation data, helping to avoid over-fitting.

After the rule induction algorithm is run in all the data sets in the meta-training set, the accuracy in the validation set and the rule lists/sets produced for all data sets are returned. These two measures can be used to calculate a fitness function. In this work, we used as the fitness function the average values of the function described in Eq.(1) over all the data sets in the meta-training set.

$$fit_i = \begin{cases} \frac{Acc_i - DefAcc_i}{1 - DefAcc_i}, & \text{if } Acc_i > DefAcc_i \\ \frac{Acc_i - DefAcc_i}{DefAcc_i}, & \text{otherwise} \end{cases} \tag{1}$$

According to the definition of fit_i, where i denotes the id of a given data set, if the accuracy obtained by the classifier is better than the default accuracy, the improvement over the default accuracy is normalized, by dividing the absolute value of the improvement by the maximum possible improvement. In the case of a drop in the accuracy with respect to the default accuracy, this difference is normalized by dividing the negative value of the difference by the maximum possible drop (the value of $DefAcc_i$). The default accuracy for a given data set is simply the accuracy obtained when using the most frequent class in the training set to classify new examples in the validation (or test) set.

The fitness values obtained by the process just described are used for selecting the best individuals in the population, and passing them onto the new generations. At the end of the evolution process, the individual with the best fitness value is returned as the GGP's final solution.

However, in order to verify if the newly created rule induction algorithm is really effective, we have to test it in a new set of data sets, which where unseen during the GGP's evolution. This new set of data sets was named meta-test set, and it is the accuracy obtained by the discovered rule induction algorithms in these data sets which has to be taken into account when evaluating the GGP system.

4.4 Evolutionary Operators

After individuals are generated and evaluated, they are selected to undergo reproduction, crossover and mutation operations, according to used defined probabilities. The reproduction operator simply copies the selected individual to the new population, without any modifications. The crossover operator, in contrast, involves two selected individuals, and swaps a selected subtree between them. The mutation operator also selects a subtree of one selected individual, and replace it by a new, randomly generated tree.

However, in GGP systems, the new individuals produced by the crossover and mutation operators have to be consistent with the grammar. For instance, when performing crossover the system cannot select a subtree with root *EvaluateRule* to be exchanged with a subtree with root *SelectCandidateRules*, because this would create an invalid individual according to the grammar.

Therefore, crossover operations have to exchange subtrees whose roots contain the same non-terminal. Mutation can be applied to a subtree rooted at a non-terminal or applied to a terminal. In the former case, the subtree undergoing mutation is replaced by a new subtree, produced by keeping the same label in the root of the subtree and then generating the rest of the subtree by a new sequence of applications of production rules, so producing a new derivation subtree. When mutating terminals, the terminal undergoing mutation is replaced by another "compatible" symbol, i.e., a terminal or non-terminal which represents a valid application of the production rule whose antecedent is that terminal's parent in the derivation tree. The probability of mutating a non-terminal is 90%, while the probability of mutating a terminal is 10%.

Figure 3 shows an example of a crossover operation. Note that just part of the individuals are shown, for the sake of simplicity. The process works as follows. Parent 1 has a node probabilistically selected for crossover. In the example illustrated, the chosen node is *RefineRule*. The node *RefineRule* is then searched in the derivation tree of parent 2. As parent 2 has a node named *RefineRule*, their subtrees are swapped, generating child 1 and child

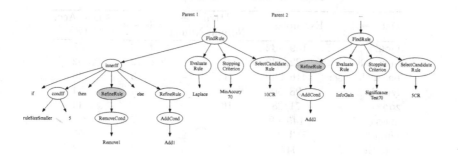

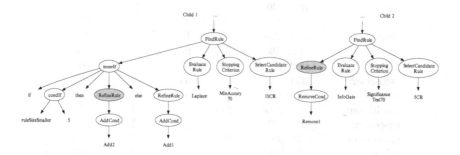

Fig. 3. Example of Crossover in the proposed GGP

2. If *RefineRule* is not present in the tree of parent 2, a new non-terminal is selected from the tree of parent 1. The GGP performs at most 10 attempts to select a node which can be found in both parents. If after 10 attempts it does not happen, both individuals undergo mutation operations.

5 Computational Results and Discussion

In order to test the effectiveness of the proposed GGP system to discover new rule induction algorithms, we have to define two different sets of parameters: (1) the parameters for the GGP system and (2) the data sets used during the training phase of the system.

Table 2 shows the 20 data sets used in the experiments. The figures in the column *Examples* indicate the number of examples present in the training and validation data sets – numbers before and after the "/", respectively, followed by the number of nominal attributes, numerical attributes and classes. The last column shows the default accuracy. It is important to note that during the evolution of the rule induction algorithm by the GGP, for each data set in the meta-training set, each candidate rule induction algorithm (i.e., each GGP individual) is trained with 70% of the examples, and then validated in the

Table 2. Data sets used by the GGP

Data set	Examples	Attributes Nomin.	Numer.	Classes	Def. Acc. (%)
monks-2	169/432	6	-	2	67
monks-3	122/432	6	-	2	52
bal-scale-discr	416/209	4	-	3	46
lymph	98/50	18	-	4	54
zoo	71/28	16	-	7	43
glass	145/69	-	9	7	35.2
pima	513/255	-	8	2	65
hepatitis	104/51	14	6	2	78
vehicle	566/280	-	18	4	26
vowel	660/330	3	10	11	9
crx	461/229	9	6	2	67.7
segment	1540/770	-	19	7	14.3
sonar	139/69	-	60	2	53
heart-c	202/101	7	6	2	54.5
ionosphere	234/117	-	34	2	64
monks-1	124/432	6	-	2	50
mushroom	5416/2708	23	-	2	52
wisconsin	456/227	9	-	2	65
promoters	70/36	58	-	2	50
splice	2553/637	63	-	3	52

remaining 30%. In contrast, in the meta-test set, the evolved rule induction algorithms are evaluated using a well-known 5-fold cross validation procedure (Witten and Frank, 2005).

As our priority was to investigate the influence the GGP parameters have in the quality of the rule induction algorithms produced, we first defined the data sets which will be used in the GGP meta-training and meta-test sets. However, it is not clear how many data sets should be used in each of these meta-sets of data, or what would be the best criteria to distribute them into these two meta-sets. Intuitively, the larger the number of data sets in the meta-training set, the more robust the evolved rule induction algorithm should be. On the other hand, the smaller the number of data sets in the meta-test set, the less information we have about the ability of the evolved rule induction algorithm to obtain a high predictive accuracy for data sets unseen during the evolution of the algorithm.

As a reasonable compromise, the data sets in Table 2 were divided into 2 groups of 10 data sets each. The top 10 sets listed in Table 2 were inserted into the meta-training set, while the bottom 10 data sets formed the meta-test set. We selected the data sets which compose the meta-training set based on the execution time of rule induction algorithms, so that we included in the meta-training set the data sets leading to faster runs of the rule induction algorithms.

After creating the meta-training and meta-test sets, we turned to the GGP parameters: population size, number of generations and crossover, mutation and reproduction rates. In all the experiments reported in this section the population size is set to 100 and the number of generations to 30. These two figures were chosen when evaluating the GGP evolution in preliminary experiments, but are not optimized. Regarding crossover, mutation and reproduction rates, GPs usually use a high rate of crossover and low rates of mutation and reproduction. However, the balance between these three numbers is an open question, and may be very problem dependent (Banzhaf *et al.*, 1998).

In previous experiments, we set the value for the reproduction rate parameter to 0.05, and run the GGP with crossover/mutation rates of 0.5/0.45, 0.6/0.35, 0.7/0.25, 0.8/0.15 and 0.9/0.05, respectively. The results obtained by the GGP when run with these different parameters configurations showed that the system was robust to these variations, producing very similar results with all the configurations. In the experiments reported in this section, the crossover rate was set to 0.7 and the mutation rate to 0.25.

The results obtained by the GGP-derived rule induction algorithms (GGP-RIs) were compared with four well-known rule induction algorithms: the ordered (Clark and Niblett, 1989) and unordered (Clark and Boswell, 1991) versions of CN2, Ripper (Cohen, 1995) and C4.5Rules (Quinlan, 1993). Out of these four algorithms, C4.5Rules is the only one which does not follow the sequential covering approach, which is the approach followed by the GGP-RIs. However, as C4.5Rules has been used as a benchmark algorithm for classification problems for many years, we also included it in our set of baseline comparison algorithms.

It is also important to observe that the current version of the grammar does not include all the components present in Ripper, but does include all the components present in both versions of CN2. In other words, the space of candidate rule induction algorithms searched by the GGP includes CN2, but it does not include C4.5Rules nor the complete version of Ripper.

Table 3 shows the average accuracy obtained by the rule induction algorithms produced by the GGP in 5 different runs, followed by the results of runs of Ordered-CN2, Unordered-CN2, Ripper and C4.5Rules (using default parameter values in all these algorithms). Note that the results reported in Table 3 are the ones obtained in the data sets belonging to the meta-test set (containing data sets unseen during the GGP evolution), and were obtained using a 5-fold cross-validation procedure for each data set. The results obtained by the GGP in the data sets belonging to the meta-training set are not reported here because, as these data sets were seen by the GGP many time during evolution, it is not fair to compare them with any other algorithms. The numbers after the symbol "±" are standard deviations. Results were compared using a statistical t-test with significance level 0.01. Cells in dark gray represent significant wins of the GGP-RIs against the corresponding baseline algorithm, while light gray cells represent significant GGP-RIs' losses.

Table 3. Comparing predictive accuracy rates (%) for the data sets in the meta-test set

Data Set	GGP-RIs	OrdCN2	UnordCN2	Ripper	C45Rules
crx	77.46±3.8	80.16 ± 1.27	80.6 ± 0.93	84.37 ± 1.21	84.82 ± 1.53
segment	95.06±0.26	95.38 ± 0.28	85.26 ± 0.87	95.44 ± 0.32	88.16 ± 7.72
sonar	72.34±1.91	70.42 ± 2.66	72.42 ± 1.4	72.88 ± 4.83	72.4 ± 2.68
heart-c	76.72±1.5	77.9 ± 1.96	77.54 ± 2.85	77.53 ± 1.1	74.2 ± 5.43
ionosphere	87.04±2.2	87.6 ± 2.76	90.52 ± 2.03	89.61 ± 1.75	89.06 ± 2.71
monks-1	99.93±0.07	100 ± 0	100 ± 0	93.84 ± 2.93	100 ± 0
mushroom	99.98±0.02	100 ± 0	100 ± 0	99.96 ± 0.04	98.8 ± 0.06
wisconsin	95.58±0.74	94.58 ± 0.68	94.16 ± 0.93	93.99 ± 0.63	95.9 ± 0.56
promoters	78.98±2.93	81.9 ± 4.65	74.72 ± 4.86	78.18 ± 3.62	83.74 ± 3.46
splice	88.68±0.31	90.32 ± 0.74	74.82 ± 2.94	93.88 ± 0.41	89.66 ± 0.78

In total, Table 3 contains 40 comparative results between GGP-RIs and baseline algorithms – 10 data sets × 4 baseline classification algorithms. Out of theses 40 cases, the accuracy of GGP-RIs was statistically better than the accuracy of a baseline algorithm in three cases, whilst the opposite was true in one case. In the other 36 cases there was no significant difference.

The GGP-RIs' predictive accuracies are statistically better than the C4.5Rules' accuracy in *mushroom* and Unordered-CN2's accuracy in *segment* and *splice*. Naturally, these three cases involve algorithms with the worst accuracy for the respective data set. It is also in a comparison among Ripper and the GGP-RIs in *splice* where the GGP-RIs obtain a significantly worse accuracy than Ripper.

Hence, these experiments lead us to conclude that the GGP-RIs can easily outperform classifiers which are not competitive with the other baseline algorithms. For example, in *splice* the predictive accuracy of Unordered-CN2 is 74.82 ± 2.94, while the other algorithms obtain accuracies close to 90%. In this case, the GGP-RIs can easily find a better accuracy than the one found by Unordered-CN2.

On the other hand, we can say that the GGP was not able to find a rule induction algorithm good enough to outperform the predictive accuracies of Ripper in *splice* because it did not have all the components necessary to do that in its grammar. However, note that the accuracy obtained by Ripper in *splice* is also statistically better than the ones obtained by C4.5Rules and Ordered-CN2 when applying a t-test with 0.01 significance level.

Finally, recall that the search space of the GGP includes both Unordered and Ordered CN2. Hence, it seems fair to expect that the GGP-RIs would never obtain a predictive accuracy significantly worse than either version of CN2. Indeed, this was the case in the experiments reported in Table 3, where the GGP-RIs significantly outperformed Unordered-CN2 in two cases (dark

---

Algorithm 2: Example of a Decision List Algorithm created by the GGP

RuleList = ∅
repeat
    bestRule = an empty rule
    candidateRules = ∅
    candidateRules = candidateRules ∪ bestRule
    while candidateRules ≠ ∅ **do**
        newCandidateRules = ∅
        for each candidateRule CR **do**
            Add 2 conditions-at-a-time to CR
            Evaluate CR using the Laplace estimation
            newCandidateRules = newCandidateRules ∪ CR
        candidateRules = 5 best rules selected from newCandidateRules
        bestRule' = best rule in candidateRules
        if Laplace(bestRule')> Laplace(bestRule) **then** bestRule = bestRule'
    if accuracy(bestRule) < 0.7 **then** break
    else RuleList = RuleList ∪ bestRule
until all examples in the training set are covered

---

gray cells in that table), and there was no case where either version of CN2 significantly outperformed the GGP-RIs.

So far we have shown that the evolved GGP-RIs are competitive to traditional human-designed rule induction algorithms. But how similar the former are to the latter? Out of the 5 GGP-RIs produced by the experiments described in this section (corresponding to 5 runs of the GGP with a different random seed in each run), 3 shared one relatively uncommon characteristic: they added two conditions instead of one condition at-a-time to an empty rule, as shown in Alg. 2. Alg. 2 starts to produce rules with an empty condition, adds two condition-at-a-time to it, evaluates the rule with the new conditions using the Laplace estimation and selects the best 5 produced rules to go on into the refinement process. The algorithm keeps inserting new conditions to the best selected rules until all the examples in the training set are covered, or while the rules found have accuracy superior to 70%.

In other words, Alg. 2 is a variation of CN2 where two conditions are added to a rule at-a-time. The other difference with respect to CN2 lies on the condition used to stop inserting rules to the model (predictive accuracy superior to 70%). But why most of the algorithms produced by the GGP are similar to CN2?

The UCI data sets (Newman *et al.*, 1998) are very popular in the machine learning community, and they have been used to benchmark classification algorithms for a long time. To a certain extent, most of the manually-designed rule induction algorithms were first designed or later modified targeting these data sets. The fact that the evolved rule induction algorithms are similar to CN2 is evidence that CN2 is actually one of the best algorithms in terms of average predictive accuracy in a set of data sets available in the UCI repository. At the same time, as the rule induction algorithms produced by the GGP showed, there are many other variations of the basic sequential covering pseudo-code which obtain accuracies competitive to the ones produced by CN2, Ripper or C4.5Rules. In general, the evolved algorithms did not obtain significantly better accuracies than the baseline classification algorithms, but the former obtained slightly better results than the latter, overall. This can be observed in Table 3, which contains three significant wins (dark gray cells) and just one significant loss (light gray cell) for the evolved algorithms.

6 Conclusions and Future Directions

This work presented a grammar-based genetic programming system which automatically discovers new sequential covering rule induction algorithms. Computational results showed that the system can effectively evolve rule induction algorithms which are competitive in terms of accuracy with well-known human designed rule induction algorithms.

This work opens a whole new area of research, and there are many other directions which could be taken. Improvements to the current work include changing the fitness of the system to use the ROC framework, and studying the impacts this change would have in the created rule induction algorithms.

A more interesting direction, which at the moment is part of our ongoing work, is to automatically create rule induction algorithms tailored to a specific application domain. In other words, we can replace the meta-training and meta-test sets of the current GGP system by a single data set, corresponding to a target application domain, and produce customized rule induction algorithms. This would be a great contribution to the area of meta-learning, in particular, which is putting many efforts into finding which algorithms are the best to mine specific data sets.

Acknowledgments

The first author is financially supported by CAPES, the Brazilian Research Council, process number 165002-5.

References

Aho, A.V., Sethi, R., Ullman, J.D, (1986), Compilers: Principles, Techniques and Tools. 1st edn. Addison-Wesley.

Banzhaf, W., Nordin, P., Keller, R.E., Francone, F.D, (1998), Genetic Programming – An Introduction; On the Automatic Evolution of Computer Programs and its Applications. Morgan Kaufmann.

Bhattacharyya, S, (1998), Direct marketing response models using genetic algorithms. In: Proc. of 4th Int. Conf. on Knowledge Discovery and Data Mining (KDD-98). 144–148.

Caruana, R., Niculescu-Mizil, A, (2004), Data mining in metric space: an empirical analysis of supervised learning performance criteria. In: Proc. of the 10th ACM SIGKDD Int. Conf. on Knowledge discovery and data mining (KDD-04), ACM Press 69–78.

Clark, P., Boswell, R., (1991), Rule induction with CN2: some recent improvements. In Kodratoff, Y., ed, EWSL-91: Proc. of the European Working Session on Learning on Machine Learning, New York, NY, USA, Springer-Verlag 151–163.

Clark, P., Niblett, T, (1989), The CN2 induction algorithm. Machine Learning **3** 261–283.

Cohen, W.W., (1995), Fast effective rule induction. In Prieditis, A., Russell, S., eds, Proc. of the 12th Int. Conf. on Machine Learning (ICML-95), Tahoe City, CA, Morgan Kaufmann 115–123.

Fawcett, T, (2003), Roc graphs: Notes and practical considerations for data mining researchers. Technical Report HPL-2003-4, HP Labs.

Flach, P, (2003), The geometry of roc space: understanding machine learning metrics through roc isometrics. In: Proc. 20th International Conference on Machine Learning (ICML-03), AAAI Press 194–201.

Freitas, A.A, (2002), Data Mining and Knowledge Discovery with Evolutionary Algorithms. Springer-Verlag.

Fürnkranz, J, (1999), Separate-and-conquer rule learning. Artificial Intelligence Review **13**(1) 3–54.

de la Iglesia, B., Debuse, J.C.W., Rayward-Smith, V.J, (1996) Discovering knowledge in commercial databases using modern heuristic techniques. In: Proc. of the 2nd ACM SIGKDD Int. Conf. on Knowledge discovery and data mining (KDD-96), 44–49.

Genetic Programming, http://www.genetic-programming.org/ (2006)

Koza, J.R, (1992), Genetic Programming: On the Programming of Computers by the means of natural selection. The MIT Press, Massachusetts.

Michalski, R.S, (1969), On the quasi-minimal solution of the general covering problem. In: Proc. of the 5th Int. Symposium on Information Processing, Bled, Yugoslavia 125–128.

Mitchell, T, (1997), Machine Learning. Mc Graw Hill.

Naur, P, (1963), Revised report on the algorithmic language algol-60. Communications ACM **6**(1) 1–17.

Newman, D.J., Hettich, S., Blake, C.L., Merz, C.J., (1998), UCI Repository of machine learning databases. University of California, Irvine, http://www.ics.uci.edu/~mlearn/MLRepository.html

Pappa, G.L., Freitas, A.A. (2006), Automatically evolving rule induction algorithms. In Fürnkranz, J., Scheffer, T., Spiliopoulou, M., eds, Proc. of the 17th European Conf. on Machine Learning (ECML-06). Volume 4212 of Lecture Notes in Computer Science., Springer Berlin/Heidelberg 341–352.

Pappa, G.L, (2007), Automatically Evolving Rule Induction Algorithms with Grammar-based Genetic Programming. PhD thesis, Computing Laboratory, University of Kent, Cannterbury, UK.

Provost, F., Fawcett, T., Kohavi, R, (1998), The case against accuracy estimation for comparing induction algorithms. In: Proc. of the 15th Int. Conf. on Machine

Learning (ICML-98), San Francisco, CA, USA, Morgan Kaufmann Publishers Inc. 445–453.

Quinlan, J.R, (1993), C4.5: programs for machine learning. Morgan Kaufmann.

Witten, I.H., Frank, E, (2005), Data Mining: Practical Machine Learning Tools and Techniques with Java Implementations. 2nd edn. Morgan Kaufmann.

Zhang, J, (1992), Selecting typical instances in instance-based learning. In: Proc. of the 9th Int. Workshop on Machine learning (ML-92), San Francisco, CA, USA, Morgan Kaufmann 470–479.

Evolutionary Design of Code-matrices for Multiclass Problems

Ana Carolina Lorena[1] and André C. P. L. F. de Carvalho[1]

[1] Centro de Matemática, Computação e Cognição
Universidade Federal do ABC
Rua Catequese, 242,09210-170,
Santo André, SP,
Brazil
ana.lorena@ufabc.edu.br

[2] Ciências de Computação
Instituto de Ciências Matemática e de Computação
Universidade de São Paulo - Campus de São Carlos
Caixa Postal 668 13560-970 São Carlos, SP, Brazil
andre@icmc.usp.br

Summary. Several real problems involve the classification of data into categories or classes. Given a dataset containing data whose classes are known, Machine Learning algorithms can be employed for the induction of a classifier able to predict the class of new data from the same domain, performing the desired discrimination. Several machine learning techniques are originally conceived for the solution of problems with only two classes. In multiclass applications, an alternative frequently employed is to divide the original problem into binary subtasks, whose results are then combined. The decomposition can be generally represented by a code-matrix, where each row corresponds to a codeword assigned for one class and the columns represent the binary classifiers employed. This chapter presents a survey on techniques for multiclass problems code-matrix design. It also shows how evolutionary techniques can be employed to solve this problem.

1 Introduction

Many problems involve the classification of data into categories or classes. Given a training dataset, Machine Learning (ML) (Mitchell, 1997) algorithms can be employed for the induction of a classifier, which should be able to predict the class of new data from the same domain.

A classification problem with only two classes is known as a binary classification problem. An example of a binary classification problem is the medical diagnostic of a particular disease. In this example, the induced classifier uses clinical information from a patient to determine if he/she has a particular disease. The classes represent the presence or absence of the disease. Many real problems, however, involve the discrimination of more than two categories or classes. Examples of such problems are the classification of handwritten digits (Knerr *et al.*, 1992), the distinction of multiple types of cancer (Statnikov *et al.*, 2005) and text categorization (Berger, 1999, Ghani, 2000).

A multiclass classification problem is intrinsically more complex than a binary problem, since the generated classifier must be able to separate the data into a larger number of categories, which also increases the chances of committing classification errors. Let us consider, for example, a balanced classification problem, with similar number of data per class, with equiprobable classes and a random classifier. If the problem is binary, the chance to obtain a correct classification is of 50%. For four classes, this chance reduces to 25%.

Several popular ML techniques are originally designed for the solution of binary classification problems. Among them, one can mention the Support Vector Machines (SVMs) (Cristianini and Shawe-Taylor, 2000) and the Adaboost algorithm (Freund and Schapire, 1997).

Two approaches have been adopted in the literature to deal with multiclass problems using binary classification techniques: adaptation of the internal operations of the classifier training algorithm and decomposition of the multiclass problem into a set of two-class classification problems.

The extension of a binary learning algorithm to a multiclass version may be either impractical or, frequently, not easy to perform (Passerini *et al.*, 2004). For SVMs, in particular, Hsu and Lin (2002) observed that the reformulation of this technique into multiclass versions leads to high cost training algorithms. Therefore, it is common to use the alternative of decomposing the multiclass problem into binary subproblems, a strategy named decomposition.

The decomposition performed can be generally represented by a code-matrix $\mathbf{M}$ (Allwein *et al.*, 2000). This matrix has k rows, representing codewords assigned to each of the k classes in the multiclass problem and the columns correspond to the desired outputs of the binary classifiers induced in the decomposition.

There are several alternatives to decompose the multiclass problem into binary subtasks (Allwein *et al.*, 2000). This chapter surveys recent developments in how to decompose multiclass problems into binary subproblems. This task can be formulated as the problem of designing code-matrices. This chapter also shows how Genetic Algorithms (GAs) (Mitchell, 1999), a search technique based on principles of genetics and natural evolution, can be used to solve the code-matrix design problem.

Initially, Section 2 introduces the code-matrix framework to solve multiclass problems. Section 3 discusses the code-matrix design problem. Section 4 describes how GAs can be used to solve the code-matrix design problem. Section 5 presents a general discussion on experimental results achieved by the described techniques and Section 6 concludes this chapter.

2 Code-matrix Decomposition of Multiclass Problems

Classification using ML techniques consists of inducing a function $f(\mathbf{x})$ from a dataset composed of pairs $(\mathbf{x}_i, y_i)$, where $y_i \in \{1, \ldots, k\}$. Some learning techniques, like the SVMs (Cristianini and Shawe-Taylor, 2000), are originally restricted to classification problems where $k = 2$, i. e., to binary classification problems.

The most common approach for the generalization of binary classification techniques to solve multiclass problems is to decompose the original problem into several binary subproblems. The learning algorithm induces a classifier for each one of these subproblems. The outputs of these classifiers are then combined to obtain the multiclass prediction.

There are several motivations for the use of decomposition strategies in multiclass solutions. Mayoraz and Moreira (1996), Masulli and Valentini (2000) and Frnkranz (2002) state that the use of a decomposition approach may reduce the complexity involved in the classes separation. Herewith, it can also benefit ML techniques whose algorithms are easily extensible to the solution of multiclass problems. Knerr *et al.* (1992), for example, observed that the classes in a digit recognition problem could be linearly separated when considered in pairs. Therefore, they opted to combine linear classifiers for all pairs of classes, an alternative considered simpler than the use of an unique classifier able to separate all classes simultaneously.

Pimenta (2005b) also points that the decomposition approach opens up new possibilities for the use of parallel processing, since the binary subproblems are independent and can be solved in different processors.

Section 2.1 reviews the main decomposition techniques from the literature. Next, Section 2.2 describes the code-matrix framework, generally used to represent the decomposition strategies.

2.1 Common Decomposition Strategies

The most straightforward decomposition strategy is the one-against-all (1AA). Given a problem with k classes, k binary classifiers are generated by using this strategy. Each classifier is responsible to distinguish a class i from the remaining classes. The final prediction is usually given by the classifier with the highest output value.

Another standard methodology, named one-against-one (1A1), consists of building $k(k-1)/2$ predictors, each differentiating a pair of classes i and j, where $i \neq j$ (Knerr *et al.*, 2000, Hastie and Tibshirani, 1998). To combine the outputs produced by these classifiers, a majority voting scheme can be applied (Kreβel, 1999). Each 1A1 classifier gives one vote to its preferred class. The final result is the class with most of the votes.

Dietterich and Bariki (1995) suggested to see the ML solution of a multiclass problem as a communication task, where the correct class of a new example must be transmitted by a channel. This channel is constituted by the example attributes, the training data and the learning algorithm. Due to errors that can be present in the attributes, in the training data and/or failures in the classifier learning process, the class information can be disrupted. To provide the system the ability to recover from these transmission errors, the class is codified by an error correcting code and each of its bits is transmitted separately, that is, through separate executions of the learning algorithm.

Herewith, a distributed output code is used to represent the k classes associated to the multiclass problem. A codeword of length l is assigned to each class. Commonly, the size of the codewords has more bits than needed in order to represent each class uniquely. The additional bits can be used to correct eventual classification errors. For this reason, this method is named error-correcting output coding (ECOC).

The generated codes are stored on a matrix $\mathbf{M} \in \{-1, +1\}^{k \times l}$. The rows of this matrix represent the codewords of each class and the columns correspond to the desired outputs of the l binary classifiers $(f_1(\mathbf{x}), ..., f_l(\mathbf{x}))$ induced.

A new pattern $\mathbf{x}$ can be classified by evaluating the predictions of the l classifiers, which generate a vector $\mathbf{f}(\mathbf{x})$ of length l. This vector is then compared to the rows of $\mathbf{M}$. The example is assigned to the class with the closest row according to the Hamming distance. This process is also named decoding.

Dietterich and Bariki (1995) proposed codewords to be designed in order to maximize their error correcting capability and presented four techniques for the construction of good error correcting codes. The choice of each technique is determined by the number of classes in the problem. These techniques are briefly described in Section 3.

2.2 Code-Matrix Framework

Allwein *et al.*(2000) presented a framework that unified the previous strategies and can be generally used to represent decomposition techniques. Throughout this framework, the decomposition strategies are reduced to code-matrix based methods. For such, a value from the set $\{-1, 0, +1\}$ is assigned to each element of the code-matrix $\mathbf{M}$. Figure 1 presents an example of code-matrix for a problem with four classes that uses four classifiers in the decomposition of the multiclass problem. It also shows, bellow this matrix, the binary partitions of classes imposed by each of the binary classifiers in the matrix columns.

Each element of the matrix assumes values in the set $\{-1, 0, +1\}$. An element m_{ij} with $+1$ value indicates that the class correspondent to row i assumes a positive label in classifier f_j induction. The -1 value designates a negative label and the 0 value indicates that the data from class i do not participate on classifier f_j induction. Binary classifiers are then trained to learn the labels represented in the columns of $\mathbf{M}$.

In the 1AA case, $\mathbf{M}$ has dimension $k \times k$, with diagonal elements equal to $+1$. The remaining elements are equal to -1. In the 1A1 decomposition, $\mathbf{M}$ has dimension $k \times k(k-1)/2$ and each column corresponds to a binary classifier

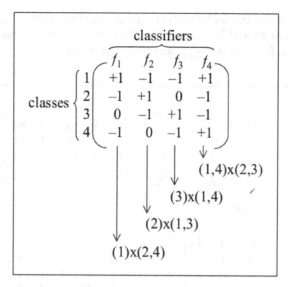

Fig. 1. Example of code-matrix for a problem with four classes

for a pair of classes (i,j). In each column representing a pair (i,j), the value of the elements corresponding to lines i and j are defined as $+1$ and -1, respectively. All other elements receive the value 0, indicating that patterns from the other classes do not participate on the induction of this particular binary classifier.

The prediction of a new pattern's class involves a decoding step, like in the ECOC strategy. Several decoding strategies have been proposed in the literature (Passerini *et al.*, 2004, Allwein *et al.*, 2000, Windeatt and Ghaderi, 2003, Escalera *et al.*, 2006, Klautau *et al.*, 2003). This chapter is concerned with the problem of decomposing the multiclass problem. For this reason, readers interested in the decoding step should look at (Passerini *et al.*, 2004, Allwein *et al.*, 2000, Windeatt and Ghaderi, 2003, Escalera *et al.*, 2006, Klautau *et al.*, 2003) and related publications.

In experimental studies, Allwein *et al.*(2000) have not verified any clear winner among different coding strategies, including 1AA, 1A1, dense random codes and sparse random codes. The authors pointed out the necessity of formulating methods to design problem specific output codes.

Next section describes the code-matrix design problem and reviews some of the main developments in this area.

3 Code-matrix Design Problem

Several alternatives can be employed in order to decompose a multiclass problem into multiple binary subproblems. The most compact decomposition of a problem with k classes can be performed with the use of $l = \lceil \log_2(k) \rceil$ binary classifiers (Mayoraz and Moreira, 1996). One example of compact matrix for a problem with four classes is presented in Figure 2a.

$$
(a)\quad
\begin{pmatrix}
+1 & +1 \\
+1 & -1 \\
-1 & +1 \\
-1 & -1
\end{pmatrix}
\qquad
(b)\quad
\begin{pmatrix}
+1 & +1 & +1 & +1 & +1 & +1 \\
-1 & -1 & -1 & -1 & +1 & +1 \\
-1 & -1 & +1 & +1 & -1 & -1 \\
-1 & +1 & -1 & +1 & -1 & +1
\end{pmatrix}
$$

$$
(c)\quad
\begin{pmatrix}
+1 & -1 & -1 & -1 \\
-1 & +1 & -1 & -1 \\
-1 & -1 & +1 & -1 \\
-1 & -1 & -1 & +1
\end{pmatrix}
\qquad
(d)\quad
\begin{pmatrix}
+1 & +1 & +1 & 0 & 0 & 0 \\
-1 & 0 & 0 & +1 & +1 & 0 \\
0 & -1 & 0 & -1 & 0 & +1 \\
0 & 0 & -1 & 0 & -1 & -1
\end{pmatrix}
$$

Fig. 2. Different code-matrices for a problem with four classes

The total number of different binary predictors for a problem with k classes is $0.5\left(3^k + 1\right) - 2^k$, considering that $f = -f$, that is, that the inversion of the positive and negative labels produces the same classifier (Mayoraz and Moreira, 1996). Among those, $2^{k-1} - 1$ include all classes simultaneously, i. e., have only the labels $+1$ and -1, without the 0 element. One example of code-matrix constituted of such classifiers for a problem with four classes is illustrated in Figure 2b.

Among the main decomposition strategies reported in the literature one can mention: 1AA, 1A1 (Knerr et al., 2000, Hastie and Tibshirani, 1998) and ECOC (Dietterich and Bariki, 1995). The 1AA and 1A1 code-matrices were already described on Section 2. Figures 2c and 2d represent the 1AA and 1A1 matrices, respectively, for a problem with four classes.

The 1AA decomposition has some disadvantages when the number of examples in one class is much smaller than number of data in other classes. This unbalance may harm the induction of a classifier with good predictive performance in the considered class. In the 1A1 case, the answer of a predictor for a pair of classes (i, j) does not provide useful information when the example does not belong to classes i or j (Alpaydin and Mayoraz, 1999).

Section 3.1 reviews some strategies used in order to obtain ECOC matrices, i. e., code-matrices with error correcting ability. Section 3.2 describes techniques able to adapt code-matrices to each multiclass problem under consideration. Section 3.3 presents other strategies employed in code-matrices obtainment. Although several authors refer to all types of code-matrices for multiclass problems as ECOCs, in this chapter, we will consider as ECOCs only code-matrices developed to have an error correcting capability.

Unless it is explicitly stated, the described works use binary code-matrices, that is, code-matrices with only +1 and −1 elements.

3.1 ECOC Design

Dietterich and Bariki (1995) enforce two characteristics necessary to ensure error correcting capability when designing ECOC matrices:

- Row separation;
- Column separation.

Where the separation is measured through Hamming distance, which is equal to the differences between different bit strings[3]. Constant columns (with only positive or negative elements) should also be avoided, since they do not represent a binary decision problem.

Let d_m designate the minimum Hamming distance between any pair of rows of $\mathbf{M}$. The final ECOC multiclass classifier is able to correct at least $\lfloor \frac{d_m-1}{2} \rfloor$ errors of the binary classifiers outputs. Since according to the Hamming distance each incorrect prediction implies in deviating one unity from the correct class codeword, committing $\lfloor \frac{d_m-1}{2} \rfloor$ errors, the closest codeword will still be that of the correct class (Dietterich and Bariki, 1995). This is the reason why a high row separation is demanded. According to this principle, the 1AA coding is unable to recover from any error, since its d_m is equal to 2. The row separation requirement is also demanded in the design of Error-Correcting Codes (ECC) in telecommunications (Alba and Chicano, 2004).

Besides, to obtain good error correcting codes for the multiclass problem solution, the errors of the binary classifiers induced must be uncorrelated. For such, a column separation is also demanded, that is, the Hamming distance among each pair of columns of $\mathbf{M}$ must be high. If in the learning algorithm the inversion of the positive and negative labels produces the same classifier $(f = -f)$, the Hamming distance between each column and the complement of the others must also be maximized.

Based on these observations, Dietterich and Bariki (1995) proposed four techniques to design code-matrices with good error-correcting capability. The choice of each one of them is determined by the number of classes in the multiclass problem. No justificative was given to how the numbers of classes were stipulated for each method.

---

[3] Recalling that in the ECOC framework, the code-matrix is constituted only of the elements +1 and −1 and the Hamming distance is used in the decoding step.

- For $k \leqslant 7$, they recommend the use of an exhaustive code, which consists on the combination of the $2^{k-1} - 1$ binary classifiers with labels $+1$ and -1, as illustrated in Figure 1b for a problem with four classes. The codeword of the first class is composed of only $+1$ values. For each other class i, where $i > 1$, it is composed of alternate runs of 2^{k-i} negative (-1) and positive $(+1)$ labels. The d_m distance in the matrix obtained through the exhaustive method is 2^{k-2}.
- If $8 \leqslant k \leqslant 11$, a method that selects columns from the exhaustive code is applied.
- For $k > 11$, there are two options: a method based on the *hill-climbing* algorithm and the generation of BCH codes (Boser and Ray-Chaudhuri, 1960), from the theory of designing good error correcting codes used in communication coding. One problem with BCH codes is that they do not ensure a good column separation.

In a recent work, Pimenta and Gama (2005) proposed an algorithm for the design of ECOCs that presented competitive predictive performance against traditional decompositions, using Decision Trees (DTs) (Quinlan, J.R., 1986) and SVMs as base classifiers. They proposed a function for the evaluation of the ECOCs quality according to their error-correcting properties. An iterative persecution algorithm (PA) was then used to construct the ECOCs. This algorithm adds or removes columns from an initial ECOC, in order to maximize its quality.

In his Msc. Dissertation, Pimenta (2005b) also employed two algorithms originally designed to obtain ECC in telecommunications in the obtainment of ECOC matrices for multiclass problems. The first is the Repulsion Algorithm (RA) (Alba and Chicano, 2004), based on the Physic behavior of equally charged particles on a sphere. Under this situation, the particles will move over the sphere until an equilibrium is reached. In the RA, each codeword is considered a charged particle, positioned in one corner of a hypercube. The movements allowed are to move from one corner to another, which corresponds to invert one bit in the binary codeword. The RA tries to maximize an evaluation function that gets higher as d_m increases. Since the row separation is not required in the design of an ECC, Pimenta adapted the evaluation function in order to penalize matrices with identical or complementary columns. Pimenta also tested an hybrid version of the RA. In this case, GAs are used to design the code-matrices, aiming to maximize the evaluation function. The RA is used in the mutation step of the GA. This hybrid algorithm is described in Section 4.

Experimentally, PA performed better on finding valid ECOCs, where the validity was measured by the criteria of avoiding equal, complementary and constant columns, while RA was the worst method. Among the valid ECOCs generated, in general PA still performed better, obtaining ECOCs with good quality according to the evaluation function proposed by Pimenta and Gama

(2005). Nevertheless, GARA (GA with RA) also designed ECOCs of good quality.

Pimenta and Gama (2005) also suggested a method to determine the number of columns in the ECOC (i. e., the number of classifiers employed in the decomposition), examining an evaluation function based on the number of errors that can be corrected by ECOCs of different sizes.

Zhang et al.(2003) proposed the use of Hadamard matrices from the ECC theory in the multiclass decomposition. They point out that these matrices can be considered optimal ECOCs, within the pool of k class codes that combine $k - 1$ base learners, where the optimality is measured according to the row and column separations criteria. Nevertheless, the Hadamard matrices are designed with numbers of rows of power two. For others numbers of classes, some rows have to be deleted. Experimentally, these ECOCs performed better than random and 1AA matrices, employing SVMs in the binary classifiers induction.

There are some studies that claim that randomly designed ECOCs show good multiclass predictive performance (Berger, 1999, Windeatt and Ghaderi, 2003, Tapia et al., 2003). Allwein et al.(2000), for example, evaluated the use of two randomly designed matrices: dense and sparse. In the dense matrix obtainment, 10,000 random matrices, with $\lceil 10*\log_2(k) \rceil$ columns and elements assuming -1 or $+1$ values with the same probability, are generated. The matrix with higher d_m and without identical or complementary columns is chosen, following the directions of Dietterich and Bariki (1995) . In the sparse matrix, which uses the ternary alphabet, the number of columns in the code-matrix is $\lceil 15\log_2 k \rceil$, and the elements are chosen as 0 with 0.5 probability and $+1$ or -1 with probability 0.25 each. Again, 10,000 random matrices are generated and the one with higher d_m is chosen.

Berger (1999) gives statistical and combinatorial arguments of why random matrices can perform well. Among these arguments, are theorems that state that random matrices are likely to show good row and column separations, specially as their number of columns increases. Nevertheless, it is assumed that the errors of the individual predictors are uncorrelated, which do not hold for real applications.

Windeatt and Ghaderi (2002) also express the desirability of equidistant codes. Equidistant codes are those for which the Hamming distance between rows is approximately constant. It was shown that if M is an equidistant code-matrix, the number of $+1$'s in different rows are the same and the number of common $+1$'s between any pair of rows is equal. They used this heuristic to select a subset of rows from BCH codes, producing equidistant code-matrices. Experimentally, they verified that equidistant codes were superior to 1AA and random codes for shorter codes (with less columns), using Multilayer Perceptron (MLP) Neural Networks (NNs) (Haykin, 1999) as base classifiers. As the length of the codes increases, the coding strategy seems to be less significant, favoring a random design.

3.2 Adapting Code-matrices to the Multiclass Problems

A common criticism to the 1AA, 1A1 and ECOC strategies is that all of them perform the multiclass problem decomposition a priori, without taking into account the properties and characteristics of each application (Allwein *et al.*, 2000, Mayoraz and Moreira, 1996, Alpaydin and Mayoraz, 1999, Mayoraz and Alpaydim, 1998, Dekel and Singer, 2003, Rätsch *et al.*, 2003, Pujol *et al.*, 2006). Besides, Allwein *et al.*(2000) point out that, although the ECOC codes have good error correcting property, several of the binary subproblems created may be difficult to learn.

Crammer and Singer (2000) presented one of the most known attempts to design code-matrices adapted to each multiclass problem considered. They argued that finding a discrete code-matrix can be considered a NP-hard problem and relaxed it allowing that M had continuous elements. As a result of their work, a version of SVMs for the direct solution of multiclass problems was obtained. Although accuracy results of this technique are comparable to those of the 1AA and 1A1 decomposition strategies used with SVMs (Hsu and Lin, 2002), the complexity of the training algorithm is higher, implying in a high computational cost.

Alpaydin and Mayoraz (1999) proposed to combine linear binary classifiers in order to obtain a non-linear multiclass classifier. In this process, a MLP NN is obtained, in which the first weight layer represents the parameters of the linear classifiers, the internal nodes correspond to the linear classifiers and the final weight layer is equivalent to the code-matrix. This NN has the architecture and second layer weights initialized according to an usual code-matrix. As a result, the code-matrix and classifiers parameters are optimized jointly in the NN training. The proposed method showed higher accuracy than those of 1AA, 1A1 and ECOC decompositions employing linear binary classifiers.

In (Dekel and Singer, 2003), an algorithm named Bunching was introduced, which, during the learning process, adapts code-matrices to the multiclass problem. In this algorithm, the training data and their labels are mapped to a common space. In this space, it is possible to define a function that measures the divergence between the data and their labels. Two matrices are used in the mapping process, one for the data and other for the labels, which is the code-matrix. These two matrices are iteratively adapted by the algorithm in order to obtain a minimum error for the training data. This error is measured by the divergence between the training data and their labels in the common space. The code-matrices are probabilistic. Given an initial code-matrix, the Bunching algorithm modifies it according to the previous procedure. Given a new example, it is mapped to the common space and the predicted class is the one closer to the example in this space. Empirically, the authors verified good results in the adaptation of code-matrices of the 1AA type and random ones, using logistic regression classifiers (Collins *et al.*, 2002).

In (Rätsch *et al.*, 2003), an optimization problem is formulated, in which the codes and weights to the binary functions used in the decomposition are determined jointly. A maximal margin approach is followed, in which the difference between the prediction vector $f(x)$ to the code of the correct class and the distance to the closer code from another class is maximized. Preliminary experimental results indicated an advantage of this method in relation to the direct use of DTs.

A heuristic method for designing ternary code-matrices based on a hierarchical partition of the classes according to a discriminative criterion was presented in (Pujol *et al.*, 2006). The criterion used was the mutual information between the feature data and its class label. Initiating with all classes, they are recursively partitioned into two subsets in order to maximize the mutual information measure, until each subset contains one class. These partitions define the binary predictors to be employed in the code-matrix. For a problem with k classes, $k - 1$ binary classifiers are generated in this process. Experimental results demonstrated the potential of the approach using DTs and Boosted Decision Stumps (BDS) (Freund and Schapire, 1997) as base classifiers. The algorithm showed competitive results against 1AA, 1A1 and random code-matrices.

In (Lorena and Carvalho, 2006), GAs were used to determine ternary code-matrices according to the performance obtained by them in the multiclass problem solution. Another goal of the implemented GA was to minimize the number of columns in the matrices, producing simpler decompositions. This work will be better described in Section 4.

3.3 Other Strategies

This section presents code-matrix design works that could not be fully characterized into one of the classes described in the previous sections, either because they employ alternative criteria in the code-matrix design or because a combination of the error-correcting and adaptiveness criteria is used.

In (Mayoraz and Moreira, 1996), an iterative algorithm to code-matrix design was presented, which takes into account three criteria. The first two are the same required by Dietterich and Bariki (1995) in the construction of ECOCs. The third criterion is that each inserted column must be pertinent, according to the positions of the classes in the input space. A binary partition of classes is considered pertinent if it is easy to learn. The largest contribution of this procedure was the use of classifiers simpler than those from ECOC.

Tapia *et al.*(2001) employed concepts from telecommunications coding theory to propose a particular class of ECOCs named Recursive ECOCs (RE-COC). The recursive codes are constructed from component subcodes of small length, which may be weak when working on their own, but strong when working together. This results in an ensemble of ECOCs, where each component subcode defines a local multiclass learner. Another interesting feature of RE-COCs, pointed by the authors, is that they allow a regulated degree of randomness in their design. Tapia *et al.*(2003) state that, according the telecommunications theory, a random code is the ideal way to protect information against noise. The decoding of RECOC is adaptive and uses information from the training error of the component subcodes in a belief propagation algorithm, allowing some degree of adaptiveness. Experimentally, the RECOCs achieved good results on a set of benchmark datasets using DTs and Boosted decision stumps (BDS) (Freund and Schapire, 1997).

Following the channel coding theory, Prez-Cruz and Arts-Rodriguez (2002) proposed to use a puncturing mechanism to prune the dependence among the binary classifiers in a code-matrix. This procedure eliminates classifiers that degrade the performance of a previously designed code-matrix, deleting columns from it. As consequence, it permits to obtain less complex multiclass schemes. A ternary coding was employed, that is, the code-matrices could have positive, negative and null elements. Experimentally, they achieved a good performance when puncturing 1A1 and BCH ECOC codes.

The design of code-matrices to maximize diversity measures from the literature on classifier ensembles is proposed in (Kuncheva, 2005). The code-matrices are constructed through the use of an evolutionary algorithm (Mitchell, 1999), which evolves matrices based on their diversity measure performance. However, the proposed framework was not evaluated experimentally on benchmark or real datasets.

In (Shen and Tan, 2005), GAs were employed to find ternary code-matrices in order to optimize an evaluation function based on the margins of separation among codes of different classes and the diversity among columns defined by Kuncheva (2005). These works will be better described in Section 4. Experimental results on multiclass classification of microarray cancer data showed encouraging results compared to other multiclass decomposition strategies, like 1AA and 1A1.

4 Evolutionary Design of Code-Matrices

The code-matrix design problem can be formulated as a search and optimization problem. As stated in the previous section, there are $0.5 \left(3^k + 1\right) - 2^k$ different binary predictors for a multiclass problem with k classes. A combinatorial number of associations of these classifiers is possible, determining different decompositions of the multiclass problem. Based on this observation, some works used Evolutionary Algorithms (EAs) (Eiben and Smith, 2003), which are search techniques based on principles of evolution and genetics, to solve the code-matrix design problem.

This section presents a review of these works. It starts with a brief introduction to the main concepts of EAs (Section 4.1). After, as in the previous section, the design of ECOCs is presented (Section 4.2), followed by a description of the design of code-matrices adapted to the solution of each multiclass problem (Section 4.3) and of other strategies employed in the matrices obtainment (Section 4.4).

4.1 Evolutionary Algorithms

According to the natural evolution theory (Darwin, 1859), organisms better adapted to their environment have higher chances to transmit their characteristics to the next generation. Thus, the environment exerts a selection among the individuals of a population, which privileges adapted individuals.

In 1900, the genetics theory was integrated to Darwin's work, introducing concepts that complemented it. One of the most important concepts is the hereditability, which defines how characteristics of an individual are transmitted to its descendants (Eiben and Smith, 2003). Two other aspects are necessary for the occurrence of the natural selection: the reproduction and the presence of variations among the characteristics of the individuals in a population, that is, the presence of genetic variability. If the genetic variability is present in a population, the natural selection may act in order to privilege individuals with characteristics that make then more adapted (or fit) to the environment. Besides, new characteristics can be introduced.

EAs employ these concepts throughout the operation of a set of possible solutions to a problem. This set is named population. The population is iteratively adapted through the application of genetic operators in order to produce solutions each time more apt to solve the problem. Throughout this process, a search procedure is performed, in which the optimal solution with maximal fitness represents the objective to be found or approximated. For this reason, EAs are regarded as search and optimization algorithms and have been applied to several problems, including applications in the areas of control, planning, combinatorial optimization and ML (Beasley, 2000).

The Genetic Algorithms (GAs) (Mitchell, 1999) can be considered one of the main research areas of EAs. They were proposed by John Holland (1975), with the initial aim of studying the adaptation mechanisms that occur in nature and incorporating them into computational systems.

Given an initial population of possible solutions to a problem, referenced as individuals, a GA seeks the global solution by an iterative process. At each iteration, also named generation, a new population is produced, which contains evolutions of individuals selected from the previous generation.

The individuals are encoded by a structure named chromosome. In the basic GA, the chromosomes are represented as bit strings. Each bit, also referenced as a gene, represents the presence (value 1) or absence (value 0) of a particular characteristic in the individual (Bäck, 2000). Nevertheless, there are several other types of encoding and the representation is normally determined according to the characteristics of the problem to be solved. The initial population is normally composed of either random solutions or solutions derived from some heuristic related to the problem.

Next, it is necessary to define how to evaluate the individuals, quantifying the fitness of each one of them to solve the problem. This evaluation is performed by a fitness function, which decodes the information in the individuals' chromosome and obtains a measure of its quality. As the encoding, this function is problem dependent.

From the evaluated population, a selection mechanism will select individuals for the next generation, which will produce offspring to a new population. The selection must privilege the fittest individuals, in accordance to the natural selection principles.

Following the concepts of hereditability, in the reproduction of the selected individuals, their characteristics are combined in order to produce descendants. This combination is performed by a genetic operator named cross-over. The cross-over is a binary operator and is applied to two individuals. These individuals, named parents, have their genes exchanged in order to produce two new individuals, the offspring. Simulating the stochastic nature of evolution, the cross-over is usually applied according to a crossover rate p_c, often in the interval $0.6 \leq p_c \leq 0.9$ (Zitzler *et al.*, 2004). For such, a random number is generated. If it is lower than p_c, the cross-over operator is applied. Otherwise, the parents are directly passed to the next generation.

After the cross-over combination, a variability is introduced to the new solutions by the application of an unary operator, named mutation. The mutation operator alters values of genes of individuals. It is also applied according to a rate p_m, which is usually small, to prevent a high alteration of the population, which would harm the GA convergence.

Other selection operator usually applied to a population is the elitism. In the elitism, a proportion p_e of the fittest individuals of the current population are directly copied into the new population. This prevents the loss of good solutions in the GA processing.

The procedures of generating a population, evaluating its individuals, selection and application of the genetic operators are iterated, and form the base of the GAs.

To stop the execution of a GA, different criteria can be used. The GA may be stopped when a maximum number of generations is reached, when the mean fitness of the population or the best individual does not change for a given number of generations, when the fitness of the individuals in the population become too alike or when a solution with the best known fitness value is found.

The use of a population approach allied to the genetic operators enhance the chance of finding the optimal solution in the search space when GAs are compared to traditional search techniques, as the hill-climbing algorithm (Michalewicz and Fogel, 2004). The GAs are also able to deal with solution spaces composed of complex and different parts, in which the impact of each part in the problem solution may be difficult to model by traditional search techniques (Mitchell, 1997). They can also take advantage of the use of parallel computation.

Nevertheless, the exploration of populations of solutions also renders the GAs a higher computational cost. GAs have also a set of parameters to be set (p_e, p_c and p_m, for example), whose definition affects their performance in the problem solution.

4.2 Evolutionary ECOC Design

There are several works in communication theory employing GAs to obtain Error Correcting Codes (for example, (Alba and Chicano, 2004, Alba *et al.*, 2002, Simn *et al.*, 2006, Wallis and Houghten, 2002, Dontas and Jong, 1990)). The ECC problem can be summarized as finding a code composed of k codewords with l bits each that corrects a given maximum number of errors, which is known to be a NP-hard optimization problem (Alba and Chicano, 2004). There are conflicting objectives in the ECC design: finding minimum length codewords (which imply in fast transmission) and maximize d_m (for a higher error-correcting capacity), which suggests to include more redundancy in the codewords (more bits and, thus, the use of larger codewords). However, the column separation and avoidance of constant columns are not required under this theory, making difficult to use them directly to find ECOCs for multiclass problems.

Pimenta (2005) adapted the GARA algorithm (Genetic Algorithm with Repulsion Algorithm) (Alba and Chicano, 2004) from the telecommunications theory to the generation of ECOC matrices. The chromosomes in this GA are kxl binary strings, formed by the concatenation of the codewords in the code-matrix $\mathbf{M}$, as illustrated in Figure 3. A binary alphabet is used is this work.

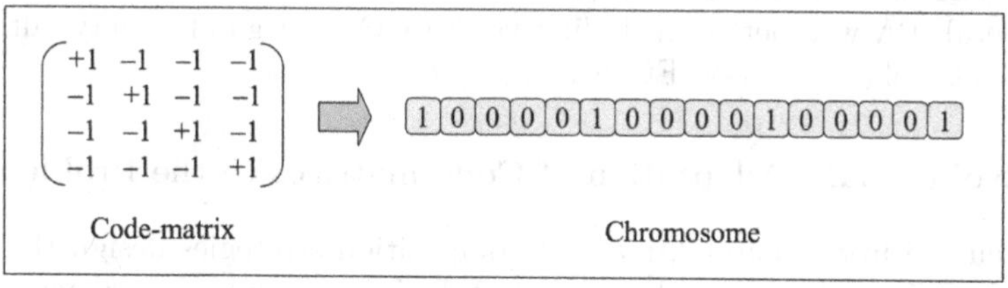

Code-matrix   Chromosome

Fig. 3. Example of chromosome in GARA (Alba and Chicano, 2004)

Defining d_{ij} as the Hamming distance between codewords i and j in the code-matrix $\mathbf{M}$ and d_m as in Section 3.1, the fitness function used that evaluates the individuals is presented in Equation 1.

$$f_e\left(\mathbf{M}\right) = \frac{1}{\sum\limits_{i=1}^{k}\sum\limits_{j=1}^{k}\frac{1}{d_{ij}^2}} + \left(\frac{d_m}{12} + \frac{d_m^2}{4} + \frac{d_m^3}{6}\right) \tag{1}$$

The first part in the sum of Equation 1 measures how well the codewords in $\mathbf{M}$ are separated in a space of l dimensions. Nevertheless, it may result in a higher value for an ECOC with a lower d_m than that of other ECOC, which is against the desired. The second term is then added to the sum to correct these cases. Overall, f_e is higher for higher d_m matrices and must be maximized by the GA.

To take into account the column separation criterion, Pimenta (2005) added a penalization term to the final fitness evaluation function, which is illustrated by Equation 2.

$$pen\,(\mathbf{M}) = 2 * f_e\,(\mathbf{M}) * p, \quad \text{where} \quad \begin{cases} p = 1 \text{ if } \mathbf{M} \text{ has equal columns} \\ p = 1 \text{ if } \mathbf{M} \text{ has complementary columns} \\ p = 0 \text{ otherwise} \end{cases}$$

(2)

The final fitness function, which should be maximized by the GA, is then given by Equation 3.

$$f_{it}\,(\mathbf{M}) = f_e\,(\mathbf{M}) - pen\,(\mathbf{M}) \tag{3}$$

The binary tournament selection chooses individuals for reproduction. The cross-over operator used was the single-point cross-over. Details about these operators may be found in (Mitchell, 1999). For mutation, an iteration of the RA was employed, as a local-search procedure. The offspring produced are inserted into a new population if they are better than its current worst individuals. The GA stops when a maximum number of generations is reached or an optimal matrix, according to the fitness function, is found.

As already reported in Section 3.1, the GARA algorithm was compared to the RA and PA algorithms in the obtainment of ECOC code-matrices. In general, PA was better in finding valid ECOCs of good quality, although GARA also obtained good ECOCs.

4.3 Evolutionary Adaptation of Code-matrices to the Problems

As discussed in Section 3.2, many decomposition strategies design the code-matrix a priori. Herewith, they do not take into account the properties and characteristics of each multiclass application.

To overcome this deficiency, a proposal involving the use of GAs to design code-matrices adapted to each multiclass problem was developed (Lorena and Carvalho, 2006). In this proposal, the GA is responsible to determine the combination of binary classifiers in a code-matrix $\mathbf{M}^*$. Herewith, the rows of $\mathbf{M}^*$, which correspond to the codewords attributed to each class, are automatically defined. The GA also determines the number of binary classifiers to be employed in the multiclass solution, that is, the number of columns contained in $\mathbf{M}^*$.

The evaluation of the matrices is based on their predictive performance in the multiclass problem solution. The GA searches for matrices that minimize the error obtained in the multiclass solution. It also aims to minimize the number of columns contained in the matrices, controlling the number of binary classifiers. This criterion represents the search for simpler solutions, and is in accordance to the Occam's razor (Mitchell, 1997), which states that, among several correct hypotheses, the simplest should be chosen. The presence of identical and complementary columns in the matrices must also be avoided, since they represent the use of identical binary classifiers in a decomposition. Columns with equal or complementary elements are denoted as equivalent in the posterior considerations.

The GA must then deal with three objectives: minimize the matrix error and its number of columns and avoid the presence of equivalent columns in the matrix. The aim is to search a code-matrix without equivalent columns with a good performance in the multiclass task and a reduced number of binary classifiers. Two variants of multi-objective GAs were employed by the authors to solve the described problem: a lexicographic, also described in (Lorena and Carvalho, 2006), and another based on the SPEA2 (Strength Pareto Evolutionary Algorithm 2) algorithm (Zitzler et al., 2002).

The chromosomes were directly represented as code-matrices, with a ternary encoding. Each individual corresponds to a possible code-matrix M with size kxl and elements in the set $\{-1, 0, +1\}$, as described in Section 2.2. This matrix representation is more intuitive to represent solutions to a multiclass problem. Wallet et al.(1996) argue that, if the problem has an inherent bidimensional structure, the GA may obtain better results with the use of matrix-codified individuals. The authors also point out that the use of this representation allows the definition of cross-over and mutation operators adequate to this problem.

To determine the number of binary classifiers in the code-matrix, the individuals in a same population had varied numbers of columns l. Herewith, this value is also determined by the GA. According to this strategy, two possible individuals for a problem with four classes are illustrated in Figure 4.

In the codified algorithms, the user limits the maximum allowed number of classifiers for the code-matrices. The generated matrices should also have at least $\lceil \log_2 k \rceil$ binary classifiers, which corresponds to the minimum necessary to divide k classes (Mayoraz and Moreira, 1996).

The initial population was implemented with the definition of random matrices with varying sizes. A consistency test was applied to these individuals, to ensure that each column of the matrices had positive and negative labels, constituting a valid binary partition. The codes of the strategies 1AA, 1A1 and ECOC (exhaustive, dense or sparse random codes) can also be provided to the initial population, adding to the search an additional information.

To evaluate each individual, the GA considers the predictive power of the set of binary classifiers, represented in its code-matrix, for the multiclass problem. For each individual, a validation error is calculated. Unknown classifications, which occur if more than one row of the code-matrix have minimum

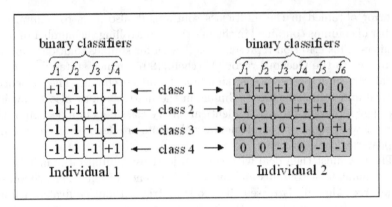

Fig. 4. Illustration of two possible individuals for a problem with four classes

distance to the prediction string, are also considered errors. This error measure should be minimized by the GA.

In the GA operation, a code-matrix may show equivalent columns. To inhibit this occurrence, each multi-objective variant employs a distinct strategy. While the lexicographic version penalizes this characteristic, the SPEA2 algorithm considers the proportion of equivalent columns in the individuals as a third objective to be minimized.

The avoiding of equivalent columns in the lexicographic version was considered a restriction of the problem. Solutions that do not violate this restriction must then be privileged. For such, the fitness of an individual is now calculated by Equation 4 (Deb, 2000). This function must be minimized, so individuals with lower values for Equation 4 are considered to be better.

$$f_{it}(i) = \begin{cases} e(i), & \text{if } i \in F \\ \max_{j \in F}(e(j)) + p_{ec}(i), & \text{if } i \in \bar{F} \end{cases} \tag{4}$$

In this equation, F denotes the set of feasible solutions, that is, solutions that do not violate the restriction and do not have equivalent columns. $\bar{F}$, on the other hand, represents non-feasible solutions, $p_{ec}(i)$ represents the proportion of equivalent columns in individual i and $e(i)$ is the validation error rate. Thus, non-feasible solutions have fitness values worst (with higher value of Equation 4) than those of the feasible ones and are compared only in terms of the intensity that they violate the restriction.

As second objective in both GAs is the minimization of the number of binary classifiers in the matrices. The lexicographic version favors the error minimization, placing the reduction of the number of binary classifiers in a second order of importance. In SPEA2, this value was considered as a second objective to be minimized using the Pareto domination relations.

To accomplish the objective ordering in the lexicographic version, first the individuals fitness are calculated using Equation 4. The traditional elitism

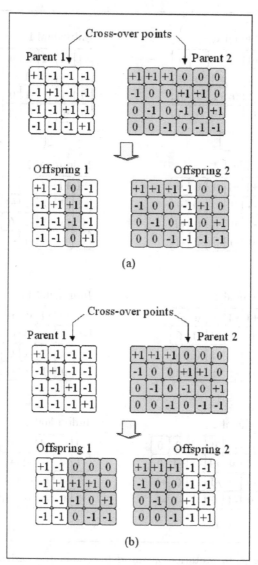

Fig. 5. Cross-over operators for code-matrix design

and selection steps are them adapted. Each time a tie occurs in these steps, the individual with the lowest number of classifiers is chosen.

The GAs stop when a maximum number of generations is reached. A binary tournament described in (Mitchell, 1999) is used in the selection step. The cross-over and mutation genetic operators were designed considering the individuals representation and the characteristics of the formulated code-matrix search problem.

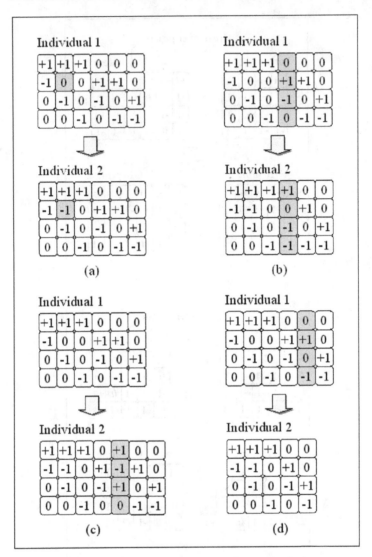

Fig. 6. Mutation operators to code-matrix design

For cross-over, two operators were defined:

- Exchange of columns between two individuals. This operation corresponds to an exchange of binary classifiers, motivated by the fact that a binary predictor can be more efficient in an alternative multiclass combination. This operator is illustrated in Figure 5a.
- Exchange of groups of columns between individuals. In this case, given two individuals, their descendants are produced by permuting all parents columns from randomly chosen points. This operator is illustrated in Fig-

ure 5b. The application of this operator allows the generation of individuals of new sizes, permitting the exploration of code-matrices of varying sizes. If one of the generated offspring has a number of columns outside the minimum and maximum established limits, it is discarded and the corresponding parent is copied into the new generation.

As mutation, four types of operators were defined:

- Change the value of a randomly chosen element of the matrix. This corresponds to the usual mutation operator and is illustrated in Figure 6a.
- New values can also be assigned to all elements in a column, as demonstrated in Figure 6b.
- Given an individual, generate a new column (binary classifier) with random elements. Figure 6c illustrates this modification. This operator can be applied to an individual only if its number of columns is inferior to the maximum value defined.
- Given an individual, remove one of its columns, as illustrated in Figure 6d. This operator can be applied only to individuals whose number of columns is higher than the minimum delimited.

The application of the first three mutation operators may generate columns without negative or positive labels. A consistency check phase must correct theses situations, defining new positive/negative labels.

As there is more than one type of cross-over and mutation operator, which one of them must be applied at each cross-over or mutation step? To opt for one of them, a criterion used in (Martí et al., 2005) was employed. Each possible operator is probabilistically selected according to its performance in the design of good code-matrices in previous generations. Using this scheme, operators that produce better solutions in previous generations have a higher chance to be applied and their importance is adapted by the GA.

At each execution of SPEA2, a set of solutions is obtained. To choose a particular solution, the distance to a reference point is considered. This point presents a null error rate, the minimum number of binary classifiers necessary to distinguish the classes and a null number of equivalent columns. The solution whose evaluations are closer to this point is chosen.

Both GAs were evaluated on a set of benchmark datasets and real multiclass problems from the Bioinformatics domain. They were employed to search for code-matrices with accuracy rates statistically similar or superior to those obtained by the 1AA decomposition (most used in practice (Rifkin and Klautau, 2004)) when using SVMs as base classifiers and with the use of less binary classifiers. The lexicographic GA was able to solve this problem, obtaining code-matrices with good accuracy results and using less binary classifiers. The SPEA2 GA was not successful in this problem. Although the obtained matrices had a low number of binary classifiers, they were not able, in general, to maintain accuracy rates comparable to those of 1AA and also showed equivalent columns.

4.4 Other Evolutionary Strategies

The decomposition framework can be regarded as an ensemble of binary classifiers for the multiclass problem solution. Based on this, Kuncheva (2005) proposed the use of diversity measures from the ensemble literature for generating code-matrices for the multiclass problems. The author argued that measuring diversity through the Hamming distance among columns is insufficient to build accurate ensembles.

The diversity measure used compromises the error-correcting capability in order to have a more diverse ensemble, which shows on average, a better performance. The disagreement measure is used to quantify diversity. It is given by Equation 5 for two codewords i and j, where N^{mn} represents the number of bits for which the codeword i has value m and the codeword j has value n ($m, n \in \{-1, +1\}$ or $\in \{0, 1\}$) and l is the number of columns of $\mathbf{M}$.

$$R_{ij} = \frac{N^{-1+1} + N^{+1-1}}{l} = \frac{\sum\limits_{s=1}^{l} |M(i, s) - M(j, s)|}{l} \tag{5}$$

R_{ij} assumes values between 0 and 1. Larger values are desirable, meaning a larger diversity. The diversity between two rows is then measured by R_{ij}.

For columns, the fact that complementary columns represent the same binary subproblem must be taken into account. The diversity between columns is then given by Equation 6.

$$C_{ij} = \min \left\{ \frac{N^{-1+1} + N^{+1-1}}{k}, \frac{N^{-1-1} + N^{+1+1}}{k} \right\}$$

$$= \min \left\{ \frac{\sum\limits_{s=1}^{k} |M(s, i) - M(s, j)|}{k}, \frac{\sum\limits_{s=1}^{k} |M(s, i) + M(s, j)|}{k} \right\} \tag{6}$$

For all rows, the total diversity measure is given by the mean of the diversities between all pairs of rows, represented in Equation 7.

$$D_r = \frac{2}{k(k-1)} \sum_{i<j} R_{ij}, \quad i, j = 1, \ldots, k \tag{7}$$

For columns, the mean is given by Equation 8.

$$D_c = \frac{2}{l(l-1)} \sum_{i<j} C_{ij}, \quad i, j = 1, \ldots, l \tag{8}$$

To obtain an unique function, Kuncheva (2005) used the average of D_r and D_c, represented in Equation 9.

$$D = \frac{1}{2}(D_r + D_c) \tag{9}$$

It is also possible to obtain a function that measures the row and column separations based on the Hamming distance, as presented in Equation 10, where H_r and H_c are the minimum distances between rows and columns, respectively, and are given by Equations 11 and 12.

$$H = \frac{H_r + H_c}{2} \tag{10}$$

$$H_r = \min_{1 \leqslant i,j \leqslant k} \{R_{ij}\} \tag{11}$$

$$H_c = \min_{1 \leqslant i,j \leqslant l} \{C_{ij}\} \tag{12}$$

EAs were then used to design code-matrices in order to maximize the diversity measure given by Equation 9. As in GARA, the chromosome is represented by a string formed by the concatenation of the codewords in the code-matrix (Figure 3). Only the mutation operator is employed, which is implemented by a bit-flip procedure. To derive a new population, the best ones are chosen from the set formed by the parents and offspring. The EA is stopped after a maximum number of generations.

The evaluation of this EA consisted of verifying whether D or H would be effectively optimized by the EA. No experiments were performed on benchmark or real multiclass datasets.

Using some ideas from the work of Kuncheva (2005), Shen and Tan (2005) also used GAs to search for code-matrices. They adapted the H and D functions to ternary code-matrices. For such, all summations in R_{ij} and C_{ij} were divided by two. Throughout this process, whenever an element is null and another is positive or negative, a value of 0.5 is summed to the computed distance. The chromosomes are again code-matrices with rows concatenated into a bit-string of length kxl.

They define the margin of separation of one class i in relation to the others by Equation 13, where d_{ij} designates the Hamming distance, adapted to the case where null elements are present in the code-matrix (when an element is null and the other is +1 or −1, the 0.5 value is added to the distance).

$$\eta_i = \min \{d_{ij}, 1 \leqslant j \leqslant k \text{ and } j \neq i\} \tag{13}$$

This margin measure is based on the rows separation criterion. To maximize all margins simultaneously, the mean of all margins is maximized. To ensure columns separation, D_c is also maximized. This is accomplished by the fitness function presented in Equation 14, which is referred as a multiple margins criterion.

$$m_g = \frac{1}{2k} \sum_{i=1}^{k} \frac{\eta_i}{l} + \frac{1}{2} D_c \tag{14}$$

The GA maximizes the m_g value. When calculating an individual's fitness, Shen and Tan previously remove equivalent or constant columns. Nevertheless, the original size l of the codewords is maintained in the fitness calculations. Throughout this process, code-matrices with these types of columns are penalized.

The GA stops if it cannot improve the fitness values for a given period of time or after a defined consecutive number of generations. The single-point cross-over, uniform mutation and roulette selection were applied (descriptions of these genetic operators may be found in (Mitchell, 1999)).

The proposed GA was evaluated experimentally on two multiclass cancer diagnosis datasets. The GA code-matrices, using linear SVMs as base classifiers, usually outperformed other code-matrices, as 1AA and 1A1, as well as direct multiclass algorithms, like k-nearest neighbor (kNN) (Mitchell, 1997) and DTs. A number of $l = \lceil 10 * \log_2(k) \rceil$ classifiers were used in the matrices. As fitness functions in the GA, they tested both H, D and m_g. The best results were verified using the m_g measure.

5 Discussion of Experimental Results

When describing the code-matrix design approaches in the previous sections, a brief discussion on experiments performed by the authors of each work was presented. The main aspects of these experiments are summarized in Table 1. This table presents, for each of the cited papers, the type of code-matrix design strategy ("CM" column), the number and types of datasets used in their experimental evaluation ("Data" column), the number of classes in the datasets investigated ("♯Classes" column), the base classification techniques used in the binary classifiers induction ("Base cl." column) and the main conclusions obtained from the experimental results. Unless explicitly mentioned, all results were compared based on accuracy or error performance.

The code-matrix design strategy can be of three types, according to the structure adopted in the description of the code-matrix design problem. The types are:

- EC: ECOC design (Sections 3.1 and 4.2);
- AD: adaptation of code-matrices for the multiclass problems (Sections 3.2 and 4.3);
- OS: other strategies (Sections 3.3 and 4.4);

  The types of datasets used can also be three, according to their nature:

- A: artificially designed datasets;
- N: natural datasets, which come from benchmarks as the UCI repository (Blake and Merz, 1998);
- R: real datasets, which come from real-world applications;

  Regarding the base classifiers, there are works using:

- DT: Decision Trees (Quinlan, J.R., 1986);

- MLP: Multilayer Perceptron Neural Network (Haykin, 1999);
- SVM: Support Vector Machines (Cristianini and Shawe-Taylor, 2000);
- AB: Adaboost (Freund and Schapire, 1997);
- NB: Nave-Bayes (Mitchell, 1997);
- Lin: linear;
- LR: Logistic Regression (Collins *et al.*, 2002);
- BDS: Boosted Decision Stumps (Freund and Schapire, 1997);
- Ran: Random;

Table 1: Summary of experimental evaluation of code-matrix design works

Paper	CM type	Data type	#Classes	Base cl.	Main conclusions
(Dietterich and Bariki, 1995)	EC	7N/1R	6, 11, 12, 19, 24, 26, 60	DT, MLP	ECOC improves DT and MLP results
(Pimenta and Gama, 2005, Pimenta, 2005)	EC	6N	4 to 6, 10	DT, SVM	Comparable or better than 1AA and 1A1
(Zhang et al., 2003)	EC	6N	6, 8, 10, 11, 26	SVM	Generally better than 1AA and random coding
(Allwein et al., 2000)	EC	13N	6 to 8, 10, 11, 19, 20, 24, 26	SVM, AB	No clear winner among 1AA, 1A1 and random coding
(Berger, 1999)	EC	4R	7, 20, 36, 41	NB	Random codes were effective on text classification
(Windeatt and Ghaderi, 2003)	EC	1A/5N	4 to 7	MLP	Equidistant codes are superior for shorter codes
(Crammer and Singer, 2002, Hsu and Lin, 2002)	AD	1A/10N	3, 4, 6, 7, 11, 26	SVM	Comparable accuracy to 1AA and 1A1 at higher cost
(Alpaydin and Mayoraz, 1999)	AD	8N	3, 7, 10, 11, 26	Lin	Comparable or better than 1AA and 1A1
(Dekel and Singer, 2003)	AD	6N/1R	6, 7, 11, 19, 26	LR	Generally outperforms 1AA and specially random codes
(Rätsch et al., 2003)	AD	2N	3, 6	DT	Could improve DT results
(Pujol et al., 2006)	AD	9N/1R	3, 6, 8, 9, 10, 28	DT, BDS	Comparable or better than 1AA, 1A1 and random codes

Continued on Next Page...

Table 1 – Continued

Paper	CM	Data type	#Classes	Base cl.	Main conclusions
(Lorena and Carvalho, 2006, Lorena, 2006)	AD	8N/4R	3, 4 to 10 and 11	SVM	Comparable to 1AA, 1A1 and ECOC with less classifiers
(Mayoraz and Moreira, 1996)	OS	4N	6, 19, 24, 26	DT	Comparable to ECOC with less binary classifiers
(Tapia et al., 2003, Tapia et al., 2001)	OS	6N	4, 6, 7, 22, 24	DT, BDS	RECOCs are suitable to multiclass problems
(Pérez-Cruz and Artés-Rodríguez, 2002)	OS	1N	11	SVM	Good performance puncturing 1A1 and BCH ECOC codes
(Kuncheva, 2005)	OS	1A	50	Rand	Evaluation of GA optimization of H and D measures
(Shen and Tan, 2005)	OS	2R	9, 14	SVM	Comparable or better than 1AA, 1A1, kNN and DTs

180 Ana Carolina Lorena and André C. P. L. F. de Carvalho

A comparison of the experimental results regarding the different strategies introduced in distinct works would bring valuable knowledge. However, it is usually difficult to perform such analysis based on the results presented on the papers. In general, different datasets are used by each author. Even when the same datasets are used, different data partitions are employed to obtain the mean accuracy/error rates reported or different learning techniques are used in the base classifiers induction, making a significant direct comparison impossible.

6 Conclusion

The solution of a multiclass classification problem can be performed through its decomposition into binary subproblems, whose results are later combined. The decomposition can be generally represented by a code-matrix M, whose rows represent codewords assigned to each class and columns represent the binary classifiers desired outputs. How to decompose the multiclass problem can then be reduced to a code-matrix design problem. This chapter surveyed some of the main developments in the design of code-matrices for multiclass problems, with special attention to those using evolutionary computation.

Two general classes of strategies can be used to obtain the codes. The first one considers the error-correcting capability of the codes. The second adapts the codes to each multiclass application. There are, however, works that use a combination of these two strategies or alternative criteria in generation of the code-matrix. Among all reviewed works, some use an evolutionary approach in order to evolve the code-matrices.

From the studies reported, it can be clearly verified that the decomposition of multiclass problems into binary subproblems is an active research area. A good deal of work can be still performed, like comparing different code-matrix design strategies and adapting the GAs in order to use alternative fitness functions.

Acknowledgements

The authors would like to thank the financial support from the Brazilian research agencies CNPq and FAPESP.

References

Alba, E., Cotta, C., Chicano, F., Nebro, A.J., (2002), Parallel evolutionary algorithms in telecommunications: two case studies. In: Proceedings of Congresso Argentino de Ciências de la Computación.

Alba, E., Chicano, J.F., (2004), Solving the error correcting code problem with parallel hybrid heuristics. In: Proceedings of 2004 ACM Symposium on Applied Computing. Volume 2. 985–989.

Allwein, E.L., Shapire, R.E., Singer, Y., (2000), Reducing multiclass to binary: a unifying approach for magin classifiers. In: Proceedings of the 17th International Conference on Machine Learning, Morgan Kaufmann 9–16.

Alpaydin, E., Mayoraz, E., (1999), Learning error-correcting output codes from data. In: Proceedings of the 9th International Conference on Neural Networks. 743–748.

Beasley, D. (2000), (Bäck et al., 2000) 4–18

Berger, A., (1999), Error-correcting output coding for text classification.

Blake, C.L., Merz, C.J., (1998), UCI repository of machine learning databases. Available at: http://www.ics.uci.edu/~mlearn/MLRepository.html.

Boser, R.C., Ray-Chaudhuri, D.K., (1960), On a class of error-correcting binary group codes. Information and Control 3 68–79.

Bäck, T., Fogel, D.B., Michalewicz, T., (2000), Evolutionary Computation 1: Basic Algorithms and Operators. Institute of Physics Publishing.

Bäck, T. (2000), (Bäck et al., 2000) 132–135

Collins, M., Shapire, R.E., Singer, Y., (2002), Logistic regression, adaboost and bregman distances. Machine Learning 47(2/3) 253–285.

Crammer, K., Singer, Y., (2002), On the learnability and design of output codes for multiclass problems. Machine Learning 47(2-3) 201–233.

Cristianini, N., Shawe-Taylor, J., (2000), An introduction to Support Vector Machines and other kernel-based learning methods. Cambridge University Press.

Darwin, C., (1859), On the origin of species by means of natural selection. John Murray, London.

Deb, K., (2000), An efficient constraint handling method for genetic algorithms. Computer Methods in Applied Mechanics and Engineering 186 311–338.

Dekel, O., Singer, Y., (2003), Multiclass learning by probabilistic embeddings. In: Advances in Neural Information Processing Systems. Volume 15., MIT Press 945–952.

Dietterich, T.G., Bariki, G., (1995), Solving multiclass learning problems via error-correcting output codes. Journal of Artificial Intelligence Research 2 263–286.

Dontas, K., Jong, K.D., (1990), Discovery of maximal distance codes using genetic algorithms. In: Proceedings of the 2nd International IEEE Conference on Tools for Artificial Intelligence, IEEE Computer Society Press 905–811.

Eiben, A.E., Smith, J.E., (2003), Introduction to Evolutionary Computing. Springer.

Escalera, S., Pujol, O., Radeva, R., (2006), Decoding of ternary error correcting output codes. In: Proceedings of the 11th Iberoamerican Congress on Pattern Recognition. Volume 4225 of Lecture Notes in Computer Science., Springer-Verlag 753–763.

Freund, Y., Schapire, R.E., (1997), A decision-theoretic generalization of on-line learning and an application to boosting. Journal of Computer and System Sciences 1(55) 119–139.

Fürnkranz, J., (2002), Round robin classification. Journal of Machine Learning Research 2 721–747.

Ghani, R., (2000), Using error correcting output codes for text classification. In: Proceedings of the 17th International Conference on Machine Learning, Morgan

182   Ana Carolina Lorena and André C. P. L. F. de Carvalho

Kaufmann 303–310.

Hastie, T., Tibshirani, R., (1998), Classification by pairwise coupling. The Annals of Statistics **2** 451–471.

Haykin, S., (1999), Neural Networks - A Compreensive Foundation. 2nd edn. Prentice-Hall, New Jersey.

Holland, J.H., (1975), Adaptation in Natural and Artificial Systems. University of Michigan Press.

Hsu, C.W., Lin, C.J., (2002), A comparison of methods for multi-class support vector machines. IEEE Transactions on Neural Networks **13**(2) 415–425.

Klautau, A., Jevtić, N., Orlistky, A., (2003), On nearest-neighbor error-correcting output codes with application to all-pairs multiclass support vector machines. Journal of Machine Learning Research **4** 1–15.

Knerr, S., Personnaz, L., Dreyfus, G., (1992), Handwritten digit recognition by neural networks with single-layer training. IEEE Transactions on Neural Networks **3**(6) 962–968.

Knerr, S., Personnaz, L., Dreyfus, G., (1990), In: Single-layer learning revisited: a stepwise procedure for building and training a neural network. Springer-Verlag, pp. 41–50

Kreβel, U., (1999), Pairwise classification and support vector machines. In Schölkopf, B., Burges, C.J.C., Smola, A.J., eds.: Advances in Kernel Methods - Support Vector Learning, MIT Press 185–208.

Kuncheva, L.I., (2005), Using diversity measures for generating error-correcting output codes in classifier ensembles. Pattern Recognition Letters **26** 83–90.

Lorena, A.C., Carvalho, A.C.P.L.F., (2006), Evolutionary design of multiclass support vector machines. Journal of Intelligent and Fuzzy Systems . Accepted, to be published..

Lorena, A.C., (2006), Investigação de estratégias para a geração de máquinas de vetores de suporte multiclasses [in portuguese], Ph.D. thesis, Departamento de Ciências de Computação, Instituto de Ciências Matemáticas e de Computação, Universidade de São Paulo, São Carlos, Brazil, http://www.teses.usp.br/teses/disponiveis/55/55134/tde-26052006-111406.

Martí, R., Laguna, M., Campos, V., (2005), Scatter search vs. genetic algorithms: An experimental evaluation with permutation problems. In Rego, C., Alidaee, B., eds.: Metaheuristic Optimization Via Adaptive Memory and Evolution: Tabu Search and Scatter Search. Kluwer Academic Publishers 263–282.

Masulli, F., Valentini, G., (2000), Effectiveness of error correcting output codes in multiclass learning problems. In: Proceedings of the 1st International Workshop on Multiple Classifier Systems. Volume 1857 of Lecture Notes in Computer Science., Springer-Verlag 107–116.

Mayoraz, E., Alpaydim, E., (1998), Support vector machines for multi-class classification. Research Report IDIAP-RR-98-06, Dalle Molle Institute for Perceptual Artificial Intelligence, Martigny, Switzerland.

Mayoraz, E., Moreira, M., (1996), On the decomposition of polychotomies into dichotomies. Research Report 96-08, IDIAP, Dalle Molle Institute for Perceptive Artificial Intelligence, Martigny, Valais, Switzerland.

Michalewicz, Z., Fogel, D.B., (2004), How to solve it: modern heuristics. Springer.

Mitchell, T., (1997), Machine Learning. McGraw Hill.

Mitchell, M., (1999), An introduction to Genetic Algorithms. MIT Press.

Passerini, A., Pontil, M., Frasconi, P., (2004), New results on error correcting output codes of kernel machines. IEEE Transactions on Neural Networks 15 45–54.

Pimenta, E., Gama, J., (2005), A study on error correcting output codes. In: Proceedings of the 2005 Portuguese Conference on Artificial Intelligence, IEEE Computer Society Press 218–223.

Pimenta, E.M.C., (2005), Abordagens para decomposição de problemas multiclasse: os códigos de correcção de erros de saída (in portuguese). Master's thesis, Departamento de Ciências de Computadores, Faculdade de Ciências da Universidade do Porto, Portugal.

Pujol, O., Tadeva, P., Vitrià, J., (2006), Discriminant ECOC: a heuristic method for application dependetn design of error correcting output codes. IEEE Transactions on Pattern Analysis and Machine Intelligence 28(6) 1007–1012.

Pérez-Cruz, F., Artés-Rodríguez, A., (2002), Puncturing multi-class support vector machines. In: Proceedings of the 12th International Conference on Neural Networks (ICANN). Volume 2415 of Lecture Notes in Computer Science., Springer-Verlag 751–756.

Quinlan, J.R., (1986), Induction of decision trees. Machine Learning 1(1) 81–106.

Rifkin, R., Klautau, A., (2004), In defense of one-vs-all classification. Journal of Machine Learning Research 5 1533–7928.

Rätsch, G., Smola, A.J., Mika, S., (2003), Adapting codes and embeddings for polychotomies. In: Advances in Neural Information Processing Systems. Volume 15., MIT Press 513–520.

Shen, L., Tan, E.C., (2005), Seeking better output-codes with genetic algorithm for multiclass cancer classification. Submitted to Bioinformatics.

Simn, M.D.J., Pulido, J.A.G., Rodrguez, M.A.V., (2006), Prez, J.M.S., Criado, J.M.G., A genetic algorithm to design error correcting codes. In: Proceedings of the 13th IEEE Mediterranean Eletrotechnical Conference 2006, IEEE Computer Society Press 807–810.

Statnikov, A., Aliferis, C.F., Tsamardinos, I., (2005), Hardin, D., Levy, S., A comprehensive evaluation of multicategory methods for microarray gene expression cancer diagnosis. Bioinformatics 21(5) 631–643.

Tapia, E., González, J.C., García-Villalba, J., Villena, J., (2001), Recursive adaptive ECOC models. In: Proceedings of the 10th Portuguese Conference on Artificial Intelligence. Volume 2258 of Lecture Notes in Artificial Intelligence., Springer-Verlag 96–103.

Tapia, E., González, J.C., García-Villalba, J., (2003), Good error correcting output codes for adaptive multiclass learning. In: Proceedings of the 4th International Workshop on Multiple Classifier Systems 2003. Volume 2709 of Lecture Notes in Computer Science., Springer-Verlag 156–165.

Wallet, B.C., Marchette, D.J., Solka, J.L., (1996), A matrix representation for genetic algorithms. In: Automatic object recognition VI, Proceedings of the International Society for Optical Engineering. 206–214.

Wallis, J.L., Houghten, S.K., (2002), A comparative study of search techniques applied to the minimum distance problem of BCH codes. Technical Report CS-02-08, Department of Computer Science, Brock University.

Windeatt, T., Ghaderi, R., (2003), Coding and decoding strategies for multi-class learning problems. Information Fusion 4(1) 11–21.

Zhang, A., Wu, Z.L., Li, C.H., Fang, K.T., (2003), On hadamard-type output coding in multiclass learning. In: Proceedings of IDEAL. Volume 2690 of Lecture

Notes in Computer Science., Springer-Verlag 397–404.

Zitzler, E., Laumanns, M., Thiele, L., (2002), SPEA2: Improving the strength pareto evolutionary algorithm. In: Evolutionary Methods for Design, Optimisation, and Control, CIMNE, Barcelona, Spain. 95–100.

Zitzler, E., Laumanns, M., Bleuler, S., (2004), A tutorial on evolutionary multiobjective optimization. In Gandibleux, X., Sevaux, M., Srensen, K., T'kindt, V., eds.: Metaheuristics for Multiobjective Optimisation. Volume 535 of Lecture Notes in Economics and Mathematical Systems., Springer-Verlag 3–37.

Part III

Fuzzy Logic Methods

The Role of Fuzzy Sets in Data Mining

Lior Rokach

Department of Information System Engineering, Ben-Gurion University, Israel
liorrk@bgu.ac.il

Summary. In this chapter we discuss how fuzzy logic extends the envelop of the main data mining tasks: clustering, classification, regression and association rules. We begin by presenting a formulation of the data mining using fuzzy logic attributes. Then, for each task, we provide a survey of the main algorithms and a detailed description (i.e. pseudo-code) of the most popular algorithms. However this chapter will not profoundly discuss neuro-fuzzy techniques, assuming that there will be a dedicated chapter for this issue.

1 Introduction

There are two main types of uncertainty in supervised learning: statistical and cognitive. Statistical uncertainty deals with the random behavior of nature and all existing data mining techniques can handle the uncertainty that arises (or is assumed to arise) in the natural world from statistical variations or randomness. While these techniques may be appropriate for measuring the likelihood of a hypothesis, they says nothing about the meaning of the hypothesis.

Cognitive uncertainty, on the other hand, deals with human cognition. Cognitive uncertainty can be further divided into two sub-types: vagueness and ambiguity.

Ambiguity arises in situations with two or more alternatives such that the choice between them is left unspecified. Vagueness arises when there is a difficulty in making a precise distinction in the world.

Fuzzy set theory, first introduced by Zadeh in 1965, deals with cognitive uncertainty and seeks to overcome many of the problems found in classical set theory.

For example, a major problem faced by researchers of control theory is that a small change in input results in a major change in output. This throws the whole control system into an unstable state. In addition there was also the problem that the representation of subjective knowledge was artificial and inaccurate. Fuzzy set theory is an attempt to confront these difficulties and in this chapter we show how it can be used in data mining tasks.

2 Basic Concepts of Fuzzy Set Theory

In this section we present some of the basic concepts of fuzzy logic. The main focus, however, is on those concepts used in the induction process when dealing with data mining. Since fuzzy set theory and fuzzy logic are much broader than the narrow perspective presented here, the interested reader is encouraged to read (Zimmermann, 2005)).

2.1 Membership function

In classical set theory, a certain element either belongs or does not belong to a set. Fuzzy set theory, on the other hand, permits the gradual assessment of the membership of elements in relation to a set.

Definition 1. *Let U be a universe of discourse, representing a collection of objects denoted generically by u. A fuzzy set A in a universe of discourse U is characterized by a membership function μ_A which takes values in the interval [0, 1]. Where $\mu_A(u) = 0$ means that u is definitely not a member of A and $\mu_A(u) = 1$ means that u is definitely a member of A.*

The above definition can be illustrated on the vague set of *Young*. In this case the set U is the set of people. To each person in U, we define the degree of membership to the fuzzy set *Young*. The membership function answers the question "to what degree is person u young?". The easiest way to do this is with a membership function based on the person's age. For example Figure 1 presents the following membership function:

$$\mu_{Young}(u) = \begin{cases} 0 & age(u) > 32 \\ 1 & age(u) < 16 \\ \frac{32-age(u)}{16} & otherwise \end{cases} \tag{1}$$

Given this definition, John, who is 18 years old, has degree of youth of 0.875. Philip, 20 years old, has degree of youth of 0.75. Unlike probability theory, degrees of membership do not have to add up to 1 across all objects and therefore either many or few objects in the set may have high membership. However, an objects membership in a set (such as "young") and the sets complement ("not young") must still sum to 1.

The main difference between classical set theory and fuzzy set theory is that the latter admits to partial set membership. A classical or crisp set, then, is a fuzzy set that restricts its membership values to $\{0, 1\}$, the endpoints of the unit interval. Membership functions can be used to represent a crisp set. For example, Figure 2 presents a crisp membership function defined as:

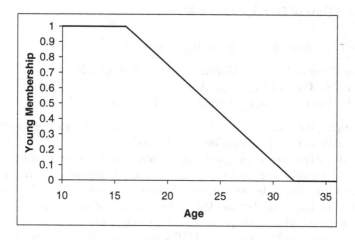

Fig. 1. Membership function for the young set.

$$\mu_{CrispYoung}(u) = \begin{cases} 0 \ age(u) > 22 \\ 1 \ age(u) \leq 22 \end{cases} \tag{2}$$

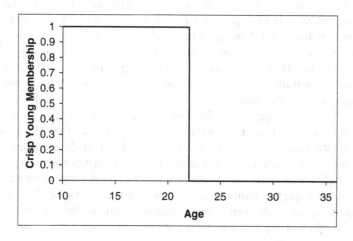

Fig. 2. Membership function for the crisp young set.

In regular classification problems, we assume that each instance takes one value for each attribute and that each instance is classified into only one of the mutually exclusive classes. To illustrate how fuzzy logic can help data mining tasks, we introduce the problem of modelling the preferences of TV viewers. In this problem there are 3 input attributes:

$A = \{$Time of Day,Age Group,Mood$\}$

and each attribute has the following values:

- $dom($Time of Day$) = \{$Morning,Noon,Evening,Night$\}$
- $dom($Age Group$) = \{$Young,Adult$\}$
- $dom($Mood$) = \{$Happy,Indifferent,Sad,Sour,Grumpy$\}$

The classification can be the movie genre that the viewer would like to watch, such as $C = \{$Action,Comedy,Drama$\}$.

All the attributes are vague by definition. For example, peoples feelings of happiness, indifference, sadness, sourness and grumpiness are vague without any crisp boundaries between them. Although the vagueness of "Age Group" or "Time of Day" can be avoided by indicating the exact age or exact time, a rule induced with a crisp decision tree may then have an artificial crisp boundary, such as "IF Age < 16 THEN action movie". But how about someone who is 17 years of age? Should this viewer definitely not watch an action movie? The viewer preferred genre may still be vague. For example, the viewer may be in a mood for both comedy and drama movies. Moreover, the association of movies into genres may also be vague. For instance the movie "Lethal Weapon" (starring Mel Gibson and Danny Glover) is considered to be both comedy and action movie.

Fuzzy concept can be introduced into a classical problem if at least one of the input attributes is fuzzy or if the target attribute is fuzzy. In the example described above , both input and target attributes are fuzzy. Formally the problem is defined as following (Yuan and Shaw, 1995):

Each class c_j is defined as a fuzzy set on the universe of objects U. The membership function $\mu_{c_j}(u)$ indicates the degree to which object u belongs to class c_j. Each attribute a_i is defined as a linguistic attribute which takes linguistic values from $dom(a_i) = \{v_{i,1}, v_{i,2}, \ldots, v_{i,|dom(a_i)|}\}$. Each linguistic value $v_{i,k}$ is also a fuzzy set defined on U. The membership $\mu_{v_{i,k}}(u)$ specifies the degree to which object u's attribute a_i is $v_{i,k}$. Recall that the membership of a linguistic value can be subjectively assigned or transferred from numerical values by a membership function defined on the range of the numerical value.

Typically, before one can incoporate fuzzy concepts into a data mining application, an expert is required to provide the fuzzy sets for the quantitative attributes, along with their corresponding membership functions. Alternatively the appropriate fuzzy sets are determined using fuzzy clustering.

2.2 Fuzzy Set Operations

Like classical set theory, fuzzy set theory includes operations union, intersection, complement, and inclusion, but also includes operations that have no classical counterpart, such as the modifiers concentration and dilation, and the connective fuzzy aggregation. Definitions of fuzzy set operations are provided in this section.

Definition 2. *The membership function of the union of two fuzzy sets A and B with membership functions μ_A and μ_B respectively is defined as the maximum of the two individual membership functions:*

$$\mu_{A \cup B}(u) = max\{\mu_A(u), \mu_B(u)\} \tag{3}$$

Definition 3. *The membership function of the intersection of two fuzzy sets A and B with membership functions μ_A and μ_B respectively is defined as the minimum of the two individual membership functions:*

$$\mu_{A \cap B}(u) = min\{\mu_A(u), \mu_B(u)\} \tag{4}$$

Definition 4. *The membership function of the complement of a fuzzy set A with membership function μ_A is defined as the negation of the specified membership function:*

$$\mu_{\overline{A}}(u) = 1 - \mu_A(u). \tag{5}$$

To illustrate these fuzzy operations, we elaborate on the previous example. Recall that John has a degree of youth of 0.875. Additionally John's happiness degree is 0.254. Thus, the membership of John in the set Young ∪ Happy would be $max(0.875, 0.254) = 0.875$, and its membership in Young ∩ Happy would be $min(0.875, 0.254) = 0.254$.

It is possible to chain operators together, thereby constructing quite complicated sets. It is also possible to derive many interesting sets from chains of rules built up from simple operators. For example John's membership in the set $\overline{Young}$ ∪ Happy would be $max(1 - 0.875, 0.254) = 0.254$

The usage of the max and min operators for defining fuzzy union and fuzzy intersection, respectively is very common. However, it is important to note that these are not the only definitions of union and intersection suited to fuzzy set theory.

Definition 5. *The fuzzy subsethood $S(A, B)$ measures the degree to which A is a subset of B.*

$$S(A, B) = \frac{M(A \cap B)}{M(A)} \tag{6}$$

where $M(A)$ is the *cardinality* measure of a fuzzy set A and is defined as

$$M(A) = \sum_{u \in U} \mu_A(u) \tag{7}$$

The subsethood can be used to measure the truth level of the rule of classification rules. For example given a classification rule such as "IF Age is Young AND Mood is Happy THEN Comedy" we have to calculate $S(Hot \cap Sunny, Swimming)$ in order to measure the truth level of the classification rule.

3 Fuzzy Supervised Learning

In this section we survey supervised methods that incoporate fuzzy sets. Supervised methods are methods that attempt to discover the relationship between input attributes and a target attribute (sometimes referred to as a dependent variable). The relationship discovered is represented in a structure referred to as a model. Usually models describe and explain phenomena, which are hidden in the dataset and can be used for predicting the value of the target attribute knowing the values of the input attributes.

It is useful to distinguish between two main supervised models: classification models (classifiers) and Regression Models. Regression models map the input space into a real-value domain. For instance, a regressor can predict the demand for a certain product given its characteristics. On the other hand, classifiers map the input space into pre-defined classes. For instance, classifiers can be used to classify mortgage consumers as good (fully payback the mortgage on time) and bad (delayed payback).

Fuzzy set theoretic concepts can be incorporated at the input, output, or into to backbone of the classifier. The data can be presented in fuzzy terms and the output decision may be provided as fuzzy membership values. In this chapter we will concentrate on fuzzy decision trees.

3.1 Growing Fuzzy Decision Tree

Decision tree is a predictive model which can be used to represent classifiers. Decision trees are frequently used in applied fields such as finance, marketing, engineering and medicine. In the opinion of many researchers decision trees gained popularity mainly due to their simplicity and transparency. Decision tree are self-explained. There is no need to be an expert in data mining in order to follow a certain decision tree.

There are several algorithms for induction of fuzzy decision trees, most of them extend existing decision trees methods. The UR-ID3 algorithm (Maher and Clair, 1993)) starts by building a strict decision tree, and subsequently fuzzifies the conditions of the tree. Tani and Sakoda (1992) use the ID3 algorithm to select effective numerical attributes. The obtained splitting intervals are used as fuzzy boundaries. Regression is then used in each subspace to form fuzzy rules. Cios and Sztandera (1992) use the ID3 algorithm to convert a decision tree into a layer of a feedforward neural network. Each neuron is represented as a hyperplane with a fuzzy boundary. The nodes within the hidden layer are generated until some fuzzy entropy is reduced to zero. New hidden layers are generated until there is only one node at the output layer.

Fuzzy-CART (Jang (1994)) is a method which uses the CART algorithm to build a tree. However, the tree, which is the first step, is only used to propose fuzzy sets of the continuous domains (using the generated thresholds). Then, a layered network algorithm is employed to learn fuzzy rules. This produces more comprehensible fuzzy rules and improves the CART's initial results.

Another complete framework for building a fuzzy tree including several inference procedures based on conflict resolution in rule-based systems and efficient approximate reasoning methods was presented in (Janikow, 1998).

Olaru and Wehenkel (2003) presented a new type of fuzzy decision trees called soft decision trees (SDT). This approach combines tree-growing and pruning, to determine the structure of the soft decision tree. Refitting and backfitting are used to improve its generalization capabilities. The researchers empirically showed that soft decision trees are significantly more accurate than standard decision trees. Moreover, a global model variance study shows a much lower variance for soft decision trees than for standard trees as a direct cause of the improved accuracy.

Peng (2004) has used FDT to improve the performance of the classical inductive learning approach in manufacturing processes. Peng proposed using soft discretization of continuous-valued attributes. It has been shown that FDT can deal with the noise or uncertainties existing in the data collected in industrial systems.

In this chapter we will focus on the algorithm proposed in (Yuan and Shaw, 1995). This algorithm can handle the classification problems with both fuzzy attributes and fuzzy classes represented in linguistic fuzzy terms. It can also handle other situations in a uniform way where numerical values can be fuzzified to fuzzy terms and crisp categories can be treated as a special case of fuzzy terms with zero fuzziness. The algorithm uses classification ambiguity as fuzzy entropy. The classification ambiguity directly measures the quality of classification rules at the decision node. It can be calculated under fuzzy partitioning and multiple fuzzy classes.

The fuzzy decision tree induction consists of the following steps:

- Fuzzifying numeric attributes in the training set.
- Inducing a fuzzy decision tree.
- Simplifying the decision tree.
- Applying fuzzy rules for classification.

Fuzzifying numeric attributes

When a certain attribute is numerical, it needs to be fuzzified into linguistic terms before it can be used in the algorithm. The fuzzification process can be performed manually by experts or can be derived automatically using some sort of clustering algorithm. Clustering groups the data instances into subsets in such a manner that similar instances are grouped together; different instances belong to different groups. The instances are thereby organized into an efficient representation that characterizes the population being sampled.

Yuan and Shaw (1995) suggest a simple algorithm to generate a set of membership functions on numerical data. Assume attribute a_i has numerical value x from the domain X. We can cluster X to k linguistic terms $v_{i,j}, j = 1, \ldots, k$. The size of k is manually predefined. For the first linguistic term $v_{i,1}$, the following membership function is used:

$$\mu_{v_{i,1}}(x) = \begin{cases} 1 & x \leq m_1 \\ \frac{m_2 - x}{m_2 - m_1} & m_1 < x < m_2 \\ 0 & x \geq m_2 \end{cases} \tag{8}$$

For each $v_{i,j}$ when $j = 2, \ldots, k-1$ has a triangular membership function as follows:

$$\mu_{v_{i,j}}(x) = \begin{cases} 0 & x \leq m_{j-1} \\ \frac{x - m_{j-1}}{m_j - m_{j-1}} & m_{j-1} < x \leq m_j \\ \frac{m_{j+1} - x}{m_{j+1} - m_j} & m_j < x < m_{j+1} \\ 0 & x \geq m_{j+1} \end{cases} \tag{9}$$

Finally the membership function of the last linguistic term $v_{i,k}$ is:

$$\mu_{v_{i,k}}(x) = \begin{cases} 0 & x \leq m_{k-1} \\ \frac{x - m_{k-1}}{m_k - m_{k-1}} & m_{k-1} < x \leq m_k \\ 1 & x \geq m_k \end{cases} \tag{10}$$

Figure 3 illustrates the creation of four groups defined on the age attribute: "young", "early adulthood", "middle-aged" and "old age". Note that the first set ("young") and the last set ("old age") have a trapezoidal form which can be uniquely described by the four corners. For example, the "young" set could be represented as $(0, 0, 16, 32)$. In between, all other sets ("early adulthood" and "middle-aged") have a triangular form which can be uniquely described by the three corners. For example, the set "early adulthood" is represented as $(16, 32, 48)$.

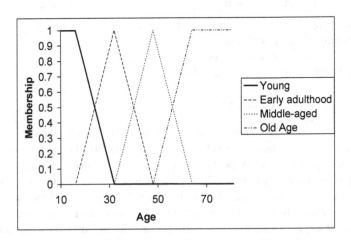

Fig. 3. Membership function for various groups in the age attribute.

The only parameters that need to be determined are the set of k centers $M = \{m_1, \ldots, m_k\}$. The centers can be found using the algorithm presented in

Algorithm 1. Note that in order to use the algorithm, a monotonic decreasing learning rate function should be provided.

Algorithm 1: Algorithm for fuzzifying numeric attributes

Input: X - a set of values, $\eta(t)$ - some monotonic decreasing scalar function representing the learning rate.

Output: $M = \{m_1, \ldots, m_k\}$

1: Initially set m_i to be evenly distributed on the range of X.
2: $t \leftarrow 1$
3: **repeat**
4:    Randomly draw one sample x from X
5:    Find the closest center m_c to x.
6:    $m_c \leftarrow m_c + \eta(t) \cdot (x - m_c)$
7:    $t \leftarrow t + 1$
8:    $D(X, M) \leftarrow \sum_{x \in X} \min_i \|x - m_i\|$
9: **until** $D(X, M)$ converges

The Induction Phase

The induction algorithm of fuzzy decision tree is presented in Algorithm 2. The algorithm measures the classification ambiguity associated with each attribute and split the data using the attribute with the smallest classification ambiguity. The classification ambiguity of attribute a_i with linguistic terms $v_{i,j}, j = 1, \ldots, k$ on fuzzy evidence S, denoted as $G(a_i|S)$, is the weighted average of classification ambiguity calculated as:

$$G(a_i \,|S) = \sum_{j='1}^{k} w(v_{i,j} \,|S) \cdot G(v_{i,j} \,|S) \tag{11}$$

where $w(v_{i,j} \,|S)$ is the weight which represents the relative size of $v_{i,j}$ and is defined as:

$$w(v_{i,j} \,|S) = \frac{M(v_{i,j} \,|S)}{\sum_k M(v_{i,k} \,|S)} \tag{12}$$

The classification ambiguity of $v_{i,j}$ is defined as $G(v_{i,j} \,|S) = g\,(\mathbf{p}\,(C \,|v_{i,j}\,))$, which is measured based on the possibility distribution vector $\mathbf{p}\,(C \,|v_{i,j}\,) = \left(p\,(c_1 \,|v_{i,j}\,), \ldots, p\left(c_{|k|} \,|v_{i,j}\,\right)\right)$.

Given $v_{i,j}$, the possibility of classifying an object to class c_l can be defined as:

$$p\left(c_l \mid v_{i,j}\right) = \frac{S(v_{i,j}, c_l)}{\max_k S(v_{i,j}, c_k)} \tag{13}$$

where $S(A, B)$ is the fuzzy subsethood that was defined in Definition 5. The function $g(\mathbf{p})$ is the possibilistic measure of ambiguity or nonspecificity and is defined as:

$$g(\mathbf{p}) = \sum_{i=1}^{|\mathbf{p}|} \left(p_i^* - p_{i+1}^*\right) \cdot \ln(i) \tag{14}$$

where $\mathbf{p}^* = \left(p_1^*, \ldots, p_{|\mathbf{p}|}^*\right)$ is the permutation of the possibility distribution $\mathbf{p}$ sorted such that $p_i^* \geq p_{i+1}^*$.

All the above calculations are carried out at a predefined significant level α. An instance will take into consideration of a certain branch $v_{i,j}$ only if its corresponding membership is greater than α. This parameter is used to filter out insignificant branches.

After partitioning the data using the attribute with the smallest classification ambiguity, the algorithm looks for nonempty branches. For each nonempty branch, the algorithm calculates the truth level of classifying all instances within the branch into each class. The truth level is caluclated using the fuzzy subsethood measure $S(A, B)$.

If the truth level of one of the classes is above a predefined threshold β then no additional partitioning is needed and the node become a leaf in which all instance will be labeled to the class with the highest truth level. Otherwise the procedure continues in a recursive manner. Note that small values of β will lead to smaller trees with the risk of underfitting. A higher β may lead to a larger tree with higher classification accuracy. However, at a certain point, higher values β may lead to overfitting.

Algorithm 2: Fuzzy decision tree induction

Input: S - Training Set A - Input Feature Set y - Target Feature
Output: Fuzzy Decision Tree
1: Create a new fuzzy tree FT with a single root node.
2: **if** S is empty OR Truth level of one of the classes $\geq \beta$ **then**
3:     Mark FT as a leaf with the most common value of y in S as a label.
4:     Return FT.
5: **end if**
6: $\forall a_i \in A$ find a with the smallest classification ambiguity.
7: **for** each outcome v_i of a **do**
8:     Recursively call procedure with corresponding partition v_i.
9:     Connect the root to the subtree with an edge that is labeled as v_i.
10: **end for**
11: Return FT

Simplifying the decision tree

Each path of branches from root to leaf can be converted into a rule with the condition part representing the attributes on the passing branches from the root to the leaf and the conclusion part representing the class at the leaf with the highest truth level classification. The corresponding classification rules can be further simplified by removing one input attribute term at a time for each rule we try to simplify . Select the term to remove with the highest truth level of the simplified rule. If the truth level of this new rule is not lower than the threshold β or the truth level of the original rule, the simplification is successful. The process will continue until no further simplification is possible for all the rules.

Using the Fuzzy Decision Tree

In a regular decision tree, only one path (rule) can be applied for every instance. In a fuzzy decision tree, several paths (rules) can be applied for one instance. In order to classify an unlabeled instance, the following steps should be performed (Yuan and Shaw, 1995):

- Step 1: Calculate the membership of the instance for the condition part of each path (rule). This membership will be associated with the label (class) of the path.
- Step 2: For each class calculate the maximum membership obtained from all applied rules.
- Step 3: An instance may be classified into several classes with different degrees based on the membership calculated in Step 2.

3.2 Soft Regression

Regressions are used to compute correlations among data sets. The "classical" approach uses statistical methods to find these correlations. Soft regression is used when we want to compare data sets that are temporal and interdependent. The use of fuzzy logic can overcome many of the difficulties associated with the classical approach. The fuzzy techniques can achieve greater flexibility, greater accuracy and generate more information in comparison to econometric modeling based on (statistical) regression techniques. In particular, the fuzzy method can potentially be more successful than conventional regression methods, especially under circumstances that severely violate the fundamental conditions required for the reliable use of conventional methods.

Soft regression techniques have been proposed in (Shnaider et al., 1991, Shnaider and Schneider, 1988).

3.3 Neuro-fuzzy

Neuro-fuzzy refers to hybrids of artificial neural networks and fuzzy logic. Neuro-fuzzy is the most visible hybrid paradigm and has been adequately investigated (Mitra and Pal, 2005)

Neuro-fuzzy hybridization can be done in two ways (Mitra, 2000): fuzzy-neural network (FNN) which is a neural network equipped with the capability of handling fuzzy information and a neural-fuzzy system (NFS) which is a fuzzy system augmented by neural networks to enhance some of its characteristics like flexibility, speed, and adaptability.

A neurofuzzy system can be viewed as a special 3layer neural network (Nauck, 1997). The first layer represents input variables, the hidden layer represents fuzzy rules and the third layer represents output variables. Fuzzy sets are encoded as (fuzzy) connection weights. Usually after learning the obtained model is interpreted as a system of fuzzy rules.

4 Fuzzy Clustering

The goal of clustering is descriptive, that of classification is predictive. Since the goal of clustering is to discover a new set of categories, the new groups are of interest in themselves, and their assessment is intrinsic. In classification tasks, however, an important part of the assessment is extrinsic, since the groups must reflect some reference set of classes.

Clustering of objects is as ancient as the human need for describing the salient characteristics of men and objects and identifying them with a type. Therefore, it embraces various scientific disciplines: from mathematics and statistics to biology and genetics, each of which uses different terms to describe the topologies formed using this analysis. From biological "taxonomies", to medical "syndromes" and genetic "genotypes" to manufacturing "group technology" — the problem is identical: forming categories of entities and assigning individuals to the proper groups within it.

Clustering groups data instances into subsets in such a manner that similar instances are grouped together, while different instances belong to different groups. The instances are thereby organized into an efficient representation that characterizes the population being sampled. Formally, the clustering structure is represented as a set of subsets $C = C_1, \ldots, C_k$ of S, such that: $S = \bigcup_{i=1}^{k} C_i$ and $C_i \cap C_j = \emptyset$ for $i \neq j$. Consequently, any instance in S belongs to exactly one and only one subset.

Traditional clustering approaches generate partitions; in a partition, each instance belongs to one and only one cluster. Hence, the clusters in a hard clustering are disjointed. Fuzzy clustering extends this notion and suggests a *soft clustering* schema. In this case, each pattern is associated with every cluster using some sort of membership function, namely, each cluster is a fuzzy set of all the patterns. Larger membership values indicate higher confidence in the assignment of the pattern to the cluster. A hard clustering can be obtained from a fuzzy partition by using a threshold of the membership value.

The most popular fuzzy clustering algorithm is the fuzzy c-means (FCM) algorithm. Even though it is better than the hard K-means algorithm at avoiding local minima, FCM can still converge to local minima of the squared error criterion. The design of membership functions is the most important problem in fuzzy clustering; different choices include those based on similarity decomposition and centroids of clusters. A generalization of the FCM algorithm has been proposed through a family of objective functions. A fuzzy c-shell algorithm and an adaptive variant for detecting circular and elliptical boundaries have been presented.

FCM is an iterative algorithm. The aim of FCM is to find cluster centers (centroids) that minimize a dissimilarity function. To accommodate the introduction of fuzzy partitioning, the membership matrix(U) is randomly initialized according to Equation 15.

$$\sum_{i=1}^{c} u_{ij} = 1, \forall j = 1, ..., n \tag{15}$$

The algorithm minimizes a dissimilarity (or distance) function which is given in Equation 16:

$$J(U, c_1, c_2, ..., c_c) = \sum_{i=1}^{c} J_i = \sum_{i=1}^{c} \sum_{j=1}^{n} u_{ij}^m d_{ij}^2 \tag{16}$$

where, u_{ij} is between 0 and 1; c_i is the centroid of cluster i; d_{ij} is the Euclidian distance between i-th centroid and j-th data point; m is a weighting exponent.

To reach a minimum of dissimilarity function there are two conditions. These are given in Equation 17 and Equation 18.

$$c_i = \frac{\sum_{j=1}^{n} u_{ij}^m x_j}{\sum_{j=1}^{n} u_{ij}^m} \tag{17}$$

$$u_{ij} = \frac{1}{\sum_{k=1}^{c} \left(\frac{d_{ij}}{d_{kj}}\right)^{2/(m-1)}} \tag{18}$$

Algorithm 3 presents the fuzzy c-means that was originally proposed in (Bezdek, 1973).

By iteratively updating the cluster centers and the membership grades for each data point, FCM iteratively moves the cluster centers to the "right" location within a data set. However, FCM does not ensure that it converges to an optimal solution. The random initilization of U might have uncancelled effect on the final performance.

There are several extensions to the basic FCM algorithm, The Fuzzy Trimmed C Prototype (FTCP) algorithm (Kim et al., 1996) increases the

---

Algorithm 3: FCM Algorithm

Input: X - Data Set
    c - number of clusters
    t - convergence threshold (termination criterion)
    m - exponential weight
Output: U - membership matrix
  1: Randomly initialize matrix U with c clusters and fulfils Eq. 15
  2: **repeat**
  3:    Calculate c_i by using Equation 17.
  4:    Compute dissimilarity between centroids and data points using Eq. 16.
  5:    Compute a new U using Eq. 18
  6: **until** The improvement over previous iteration is below t.

---

robustness of the clusters by trimming away observations with large residuals. The Fuzzy C Least Median of Squares (FCLMedS) algorithm (Nasraoui and Krishnapuram, 1997) replaces the summation presented in Equation 16 with the median.

5 Fuzzy Association Rules

Association rules are rules of the kind "70% of the customers who buy vine and cheese also buy grapes". While the traditional field of application is market basket analysis, association rule mining has been applied to various fields since then, which has led to a number of important modifications and extensions.

In this section, an algorithm based on the *apriori* data mining algorithm is described to discover large itemsets. Fuzzy sets are used to handle quantitative values, as described in (Hong et al., 1999). Our algorithm is applied with some differences. We will use the following notation:

- n – number of transactions in the database.
- m – number of items (attributes) in the database.
- d_i – the i-th transaction.
- I_j – the j-th attribute.
- I_{ij} – the value of I_j for d_i.
- μ_{ijk} – the membership grade of I_{ij} in the region k.
- R_{jk} – the k-th fuzzy region of the attribute I_j.
- $num(R_{jk})$ – number of occurrences of the attribute region R_{jk} in the whole database, where $\mu_{ijk} > 0$.
- C_r – the set of candidate itemsets with r attributes.
- c_r – candidate itemset with r attributes.
- f_j^i – the membership value of d_i in region s_j.
- f_{cr}^i – the fuzzy value of the itemset c_r in the transaction d_i.

Algorithm 4: Fuzzy Association Rules Algorithm

1: **for all** transaction i **do**
2:     **for all** attribute j **do**
3:         $I_{ij}^f = (\mu_{ij1}/R_{j1} + \mu_{ij2}/R_{j2} + \ldots + \mu_{ijk}/R_{jk})$ {where the superscript f denotes fuzzy set}
4:     **end for**
5: **end for**
6: For each attribute region R_{jk}, count the number of occurrences, where $\mu_{ijk} > 0$, in the whole database. The output is $num(R_{jk})$.

$$num(R_{jk}) = \sum_{i=1}^{n} 1\{\mu_{ijk}/R_{jk} \neq 0\}$$

7: $L_1 = \{R_{jk} | num(R_{jk}) \geq minnum, 1 \leq j \leq m, 1 \leq k \leq numR(I_j)\}$.
8: $r=1$ (r is the number of items that composed the large itemsets in the current stage).
9: Generate the candidate set C_{r+1} from L_r
10: **for all** newly formed candidate itemset c_{r+1} in C_{r+1}, that is composed of the items $(s_1, s_2, \ldots, s_{r+1})$ **do**
11:     For each transaction d_i calculate its intersection fuzzy value as: $f_{(cr+1)}^i = f_1^i \cap f_2^i \cap \ldots \cap f_{r+1}^i$.
12:     Calculate the frequency of c_{r+1} on the transactions, where $f_{(cr+1)}^i > 0$. $num(c_{r+1})$ is output.
13:     If the frequency of the itemset is larger than or equal to the predefined number of occurrences minnum, put it in the set of large r+1-itemsets L_{r+1}.
14: **end for**
15: **if** L_{r+1} is not empty **then**
16:     $r = r + 1$
17:     go to Step 9.
18: **end if**
19: **for all** large itemset l_r, $r \geq 2$ **do**
20:     Calculate its support as: $\sup(l_r) = \Sigma f_{(lr)}^i$.
21:     Calculate its strength as: $str(l_r) = \sup(l_r)/num(l_r)$.
22: **end for**
23: For each large itemset l_r, $r \geq 2$, generate the possible association rules as in (Agrawal et al., 1993).
24: For each association rule $s_1, s_2, \ldots, s_n \geq s_{n+1}, \ldots, s_r$, calculate its confidence as: $num(s_1, s_2 \ldots s_n, s_{n+1} \ldots s_r)/num(s_1, s_2 \ldots s_n)$.
25: **if** the confidence is higher than the predefined threshold minconf **then**
26:     output the rule as an association rule.
27: **end if**
28: For each association rule $s_1, s_2, \ldots, s_n \geq s_{n+1}, \ldots, s_r$, record its strength as $str(s_1, s_2 \ldots s_n, s_{n+1} \ldots s_r)$, and its support as $\sup(l_r)$.

- L_r – the set of large itemsets with r items.
- l_r – a large itemset with r items.
- $num(I_1, \ldots, I_s)$ – the occurrences number of the itemset $(I_1, \ldots, I_s)$.
- $numR(I_j)$ – the number of the membership function regions for the attribute I_j.

Algorithm 4 presents the fuzzy association algorithm proposed in (Komem and Schneider, 2005). The quantitative values are first transformed into a set of membership grades, by using predefined membership functions. Every membership grade represents the agreement of a quantitative value with a linguistic term. In order to avoid discriminating the importance level of data, each point must have membership grade of 1 in one membership function; Thus, the membership functions of each attribute produce a continuous line of $\mu = 1$. Additionally, in order to diagnose the bias direction of an item from the center of a membership function region, almost each point get another membership grade which is lower than 1 in other membership functions region. Thus, each end of membership function region is touching, close to, or slightly overlapping an end of another membership function (except the outside regions, of course).

By this mechanism, as point "a" moves right, further from the center of the region "middle", it gets a higher value of the label "middle-high", additionally to the value 1 of the label "middle".

6 Conclusion

This chapter discussed how fuzzy logic can be used to solve several different data mining tasks, namely classification clustering, and discovery of association rules. The discussion focused mainly one representative algorithm for each of these tasks.

There are at least two motivations for using fuzzy logic in data mining, broadly speaking. First, as mentioned earlier, fuzzy logic can produce more abstract and flexible patterns, since many quantitative features are involved in data mining tasks. Second, the crisp usage of metrics is better replaced by fuzzy sets that can reflect, in a more natural manner, the degree of belongingness/membership to a class or a cluster.

References

R. Agrawal, T. Imielinski and A. Swami: Mining Association Rules between Sets of Items in Large Databases. Proceeding of ACM SIGMOD, 207-216. Washington, D.C, 1993.

J. C. Bezdek. Fuzzy Mathematics in Pattern Classification. PhD Thesis, Applied Math. Center, Cornell University, Ithaca, 1973.

Cios K. J. and Sztandera L. M., Continuous ID3 algorithm with fuzzy entropy measures, Proc. IEEE Internat. Con/i on Fuzz)' Systems,1992, pp. 469-476.

T.P. Hong, C.S. Kuo and S.C. Chi: A Fuzzy Data Mining Algorithm for Quantitative Values. 1999 Third International Conference on Knowledge-Based Intelligent Information Engineering Systems. Proceedings. IEEE 1999, pp. 480-3.

T.P. Hong, C.S. Kuo and S.C. Chi: Mining Association Rules from Quantitative Data. Intelligent Data Analysis, vol.3, no.5, nov. 1999, pp363-376.

Jang J., "Structure determination in fuzzy modeling: A fuzzy CART approach," in Proc. IEEE Conf. Fuzzy Systems, 1994, pp. 480485.

Janikow, C.Z., Fuzzy Decision Trees: Issues and Methods, IEEE Transactions on Systems, Man, and Cybernetics, Vol. 28, Issue 1, pp. 1-14. 1998.

Kim, J., Krishnapuram, R. and Dav, R. (1996). Application of the Least Trimmed Squares Technique to Prototype-Based Clustering, Pattern Recognition Letters, 17, 633-641.

Joseph Komem and Moti Schneider, On the Use of Fuzzy Logic in Data Mining, in The Data Mining and Knowledge Discovery Handbook, O. Maimon, L. Rokach (Eds.), pp. 517-533, Springer, 2005.

Maher P. E. and Clair D. C, Uncertain reasoning in an ID3 machine learning framework, in Proc. 2nd IEEE Int. Conf. Fuzzy Systems, 1993, pp. 712.

S. Mitra, Y. Hayashi, "Neuro-fuzzy Rule Generation: Survey in Soft Computing Framework." IEEE Trans. Neural Networks, Vol. 11, N. 3, pp. 748-768, 2000.

S. Mitra and S. K. Pal, Fuzzy sets in pattern recognition and machine intelligence, Fuzzy Sets and Systems 156 (2005) 381386

Nasraoui, O. and Krishnapuram, R. (1997). A Genetic Algorithm for Robust Clustering Based on a Fuzzy Least Median of Squares Criterion, Proceedings of NAFIPS, Syracuse NY, 217-221.

Nauck D., Neuro-Fuzzy Systems: Review and Prospects Paper appears in Proc. Fifth European Congress on Intelligent Techniques and Soft Computing (EUFIT'97), Aachen, Sep. 8-11, 1997, pp. 1044-1053

Olaru C., Wehenkel L., A complete fuzzy decision tree technique, Fuzzy Sets and Systems, 138(2):221–254, 2003.

Peng Y., Intelligent condition monitoring using fuzzy inductive learning, Journal of Intelligent Manufacturing, 15 (3): 373-380, June 2004.

E. Shnaider and M. Schneider, Fuzzy Tools for Economic Modeling. In: Uncertainty Logics: Applications in Economics and Management. Proceedings of SIGEF'98 Congress, 1988.

Shnaider E., M. Schneider and A. Kandel, 1997, A Fuzzy Measure for Similarity of Numerical Vectors, Fuzzy Economic Review, Vol. II, No. 1, 1997, pp. 17 - 38. -2Nkmg cnycau qfgf ockoqp fkf pqv tgcf gxgp qpg rcig qh vjku dqqm0 Jg tghwugf vq jgnr dwv jcf pq rtqdngo vq ytkvg jku qyp pcog qp vjg dqqm cpf vgnn gxgtaqpg jg ku yqtmkpi jctf0-2

Tani T. and Sakoda M., Fuzzy modeling by ID3 algorithm and its application to prediction of heater outlet temperature, Proc. IEEE Internat. Conf. on Fuzzy Systems, March 1992, pp. 923-930.

Yuan Y., Shaw M., Induction of fuzzy decision trees, Fuzzy Sets and Systems 69(1995):125-139.

Zimmermann H. J., Fuzzy Set Theory and its Applications, Springer, 4th edition, 2005.

Support Vector Machines and Fuzzy Systems

Yixin Chen

Department of Computer and Information Science
The University of Mississippi
University, MS 38655
ychen@cs.olemiss.edu

Summary. Fuzzy set theory and fuzzy logic provide tools for handling uncertainties in data mining tasks. To design a fuzzy rule-based classification system (fuzzy classifier) with good generalization ability in a high dimensional feature space has been an active research topic for a long time. As a powerful machine learning approach for data mining and pattern recognition problems, support vector machine (SVM) is known to have good generalization ability. More importantly, an SVM can work very well on a high (or even infinite) dimensional feature space. This chapter presents a survey of the connection between fuzzy classifiers and kernel machines. A significant portion of the chapter is built upon material from articles we have written, in particular (Chen and Wang, 2003a, Chen and Wang, 2003b).

1 Introduction

As powerful tools for managing uncertainties inherent in complex systems, fuzzy set theory and fuzzy logic have been successfully applied to a variety of areas including data mining, system identification and control, signal and image processing, pattern classification, and information retrieval (Klawon and Klement, 1997, Klir and Yuan, 1995, Zimmermann, 1991). A fuzzy classifier (FC) is a fuzzy rule-based classification system, which makes decisions based on fuzzy inference–a fusion of natural languages and computation with fuzzy variables. Although fuzzy rules may provide intuitive linguistic interpretations of the concept underneath a classification problem (Zadeh, 1996), the FCs were regarded as methods that "are cumbersome to use in high dimensions or on complex problems or in problems with dozens or hundreds of features (pp. 194, (Duda *et al.*, 2000))".

Kernel machines and the associated learning methods, especially the support vector machine (SVM) approach (Vapnik, 1998), represent one of the most important directions both in theory and application of machine learning. With proper learning methods, kernel machines are known to have good generalization abilities and, more importantly, perform very well on high (or even infinite) dimensional feature spaces. In recent years, efforts have been made to analyze the relationship between fuzzy rule-based systems and kernel machines (Lin and Wang, 2002, Chen and Wang, 2003a, Chen and Wang, 2003b, Leski, 2005, Moser, 2006). In this chapter, we demonstrate that, under a general assumption on membership functions, an additive FC is equivalent to a kernel machine in terms of decision boundaries. Consequently, various learning algorithms for kernel machines are applicable to the class of FCs. Moreover, techniques originated in the fuzzy systems literature may also enrich the toolbox of kernel machines.

1.1 Traditional Approaches to Building a Fuzzy System

In general, building a fuzzy system consists of three basic steps:

- Structure identification
  It includes variable selection, partitioning input and output spaces, specifying the number of fuzzy rules, and choosing a parametric/nonparametric form of membership functions.
- Parameter estimation
  It obtains unknown parameters in fuzzy rules via optimizing a given criterion.
- Model validation
  It involves performance evaluation and model simplification.

Deciding the number of input variables is referred to as the problem of variable selection, i.e., selecting input variables that are most predictive of a given outcome. It is related to the problems of input dimensionality reduction and parameter pruning. Emami et al. (Emami *et al.*, 1998) presented a simple method of identifying non-significant input variables in a fuzzy system based on the distribution of degree of memberships over the domain. Silipo et al. (Silipo and Berthold, 2000) proposed a method that quantifies the discriminative power of the input features in a fuzzy model based on information gain. Selecting input variables according to their information gains may improve the prediction performance of the fuzzy system and provides a better understanding of the underlying concept that generates the data.

Given a set of input and output variables, a fuzzy partition associates fuzzy sets (or linguistic labels) with each variable. There are roughly two ways of doing it: data independent partition and data dependent partition. The former approach partitions the input space in a predetermined fashion. The partition of the output space then follows from supervised learning. One of the commonly used strategies is to assign a fixed number of linguistic labels to each input variable (Wang and Mendel, 1992). Although this scheme is not difficult to implement, it has two serious drawbacks:

- The information in the given data (patterns) is not fully exploited. The performance of the resulting system may be poor if the input space partition is quite distinct from the true distribution of data. Optimizing output space partition alone is not sufficient.

- The scheme suffers from the curse of dimensionality. If each input variable is allocated m fuzzy sets, a fuzzy system with n inputs and one output needs on the order of m^n rules.

Various data dependent partition methods have been proposed to alleviate these drawbacks. Dickerson et al. (Dickerson and Kosko, 1996) used an unsupervised competitive learning algorithm to find the mean and covariance matrix of each data cluster in the input/output space. Each data cluster forms an ellipsoidal fuzzy rule patch. Thawonmas et al. (Thawonmas and Abe, 1999) described a simple heuristic for unsupervised iterative data partition. At each iteration, an input dimension, which gives the maximum intra-class dierence between the maximum and the minimum values of the data along that dimension, is selected. The partition is performed perpendicular to the selected dimension. Two data group representations, hyper-box and ellipsoidal representations, are compared. In (Setnes, 2000), a supervised clustering algorithm is used to group input/output data pairs into a predetermined number of fuzzy clusters. Each cluster corresponds to a fuzzy IF-THEN rule. Univariate membership functions can then be obtained by projecting fuzzy clusters onto corresponding coordinate axes.

Although a fuzzy partition can generate fuzzy rules, results are usually very coarse with many parameters to be learned and tuned. Various optimization techniques are proposed to solve this problem. Genetic algorithms (Chiang et al., 1997, Tang et al., 1998, Wong and Chen, 2000) and artificial neural networks (Jang and Sun, 1993, Kasabov, 1996, Wu et al., 2001) are two of the most popular and effective approaches.

1.2 Generalization Performance

After going through the long journey of structure identification and parameter estimation, can we infer that we get a good fuzzy model? In order to draw a conclusion, the following two questions must be answered:

- How capable can a fuzzy model be?
- How well can the model, built on finite amount of data, capture the concept underlying the data?

The first question could be answered from the perspective of function approximation. Several types of fuzzy models are proven to be "universal approximators" (Kosko, 1994, Rovatti, 1998, Wang , 1999, Ying, 1998), i.e., we can always find a model from a given fuzzy model set so that the model can uniformly approximate any continuous function on a compact domain to any degree of accuracy. The second question is about the generalization performance, which is closely related to several well-known problems in the statistics and machine learning literature, such as the structural risk minimization (Vapnik, 1982), the bias variance dilemma (Geman et al., 1992), and the overfitting phenomena (Bartlett, 1997). Loosely speaking, a model, build on finite amount of given data (training patterns), generalizes the best if the right tradeoff is found between the training (learning) accuracy and the "capacity" of the model set from which the model is chosen. On one hand, a low "capacity" model set may not contain any model that fits the training data well. On the other hand, too much freedom may eventually generate a model behaving like a refined look-up-table: perfect for the training data but (maybe) poor on generalization.

Researchers in the fuzzy systems community attempt to tackle this problem with roughly two approaches:(1) use the idea of cross-validation to select a model that has the best ability to generalize (Sugeno and Kang, 1998); (2) focus on model reduction, which is usually achieved by rule base reduction (Setnes and Babuška, 2001, Yen and Wang, 1998), to simplify the model.

1.3 A Kernel Method for Fuzzy Systems

In the statistical learning literature, the Vapnik-Chervonenkis (VC) theory (Vapnik, 1995, Vapnik, 1998) provides a general measure of model set complexity. Based on the VC theory, support vector machines (SVM) (Vapnik, 1995, Vapnik, 1998) can be designed for classification problems. In many real applications, the SVMs give excellent performance (Cristianini and Shawe-Taylor, 2000).

In this chapter, we relate additive fuzzy systems to kernel machines, and demonstrate that, under a general assumption on membership functions, an additive fuzzy rule-based classification system can be constructed directly from the given training samples using the support vector learning approach. Such additive fuzzy rule-based classification systems are named the positive definite fuzzy classifiers (PDFC). Using the SVM approach to build PDFCs has following advantages:

- Fuzzy rules are extracted directly from the given training data. The number of fuzzy rules is irrelevant to the dimension of the input space. It is no greater (usually much less) than the number of training samples. In this sense, we avoid the "curse of dimensionality."
- The VC theory establishes the theoretical foundation for good generalization of the resulting PDFC.
- The global solution of an SVM optimization problem can be found efficiently using specifically designed quadratic programming algorithms.

1.4 An Outline of the Chapter

The remainder of the chapter is organized as follows. Section 2 describes the class of FCs to be studied: additive FCs with positive definite reference functions, product fuzzy conjunction operator, and center of area (COA) defuzzification with thresholding unit. These FCs are named positive definite FCs.

The equivalence between a PDFC and a kernel machine is proven. Based on a support vector learning method, Section 3 proposes a learning algorithm to construct PDFCs from training samples. Experimental results are provided in Section 4. And finally, we conclude in Section 5 together with a discussion of relevant and future work.

2 Additive Fuzzy Classifiers and Positive Definite Fuzzy Classifiers

This section starts with a short description of an additive fuzzy model, based on which binary FCs and standard binary FCs are defined. We then introduce the concept of positive definite functions, and define positive definite FC (PDFC) accordingly. Finally, some nice properties of the PDFCs are discussed.

2.1 Additive Fuzzy Classifiers

Depending on the THEN-part of fuzzy rules and the way to combine fuzzy rules, an FC can take many different forms (Kuncheva, 2000). In this chapter, we consider the additive fuzzy model with constant THEN-parts. Given m fuzzy rules of the form

$$\text{Rule } j: \quad \text{IF } \mathbf{A}_j^1 \text{ AND } \mathbf{A}_j^2 \text{ AND } \cdots \text{ AND } \mathbf{A}_j^n \text{ THEN } b_j \tag{1}$$

where $\mathbf{A}_j^k$ is a fuzzy set with membership function $a_j^k : \mathbb{R} \to [0,1]$, $j = 1, \cdots, m$, $k = 1, \cdots, n$, $b_j \in \mathbb{R}$, if we choose product as the fuzzy conjunction operator, addition for fuzzy rule aggregation (that is what "additive" means), and COA defuzzification, then the input output mapping, $F : \mathbb{R}^n \to \mathbb{R}$, of the model is defined as

$$F(\mathbf{x}) = \frac{\sum_{j=1}^m b_j \prod_{k=1}^n a_j^k(x_k)}{\sum_{j=1}^m \prod_{k=1}^n a_j^k(x_k)} \tag{2}$$

where $\mathbf{x} = [x_1, \cdots, x_n]^T \in \mathbb{R}^n$ is the input. Note that (2) is not well-defined on $\mathbb{R}^n$ if $\sum_{j=1}^m \prod_{k=1}^n a_j^k(x_k) = 0$ for some $\mathbf{x} \in \mathbb{R}^n$, which could happen if the input space is not fully covered by fuzzy rule "patches". However, there are several easy fixes for this problem. For example, we can force the output to some constant when $\sum_{j=1}^m \prod_{k=1}^n a_j^k(x_k) = 0$, or add a fuzzy rule so that the denominator $\sum_{j=1}^m \prod_{k=1}^n a_j^k(x_k) > 0$ for all $\mathbf{x} \in \mathbb{R}^n$. Here we take the second approach for analytical simplicity. The following rule is added:

$$\text{Rule } 0: \quad \text{IF } \mathbf{A}_0^1 \text{ AND } \mathbf{A}_0^2 \text{ AND } \cdots \text{ AND } \mathbf{A}_0^n \text{ THEN } b_0 \tag{3}$$

where $b_0 \in \mathbb{R}$, the membership functions $a_0^k(x_k) \equiv 1$ for $k = 1, \cdots, n$ and any $x_k \in \mathbb{R}$. Consequently, the input output mapping becomes

$$F(\mathbf{x}) = \frac{b_0 + \sum_{j=1}^{m} b_j \prod_{k=1}^{n} a_j^k(x_k)}{1 + \sum_{j=1}^{m} \prod_{k=1}^{n} a_j^k(x_k)} \quad . \tag{4}$$

A classifier associates class labels with input features, i.e., it is essentially a mapping from the input space to the set of class labels. In binary case, thresholding is one of the simplest ways to transform $F(\mathbf{x})$ to class labels $+1$ or -1. In this article, we are interested in binary FCs defined as follows.

Definition 2.1 *(Binary FC) Consider a fuzzy system with $m+1$ fuzzy rules where Rule 0 is given by (3), Rule $j, j = 1, \cdots, m$, has the form of (1). If the system uses product for fuzzy conjunction, addition for rule aggregation, and COA defuzzification, then the system induces a binary FC, f, with decision rule,*

$$f(\mathbf{x}) = \text{sign}\,(F(\mathbf{x})) \tag{5}$$

where $F(\mathbf{x})$ is defined in (4).

The membership functions for a binary FC defined above could be any function from $\mathbb{R}$ to $[0,1]$. However, too much flexibility on the model could make effective learning (or training) infeasible. So we narrow our interests to the class of membership functions that are generated from location transformation of reference functions (Dubois D and Prade H (1978)), and the classifiers defined on them.

Definition 2.2 *(Reference Function, (Dubois D and Prade H (1978))) A function $\mu : \mathbb{R} \to [0,1]$ is a reference function if and only if: 1) $\mu(x) = \mu(-x)$; 2) $\mu(0) = 1$; and, 3) μ is non-increasing on $[0, \infty)$.*

Definition 2.3 *(Standard Binary FC) A binary FC given by Definition 2.1 is a standard binary FC if for the kth input, $k \in \{1, \cdots, n\}$, the membership functions, $a_j^k : \mathbb{R} \to [0,1]$, $j = 1, \cdots, m$, are generated from a reference function a^k through location transformation, i.e., $a_j^k(x_k) = a^k(x_k - z_j^k)$ for some location parameter $z_j^k \in \mathbb{R}$. (Note that different inputs can have different reference functions.)*

Corollary 2.4 *The decision rule of a standard binary FC given by Definition 2.3 can be written as*

$$f(\mathbf{x}) = \text{sign}\left(\sum_{j=1}^{m} b_j K(\mathbf{x}, \mathbf{z}_j) + b_0\right) \tag{6}$$

where $\mathbf{x} = [x_1, x_2, \cdots, x_n]^T \in \mathbb{R}^n$, $\mathbf{z}_j = [z_j^1, z_j^2, \cdots, z_j^n]^T \in \mathbb{R}^n$ contains the location parameters of a_j^k, $k = 1, \cdots, n$, $K : \mathbb{R}^n \times \mathbb{R}^n \to [0,1]$ is a translation *invariant kernel*[1] *defined as*

$$K(\mathbf{x}, \mathbf{z}_j) = \prod_{k=1}^{n} a^k(x_k - z_j^k) \; . \tag{7}$$

Proof: From (4), (5), and the fact that $1 + \sum_{j=1}^{m} \prod_{k=1}^{n} a_j^k(x_k) > 0$, we have

$$f(\mathbf{x}) = \text{sign}\left(b_0 + \sum_{j=1}^{m} b_j \prod_{k=1}^{n} a_j^k(x_k) \right) \; ,$$

which transforms to (6) using Definition 2.3. $\square$

2.2 Positive Definite Fuzzy Classifiers

Corollary 2.4 presents a novel kernel perspective on standard binary FCs. One particular kind of kernel, Mercer kernel, has received considerable attention in the machine learning literature (Cristianini and Shawe-Taylor, 2000, Genton, 2001, Vapnik, 1998) because it is an efficient way of extending linear learning machines to nonlinear ones. Is the kernel defined by (7) a Mercer kernel? A kernel satisfying the Mercer conditions (Cristianini and Shawe-Taylor, 2000) is named a Mercer kernel. An equivalent form of the Mercer condition, which proves most useful in constructing Mercer kernels, is given by the following lemma (Cristianini and Shawe-Taylor, 2000).

Lemma 2.5 *(Positivity Condition for Mercer Kernels (Cristianini and Shawe-Taylor, 2000)) A kernel $K : \mathbb{R}^n \times \mathbb{R}^n \to \mathbb{R}$ is a Mercer kernel if and only if the matrix $[K(\mathbf{x}_i, \mathbf{x}_j)] \in \mathbb{R}^{n \times n}$ is positive semi-definite for all choices of points $\{\mathbf{x}_1, \cdots, \mathbf{x}_n\} \subset \mathbb{X}$ ($\mathbb{X}$ is a compact subset of $\mathbb{R}^n$) and all $n = 1, 2, \cdots \cdots$.*

For most nontrivial kernels, directly checking the positivity condition in Lemma 2.5 is not an easy task. Nevertheless, for the class of translation invariant kernels, to which the kernels defined by (7) belong, there is an equivalent yet practically more powerful criterion based on the spectral property of the kernel (Smola *et al.*, 1998).

Lemma 2.6 *(Positivity Condition for Translation Invariant Kernels (Smola et al., 1998)) A translation invariant kernel $K(\mathbf{x}, \mathbf{z}) = K(\mathbf{x} - \mathbf{z})$ is a Mercer kernel if and only if the Fourier transform*

$$\mathcal{F}[K](\boldsymbol{\omega}) = \frac{1}{(2\pi)^{\frac{n}{2}}} \int_{\mathbb{R}^n} K(\mathbf{x}) e^{-i\langle \boldsymbol{\omega}, \mathbf{x} \rangle} dx$$

is nonnegative.

---

[1] A kernel $K(\mathbf{x}, \mathbf{z})$ is translation invariant if $K(\mathbf{x}, \mathbf{z}) = K(\mathbf{x} - \mathbf{z})$, i.e., it depends only on $\mathbf{x} - \mathbf{z}$, but not on $\mathbf{x}$ and $\mathbf{z}$ themselves.

Kernels defined by (7) do not, in general, have nonnegative Fourier transforms. However, if we assume that the reference functions are positive definite functions, which are defined by the following definition, we do get a Mercer kernel (given in Theorem 2.9).

Definition 2.7 *(Positive Definite Function (Horn and Johnson, 1985)) A function $f : \mathbb{R} \to \mathbb{R}$ is said to be a positive definite function if the matrix $[f(x_i - x_j)] \in \mathbb{R}^{n \times n}$ is positive semi-definite for all choices of points $\{x_1, \cdots, x_n\} \subset \mathbb{R}$ and all $n = 1, 2, \cdots \cdots$.*

Corollary 2.8 *A function $f : \mathbb{R} \to \mathbb{R}$ is positive definite if and only if the Fourier transform*

$$\mathcal{F}[f](\omega) = \frac{1}{\sqrt{2\pi}} \int_{-\infty}^{\infty} f(x) e^{-i\omega x} dx$$

is nonnegative.

Proof: Given any function $f : \mathbb{R} \to \mathbb{R}$, we can define a translation invariant kernel $K : \mathbb{R} \times \mathbb{R} \to \mathbb{R}$ as

$$K(x, z) = f(x - z) \ .$$

From Lemma 2.6, K is a Mercer kernel if and only if the Fourier transform of f is nonnegative. Thus from Lemma 2.5 and Definition 2.7, we conclude that f is a positive definite function if and only if its Fourier transform is nonnegative. $\square$

Theorem 2.9 *(Positive Definite FC, PDFC) The translation invariant kernel (7) is a Mercer kernel if the reference functions, $a^k : \mathbb{R} \to [0, 1]$, $k = 1, \cdots, n$, are positive definite functions. The corresponding standard binary FC is named a PDFC.*

Proof: From Lemma 2.6, it suffices to show that the translation invariant kernel defined by (7) has nonnegative Fourier transform. Rewrite (7) as

$$K(\mathbf{x}, \mathbf{z}) = K(\mathbf{u}) = \prod_{k=1}^{n} a^k(u_k)$$

where $\mathbf{x} = [x_1, \cdots, x_n]^T$, $\mathbf{z} = [z_1, \cdots, z_n]^T \in \mathbb{R}^n$, $\mathbf{u} = [u_1, \cdots, u_n]^T = \mathbf{x} - \mathbf{z}$. Then

$$\mathcal{F}[K](\omega) = \frac{1}{(2\pi)^{\frac{n}{2}}} \int_{\mathbb{R}^n} e^{-i\langle \omega, \mathbf{u} \rangle} \prod_{k=1}^{n} a^k(u_k) d\mathbf{u} = \prod_{k=1}^{n} \frac{1}{\sqrt{2\pi}} \int_{\mathbb{R}} a^k(u_k) e^{-i\omega_k u_k} du_k \ ,$$

which is nonnegative since a^k, $k = 1, \cdots, n$, are positive definite functions. $\square$

It might seem that the positive definite assumption on reference functions is quite restrictive. In fact, many commonly used reference functions are indeed positive definite. An incomplete list includes

- Symmetric triangle

$$\mu(x) = \max(1 - d\,|x|\,, 0)$$

- Gaussian

$$\mu(x) = e^{-dx^2}$$

- Cauchy

$$\mu(x) = \frac{1}{1 + dx^2}$$

- Laplace

$$\mu(x) = e^{-d|x|}$$

- Hyperbolic secant

$$\mu(x) = \frac{2}{e^{dx} + e^{-dx}}$$

- Squared sinc

$$\mu(x) = \frac{\sin^2(dx)}{d^2 x^2}$$

where $d > 0$.

Note that the Gaussian reference function corresponds to the commonly used Gaussian kernel. More generally, the weighted summation (with positive weights) and the product of positive definite functions are still positive definite (a direct conclusion from the linearity and product/convolution properties of the Fourier transform). So we can get a class of positive definite reference functions from those listed above. It is worthwhile noting that the asymmetric triangle and the trapezoid reference functions are not positive definite.

2.3 Some Remarks on PDFCs

A Mercer kernel implicitly defines a nonlinear mapping, $\Phi : \mathbb{X} \to \mathbb{F}$, such that the kernel computes the inner product in $\mathbb{F}$, i.e., $K(\mathbf{x}, \mathbf{z}) = \langle \Phi(\mathbf{x}), \Phi(\mathbf{z}) \rangle_{\mathbb{F}}$ where $\mathbb{X}$ is the input space, $\langle \cdot, \cdot \rangle_{\mathbb{F}}$ is an inner product in the new feature space $\mathbb{F}$ (its dimension can be infinite). Therefore, from Corollary 2.4 and Theorem 2.9 the decision rule of a PDFC can be equivalently written as

$$f(\mathbf{x}) = \text{sign} \left(\left\langle \sum_{j=1}^{m} b_j \Phi(\mathbf{z}_j), \Phi(\mathbf{x}) \right\rangle_{\mathbb{F}} + b_0 \right). \tag{8}$$

Remark 2.10 *Equation (8) relates the decision boundary of a PDFC in* $\mathbb{X}$ *to a hyperplane in* $\mathbb{F}$ *(with normal direction* $\mathbf{w} = \sum_{j=1}^{m} b_j \Phi(\mathbf{z}_j)$*). It implies that for any hyperplane in* $\mathbb{F}$*, if the normal direction is a linear combination of vectors that have pre-images (under* Φ*) in* $\mathbb{X}$*, then the hyperplane transforms to a decision boundary of a PDFC. Conversely, given a PDFC, one can find a hyperplane in* $\mathbb{F}$ *that transforms to the decision boundary of the given PDFC. Therefore, we can alternatively think of the decision boundary of a PDFC as a hyperplane in* $\mathbb{F}$*. Constructing a PDFC is then converted to finding a hyperplane in* $\mathbb{F}$*.*

Remark 2.11 *A hyperplane in* $\mathbb{F}$ *is defined by its normal direction* $\mathbf{w}$ *and the distance to the origin. According to (8), the IF-part and THEN-part of fuzzy rules play different roles in modeling the hyperplane. Once we have the IF-part parameters,* $\{\mathbf{z}_1, \cdots, \mathbf{z}_m\}$*, the set of feasible orientations of the hyperplanes is given by* $\mathbb{W} = \mathrm{Span}\{\Phi(\mathbf{z}_1), \cdots, \Phi(\mathbf{z}_m)\}$*. Finding the THEN-part parameters* $\{b_1, \cdots, b_m\}$ *is essentially selecting an orientation from* $\mathbb{W}$ *as* $\sum_{j=1}^{m} b_j \Phi(\mathbf{z}_j)$*. The distance of the hyperplane to the origin is then decided by* b_0*, which is the THEN-part of Rule 0.*

3 Support Vector Learning for Positive Definite Fuzzy Classifiers

A PDFC with n inputs is parameterized by n, possibly different, positive definite reference functions ($a^k : \mathbb{R} \to [0,1]$, $k = 1, \ldots n$), a set of location parameters ($\{\mathbf{z}_1, \cdots, \mathbf{z}_m\} \subset \mathbb{X}$) for the membership functions of the IF-part fuzzy rules, and a set of real numbers ($\{b_0, \cdots, b_m\} \subset \mathbb{R}$) for the constants in the THEN-part fuzzy rules where m is unknown. Which reference functions to choose is an interesting research topic by itself (Mitaim and Kosko, 2001). PDFCs with different reference functions are empirically compared in Section 4. Here we assume that the reference functions $a^i : \mathbb{R} \to [0,1]$, $i = 1, \cdots, n$ are predetermined. Thus the problem is how to extract a set of fuzzy rules ($\{\mathbf{z}_1, \cdots, \mathbf{z}_m\}$ and $\{b_0, \cdots, b_m\}$) from training samples so that the PDFC has good generalization ability.

In the previous section, we demonstrate the equivalence (in terms of decision boundaries) between PDFCs and kernel machines. So any learning algorithm for kernel machines can potentially be applied to construct PDFCs. As a universal learning machine for pattern recognition problems, the SVM is known to have good generalization ability because the SVM learning approach tries to decrease an upper bound on the expected risk by reducing the empirical risk and, at the same time, controlling the VC dimension of the model set (Cristianini and Shawe-Taylor, 2000, Vapnik, 1998). Here we propose a learning algorithm for PDFCs based on the SVM learning approach. The learning algorithm first construct an SVM from training samples, then convert support vectors to fuzzy rules such that the PDFC and SVM have identical decision rules. The whole procedure is described by the following algorithm.

Algorithm 1: SVM Learning for PDFC

Inputs: Positive definite reference functions $a^k(x_k)$, $k = 1, \cdots, n$, associated with n input variables, and a set of training samples $\{(\mathbf{x}_1, y_1), \cdots, (\mathbf{x}_l, y_l)\} \subset \mathbb{X} \times \{+1, -1\}$ where y_i is the class label associated with feature vector $\mathbf{x}_i$.

Outputs: A set of fuzzy rules parameterized by $\mathbf{z}_j$, b_j, and m. $\mathbf{z}_j$ $(j = 1, \cdots, m)$ contains the location parameters of the IF-part membership functions of the jth fuzzy rule, b_j $(j = 0, \cdots, m)$ is the THEN-part constant of the jth fuzzy rule, and $m + 1$ is the number of fuzzy rules.

Steps:

  1 Construct a Mercer kernel, K, from the given positive definite reference functions according to (7).

  2 Construct an SVM to get a decision rule of the form
$$y = \text{sign}\left(\sum_{i=1}^{l} y_i \alpha_i K(\mathbf{x}_j, \mathbf{x}_i) + b \right)$$
where $\alpha_i \geq 0$, $i = 1, \cdots, l$, are the Lagrange multipliers obtained by solving the SVM quadratic programming problem[2].

  3 Extract fuzzy rules from the above SVM decision rule:
$b_0 \leftarrow b$
$j \leftarrow 1$
FOR $i = 1$ **TO** l
  IF $\alpha_i > 0$
    $\mathbf{z}_j \leftarrow \mathbf{x}_i$
    $b_j \leftarrow y_i \alpha_i$
    $j \leftarrow j + 1$
  END IF
END FOR
$m \leftarrow j - 1$

Clearly the number of fuzzy rules equals the number of nonzero Lagrange multipliers, and is irrelevant to the dimension of the input space. In this sense, the "curse of dimensionality" (the number of fuzzy rules increases exponentially with the increasing of input dimension) is avoided. In addition, due to the sparsity of the Lagrange multipliers, the number of fuzzy rules is usually much less than the number of training samples. There is a one-to-one correspondence between support vectors and fuzzy rules. Each fuzzy rule is parameterized by a support vector $\mathbf{x}_j$, class label y_j, and the associated nonzero Lagrange multiplier α_j where $\mathbf{x}_j$ specifies the location of the IF-part membership functions, $y_j \alpha_j$ gives the THEN-part constant. Therefore, we can alternatively view a PDFC as an SVM with the kernel constructed from positive definite reference functions.

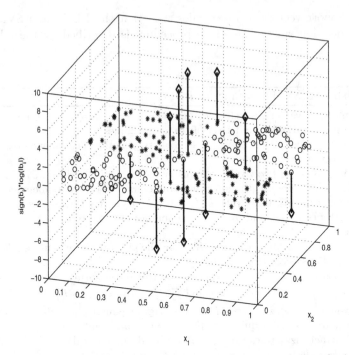

Fig. 1. Checkerboard problem. The training samples are marked with *'s and o's. Each rule of PDFC is represented by a vertical line pointing from a sample to a ◇ where the sample corresponds to the location of the rule. The signed length of the line segment is defined by $sign(b_j)log(|b_j|)$ where b_j is the THEN part of a rule.

Figure 1 shows a binary classification problem and the fuzzy rules obtained from the above algorithm. The samples are generated from a checkerboard distribution with the positive and negative classes denoted by $*$ and $\circ$, respectively. The PDFC is constructed from 100 positive and 100 negative training samples. The reference function is selected to be the Gaussian function with $\sigma = \frac{\sqrt{3}}{3}$. Figure 1 shows the 10 rules learnt from the training data. The location of each rule is indicated by the projection of the ◇ onto the x_1-x_2 plane. The THEN part of each rule, b_j, is marked by a vertical line pointing from a sample to a ◇. The vertical axis indicates $sign(b_j)log(|b_j|)$. The PDFC achieves 98.5% accuracy on an independent test set of 100 positive and 100 negative samples.

4 Experimental Results

In this section, PDFCs with different choices of reference functions are compared on the USPS data set [3], which contains 9298 grayscale images of hand-

---

[3] The USPS data set is available at http://www.kernel-machines.org/data.

Table 1. The maximal classification rate and the number of fuzzy rules for different reference functions using the USPS data set.

Reference Function	Gaussian	Cauchy	Laplace	S-Triangle	H-Secant	Sinc^2
d	$\frac{1}{128}$	$\frac{1}{128}$	$\frac{1}{64}$	$\frac{1}{64}$	$\frac{1}{8}$	$\frac{1}{8}$
Classification Rate	99.55%	99.55%	99.40%	99.40%	99.55%	99.30%
Number of Fuzzy Rules	464	462	835	841	462	352

written digits. The images are size normalized to fit in a 16×16 pixel box while preserving their aspect ratio. The data set is divided into a training set of 7291 samples and a testing set of 2007 samples. For each sample, the input feature vector consists of 256 grayscale values. We test the performance of PDFCs for six positive definite reference functions listed in Section 2.1, namely symmetric triangle, Gaussian, Cauchy, Laplace, hyperbolic secant, and squared sinc. For different input variables, the reference functions are chosen to be identical (otherwise, there will be too many cases to compare). Due to space limitation, we only present the results of separating digit 0 from the rest 9 digits. Similar results have been observed for the other 9 cases. In the dual formulation of the SVM optimization problem (the 1-norm soft margin problem is solved here [4]), the upper bound of the Lagrange multipliers is sent to be 1000. The d parameter for all reference functions takes discrete values from $\{\frac{1}{2^n} : n = 3, \cdots, 20\}$. We pick the maximal classification rates for all six reference functions, and list them in Table 3 together with the corresponding d values and the number of fuzzy rules.

It is interesting to see that the maximal classification rates, varying from 99.30% (14 misclassified validation samples out of 2007 validation samples) to 99.55% (9 misclassified validation samples out of 2007 validation samples), are very close. The Gaussian, Cauchy, and hyperbolic secant give the same best classification rate of 99.55%, but the number of fuzzy rules need by the Gaussian reference function, which is 464, is slightly greater than 462, the number of fuzzy rules required by the latter two reference functions. The computational cost for the Cauchy reference function is lower than that of the hyperbolic secant reference function because there is no need to compute an exponential term in evaluating the Cauchy reference function. Although the squared sinc gives the worst (not significant though) classification rate (99.30%), it requires significantly less number of fuzzy rules. Figure 2 shows the misclassified validation samples for all reference functions with values of d given by Table 3. Some of those samples are very ambiguous, but several are identifiable by humans, although they are written in an under-represented style.

---

[4] The SVMLight (Joachims, 1999) is used to implement the SVMs.

(a) Gaussian, Cauchy, and hyperbolic secant reference functions.

(b) Laplace and symmetric triangle reference functions.

(c) Squared sinc reference function.

Fig. 2. The testing samples misclassified by PDFCs using different reference functions. From left to right, the correct labels for the images are (a) 000500030, (b) 080000500000, and (c) 08820023500030.

5 Discussion and Future Work

In this chapter, we exhibit the connection between fuzzy classifiers and kernel machines, and propose a support vector learning approach to construct fuzzy classifiers so that a fuzzy classifier can have good generalization ability in a high dimensional feature space.

5.1 The Relationship between PDFC kernels and RBF Kernels

In the literature, it is well-known that a Gaussian RBF network can be trained via support vector learning using a Gaussian RBF kernel (Schölkopf *et al.*, 1997). While the functional equivalence between fuzzy inference systems and Gaussian RBF networks is established in (Jang and Sun, 1993) where the membership functions within each rule must be Gaussian functions with identical variance. So connection between such fuzzy systems and SVMs with Gaussian RBF kernels can be established. The following discussion compares the kernels defined by PDFCs and RBF kernels commonly used in SVMs.

The kernels of PDFCs are constructed from positive definite reference functions. These kernels are translation invariant, symmetric with respect to a set of orthogonal axes, and tailing off gradually. In this sense, they appear to be very similar to the general RBF kernels (Genton, 2001). In fact, the Gaussian reference function defines the Gaussian RBF kernel. However, in general, the kernels of PDFCs are not RBF kernels. According to the definition, an RBF kernel, $K(\mathbf{x}, \mathbf{z})$, depends only on the norm of $\mathbf{x} - \mathbf{z}$, i.e., $K(\mathbf{x} - \mathbf{z}) = K_{RBF}(\|\mathbf{x} - \mathbf{z}\|)$. It can be shown that for a kernel, $K(\mathbf{x}, \mathbf{z})$, defined by (7) using symmetric triangle, Cauchy, Laplace, hyperbolic secant, or squared sinc reference functions (even with identical d for all input variables), there exists $\mathbf{x}_1$, $\mathbf{x}_2$, $\mathbf{z}_1$, and $\mathbf{z}_2$ such that $\|\mathbf{x}_1 - \mathbf{z}_1\| = \|\mathbf{x}_2 - \mathbf{z}_2\|$ and $K(\mathbf{x}_1, \mathbf{z}_1) \neq K(\mathbf{x}_2, \mathbf{z}_2)$. Moreover, a general RBF kernels (even if it is a Mercer kernel) may not be a PDFC kernel, i.e., it can not be in general decomposed as product of positive definite reference functions. It is worth noting that the kernel defined by symmetric triangle reference functions is identical to the B_n-splines (or order 1) kernel that is commonly used in the SVM literature (Vapnik et al., 1997).

5.2 Advantages of Connecting Fuzzy Systems to Kernel Machines

Kernel methods represent one of the most important directions both in theory and application of machine learning. While fuzzy classifier was regarded as a method that "are cumbersome to use in high dimensions or on complex problems or in problems with dozens or hundreds of features (pp. 194, (Duda et al., 2000))." Establishing the connection between fuzzy systems and kernel machines has the following advantages:

- A novel kernel perspective of fuzzy classifiers is provided. Through reference functions, fuzzy rules are related to translation invariant kernels. Fuzzy inference on the IF-part of a fuzzy rule is equivalent to evaluating the kernel. If the reference functions are restricted to the class of positive definite functions then the kernel turns out to be a Mercer kernel, and the corresponding fuzzy classifier becomes a PDFC. Since Mercer kernel induces a feature space, we can consider the decision boundary of a PDFC as a hyperplane in that space. The design of a PDFC is then equivalent to finding an "optimal" hyperplane.

- A new approach to build fuzzy classifiers is proposed. Based on the link between fuzzy systems and kernel machines, a support vector learning approach is proposed to construct PDFCs so that a fuzzy classifier can have good generalization ability in a high dimensional feature space. The resulting fuzzy rules are determined by support vectors, corresponding Lagrange multipliers, and associated class labels.

- It points out a future direction of applying techniques in fuzzy systems literature to improve the performance of kernel methods. The link between fuzzy systems and kernel machines implies that a class of kernel machines, such as those using Gaussian kernels, can be interpreted by a set of fuzzy IF-THEN rules. This opens interesting connections between fuzzy rule base reduction techniques (Setnes, 2000) and computational complexity issues in SVMs (Burges and Schölkopf, 1997) and kernel PCA (principal component analysis) (Schölkopf et al., 1998):

  - The computational complexity of an SVM scales with the number of support vectors. One way of decreasing the complexity is to reduce the number of support-vector-like vectors in the decision rule (6). For the class of kernels, which can be interpreted by a set of fuzzy IF-THEN rules, this can be viewed as fuzzy rule base simplification.

  - In kernel PCA (Schölkopf et al., 1998), given a test point $\mathbf{x}$, the kth nonlinear principal component, β_k, is computed by $\beta_k = \sum_{i=1}^{l} \alpha_i^k K(\mathbf{x}, \mathbf{x}_i)$ where l is the number of data points in a given data set (details of calculating $\alpha_i^k \in \mathbb{R}$ can be found in (Schölkopf et al., 1998)). Therefore, the computational complexity of computing β_k scales with l. For the class of kernels discussed in this chapter, it is not difficult to derive that β_k can be equivalently viewed as the output of an additive fuzzy system using first order moment defuzzification without thresholding unit. Here $\mathbf{x}_i$ and α_i^k parameterize the IF-part and THEN-part of the ith fuzzy rule ($i = 1, \cdots, l$), respectively. As a result, fuzzy rule base reduction techniques may be applied to increase the speed of nonlinear principal components calculation.

5.3 Future Directions

As future work, the following directions can be explored:

- The requirement that all membership functions associated with an input variable are generated from the same reference function maybe somewhat restrictive. However, it can be shown that this constraint can be relaxed;
- The positivity requirement on reference functions can also be relaxed. In that case, the kernel in general will not be a Mercer kernel. But the fuzzy classifiers can still be related to the generalized support vector machines (Mangasarian, 2000);
- Although our work focuses on the classification problem, it is not difficult to extend the results to function approximations. Fuzzy function approximation (using positive definite reference functions) is equivalent to support vector regression (Vapnik *et al.*, 1997) using the kernel defined by reference functions;
- Apply fuzzy rule base reduction techniques to reduce computational complexities of the SVM and kernel PCA.

Acknowledgments

The work is supported by the University of Mississippi. The author would also like to thank James Z. Wang and Yongyi Chen for discussions on the topic.

References

Bartlett PL (1997) For valid generalization, the size of the weights is more important than the size of the network, Advances in Neural Information Processing Systems 9, 134-140

Burges CJC, Schölkopf B (1997) Improving the accuracy and speed of support vector machines, Advances in Neural Information Processing Systems 9, 375–381

Chen Y, Wang JZ (2003a) Support vector learning for fuzzy rule-based classification systems, IEEE Transactions on Fuzzy Systems, 11(6):716–728

Chen Y, Wang JZ (2003b) Kernel machines and additive fuzzy systems: classification and function approximation, Proc. IEEE International Conference on Fuzzy Systems, 789–795

Chiang CK, Chung HY, Lin JJ (1997) A self-learning fuzzy logic controller using genetic algorithms with reinforcements, IEEE Transactions on Fuzzy Systems, 5(3):460–467

Cristianini N., Shawe-Taylor J. (2000) An Introduction to Support Vector Machines and Other Kernel-Based Learning Methods. Cambridge University Press

Dickerson JA, Kosko B (1996) Fuzzy function approximation with ellipsoidal rules, IEEE Transactions on Systems, Man, and Cybernetics, Part B: Cybernetics, 26(4):542–560

Dubois D and Prade H (1978) Operations on fuzzy numbers, International Journal of Systems Science, 9(6):613–626

Duda RO, Hart PE, Stork DG (2000) Pattern classification, Second Edition. John Wiley and Sons, Inc.

Emami MR, Türksen IB, Goldenberg AA (1998) Development of a systematic methodology of fuzzy logic modeling, IEEE Transactions on Neural Networks, 6(3):346–361

Geman S, Bienenstock E, Doursat R (1992) Neural networks and the Bias/Variance dilemma, Neural Computation, 4(1):1–58

Genton MG (2001) Classes of kernels for machine learning: a statistics perspective, Journal of Machine Learning Research, 2:299–312

Horn RA, Johnson CR (1985) Matrix Analysis. Cambridge University Press

Jang JSR, Sun CT (1993) Functional equivalence between radial basis function networks and fuzzy inference systems, IEEE Transactions on Neural Networks, 4(1):156–159

Jang JSR, Sun CT (1995) Neuro-fuzzy modeling and control, Proceedings of the IEEE, 83(3):378–406

Joachims T (1999) Making large-scale SVM learning practical, Advances in Kernel Methods - Support Vector Learning, Cambridge, MA: MIT Press, 169-184

Kasabov NK (1996) Learning fuzzy rules and approximate reasoning in fuzzy neural networks and hybrid systems, Fuzzy Sets and Systems, 82(2):135–149

Klawon F, Klement PE (1997) Mathematical analysis of fuzzy classifiers, Lecture Notes in Computer Science 1280:359–370

Klir G, Yuan B (1995) Fuzzy sets and fuzzy logic: theory and applications. Prentice Hall

Kosko B (1994) Fuzzy systems as universal approximators, IEEE Transactions on Computers, 43(11):1329–1333

Kuncheva LI (2000) How good are fuzzy if-then classifiers, IEEE Transactions on Systems, Man, and Cybernetics-Part B: Cybernetics, 30(4):501–509

Leski JM (2005) TSK-Fuzzy modeling based on ϵ-insensitive learning, IEEE Transactions on Fuzzy Systems, 13(2):181–193

Lin CF, Wang SD (2002) Fuzzy support vector machines, IEEE Transactions on Neural Networks, 13(2):464–471

Mangasarian OL (2000) Generalized support vector machines, Advances in Large Margin Classifiers, 135–146

Mitaim S, Kosko B (2001) The shape of fuzzy sets in adaptive function approximation, IEEE Transactions on Fuzzy Systems, 9(4):637–656

Moser B (2006) On representing and generating kernels by fuzzy equivalence relations, Journal of Machine Learning Research, 7:2603–2620

Rovatti R (1998) Fuzzy piecewise multilinear and piecewise linear systems as universal approximators in Sobolev norms, IEEE Transactions on Fuzzy Systems,

6(2):235–249

Schölkopf B, Smola AJ, Müller KR, Nonlinear component analysis as a kernel eigenvalue problem, Neural Computation, 10:1299–1319

Schölkopf B, Sung KK, Burges C, Girosi F, Niyogi P., Poggio T., Vapnik V (1997) Comparing support vector machines with Gaussian kernels to radial basis function classifiers, IEEE Transactions on Signal Processing, 45(11):2758–2765

Setnes M (2000) Supervised fuzzy clustering for rule extraction, IEEE Transactions on Fuzzy Systems, 8(4):416–424

Setnes M, Babuška R (2001) Rule base reduction: some comments on the use of orthogonal transforms, IEEE Transactions on Systems, Man, and Cybernetics-Part C: Applications and Reviews, 31(2):199–206

Silipo R, Berthold MR, (2000) Input features' impact on fuzzy decision process, IEEE Transactions on Systems, Man, and Cybernetics, Part B: Cybernetics, 30(6):821–834

Smola AJ, Schölkopf B, Müller KR (1998) The connection between regularization operators and support vector kernels, Neural Networks, 11(4):637–649

Sugeno M, Kang GT (1998) Structure identification of fuzzy model, Fuzzy Sets and Systems, 28:15–33

Tang K, Man K, Liu Z, Kwong S (1998) Minimal fuzzy memberships and rules using hierarchical genetic algorithms, IEEE Transactions on Industrial Electronics, 45(1):162–169

Thawonmas R, Abe S (1999) Function approximation based on fuzzy rules extracted from partitioned numerical data, IEEE Transactions on Systems, Man, and Cybernetics, Part B: Cybernetics, 29(4):525–534

Vapnik V (1982) Estimation of dependences based on empirical data. Springer Verlag, New York

Vapnik V (1995) The Nature of Statistical Learning Theory. Springer-Verlag, New York

Vapnik V (1998) Statistical learning theory. John Wiley and Sons, Inc., New York

Vapnik V, Golowich SE, Smola A (1997) Support vector method for function approximation, regression estimation, and signal processing, Advances in Neural Information Processing Systems 9, 281–287

Wang LX (1999) Analysis and design of hierarchical fuzzy systems, IEEE Transactions on Fuzzy Systems, 7(5):617–624

Wang L, Mendel JM (1992) Fuzzy basis functions, universal approximation, and orthogonal least-squares learning, IEEE Transactions on Neural Networks, 3(5):807–814

Wong CC, Chen CC (2000) A GA-based method for constructing fuzzy systems directly from numerical data, IEEE Transactions on Systems, Man, and Cybernetics, Part B: Cybernetics, 30(6):904–911

Wu S, Er MJ, Gao Y (2001) A fast approach for automatic generation of fuzzy rules by generalized dynamic fuzzy neural networks, IEEE Transactions on Fuzzy Systems, 9(4):578–594

Yen J, Wang L (1998) Application of statistical information criteria for optimal fuzzy model construction, IEEE Transactions on Fuzzy Systems, 6(3):362–372

Ying H (1998) General SISO Takagi-Sugeno fuzzy systems with linear rule consequent are universal approximators, IEEE Transactions on Fuzzy Systems, 6(4):582–587

Zadeh LA (1996) Fuzzy logic = computing with words, IEEE Transactions on Fuzzy Systems, 4(2):103–111

Zimmermann HJ (1991) Fuzzy set theory and its applications. Kluwer Academic Publishers

KDD in Marketing with Genetic Fuzzy Systems

Jorge Casillas[1] and Francisco J. Martínez-López[2]

[1] Department of Computer Science and Artificial Intelligence, University of Granada, Spain casillas@decsai.ugr.es
[2] Department of Marketing, University of Granada, Spain fjmlopez@ugr.es

Summary. This publication is the fruit of a collaborative research between academics from the marketing and the artificial intelligence fields. It presents a brand new methodology to be applied in marketing (causal) modeling. Specifically, we apply it to a consumer behavior model used for the experimentation. The characteristics of the problem (with uncertain data and available knowledge from a marketing expert) and the multiobjective optimization we propose make genetic fuzzy systems a good tool for tackling it. In sum, by applying this methodology we obtain useful information patterns (fuzzy rules) which help to better understand the relations among the elements of the marketing system (causal model) being analyzed; in our case, a consumer model.

1 Introduction

The field of Knowledge Discovery in Databases (KDD) has lots of potential to support current marketing decision problems. Several academics have recently noted this question, when emphasizing the logical evolution that marketing modeling methods must describe towards systems based on Artificial Intelligence and KDD methodologies (Shim *et al.* 2002; Wedel *et al.* 2000). Our work in the last years has aimed to contribute to the rapprochement of these fields. Specifically, this paper presents a KDD methodology developed *ad hoc* to be applied in marketing (causal) modeling. A *descriptive rule induction* method is posed to discover individual rules which show information patterns of especial interest in the data. To do this, we consider fuzzy association rules, but previously setting antecedents' and consequents' variables; i.e. we use a theoretic (causal) model of reference, which is used to supervise the machine learning process. Extraction is realized by genetic fuzzy systems. In this respect, two questions may arise, whose answers are convenient at this introductory section: why fuzzy rules? and, why genetic algorithms (GAs)? In other words, why use these tools of representation and learning instead of others widely used in KDD?

The use of fuzzy rules (instead of interval rules, decision trees, etc.) is mainly justified by the type of data we work with (see section 2.1). In our case, each element/construct of the marketing model is determined by a set of indicators (observed variables) which give partial information to describe it. This adds uncertainty to the data that it can be easily treated with fuzzy rules. Also, it is possible to express the available knowledge of a marketing expert by means of linguistic semantics. Finally, fuzzy rules obtained present high legibility, an important question in KDD.

With respect to the use of GAs to induce fuzzy rules instead of other machine learning techniques, it is due to the following aspects. On the one hand, as the quality of the different fuzzy rules is valued by contradictory objectives – such as support and confidence –, we opt for a multiobjective optimization to treat them adequately. This is currently one of the alternatives with more potential, as well as one of the signs of identity, in AGs, where it stands out due to its superior performance when compared with other techniques. Furthermore, to achieve higher compacity, thus interpretability, we consider a flexible representation of the fuzzy rules which can be easily handled with GAs.

The paper is structured as follows. Section 2 introduces our KDD methodology proposal (a brief extract). In Section 3 we empirically apply the methodology on a consumer model. Then, some rules are commented on to illustrate the kind of results we can obtain by this methodology. Finally, we give some concluding remarks.

2 Consumer Behavior Modeling with Fuzzy Rules: A Knowledge Discovery Methodology

The proposed KDD methodology to estimate the consumer behavior consists of three different parts: data gathering and preparation (pre-processing), data mining, and knowledge interpretation (post-processsing). This section introduces the two first stages, while the latter one is illustrated with an experimental example in the next section.

2.1 Data Gathering

First step is to collect the data related to the variables defining the theoretic consumer behavior model of reference. In this sense, as it has been traditionally done in marketing, data are obtained by means of a questionnaire. Thus, firstly, attention should be paid to how consumer behavior modelers face and develop the measurement process of variables that complex behavioral models contain; i.e. usually, latent/unobserved variables. Its understanding is necessary in order to adequately approach the starting point of the KDD process, so to give suitable and adapted solutions to the specific data we find in consumer behavior modeling

It can be said that measuring streams for these latent variables in marketing modeling can be classified into two groups depending on if they state that these constructs can or cannot be perfectly measured by means of observed variables (indicators); i.e., the existence or not of a one-to-one correspondence between a construct and its measurement. Certainly, though consumer behavior modelers tended to make use in the beginning of what was known as the *operational definition philosophy*, a more convenient and reasonable position is that ulteriorly based on the *partial interpretation philosophy* which distinguished between unobserved (constructs) and observed (indicators) variables. This latter approach of measurement, being currently predominant in the marketing modeling discipline, poses to jointly consider multiple indicators – imperfect when considered individually, though reliable when considered altogether – of the subjacent construct to obtain valid measures (Steenkamp and Baumgartner 2000). Hence, we will take this measurement approach into account when facing how to process the data.

To illustrate the data gathering process, we will consider a simple measurement (causal) model depicted in Figure 1, compounded by three construct or latent variables (depicted by circles), two exogenous and one endogenous: (1) *convenience orientation*, (2) *risk averseness*, and (3) *consumer attitude toward virtual stores*.

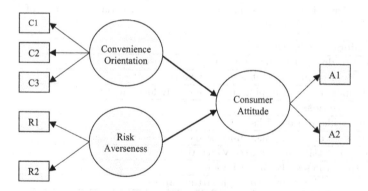

Fig. 1. Example of a simple measurement (causal) model – partial model extracted from the full Lee's (2007) conceptual model.

Likewise, with respect to the measurement scales, imagine that the three constructs have been measured by means of several nine-points interval scales (e.g. Likert type or semantic differential scales). Specifically, in Table 2.2 we show an example of the set of items – i.e. observed variables – that could have been used for measuring each construct. The model for this illustration and the respective items has been extracted from Lee (2007). Finally, Table 2.2 shows an example of data set available for this problem, which consists of three variables, each of them composed by a set of values (items). There are just four instances (i.e. four consumer's responses), what it is not realistic at all – i.e. think that a consumer database has usually hundreds or even thousands of individuals' responses gathered –, though it is useful for our illustrative purpose.

2.2 Data Processing

Next, it is necessary to adapt the collected data to a scheme easily tractable by fuzzy rule learning methods. Therefore, our methodological approach should be aware of the special features of the available data (with several items or indicators to describe a specific variable) when adapting the observed variables to a fuzzy rule learning method. An intuitive approach could directly reduce the items of certain variables to a single value (e.g., by arithmetic mean) (Casillas *et al.* 2004). Another possibility would be to expand any multi-item example (the result of a questionnaire filled out by a consumer) to several single-item examples and, subsequently, reduce the data size with some instance selection process.

Table 1. Questionnaire associated to the observed variables (items) of the model shown in Figure 1 (Lee, 2007)

Convenience Orientation
C1: I try to do most of my shopping in one store to save time
C2: I shop in many different ways to save time
C3: I do most of my shopping in conveniently located stores
Risk Averseness
R1: I don't like to take risks
R2: I have no desire to take unnecessary chances on things
Consumer Attitude toward Virtual Stores
A1: Virtual stores make me feel good
A2: I enjoy buying things through virtual stores

The problem of these approaches is that the data must be transformed, so relevant information may be lost. We propose a more sophisticated process that allows working with the original format without any pre-processing stage: the *multi-item fuzzification*. Thus, a *T-conorm* operator (e.g., maximum), traditionally used in fuzzy logic to develop the union of fuzzy sets, is applied to aggregate the partial information given by each item during the inference process. Since it is not pre-processing data but a component of the machine learning design, the details of that treatment of the items is described in Section 2.4.

Table 2. Example of available data set from four responses about the items shown in Table 2.2

Cases	Convenience Orientation			Risk Averseness		Consumer Attitude	
	C1	C2	C3	R1	R2	A1	A2
Consumer 1	2	3	2	6	7	2	2
Consumer 2	6	6	7	3	2	8	7
Consumer 3	8	8	9	2	3	9	9
Consumer 4	5	5	5	3	3	4	4

2.3 Representation and Inclusion of Expert Knowledge

Several issues should be tackled at this step: the set of variables to be modeled, the transformation of marketing scales used for measuring such variables into fuzzy semantic and the fuzzy rule structure (relations among constructs). We suggest some approaches to fix these components. All of them are based on the marketing expert's capability to express his knowledge in a humanly understandable format by fuzzy logic.

Fuzzy Semantics from Expert Knowledge

Once the marketing modeler has finally determined both, the theoretical constructs and the observed variables associated with each one (i.e. the measurement model), a transformation of the original marketing scales used for measuring those observed variables into linguistic terms should be done. At this point, several marketing scale types can be used for its measurement. With the aim of simplifying the problem, in this paper we focus on Likert-type[3], differential semantic and rating scales, which are the most commonly used in these models. The transformation should be practiced taking into account three main questions:

The *number of linguistic terms* to be used for each variable must be defined. An odd number seems to be a good approach since in our case it is useful to linguistically express the "medium" or "unconcerned" concept. Since traditional interval scales used in marketing usually present between 5 to 9 different degrees (i.e. points of the scale), the use of three or five linguistic terms (fuzzy sets) is enough to map these values.

The *membership function type* defining the behavior of certain fuzzy variables should be also defined. In this sense, such behavior can be broadly

---

[3] A Likert-type measurement scale is a scale usually used in marketing surveys, and in Social Sciences' surveys in general, which takes as a basis the philosophy of the original Likert scale format of 5 points. Specifically, individuals are asked to show their degree of agreement or disagreement on a symmetric agree-disagree scale for certain item.

treated considering the use of linear (trapezoidal or triangular) vs. non linear (Gaussian) membership functions to characterize the fuzzy sets. In this respect, we pose that it is more appropriate to use linear functions, inasmuch as it facilitates the latter interpretation of relations.

The *membership function shapes* should also be fixed. In this respect, we propose to impose some properties in order to ensure good interpretability. Extreme values of the interval should have a membership degree 1 to extreme labels. Mean value of the interval should have membership 1 to medium label. Likewise, we consider strong Ruspini's fuzzy partitions (Ruspini, 1969) – where the sum of the membership degrees of every value to the set of linguistic terms is 1 – in order to ensure good interpretability. Finally, in order to statistically unbias the significance of every linguistic term, we impose the same covering degree. Thus, we define the membership function shapes where, given the set S = {min,...,max} defining the interval, they hold the following condition:

$$\sum_{k \in S} \mu_{A_i}(k) = \frac{\max - \min}{l}, \quad \forall A_i \in A, \tag{1}$$

with l being the number of linguistic terms and $A = \{A_1, \ldots, A_l\}$ the set of them.

To sum up, Figure 2 shows an example based on the transformation of a nine-point rating scale (a typical marketing scale used to measure the observed variables/indicators related to certain construct) into a fuzzy semantic with the three linguistic terms *Low*, *Medium*, and *High*.

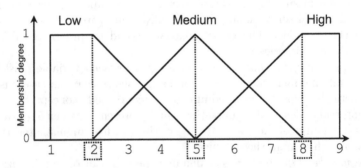

Fig. 2. Fuzzy semantic from a transformation of a 9-point marketing scale (rating scale)

Input/Output Linguistic Variables from Expert Knowledge

Furthermore, once the structure of the model has been fixed by the marketing expert under the base of the theoretic model, fuzzy rules are used to relate input (antecedents) with output (consequents) variables. Obviously, hypotheses contained in the model can be directly used to define IF-THEN structures by considering the dependencies shown among the variables. Thus, we obtain a fuzzy rule base for each consequent (endogenous construct) considered and its respective set of antecedents.

For example, if we take for illustrative purposes the model depicted in Figure 1, the fuzzy rule structure that represents the relations between the elements "Convenience Orientation" and "Risk Averseness" with the consequent "Consumer Attitude" will have the following form:

IF *Convenience Orientation* is A_1 and *Risk Averseness* is A_2 **THEN** *Consumer Attitude* is B

2.4 Data Mining Process

Once the linguistic variables that properly represent the tackled information have been fixed, a machine learning process must be used to automatically extract the knowledge existing in the database. This process is, without any doubt, the most important issue from the KDD point of view.

As mentioned in Section 1, in this paper we are interested in descriptive induction. Therefore, we will use GAs Michigan-style to obtain rules individually relevant. We consider two quality criteria, support (degree of representativity of the rule with respect to the set of data) and confidence (degree of accuracy of the relation shown by the rule). It is intuitive to check that the higher the support, the higher the difficulty to maintain high degrees of confidence. To jointly consider both criteria, we propose the use of *multiobjective GAs*, as they offer good results when working with multiple contradictory objectives. The next section describes the main elements of this method we propose.

Fuzzy Rule Structure

In data mining it is crucial to use a learning process with a high degree of interpretability. To do that, we opt for a compact description based on the disjunctive normal form (DNF). This kind of fuzzy rule structure has the following form:

IF X_1 is $\tilde{A}_1$ and ... and X_n is $\tilde{A}_n$ **THEN** Y_1 is B

where each input variable X_i, $i \in \{1, \ldots, n\}$ takes as a value a set of linguistic terms $\tilde{A}_i = \{A_{i1}$ or ... or $A_{in_i}\}$, whose members are joined by a disjunctive operator. We use the bounded sum min $\{1, a + b\}$ as $T\text{-}conorm^4$. The structure is a natural support to allow the absence of some input variables in each rule, simply making $\tilde{A}_i$ to be the whole set of linguistic terms available.

Multi-item Fuzzification

In order to properly consider the set of indicators available for each input/output variable (as discussed in Section 2.2), we propose an extension of the membership degree computation, the so-called *multi-item fuzzification*. The process is based on a union of the partial information provided by each item. Given X_i and Y_j measured by the vectors of items $\mathbf{x}_i = (x_1^{(i)}, \ldots, x_{h_i}^{(i)}, \ldots, x_{p_i}^{(i)})$ and $\mathbf{y} = (y_1, \ldots, y_t, \ldots, y_q)$, respectively, the fuzzy propositions X_i is $\tilde{A}_i$ and Y is B are respectively interpreted as follows:

$$\mu_{\tilde{A}_i}(\mathbf{x}_i) = \min \left\{ 1, \bigcup_{h_i=1}^{p_i} \sum_{A \in \tilde{A}_i} \mu_A(x_{h_i}^{(i)}) \right\} \tag{2}$$

$$\mu_B(\mathbf{y}) = \bigcup_{t=1}^{q} \mu_B(y_t), \tag{3}$$

with $\cup$ being a T-conorm (the maximum in this paper).

Subgroup Discovery

To do the descriptive rules induction process, we have applied a method with certain similarities to the subgroups discovery technique – widely used in classification learning rules (Lavrac 2004) –, where the property of interest is the class associated with the variables of the consequent. Therefore, we try to group the set of data into differentiated subgroups, including in each of them those examples represented by the consequent with the aim of discovering a representative set of rules for each subgroup. In this regard, the most usual approach is based on running the algorithm designed for each subgroup of data which satisfies the property set for the consequent.

However, instead of this approach, we carry out a simultaneous subgroup discovery in the algorithm we propose. This variant allows us to form niches of fuzzy rules differentiated by the consequent which are optimized in parallel to finally generate a set of suboptimal solutions for each class of the consequent. With the aim of developing this simultaneous process, as it is shown in the next sections, we vary the concept of multiobjective dominance by making the genetic operators act only on the antecedents of the rules.

---

[4] This family of binary operators is used in fuzzy logic to interpret the disjunction 'or'

Coding Scheme

Each individual of the population represents a fuzzy rule; i.e. a Michigan-style genetic algorithm. The coding scheme will be binary to represent the antecedent and whole for the consequent. Thus, the allele "1" in the antecedent part means that the linguistic term related to the gene is used in the corresponding variable. For the consequent, we will directly code the index of the linguistic term used. Hence, the size to code a DNF fuzzy rule is equal to the sum of the number of linguistic terms employed in each input variable (antecedent) plus the number of output variables. For instance, if we had three linguistic terms for each variable, the rule [IF X1 is Small and X2 is {Medium or High} THEN Y is Medium], would be coded as [100 011|2].

Objective Functions

In this algorithm, we consider the two criteria most frequently used to value the quality of the association rules (Dubois *et al.* 2005): support and confidence. However, we adapt the calculus of these criteria to fuzzy association rules, also considering the especial characteristics of the multi-item variables (elements of the model) which we work with.

Support. This objective function values the degree of representation of certain fuzzy rule on the set of data analyzed. It is calculated as the average degree covered by the rule considering every one of these data (individuals' responses). To obtain the degree of cover we conjointly consider the membership degrees in relation to the diverse variables; i.e. the set of antecedents as well as the consequent. The measure of support (for maximization) for a fuzzy rule R comes defined as follows:

$$Support(R) = \frac{1}{N} \sum_{e=1}^{N} T(\mu_A(\mathbf{x}^{(e)}), \mu_B(\mathbf{y}^{(e)})), \qquad (4)$$

where N is the size of the database (the sample size or number of respondents), $\mathbf{x}^{(e)} = (\mathbf{x}_1^{(e)}, \ldots, \mathbf{x}_n^{(e)})$ and $\mathbf{y}^{(e)}$ is the *e*th instance multi-item of input and output respectively, T the *product* T-norm, and

$$\mu_A(\mathbf{x}^{(e)}) = \min_{i \in \{1,\ldots,n\}} \mu_{\tilde{A}_i}(\mathbf{x}_i^{(e)}) \qquad (5)$$

the coverage degree of the antecedent of the rule R for this example (i.e. it is considered the T-norm of the minimum to interpret the connector "and" of the fuzzy rule). Also, it is convenient to point out that we employ the multi-item fuzzification shown in section 2.4 to calculate $\mu_{\tilde{A}_i}(\mathbf{x}_i^{(e)})$ and $\mu_B(\mathbf{y}^{(e)})$.

Confidence. This objective function measures the reliability of the relationship between antecedent and consequent described by the analyzed fuzzy rule. We have used a confidence degree that avoids accumulation of low cardinalities (Dubois *et al.* 2005). It is computed (for maximizing) as follows:

$$Confidence(R) = \frac{\sum_{e=1}^{N} T(\mu_A(\mathbf{x}^{(e)}), I(\mu_A(\mathbf{x}^{(e)}), \mu_B(\mathbf{y}^{(e)})))}{\sum_{e=1}^{N} \mu_A(\mathbf{x}^{(e)})}, \qquad (6)$$

The Dienes' S-implication $I(a, b) = \max\{1 - a, b\}$ is used. We consider again T-norm of product and multi-fuzzification.

Evolutionary Scheme

A generational approach with the multi-objective NSGA-II replacement strategy (Deb et al. 2002) is adopted. Crowding distance in the objective function space is used. Binary tournament selection based on the nondomination rank (or the crowding distance when both solutions belong to the same front) is applied.

To correctly develop the simultaneous subgroup discovery we will need to redefine the concept of dominance. In order to do this, one solution (rule) will dominate another when, besides being better or equal in all the objectives and better in at least one of them, it presents the same consequent as the other rule. Hence, those rules with different consequents do not dominate each other. Consequently, we force the algorithm to form so many niches of search (Pareto sets) as diverse consequents (subgroups) are considered.

Genetic Operators

The initial population is built defining so many groups (equal in size) as there are different consequents. In each of them, chromosomes are generated fixing such consequents and randomly building a simple antecedent where each input variable is related to a linguistic term. The two operators of reproduction only act in the part of the antecedent of the rule. This fact ensures that the size of every subgroup in the population is constant. In this way, we allow the algorithm to independently explore, but simultaneously, each group.

We employ a multipoint crossover operator which selects two crossover points (in the part of the antecedent) and interchanges the central sub-chain. The operator of mutation randomly selects a variable of the antecedent of the fuzzy rule coded in the chromosome and carries out some of the three following operations: *expansion*, which flips to 1 a gene of the selected variable; *contraction*, which flips to 0 a gene of the selected variable; or *shift*, which flips to 0 a gene of the variable and flips to 1 the gene immediately before or after it. The selection of one of these mechanisms is made randomly among the available choices (e.g., contraction cannot be applied if only a gene of the selected variable has the allele 1).

3 Experimental Results and Knowledge Interpretation

The experimentation of the descriptive rule induction method we present has been made based on a causal model already proposed by Novak et al. (2000). It analyzes the consumer's flow state in interactive computer-mediated environments. As the authors allow the use of their database for academic purposes, we have opted for experimenting our methodology with a consumer model already validated and widely known by the academics. This is a plausible and orthodox alternative, as we can see by analyzing other research previously developed (see, as e.g.: Beynon *et al.* 2001; Fish *et al.* 2004; Hurtley *et al.* 1995; Levy and Yoon 1995; Rhim and Cooper 2005).

3.1 Some Theoretical Notes about the Model Used for the Experimentation

In order to briefly introduce this concept, so the reader better understands the variable we want to explain in this empirical application of our methodology, we now synthetically present some ideas about it. *Flow* has been recently imported from motivational psychology and successfully adapted to explain consumer behavior phenomena on the Web (Hoffman and Novak 1996; Korzan 2003; Luna *et al.* 2002; Novak *et al.* 2000; Novak *et al.* 2003). In general terms, *flow* state is defined as "the process of optimal experience" or the mental state that individuals sometimes experience when they are deeply immersed in certain events, objects or activities (Csikszentmihalyi 1975, 1977). This concept has been adapted to the Web environment. In this context, *flow* state is achieved when the consumer is so deeply involved in the process of navigation on the Web that "nothing else seems to matter" (Hoffman and Novak 1996, p. 57).

Though the model we consider for the experimentation has 12 elements (constructs) interconnected, with 6 fuzzy rule based systems, due to the space constraints, in this paper we focus on that system which considers the four primary antecedents of the consumer's *flow*. Specifically, we consider the following four constructs, as antecedents of the consumer's flow state (consequent):

- *speed of interaction* refers to the user's perception about how quick is the process of interaction when using the Web
- *skill/control* gathers the consumer's opinion regarding his own capacity to develop successful navigating process on the Web
- *challenge/arousal* gathers how challenging and stimulating is surfing the Web
- *telepresence/time distortion* is also a compound construct which refers to the consumer's perception about the predominance of the computer virtual (Web) environment over the physical environment where the consumer is placed when surfing the Web, as well as to the lost of the consumer's self consciousness on the notion of time when developing such process of navigation.

Novak *et al.* (2000) hypothesized that these four elements are positively related to this central construct of the model.

All these constructs were gathered by multi-item Likert-type scales with 9 points; i.e. metric scales. The fuzzy semantic we have applied to all the variables is shown in Figure 2.

Training data are composed of 1,154 examples (consumers' responses). We have run the algorithm 10 times, obtaining the following values for the parameters: 300 generations, size of the population 100, crossover probability 0.7 and the probability of mutation per chromosome 0.1.

3.2 Analysis of the Pareto Front

The Pareto front we have obtained is shown in Figure 3. With respect to the value taken by the consequent *flow* in the rules generated, it can be easily observed that the most plausible output is "medium." Indeed, there is a clear supremacy of the rules with this label in the consequent over the two other outputs in terms of support and confidence. This fact is intensified as the support of the rules grows, without noticing a relevant loss of reliability in the rules which represent medium *flow* states. Therefore, it can be inferred that the most representative state of *flow*, for the whole consumers' database, is moderate.

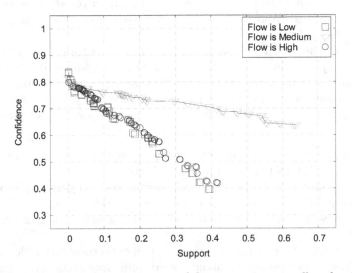

Fig. 3. Sub-Pareto fronts for every output of the consequent, as well as the absolute Pareto front (the best rules from the whole set of rules) joined by a line.

3.3 Illustrative Analysis of the Rules

An individual analysis of the rules generated by this descriptive method is very useful to better understand the consumer behavior being analyzed. Specifically, it is recommendable to do a selection of rules from the whole set compounding the absolute Pareto front, paying attention to its support (degree of representativity of the consumers' database) and, especially, to its confidence (degree of reliability of the information pattern shown by the rule). In this regard, we have done an illustrative selection shown in Table 3.3.

Table 3. Illustrative selection of rules from the absolute Pareto front. L stands for Low, M stands for medium, H stands for high.

	Speed of Interaction		Skill/Control		Challenge/Arousal		Telepresence/Time Distort.		Flow	Sup	Conf
R_1	L	H	M				L		L	0.0104	0.7980
R_2		M	L	H		H	M		M	0.0102	0.7937
R_3		M					M	H	M	0.3947	0.7051

Considering the absolute Pareto front, R_1 is the rule with highest confidence, associated with low states of *flow*. Likewise, R_2 represents the most reliable rule from those with moderate *flow* states. Finally, we have also considered the rule R_3, being the one with highest support among the whole set of rules with confidence higher than 0.7; i.e. the confidence threshold value we have set to give reliability to the information patterns shown by the rules.

Synthetically, from the four antecedents considered, it highlights the influence of the perception about *telepresence/time distortion* (TP/TD) in determining consumers' states of *flow*; it can be observed how its value is determinant in explaining low (R_1) or moderate (R_2 and R_3) states of *flow*. Likewise, the rest of the antecedents seem to exert a poor or null influence on the consequent. This fact can also be due to the element TP/TD that eclipses the influence of the rest. In any case, it conforms to the main idea we extracted when the Pareto front was analyzed; i.e. a non existence of combinations of antecedents (rules) producing high states of *flow*, with significant levels of reliability and representativity. In this sense, it is quite illustrative to see how even when the most influential antecedent – i.e. TP/TD – takes high values, the consumer's *flow* state in the process of navigation tends to remain moderate.

4 Concluding Remarks

We have faced an interesting problem of KDD in relation to marketing causal modeling and its resolution by genetic fuzzy systems. The problem presents a specific type of data with uncertainty which justifies the use of fuzzy rules. Furthermore, we have practiced a multi-objective optimization in order to obtain rules with high degrees of support and confidence. The KDD methodology proposed has been successfully applied to a real problem of consumer behavior in online environments.

In our research agenda, we have the use of other metrics such as consistency and interest of the rules. Also, the unsupervised learning of fuzzy association rules, i.e. without using any antecedent or consequent previously fixed by the marketing expert.

Acknowledgements

Research supported in part by the Spanish Ministry of Education and Science under project no. TIN2005-08386-C05-01

References

Beynon M, Curry B, Morgan P. (2001) Knowledge discovery in marketing. An approach through rough set theory. European Journal of Marketing 35(7/8): 915–935.

Casillas J, Martínez-López FJ, Martínez FJ (2004) Fuzzy association rules for estimating consumer behaviour models and their application to explaining trust in Internet shopping. Fuzzy Economic Review IX(2): 3–26.

Csikszentmihalyi M (1975) Play and intrinsic rewards. Journal of Humanistic Psychology 15(3): 41–63.

Csikszentmihalyi M (1977) Beyond boredom and anxiety (Second edition). San Francisco: Jossey-Bass.

Deb K, Pratap A, Agarwal S, Meyarevian T (2002) A fast and elitist multiobjective genetic algorithm: NSGA-II. IEEE Transactions on Evolutionary Computation 6(2): 182–197.

Dubois D, Prade H, Sudkamp T (2005) On the representation, measurement, and discovery of fuzzy associations. IEEE Transactions on Fuzzy Systems 13(2): 250–262.

Fish KE, Johnson JD, Dorsey RE, Blodgett JG (2004) Using an artificial neural network trained with a genetic algorithm to model brand share. Journal of Business Research 57 (1): 79–85.

Gatignon H (2000) Commentary on Peter Leeflang and Dick Wittink's "Building models form marketing decisions: past, present and future". International Journal of Research in Marketing 17: 209–214.

Hoffman D, Novak T (1996) Marketing in hypermedia computer-mediated environments: conceptual foundations Journal of Marketing 60 (July): 50–68.

Hurley S, Moutinho L, Stephens NM (1995) Solving marketing optimization problems using genetic algorithms. European Journal of Marketing 29 (4): 39–56.

Korzaan ML (2003) Going with the flow: predicting online purchase intentions. Journal of Computer Information Systems (Summer): 25–31.

Lavrac N, Cestnik B, Gamberger D, Flach P (2004) Decision support through sub-group discovery: three case studies and the lessons learned. Machine Learning 57 (1–2): 115–143.

Lee, B.C.Y. (2007) Consumer attitude toward virtual stores and its correlates: Journal of Retailing and Consumer Services 14(3): 182-191.

Levy JB, Yoon E (1995) Modeling global market entry decision by fuzzy logic with an application to country risk assessment. European Journal of Operational Research 82: 53–78.

Luna D, Peracchio LA, De Juan MD (2002) Cross-cultural and cognitive aspects of Web site navigation. Journal of the Academy of Marketing Science 30(4): 397–410.

Novak T, Hoffman D, Duhachek A (2003) The influence of goal-directed and experiential activities on online flow experiences. Journal of Consumer Psychology 13 (1/2): 3–16.

Novak T, Hoffman D, Yung Y (2000) Measuring the customer experience in online environments: A structural modeling approach. Marketing Science 19 (1): 22–42.

Rhim H, Cooper LG (2005) Assessing potential threats to incumbent brands: New product positioning under price competition in a multisegmented market. International Journal of Research in Marketing 22: 159–182.

Ruspini E (1969) A new approach to clustering, Information and Control 15: 22-32.

Shim JP, Warkentin M, Courtney JF, Power, DJ, Sharda R, Carlsson C (2002) Past, present and future of decision support technology. Decision Support Systems 33: 111–126.

Steenkamp J, Baumgartner H (2000) On the use of structural equation models for marketing modeling. International Journal of Research in Marketing 17: 195–202.

Wedel M, Kamakura W. Böckenholt U (2000) Marketing data, models and decisions. International Journal of Research in Marketing 17: 203–208.

Knowledge Discovery in a Framework for Modelling with Words

Zengchang Qin[1] and Jonathan Lawry[2]

[1] Berkeley Initiative in Soft Computing (BISC), Computer Science Division, EECS Department, University of California, Berkeley, CA 94720, US.
zqin@eecs.berkeley.edu
[2] Artificial Intelligence Group, Department of Engineering Mathematics, University of Bristol, BS8 1TR, UK.
j.lawry@bris.ac.uk

Summary. The learning of transparent models is an important and neglected area of data mining. The data mining community has tended to focus on algorithm accuracy with little emphasis on the knowledge representation framework. However, the transparency of a model will help practitioners greatly in understanding the trends and idea hidden behind the system. In this chapter, a random set based knowledge representation framework for learning linguistic models is introduced. This framework is referred to as label semantics and a number of data mining algorithms are proposed. In this framework, a vague concept is modelled by a probability distribution over a set of appropriate fuzzy labels which is called as mass assignment. The idea of mass assignment provides a probabilistic approach for modelling uncertainty based on pre-defined fuzzy labels.

1 Introduction

Fuzzy Logic was first proposed by Zadeh (Zadeh, 1965) as an extension of traditional binary logic. In contrast to a classical set, which has a crisp boundary, the boundary of a fuzzy set is blurred and the transition is characterized by *membership functions*. In early research fuzzy logic was successfully applied in control systems and expert systems where the linguistic interpretation fuzzy sets allowed for an interface between the human user and a computer system. Because our language is fuzzy, the concepts represented by language is full of uncertainty and impreciseness. Therefore, fuzzy sets can be used to model language. This idea also motivates related research into Computing with Words (Zadeh, 1996) and Perception-based Reasoning (Zadeh, 2002).

Almost all the labels we give to characterize a group of objects are fuzzy. Given a fuzzy set, an object may belong to this set with a certain *membership value*. In traditional set theory, this membership value only has two possible values, 1 and 0, representing the case where the object belongs to or does not belong to the set, respectively. In a fuzzy set, the membership values are continuous real values from 0 to 1. We use a fuzzy term such as 'big' to label a particular group, because they share the property of objects within this group (i.e., they are big). The objects within this group will have different membership values varying from 0 to 1 qualifying the degree to which they satisfy the concept 'big'. An object with membership of 0.8 is more likely to be described as 'big' than an object with membership of 0.4. If we consider this problem in another way. Given an object, label 'big' can be used to describe this object with some appropriateness degrees. Follow this idea, we discuss a new approach based on random set theory to interpret imprecise concepts. This framework, first proposed by Lawry (Lawry, 2001) and is referred to as *Label Semantics*, can be regarded as an approach to Modelling with Words (Lawry *et al.*, 2003).

Modeling with Words is a new research area which emphasis "modelling" rather than "computing". For example, Zadeh's theories on Perception-based Computing (Zadeh, 2002) and Precisiated Natural Language (Zadeh, 2005) are the approaches of "computing". However, the relation between it and Computing with Words (Zadeh, 1996) is close is likely to become even closer (Zadeh, 2003). Both of the research areas are aimed at enlarging the role of natural languages in scientific theories, especially, in knowledge management, decision and control. In this chapter, the framework is mainly used for modelling and building intelligent machine learning and data mining systems. In such systems, we use words or fuzzy labels for modelling uncertainty. Therefore, the research presented here is considered as a framework for modelling with words.

This chapter is organized as follows: A systematic introduction on label semantics is given in the first section. Based on the framework we introduced, we will give the details of several data mining models based on label semantics: Linguistic Decision Trees in section 3, Label semantics based Bayesian estimation in section 4, and Linguistic Rule Induction in section 5. Finally, we give the summary and discussions in the final section.

2 Label Semantics

Vague or imprecise concepts are fundamental to natural language. Human beings are constantly using imprecise language to communicate each other. We usually say 'Peter is tall and strong' but not 'Peter is exactly 1.85 meters in height and he can lift 100kg weights'. We will focus on developing an understanding of how an intelligent agent can use vague concepts to convey information and meaning as part of a general strategy for practical reasoning and decision making. Such an agent can could be an artificial intelligence program or a human, but the implicit assumption is that their use of vague concepts is governed by some underlying internally consistent strategy or algorithm. We may notice that *labels* are used in natural language to describe what we see, hear and feel. Such labels may have different degrees of vagueness (i.e., when we say Peter is *young* and he is *male*, the label *young* is more vague than the label *male* because people may have more widely different opinions on being *young* than being *male*. For a particular concept, there could be more than one label that is appropriate for describing this concept, and some labels could be more appropriate than others. Here, we will use a random set framework to interpret these facts. *Label Semantics*, proposed by Lawry (Lawry, 2001), is a framework for modelling with linguistic expressions, or labels such as *small, medium* and *large*. Such labels are defined by overlapping fuzzy sets which are used to cover the universe of continuous variables.

2.1 Mass Assignment on Fuzzy Labels

For a variable x into a domain of discourse Ω we identify a finite set of linguistic labels $\mathcal{L} = \{L_1, \cdots, L_n\}$ with which to label the values of x. Then for a specific value $x \in \Omega$ an individual I identifies a subset of $\mathcal{L}$, denoted D_x^I to stand for the description of x given by I, as the set of labels with which it is appropriate to label x. The underlying question posed by label semantics is how to use linguistic expressions to label numerical values. If we allow I to vary across a population V with prior distribution P_V, then D_x^I will also vary and generate a random set denoted D_x into the power set of $\mathcal{L}$ denoted by S. We can view the random set D_x as a description of the variable x in terms of the labels in $\mathcal{L}$. The frequency of occurrence of a particular label, say S, for D_x across the population then gives a distribution on D_x referred to as a mass assignment on labels. More formally,

Definition 1 (*Label Description*) *For $x \in \Omega$ the label description of x is a random set from V into the power set of $\mathcal{L}$, denoted D_x, with associated distribution m_x, which is referred to as mass assignment:*

$$\forall S \subseteq \mathcal{L}, \quad m_x(S) = P_V(\{I \in V | D_x^I = S\}) \tag{1}$$

where P_V is the prior distribution of population V. $m_x(S)$ is called the mass associated with a set of labels S and

$$\sum_{S \subseteq \mathcal{L}} m_x(S) = 1 \tag{2}$$

Intuitively mass assignment is a distribution on appropriate label sets and $m_x(S)$ quantifies the evidence that S is the set of appropriate labels for x.

For example, given a set of labels defined on the temperature outside: $\mathcal{L}_{Temp} = \{low, medium, high\}$. Suppose 3 of 10 people agree that '*medium* is the only appropriate label for the temperature of $15°$ and 7 agree 'both *low* and *medium* are appropriate labels'. According to def. 1,

$$m_{15}(medium) = 0.3 \ and \ m_{15}(low, medium) = 0.7$$

so that the mass assignment for $15°$ is $m_{15} = \{medium\} : 0.3, \{low, medium\}:$ 0.7. More details about the theory of mass assignment can be found in (Baldwin *et al.*, 1995).

2.2 Appropriateness Degrees

Consider the previous example, can we know how appropriate for a single label, say *low*, to describe $15°$? In this framework, *appropriateness degrees* are used to evaluate how appropriate a label is for describing a particular value of variable x. Simply, given a particular value α of variable x, the appropriateness degree for labeling this value with the label L, which is defined by fuzzy set F, is the membership value of α in F. The reason we use the new term 'appropriateness degrees' is partly because it more accurately reflects the underlying semantics and partly to highlight the quite distinct calculus based on this framework (Lawry, 2001). This definition provides a relationship between mass assignments and appropriateness degrees.

Definition 2 (*Appropriateness Degrees*)

$$\forall x \in \Omega, \ \forall L \in \mathcal{L} \quad \mu_L(x) = \sum_{S \subseteq \mathcal{L}: L \in S} m_x(S)$$

Consider the previous example, we then can obtain $\mu_{medium}(15) = 0.7 + 0.3 = 1$, $\mu_{low}(15) = 0.7$. It is also important to note that, given definitions for the appropriateness degrees on labels, we can isolate a set of subsets of $\mathcal{L}$ with non-zero masses. These are referred to as *focal sets* and the appropriate labels with non-zero masses as *focal elements*, more formally,

Definition 3 (*Focal Set*) *The focal set of $\mathcal{L}$ is a set of focal elements defined as:*

$$\mathcal{F} = \{S \subseteq \mathcal{L} | \exists x \in \Omega, m_x(S) > 0\}$$

Given a particular universe, we can then always find the unique and consistent translation from a given data element to a mass assignment on focal elements, specified by the function $\mu_L : L \in \mathcal{L}$.

2.3 Linguistic Translation

Based on the underlying semantics, we can translate a set of numerical data into a set of mass assignments on appropriate labels based on the reverse of definition 2 under the following assumptions: consonance mapping, full fuzzy covering and 50% overlapping (Qin and Lawry, 2005b). Consonance assumption implies that voters are agreed with the natural order of fuzzy labels. A voter won't set 'small' and 'large' as appropriate labels without 'medium'. These assumptions are fully described in (Qin and Lawry, 2005b) and justified in (Lawry, 2004). These assumptions guarantee that there is unique mapping from appropriate degrees to mass assignments on labels. For example, Figure 1 shows the universes of two variables x_1 and x_2 which are fully covered by 3 fuzzy sets with 50% overlap, respectively. For x_1, the following focal elements occur:

$$\mathcal{F}_1 = \{\{small_1\}, \{small_1, medium_1\}, \{medium_1\}, \{medium_1, large_1\}, \{large_1\}\}$$

Since $small_1$ and $large_1$ do not overlap, the set $\{small_1, large_1\}$ cannot occur as a focal element according to def. 3. We can always find a unique translation from a given data point to a mass assignment on focal elements, as specified by the function μ_L. Given a particular data element, the sum of associated mass is 1. This is referred to as *linguistic translation*. Suppose we are given a numerical data set $\mathcal{D} = \{\langle x_1(i), \ldots, x_n(i)\rangle | i = 1, \ldots, N\}$ and focal set on attribute j: $\mathcal{F}_j = \{F_j^1, \ldots, F_j^{h_j} | j = 1, \ldots, n\}$, we can obtain the following new data base by applying linguistic translation described in Algorithm 1.

Algorithm 1: Linguistic translation

    input   : Given a database $\mathcal{D} = \{\langle x_1(i), \cdots, x_n(i)\rangle | i = 1, \cdots, |\mathcal{D}|\}$ with associated classes $\mathcal{C} = \{C_1, \cdots, C_{|\mathcal{C}|}\}$
    output: Linguistic dataset $\mathcal{LD}$

1 **for** $j \leftarrow 1$ **to** n **do**
2   **foreach** x_j **do** : Cover the universe of x_j with N_F trapezoidal fuzzy sets with 50% overlap.
3   **for** $i \leftarrow 1$ **to** $|\mathcal{D}|$ **do**
4   **foreach** *Data element* $x_j(i)$ **do**
5   Read appropriateness degrees for $x_j(i)$ from corresponding fuzzy set.
6   Calculating corresponding mass assignments:
        $\mathcal{LD}_{i,j} = \langle m_{x(i)}(F_j^1), \cdots, m_{x(i)}(F_j^{h_j})\rangle$ on focal elements from appropriateness degrees.

7 Save dataset $\mathcal{LD}$ where $\mathcal{LD} = \{\mathcal{LD}_{i,j} | i = 1, \cdots, |\mathcal{D}|, j = 1, \cdots, n\}$

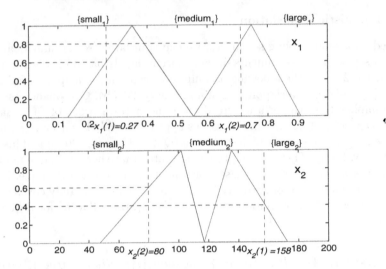

Fig. 1. A full fuzzy covering (discretization) using three fuzzy sets with 50% overlap on two attributes x_1 and x_2, respectively.

For a particular attribute with an associated focal set, linguistic translation is a process of replacing its data elements with the focal element masses of these data elements. See figure 1. $\mu_{small_1}(x_1(1) = 0.27) = 1$, $\mu_{medium_1}(0.27) = 0.6$ and $\mu_{large_1}(0.27) = 0$. They are simply the memberships read from the fuzzy sets. We then can obtain the mass assignment of this data element according to def. 2 under the consonance assumption (Qin and Lawry, 2005b): $m_{0.27}(small_1) = 0.4$, $m_{0.27}(small_1, medium_1) = 0.6$. Similarly, the linguistic translations for two data:

$$\mathbf{x}_1 = \langle x_1(1) = 0.27 \rangle, \langle x_2(1) = 158 \rangle$$

$$\mathbf{x}_2 = \langle x_1(2) = 0.7 \rangle, \langle x_2(2) = 80 \rangle$$

are illustrated on each attribute independently as follows:

$$\begin{bmatrix} x_1 \\ \hline x_1(1) = 0.27 \\ x_1(2) = 0.7 \end{bmatrix} \overset{LT}{\rightarrow} \begin{bmatrix} m_x(\{s_1\}) & m_x(\{s_1, m_1\}) & m_x(\{m_1\}) & m_x(\{m_1, l_1\}) & m_x(\{l_1\}) \\ \hline 0.4 & 0.6 & 0 & 0 & 0 \\ 0 & 0 & 0.2 & 0.8 & 0 \end{bmatrix}$$

$$\begin{bmatrix} x_2 \\ \hline x_2(1) = 158 \\ x_2(2) = 80 \end{bmatrix} \overset{LT}{\rightarrow} \begin{bmatrix} m_x(\{s_2\}) & m_x(\{s_2, m_2\}) & m_x(\{m_2\}) & m_x(\{m_2, l_2\}) & m_x(\{l_2\}) \\ \hline 0 & 0 & 0 & 0.4 & 0.6 \\ 0.4 & 0.6 & 0 & 0 & 0 \end{bmatrix}$$

Therefore, we can obtain:

$$\mathbf{x}_1 \rightarrow \langle \{s_1\} : 0.4, \{s_1, m_1\} : 0.6 \rangle, \langle \{m_2, l_2\} : 0.4, \{l_2\} : 0.6 \rangle$$

$$\mathbf{x}_2 \rightarrow \langle \{m_1\} : 0.2, \{m_1, l_1\} : 0.8 \rangle, \langle \{s_2\} : 0.4, \{s_2, m_2\} : 0.6 \rangle$$

We may notice that the new mass assignment based data generated by linguistic translation is depending on the way of universe discretization. Different discretizations may result in different data. Since we will use the new data for training data mining models in the following sections. We hope our data could be as discriminate as possible. A few empirical experiments have been done in (Qin and Lawry, 2005b) and the percentile-based (or equal point) discretization is a fairly good method where each fuzzy label covers approximately the same number of data points. In this chapter, unless otherwise stated, we will use this method for discretizing the continuous universe.

2.4 Linguistic Reasoning

As a high-level knowledge representation language for modelling vague concepts, label semantics allows linguistic reasoning. Given a universe of discourse Ω containing a set of objects or instances to be described, it is assumed that all relevant expressions can be generated recursively from a finite set of basic labels $\mathcal{L} = \{L_1, \ldots, L_n\}$. Operators for combining expressions are restricted to the standard logical connectives of negation "$\neg$", conjunction "$\wedge$", disjunction "$\vee$" and implication "$\rightarrow$". Hence, the set of logical expressions of labels can be formally defined as follows:

Definition 4 (*Logical Expressions of Labels*) *The set of logical expressions, LE, is defined recursively as follows:*

(i) $L_i \in LE$ *for* $i = 1, \ldots, n.$
(ii) If $\theta, \varphi \in LE$ *then* $\neg \theta, \theta \wedge \varphi, \theta \vee \varphi, \theta \rightarrow \varphi \in LE$

Basically, we interpret the main logical connectives as follows: $\neg L$ means that L is not an appropriate label, $L_1 \wedge L_2$ means that both L_1 and L_2 are appropriate labels, $L_1 \vee L_2$ means that either L_1 or L_2 are appropriate labels, and $L_1 \rightarrow L_2$ means that L_2 is an appropriate label whenever L_1 is. As well as labels for a single variable, we may want to evaluate the appropriateness degrees of a complex logical expression $\theta \in LE$. Consider the set of logical expressions LE obtained by recursive application of the standard logical connectives in $\mathcal{L}$. In order to evaluate the appropriateness degrees of such expressions we must identify what information they provide regarding the the appropriateness of labels. In general, for any label expression θ we should be able to identify a maximal set of label sets, $\lambda(\theta)$ that are consistent with θ so that the meaning of θ can be interpreted as the constraint $D_x \in \lambda(\theta)$.

Definition 5 (*λ-function*) *Let* θ *and* φ *be expressions generated by recursive application of the connectives* $\neg, \vee, \wedge$ *and* $\rightarrow$ *to the elements of* $\mathcal{L}$ *(i.e.*

$\theta, \varphi \in LE$). Then the set of possible label sets defined by a linguistic expression can be determined recursively as follows:

(i) $\lambda(L_i) = \{S \subseteq \mathcal{F} | \{L_i\} \subseteq S\}$
(ii) $\lambda(\neg\theta) = \overline{\lambda(\theta)}$
(iii) $\lambda(\theta \wedge \varphi) = \lambda(\theta) \cap \lambda(\varphi)$
(iv) $\lambda(\theta \vee \varphi) = \lambda(\theta) \cup \lambda(\varphi)$
(v) $\lambda(\theta \rightarrow \varphi) = \overline{\lambda(\theta)} \cup \lambda(\varphi)$

It should also be noted that the λ-function provides us with notion of logical equivalence '$\equiv_L$' for label expressions

$$\theta \equiv_L \varphi \Longleftrightarrow \lambda(\theta) = \lambda(\varphi)$$

Basically, the λ-function provides a way of transferring logical expressions of labels (or linguistic rules) to random set descriptions of labels (i.e. focal elements). $\lambda(\theta)$ corresponds to those subsets of $\mathcal{F}$ identified as being possible values of D_x by expression θ. In this sense the imprecise linguistic restriction 'x is θ' on x corresponds to the strict constraint $D_x \in \lambda(\theta)$ on D_x. Hence, we can view label descriptions as an alternative to linguistic variables as a means of encoding linguistic constraints.

2.5 High Level Label Description

In this section, we will consider how to use a high level fuzzy label to describe another fuzzy label. Here the term *high level* does not mean a hierarhial structure. We will actually consider two set of fuzzy labels which are independently defined on the same universe. If the cardinality of a set of labels $\mathcal{L}$ is denoted by $|\mathcal{L}|$. We then can say $\mathcal{L}_1$ higher level labels of $\mathcal{L}_2$ if $\mathcal{L}_1 < \mathcal{L}_2$. We will acutally consider the methodology of using one set of fuzzy labels to represent the other set of fuzzy labels.

For example, a fuzzy concept *about_m* is defined by an interval on [a, b] (see the left-hand side figure of fig. 2), so that the appropriateness degree of using fuzzy label *small* to label *about_m* is:

$$\mu_{small}(about\_m) = \frac{1}{b-a} \int_a^b \mu_{small}(u) du \qquad (3)$$

If the vagueness of the concept *about_m* depends on the interval denoted by δ where the length of the interval $|\delta| = b - a$. We then can obtain:

$$\mu_{small}(about\_m) = \frac{1}{|\delta|} \int_{u \in \delta} \mu_{small}(u) du \qquad (4)$$

If *about_m* is defined by other fuzzy labels rather than an interval, for example, a triangular fuzzy set (e.g., the right-hand side figure of fig. 2). How can we define the appropriateness degrees?

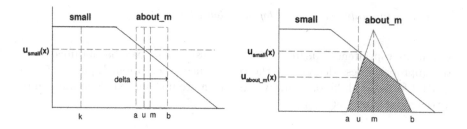

Fig. 2. The appropriateness degree of using *small* to label vague concept *about_m* is defined by the ratio of the area covered by both labels to the area covered by *about_m* only.

We begin by considering a data element $x \in [a, b]$, the function $\mu_{about\_m}(x)$ represents the degree of x belonging to the fuzzy label F. Function $\mu_{small}(x)$ defines the appropriateness degrees of using label *small* to describe x [3]. We essentially hope to obtain the appropriateness degrees of using *small* to label *about_m*. We then consider the each elements belonging to *about_m*. If $\mu_{about\_m}(x) = 1$, which means x is absolutely belonging to *about_m*, then the appropriateness degree is just $\mu_{small}(x)$. However, if $\mu_{about\_m} < \mu_{small}(x)$, we can only say it is belonging to *about_m* in certain degrees. Logically, fuzzy operation AND is used, and in practical calculation, the $\min(\cdot)$ function is employed. The appropriateness is then defined by:

$$\mu_{small}(about\_m) = \frac{\int_{u \in \delta} \min(\mu_{small}(u), \mu_{about\_m}(u)) du}{\int_{u' \in \delta} \mu_{about\_m}(u') du'} \tag{5}$$

where function $\min(x, y)$ returns the minimum value between x and y. Equation 4 is a special case of equation 5 where the following equations always hold:

$$\mu_{small}(u) = \min(\mu_{small}(u), \mu_{about\_m}(u))$$

$$|\delta| = \int_{u \in \delta} \mu_{about\_m}(u) du$$

Definition 6 *Given a vague concept (or a fuzzy label) F and a set of labels $\mathcal{L} = \{L_1, \ldots, L_m\}$ defined on a continuous universe Ω. The appropriateness degrees of using label L ($L \in \mathcal{L}$) to describe F is:*

---

[3] Here we interpret $\mu(\cdot)$ in different manners: membership function and appropriateness degrees, though they are mathematically the same.

$$\mu_L(F) = \frac{\int_{u \in \delta} \min(\mu_L(u), \mu_F(u)) du}{\int_{u' \in \delta} \mu_F(u') du'} \quad (6)$$

where δ is the universe covered by fuzzy label F.

Given appropriateness degrees, the mass assignment can be obtained from the appropriateness degrees by the consonance assumption. Equation 5 is a general form for all kinds of fuzzy sets which are not limited to an interval or a triangular fuzzy sets.

3 Linguistic Decision Tree

Tree induction learning models have received a great deal of attention over recent years in the fields of machine learning and data mining because of their simplicity and effectiveness. Among them, the ID3 (Quinlan, 1986) algorithm for decision trees induction has proved to be an effective and popular algorithm for building decision trees from discrete valued data sets. The C4.5 (Quinlan, 1990) algorithm was proposed as a successor to ID3 in which an entropy based approach to crisp partitioning of continuous universes was adopted. One inherent disadvantage of crisp partitioning is that it tends to make the induced decision trees sensitive to noise. This noise is not only due to the lack of precision or errors in measured features but is often present in the model itself since the available features may not be sufficient to provide a complete model of the system. For each attribute, disjoint classes are separated with clearly defined boundaries. These boundaries are 'critical' since a small change close to these points will probably cause a complete change in classification. Due to the existence of uncertainty and imprecise information in real-world problems, the class boundaries may not be defined clearly. In this case, decision trees may produce high misclassification rates in testing even if they perform well in training. To overcome this problems, many fuzzy decision tree models have been proposed (Baldwin *et al.*, 1997, Janikow, 1998, Olaru and Wehenkel, 2003, Peng and Flach, 2001).

Linguistic decision tree (LDT) (Qin and Lawry, 2005b) is a tree-structured classification model based on label semantics. The information heuristics used for building the tree are modified from Quinlan's ID3 (Quinlan, 1986) in accordance with label semantics. Given a database of which each instance is labeled by one of the classes: $\{C_1, \cdots, C_M\}$. A linguistic decision tree with S consisting branches built from this database can be defined as follows:

$$T = \{\langle B_1, P(C_1|B_1), \cdots, P(C_M|B_1)\rangle, \cdots \langle B_S, P(C_1|B_S), \cdots, P(C_M|B_S)\rangle\}$$

where $P(C_k|B)$ is the probability of class C_k given a branch B. A branch B with d nodes (i.e., the length of B is d) is defined as: $B = \langle F_1, \cdots, F_d \rangle$, where

$d \leq n$ and $F_j \in \mathcal{F}_j$ is one of the focal elements of attribute j. For example, consider the branch: $\langle\langle\{small_1\}, \{medium_2, large_2\}\rangle, 0.3, 0.7\rangle$. This means the probability of class C_1 is 0.3 and C_2 is 0.7 given attribute 1 can only be described as *small* and attribute 2 can be described as both *medium* and *large*.

These class probabilities are estimated from a training set $\mathcal{D} = \{\mathbf{x}_1, \cdots, \mathbf{x}_N\}$ where each instance $\mathbf{x}$ has n attributes: $\langle x_1, \cdots, x_n \rangle$. We now describe how the relevant branch probabilities for a LDT can be evaluated from a database. The probability of class C_k $(k = 1, \cdots, M)$ given B can then be evaluated as follows. First, we consider the probability of a branch B given $\mathbf{x}$:

$$P(B|\mathbf{x}) = \prod_{j=1}^{d} m_{x_j}(F_j) \tag{7}$$

where $m_{x_j}(F_j)$ for $j = 1, \cdots, d$ are mass assignments of single data element x_j. For example, suppose we are given a branch $B = \langle\{small_1\}, \{medium_2, large_2\}\rangle$ and data $\mathbf{x} = \langle 0.27, 158 \rangle$ (the linguistic translation of $\mathbf{x}_1$ was given in section 2.3). According to eq. 7:

$$P(B|\mathbf{x}) = m_{x_1}(\{small_1\}) \times m_{x_2}(\{medium_2, large_2\}) = 0.4 \times 0.4 = 0.16$$

The probability of class C_k given B can then be evaluated by:

$$P(C_k|B) = \frac{\sum_{i \in \mathcal{D}_k} P(B|\mathbf{x}_i)}{\sum_{i \in \mathcal{D}} P(B|\mathbf{x}_i)} \tag{8}$$

where $\mathcal{D}_k$ is the subset consisting of instances which belong to class k. In the case where the denominator is equals to 0, which may occur when the training database for the LDT is small, then there is no non-zero linguistic data covered by the branch. In this case, we obtain no information from the database so that equal probabilities are assigned to each class. $P(C_k|B) = \frac{1}{M}$ for $k = 1, \cdots, M$. In the case that a data element appears beyond the range of training data set, we then assign the appropriateness degrees of the minimum or maximum values of the universe to the data element depending on which side of the range it appears.

According to the Jeffrey's rule (Jeffrey, 1965) the probabilities of class C_k given a LDT with S branches are evaluated as follows:

$$P(C_k|\mathbf{x}) = \sum_{s=1}^{S} P(C_k|B_s)P(B_s|\mathbf{x}) \tag{9}$$

where $P(C_k|B_s)$ and $P(B_s|\mathbf{x})$ are evaluated based on equations 7 and 8.

3.1 Linguistic ID3 Algorithm

Linguistic ID3 (LID3) is the learning algorithm we propose for building the linguistic decision tree based on a given linguistic database. Similar to the ID3 algorithm (Quinlan, 1986), search is guided by an information based heuristic, but the information measurements of a LDT are modified in accordance with label semantics. The measure of information defined for a branch B and can be viewed as an extension of the entropy measure used in ID3.

Definition 7 (Branch Entropy) *The entropy of branch B given a set of classes $\mathcal{C} = \{C_1, \ldots, C_{|\mathcal{C}|}\}$ is*

$$E(B) = -\sum_{t=1}^{|\mathcal{C}|} P(C_t|B) \log_2 P(C_t|B) \tag{10}$$

Now, given a particular branch B suppose we want to expand it with the attribute x_j. The evaluation of this attribute will be given based on the *Expected Entropy* defined as follows:

$$EE(B, x_j) = \sum_{F_j \in \mathcal{F}_j} E(B \cup F_j) \cdot P(F_j|B) \tag{11}$$

where $B \cup F_j$ represents the new branch obtained by appending the focal element F_j to the end of branch B. The probability of F_j given B can be calculated as follows:

$$P(F_j|B) = \frac{\sum_{i \in D} P(B \cup F_j|\mathbf{x}_i)}{\sum_{i \in D} P(B|\mathbf{x}_i)} \tag{12}$$

We can now define the *Information Gain (IG)* obtained by expanding branch B with attribute x_j as:

$$IG(B, x_j) = E(B) - EE(B, x_j) \tag{13}$$

The pseudo-code is listed in Algorithm 2. The goal of tree-structured learning models is to make subregions partitioned by branches be less "impure", in terms of the mixture of class labels, than the unpartitioned dataset. For a particular branch, the most suitable free attribute for further expanding (or partitioning), is the one by which the "pureness" is maximally increased with expanding. That corresponds to selecting the attribute with maximum information gain. As with ID3 learning, the most informative attribute will form the root of a linguistic decision tree, and the tree will expand into branches associated with all possible focal elements of this attribute. For each branch, the free attribute with maximum information gain will be the next node, from level to level, until the tree reaches the maximum specified depth has been reached.

3.2 Degrees of Fuzziness

Through linguistic translation, all numerical data can be represented as mass assignments based on a predefined fuzzy discretization method. In this section,

---

Algorithm 2: Decision Tree Learning

    input : $\mathcal{LD}$: Linguistic dataset obtained from Algorithm 1.

    output: LDT: Linguistic Decision Tree

1 Set a maximum depth M_{dep} and a threshold probability T.

2 **for** $l \leftarrow 0$ **to** M_{dep} **do**

3      $\mathcal{B} \leftarrow \emptyset$ when $l = 0$

4   The set of branches of LDT at depth l is $\mathcal{B}_l = \{B_1, \cdots, B_{|\mathcal{B}_l|}\}$

5   **for** $v \leftarrow 1$ **to** $|\mathcal{B}|$ **do**

6   **foreach** B_v **do** :

7   **for** $t \leftarrow 1$ **to** $|\mathcal{C}|$ **do**

8   **foreach** t **do** Calculating conditional probabilities:

                 $P(C_t|B_v) = \sum_{i \in \mathcal{D}_t} P(B_v|\mathbf{x}_i) / \sum_{i \in \mathcal{D}} P(B_v|\mathbf{x}_i)$

9   **if** $P(C_t|B_v) \geq T$ **then**

10   break (step out the loop)

11   **if** $\exists\, x_j : x_j$ *is free attribute* **then**

12   **foreach** x_j **do** : Calculate: $IG(B_v, x_j) = E(B_v) - EE(B_v, x_j)$

13              $IG_{max}(B_v) = \max_{x_j}[IG(B_v, x_j)]$

14   Expanding B_v with x_{max} where x_{max} is the free attribute we can obtain the maximum IG value IG_{max}.

15              $\mathcal{B}'_v \leftarrow \bigcup_{F_j \in \mathcal{F}_j} \{B_v \cup F_j\}$.

16   **else**

17   exit;

18      $\mathcal{B}_{l+1} \leftarrow \bigcup_{r=1}^{s} \mathcal{B}'_r$.

19 $LDT = \mathcal{B}$

---

unless otherwise stated, we will use a percentile-based (or equal points) discretization. The idea is to cover approximately the same number of data points for each fuzzy label. The justification for using this discretization method is given in (Qin and Lawry, 2005b).

Basically, fuzzy discretization provides an interpretation between numerical data and their corresponding linguistic data based on label semantics. We may notice that different fuzzy discretization may result in different linguistic data. We introduce a new parameter PT by which to measure the degrees of overlapping between fuzzy labels. As we can see from figure 3, given two fuzzy labels F and G, m is the distance between the weighting centers of a fuzzy labels to the meeting point of their membership functions. a is actually the length of the overlapping area. PT is calculated as follows:

$$PT = a/2m \tag{14}$$

$PT = 0.5$ represents 50% of overlapping between each two neighboring fuzzy labels (e.g., figure 3-A). $PT = 0$ represents no overlapping at all (figure 3-C), i.e., the labels are discrete but not fuzzy. Figure 3-B shows a situation that

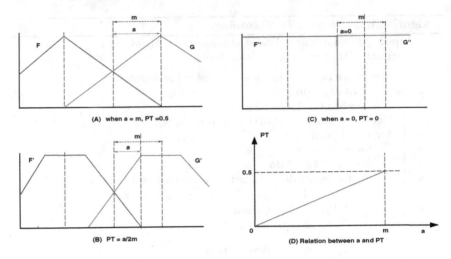

Fig. 3. A schematic illustration of calculating the overlap parameter PT given different degrees of overlaps.

the degree of overlapping is between 0 and 0.5. Figure 3-D also shows the linear relation of parameter a and PT.

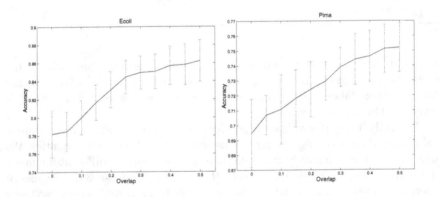

Fig. 4. Monotonically increased performance for linguistic decision trees with increasing degrees of fuzziness.

As we can see from these two figures, the performance these two datesets are roughly monotonic increased with the increase of PT. It implies that more fuzziness tends to increase the robustness of the LDT model and get better performance. From all the results, we can see that LDTs with fuzzy labels generally outperform the ones with discrete labels (where $PT = 0$). Due to the page limit, we cannot put all the results but they are available in (Qin and Lawry, 2007). Therefore, in summary, for the case of LDT model, we can say that fuzziness will bring greater performance. The increase is almost monotonically. But the optimal overlapping degrees are depends on the dataset you tested.

3.3 Linguistic Constraints

Here we assume that the linguistic constraints take the form of $\theta = \langle x_1$ is $\theta_1, \ldots, x_n$ is $\theta_n \rangle$, where θ_j represents a label expression based on $\mathcal{L}_j : j = 1, \ldots, n$. Consider the vector of linguistic constraint $\boldsymbol{\theta} = \langle \theta_1, \cdots, \theta_n \rangle$, where θ_j is the linguistic constraints on attribute j. We can evaluate a probability value for class C_t conditional on this information using a given linguistic decision tree as follows. The mass assignment given a linguistic constraint θ is evaluated by

$$\forall F_j \in \mathcal{F}_j \quad m_{\theta_j}(F_j) = \begin{cases} \frac{pm(F_j)}{\sum_{F_j \in \lambda(\theta_j)} pm(F_j)} & if : F_j \in \lambda(\theta_j) \\ 0 & otherwise \end{cases} \tag{15}$$

where $pm(F_j)$ is the prior mass for focal elements $F_j \in \mathcal{F}_j$ derived from the prior distribution $p(x_j)$ on Ω_j as follows:

$$pm(F_j) = \int_{\Omega_j} m_x(F_j) p(x_j) dx_j \tag{16}$$

Usually, we assume that $p(x_j)$ is the uniform distribution over Ω_j so that

$$pm(F_j) \propto \int_{\Omega_j} m_x(F_j) dx_j \tag{17}$$

For branch B with s nodes, the probability of B given $\boldsymbol{\theta}$ is evaluated by

$$P(B|\boldsymbol{\theta}) = \prod_{r=1}^{|B|} m_{\theta_{j_r}}(F_{j_r}) \tag{18}$$

and therefore, by Jeffrey's rule (Jeffrey, 1965)

$$P(C_t|\boldsymbol{\theta}) = \sum_{v=1}^{|LDT|} P(C_t|B_v) P(B_v|\boldsymbol{\theta}) \tag{19}$$

The methodology for classification under linguistic constraints allows us to fuse the background knowledge in linguistic form into classification. This is one of the advantages of using high-level knowledge representation language models such as label semantics.

3.4 Classification given fuzzy data

In previous sections LDTs have only been used to classify crisp data where objects are described in terms of precise attribute values. However, in many real-world applications limitations of measurement accuracy means that only imprecise values can be realistically obtained. In this section we introduce the idea of fuzzy data and show how LDTs can be used for classification in this context. Formally, a fuzzy database is defined to be a set of elements or objects each described by linguistic expressions rather than crisp values. In other words

$$\mathcal{FD} = \{\langle \theta_1(i), \ldots, \theta_n(i) \rangle : i = 1, \ldots, N\}$$

Currently there are very few benchmark problems of this kind with fuzzy attribute values. This is because, traditionally only crisp data values are recorded even in cases where this is inappropriate. Hence, we have generated a fuzzy database from a toy problem where the aim is to identify the interior of a figure of eight shape. Specifically, a figure of eight shape was generated according to the equation $x = 2^{(-0.5)}(sin(2t) - sin(t))$ and $y = 2^{(-0.5)}(sin(2t) + sin(t))$ where $t \in [0, 2\pi]$. (See figure 5). Points in $[-1.6, 1.6]^2$ are classified as legal if they lie within the 'eight' shape (marked with $\times$) and illegal if they lie outside (marked with points).

To form the fuzzy database we first generated a crisp database by uniformly sampling 961 points across $[-1.6, 1.6]^2$. Then each data vector $\langle x_1, x_2 \rangle$ was converted to a vector of linguistic expressions $\langle \theta_1, \theta_2 \rangle$ as follows: $\theta_j = \theta_{R_j}$ where $R_j = \{F \in \mathcal{F}_j : m_{x_j}(F) > 0\}$ A LDT was then learnt by applying the LID3 algorithm to the crisp database. This tree was then used to classify both the crisp and fuzzy data.

Suppose a LDT is trained on the 'eight' database where each attribute is discretized by five fuzzy sets uniformly: $verysmall$ (vs), $small$ (s),$medium$ (m), $large$ (l) and $verylarge$ (vl). Further, suppose we are given the following description of data points:

$\theta_1 = \langle x$ is $vs \lor s \land \neg m, y$ is $vs \lor s \land \neg m \rangle$
$\theta_2 = \langle x$ is $m \land l, y$ is $s \land m \rangle$
$\theta_3 = \langle x$ is $s \land m, y$ is $l \lor vl \rangle$

Experimental results obtained based on the approach introduced in 3.3 are as follows:

$Pr(C_1|\theta_1) = 1.000$ $Pr(C_2|\theta_1) = 0.000$
$Pr(C_1|\theta_2) = 0.000$ $Pr(C_2|\theta_2) = 1.000$
$Pr(C_1|\theta_3) = 0.428$ $Pr(C_2|\theta_3) = 0.572$

As we can see from figure 5, the above 3 linguistic constraints roughly correspond to the area 1, 2 and 3, respectively. By considering the occurrence of legal and illegal examples within these areas, we can verify the correctness of our approach.

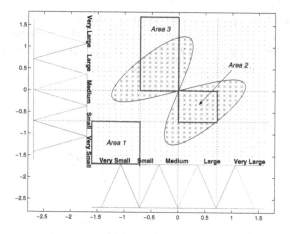

Fig. 5. Testing on the 'eight' problem with linguistic constraints θ, where each attribute is discretized by 5 trapezoidal fuzzy sets: *very small, small, medium, large and very large.*

3.5 Linguistic Decision Trees for Predictions

Consider a database for prediction:
$$\mathcal{D} = \{\langle x_1(i), \cdots, x_n(i), x_t(i)\rangle \, |i = 1, \cdots, |\mathcal{D}|\}$$
where $x_1, \cdots, x_n$ are potential explanatory attributes and x_t is the continuous target attribute. Unless otherwise stated, we use trapezoidal fuzzy sets with 50% overlap to discretized each continuous attribute individually (x_t) universe and assume the focal sets are $\mathcal{F}_1, \cdots, \mathcal{F}_n$ and $\mathcal{F}_t$. For the target attribute x_t: $\mathcal{F}_t = \{F_t^1, \cdots, F_t^{|\mathcal{F}_t|}\}$. For other attributes: x_j: $\mathcal{F}_j = \{F_j^1, \ldots, F_j^{|\mathcal{F}_j|}\}$. The inventive step is, to regard the focal elements for the target attribute as class labels. Hence, the LDT[4] model for prediction has the following form: A linguistic decision tree for prediction is a set of branches with associated probability distribution on the target focal elements of the following form:

$$LDT = \{\langle B_1, P(F_t^1|B_1), \cdots, P(F_t^{|\mathcal{F}_t|}|B_1)\rangle, \cdots,$$
$$\langle B_{|LDT|}, P(F_t^1|B_{|LDT|}), \cdots, P(F_t^{|\mathcal{F}_t|})|B_{|LDT|})\rangle\}$$

where $F_t^1, \cdots, F_t^{|\mathcal{F}_t|}$ are the target focal elements (i.e. the focal elements for the target attribute or the output attribute).

$$P(F_t^j|\mathbf{x}) = \sum_{v=1}^{|LDT|} P(F_t^j|B_v)P(B_v|\mathbf{x}) \tag{20}$$

---

[4] We will use the same name 'LDT' for representing both linguistic decision trees (for classification) and linguistic prediction trees.

Given value $\mathbf{x} = \langle x_1, \cdots, x_n \rangle$ we need to estimate the target value $\widehat{x}_t$ (i.e. $\mathbf{x}_i \rightarrow \widehat{x}_t$). This is achieved by initially evaluating the probabilities on target focal elements: $P(F_t^1|\mathbf{x}), \cdots, P(F_t^{|\mathcal{F}_t|}|\mathbf{x})$ as described above. We then take the estimate of x_t, denoted $\widehat{x}_t$, to be the expected value:

$$\widehat{x}_t = \int_{\Omega_t} x_t \, p(x_t|\mathbf{x}) \, dx_t \tag{21}$$

where:

$$p(x_t|\mathbf{x}) = \sum_{j=1}^{|\mathcal{F}_t|} p(x_t|F_t^j) \, P(F_t^j|\mathbf{x}) \tag{22}$$

and

$$p(x_t|F_t^j) = \frac{m_{x_t}(F_t^j)}{\int_{\Omega_t} m_{x_t}(F_t^j) \, dx_t} \tag{23}$$

so that, we can obtain:

$$\widehat{x}_t = \sum_j P(F_t^j|\mathbf{x}) \, E(x_t|F_t^j) \tag{24}$$

where:

$$E(x_t|F_t^j) = \int_{\Omega_t} x_t \, p(x_t|F_t^j) \, dx_t = \frac{\int_{\Omega_t} x_t \, m_{x_t}(F_t^j) \, dx_t}{\int_{\Omega_t} m_{x_t}(F_t^j) \, dx_t} \tag{25}$$

We test our model on a toy problem of surface regression: 529 points were *uniformly* generated describing a surface defined by equation $z = sin(x \times y)$ where $x, y \in [0, 3]$. 2209 points are sampled uniformly as the test set. The attributes are discretized uniformly by fuzzy labels, the detailed results with different number of fuzzy labels are available in (Qin and Lawry, 2005c). We compared the prediction surface by the LDT model and the original surface in figure in 6. As we can see from the figures that these results are quite comparable though LDT didn't capture the small change at the tail. In this experiment, we use 7 fuzzy labels for discretization. If we use more labels, we can get the results as good as as we want, but it just needs more computational time.

4 Bayesian Estimation Based on Label Semantics

Bayesian reasoning provides a probabilistic approach to inference based on the Bayesian theorem. Given a test instance, the learner is asked to predict its class according to the evidence provided by the training data. The classification of unknown example $\mathbf{x}$ by Bayesian estimation is on the basis of the following probability,

$$P(C_k|\mathbf{x}) = \frac{P(\mathbf{x}|C_k)P(C_k)}{P(\mathbf{x})} \tag{26}$$

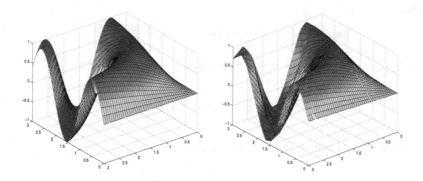

Fig. 6. Left-hand: the surface of $z = sin(x \times y)$. Right-hand: the prediction surface by linguistic decision trees.

Since the denominator in eq. 26 is invariant across classes, we can consider it as a normalization parameter. So, we obtain:

$$P(C_k|\mathbf{x}) \propto P(\mathbf{x}|C_k)P(C_k) \tag{27}$$

Now suppose we assume for each variable x_j that its outcome is independent of the outcome of all other variables given class C_k. In this case we can obtain the so-called naive Bayes classifier as follows:

$$P(C_k|\mathbf{x}) \propto \prod_{j=1}^{n} P(x_j|C_k)P(C_k) \tag{28}$$

where $P(x_j|C_k)$ is often called the likelihood of the data x_j given C_k. For a qualitative attribute, it can be estimated from corresponding frequencies. For a quantitative attribute, either probability density estimation or discretization can be employed to estimate its probabilities.

4.1 Fuzzy Naive Bayes

In label semantics framework, suppose we are given focal set $\mathcal{F}_j$ for each attribute j. Assuming that attribute x_j is numeric with universe Ω_j, then the likelihood of x_j given C_k can be represented by a density function $p(x_j|C_k)$ determine from the database $\mathcal{D}_k$ and prior density according to Jeffrey's rule (Jeffrey, 1965).

$$p(x_j|C_k) = \sum_{F \in \mathcal{F}_j} p(x_j|F)P(F|C_k) \tag{29}$$

From Bayes theorem, we can obtain:

$$p(x_j|F) = \frac{P(F|x_j)p(x_j)}{P(F)} = \frac{m_{x_j}(F)p(x_j)}{pm(F)} \tag{30}$$

where,

$$pm(F) = \int_{\Omega_j} P(F|x_j)p(x_j)dx_j = \frac{\sum_{\mathbf{x}\in\mathcal{D}} m_{x_j}(F)}{|\mathcal{D}|} \qquad (31)$$

Substituting equation 30 in equation 29 and re-arranging gives

$$p(x_j|C_k) = p(x_j) \sum_{F\in\mathcal{F}_j} m_{x_j}(F)\frac{P(F|C_k)}{pm(F)} \qquad (32)$$

where $P(F|C_k)$ can be derived from $\mathcal{D}_k$ according to

$$P(F|C_k) = \frac{\sum_{\mathbf{x}\in\mathcal{D}_k} m_{x_j}(F)}{|\mathcal{D}_k|} \qquad (33)$$

This model is called fuzzy Naive Bayes (FNB). If we weaken the independence assumption, we can obtain a fuzzy semi-Naive Bayes (FSNB). More details of FNB and FSNB can be found in (Randon and Lawry, 2006).

4.2 Fuzzy Semi-Naive Bayes

The main advantage of using Semi-Naive Bayes over Naive Bayes is that it allows us to solve non-decomposable problems such as XOR by weakening the independence assumption of Naive Bayes. However, in order to utilize Semi-Naive Bayes it is necessary to find effective groupings of attributes within which dependencies must be taken into account. In this chapter, we present and evaluate a number of heuristic search algorithms for finding such groups of attributes.

Given a set of attributes: $x_1, x_2, \cdots, x_n$, they are partitioned into subsets $S_1, \cdots, S_w$ where $w \geq n$ and for each S_i a joint mass assignment $m_{i,j}$ is determined as follows: suppose, w.l.o.g $S_i = \{x_1, \cdots, x_v\}$ then the join mass assignment is

$$\forall T_1 \times \cdots \times T_v \in 2^{LA_1} \times \cdots \times 2^{LA_v} \qquad (34)$$

$$m_{i,j}(T_1, \cdots, T_v) = \frac{1}{|DB_j|} \sum_{k\in\mathcal{D}} \prod_{r=1}^{w} m_{r,j}(T_i : x_i \in S_r) \qquad (35)$$

Hence the prototype describing C_j is defined as $\langle m_{i,j}, \cdots, m_{w,j} \rangle$. A prototype of this form naturally defines a joint mass assignment m_j on the whole cross product space $2^{LA_1} \times \cdots \times 2^{LA_n}$ conditional on C_j as follows:

$$\forall T_1 \times \cdots \times T_n \in 2^{LA_1} \times \cdots \times 2^{LA_n} \; m_j(T_1, \cdots, T_n) = \prod_{r=1}^{w} m_{r,j}(T_i : x_i \in S_r) \quad (36)$$

In this formulation we are encoding variable dependence within the variable groupings $S_i : i = 1, \cdots w$ and assuming independence between the groups.

In order to estimate classification probabilities given input vectors of rea attribute values we need a mechanism for mapping from mass assignments on label space onto density functions on attribute space.

Definition 8 (Conditional Density Given a Mass Assignment) *Let x be a variable into Ω with prior distribution $p(x)$, LA be a set of labels for x and m be a posterior mass assignment for the set of appropriate labels of x inferred from some database $\mathcal{D}$. Then the posterior distribution of x conditional on m is given by*

$$\forall x \in \Omega, \ p(x|m) = p(x) \sum_{S \subseteq LA} \frac{m(S)}{pm(S)} m_x(S) \tag{37}$$

where $pm(S)$ is the prior mass assignment generated by the prior distribution $p(x)$ according to

$$pm(S) = \int_{\Omega} m_x(S) p(x) dx \tag{38}$$

This definition is motivated by the following argument based on the theorem of total probability which for a mass assignment, describing variables x on Ω.

We now consider methods for finding attribute groupings that increase discrimination in the model. Two measures has been proposed in (Randon and Lawry, 2006):

Definition 9 (Importance Measure) *Let the joint mass assignment for S_i given C_j be denoted $m_{i,j}$. For any input vector S_i the probability of cloass C_j can be estimated using Bayes theorem where*

$$P(C_j|S_i) = \frac{p(S_i|m_{i,j})|C_j|}{p(S_i|m_{i,j})|C_j| + p(S_i|m_{i,\neg j})|C_{\neg j}|} \tag{39}$$

where $m_{i,\neg j}$ denotes the mass assignments for S_j given $\neg C_j$. The importance measured of group S_i for class C_j is then defined by

$$IM_j(S_i) = \frac{\sum_{k \in \mathcal{D}_j} P(C_j|S_i(k))}{\sum_{k \in \mathcal{D}} P(C_j|S_i(k))} \tag{40}$$

Effectively, $IM_j(S_i)$ is a measure of the importance of the set of variables S_i as discriminators of C_j from the other classes.

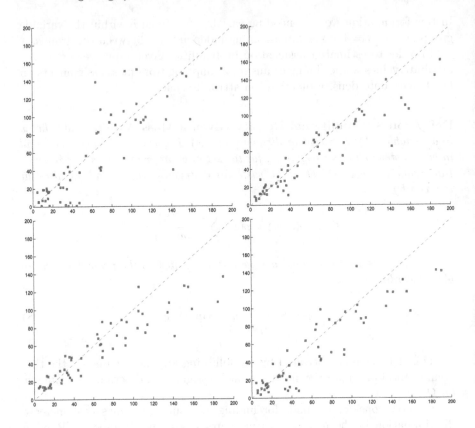

Fig. 7. Scatter plot showing original data verses prediction data on sunspot prediction problems. Upper left: Fuzzy Naive Bayes; upper right: Support Vector Regression; lower left: non-merged LDT with 5 fuzzy labels; lower right: Semi-naive Bayes.

Definition 10 (Correlation Measure) *Let $\mathcal{F}_1$ be the focal sets for S_1 and $\mathcal{F}_2$ the focal sets for S_2. Now let $m_{1,2,j}$ be the joint mass of $S_1 \cup S_2$ given C_j*

$$C(S_1, S_2) = \sqrt{\frac{1}{|\mathcal{F}_1||\mathcal{F}_1|} \sum_{R \subseteq \mathcal{F}_1} \sum_{T \subseteq \mathcal{F}_2} (m_{1,2,j}(R,T) - m_{1,j}(R)m_{2,j}(T))^2} \quad (41)$$

Here a threshold must be used to determine whether attributes should be grouped. The nearer the correlation measure gets to 1 the higher the correlation between attribute groups.

We tested our models with a real-world problem taken from the Time Series Data Library (Hyndman and Akram, 2007) and contains data of sunspot numbers between the years 1700-1979. The input attributes are x_{T-12} to x_{T-1}

(the data for previous 12 years) and the output (target) attribute is x_T, i.e. one-year-ahead. The experimental results for LID3, Fuzzy Naive Bayes, Semi-Naive Bayes and ε-SVR (Gunn, 1998) are compared in figure 7. We can see the results are quite comparable. In these graphs, for an error free prediction all points will fall on the line defined by $y = x$. Roughly, from the illustration, we can see that SVR and non-merged LDT have better performance, because predicted values distributed closer to $y = x$ than other two models.

4.3 Hybrid Bayesian Estimation Tree

Based on previous two linguistic models, a hybrid model was proposed in (Qin and Lawry, 2005a). Given a decision tree T is learnt from a training database $\mathcal{D}$. According to the Bayesian theorem: A data element $\mathbf{x} = \langle x_1, \ldots, x_n \rangle$ can be classified by:

$$P(C_k|\mathbf{x}, T) \propto P(\mathbf{x}|C_k, T)P(C_k|T) \tag{42}$$

We can then divide the attributes into 2 disjoint groups denoted by $\mathbf{x}_T = \{x_1, \cdots, x_m\}$ and $\mathbf{x}_B = \{x_{m+1}, \cdots, x_n\}$, respectively. $\mathbf{x}_T$ is the vector of the variables that are contained in the given tree T and the remaining variables are contained in $\mathbf{x}_B$. Assuming conditional independence between $\mathbf{x}_T$ and $\mathbf{x}_B$ we obtain:

$$P(\mathbf{x}|C_k, T) = P(\mathbf{x}_T|C_k, T)P(\mathbf{x}_B|C_k, T) \tag{43}$$

Because $\mathbf{x}_B$ is independent of the given decision tree T and if we assume the variables in $\mathbf{x}_B$ are independent of each other given a particular class, we can obtain:

$$P(\mathbf{x}_B|C_k, T) = P(\mathbf{x}_B|C_k) = \prod_{j \in \mathbf{x}_B} P(x_j|C_k) \tag{44}$$

Now consider $\mathbf{x}_T$. According to Bayes theorem,

$$P(\mathbf{x}_T|C_k, T) = \frac{P(C_k|\mathbf{x}_T, T)P(\mathbf{x}_T|T)}{P(C_k|T)} \tag{45}$$

Combining equation 43, 44 and 45:

$$P(\mathbf{x}|C_k, T) = \frac{P(C_k|\mathbf{x}_T, T)P(\mathbf{x}_T|T)}{P(C_k|T)} \prod_{j \in \mathbf{x}_B} P(x_l|C_k) \tag{46}$$

Combining equation 42 and 46

$$P(C_k|\mathbf{x}, T) \propto P(C_k|\mathbf{x}_T, T)P(\mathbf{x}_T|T) \prod_{j \in \mathbf{x}_B} P(x_j|C_k) \tag{47}$$

Further, since $P(\mathbf{x}_T|T)$ is independent from C_k, we have that:

$$P(C_k|\mathbf{x}, T) \propto P(C_k|\mathbf{x}_T, T) \prod_{j \in \mathbf{x}_B} P(x_j|C_k) \tag{48}$$

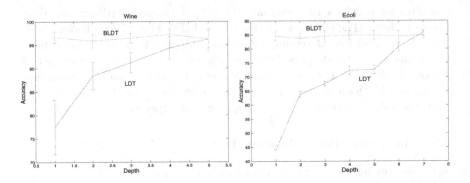

Fig. 8. Results for single LDT with Bayesian estimation: average accuracy with standard deviation on each dataset against the depth of the tree.

where $P(x_j|C_k)$ is evaluated according to eq. 32 and $P(C_k|\mathbf{x}_T, T)$ is just the class probabilities evaluated from the decision tree T according to equation 9.

We tested this new model with a set of UCI (UCI, 2007) data sets. Figure 8 is a simple result. More results are available in (Qin and Lawry, 2005a). From figures 8, we can see that the BLDT model generally performs better at shallow depths than LDT model. However, with the increasing of the tree depth, the performance of the BLDT model remains constant or decreases, while the accuracy curves for LDT increase. The basic idea of using Bayesian estimation given a LDT is to use the LDT as one estimator and the rest of the attributes as other independent estimators. Consider the two extreme cases for eq. 48. If all the attributes are used in building the tree (i.e. $\mathbf{x}_T = \mathbf{x}$), the probability estimations are from the tree only, that is:

$$P(C_k|\mathbf{x}, T) \propto P(C_k|\mathbf{x}_T, T)$$

If none of the attributes are used in developing the tree (i.e. $\mathbf{x} = \mathbf{x}_B$), the probability estimation will become:

$$P(C_k|\mathbf{x}, T) \propto \prod_{j \in \mathbf{x}_B} P(x_j|C_k)$$

which is simply a Naive Bayes classifier.

4.4 Bayesian Estimation From a Set of Trees

Given a training dataset, a small-sized tree (usually the depth is less than 3) can be learnt based on the method we discussed in section 3. We then learn another tree with the same size based on the remaining attributes, i.e., the attributes which have not been used in previous trees. In this manner, a set of trees can successively be built from training set. We denote this set of trees by $\mathcal{T} = \langle T_1, \ldots, T_W \rangle$ and where the set of attributes $\mathbf{x}_{T_w}$ for $w = 1, \ldots, W$ for a partition of $\{x_1, \ldots, x_n\}$ (see fig. 9 for a schematic illustration). For a given unclassified data element $\mathbf{x}$, we can partition it into W groups of disjoint set of attributes $\langle \mathbf{x}_{T_1}, \ldots, \mathbf{x}_{T_W} \rangle$. If we assume:

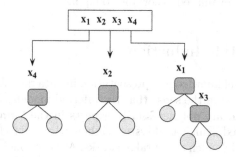

Fig. 9. An schematic illustration of Bayesian estimation from a set of linguistic decision trees.

$$P(C_t|\mathbf{x}) = P(C_t|\mathbf{x}_{T_1}, \ldots, \mathbf{x}_{T_W}) \approx P(C_t|T_1, \ldots, T_W) \qquad (49)$$

Then, according to the Bayes theorem:

$$P(C_t|\mathcal{T}) = P(C_t|T_1, \ldots, T_W) = \frac{P(T_1, \ldots, T_W|C_t)P(C_t)}{P(T_1, \ldots, T_W)} \qquad (50)$$

Assuming that the trees are generated independently then it is reasonable to assume that the groups of attributes are conditionally independent of each other. Hence,

$$P(T_1, \ldots, T_W|C_t) = \prod_{w=1}^{W} P(T_w|C_t) \qquad (51)$$

For a particular tree T_w for $w = 1, \ldots, W$, we have

$$P(T_w|C_t) = \frac{P(C_t|T_w)P(T_w)}{P(C_t)} \qquad (52)$$

So that,

$$\prod_{w=1}^{W} P(T_w|C_t) = \frac{\prod_{w=1}^{W} P(C_t|T_w) \prod_{i=1}^{W} P(T_w)}{P(C_t)^W} \qquad (53)$$

Combining eq. 50, 51 and 53, we obtain

$$P(C_t|\mathcal{T}) \propto \frac{\prod_{w=1}^{W} P(C_t|T_w) \prod_{w=1}^{W} P(T_w)}{P(C_t)^{W-1}} \qquad (54)$$

Since $\prod_{w=1}^{W} P(T_w)$ is independent from C_t, we finally obtain:

$$P(C_t|T) \propto \frac{\prod_{w=1}^{W} P(C_t|T_w)}{P(C_t)^{W-1}} \tag{55}$$

where $P(C_t|T_w)$ is evaluated according to eq. 9.

5 Linguistic Rule Induction

The use of high-level knowledge representation in data modelling allows for enhanced transparency in the sense that the inferred models can be understood by practioners who are not necessarily experts in the formal representation framework employed. Rule based systems inherently tend to be more transparent than other models such as neural networks. A set of concise understandable rules can provide a better understanding of how the classification or prediction is made. Generally, there are two general types of algorithms for rule induction, *top down* and *bottom up* algorithms. Top-down approaches start from the most general rule and specialize it gradually. Bottom-up methods star from a basic fact given in training database and generalize it. In this paper we will focus on a top-down model for generating linguistic rules based on Quinlan's *First-Order Inductive Learning* (FOIL) Algorithm (Quinlan, 1990).

The FOIL algorithm is based on classical binary logic where typically attributes are assumed to be discrete. Numerical variables are usually discretized by partitioning the numerical domain into a finite number of intervals. However, because of the uncertainty involved in most real-world problems, sharp boundaries between intervals often lead to a loss of robustness and generality. Fuzzy logic has been used to solve the problem of sharp transitions between two intervals. Fuzzy rule induction research has been popular in both fuzzy and machine learning communities as a means to learning robust transparent models. Many algorithms have been proposed including simple fuzzy logic rule induction (Baldwin and Xie, 2004), fuzzy association rule mining (Xie, 2005) and first-order fuzzy rule induction based on FOIL (Drobics *et al.*, 2003, Prade *et al.*, 2003). In this paper, we will focus on an extension to the FOIL algorithm based on label semantics.

5.1 Generalized Appropriateness Measures

Based on definition 5, we can evaluate the appropriateness degree of $\theta \in LE$ is to aggregate the values of m_x across $\lambda(\theta)$. This motivates the following general definition of appropriateness measures.

Definition 11 (*Appropriateness Measures*) $\forall \theta \in LE$, $\forall x \in \Omega$ the measure of appropriateness degrees of θ as a description of x is given by:

$$\mu_\theta(x) = \sum_{S \in \lambda(\theta)} m_x(S)$$

Appropriateness degrees (def. 2) introduced at the beginning of this chapter are only a special case of the appropriateness measures where $\theta = L$ for $L \in \mathcal{L}$.

Given a continuous variable x: $\mathcal{L} = \{small, medium, large\}$, $\mathcal{F} = \{\{small\}, \{small, medium\}, \{medium\}, \{medium, large\}, \{large\}\}$. Suppose we are told that "x is **not large** but it is **small or medium**". This constraint can be interpreted as the logical expression

$$\theta = \neg large \wedge (small \vee medium)$$

According to definition 5, the possible label sets of the given logical expression θ are calculated as follows:

$$\lambda(\neg large) = \{\{small\}, \{small, medium\}, \{medium\}\}$$

$$\lambda(small) = \{\{small\}, \{small, medium\}\}$$

$$\lambda(medium) = \{\{small, medium\}, \{medium\}, \{medium, large\}\}$$

So that we can obtain:

$$\lambda(\theta) = \lambda(\neg large \wedge (small \vee medium)) = \{\{small\}, \{small, medium\}, \{medium\}\} \wedge (\{\{small\}, \{small, medium\}\} \vee \{\{small, medium\}, \{medium\}, \{medium, large\}\}) = \{\{small\}, \{small, medium\}, \{medium\}\}$$

If a prior distribution on focal elements of variable x are given as follows:

$$\{small\} : 0.1, \{small, med.\} : 0.3, \{med.\} : 0.1, \{med., large\} : 0.5, \{large\} : 0.0$$

The appropriateness measure for $\theta = \neg large \wedge (small \vee medium)$ is:

$$\mu_\theta(x) = \sum_{S \in \lambda(\theta)} m_x(S)$$
$$= m_x(\{small\}) + m_x(\{small, medium\}) + m_x(\{medium\})$$
$$= 0.1 + 0.3 + 0.1 = 0.5$$

5.2 Linguistic Rules in Label Semantics

In sections 2 and 3, a basic introduction of label semantics is given and how it can be used for data modelling is discussed. In this section, we will describe a linguistic rule induction model based on label semantics. Now, we begin by clarifying the definition of a linguistic rule. Based on def. 4, a linguistic rule is a rule can be represented as a multi-dimensional logical expressions of fuzzy labels.

Definition 12 (*Multi-dimensional Logical Expressions of Labels*) $MLE^{(n)}$ *is the set of all multi-dimensional label expressions that can be generated from the logical label expression LE_j: $j = 1, \ldots, n$ and is defined recursively by:*

(i)   If $\theta \in LE_j$ for $j = 1, \ldots, n$ then $\theta \in MLE^{(n)}$
(ii) If $\theta, \varphi \in MLE^{(n)}$ then $\neg\theta$, $\theta \wedge \varphi$, $\theta \vee \varphi$, $\theta \to \varphi \in MLE^{(n)}$

Any n-dimensional logical expression θ identifies a subset of $2^{\mathcal{L}_1} \times \ldots \times 2^{\mathcal{L}_n}$, denoted $\lambda^{(n)}(\theta)$, constraining the cross product of logical descriptions on each variable: $D_{x_1} \times \ldots \times D_{x_1}$. In such a way the imprecise constraint θ on n variables can be interpret as the precise constraint $D_{x_1} \times \ldots \times D_{x_1} \in \lambda^{(n)}(\theta)$

Given a particular data, how can we evaluated if a linguistic rule is appropriate for describing it? Based on the one-dimensional case, we now extend the concepts of appropriateness degrees to the multi-dimensional case as follows:

Definition 13 (*Multi-dimensional Appropriateness Degrees*) *Given a set of n-dimensional label expressions $MLE^{(n)}$:*

$$\forall\, \theta \in MLE^{(n)}, \forall x_j \in \Omega_j : j = 1, \cdots, n$$

$$\mu_\theta^n(\mathbf{x}) = \mu_\theta^n(x_1, \cdots, x_n) = \sum_{\langle F_1, \cdots, F_n \rangle \in \lambda^{(n)}(\theta)} (F_1, \cdots, F_n)$$

$$= \sum_{\langle F_1, \cdots, F_n \rangle \in \lambda^{(n)}(\theta)} \prod_{j=1}^{n} m_{x_j}(F_j)$$

The appropriateness degrees in one-dimension are for evaluating a single label for describing a single data element, while in multi-dimensional cases they are for evaluating a linguistic rule for describing a data vector.

Consider a modelling problem with two variables x_1 and x_2 for which $\mathcal{L}_1 = \{small\ (s),\ medium\ (med),\ large(lg)\}$ and $\mathcal{L}_2 = \{low(lo),\ moderate\ (mod),\ high(h)\}$. Also suppose the focal elements for $\mathcal{L}_1$ and $\mathcal{L}_2$ are:

$$\mathcal{F}_1 = \{\{s\}, \{s, med\}, \{med\}, \{med, lg\}, \{lg\}\}$$

$$\mathcal{F}_2 = \{\{lo\}, \{lo, mod\}, \{mod\}, \{mod, h\}, \{h\}\}$$

According to the multi-dimensional generalization of definition 5 we have that

$$\lambda^{(2)}((med \wedge \neg s) \wedge \neg lo) = \lambda^{(2)}(med \wedge \neg s) \cap \lambda^{(2)}(\neg lo)$$

$$= \lambda(med \wedge \neg s) \times \lambda(\neg lo)$$

Now, the set of possible label sets is obtained according to the λ-function:

$$\lambda(med \wedge \neg s) = \{\{med\}, \{med, lg\}\}$$

$$\lambda(\neg lo) = \{\{mod\}, \{mod, h\}, \{h\}\}$$

Hence, based on def. 5 we can obtain:

$$\lambda^{(2)}((med \wedge \neg s) \wedge \neg lo) = \{\langle\{med\}, \{mod\}\rangle, \langle\{med\}, \{mod, h\}\rangle,$$

$$\langle\{med\}, \{h\}\rangle, \langle\{med, lg\}, \{mod\}\rangle, \langle\{med, lg\}, \{mod, h\}\rangle, \langle\{med, lg\}, \{h\}\rangle\}$$

The above calculation on random set interpretation of the given rule based on λ-function is illustrated in fig. 10: given focal set $\mathcal{F}_1$ and $\mathcal{F}_2$, we can construct a 2-dimensional space where the focal elements have corresponding focal cells. Representation of the multi-dimensional λ-function of the logical expression of the given rule are represented by grey cells.

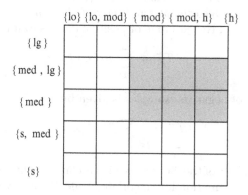

Fig. 10. Representation of the multi-dimensional λ-function of the logical expression $\theta = (med \wedge \neg s) \wedge \neg lo$ showing the focal cells $\mathcal{F}_1 \times \mathcal{F}_2$.

Given $\mathbf{x} = \langle x_1, x_2 \rangle = \langle x_1 = \{med\} : 0.6, \{med, lg\} : 0.4 \rangle, \langle x_2 = \{lo, mod\} : 0.8, \{mod\} : 0.2 \rangle$, we obtain:

$$\mu_\theta(\mathbf{x}) = (m(\{med\}) + m(\{med, lg\})) \times (m(\{mod\}) + m(\{mod, h\}) + m(\{h\}))$$

$$= (0.6 + 0.4) \times (0.2 + 0 + 0) = 0.2$$

And according to def. 5:

$$\mu^n_{\neg\theta}(\mathbf{x}) = 1 - \mu_\theta(\mathbf{x}) = 0.8$$

In another words, we can say that the linguistic expression θ covers the data $\mathbf{x}$ to degree 0.2 and θ can be considered as a linguistic rule. This interpretation of appropriateness is highlighted in next section on rule induction.

5.3 Information Heuristics for LFOIL

In the last section, we have shown how to evaluate the appropriateness of using a linguistic rule to describe a data vector. In this section, a new algorithm for learning a set of linguistic rules is proposed based on the FOIL algorithm (Quinlan, 1990), it is referred to as *Linguistic FOIL* (LFOIL). Generally, the heuristics for a rule learning model are for assessing the usefulness of a literal as the next component of the rule. The heuristics used for LFOIL are similar but modified from the FOIL algorithm (Quinlan, 1990) so as to incorporate linguistic expressions based on labels semantics. Consider a classification rule of the form:

$$R_i = \theta \rightarrow C_k \ \ where \ \ \theta \in MLE^{(n)}$$

Given a data set $\mathcal{D}$ and a particular class C_k, the data belonging to class C_k are referred to as *positive examples* and the rest of them are *negative examples*. For the given rule R_i, the coverage of positive data is evaluated by

$$T_i^+ = \sum_{l \in \mathcal{D}_k} \mu_\theta(\mathbf{x}_l) \tag{56}$$

and the coverage of negative examples is given by

$$T_i^- = \sum_{l \in (\mathcal{D} - \mathcal{D}_k)} \mu_\theta(\mathbf{x}_l) \tag{57}$$

where $\mathcal{D}_k$ is the subset of the database which is consisted by the data belonging to class C_k. The information for the original rule R_i can by evaluated by

$$I(R_i) = -\log_2 \left(\frac{T_i^+}{T_i^+ + T_i^-} \right) \tag{58}$$

Suppose we then propose to another label expression φ to the body of R_i to generate a new rule

$$R_{i+1} = \varphi \wedge \theta \rightarrow C_k$$

where $\varphi, \theta \in MLE^{(n)}$. By adding the new literal φ, the positive and negative coverage becomes:

$$T_{i+1}^+ = \sum_{l \in \mathcal{D}_k} \mu_{\theta \wedge \varphi}(\mathbf{x}_l) \tag{59}$$

$$T_{i+1}^- = \sum_{l \in (\mathcal{D} - \mathcal{D}_k)} \mu_{\theta \wedge \varphi}(\mathbf{x}_l) \tag{60}$$

Therefore, the information becomes,

$$I(R_{i+1}) = -\log_2 \left(\frac{T_{i+1}^+}{T_{i+1}^+ + T_{i+1}^-} \right) \tag{61}$$

Then we can evaluate the information gain from adding expression φ by:

$$G(\varphi) = T_{i+1}^+(I(R_i) - I(R_{i+1})) \tag{62}$$

We can see that the measure of information gain consists of two components. T_{i+1}^+ is the coverage of positive data by the new rule R_{i+1} and $(I(R_i)-I(R_{i+1}))$ is the increase of information. The probability of C_k given a linguistic rule R_i is evaluated by:

$$P(C_k|R_i) = \frac{\sum_{l \in \mathcal{D}_k} \mu_\theta(\mathbf{x}_l)}{\sum_{l \in \mathcal{D}} \mu_\theta(\mathbf{x}_l)} = \frac{T_i^+}{T_i^+ + T_i^-} \tag{63}$$

when $P(C_k|R_{i+1}) > P(C_k|R_i)$ (i.e., by appending a new literal, more positive examples are covered), we can obtain that $(I(R_i) - I(R_{i+1})) > 0$. By choosing a literal φ with maximum G value, we can form the new rule which covers more positive examples and thus increasing the accuracy of the rule.

5.4 Linguistic FOIL

We define a prior knowledge base $KB \subseteq MLE^{(n)}$ and a probability threshold $PT \in [0,1]$. KB consists of fuzzy label expressions based on labels defined on each attribute. For example, given fuzzy labels $\{small_1 \ large_1\}$ to describe attribute 1 and $\{small_2 \ large_2\}$ to describe attribute 2. A possible knowledge base for the given two variables is: $KB = \{small_1, \neg small_1, large_1, \neg large_1, small_2, \neg small_2, large_2, \neg large_2\}$.

The idea for FOIL is as follows: from a general rule, we specify it by adding new literals in order to cover more positive and less negative examples according to the heuristics introduced in last section. After developing one rule, the positive examples covered by this rule are deleted from the original database. We then need to find a new rule based on this reduced database until all positive examples are covered. In this paper, because of the fuzzy linguistic nature of the expressions employed, typically data will be only partially covered by a given rule. For this reason we need a probability threshold PT as part of the decision process concerning rule coverage.

A pseudo-code of LFOIL are consists of two parts which are described follows:

Generating a Rule

- Let rule $R_i = \theta_1 \wedge \cdots \wedge \theta_d \to C_k$ be the rule at step i, we then find the next literal $\theta_{d+1} \in KB - \{\theta_1, \cdots, \theta_d\}$ for which $G(\theta_{d+1})$ is maximal.

- Replace rule R_i with $R_{i+1} = \theta_1 \wedge \cdots \wedge \theta_d \wedge \theta_{d+1} \to C_k$

- If $P(C_k|\theta_1 \wedge \cdots \wedge \theta_{i+1}) \geq PT$ then terminate else repeat.

Generating a Rule Base

Let $\Delta_i = \{\varphi_1 \to C_k, \cdots, \varphi_t \to C_k\}$ be the rule base at step i where $\varphi \in MLE$. We evaluate the coverage of Δ_i as follows:

$$CV(\Delta_i) = \frac{\sum_{l \in \mathcal{D}_k} \mu_{\varphi_1 \vee \cdots \vee \varphi_t}(\mathbf{x}_l)}{|\mathcal{D}_k|} \tag{64}$$

We define a coverage function $\delta : \Omega_1 \times \cdots \times \Omega_n \to [0, 1]$ according to:

$$\delta(\mathbf{x}|\Delta_i) = \mu_{\neg \Delta_i}(\mathbf{x}) = \mu_{\neg(\varphi_1 \vee \cdots \vee \varphi_t)}(\mathbf{x}) \tag{65}$$

$$= 1 - \mu_{(\varphi_1 \vee \cdots \vee \varphi_t)}(\mathbf{x}) = 1 - \sum_{w=1}^{t} \mu_{R_w}(\mathbf{x})$$

where $\delta(\mathbf{x}|\Delta_i)$ represents the degree to which $\mathbf{x}$ is *not* covered by a given rule base Δ_i. If CV is less than a predefined coverage threshold $CT \in [0, 1]$:

$$CV(\Delta_i) < CT$$

then we generate a new rule for class C_k according to the above rule generation algorithm to form a new rule base Δ_{i+1} but where the entropy calculations are amended such that for a rule $R = \theta \to C_k$,

$$T^+ = \sum_{l \in \mathcal{D}_k} \mu_\theta(\mathbf{x}_l) \times \delta(\mathbf{x}_l|\Delta_i) \tag{66}$$

$$T^- = \sum_{l \in (\mathcal{D} - \mathcal{D}_k)} \mu_\theta(\mathbf{x}_l) \tag{67}$$

The algorithm terminates when $CV(RB_{i+1}) \geq CT$ or $CV(RB_{i+1}) - CV(RB_i) < \epsilon$ where $\epsilon \in [0, 1]$ is a very small value, i.e., if there are no improvements in covering positive examples, we will stop the algorithm to avoid an infinite-loop calculation.

Given a rule base $\Delta_i = \{\varphi_1 \to C_k, \cdots, \varphi_t \to C_k\}$ and an unclassified data $\mathbf{x}$, we can estimate the probability of C_k, $P(C_k|\mathbf{x})$, as follows: Firstly, we determine the rule $R_{max} = \varphi_j \to C_k$ for which $\mu_{\varphi_j}(\mathbf{x})$ is maximal:

$$\varphi_j = \arg\max_{k \in \Delta_i} \mu_{\varphi_k} \tag{68}$$

Therefore, given the unclassified data $\mathbf{x}$, rule R_{max} is the most appropriate rule from the rule base we learned. For the rule $R_{max} \to C_k$ we evaluate two probabilities p_{max} and q_{max} where:

$$p_{max} = P(C_k|\varphi_j) \tag{69}$$

$$q_{max} = P(C_k|\neg\varphi_j) \tag{70}$$

We then use Jeffrey's rule (Jeffrey, 1965) to evaluate the class probability by:

$$P(C_k|\mathbf{x}) = p_{max} \times \mu_{\varphi_j}(\mathbf{x}) + q_{max} \times (1 - \mu_{\varphi_j}(\mathbf{x})) \tag{71}$$

We tested this rule learning algorithms with some toy problems and some real-world problems. Although it does not give us very good accuracy but we obtained some comparable performance to decision tree but with much better transparency. More details are available in (Qin and Lawry, 2005d).

6 Conclusions and Discussions

In this chapter, label semantics, a higher level knowledge representation language, was used for modeling imprecise concepts and building intelligent data mining systems. In particular, a number of linguistic data mining models have been proposed including: Linguistic Decision Trees (LDT) (for both classification and prediction), Bayesian estimation models (Fuzzy Naive Bayes, Semi-Naive Bayes, Bayesian Estimation Trees) and Linguistic Rule Induction (Linguistic FOIL).

Through previous empirical studies, we have shown that in terms of accuracy the linguistic decision tree model tends to perform significantly better than both C4.5 and Naive Bayes and has equivalent performance to that of the Back-Propagation neural networks (Qin and Lawry, 2005b). However, it is also the case that this model has much better transparency than other algorithms. Linguistic decision trees are suitable for both classification and prediction. Some benchmark prediction problems have been tested with the LDT model and we found that it has comparable performance to a number of state-of-art prediction algorithms such as support vector regression systems. Furthermore, a methodology for classification with linguistic constraints has been proposed within the label semantics framework.

In order to reduce complexity and enhance transparency, a forward merging algorithm has been proposed to merge the branches which give sufficiently similar probability estimations. With merging, the partitioning of the data space is re-constructed and more appropriate granules can be obtained. Experimental studies show that merging reduces the tree size significantly without a significant loss of accuracy. In order to obtain a better estimation, a new hybrid model combining the LDT model and Fuzzy Naive Bayes has been investigated. The experimental studies show that this hybrid model has comparable performance to LID3 but with much smaller trees. Finally, a FOIL based rule learning system has been introduced within label semantics framework. In this approach, the appropriateness of using a rule to describe a data element is represented by multi-dimensional appropriateness measures. Based on the FOIL algorithm, we proposed a new linguistic rule induction algorithm according to which we can obtain concise linguistic rules reflecting the underlying nature of the system.

It is widely recognized that most natural concepts have non-sharp boundaries. These concepts are vague or fuzzy, and one will usually only be willing to agree to a certain degree that an object belongs to a concept. Likewise, in machine learning and data mining, the patterns we are interested in are often vague and imprecise. To model this, in this chapter, we have discretized numerical attributes with fuzzy labels by which we can describe real values. Hence, we can use linguistic models to study the underlying relationships hidden in the data.

One of the distinctive advantages of linguistic models is that they allow for information fusion. In this chapter, we discussed methods for classification with linguistic constraints and classification for fuzzy data. Other information fusion methods are discussed in (Lawry, 2004). How to efficiently use background knowledge is an important challenge in machine learning. For example, Wang (Wang, 2004) argues that Bayesian learning has limitations in combining the prior knowledge and new evidence. We also need to consider the inconsistency between the background knowledge and new evidence. We believe that it will become a popular research topic in approximate reasoning.

Acknowledgements

The authors thank Prof Lotfi Zadeh for some insightful comments on this research. The first author also thanks Masoud Nikravesh, Marcus Thint, Ben Azvine and Trevor Martin for their interests in this research and support. The writing of this chapter is partly funded BT/BISC fellowship.

References

J.F. Baldwin, T.P. Martin and B.W. Pilsworth (1995), *Fril-Fuzzy and Evidential Reasoning in Artificial Intelligence*. John Wiley & Sons Inc, 1995.

J. F. Baldwin, J. Lawry and T.P. Martin (1997), Mass assignment fuzzy ID3 with applications. *Proceedings of the Unicom Workshop on Fuzzy Logic: Applications and Future Directions*, London pp. 278-294, 1997.

J. F. Baldwin and D. Xie (2004), Simple fuzzy logic rules based on fuzzy decision tree for classification and prediction problem, *Intelligent Information Processing II*, Z. Shi and Q. He (Ed.), Springer, 2004.

C. Blake and C.J. Merz (2007). UCI machine learning repository. http://www.ics.uci.edu/~mlearn/MLRepository.html, 2007.

M. Drobics, U. Bodenhofer and E. P. Klement (2003), FS-FOIL: an inductive learning method for extracting interpretable fuzzy descriptions, *International Journal of Approximate Reasoning*, 32: pp. 131-152, 2003.

S. R. Gunn (1998), Support vector machines for classification and regression. Technical Report of Dept. of Electronics and Computer Science, University of Southampton, 1998.

E. Hullermeier (2005), Fuzzy methods in machine learning and data mining: status and prospects, to appear in *Fuzzy Sets and Systems*, 2005.

R. Hyndman and M Akram (2005), Time series Data Library. Monash University, 2007.

C. Z. Janikow (1998), Fuzzy decision trees: issues and methods. *IEEE Trans. on Systems, Man, and Cybernetics-Part B: Cybernetics*, Vol. 28, No. 1, 1998.

R. C. Jeffrey (1965), *The Logic of Decision*, Gordon & Breach Inc., New York, 1965.

J. Lawry, J. Shanahan, and A. Ralescu (2003), *Modelling with Words: Learning, fusion, and reasoning within a formal linguistic representation framework.* LNAI 2873, Springer-Verlag, 2003.

J. Lawry (2001), Label semantics: A formal framework for modelling with words. *Symbolic and Quantitative Approaches to Reasoning with Uncertainty*, LNAI 2143: pp. 374-384, Springer-Verlag, 2001.

J. Lawry (2004), A framework for linguistic modelling, *Artificial Intelligence*, 155: pp. 1-39, 2004.

J Lawry (2006), *Modelling and Reasoning with Vague Concepts*, Springer, 2006.

C. Olaru and L. Wehenkel (2003), A complete fuzzy decision tree technique. *Fuzzy Sets and Systems.* 138: pp.221-254, 2003.

Y. Peng, P. A. Flach (2001), Soft discretization to enhance the continuous decision trees. *ECML/PKDD Workshop: IDDM.*

H. Prade, G. Richard, and M. Serrurier (2003), Enriching relational learning with fuzzy predicates, N. Lavrac, et. al (Eds.): *Proceedings of PKDD*, LNAI 2838, pp. 399-410.

Z. Qin and J. Lawry (2004), A tree-structured model classification model based on label semantics, *Proceedings of the 10th International Conference on Information Processing and Management of Uncertainty in Knowledge-based Systems (IPMU-04)*, pp. 261-268, Perugia, Italy.

Z. Qin and J. Lawry (2005a), Hybrid Bayesian estimation trees based on label semantics, L. Godo (Ed.), *Proceedings of Eighth European Conference on Symbolic and Quantitative Approaches to Reasoning with Uncertainty*, Lecture Notes in Artificial Intelligence 3571, pp. 896-907, Springer.

Z. Qin and J. Lawry (2005b), Decision tree learning with fuzzy labels, *Information Sciences*, Vol. 172/1-2: pp. 91-129.

Z. Qin and J. Lawry (2005c), Prediction trees using linguistic modelling, *the Proceedings of International Fuzzy Association World Congress-05*, Beijing, China, September.

Z. Qin and J. Lawry (2005d), Linguistic rule induction based on a random set semantics, *the Proceedings of International Fuzzy Association World Congress-05*, Beijing, China.

Z. Qin and J. Lawry (2007), Fuzziness and performance: an empirical study with linguistic decision trees. To appear in IFSA-2007, Cuncun, Mexico.

J. R. Quinlan (1986), Induction of decision trees, *Machine Learning*, Vol 1: pp. 81-106.

J. R. Quinlan (1993), *C4.5: Programs for Machine Learning*, San Mateo: Morgan Kaufmann.

J. R. Quinlan (1990), Learning logical definitions from relations, *Machine Learning*, 5: 239-266.

N. J. Randon and J. Lawry (2006), Classification and query evaluation using modelling with words, Information Sciences, Special Issue - Computing with Words: Models and Applications, Vol. 176: pp 438-464.

Pei Wang (2004), The limitation of Bayesianism, Artificial Intelligence 158(1): pp. 97-106.

D. Xie (2005), Fuzzy associated rules discovered on effective reduced database algorithm, *Proceedings of IEEE-FUZZ*, pp. 779-784, Reno, USA, 2005.

L. A. Zadeh (1965), Fuzzy sets, *Information and Control*, Vol 8: pp. 338-353.

L. A. Zadeh (1996), Fuzzy logic = computing with words, *IEEE Transaction on Fuzzy Systems*. Vol. 4, No. 2: pp. 103-111.

L. A. Zadeh, Toward a perception-based theory of probabilistic reasoning with imprecise probabilities, Journal of Statistical Planning and Inference, Vol. 105: pp. 233264.

L.A. Zadeh (2003), Foreword for modelling with words, *Modelling with Words*, LNAI 2873, Ed., J. Lawry, J. Shanahan, and A.Ralescu, Springer.

L.A. Zadeh (2005), Toward a generalized theory of uncertainty (GTU) an outline, Information Sciences, Vol. 172/1-2, pp. 1-40.

Part IV

Advanced Soft Computing Methods and Areas

Swarm Intelligence Algorithms for Data Clustering

Ajith Abraham[1], Swagatam Das[2], and Sandip Roy[3]

[1] Center of Excellence for Quantifiable Quality of Service (Q2S), Norwegian
  University of Science and Technology, Trondheim, Norway
  ajith.abraham@ieee.org
[2] Department of Electronics and Telecommunication Engineering, Jadavpur
  University, Kolkata 700032, India.
[3] Department of Computer Science and Engineering, Asansol Engineering College,
  Asansol-713304, India.

Summary. Clustering aims at representing large datasets by a fewer number of
prototypes or clusters. It brings simplicity in modeling data and thus plays a central role in the process of knowledge discovery and data mining. Data mining tasks,
in these days, require fast and accurate partitioning of huge datasets, which may
come with a variety of attributes or features. This, in turn, imposes severe computational requirements on the relevant clustering techniques. A family of bio-inspired
algorithms, well-known as Swarm Intelligence (SI) has recently emerged that meets
these requirements and has successfully been applied to a number of real world clustering problems. This chapter explores the role of SI in clustering different kinds of
datasets. It finally describes a new SI technique for partitioning any dataset into an
optimal number of groups through one run of optimization. Computer simulations
undertaken in this research have also been provided to demonstrate the effectiveness
of the proposed algorithm.

1 Introduction

Clustering means the act of partitioning an unlabeled dataset into groups
of similar objects. Each group, called a 'cluster', consists of objects that are
similar between themselves and dissimilar to objects of other groups. In the
past few decades, cluster analysis has played a central role in a variety of
fields ranging from engineering (machine learning, artificial intelligence, pattern recognition, mechanical engineering, electrical engineering), computer sciences (web mining, spatial database analysis, textual document collection, image segmentation), life and medical sciences (genetics, biology, microbiology,
paleontology, psychiatry, pathology), to earth sciences (geography. geology, remote sensing), social sciences (sociology, psychology, archeology, education),

and economics (marketing, business) (Evangelou *et al.*, 2001, Lillesand and Keifer, 1994, Rao, 1971, Duda and Hart, 1973, Fukunaga, 1990, Everitt, 1993).

From a machine learning perspective, clusters correspond to the hidden patterns in data, the search for clusters is a kind of unsupervised learning, and the resulting system represents a *data concept*. The problem of data clustering has been approached from diverse fields of knowledge like statistics (multivariate analysis) (Forgy, 1965), graph theory (Zahn, 1971), expectation maximization algorithms (Mitchell, 1997), artificial neural networks (Mao and Jain, 1995, Pal *et al.*, 1993, Kohonen, 1995), evolutionary computing (Falkenauer, 1998, Paterlini and Minerva, 2003) and so on. Researchers all over the globe are coming up with new algorithms, on a regular basis, to meet the increasing complexity of vast real-world datasets. A comprehensive review of the state-of-the-art clustering methods can be found in (Xu and Wunsch, 2005) and (Rokach and Maimon, 2005).

Data mining is a powerful new technology, which aims at the extraction of hidden predictive information from large databases. Data mining tools predict future trends and behaviors, allowing businesses to make proactive, knowledge-driven decisions. The process of knowledge discovery from databases necessitates fast and automatic clustering of very large datasets with several attributes of different types (Mitra *et al.*, 2002). This poses a severe challenge before the classical clustering techniques. Recently a family of nature inspired algorithms, known as *Swarm Intelligence* (SI), has attracted several researchers from the field of pattern recognition and clustering. Clustering techniques based on the SI tools have reportedly outperformed many classical methods of partitioning a complex real world dataset.

Swarm Intelligence is a relatively new interdisciplinary field of research, which has gained huge popularity in these days. Algorithms belonging to the domain, draw inspiration from the collective intelligence emerging from the behavior of a group of social insects (like bees, termites and wasps). When acting as a community, these insects even with very limited individual capability can jointly (cooperatively) perform many complex tasks necessary for their survival. Problems like finding and storing foods, selecting and picking up materials for future usage require a detailed planning, and are solved by insect colonies without any kind of supervisor or controller. An example of particularly successful research direction in swarm intelligence is Ant Colony Optimization (ACO) (Dorigo *et al.*, 1996, Dorigo and Gambardella, 1997), which focuses on discrete optimization problems, and has been applied successfully to a large number of NP hard discrete optimization problems including the traveling salesman, the quadratic assignment, scheduling, vehicle routing, etc., as well as to routing in telecommunication networks. Particle Swarm Optimization (PSO) (Kennedy and Eberhart, 1995) is another very popular SI algorithm for global optimization over continuous search spaces. Since its advent in 1995, PSO has attracted the attention of several researchers all over the world resulting into a huge number of variants of the basic algorithm as well as many parameter automation strategies.

In this Chapter, we explore the applicability of these bio-inspired approaches to the development of self-organizing, evolving, adaptive and autonomous clustering techniques, which will meet the requirements of next-generation data mining systems, such as diversity, scalability, robustness, and resilience. The next section of the chapter provides an overview of the SI paradigm with a special emphasis on two SI algorithms well-known as Particle Swarm Optimization (PSO) and Ant Colony Systems (ACS). Section 3 outlines the data clustering problem and briefly reviews the present state of the art in this field. Section 4 describes the use of the SI algorithms in both crisp and fuzzy clustering of real world datasets. A new automatic clustering algorithm, based on PSO, has been outlined in this Section. The algorithm requires no previous knowledge of the dataset to be partitioned, and can determine the optimal number of classes dynamically. The new method has been compared with two well-known, classical fuzzy clustering algorithms. The Chapter is concluded in Section 5 with possible directions for future research.

2 An Introduction to Swarm Intelligence

The behavior of a single ant, bee, termite and wasp often is too simple, but their collective and social behavior is of paramount significance. A look at National Geographic TV Channel reveals that advanced mammals including lions also enjoy social lives, perhaps for their self-existence at old age and in particular when they are wounded. The collective and social behavior of living creatures motivated researchers to undertake the study of today what is known as *Swarm Intelligence*. Historically, the phrase Swarm Intelligence (SI) was coined by Beny and Wang in late 1980s (Beni and Wang, 1989) in the context of cellular robotics. A group of researchers in different parts of the world started working almost at the same time to study the versatile behavior of different living creatures and especially the social insects. The efforts to mimic such behaviors through computer simulation finally resulted into the fascinating field of SI. SI systems are typically made up of a population of simple agents (an entity capable of performing/executing certain operations) interacting locally with one another and with their environment. Although there is normally no centralized control structure dictating how individual agents should behave, local interactions between such agents often lead to the emergence of global behavior. Many biological creatures such as fish schools and bird flocks clearly display structural order, with the behavior of the organisms so integrated that even though they may change shape and direction, they appear to move as a single coherent entity (Couzin *et al.*, 2002). The main properties of the collective behavior can be pointed out as follows and is summarized in Figure 1.

Homogeneity: every bird in flock has the same behavioral model. The flock moves without a leader, even though temporary leaders seem to appear.

Locality: its nearest flock-mates only influence the motion of each bird. Vision
is considered to be the most important senses for flock organization.
Collision Avoidance: avoid colliding with nearby flock mates.
Velocity Matching: attempt to match velocity with nearby flock mates.
Flock Centering: attempt to stay close to nearby flock mates

Individuals attempt to maintain a minimum distance between themselves
and others at all times. This rule is given the highest priority and corresponds
to a frequently observed behavior of animals in nature (Krause and Ruxton,
2002). If individuals are not performing an avoidance maneuver they tend to
be attracted towards other individuals (to avoid being isolated) and to align
themselves with neighbors (Partridge and Pitcher, 1980, Partridge, 1982).

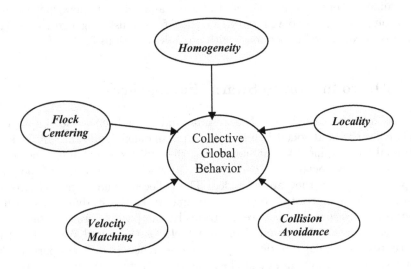

Fig. 1. Main traits of collective behavior

Couzin et al. identified four collective dynamical behaviors (Couzin et al.,
2002) as illustrated in Figure 2:

Swarm: an aggregate with cohesion, but a low level of polarization (parallel
alignment) among members
Torus: individuals perpetually rotate around an empty core (milling). The
direction of rotation is random.
Dynamic parallel group: the individuals are polarized and move as a coherent
group, but individuals can move throughout the group and density and
group form can fluctuate (Partridge and Pitcher, 1980, Major and Dill,
1978).
Highly parallel group: much more static in terms of exchange of spatial positions within the group than the dynamic parallel group and the variation
in density and form is minimal.

As mentioned in (Grosan *et al.*, 2006) at a high-level, a swarm can be viewed as a group of agents cooperating to achieve some purposeful behavior and achieve some goal (Abraham *et al.*, 2006). This collective intelligence seems to emerge from what are often large groups:

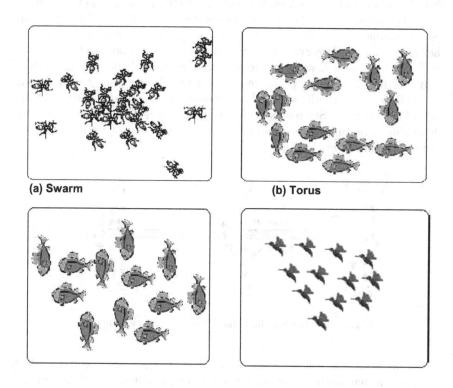

(a) Swarm   **(b) Torus**

Fig. 2. Different models of collective behavior (Grosan *et al.*, 2006)

According to Milonas, five basic principles define the SI paradigm (Milonas, 1994). First is the the proximity principle: the swarm should be able to carry out simple space and time computations. Second is the quality principle: the swarm should be able to respond to quality factors in the environment. Third is the principle of diverse response: the swarm should not commit its activities along excessively narrow channels. Fourth is the principle of stability: the swarm should not change its mode of behavior every time the environment changes. Fifth is the principle of adaptability: the swarm must be able to change behavior mote when it is worth the computational price. Note that principles four and five are the opposite sides of the same coin. Below we discuss in details two algorithms from SI domain, which have gained wide popularity in a relatively short span of time.

2.1 The Ant Colony Systems

The basic idea of a real ant system is illustrated in Figure 4. In the left picture, the ants move in a straight line to the food. The middle picture illustrates the situation soon after an obstacle is inserted between the nest and the food. To avoid the obstacle, initially each ant chooses to turn left or right at random. Let us assume that ants move at the same speed depositing pheromone in the trail uniformly. However, the ants that, by chance, choose to turn left will reach the food sooner, whereas the ants that go around the obstacle turning right will follow a longer path, and so will take longer time to circumvent the obstacle. As a result, pheromone accumulates faster in the shorter path around the obstacle. Since ants prefer to follow trails with larger amounts of pheromone, eventually all the ants converge to the shorter path around the obstacle, as shown in Figure 3.

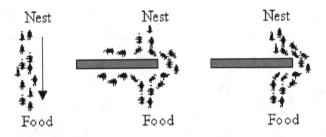

Fig. 3. Illustrating the behavior of real ant movements.

An artificial Ant Colony System (ACS) is an agent-based system, which simulates the natural behavior of ants and develops mechanisms of cooperation and learning. ACS was proposed by Dorigo *et al.* (Dorigo and Gambardella, 1997) as a new heuristic to solve combinatorial optimization problems. This new heuristic, called Ant Colony Optimization (ACO) has been found to be both robust and versatile in handling a wide range of combinatorial optimization problems.

The main idea of ACO is to model a problem as the search for a minimum cost path in a graph. Artificial ants as if walk on this graph, looking for cheaper paths. Each ant has a rather simple behavior capable of finding relatively costlier paths. Cheaper paths are found as the emergent result of the global cooperation among ants in the colony. The behavior of artificial ants is inspired from real ants: they lay pheromone trails (obviously in a mathematical form) on the graph edges and choose their path with respect to probabilities that depend on pheromone trails. These pheromone trails progressively decrease by evaporation. In addition, artificial ants have some extra features not seen in their counterpart in real ants. In particular, they live in a discrete world (a graph) and their moves consist of transitions from nodes to nodes.

Below we illustrate the use of ACO in finding the optimal tour in the classical Traveling Salesman Problem (TSP). Given a set of n cities and a set of distances between them, the problem is to determine a minimum traversal of the cities and return to the home-station at the end. It is indeed important to note that the traversal should in no way include a city more than once. Let r (C_x, C_y)be a measure of cost for traversal from city C_x to C_y. Naturally, the total cost of traversing n cities indexed by $i_1, i_2, i_3, \ldots, i_n$ in order is given by the following expression:

$$Cost(i_1, i_2, \ldots, i_n) = \sum_{j=1}^{n-1} r(Ci_j, Ci_{j+1}) + r(Ci_n, Ci_1) \tag{1}$$

The ACO algorithm is employed to find an optimal order of traversal of the cities. Let τ be a mathematical entity modeling the pheromone and $\eta_{ij} = 1/r$ (i , j) is a local heuristic. Also let allowed$_k(t)$ be the set of cities that are yet to be visited by ant k located in city$i$. Then according to the classical ant system (Everitt, 1993) the probability that ant k in city i visits city j is given by:

$$p_{ij}^k(t) = \frac{[\tau_{ij}(t)]^\alpha [\eta_{ij}]^\beta}{\sum_{h \in allowed_k(t)} [\tau_{ih}(t)]^\alpha [\eta_{ih}]^\beta} \quad if \; h \in allowed_k(t) \atop 0 \qquad\qquad\qquad\qquad otherwise \tag{2}$$

In Equation 2 shorter edges with greater amount of pheromone are favored by multiplying the pheromone on edge (i, j) by the corresponding heuristic value $\eta(i, j)$. Parameters α (ξ 0) and β (ξ 0) determine the relative importance of pheromone versus cost. Now in ant system, pheromone trails are updated as follows. Let D_k be the length of the tour performed by ant k, $\Delta\tau_k$ (i , j)= $1/D_k$ if (i,j) $\in$ tour done by ant $k$and = 0 otherwise and finally let ρ $\in$ [0,1] be a pheromone decay parameter which takes care of the occasional evaporation of the pheromone from the visited edges. Then once all ants have built their tours, pheromone is updated on all the ages as,

$$\tau(i,j) = (1 - \rho).\tau(i,j) + \sum_{k=1}^{m} \Delta\tau_k(i,j) \tag{3}$$

From Equation (3), we can guess that pheromone updating attempts to accumulate greater amount of pheromone to shorter tours (which corresponds to high value of the second term in (3) so as to compensate for any loss of pheromone due to the first term). This conceptually resembles a reinforcement-learning scheme, where better solutions receive a higher reinforcement.

The ACO differs from the classical ant system in the sense that here the pheromone trails are updated in two ways. Firstly, when ants construct a tour they locally change the amount of pheromone on the visited edges by a local updating rule. Now if we let γ to be a decay parameter and $\Delta\tau(i, j) = \tau_0$ such that τ_0 is the initial pheromone level, then the local rule may be stated as,

$$\tau(i,j) = (1 - \gamma).\tau(i,j) + \gamma.\Delta\tau(i,j) \tag{4}$$

Secondly, after all the ants have built their individual tours, a global updating rule is applied to modify the pheromone level on the edges that belong to the best ant tour found so far. If κ be the usual pheromone evaporation constant, D_{gb} be the length of the globally best tour from the beginning of the trial and
$\Delta\tau'(i , j) = 1/ D_{gb}$ only when the edge (i,j) belongs to global-best-tour and zero otherwise, then we may express the global rule as follows:

$$\tau(i,j) = (1 - \kappa).\tau(i,j) + \kappa.\Delta\tau'(i,j) \tag{5}$$

The main steps of ACO algorithm are presented in Algorithm 1.

Algorithm 1: Procedure ACO

1: Initialize pheromone trails;
2: **repeat** {at this stage each loop is called an iteration}
3:    Each ant is positioned on a starting node
4:    **repeat** {at this level each loop is called a step}
5:       Each ant applies a *state transition rule like rule (2)* to incrementally build a solution and a *local pheromone-updating rule like rule (4)*;
6:    **until** all ants have built a complete solution
7:    global pheromone-updating rule like rule (5) is applied.
8: **until** terminating condition is reached

2.2 The Particle Swarm Optimization (PSO)

The concept of Particle Swarms, although initially introduced for simulating human social behaviors, has become very popular these days as an efficient search and optimization technique. The Particle Swarm Optimization (PSO) (Kennedy and Eberhart, 1995,Kennedy et al., 2001), as it is called now, does not require any gradient information of the function to be optimized, uses only primitive mathematical operators and is conceptually very simple.

In PSO, a population of conceptual 'particles' is initialized with random positions X_i and velocities V_i, and a function, f, is evaluated, using the particle's positional coordinates as input values. In an n-dimensional search space, $X_i = (x_{i1}, x_{i2}, x_{i3},...,x_{in})$ and $V_i = (v_{i1}, v_{i2}, v_{i3},...,v_{in})$. Positions and velocities are adjusted, and the function is evaluated with the new coordinates at each time-step. The basic update equations for the d-th dimension of the i-th particle in PSO may be given as

$$V_{id}(t+1) = \omega.V_{id}(t) + C_1.\varphi_1.(P_{lid} - X_{id}(t)) + C_2.\varphi_2.(P_{gd} - X_{id}(t))$$
$$X_{id}(t+1) = X_{id}(t) + V_{id}(t+1) \tag{6}$$

The variables ϕ_1 and ϕ_2 are random positive numbers, drawn from a uniform distribution and defined by an upper limit ϕ_{max}, which is a parameter of the system. C_1 and C_2 are called acceleration constants whereas ω is called inertia weight. P_{li} is the local best solution found so far by the i-th particle, while P_g represents the positional coordinates of the fittest particle found so far in the entire community. Once the iterations are terminated, most of the particles are expected to converge to a small radius surrounding the global optima of the search space. The velocity updating scheme has been illustrated in Figure 4 with a humanoid particle.

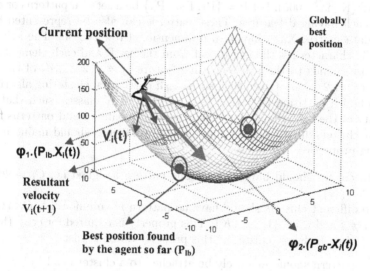

Fig. 4. Illustrating the velocity updating scheme of basic PSO

A pseudo code for the PSO algorithm is presented in Algorithm 2.

3 Data Clustering – An Overview

In this section, we first provide a brief and formal description of the clustering problem. We then discuss a few major classical clustering techniques.

3.1 Problem Definition

A *pattern* is a physical or abstract structure of objects. It is distinguished from others by a collective set of attributes called *features*, which together represent

---

Algorithm 2: The PSO Algorithm

Input: Randomly initialized position and velocity of the particles: $\mathbf{X}_i(0)$ and $\mathbf{V}_i(0)$

Output: Position of the approximate global optima $\mathbf{X}^*$

1: **while** terminating condition is not reached **do**
2:    **for** $i = 1$ to *numberofparticles* **do**
3:       Evaluate the fitness: $= f(\mathbf{X}_i(t))$;
4:       Update $\mathbf{P}(t)$ and $\mathbf{g}(t)$;
5:       Adapt velocity of the particle using Equation 3;
6:       Update the position of the particle;
7:    **end for**
8: **end while**

---

a pattern (Konar, 2005). Let $P = \{P_1, P_2 \ldots P_n\}$ be a set of n patterns or data points, each having d features. These patterns can also be represented by a profile data matrix $\mathbf{X}_{n \times d}$ having n d-dimensional row vectors. The i-th row vector $\mathbf{X}_i$ characterizes the i-th object from the set P and each element $X_{i,j}$ in $\mathbf{X}_i$ corresponds to the j-th real value feature ($j = 1, 2, \ldots, d$) of the i-th pattern (i =1,2,...., n). Given such an $\mathbf{X}_{n \times d}$, a partitional clustering algorithm tries to find a partition $C = \{C_1, C_2, \ldots, C_K\}$ of K classes, such that the similarity of the patterns in the same cluster is maximum and patterns from different clusters differ as far as possible. The partitions should maintain the following properties:

1. Each cluster should have at least one pattern assigned i.e. $C_i \neq \Phi \forall i \in \{1, 2, ..., K\}$.
2. Two different clusters should have no pattern in common. i.e. $C_i \cap C_j = \Phi, \forall i \neq j$ and $i, j \in \{1, 2, ..., K\}$. This property is required for crisp (hard) clustering. In Fuzzy clustering this property doesn't exist.
3. Each pattern should definitely be attached to a cluster i.e. $\bigcup\limits_{i=1}^{K} C_i = P$.

Since the given dataset can be partitioned in a number of ways maintaining all of the above properties, a fitness function (some measure of the adequacy of the partitioning) must be defined. The problem then turns out to be one of finding a partition $\mathbf{C}^*$ of optimal or near-optimal adequacy as compared to all other feasible solutions $\mathbf{C} = \{ \mathbf{C}^1, \mathbf{C}^2, \ldots, \mathbf{C}^{N(n,K)}\}$ where,

$$N(n, K) = \frac{1}{K!} \sum_{i=1}^{K} (-1)^i \binom{K}{i}^i (K - i)^i \tag{7}$$

is the number of feasible partitions. This is same as,

$$\underset{C}{Optimize} f(X_{n \times d}, C) \tag{8}$$

where C is a single partition from the set $\mathbf{C}$ and f is a statistical-mathematical function that quantifies the goodness of a partition on the basis of the similarity measure of the patterns. Defining an appropriate similarity measure plays fundamental role in clustering (Jain *et al.*, 1999). The most popular way to evaluate similarity between two patterns amounts to the use of *distance measure*. The most widely used distance measure is the Euclidean distance, which between any two d-dimensional patterns $\mathbf{X}_i$ and $\mathbf{X}_j$ is given by,

$$d(\mathbf{X}_i, \mathbf{X}_j) = \sqrt{\sum_{p=1}^{d} (X_{i,p} - X_{j,p})^2} = \|\mathbf{X}_i - \mathbf{X}_j\| \tag{9}$$

It has been shown in (Brucker, 1978) that the clustering problem is NP-hard when the number of clusters exceeds 3.

3.2 The Classical Clustering Algorithms

Data clustering is broadly based on two approaches: *hierarchical* and *partitional* (Frigui and Krishnapuram, 1999, Leung *et al.*, 2000). Within each of the types, there exists a wealth of subtypes and different algorithms for finding the clusters. In hierarchical clustering, the output is a tree showing a sequence of clustering with each cluster being a partition of the data set (Leung *et al.*, 2000). Hierarchical algorithms can be agglomerative (bottom-up) or divisive (top-down). Agglomerative algorithms begin with each element as a separate cluster and merge them in successively larger clusters. Divisive algorithms begin with the whole set and proceed to divide it into successively smaller clusters. Hierarchical algorithms have two basic advantages (Frigui and Krishnapuram, 1999). Firstly, the number of classes need not be specified a priori and secondly, they are independent of the initial conditions. However, the main drawback of hierarchical clustering techniques is they are static, i.e. data-points assigned to a cluster can not move to another cluster. In addition to that, they may fail to separate overlapping clusters due to lack of information about the global shape or size of the clusters (Jain *et al.*, 1999).

Partitional clustering algorithms, on the other hand, attempt to decompose the data set directly into a set of disjoint clusters. They try to optimize certain criteria. The criterion function may emphasize the local structure of the data, as by assigning clusters to peaks in the probability density function, or the global structure. Typically, the global criteria involve minimizing some measure of dissimilarity in the samples within each cluster, while maximizing the dissimilarity of different clusters. The advantages of the hierarchical algorithms are the disadvantages of the partitional algorithms and vice versa. An extensive survey of various clustering techniques can be found in (Jain *et al.*, 1999). The focus of this chapter is on the partitional clustering algorithms.

Clustering can also be performed in two different modes: crisp and fuzzy. In crisp clustering, the clusters are disjoint and non-overlapping in nature.

Any pattern may belong to one and only one class in this case. In case of fuzzy clustering, a pattern may belong to all the classes with a certain fuzzy membership grade (Jain *et al.*, 1999).

The most widely used iterative K-means algorithm (MacQueen, 1967) for partitional clustering aims at minimizing the ICS (Intra-Cluster Spread) which for K cluster centers can be defined as

$$ICS(C_1, C_2, ..., C_K) = \sum_{i=1}^{K} \sum_{\mathbf{X}_i \in C_i} \|\mathbf{X}_i - \mathbf{m}_i\|^2 \tag{10}$$

The K-means (or hard c-means) algorithm starts with K cluster-centroids (these centroids are initially selected randomly or derived from some a priori information). Each pattern in the data set is then assigned to the closest cluster-centre. Centroids are updated by using the mean of the associated patterns. The process is repeated until some stopping criterion is met.

In the c-medoids algorithm (Kaufman and Rousseeuw, 1990), on the other hand, each cluster is represented by one of the representative objects in the cluster located near the center. Partitioning around medoids (PAM) (Kaufman and Rousseeuw, 1990) starts from an initial set of medoids, and iteratively replaces one of the medoids by one of the non-medoids if it improves the total distance of the resulting clustering. Although PAM works effectively for small data, it does not scale well for large datasets. Clustering large applications based on randomized search (CLARANS) (Ng and Han, 1994), using randomized sampling, is capable of dealing with the associated scalability issue.

The fuzzy c-means (FCM) (Bezdek, 1981) seems to be the most popular algorithm in the field of fuzzy clustering. In the classical FCM algorithm, a *within cluster sum* function J_m is minimized to evolve the proper cluster centers:

$$J_m = \sum_{j=1}^{n} \sum_{i=1}^{c} (u_{ij})^m \|\mathbf{X}_j - \mathbf{V}_i\|^2 \tag{11}$$

where $\mathbf{V}_i$ is the i-th cluster center, $\mathbf{X}_j$ is the j-th d-dimensional data vector and $\| \, . \, \|$ is an inner product-induced norm in d dimensions. Given c classes, we can determine their cluster centers $\mathbf{V}_i$ for i=1 to c by means of the following expression:

$$\mathbf{V}_i = \frac{\sum\limits_{j=1}^{n} (u_{ij})^m \mathbf{X}_j}{\sum\limits_{j=1}^{n} (u_{ij})^m} \tag{12}$$

Here m (m¿1) is any real number that influences the membership grade. Now differentiating the performance criterion with respect to $\mathbf{V}_i$ (treating u_{ij} as constants) and with respect to u_{ij} (treating $\mathbf{V}_i$ as constants) and setting them to zero the following relation can be obtained:

$$u_{ij} = \left[\sum_{k=1}^{c} \left(\frac{\|\mathbf{X}_j - \mathbf{V}_i\|^2}{\|\mathbf{X} - \mathbf{V}_i\|^2} \right)^{1/(m-1)} \right]^{-1} \tag{13}$$

Several modifications of the classical FCM algorithm can be found in (Hall et al., 1999, Gath and Geva, 1989, Bensaid et al., 1996, Clark et al., 1994, Ahmed et al., 2002, Wang et al., 2004).

3.3 Relevance of SI Algorithms in Clustering

From the discussion of the previous section, we see that the SI algorithms are mainly stochastic search and optimization techniques, guided by the principles of collective behaviour and self organization of insect swarms. They are efficient, adaptive and robust search methods producing near optimal solutions and have a large amount of implicit parallelism. On the other hand, data clustering may be well formulated as a difficult global optimization problem; thereby making the application of SI tools more obvious and appropriate.

4 Clustering with the SI Algorithms

In this section we first review the present state of the art clustering algorithms based on SI tools, especially the ACO and PSO. We then outline a new algorithm which employs the PSO model to automatically determine the number of clusters in a previously unhandled dataset. Computer simulations undertaken for this study have also been included to demonstrate the elegance of the new dynamic clustering technique.

4.1 The Ant Colony Based Clustering Algorithms

Ant colonies provide a means to formulate some powerful nature-inspired heuristics for solving the clustering problems. Among other social movements, researchers have simulated the way, ants work collaboratively in the task of grouping dead bodies so, as to keep the nest clean (Bonabeau et al., 1999). It can be observed that, with time the ants tend to cluster all dead bodies in a specific region of the environment, thus forming piles of corpses.

Larval sorting and corpse cleaning by ant was first modeled by Deneubourg et al. for accomplishing certain tasks in robotics (Deneubourg et al., 1991). This inspired the Ant-based clustering algorithm (Handl et al., 2003). Lumer and Faieta modified the algorithm using a dissimilarity-based evaluation of the local density, in order to make it suitable for data clustering (Lumer and Faieta, 1994). This introduced standard Ant Clustering Algorithm (ACA). It has subsequently been used for numerical data analysis (Lumer and Faieta,

1994), data-mining (Lumer and Faieta, 1995), graph-partitioning (Kuntz and Snyers, 1994, Kuntz and Snyers, 1999, Kuntz et al., 1998) and text-mining (Handl and Meyer, 2002, Hoe et al., 2002, Ramos and Merelo, 2002). Many authors (Handl and Meyer, 2002, Ramos et al., 2002) proposed a number of modifications to improve the convergence rate and to get optimal number of clusters. Monmarche et al. hybridized the Ant-based clustering algorithm with K-means algorithm (Monmarche et al., 1999) and compared it to traditional K-means on various data sets, using the classification error for evaluation purposes. However, the results obtained with this method are not applicable to ordinary ant-based clustering since it differs significantly from the latter.

Like a standard ACO, ant-based clustering is a distributed process that employs positive feedback. Ants are modeled by simple agents that randomly move in their environment. The environment is considered to be a low dimensional space, more generally a two-dimensional plane with square grid. Initially, each data object that represents a multi-dimensional pattern is randomly distributed over the 2-D space. Data items that are scattered within this environment can be picked up, transported and dropped by the agents in a probabilistic way. The picking and dropping operation are influenced by the similarity and density of the data items within the ant's local neighborhood. Generally, the size of the neighborhood is 3×3. Probability of picking up data items is more when the object are either isolated or surrounded by dissimilar items. They trend to drop them in the vicinity of similar ones. In this way, a clustering of the elements on the grid is obtained.

The ants search for the feature space either through random walk or with jumping using a short term memory. Each ant picks up or drops objects according to the following local probability density measure:

$$f(\mathbf{X}_i) = \max\{0, \frac{1}{s^2} \sum\nolimits_{\mathbf{X}_j \in N_{s \times s}(r)} [1 - \frac{d(\mathbf{X}_i, \mathbf{X}_j)}{\alpha(1 + \frac{\nu - 1}{\nu_{max}})} \tag{14}$$

In the above expression, $N_{s \times s}(r)$ denotes the local area of perception surrounding the site of radius r, which the ant occupies in the two-dimensional grid. The threshold αg cales the dissimilarity within each pair of objects, and the moving speed v controls the step-size of the ant searching in the space within one time unit. If an ant is not carrying an object and finds an object $\mathbf{X}_i$ in its neighborhood, it picks up this object with a probability that is inversely proportional to the number of similar objects in the neighborhood. It may be expressed as:

$$P_{pick-up}(\mathbf{X}_i) = [\frac{k_p}{k_p + f(\mathbf{X}_i)}]^2 \tag{15}$$

If however, the ant is carrying an object x and perceives a neighbor's cell in which there are other objects, then the ant drops off the object it is carrying with a probability that is directly proportional to the object's similarity with the perceived ones. This is given by:

$$P_{drop}(\mathbf{X}_i) = \begin{array}{ll} 2.f(\mathbf{X}_i) & if f(\mathbf{X}_i) < k_d \\ 1 & if f(\mathbf{X}_i) \geq k_d \end{array}$$

The parameters k_p and k_d are the picking and dropping constants (Gath and Geva, 1989) respectively. Function $f(\mathbf{X}_i)$ provides an estimate of the density and similarity of elements in the neighborhood of object $\mathbf{X}_i$. The standard ACA pseudo-code is summarized in Algorithm 3.

Algorithm 3: Procedure ACA

1: Place every item $\mathbf{X}_i$ on a random cell of the grid;
2: Place every ant k on a random cell of the grid unoccupied by ants;
3: iteration_count ← 1;
4: **while** iteration_count < maximum_iteration **do**
5:    **for** $i = 1$ to no_of_ants **do**
6:      if unladen ant and cell occupied by item $\mathbf{X}_i$ **then**
7:        compute $f(\mathbf{X}_i)$ and $P_{pick-up}(\mathbf{X}_i)$;
8:      else
9:        if ant carrying item xi and cell empty **then**
10:          compute $f(\mathbf{X}_i)$ and $P_{drop}(\mathbf{X}_i)$;
11:          drop item $\mathbf{X}_i$ with probability $P_{drop}(\mathbf{X}_i)$;
12:        **end if**
13:      **end if**
14:      move to a randomly selected, neighboring and unoccupied cell ;
15:    **end for**
16:    t ← t + 1
17: **end while**
18: print location of items;

Kanade and Hall (Kanade and Hall, 2003) presented a hybridization of the ant systems with the classical FCM algorithm to determine the number of clusters in a given dataset automatically. In their fuzzy ant algorithm, at first the ant based clustering is used to create raw clusters and then these clusters are refined using the FCM algorithm. Initially the ants move the individual data objects to form heaps. The centroids of these heaps are taken as the initial cluster centers and the FCM algorithm is used to refine these clusters. In the second stage the objects obtained from the FCM algorithm are hardened according to the maximum membership criteria to form new heaps. These new heaps are then sometimes moved and merged by the ants. The final clusters formed are refined by using the FCM algorithm.

A number of modifications have been introduced to the basic ant based clustering scheme that improve the quality of the clustering, the speed of convergence and, in particular, the spatial separation between clusters on the grid, which is essential for the scheme of cluster retrieval. A detailed description of the variants and results on the qualitative performance gains afforded by these extensions are provided in (Tsang and Kwong, 2006).

4.2 The PSO Based Clustering Algorithms

Research efforts have made it possible to view data clustering as an optimization problem. This view offers us a chance to apply PSO algorithm for evolving a set of candidate cluster centroids and thus determining a near optimal partitioning of the dataset at hand. An important advantage of the PSO is its ability to cope with local optima by maintaining, recombining and comparing several candidate solutions simultaneously. In contrast, local search heuristics, such as the simulated annealing algorithm (Selim and Alsultan, 1991) only refine a single candidate solution and are notoriously weak in coping with local optima. Deterministic local search, which is used in algorithms like the K-means, always converges to the nearest local optimum from the starting position of the search.

PSO-based clustering algorithm was first introduced by Omran *et al.* in (Omran *et al.*, 2002). The results of Omran *et al.* (Omran *et al.*, 2002, Omran *et al.*, 2005a) showed that PSO based method outperformed K-means, FCM and a few other state-of-the-art clustering algorithms. In their method, Omran *et al.* used a quantization error based fitness measure for judging the performance of a clustering algorithm. The quantization error is defined as:

$$J_e = \frac{\sum_{i=1}^{K} \sum_{\forall \mathbf{X}_j \in C_i} d(\mathbf{X}_j, \mathbf{V}_i)/n_i}{K} \tag{16}$$

where C_i is the i-th cluster center and n_i is the number of data points belonging to the i-th cluster. Each particle in the PSO algorithm represents a possible set of K cluster centroids as:

$$\vec{Z}_i(t) = \quad \boxed{\begin{array}{|c|c|c|c|} \vec{V}_{i,1} & \vec{V}_{i,2} & \text{.......} & \vec{V}_{i,K} \end{array}}$$

where $\mathbf{V}_{i,p}$ refers to the p-th cluster centroid vector of the i-th particle. The quality of each particle is measured by the following fitness function:

$$f(\mathbf{Z}_i, M_i) = w_1 \bar{d}_{\max}(M_i, \mathbf{X}_i) + w_2(R_{\max} - d_{\min}(\mathbf{Z}_i)) + w_3 J_e \tag{17}$$

In the above expression, R_{max} is the maximum feature value in the dataset and $\mathbf{M}_i$ is the matrix representing the assignment of the patterns to the clusters of the i-th particle. Each element $m_{i,k,p}$ indicates whether the pattern $\mathbf{X}_p$ belongs to cluster C_k of i-th particle. The user-defined constants w_1, w_2, and w_3 are used to weigh the contributions from different sub-objectives. In addition,

$$\bar{d}_{\max} = \max_{k \in 1,2,\ldots,K} \left\{ \sum_{\forall \mathbf{X}_p \in C_{i,K}} d(\mathbf{X}_p, \mathbf{V}_{i,k})/n_{i,k} \right\} \tag{18}$$

and,

$$d_{\min}(\mathbf{Z}_i) = \min_{\forall p,q,p \neq q} \{ d(\mathbf{V}_{i,p}, \mathbf{V}_{i,q}) \} \tag{19}$$

is the minimum Euclidean distance between any pair of clusters. In the above, $n_{i,k}$ is the number of patterns that belong to cluster $\mathbf{C}i,k$ of particle i. he fitness function is a multi-objective optimization problem, which minimizes the intra-cluster distance, maximizes inter-cluster separation, and reduces the quantization error. The PSO clustering algorithm is summarized in Algorithm 4.

Algorithm 4: The PSO Clustering Algorithm

1: Initialize each particle with K random cluster centers.
2: **for** iteration_count = 1 to maximum_iterations **do**
3:     **for all** particle i **do**
4:         **for all** pattern $\mathbf{X}_p$ in the dataset **do**
5:             calculate Euclidean distance of $\mathbf{X}_p$ with all cluster centroids
6:             assign $\mathbf{X}_p$ to the cluster that have nearest centroid to $\mathbf{X}_p$
7:         **end for**
8:         calculate the fitness function $f(\mathbf{Z}_i, M_i)$
9:     **end for**
10:    find the personal best and global best position of each particle.
11:    Update the cluster centroids according to velocity updating and coordinate updating formula of PSO.
12: **end for**

Van der Merwe and Engelbrecht hybridized this approach with the k-means algorithm for clustering general dataets (van der Merwe and Engelbrecht, 2003). A single particle of the swarm is initialized with the result of the k-means algorithm. The rest of the swarm is initialized randomly. In 2003, Xiao et al used a new approach based on the synergism of the PSO and the Self Organizing Maps (SOM) (Xiao et al., 2003) for clustering gene expression data. They got promising results by applying the hybrid SOM-PSO algorithm over the gene expression data of Yeast and Rat Hepatocytes. Paterlini and Krink (Paterlini and Krink, 2006) have compared the performance of K-means, GA (Holland, 1975, Goldberg, 1975), PSO and Differential Evolution (DE) (Storn and Price, 1997) for a representative point evaluation approach to partitional clustering. The results show that PSO and DE outperformed the K-means algorithm.

Cui et al. (Cui and Potok, 2005) proposed a PSO based hybrid algorithm for classifying the text documents. They applied the PSO, K-means and a hybrid PSO clustering algorithm on four different text document datasets. The results illustrate that the hybrid PSO algorithm can generate more compact clustering results over a short span of time than the K-means algorithm.

4.3 An Automatic Clustering Algorithm Based on PSO

Tremendous research effort has gone in the past few years to evolve the clusters in complex datasets through evolutionary computing techniques. However, little work has been taken up to determine the optimal number of clusters at the same time. Most of the existing clustering techniques, based on evolutionary algorithms, accept the number of classes K as an input instead of determining the same on the run. Nevertheless, in many practical situations, the appropriate number of groups in a new dataset may be unknown or impossible to determine even approximately. For example, while clustering a set of documents arising from the query to a search engine, the number of classes K changes for each set of documents that result from an interaction with the search engine. Also if the dataset is described by high-dimensional feature vectors (which is very often the case), it may be practically impossible to visualize the data for tracking its number of clusters.

Finding an optimal number of clusters in a large dataset is usually a challenging task. The problem has been investigated by several researches (Halkidi et al., 2001, Theodoridis and Koutroubas, 1999) but the outcome is still unsatisfactory (Rosenberger and Chehdi, 2000). Lee and Antonsson (Lee and Antonsson, 2000) used an Evolutionary Strategy (ES) (Schwefel, 1995) based method to dynamically cluster a dataset. The proposed ES implemented variable-length individuals to search for both centroids and optimal number of clusters. An approach to classify a dataset dynamically using Evolutionary Programming (EP) (Fogel et al., 1966) can be found in Sarkar (Sarkar et al., 1997) where two fitness functions are optimized simultaneously: one gives the optimal number of clusters, whereas the other leads to a proper identification of each cluster's centroid. Bandopadhyay et al. (Bandyopadhyay and Maulik, 2000) devised a variable string-length genetic algorithm (VGA) to tackle the dynamic clustering problem using a single fitness function. Very recently, Omran et al. came up with an automatic hard clustering scheme (Omran et al., 2005c). The algorithm starts by partitioning the dataset into a relatively large number of clusters to reduce the effect of the initialization. Using binary PSO (Kennedy and Eberhart, 1997), an optimal number of clusters is selected. Finally, the centroids of the chosen clusters are refined through the K-means algorithm. The authors applied the algorithm for segmentation of natural, synthetic and multi-spectral images.

In this section we discuss a new fuzzy clustering algorithm (Das et al., 2006), which can automatically determine the number of clusters in a given dataset. The algorithm is based on a modified PSO algorithm with improved convergence properties.

The Modification of the Classical PSO

The canonical PSO has been subjected to empirical and theoretical investigations by several researchers (Eberhart and Shi, 2001, Clerc and Kennedy, 2002). In many occasions, the convergence is premature, especially if the swarm uses a small inertia weight ω or constriction coefficient (Clerc and Kennedy, 2002). As the global best found early in the searching process may be a poor local minima, we propose a multi-elitist strategy for searching the global best of the PSO. We call the new variant of PSO the MEPSO. The idea draws inspiration from the works reported in (Deb *et al.*, 2002). We define a growth rate β for each particle. When the fitness value of a particle of t-th iteration is higher than that of a particle of (t-1)-th iteration, the β will be increased. After the local best of all particles are decided in each generation, we move the local best, which has higher fitness value than the global best into the candidate area. Then the global best will be replaced by the local best with the highest growth rate β. Therefore, the fitness value of the new global best is always higher than the old global best. The pseudo code about MEPSO is described in Algorithm 5.

Algorithm 5: The MEPSO Algorithm

1: **for** $t = 1$ to t_{max} **do**
2: **if** $t < t_{max}$ **then**
3:   **for** $j = 1$ to N **do** {swarm size is N}
4:    **if** the fitness value of *particle$_j$* in t-th time-step > that of *particle$_j$* in $(t-1)$-th time-step **then**
5:     $\beta_j = \beta_j + 1$;
6:    **end if**
7:    Update Local *best$_j$*.
8:    **if** the fitness of Local *best$_j$* > that of Global best now **then**
9:     Choose Local *best$_j$* put into candidate area.
10:    **end if**
11:   **end for**
12:   Calculate β of every candidate, and record the candidate of β_{max} .
13:   Update the Global best to become the candidate of β_{max}.
14: **else**
15:   Update the Global best to become the particle of highest fitness value.
16: **end if**
17: **end for**

Particle Representation

In the proposed method, for n data points, each p-dimensional, and for a user-specified maximum number of clusters c_{max}, a particle is a vector of real numbers of dimension $c_{max} + c_{max} \times p$. The first c_{max} entries are positive floating-point numbers in (0, 1), each of which controls whether the corresponding cluster is to be activated (i.e. to be really used for classifying the data) or not. The remaining entries are reserved for c_{max} cluster centers, each p-dimensional. A single particle can be shown as:

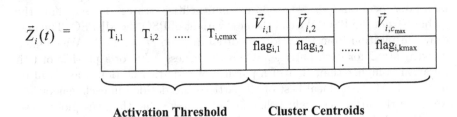

$$\bar{Z}_i(t) =$$

| $T_{i,1}$ | $T_{i,2}$ | ..... | $T_{i,cmax}$ | $\vec{V}_{i,1}$ $flag_{i,1}$ | $\vec{V}_{i,2}$ $flag_{i,2}$ | ...... | $\vec{V}_{i,c_{max}}$ $flag_{i,kmax}$ |

Activation Threshold   **Cluster Centroids**

Every probable cluster center $m_{i,j}$ has p features and a binary $flag_{i,j}$ associated with it. The cluster center is active (i.e., selected for classification) if $flag_{i,j} = 1$ and inactive if $flag_{i,j} = 0$. Each flag is set or reset according to the value of the activation threshold $T_{i,j}$. Note that these flags are latent information associated with the cluster centers and do not take part in the PSO-type mutation of the particle. The rule for selecting the clusters specified by one particle is:

$$If T_{i,j} > 0.5 Then flag_i, j = 1 Else flag_{i,j} = 0 \qquad (20)$$

Note that the flags in an offspring are to be changed only through the T_{ij}'s (according to the above rule). When a particle jumps to a new position, according to (8), the T values are first obtained which then are used to select (via equation (6)) the m values. If due to mutation some threshold T in a particle exceeds 1 or becomes negative, it is fixed to 1 or zero, respectively. However, if it is found that no flag could be set to one in a particle (all activation thresholds are smaller than 0.5), we randomly select 2 thresholds and re-initialize them to a random value between 0.5 and 1.0. Thus the minimum number of possible clusters is 2.

Fitness Function

The quality of a partition can be judged by an appropriate cluster validity index. Cluster validity indices correspond to the statistical-mathematical functions used to evaluate the results of a clustering algorithm on a quantitative basis. Generally, a cluster validity index serves two purposes. First, it can be used to determine the number of clusters, and secondly, it finds out the corresponding best partition. One traditional approach for determining the optimum number of classes is to run the algorithm repeatedly with different number of classes as input and then to select the partitioning of the data resulting in the best validity measure (Halkidi and Vazirgiannis, 2001). Ideally, a validity index should take care of the following aspects of the partitioning:

1. *Cohesion*: Patterns in one cluster should be as similar to each other as possible. The fitness variance of the patterns in a cluster is an indication of the cluster's cohesion or compactness.
2. *Separation*: Clusters should be well separated. The distance among the cluster centers (may be their Euclidean distance) gives an indication of cluster separation.

In the present work we have based our fitness function on the Xie-Benni index. This index, due to (Xie and Beni, 1991), is given by:

$$XB_m = \frac{\sum\limits_{i=1}^{c} \sum\limits_{j=1}^{n} u_{ij}^2 \|\mathbf{X}_j - \mathbf{V}_i\|^2}{n \times \min_{i \neq j} \|\mathbf{V}_i - \mathbf{V}_j\|^2} \tag{21}$$

Using XB_m the optimal number of clusters can be obtained by minimizing the index value. The fitness function may thus be written as:

$$f = \frac{1}{XB_i(c) + eps} \tag{22}$$

where XB_i is the Xie-Benni index of the i-th particle and eps is a very small constant (we used 0.0002). So maximization of this function means minimization of the XB index.

We have employed another famous validity index known as the partition entropy in order to judge the accuracy of the final clustering results obtained by MEPSO and its competitor algorithms in case of the image pixel classification. The partition entropy (Bezdek, 1981) function is given by,

$$V_{pe} = \frac{-\sum\limits_{j=1}^{n} \sum\limits_{i=1}^{c} [u_{ij} \log u_{ij}]}{n} \tag{23}$$

The idea of the validity function is that the partition with less fuzziness means better performance. Consequently, the best clustering is achieved when the value V_{pe} is minimal.

4.4 Avoiding Erroneous particles with Empty Clusters or Unreasonable Fitness Evaluation

There is a possibility that in our scheme, during computation of the XB index, a division by zero may be encountered. This may occur when one of the selected cluster centers is outside the boundary of distributions of the data set. To avoid this problem we first check to see if any cluster has fewer than 2 data points in it. If so, the cluster center positions of this special chromosome are re-initialized by an average computation. We put n/c data points for every individual cluster center, such that a data point goes with a center that is nearest to it.

4.5 Combining All Together

The clustering method described here, is a two-pass process at each iteration or time step. The first pass amounts to calculating the active clusters as well as the membership functions for each particle in the spectral domain. In the second pass, the membership information of each pixel is mapped to the spatial domain, and the spatial function is computed from that. The MEPSO iteration proceeds with the new membership that is incorporated with the spatial function. The algorithm is stopped when the maximum number of time-steps t_{max} is exceeded. After the convergence, de-fuzzification is applied to assign each data item to a specific cluster for which the membership is maximal.

4.6 A Few Simulation Results

The MEPSO-clustering algorithm has been tested over a number of synthetic and real world datasets as well as on some image pixel classification problems. The performance of the method has been compared with the classical FCM algorithm and a recently developed fuzzy clustering algorithm based on GA. The later algorithm is referred in literature as Fuzzy clustering with Variable length Genetic Algorithm (FVGA) the details of which can be found in (Pakhira et al., 2005). In the present chapter, we first provide the simulation results obtained over four well-chosen synthetic datasets (Bandyopadhyay and Maulik, 2000) and two real world datasets. The real world datasets used are the glass and the Wisconsin breast cancer data set, both of which have been taken from the UCI public data repository (Blake et al., 1998). The glass data were sampled from six different type of glass: building windows float processed (70 objects), building windows non float processed (76 objects), vehicle windows float processed (17 objects), containers (13 objects), tableware (9 objects), headlamps (29 objects) with nine features each. The Wisconsin breast cancer database contains 9 relevant features: clump thickness, cell size uniformity, cell shape uniformity, marginal adhesion, single epithelial cell size, bare nuclei, bland chromatin, normal nucleoli and mitoses. The dataset has two classes. The objective is to classify each data vector into benign (239 objects) or malignant tumors (444 objects).

Performance of the MEPSO based algorithm on four synthetic datasets has been shown in Figures 5 through 8. In Table 1, we provide the mean value and standard deviation of the Xie Beni index evaluated over final clustering results, the number of classes evaluated and the number of misclassified items with respect to the nominal partitions of the benchmark data, as known to us. For each data set, each run continues until the number of function evaluations (FEs) reaches 50,000. Twenty independent runs (with different seeds for the random number generator) have been taken for each algorithm. The results have been stated in terms of the mean *best-of-run* values and standard deviations over these 20 runs in each case. Only for the FCM, correct number of classes has been provided as input. Both FVGA and MEPSO determine the number of classes automatically on the run.

From Tables 1 and 2, one may see that our approach outperforms the state-of-the-art FVGA and the classical FCM over a variety of datasets in a statistically significant manner. Not only does the method find the optimal number of clusters, it also manages to find better clustering of the data points in terms of the two major cluster validity indices used in the literature.

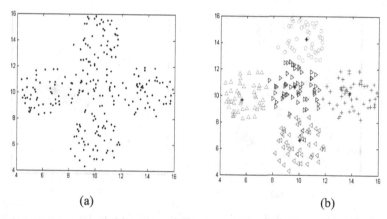

(a)   (b)

Fig. 5. (a) The unlabeled synthetic dataset 1 (b) Automatic Clustering with the MEPSO

4.7 Image Segmentation through Clustering

Image segmentation may be defined as the process of dividing an image into disjoint homogeneous regions. These homogeneous regions usually contain similar objects of interest or part of them. The extent of homogeneity of the segmented regions can be measured using some image property (e.g. pixel intensity (Jain *et al.*, 1999)). Segmentation forms a fundamental step towards several complex computer-vision and image analysis applications including digital mammography, remote sensing and land cover study. Image segmentation can be treated as a clustering problem where the features describing each pixel correspond to a pattern, and each image region (i.e., segment)

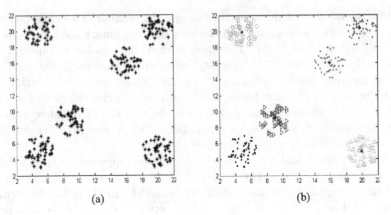

Fig. 6. (a) The unlabeled synthetic dataset 1 (b) Automatic Clustering with the MEPSO

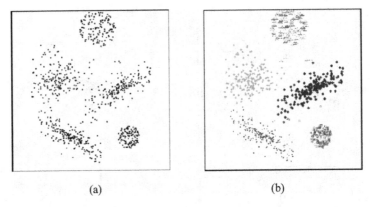

Fig. 7. (a) The unlabeled synthetic dataset 1 (b) Automatic Clustering with the MEPSO

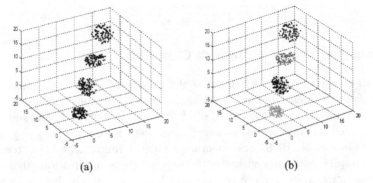

Fig. 8. (a) The unlabeled synthetic dataset 1 (b) Automatic Clustering with the MEPSO

Table 1. Final solution (mean and standard deviation over 20 independent runs) after each algorithm was terminated after running for 50,000 function evaluations (FE) with DB Measure based fitness function.

Problem	Algorithm	Average no. of clusters found	Final DB measure	Mean No. of misclassified Items
Synthetic Data 1	MEPSO	**5.05±0.0931**	**3.0432±0.021**	**5.25±0.096**
	VGA	8.15±0.0024	4.3432±0.232	15.75±0.154
	FCM	NA	5.3424±0.343	19.50±1.342
Synthetic Data 2	MEPSO	**6.45±0.0563**	**1.4082±0.006**	**4.50±0.023**
	VGA	6.95±0.021	1.5754±0.073	10.25±0.373
	FCM	NA	1.6328±0.002	26.50±0.433
Synthetic Data 3	MEPSO	**5.25±0.0241**	**0.9224±0.334**	**9.15±0.034**
	VGA	5.75±0.0562	1.2821±0.009	15.50±0.048
	FCM	NA	2.9482±0.028	17.25±0.275
Synthetic Data 4	MEPSO	**4.00±0.00**	**1.0092±0.083**	**1.50±0.035**
	VGA	4.75±0.0193	1.5152±0.073	4.55±0.05
	FCM	NA	1.8371±0.034	8.95±0.15
Glass	MEPSO	**6.05±0.0248**	**1.0802±0.083**	**8.35±0.662**
	FVGA	5.95±0.0193	1.5152±0.073	14.35±0.26
	FCM	NA	1.8371±0.034	18.65±0.85
Breast Cancer	MEPSO	2.05±0.0563	0.5003±0.006	**25.00±0.09**
	FVGA	2.50±0.0621	0.5754±0.073	26.50±0.80
	FCM	NA	0.6328±0.002	30.23±0.46

corresponds to a cluster (Jain et $al.$, 1999). Therefore, many clustering algorithms have widely been used to solve the segmentation problem (e.g., K-means (Tou and Gonzalez, 1974), Fuzzy C-means (Trivedi and Bezdek, 1986), ISODATA (Ball and Hall, 1967), Snob (Wallace and Boulton, 1968) and recently the PSO and DE based clustering techniques (Omran et $al.$, 2005a, Omran et $al.$, 2005b)).

Here we illustrate the automatic soft segmentation of a number of grey scale images by using our MEPSO based clustering algorithm. An important characteristic of an image is the high degree of correlation among the neighboring pixels. In other words, these neighboring pixels possess similar feature values, and the probability that they belong to the same cluster is great. This spatial relationship (Ahmed et $al.$, 2002) is important in clustering, but it is not utilized in a standard FCM algorithm. To exploit the spatial information, a spatial function is defined as:

$$h_{ij} = \sum_{k \in \delta(\mathbf{X}_j)} u_{ik} \tag{24}$$

where $\delta(\mathbf{X}_j)$ represents a square window centered on pixel (i.e. data point) $\mathbf{X}_j$ in the spatial domain. A 5×5 window was used throughout this work. Just like the membership function, the spatial function h_{ij} represents the probability that pixel $\mathbf{X}_j$ belongs to i-th cluster. The spatial function of a pixel for a cluster is large if the majority of its neighborhood belongs to the same clusters. We incorporate the spatial function into membership function as follows:

$$u'_{ij} = \frac{u^r_{ij} h^t_{ij}}{\sum\limits_{k=1}^{c} u^r_{kj} h^t_{kj}} \tag{25}$$

Here in all the cases we have used r = 1, t = 1after considerable trial and errors.

Although we tested our algorithm over a large number of images with varying range of complexity, here we show the experimental results for three images only, due to economy of space. Figures 4.7 to 4.7 show the three original images and their segmented counterparts obtained using the FVGA algorithm and the MEPSO based method. In these figures the segmented portions of an image have been marked with the grey level intensity of the respective cluster centers. In Table 2, we report the mean value the DB measure and partition entropy calculated over the 'best-of-run' solutions in each case. One may note that the MEPSO meets or beats the competitor algorithm in all the cases. Table 3 reports the mean time taken by each algorithm to terminate on the image data. Finally, Table 4 contains the mean and standard deviations of the number of classes obtained by the two automatic clustering algorithms.

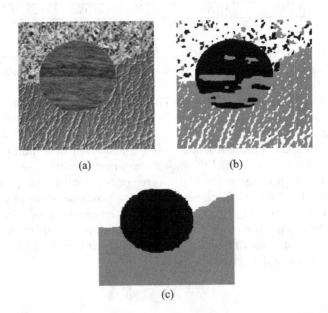

(a)   (b)

(c)

Fig. 9. (a) The original Texture image. (b) Segmentation by FVGA (c= 3) (c) Segmentation by MEPSO based method (c = 3)

Fig. 10. (a) The original Pepper image. (b) Segmentation by FVGA (c= 7) (c) Segmentation by MEPSO based method (c = 7)

Table 2. Automatic clustering result for three real life grayscale images (over 20 runs; each run continued up to 50,000 FE)

Image	Validity Index	Mean and Std Dev of the validity indices over the final clustering results of 20 independent runs		
		AFDE	FVGA	FCM
Texture	Xie-Beni	**0.7283**	0.7902	0.7937
		(0.0001)	(0.0948)	(0.0013)
	Partition Entropy	**2.6631**	2.1193	2.1085
		(0.7018)	(0.8826)	(0.0043)
MRI Image	Xie-Beni of Brain	**0.2261**	0.2919	0.3002
		(0.0017)	(0.0583)	(0.0452)
	Partition Entropy	**0.1837**	0.1922	0.1939
		(0.0017)	(0.0096)	(0.0921)
Pepper Image	Xie-Beni	**0.05612**	0.09673	0.09819
		(0.0092)	(0.0043)	(0.0001)
	Partition Entropy	**0.8872**	1.1391	1.1398
		(0.0137)	(0.0292)	(0.0884)

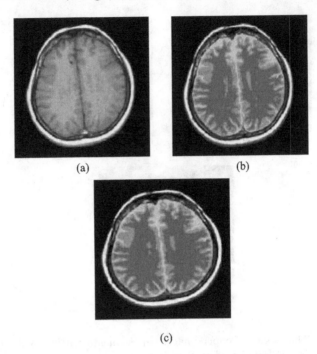

(a)   (b)

(c)

Fig. 11. (a) The original MRI image. (b) Segmentation by FVGA (c= 5) (c) Segmentation by MEPSO (c = 5)

Table 3. Comparison among the mean execution time taken by the different algorithms

Image	Optimal No. of Clusters	Mean and Std Dev of the number of classes estimated by the competitor algorithms	
		FVGA	MEPSO
Texture	3	3.75±0.211	3.05±0.132
MRI	5	5.05±0.428	5.25±0.212
Pepper	7	8.15±0.772	6.95±0.982

Table 4. Automatic clustering results for the three real-life grayscale images (over 20 runs; each runs continued for 50,000 FE)

Image	Mean and Std Dev of the execution time (in seconds) taken by the competitor algorithms	
	FVGA	MEPSO
Texture	32.05±0.076	47.25±0.162
MRI	24.15±0.016	34.65±0.029
Pepper	49.20±0.201	67.85±0.817

5 Conclusion and Future Directions

In this Chapter, we introduced some of the preliminary concepts of Swarm Intelligence (SI) with an emphasis on particle swarm optimization and ant colony optimization algorithms. We then described the basic data clustering terminologies and also illustrated some of the past and ongoing works, which apply different SI tools to pattern clustering problems. We proposed a novel fuzzy clustering algorithm, which is based on a deviant variety of the PSO. The proposed algorithm can automatically compute the optimal number of clusters in any dataset and thus requires minimal user intervention. Comparison with a state of the art GA based clustering strategy, reveals the superiority of the MEPSO-clustering algorithm both in terms of accuracy and speed.

Despite being an age old problem, clustering remains an active field of interdisciplinary research till date. No single algorithm is known, which can group all real world datasets efficiently and without error. To judge the quality of a clustering, we need some specially designed statistical-mathematical function called the clustering validity index. But a literature survey reveals that, most of these validity indices are designed empirically and there is no universally good index that can work equally well over any dataset. Since, majority of the PSO or ACO based clustering schemes rely on a validity index to judge the fitness of several possible partitioning of the data, research effort should be spent for defining a reasonably good index function and validating the same mathematically.

Feature extraction is an important preprocessing step for data clustering. Often we have a great number of features (especially for a high dimensional dataset like a collection of text documents) which are not all relevant for a given operation. Hence, future research may focus on integrating the automatic feature-subset selection scheme with the SI based clustering algorithm. The two-step process is expected to automatically project the data to a low dimensional feature subspace, determine the number of clusters and find out the appropriate cluster centers with the most relevant features at a faster pace.

Gene expression refers to a process through which the coded information of a gene is converted into structures operating in the cell. It provides the physical evidence that a gene has been "turned on" or activated for protein synthesis (Lewin, 1995). Proper selection, analysis and interpretation of the gene expression data can lead us to the answers of many important problems in experimental biology. Promising results have been reported in (Xiao et al., 2003) regarding the application of PSO for clustering the expression levels of gene subsets. The research effort to integrate SI tools in the mechanism of gene expression clustering may in near future open up a new horizon in the field of bioinformatic data mining.

Hierarchical clustering plays an important role in fields like information retrieval and web mining. The self-assembly behavior of the real ants may be exploited to build up new hierarchical tree-structured partitioning of a

data set according to the similarities between those data items. A description
of the little but promising work already been undertaken in this direction
can be found in (Azzag *et al.*, 2006). But a more extensive and systematic
research effort is necessary to make the ant based hierarchical models superior
to existing algorithms like Birch (Zhang *et al.*, 1997).

References

A. Abraham, C. Grosan and V. Ramos (2006) (Eds.), Swarm Intelligence and
    Data Mining, Studies in Computational Intelligence, Springer Verlag, Germany,
    pages 270, ISBN: 3-540-34955-3.
Ahmed MN, Yaman SM, Mohamed N, (2002), Farag AA and Moriarty TA, Modi-
    fied fuzzy c-means algorithm for bias field estimation and segmentation of MRI
    data. IEEE Trans Med Imaging, 21, pp. 193–199.
Azzag H, Guinot C and Venturini G, Data and text mining with hierarchical clus-
    tering ants, in *Swarm Intelligence in Data Mining*, Abraham A, (2006), Grosan
    C and Ramos V (Eds), Springer, pp. 153-186.
Ball G and Hall D, (1967), A Clustering Technique for Summarizing Multivariate
    Data, Behavioral Science 12, pp. 153-155.
Bandyopadhyay S and Maulik U, (2000), Genetic clustering for automatic evolution
    of clusters and application to image classification, Pattern Recognition, 35, pp.
    1197-1208.
Beni G and Wang U, (1989), Swarm intelligence in cellular robotic systems. In
    NATO Advanced Workshop on Robots and Biological Systems, Il Ciocco, Tus-
    cany, Italy.
Bensaid AM, Hall LO, Bezdek JC.and Clarke LP, (1996), Partially supervised
    clustering for image segmentation. Pattern Recognition, vol. 29, pp. 859-871.
Bezdek JC, (1981), Pattern recognition with fuzzy objective function algorithms.
    New York: Plenum.
Blake C, Keough E and Merz CJ, (1998), UCI repository of machine learning
    database http://www.ics.uci.edu/~mlearn/MLrepository.html.
Bonabeau E, Dorigo M and Theraulaz G, (1999), *Swarm Intelligence: From Natural
    to Artificial Systems.* Oxford University Press, New York.
Brucker P, (1978), On the complexity of clustering problems. Beckmenn M and
    Kunzi HP(Eds.), *Optimization and Operations Research*, Lecture Notes in Eco-
    nomics and Mathematical Systems, Berlin, Springer, vol.157, pp. 45-54.
Clark MC, Hall LO, Goldgof DB, Clarke LP, (1994), Velthuizen RP and Silbiger
    MS , MRI segmentation using fuzzy clustering techniques. IEEE Eng Med Biol,
    13, pp.730–742.
Clerc M and Kennedy J. (2002), The particle swarm - explosion, stability, and
    convergence in a multidimensional complex space, In IEEE Transactions on
    Evolutionary Computation, 6(1):58-73.
Couzin ID, Krause J, James R, Ruxton GD, Franks NR, (2002), Collective Memory
    and Spatial Sorting in Animal Groups, Journal of Theoretical Biology, 218, pp.
    1-11.
Cui X and Potok TE, (2005), Document Clustering Analysis Based on Hybrid
    PSO+Kmeans Algorithm, Journal of Computer Sciences (Special Issue), ISSN
    1549-3636, pp. 27-33.

Das S, Konar A and Abraham A, (2006), Spatial Information based Image Segmentation with a Modified Particle Swarm Optimization, in proceedings of Sixth International Conference on Intelligent System Design and Applications (ISDA 06) Jinan, Shangdong, China, IEEE Computer Society Press.

Deb K, Pratap A, Agarwal S, and Meyarivan T (2002), A fast and elitist multiobjective genetic algorithm: NSGA-II, IEEE Trans. on Evolutionary Computation, Vol.6, No.2.

Deneubourg JL, Goss S, Franks N, Sendova-Franks A, (1991), Detrain C and Chetien L , The dynamics of collective sorting: Robot-like ants and ant-like robots. In Meyer JA and Wilson SW (Eds.) *Proceedings of the First International Conference on Simulation of Adaptive Behaviour: From Animals to Animats 1*, pp. 356–363. MIT Press, Cambridge, MA.

Dorigo M and Gambardella LM, (1997), Ant colony system: A cooperative learning approach to the traveling salesman problem, IEEE Trans. Evolutionary Computing, vol. 1, pp. 53–66.

Dorigo M, Maniezzo V and Colorni A, (1996), The ant system: Optimization by a colony of cooperating agents, IEEE Trans. Systems Man and Cybernetics – Part B, vol. 26.

Duda RO and Hart PE, (1973), *Pattern Classification and Scene Analysis.* John Wiley and Sons, USA.

Eberhart RC and Shi Y, (2001), Particle swarm optimization: Developments, applications and resources, In Proceedings of IEEE International Conference on Evolutionary Computation, vol. 1, pp. 81-86.

Evangelou IE, Hadjimitsis DG, Lazakidou AA, (2001), Clayton C, Data Mining and Knowledge Discovery in Complex Image Data using Artificial Neural Networks, Workshop on Complex Reasoning an Geographical Data, Cyprus.

Everitt BS, (1993), *Cluster Analysis.* Halsted Press, Third Edition.

Falkenauer E, (1998), *Genetic Algorithms and Grouping Problems*, John Wiley and Son, Chichester.

Fogel LJ, Owens AJ and Walsh MJ, (1966), Artificial Intelligence through Simulated Evolution. New York: Wiley.

Forgy EW, (1965), Cluster Analysis of Multivariate Data: Efficiency versus Interpretability of classification, Biometrics, 21.

Frigui H and Krishnapuram R, (1999), A Robust Competitive Clustering Algorithm with Applications in Computer Vision, IEEE Transactions on Pattern Analysis and Machine Intelligence 21 (5), pp. 450-465.

Fukunaga K, (1990), Introduction to Statistical Pattern Recognition. Academic Press.

Gath I and Geva A, (1989), Unsupervised optimal fuzzy clustering. IEEE Transactions on PAMI, 11, pp. 773-781.

Goldberg DE, (1975), Genetic *Algorithms in Search, Optimization and Machine Learning*, Addison-Wesley, Reading, MA.

Grosan C, Abraham A and Monica C, Swarm Intelligence in Data Mining, in *Swarm Intelligence in Data Mining*, Abraham A, (2006), Grosan C and Ramos V (Eds), Springer, pp. 1-16.

Halkidi M and Vazirgiannis M, (2001), Clustering Validity Assessment: Finding the Optimal Partitioning of a Data Set. Proceedings of the 2001 IEEE International Conference on Data Mining (ICDM 01), San Jose, California, USA, pp. 187-194.

Halkidi M, Batistakis Y and Vazirgiannis M, (2001), On Clustering Validation Techniques. Journal of Intelligent Information Systems (JIIS), 17(2-3), pp. 107-145.

Handl J and Meyer B, (2002), Improved ant-based clustering and sorting in a document retrieval interface. In Proceedings of the Seventh International Conference on Parallel Problem Solving from Nature (PPSN VII), volume 2439 of LNCS, pp. 913–923. Springer-Verlag, Berlin, Germany.

Handl J, Knowles J and Dorigo M, (2003), Ant-based clustering: a comparative study of its relative performance with respect to k-means, average link and 1D-som. Technical Report TR/IRIDIA/2003-24. IRIDIA, Universite Libre de Bruxelles, Belgium.

Hoe K, Lai W, and Tai T, (2002), Homogenous ants for web document similarity modeling and categorization. In *Proceedings of the Third International Workshop on Ant Algorithms (ANTS 2002)*, volume 2463 of *LNCS*, pp. 256–261. Springer-Verlag, Berlin, Germany.

Holland JH, (1975), *Adaptation in Natural and Artificial Systems*, University of Michigan Press, Ann Arbor.

Jain AK, Murty MN and Flynn PJ, (1999), Data clustering: a review, ACM Computing Surveys, vol. 31, no.3, pp. 264—323.

Kanade PM and Hall LO, (2003), Fuzzy Ants as a Clustering Concept. In Proceedings of the 22nd International Conference of the North American Fuzzy Information Processing Society (NAFIPS03), pp. 227-232.

Kaufman, L and Rousseeuw, PJ, (1990), *Finding Groups in Data: An Introduction to Cluster Analysis*. John Wiley & Sons, New York.

Kennedy J and Eberhart R, (1995), Particle swarm optimization, In Proceedings of IEEE International conference on Neural Networks, pp. 1942-1948.

Kennedy J and Eberhart RC, (1997), A discrete binary version of the particle swarm algorithm, Proceedings of the 1997 Conf. on Systems, Man, and Cybernetics, IEEE Service Center, Piscataway, NJ, pp. 4104-4109.

Kennedy J, Eberhart R and Shi Y, (2001), *Swarm Intelligence*, Morgan Kaufmann Academic Press.

Kohonen T, (1995), *Self-Organizing Maps*, Springer Series in Information Sciences, Vol 30, Springer-Verlag.

Konar A, (2005), Computational Intelligence: Principles, Techniques and Applications, Springer.

Krause J and Ruxton GD, (2002), Living in Groups. Oxford: Oxford University Press.

Kuntz P and Snyers D, (1994), Emergent colonization and graph partitioning. In *Proceedings of the Third International Conference on Simulation of Adaptive Behaviour: From Animals to Animats 3*, pp. 494– 500. MIT Press, Cambridge, MA.

Kuntz P and Snyers D, (1999), New results on an ant-based heuristic for highlighting the organization of large graphs. In *Proceedings of the 1999 Congress on Evolutionary Computation*, pp. 1451–1458. IEEE Press, Piscataway, NJ.

Kuntz P, Snyers D and Layzell P, (1998), A stochastic heuristic for visualising graph clusters in a bi-dimensional space prior to partitioning. *Journal of Heuristics*, 5(3), pp. 327–351.

Lee C-Y and Antonsson EK, (2000), Self-adapting vertices for mask layout synthesis Modeling and Simulation of Microsystems Conference (San Diego, March

27–29) eds. M Laudon and B Romanowicz. pp. 83–86.

Leung Y, Zhang J and Xu Z, (2000), Clustering by Space-Space Filtering, IEEE Transactions on Pattern Analysis and Machine Intelligence 22 (12), pp. 1396-1410.

Lewin B, (1995), *Genes VII.* Oxford University Press, New York, NY.

Lillesand T and Keifer R, (1994), *Remote Sensing and Image Interpretation*, John Wiley & Sons, USA.

Lumer E and Faieta B, (1994), Diversity and Adaptation in Populations of Clustering Ants. In Proceedings Third International Conference on Simulation of Adaptive Behavior: from animals to animates 3, Cambridge, Massachusetts MIT press, pp. 499-508.

Lumer E and Faieta B, (1995), Exploratory database analysis via self-organization, Unpublished manuscript.

MacQueen J, (1967), Some methods for classification and analysis of multivariate observations, Proceedings of the Fifth Berkeley Symposium on Mathematical Statistics and Probability, pp. 281-297.

Major PF, Dill LM, (1978), The three-dimensional structure of airborne bird flocks. Behavioral Ecology and Sociobiology, 4, pp. 111-122.

Mao J and Jain AK, (1995), Artificial neural networks for feature extraction and multivariate data projection. IEEE Trans. Neural Networks.vol. 6, 296–317.

Milonas MM, (1994), Swarms, phase transitions, and collective intelligence, In Langton CG Ed., Artificial Life III, Addison Wesley, Reading, MA.

Mitchell T, (1997), *Machine Learning.* McGraw-Hill, Inc., New York, NY.

Mitra S, Pal SK and Mitra P, (2002), Data mining in soft computing framework: A survey, IEEE Transactions on Neural Networks, Vol. 13, pp. 3-14.

Monmarche N, Slimane M and Venturini G, (1999), Ant Class: discovery of clusters in numeric data by a hybridization of an ant colony with the k means algorithm. Internal Report No. 213, E3i, Laboratoire d'Informatique, Universite de Tours.

Ng R and Han J, (1994), Efficient and effective clustering method for spatial data mining. In: Proc. 1994 International Conf. Very Large Data Bases (VLDB'94). Santiago, Chile, September pp. 144–155.

Omran M, Engelbrecht AP and Salman A, (2005), Particle Swarm Optimization Method for Image Clustering. *International Journal of Pattern Recognition and Artificial Intelligence*, 19(3), pp. 297–322.

Omran M, Engelbrecht AP and Salman A, (2005), Differential Evolution Methods for Unsupervised Image Classification, Proceedings of Seventh Congress on Evolutionary Computation (CEC-2005). IEEE Press.

Omran M, Salman A and Engelbrecht AP, (2002), Image Classification using Particle Swarm Optimization. In *Conference on Simulated Evolution and Learning*, volume 1, pp. 370–374.

Omran M, Salman A and Engelbrecht AP, (2005), Dynamic Clustering using Particle Swarm Optimization with Application in Unsupervised Image Classification. Fifth World Enformatika Conference (ICCI 2005), Prague, Czech Republic.

Pakhira MK, Bandyopadhyay S and Maulik, U, (2005), A Study of Some Fuzzy Cluster Validity Indices, Genetic clustering And Application to Pixel Classification, Fuzzy Sets and Systems 155, pp. 191–214.

Pal NR, Bezdek JC and Tsao ECK, (1993), Generalized clustering networks and Kohonen's self-organizing scheme. IEEE Trans. Neural Networks, vol 4, 549–557.

Partridge BL, (1982), The structure and function of fish schools. Science American, 245, pp. 90-99.

Partridge BL, Pitcher TJ, (1980), The sensory basis of fish schools: relative role of lateral line and vision. Journal of Comparative Physiology, 135, pp. 315-325.

Paterlini S and Krink T, (2006), Differential Evolution and Particle Swarm Optimization in Partitional Clustering. *Computational Statistics and Data Analysis*, vol. 50, pp. 1220– 1247.

Paterlini S and Minerva T, (2003), Evolutionary Approaches for Cluster Analysis. In Bonarini A, Masulli F and Pasi G (eds.) *Soft Computing Applications*. Springer-Verlag, Berlin. 167-178.

Ramos V and Merelo JJ, (2002), Self-organized stigmergic document maps: Environments as a mechanism for context learning. In *Proceedings of the First Spanish Conference on Evolutionary and Bio-Inspired Algorithms (AEB 2002)*, pp. 284–293. Centro Univ. M'erida, M'erida, Spain.

Ramos V, Muge F and Pina P, (2002), Self-Organized Data and Image Retrieval as a Consequence of Inter-Dynamic Synergistic Relationships in Artificial Ant Colonies. Soft Computing Systems: Design, Management and Applications. 87, pp. 500–509.

Rao MR, (1971), Cluster Analysis and Mathematical Programming,. Journal of the American Statistical Association, Vol. 22, pp 622-626.

Rokach, L., Maimon, O. (2005), Clustering Methods, Data Mining and Knowledge Discovery Handbook, Springer, pp. 321-352.

Rosenberger C and Chehdi K, (2000), Unsupervised clustering method with optimal estimation of the number of clusters: Application to image segmentation, in Proc. IEEE International Conference on Pattern Recognition (ICPR), vol. 1, Barcelona, pp. 1656-1659.

Sarkar M, Yegnanarayana B and Khemani D, (1997), A clustering algorithm using an evolutionary programming-based approach, Pattern Recognition Letters, 18, pp. 975–986.

Schwefel H-P, (1995), *Evolution and Optimum Seeking*. New York, NY: Wiley, 1st edition.

Selim SZ and Alsultan K, (1991), A simulated annealing algorithm for the clustering problem. Pattern recognition, 24(7), pp. 1003-1008.

Storn R and Price K, (1997), Differential evolution – A Simple and Efficient Heuristic for Global Optimization over Continuous Spaces, Journal of Global Optimization, 11(4), pp. 341–359.

Theodoridis S and Koutroubas K, (1999), Pattern recognition, Academic Press.

Tou JT and Gonzalez RC, (1974), Pattern Recognition Principles. London, Addison-Wesley.

Trivedi MM and Bezdek JC, (1986), Low-level segmentation of aerial images with fuzzy clustering, IEEE Trans.on Systems, Man and Cybernetics, Volume 16.

Tsang W and Kwong S, Ant Colony Clustering and Feature Extraction for Anomaly Intrusion Detection, in *Swarm Intelligence in Data Mining*, Abraham A, (2006), Grosan C and Ramos V (Eds), Springer, pp. 101-121.

van der Merwe DW and Engelbrecht AP, (2003), Data clustering using particle swarm optimization. In: Proceedings of the 2003 IEEE Congress on Evolutionary Computation, pp. 215-220, Piscataway, NJ: IEEE Service Center.

Wallace CS and Boulton DM, (1968), An Information Measure for Classification, Computer Journal, Vol. 11, No. 2, 1968, pp. 185-194.

Wang X, Wang Y and Wang L, (2004), Improving fuzzy c-means clustering based on feature-weight learning. Pattern Recognition Letters, vol. 25, pp. 1123–32.

Xiao X, Dow ER, Eberhart RC, Miled ZB and Oppelt RJ, (2003), Gene Clustering Using Self-Organizing Maps and Particle Swarm Optimization, Proc of the 17th International Symposium on Parallel and Distributed Processing (PDPS '03), IEEE Computer Society, Washington DC.

Xie, X and Beni G, (1991), Validity measure for fuzzy clustering. IEEE Trans. Pattern Anal. Machine Learning, Vol. 3, pp. 841–846.

Xu, R., Wunsch, D. (2005), Survey of Clustering Algorithms, IEEE Transactions on Neural Networks, Vol. 16(3): 645-678.

Zahn CT, (1971), Graph-theoretical methods for detecting and describing gestalt clusters, IEEE Transactions on Computers C-20, 68–86.

Zhang T, Ramakrishnan R and Livny M, (1997), BIRCH: A New Data Clustering Algorithm and Its Applications, Data Mining and Knowledge Discovery, vol. 1, no. 2, pp. 141-182.

Hall LO, Özyurt IB and Bezdek JC, (1999), Clustering with a genetically optimized approach, IEEE Trans. Evolutionary Computing 3 (2) pp. 103–112.

A Diffusion Framework
for Dimensionality Reduction

Alon Schclar[1]

School of Computer Science, Tel Aviv University, Tel Aviv 69978, Israel
shekler@post.tau.ac.il

Summary. Many fields of research deal with high-dimensional data sets. Hyper-spectral images in remote sensing and in hyper-spectral microscopy, transactions in banking monitoring systems are just a few examples for this type of sets. Revealing the geometric structure of these data-sets as a preliminary step facilitates their efficient processing. Often, only a small number of parameters govern the structure of the data-set. This number is the true dimension of the data-set and is the motivation to reduce the dimensionality of the set. Dimensionality reduction algorithms try to discover the true dimension of a data set.

In this chapter, we describe a natural framework based on diffusion processes for the multi-scale analysis of high-dimensional data-sets (Coifman and Lafon, 2006). This scheme enables us to describe the geometric structures of such sets by utilizing the Newtonian paradigm according to which a global description of a system can be derived by the aggregation of local transitions. Specifically, a Markov process is used to describe a random walk on the data set. The spectral properties of the Markov matrix that is associated with this process are used to embed the data-set in a low-dimensional space. This scheme also facilitates the parametrization of a data-set when the high dimensional data-set is not accessible and only a pair-wise similarity matrix is at hand.

1 Introduction

In the following, we describe the reason why diffusion processes are suitable for the analysis of data-sets. We also give a brief introduction to Markov processes. A more comprehensive introductory to random processes can be found in (Sheldon, 1983).

1.1 Why diffusion ?

Let $\{x_k\}_{k=1}^m$ be a data-set of points. Suppose we wish to *randomly walk* between these points starting arbitrarily from one of the points. At each time t we choose our next point in the path according to a given probability. We denote the probability to move from point x_i to point x_j by p_{ij} and refer to a single move as a *transition*. We look into the the simple case where p_{ij} is inversely proportional to the Euclidean distance between x_i and x_j and where the data-set can be divided into two well separated clusters. This means that the probability to travel within a cluster is much higher than that of traveling between the clusters. Consequently, after a large number of steps we will most probably end up in the cluster we began our walk.

Contrary to this example, in most cases the structure of the data-set is unknown and we need to reveal it. This can be done by calculating for every point x_i the probability we will end up there after traveling between the points for a *long time*. (formally, we look into the asymptotic behavior of the random walk). Points that are clustered together will have similar probabilities.

1.2 Markov processes

The random walk we described above is a special case of a *Markov process*. The general Markov framework describes a random walk between a set of states $\{s_k\}_{k=1}^m$. The transition probabilities are given by a $m \times m$ matrix $P = (p_{ij})$ where the i-th row contains the transition probabilities from state s_i to all the other states. In our model we choose the sum of each row to be equal to one. Furthermore, we use a *memoryless* process i.e. the probability to move at time $t+1$ from the current state s_i to the next state s_j depends only on s_i and the transition probability p_{ij}. If we denote the probability to be in state s_i at time t by $p_t(s_i)$, then the *memoryless* property can be described as:

$$p_{t+1}(s_j \mid s_i) = p_t(s_i) \cdot p_{ij}$$

A Markov process can also be modeled by a weighted graph $G = (V, E)$ in which the nodes correspond to the states, the edges to transitions and the edge weights to the transition probabilities. We will use this model to describe the diffusion maps algorithm.

2 The diffusion maps algorithm

As mentioned above, the diffusion maps algorithm is used to analyze a given a set of data points

$$\Gamma = \{x_i\}_{i=1}^m, \; x_i \in \mathbb{R}^n \tag{1}$$

It includes the following steps:

1. Construction of an undirected graph G on Γ with a weight function w_ε that corresponds to the *local* point-wise similarity between the points in Γ^1.

---

[1] This step is skipped in case the set Γ is not accessible and we are only given w_ε.

2. Construction of a random walk on the graph G via a Markov transition matrix P that is derived from w_ε.
3. Eigen-decomposition of P.

The graph weights are chosen to be proportional to the similarity between the points i.e. the similar a pair of points is, the higher is the edge weight connecting the pair. This similarity depends on the application that requires the analysis of Γ and on the nature of the data-set at hand. In many situations, however, each data point is a collection of numerical measurements and thus can be thought of as a point in an Euclidean space. In this case, similarity can be measured in terms of closeness in this space and it is chosen to be inverse-proportional to the Euclidian distance between x_i and x_j. This construction captures the local geometry of the data-set and it reflects the quantities of interest.

A diffusion process is used to propagate the local geometry in order to discover the global geometry of the data-set. Specifically, we build a diffusion operator whose eigen-decomposition enables the embedding of Γ into a space S of substantially lower dimension. The Euclidean distance between a pair of points in the dimension-reduced space defines a *diffusion metric* that measures the proximity of points in terms of their connectivity in the original space. Specifically, the Euclidean distance between a pair of points, in S, is equal to the random walk distance between the corresponding pair of points in the original space. The embedding of the data points into the low-dimension space provides coordinates on the data set that reorganize the points according to this metric.

The eigenvalues and eigenfunctions of P define a natural embedding of the data through the diffusion map and the study of the eigenvalues allows us to use the eigenfunctions for dimensionality reduction.

2.1 Building the graph G and the weight function w_ε

Let Γ be a set of points in $\mathbb{R}^n$ as defined in (1). We construct the graph $G(V, E)$, $|V| = m$, $|E| \ll m^2$, on Γ in order to study the intrinsic geometry of this set. A weight function $w_\varepsilon(x_i, x_j)$ which measures the pairwise similarity between the points is introduced.

For all $x_i, x_j \in \Gamma$, the weight function is chosen to obey the following properties:

- symmetry: $w_\varepsilon(x_i, x_j) = w_\varepsilon(x_j, x_i)$
- non-negativity: $w_\varepsilon(x_i, x_j) \geq 0$
- fast decay: given a scale parameter $\varepsilon > 0$, $w_\varepsilon(x_i, x_j) \to 0$ when $\|x_i - x_j\| \gg \varepsilon$ and $w_\varepsilon(x_i, x_j) \to 1$ when $\|x_i - x_j\| \ll \varepsilon$. .

Note that the parameter ε defines a notion of neighborhood i.e. for every point x_i, the weights $w_\varepsilon(x_i, x_j)$ are numerically significant only if x_j is ε-close to

x_i. In this sense, w_ε captures the local geometry of Γ by providing a first-order pairwise similarity measure for ε-neighborhood of every point x_i i.e it defines the nearest neighbor structures in the graph. This corresponds to the assumption that the only relevant information lies in local neighborhoods. Consequently, the matrix that represents w_ε is sparse.

One of the common choices for w_ε is

$$w_\varepsilon\left(x_i, x_j\right) = \exp\left(-\frac{\|x_i - x_j\|^2}{\varepsilon}\right). \tag{2}$$

Indeed, x_i and x_j will be numerically significant if they are sufficiently close. In the case of a data set approximately lying on a submanifold, this choice corresponds to an approximation of the heat kernel on the submanifold (see (Belkin and Niyogi, 2003)). Furthermore, this result was extended in (Coifman and Lafon, 2006) where it was shown that any weight of the form $f\left(\|x_i - x_j\|\right)$ where f decays sufficiently fast at infinity allows to approximate the heat kernel . Thus, other application dependant weight functions can be used. Accordingly, this choice should take into account any prior knowledge on the data. For example, if the the data points are binary, the Hamming distance can be used instead of the Euclidean distance.

The choice of ε in (2) is extremely important since it defines the scale of the neighborhood. General guidelines as well as some data-driven heuristics for choosing ε are described later in this chapter.

2.2 Construction of the normalized graph Laplacian

The non-negativity property of w_ε allows us to normalize it into a Markov transition matrix P where the states of the corresponding Markov process are the data points. This enables to analyze Γ via a random walk. The construction of P is known as the *normalized graph Laplacian* (Chung, 1997).

Formally, $P = \{p\left(x_i, x_j\right)\}_{i,j=1,\dots,m}$ is constructed as follows:

$$p\left(x_i, x_j\right) = \frac{w_\varepsilon\left(x_i, x_j\right)}{d\left(x_i\right)} \tag{3}$$

where

$$d\left(x_i\right) = \sum_{j=1}^{m} w_\varepsilon\left(x_i, x_j\right) \tag{4}$$

is the degree of x_i. P is a Markov matrix since the sum of each row in P is 1 and $p\left(x_i, x_j\right) \geq 0$. Thus, $p\left(x_i, x_j\right)$ can be viewed as the probability to move from x_i to x_j in a *single* time step. Raising this quantity to a power t advances the walk in time i.e. this probability is propagated to nodes in the neighborhood of x_i and x_j and the result is the probability to move from x_i to x_j in t time steps. We denote this probability by $p_t\left(x_i, x_j\right)$. These probabilities measure the connectivity of the points within the graph. The parameter t controls the scale of the neighborhood in addition to the scale control provided by ε.

2.3 Eigen-decomposition

As mentioned above the asymptotic behavior of the random walk entails the geometrical structure of the data set Γ. The close relation between the asymptotic behavior of P, i.e. the properties of its eigen-decomposition and the clusters that are inherent in the data, was explored in (Chung, 1997, Fowlkes *et al.*, 2004). As suggested in the example above, this behavior can be used to find clusters in the data set (Weiss, 1999, Shi and Malik, 2000), by using the first non-constant eigenvector to separate a data set into two clusters. One can separate to more than two clusters by using additional eigenvectors (Lafon and Lee, 2006, Meila and Shi, 2001, Yu and Shi, 2003).

Let $\{\mu_k\}_{k=1}^m$ and $\{\nu_k\}_{k=1}^m$ be the left and the right biorthogonal eigenvectors of P, respectively and let $\{\lambda_k\}_{k=1}^m$ be their corresponding eigenvalues where $|\lambda_1| \geq |\lambda_2| \geq ... \geq |\lambda_m|$.

Proposition 1. *If G is connected than the asymptotic behavior of the Markov process is dominated by a stationary distribution which is given by*

$$\lim_{t \to \infty} p_t (x_i, x_j) = \mu_1 (x_j)$$

where μ_1 is the left eigenvector that corresponds to the highest eigenvalue.

Proof. Essentially, we need to prove that the stationary distribution exists and is equal to μ_1. First, it is easy to see that the state space of the Markov chain at hand is finite. This is since our data set is finite. Second, according to the Perron–Frobenius theorem, it is enough to show that the chain is irreducible and aperiodic.

Irreducibility: Let x_i and x_j be two data points. We denote by l the length of the path between them. The connectivity of the graph implies that l is finite and thus $p_l (x_i, x_j) > 0$. Thus, the chain is irreducible.

Aperiodicity: Although we require the weight function to be non-negative, most weight functions are actually positive and thus we get $w_\varepsilon (x_i, x_j) > 0$ which implies aperiodicity since $p (x_i, x_j) > 0$ as well. $\square$

Proposition 2. *I. The eigenvector μ_1 can be derived from*

$$\mu_1 (x_i) = \frac{d (x_i)}{\sum_{j=1}^m d (x_j)}.$$

II. From a pre-asymptotic point of view, for a finite time t we have

$$p_t (x_i, x_j) = \sum_{k=1}^m \lambda_k^t \nu_k (x_i) \mu_k (x_j). \tag{5}$$

Proof. In order to prove this proposition construct a *symmetric* matrix A that is conjugate (see (Chung, 1997)) to P. The entries of A are obtained from the entries of P by

$$a\left(x_i, x_j\right) = \sqrt{\frac{d\left(x_i\right)}{d\left(x_j\right)}} p\left(x_i, x_j\right) = \frac{w_\varepsilon\left(x_i, x_j\right)}{\sqrt{d\left(x_i\right) d\left(x_j\right)}}.$$

We denote the eigenvectors of A by $\xi_1, \ldots, \xi_m$ and have

$$a\left(x_i, x_j\right) = \sum_{k=1}^{m} \lambda_k \xi_k\left(x_i\right) \xi_k\left(x_j\right) \tag{6}$$

It can be verified that A and P share the same eigenvalues and that their eigenvectors are connected by:

$$\mu_k\left(x_j\right) = \xi_k\left(x_j\right) \xi_1\left(x_j\right) \tag{7}$$

$$\nu_k\left(x_i\right) = \xi_k\left(x_j\right) / \xi_1\left(x_j\right) \tag{8}$$

for $i, j = 1, \ldots m$.

Furthermore, it is easy to check that $\xi_1\left(x_i\right) = \frac{\sqrt{d(x_i)}}{\sqrt{\sum_{j=1}^{m} d(x_j)}}$ which implies that $\nu_1\left(x_i\right) = 1$ and proves I:

$$\mu_1\left(x_i\right) = \frac{d\left(x_i\right)}{\sum_{j=1}^{m} d\left(x_j\right)}.$$

Combining (6), (7), (8) with

$$\mu_1\left(x_i\right) \nu_k\left(x_i\right) = \mu_k\left(x_i\right) \tag{9}$$

and raising A to the power t proves II

$$p_t\left(x_i, x_j\right) = \sum_{k=1}^{m} \lambda_k^t \nu_k\left(x_i\right) \mu_k\left(x_j\right)$$

with the following biorthogonality relation

$$\sum_{k=1}^{m} \nu_i\left(x_k\right) \mu_j\left(x_k\right) = \delta_{ij} \tag{10}$$

for $i, j = 1, \ldots m$, where δ_{ij} is the Kronecker symbol (Stewart, 2002). $\square$

The matrix A plays an important role in the actual calculation of $\{\mu_k\}_{k=1}^{m}$, $\{\nu_k\}_{k=1}^{m}$ and $\{\lambda_k\}_{k=1}^{m}$. Algorithms for the eigen-decomposition of symmetric matrices are more accurate than those for non-symmetric matrices. Using (7) and (8) along with the fact that the eigenvalues of A and P are the same enables to perform the eigen-decomposition on A instead of P.

An appropriate choice of ε achieves a fast decay of $\{\lambda_k\}$. Thus, in order to achieve a relative accuracy $\delta > 0$, only a small number $\eta(\delta)$ of terms are required in the sum in (5). This enables us to introduce a *diffusion metric* based upon the following *diffusion distance* ((Coifman and Lafon, 2006))

$$D_t^2(x_i, x_j) = \sum_{k=1}^{m} \frac{(p_t(x_i, x_k) - p_t(x_j, x_k))^2}{\mu_1(x_k)}. \tag{11}$$

This formulation is derived from the known random walk distance in Potential Theory:

$$D_t^2(x_i, x_j) = p_t(x_i, x_i) + p_t(x_j, x_j) - 2p_t(x_i, x_j)$$

where the factor 2 is due to the fact that G is undirected.

The diffusion distance averages all the paths from x_i to x_j. Doing so measures the interaction of x_i and x_j with the rest of the graph by taking into account the connectivity of the points in the graph. This metric is more robust to noise and topological short-circuits than the geodesic distance or the shortest-path distance since it involves an integration along all paths of length t between x_i and x_j. Furthermore, classical graph theory notions such as mixing time and clusterness (Diaconis and Stroock, 1991) are also incorporated into this metric.

Finally, the low dimensional embedding is facilitated by the following proposition:

Proposition 3. *The diffusion distance can be expressed in terms of the right eigenvectors of P:*

$$D_t^2(x_i, x_j) = \sum_{k=1}^{m} \lambda_k^{2t} (\nu_k(x_i) - \nu_k(x_j))^2.$$

Proof. Combining (9) with (10) we get

$$\sum_{k=1}^{m} \frac{\mu_i(x_k)\mu_j(x_k)}{\mu_1(x_k)} = \delta_{ij}. \tag{12}$$

for $i, j = 1, \ldots m$. This implies that $\{\mu_i\}_{i=1}^{m}$ is an orthonormal system in the metric space $L_2(\Gamma, 1/\mu_1)$. By fixing x_k, we can view (5) as the decomposition of $p_t(x_i, \cdot)$ in this system where the decomposition coefficients are given by $\{\lambda_k^t \nu_k(x_i)\}_{k=1}^{m}$. This allows to rewrite (11) as

$$D_t^2(x_i, x_j) = \|p_t(x_i, \cdot) - p_t(x_j, \cdot)\|_{L_2(\Gamma, 1/\mu_1)}$$

which yields

$$D_t^2(x_i, x_j) = \sum_{k=1}^{m} \lambda_k^{2t} (\nu_k(x_i) - \nu_k(x_j))^2 \quad \square \tag{13}$$

Notice that the sum in (13) can start from 2 since $\nu_1(x_i) = 1$ as it was seen in proposition 1, and therefore does not help to differentiate between two distances. It follows that in order to compute the diffusion distance, one can simply use the right eigenvectors of P. Moreover, this facilitates the embedding of the original points in a Euclidean space $\mathbb{R}^{\eta(\delta)-1}$ by:

$$\Xi_t : x_i \rightarrow \left(\lambda_2^t \nu_2(x_i), \lambda_3^t \nu_3(x_i), \ldots, \lambda_{\eta(\delta)}^t \nu_{\eta(\delta)}(x_i) \right).$$

This also provides coordinates on the set Γ. Essentially, $\eta(\delta) \ll n$ due to the fast decay of the eigenvalues decay of P and it depends only on the primary intrinsic variability of the data as captured by the random walk and not on the original dimensionality of the data. Furthermore, this data-driven method enables the parametrization of any set of points – abstract or not – provided the similarity matrix of the points w_ε is available.

Figure 1 illustrates the results of the diffusion maps algorithm applied on a data-set of digit images. The data-set consisted of five hundreds 30×20 binary images of the digit nine. Each vector in this data-set was in $\mathbb{R}^{600}$. The data-set was embedded into $\mathbb{R}^2$ and recovered two governing features of the digit: the *rotation angle* of the digit, which is given by the x-axis, and the *height* of the digit, which is given by the y-axis.

An example of data clustering using diffusion maps is given in Fig. 2. The diffusion maps algorithm was applied on a data set consisting of five hundreds 30×20 binary images of the digit nine and five hundreds 30×20 binary images of the digit zero. The embeddings of the digit nine are illustrated by circles while the embeddings of the digit zero are illustrated by plus signs.

3 Choosing ε

The size of the local neighborhood of each point is determined by ε. A large ε defines a wide neighborhood and thus producing a coarse analysis of the data since most neighborhoods will contain a large number of points. In contrast, for a small ε many neighborhoods will contain a single point. Clearly, an appropriate ε should be between these two cases and should stem from the data. Let $D = \{d_{ij}\}_{i,j=1,\ldots,m}$ be the pairwise Euclidean distance matrix between the points in Γ. Two heuristics are proposed:

The median heuristic: $\varepsilon = median\{d_{ij}\}_{i,j=1,\ldots,m}$.

The median of D provides an estimate to the average pairwise distance that is robust to outliers.

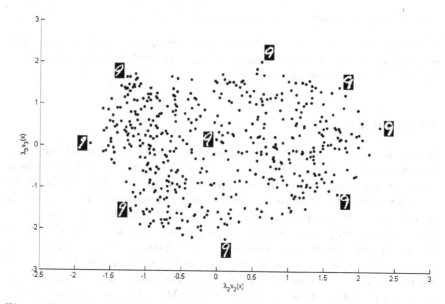

Fig. 1. Embedding of five hundreds 30×20 binary images of the digit nine (each is in $\mathbb{R}^{600}$) into $\mathbb{R}^2$. The *rotation angle* of the digit is given by the x-axis and the *height* of the digit is given by the y-axis

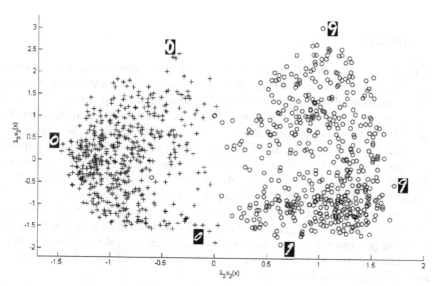

Fig. 2. Embedding of five hundreds 30×20 binary images of the digit nine and five hundreds 30×20 binary images of the digit zero into $\mathbb{R}^2$. The embeddings of the digit zero are illustrated by plus signs while the embeddings of the digit nine are illustrated by circles

The max-min heuristic: $\varepsilon = \alpha \cdot \max_i \min_j D$

In this case, $\min_j D$ denotes a column vector consisting of the distance of each point to its closest neighbor. Taking $\alpha \geq 1$, verifies that each neighborhood contains at least one neighbor.

4 Conclusion

In this chapter we saw that diffusion processes prove to be an effective tool for data analysis. Given a data set, a Markov process is constructed where the states are composed of the data points and the transition probabilities are determined according to a pairwise similarity measure. The similarities are only locally determined and they are propagated via the diffusion process. Using the spectral properties of the Markov matrix that is associated with the Markov process, we are able to reduce the dimensionality of the original data set and embed it into a space of substantially lower dimension. The diffusion distance that was introduced in this chapter measures the level of connectivity between a pair of points in the original space. After the dimensionality reduction, the Euclidean distance between a pair of points in the lower dimensional space approximates the diffusion distance between these points in the original space.

5 Further reading

A more comprehensive description of the diffusion maps scheme can be found in (Coifman and Lafon, 2006, Coifman *et al.*, 2005). A few of the successful application of the diffusion maps algorithm include lip reading (Lafon *et al.*, 2006), text classification (Lafon and Lee, 2006), segmentation of multi-contrast MRI images (Shtainhart *et al.*, 2007). The Diffusion bases algorithm – a dual algorithm to the diffusion maps algorithm – was recently introduced in (Schclar and Averbuch, 2007). Laplacian eigenmaps – a dimensionality reduction algorithm that is closely related to the diffusion maps – is described in (Belkin and Niyogi, 2003). Several papers explored the connections and applications of the graph Laplacian to machine learning (for example, (Kondor and Lafferty, 2002)). A generalization of classical wavelets which is based on diffusion processes, allowing multiscale analysis of general structures, such as manifolds, graphs and point clouds in Euclidean space, is introduced in (Coifman and Maggioni, 2006).

References

M. Belkin and P. Niyogi. (2003), Laplacian eigenmaps for dimensionality reduction and data representation. *Neural Computation*, 15(6):1373–1396.

F. R. K. Chung. (1997), *Spectral Graph Theory.* AMS Regional Conference Series in Mathematics, 92.

R. R. Coifman, S. Lafon, A. Lee, M. Maggioni, B. Nadler, F. Warner, and S. Zucker. (2005), Geometric diffusions as a tool for harmonics analysis and structure definition of data: Diffusion maps. In *Proceedings of the National Academy of Sciences,* volume 102, pages 7432–7437.

R. R. Coifman and S. Lafon. (2006), Diffusion maps. *Applied and Computational Harmonic Analysis: special issue on Diffusion Maps and Wavelets,* 21:5–30.

R. R. Coifman and M. Maggioni R. R. Coifman and M. Maggioni. (2006) Diffusion wavelets. *Applied and Computational Harmonic Analysis: special issue on Diffusion Maps and Wavelets,* 21(1):53–94.

P. Diaconis and D. Stroock. (1991), Geometric bounds for eigenvalues of markov chains. *The Annals of Applied Probability,* 1(1):36–61.

C. Fowlkes, S. Belongie, F. Chung, and J. Malik. (2004), Spectral grouping using the nyström method. *IEEE Transactions on Pattern Analysis and Machine Intelligence,* 26(2):214–225.

R. I. Kondor and J. D. Lafferty. (2002), Diffusion kernels on graphs and other discrete input spaces. In *Proceedings of the 19th International Conference on Machine Learning (ICML 02),* pages 315–322.

S. Lafon Y. Keller and R. R. Coifman. (2006), Data fusion and multi-cue data matching by diffusion maps. *IEEE Transactions on Pattern Analysis and Machine Intelligence,* 28(11):1784–1797.

S. Lafon and A. Lee. (2006), Diffusion maps and coarse-graining: A unified framework for dimensionality reduction, graph partitioning, and data set parameterization. *IEEE Transactions on Pattern Analysis and Machine Intelligence,* 28(9):1393–1403.

M. Meila and J. Shi. (2001), A random walk's view of spectral segmentation. In *Proceedings of the International Workshop on Artifical Intelligence and Statistics.*

A. Schclar and A. Averbuch. (2007), Hyper-spectral segmentation via diffusion bases. *Technical report, Tel Aviv University.*

S. M. Sheldon. (1983), *Stochastic Processes.* John Wiley & Sons.

J. Shi and J. Malik. (2000), Normalized cuts and image segmentation. *IEEE Transactions on Pattern Analysis and Machine Intelligence,* 22(8):888–905.

A. Shtainhart, A. Schclar, and A. Averbuch. (2006), Neuronal tissues sub-nuclei segmentation using multi-contrast mri. *Technical report, Tel Aviv University.*

J. Stewart. (2002), *Calculus.* Brooks Cole, 5th edition.

Y. Weiss. (1999), Segmentation using eigenvectors: A unifying view. In *ICCV (2),* pages 975–982.

S. X. Yu and J. Shi. (2003), Multiclass spectral clustering. In *Proceedings of the IEEE International Conference on Computer Vision,* pages 313–319.

Data Mining and Agent Technology: a fruitful symbiosis

Christos Dimou[1], Andreas L. Symeonidis[1,2], and Pericles A. Mitkas[1,2]

[1] Electrical and Computer Engineering Dept.
  Aristotle University of Thessaloniki, 54 124, Thessaloniki, Greece
[2] Intelligent Systems and Software Engineering Laboratory,
  Informatics and Telematics Institute/CERTH, 57 001, Thessaloniki, Greece
  cdimou@issel.ee.auth.gr, asymeon@iti.gr, mitkas@eng.auth.gr

Summary. Multi-agent systems (MAS) have grown quite popular in a wide spectrum of applications where argumentation, communication, scaling and adaptability are requested. And though the need for well-established engineering approaches for building and evaluating such intelligent systems has emerged, currently no widely accepted methodology exists, mainly due to lack of consensus on relevant definitions and scope of applicability. Even existing well-tested evaluation methodologies applied in traditional software engineering, prove inadequate to address the unpredictable emerging factors of the behavior of intelligent components. The following chapter aims to present such a unified and integrated methodology for a specific category of MAS. It takes all constraints and issues into account and denotes the way knowledge extracted with the use of Data mining (DM) techniques can be used for the formulation initially, and the improvement, in the long run, of agent reasoning and MAS performance. The coupling of DM and Agent Technology (AT) principles, proposed within the context of this chapter is therefore expected to provide to the reader an efficient gateway for developing and evaluating highly reconfigurable software approaches that incorporate domain knowledge and provide sophisticated Decision Making capabilities. The main objectives of this chapter could be summarized into the following: a) introduce Agent Technology (AT) as a successful paradigm for building Data Mining (DM)-enriched applications, b) provide a methodology for (re)evaluating the performance of such DM-enriched Multi-Agent Systems (MAS), c) Introduce Agent Academy II, an Agent-Oriented Software Engineering framework for building MAS that incorporate knowledge model extracted by the use of (classical and novel) DM techniques and d) denote the benefits of the proposed approach through a real-world demonstrator. This chapter provides a link between DM and AT and explains how these technologies can efficiently cooperate with each other. The exploitation of useful knowledge extracted by the use of DM may considerably improve agent infrastructures, while also increasing reusability and minimizing customization costs. The synergy between DM and AT is ultimately expected to provide MAS with higher levels of autonomy, adaptability and accuracy and, hence, intelligence.

1 Introduction

Large amounts of data are being produced and made available online every day, pushing user needs towards a more knowledge-demanding direction. Today's applications are therefore required to extract knowledge from large, often distributed, repositories of text, multimedia or hybrid content. The nature of this quest makes it impossible to use traditional deterministic computing techniques. Instead, various soft computing techniques are employed to meet the challenge for more sophisticated solutions in knowledge discovery. Most notably, Data Mining (DM) is thought of as one of the state-of-the-art paradigms. DM produces useful patterns and associations from large data repositories that can later be used as *knowledge nuggets*, within the context of any application.

Individual facets of knowledge discovery, introduced by DM techniques, often need to be orchestrated, integrated and presented to end users in a unified way. Moreover, knowledge has to be exploited and embodied in autonomous software for learning purposes and, hence, a more increased performance (Figure 1). Agent Technology (AT) proves to be a promising paradigm that is suitable for modelling and implementing the unification of DM tasks, as well as for providing autonomous entity models that dynamically incorporate and use existing knowledge. Indeed, a plethora of multi-agent systems (MAS) and other agent-related solutions for knowledge-based systems can be found in the literature, and more specifically in the area of agent-based DM, as it is explained in detail in Section 3 of this chapter.

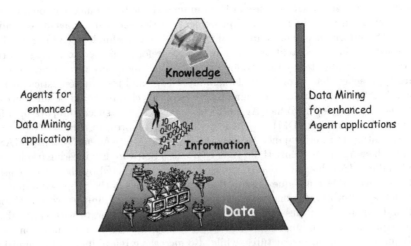

Fig. 1. Mining for intelligence

A numerous related agent development methodologies deal with most of the steps of the development lifecycle. However, there is a remarkable lack of generalized evaluation methodologies for the systems in question. The evaluation of performance is a fundamental step of any development methodology, which provides developers with countable, qualitative and verifiable attributes in an effort to better comprehend the nature of the system at hand. Additionally, generalized and standardized evaluation procedures allow third parties to safely verify the acclaimed properties of deployed systems or newly discovered scientific results.

Existing evaluation approaches address either the DM algorithmic issues or the overall system performance. Both approaches come short in the case of AT and DM integration, due to the complex and dynamic nature of the produced systems. In the case of DM evaluation, focus is given on the statistical performance of individual techniques, in terms of precision and recall, ignoring the actual impact of the extracted knowledge to the application level. In the case of overall system evaluation, existing methods fail to deal satisfactorily with emergent agent behaviors that may not be known at design time.

In this chapter, we present an integrated software engineering approach for developing DM-enriched MAS. Having *Agent Academy II* as the basic designing, development and agent training framework for MAS that employ DM, we provide a generalized methodology for evaluating the performance of a developed system. A set of consice methodological steps is presented, focusing on three fundamental evaluation aspects, namely the selection of a) metrics, b) measurement method, and c) aggregation methods. The proposed methodology is designed to assist developers as an off-the-shelf tool that can be integrated in the overall system development methodology.

The remainder of this chapter is organized as follows: in Section 2 an overview of the basic primitives of AT and DM is provided; Section 3 reviews the related literature in DM and MAS integration and evaluation; Section 4 presents the core development and evaluation methodology, by outlining the appropriate theoretical and software tools; in Section 5, Agent Academy II, a development framework for DM-enriched MAS is presented; finally, Section 6 summarizes and discusses related concluding remarks.

2 Agent Technology and Data Mining

AT and DM have been incorporated and integrated in numerous research efforts. However, the disparity of applications and the notable diversity of the nature of these technologies motivate us to provide thorough definitions of relevant terms and present our point of view over their symbiosis.

2.1 Agents

The term "software agent" has been coined since the early years of Artificial Intelligence, in order to denote any software module that exhibits intelligent behavior. This vague definition, in combination with the unfeasible visions of early AI, has resulted into unsatisfactory applications and has decreased agent computing popularity for many years. It is only until recently that interest in software agents has revived within the context of complex systems' engineering. Agents appear as a handy modelling concept for autonomous, decentralized entities, cooperating towards a common goal or competing on limited resources. Moreover, the advent of many popular, highly distributed internet applications has reinforced agents' position as a promising paradigm for addressing the emerging engineering problems (Weiss (2001)) (Jennings (2001)) (Foster et al.(2004)) (Greenwald and Stone (2001)).

In practice, however, no single universally agreed-upon definition of a software agent exists. This problem occurs due to the horizontal nature of agents. Agents can be either abstract tools for modelling complex systems or actual implemented software modules that may perform any task. The vast disparity of application domains on which agents have been applied reinforces the definition difficulties. In some sets of applications agents may need to exhibit decision making behaviors, whereas in other cases agents may be assigned routine, predefined tasks. Various abstract definitions for agents have been proposed, focusing on one or more agent characteristics with respect to one or more application domains. Woolridge and Jennings, for example, define a software agent with respect to situatedness, autonomy and goal-orientation.

In general, an agent is a software entity that exhibits some or all of the following characteristics:

1. *Autonomy*: Considered as one of the most fundamental features of agency, autonomy implies the degree of control that an agents poses on its own execution thread. Autonomy is usually a strong requirement in many application domains and therefore agents often employ relevant techniques for task-wise decision making in their effort to accomplish their goals.

2. *Interactivity*: Agents are seldom stand alone. They most often rely in information rich and eventful environments with other agents, services or human users. It is therefore required for agents to possess corresponding sensors for perceiving information and actuators for changing the environment. Moreover, interactivity emerges as a result of a more complex intrinsic behavioral processing of the environmental input. Therefore, agents may either respond to occurring events (*reactiveness*) or take initiative and act in order to accomplish predefined goals (*proactiveness*).

3. *Adaptability*: In dynamically changing environments, agents need to be able to change their internal states and consequent actions, to better match the ever-changing conditions.

4. *Sociability*: A product of interactivity, sociability is based on relative human social skills, such as the ability to determine trusted parties or form coalitions in unknown environments.

5. *Cooperativity*: In applications such as distributed problem solving, agents are often required to collaborate with each other in order to reach a common goal that otherwise would be impossible or impractical to reach.

Cooperation may be coordinated by dedicated agents or, in more open environments, emerge via agent communication.

6. *Competitiveness*: Agents are often programmed to allocate certain resources in well-defined environments. Like in similar real-world scenaria, the resources are limited and therefore agents need to compete against each other in order to allocate such resources. Agents employ strategies and action plans for prevailing in such competitive environments.

7. *Mobility*: Transition between different environments is a desired property of agents in applications such as data gathering, web crawling etc.

8. *Character*: Human-centered characteristics can be summarized as a character that is embodied in agents, most often in interface, personal, or assisting agents.

9. *Learning*: Learning is an all-encompassing term that utilizes some or all of the above properties, so that agents observe the impact of theirs or other agents' actions on the environment and predict the optimal behavior, that is activated in similar situations in the future.

Alternative definition approaches attempt to classify agents with respect to their application domain. Such domains may include *inter alia* searching and filtering of information, monitoring conditions, alerting, proxing, coordinating network tasks and managing resources.

A robust classification of agents is provided by (Nwana (1996)). According to this approach, agents can be classified with respect to the following dimensions:

1. *Mobility*, that differentiates agents into *static* and *mobile*
2. The *logic paradigm* they employ, which classifies them as either *deliberative* or *reactive*
3. The *fundamental characteristic* that describe the agent (autonomy, cooperativity, learning). Based on these axes, agents can be classified as (Figure 2):
   - collaborative agents
   - collaborative learning agents
   - interface agents
   - smart agents

In this work, we have adopted Nwana's classification scheme, since it covers successfully a wide area of agent-related applications, as well as it proves to be robust enough to meet the needs of a large number of researchers in the AT field.

2.2 Multi-Agent Systems (MAS)

The promising properties of agents discussed above can only be fully exploited in complex architectures that are deployed in a systematic way. *Agent Oriented Software Engineering* (AOSE) (Jennings (1999)) (Perini et al. (2001)) tackles

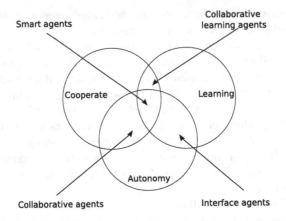

Fig. 2. Nwana's classification of agents

this challenge by providing high level abstraction, modelling and development tools, grouped under the umbrella term of Multi-Agent Systems (MAS). A MAS is as a systematic solution to inherently distributed problems by utilizing autonomous interacting agents and appropriate communication protocols. MAS integrate the above mentioned agent properties and provide new system features that would otherwise be impossible to achieve using monolithic systems. Such characteristics include:

- Increased *performance, reliability* and *maintenability.*
- *Modularity, flexibility* and *extensibility.*
- Overcome of *limited scope* and *capacity* of single agents in terms of knowledge and tasks.
- Better support for *dynamic, unpredictable environments.*
- Introduction of *collective intelligence,* that is the augmentation of intelligence of many simple, not-so-smart interacting entities in contradiction to single, centralized sophisticated modules.

Distributed systems, in the above sense, are modelled as a network of autonomous entities that regulate, control and organize all activities within the distributed environment. In the recent years, a plethora of such distributed systems has emerged. Most notably, the Grid paradigm (Foster et al.(2001)) that envisions a transparent infrastructure of high performance computer resources or knowledge resources that is scattered throughout the globe. Since the conceptualization of the Grid, it has become apparent that MAS may play a pivotal role in the modelling and implementation of such systems (Foster et al.(2004)) (Tang and Zhang (2006)). Other agent-based popular applications include Web Services (Gibbins et al. (2003)) (Muller et al. (2006)) (Negri et al. (2006)), Web Crawling (Jansen et al. (2006)) (Dimou et al.(2006)), environmental monitoring (Athanasiadis and Mitkas (2005)) (Purvis et al. (2003))

and virtual market places (Wurman et al. (1998)) (Wellman and Wurman (1998)).

MAS Characteristics

In general, MAS adhere to the following three primitives. First, MAS must specify appropriate communication and interaction protocols. Despite agents being the building blocks of a problem solving architecture, no individual problem could be effectively solved if no common communication ground, and no action protocol exists.

Secondly, MAS must be open and decentralized. No prior knowledge of, for example, number of participants or static behaviors are always known to the system developer. In a running MAS, new agents may join at any time having only to comform to the communication protocol, being able to act on the way they choose, often in unpredictable manner.

Finally, MAS must consist of possibly heterogeneous agents that are scattered around the environment and act autonomously or in collaboration.

2.3 Data Mining

The need for methods for discovering useful information in large data volumes has been a vivid research topic for many years. Especially nowdays, this need is imperative due to the increasing rate of data production, intensified by the ever-increasing demand for information. DM is a relatively new approach to this problem, often denoted as Knowledge Discovery in Databases (KDD), deals with this exact problem: "the extraction of interesting, non-trivial, implicit, previously unknown and potentially useful information or patterns from data in large databases" (Fayyad et al.(1996)). Though a large number of patterns may arise from the application of DM on datasets, only interesting ones are selected, that is patterns that can be easily understood by humans and suitable for validating a user hypothesis.

Other researchers argue that DM is only "the most important step in the KDD process and involves the application of data analysis and discovery algorithms that, under acceptable computational efficiency limitations, produce a particular enumeration of patterns of data" (Allard and Fraley (1997)). Either approach adopted, in essence DM and KDD address the same problem of extracting useful knowledge and, within the context of this chapter, integrate this knowledge into MAS.

KDD process

KDD is the iterative traversal of the list of steps presented in Table 1

One or more steps of the KDD process may be repeated as many times deemed necessary, in order to come up with desirable outcome.

Table 1. Steps of the KDD process

1. Identify the goal of the KDD process
2. Create a target dataset
3. Clean and preprocess data
4. Reduce and project data
5. Identify the appropriate DM method
6. Select a DM algorithm
7. Apply DM
8. Evaluate DM results
9. Consolidate discovered knowledge

Data Mining Techniques

DM techniques may be applied on large data sets either for validation of a hypothesis or for discovering new patterns. The latter case is further divided into prediction of future trends of the data fluctuation and to a more detailed description and understanding of already extracted patterns. Within the scope of this chapter, focus is given on discovering new patterns and the associated DM techniques include (Fayyad et al.(1996)):

1. *Classification*: the discovery of knowledge model that classifies new data into one of the existing pre-specified classes.
2. *Characterization and Discrimination*: the discovery of a valid description for a part of the dataset.
3. *Clustering*: the identification of finite number of clusters that group data based on their similarities and differences.
4. *Association-Correlation*: the extraction of association rules, which indicate cause-effect relations between the attributes of a dataset.
5. *Outlier analysis*: the identification and exclusion of data that do not abide by the behavior of the rest of the data records.
6. *Trend and evolution analysis*: the discovery of trends and diversions and the study of the evolution of an initial state/hypothesis throughout the course of time.

2.4 Integrating Agent Technology and Data Mining

AT and DM are two separate vessels that each, as derived from the above, has its own scope and applicability. The idea of combining these diverse technologies is emerged by the need to either a) enrich autonomous agents by employing knowledge derived from DM or b) utilize software agents to assist the data extraction process. Both aspects are intriguing and challenging, mainly because of the disparity of AT and DM, since:

1. Despite logic being their common denominator, AT and DM employ two complementary logic paradigms. Agent reasoning is usually based on deductive logic, whereas DM embraces inductive logic.

2. Categorization of MAS with respect to DM-extracted knowledge is complicated due to the wide application range of both technologies.

Logic paradigms

In deductive inference, conclusions are drawn by the combination of a number of premises. Thus, knowledge models are applied to data producing knowledge information (Fernandes(2000)). Under the assumption that these premises are true, deductive logic is truth preserving. In MAS applications, deduction is used by agents in a form of predefined rules and procedures usually defined by domain experts. These rules specify agent actions with respect to the input sensed. Nevertheless, deduction proves inefficient in complex and versatile environments (Arthur (1994)) (Wooldridge (1999)).

Inductive inference, on the other hand, attempts to transform specific data and information into concrete, generalized knowledge models. During the induction process, new rules and correlations are being produced aiming at validating each hypotheses. In contradiction to deduction, induction may lead to invalid conclusions, as it only uses progressive generalizations of specific examples (Kodratoff (1988)).

It becomes evident that the coupling of the above two approaches under the combination of the carrying technologies leads to enhanced and more efficient reasoning systems as proved by (Symeonidis and Mitkas (2005)). Indeed, this combination overcomes the limitations of both paradigms by using deduction for well-known procedures and induction of discovering previously unknown knowledge. The processes of agent training and knowledge diffusion are further explained in the remainder of this section.

Agent modelling

Knowledge extraction capabilities must be present in agent design, as early as in the agent modelling phase. During this process, the intended DM techniques employed shape the nature of the reference engine and provide the knowledge model of the agent with required useful patterns. Every agent exhibiting such reasoning capabilities is required to have the internal structure outlined below.

- Application domain
- Domain ontology
- Agent shell
- Agent type
- Behavior type
- Knowledge Model
- Reasoning engine

When the DM-generated knowledge model is incorporated to the otherwise dummy agent, the outer layers, namely domain ontology, agent shell, agent type and behavior type consist the functional parts of the agent that are influenced in corresponding manners.

The process of dynamically incorporating DM-extracted knowledge models (KM) into agents and MAS is defined as "agent training" while the process of revising in order to improve the knowledge model of agents by reapplying DM techniques is defined as retraining. Finally, "knowledge diffusion" is defined as the outcome of the incorporation of DM extracted knowledge to agents.

Three levels of diffusion

Knowledge diffusion is instantiated in three different ways, with respect to the alternative targets of DM:

1. *DM on the application level of MAS.* DM is applied in order to find useful rules and associations in application data, in order to provide knowledge nuggets to the end user, independently of the internal architecture.
2. *DM on the behavioral level of MAS.* DM is applied on behavioral data, usually log files with past agent actions, in order to predict future agent behaviors.
3. *DM on the evolutionary agent communities.* Evolutionary DM is performed on agent communities in order to study agent societal issues. According to this societal point of view, the goals that need to be satisfied are not atomic but collective and, therefore, knowledge is fused into agents that share common goals.

3 Related work

3.1 MAS and DM

The integration of AT and DM is a subject of a number of research efforts that can be found in the literature. In (Galitsky and Pampapathi(2003)), a combination of inductive and deductive logic for reasoning purposes is proposed for improved customer relationship management. In this work, deduction is used when complete information is available, whereas induction is employed to forecast behaviors of customers when the available information is incomplete. (Fernandes(2000)) provides an implementation of a single inference engine for agents that uses both inductive and deductive reasoning. In this work, logic terms of model data, information and knowledge are incorporated and processed by deductive agents. Finally, an integration of deductive database queries and inductive analysis on these queries and their produced knowledge is presented in (Kero et al. (1995)).

It is a frequent observation in MAS applications that a tradeoff between inference (either inductive or deductive), complexity and development cost arises. However, in more dynamic environments, where both requirements and agent behaviors need constant modification, a systematic approach is compulsory. Symeonidis and Mitkas (Symeonidis and Mitkas (2005)) present a unified methodology for transferring DM extracted knowledge into newly created agents. Knowledge models are generated through DM on the various levels of knowledge diffusion and are dynamically incorporated in agents. The iterative process of retraining through DM on newly acquired data is employed, in order to enhance the efficiency of intelligent agent behavior. The suggested methodology is thoroughly tested on three diverse case studies.

3.2 Evaluation

Although promising, the integration of DM results into MAS functionality arises interesting and some times crucial issues, as far as safety and soundness is concerned. Seeking to extend the work of (Symeonidis and Mitkas (2005)) and provide an evaluation framework for agent efficiency, we present a literature review on intelligent agent evaluation.

Evaluation is a vital step in any complete scientific and engineering methodology. It is defined as "the process of examining a system or a system component to determine the extend to which specified properties are present"[1]. It is the most powerful and sound tool for researchers to assess the quality and applicability of their findings, as well as to set the limits and the optimal environmental or intrinsic system parameters for optimal performance.

Within the Soft Computing paradigm, evaluation is an all encompassing term that may address any component of the system at hand, heavily depending on the developer's aims. It is therefore the researcher's choice to focus on: a) algorithmic issues, b) system performance evaluation, or c) observable intelligence of the implemented system. By addressing one or more of the above, a researcher is able to isolate theoretical shortcoming or implementation malpractices, comprehend the intrinsic characteristics of the system and improve it in the most beneficial manner.

Algorithmic performance and quality evaluation in the context of Soft Computing has been an issue covered by a large corpus of work in the literature, that especially draws from the information retrieval theory primitives. In such cases, the algorithm employed is assessed against its ability to extract the largest percent possible of useful information. Common metrics in this direction include precision, recall, fallout, F-measure and mean average precision. Other Soft Computing approaches use other appropriate metrics or aggregation techniques, depending on the case, including ROC curves, fitness functions and composite figure of merits. Algorithmic evaluation is an important tool that gives a summary of the black box implementation of any algorithm.

---

[1] The Free Online Dictionary of Computing, September 2003
(http://www.foldoc.com)

In the case of intelligent systems, such as MAS, instead of evaluating individual algorithms, we need to assess the actual impact of the employed techniques with respect to other engineering aspects, such as integration issues, performance issues and impact of the selected techniques to the overall quality of the outcome. Moreover, emergent, unpredictable and intelligent behavior that often is exhibited by such systems complicates the process of defining and realizing evaluation procedures. For instance, a bidding agent may use a DM knowledge extraction algorithm from historical data. Despite the satisfaction of high algorithmic precision, the agent may end up losing all auctions because of inefficiency in timing and/or overall strategy. We, therefore, need to regard the system at hand as an integrated intelligent system that consists of modules, exhibits certain behaviors and aims at the accomplishment of specific goals.

In the literature, two general research approaches towards the direction of engineering aspects evaluation exist: a) bottom-up and b) top-down. The first approach represents the strong AI perspective on the problem, indicating that intelligent systems may exhibit any level of intelligence comparable to human abilities. Zadeh (Zadeh (2002)) argues that evaluating such systems is infeasible today, due to the lack of powerful formal languages for defining intelligence and appropriate intelligent metrics. The second approach represents the weak AI or engineering perspective, according to which intelligent systems are systems of increased complexity that are nevertheless well-defined in specific application domains, designed for solving specific problems. Albus (Albus et al. (2000)) suggests that intelligent performance can be effectively evaluated after a concise decomposition of the problem scope and definitions of relative metrics and measurement procedures. Driven by the urging need to evaluate and compare existing or emergent applications, we adopt the top-down approach.

It should be denoted at this point that no general, complete methodology for evaluating engineering applications exists. Instead, researchers often have to devise their own ad-hoc metrics and experimental procedures. In fact, in some cases, the chosen parameters or input data are chosen so as to produce the best results for the -each time presented- method. Moreover, the findings are often supported by qualitatively arguments only, in favor of the proposed system and no debate with respect to its drawbacks is provided. Consequently, it is impossible for a third party to repeat the evaluation procedure and validate the quality of the proposed solution by concluding to similar results. The need for a generalized evaluation framework is, thus, evident.

The requirements of such a methodology is to address both system performance issues as well as emergent, intelligent atomic and social behavior. To answer this challenge, we must devise a methodology that focuses on the following:

- *Re-usability*: The provided methodology must be domain independent and must be available for reuse under different application scenaria, always taking into account possible inherent or emergent heterogeneity in different implementations.

- *Qualitative comparability*: Different implementations in a specific application domain must be liable to comparison with respect to a set of selected qualitative features.
- *Quantitative assessment*: Different implementations in a specific application domain must also be liable to comparison with respect to a set of selected quantitative criteria. Additionally, there must be the opportunity of defining optimal or desired performance, against which one or more implementations may be compared.

Software engineering evaluation, as a well established field, consists a major source of background theory and tools towards this direction. Complete methodologies with quantitative and qualitative metrics have been developed and used in actual software projects. Although subsets of metrics and methods may be adopted, these approaches do not suffice for evaluating intelligent systems, since standard software evaluation processes focus in product features and do not always take into account emergent and unpredictable system behavior.

Ongoing efforts for generalized metrics and evaluation methodologies exist in application fields, such as robotics and autonomic computing. In robotics, evaluation efforts span from autonomous vehicle navigation (Nelson et al. (2002)) (Hu and Zeigler (2002)) (Zimmerman et al. (2002)) to hybrid human-robot control systems (Scholtz et al. (2002)) (Burke et al.(2002)) (Goodrich et al. (2002)). In autonomic computing, emphasis is given to the quality assessment of the selected self-managing techniques (Huebscher and McCann (2004)). Both fields provide us with usefull metrics and thorough methodological steps. However, neither of the above approaches are complete and mature nor do they provide us with relevant tools for the case of knowledge infusion in autonomous entities.

4 A methodology for designing and evaluating DM-enriched applications

In this section we present a generalized methodology for comprehensive development of DM-enriched Multi-Agent Systems. While a typical designing methodology comprises many parts, we focus mainly on the evaluation part of our methodology, for two reasons. First, a multiplicity of designing methodologies exists in the area of MAS and any of them could be used and tailored to model and implement DM enriched applications. Second, there is a remarkable lack of evaluation methods and tools in the area of MAS. By first outlining the evaluation requirements of our proposed approach, we imply the designing requirements that can be met by some of the existing designing methodologies.

The proposed evaluation methodology serves as an off-the-shelf tool for researchers and developers in this field. Composed of both theoretical analysis and software tools, it provides guidelines and techniques that can be used, adopted or extended for the application domain at hand. We follow the top-down engineering perspective, as proposed by Albus (Albus et al. (2000)) and described in the previous section. The methodology is therefore applicable to existing applications or applications that meet current agent oriented engineering concepts and follow the definitions for agent systems and DM terms provided in previous sections.

In our approach, evaluation derives from the observable behavior of agents within MAS. We therefore consider agents to be black boxes at different levels of granularity, depending on the application scope and the evaluation needs of the designer. In a *fine-grained* level, it is desirable to isolate single agents and observe their efficiency and impact of their actions on their environment. In a *coarse-grained* level, we focus on the overall behavior of an agent society and the outcome of transparent collaborative problem solving, competition or negotiation. In the former case, we consider each participating agent as a black box, whereas in the latter case we view the entire MAS as a black box. In both cases, the methodology isolates and measures certain characteristics of the observable behavior of each black box.

By this approach, we assess the impact of the actual performance of agents and MAS, bypassing the methods of implementation, algorithms and other intrinsic characteristics. This implementation independence of our methodology, makes it a powerful tool for measuring both directly the actual efficacy of a system as a whole and indirectly the performance of the intrinsic methods employed. In other words, the algorithmic decisions are indirectly handled and revised in an iterative manner, if and only if the results of the observable behavior evaluation are not within accepted limits. Moreover, two differently implemented systems can be compared against each other, solely in terms of efficiency, having the underlying mechanisms implicitly compared at the same time.

For establishing an evaluation framework that meets the above characteristics, we define:

- *Horizontal aspects*, the essential methodological steps, that if followed sequentially in an iterative manner, will comprise a complete evaluation methodology. The horizontal aspects of our methodology are:
  - *Definitions and theoretical background* on evaluation terms and relevant techniques.
  - *Theoretical tools* that can help designers chose what to measure, how to measure and how to integrate specific findings.
  - *Software tools* that assist designers in their experimental measurements.

- *Vertical aspects* are specific techniques that may be part of any of the above horizontal aspects and deal with the following three terms (Shih (2000)):
  - *Metrics* that correspond to system features to be measured.
  - *Measurement methods* that define the actual experimental procedure of assigning measurement values to the selected metrics.
  - *Aggregation* of the metric-measurement pairs in single characterizations for the system.

In the remainder of this section, we examine the above mentioned horizontal aspects in turn, analyzing each of their vertical aspects accordingly.

4.1 Definitions and theoretical background

The definitions of relevant terms and the corresponding theoretical background is of vital importance, in order to determine the scope and goals of evaluation. Any developer, before actually initiating his/her experiments, must have full grasp of what can and what cannot be evaluated. We, hereinafter, present relevant definitions and background theory with respect to: a) metrics, b) measurement methods, and c) aggregation.

Metrics

Metrics are standards that define measurable attributes of entities, their units and their scopes. Metrics are the essential building blocks of any evaluation process, since they allow the establishment of specific goals for improvement. A specific metric provides an indication of the degree to which a specific system attribute has met its defined goal. Deviation from the desired range of values indicates that improvement is needed in the related parts or modules of the system. With respect to a complete evaluation methodology, a metric is the answer to the question: *"What should I evaluate?"*.

It must be noted that in software engineering (SE) the term metric is often used interchangeably with the term measurement to denote specific measured values for an attribute. In this work, however, we distinguish the two terms, in order to separate the metrics selection process from the actual measurement data collection.

A metric is defined by: a) its relationship to the corresponding features of the evaluated system, and b) the selected scale of measurement. The former consists of actual parameters or attributes of the system. For example, in auction environments, typical attributes would be the starting and ending time of an auction, as well as the winning bid. The latter term refers to the unit of measurement for this attribute. In the above example, a timestamp in milliseconds or an amount in Euros would suffice to describe the scale of the selected attributes. Typical types of scales include nominal and ordinal values, intervals and ratio scales.

In SE more than 300 metrics have been defined and used in various evaluation methodologies. Metrics are organized in categories, including technical, performance, business, productivity and end-user metrics (Fenton(1991)). However, in this work, we focus only on performance metrics, since DM for MAS is a relatively new technology that has not yet reached the maturity of software products. The proposed evaluation methodology, however, is expandable so that other aspects besides performance may be covered as well.

A requirement of our methodology with respect to metrics is to be able to provide a set of appropriate metrics and a comprehensive organization of this set in terms of similarity and cohesion. This taxonomy of metrics should also be extensible so that it is applicable to any application. A user will ideally be able to parse this taxonomy and select the metrics that are desirable for the system at hand.

Measurement

Measurement is defined as "the process of ascertaining the attributes, dimensions, extend, quantity, degree of capacity of some object of observation and representing these in the qualitative or quantitative terms of a data language" (Krippendorff (1986)). Having selected the appropriate metrics, measurement is the next fundamental methodological step that systematically assigns specific values to these metrics. Typical measurement methods consists of experimental design and data collection. A measurement method is the answer to the question "*How should I perform the experimental evaluation?*".

Among the three distinct steps of the proposed methodology, measurement is the most dependent on the implementation details of the application. Indeed, a generalized evaluation methodology cannot indicate precise steps of carrying out a specific measurement procedure. From this point of view, the key requirement of our methodology is to provide a set of measurement methods, so that the user may choose from a variety of options the most appropriate on to tackle the application domain at hand. Our methodology also provides a guideline list for conducting experimental design and data collection, as derived from traditional SE evaluation paradigms.

Aggregation

Aggregation, or composition, is the process of summarizing multiple measurements into a single measurement is such a manner that the output measurement will be characteristic of the system performance. Aggregation groups and combines the collected measurements, possibly by the use of weights of importance, in order to conclude to atomic characterization for the evaluated system. For example, an evaluated system may perform exceptionally well in terms of response time metrics (timeliness), but these responses may be far from correct (accuracy). An aggregation process must weightedly balance contradicting measures and provide an overall view of parts or the whole of the system, within boundaries of acceptable performance. Aggregation is the answer to the question: *"What is the outcome of the evaluation procedure?"*.

A plethora of diverse aggregation techniques exist. Most commonly, aggregation is accomplished with the assistance of mathematical representation of multi-dimensional vectors and methods of either comparing sets of such vectors or comparing single vectors against predefined ideal vectors. The field of multi-criteria decision making provides us with a rich literature on this issue. Approaches in this field vary from simple sum, average, triangulation or other weighted functions to multi-dimensional vector comparison and vector distance. Especially in the field of intelligent system evaluation, vectors play a crucial role, in the form of Vector of Performance (VoP) or Vectors of Intelligence (VoI) (Szuba (2002)).

A requirement of our methodology with respect to aggregation is to provide with the user with appropriate aggregation theory and techniques in order to combine any specific measurements into conclusive characterizations of the evaluated system.

4.2 Theoretical Tools

We next present a set of theoretical tools that aim to assist users throughout the designing of the evaluation procedure, by providing sets of options and guidelines for intelligent performance assessment.

Metrics

Motivated by the requirements for metrics presented above, we introduce a theoretical tool for metric categorization in the form of an acyclic directed graph. The graph is organized in layers or *views* of granularity from general to specific, as further explained below. A user may traverse the graph in a top-down manner and, depending on the choices made, he/she shall conclude to a set of suitable metrics. After finalizing the measurement and aggregation methodology, as presented in the following sections, the developer will be able to traverse the graph upwards in order to provide single characterization for the system at each view. The graph is designed to be general, but also provides the option of extensibility for necessary domain specific metrics.

This tool was inspired by numerous related efforts in the traditional SE field, that provide comprehensive taxonomies of metrics (e.g. (de los Angeles Martin and Olsina (2003)). Besides dealing with predictable, deterministic, closed and non-dynamic software, the above approaches also come short because of the flat categorization of metrics at a single level of granularity.

In the proposed approach, we organize a metrics graph into four views, as depicted in Figure 3:

These views include:

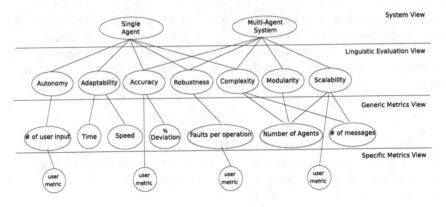

Fig. 3. Metrics graph

1. *System view*: At the top-most level, the class of the application is selected. A user may chose between single-agent, multi-agent society and multi-agent competition, depending on the scope and focus of the evaluation effort.
2. *Linguistic evaluation view*: At this level, a user chooses the appropriate verbal characterizations of system aspects, such as accuracy, timeliness, robustness and scalability. These abstract high level characterizations exclude parts of the underlying metrics, while focusing on the aspects of interest to the evaluator.
3. *Generic metrics view*: This level consists of metrics that are general and independent of the application field, such as response time, number of agents and message exchange frequency. The user may either use directly these metrics or refine them by continuing to the next level.
4. *Specific metrics view*: The final level consists of metrics that are specific to the application field. These metrics are only defined by the user, since they are not known *a priori* to a generalized evaluation methodology. Newly defined metrics must conform to the metric definition and parametrization presented in the previous section. Finally, they must be appended to one of the graph nodes of the above levels with directed arcs.

After selecting the metrics from this graph, the user is requested to define a set of parameters for each metric, including the preferred scale of measurement and other attributes, such as frequency of measurement, time intervals etc.

Measurement methods

Before implementing the actual measurement process, one must define the measurement method. Kitchenham (Kitchenham (1996)) provides a categorization of measurement techniques, with respect to the types of properties employed and the nature of the experimental technique. Inspired by this work, we provide the categorization displayed in the Table 2.

Table 2. Categorization of measurement methods

Experiment Type	Description
Quantitative experiment	An investigation of the quantitative impact of methods/tools organized as a formal experiment
Quantitative case study	An investigation of the quantitative impact of methods/tools organized as a case study
Quantitative survey	An investigation of the quantitative impact of methods/tools organized as a survey
Qualitative screening	A feature-based evaluation done by a single individual who not only determines the features to be assessed and their rating scale but also does the assessment. For initial screening, the evaluations are usually based on literature describing the software method/tools rather than actual use of the methods/tools
Qualitative experiment	A feature-based evaluation done by a group of potential user who are expected to try out the methods/tools on typical tasks before making their evaluations
Qualitative case study	A feature-based evaluation performed by someone who has used the method/tool on a real project
Qualitative survey	A feature-based evaluation done by people who have had experience of using the method/tool, or have studied the method/tool. The difference between a survey and an experiment is that participation in a survey is at the discretion of the subject
Qualitative effects analysis	A subjective assessment of the quantitative effect of methods and tools, based on expert opinion
Benchmarking	A process of running a number of standard tests using alternative tools/methods (usually tools) and assessing the relative performance of the tools against those tests

Having selected the measurement method, one must thoroughly provide an experimental design prototype and a data collection procedure. As stated earlier, our methodology can only provide a set of guidelines that any designer may adjust to their specific application. A typical experimental design procedure must describe thoroughly the objectives of the experiments and ensure that these objectives can be reached using the specified techniques.

The last step of the measurement methodology is to carry out the data collection process. Here, the basic guidelines for the designer to follow are to ensure that the data collection process is well defined and monitor the data collection and watch for deviations from the experiment design.

Aggregation

Following the collection of measurement values and the construction of metric-measurement pairs, the problem of aggregation arises. In the evaluation process, aggregation occurs naturally in order to summarize the experimental findings into a single characterization of the performance, either of single modules, or the system as a whole. In the case of the metrics graph of the proposed methodology, after having the measurements collected, the user must traverse the graph in a bottom-up manner. From the *specific metrics view* and the *general metrics view*, he/she must proceed upwards and, at each view, apply aggregation techniques to provide single characterizations for every parent node.

For example, assume that the simplified subtree, depicted in Figure 4, has been used for measuring the performance of a single agent. It must be noted that in this example, no user specified metrics have been included and therefore the *Specific Metrics View* layer is omitted.

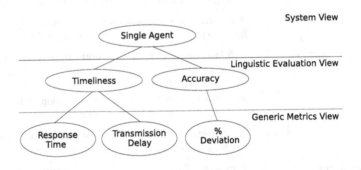

Fig. 4. Example metrics graph for aggregation

We assume that we already have obtained measurement values for the metrics at the general metrics view. In this example, the aggregation process consists of two steps. The first step concludes to a single measurement or characterization for each of the two selected linguistic terms, namely timeliness and accuracy, by weightedly combining the available measurements. The second step combines the linguistic characterization into a single characterization for the single agent system.

It becomes apparent from the above example, that a natural method for combining diverse and heterogeneous measurement information and linguistic characterizations is needed. We argue that *fuzzy aggregation* provides us with the appropriate natural functionality for this purpose. The term *natural* refers to the ability of the evaluator to express the evaluation findings in a manner that is coherent to their natural language. In other words, the fuzzy aggregation process translates the problem of combining numerical, ordinal or other measures into a collection of verbal characterizations for the system performance.

The proposed fuzzy aggregation method consists of four steps:

1. *Define weights in the metrics graph.* This process determines the importance of each node in the metrics graph with respect to the overall system performance. This decision relies heavily on the application domain as well as the requirements of each application. Hence, the determination of the weights may occur either a) semi-automatically, in case historical data on the importance of each node are available, possibly by an expert system, or b) directly by an expert user, the system designers in most cases.

2. *Define corresponding fuzzy scales for each metric.* The next step deals with the definition of fuzzy scales for the selected metrics. Fuzzy scales are defined by ordinal linguistic variables, such as *low, moderate, high* and membership functions that map numerical values to the above variables. Having the scales defined, one may already have scales for *natural* characterizations of performance, such as *high response time* or *moderate accuracy*, with respect to desired values.

3. *Convert actual measurements to fuzzy scales.* The conversion is a simple import of the selected measurements to the membership functions defined in the previous step.

4. *Apply a corresponding fuzzy aggregation operator at each view of the graph.* A wide variety of fuzzy aggregation operators exists (Grabisch et al. (1998)), which can be categorized in:

   - Conjunctive operators, that perform aggregation with the logical "and" connection.
   - Disjunctive operators, that perform aggregation with the logical "or" connection.
   - Compensative operators, which are comprised between minimum and maximum, such as mean or median operators.
   - Non-compensative operators, that do not belong to any of the above categories, such as symmetric sums.

Theoretical tools: Summary

In Table 3, we summarize the required methodological steps with respect to the theoretical tools, which take place at the evaluation process of a development methodology. In section 5.2, we present a real world case study on which the presented methodology is thoroughly applied.

Table 3. Summarization of methodological steps

1. Traverse metrics graph and select metrics
2. Provide domain specific metrics (optionally)
3. Determine metrics parameters
4. Specify measurement method and parameters
5. Execute experiments
6. Define weights in the graph
7. Define fuzzy scales and convert measurements accordingly
8. Select and apply aggregation operators on the collected measurements

4.3 Software Tools

In addition to the above presented theoretical tools, a complete off-the-shelf evaluation methodology must contain specifically implemented software tools that assist the evaluation procedure. In this section, we sketch the outline of such a software evaluation tool and the corresponding design guidelines that can be adopted by other similar tools.

The proposed evaluator tool is required to provide semi-automated assistance to the user throughout the following phases of evaluation:

- design
- run-time experimental procedure
- evaluation data summarization
- presentation of the results

A key requirement for this tool is that there must be minimum intervention to the code of an existing system and minimum prior knowledge of the system developer with respect to evaluation aspects. This requirement allows such software tools to apply to existing applications as an evaluation plug-in using dynamic code generation. Figure 5 depicts the six stages of assistance to the evaluation procedure.

1. *Selection of Metrics*: The first component of the proposed tool, is a Graphical User Interface that presents a metrics graph to the user and provides him/her with edit operations. According to the needs of the application, the user selects paths that lead to useful metric nodes and deletes paths and nodes that are unnecessary. As a result, the user determines a subset of the initial graph that is specific to the initiated evaluation procedure. Finally, the parameters of each selected metric as well as corresponding aggregation weights are defined.

2. *Dynamic Interface Generation*: Having the metrics subtree that has been produced in the previous stage, the tool dynamically generates a Java programming interface that corresponds to this evaluation procedure. Elements of agent behavior, communication and interaction are incorporated to implement essential abstract methods that are instantiated in the next stage.

Architecture of the proposed Evaluation Tool

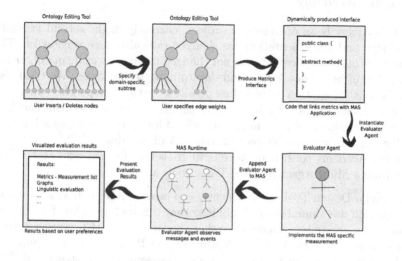

Fig. 5. Outline of the proposed Agent Evaluator Software Tool

3. *Implementation of Evaluator Agent:*Based on the produced programming interface, the user of the tool provide the necessary code for an Evaluator Agent that implements this interface, taking into account all the application-specific details.

4. *Attachment of Evaluator Agent to a MAS at run-time:* The Evaluator Agent is imported to the running system at run-time, executing observation operations on actions, events and messages that relate to the selected metrics.

5. *Data Collection:* The Evaluator Agent records all the observed actions into a log file.

6. *Presentation of Results:* After completion of the system execution or the ellapse of a predefined interval, the proposed tool presents the outcome of the evaluation process to the user, by processing the log files, deriving appropriate measurements from recorded events and messages and aggregates the results accordingly.

5 Agent Academy II: an Agent-Oriented Software Engineering tool for building DM-enriched MAS

5.1 Agent Academy II

Agent Academy is an open-source project, currently in the second version[1]. The design and implementation has changed radically since version 1.0. The initial goals of the application have not changed though, focusing mainly in the integration of agent developing and data mining technologies. We tried also to make this integration as broad as possible. In this perspective, we added features we find valuable to developers such as project management capabilities or java editing tools. Agent Academy enables users to reuse existing code by allowing a user to simply paste it into AA directories.

Agent Academy consists of three basic tools that form also an abstraction of creating a Multi Agent System. These tools are:

- Behavior Design Tool, where the user can create JADE behaviors, compile them and use a number of capabilities that this tool provides (for example users can create java source code that sends/receives ACL messages using a simple GUI etc) A central feature of the BDT is that it supplies to the users an intuitive tool for keeping the source code structured. The idea behind this feature is that users can create blocks of code of any size (i.e. it can span in an entire method). These blocks have a description, a body (the source code) and the method in which they belong. All these attributes can change dynamically allowing the users to add the same block of code in many methods or create a high-level description of the source file by summing up all the blocks descriptions. Implementing these blocks as static variables enables users to exchange blocks among multiple source files.
- Agent Design Tool, with which the developers can create software agents and add the designed behaviors as the agents execution tasks. We think agent functionality should reside in the agents behaviors, so ADT has not extended capabilities. ADT is equipped with a number of capabilities that we think are really important to agent developers. We are going to briefly mention them here and describe them in greater detail later. The first among them is the debugging tool (aka Graphical Monitor Agent Execution) that its use can save lot of debugging time. By means of this monitor, users can watch the execution of agent behaviors. This process is dynamic, meaning that behaviors that are added to the agent long after agent initialization can also be monitored. A tool that is also available from other Agent Academy modules is the Data Mining Module. Users can launch this tool, create a data mining model in the fly and add it to agent code just like any other JADE behavior.

---

[1] Available at http://sourceforge.net/projects/agentacademy

- Multi-Agent System Design Tool, is the tool that developers can use to create Multi-Agent Systems. The functionality of this tool is limited, constrained mainly in the easy, user-friendly definition of the participants in the MAS being designed.

Agent Academy users are encouraged to implement the MAS creation process following steps that correspond to the order the AA tools were presented, although other approaches can also be effective. Beyond this agent-oriented functionality, Agent Academy comes with a set of tools for a small/medium scale Project Management. In more detail, users are given the possibility to keep a small account of their projects components by using the Project Notepad that is matrix in which they can store the agents and behaviors created inside their project. Users can also use standard clean/build/run project capabilities from the Agent Academy main window.

5.2 A real world demonstrator

For validating the proposed methodology, we have selected Supply Chain Management (SCM) as a representative domain for testing agents that utilize DM techniques. We have implemented an SCM agent under the name Mertacor that has successfully participated in past Trading Agent SCM Competitions. Mertacor combines agent features with DM techniques. In the remainder of this section, we provide an overview of the SCM domain, the competition scenario and Mertacor's architecture. We conclude by applying the proposed evaluation methodology to different implementations of Mertacor.

Supply Chain Management

SCM tasks comprise the management of materials, information and finance in a network consisting of suppliers, manufacturers, distributors and customers. SCM strategies target at the efficient orchestration of the sequence of tasks, from raw materials to end-user service. Traditional SCM relied heavily on rigid and predefined contracts between participating parties. However, the need for dynamic configuration of the supply chain, as indicated nowaydays by global markets, became imperative. Modern SCM approaches focus on the integration, optimization and management of the entire process of material sourcing, production, inventory management and distribution to customers.

The core design primitives for coping with SCM are a) coordination of distributed, heterogeneous information,b) efficient negotiation between participating entities and c) functional resource allocation. MAS are an ideal modelling and implementation solution to this inherently distributed problem (Ferber(1999)) (Wu et al. (2000)). Moreover, DM techniques have been successfully applied for SCM purposes in the past. DM has efficiently addresses issues of customer and supplier profiling, inventory scheduling and market based analysis.

SCM Trading Agent Competition Game

The Trading Agent Competition (TAC) is an annual, international competition that consists of two games: a) TAC Classic and b) TAC SCM. In the latter, the game scenario, as described in (Collins and Janson (2004)), consists of groups of six competing agents, each of which represents a PC assembler with limited production capacity an competes with other agents in selling PC units to customers. The agents' task is to efficiently manage a part of the supply chain, namely to negotiate on supply contracts, bid for customer offers, manage daily assembly activities and ship completed offers to customers. Negotiations with manufacturers and customers are performed through a Request-For-Quote (RFQ) mechanism, which proceeds in three steps:

- Buyer issues RFQs to one or more sellers
- Sellers respond to RFQs with offers
- Buyers accept or reject offers. An accepted offer becomes an order.

In order to get paid, the agent must deliver on-time, otherwise it is charged with a penalty. At the end of the game, the agent with the greatest revenue is declared winner. For more information on the game, read the game specification provided by (Collins and Janson (2004)).

Mertacor Architecture

Mertacor, as introduced in (Kontogounis et al. (2006)), consists of four cooperating modules (Figure 6):

1. the *Inventory Module*(IM). Mertacor introduces an assemble-to-order (ATO) strategy, which is a combination of two popular inventory strategies, namely *make-to-order* and *make-to-stock*.
2. the *Procuring Module*(PM). This module predicts future demand and orders affordable components, balancing between cheap procurement and running needs in the assembly line.
3. the *Factory Module*(FM). This module constructs assembly schedules and provides the Bidding Module with information on the factory production capacity, based on simulation of customer demand for the next 15 game days.
4. the *Bidding Module*(BM). This module attempts to predict a winning bid for each order, by performing DM on logs of past games, and makes respective offers for incoming orders.

Mertacor's core integrates these modules into a transparently robust unit that handles negotiations with both customers and suppliers. This architecture provides flexibility and extensibility, permitting the application of Mertacor's strategy to other real-life SCM environments.

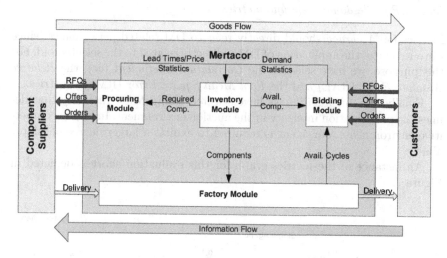

Fig. 6. Overview of Mertacor's architecture

Evaluating Mertacor's performance

In the remainder of this section, we apply the proposed evaluation methodology to various implementations of Mertacor. In our effort to assess the impact of DM in Mertacor's performance, we require that the experiments are planned is such way that deals with both DM algorithmic-specific efficacy and their impact on overall agent performance. We follow the methodological steps defined in Table 3.

Step 1: Traverse metrics graph and select metrics

Starting from the *System view*, we select the *Single Agent* node and its corresponding path. This choice is attributed to the nature of auctioning environments; we, being the developers of Mertacor, have complete control only on the agent's executing thread and observe the auctioning world only through Mertacor's perspective. We, therefore, need to focus on performance aspects that exclusively deal with this single agent.

At the *Linguistic Evaluation View*, we select the linguistic metrics of *Accuracy*, *Timeliness* and *Adaptability*. Indeed, from our experience in SCM auctions, these three characteristics are the most significant ones, since the outcome of each auction is heavily dependent on the deviation of the forecasted bid, the on-time delivery of the bid and the ability of the agent to adapt in dynamic environments, respectively.

At the *Generic Metrics View* we only select *Time*, as the standard metric for *Timeliness*. The rest of the metrics are domain specific and are, therefore, defined in the next methodological step.

Step 2: Provide domain specific metrics

Metrics for *Accuracy* should directly refer to DM related performance, since the outcome of the application of DM is directly related to the selected bid. For this purpose, we have selected the *Correlation Coefficient* (cc), the *Relative Absolute Error* (RAE) and the *Root Mean Square Error* (RMSE) metrics.

Finally, for *Adaptability*, we have selected *Competition Intensity* that defines the participation intensity in the auction environment. In highly competitive environments, our agent is required to exhibit a larger degree of adaptability.

An instance of the metrics graph for this evaluation effort is depicted in Figure 7.

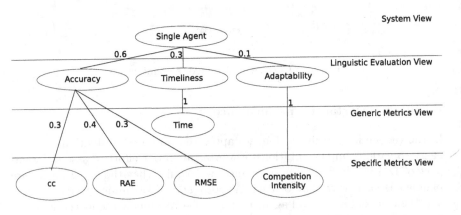

Fig. 7. Resulted metrics graph for Mertacor evaluation

Step 3: Determine metrics parameters

We now continue by defining the scale of each metric. For the three linguistic metrics, *Accuracy*, *Timeliness* and *Adaptability*, we define the corresponding fuzzy scales in *Step 7* of the methodology. For the generic and specific metrics, we provide the following scales:

1. *CC*: The correlation coefficient is the degree at which the forecasted bid and the resulted price are correlated. The *cc* lies in the [-1,1] interval.
2. *RAE*: The *Relative Absolute Error* is a percentage indicator for the deviation of the above mentioned variables.
3. *RMSE*: The *Root Mean Square Error* is another well-known DM metric for the above mentioned variables.
4. *Time*: In TAC SCM auctions, bids are normally submitted just before the end of each predefined auction interval. One could argue that, since this time constraint exists, all agents have a time barrier to bid and therefore

all bidding calculation procedures should be characterized either as successful or failed. In that context, timeliness is only a binary metric that provides no further performance indication. However, due to the modular architecture of Mertacor, the earliest possible decision on the bid, allows the agent to perform other game-related tasks in this interval. We therefore define *Time* as the time interval between the first call of the related bidding API function and the determination of the bidding value, in milliseconds.

5. *Competition Intensity*: We have selected two different competing environments that affect *Adaptability*: a) Finals, where the competition intensity is high, and b) Second finals, where the competition intensity is low.

Step 4: Specify measurement method and parameters

Estimation of the winning price of the bids can be modeled as a regression problem, where the desired output is the agent's bidding price for clients' RFQs and the inputs are the parameters related to the bid that are known to the agent. The initial set of attributes considered are the demand (Total PCs requested each day), the demand in the product's market range, the due date of the order, the reserve price of components, and the maximum and minimum prices of same type PCs sold in the last days (2 previous days for maximum 4 for minimum), as shown in Table 4.

Table 4. Set of SCM auction attributes for DM

Attribute description	Attribute name
Demand (Total PCs requested the day the RFQ was issued)	demandAll
Demand in the product's market range	demandRange
Duedate	dueDate
Reserve price	reservePrice
Maximum price of PCs of same type sold in the last 1 day	max1
Maximum price of PCs of same type sold in the last 2 days	max2
Minimum price of PCs of same type sold in the last 1 day	min1
Minimum price of PCs of same type sold in the last 2 days	min2
Minimum price of PCs of same type sold in the last 3 days	min3
Minimum price of PCs of same type sold in the last 4 days	min4
Winning price of the bid	price

Available data was split into three subsets, each one representing a different market range (LOW - MEDIUM - HIGH), both for the finals and second finals of the game, resulting to six different datasets (finalsLOWMEDIUMHIGH and secondFinalsLOWMEDIUMHIGH).

The instances within the initial datasets ranged from 45000 to 230000 instances. Analysis was performed on all datasets. Nevertheless, due to space limitation we shall discuss only one case (finalsLOW dataset), while analysis on the other cases was performed in an analogous manner. The initial dataset contained 156228 records of bids. In order to remove redundant information and enable quicker and more accurate training, a number of pre-processing filters were tested against the dataset. In particular, we applied the CfsSubsetEval1 (Hall (1998)) WrapperSubsetEval2 (Kohavi and John (1997)), and ReliefFAttributeEva3l (Sikonja and Kononenko (1997)) filters for attribute selection, using the GreedyStepwise and RandomSearch search methods. The trimmed dataset contained the following attributes as input: the demand, the reserve price for components, the maximum price of same type PCs for the two previous days and the minimum price for the previous day, while price was the output attribute. In order to reduce the number of instances for training, and since the class attribute (price) is numeric, the StratifiedRemoveFolds4 (Breiman and Stone (1984)) method was selected. Two datasets were finally produced, containing the one third (1/3) and one eighth (1/8) of the initial instances respectively.

Finally, for training purposes, four different classification (regression) and two meta-classification schemes were applied, in order to decide on the one that optimally meets the problem of predicting the winning bid of an order:

1. Linear Regression
2. Neural Networks
3. SMOreg (Support Vector Machines)
4. the M5' algorithm
5. Additive Regression
6. Bagging

Step 5: Execute experiments

In order to experiment on the data with a variety of training techniques and algorithms, the WEKA (Witten and Frank (2005)) was selected, providing with a wide range of filters for pre-processing, model evaluation, visualization and post-processing. The results of the experimental procedures are presented in Table 5 and Table 6, for low and high *Competition Intensity* values, respectively.

Step 6: Define weights in the graph

This step requires a subjective, expert-initiated attribution of weights to the corresponding edges of the metrics graph. Driven by our experience in the field, we assign a higher weight to *Accuracy* (0.6) and lesser weights to *Timeliness* (0.3) and *Adaptability* (0.1). The corresponding weights are illustrated in Figure 7.

Step 7: Define fuzzy scales and convert measurements accordingly

We provide the following fuzzy sets for the selected metrics:

Table 5. Results of experiments for low Competition Intensity

Algorithm	CC	RAE (%)	RMSE	Time	Data Subset
Linear Regression	0.93	28.99	90.17	108	LOW
Neural Networks	0.93	32.91	94.69	111	LOW
Support Vector Machines	0.93	26.47	89.08	157	LOW
M5'	0.95	22.77	61.09	140	LOW
Additive Regr.	1.00	3.21	22.12	192	LOW
Bagging	0.98	14.89	52.02	201	LOW
Linear Regression	0.94	26.50	112.71	129	MEDIUM
Neural Networks	0.95	24.85	105.69	133	MEDIUM
Support Vector Machines	0.93	28.66	109.61	182	MEDIUM
M5'	0.97	19.30	86.90	168	MEDIUM
Additive Regr.	1.00	3.01	23.53	230	MEDIUM
Bagging	0.98	13.26	65.52	237	MEDIUM
Linear Regression	0.94	26.78	105.51	140	HIGH
Neural Networks	0.95	27.83	105.21	144	HIGH
Support Vector Machines	0.94	25.82	103.32	204	HIGH
M5'	0.96	21.29	87.14	183	HIGH
Additive Regr	1.00	2.98	24.70	249	HIGH
Bagging	0.98	15.13	65.69	260	HIGH

Table 6. Results of experiments for high Competition Intensity

Algorithm	CC	RAE (%)	RMSE	Time	Data Subset
Linear Regression	0.98	14.34	63.40	110	LOW
Neural Networks	0.97	21.26	64.82	112	LOW
Support Vector Machines	0.96	17.48	72.84	155	LOW
M5'	0.98	13.49	56.79	145	LOW
Additive Regr.	0.97	19.24	67.51	189	LOW
Bagging	0.99	5.62	27.76	199	LOW
Linear Regression	0.97	16.95	74.33	133	MEDIUM
Neural Networks	0.97	20.21	75.20	132	MEDIUM
Support Vector Machines	0.97	17.54	73.81	193	MEDIUM
M5'	0.99	9.91	46.93	172	MEDIUM
Additive Regr.	0.96	25.98	92.30	227	MEDIUM
Bagging	1.00	4.84	31.38	233	MEDIUM
Linear Regression	0.97	16.55	68.14	142	HIGH
Neural Networks	0.98	18.94	71.91	144	HIGH
Support Vector Machines	0.97	16.27	72.31	208	HIGH
M5'	0.99	10.03	45.35	178	HIGH
Additive Regr.	0.95	28.26	94.68	242	HIGH
Bagging	0.99	5.70	34.90	263	HIGH

- Fuzzy variables *very low,low,medium,high* and *very high* for the *RAE* and *RMSE* metrics
- Fuzzy variables *low* and *high* for the *CC* and *Competition Intensity* metrics
- Fuzzy variables *low, medium* and *high* for the *Time* metric

The corresponding fuzzy membership functions for *CC, RAE, RMSE* and *Time* are depicted in Figure 8.

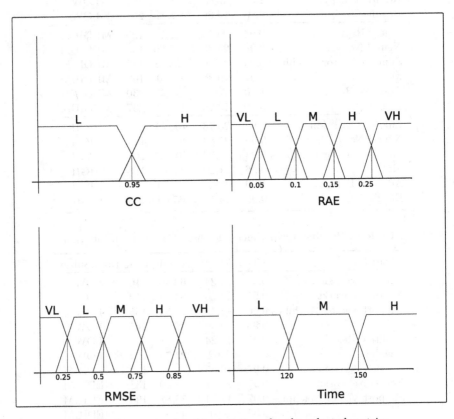

Fig. 8. Fuzzy membership functions for the selected metrics

Step 8: Select and apply aggregation operators on the collected measurements

The final step of the methodology consists of the application of the selected aggregation method. As described in (Grabisch et al. (1998)), the application of weighted operators result into a single characterization for every linguistic metric. After summarizing the results it can be seen that *Additive Regression* exhibit the best performance for all data subsets, as it balances between large accuracy and adequate time responses, for both high and low *Competition Intensity*.

6 Concluding remarks

As the number of application that integrate DM and AT increase, the need for assessing the overall system performance is imperative. In this work, we have presented a generalized methodology for evaluating agents and MAS that employ DM techniques for knowledge extraction and knowledge model generation. The proposed methodology comprises a set of concise steps that guide an evaluator through the evaluation process. A novel theoretical representation tool introduces a metrics graph and appropriate selection guidelines for measurement and aggregation methods. A real world DM-enriched agent in the field of Supply Chain Management has used to demonstrate the applicability of the proposed methodology. Future work in this direction include the specification of a unique metrics ontology for the proposed metrics representation graph and the expansion of the graph with a complete set of real world metrics, borrowed either from the software engineering discipline or existing, ad-hoc efforts in intelligent systems evaluation. Finally, the proposed methodology must be thoroughly tested in a number of diverse and representative case studies.

References

James Albus, Elena R. Messina, and John M. Evans. (2000), Performance metrics for intelliget systems (permis) white paper. In *Proc. of the First International Workshop on Performance Metrics for Intelligent Systems (PERMIS)*.

Dennis Allard and Chris Fraley. (1997), Non parametric maximum likelihood estimation of features in saptial point process using voronoi tessellation. *Journal of the American Statistical Association*.

Brian W. Arthur. (1994), Inductive reasoning and bounded rationality. *American Economic Review*, 84:406–411.

Ioannis N. Athanasiadis and Pericles A. Mitkas. (2005), Social influence and water conservation: An agent-based approach. *Computing in Science and Engg.*, 7 (1):65–70, 2005. ISSN 1521-9615.

Friedman J.H. unsrt Olshen R.A. Breiman, L. and C.J. Stone. (1984), *Classification and Regression Trees*. Chapman and Hall, New York.

J. L. Burke, R.R. Murphy, D. R. Riddle, and T. Fincannon. (2002), Task performance metrics in human-robot interaction: Taking a systems approach. In *Proc. of the Fourth International Workshop on Performance Metrics for Intelligent Systems (PERMIS)*.

Arunachalam R. Sadeh N. Ericsson J. Finne N. Collins, J. and S. Janson. (2004), The supply chain management game for the 2005 trading agent competition. Technical report, CMU.

M. de los Angeles Martin and Luis Olsina. (2003), Towards an ontology for software metrics and indicators as the foundation for a cataloging web system. In *LA-WEB '03: Proceedings of the First Conference on Latin American Web Congress*, page 103, Washington, DC, USA, 2003. IEEE Computer Society. ISBN 0-7695-2058-8.

Christos Dimou, Alexandros Batzios, Andreas L. Symeonidis, and Pericles A. Mitkas. (2006), A multi-agent simulation framework for spiders traversing the semantic web. In *Web Intelligence*, pages 736–739. IEEE Computer Society, 2006. ISBN 0-7695-2747-7.

Usama M. Fayyad, Gregory Piatetsky-Shapiro, and Padhraic Smyth. (1996), Knowledge discovery and data mining: Towards a unifying framework. In *KDD*, pages 82–88.

Norman E. Fenton. (1991), *Software Metrics: A Rigorous Approach*. Chapman & Hall, Ltd., London, UK, ISBN 0442313551.

Jacques Ferber. (1999), *Multi-Agent Systems: An Introduction to Distributed Artificial Intelligence*. Addison-Wesley Longman Publishing Co., Inc., Boston, MA, USA, ISBN 0201360489.

A. A. A. Fernandes. (2000), Combining inductive and deductive inference in knowledge management tasks. In *DEXA '00: Proceedings of the 11th International Workshop on Database and Expert Systems Applications*, page 1109, Washington, DC, USA, IEEE Computer Society. ISBN 0-7695-0680-1.

Ian T. Foster, Carl Kesselman, and Steven Tuecke. (2001), The anatomy of the grid - enabling scalable virtual organizations. *CoRR*, cs.AR/0103025.

Ian T. Foster, Nicholas R. Jennings, and Carl Kesselman. (2004), Brain meets brawn: Why grid and agents need each other. In *AAMAS*, pages 8–15.

Boris Galitsky and Rajesh Pampapathi (2003), Deductive and inductive reasoning for processing the claims of unsatisfied customers. In Paul W. H. Chung, Chris J. Hinde, and Moonis Ali, editors, *IEA/AIE*, volume 2718 of *Lecture Notes in Computer Science*, pages 21–30. Springer, ISBN 3-540-40455-4.

Nicholas Gibbins, Stephen Harris, and Nigel Shadbolt (2003), Agent-based semantic web services. In *WWW '03: Proceedings of the 12th international conference on World Wide Web*, pages 710–717, New York, NY, USA, 2003. ACM Press. ISBN 1-58113-680-3.

M.A. Goodrich, E.R. Boer, J. W. Crandall, R.W. Ricks, and M.L. Quigley (2002), Behavioral entropy in human-robot interaction. In *Proc. of the Fourth International Workshop on Performance Metrics for Intelligent Systems (PERMIS)*.

Michel Grabisch, Sergei A. Orlovski, and Ronald R. Yager (1998), Fuzzy aggregation of numerical preferences. pages 31–68.

Amy R. Greenwald and Peter Stone. (2001), Autonomous bidding agents in the trading agent competition. *IEEE Internet Computing*, 5(2):.

M. A Hall. (1998), Correlation-based feature subset selection for machine learning. Technical report, Thesis submitted in partial fulfilment of the requirements of the degree of Doctor of Philosophy at the University of Waikato.

X. Hu and B. Zeigler. (2002), Measuring cooperative robotic systems using simulation-based virtual environment. In *Proc. of the Fourth International Workshop on Performance Metrics for Intelligent Systems (PERMIS)*.

Markus C. Huebscher and Julie A. McCann. (2004), Evaluation issues in autonomic computing. In *Proceedings of Grid and Cooperative Computing Workshops (GCC)*, pages 597–608.

Bernard J. Jansen, Tracy Mullen, Amanda Spink, and Jan Pedersen (2006), Automated gathering of web information: An in-depth examination of agents interacting with search engines. *ACM Trans. Inter. Tech.*, 6(4):442–464, 2006. ISSN 1533-5399.

Nicholas R. Jennings. (2001), An agent-based approach for building complex software systems. *Commun. ACM*, 44(4):35–41, 2001. ISSN 0001-0782.

Nicholas R. Jennings. (1999) Agent-oriented software engineering. In Ibrahim F. Imam, Yves Kodratoff, Ayman El-Dessouki, and Moonis Ali, editors, *IEA/AIE*, volume 1611 of *Lecture Notes in Computer Science*, pages 4–10, ISBN 3-540-66076-3.

Bob Kero, Lucian Russell, Shalom Tsur, and Wei-Min Shen. (1995) An overview of database mining techniques. In *KDOOD/TDOOD*, pages 1–8.

Barbara Ann Kitchenham. Evaluating software engineering methods and tool, part 2: selecting an appropriate evaluation method technical criteria. *SIGSOFT Softw. Eng. Notes*, 21(2):11–15, 1996. ISSN 0163-5948.

Y. Kodratoff. (1988), *Introduction to machine learning*. Pitman Publishing.

R. Kohavi and G. John. (1997), Wrappers for feature subset selection. *Artificial Intelligence journal, special issue on relevance*, 97(1-2):273–324.

I. Kontogounis, Chatzidimitriou, A. K., Symeonidis, and P.A. Mitkas. (2006), A robust agent design for dynamic scm environments. In *LNAI, Vol. 3955*, pages 127–136. Springer-Verlag.

Klaus Krippendorff, (1986), *A Dictionary of Cybernetics*. The American Society of Cybernetics, Norfolk, VA, USA.

Ingo Muller, Ryszard Kowalczyk, and Peter Braun (2006), Towards agent-based coalition formation for service composition. In *IAT '06: Proceedings of the IEEE/WIC/ACM International Conference on Intelligent Agent Technology (IAT 2006 Main Conference Proceedings) (IAT'06)*, pages 73–80, Washington, DC, USA, 2006. IEEE Computer Society. ISBN 0-7695-2748-5.

A. Negri, A. Poggi, M. Tomaiuolo, and P. Turci (2006), Agents for e-business applications. In *AAMAS '06: Proceedings of the fifth international joint conference on Autonomous agents and multiagent systems*, pages 907–914, New York, NY, USA, 2006. ACM Press. ISBN 1-59593-303-4.

A. L. Nelson, E. Grant, and T. C. Henderson. (2002), Competitive relative performance evaluation of neural controllers for competitive game playing with teams of real mobile robots. In *Proc. of the Third International Workshop on Performance Metrics for Intelligent Systems (PERMIS)*.

Hyacinth S. Nwana. (1996), Software agents: An overview. *Knowledge Engineering Review*, 11(3):1–40.

Anna Perini, Paolo Bresciani, Paolo Giorgini, Fausto Giunchiglia, and John Mylopoulos. (2001), Towards an agent oriented approach to software engineering. In Andrea Omicini and Mirko Viroli, editors, *WOA*, pages 74–79. Pitagora Editrice Bologna, 2001. ISBN 88-371-1272-6.

Martin K. Purvis, Stephen Cranefield, Roy Ward, Mariusz Nowostawski, Daniel Carter, and Geoff Bush. (2003), A multi-agent system for the integration of distributed environmental information. *Environmental Modelling and Software*, 18(6):565–572.

J. Scholtz, B. Antonishek, and J. Young. (2002) Evaluation of human-robot interaction in the nist reference search and rescue test arenas. In *Proc. of the Fourth International Workshop on Performance Metrics for Intelligent Systems (PERMIS)*.

T. K. Shih. (2000) Evolution of mobile agents. In *Proc. of the First International Workshop on Performance Metrics for Intelligent Systems (PERMIS)*.

M.R. Sikonja and I. Kononenko. (1997) An adaptation of relief for attribute esti-mation on regression. machine learning. In *Proceedings of 14th International Conference on Machine Learning D., Fished (ed.)*, Nashville, TN, USA.

Andreas L. Symeonidis and Pericles A. Mitkas. (2005), *Agent Intelligence Through Data Mining*. Springer Science and Business Media.

Tadeusz Szuba. (2002), Universal formal model of collective intelligence and its iq measure. In *CEEMAS '01: Revised Papers from the Second International Workshop of Central and Eastern Europe on Multi-Agent Systems*, pages 303–312, London, UK, 2002. Springer-Verlag. ISBN 3-540-43370-8.

Jia Tang and Minjie Zhang. (2006), An agent-based peer-to-peer grid comput-ing architecture: convergence of grid and peer-to-peer computing. In *ACSW Frontiers '06: Proceedings of the 2006 Australasian workshops on Grid com-puting and e-research*, pages 33–39, Darlinghurst, Australia, Australia, 2006. Australian Computer Society, Inc. ISBN 1-920-68236-8.

Gerhard Weiss. (2001) Agent orientation in software engineering. *Knowl. Eng. Rev.*, 16(4):349–373, 2001. ISSN 0269-8889.

Michael P. Wellman and Peter R. Wurman. (1998), Market-aware agents for a multiagent world. *Robotics and Autonomous Systems*, 24(3-4):115–125.

Ian H. Witten and Eibe Frank. (2005), *Data Mining: Practical machine learning tools and techniques*. Morgan Kaufmann, San Francisco.

Michael Wooldridge. (1999), Intelligent agents. In G. Weiss, editor, *Multiagent Systems*. The MIT Press.

J. Wu, M. Ulieru, M. Cobzaru, and D. Norrie. (2000), Supply chain management systems: state of the art and vision. In *9th International Conference on Man-agement of Innovation and Technology*, pages 759–764. IEEE Press, 2000. ISBN 3-540-43370-8.

Peter R. Wurman, Michael P. Wellman, and William E. Walsh. (1998), The michi-gan internet auctionbot: a configurable auction server for human and software agents. In *AGENTS '98: Proceedings of the second international conference on Autonomous agents*, pages 301–308, New York, NY, USA, 1998. ACM Press. ISBN 0-89791-983-1.

Lotfi A. Zadeh. (2002), In quest of performance metrics for intelligent systemsa challenge that cannot be met with existing methods. In *Proc. of the Third Inter-national Workshop on Performance Metrics for Intelligent Systems (PERMIS)*.

N. Zimmerman, C. Schlenoff, S. Balakirsky, and R. Wray. (2002), Performance evaluation of tools and techniques for representing cost-based decision crite-ria for on-road autonomous navigation. In *Proc. of the Third International Workshop on Performance Metrics for Intelligent Systems (PERMIS)*.

Approximate Frequent Itemset Mining In the Presence of Random Noise

Hong Cheng[1], Philip S. Yu[2] and Jiawei Han[1]

[1] University of Illinois at Urbana-Champaign {hcheng3,hanj}@cs.uiuc.edu
[2] IBM T. J. Watson Research Center psyu@us.ibm.com

Summary. Frequent itemset mining has been a focused theme in data mining research and an important first step in the analysis of data arising in a broad range of applications. The traditional exact model for frequent itemset requires that every item occur in each supporting transaction. However, real application data is usually subject to random noise or measurement error, which poses new challenges for the efficient discovery of frequent itemset from the noisy data.

Mining approximate frequent itemset in the presence of noise involves two key issues: the definition of a noise-tolerant mining model and the design of an efficient mining algorithm. In this chapter, we will give an overview of the approximate itemset mining algorithms in the presence of random noise and examine several noise-tolerant mining approaches.

Key words: error-tolerant itemset, approximate frequent itemset, core pattern recovery

1 Introduction

Frequent itemset mining has been a focused theme in data mining research with a large number of scalable mining methods proposed (Agrawal et al., 1993 , Agrawal and Srikant, 1994, Han et al., 2000, Zaki et al., 2000) and various extensions including closed itemsets, maximal itemsets and so on (Pei et al., 2000, Zaki and Hsiao, 2002, Bayardo, 1998, Burdick et al., 2001). Frequent patterns have found broad applications in areas like association rule mining (Agrawal et al., 1993), indexing (Yan et al., 2004), classification (Liu et al., 1998, Li et al., 2001, Cong et al., 2005, Cheng et al., 2007) and clustering (Wang et al., 1999). In these applications, the ultimate goal is to discover interesting associations between objects and attribute subsets, rather than association among attributes alone. One important experimental application of frequent itemset mining is the exploration of gene expression data, where the

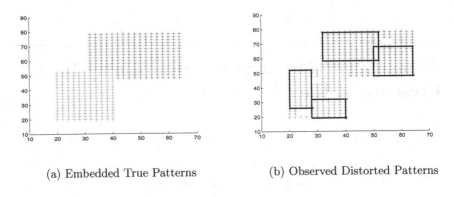

(a) Embedded True Patterns   (b) Observed Distorted Patterns

Fig. 1. Patterns with and without Random Noise

joint discovery of both the set of conditions that significantly affect gene regulation and the set of co-regulated genes is of great interest. Another important application of frequent itemset mining is frequent pattern-based classification, where the associations between attributes and their relation to the class labels or functions are explored.

Despite the exciting progress in the field of frequent itemset mining and its extensions, an intrinsic problem with the exact frequent itemset mining is the rigid definition of support. An itemset x is supported by a transaction t, if each item of x exactly appears in t. An itemset x is frequent if the number of transactions supporting it is no less than a user-specified minimum support threshold (denoted as *min_sup*). However, in real applications, a database is typically subject to random noise or measurement error, which poses new challenges for the discovery of frequent itemsets. For example, in a customer transaction database, random noise could be caused by an out-of-stock item, promotions or some special event like the world cup, holidays, *etc.*. Measurement error could be caused by noise from experiments, uncertainty involved in discretizing continuous values, stochastic nature of the study field, *etc.*. In privacy-preserving data mining (Agrawal and Srikant, 2000, Verykios *et al.*, 2004), random noise is added to perturb the true values of the original database. Such random noise can distort the true underlying patterns. Theoretical analysis by (Liu *et al.*, 2006) shows that in the presence of even low levels of noise, large frequent itemsets are broken into fragments of logarithmic size, thus the itemsets cannot be recovered by the exact frequent itemset mining algorithms. Figure 1 shows two transaction databases. The x-axis represents items and the y-axis represents the transactions. Figure 1 (a) shows the embedded true patterns in the database without random noise while (b) shows the observed distorted patterns in the presence of random noise (several "holes" appear in the embedded patterns due to random noise). If the exact frequent itemset mining algorithms are applied to a database subject to random noise, as in Figure 1 (b), the original embedded true patterns will be fragmented into several smaller ones which are highlighted by the bounding boxes.

In this chapter, we will give an overview of approximate itemset mining algorithms in the presence of random noise and examine three different approaches: (1) a heuristic error-tolerant itemset (ETI) approach (Yang *et al.*, 2001), (2) an apriori-based approximate frequent itemset (AFI) approach (Liu *et al.*, 2006) and (3) a core pattern recovery (AC-Close) approach (Cheng *et al.*, 2006) to solve this problem.

2 Preliminary Concepts

Let a transaction database D take the form of an $n \times m$ binary matrix. Let $I = \{i_1, i_2, \ldots, i_m\}$ be the set of all items and $T = \{t_1, t_2, \ldots, t_n\}$ be the set of all transactions in D. A subset of I is called an *itemset*. Each row of D is a transaction $t \in T$ and each column is an item $i \in I$. A transaction t supports an itemset x, if for each item $i \in x$, the corresponding entry $D(t, i) = 1$. An itemset x is *frequent* if the fraction of transactions supporting it is no less than a user-specified threshold *min_sup*.

An intuitive approach for handling errors is to relax the requirement that a sub-matrix determined by the frequent itemset consists entirely of 1s, and allow it instead to contain a large fraction of 1s and a small fraction of 0s. Based on the same philosophy, different studies proposed different mining models and constraints on top of which, efficient mining algorithms and search/pruning strategies have been developed. Since each study has some variations of the mining model, the specific definitions and concepts are introduced with each approach in the following sections respectively.

Table 1 summarizes and compares the characteristics of the three different mining approaches in four aspects. Although the model definition and algorithmic properties will be provided in the following sections in detail, we give a brief explanation for Table 1. The first criterion *error control* describes how each noise-tolerant model defines the fraction of errors allowed. The ETI model controls the fraction of errors in each row or in the sub-matrix formed by the itemset; while the AFI model and the AC-Close model control the fraction of errors in both rows and columns. In addition, AC-Close enforces a core pattern constraint which will be explained later. For *mining methodology*, both ETI and AFI work in a bottom-up way *i.e.*, generating itemsets in a size-increasing order; while AC-Close works in a top-down fashion, *i.e.*, generating itemsets in a size-decreasing order. All three methods search for the itemsets in a breadth-first manner. As for the *result quality* criterion, it is assessed through simulation experiments: given a noise-free dataset D_t and known embedded patterns F_{true}, random noise is added to D_t to derive a noisy dataset D. Then noise-tolerant mining algorithms are applied on D to recover the true patterns. By knowing the true patterns, the quality of mining results could be evaluated. Two criteria are used for the evaluation purpose: *recall* (or *recoverability*) and *precision* (or *spuriousness*). According to the performance study in (Liu *et al.*, 2006, Cheng *et al.*, 2006), AFI outperforms ETI on both criteria of recall and precision. AC-Close achieves a similar or slightly lower recall than AFI while having a much higher precision than AFI. As for mining *efficiency* and *scalability*, AFI is shown to outperform ETI by an order of magnitude; while AC-Close is shown to outperform AFI by at least two orders of magnitude.

Table 1. Algorithm Characteristics Comparison

Criterion	ETI	AFI	AC-Close
Error Control	row or sub-matrix	row and column	row and column core pattern constraint
Mining Methodology	bottom-up breadth-first	bottom-up breadth-first	top-down breadth-first
Result Quality	low	moderate	high
Efficiency/Scalability	low	moderate	high

3 A Heuristic Mining Approach

(Yang *et al.*, 2001) was a pioneer study which generalizes the frequent itemsets allowing for the notion of errors in the itemset definition. It proposed an error-tolerant model (ETI) and developed a heuristic mining algorithm that identifies the error-tolerant frequent clusters of items in transactional databases. The proposed ETI algorithm was also applied to three application scenarios: (1) clustering high dimensional data; (2) query selectivity estimation; and (3) collaborative filtering.

3.1 An Error-Tolerant Itemset Model

In the binary matrix representation of the data, an error-tolerant frequent itemset is represented as a set of dimensions (called *defining dimensions* or DD in short) where 1 appears with high probability among a set of rows. Two constraints are enforced: *min_sup* and an error threshold ϵ. With different degrees of relaxation, two slightly different error-tolerant itemset models are proposed: strong ETI and weak ETI.

Definition 1. *Given min_sup = s and error threshold ϵ, a strong ETI consists of a set of items, called defining dimensions $DD \subseteq I$, such that there exists a subset of transactions $R \subseteq T$ consisting of at least $s|T|$ transactions* and, for each $t \in R$, the fraction of items in DD which are present in t is at least $1 - \epsilon$.

Definition 2. *Given* $min\_sup = s$ *and error threshold* ϵ, *a weak ETI consists of a set of items, called defining dimensions* $DD \subseteq I$, *such that there exists a subset of transactions* $R \subseteq T$, $|R| \geq s|T|$, *and*

$$\frac{\sum_{t \in R} \sum_{d \in DD} D(t,d)}{|R| \cdot |DD|} \geq (1 - \epsilon) \tag{1}$$

The strong ETI controls the fraction of errors in each supporting transaction to be no greater than ϵ; while the weak ETI only requires the sub-matrix formed by R and DD contains a fraction of errors to be no greater than ϵ. It is clear that anything that satisfies the strong definition also satisfies the weak definition, but not vice versa.

3.2 ETI Mining Algorithm

Based on the ETI models and their properties, (Yang *et al.*, 2001) first proposed an exhaustive mining algorithm to discover the strong or weak ETIs, as presented in Algorithm 1.

Algorithm 1: Exhaustive ETI Mining Algorithm

1: Find all dimensions d_i where the global count of 1s is at least $s|T|(1 - \epsilon)$. Each of these dimensions forms a singleton weak ETI. Each of these singleton sets is called a "seed". Set $i = 1$.

2: For every seed that contains i dimensions, grow it by adding a new dimension so that the new seed still forms a weak ETI. If one or more such dimensions can be found, keep all the new seeds.

3: Increment i and repeat step 2 until no more growing is possible.

4: Among all seeds, pick those satisfying the strong ETI definition.

The algorithm mines the complete set of weak or strong ETIs. Thus the time complexity of this algorithm is exponential in the maximum number of ETI defining dimensions. To reduce time complexity, a polynomial time greedy algorithm was proposed that finds most of the ETIs by exploiting several heuristics. These heuristics are applied to step 2 in Algorithm 1 and summarized as follows.

Heuristics to Reduce Complexity

1. When looking for a dimension to grow a seed, consider only those dimensions that have been picked in step 1.

2. When testing whether a dimension can be added to a seed, the expanded seed should still define a weak ETI, and that the new dimension have at most a fraction of ϵ 0s within the weak ETI.

3. When two or more dimensions are candidates for seed growth, keep only one. Throw away the old seed once it has been grown to a new seed.

These three heuristics can greatly reduce the mining time complexity by growing greedily with the most "promising" dimensions. As a result, these heuristics also cause some ETIs to be missed. To alleviate this problem, an iterative scheme is used to heuristically search the missed ETIs.

4 An Apriori-based Approach

Recently, (Liu et al., 2006) proposed a different noise-tolerant itemset model: approximate frequent itemset model. According to the model, an apriori-based mining algorithm AFI was proposed. The algorithm takes a candidate generate-and-test approach, using the apriori property to prune the search space and generating the approximate frequent itemsets in a level-wise breadth-first manner.

4.1 An Approximate Frequent Itemset Model

In the approximate frequent itemset model, besides min_sup constraint, two additional constraints are proposed: *row error threshold* and *column error threshold*, to control the fraction of noise in both dimensions of transactions and items, respectively. The row error threshold indicates that, for a given itemset, a supporting transaction should contain most of the items. Similarly, the column error threshold guarantees that an associated item has to appear in most of the supporting transactions in order to be included in an itemset.

The definition of approximate frequent itemset is given as follows.

Definition 3. *Let* $min\_sup = s$, $\epsilon_r, \epsilon_c \in [0,1]$ *and the transaction database be* D. *An itemset* $x \subseteq I$ *is an approximate frequent itemset if there exists a set of transactions* $T_a(x) \subseteq T$ *with* $|T_a(x)| \geq s|T|$, *and the following two conditions hold:*

$$1.\ \forall i \in T_a(x),\ \frac{1}{|x|} \sum_{j \in x} D(i,j) \geq (1 - \epsilon_r)$$

$$2.\ \forall j \in x,\ \frac{1}{|T_a(x)|} \sum_{i \in T_a(x)} D(i,j) \geq (1 - \epsilon_c)$$

ϵ_r *and* ϵ_c *are referred to as row error threshold and column error threshold, respectively. For the approximate itemset* x, *its supporting transaction set is denoted as* $T_a(x)$ *where each* $t \in T_a(x)$ *approximately supports* x. *The support is denoted as* $sup_a(x) = \frac{|T_a(x)|}{|T|}$ *and the absolute count is denoted as* $sup\_cnt_a(x) = |T_a(x)|$.

4.2 AFI Mining Algorithm

Mining approximate frequent itemsets poses a number of algorithmic challenges beyond those faced when mining exact itemsets. The foremost difficulty is that noise-tolerant itemset mining cannot employ the anti-monotone property that has led to the success of frequent itemset mining. An important contribution by (Liu et al., 2006) is the noise-tolerant Apriori property derived, which effectively enforces the anti-monotone property in the approximate itemset mining and therefore limits the search space. Another challenge is that the approximate frequent itemset criterion allows the number of errors to increase with the size of the itemset. It is therefore critical to take account of the additional errors in an itemset as its dimensionality increases while collecting the supporting transactions. These two issues and proposed solutions by (Liu et al., 2006) are presented as follows respectively.

Noise-Tolerant Support Pruning

The anti-monotone property of exact frequent itemsets is the key to minimizing exponential searches in frequent itemset mining. In particular, the anti-monotone property ensures that a $(k + 1)$ exact itemset can not be frequent if any one of its k sub-itemsets is not frequent. However, this property is no longer true for the approximate frequent itemsets.

(Liu et al., 2006) derived a noise-tolerant support to serve as the Apriori pruning threshold, which prunes the search space effectively.

Definition 4. *Given ϵ_r and ϵ_c and* min_sup, *the noise-tolerant pruning support for a length-k itemset is*

$$min\_sup^k = max\{0, min\_sup \cdot \left(1 - \frac{k\epsilon_c}{\lfloor k\epsilon_r \rfloor + 1}\right)\} \qquad (2)$$

The noise-tolerant support threshold is used as the basis of a pruning strategy for the approximate itemset mining. It removes the supersets of a size-k approximate itemset x from further consideration when the frequency of x is less than min_sup^k.

0/1 Extensions

Starting with single items, the AFI algorithm generates size-$(k + 1)$ itemsets from size-k itemsets in a level-wise way. The number of 0s allowed in an itemset grows with the length of the itemset in a discrete manner. If $\lfloor (k + 1)\epsilon_r \rfloor > \lfloor k\epsilon_r \rfloor$, then transactions supporting the $(k+1)$-itemset are permitted one more zero than transactions supporting the k-itemset. If $\lfloor (k + 1)\epsilon_r \rfloor = \lfloor k\epsilon_r \rfloor$, no additional zeros are allowed at level $(k + 1)$ compared with level k. In the first case, if an additional zero is allowed at level $(k+1)$, any transaction supporting a k-itemset should also support its $(k+1)$ superset. On the other hand, for the second case when no additional zeros are allowed at level $(k+1)$, a transaction that does not support k-itemset will not have enough 1s to support its $(k+1)$ superset. These two properties are formally addressed by (Liu *et al.*, 2006) as follows.

Lemma 1. *(1-Extension) If* $\lfloor (k+1)\epsilon_r \rfloor = \lfloor k\epsilon_r \rfloor$, *then any transaction that does not support a k-itemset will not support its $(k+1)$ superset.*

In the case of 1-extension, the transaction set of a $(k+1)$-itemset is the *intersection* of the transaction sets of its length k subsets.

Lemma 2. *(0-Extension) If* $\lfloor (k+1)\epsilon_r \rfloor = \lfloor k\epsilon_r \rfloor + 1$, *then any transaction that supports a k-itemset also supports its $(k+1)$ superset.*

In the case of 0-extension, the transaction set of a $(k+1)$-itemset is the *union* of the transaction sets of its length k subsets.

0-extension and 1-extension suggest two basic steps to be taken for efficient computation and maintenance of the supporting transactions. They allow the algorithm to obtain the supporting transactions of an itemset from its subsets while avoiding the repeated scans of the original database.

AFI Mining Algorithm

The AFI algorithm uses the 0-extension and 1-extension techniques together with the noise-tolerant support-based pruning strategy to perform the mining of approximate frequent itemsets. The algorithm is presented as follows.

The level-wise mining process generates a superset of the approximate frequent itemsets AFI_p. Line 14 in Algorithm 2 further checks the generated approximate frequent itemsets w.r.t. *min_sup* and ϵ_c and filters those itemsets which fail to satisfy *min_sup* or ϵ_c. This post-processing can be done separately from the level-wise generation since it will neither benefit nor prohibit the traversing of the search space.

5 A Core Pattern Recovery Approach

5.1 Motivation

The approximate frequent itemset model proposed by (Liu *et al.*, 2006) can effectively control the percentage of noise in both dimensions of transactions and items, and the proposed AFI algorithm can successfully discover some true patterns which are distorted by the random noise. However, a large number of "uninteresting" candidates are explored during the mining process. Such candidates are uninteresting in the sense that they are spurious: they correspond to no true frequent patterns in the unobserved true transaction database. They are generated as a result of indiscriminative combination of items and

---
Algorithm 2: AFI Mining Algorithm

Input: D, ϵ_r, ϵ_c, min_sup
Output: The set of approximate frequent itemsets

1: **for** $i = 1$ to m **do**
2:     $T(i)$=genSupport(D,i);
3: $k = 1$;
4: $L_1 = \bigcup_{i>0}^{m}\{i\}$;
5: **repeat**
6:     $k := k + 1$;
7:     $L_k :=$GenCandidateItemset(L_{k-1}, min_sup^{k-1});
8:     **if** ($\lfloor (k+1)\epsilon_r \rfloor = \lfloor k\epsilon_r \rfloor$)
9:         $T(L_k) :=$1-extension(I, L_{k-1});
10:     **else**
11:         $T(L_k) :=$0-extension(I, L_{k-1});
12:     $AFI_p := AFI_p \cup L_k$;
13: **until** $L_k = \phi$
14: $AFI :=$filter(AFI_p, min_sup, ϵ_c);
15: **return** AFI;

---

relaxed mining methods. Although some of the candidates are filtered by the error thresholds, others which pass the error check are output together with the recovered true patterns. Let's first examine Example 1.

Example 1. Table 2 shows a transaction database D. Let $min\_sup = 3$, $\epsilon_r = 1/3$ and $\epsilon_c = 1/2$.

Table 2. A Sample Purchase Database D

TID	Burger	Coke	Diet Coke
0	1	1	0
1	1	1	0
2	1	0	1
3	1	0	1

According to the approximate frequent itemset model in (Liu *et al.*, 2006), {*burger, coke, diet coke*} is discovered as an approximate frequent itemset with support 4. However, the exact support of {*burger, coke, diet coke*} in D is 0. This pattern would be deemed uninteresting since *coke* and *diet coke* are seldom purchased together in reality. Those 0s in D are not caused by random noise, but reflect the real data distribution. However, with the user-specified parameters ϵ_r and ϵ_c, it is recovered as an approximate frequent itemset by the AFI algorithm.

If the set of true frequent itemsets is treated as the ground truth, such uninteresting patterns which are excluded from the true set, are deemed as *false positive*. (Liu et al., 2006) discovers a complete set of approximate frequent itemsets satisfying the error thresholds. A large number of false-positive patterns can be generated due to the exponential combinations, which make the problem computationally intractable. Even worse, if such false-positive candidates pass the error threshold check and are output as the final result, it is hard for an end user to distinguish the recovered true patterns from these false positives.

To tackle such a problem, (Cheng et al., 2006) proposed a core pattern model and recovered the approximate frequent itemsets from core patterns. Intuitively, an itemset x is a core pattern if its exact support in the noisy database D is no less than αs, where $\alpha \in [0, 1]$ is a *core pattern factor*, and s is the *min_sup* threshold. A probability model was derived to estimate the probability of a true frequent pattern (in the noise-free database) remaining as a core pattern in D in the presence of noise. With some realistic parameter settings, it was shown that such true patterns remain as core patterns in the noisy database with high probability.

With the core pattern constraint, the set of core patterns are used as initial seeds for approximate itemset generation. To further reduce the output size, the concept of *approximate closed itemset* was proposed. An efficient algorithm AC-Close was developed to mine the approximate closed itemsets. A *top-down* mining strategy is exploited where the large-size approximate itemsets are discovered before the small-size ones, which makes full use of the pruning power of *min_sup* and closeness and thus, narrows down the search space dramatically.

5.2 A Core Pattern Recovery Model

First, the core pattern is defined as follows.

Definition 5. *An itemset x is a core pattern in the noisy database D if the exact support of x, $sup_e(x) \geq \alpha s$, where $\alpha \in [0, 1]$ is the core pattern factor and s is the min_sup threshold.*

Accordingly, the core pattern recovery model is proposed for mining the approximate frequent itemsets.

Definition 6. *Let $min\_sup = s$, ϵ_r, $\epsilon_c \in [0, 1]$ and the transaction database be D. An approximate frequent itemset x is (1) a core pattern with $sup_e(x) \geq \alpha s$, and (2) if there exists a set of transactions $T_a(x) \subseteq T$ with $|T_a(x)| \geq s|T|$, and the following two conditions hold:*

$$1. \; \forall i \in T_a(x), \; \frac{1}{|x|} \sum_{j \in x} D(i,j) \geq (1 - \epsilon_r)$$

$$2. \; \forall j \in x, \; \frac{1}{|T_a(x)|} \sum_{i \in T_a(x)} D(i,j) \geq (1 - \epsilon_c)$$

ϵ_r and ϵ_c are referred to as row error threshold and column error threshold, respectively.

To further reduce the number of approximate frequent itemsets discovered, a new concept of *approximate closed itemsets* was proposed.

Definition 7. *An approximate frequent itemset x is closed if there exists no itemset y such that (1) y is a proper superset of x, and (2) $sup_a(y) \geq sup_a(x)$.*

An important difference between the closeness definition for approximate itemset and that for exact itemset (Pei *et al.*, 2000, Zaki and Hsiao, 2002) is the second condition in Definition 7. From the AFI algorithm, one should note that, given two approximate frequent itemsets x and y where $x \subseteq y$, either of the following two conditions holds: (1) $sup_a(x) \geq sup_a(y)$, and (2) $sup_a(x) < sup_a(y)$. The second condition holds because of the "0-extension" effect, *i.e.*, compute a size-k itemset's supporting transactions by taking the *union* of all supporting transactions of its size-$(k-1)$ sub-itemsets. Considering such a factor, an approximate frequent itemset x is non-closed if there is a superset y such that $sup_a(y) \geq sup_a(x)$. The itemset x, to some extent, is deemed less interesting, since there exists a super-pattern y which subsumes x in both directions of items and transactions.

The problem of *approximate closed itemset* mining from core patterns is the mining of all itemsets which are (1) core patterns w.r.t. α; (2) approximate frequent itemsets w.r.t. ϵ_r, ϵ_c and *min_sup*; and (3) closed.

5.3 Approximate Closed Itemsets Mining

First of all, some theoretical analysis of the core pattern recovery model is provided, by modelling the probability of a true frequent pattern being recovered as a core pattern in the database with random noise. This model shows that, the core pattern recovery mechanism can effectively recover the true patterns with high probability, at some realistic noise level. We will discuss how to generate the candidate approximate itemsets from the core patterns with ϵ_r, ϵ_c and *min_sup*, and develop several pruning strategies as well.

A Probabilistic Model

With the core pattern constraint, a set of core patterns (denoted as $\mathcal{C}$) can be discovered as the initial seeds for approximate itemset generation. Each core pattern $x \in \mathcal{C}$ is extended into an approximate one by allowing some noise. Before developing the techniques for generating approximate itemsets, we address the question of whether it is reasonable to assume the core pattern constraint. Since it is possible that a true frequent pattern x fails the core pattern requirement $(sup_e(x) \geq \alpha s)$, and thus is excluded from the final result set, this approach could miss certain true frequent patterns. One may ask, how likely is it to miss a true frequent pattern by focusing on the core pattern only? The following lemma provides an answer to this question.

Lemma 3. *Assume an unobserved true database D_t has N transactions and $min\_sup = s$. A true frequent pattern x of size l, has exact support count $sup\_cnt_e(x, D_t) = n \geq sN$. Assume the core pattern factor is α. If, in the presence of random noise, each entry in D_t is flipped independently from 1 to 0 with a probability p, resulting in the noisy database D. Then the probability of x remaining in D with $sup_e(x) \geq \alpha s$ is*

$$P(sup_e(x) \geq \alpha s) = I_{(1-p)^l}(\alpha sN, n - \alpha sN + 1)$$

where $I_{(1-p)^l}(\alpha sN, n - \alpha sN + 1)$ is the regularized incomplete beta function (Abramowitz and Stegun, 1964, Press et al., 1992).

Proof. For each transaction t out of the n which supports x, the probability of t still supporting x, in the presence of noise, is $(1-p)^l$ and the probability of not supporting x is $1 - (1-p)^l$. Each such transaction flipping is a Bernoulli trial. Obtaining k supporting transactions out of n where $\alpha sN \leq k \leq n$ corresponds to $sup\_cnt_e(x, D) = k$, $k \in [\alpha sN, n]$. Then the probability of $sup\_cnt_e(x, D) = k$ is

$$P(sup\_cnt_e(x, D) = k) = \binom{n}{k}(1-p)^{kl}(1 - (1-p)^l)^{(n-k)} \qquad (3)$$

Eq. (3) follows a binomial distribution. Summing over all $k \in [\alpha sN, n]$ on Eq. (3) derives the probability of $sup_e(x) \geq \alpha s$ in D, as follows.

$$
\begin{aligned}
P(sup_e(x) \geq \alpha s) &= \sum_{k=\alpha sN}^{n} P(sup\_cnt_e(x, D) = k) \\
&= \sum_{k=\alpha sN}^{n} \binom{n}{k}(1-p)^{kl}(1 - (1-p)^l)^{(n-k)} \\
&= I_{(1-p)^l}(\alpha sN, n - \alpha sN + 1) \\
&= \frac{B((1-p)^l; \alpha sN, n - \alpha sN + 1)}{B(\alpha sN, n - \alpha sN + 1)}
\end{aligned}
$$

where $B(\alpha sN, n - \alpha sN + 1)$ is the beta function and $B((1-p)^l; \alpha sN, n - \alpha sN + 1)$ is the incomplete beta function (Abramowitz and Stegun, 1964, Press et al., 1992).

An application of Lemma 3 to some realistic assumption over some transaction database clearly shows, it is with high probability that a true frequent pattern x still appears in D with $sup_e(x) \geq \alpha s$ in the presence of random noise. For example, for $N = 1,000,000$, $s = 0.01$, $n = 12,000$, $l = 5$, and $p = 0.05$. For $\alpha \leq 0.9$, $P(sup_e(x) \geq \alpha s) = 99.99\%$; for $\alpha = 0.92$, $P(sup_e(x) \geq \alpha s) = 96.92\%$. Therefore, with the random noise level of $p = 0.05$, an itemset x has exact count no less than 9,000 in D with probability 99.99%, and has exact count no less than 9,200 with probability 96.92%.

Candidate Approximate Itemset Generation

Based on Lemma 3, an efficient algorithm can be designed to discover the approximate frequent itemsets from core patterns. It first mines the set of core patterns from D with $min\_sup = \alpha s$. These patterns are treated as the initial seeds for possible further extension to approximate frequent itemsets. In this section, we discuss how to generate the candidate approximate frequent itemsets from the set of core patterns.

Assume we have discovered a set of core patterns with $min\_sup = \alpha s$. Let C be the set of core patterns. A lattice $\mathcal{L}$ is built over C. Example 2 is used to illustrate the process.

Example 2. Table 3 shows a sample transaction database D with 7 transactions and 4 items $\{a, b, c, d\}$. Let $\epsilon_r = 0.5$, $\epsilon_c = 0.5$, the absolute $min\_sup = 3$, and $\alpha = 1/3$.

Table 3. A Transaction Database D

TID	a	b	c	d
0	1	1	1	0
1	1	0	0	0
2	1	1	1	1
3	0	0	1	1
4	1	1	0	0
5	1	0	1	1
6	0	1	1	1

Mining the core patterns from D with the absolute support $\alpha*min\_sup = 1$ generates 15 core patterns. Figure 2 shows the lattice of core patterns, where the closed core patterns are in bold.

First, for the size-4 core pattern $\{a, b, c, d\}$, the number of 0s allowed in a supporting transaction is $\lfloor 4 * 0.5 \rfloor = 2$ given $\epsilon_r = 0.5$. Traverse upward in the lattice for 2 levels (*i.e.*, levels 2 and 3), which constitute the *extension space* for $\{a, b, c, d\}$. The extension space for a core pattern is defined as follows.

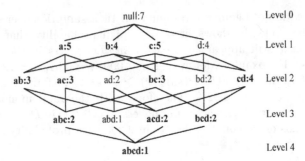

Fig. 2. The Lattice $\mathcal{L}$ of Core Patterns

Definition 8. *For a core pattern y with size l, the extension space, denoted as $ES(y)$, is a set of sub-patterns of y from level $(\lceil l * (1 - \epsilon_r) \rceil)$ to level $(l - 1)$ in the lattice, given $\epsilon_r \in [0, 1]$.*

Because of the ϵ_r fraction of errors allowed in a transaction, for a core itemset y and each sub-pattern $x \in ES(y)$, any transaction supporting x also approximately supports y. According to this property, the transaction set $T_a(y)$ of y is the *union* of the exact transaction set $T_e(x)$ of each sub-pattern $x \in ES(y)$. Thus, for $\{a, b, c, d\}$, its transaction set $T_a(\{a, b, c, d\})$ is the union of the exact transaction sets of all 10 itemsets at levels 2 and 3 of Figure 2.

To optimize the union operation, only the closed core patterns in the extension space are included, while those non-closed ones are excluded for union. This is because, the exact transaction sets of non-closed sub-patterns will not contribute to the approximate transaction set of the core pattern. For the non-closed itemset $\{a, b, d\}$ at level 3, $T_e(\{a, b, d\}) = T_e(\{a, b, c, d\}) = \{2\}$. So it will not contribute any additional transactions to $T_a(\{a, b, c, d\})$ through the union operation. It is the same for $\{a, d\}$ and $\{b, d\}$ at level 2, since they are subsumed by $\{a, c, d\}$ and $\{b, c, d\}$, respectively. This property is stated formally in Lemma 4.

Lemma 4. *For a candidate approximate itemset y and each closed core pattern $x \in ES(y)$, the approximate transaction set $T_a(y)$ is computed by taking the union of the exact transaction set $T_e(x)$ of x.*

By taking the union of the exact transaction sets of the 7 closed patterns at levels 2 and 3, the approximate transaction set $T_a(\{a, b, c, d\}) = \{0, 2, 3, 4, 5, 6\}$. Thus, $\{a, b, c, d\}$ is a candidate approximate itemset since it satisfies *min_sup* and ϵ_r. It needs to be checked w.r.t. ϵ_c and closeness, which will be discussed separately.

To summarize, the steps to identify candidate approximate itemsets include:

1. For each core pattern y in the lattice, identify its extension space $ES(y)$ according to ϵ_r;

2. Pick the closed sub-patterns of y from $ES(y)$, take the union of the exact transaction sets of them;

3. Check against *min_sup*. Keep those which satisfy *min_sup* as candidate approximate frequent itemsets.

Pruning by ϵ_c

After the candidate generation, all the candidate approximate itemsets are identified which satisfy *min_sup* and ϵ_r. The next step is to check a candidate approximate itemset x w.r.t. the column error threshold ϵ_c. According to the second condition in Definition 3, to check the ϵ_c constraint, it needs to scan the approximate transaction set $T_a(x)$ and accumulate the count of each item in x. However, a pruning strategy, referred to as ϵ_c *early pruning*, allows us to identify some candidates which violate the ϵ_c constraint without scanning $T_a(x)$. This pruning strategy is stated as follows.

Lemma 5. *Let $x = i_1...i_n$ be an itemset and the exact support of a single item $i_k \in x$ in D be $sup_e(i_k)$, $k \in [1, n]$. Let the support of the approximate pattern x be $sup_a(x)$. If*

$$\exists i_k \in x, \frac{sup_e(i_k)}{sup_a(x)} < (1 - \epsilon_c)$$

satisfies, then x cannot pass the ϵ_c check.

Proof. Let the exact support count of item i_k in the transaction set T_a be $sup\_cnt_e(i_k, T_a)$, then

$$\frac{sup\_cnt_e(i_k, T_a)}{|T_a|} \leq \frac{sup\_cnt_e(i_k, D)}{|T_a|} = \frac{sup_e(i_k)}{sup_a(x)}$$

If $\frac{sup_e(i_k)}{sup_a(x)} < (1 - \epsilon_c)$, then $\frac{sup\_cnt_e(i_k, T_a)}{|T_a|} < (1 - \epsilon_c)$, which violates Definition 2. As a result, item i_k cannot pass the ϵ_c check. The ϵ_c early pruning is effective especially when ϵ_c is small, or there exists an item in x with very low exact support in D. If the pruning condition is not satisfied, a scan on $T_a(x)$ is performed for the ϵ_c check.

For a candidate pattern x which violates the ϵ_c constraint, we can either prune it or find a maximal subset of $T_a(x)$ which satisfies ϵ_c. A heuristic algorithm for finding a maximal AFI is introduced in (Liu *et al.*, 2005).

Top-down Mining and Pruning by Closeness

The previous steps focus on how to generate the individual candidate approximate itemset. In this part, an efficient *top-down* search strategy is designed as the mining framework, which enables effective pruning by the closeness definition and the *min_sup* threshold.

A top-down mining strategy is taken over the lattice $\mathcal{L}$, such that the mining starts with the largest pattern in $\mathcal{L}$ and proceeds level by level, in the size decreasing order of core patterns. Let's look at an example.

Example 3. Mining on the lattice $\mathcal{L}$ in Figure 2 starts with the size-4 pattern $\{a, b, c, d\}$. Since the number of 0s allowed in a transaction is $\lfloor 4 * 0.5 \rfloor = 2$, its extension space includes closed patterns at levels 2 and 3, i.e., $ES(\{a, b, c, d\}) = \{abc : 2, acd : 2, bcd : 2, ab : 3, ac : 3, bc : 3, cd : 4\}$. The transaction set $T_a(\{a, b, c, d\})$ is computed by taking the union of the transaction sets of the above 7 patterns. Further checking shows that $\{a, b, c, d\}$ satisfies *min_sup* and ϵ_c as well. Since $\{a, b, c, d\}$ is the approximate itemset of the largest size, it is an approximate closed itemset.

When the mining proceeds to level 3, for example, the size-3 pattern $\{a, b, c\}$. The number of 0s allowed in a transaction is $\lfloor 3 * 0.5 \rfloor = 1$, so its extension space includes its closed sub-patterns at level 2, i.e., $ES(\{a, b, c\}) = \{ab : 3, ac : 3, bc : 3\}$. The transaction set $T_a(\{a, b, c\})$ is computed by taking the union of the transaction sets of the above 3 patterns.

Since $ES(\{a, b, c\}) \subseteq ES(\{a, b, c, d\})$ holds, $T_a(\{a, b, c\}) \subseteq T_a(\{a, b, c, d\})$ holds too. In this case, after the computation on $\{a, b, c, d\}$, we can prune $\{a, b, c\}$ without actual computation with either of the following two conclusions: (1) if $\{a, b, c, d\}$ satisfies the *min_sup* threshold and the ϵ_c constraint, then no matter whether it is closed or non-closed, $\{a, b, c\}$ can be pruned because it will be a non-closed approximate itemset; or (2) if $\{a, b, c, d\}$ does not satisfy the *min_sup* threshold, then $\{a, b, c\}$ can be pruned because it will not satisfy the *min_sup* threshold either. In the first condition, we say *no matter whether $\{a, b, c, d\}$ is closed or non-closed, $\{a, b, c\}$ is non-closed*. This is because, if $\{a, b, c, d\}$ is closed, then $\{a, b, c\}$ is subsumed by $\{a, b, c, d\}$ and thus is non-closed; if $\{a, b, c, d\}$ is non-closed, then there must exist a closed approximate super-pattern which subsumes $\{a, b, c, d\}$, and then subsumes $\{a, b, c\}$ as well. Thus $\{a, b, c\}$ is non-closed.

Similarly, the other three core patterns at level 3, $\{abd : 1, acd : 2, bcd : 2\}$ can be pruned after the computation on $\{a, b, c, d\}$.

We refer to the pruning technique in Example 3 as *forward pruning*, which is formally stated in Lemma 6.

Lemma 6. *If $\lfloor (k+1) \cdot \epsilon_r \rfloor = \lfloor k \cdot \epsilon_r \rfloor + 1$, after the computation on a size-$(k+1)$ pattern is done, all its size-k sub-patterns in the lattice $\mathcal{L}$ can be pruned with either of the following two conclusions: (1) if the size-$(k + 1)$ pattern satisfies min_sup and ϵ_c, then the size-k patterns can be pruned because they are non-closed; or (2) if the size-$(k + 1)$ pattern does not satisfy min_sup, then the size-k patterns can be pruned because they do not satisfy min_sup either.*

Forward pruning, naturally integrated with the top-down mining, can reduce the search space dramatically due to the *min_sup* threshold and the closeness constraint.

Another pruning strategy, called *backward pruning*, is proposed as well to ensure the closeness constraint. Let's look at an example before stating it formally.

Example 4. When the mining proceeds to level 2, for example, the core pattern $\{a, d\}$ is extended to a candidate approximate pattern, with the transaction set $T_a(\{a, d\}) = \{0, 1, 2, 3, 4, 5, 6\}$. Since it satisfies *min_sup* and ϵ_c, it has to be checked against all its approximate closed super-patterns for its closeness. In this case, the approximate closed super-pattern $\{a, b, c, d\}$ is checked with $T_a(\{a, b, c, d\}) = \{0, 2, 3, 4, 5, 6\}$. Since $|T_a(\{a, d\})| > |T_a(\{a, b, c, d\})|$, $\{a, d\}$ is an approximate closed itemset.

Lemma 7 formally states the backward pruning technique.

Lemma 7. *If a candidate approximate pattern x satisfies min_sup, ϵ_r and ϵ_c, it has to be checked against each approximate closed itemset y where $x \subseteq y$. If there exists no approximate closed itemset y such that $x \subseteq y$ and $sup_a(x) \leq sup_a(y)$, then x is an approximate closed itemset.*

5.4 AC-Close Algorithm

Integrating the top-down mining and the various pruning strategies, an efficient algorithm AC-Close was developed in (Cheng *et al.*, 2006) to mine the approximate closed itemsets from the core patterns, presented in Algorithm 3.

In Algorithm 3, *ACI* represents the final set of approximate closed itemsets, $T_a(x)$ is the approximate transaction set of an itemset x, C_k is the set of size-k candidate approximate itemsets, and L_k is the set of size-k approximate closed itemsets. $forwardPrune(C_{k-1}, x)$ prunes the sub-patterns of x from the size-$(k-1)$ candidate set before computation proceeds to them, according to Lemma 6. $backwardPrune(C_k, ACI)$ prunes the non-closed approximate itemsets from C_k, according to Lemma 7. "*" at line 9 means the ϵ_c early pruning is applied for checking the ϵ_c constraint. If it applies, there is no need to scan the transaction set $T_a(x)$ for the ϵ_c checking.

6 Experimental Study

In this section, experimental results reported by (Cheng *et al.*, 2006) are presented to compare different mining algorithms. Since it is shown by (Liu *et al.*, 2006) that AFI systematically outperforms ETI in terms of both efficiency and result quality, the comparison between AFI and ETI is omitted. The results reported in this section focus on the comparison between AFI and AC-Close. For a detailed experimental results between AFI and ETI please refer to (Liu *et al.*, 2006).

Algorithm 3: The AC-Close Algorithm

Input: D, $min\_sup = s$, ϵ_r, ϵ_c, α
Output: ACI: approximate closed itemsets

1: $\mathcal{C} = \text{genFreqItemset}(D, \alpha s)$;
2: $\mathcal{L} = \text{buildLattice}(\mathcal{C})$;
3: $k = $ max level of $\mathcal{L}$;
4: $C_k = \{x | x \in \mathcal{L} \text{ and } size(x) = k\}$;
5: **repeat**
6:     **for** $x \in C_k$
7:         $ES = \text{genExtensionSpace}(x, \mathcal{L})$;
8:         $T_a(x) = \text{unionTransaction}(ES)$;
9:         **if** (x not satisfies s or ϵ_c)*
10:           $C_k = C_k - \{x\}$;
11:         **if**($\lfloor k \cdot \epsilon_r \rfloor = \lfloor (k-1) \cdot \epsilon_r \rfloor + 1$)
12:           $C_{k-1} = \text{forwardPrune}(C_{k-1}, x)$;
13:     **end for**
14:     $L_k = \text{backwardPrune}(C_k, ACI)$;
15:     $ACI = ACI \cup L_k$;
16:     $k = k - 1$;
17: **until** $k = 0$
18: **return** ACI

Experiment is carried out both on synthetic datasets and the UCI datasets. Efficiency and result quality of both algorithms are evaluated and reported. Both algorithms are coded in Microsoft Visual C++ and experiments were run on a 3GHz PC with 2GB memory.

Three groups of experiments were conducted for the performance comparisons. The first tested the efficiency and scalability of AFI and AC-Close w.r.t. various parameters. The second group tested the result quality of AFI and AC-Close on synthetic datasets with a controlled fraction of random noise embedded and with known underlying patterns. Finally, both algorithms were applied to a UCI dataset with known underlying patterns.

6.1 Scalability

The IBM synthetic data generator is used to generate synthetic datasets for the scalability test. A dataset T10.I100.D20K (Agrawal and Srikant, 1994) is generated with 20K transactions, 100 distinct items and an average of 10 items per transaction.

Figure 3 shows the running time of both algorithms by varying min_sup. The three figures show the performance with $\epsilon_r = \epsilon_c = 0.15$, 0.20, 0.25 respectively. $\alpha = 0.8$ is used in AC-Close. In all three cases, AC-Close runs

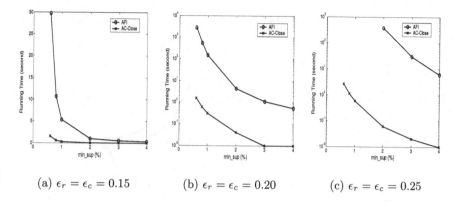

(a) $\epsilon_r = \epsilon_c = 0.15$ (b) $\epsilon_r = \epsilon_c = 0.20$ (c) $\epsilon_r = \epsilon_c = 0.25$

Fig. 3. Running Time of AFI and AC-Close, varying *min_sup*, on T10.I100.D20K

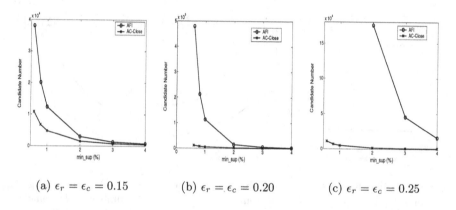

(a) $\epsilon_r = \epsilon_c = 0.15$ (b) $\epsilon_r = \epsilon_c = 0.20$ (c) $\epsilon_r = \epsilon_c = 0.25$

Fig. 4. Number of Candidates Generated by AFI and AC-Close, varying *min_sup*, on T10.I100.D20K

much faster than AFI. In addition, the time difference increases as ϵ_r and ϵ_c increase.

Figure 4 shows the number of candidate approximate frequent itemsets generated by both algorithms during the same experiment in Figure 3. In AFI, the candidates are the patterns generated during the mining process where the size-k candidates satisfy the noise-tolerant pruning support min_sup^k. In AC-Close, the candidates are the core patterns. In all three cases, AFI consistently generates far more candidates than AC-Close. This result shows that AFI has a much larger search space than AC-Close.

Figure 5 shows the running time of both algorithms by varying ϵ_r, ϵ_c and α respectively. To reduce the parameter space, in Figure 5 (a), we set $\epsilon = \epsilon_r = \epsilon_c$. $min\_sup = 0.8\%$ and $\alpha = 0.8$ are used in this experiment. The

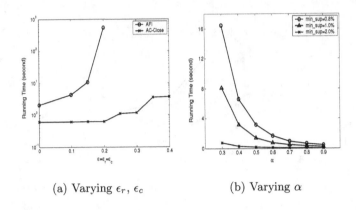

(a) Varying ϵ_r, ϵ_c (b) Varying α

Fig. 5. Running Time of AFI and AC-Close, varying ϵ_r, ϵ_c and α, on T10.I100.D20K

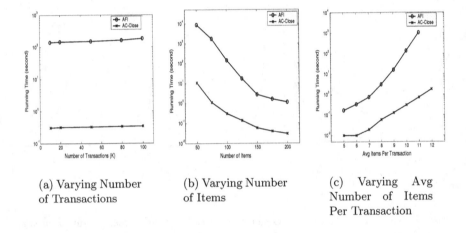

(a) Varying Number of Transactions   (b) Varying Number of Items   (c) Varying Avg Number of Items Per Transaction

Fig. 6. Other Scalability Tests

running time of AFI increases very quickly as ϵ increases while the efficiency of AC-Close is not affected too much by ϵ. The size of approximate itemsets increases by allowing more noise in an itemset. So more candidate itemsets are generated by AFI and the computation time increases exponentially w.r.t. the itemset size. Since AC-Close still focuses on mining the core pattern set as ϵ increases, the candidate set remains the same.

Figure 5 (b) shows the running time of AC-Close by varying the core pattern factor α. $\epsilon_r = \epsilon_c = 0.20$ is used. As α decreases, the core pattern set becomes larger. Therefore, more candidates are generated for approximate itemset mining and the computation time increases. Nevertheless, AC-Close is shown to be very efficient even when α is set to as low as 0.3.

Figure 6 shows the scalability tests by varying different statistics of the transaction database. In all three experiments, $min\_sup = 1\%$, $\epsilon_r = \epsilon_c = 0.20$ and $\alpha = 0.8$ are used.

Figure 6 (a) shows the running time by varying the number of transactions. The number of distinct items is 100 and the average items per transaction is 10. Since both algorithms only perform the union or intersection operations on the transaction id lists without scanning the database repeatedly, increasing the transaction number does not affect the performance much.

Figure 6 (b) shows the running time by varying the number of distinct items in the database. The number of transactions is 10K and the average transaction length is 10. When the number of items is large, the database becomes sparse. So both algorithms run more efficiently. As the number of items decreases, the database becomes dense and the number of qualified approximate frequent itemsets increases. Figure 6 (b) shows that the running time of AFI increases more rapidly than that of AC-Close.

Figure 6 (c) shows the running time by varying the average number of items per transaction. The number of transactions is 10K and the number of distinct items is 100. As the average transaction length increases, the combination between items increases exponentially. The figure shows that the running time of AFI increases much faster.

6.2 Quality

Besides the scalability tests, the quality of mining results are also compared between AFI and AC-Close. A synthetic dataset D_t, T10.I100.D20K, is used as the noise-free dataset. Noise is introduced to flip each entry of D_t with a probability p. The noisy dataset is denoted as D. Exact frequent pattern mining is applied to D_t and the exact frequent itemsets are treated as the ground truth, denoted as F_{true}. In addition, AFI and AC-Close are applied to the noisy dataset D and the approximate itemsets are treated as the recovered patterns, denoted as F_{apr}. For comparison purpose, AC-Close outputs the approximate frequent itemsets instead of the closed ones. Two evaluation metrics *precision* and *recall* are used as the measure, as defined below.

$$precision = \frac{|F_{true} \cap F_{apr}|}{|F_{apr}|}, \quad recall = \frac{|F_{true} \cap F_{apr}|}{|F_{true}|}$$

Tables 4 and 5 show the quality comparison between AFI and AC-Close, with $p = 0.05$ and $p = 0.20$ respectively. $\epsilon_r = \epsilon_c = 0.20$ and $\epsilon_r = \epsilon_c = 0.25$ are set in the two cases respectively. In both cases, $\alpha = 0.8$ is used.

In Table 4, AFI achieves the same recall values as AC-Close but AFI also generates some false positive patterns which do not appear in the true pattern set. In contrast, the precision of AC-Close is 100%. This shows that the core pattern approach can effectively recover the true patterns from the noisy dataset.

Table 4. Precision and Recall of Mining Result by AFI and AC-Close, Noise Level $p = 0.05$

min_sup(%)	Precision		Recall	
	AFI	AC-Close	AFI	AC-Close
0.6	90.04	100	76.70	76.70
0.8	90.46	100	78.61	78.61
1.0	91.69	100	78.30	78.30
2.0	97.52	100	81.71	81.71
3.0	99.40	100	81.61	81.61
4.0	100	100	81.27	81.27

Table 5. Precision and Recall of Mining Result by AFI and AC-Close, Noise Level $p = 0.20$

min_sup(%)	Precision		Recall	
	AFI	AC-Close	AFI	AC-Close
0.6	60.51	100	33.64	33.13
0.8	63.22	100	34.68	34.35
1.0	62.84	100	35.56	35.52
2.0	80.87	100	40.18	40.18
3.0	87.37	100	40.89	40.89
4.0	89.66	100	44.96	44.96

In Table 5, the noise level $p = 0.20$ is higher. To recover the true patterns, the error threshold $\epsilon_r = \epsilon_c$ is set to 0.25. In all cases, the recall of AC-Close is either the same or very close to that of AFI. However, with the error threshold setting, AFI generates many more false positives, as indicated by the precision measure.

Table 6. Precision and Recall of the Mining Result by AC-Close, varying α, $p = 0.05$

α	min_sup=0.8%		min_sup=1.0%	
	Precision	Recall	Precision	Recall
0.9	100	78.61	100	78.30
0.8	100	78.61	100	78.30
0.7	100	78.61	100	78.30
0.6	100	78.61	100	78.30
0.5	100	78.61	100	78.30
0.4	99.96	78.61	100	78.30
0.3	99.81	78.61	99.94	78.30
AFI	90.46	78.61	91.69	78.30

Table 7. Precision and Recall of the Mining Result by AC-Close, varying α, $p = 0.20$

α	$min\_sup=0.8\%$		$min\_sup=1.0\%$	
	Precision	Recall	Precision	Recall
0.9	100	34.35	100	35.52
0.8	100	34.35	100	35.52
0.7	100	34.35	100	35.52
0.6	100	34.35	100	35.52
0.5	100	34.38	100	35.52
0.4	99.95	34.61	99.93	35.54
0.3	99.11	34.68	98.67	35.56
AFI	63.22	34.68	62.84	35.56

Tables 6 and 7 show the result quality of AC-Close at different α values, on T10.I100.D20K, at a noise level $p = 0.05$ and $p = 0.20$ respectively. $\epsilon_r = \epsilon_c = 0.20$ and $\epsilon_r = \epsilon_c = 0.25$ are used in the two cases accordingly. At the bottom row of each table, the precision and recall of AFI is shown as the comparison baseline. In Table 6 when the noise level is low, a low α value does not increase the recall (*i.e.*, discover more true patterns), but generates some false positive. This is because, the true patterns and their support are not affected much by the noise. Therefore, with a low level of random noise, it is not necessary to try a low α value. In Table 7 when the noise level is higher, a low α slightly increases the recall, but also generates some false positives. In both cases, the recall is either the same or very close to that of AFI but the precision is much higher than that of AFI.

6.3 Zoo Dataset

In this experiment, AFI and AC-Close are applied to the Zoo dataset from the UCI Machine Learning Repository (UCI, 2007). The Zoo dataset contains 101 instances and each instance has 15 boolean attributes and a class label (*mammal, bird, etc.*). The 15 boolean attributes including *hair, feathers* and *eggs* are used as items.

One mining task is to discover the common features of a set of animals in the same class. For example, mammals produce milk, are covered in hair, are toothed and grow tails. However, not every mammal exhibits these common features: platypuses lack teeth and dolphins are hairless. If such exceptions are not tolerated, it is hard to find the complete set of features that characterize a class.

For testing purposes, we adopted the 7 classes into which the instances were already categorized as the true underlying pattern. Then we examined how well the competing mining methods recovered these classes. We focused on the 4 classes with at least 5 instances.

Both AFI and AC-Close are tested in terms of the running time and result quality. $\epsilon_r = 0.25$, $\epsilon_c = 0.30$ and the absolute $min\_sup = 12$ are used. The core pattern factor is set to $\alpha = 0.5$. The running time of AFI is $1,471.973$ seconds and that of AC-Close is 1.594 seconds, almost 1000 times faster than AFI.

To measure the result quality, for each approximate pattern x discovered, we compare its supporting transaction set $T_a(x)$ against the transactions of the true class. The approximate pattern with the highest similarity to the true class is presented. Table 8 shows the transaction size (denoted as $|T_c|$) of each class and the transaction size (denoted as $|T_a|$) of the approximate patterns. For example, in Table 8, the true class of *mammal* has 41 instances, which correspond to the 41 transactions in the Zoo data belonging to the mammal class. Both AFI and AC-Close can discover an approximate frequent itemset which is approximately supported by the 41 transactions. As shown in Table 8, both algorithms can discover three classes with 100% match. For the fourth class, the approximate pattern of AFI has 12 transactions while that of AC-Close has 13 transactions.

Table 8. True Pattern Recovery in Zoo Dataset

Class	True Pat	AFI	AC-Close
mammal	41	41	41
bird	20	20	20
fish	13	13	13
sea creature	10	12	13

7 Related Work on Approximate Frequent Itemset

Other related studies on approximate frequent patterns include (Mannila and Toivonen, 1996, Boulicaut *et al.*, 2000, Pei *et al.*, 2003, Seppänen and Mannila, 2004, Steinbach *et al.*, 2004, Zhu *et al.*, 2007, Yan *et al.*, 2007). (Mannila and Toivonen, 1996) showed that approximate association rules are interesting and useful. (Boulicaut *et al.*, 2000) proposed the concept of free-sets and led to an error-bound approximation of frequencies.

The goal of (Pei *et al.*, 2003) is to derive a *condensed frequent pattern base*, a compact representation from which the support of all other frequent patterns can be approximated within some fixed error bound. This work emphasizes more on the compression issue of frequent patterns.

Seppänen and Mannila (Seppänen and Mannila, 2004) proposed to mine the dense itemsts in the presence of noise. A dense itemset is an itemset with a sufficiently large sub-matrix that exceeds a given density threshold of attributes present.

The support envelope technique proposed by Steinbach et al. (Steinbach *et al.*, 2004) identifies regions of the data matrix where each transaction contains at least a given number of items and each item appears in at least a given number of transactions. The support envelope is a tool for exploration and visualization of the high-level structures of association patterns in a transaction database. A symmetric ETI model is proposed such that the same fraction of errors are allowed in both rows and columns. However, no additional properties or algorithms are proposed to mine the symmetric ETIs.

A recent study by Zhu et al. (Zhu *et al.*, 2007) aimed at mining the *colossal* frequent patterns which are frequent itemsets of rather large size. The problem formulation in this study is not itemset recovery from noise, but efficient discovery of colossal patterns. A novel mining approach called *Pattern-Fusion* was proposed to efficiently find a good approximation to the colossal patterns. With this approach, a colossal pattern is discovered by fusing its small core patterns in one step, whereas the incremental pattern-growth mining strategies, such as those adopted in Apriori or FP-growth, have to examine a large number of mid-sized ones.

Yan et al. (Yan *et al.*, 2007) proposed a noise-tolerant model for mining frequent dense subgraphs across multiple graphs. This approach is applied for efficiently and systematically identifying frequent coexpression clusters. Given m microarray datasets, they model each microarray dataset as a coexpression graph, and search for densely connected subgraphs. Due to the noise and outliers in data and the unavoidable cutoff selection for edge construction, the exact match criterion is relaxed, otherwise pursuing exact match would overlook some coexpressed clusters. Therefore, instead of requiring the recurrence of the exact dense subgraph, it only requires the connectivity among the gene set to be higher than a threshold.

8 Conclusions

Frequent itemset mining is one of the fundamental tasks in data mining. In real applications where the data is typically subject to random noise or measurement error, exact frequent itemset mining no longer meets the needs of discovering the true patterns from the noisy dataset. A noise-tolerant mining model is the key solution in this application scenario.

In this chapter, we overview several different noise-tolerant mining models and the methodologies for efficient mining of approximate frequent itemsets. Our experimental study compares the mining efficiency and result quality of different mining approaches.

There are still many interesting issues to be further studied in the noise-tolerant mining models and their applications, including depth-first mining methods for approximate frequent itemsets; design of noise-tolerant models for more complicated patterns such as sequences or structures; subspace clustering in high-dimensional data and gene expression data as well as approximate itemset-based classification models in the presence of noise.

References

M. Abramowitz and I. A. Stegun. *Handbook of Mathematical Functions with Formulas, Graphs, and Mathematical Tables*. Dover, 1964.

R. Agrawal, T. Imielinski, and A. Swami. Mining association rules between sets of items in large databases. In *Proc. SIGMOD'93*, pages 207–216, May 1993.

R. Agrawal and R. Srikant. Fast algorithms for mining association rules. In *Proc. VLDB'94*, pages 487–499, Sept. 1994.

R. Agrawal and R. Srikant. Privacy-preserving data mining. In *Proc. of SIGMOD*, pages 439–450, 2000.

R. J. Bayardo. Efficiently mining long patterns from databases. In *Proc. SIGMOD'98*, pages 85–93, June 1998.

J.F. Boulicaut, A. Bykowski, and C. Rigotti. Approximation of frequency queries by means of free-sets. In *Principles of Data Mining and Knowledge Discovery*, pages 75–85, 2000.

D. Burdick, M. Calimlim, and J. Gehrke. MAFIA: A maximal frequent itemset algorithm for transactional databases. In *Proc. ICDE'01*, pages 443–452, April 2001.

H. Cheng, X. Yan, J. Han, and C. Hsu. Discriminative frequent pattern analysis for effective classification. In *Proc. 2007 Int. Conf. Data Engineering (ICDE'07)*, Istanbul, Turkey, April 2007.

H. Cheng, P. S. Yu, and J. Han AC-Close: Efficiently Mining Approximate Closed Itemsets by Core Pattern Recovery. In *Proc. of ICDM*, pages 839–844, 2006.

G. Cong, K. Tan, A. Tung, and X. Xu. Mining top-k covering rule groups for gene expression data. In *Proc. of SIGMOD*, pages 670–681, 2005.

FIMI: Frequent itemset mining implementations repository. http://fimi.cs.helsinki.fi, 2003.

J. Han, J. Pei, and Y. Yin. Mining frequent patterns without candidate generation. In *Proc. SIGMOD'00*, pages 1–12, May 2000.

W. Li, J. Han, and J. Pei. CMAR: Accurate and efficient classification based on multiple class-association rules. In *Proc. of ICDM*, pages 369–376, 2001.

B. Liu, W. Hsu, and Y. Ma. Integrating classification and association rule mining. In *Proc. of KDD*, pages 80–86, 1998.

J. Liu, S. Paulsen, W. Wang, A. Nobel, and J. Prins. Mining approximate frequent itemset from noisy data. In *Technical report, Department of Computer Science, TR05-015*, 2005.

J. Liu, S. Paulsen, X. Sun, W. Wang, A. Nobel, and J. Prins. Mining approximate frequent itemsets in the presence of noise: Algorithm and analysis. In *Proc. SDM'06*, pages 405–416, April 2006.

H. Mannila and H. Toivonen. Multiple uses of frequent sets and condensed representations. In *Knowledge Discovery and Data Mining*, pages 189–194, 1996.

J. Pei, G. Dong, W. Zou, and J. Han. Mining condensed frequent pattern bases. In *Knowledge and Information Systems*, volume 6 of *5*, pages 570–594, 2004.

J. Pei, J. Han, and R. Mao. CLOSET: An efficient algorithm for mining frequent closed itemsets. In *Proc. DMKD'00*, pages 11–20, May 2000.

W. H. Press, B. P. Flannery, S. A. Teukolsky, and W. T. Vetterling. *Numerical Recipes in C*. Cambridge, 2nd edition, 1992.

J. Seppänen and H. Mannila. Dense itemsets. In *Proc. of KDD*, pages 683–688, 2004.

M. Steinbach, P. Tan, and V. Kumar. Support envelopes: A technique for exploring the structure of association patterns. In *Proc. KDD'04*, pages 296–305, Aug. 2004.

UCI: machine learning repository. http://www.ics.uci.edu/~mlearn/MLSummary.html, 2007.

V. Verykios, E. Bertino, I. Fovino, L. Provenza, Y. Saygin, and Y. Theodoridis. State-of-the-art in privacy preserving data mining. *SIGMOD Record*, 3:50–57, 2004.

K. Wang, C. Xu, and B. Liu. Clustering transactions using large items. In *Proc. of CIKM*, pages 483–490, 1999.

X. Yan, M. R. Mehan, Y. Huang, M. S. Waterman, P. S. Yu, and X. J. Zhou. A graph-based approach to systematically reconstruct human transcriptional regulatory modules. In *Proc. of ISMB*, 2007.

X. Yan, P. S. Yu, and J. Han. Graph Indexing: A frequent structure-based approach. In *Proc. of SIGMOD*, pages 335–346, 2004.

C. Yang, U. Fayyad, and P. S. Bradley. Efficient discovery of error-tolerant frequent itemsets in high dimensions. In *Proc. KDD'01*, pages 194–203, Aug. 2001.

M. J. Zaki. Scalable algorithms for association mining. *IEEE Trans. Knowledge and Data Engineering*, 12:372–390, 2000.

M. J. Zaki and C. J. Hsiao. CHARM: An efficient algorithm for closed itemset mining. In *Proc. SDM'02*, pages 457–473, April 2002.

F. Zhu, X. Yan, J. Han, P. S. Yu, and H. Cheng. Mining colossal frequent patterns by core pattern fusion. In *Proc. 2007 Int. Conf. Data Engineering (ICDE'07)*, Istanbul, Turkey, April 2007.

The Impact of Overfitting and Overgeneralization on the Classification Accuracy in Data Mining

Huy Nguyen Anh Pham[1] and Evangelos Triantaphyllou[1]

Department of Computer Science, 298 Coates Hall, Louisiana State University, Baton Rouge, LA 70803 hpham15,trianta@lsu.edu

Summary. Many classification studies often times conclude with a summary table which presents performance results of applying various data mining approaches on different datasets. No single method outperforms all methods all the time. Furthermore, the performance of a classification method in terms of its false-positive and false-negative rates may be totally unpredictable. Attempts to minimize any of the previous two rates, may lead to an increase on the other rate. If the model allows for new data to be deemed as unclassifiable when there is not adequate information to classify them, then it is possible for the previous two error rates to be very low but, at the same time, the rate of having unclassifiable new examples to be very high. The root to the above critical problem is the overfitting and overgeneralization behaviors of a given classification approach when it is processing a particular dataset. Although the above situation is of fundamental importance to data mining, it has not been studied from a comprehensive point of view. Thus, this chapter analyzes the above issues in depth. It also proposes a new approach called the Homogeneity-Based Algorithm (or HBA) for optimally controlling the previous three error rates. This is done by first formulating an optimization problem. The key development in this chapter is based on a special way for analyzing the space of the training data and then partitioning it according to the data density of different regions of this space. Next, the classification task is pursued based on the previous partitioning of the training space. In this way, the previous three error rates can be controlled in a comprehensive manner. Some preliminary computational results seem to indicate that the proposed approach has a significant potential to fill in a critical gap in current data mining methodologies.

Key words: classification, prediction, overfitting, overgeneralization, false-positive, false-negative, homogenous set, homogeneity degree, optimization

1 Introduction

The importance of collecting enormous amounts of data related to science, engineering, business, governance, and almost any endeavor of human activity or the natural world is well recognized today. Powerful mechanisms for collecting and storing data and managing them in large datasets are in place in many large and mid-range companies, not to mention research labs and various agencies. There is, however, a serious challenge in making good use of such massive datasets and trying to learn new knowledge of the system or phenomenon that created these data. Human analysts cannot process and comprehend such datasets unless they have special computational tools at their disposal.

The emerging field of data mining and knowledge discovery seeks to develop reliable and effective computational tools for analyzing large datasets for the purpose of extracting new knowledge from the data. Such new knowledge can be derived in the form of patterns that are embedded in the data.

Many applications of data mining involve the analysis of data that describe the state of nature of a hidden system of interest to the analyst. Such a system could be a natural or artificial phenomenon (such as the state of the weather or the result of a scientific experiment), a mechanical system (such as the engine of a car), an electronic system (such as an electronic device), and so on. Each data point describes the state of the phenomenon or system in terms of *a number of attributes* and *their values* for a given realization of the phenomenon or system. Furthermore, each data point is associated with *a class value* which describes a particular state of nature of this phenomenon or system.

For instance, a bank administrator could be interested in knowing whether a loan application should be approved or not based on some characteristics of applicants for credit. Here the two classes are: "approve" or "do not approve". Attributes in this hypothetical scenario could be the age of the applicant, the income level of the applicant, the education level, whether he/she has a permanent job, etc. Then, the goal of the data mining process might be to extract any patterns that might be present in the data of successful credit applicants and also patterns that might be present in the data of non-successful applicants. By "successful applicants" we mean here those who can repay their loans without any negative complications, while with "non-successful applicants" we mean those who default their loans.

There could be many questions to be asked, but only a few of them would be important for the decision. With the abundance of the data available in this area, a careful analysis could provide a *pattern* that exposes the main characteristics of reliable loan applicants. Then, the data mining analyst would like to identify such patterns from past data for which we know the final outcome and use those patterns to decide whether a new application for credit should be approved or not.

In other words, many applications of data mining involve the analysis of data for which we know the class value of each data point. We wish to infer some patterns from these data which in turn could be used to infer the class value of new points for which we do not know their class value. These patterns may be defined on the attributes used to describe the available data (also known as the *training data*). For instance, for the previous bank example the patterns may be defined on the level of education, years on the same job, level of income, of the applicants.

This kind of data mining analysis is called *classification* or *class prediction* of new data points because it uses patterns inferred from training data to aid in the correct classification/class prediction of new data points for which we do not know their class value. We only know the values of the attributes (perhaps not all of them) of the new data points. This description implies that this type of data mining analysis, besides the typical data definition, data collection, and data cleaning steps, involves the inference of a model of the phenomenon or system of interest to the analyst. This model is the patterns mentioned above. The data involved in deriving this model are the training data. Next, this model is used to infer the class value of new points.

There have been many theoretical and practical developments in the last two decades in this field. Most recent methods include the Statistical Learning Theory (Vapnik, 1998), Artificial Neural Networks (ANNs) (Hecht-Nielsen, 1989) and (Abdi, 2003), Decision Trees (DTs) (Quinlan, 1993), logic-based methods (Hammer and Boros, 1994), (Triantaphyllou, 1994; and 2007), and Support Vector Machines (SVMs) (Vapnik, 1979; and 1998) and (Cristianini and John, 2003).

In many real-life or experimental studies of data mining, some classification approaches work better with some datasets, while they work poorly with other datasets for no apparent reason. For instance, DTs had some success in the medical domain (Zavrsnik et. al., 1995). However, they also have had some certain limitations when they were used in this domain, as described for instance in (Kokol et. al., 1998) and (Podgorelec, 2002). Furthermore, the success of SVMs has been shown in bioinformatics, such as in (Byvatov, 2003) and (Huzefa et. al., 2005). At the same time, SVMs also did poorly in this field (Spizer et. al., 2006). If the data mining approach is accurate, then the people praise the mathematical model and claim that it is a good model. However, there is no good understanding of why such models are accurate or not. Their performance is often times coincidental.

A growing belief is that overfitting and overgeneralization problems may cause poor performance of the classification/class prediction model. Overfitting means that the extracted model describes the behavior of known data very well but does poorly on new data points. Overgeneralization occurs when the system uses the available data and then attempts to analyze vast amounts of data that has not seen yet.

Assume that there are two classes which, arbitrarily, we will call the positive and the negative class. Then, one may infer the following two classification models. The first model (which we will call the "positive" model) describes patterns embedded in the positive examples and which do not exist in the negative examples. In a similar manner, we define the "negative" model. For instance, when developing a diagnosis system for some types of cancer one may want to derive two models that can classify a new patient to either, positive (which means has cancer) or negative (which means does not have cancer) cases.

The analyst may want one of the previous two models to be more "conservative" while the other model to be more "liberal". If both models are ultra "conservative" then the implication is that they would only classify new cases that are very closely related to cases they already have seen in the training data. In this situation, the net effect would be many cases to be left as *unclassifiable* by both systems. Similarly, if both systems are classifying new data in a "liberal" manner, then they may contradict each other too often when they are presented with new cases. Again, this situation might be undesirable. Thus, a "liberal" behavior by a classification model means that the model has a tendency for overgeneralization. A similar relationship exists between the concept of "conservative" and overfitting

This chapter aims at finding a way to balance both fitting and generalization in order to minimize the total misclassification cost of the final system. By doing so, it is hoped that the classification/prediction accuracy of the inferred models will be very high or at least as high as it can be achieved with the available training data. We plan to achieve this by balancing the previous two conflicting behaviors of the extracted systems.

The next section provides a preliminary description of the main research problem. The third section gives a summary of the main developments in the related literature. The proposed methodology is highlighted in the fourth section. That section shows how a balance between fitting and generalization has the potential to improve many existing classification algorithms. The fifth section discusses some promising preliminary results. These pilot results give an early indication of how this methodology may improve the performance of existing classification algorithms. Finally, this chapter ends with some conclusions.

2 Formal Problem Description

2.1 Some Basic Definitions

In order to help fix ideas, we first consider the hypothetical sample data depicted in Figure 1. Let us assume that the "circles" and "squares" in this figure correspond to sampled observations from two classes defined in 2-D.

In general, a *data point* is a vector defined on n variables along with their values. In the above figure, n is equal to 2 and the two variables are indicated by the X and Y axis. Not all values may be known for a given data point.

Data points describe the behavior of the system of interest to the analyst. For instance, in the earlier bank application a given data point may describe the level of education, years on the same job, level of income of a particular applicant, etc. The variables may be continuous, binary, or categorical, etc. All data are assumed to be deterministic and numeric at this point. The *state space* is the universe of all possible data points. In terms of Figure 1, the state space is any point in the X-Y plane.

We assume that there are only two classes. Arbitrarily, we will call one of them the *positive* class while the other the *negative* class. Thus, a *positive data point*, also known as a *positive example*, is a data point that has been evaluated to belong to the positive class. A similar definition exists for *negative data points* or *negative examples*.

Given a set of positive and negative examples, such as the ones depicted in Figure 1, this set is called the *training data* (examples) or the *classified examples*. The remaining of the data from the state space is called the *unclassified data* (examples).

2.2 Problem Description

We start the problem description with a simple analysis on the sample data depicted in Figure 1. Suppose that a data mining approach (such as a DT, ANN, or SVM) has been applied on these data. Next we assume that two classification systems have been inferred from these data. Usually, such classification systems arrange the training data into groups described by the parts of a decision tree or classification rules. In a way, these groups of training data define the patterns inferred from the data after the application of a data mining algorithm. For this hypothetical scenario, we assume that the data mining algorithm has inferred the system patterns depicted in Figure 2.(a).

In general, one classification system describes the positive data (and thus we will call it the *positive system*) while the other system describes the negative data (and thus we will call it the *negative system*). In Figure 2.(a) the positive system corresponds to sets A and B (which define the positive pattern) while sets C and D correspond to the negative system (and thus they define the negative pattern).

In many real-life applications, there are two different penalty costs if one erroneously classifies a true positive point as negative or if one classifies a true negative point as positive. The first case is known as false-positive, while the second case is known as false-negative. Furthermore, a closer examination of Figure 2.(a) indicates that there are some unclassifiable points which either are not covered by any of the patterns or are covered by patterns that belong to both classes. For instance, point N (indicated as a triangle) is not covered by any of the patterns, while point M (also a triangle) is covered by sets A and C which belong to the positive and the negative patterns, respectively.

For the first case, as point N is not covered by any of the patterns, the inferred system may declare it as an *unclassifiable* point. In the second case,

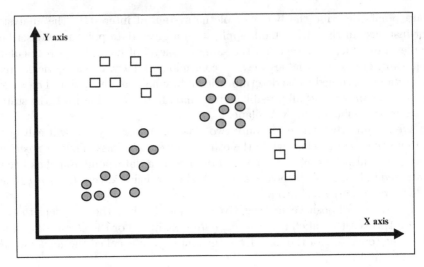

Fig. 1. Sample data from two classes in 2-D.

there is a direct disagreement by the inferred system as the new point (i.e., point M) is covered simultaneously by patterns of both classes. Again, such a point may be also declared as *unclassifiable*. Thus, in many real-life applications of data mining one may have to consider three different penalty costs as follows: one cost for the false-positive case, one cost for the false-negative case, and one cost for the unclassifiable case.

Next consider Figure 2.(b). Suppose that all patterns A, B, C and D have been reduced significantly but still cover the original training data. A closer examination of this figure indicates that now both points M and N are not covered by any of the inferred patterns. In other words, these points and several additional points which were classified before by the inferred systems now become unclassifiable.

Furthermore, the data points which before were simultaneously covered by patterns from both classes, and thus were unclassifiable, are now covered by only one type of pattern or none at all. Thus, it is very likely that the situation depicted in Figure 2.(b) may have a higher total penalty cost than the original situation depicted in Figure 2.(a). If one takes this idea of reducing the covering sets as much as possible to the extreme, then there would be one pattern (i.e., just a small circle) around each individual training data point. In this extreme case, the total penalty cost due to unclassifiable points would be maximum as the system would be able to classify the training data only and nothing else. The previous scenarios are known as *overfitting* of the training data.

On the other hand, suppose that the original patterns depicted as sets A, B, C and D (as shown in Figure 2.(a)) are now expanded significantly as in Figure 2.(c). A closer examination of this figure demonstrates that points M and N are now covered simultaneously by patterns of both classes. Also, more points are now covered simultaneously by patterns of both classes. Thus, under this scenario we also have lots of unclassifiable points because this scenario creates lots of cases of disagreement between the two classification systems (i.e., the positive and the negative systems). This realization means that the total penalty cost due to unclassifiable points will also be significantly higher than under the scenario depicted in Figure 2.(a). This scenario is known as *overgeneralization* of the training data.

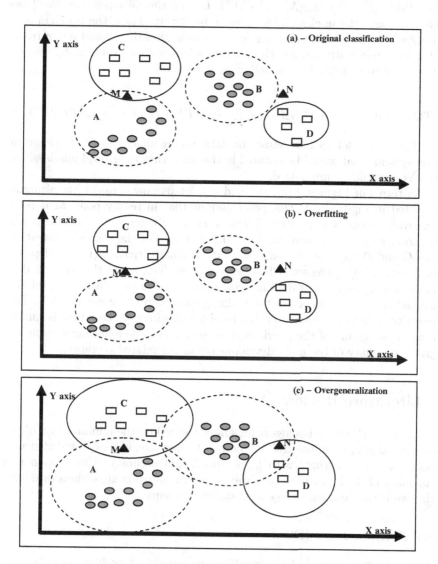

Fig. 2. An illustrative example of overfitting and overgeneralization.

Thus, we cannot separate the control of fitting and generalization into two independent studies. That is, we need to find a way to simultaneously balance fitting and generalization by adjusting the inferred systems (i.e., the positive and the negative systems) obtained from a classification algorithm. The balance of the two systems will target at minimizing the total misclassification costs of the final system.

In particular, let us denote C_{FP}, C_{FN}, and C_{UC} as the penalty costs for the false-positive, the false-negative, and the unclassifiable cases, respectively. Let $RATE\_FP$, $RATE\_FN$, and $RATE\_UC$ be the false-positive, the false-negative, and the unclassifiable rates, respectively. Then, the problem is to achieve a balance between fitting and generalization that would minimize, or at least significantly reduce, the total misclassification cost denoted as TC. The problem is defined in the following expression:

$$TC = \min \left(C_{FP} \times RATE\_FP + C_{FN} \times RATE\_FN + C_{UC} \times RATE\_UC \right) \quad (1)$$

This methodology may assist the data mining analyst to create classification systems that would be optimal in the sense that their total misclassification cost would be minimized.

In terms of Figures 2.(a), (b) and (c), let us now consider the situation depicted in Figure 3. At this point assume that in reality point M is negative while point N is positive. Figure 3 shows different levels of fitting and generalization for the two classification systems. For the sake of illustration, sets C and D are kept the same as in the original situation (i.e., as depicted in Figure 2.(a)) while set A has been reduced (i.e., it fits the training data more closely) and now it does not cover point M. On the other hand, set B is expanded (i.e., it generalizes the training data more) to cover point N. This new situation may correspond to a total misclassification cost that is smaller than those by any of the previous three scenarios. The following section will give a summary of the main developments in the related literature.

3 Literature Review

Most of the classification algorithms have focused on the minimization of the classification error of the training points. In this way, it is expected that new points will be classified with higher prediction accuracy. This section is a summary of the literature about ways that classification algorithms deal with the overfitting and the overgeneralization problems.

3.1 Decision Trees (DTs)

There are two methods for controlling the overfitting problem in DTs: pre-pruning methods in which the growing tree approach is halted by some early stopping rules before generating a fully grown tree, and post-pruning in which the DT is first grown to its maximum size and then we trim some partitions of the tree.

There was recently a lot of effort which has focused on improving the pre-pruning methods. (Kohavi, 1996) proposed the NBTree (a hybrid of decision-tree and naive- classifiers). The NBTree provides some early stopping rules by comparing two alternatives: partitioning the instance-space further on (i.e., continue splitting the tree based on some gain ratio stopping criteria) versus stopping the partition and producing a single Naïve Bayes classifier. (Zhou and Chen, 2002) suggested the hybrid DT approach for growing a binary DT. A feed-forward neural network is used to subsequently determine some early stopping rules. (Rokach et. al., 2005) proposed the cluster-based concurrent decomposition (CBCD) algorithm. That algorithm first decomposes the training set into mutually exclusive sub-samples and then uses a voting scheme to combine these sub-samples for the classifier's predictions. Similarly, (Cohen et. al., 2007) proposed an approach for building a DT by using a homogeneity criterion for splitting the space. However, the above approaches have a difficulty in choosing the threshold value for early termination. A value which is too high may result in underfitting models, while a too low threshold value may not be sufficient to overcome overfitting models.

Under the post-pruning approaches described in (Breiman et. al., 1984) and (Quinlan, 1987), the pruning process eliminates some partitions of the tree. The reduction on the number of partitions makes the remaining tree more general. In order to help fix the main idea, we consider the simple example depicted in Figure 4. Suppose that Figure 4.(a) shows a DT inferred from some training examples. The pruning process eliminates some of the DT's nodes as depicted in Figure 4.(b). The remaining part of the DT, as shown in Figure 4.(c), implies some rules which are more general. For instance, the left most branch of the DT in Figure 4.(a) implies the rule "if $D \wedge A \wedge B \wedge C$, then ..." On the order hand, Figure 4.(c) implies the more general rule "if $D \wedge A$, then ..."

However, more generalization is not always required nor is it always beneficial. A more complex arrangement of partitions has been proved to increase the complexity of DTs in some applications. Furthermore, the treatment of generalization of a DT may lead to overgeneralization since pruning conditions are based on localized information.

Instead of the pruning methods, there have been some other developments to improve the accuracy of DTs. (Webb, 1996) attempted to graft additional leaves to a DT after its induction. This method does not leave any area of the instance space in conflict, because each data point belongs to only one class. Obviously, the overfitting problem may arise from this approach. (Mansour et. al., 2000) proposed another way to deal with the overfitting problem by using the learning theoretical method. In that method, the bounds on the error rate for DTs depend both on the structure of the tree and on the specific sample. (Kwok and Carter, 1990), (Schapire, 1990), (Wolpert, 1992), (Dieterich and

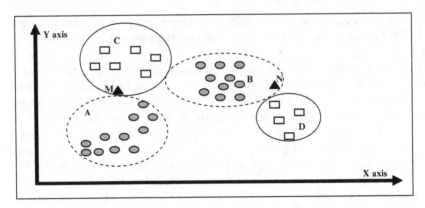

Fig. 3. An illustrative example of a better classification.

Bakiri, 1994), (Ali *et. al.*, 1994), (Oliver and Hand, 1995), (Nock and Gascuel, 1995) and (Breiman, 1996) allowed multiple classifiers used in a conjunction. This method is similar to using a Disjunctive Normal Form (DNF) Boolean function. Furthermore, (Breiman, 2001) also used the so-called random forest approach for multiple classifiers. However, the above approaches might create conflicts between the individual classifiers' partitions, as in the situation presented in C4.5 (Quinlan, 1993).

3.2 Rule-Based Classifiers

A rule-based classifier uses a collection of "if ... then ..." rules that identify key relationships between the attributes and the class values of a dataset. There are two methods which infer classification rules: direct methods which infer classification rules directly from the data, and indirect methods which infer classification rules from other classification methods such as DTs, SVMs, or ANNs and then they translate the final model into a set of classification rules (Tan *et. al.*, 2005). An extensive survey of rule-based methods can be found in (Triantaphyllou and Felici, 2006). A new rule-based approach, which is based on mathematical logic, is described in (Triantaphyllou, 2007).

A well-known algorithm of direct methods is the Sequence Covering algorithm and its later enhancement, the CN2 algorithm (Clark and Niblett, 1989). To control the balance of fitting and generalization while generating rules, these algorithms first use two strategies for growing the classification rules: general-to-specific or specific-to-general. Then, the rules are refined by using the pre and post-pruning methods mentioned in DTs.

Under the general-to-specific strategy, a rule is created by finding all possible candidates and use a greedy approach to choose the new conjuncts to be added into the rule antecedent part in order to improve its quality. This approach ends when some stopping criteria are met.

Under the specific-to-general strategy, a classification rule is initialized by randomly choosing one of the positive points as the initial step. Then, the rule is refined by removing one of its conjuncts so that this rule can cover more positive points. This refining approach ends when certain stopping criteria are met. A similar way exists for the negative points.

There are some related developments regarding these strategies. Such developments include a beam search approach (Clark and Boswell, 1991) which avoids the overgrowing of rules as result of the greedy behavior, the RIPPER algorithm (Cohen, 1995) which uses a rule induction algorithm. However, the use of the two strategies for growing classification rules has their drawbacks. The complexity for finding optimal rules is of exponential size of the search space. Although some rule pruning methods are used to improve their generalization error, they also leave drawbacks as mentioned in the case of DTs.

3.3 K-Nearest Neighbor Classifiers

While DTs and rule-based classifiers are examples of eager learners, K-Nearest Neighbor Classifiers (Cover, Hart, 1967) and (Dasarathy, 1979) are known as lazy learners. That is, this approach finds K training points that are relatively similar to attributes of a testing point to determine its class value.

The importance of choosing the right value for K directly affects the accuracy of this approach. A wrong value for K may lead to the overfitting or the overgeneralization problems (Tan *et. al.*, 2005). One way to reduce the impact of K is to weight the influence of the nearest neighbors according to their distance to the testing point. One of the most well-known schemes is the distance-weighted voting scheme (Dudani, 1976) and (Keller, Gray and Givens, 1985).

However, the use of K-nearest neighbor classifiers has their drawbacks. Classifying a test example can be quite expensive since we need to compute a similarity degree between the test point and each training point. They are unstable since they are based on localized information only. Finally, it is difficult to find an appropriate value for K to avoid model overfitting or overgeneralization.

3.4 Bayes Classifiers

This approach uses the modeling probabilistic relationships between the attribute set and the class variable for solving classification problems. There are two well known implementations of Bayesian classifiers: Naïve Bayes (NBs) and Bayesian Belief Networks (BBNs).

NBs assume that all the attributes are independent of each other and then they estimate by using the class conditional probability. This independence assumption, however, is obviously problematic because often times in many

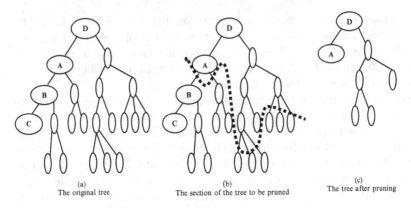

(a)
The original tree

(b)
The section of the tree to be pruned

(c)
The tree after pruning

Fig. 4. An illustrative example of the DT pruning.

real applications there are strong conditional dependencies between the attributes. Furthermore, when using the independence assumption, NBs may suffer of overfitting since they are based on localized information.

Instead of requiring all attributes to be conditionally independent given a class, a BBN (Duda and Hart, 1973) allows only for pairs of attributes to be conditionally independent. We introduce this approach by discussing an illustrative example. Suppose that we have a training dataset consisting of the attributes: age, occupation, income, buy (i.e., buy some product X), and interest (i.e., "interest in purchasing insurance for this product"). The attributes age, occupation and income may determine if a customer will buy some product X. Given is a customer who has bought product X. There is an interest in buying insurance when we assume this is independent of age, occupation, and income. These constraints are presented by the BBN depicted in Figure 5. Thus, for a certain data point described by a 5-tuple (age, occupation, income, buy, interest), its probability based on the BBN should be:

P(age, occupation, income, buy, interest) =

$$P(\text{age}) \times P(\text{occupation}) \times P(\text{income}) \times P(\text{buy} \mid \text{age, occupation, income}) \times P(\text{interest} \mid \text{buy}).$$

There was a lot of effort which has focused on improving BBNs. This effort follows two general approaches: selecting a feature subset (Langley and Sage, 1994), (Pazzani, 1995), and (Kohavi and John, 1997) and relaxing the independence assumptions (Kononenko, 1991) and (Friedman *et. al.*, 1997). However, these developments have the following drawbacks:

They require a large amount of effort when constructing the network.

They quietly degrade to overfitting because they combine probabilistically the data with prior knowledge.

3.5 Artificial Neural Networks (ANNs)

Recall that an ANN is a model that is an assembly of inter-connected nodes and weighted links. The output node sums up each of its input values according to the weights of its links. The output node is compared against a threshold value t. Such a model is illustrated in Figure 6. The ANN in this figure consists of the three input nodes X_1, X_2, and X_3 which correspond to the weighted links w_1, w_2, and w_3, respectively, and one output node Y. The sum of the input nodes can be $Y = \text{sign} \sum_i (X_i w_i - t)$, called the perceptron model (Abdi, 2003).

In general, an ANN has a set of input nodes X_1, X_2, ..., X_m and one output node Y. Given are n values for the m-tuple $(X_1, X_2, \ldots, X_m)$. Let $\hat{Y}_1$, $\hat{Y}_2$, ..., $\hat{Y}_n$ be the predicted outputs and Y_1, Y_2, ..., Y_n be the expected outputs from the n values, respectively. Let $E = \sum_{i=1}^{n} [Y_i - \hat{Y}_i]^2$ denote the total sum of the squared differences between the expected and the predicted outputs. The goal of the ANN is to determine a set of the weights in order to minimize the value of E. During the training phase of an ANN, the weight parameters are adjusted until the outputs of the perceptron become consistent with the true outputs of the training points. In the weight update process, the weights should not be changed too drastically because E is computed only for the current training point. Otherwise, the adjustments made during earlier iterations may be undone.

In order to avoid overgeneralization or overfitting, the design for an ANN must be considered. A network that is not sufficiently complex may fail to fully detect the input in a complicated dataset, leading to overgeneralization. On the other hand, a network that is too complex may not only fit the input but also the noisy points, thus leading to overfitting. According to (Geman, Bienenstock, and Doursat, 1992) and (Smith, 1996), the complexity of a network is related both to the number of the weights and to the size of the weights. Geman and Smith were directly or indirectly concerned with the number and size of the weights. That is, the number of the weights relates to the number of hidden units and layers. The more weights there are, relative to the number of the training cases, the more overfitting amplifies noise in the classification systems (Moody, 1992). Reducing the size of the weights may reduce the effective number of the weights leading to weight decay (Moody, 1992) and early stopping (Weigend, 1994). In summary, ANNs have the following drawbacks:

It is difficult to find an appropriate network topology for a given problem in order to avoid model overfitting and overgeneralization.

It takes lots of time to train an ANN when the number of hidden nodes is large.

3.6 Support Vector Machines (SVMs)

Another classification technique that has received considerable attention is known as SVMs (Vapnik, 1995). The basic idea behind SVMs is to find a maximal margin hyperplane, θ, that will separate points considered as vectors in an m-dimensional space. The maximum margin hyperplane can be essentially represented as a linear combination of the training points. Consequently, the decision function for classifying new data points with respect to the hyperplane only involves dot products between data points and the hyperplane.

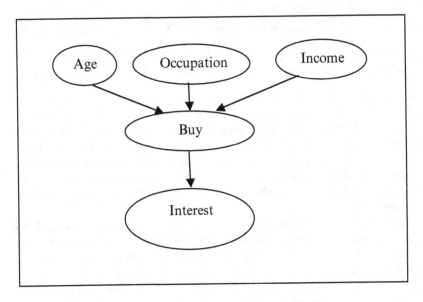

Fig. 5. An illustrative example of a BBN (Rada, 2004).

In order to help fix ideas, we consider the simple illustrative example depicted in Figure 7. Suppose that we have a training dataset defined on two given classes (represented by the squares and circles) in 2-D. In general, the approach can find many hyperplanes, such as B_1 or B_2, separating the training dataset into the two classes. The SVM, however, chooses B_1 to classify this training dataset since B_1 has the maximum margin. Roughly speaking it is in the middle of the distance between the two groups of training examples.

Decision boundaries with maximal margins tend to lead to better generalization. Furthermore, SVMs attempt to formulate the learning problem as a convex optimization problem in which efficient algorithms are available to find a global solution. For many datasets, however, an SVM may not be able to formulate the learning problem as a convex optimization problem because

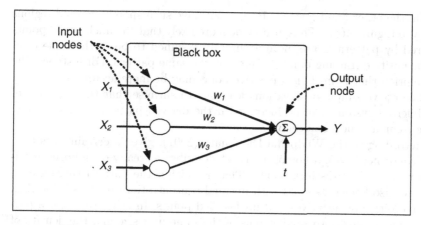

Fig. 6. An illustrative example of an ANN (Tan et. al., 2005).

it may be the cause of too many misclassifications. Thus, the attempts for formulating the learning problem may lead to overgeneralization.

4 Proposed Methodology – The Homogeneity-Based Algorithm (HBA)

4.1 Some Key Observations

In order to help motivate the proposed methodology, we first consider the situation depicted in Figure 8.(a). This figure presents two inferred patterns. These are the circular areas that surround groups of training data (shown as small circles). Actually, these data are part of the training data shown earlier in Figure 1 (please recall that the circles in Figure 1 represent positive points). Moreover, in Figure 8.(a) there are two additional data points shown as small triangles and are denoted as points P and Q. At this situation, it is assumed that we do not know the actual class values of these two new points. We would like to use the available training data and inferred patterns to classify these two points. Because points P and Q are covered by patterns A and B, respectively, both of these points may be assumed to be positive examples.

Let us look more closely at pattern A. This pattern covers regions of the state space that are not adequately populated by positive training points. Such regions, for instance, exist in the upper left corner and the lower part of pattern A (see also Figure 8.(a)). It is possible that the unclassified points which belong to such regions are erroneously assumed to be of the same class as the positive training points covered by pattern A. Point P is in one of these sparely covered regions under pattern A. Thus, the assumption that point P is a positive point may not be very accurate.

On the other hand, pattern B does not have such sparely covered regions (see also Figure 8.(a)). Thus, it may be more likely that the unclassified points covered by pattern B are more accurately assumed to be of the same class as the positive training points covered by the same pattern. For instance, the assumption that point Q is a positive point may be more accurate.

The above simple observations lead one to surmise that the accuracy of the inferred systems can be increased if the derived patterns are, somehow, more compact and homogenous.

According to the Wikipedia Dictionary (2007), given a certain class (i.e., positive or negative), a homogenous set describes a steady or uniform distribution of a set of distinct points. That is, within the pattern there are no regions (also known as *bins*) with unequal concentrations of classifiable (i.e., either positive or negative) and unclassified points. In other words, if a pattern is partitioned into smaller bins of the same unit size and the density of these bins is almost equal to each other (or, equivalently, the standard deviation is small enough), then this pattern is a homogenous set. An axiom and a theorem are derived from the definition of a homogenous set as follows:

Axiom 1. Given is an inferred pattern C of size one. Then, C is a homogenous set.

This axiom is used later in Section 4.4.

Theorem 1. *Let us consider a homogenous set C. If C is divided into two parts, C_1 and C_2, then the two parts are also homogenous sets.*

Proof. We prove Theorem 1 by using contradiction. Since C is a homogenous set, there is a uniform random variable Z that represents the distribution of points in C. Similarly, Z_1 and Z_2 are the two random variables that represent the distribution of points in C_1 andC_2, respectively. Obviously, Z is the sum of Z_1 and Z_2. Assume that either Z_1 or Z_2 is a non homogenous set. Thus, $Z_1 + Z_2$ is not a uniform random variable. This contradicts the fact that Z is a uniform random variable.

The pattern which is represented by the non homogenous A can be replaced by two more homogenous sets denoted as A_1 and A_2 as in Figure 8.(b). Now the regions covered by the two new smaller patterns A_1 and A_2 are more homogenous than the area covered by the original pattern A. Given these considerations, point P may be assumed to be an unclassifiable point while point Q is still a positive point.

As presented in the previous paragraphs, the homogenous property of patterns may influence the number of misclassification cases of the inferred classification systems. Furthermore, if a pattern is a homogenous set, then the number of training points covered by this pattern may be another factor which affects the accuracy of the overall inferred systems. For instance, Figure 9 shows the case discussed in Figure 8.(b) (i.e., pattern A has been replaced by

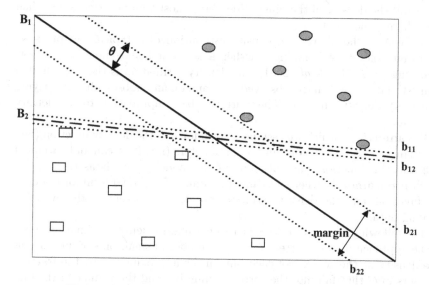

Fig. 7. An illustrative example of an SVM (Tan et. al., 2005).

two more homogenous sets denoted as A_1 and A_2). Suppose that all patterns A_1, A_2 and B are homogenous sets and a new point S (indicated as a triangle) is covered by pattern A_1.

A closer examination of this figure shows that the number of points in B is higher than those in A_1. Although both points Q and S are covered by homogenous sets, the assumption that point Q is a positive point may be more accurate than the assumption that point S is a positive point. The above simple observation leads one to surmise that the accuracy of the inferred systems may also be affected by a *density* measure. Such a density could be defined as the number of points in each inferred pattern per unit of area or volume. Therefore, this density will be called the *homogeneity degree*.

In summary, a fundamental assumption here is as follows: if an unclassified point is covered by a pattern that is a homogenous set which also happens to have a high homogeneity degree, then it may be more accurately assumed to be of the same class as the points covered by that pattern. On the other hand, the accuracy of the inferred systems may be increased when their patterns are more homogenous and have high homogeneity degrees.

4.2 Non Parametric Density Estimation

Please recall that a pattern C of size n is a homogenous set if the pattern can be partitioned into smaller bins of the same unit size h and the density of these bins is almost equal to each other (or, equivalently, the standard deviation is small enough). In other words, if C is superimposed by a hypergrid of unit size h and the density of the bins inside C is almost equal to each other, then C is a homogenous set.

As seen in the above, the density estimation of a typical bin plays an important role in determining whether a set is a homogenous set or not. According to (Duda $et.\ al.$, 2001), the density estimation is the construction of an estimate, based on the observed data and on an unobservable underlying probability density function. There are two basic approaches to the density estimation:

Parametric in which we assume a given form of the density function (i.e., Gaussian, normal, and so on) and its parameters (i.e., its mean and variance) such that this function may optimally fit the model to the dataset.

Non parametric where we cannot assume a functional form for the density function, and the density estimates are driven entirely by the available training data.

The following sections will use the non parametric density estimation. That is, the approach divides pattern C into a number of small bins of unit size h. The density at the center x of each bin can be approximated by the fraction of points in C that fall into the corresponding bin and the volume of the bin. For instance, a bin in 3-D can be a cube of unit size h as depicted in Figure 10. Let n be the number of points in C and $d(x)$ denote the x's density, then:

$$d(x) = \frac{1}{n}[\frac{the\ number\ of\ examples\ falling\ in\ the\ bin\ with\ center\ x}{volume\ of\ the\ bin}]. \quad (2)$$

The basic idea behind computing $d(x)$ relies on the probability p that a data point x, drawn from a distribution function, will fall in bin R. By using this idea we arrive at the following obvious estimate for $d(x)$:

$$d(x) \approx \frac{k}{n \times V}, \quad (3)$$

where x is a point within R; k is the number of points which fall in R; and V is the volume enclosed by R.

The Parzen Windows approach (Duda and Hart, 1973) was introduced as the most appropriate approach for the density estimation. That is, it temporarily assumes that the region R is a D-dimensional hypercube of unit size h. To find the number of points that fall within this region, the Parzen Windows approach defines a kernel function $\varphi(u)$ as follows:

$$\varphi(u) = \begin{cases} 1, & |u| \leq 1/2. \\ 0, & otherwise. \end{cases} \quad (4)$$

It follows that the quantity $\varphi(\frac{x-x_i}{h})$ is equal to unity if the point x_i is inside the hypercube of unit size h and centered at x, and zero otherwise. Therefore, k, the number of points in the hypercube is given by:

$$k = \sum_{i=1}^{n} \varphi(\frac{x - x_i}{h}) \tag{5}$$

In the D-dimensional space, the kernel function can be presented as follows:

$$\varphi(\frac{x - x_i}{h}) = \prod_{m=1}^{D} \varphi(\frac{x^m - x_i^m}{h}). \tag{6}$$

By using (6) in Equation (3), one gets:

$$d(x) \approx \frac{1}{n \times h^D} \sum_{i=1}^{n} \prod_{m=1}^{D} \varphi(\frac{x^m - x_i^m}{h}). \tag{7}$$

Usually, but not always, $\varphi(u)$ will be radically symmetric. Thus, the unimodal probability density function, for instance the multivariate Gaussian density function, may be used to compute $\varphi(u)$:

$$\varphi(u) = \frac{1}{(2 \times \pi)^{\frac{D}{2}}} \exp(-\frac{1}{2}u^t u). \tag{8}$$

Choosing a value for h plays the role of a smoothing parameter in the density estimation. That is, if $h \to \infty$, then the density at point x in C, $d(x)$, approaches a false density. As $h \to 0$, then the kernel function approaches the Dirac Delta Function and $d(x)$ approaches to the true density (Bracewell, 1999).

Suppose that we determine all distances between all possible pairs formed by taking any two points from pattern C. For easy illustration, assume that for pattern C which contains 5 points these distances are as follows: 6, 1, 2, 2, 1, 5, 2, 3, 5, 5. Then, we define S as a set of the distances which have the highest frequency. For the previous illustrative example, we have set S equal to $\{2, 5\}$ as both distances 2 and 5 occur with frequency equal to 3. By using the concept of the previous set S, Heuristic Rule 1 proposes a way for finding an appropriate value for h when we estimate the density $d(x)$. In particular, it uses the minimum value in S (which is equal to 2 in this illustration) as follows:

Heuristic Rule 1: *If h is set equal to the minimum value in set S and this value is used to compute $d(x)$ by using Equation (7), then $d(x)$ approaches to a true density.*

This heuristic rule is reasonable for the following reason. In practice, since pattern C has a finite number of points the value for h cannot be made arbitrarily small. Obviously, an appropriate value for h is between the maximum and the minimum distances that are computed by all pairs of points in pattern C. If the value for h is the maximum distance, then C would be inside a single bin. Thus, $d(x)$ approaches to a false density. In contrast, if the value for h is the minimum distance, then the set of the bins would degenerate to the set of the single points in C. This situation also leads to a false density.

According to (Bracewell, 1999), as $h \to 0$, then $d(x)$ approaches to the true density. Furthermore, a small value for h would be appropriate to approach to the true density (Duda *et. al.*, 2001). Thus, the value for h described in Heuristic Rule 1 is a reasonable selection because it is close to the minimum distance but simultaneously the bins would not degenerate to the single points in C.

4.3 The Proposed Approach

Recall that in optimizing the total misclassification cost as defined in Equation (1) for classification algorithms, one cannot separate the control of fitting and generalization into two independent studies. Instead of this, the key idea of the proposed methodology is to simultaneously balance both fitting and generalization by adjusting the inferred systems through the use of the concept of homogenous sets and the homogeneity degree. The proposed methodology can be summarized in terms of the following three phases:

- **Phase #1**: Apply a classification approach (such as a DT, ANN, or SVM) to infer the two classification systems (i.e., the positive and the negative classification systems). Suppose that each classification system consists of a set of patterns. Next, break the inferred patterns into hyperspheres.
- **Phase #2**: Determine whether the hyperspheres derived in Phase #1 are homogenous sets or not. If so, then go to Phase #3. Otherwise, break a non homogenous set into smaller hyperspheres. Repeat Phase #2 until all of the hyperspheres are homogenous sets.
- **Phase #3**: For each homogenous set, if its homogeneity degree is greater than a certain breaking threshold value, then expand it. Otherwise, break it into smaller homogenous sets. The approach stops when all of the homogenous sets have been processed.

Suppose that given is a homogenous set C. Let $HD(C)$ denote its homogeneity degree. There are five parameters which are used in the proposed methodology:

- Two expansion threshold values α^+ and α^- to be used for expanding the positive and the negative homogenous sets, respectively.
- Two breaking threshold values β^+ and β^- to be used for breaking the positive and the negative patterns, respectively.
- A density threshold value γ to be used for determining whether either a positive or a negative hypersphere is approximately a homogenous set or not.

These three phases are also described in Algorithm 1 where they lead to the formulation of six sub-problems as follows:

Algorithm 1: The main algorithm.

Input: The training sets with the positive and the negative points.
A given classification algorithm.
Values of the control parameters α^+, α^-, β^+, β^-, and γ.
Output: New positive and negative classification systems.
1: Call **Sub-Problem #1**. {Phase #1}
2: Call **Sub-Problem #2**.
3: **for all** hypersphere C **do** {Phase #2}
4:    Call **Sub-Problem #3** with inputs C and γ.
5:    **if** C is a non homogenous set **then**
6:       Call **Sub-Problem #4**
7:       Go To Step 3
8:    **end if**
9: **end for**
10: Sort the homogeneity degrees in decreasing order.
11: **for all** homogenous set C **do** {Phase #3}
12:    **if** $HD(C) \geq \beta^+$ (for positive sets) or $HD(C) \geq \beta^-$ (for negative sets) **then**
13:       Call **Sub-Problem #5** with inputs $HD(C)$ and α^+ or α^-.
14:    **else**
15:       Call **Sub-Problem #6**.
16:    **end if**
17: **end for**

- **Sub-Problem #1:** Apply a data mining approach (such as a DT, ANN, SVM) to infer the two classification systems.
- **Sub-Problem #2:** Break the inferred patterns into hyperspheres.
- **Sub-Problem #3:** Determine whether a hypersphere is a homogenous set or not. If so, then its homogeneity degree is estimated.
- **Sub-Problem #4:** If a hypersphere is not a homogenous set, then break it into smaller hyperspheres.
- **Sub-Problem #5:** Expand a homogenous set C by using the notion of its homogeneity degree $HD(C)$ and the corresponding expansion threshold value plus some stopping conditions.
- **Sub-Problem #6:** Break a homogenous set C into smaller homogenous sets.

To solve Sub-Problem #1, one simply applies a classification algorithm and then derives the classification patterns. Furthermore, a solution to Sub-Problem #2 is similar to solutions for Sub-Problem #4. Therefore, the following sections present some procedures for solving Sub-Problems #2, #3, #5, and #6.

4.4 Solving Sub-Problem # 2

In order to help motivate the solution to Sub-Problem #2, we first consider the situation depicted in Figure 11.(a). This figure presents a set of positive

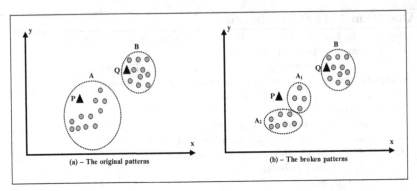

Fig. 8. Pattern B is a homogenous set while pattern A is a non homogenous set. Pattern A can be replaced by the two homogenous sets A_1 and A_2 as shown in part (b).

training points and a set of negative training points in 2-D. Suppose that Sub-Problem #1 has applied a DT algorithm on these sample data to infer a decision tree as depicted in Figure 11.(b). This decision tree separates the training data into the four groups described by the two solid lines depicted in Figure 11.(c).

Next for each pattern somehow Sub-Problem #2 finds the minimum number of hyperspheres which cover all the points in the original patterns. For instance, the above situation is depicted in Figure 11.(d) in which the positive patterns and the bottom negative pattern are covered by the circles (please note that in 2-D hyperspheres are circles): B, D and C, respectively. The top negative pattern is covered by the two circles A and E.

The problem of finding the minimum number of hyperspheres that can cover a pattern C of size N is similar to a form of the *set cover problem,* an NP-complete problem (Karp, 1972). In this research, a heuristic algorithm is proposed as depicted in Algorithm 2.

The algorithm starts by first estimating the densities of the N points by using Equation (7). Assume that the value for K is going from 1 to N. The algorithm will pick K points in C with the highest densities. Next, it uses these K points as centroids in the K-means clustering approach. If the K hyperspheres which are obtained from the clustering approach cover C, then the algorithm will stop. Otherwise, we repeat the algorithm with the value for K increased by one. Obviously, the algorithm will stop after some iterations because of Axiom 1. For instance, in Figure 11.(d) the algorithm determines at least two circles which can cover the two positive patterns while it uses three circles for the two negative patterns.

Recall that Sub-Problem #4 is to decompose a non homogenous set C into smaller hyperspheres in order to minimize the number of the hyperspheres which cover pattern C. We can use a similar algorithm as the one depicted in Algorithm 2.

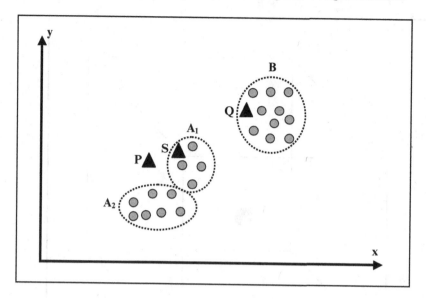

Fig. 9. An illustrative example of homogenous sets.

Algorithm 2: The algorithm for Sub-Problem 2

Input: Pattern C of size N.
Output: K hyperspheres.
1: Estimate the densities of the N points by using Equation (7).
2: **for** $K=1$ to N **do**
3:    Pick K points in C with the highest densities.
4:    Use the K-means clustering approach to find K hyperspheres.
5:    **if** the K hyperspheres cover C **then**
6:       STOP
7:    **else**
8:       $K = K + 1$
9:    **end if**
10: **end for**

4.5 Solving Sub-Problem #3

Let consider some hypersphere C. Sub-Problem #3 determines whether or not hypersphere C is a homogenous set. By using the idea of the non parametric density estimation described in Section 4.2, C is divided into a number of small bins of unit size h and approximates the density at the center x of each bin. If the densities at the centers are approximately equal to each other, then C is a homogenous set.

In order to help motivate the algorithm for Sub-Problem #3, we first consider the situation depicted in Figure 12. The left side of this figure presents two positive circles, called A and B in 2-D.

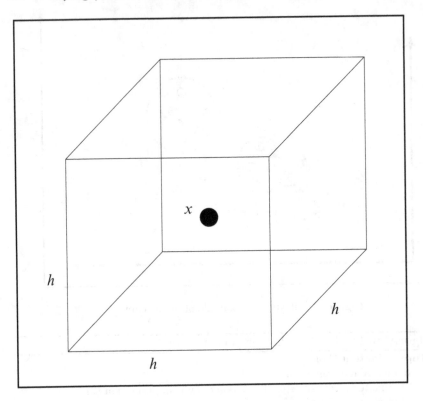

Fig. 10. A bin of unit size h and the center x in 3-D.

Algorithm 3: The algorithm for Sub-Problem 3

Input: Hypersphere C and density threshold value γ.

Output: Decide whether or not hypersphere C is a homogenous set.

1: Compute the distances between all pairs of points in C.

2: Let h be the distance mentioned in Heuristic Rule 1.

3: Superimpose C into hypergrid V of unit size h.

4: Approximate the density at the center x of each bin.

5: Compute the standard deviation of the densities at the centers of the bins.

6: **if** the standard deviation is ≤ess than or equal to γ, **then**

7:     C is a homogenous set and its homogeneity degree $HD(C)$ is computed by using Equation (9).

8: **else**

9:     C is not a homogenous set.

10: **end if**

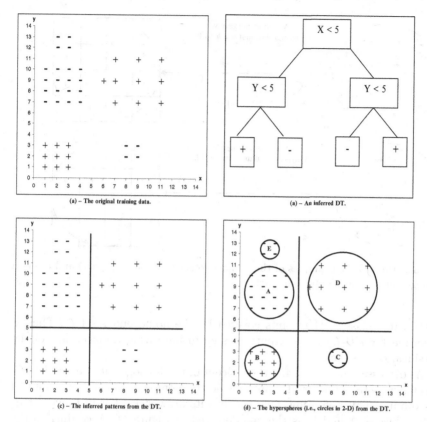

(a) – The original training data.

(a) – An inferred DT.

(c) – The inferred patterns from the DT.

(d) – The hyperspheres (i.e., circles in 2-D) from the DT.

Fig. 11. An Illustrative example of Phase 1

Suppose that both circles A and B are superimposed by the same hypergrid V of unit size h equal to one. This situation is depicted in the right side of Figure 12. By using Equation (7), the right figures show that all bins in circle A are of the same density equal to $\frac{1}{16 \times 1^2}$ =0.0625. In contrast, the density of some of the bins in circle B is equal to $\frac{0}{16 \times 1^2}$ =0. Thus, circle A is a homogenous set while circle B is not.

Furthermore, instead of the strict condition which requires the same density at the centers of the bins, we may apply a softer condition. That is, if the standard deviation of the densities at the centers of the bins is approximately less or equal to γ, say for $\gamma = 0.01$, then hypersphere C may be considered to be a homogenous set. The algorithm for Sub-Problem #3 is given in Algorithm 3.

As mentioned in Section 4.1, the homogeneity degree $HD(C)$ is a factor that may affect the total misclassification cost of the inferred classification systems. If an unclassified point is covered by a homogenous set C which has a higher homogeneity degree, then it may more accurately be assumed to be

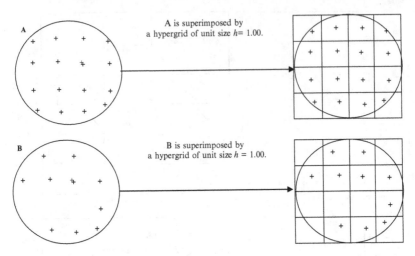

Fig. 12. Illustrative examples of the homogenous set (at the top part) and the non homogenous set (at the bottom part).

of the same class as the points covered by the homogenous set C. Thus, a definition for $HD(C)$ is an important step in improving the accuracy of the classification systems.

As discussed in Section 4.1, the concept of the homogeneity degree $HD(C)$ is defined as the number of points inside the homogenous set C per unit of C's volume. This definition, however, has its drawbacks. For instance, let us look at circles A and E as the one depicted in Figure 11. According to the above definition, $HD(\text{A})$ is equal to $\frac{16}{2 \times 1.5^2 \times \pi} \approx 1.1318$, while $HD(\text{E})$ is equal to $\frac{4}{2 \times 0.5^2 \times \pi} \approx 2.5465$. This means that pattern E is denser than pattern A. This is an apparent contradiction since in reality pattern A has more points and covers a wider region than pattern E. Thus, we need to find an appropriate definition for the homogeneity degree.

Intuitively, $HD(C)$ depends on the value h defined in Heuristic Rule 1 and the number of points in C, denoted by n_C. If n_C increases, then $HD(C)$ would slightly increase since the volume of C does not change and C has more points. Furthermore, if h increases, then the average distance between pairs of points in homogenous set C increases. Obviously, this leads to; $D(C)$ decreases. Hence, $HD(C)$ is inversely proportional to h while is directly proportional to n_C. We use the function $\ln(n_C)$ to show the slight effect of n_C to $HD(C)$.

$$HD(C) = \frac{\ln(n_C)}{h}. \tag{9}$$

For instance, $HD(\text{A})$ as depicted in Figure 12 is equal to $\frac{\ln(16)}{1} \approx 2.77$. Let us consider the illustrative example depicted in Figure 11. Now we have

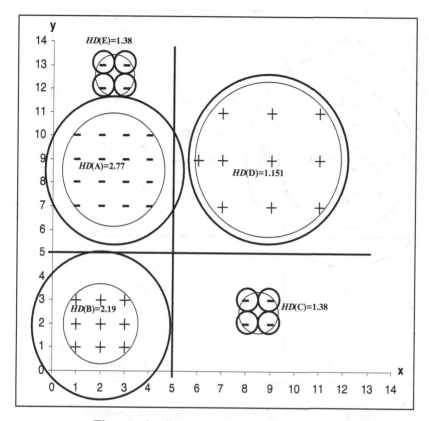

Fig. 13. An illustrative example of Sub-Problem 5.

$HD(\text{A})$ equal to $\frac{\ln(16)}{1} \approx 2.77$, $HD(\text{B})$ equal to $\frac{\ln(9)}{1} \approx 2.19$, $HD(\text{C}) = HD(\text{E})$ equal to $\frac{\ln(4)}{1} \approx 1.38$, and $HD(\text{D})$ equal to $\frac{\ln(10)}{2} \approx 1.151$.

4.6 Solving Sub-Problem #5

Recall that the control of fitting and generalization for classification systems may be achieved by expanding or breaking the inferred homogenous sets by using their homogeneity degrees. Suppose that we are given a positive homogenous set F with its homogeneity degree $HD(F)$, the breaking threshold value β^+, and the expansion threshold value α^+. A similar definition exists for a negative homogenous set. According to the main algorithm depicted in Algorithm 1, if $HD(F)$ is greater than or equal to β^+, then the homogenous set F will be expanded by using the expansion threshold value α^+. Otherwise, we will break the homogenous set F into smaller hyperspheres.

In order to help motivate this stage, we consider the example depicted in Figure 11. Please recall that the homogeneity degrees of circles A, B, C, D,

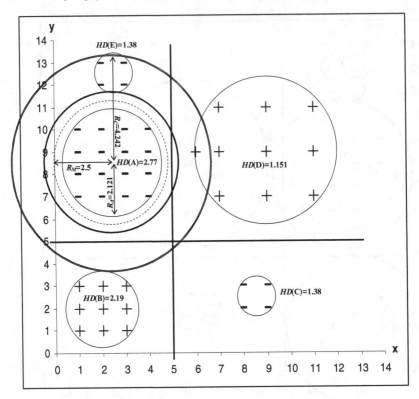

Fig. 14. An illustrative example of the radial expansion.

and E are $HD(A)=2.77$, $HD(B)=2.19$, $HD(C)=1.38$, and $HD(D)=1.15$, and $HD(E)=1.38$, respectively. Suppose that the two breaking threshold values β^+ and β^- are equal to 1.00 and 1.50, respectively. Furthermore, let the two expansion threshold values α^+ and α^- be equal to 2.00. As depicted in Figure 13, the homogenous sets A, B, and D are expanded (the expanded regions are indicated by the solid line circles), while C and E are broken into four smaller circles (the broken regions are indicated by the small solid line circles). Please note that the breaking

approach, i.e., Sub-Problem #6, is described in Section 4.7.

There are two types of expansion: a radial expansion in which a homogenous set F is expanded in all directions and a linear expansion in which a homogenous set F is expanded in a certain direction. For instance, in Figure 13 the homogenous sets A, B, and D have used the radial expansion approach. The following sections discuss in detail these two expansion types.

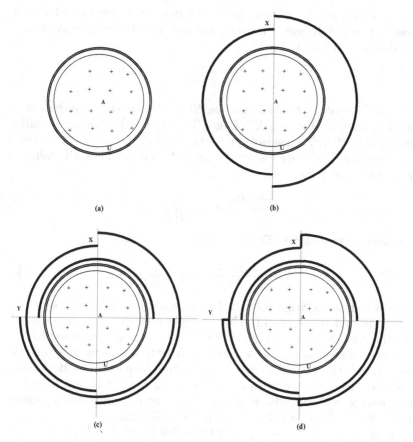

Fig. 15. An illustrative example of the linear expansion.

Radial Expansion

In the radial type, a homogenous set F is expanded in all directions. Let M be a region expanded from F. Let R_F and R_M denote the radiuses of F and M, respectively. In the radial expansion approach R_F is increased by a certain amount denoted as T, called a *step-size increase*. Thus, one gets:

$$R_M = R_F + T \tag{10}$$

Following a dichotomous search methodology, we assume that there exists a hypersphere G which covers the homogenous set F. Furthermore, without loss of generality, let us assume that the radius R_G may be computed by:

$$R_G = 2 \times \quad R_F \tag{11}$$

By using R_G and R_F, we can derive the step-size increase T. That is, T must depend on the difference between R_G and R_F. One of the ways that T may be determined is as follows:

$$T = \frac{R_G - R_F}{2}. \tag{12}$$

At the same time, T should depend on $HD(F)$ because of the dichotomous search methodology. That is, if $HD(F)$ gets higher, then T should get smaller. This means that $HD(F)$ is inversely proportional to T. We may use a threshold value L to ensure that $HD(F)$ is always greater than one. Thus, the value for T may be defined as follows:

$$T = \frac{R_G - R_F}{2} \times \frac{1}{L \times HD(F)}. \tag{13}$$

If we substitute back into Equation (10), R_M becomes:

$$R_M = R_F + \frac{R_G - R_F}{2} \times \frac{1}{L \times HD(F)}. \tag{14}$$

In order to help motivate the radial expansion algorithm, we consider the example indicated in Figure 14. This example uses the same hypothetical data as the ones depicted in Figure 11.(d). Assume that L is equal to one. A closer examination of Figure 14 indicates that the hypersphere A (i.e., the one-line circle with $R_A=2.121$) is covered by the three circles: a double-line circle which depicts circle G with $R_G = 2.121 \times 2 = 4.242$, a solid line circle which shows the final expanded region, and a dotted line circle which presents the hypersphere M whose radius is computed as follows:

$R_M = R_F + \frac{R_G - R_M}{2} \times \frac{1}{L \times w(A)} = 2.121 + \frac{4.242 - 2.121}{2} \times \frac{1}{1 \times 2.77} \approx 2.5.$

Similarly, Equation (14) computes the following values for R_M in four iterations: 2.8, 3.06, 3.23, and 3.25, respectively, until R_M satisfies the stopping conditions mentioned next in Section 4.6. The final expanded region is the solid line circle depicted in Figure 14. Furthermore, this figure also shows that a part of the state space which has been inferred as a positive region by the DT algorithm. However, now it is derived as a negative region after using the HBA. This illustration indicates that the HBA may derive better classification systems. The radial expansion algorithm is depicted in Algorithm 4.

Linear Expansion

The linear approach expands a homogenous set F in a certain direction. There is a difference between the method presented in the previous section and the one presented in this section (i.e., linear vs. radial). That is, now the homogenous set F is first expanded to hypersphere M by using the radial expansion. Then, hypersphere M is expanded in a given direction by using

Algorithm 4: The algorithm for the radial expansion.
Input: Homogenous set F with $HD(F)$, R_F, and α^+
Output: An expanded region E.
1: Set $M = F$ (i.e., $R_F = R_M$).
2: Set hypersphere G covering M with radius $R_G = 2 \times R_M$.
3: **repeat**
4:    Set $E = M$ (i.e., $R_E = R_M$).
5:    Expand M by using Equation (14).
6: **until** R_M satisfies stopping conditions discussed in Section 4.6 or $R_M = R_G$.
7: **if** R_M satisfies stopping conditions **then**
8:    STOP.
9: **else**
10:    go to Step 2.
11: **end if**

the radial approach until it satisfies the stopping conditions mentioned next in Section 4.6. The final region is the union of all the expanded regions.

In order to help motivate the linear expansion approach, we consider the homogenous set A depicted in Figure 15. Suppose that by using the radial expansion for the homogenous set A with the expansion threshold value equal to 2.00, we get the hypersphere U (i.e., the two-line circle depicted in Figure 15.(a)). Next, we divide the hypersphere U in the X axis into two parts. The radial expansion approach would expand each one of the parts as the solid lines depicted in Figure 15.(b). A similar approach exists for the Y axis depicted in Figure 15.(c). The final expanded region is the region which is defined by the union of the solid lines depicted in Figure 15.(d).

Description of the Stopping Conditions

This section presents the stopping conditions for the radial expansion approach for expanding a homogenous set F. That is, the stopping conditions must satisfy the following requirements:

Depend on the homogeneity degree. This has been mentioned in the fundamental assumption of the proposed approach.

Stop when an expanded region reaches other patterns. We can use a softer condition in which the expanded region can accept several noisy data points. If the homogeneity degree is high, then the expanded region can accept more noisy data.

To address the first stopping condition, an upper bound for R_M should be directly proportional to the homogeneity degree $HD(F)$, the expansion threshold value α^+, and the original radius R_F. The second stopping condition can be determined while expanding. Furthermore, an upper bound on the number of noisy points should be directly proportional to $HD(F)$ and the size of F, which is denoted as n_F. The stopping conditions are summarized as follows (a similar way exists for the expansion threshold value α^-):

$$R_M \leq HD(F) \times R_F \times \alpha^+ \text{ and } \textit{the number of noisy points} \leq \frac{HD(F) \times \alpha^+}{n_F}$$
$$(15)$$

4.7 Solving Sub-Problem #6

Suppose that given is a positive homogenous set F. Recall that if its homogeneity degree $HD(F)$ is less than β^+, then the homogenous set F is broken into sub-patterns. According to Theorem 1, the sub-patterns are also homogenous sets. Thus, they can be expanded or broken down even more.

In order to help motivate this problem, we consider the example depicted in Figure 13. In this figure the two threshold values β^+ and β^- are equal to 1.00 and 1.50, respectively. Therefore, the homogenous sets C and E are broken down into four smaller circles for each set. Then, these smaller circles are considered to be homogenous sets with their homogeneity degrees equal to zero. Thus, they should not be expanded.

5 Some Computational Results

5.1 Datasets and Parametric Analysis

Please recall that this chapter aims at better understanding the performance of the HBA in balancing both fitting and generalization by adjusting the inferred systems through the use of the concept of homogenous sets and the homogeneity degree. The balance will target at minimizing the total misclassification costs, TC, of the final system:

$$TC = \min\left(C_{FP} \times RATE\_FP + C_{FN} \times RATE\_FN + C_{UC} \times RATE\_UC\right).$$

Please note that the penalty costs: C_{FP}, C_{FN}, and C_{UC} depend on each individual application. In the following experiments, we used some 2-D synthetic datasets which were divided into a training set and a testing set as described in Table 1. These data points were determined as follows. At first the map of VietNam was considered. Next some data points were generated randomly in 2-D. A data point would be a positive point, if it fell inside the map of VietNam. Otherwise, that point was defined as a negative point. The HBA attempted to use the training set to infer the map of VietNam (i.e., the positive and the negative systems). Then, we used the inferred map to test the testing set. The four parameters used in the HBA are as follows:

- Two expansion threshold values α^+ and α^- to be used for expanding the positive and the negative homogenous sets, respectively.

Table 1. Characteristics of the 2-D synthetic datasets

Name	Number of training points	Number of testing points
D_1	63	16
D_2	89	28
$D_3 = D_1 \cup D_2$	144	44

- Two breaking threshold values β^+ and β^- to be used for breaking the positive and the negative patterns, respectively.

Furthermore, it was also assumed that β^+ and β^- were in $[0, 2]$ while α^+ and α^- were in $[0, 10]$. Given is a certain 3-tuple of the penalty costs (C_{FP}, C_{FN}, C_{UC}). By using exhaustive search in the above ranges the HBA found the optimal combinations of α^+, α^-, β^+, and β^- in order to minimize the TC value. On the other hand, given are different values for the 3-tuple (C_{FP}, C_{FN}, C_{UC}). We expect that the value for TC after controlling the fitting and generalization problems would be less than or at most equal to what was achieved by the original algorithms.

5.2 Experimental Results

The experiments were ran on a PC with 2.8GHZ speed and 1GB RAM under the Windows XP operating system. The original classification algorithms used in these experiments are based on SVMs, ANNs, and DTs. There were thirteen experiments done on the three datasets D_1, D_2, and D_3 with different values for the 3-tuple (C_{FP}, C_{FN}, C_{UC}). Furthermore, we used the libraries in Neural Network Toolbox 6.0 and Statistics Toolbox 6.0 (Matlab, 2004) for implementing the classification algorithms, the K-means clustering algorithm, and the density estimation approach. The experimental details are as follows:

Case 1: At first we studied the case of a 3-tuple (C_{FP}, C_{FN}, C_{UC}) in which the application would penalize much more for the false-positive cases than for the other types of error. Thus, the objective function in this case was assumed to be:

$$TC = 6 \times RATE\_FP + 3 \times RATE\_FN + RATE\_UC.$$

Next, we ran the HBA on D_1 with β^+ and β^- divided into $\{0, 1, 2\}$ and α^+ and α^- divided into $\{0, 2, 4, 6, 8, 10\}$. Recall that $RATE\_FP$, $RATE\_FN$, and $RATE\_UC$ are the false-positive, the false-negative, and the unclassifiable rates, respectively. Table 2 shows these three rates and the value of TC obtained from the algorithms. The notation "SVM-HBA" means that the HBA used the classification models first obtained by using the SVM algorithm before controlling the fitting and generalization problems. The two similar notations exist for DT-HBA (the Decision Tree algorithm and the HBA) and

Table 2. Results for minimizing TC = 6×RATE_FP + 3×RATE_FN + RATE_UC on D_1.

Algorithm	$RATE\_FP$	$RATE\_FN$	$RATE\_UC$	TC
SVM	1	0	7	13
DT	3	0	5	23
ANN	1	0	7	13
SVM-HBA	0	1	5	8
DT-HBA	0	1	5	8
ANN-HBA	0	1	5	8

ANN-HBA (the Artificial Neural Network algorithm and the HBA). Table 2 presents that SVM-HBA, DT-HBA, and ANN-HBA found the optimal TC to be equal to 8. This value was less than the value of TC achieved by the original algorithms (i.e., the SVM, DT, and ANN) by about 39%.

Table 3 presents information for the four specific parameter values when SVM-HBA found the optimal TC. The execution time in this case was approximately equal to 1 hour and 3 minutes.

Table 3. Values for the four parameters when the SVM-HBA ran on D_1 and found the optimal TC.

β^+	α^-	β^-	α^+
1	10	2	4
1	10	2	6
1	10	2	8
1	10	2	10

An even lower TC was found once we divided β^+ and β^- into $\{0, 1, 2\}$ and divided α^+ and α^- into $\{0$ to$10\}$. These results are presented in Table 4.

Table 4. Results for minimizing TC = 6×RATE_FP + 3×RATE_FN + RATE_UC on D_1 with the smaller ranges.

Algorithm	$RATE\_FP$	$RATE\_FN$	$RATE\_UC$	TC
SVM	1	0	7	13
DT	3	0	5	23
ANN	1	0	7	13
SVM-HBA	0	0	7	7
DT-HBA	0	0	7	7
ANN-HBA	0	0	7	7

Table 4 shows that if we split the four parameters into smaller ranges, then the HBA could find a lower TC. This may lead to a new strategy in which one can develop an approach for determining optimal combinations of the four parameter values by successively considering higher resolution.

Case 2: Now we consider a case in which the application would penalize much more for the unclassifiable cases than for the other types of error. Thus, the objective function in this case was assumed to be:

$$TC = RATE\_FP + 3 \times RATE\_FN + 6 \times RATE\_UC.$$

We ran the HBA on D_1 with β^+ and β^- divided into $\{0, 1, 2\}$ and α^+ and α^- divided into $\{0$ to $10\}$. Table 5 shows that SVM-HBA, DT-HBA, and ANN-HBA found an optimal TC which was less than the value of TC achieved by the original algorithms by about 53%.

Table 5. Results for minimizing TC = RATE_FP + 3×RATE_FN +6×RATE_UC on D_1.

Algorithm	$RATE\_FP$	$RATE\_FN$	$RATE\_UC$	TC
SVM	1	0	7	43
DT	3	0	5	33
ANN	1	0	7	43
SVM-HBA	1	1	4	28
DT-HBA	2	1	2	17
ANN-HBA	1	1	4	28

Case 3: Now we consider a case in which the application would penalize the same way for the false-positive, the false-negative, and the unclassifiable cases. Thus, the objective function in this case was assumed to be:

$$TC = 3.3 \times RATE\_FP + 3.3 \times RATE\_FN + 3.3 \times RATE\_UC.$$

We ran the HBA on D_1 with β^+ and β^- divided into $\{0, 1, 2\}$ and α^+ and α^- divided into $\{0, 2, 4, 6, 8, 10\}$. Table 6 shows that SVM-HBA, DT-HBA, and ANN-HBA found two possible cases for each algorithm where the optimal value for TC was less than the value of TC achieved by the original algorithms by about 33%.

A similar result for TC once we ran the HBA on D_3, which had more training points, also divided β^+ and β^- into $\{0, 1, 2\}$, and α^+ and α^- into $\{0, 2, 4, 6, 8, 10\}$. These results are presented in Table 7.

Table 7 shows that SVM-HBA, DT-HBA, and ANN-HBA found the optimal TC which was less than the value of TC achieved by the original algorithms by about 47%. The execution time in this case was approximately equal to 12 hours and 50 minutes.

Table 6. Results for minimizing TC = 3.3×RATE_FP + 3.3×RATE_FN +3.3×RATE_UC on D_1.

Algorithm	RATE_FP	RATE_FN	RATE_UC	TC
SVM	1	0	7	26.4
DT	3	0	5	26.4
ANN	1	0	7	26.4
SVM-HBA	0	1	5	19.8
	1	1	4	19.8
DT-HBA	1	1	3	16.5
	2	1	2	16.5
ANN-HBA	0	1	5	19.8
	1	1	4	19.8

Table 7. Results for minimizing TC = 3.3×RATE_FP + 3.3×RATE_FN + 3.3RATE_UC on D_3

Algorithm	RATE_FP	RATE_FN	RATE_UC	TC
SVM	5	3	26	112.2
DT	8	3	24	115.5
ANN	5	2	27	112.2
SVM-HBA	4	7	7	59.40
DT-HBA	7	7	9	75.90
ANN-HBA	4	7	7	59.40

<u>Case 4:</u> Now we consider a case in which the application would penalize much more for the false-negative cases than for the other types of error. Furthermore, the penalty cost for unclassifiable cases was equal to zero Thus, the objective function in this case was assumed to be:

$$TC = 2 \times RATE\_FP + 20 \times RATE\_FN + 0 \times RATE\_UC.$$

We ran the HBA on D_2 with β^+ and β^- divided into {0, 1, 2} and α^+ and α^- divided into {0, 2, 4, 6, 8, 10}. Table 8 shows that SVM-HBA, DT-HBA, and ANN-HBA found an optimal TC equal to 0. This value was equal to the value of TC achieved by the original algorithms. However, SVM-HBA achieved an unclassifiable rate of 21 versus 28 for the original algorithms. A similar result existed for DT-HBA and ANN-HBA. The execution time in this case was approximately equal to 5 hours and 24 minutes.

We also experimented with the following different objective functions on the dataset D_1:

$$TC = 6 \times RATE\_FP + 2 \times RATE\_FN + 2 \times RATE\_UC,$$

$$TC = 4 \times RATE\_FP + 2 \times RATE\_FN + 4 \times RATE\_UC, \text{ and}$$

Table 8. Results for minimizing TC = 2×RATE_FP +20×RATE_FN on D$_2$.

Algorithm	RATE_FP	RATE_FN	RATE_UC	TC
SVM	0	0	28	0
DT	0	0	28	0
ANN	0	0	28	0
SVM-HBA	0	0	21	0
DT-HBA	0	0	24	0
ANN-HBA	0	0	22	0

$$TC = 3 \times RATE\_FP + 6 \times RATE\_FN + 1 \times RATE\_UC.$$

Similarly, we experimented with the following different objective functions on the dataset D$_2$:

$$TC = 2 \times RATE\_FP + 20 \times RATE\_FN + 0 \times RATE\_UC,$$

$$TC = 6 \times RATE\_FP + 3 \times RATE\_FN + 1 \times RATE\_UC, \text{ and}$$

$$TC = 50 \times RATE\_FP + 60 \times RATE\_FN + 1 \times RATE\_UC.$$

We also experimented with the following different objective functions on the dataset D$_3$:

$$TC = RATE\_FP + 3 \times RATE\_FN + 6 \times RATE\_UC, \text{ and}$$

$$TC = 20 \times RATE\_FP + 2 \times RATE\_FN + 0 \times RATE\_UC.$$

In all these tests we concluded that the HBA always found the optimal combinations of α^+, α^-, β^+, and β^- in order to minimize the value of TC. Furthermore, the value for TC in all these cases was significantly less than or at most equal to what was achieved by the original algorithms.

6 Conclusions

The performance of a classification method in terms of the false-positive, the false-negative, and the unclassifiable rates may be totally unpredictable and depend on the application at hand. Attempts to minimize one of the previous rates, lead to increases on the other two rates. The root to the above critical problems is the overfitting and overgeneralization behaviors of a given classification approach when it is processing a particular dataset. This chapter identified a gap between fitting and generalization with current algorithms and also defined the desired goal as an optimization problem. Next, it provided a new approach, called the Homogeneity-Based Algorithm (HBA), which appears to be very promising. There are some future research goals. For example, the HBA needs to be tested with higher dimensions and more data. This is ongoing research by our group. Currently we are implementing a GA (Genetic Algorithm) for finding the optimal values of the controlling threshold values α^+, α^-, β^+, and β^-. Some preliminary results seem to suggest that by using the GA one can achieve even better values for the various objectives functions at a fraction of the original CPU time (often times by spending between 50% to 80%).;

References

Abdi, H., (2003), "*A neural network primer,*" Journal of Biological Systems, vol. 2, pp. 247-281.

Ali, K., C. Brunk, and M. Pazzani, (1994), "*On learning multiple descriptions of a concept,*" Proceedings of Tools with Artificial Intelligence, New Orleans, LA, USA, pp. 476-483.

Artificial Neural Network Toolbox 6.0 and Statistics Toolbox 6.0, Matlab Version 7.0, website: http://www.mathworks.com/products/

Boros, E., P. L. Hammer, and J. N. Hooker, (1994), "*Predicting Cause-Effect Relationships from Incomplete Discrete Observations,*" Journal on Discrete Mathematics, vol. 7, no. 4, pp. 531-543.

Bracewell, R., (1999), "*The Impulse Symbol,*" Chapter 5 in The Fourier Transform and Its Applications, 3rd ed. New York: McGraw-Hill, pp. 69-97.

Breiman, L., (1996), "*Bagging predictors,*" Journal of Machine Learning, vol. 24, pp. 123-140.

Breiman, L., (2001), "*Random forests,*" Journal of Machine Learning, vol. 45, no. 1, pp. 5–32.

Breiman, L., J. H. Friedman, R. A. Olshen, and C. J. Stone, (1984), "*Classification and Regression Trees,*" Chapman Hall/CRC Publisher, pp. 279-293.

Byvatov, E., and G. Schneider, (2003), "*Support vector machine applications in bioinformatics,*" Journal of Application Bioinformatics, vol. 2, no.2, pp. 67-77.

Clark, P., and R. Boswell, (1991), "*Rule induction with CN2: Some recent improvements,*" Y. Kodratoff, editor, Machine Learning - EWSL-91, Berlin, Springer-Verlag, pp. 151-163.

Clark, P., and T. Niblett, (1989), "*The CN2 Algorithm,*" Journal of Machine Learning, vol. 3, pp. 261-283.

Cohen S., L. Rokach, O. Maimon, (2007), "*Decision-tree instance-space decomposition with grouped gain-ratio,*", Information Science, Volume 177, Issue 17, pp. 3592-3612.

Cohen, W. W., (1995), "*Fast effective rule induction,*" Machine Learning: Proceedings of the Twelfth International Conference, Tahoe City, CA., USA, pp. 115-123.

Cortes, C., and V. Vapnik, (1995), *"Support-vector networks,"* Journal of Machine Learning, vol. 20, no. 3, pp. 273-297.

Cover, T. M., and P. E. Hart, (1967), *"Nearest Neighbor Pattern Classification,"* Institute of Electrical and Electronics Engineers Transactions on Information Theory, vol. 13, no. 1, pp. 21-27.

Cristianini, N., and S. T. John, (2000), *"An Introduction to Support Vector Machines and other kernel-based learning methods,"* Cambridge University Press.

Dasarathy, B. V., and B. V. Sheela, (1979), *"A Composite Classifier System Design: Concepts and Methodology,"* Proceedings of the IEEE, vol. 67, no. 5, pp. 708-713.

Dietterich, T. G., and G. Bakiri, (1994), *"Solving multiclass learning problems via error-correcting output codes,"* Journal of Artificial Intelligence Research, vol. 2, pp. 263-286.

Duda, R. O., and P. E. Hart, (1973), *"Pattern Classification and Scene Analysis,"* Wiley Publisher, pp. 56-64.

Duda. O. R., E. H. Peter, G. S. David , (2001), *"Pattern Classification,"* Chapter 4: Nonparametric Techniques in Wiley Interscience Publisher, pp. 161-199.

Dudani, S., (1976), *"The Distance-Weighted k-Nearest-Neighbor Rule,"* IEEE Transactions on Systems, Man and Cybernetics, vol. 6, no. 4, pp. 325-327.

Friedman, N., D. Geiger, and M. Goldszmidt, (1997), *"Bayesian Network Classifiers,"* Journal of Machine Learning, vol. 29, pp. 131-161.

Geman, S., E. Bienenstock, and R. Doursat, (1992), *"Neural Networks and the Bias/Variance Dilemma,"* Journal of Neural Computation, vol. 4, pp. 1-58.

Hecht-Nielsen, R., (1989), *"Theory of the Backpropagation neural Network,"* International Joint Conference on neural networks, Washington, DC, USA, pp. 593-605.

Huzefa, R., and G. Karypis, (2005), *"Profile Based Direct Kernels for Remote Homology Detection and Fold Recognition,"* Journal of Bioinformatics, vol. 31, no. 23, pp. 4239-4247.

Karp, R. M., (1972), *"Reducibility Among Combinatorial Problems,"* Proceedings of Sympos. IBM Thomas J. Watson Res. Center, Yorktown Heights, New York: Plenum, pp. 85-103.

Keller, J. M., M. R. Gray, and J. A. Givens, Jr, (1985), *"A Fuzzy K-Nearest Neighbor Algorithm,"* Journal of IEEE Transactions on Systems, Man, and Cybernetics, vol. 15, no. 4, pp. 580-585.

Kohavi R., (1996), *"Scaling up the accuracy of naive-Bayes classifiers: a decision-tree hybrid,"* Proceedings of the Second International Conference on Knowledge Discovery and Data Mining, Portland, OR, USA, pp. 202-207.

Kohavi, R., and G. John, (1997), *"Wrappers for Feature Subset Selection,"* Journal of Artificial Intelligence: special issue on relevance, vol. 97, no. 1-2, pp. 273-324.

Kokol, P., M. Zorman, M. M. Stiglic, and I. Malcic, (1998), *"The limitations of decision trees and automatic learning in real world medical decision making,"* Proceedings of the 9th World Congress on Medical Informatics MEDINFO'98, vol. 52, pp. 529-533.

Kononenko, I., (1991), *"Semi-naïve Bayesian classifier,"* Y. Kodratoff Editor, Proceedings of sixth European working session on learning, Springer-Verlag, pp. 206-219.

Kwok, S., and C. Carter, (1990), *"Multiple decision trees: uncertainty,"* Journal of Artificial Intelligence, vol.4, pp. 327-335.

Langley, P., and S. Sage, (1994), *"Induction of Selective Bayesian Classifiers,"* Proceedings of UAI-94, Seattle, WA, USA, pp. 399-406.

Mansour, Y., D. McAllester, (2000), *"Generalization Bounds for Decision Trees,"* Proceedings of the 13th Annual Conference on Computer Learning Theory, San Francisco, Morgan Kaufmann, USA, pp. 69–80.

Moody, J. E., (1992), *"The Effective Number of Parameters: An Analysis of Generalization and Regularization in Nonlinear Learning Systems,"* Journal of Advances in Neural Information Processing Systems, vol. 4, pp. 847-854.

Nock, R., and O. Gascuel, (1995), *"On learning decision committees,"* Proceedings of the Twelfth International Conference on Machine Learning, Morgan Kaufmann, Taho City, CA., USA, pp. 413-420.

Oliver, J. J., and D. J.Hand, (1995), *"On pruning and averaging decision trees,"* Proceedings of the Twelfth International Conference on Machine Learning, Morgan Kaufmann, Taho City, CA., USA, pp. 430-437.

Pazzani, M.J., (1995), *"Searching for dependencies in Bayesian classifiers,"* Proceedings of AI STAT'95, pp. 239-248.

Podgorelec, V., P. Kokol, B. Stiglic, and I. Rozman, (2002), *"Decision trees: an overview and their use in medicine,"* Journal of Medical Systems, Kluwer Academic/Plenum Press, vol. 26, no. 5, pp. 445-463

Quinlan, J. R., (1987), *"Simplifying decision trees,"* International Journal of Man-Machine Studies, vol. 27, pp. 221-234.

Quinlan, J. R., (1993), *"C4.5: Programs for Machine Learning,"* Morgan Kaufmann Publisher San Mateo, CA., USA, pp. 35-42.

Rada, M., (2004), *"Seminar on Machine Learning,"* a presentation of a course taught at University of North Texas.

Rokach L., O. Maimon, O. Arad, (2005), *"Improving Supervised Learning by Sample Decomposition,"* Journal of Computational Intelligence and Applications, vol. 5, no. 1, pp. 37-54.

Sands D., (1998), *"Improvement theory and its applications,"* Gordon A. D., and A. M. Pitts Editors, Higher Order Operational Techniques in Semantics, Publications of the Newton Institute, Cambridge University Press, pp. 275-306.

Schapire, R. E, (1990), *"The strength of weak learnability,"* Journal of Machine Learning, vol. 5, pp. 197-227.

Shawe-Taylor. J., and C. Nello, (1999), *"Further results on the margin distribution,"* Proceedings of COLT99, Santa Cruz, CA., USA, pp. 278-285.

Smith, M., (1996), *"Neural Networks for Statistical Modeling,"* Itp New Media Publisher, ISBN 1-850-32842-0, pp. 117–129.

Spizer, M., L. Stefan, C. Paul, S. Alexander, and F. George, (2006), *"IsoSVM – Distinguishing isoforms and paralogs on the protein level,"* Journal of BMC Bioinformatics, vol. 7:110, website: http://www.biomedcentral.com/content/pdf/1471-2105-7-110.pdf.

Tan, P. N., S. Michael, and K. Vipin, (2005), *"Introduction to Data Mining,"* Chapters 4 and 5, Addison-Wesley Publisher, pp. 145-315.

Triantaphyllou, E., (2007), *"Data Mining and Knowledge Discovery Via a Novel Logic-Based Approach,"* A monograph, Springer, Massive Computing Series, 420 pages, (in print).

Triantaphyllou, E., and G. Felici, (Editors), (2006), *"Data Mining and Knowledge Discovery Approaches Based on Rule Induction Techniques,"* Springer, Massive Computing Series, 796 pages.

Triantaphyllou, E., L. Allen, L. Soyster, and S. R. T. Kumara, (1994), *"Generating Logical Expressions From Positive and Negative Examples via a Branch-and-Bound approach,"* Journal of Computers and Operations Research, vol. 21, pp. 783-799.

Vapnik, V., (1998), *"Statistical Learning Theory,"* Wiley Publisher, pp. 375-567.

Webb, G. I., (1996), *"Further experimental evidence against the utility of Occam's razor,"* Journal of Artificial Intelligence Research, vol. 4, pp. 397-417.

Webb, G. I., (1997), *"Decision Tree Grafting,"* Proceedings of the 15th International Joint Conference on Artificial Intelligence (IJCAI'97), vol. 2, pp. 23-29.

Weigend, A., (1994), *"On overfitting and the effective number of hidden units,"* Proceedings of the 1993 Connectionist Models Summer School, pp. 335-342.

Wikipedia Dictionary, (2007), website: http://en.wikipedia.org/wiki/Homogenous.

Wolpert, D. H, (1992), *"Stacked generalization,"* Journal of Neural Networks, vol. 5, pp. 241-259.

Zavrsnik, J., P. Kokol, I. Maleiae, K. Kancler, M. Mernik, and M. Bigec, (1995), *"ROSE: decision trees, automatic learning and their applications in cardiac medicine,"* MEDINFO'95, Vancouver, Canada, pp. 201-206.

Zhou Z. and C. Chen, (2002), *"Hybrid decision tree,"* Journal of Knowledge-Based Systems, vol. 15, pp. 515 - 528.

Index